Free study resources for your American History course—*available online!*

Primary source documents, video and audio clips, activities, and self-quizzing—all FREE to you when you purchase this text!

American Journey Online

http://ajaccess.wadsworth.com

FREE access with every new copy of the text!

American Journey Online comprises 16 primary source collections that capture the landmark events and major themes of the American experience—through images and the words of those who lived it. Discover hundreds of rare documents, pictures, and archival audio and video, along with essays, headnotes, and captions that set the sources in context. Full-text searchability and extensive hyperlinking make searching and cross-referencing easy. Your passcode is included when you purchase a new copy of this text!

InfoTrac® College Edition

http://www.infotrac-college.com

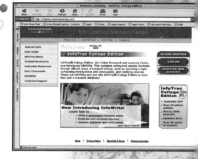

FREE access with every new copy of the text!

You also receive four months of free access to **InfoTrac College Edition**, the online database that puts cutting-edge research and the latest headlines at your fingertips! This database offers more than 10 million articles from thousands of academic journals, newsletters, and up-to-the-minute periodicals—available 24 hours a day from any computer with Internet access. **InfoTrac College Edition** makes research so easy, you will want to use it to enhance your work in *every* course. **NEW!** Your subscription includes instant access to critical-thinking and paper-writing tools through **InfoWrite**.

Journals subject to change.

Book Companion Web Site

At the Thomson Wadsworth History Resource Center

http://history.wadsworth.com/murrin_LEP4e

Exciting and interactive, this text's **Book Companion Web Site** features a wide variety of study aids that will help you make the most of your course! These include:

*Chapter outlines and summaries • Tutorial quizzes • A final exam that incorporates all the quizzes by chapter • A glossary that includes flashcards with audio • Simulations—interactive, detailed accounts paired with critical thinking and multiple choice quizzes • **American Journey Online** activities and video exercises • An "At the Movies" feature, which provides descriptions, critical thinking questions, and Web links for major films throughout American history • Crossword puzzles • The U.S. Image Bank, featuring images and maps that can be put into multimedia presentations • Interactive maps with questions • Primary sources • And much more!*

To access the **Book Companion Web Site**, simply visit the URL listed above or click on "Student Book Companion Sites" at the Thomson Wadsworth History Resource Center home page (http://history.wadsworth.com). Click on your book cover, and you're there!

How to Use Maps in This Textbook

Here are some basic map concepts and simple tips to help you get the most from the maps in this textbook.

● There are many different types of maps intended to illustrate different types of information. A few of the kinds most frequently used in history books are political, demographic, topographic, and military maps.

   ● **Political maps** traditionally show territorial boundaries (such as state and country borders).
   ● **Demographic maps** use shading or cross-hatching to show trends relating to population density and distribution.
   ● **Topographic maps** illustrate both natural and man-made surface features, such as mountain ranges, rivers, and dams.
   ● **Military maps** zoom in on a specific battlefield or show a broad theater of war, and illustrate troop movements over a period of time.

   Many maps, such as the one in this foldout, combine multiple features into one document, illustrating more than one kind of information.

● Always look at the scale, which allows you to determine the distance, in miles or kilometers, between locations on the map.

● Examine the legend carefully (it's usually contained in a boxed inset). It explains the colors, shading, and symbols used on the map.

● If the map is accompanied by a caption, read it thoroughly. Captions usually provide clues to what the author thinks is important about the geography, and offer additional interesting details that may not be covered in the surrounding text.

● Note the mountains, rivers, oceans and other topographic features and consider how these features would affect human activities such as agriculture, trade, communication, travel, and warfare during the period being discussed.

● Refer often to the maps as you read surrounding text, and go back to study them after you have finished reading. Maps can enhance your understanding of events and places discussed.

WADSWORTH ™   Australia • Canada • Mexico • Singapore • Spain
United Kingdom • United States

THOMSON

✦

WADSWORTH

Publisher: Clark Baxter
Senior Development Editor: Margaret McAndrew Beasley
Senior Assistant Editor: Julie Yardley
Editorial Assistant: Anne Gittinger
Senior Technology Project Manager: Melinda Newfarmer
Executive Marketing Manager: Caroline Croley
Marketing Assistant: Mary Ho
Advertising Project Manager: Brian Chaffee
Project Manager, Editorial Production: Kimberly Adams
Print/Media Buyer: Barbara Britton
Permissions Editor: Joohee Lee
Production Service: Lachina Publishing Services

Text Designer: Norman Baugher
Photo Researcher: Lili Weiner
Musical Consultant: Harvey Cohen
Copy Editor: Ginjer Clarke
Production Specialist: Sona Lachina
Cover Designer: John Walker and Lisa Devenish
Cover Image: Detroit Industry, North Wall, 1932–1933, Diego M. Rivera, Gift of Edsel B. Ford, Photograph © 2001 The Detroit Institute of Arts
Printer: Quebecor World/Versailles
Compositor: Lachina Publishing Services

Printed in the United States of America
1 2 3 4 5 6 7 08 07 06 05 04

Library of Congress Control Number: 2003116388
Student Edition: ISBN 0-534-62730-7
Instructor's Edition: ISBN 0-534-62735-8

Wadsworth/Thomson Learning
10 Davis Drive
Belmont, CA 94002-3098
USA

Asia
Thomson Learning
5 Shenton Way #01-01
UIC Building
Singapore 068808

Australia/New Zealand
Thomson Learning
102 Dodds Street
Southbank, Victoria 3006
Australia

Canada
Nelson
1120 Birchmount Road
Toronto, Ontario M1K 5G4
Canada

Europe/Middle East/Africa
Thomson Learning
High Holborn House
50/51 Bedford Row
London WC1R 4LR
United Kingdom

Latin America
Thomson Learning
Seneca, 53
Colonia Polanco
11560 Mexico D.F.
Mexico

Spain/Portugal
Paraninfo
Calle Magallanes, 25
28015 Madrid, Spain

About the Authors

THE AUTHOR TEAM

From left: Norman Rosenberg, Emily Rosenberg, Paul Johnson, Gary Gerstle, John Murrin, and Jim McPherson.

One of the pleasures of this textbook project, now 15 years old, is the opportunity it has given us to work with each other. Before starting work on a new edition, we all gather for a lengthy period of time to evaluate past editions, discuss reviews that we have solicited from our textbook readers, and brainstorm about ways to improve our book and to make our history more lively, accurate, and up to date. These meetings are always interesting and energizing. After we scatter, the discussions continue through extensive e-mail and phone conversations in which we test and refine the initiatives that we have developed. The volume and richness of this communication over the years have deepened the collective nature of our endeavor and strengthened the quality of the history that we write. We are all proud to be part of the *Liberty, Equality, Power* author team.

JOHN M. MURRIN *Princeton University, Emeritus*
John M. Murrin is a specialist in American colonial and revolutionary history and the early republic. He has edited one multivolume series and five books, including two co-edited collections, *Colonial America: Essays in Politics and Social Development,* Fifth Edition (2001), and *Saints and Revolutionaries: Essays in Early American History* (1984). His own essays on early American history range from ethnic tensions, the early history of trial by jury, the rise of the legal profession, and the political culture of the colonies and the new nation, to the rise of professional baseball and college football in the 19th century. Professor Murrin

served as president of the Society for Historians of the Early American Republic in 1998–99.

PAUL E. JOHNSON *University of South Carolina*
A specialist in early national social and cultural history, Paul E. Johnson is also the author of *Sam Patch, the Famous Jumper* (2003); *A Shopkeeper's Millennium: Society and Revivals in Rochester, New York, 1815–1837,* 25th Anniversary Edition (2004); co-author (with Sean Wilentz) of *The Kingdom of Matthias: Sex and Salvation in 19th-Century America* (1994); and editor of *African-American Christianity: Essays in History* (1994). He has been awarded

the Merle Curti Prize of the Organization of American Historians (1980), the Richard P. McCormack Prize of the New Jersey Historical Association (1989), a John Simon Guggenheim Memorial Fellowship (1995), and the Gilder Lehrman Fellowship (2001).

JAMES M. McPHERSON *Princeton University*
James M. McPherson is a distinguished Civil War historian and was president of the American Historical Association in 2003. He won the 1989 Pulitzer Prize for his book *Battle Cry of Freedom: The Civil War Era.* His other publications include *Marching Toward Freedom: Blacks in the Civil War,* Second Edition (1991); *Ordeal by Fire: The Civil War and Reconstruction,* Third Edition (2001); *Abraham Lincoln and the Second American Revolution* (1991); *For Cause and Comrades: Why Men Fought in the Civil War* (1997), which won the Lincoln Prize in 1998; and *Crossroads of Freedom: Antietam* (2002).

GARY GERSTLE *University of Maryland*
Gary Gerstle—a specialist in labor, immigration, and political history—has published four books: *Working-Class Americanism: The Politics of Labor in a Textile City, 1914–1960* (1989); *The Rise and Fall of the New Deal Order, 1930–1980* (1989); *American Crucible: Race and Nation in the Twentieth Century* (2001), which won the Saloutos Prize in 2001 for the best work in immigration and ethnic history; and *E Pluribus Unum: Immigrants, Civic Culture, and Political Incorporation* (2001). His articles have appeared in the *American Historical Review, Journal of American History, American Quarterly,* and other journals.

His honors include a National Endowment for the Humanities Fellowship for University Teachers and a John Simon Guggenheim Memorial Fellowship.

EMILY S. ROSENBERG *Macalester College*
Emily S. Rosenberg specializes in U.S. foreign relations in the 20th century and is the author of *Spreading the American Dream: American Economic and Cultural Expansion, 1890–1945* (1982); *Financial Missionaries to the World: The Politics and Culture of Dollar Diplomacy* (1999), which won the Ferrell Book Award; and *Pearl Harbor in American Memory* (2004). Her other publications include (with Norman L. Rosenberg) *In Our Times: America Since 1945,* Seventh Edition (2003), and numerous articles dealing with foreign relations in the context of international finance, American culture, and gender ideology. She has served on the board of the Organization of American Historians, on the board of editors of the *Journal of American History,* and as president of the Society for Historians of American Foreign Relations.

NORMAN L. ROSENBERG *Macalester College*
Norman L. Rosenberg specializes in legal history with a particular interest in legal culture and First Amendment issues. His books include *Protecting the "Best Men": An Interpretive History of the Law of Libel* (1990) and (with Emily S. Rosenberg) *In Our Times: America Since 1945,* Seventh Edition (2003). He has published articles in the *Rutgers Law Review, UCLA Law Review, Constitutional Commentary, Law & History Review,* and many other journals and law-related anthologies.

Contents in Brief

Contents in Detail

CHAPTER 3
England Discovers Its Colonies: Empire, Liberty, and Expansion 82

Features

Maps

Americans Abroad

History through Film

Link to the Past

Musical Link to the Past

To the Student: Why Study History?

WHY TAKE A COURSE in American history? This is a question that many college and university students ask. In many respects, students today are like the generations of Americans who have gone before them: optimistic and forward looking, far more eager to imagine where we as a nation might be going than to reflect on where we have been. If anything, this tendency has become more pronounced in recent years, as the Internet revolution has accelerated the pace and excitement of change and made even the recent past seem at best quaint, at worst uninteresting and irrelevant.

But it is precisely in these moments of great change that a sense of the past can be indispensable in terms of guiding our actions in the present and future. We can find, in other periods of American history, moments, like our own, of dizzying technological change and economic growth, rapid alterations in the concentration of wealth and power, and basic changes in patterns of work, residence, and play. How did Americans at those times create, embrace, and resist these changes? In earlier periods of American history, the United States was home, as it is today, to a remarkably diverse array of ethnic and racial groups. How did earlier generations of Americans respond to the cultural conflicts and misunderstandings that often arise from conditions of diversity? How did immigrants perceive their new land? How and when did they integrate themselves into American society? To study how ordinary Americans of the past struggled with these issues is to gain perspective on the opportunities and problems that we face today.

History also provides an important guide to affairs of state. What should the role of America be in world affairs? Should we participate in international bodies such as the United Nations or insist on our ability to act autonomously and without the consent of other nations? What is the proper role of government in economic and social life? Should the government regulate the economy? To what extent should the government enforce morality regarding religion, sexual practices, drinking and drugs, movies, TV, and other forms of mass culture? And what are our responsibilities as citizens to each other and to the nation? Americans of past generations have debated these issues with verve and conviction. Learning about these debates and how they were resolved will enrich our understanding of the policy possibilities for today and tomorrow.

History, finally, is about stories—stories that we all tell about ourselves; our families; our communities; our ethnicity, race, region, and religion; and our nation. They are stories of triumph and tragedy, of engagement and flight, and of high ideals and high comedy. When telling these stories, "American history" is often the furthest thing from our minds. But, often, an implicit sense of history informs what we say about grandparents who immigrated many years ago; the suburb in which we live; the church, synagogue, or mosque that we attend; or the ethnic or racial group to which we belong. But how well do we really understand these individuals, institutions, and groups? Do we tell the right stories about them, ones that capture the complexities of their past? Or have we wittingly or unwittingly simplified, altered, or flattened them? A study of American history first helps us to ask these questions and then to answer them. In the process, we can engage in a fascinating journey of intellectual and personal discovery and situate ourselves more firmly than we had ever thought possible in relation to those who came before us. We can gain firmer self-knowledge and a greater appreciation for the richness of our nation and, indeed, of all humanity.

Preface

W E ARE PLEASED to present the fourth edition of *Liberty, Equality, Power*. Like the first three editions, this one captures the drama and excitement of America's past, from the pre-Columbian era through our own time. It integrates social and cultural history into a political story that is organized around the themes of liberty, equality, and power, and synthesizes the finest older historical scholarship with the best of the new to create a narrative that is balanced, lively, and accessible to a broad range of students.

The *Liberty, Equality, Power* Approach

In this book, we tell many small stories, and one large one: how America transformed itself, in a relatively brief era of world history, from a land inhabited by hunter-gatherer and agricultural Native American societies into the most powerful industrial nation on earth. This story has been told many times before, and those who have told it in the past have usually emphasized the political experiment in liberty and equality that took root here in the 18th century. We, too, stress the extraordinary and transformative impact that the ideals of liberty and equality exerted on American politics, society, and economics during the American Revolution and after.

We show how the creation of a free economic environment—one in which entrepreneurial spirit, technological innovation, and industrial production have flourished—underpinned American industrial might. We have emphasized, too, the successful struggles for freedom that, over the course of the last 225 years, have brought—first to all white men, then to men of color, and finally to women—rights and opportunities that they had not previously known.

But we have also identified a third factor in this pantheon of American ideals—that of power. We examine power in many forms: the accumulation of vast economic fortunes that dominated the economy and politics; the dispossession of American Indians from land that they regarded as theirs; the enslavement of millions of Africans and their African American descendants for a period of almost 250 years; the relegation of women and of racial, ethnic, and religious minorities to subordinate places in American society; and the extension of American control over foreign peoples, such as Latin Americans and Filipinos, who would have preferred to have been free and self-governing. We do not mean to suggest that American power has always been turned to these negative purposes. Subordinate groups have themselves marshaled power to combat oppression, as in the abolitionist and civil-rights crusades, the campaign for woman suffrage, and the labor movement. The state has used its power to moderate poverty and to manage the economy in the interests of general prosperity. And it has used its military power to defeat Nazi Germany, World War II Japan, the Cold War Soviet Union, and other enemies of freedom.

The invocation of power as a variable in American history forces us to widen the lens through which we look at the past and to complicate the stories we tell. Ours has been a history of freedom and domination; of progress toward realizing a broadly democratic polity and of delays and reverses; of abundance and poverty; of wars for freedom and justice and for control of foreign markets. In complicating our master narrative in this way, we think we have rendered American history more exciting and intriguing. Progress has not been automatic, but the product of ongoing struggles.

In this book, we have also tried to capture the diversity of the American past, both in terms of outcomes and in terms of the variety of groups who have participated in America's making. American Indians, in this book, are not presented simply as the victims of European aggression but as a people remarkably diverse in their own ranks, with a variety of systems of social organization and cultural expression. We give equal treatment to the industrial titans of American history—the likes of Andrew Carnegie and John D. Rockefeller—and to those, such as small farmers and poor workers, who resisted the corporate reorganization of economic life. We celebrate the great moments of 1863, when African Americans were freed from slavery, and of 1868, when they were made full citizens of the United States. But we also note how a majority of African Americans had to wait another 100 years, until the civil-rights movement of the 1960s, to gain full access to American freedoms. We tell similarly complex

stories about women, Latinos, and other groups of ethnic Americans.

Political issues, of course, are only part of America's story. Americans have always loved their leisure and have created the world's most vibrant popular culture. They have embraced technological innovations, especially those promising to make their lives easier and more fun. We have, therefore, devoted considerable space to a discussion of American popular culture, from the founding of the first newspapers in the 18th century and the rise of movies, jazz, and the comics in the early 20th century, to the cable television and Internet revolutions in recent years. We have pondered, too, how American industry has periodically altered home and personal life by making new products—such as clothing, cars, refrigerators, and computers—available to consumers.

In such ways, we hope to give our readers a rich portrait of how Americans lived at various points in our history.

New to the Fourth Edition

The third edition won praise for its successful integration of political, cultural, and social history; its thematic unity; its narrative clarity and eloquence; its extraordinary coverage of pre-Columbian America; its extended treatment of the Civil War; its history of economic growth and change; and its excellent map and illustration programs. It also received high marks for its History through Film series, which discusses 31 different films (one per chapter) that treat important aspects of the American past. This very popular feature encourages students to think critically about what they see on screen and allows instructors to stimulate students' historical interest through a medium that they enjoy. The third edition earned plaudits, finally, for the inclusion of chapter outlines and focus questions at the beginning of each chapter and for the decision to move the Chronology boxes to each chapter's fore. We have preserved and enhanced all these strengths of the third edition in the fourth, and are pleased to announce that our History through Film series includes discussions of two new films, *The Gangs of New York* and *High Noon*. In preparing for this revision, we solicited feedback from professors and scholars throughout the country, many of whom have used the third edition of *Liberty, Equality, Power* in their classrooms. Their comments proved most helpful, and many of their suggestions have been incorporated into the fourth edition. For example, in response to reviewer comments, we have added captions to our outstanding map program, so that each map now comes with a brief commentary on how to interpret the geographical

and topographical data it contains. Many of the maps are now animated on the Companion Web Site. We have also updated and condensed Suggested Readings and moved them to each chapter's end. Extensive bibliographic essays for each chapter are still available on the Web site. We have revised our Link to the Past feature so that the text of each focuses more on specific primary sources, offering quotes, commentary, and questions while still linking these sources to online documents, images, or video or sound recordings. We think these improvements in the Links will add to their appeal.

In addition to making these pedagogical changes, we scrutinized each page of the textbook, making sure our prose was clear, the historical issues well presented, and the scholarship up to date. This review, guided by the scholarly feedback we received, caused us to make numerous revisions and additions throughout the textbook. We have also worked hard to bring our story to the present. Because of the changes in the final chapters, we now offer students historical perspective on such important recent events as George W. Bush's election in 2000, the destruction of the World Trade Center towers on September 11, 2001, and the war on terrorism and against Iraq.

Although a list of all the notable substantive changes appears below, we want to highlight one concentrated area of revision—the period from the 1880s through the 1930s, encompassing chapters 18–25. Although reviewers praised the high quality of the political history contained in these pages, some asked us to add more cultural and social history to the narrative mix. We have taken this request seriously, and have introduced more than 5,000 words of social and cultural commentary, much of it focusing on the following topics: the growth of the American middle class in both white and African American communities during the Gilded Age; middle-class patterns of urban living and consumption; the significance of the Philadelphia Centennial Exposition of 1876, the Chicago World's Fair of 1893, and museum exhibitions to late 19th century culture; turn-of-the-century changes in literary culture; the changing circumstances of women; Chinese and Japanese immigration to the United States in the late 19th and early 20th centuries; the decline of feminism in the 1920s; and the effects of the Great Depression on literary, cinematic, and musical culture during the 1930s. So as not to make the chapters in this time period overly long, we have made careful cuts in those chapters' political coverage; the net addition of text is much less than 5,000 words. The result, we believe, is a balanced and integrated political, social, and cultural history of the United States between the Civil War and the Second World War.

New Feature: Americans Abroad

We have also gone beyond our reviewers' suggestions and, in our group meetings to prepare for the fourth edition, committed ourselves to two new features for the textbook. The first, Americans Abroad, appearing in each chapter, focuses on an American who spent a significant portion of his or her life abroad. Some of those profiled carried U.S. political and cultural influence to other countries, while others became conduits through which foreign ideas and influences entered the United States. With our 31 features on both kinds of individuals, we wish to stress the interconnections between American history and world history, and examine the people who forged them. We have chosen a broad range of interesting and important figures—from Pocahontas to Thomas Jefferson, from the explorer Henry Morton Stanley to the anthropologist Margaret Mead, from the American industrialist Francis Cabot Lowell to the African American entertainer Josephine Baker, and from Civil War general Daniel Sickles to Secretary of State Madeleine Albright. We think students will both enjoy learning about these fascinating Americans, their travels, and their influence, and begin to develop, through such knowledge, a sense for the international context in which U.S. history has always unfolded. In the past, Americans (historians among them) have often ignored that context. But, as the events of September 11, 2001, tragically demonstrated, we ignore that context at our peril.

New Feature: Musical Link to the Past

Across their 200 plus years as a people, Americans have produced an extraordinarily rich and varied musical heritage. With the second new feature, Musical Link to the Past, we have embarked on a special effort to make aspects of this musical heritage integral to the history we present to our readers. In 15 features, we examine songs—the lyrics, the music, the performers, the historical context—from the middle of the 18th century to the present. These pieces range from revolutionary era odes to American liberty to 20th century country music laments about women's domestic burdens. Represented in this textbook are pieces by artists as diverse as Stephen Foster and Joni Mitchell, John Philip Sousa and Bob Dylan, Duke Ellington and Grandmaster Flash. All have made important contributions to the history of American music and enriched our musical heritage.

We hope that instructors and students alike will respond enthusiastically to our Musical Links to the Past. To make this feature come alive in classrooms, we have assembled a CD containing the musical selections that we discuss. All instructors who adopt our textbook will, upon request, receive a free copy of this CD, and will, as a result, be able to play the music in their classrooms. For a small fee, students will be able to acquire their own CD copy.

In preparing this feature, we turned to Dr. Harvey Cohen, a cultural historian and music expert who teaches U.S. history at the University of Maryland. Possessing an extraordinary knowledge of the history of American music, and being an accomplished musician in his own right, Harvey was the ideal scholar to guide our choice of songs. He also drafted the texts of the 15 features, and, in the process, labored hard and imaginatively to turn his musical knowledge into history that, we think, will appeal to students. His work has been indispensable to us, and we are deeply grateful to him.

Specific Revisions to Content and Coverage

Chapter 2 New discussions of 1) how New France's Indian alliances drew the colony into the Indian slave trade by the early 18th century; 2) the recovery of the Massachusetts economy from the disastrous slump of 1641; and 3) the Indian slave trade in South Carolina.

Chapter 3 New material on the origins of the Yamasee War of 1715–17 that almost destroyed South Carolina. This chapter also contains new arguments about the contrasting origins and development of racism toward Indians and Africans in the southern colonies.

Chapter 4 New material on the Virginia slave revolt of 1730, the biggest one in the colony's history.

Chapter 18 New material on 1) the Native American perspective on destruction of the buffalo and the resulting effects on traditional Indian lifestyle; 2) how reality of life in the West differed from the myths and romanticized versions of "cowboys and Indians" popularized in fiction and traveling shows such as Buffalo Bill's Wild West show; and 3) how southern whites began to rebuild their way of life in the decades following the end of Reconstruction.

Chapter 19 Major new sections on American middle-class society and culture, the Columbian Exposition of 1893, and the New Woman.

Chapter 20 Major new section on Chinese and Japanese immigrants to the United States.

Chapter 24 Major new section on the decline of feminism in the 1920s; new material on Josh Gibson and the National Negro League.

Chapter 25 Major new section on the culture of the 1930s, covering the work of such artists as Studs Lonigan, Nathaniel West, and the Marx Brothers; new material on Woody Guthrie.

Chapter 27 Material on Eisenhower and on gender and women moved to chapter 28; more emphasis on race and gender in Cold War policies and the relationship of the economy to the Cold War.

Chapter 28 Section on women reorganized and strengthened.

Chapter 30 Reorganized through the removal of material on presidential administrations, which has now been placed in chapter 31.

Chapter 31 Brings American history to 2004, and includes full accounts of the first three years of the Bush administration; September 11, 2001, and its aftermath; and the war on terrorism and in Afghanistan and Iraq.

Supplements

For the Instructor

Instructor's Manual/Test Bank, Vols. I & II The Instructor's Manual portion contains Chapter Outlines, Chronologies, Thematic Topics for Enrichment (critical thinking questions that could be used for classroom discussion or exams), Suggested Essay Topics, Comprehensive Lecture Outlines, and a Teaching Resources section that provides video ideas for lecture enrichment. The Test Bank section includes for each chapter: 50 multiple choice questions, 40 true/false questions, and approximately 10 fill-in-the-blank questions. All three of these question types are classified by type of question, whether they are analytical or factual, and the level of difficulty. Also included in the Test Bank are approximately 10 identification questions per chapter as well as five to seven short essays and two to four long essay questions with answers provided. The IM/TB is also available electronically on the Instructor's Resource CD and the pin-coded text Web site.

Instructor's Resource CD with ExamView (Windows/ Macintosh) Includes the Instructor's Manual, Resource Integration Grid, ExamView® testing, and PowerPoint® slides with lecture outlines and images that can be used as offered, or customized by importing personal lecture slides or other material. ExamView allows you to create, deliver, and customize tests and study guides (both print and online) in minutes with this easy-to-use assessment and tutorial system. It offers both a Quick Test Wizard and an Online Test Wizard that guide you step by step through the process of creating tests, while its "what you see is what you get" capability allows you to see the test you are creating on the screen exactly as it will print or display online. You can build tests of up to 250 questions using up to 12 question types. Using ExamView's complete word processing capabilities, you can enter an unlimited number of new questions or edit existing questions.

New! Musical Links to the Past CD Available free to adopters and for a small fee to students, this CD contains audio recordings of nearly all of the musical selections from the text's new Musical Link to the Past feature.

WebTutor Toolbox on WebCT or Blackboard This online ancillary helps students succeed by taking the course beyond classroom boundaries to a virtual environment rich with study and mastery tools, communication tools, and course content. Professors can use WebTutor to provide virtual office hours, post their syllabi, set up threaded discussions, and track student progress with the quizzing material. For students, WebTutor offers real-time access to a full array of study tools, including flashcards (with audio), practice quizzes and tests, online tutorials, exercises, discussion questions, Web links, and a full glossary. Professors can customize the content in any way they choose, from uploading images and other resources, to adding Web links, to creating their own practice materials.

Transparency Acetates with Commentary for U.S. History Contains more than 150 four-color map images from all of Wadsworth's U.S. History Texts. Packages are three-hole punched and shrink-wrapped. Correlation Guides for specific texts are included.

Wadsworth History Resource Center & *Liberty, Equality, Power* **Companion Web Site**

http://history.wadsworth.com/murrin_LEP4e

Provocative, exciting, and interactive, this site has something for everyone: instructors, students, and U.S. history buffs. Includes a wealth of documents and visuals with related activities, interactive maps (Timeline Maps and Discovery Maps), tutorial quiz questions, hyperlinks, and Internet and InfoTrac® College Edition exercises for each chapter. Also features activities utilizing American Journey Online for each chapter of the text. Each chapter includes Chapter Outlines, Learning Objectives, Glossaries (includ-

ing flashcards with audio), Tutorial Quizzes (20 multiple choice, 5 to 10 fill-in-the-blank or true/false, and 5 essay/ short answers per chapter), Final Exam (incorporates all the quizzes by chapter into one "final" exam), Internet Exercises (centered around the *Liberty, Equality, Power* theme), InfoTrac Exercises, and Web Links.

Online Instructor's Resources include detailed plans and instructions for three Group Projects for classroom use: 1) Re-creating the '60s: Teaching History through Teach-ins; 2) Commemorating the Boston Massacre: Teaching History through Public Memory; and 3) Reconstruction and the Meaning of Freedom: Teaching History through Public Debate. In each of the projects, students examine the choices facing people in a particular era from the various perspectives of the different groups involved in the historical event.

Core Concept Lecture Launcher Videos The Core Concept video package was created exclusively for *Liberty, Equality, Power* by Films for the Humanities. Each video contains eight segments that include introductions by the respective author, concept clues, brief video segments, and concluding questions that take the student from image to text. Video segments are arranged chronologically and relate to topics of importance in the text. The video package is available free to instructors with adoption of the text.

Supplements are available to qualified adopters. Please consult your local sales representative for details.

For the Student

History Interactive: A Study Tool for *Liberty, Equality, Power* This valuable resource for students includes chapter summaries, chapter outlines, identification terms and definitions, fill-in-the-blank and multiple choice quizzes, and extensive bonus materials including source readings, maps, and images. Also included are interactive versions of the text's maps plus Link to the Past and Americans Abroad features; two HistoryNOW modules; and a complete catalog of HistoryNOW interactive modules available for students and correlated chapter by chapter to *Liberty, Equality, Power.*

U.S. History Atlas An invaluable collection of more than 50 clear and colorful historical maps covering all major periods in American history.

Wadsworth History Resource Center & *Liberty, Equality, Power* Companion Web Site

http://history.wadsworth.com/murrin_LEP4e

See description above.

American Journey Online Database

http://ajaccess.wadsworth.com

This text comes with free access to American Journey Online—16 primary source collections that capture the landmark events and major themes of the American experience through words and images from those who lived it. Each key topic in American history and culture addressed by the series encompasses hundreds of carefully selected rare documents, pictures, and archival audio and video, while essays, headnotes, and captions by scholars set the sources in context. Full text searchability and extensive hyperlinking provide fast and easy access and cross referencing. A new module on the Second World War is now available. For more information on how to search the database, please download the free User Guide, which highlights key features of American Journey Online including search tips for each module, exercises, activities, and more.

U.S. History Documents Package The Documents Package, edited by Mark W. Beasley of Hardin-Simmons University, has been expanded to include more than 250 primary source documents interspersed with political cartoons and advertisements. Chapter openers and notes for each selection introduce the documents, provide essential background, and tie in the themes of liberty, equality, and power. Chapter discussion questions ask students to think critically about the ways the documents relate to each other and the text. The two-volume package is available to bundle with the textbook.

WebTutor Toolbox on WebCT or Blackboard See description above.

Acknowledgments

We recognize the contributions of reviewers who read portions of the manuscript in various stages:

William Allison, Weber State University
Angie Anderson, Southeastern Louisiana University
Kenneth G. Anthony, University of North Carolina, Greensboro
Paul R. Beezley, Texas Tech University
David Bernstein, California State University at Long Beach
Michael R. Bradley, Motlow College
Betty Brandon, University of South Alabama
Daniel Patrick Brown, Moorpark College
Ronald G. Brown, College of Southern Maryland
Phil Crow, North Harris College
Lorenzo M. Crowell, Mississippi State University

Amy E. N. Darty, University of Central Florida
Thomas M. Deaton, Dalton State College
Norman C. Delaney, Del Mar College
Ted Delaney, Washington and Lee University
Andrew J. DeRoche, Front Range Community College
Bruce Dierenfield, Canisius College
Brian R. Dirck, Anderson University
Maura Doherty, Illinois State University
R. Blake Dunnavent, Lubbock Christian University
Eileen Eagan, University of Southern Maine
Derek Elliott, Tennessee State University
B. Jane England, North Central Texas College
Van Forsyth, Clark College
Michael P. Gabriel, Kutztown University of Pennsylvania
Gary Gallagher, Pennsylvania State University
Gerald Ghelfi, Santa Ana College
Michael Goldberg, University of Washington, Bothell
David E. Hamilton, University of Kentucky
Michael J. Haridopolos, Brevard Community College
Mark Harvey, North Dakota State University
Mark Huddle, University of Georgia
Samuel C. Hyde, Jr., Southeastern Louisiana University
Thomas N. Ingersoll, Ohio State University
Frank Karpiel, Ramapo College of New Jersey
Michael Kazin, American University
Michael King, Moraine Valley Community College
Michael Krenn, Appalachian State
Frank Lambert, Purdue University
Pat Ledbetter, North Central Texas College
Jan Leone, Middle Tennessee State University
Craig Livingston, Montgomery College
Robert F. Marcom, San Antonio College
Suzanne Marshall, Jacksonville State University
Jimmie McGee, South Plains College
Nora E. McMillan, San Antonio College
Jerry Mills, Midland College
Charlene Mires, Villanova University
Rick Moniz, Chabot College
Michael R. Nichols, Tarrant County College, Northwest
Linda Noel, University of Maryland
Richard B. Partain, Bakersfield College
William Pencak, Penn State University, University Park Campus
Teresa Thomas Perrin, Austin Community College
David Poteet, New River Community College
Jonathan Rees, University of Southern Colorado
Anne Richardson, Texas Christian University
Lelia M. Roeckell, Molloy College
Roy Scott, Mississippi State University
Reynolds J. Scott-Childress, University of Maryland
Katherine A. S. Sibley, St. Joseph's University
Herb Sloan, Barnard College

John Smolenski, University of California, Davis
Jennifer Stollman, University of Mississippi
Siegfried H. Sutterlin, Indian Hills Community College
John Wood Sweet, The Catholic University of America
Xiansheng Tian, Metro State College of Denver
Vincent Vinikas, University of Arkansas, Little Rock
Vernon Volpe, University of Nebraska
Harry L. Watson, The University of North Carolina at Chapel Hill
William Benton Whisenhunt, College of DuPage
Laura Matysek Wood, Tarrant County College, Northwest

We wish to thank the members of the Wadsworth staff who embraced our textbook wholeheartedly when they inherited it from Harcourt and who have expertly guided the production of this fourth edition. Marcus Boggs, vice president and editor-in-chief, made it clear to us from the moment of acquisition that Wadsworth's support for this textbook would be strong. Clark Baxter, publisher, has brought great vision, enthusiasm, and savvy to this project and kept watch on the many different individuals in various locations who had responsibilities to this edition. Caroline Croley, executive marketing manager, has proven to be shrewd and imaginative in her efforts to make the match between our book and teachers of U.S. history a good one. Jennifer Ellis and Melinda Newfarmer, technology project managers, have helped us to glimpse vistas of multimedia use that we did not know existed. Kim Adams, production project manager, has expertly guided this book through the necessary stages from manuscript to finished book, while Ronn Jost, a project editor at Lachina Publishing Services, Inc., has expeditiously handled the complicated and seemingly endless tasks of copyediting, composition, proofreading, and indexing. Finally, a big thanks to all the Wadsworth salesmen and women who, from the moment we first presented our book to them in September 2001, have worked hard and creatively to generate interest in our book among university, college, and high school teachers across America. May this be one of many editions that we produce under the Wadsworth imprint.

We have been fortunate to be able, in this edition, to keep working with two freelancers who have made important contributions to several previous editions. Our photo editor, Lili Weiner, continues to dig up scores of new and interesting photographs and illustrations for us to examine. And our longtime developmental editor, Margaret McAndrew Beasley, has provided indispensable continuity and calm in a complicated time of transition. Margaret's editing skills, organizational expertise, good sense, and belief in this book and its authors keep us going.

In addition, each of us would like to offer particular thanks to those historians, friends, and family members who helped to bring this project to a successful conclusion.

JOHN M. MURRIN Mary R. Murrin has read each chapter, offered numerous suggestions, and provided the kind of moral and personal support without which this project would never have been completed. James Axtell and Gregory Evans Dowd saved me from many mistakes about Indians. John E. Selby and the late Eugene R. Sheridan were particularly helpful on what are now chapters 5 and 6. At an early phase, William J. Jackson and Lorraine E. Williams offered some very useful suggestions. Fred Anderson and Virginia DeJohns Anderson offered many acute suggestions for improvement. I am deeply grateful for their advice. Several colleagues and graduate students also have contributed in various ways, especially Stephen Aron, Ignacio Gallup-Diaz, Evan P. Haefeli, Geoffrey Plank, Nathaniel J. Sheidley, Jeremy Stern, and Beth Lewis Pardse.

PAUL E. JOHNSON My greatest debt is to the community of scholars who write about the United States between the Revolution and the Civil War. Closer to home, I owe thanks to the other writers of this book—particularly to John Murrin. The Department of History at the University of South Carolina provided time to work, while my wife, Kasey Grier, and a stray dog we named Lucy provided the right kinds of interruptions.

JAMES M. McPHERSON My family provided an environment of affection and stability that contributed immeasurably to the writing of my chapters, while undergraduate students at Princeton University who have taken my courses over the years provided feedback, questions, and insights that helped me to understand what students know and don't know, and what they need to know.

GARY GERSTLE When first drafting my parts of this textbook, I benefited enormously from the input of Roy Rosenzweig and Tom Knock, who gave each of my chapters an exceptionally thorough, thoughtful, and insightful critique. Kathleen Trainor was a gifted research assistant: She researched subjects I knew too little about, contributed to the design of charts and maps, checked facts, and solved countless thorny problems. To all these tasks she brought imagination, efficiency, and good cheer. Jerald Podair helped me to compile chapter bibliographies, offered me excellent ideas for maps and tables, and, on numerous occasions (and at all hours of the day and night), allowed me to draw on his encyclopedic knowledge of American history.

Reynolds Scott-Childress wrote the initial drafts for the new sections on cultural and social history in chapters 18 and 19 (and for the latter's Americans Abroad feature), while Linda Noel helped to research and write the Americans Abroad features for chapters 20–25. Kelly Ryan helped me to assemble the Link to the Past features, while Robert Chase worked to streamline and update the bibliographies. Marcy Wilson helped me out in a pinch with some quick and careful proofreading. All of the last five individuals acknowledged are either recent Ph.D.s at the University or Maryland or soon will finish their degrees there. Four of them have taught for me in my U.S. history survey at Maryland and have used *Liberty, Equality, Power* in their sections. They know the book well (too well, some of them would say!), and the feedback they have given me over the years has helped to guide revisions. I thank them for their many contributions to this book. Finally, I thank my fellow authors for their intelligence, wit, and deep commitment to this project. By the time this book comes out, we will have been a team for 15 years. It has been an interesting, challenging, and satisfying journey.

EMILY AND NORMAN ROSENBERG We would like to thank our children—Sarah, Molly, Ruth, and Joe, who provided expert assistance on our charts. Students at Macalester College also deserve thanks, especially Sonya Michlin, Lorenzo Nencioli, Katie Kelley, Justin Brandt, Jessica Ford, and Mariah Howe. Paul Solon, a colleague at Macalester, provided his expertise in commenting on the maps. Anthony Todd, our research assistant at Macalester, made many important contributions to the fourth edition. We also want to acknowledge all of the people who offered their responses to the previous editions, including the historians who adopted the book and the students, especially those at San Diego State University, who read and evaluated it. Gary Gerstle, our collaborator, the late Richard Steele, a colleague at San Diego State, and Bruce Dierenfield provided wonderfully critical readings, and this edition is much better for their assistance.

Finally, no project of this scope is completely error free. We welcome all corrections and suggestions for improvement. Please send comments to:

Clark Baxter, Publisher
Wadsworth-Thomson
27R West Street #8
Beverly Farms, MA 01915

John M. Murrin, Paul E. Johnson, James M. McPherson, Gary Gerstle, Emily S. Rosenberg, Norman L. Rosenberg

LIBERTY

EQUALITY

POWER

Chapter 1

When Old Worlds Collide: Contact, Conquest, Catastrophe

HISTORY ON CANVAS

Cortés Scuttles Ship (left), by O. Graeff, circa 1805. Nezahualcoyotzin (right), ruler of Texcoco from approximately 1431 to 1472, painted in battle array by a late 16th- or early 17th-century Mexican Indian who had mastered European artistic techniques.

CHAPTER OUTLINE

Whc Christopher Columbus crossed the Atlantic, he did not know where he was going, and he died without realizing where he had been. Yet he changed history forever. In the 40 years after 1492, European navigators mastered the oceans of the world, joining together societies that had lived in isolation for thousands of years. European invaders conquered the Americas, not just with sails, gunpowder, and steel, but also with their plants and livestock and, most of all, their diseases. They brought staple crops and slavery with them as well. By 1600, they had created the first global economy in the history of humankind and had inflicted upon the native peoples of the Americas—unintentionally, for the most part—the greatest known catastrophe that human societies have ever experienced.

In the 15th century, when all of this started, the Americas were in some ways a more ancient world than Western Europe. For example, the Portuguese, Spanish, French, and English languages were only beginning to assume their modern forms during the century or two before and after Columbus's voyage. Centuries earlier, when Rome was falling into ruins and Paris and London were little more than hamlets, huge cities were thriving in the Andes and Mesoamerica (the area embracing Central America and southern and central Mexico). Which world was old and which was new is a matter of perspective. Each already had its own distinctive past.

CHAPTER FOCUS

♦ What enabled relatively backward European societies to establish dominance over the oceans of the world?

♦ Why were the native peoples of the Americas extremely vulnerable to European diseases, instead of the other way around?

♦ Why did Western Europe, a free-labor society, generate systems of unfree labor overseas?

♦ What was the Columbian Exchange, and how important has it been?

Peoples in Motion

Like all other countries of North and South America, the United States is a nation of immigrants. Even the native peoples were once migrants who roamed their way through a strange new land.

Long before Europeans discovered and explored the wide world around them, many different peoples had migrated thousands of miles over thousands of years across oceans and continents. Before Columbus sailed west from Spain in 1492, five distinct waves of immigrants had already swept over the Americas. Three came from Asia. The fourth, from the Pacific Islands, or Oceania, may have just brushed America. The last, from northern Europe, decided not to stay.

From Beringia to the Americas

Before the most recent Ice Age ended about 12,000 years ago, glaciers covered huge portions of the Americas, Europe, and Asia. The ice captured so much of the world's water that sea level fell drastically and created a land bridge 600 miles wide across the Bering Strait between Siberia and Alaska. For more than 10,000 years after 23,000 B.C., this exposed area—geographers call it Beringia—was dry land on which plants, animals, and humans could live. Starting about 14,000 years ago, people drifted in small bands from Asia to North America. No doubt many generations lived on Beringia, although the harsh environment of this land on the edge of the Arctic Circle would have required unusual skills just to survive. These first humans to reach the Americas hunted animals for meat and furs and probably built small fishing vessels that could weather the Arctic storms. Faced with impassable glaciers to the north and east, they made snug homes to keep themselves warm through the fierce winters. Their numbers were, in all likelihood, quite small.

By 12,000 B.C., humans definitely were living in eastern Siberia, western Alaska, and Beringia. (Because Berin-

CHRONOLOGY

12,000 B.C. Migration to the Americas begins

9000 B.C. Shenandoah Valley occupied

9000–7000 B.C. Most large American mammals become extinct

5000–700 B.C. Cultures of the Red Paint People and the Louisiana mound builders thrive

1600 B.C. Polynesian migrations begin (reaching Hawaii by A.D. 100)

500 B.C.–A.D. 400 Adena-Hopewell mound builders emerge in Ohio River valley

874 Norsemen reach Iceland

900–1250 Toltecs dominate the Valley of Mexico • Cahokia becomes largest Mississippian mound builders' city • Anasazi culture thrives in American Southwest

982 Norse settle Greenland

1001–14 Norse found Vinland on Newfoundland

1400s Incas begin to dominate the Andes; Aztecs begin to dominate Mesoamerica (1400–50) • Cheng Ho makes voyages of exploration for China (1405–34) • Portuguese begin to master the Atlantic coast of Africa (1434) • First Portuguese slave factory established on African coast (1448) • Dias reaches Cape of Good Hope (1487) • Columbus reaches the Caribbean (1492) • Treaty of Tordesillas divides non-Christian world between Portugal and Spain (1494) • da Gama rounds Cape of Good Hope and reaches India (1497–99)

1500s Portuguese discover Brazil (1500) • Balboa crosses Isthmus of Panama to the Pacific (1513) • Magellan's fleet circumnavigates the globe; Cortés conquers the Aztec empire (1519–22) • de Vaca makes overland journey from Florida to Mexico (1528–36) • Pizarro conquers the Inca empire (1531–32) • de Soto's expedition explores the American Southeast (1539–43) • Coronado's expedition explores the American Southwest (1540–42) • Jesuit mission established at Chesapeake Bay (1570–71) • Philip II issues Royal Order for New Discoveries (1573) • Philip II unites Spanish and Portuguese empires (1580)

gia is once again under water, it cannot be easily studied, although fossils of mammoths have been found on the ocean floor.) As the glaciers receded for the last time, these people spread throughout the Americas. By 8000 B.C., they had reached all the way to Tierra del Fuego off the southern tip of South America. Near the eastern coast of North America, the Thunderbird dig in Virginia's Shenandoah Valley shows signs of continuous human occupation from before 9000 B.C. until the arrival of Europeans.

These Asians probably came in three waves. Those in the first wave spread over most of the two continents and spoke "Amerind," the forerunner of most American

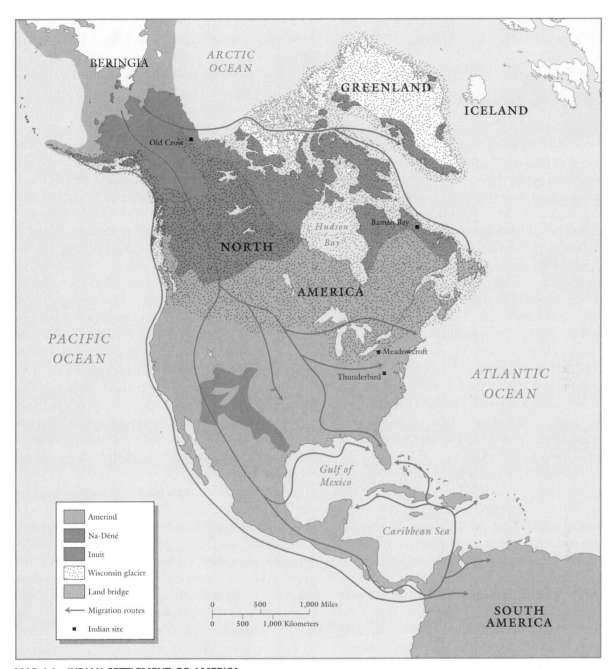

MAP 1.1 INDIAN SETTLEMENT OF AMERICA
The probable routes that people followed after they left Beringia and spread throughout the Americas.

Indian languages on both continents. The Algonquian, Iroquoian, Muskogean, Siouan, Nahuatl (Aztec), Mayan, and all South American tongues derive from this source. Those in the middle wave, which came a few thousand years later, spoke what linguists call "Na-Déné," which eventually gave rise to the various Athapaskan languages of the Canadian Northwest as well as the Apache, Navajo, and related tongues in the American Southwest. The last to arrive, the ancestors of the Inuits (called Eskimos by other Indians), crossed after 7000 B.C., when Beringia was again under

water. About 4,000 years ago, these people began to migrate from the Aleutian Islands and Alaska to roughly their present sites in the Americas. Unlike their predecessors, they found the Arctic environment to their liking and migrated across the northern rim of North America and then across the North Atlantic to Greenland, where they encountered the first Europeans migrating westward—the Norsemen. Somehow, the Inuits maintained at least limited contact with one another across 6,000 miles of bleak Arctic tundra. The Thule, or final pre-Columbian phase of

Inuit culture, lasted from A.D. 1000 to 1700 and sustained similar folkways from Siberia to Greenland.

The Great Extinction and the Rise of Agriculture

As the glaciers receded and the climate warmed, the people who had wandered south and east found an attractive environment teeming with game. Imperial mammoths, huge mastodons, woolly rhinoceroses, a species of enormous bison, and giant ground sloths roamed the plains and forests, along with camels and herds of small horses. These animals had thrived in a frigid climate, but they had trouble adjusting to hot weather. They also had no instinctive fear of the two-legged intruders, who became ever more skillful at hunting them. A superior spear point, the Clovis tip, appeared in the area of present-day New Mexico and Texas some time before 9000 B.C., and within a thousand years its use had spread throughout North and South America. As it spread, the big game died off along with horses, which were small and valued only as food. Overhunting cannot explain the entire extinction, but it was a major factor, along with climatic change. Mammoths, for example, survived until 2000 B.C. on uninhabited Wrangell Island near Alaska. Most large animals of the Americas disappeared about 9,000 years ago.

Their passing left the hemisphere with a severely depleted number of animal species. Nothing as big as the elephant survived. The largest beasts left were bears, bison, and moose; the biggest cat was the jaguar. The human population had multiplied and spread with ease so long as the giant species lasted. Their extinction probably led to a sharp decline in population as people scrambled for new sources of food. Some Indians raised guinea pigs, turkeys, or ducks, but apart from dogs on both continents, they domesticated no large animals except in South America, where they used llamas to haul light loads in mountainous terrain and raised alpacas for their wool. In Eurasia, with its numerous domesticated animals, the killer diseases such as smallpox and bubonic plague took hold first among domestic animals and then spread among humans. Disease by disease, the survivors developed immunities over a long period of time. No comparable process occurred in the Americas, where few animals were domesticated.

One North American culture, adapting to the new demands of a world with few large animals, displayed an energy that archaeologists are only now beginning to recognize. About 5000 B.C., along the northeast coast, a gifted maritime people emerged who ventured onto the Atlantic to catch swordfish and, probably, whales. They carried on a vigorous trade from Labrador to Maine and perhaps as far south as New Jersey, spanning a coastline of more than 1,500 miles. They are sometimes called the Red Paint People (a more technical term is Maritime Archaic) because of their use of red ocher in funeral ceremonies. Their burial mounds are the oldest yet found in America. They lived in multiroom houses up to 100 yards long. Most remarkable of all, the motifs on their religious monuments—mounds and stone markers—resemble others found in Brittany and Norway, but the American monuments are several hundred years older than the most ancient ones yet found in Europe. It is barely possible that these North American seafarers followed the Gulf Stream across the Atlantic to Europe thousands of years before Europeans voyaged to America. This culture collapsed 4,000 years ago. No one knows why.

Some native peoples settled down without becoming farmers. Those in the Pacific Northwest developed complex art forms that fascinate modern collectors and sustained themselves through fishing, hunting, and the gathering of nuts, berries, and other edible plants. Men fished and hunted; women gathered. California peoples sustained some of the densest populations north of Mexico by collecting acorns and processing them into meal, which they baked into cakes. In the rain forests of Brazil, in south and central Florida, and in the cold woodlands of northern New England, hunter-gatherers also got along without becoming farmers.

Most North Americans could not depend solely on hunting and gathering food, however. In a few places, some of them, probably women, began to plant and harvest crops instead of simply gathering and eating what they found. In Asia and Africa, this practice was closely linked to the domestication of animals and happened quickly enough to be called the Neolithic (new or late Stone Age) revolution. But in the Americas the rise of farming had little to do with animals, occurred gradually, and might better be termed the Neolithic *evolution*. For the first 3,500 years, farming supplemented a diet that still depended mostly on fishing and hunting, although now of smaller animals. Somewhere between 4000 and 1500 B.C., permanent farm villages began to dominate parts of Peru, south-central Mexico, northeast Mexico, and the southwestern United States. Their crops were different from those of Europe, the Middle East, or East Asia. The first American farmers grew amaranth (a cereal), manioc (familiar to modern Americans as tapioca), chili peppers, pumpkins, sweet potatoes, several varieties of beans, and, above all, maize, or Indian corn, which slowly became a staple throughout most of the Americas. Indians also raised white potatoes and tomatoes. The spread of these crops launched another population surge that was great enough to support cities in some areas.

The Polynesians and Hawaii

Asians migrating across Beringia were not the only people on the move. Polynesians sailed out from Southeast Asia into the Pacific about 1600 B.C., and during the next 2,000 years, they settled hundreds of islands scattered across more than 30 million square miles of ocean. Their ability to carry families and plants safely across thousands of miles of open sea in what were essentially large dugout canoes with sails and attached outriggers was the greatest maritime feat of the era. Nearly all of their settlements were on tropical islands. By the first century A.D., Fiji had become a kind of cultural and linguistic center, and the Polynesians had reached as far as Hawaii, nearly 2,500 miles to the northeast. By A.D. 300, they had colonized Easter Island, more than 4,000 miles to the east and only 2,000 miles off the coast of South America. Before A.D. 1000, they had also settled New Zealand, far to the south of Fiji. Hawaii's population, organized into stratified societies and multiple chiefdoms, would grow to 800,000 before the first Europeans arrived in the 1770s.

Did Polynesians ever reach the American mainland in prehistoric times? It seems hard to believe that such daring mariners would not have sailed on beyond Hawaii and Easter Island. And yet, if some of them did reach the Americas, they left no discernible influence on the Indian societies already there. Someone—either an Indian or a Polynesian—must have brought the sweet potato from South America to Easter Island. Yet the culture of Easter Island was Polynesian, whereas those of South America remained thoroughly Indian.

The Norsemen

About the time that Polynesians were settling Easter Island, Europeans also began trekking long distances. Pushed by fierce invaders from central Asia, various Germanic tribes overran the western provinces of the Roman Empire. The Norse, a Germanic people who had occupied Scandinavia, were among the most innovative of these invaders. For centuries their Viking warriors raided the coasts of the British Isles and France. Their sleek longboats, propelled by both sails and oars, enabled them to challenge the contrary currents of the north Atlantic. Some of them began to gaze westward across the ocean.

Beginning in A.D. 874, Vikings occupied Iceland. In 982 and 983, Erik the Red, who had been accused of manslaughter in Norway and outlawed for committing more mayhem in Iceland, led his Norse followers farther west to Greenland. There the Norse made Europe's first contact with Inuits and established permanent settlements.

Leif, Erik's son, sailed west from Greenland in 1001 and began to explore the coast of North America. He made three more voyages, the last in 1014, and started a colony that he called "Vinland" on the northern coast of Newfoundland at a place now named L'Anse aux Meadows. The local Indians (called "Skrellings" by the Norse, which means "barbarians" or "weaklings") resisted vigorously. In one engagement, just as the Norse were about to be routed, Freydis, the bastard daughter of old Erik, and the first European woman known to North American history, saved the day by baring her breasts, slapping them with a sword, and screaming ferociously. Awed, the Skrellings fled. Nevertheless, the Norse soon quarreled among themselves and destroyed the colony. During the 1014 voyage, Freydis and her husband murdered her brother and seized his ship. When Leif found out, he cursed Freydis's offspring, who, Norse poets assure us, never amounted to anything after that. The Norse abandoned Vinland, but they continued to visit North America for another century, probably to get wood. A 12th-century Norse coin, recovered from an Indian site in Maine, gives proof of their continuing contact with North America.

About 500 years after Erik the Red's settlement, the Norse also lost Greenland. There, not long before Columbus sailed in 1492, the last Norse settler died a lonely death. In the chaos that followed the Black Death in Europe and Greenland after 1350, the colony had suffered a severe population decline, gradually lost regular contact with the homeland, and slowly withered away. Despite their spectacular exploits, the Norse had no impact on the later course of American history. They had reached a dead end.

◉ Europe and the World in the 15th Century

Nobody in the year 1400 could have foreseen the course of European expansion that was about to begin. Europe stood at the edge, not the center, of world commerce. It desired much that others possessed but made little that those others wished to have.

China: The Rejection of Overseas Expansion

By just about every standard, China under the Ming dynasty was the world's most complex culture. In the 15th century, the government of China, staffed by well-educated bureaucrats, ruled 100 million people, a total half again as large as the combined populations of all European states west of Russia. The Chinese had invented

the compass, gunpowder, and early forms of printing and paper money. Foreigners coveted the silks, teas, and other fine products available in China, but they had little to offer in exchange. Most of what Europe knew about China came from *The Travels of Marco Polo*, written by a merchant from the Italian city-state of Venice who at age 17 journeyed overland with his father and uncle to the Chinese court, which he reached in 1271, and then served the emperor, Kublai Khan, for the next 20 years. This "Great Khan is the mightiest man, whether in respect of subjects or of territory or of treasure, who is in the world today or who ever has been, from Adam our first parent down to the present moment," Marco assured Europe. The Khan's capital city (today's Beijing) was the world's largest and grandest, Marco insisted, and received 1,000 cartloads of silk a day. In brief, China outshone Europe and all other cultures.

The Chinese agreed. Between 1405 and 1434, a royal eunuch, Cheng Ho, led six large fleets from China to the East Indies and the coast of East Africa, trading and exploring along the way. His biggest ships, 400 feet long, displaced 1,500 tons and were certainly large enough to sail around the southern tip of Africa and "discover" Europe. Had China thrown its resources and talents into overseas expansion, the subsequent history of the world would have been vastly different, but most of what the Chinese learned about the outside world merely confirmed their belief that other cultures had little to offer their Celestial Kingdom. No one followed Cheng Ho's lead after he died. Instead, the emperor banned the construction of ocean-going ships and later forbade anyone to own a vessel with more than two masts. China, a self-contained economic and political system, turned inward. It did not need the rest of the world.

Europe versus Islam

Western Europe was a rather backward place in 1400. Compared with China or the Islamic world, it suffered severe disadvantages. Its location on the Atlantic rim of the Eurasian continent had always made access to Asian trade difficult and costly. Islamic societies controlled overland trade with Asia and the only known seaborne route to Asia through the Persian Gulf. As of 1400, Arab mariners were the world's best.

Europeans desired the fine silks of China. They also coveted East Indian spices to enliven their food and help preserve it through the long winters. But because Europeans produced little that Asians wished to buy, they had to pay for these imports with silver or gold, both of which were scarce.

In fact, while Europe's sphere of influence was shrinking and while China seemed content with what it already had, Islamic states were well embarked on another great phase of expansion. Europe's mounted knights in heavy armor failed to stop the Ottoman Turks, who took Constantinople in 1453, overran the Balkans by the 1520s, and even threatened Vienna. The Safavid Empire in Iran (Persia) rose to new splendor at the same time. Other Moslems carried the Koran to Indonesia and northern India, where their powerful Mogul empire formed the basis for the modern states of Pakistan and Bangladesh.

Yet Europe had certain advantages, too. The European economy had made impressive gains in the Middle Ages, primarily because of agricultural advances, such as improved plows, that also fostered population growth. By 1300, more than 100 million people were living in Europe. Europe's farms could not sustain further growth, however. Lean years and famines ensued, leaving people undernourished. In the late 1340s, the Black Death (bubonic plague) reduced the population by more than one-third. Recurring bouts of plague kept population low until about 1500, when vigorous growth resumed. But during the long decline of the 15th century, overworked soil regained its fertility, and per capita income rose considerably among people who now had stronger immunities to disease.

By then, European metallurgy and architecture were quite advanced. The Renaissance, which revived interest in the literature of ancient Greece and Rome, also gave a new impetus to European culture, especially after Johannes Gutenberg invented the printing press and movable type in the 1430s. Soon information began to circulate more rapidly in Europe than anywhere else in the world. This revolution in communications permitted improvements in ship design and navigational techniques to build on each other and become a self-reinforcing process. The Arabs, by contrast, had borrowed block printing from China in the 10th century, only to give it up by 1400.

Unlike China, none of Europe's kingdoms was a self-contained economy. All had to trade with one another and with the non-Christian world. Although in 1400 this need was a drawback, between the 15th and 17th centuries it slowly became an asset. No single state had a monopoly on the manufacture of firearms or on the flow of capital, and European societies began to compete with one another in gaining access to these resources and in mastering new maritime and military techniques. European armies were far more formidable in 1520 than they had been in 1453, and by then European fleets could outsail and outfight all rivals.

The Legacy of the Crusades

Quite apart from the Norse explorers, Europe had a heritage of expansion that derived from the efforts of the crusaders to conquer the Holy Land from Islam. Crusaders

had established their own Kingdom of Jerusalem, which survived for more than a century but was finally retaken in 1244. Thereafter, while a new wave of Islamic expansion seemed about to engulf much of the world, Christian Europe gained only a few Mediterranean and Atlantic islands before 1492 but learned some important lessons in the process. To make Palestine profitable, the crusaders had taken over sugar plantations already there and had worked them with a combination of free and slave labor. After they were driven from the Holy Land, they retreated to the Mediterranean islands of Cyprus, Malta, Crete, and Rhodes, where they used slaves to grow sugar cane or grapes.

Long before Columbus, these planters had created the economic components of overseas expansion. They assumed that colonies should produce a staple crop, at least partly through slave labor, for sale in Europe. The first slaves were Moslem captives. In the 14th and 15th centuries, planters turned to pagan Slavs (hence the word *slave*) from the Black Sea area and the Adriatic. Some black Africans were also acquired from Arab merchants who controlled the caravan trade across the Sahara Desert, but these early plantations never exploited their laborers with the intensity that would later become routine in the Americas.

The Unlikely Pioneer: Portugal

It seemed highly improbable in 1400 that Europe was standing on the threshold of a dramatic expansion. That Portugal would lead the way seemed even less likely. Portugal, a small kingdom of fewer than a million people, had been united for less than a century. Lisbon, with 40,000 people, was the only city of any size. Portugal's maritime traditions lagged well behind those of the Italian states, France, and England. Its merchant class was tiny, and it had little capital.

Yet Portugal had some advantages. It enjoyed internal peace and an efficient government at a time when its neighbors were beset by war and internal upheaval. Moreover, Portugal's location at the intersection of the Mediterranean and Atlantic worlds prompted its mariners to ask how they could transform the Atlantic from a barrier into a highway.

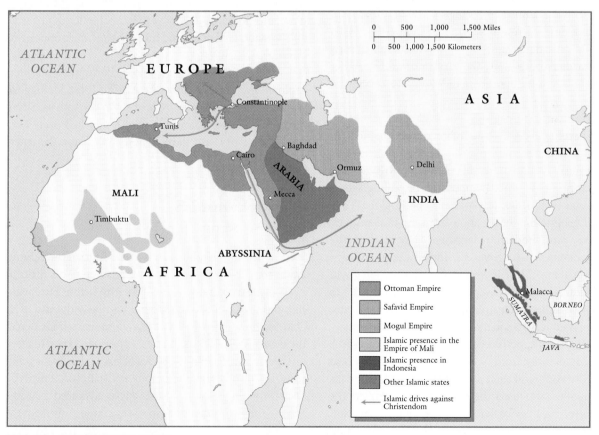

MAP 1.2 EXPANSION OF ISLAM

While Europeans were beginning to move overseas, Islam was also expanding into southeastern Europe, various parts of Africa, the Indian subcontinent, and the East Indies.

At first, they were interested in short-term gains, rather than in some all-water route to Asia. The Portuguese knew that Arab caravans crossed the Sahara to bring gold, slaves, and ivory from black Africa to Europe. Arab traders spoke of how King (or *Mansa*) Musa (d. 1332) of the Mandingo empire of Mali controlled more gold than any other ruler in the world and of how he could field an army of 100,000 men. These reports reached Europe, where Musa was described as "the richest and most noble lord of all this region on account of the abundance of gold which is gathered in his kingdom." The Portuguese believed that an Atlantic voyage to coastal points south of the Sahara would undercut Arab traders and bring large profits. The greatest problem they faced in this quest was Cape Bojador, with its treacherous shallows, awesome waves, and strong northerly winds. Several bold captains had sailed around the cape, but none had returned.

A member of the Portuguese royal family, Prince Henry, challenged this barrier. In 1420, he became head of the crusading Order of Christ and used its revenues to sponsor 15 voyages along the African coast. In 1434, one of his captains, Gil Eannes, finally succeeded. After passing the cape and exploring the coastline, Eannes sailed west into the Atlantic beyond the sight of land until he met favorable winds and currents that carried him back to Europe. Having launched Portugal's era of expansion, Henry soon lost interest in it. While he indulged in costly and futile crusades against Morocco, less exalted men pushed farther south along the African coast. Only after they made it beyond the Sahara did their efforts begin to pay off.

During the 15th century, Portugal vaulted past all rivals in two major areas—the ability to navigate the high seas beyond sight of land, and the capacity to defeat any non-European fleet on the world's oceans. Portuguese (and later Spanish) navigators mapped the prevailing winds and currents on the high seas over most of the globe. They collected geographic information from classical sources, foreigners, and modern navigators. They studied the superior designs of Arab vessels, copied them, and improved on them. They increased the ratio of length to beam (width at the broadest point of the hull) from 2:1 to 3:1, borrowed the lateen (triangular) sail from the Arabs, and combined it with square rigging in the right proportion to produce a superb oceangoing vessel, the caravel. A caravel could make from 3 to 12 knots and could beat closer to a head wind than any other sailing ship. Portuguese captains also used the compass and adopted the Arabs' astrolabe, a device that permits accurate calculation of latitude, or distances north and south. (The calculation of longitude—distances east and west—is much more

THE CARAVEL: A SWIFT OCEANGOING VESSEL
This caravel is a modern reconstruction of the 15th-century *Niña,* which crossed the Atlantic with Columbus in 1492.

difficult and was not mastered until the 18th century.) As they skirted the African coast, these Portuguese sailors made precise charts and maps that later mariners could follow.

The Portuguese also learned how to mount heavy cannon on the decks of their ships—a formidable advantage in an age when others fought naval battles by grappling and boarding enemy vessels. Portuguese ships were able to stand farther off and literally blow their opponents out of the water.

As the 15th century advanced, Portuguese mariners explored ever farther along the African coast, looking for wealth and eventually a direct, cheap route to Asia. South of the Sahara they found the wealth they had been seeking—gold, ivory, and slaves. These riches kept the enterprise alive.

Africa, Colonies, and the Slave Trade

West Africa was inhabited by a mostly agricultural population that also included skilled craftsmen. West Africans probably learned how to use iron long before Europeans did, and they had been supplying Europe with most of its gold for hundreds of years through indirect trade across the desert. West Africa's political history had been marked by the rise and decline of a series of large inland states. The most recent of these, the empire of Mali, was already in decline by 1450. As the Portuguese advanced past the Sahara, their commerce began to pull trade away from the desert caravans, which further weakened Mali and other interior states. By 1550, the empire had fallen apart.

The Portuguese also founded offshore colonies along the way. They began to settle the uninhabited Madeira Islands in 1418, took possession of the Azores between 1427 and 1450, occupied the Cape Verde group in the 1450s, and took over São Tomé in 1470. Like exploration, colonization also turned a profit. Lacking investment capital and experience in overseas settlement, the Portuguese drew on Italian merchants for both. In this way, the plantation complex of staple crops and slavery migrated from the Mediterranean to the Atlantic. Beginning in the 1440s, Portuguese island planters produced sugar or wine, increasingly with slave labor imported from nearby Africa. Some plantations, particularly on São Tomé, kept several hundred slaves at work growing and processing sugar.

At first, the Portuguese acquired their slaves by landing on the African coast, attacking agricultural villages, and carrying off everyone they could catch, but these raids enraged coastal peoples and made other forms of trade more difficult. In the decades after 1450, the slave trade assumed its classic form. The Portuguese established small posts, or "factories," along the coast or, ideally, on small offshore islands, such as Arguin Island near Cape Blanco, where they built their first African fort in 1448. Operating out of these bases, traders would buy slaves from the local rulers, who usually acquired them by waging war. During the long history of

© Genevieve Leaper; Ecoscene/Corbis.

MADEIRA

This modern photograph of Madeira conveys something of what the Portuguese saw when they first visited the island in the early 15th century— an uninhabited, mountainous, and heavily forested landscape.

the Atlantic slave trade, nearly every African shipped overseas had first been enslaved by other Africans.

Slavery had long existed in Africa, but in a form less brutal than that which the Europeans would impose. When the Atlantic slave trade began, no African middleman could have foreseen how the enslavement of Africans by Europeans would differ from the enslavement of Africans by Africans. These differences were crucial. In Africa, slaves were not forced to toil endlessly to produce staple crops, and their descendants often became fully assimilated into the captors' society. Slaves were not isolated as a separate caste. By the time African middlemen learned about the cruel conditions of slavery under European rule, the trade had become too lucrative to stop, although several African societies tried. They discovered, however, that those who refused to participate in the trade were likely to become its victims. When the rulers of the Kongo embraced Catholicism in the 16th century, they protested against the Atlantic slave trade, only to see their own people become vulnerable to enslavement by others. The non-Christian kingdom of Benin learned the same lesson.

The Portuguese made the slave trade profitable by exploiting rivalries among the more than 200 small states of West and Central Africa. This part of Africa was divided into more language groups and small states than Europeans would find anywhere else in the world. Despite many cultural similarities among these groups, West Africans had never thought of themselves as a single people. Nor did they share a universal religion that might have restrained them from selling other Africans into slavery.

© Werner Forman/Art Resource, NY.

THE PORTUGUESE SLAVE-TRADING FORTRESS OF ELMINA

Located on the Gold Coast of West Africa, the fortress was built in 1481.

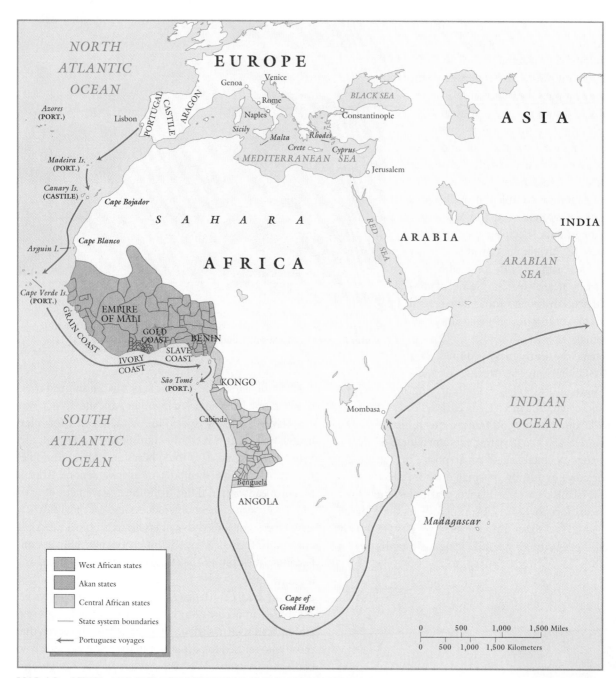

MAP 1.3 AFRICA AND THE MEDITERRANEAN IN THE 15TH CENTURY

The Mediterranean islands held by Europeans in the late Middle Ages, the Atlantic islands colonized by Portugal and Spain in the 15th century, the part of West Africa from Cape Blanco to Angola that provided the main suppliers of the Atlantic slave trade, and the Portuguese all-water route to India after 1497.

 View an animated version of this map or related maps at **http://history.wadsworth.com/murrin_LEP4e**.

Moslems believed it sinful to enslave a fellow believer. Western Europeans, although they were quite capable of waging destructive wars against one another, strongly believed that enslaving fellow Christians was immoral. Enslaving pagan or Moslem Africans was another matter. Some Europeans even persuaded themselves that they were doing Africans a favor by buying them and making their souls eligible for salvation.

Portugal's Asian Empire

Portuguese exploration continued, paying for itself through gold, ivory, and slaves. In the 1480s, the government decided to support the quest for an all-water route to Asia. In 1487, Bartolomeu Dias reached the Cape of Good Hope at the southern tip of Africa and headed east toward the Indian Ocean, but his crew rebelled in those

stormy waters, and he turned back. Ten years later, Vasco da Gama led a small fleet around the Cape of Good Hope and sailed on to the Malibar Coast of southwestern India. In a voyage that lasted more than two years (1497–99), da Gama bargained and fought for spices that yielded a 20-to-1 profit for his investors.

Da Gama opened the way for Portugal's empire in the East. To secure their Asian trade, the Portuguese established a chain of naval bases that extended from East Africa to the mouth of the Persian Gulf, then to Goa on the west coast of India, and from there to the Moluccas, or East Indies. Portuguese missionaries even penetrated Japan. The Moluccas became the Asian center of the Portuguese seaborne empire, with their spices yielding most of the wealth that Portugal extracted from its eastern holdings. As early as 1515, African and Asian trade was providing two-thirds of Portugal's state revenues.

Beyond assuring its continued access to spices, Portugal made little effort to govern its holdings, and thus its eastern empire never became colonies of settlement. In all of their Asian holdings, the Portuguese remained heavily outnumbered by native peoples. Only in the Western Hemisphere—in Brazil, which was discovered accidentally by Pedro Álvares Cabral in 1500 when he was blown off course while trying to round the Cape of Good Hope—had settlement become a major goal by the late 16th century.

Early Lessons

As the Norse failure showed, the ability to navigate the high seas, although an impressive feat in itself, gave no guarantee of lasting success. Sustained expansion overseas required the support of a home government and ready access to what other states had learned. Italian merchants in nearby Rhodes or Cyprus passed their experiences on to the Portuguese to be applied in the Atlantic islands of Madeira or the Azores. And the lessons learned there were then relayed to distant Brazil. The Portuguese drew on Italian capital and maritime skills, as well as on Arab learning and technology, in launching their ventures. Spaniards, in turn, would learn much from the Portuguese, and the French, Dutch, and English would borrow from Italians, Portuguese, and Spaniards.

© Archivo Iconografico, S.A./Corbis.

THE LISBON WATERFRONT IN THE 16TH CENTURY
Although other European cities were larger than Lisbon, it became the first port to establish direct trade between Europe, Africa, South and East Asia, and the Americas.

The economic impulse behind colonization was thus in place long before Columbus sailed west. The desire for precious metals provided the initial stimulus, but staple crops and slavery kept that impetus alive. Before the 19th century, more than two-thirds of the people who crossed the Atlantic were slaves who were brought to America to grow sugar or other staples. The Atlantic slave trade was not some unfortunate exception to a larger story of liberty. For three and a half centuries, it was the norm.

Few Europeans who crossed the ocean expected to work. Early modern Europe was a hierarchical society in which men with prestige and wealth did virtually no physical labor. Upward social mobility meant advancing toward the goal of "living nobly," without the need to labor. In both Portugal and Spain, the social barriers between aristocrats and commoners had been flexible for some time. Professional men, famous soldiers, and rich merchants could acquire titles and begin to "live nobly." The opening of the Americas offered even greater possibilities for men to succeed by forcing others to toil for them.

⦿ Spain, Columbus, and the Americas

While the Portuguese surged east, Spaniards moved more sluggishly to the west. Just as Portugal gained experience by colonizing Madeira and the Azores, the Spanish kingdom of Castile sent its first settlers to the Canary Islands shortly after 1400. They spent the last third of the 15th century conquering the local inhabitants, the Guanches, a Berber people who had left North Africa before the rise of Islam and had been almost completely cut off from Africa and Europe for a thousand years. By the 1490s, the Spanish had all but exterminated them, the first people to face virtual extinction in the wake of European expansion.

Except for seizing the Canaries, the Spaniards devoted little attention to exploration or colonization. Instead, for most of the 15th century, the Iberian kingdoms of Aragon and Castile warred with other powers, quarreled with each other, or dealt with internal unrest. But in 1469, Prince Ferdinand of Aragon married Princess Isabella of Castile. They soon inherited their respective thrones and formed the modern kingdom of Spain, which had a population of about 4.9 million by 1500. Aragon, a Mediterranean society, had made good on an old claim to the Kingdom of Naples and Sicily and thus already possessed a small imperial bureaucracy

with experience in administering overseas possessions. Castile, landlocked on three sides, was larger than Aragon but in many ways more parochial. Its people, although suspicious of foreigners, had turned over much of their small overseas trade to merchants and mariners from Genoa in northern Italy who had settled in the port of Seville. Crusading Castilians, not traders, had taken the lead in expelling the Moors from the Iberian peninsula. Castilians, who were more likely than the Portuguese to identify expansion with conquest instead of trade, would lead Spain overseas.

In January 1492, Isabella and Ferdinand completed the reconquest of Spain by taking Granada, the last outpost of Islam on the Iberian peninsula. Flush with victory, they gave unconverted Jews six months to become Christians or be expelled from Spain. Just over half of Spain's 80,000 Jews fled, mostly to nearby Christian lands, including Portugal, that were more tolerant than Spain. A decade later, Ferdinand and Isabella also evicted all unconverted Moors. Spain entered the 16th century as Europe's most fiercely Catholic society, and this attitude accompanied its soldiers and settlers to America.

Columbus

A talented navigator from Genoa named Christopher Columbus promptly sought to benefit from the victory at Granada. He had served the Portuguese Crown for several years, had engaged in the slave trade between Africa and the Atlantic islands, had married the daughter of a promi-

Leonardo Torriani, *Die Kanarischen Inseln und Ihre Urbewohner* (1590). ed. Dominik Wölfel (Leipzig: K. F. Koehler, 1940). Plate X.

TWO GUANCHES

In the late 15th century, Spaniards all but exterminated these people, of Berber descent, on the Canary Islands.

nent Madeira planter, and may even have sailed to Iceland. He had been pleading for years with the courts of Portugal, England, France, and Spain to give him the ships and men to attempt an unprecedented feat: He believed he could reach eastern Asia by sailing west across the Atlantic.

Columbus's proposed voyage was controversial, but not because he assumed the earth was round. Learned men at that time agreed on that point, but they disagreed about the earth's size. Columbus put its circumference at only 16,000 miles. He proposed to reach Japan or China by sailing west a mere 3,000 miles. The Portuguese scoffed at his reasoning. They put the planet's circumference at about 26,000 miles, and they warned Columbus that he would perish on the vast ocean if he tried his mad scheme. Their calculations were, of course, far more accurate than those of Columbus; the circumference of the earth is about 25,000 miles at the equator. Even so, the fall of Granada gave Columbus another chance to plead his case. Isabella, who now had men and resources to spare, grew

more receptive to his request. She put him in charge of a fleet of two caravels, the *Niña* and the *Pinta*, together with a larger, square-rigged vessel, the *Santa María*, which Columbus made his flagship.

Columbus's motives were both religious and practical. He believed that the world was going to end soon, perhaps in 1648, but that God would make the Gospel available to all humankind before the last days. As the "Christ-bearer" (the literal meaning of his first name), Columbus was convinced that he had a role to play in bringing on the Millennium, the period at the end of history when Jesus would return and rule with his saints for 1,000 years; however, he was not at all averse to acquiring wealth and glory along the way.

Embarking from the port of Palos in August 1492, Columbus headed south to the Canaries, picked up provisions, and sailed west across the Atlantic. He kept two ship's logs, one to show his men, in which he underestimated the distance they had traveled, and the other for his

---

L I N K   T O   T H E   P A S T

Misunderstanding Columbus

On Christopher Columbus's third voyage to the Americas (1498–1500), he was sailing near a Caribbean island, possibly Trinidad, when he encountered a canoe manned by 24 Indians. His effort to bring the canoe close enough to trade with its occupants indicates how wide were the cultural misunderstandings between these two very different peoples.

As this canoe approached, they shouted to us from a distance, but neither I nor anyone else understood them. I gave orders, however that they should be signalled to approach, and more than two hours passed in this way. Each time they came a little nearer, they immediately sheered off again. I ordered pans and other shining objects to be displayed in order to attract them and bring them closer, and after a while they came nearer. . . . I greatly desired conversation with them, but it seemed that I had nothing left to show them which would induce them to come nearer still. So I had a tambourine brought up to the poop [deck] and played, and made some of the young men dance, imagining that the Indians would draw closer to see the festivities. On observing the music and dancing, however, they dropped their oars, and picked up their bows, and strung them. Each one seized

his shield, and they began to shoot arrows at us. I immediately stopped the music and dancing and ordered some crossbows to be fired. The Indians then put off, making for another caravel, and hastily sheltered under its stern. The pilot hailed them and gave a coat and hat to the man who seemed to be their chief, and arranged with him that he would meet and talk with them on the beach, to which they immediately rowed their canoe to await him. But he did not wish to go without my permission. When they saw him come to my ship in his boat, they got back into their canoe and rowed away, and I never saw them again or any other inhabitant of this island.

From Columbus's account of his third voyage, in *The Life of the Admiral by his Son, Hernando Colon*

1. Why do you suppose the Indians failed to connect the crew of the other European vessel with Columbus, and what do you think they were most afraid of?

For additional sources related to this feature, visit the *Liberty, Equality, Power* Web site at:

http://history.wadsworth.com/murrin_LEP4e

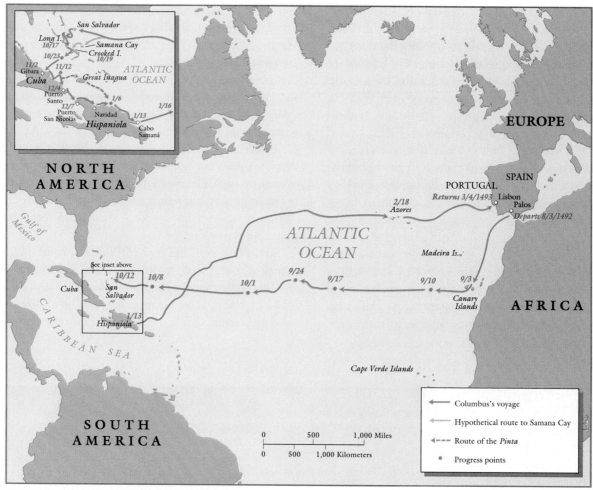

MAP 1.4 COLUMBUS'S FIRST VOYAGE, 1492

The route taken by Columbus from Palos, Spain, to the Canary Islands, then to San Salvador or possibly Samana Cay (see insert map), and finally back to Europe.

eyes only. (Ironically, the false log turned out to be more accurate than the official one.) He promised a prize to the first sailor to sight land. Despite his assurances that they had not sailed far, the crews grew restless in early October. Columbus pushed on. When land was spotted, on October 12, he claimed the prize for himself. He said he had seen a light in the distance the previous night.

The Spaniards splashed ashore on San Salvador, now Watling's Island in the Bahamas. (A few historians argue for Samana Cay, 60 miles south of San Salvador, as the site of the first landfall.) Convinced that he was somewhere in the East Indies, near Japan or China, Columbus called the local inhabitants "Indians," a word that meant nothing to them but one that has endured. When the peaceful Tainos (or Arawaks) claimed that the Carib Indians on nearby islands were cannibals, Columbus interpreted their word for "Carib" to mean the great "Khan" or emperor of China, known to him through Marco Polo's *Travels.* Columbus set out to find the Caribs. For several months he poked

about the Caribbean, mostly along the coasts of Cuba and Hispaniola. Then, on Christmas, the *Santa María* ran onto rocks and had to be abandoned. A few weeks later, Columbus sailed for Spain on the *Niña.* Some historians speculate that he had arranged the Christmas disaster as a way of forcing some of the crew to stay behind as a garrison on Hispaniola, but by then even the gentle Tainos had seen enough. By the time Columbus returned on his second voyage in late 1493, they had killed every man he had left.

The voyage had immediate consequences. In 1493, Pope Alexander VI (a Spaniard) issued a bull, *Inter Caeteras,* which divided all non-Christian lands between Spain and Portugal. A year later, in the Treaty of Tordesillas, the two kingdoms adjusted the dividing line, with Spain eventually claiming most of the Western Hemisphere, plus the Philippines, and Portugal most of the Eastern Hemisphere, including the African coast, plus Brazil. As a result, Spain never acquired direct access to the African slave trade.

Columbus made three more voyages in quest of China and also served as governor of the Spanish Indies. But Castilians never really trusted this Genoese opportunist, who spoke their language with a Portuguese accent and was a poor administrator to boot. The colonists often defied him, and after his third voyage, they shipped him back to Spain in chains in 1500. Although later restored to royal favor, he died in 1506, a bitter, disappointed man.

Spain and the Caribbean

By then, overseas settlement had acquired a momentum of its own as thousands of ex-soldiers, bored *hidalgos* (minor nobles with little wealth), and assorted adventurers drifted across the Atlantic. They carried with them seeds for Europe's cereal crops and livestock, including horses, cows, sheep, goats, and pigs. On islands without fences, the animals roamed freely, eating everything in sight, and soon threatened the Tainos' food supply. Unconcerned, the Spaniards forced the increasingly malnourished Indians to work for them, mostly panning for gold. Under these pressures, even before the onset of major infectious diseases, the native population fell catastrophically throughout the Caribbean. By 1514, only 22,000 able-bodied adults remained on Hispaniola, from an initial population of perhaps one million. The native people died even more rapidly than the meager supply of placer gold disappeared. This story was soon repeated on Cuba, Jamaica, and other islands. A whole way of life all but vanished from the earth to be replaced by sugar, slaves, and livestock as the Spaniards despaired of finding other forms of wealth. African slaves, acquired from the Portuguese, soon arrived to replace the dead Indians as a labor force.

The Spaniards continued their New World explorations: Juan Ponce de León tramped through Florida in quest of a legendary fountain of youth, shrewdly calculating that such an elixir would bring a handsome price in Europe. Vasco Núñez de Balboa became the first European to reach the Pacific Ocean, after crossing the Isthmus of Panama in 1513. Even so, as late as 1519—a full generation after Columbus's first voyage—Spain had gained little wealth from these new possessions, whatever and wherever they turned out to be. One geographer concluded that Spain had found a whole new continent, which he named "America" in honor of his informant, the explorer Amerigo Vespucci. For those who doubted this claim, Ferdinand Magellan, a Portuguese mariner serving the king of Spain, settled the issue when his fleet sailed around the world between 1519 and 1522. Magellan himself never completed the voyage. He was killed in the Philippines.

During the same three years, Hernán Cortés sailed from Cuba, invaded Mexico, and found the treasure that

Spaniards had been seeking. In 1519, he landed at a place he named Veracruz (The True Cross) and over the next several months succeeded in tracking down the fabulous empire of the Aztecs, high in the Valley of Mexico. When his small army of 400 men first laid eyes on the Aztec capital of Tenochtitlán (a metropolis of 200,000, much larger than any city in Western Europe), they wondered if they were dreaming. But they marched on. Moctezuma (or Montezuma II), the Aztec "speaker," or ruler, sent rich presents to persuade the Spaniards to leave, but the gesture had the opposite effect. "They picked up the gold and fingered it like monkeys," an Aztec later recalled, "Their bodies swelled with greed, and their hunger was ravenous.... They snatched at the golden ensigns, waved them from side to side and examined every inch of them." Cortés had stumbled upon a wholly different world in the Americas, one with its own long and varied past.

☀ The Emergence of Complex Societies in the Americas

The high cultures of the Americas had been developing for thousands of years before Cortés found one of them. Their ways were ancient, and they were proud of their past. Their wealth fired the imagination of Europe and aroused the envy of Spain's enemies. The fabulous Aztec and Inca empires became the magnets that turned European exploration into rival empires of permanent settlement.

The Rise of Sedentary Cultures

After 4000 B.C., agriculture transformed the lives of most Indians. As farming slowly became the principal source of food in the Americas, settled villages in a few locations grew into large cities. Most of them appeared in the Valley of Mexico, Central America, or the Andes. For centuries, however, dense settlements also thrived in Chaco Canyon in present-day New Mexico and in the Mississippi River valley. Meanwhile, farming continued to spread. By the time Columbus sailed, most Indians were raising crops.

Indians became completely sedentary (nonmigratory) only in the most advanced cultures. Most of those north of Mexico lived a semisedentary life—that is, they were migratory for part of each year. After a tribe chose a site, the men chopped down some trees, girded others, burned away the underbrush, and often planted tobacco, a mood-altering sacred crop grown exclusively by men. Burning the underbrush fertilized the soil with ash and gave the community years of high productivity. Meanwhile, women

LONGHOUSE, WIGWAM, AND TEPEE

The longhouse (top right), made from bark or mats stretched over a wooden frame, was the standard communal dwelling of the Iroquois and Huron peoples. Most Algonquian peoples of the eastern woodlands lived in wigwams (top left), such as this undated example. Wigwams were made by bending the boughs of trees into a frame to be covered with animal skins. West of the Mississippi, most Plains Indians lived in small but strong tepees (bottom left), which were usually made from poles covered with buffalo hides. All of these dwellings were constructed by women.

erected the dwellings (longhouse, wigwam, tepee) and planted and harvested food crops, especially corn. Planting beans among the corn helped maintain good crop yields. In the fall, either the men alone or entire family groups went off hunting or fishing.

Under this "slash and burn" system of agriculture, farming became women's work, beneath the dignity of men, whose role was to hunt, fish, and make war. Because this system slowly depleted the soil, the whole tribe had to move to new fields after a decade or two, often because accessible firewood had been exhausted. In this semi-sedentary way of life, few Indians cared to acquire more personal property than the women could carry from one place to another, either during the annual hunt or when the whole community had to move. This limited interest in consumption would profoundly condition their response to capitalism after contact with Europeans.

Even sedentary Indians did not own land as individuals. Clans or families guarded their "use rights" to land that had been allocated to them by their chiefs. In sedentary societies, both men and women worked in the fields, and families accumulated surpluses for trade. Not all sedentary peoples developed monumental architecture and elaborate state forms. The Tainos of the Greater Antilles in the Caribbean were fully sedentary, for example, but they never erected massive temples or created powerful states. But, with a few striking exceptions, such examples of cultural complexity emerged primarily among sedentary populations. In Mesoamerica and the Andes, intensive farming, cities, states, and monumental architecture came together at several different times to produce distinctive high cultures.

The spread of farming produced another population surge among both sedentary and semisedentary peoples. Estimates vary greatly, but according to the more moderate ones, at least 50 million people were living in the Western Hemisphere by 1492—and perhaps as many as 70 million, or one-seventh of the world's population. High estimates exceed 100 million. The Valley of Mexico in 1500 was one of the most densely inhabited regions on Earth.

Despite their large populations, even the most complex societies in the Americas remained Stone Age cultures in their basic technology. The urban societies of Mesoamerica and the Andes became the largest and most complex Stone Age cultures in the history of the world. The Indians made some use of metals, although more for decorative than practical purposes. This metalworking skill originated in South America and spread to Mesoamerica a few centuries before Columbus. By 1520, Indians had amassed enough gold and silver to provide dozens of plundering Europeans with princely fortunes. As far north as the Great Lakes, copper had been discovered and fashioned into fishing tools and art objects since the first millennium B.C. Copper was traded over large areas of North

INDIAN WOMEN AS FARMERS

In this illustration, a French artist depicted 16th-century Indian women in southeastern North America.

Courtesy of the John Carter Brown Library at Brown University.

America, but Indians had not learned how to make bronze (a compound of copper and tin) nor found any use for iron. Nearly all of their tools were made of stone or bone, and their sharpest weapons were made from obsidian, a hard, glassy, volcanic rock. Nor did they use the wheel or devices based on the wheel, such as pulleys or gears. They knew how to make a wheel—they had wheeled toys—but they never found a practical purpose for this invention, probably because North America had no draft animals, and South Americans used llamas mostly in steep, mountainous areas where wheeled vehicles would have made no sense.

The Andes: Cycles of Complex Cultures

Despite these technological limitations, Indians accomplished a great deal. During the second millennium B.C., elaborate urban societies began to take shape both in the Andes and along Mexico's gulf coast. Because no Andean culture had become literate before the Europeans arrived, we know much less about events there than we do about Mesoamerica, but we do know that ancient Andean societies devised extremely productive agricultural systems at 12,000 feet above sea level, far above the altitude at which anyone else has ever been able to raise crops. In the 1980s, when archaeologists rebuilt part of the prehistoric Andean irrigation system according to ancient specifications, they discovered that it was far more productive than a system using modern fertilizers and machines. The Andean system could produce 10 metric tons of potatoes per hectare

MESOAMERICAN TOY DEER

This sketch of a toy deer shows that Mesoamerican people did understand the principle of the wheel, but they found no practical use for it.

(about 2.4 acres), as against 1 to 4 tons on nearby modern fields. Lands using the Andean canal system never had to lie fallow. This type of irrigation took hold around Lake Titicaca about 1000 B.C. and spread throughout the region. It was abandoned around A.D. 1000, apparently in response to a monster drought that endured, with only brief intermissions, for two centuries.

Monumental architecture and urbanization appeared in the Andes even before the canal system at Lake Titicaca was created. Between 3000 and 2100 B.C., both took hold along the Peruvian coast and in the interior. The new

COMPLEX CULTURES OF PRE-COLUMBIAN AMERICA

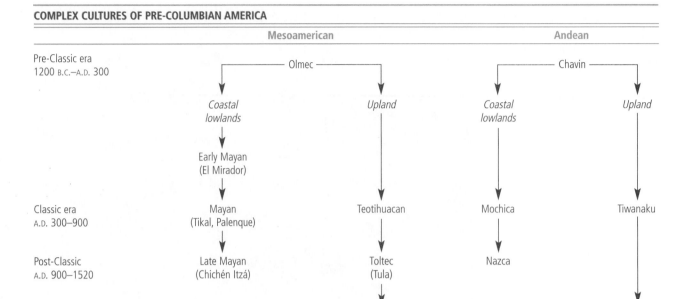

	Mesoamerican		Andean	
Pre-Classic era 1200 B.C.–A.D. 300	Olmec		Chavin	
	Coastal lowlands	*Upland*	*Coastal lowlands*	*Upland*
	Early Mayan (El Mirador)			
Classic era A.D. 300–900	Mayan (Tikal, Palenque)	Teotihuacan	Mochica	Tiwanaku
Post-Classic A.D. 900–1520	Late Mayan (Chichén Itzá)	Toltec (Tula)	Nazca	
		Aztecs (Tenochtitlán)		Incas (Cuzco)

communities were built around a U-shaped temple about three stories high. Some of the earliest temples were pyramids, the oldest of which are as ancient as those of Egypt. In later centuries, as more people moved into the mountains, some pyramids became immense. The one at Sechin Alto near Lima, more than 10 stories high, was built between 1800 and 1500 B.C. Eventually, these accomplishments merged into what archaeologists call the Pre-Classic Chavin culture, which was well established by 1000 B.C., only to collapse suddenly about 300 B.C. In all probability, no single state ever dominated this culture.

Chavin culture had two offshoots: one on the coast and one in the mountains. Together they constitute the Classic phase of pre-Columbian history in South America. The Mochica culture, which emerged about A.D. 300 on the northwest coast of Peru, produced finely detailed pottery, much of it erotic, and built pyramids as centers of worship. At about the same time, another Classic culture arose in the mountains around the city of Tiwanaku, 12,000 feet above sea level. The people of this society grew a great variety of food plants, both tropical and temperate. Terraces, laid out at various altitudes on the mountainside, enabled the community to raise crops from different climatic zones, all a few hours distant from one another. At the lowest levels, Tiwanakans planted cotton in the hot, humid air. Farther up the mountain, they raised maize (corn) and other crops suitable to a temperate zone. At still higher elevations, they grew potatoes and grazed their alpacas and llamas. They even invented freeze-dried food

TERRACED AGRICULTURE OF THE ANDES

This example is from the Incas, but the technology was much older than the Inca civilization.

by carrying it far up the mountains to take advantage of the frost that fell most nights of the year.

The Tiwanaku Empire, with its capital on the southern shores of Lake Titicaca, flourished until even its sophisticated irrigation system could not survive the horrendous drought that began at the end of the 10th century A.D. The Classic Andean cultures collapsed between

the 6th and 11th centuries A.D., possibly after a conquest of the Mochica region by the Tiwanakans, who provided water to the coastal peoples until they too were overwhelmed by the drought.

The disruption that followed this decline was temporary because complex Post-Classic cultures soon thrived both north and west of Tiwanaku. The coastal culture of the Nazca people has long fascinated both scholars and tourists because of its exquisite textiles, and above all because of a unique network of lines they etched in the desert. Some lines form the outlines of birds or animals, but others simply run straight for miles until they disappear at the horizon. Only from the air are these patterns fully visible.

Inca Civilization

Around A.D. 1400, the Inca (the word applied both to the ruler and to the empire's dominant nation) emerged as the new imperial power in the Andes. They built their capital at Cuzco, high in the mountains. From that upland center, the Incas controlled an empire that eventually extended more than 2,000 miles from south to north, and they bound it together with an efficient network of roads and

INCA *QUIPU*

The accounting device pictured here is based on a decimal system developed by the Incas.

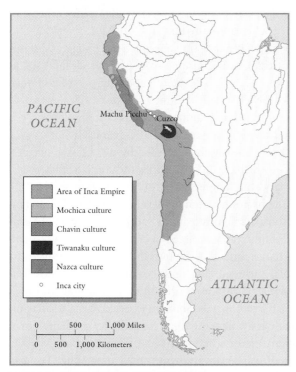

MAP 1.5   INCA EMPIRE AND PRINCIPAL EARLIER CULTURES

The Pacific coast of South America showing the location of the Mochica, Chavin, Tiwanaku, and Nazca cultures and finally the Inca empire, which covered a much larger area.

suspension bridges. Along these roads, the Incas maintained numerous storehouses for grain. They had no written language, but high-altitude runners, who memorized the Inca's oral commands with perfect accuracy, raced along the roads to relay their ruler's decrees over vast distances. The Incas also invented a decimal system and used it to keep records of the tribute they levied upon subject peoples. They used a device they called a *quipu*. By 1500, the Inca empire ruled perhaps 8 to 12 million people. No other nonliterate culture has ever matched that feat.

Mesoamerica: Cycles of Complex Cultures

Mesoamerica experienced a similar cycle of change, but over a somewhat shorter period. Its own Pre-Classic, Classic, and Post-Classic cultures also comprised both upland and lowland societies.

The Olmecs, who appeared along the Gulf Coast about 1200 B.C., became the parent culture for the region. It centered on three cities. The oldest, San Lorenzo (names are modern, as is "Olmec," which means "people of rubber," for the rubber trees that thrive in this tropical region), flourished from 1200 to 900 B.C., when it was conquered by invaders. Olmec influence reached its zenith during the

domination of La Venta, which became an urban center about 1100 B.C., reached its peak 300 years later, and declined. After La Venta was demolished between 500 and 400 B.C., leadership passed to the city of Tres Zapotes, which thrived for another four centuries.

These three Olmec centers, with permanent populations of only about 1,000, were too small to sustain large armies. The colossal stone heads that honored their rulers were the most distinctive Olmec artifacts, but they appeared only in the homeland. Other aspects of Olmec culture became widely diffused throughout Mesoamerica. The Olmecs built the first pyramids and the first ballparks in Mesoamerica. Their game, played with a heavy rubber ball, spread into what is now the southwestern United States. The losers were, at least on certain religious occasions, beheaded.

The Olmecs also learned how to write and developed a dual calendar system that endured through the Aztec era. At the end of a 52-year cycle, the first day of the "short" calendar would again coincide with the first day of the "long" one. Olmecs faced the closing days of each cycle with dread, lest the gods allow the sun and all life on earth to be destroyed—something that, Olmecs believed, had already happened several times. They believed that the sacrifice of a god had been necessary to set the sun in motion

EL CARACOL, A LATE MAYAN OBSERVATORY AT CHICHÉN ITZÁ

Astronomy was highly developed in all of the pre-Columbian high cultures of Mesoamerica; however, if the Mayans used any specialized instruments to study the heavens, we do not know what they were.

in each new creation cycle and that only the blood of human sacrifice could placate the gods and keep the sun moving.

These beliefs endured in Mesoamerica for perhaps 3,000 years, regardless of the rise and fall of empires and cities. The essentials may even be older than Olmec culture. The creation myths of both Mesoamerican and Andean peoples are similar, which may suggest a common origin in the distant past, perhaps as far back as Beringia, where the sun did disappear for part of each year. Olmec beliefs retained immense power. The arrival of Cortés created a religious as well as a political crisis, because 1519 marked the end of a 52-year cycle.

The Olmecs were succeeded by two Classic cultures, both of which created great cities and studied the heavens. The city and empire of Teotihuacan emerged in the mountains not far from modern Mexico City. Mayan culture took shape mostly in the southern lowlands of Yucatán. Teotihuacan was already a city of 40,000 by A.D. 1 and grew to five times that size over the next three centuries. Its temples included enormous pyramids, but its most impressive art form was its brightly painted murals, of which only a few survive. Teotihuacan invested resources in comfortable apartment dwellings for ordinary residents, not in monuments or inscriptions to rulers. It probably had a form of senate government, not a monarchy. The city extended its influence throughout Mesoamerica and remained a powerful force until its sudden destruction in about A.D. 750, apparently by conquest because its shrines were toppled and the city was abandoned. In all likelihood, Teotihuacan's growth had so depleted the resources

OLMEC STONE HEAD
This giant head of stone is 9 feet 4 inches tall.

Reconstruction by Tatiana Proskouriakoff. From the Fall of the Ancient Maya by David Webster, published by Thames & Hudson, London and New York.

COPAN'S TEMPLE OF THE HIEROGLYPHIC STAIRWAY

It is an exceptional example both of Mayan architecture and Mayan literacy.

© Boltin Picture Library.

THE TEMPLE OF THE SUN AT TEOTIHUACAN

The giant, stepped pyramid shown here is one of pre-Columbian America's most elegant pyramids.

of the area that the city could not have sustained itself much longer. Modern beliefs to the contrary, Indians enjoyed no mystical protection from ecological disasters.

In the lowlands, Classic Mayan culture went through a similar cycle from expansion to ecological crisis. It was also urban but less centralized than that of Teotihuacan, although some Mayan temples were just as monumental. For more than 1,000 years, Mayan culture rested on a network of competing city-states, which, as in ancient Greece, shared similar values. One of the largest Mayan cities, Tikal, arose on the plateau separating rivers flowing into the Caribbean from rivers emptying into the Gulf of Mexico. It controlled commerce with Teotihuacan. Tikal housed 100,000 at its peak before A.D. 800. Twenty other cities, most about one-fourth the size of Tikal, flourished throughout the region. Mayan engineers built canals to water the crops needed to support this urban system, which was well established by the first century B.C. The Danta pyramid, completed in the second century B.C. at the Pre-Classic city of El Mirador, was probably the most massive architectural structure in pre-Columbian Mesoamerica. El Mirador declined before the Classic era began.

The earliest Mayan writings date to 50 B.C., but few survive from the next 300 years. About A.D. 300, Mayans began to record their history in considerable detail. Since 1960, scholars have deciphered most Mayan inscriptions, which means that the Classic phase of Mayan culture is completing a shift from a prehistoric to a historic (or written) past. Mayan texts are now studied much like those of Europe. Mayan art and writings reveal the religious beliefs of these people, including the place of human sacrifice in their cosmos and the role of ritual self-mutilation, particularly among the elite, in their worship. Scholars have learned, for example, about the long reign of Pacal the Great, king (or "Great Sun") of the elegant city of Palenque, who was born on March 26, 603, and died on August 31, 683. His sarcophagus lists his ancestors through six generations. Other monuments tell of the Great Suns of other cities whom Pacal vanquished and sacrificed to the gods.

Classic Mayan culture began to collapse about 50 years after the fall of Teotihuacan, which disrupted Mayan trade with the Valley of Mexico. The crisis spread rapidly. Palenque and a half-dozen other cities were abandoned between 800 and 820. The last date recorded at Tikal was in 869; the last in

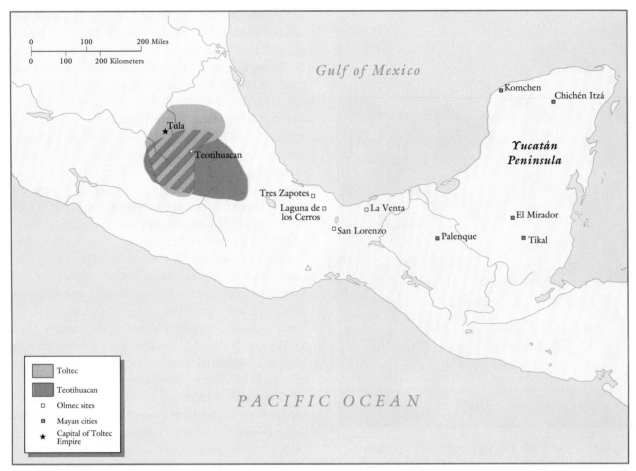

MAP 1.6   ANCIENT MESOAMERICA
The location of the three principal Olmec cities, Teotihuacan, several major Mayan cities, and the Toltec capital of Tula.

the southern lowlands came 40 years later. The Mayan aristocracy had grown faster than the commoners could support it, until population outstripped local resources and generated irreversible ecological decay. Frequent wars hastened the decline. Trade with the Valley of Mexico, although diminished, shifted north to other cities. With the collapse of the southern cities, the population of the region fell drastically, partly through emigration northward.

After A.D. 900, the Post-Classic era saw a kind of Mayan renaissance in the northern lowlands of the Yucatán, where many refugees from the south had fled. Chichén Itzá, a city that had existed for centuries, preserved many distinctive Mayan traits but merged them with new influences from the Valley of Mexico, where the Toltecs had become dominant in the high country and may even have conquered Chichén Itzá. The Toltecs were a fierce warrior people whose capital at Tula, with 40,000 people, was one-fifth as large as Teotihuacan at its peak. They prospered from the cocoa trade with tropical low-

lands but otherwise did nothing to expand the region's food supply. They controlled the Valley of Mexico for almost three centuries, until about A.D. 1200, when they too declined. They left a legacy of conquest to later rulers in the valley, all of whom claimed descent from Toltec kings.

The Aztecs and Tenochtitlán

By 1400, power in the Valley of Mexico was passing to the Aztecs, a warrior people who had migrated from the north about two centuries earlier and had settled, with the bare sufferance of their neighbors, on the shore of Lake Texcoco. They built a great city, Tenochtitlán, out on the lake. Its only connection with the mainland was by several broad causeways. The Aztecs raised their agricultural productivity by creating highly productive *chinampas,* or floating gardens, right on the lake. Yet their mounting population strained the food supply. In the 1450s, the threat of famine was severe.

Image taken from exhibit produced by the Florida Museum of Natural History.

© Bottin Picture Library.

WALL PAINTINGS AT BONAMPAK

The wall paintings at Bonampak from the Teotihuacan era are a spectacular example of pre-Columbian art.

MAYAN SACRIFICIAL VICTIM

Human sacrifice played a major role in Mesoamerican religion. The artist who crafted this disemboweled man recognized the agony of the victim.

Tenochtitlán, with a population of something over 200,000, had forged an alliance with Texcoco and Tlacopan, two smaller lakeside cities. Together they dominated the area, but by the second quarter of the 15th century, leadership was clearly passing to the Aztecs. As newcomers to the region, the Aztecs felt a need to prove themselves worthy heirs to Teotihuacan, Tula, and the ancient culture of the Valley of Mexico. They adopted the old religion but practiced it with a terrifying intensity. They waged perpetual war, usually with neighboring cities, to gain captives for their ceremonies. They built and constantly rebuilt and enlarged their Great Pyramid of the Sun. At its dedication in 1487, they sacrificed—if we can believe later accounts—about 14,000 people in a ceremony that went on for four days until the priests dropped from exhaustion. Each captive climbed the steep steps of the pyramid and was held by his wrists and ankles over the sacrificial slab while a priest cut open his breast, ripped out his heart, held it up

to the sun, placed it inside the statue of a god, and then rolled the carcass down the steps so that parts of the body could be eaten, mostly by members of the captor's family, but never by the captor. He fasted instead and mourned the death of a worthy foe.

Human sacrifice was an ancient ritual in Mesoamerica, familiar to everyone, but the Aztecs practiced it on a scale that was unparalleled anywhere else in the world. The need for thousands of victims each year created potential enemies everywhere. Although neighboring peoples shared the religious beliefs of the Aztecs, they nevertheless hated these conquerors from the north. After 1519, many Indians in Mesoamerica would help the Spaniards bring down the Aztecs. By contrast, the Spanish found few allies in the Andes, where resistance in the name of the Inca would persist for most of the 16th century and would even revive in the late 18th century, 250 years after the conquest.

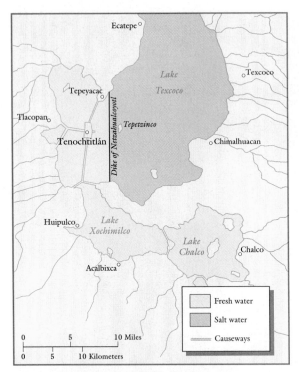

MAP 1.7   VALLEY OF MEXICO, 1519
Lake Texcoco and its principal cities, especially Tenochtitlán (built on the lake itself) and its allies, Tlacopan and Texcoco.

North American Mound Builders

North of Mexico, from 3000 B.C. to about A.D. 1700, three distinct cultures of "mound builders" succeeded each other and exerted a powerful influence over the interior of North America. Named for the huge earthen mounds they erected, these cultures arose near the Ohio and Mississippi rivers and their tributaries. The earliest mound builders became semisedentary even before learning to grow crops.

WOODCUT OF A QUEEN, OR THE WIFE OF A "GREAT SUN" OF THE MISSISSIPPI MOUND BUILDERS, BEING CARRIED ON A LITTER
This 16th-century engraving is by Theodore de Bry.

Fish, game, and the lush vegetation of the river valleys sustained them for most of the year and enabled them to erect permanent dwellings.

The oldest mound-building culture appeared among a preagricultural people in what is now northeastern Louisiana about 3400 B.C., at a site called Watson Break. Later, just 40 miles away, early mound builders flourished from 1500 B.C. to 700 B.C. at Poverty Point (named for a 19th-century plantation), a center that contained perhaps 5,000 people at its peak in about 1000 B.C. The second mound-building culture, the Adena-Hopewell, emerged between 500 B.C. and A.D. 400 in the Ohio River valley. Its mounds were increasingly elaborate burial sites, indicating belief in an afterlife. Mound-building communities participated in a commerce that spanned most

THE GREAT SERPENT MOUND
Located near Chillicothe, Ohio, this mound is about 1,200 feet long and is one of the most spectacular mounds to survive from the Adena-Hopewell era.

of the continent between the Appalachians and the Rockies, the Great Lakes and the Gulf of Mexico. Obsidian from the Yellowstone Valley in the Far West, copper from the Great Lakes basin, and shells from the Gulf of Mexico have all been found buried in the Adena-Hopewell mounds. Both the mound building and the long-distance trade largely ceased after A.D. 400, for reasons that remain unclear. The people even stopped growing corn for a few centuries. Yet the mounds were so impressive that when American settlers found them after the Revolution, they refused to believe that "savages" could have built them.

Mound building revived in a third and final Mississippian phase between A.D. 1000 and 1700. This culture dominated the Mississippi River valley from modern St. Louis to Natchez, with the largest center at Cahokia in present-day Illinois and another important one at Moundville in Alabama. Ordinary people became "stinkards" in this culture, while some families had elite status. The "Great Sun" ruled with authority and was transported by litter from place to place. When he died, some of his wives, relatives, and retainers even volunteered to be sacrificed at his funeral and join him in the afterlife. Burial mounds thus became much grander in Mississippian communities. The Indians topped the mounds in which their rulers were interred with elaborate places of worship and residences for the priests and Great Suns of these highly stratified societies.

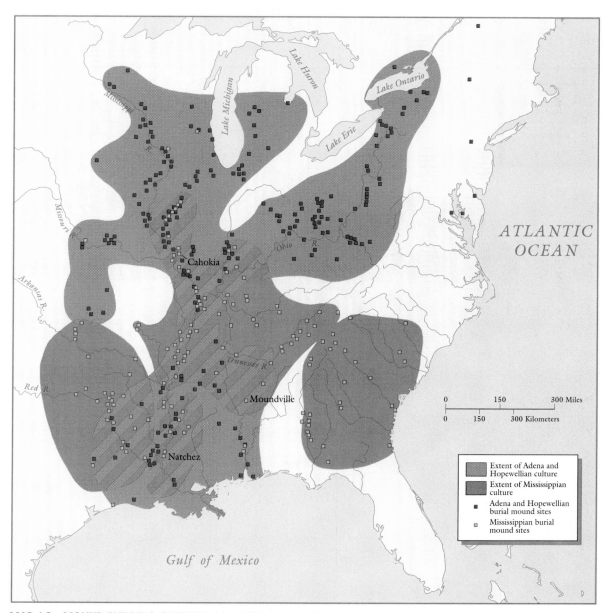

MAP 1.8   MOUND-BUILDING CULTURES OF NORTH AMERICA
Early Adena and Hopewell burial sites and later Mississippian sites and the areas that these cultures influenced.

Painting by Lloyd K. Townsend. Cahokia Mounds Historic Site.

CAHOKIA

The largest Mississippian mound-building site was Cahokia, in Illinois near St. Louis. Depicted here is the city's sacred, ceremonial center facing toward Monk Mound in the distance.

The city of Cahokia, near modern St. Louis, flourished from A.D. 900 to 1250 and may have had 30,000 residents at its peak, making it the largest city north of Mexico and almost as populous as the contemporary Toltec capital at Tula. Cahokia's enormous central mound, 100 feet high, is the world's largest earthen work. Similarities with Mesoamerican practices and artifacts have led many scholars to look for direct links between the two cultures. Yet although travel was possible between Mesoamerica and the Mississippi valley, no Mesoamerican artifacts have been found in the southeastern United States.

Urban Cultures of the Southwest

Other complex societies emerged in North America's semi-arid Southwest—among them the Hohokam, the Anasazi,

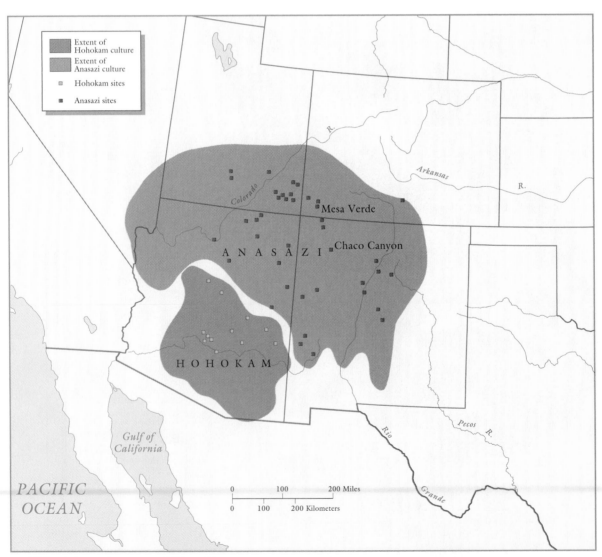

MAP 1.9   HOHOKAM AND ANASAZI SITES

These cultures in the Southwest combined irrigation and road building with sophisticated architecture.

and the Pueblo. The Hohokam Indians settled in what is now central Arizona somewhere between 300 B.C. and A.D. 300. Their irrigation system, consisting of several hundred miles of canals, produced two harvests per year. They wove cotton cloth and made pottery with a distinctive red color. They traded with places as distant as California and Mesoamerica and even imported a version of the Mesoamerican ball game. Perhaps because unceasing irrigation had increased the salinity of the soil, this culture, after enduring for more than 1,000 years, had gone into irreversible decline by 1450.

Even more tantalizing and mysterious is the brief flowering of the Anasazi (a Navajo word meaning "the ancient ones"), a cliff-dwelling people who have left behind some remarkable artifacts at Chaco Canyon in New Mexico, at Mesa Verde in Colorado, and at other sites. In their caves and cliffs, they constructed apartment houses five stories high with as many as 500 dwellings and with elegant and spacious *kivas,* or meeting rooms for religious functions. The Anasazi were superb astronomers. Through an arrangement of rock slabs, open to the sun and moon at the mouth of a cave, and of spirals on the interior wall that plotted the movement of the sun and moon, they created a calendar that could track the summer and winter solstices and even the 19-year cycles of the moon, an astronomical refinement Europeans had not yet achieved. They traveled to their fields and brought in lumber and other distant supplies on a network of roads that ran for scores of miles in several directions. They achieved most of these feats over a period of about two centuries, although Anasazi pottery has been found that dates from much earlier times. In the last quarter of the 13th century, apparently overwhelmed by a prolonged drought and by hostile invaders, they abandoned their principal sites. Pueblo architecture resembles that of the Anasazi, and the Pueblo Indians claim descent from them.

Contact and Cultural Misunderstanding

After the voyage of Columbus, the peoples of Europe and America, both with ancient pasts, confronted each other. Mutual understanding was unlikely except on a superficial level. Nothing in the histories of Europeans or Indians had prepared either of them for the encounter. The humanists of Renaissance Europe, avidly studying ancient Greece and Rome, were uncovering the huge differences between those pagan cultures and the Christian values of the Middle Ages and were developing a strong sense of history, an awareness that their past had been quite different from their present. They were also used to dealing with Moslem "infidels," whom they regarded as terribly alien but whose monotheistic beliefs were not all that different from their own. They also understood that East Asia was neither classical nor Christian, not Islamic or "barbaric." Even so, none of this experience prepared them for what they found in America.

Religious Dilemmas

Christians had trouble understanding how Indians could exist at all. The Bible, they were certain, recorded the creation of all humankind, but it never mentioned the Indians. From which of the sons of Noah had they descended? Were they the "lost 10 tribes" of Israel, perhaps? This idea was first suggested by Spanish missionaries and would later appeal to British Protestants. Some theologians, such as Spaniard Juan Ginés de Sepúlveda, tried to resolve this dilemma by arguing that Indians were animals without souls, not human beings at all. The pope and the royal courts of Portugal and Spain listened instead to a Dominican missionary, Fray Bartolomé de Las Casas, who insisted on the Indians' humanity. But, asked Europeans, if Indians (and Asians) did possess immortal souls, would a compassionate God have left them in utter darkness for centuries without making the Gospel known to them? Rejecting that possibility, some early Catholic missionaries concluded that one of the apostles must have visited America (and India) and that the Indians must have

MODERN RESTORATION OF AN ANASAZI *KIVA*

This *kiva,* or meeting room of the Anasazi, was located underground and was accessed by a ladder through a hole in the ceiling.

© David Muench.

North Wind Picture Archives.

TENOCHTITLÁN

This painting by Ignacio Marquina conveys a sense of the city's spectacular size and its monumental architecture.

rejected his message. The Portuguese announced in the 1520s that they had discovered the tomb of St. Thomas the Doubter in India, and then in 1549, a Jesuit claimed to have found Thomas's footprint in Brazil. If only to satisfy the spiritual yearnings of Europeans overseas, St. Thomas got around!

To Europeans, the sacrificial temples, skull racks, and snake motifs of Mesoamerica led to only one conclusion: The Aztecs worshiped Satan. Their statues and even their writings had to be destroyed. Human sacrifice and ritual cannibalism were widespread throughout the Americas, although nowhere else on the two continents did the scale approach that practiced by the Aztecs. The Incas, whose creation myth resembled that of Mesoamerica, offered an occasional victim to the sun or to some other god. The Indians of eastern North America frequently tortured to death their adult male captives, and every Indian warrior learned from boyhood how to endure such torments. Christians were shocked by human sacrifice and found cannibalism revolting, but Indians regarded certain European practices with equal horror. Between 1500 and 1700, Europeans burned or hanged perhaps 50,000 to 100,000 people, usually old women, for conversing with the wrong

spirits—that is, for witchcraft. The Spanish Inquisition burned thousands of heretics. To the Indians, such executions looked like human sacrifices to placate an angry Christian God.

The dilemma that Indians posed for Europeans emerged almost at once. On his second voyage, Columbus brought the first missionaries to the Americas. After one of them preached to a group of Tainos and presented them with some holy images, the Indians, records relate, "left the chapel, . . . flung the images to the ground, covered them with a heap of earth, and pissed upon it." The governor, a brother of Columbus, had them burned alive. The Indians probably saw this punishment as a form of human sacrifice to a vengeful god. They had no way of grasping the Christian distinction between human sacrifice and punishment for desecration.

Even the Christians' moral message was ambiguous. Missionaries eagerly brought news of the Christ, how he had died to save humankind from sin. Catholic worship, then as now, centered on the Mass and the Eucharist, in which a priest transforms bread and wine into the literal body and blood of Christ. "Except ye eat the flesh of the Son of man, and drink his blood," Jesus told his disciples

(John 6:53), "ye have no life in you." Most Protestants also accepted this sacrament but interpreted it symbolically, not literally. To the Indians, Christians seemed to be a people who ate their own god but grew outraged at the lesser matter of sacrificing a human being to please an Indian god.

When Europeans tried to convert Indians to Christianity, the Indians concluded that the converts would spend the afterlife with the souls of Europeans, separated forever from their own ancestors, whose memory they revered. Neither side fully recognized these obstacles to mutual understanding. Although early Catholic missionaries converted thousands of Indians, the results were mixed at best. Some Indians willingly abandoned their old beliefs, but others resisted Christian doctrines. Most converts adopted some Christian practices and continued many of their old rituals, often in secret.

AZTEC SKULL RACK ALTAR

This rack held the skulls of hundreds of sacrificial victims and shocked the invading Spaniards.

War as Cultural Misunderstanding

Such misunderstandings multiplied as Indians and Europeans came into closer contact. Both waged war, but with different objectives. Europeans tried to settle matters on the battlefield and expected to kill many enemies. Indians fought mostly to obtain captives, whether for sacrifice (as with the Aztecs) or to replace tribal losses through adoption (as with the Iroquois). To them, massive deaths on the battlefield were almost a blasphemy, an appalling waste of life that could in no way appease the gods. Europeans and Indians also differed profoundly on what acts constituted atrocities. The torture and ritual sacrifice of captives horrified Europeans; the slaughter of women and children, which Europeans brought to America, appalled Indians.

Gender and Cultural Misunderstanding

Indian social organization also differed fundamentally from that of Europeans. European men owned almost all property, set the rules of inheritance, farmed the land, and performed nearly all public functions. Among many Indian peoples, especially those first encountered by Europeans north of Mexico, descent was matrilineal (traced through the maternal line), and women owned nearly all movable property. European men felt incomplete unless they acquired authority over other people, especially the other members of their households. They also expected social inferiors to obey superiors. Indian men had none of these patriarchal ambitions. Chiefs governed more through persuasion and example than through command. Women did the farming in semisedentary Indian cultures, and they often could demand a war or try to prevent one, although the final decision rested with men. When Europeans tried to change warriors into farmers, Indian males protested that they were being turned into women. Only over fully sedentary peoples could Europeans impose direct rule by building on the social hierarchy, division of labor, and system of tribute already in place.

Conquest and Catastrophe

Spanish *conquistadores*, or conquerors, led small armies that rarely exceeded 1,000 men. Yet, because they were also able to raise large Indian armies as allies, they subdued two empires much larger than Spain and then looked around for more worlds to overrun. There, beyond the great empires, Indians had more success in resisting them.

The Conquest of Mexico and Peru

When Cortés entered Tenochtitlán in 1519, he seized Moctezuma, the Aztec ruler, as prisoner and hostage. Although overwhelmingly outnumbered, Cortés and his

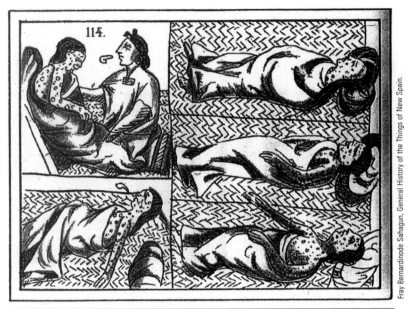

Fray Bernardino de Sahagun, General History of the Things of New Spain.

THE RAVAGES OF SMALLPOX

These drawings show the devastation of smallpox among the Aztecs, as depicted in the Aztec Codex, one of the few surviving collections of Aztec writing.

destroyed Tenochtitlán. He had hoped to leave the great city intact, not wreck it, but he and the Aztecs found no common understanding that would enable them to stop fighting before the city lay in ruins. "We have chewed dry twigs and salt grasses," mourned one Aztec poet after the fall of the city; "we have filled our mouths with dust and bits of adobe; we have eaten lizards, rats and worms." With royal support from Spain, the *conquistadores* established themselves as new imperial rulers in Mesoamerica, looted all the silver and gold they could find, and built Mexico City on the ruins of Tenochtitlán.

Rumors abounded about an even richer civilization far to the south, and in 1531 and 1532, Francisco Pizarro finally located the Inca empire high in the Andes. Smallpox had preceded him and killed the reigning Inca. In the civil war that followed, Atahualpa had defeated his brother to become the new Inca. Pizarro captured Atahualpa, held him hostage, and managed to win a few allies from among the Inca's recent enemies. Atahualpa filled his throne room with precious metals as a truly royal ransom, but Pizarro had him strangled anyway. Tens of thousands of angry Indians besieged the Spaniards for months in Cuzco, the Inca capital, but Pizarro, although vastly outnumbered, managed to hold out and finally prevailed. After subduing the insurgents, the Spanish established a new capital at Lima on the coast.

men began to destroy Aztec religious objects, replacing them with images of the Virgin Mary or other Catholic saints. In response, while Cortés was away, the Aztecs rose against the intruders, Moctezuma was killed, and the Spaniards were driven out with heavy losses. But then, the smallpox the Spaniards left behind soon began killing Aztecs by the thousands. Cortés found refuge with the nearby Tlaxcalans, a proudly independent people who had never submitted to Aztec rule. With thousands of their warriors, he returned the next year, built several warships armed with cannon to dominate Lake Texcoco, and

Folding Screen: The Encounter of Cortes and Moctezuma (obverse); The Four Continents (reverse). Collection Banco Nacional de Mexico, Mexico City.

THE ENCOUNTER OF CORTÉS AND MOCTEZUMA

Spain understood that the conquest of Mexico dramatically changed the history of the world and made possible a global empire. Juan Correa, a Mexican artist, painted this scene on a Japanese *biamba,* or folding screen, sometime between 1645 and 1650. On the other side of the screen he painted *The Four Continents* (Europe, Asia, Africa, and America).

TRIBUTE LABOR (*MITA*) IN THE SILVER MINES

The silver mines of Potosí, in the Andes, are about two miles above sea level. The work, as depicted in this 1603 engraving by Theodore de Bry, was extremely onerous and often dangerous.

New York Public Library. Astor, Lenox and Tilden Foundations, Rare Book Division.

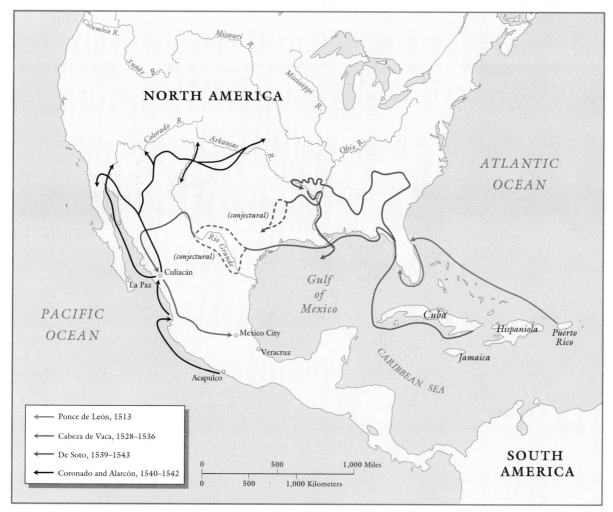

Ponce de León, 1513

Cabeza de Vaca, 1528–1536

De Soto, 1539–1543

Coronado and Alarcón, 1540–1542

MAP 1.10   PRINCIPAL SPANISH EXPLORATIONS OF NORTH AMERICA

Four Spanish expeditions marched through much of the interior of North America between 1513 and 1543.

 View an animated version of this map or related maps at http://history.wadsworth.com/murrin_LEP4e.

In a little more than 10 years, some hundreds of Spanish soldiers with thousands of Indian allies had conquered two enormous empires with a combined population perhaps five times greater than that of all Spain. But only in the 1540s did the Spanish finally locate the bonanza they had been seeking. The fabulous silver mines at Potosí in present-day Bolivia and other smaller lodes in Mexico became the source of Spain's wealth and power for the next 100 years. So wondrous did the exploits of the *conquistadors* seem by then that anything became believable, including rumors that cities of pure gold lay somewhere in the interior of North America.

North American *Conquistadores* and Missionaries

Alvar Núñez Cabeza de Vaca was one of four survivors of Pánfilo de Narváez's disastrous 1528 expedition to Florida. Cabeza de Vaca made his way back to Mexico City in 1536 after an overland journey that took him from Florida through Texas and northern Mexico. In a published account of his adventures, he briefly mentioned Indian tales of great and populous cities to the north, and this reference soon became stories of "golden cities." Hernando de Soto landed in Florida in 1539 and roamed through much of the southeastern United States in quest of these treasures, leaving disease and mayhem in his wake. He crossed the Mississippi in 1541, wandered through the Ozarks and eastern Oklahoma, and marched back to the great river. He died there in 1542. His companions continued to explore for another year before returning to Spanish territory. Farther west, Francisco Vasquez de Coronado marched into New Mexico and Arizona, where he encountered several Pueblo towns but no golden cities. The expedition reached the Grand Canyon, then headed east into Texas and as far north as Kansas before returning to Mexico in 1542. North of Mexico, Indians menaced and sometimes even defeated Spanish soldiers, who finally gave up, but left their diseases behind. There were no cities of gold.

H I S T O R Y   T H R O U G H   F I L M

The Mission (1986)

This film passionately portrays the destruction of the Jesuit missions in 18th-century Paraguay. Their success and communal prosperity (which included abolishment of private property) aroused the envy and the enmity of neighboring Portuguese settlers. Some of their churches were as large and as beautifully adorned as European cathedrals. When the Crown of Spain transferred the Guaraní territory to the Crown of Portugal in a 1750 treaty, the settlers and the government of Brazil got their chance to move against the missions. Loosely based on the Portuguese war against the Guaraní in the 1750s, the film is really a tribute to the dedication and sincerity of the Jesuit order, the colonial era's most successful missionary organization in either North or South America.

The screenplay by Robert Bolt, well known for his play and film of *A Man for All Seasons* (1966) and his film script for *Dr. Zhivago* (1965), telescopes the events of one and a half centuries into what seems to be only a year or so. In the

Directed by Roland Joffé. Starring Jeremy Irons (Father Gabriel), Robert De Niro (Mendoza), and Liam Neeson (Father Fielding).

17th century, Portuguese slavers raided even Jesuit missions and carried off thousands of Indians to a life of toil in Brazil. The Guaraní War was not about enslavement but about the campaign to seize the native inhabitants' land and communal property. Bolt puts both events in the 18th century and provides a dramatic climax.

The film stars Jeremy Irons as Gabriel, a Spanish Jesuit missionary who uses the Guaraní Indians' love of music as a means of converting them. Robert De Niro plays Mendoza, a reformed slaver who has killed his own brother in a lovers' quarrel and then repents by joining Father Gabriel's mission. When the European courts and even the Jesuit order command the missionaries not to resist the Portuguese takeover, the missionaries refuse to leave their people but split over how to resist. Gabriel chooses nonviolence. Mendoza and Father Fielding (Liam Neeson) take up arms. All of them are killed. Jesuit involvement in the Guaraní War gave the Catholic monarchs of Europe the

After the *conquistadores* departed, Spanish priests did their best to convert thousands of North American Indians to the Catholic faith. These efforts extended well north of New Spain (Mexico). In 1570, the Jesuits even established a mission in what is now Virginia, but local Indians soon wiped it out.

After the failure of the Jesuit mission, Spain decided to treat the Indians of Florida and New Mexico with decency and fairness and eventually came to rely on these missions for protection against English and French intruders. The Jesuits withdrew, and Franciscans took their place. In 1573, King Philip II (1556–98) issued the Royal Orders for New Discoveries, which made it illegal to enslave Indians or even attack them. Instead, unarmed priests were to bring Indians together in missions and convert them into peaceful Catholic subjects of Spain. The Franciscans quickly discovered that, without military support, they were more likely to win martyrdom than converts. They reluctantly accepted military protection, but they tried to make sure that none of

the few soldiers who accompanied them behaved like *conquistadores*.

Missionary work demanded commitment and faith. The Franciscans had both. A belief in miracles also sustained them. In 1631, a mystical nun in Castile, María de Jesús de Agreda, claimed that angels had carried her across the Atlantic, where she preached to Indians in their own languages. When Pueblo Indians reported that a "Lady in Blue" once preached to them, the Franciscans put the two accounts together into a miraculous event that enchanted thousands for a century, even though the nun retracted most of her story in 1650.

Franciscans had no success among the nomadic residents of central and southern Florida. They had to build their missions within the permanent villages of northern Florida or the Pueblo communities of New Mexico. The Spanish incursion into New Mexico began quite badly with the slaughter of perhaps 800 Indian men, women, and children in 1599, but then relations softened. At first, Indian women willingly supplied the labor needed to

excuse they needed to expel the Jesuits from their kingdoms and then to persuade the pope to disband the order.

By telescoping events that occurred decades apart into a short period, Bolt intensifies the drama but also suggests that some Europeans, especially Jesuits, did consistently and over a long period place the welfare of Indians above all other values. In a poignant final scene, many mission children, now completely naked, are rowing back into the wilderness to escape enslavement. The settlers, Bolt insists, would not allow them to become civilized.

Filmed on location above and below magnificent Agazzu Falls, one of the most spectacular sights in South America, the film won the 1986 Cannes Film Festival's award for best picture and an Oscar for best cinematography. British director Roland Joffé had already earned acclaim for *The Killing Fields* (1983), a stark depiction of the near-genocidal atrocities in Cambodia after the Vietnam War. He later directed *Fatman and Little Boy* (1989), a dramatization of the birth of the atomic bomb.

In this scene, Father Gabriel plays the flute to attract a Guaraní audience.

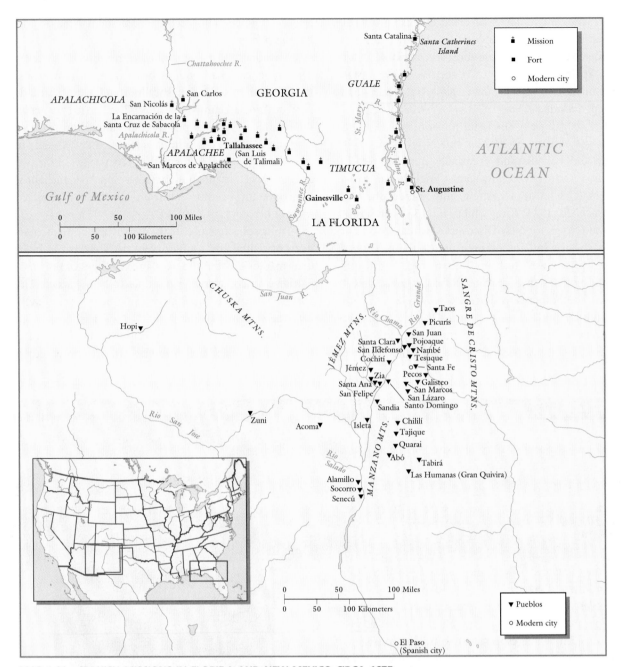

MAP 1.11   SPANISH MISSIONS IN FLORIDA AND NEW MEXICO CIRCA 1675
Franciscan friars established missions in Florida from the Atlantic to the Gulf of Mexico and in New Mexico along the
Rio Grande Valley and, in a few cases, farther inland.

build and sustain these missions. By 1630, about 86,000
Pueblo, Apache, and Navajo Indians of New Mexico had
accepted baptism. They lived in a chain of missions north
and south of Santa Fe, 1,500 arduous and dusty miles
from the colonial capital at Mexico City. By midcentury,
30 missions in Florida contained about 26,000 baptized
Indians and covered an area extending some 250 miles
from the Atlantic coast of what is now Georgia westward
into the Florida panhandle. The Franciscans also urged
their converts, with limited success, to wear European cloth-

ing. In 1671, when a bishop counted 4,081 newly converted women in Florida who went about topless and with
their lower legs exposed, he ordered them to cover up.

The Spanish Empire and Demographic Catastrophe

By the late 16th century, the Spanish Empire had emerged
as a system of direct colonial rule in Mexico and Peru,
where the conquerors took over and used existing systems

A Chesapeake Warrior Challenges the Spanish Empire

In 1561, an Algonquian Indian chief brought his son aboard a Spanish vessel trading in Chesapeake Bay. The teenager seemed of such "fine presence and bearing" that the Spaniards asked to take him to Spain and present him to the royal court. They promised to return him with wealth and honors. In Spain, the expedition's commander, Pedro Menéndez de Avilés, introduced him as a "*cacique* or important lord from Florida." The young man learned Spanish, studied Christianity, and was baptized as Don Luis de Velasco in honor of the Spanish viceroy in Mexico, who became his godfather. Don Luis sailed to Mexico with Menéndez in 1563, then returned to Spain, and this time Don Luis studied with the Jesuits, whom Menéndez had been urging to establish a mission in the Chesapeake Bay region.

In September 1570, with Father Juan Baptista de Segura in charge, two priests, three brothers, three novices, a boy, and Don Luis, who was expected to act as interpreter, landed, probably near modern Williamsburg. The missionaries assumed that the young Indian had been appropriately awed by Spanish might. After 10 years' absence, his relatives were astonished to see him and at first believed that the Jesuits had awakened him from the dead. But this initial awe quickly turned sour because the newcomers expected the Indians to feed them after a season of drought. A younger brother of Don Luis had become chief and offered to yield the position to him, but Don Luis declined the honor. He soon reverted to Indian folkways by agreeing to take several wives. When Segura publicly humiliated him for engaging in these sinful practices, Don Luis deserted the mission in October. After four months, the Spaniards sent a small expedition to find him. He promised to come back, but instead, accompanied by several warriors, he followed the party and killed its members on February 4, 1571. Five days later, his men wiped out all of the survivors

except the boy. Don Luis had been impressed by Spanish power, but the result was not what the missionaries had hoped.

Menéndez took fearful vengeance in 1572. A barrage of harquebuses tore into a crowd of Indians. After the survivors refused to surrender Don Luis to Spanish justice, Menéndez hanged eight Indian hostages. Don Luis was very likely related to Powhatan and Opechancanough, the paramount sachems of the Powhatan Indians of "Virginia" between the founding of Jamestown in 1607 and Opechancanough's death in 1646. One historian has even argued that Don Luis was Opechancanough, an Algonquian word that meant "he whose soul is white" and who was described in the 1640s as more than a hundred years old. But if Opechancanough had lived among Europeans for 10 years as Don Luis, he would hardly have been so fascinated with a lock and key as to lock and unlock it a hundred times a day, according to an English missionary, for "he thought no device in all the world comparable to it."

© Hulton Archive/Getty Images.

DON LUIS DE VELASCO MURDERING THE JESUITS, 1571

This engraving by Melchior Küssell was published in 1675 and portrays the victims as martyrs who died for their faith. There is no reason to assume that the artist knew what Don Luis looked like.

of tribute. These core holdings were protected by a strong defensive perimeter in the Caribbean and surrounded by a series of frontier missions, extending in the north into Florida and New Mexico. The Spaniards also brought new systems of labor and new religious institutions to their overseas colonies, although in time both were altered by local conditions.

The first Spanish rulers in Mexico and Peru relied on a form of labor tribute that had helped to depopulate the West Indies. Called *encomienda,* this system permitted the holder, or *encomendero,* to claim labor from an Indian district for a stated period. *Encomienda* worked because it resembled the way the Aztecs and the Incas had routinely levied labor for their own massive public buildings and irrigation projects. In time, the king intervened to correct abuses and to limit labor tribute to projects that the Crown initiated, such as mining and the construction of churches or other public buildings. Spanish settlers resisted the reforms at first but slowly shifted from demanding labor to claiming land. In the countryside, the *hacienda,* a large estate with its own crops and herds, became a familiar institution.

Although the Church never had enough clergy to meet its needs, it became a massive presence during the 16th century. Yet America changed it, too. As missionaries acquired land and labor, they began to exhibit less zeal for Indian souls. The Franciscans—in Europe, the gentlest of Catholic religious orders—brutally and systematically tortured their Mayan converts in the 1560s whenever they caught them worshiping their old gods. To the Franciscans, the slightest lapse could signal a reversion to Satan worship, with human sacrifice a likely consequence. They did not dare to be kind.

Most important, the Spaniards brought deadly microbes with them. Smallpox, which could be fatal but which most Europeans survived in childhood, devastated the Indians, who had almost no immunity to it. Even measles could be fatal, and common colds easily turned into pneumonia. When Cortés arrived in 1519, the native population of Mexico probably exceeded 15 million. In the 1620s, after waves of killing epidemics, it bottomed out at 700,000 and did not regain its pre-Spanish level until the 1950s. Peru suffered nearly as horribly. Its population fell from about 10 million in 1525 to 600,000 a century later. For the hemisphere as a whole, any given region probably lost 90 or 95 percent of its population within a century of sustained contact with Europeans. Lowland tropical areas usually suffered the heaviest casualties; in some of these places, all of the Indians died. Highland areas and sparsely settled regions fared somewhat better.

The Spanish Crown spent much of the 16th century trying to keep abreast of these changes, but eventually it imposed administrative order on the unruly *conquistadores* and brought peace to its colonies. At the center of the imperial bureaucracy, in Seville, stood the Council of the Indies. The council administered the three American viceroyalties of New Spain, Peru, and eventually New Granada, which were further subdivided into smaller *audiencias,* executive and judicial jurisdictions supervised by the viceroys. The Council of the Indies appointed the viceroys and other major officials, who ruled from the new cities that the Spaniards built with local labor at Havana, Mexico City, Lima, and elsewhere. Although centralized and autocratic in theory, the Spanish Empire allowed local officials a fair degree of initiative, if only because months or even years could elapse in trying to communicate across its immense distances. "If death came from Spain," mused one official, "we should all live long lives."

Brazil

Portuguese Brazil was theoretically autocratic, too, but it was divided into 14 "captaincies," or provinces, and thus was far less centralized. The Portuguese invasion did not lead to the direct rule of native societies but to their displacement or enslavement. After the colonists on the northeast coast turned to raising sugar in the late 16th century, Brazilian frontiersmen, or *bandeirantes,* foraged deep into the continent to enslave more Indians. They even raided remote Spanish Andean missions, rounded up the converts, and dragged them thousands of miles across mountains and through the jungle to be worked to death on the sugar plantations. On several occasions, while Brazil was ruled by Spain (see the discussion that follows), outraged missionaries persuaded the king to abolish slavery altogether. Not even absolutism could achieve that goal. Slavery continued without pause, and Africans gradually replaced Indians as the dominant labor force. Brazil was the major market for African slaves until the 1640s, when demand in West Indian sugar islands became even greater.

Global Colossus, Global Economy

American silver made the king of Spain the most powerful monarch in Christendom. Philip II commanded the largest army in Europe, held the Turks in check in the Mediterranean, and tried to crush the Protestant Reformation in northern Europe (see chapter 2). He had other ambitions as well. In 1580, after the king of Portugal died with no direct heir, Philip claimed his throne, thus uniting under his own rule Portugal's Asian empire, Brazil, Spain's American possessions, and the Philippines. This colossus was the greatest empire the world had ever seen. It also sustained the first truly global economy, because the Por-

tuguese used Spain's American silver to pay for the spices and silks they imported from Asia. The union of Spain and Portugal lasted until the 1640s, when Portugal revolted and regained its independence.

The Spanish colossus became part of an even broader economic pattern. Serfdom, which tied peasants to their lords and to the land, had been Europe's predominant labor system in the early Middle Ages. Although peasants could not move, neither could they be sold; they were not slaves. Serfdom had been declining in Western Europe since the 12th century and was nearly gone by 1500. A system of free labor arose in its place, and overseas expansion strengthened that trend within Western Europe. Although free labor prevailed in the Western European homeland, unfree labor systems took root all around Europe's periphery, both overseas and in Eastern Europe, and the two systems were structurally linked. In general, free labor reigned where populations were dense and still growing. Large pools of labor kept wages low, but around the periphery of Western Europe, where land was cheap and labor expensive, coercive systems became the only efficient way for Europeans to extract from those areas the goods they desired.

The forms of unfree labor varied greatly across space and time, from slavery to less brutal systems. In New Spain, as the native population dwindled, the practice of *encomienda* slowly yielded to debt peonage. Unpayable debts kept Indians tied to the *haciendas* of the countryside. The mining of precious metals, on the other hand, was so dangerous and unpleasant that it almost always required a large degree of physical coercion, a system of labor tribute called *mita* in the Andes. Similarly, any colonial region that devoted itself to the production of staple crops for sale in Europe also turned to unfree labor and eventually to overt slavery. Sugar production first reduced Indians to bondage in the Caribbean and Brazil and later, as they died off, led to the importation of African slaves by the millions. Other staples—tobacco, rice, cotton, coffee— later followed similar patterns. At first these crops were considered luxuries and commanded high prices, but as they became widely available on the world market, their prices fell steeply, profit margins contracted, and planters turned overwhelmingly to coerced labor. Even in Eastern Europe, which began to specialize in producing cereal crops for sale in the more diversified West, serfdom revived. In Russia, where the Orthodox Church never condemned the enslavement of fellow Christians, the condition of a serf came to resemble that of a slave in one of the Atlantic empires. Some serfs were even bought and sold.

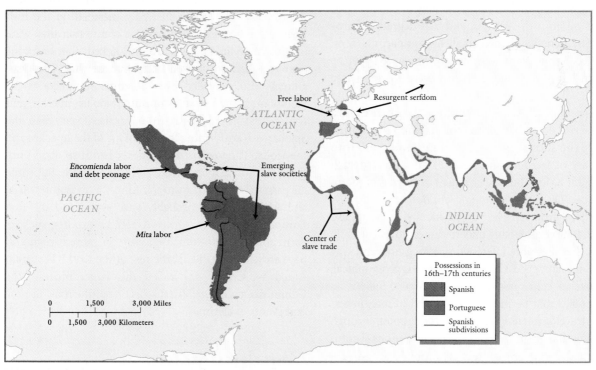

MAP 1.12 SPANISH EMPIRE AND GLOBAL LABOR SYSTEM

While Western European states were becoming free-labor societies, they created or encouraged the establishment of societies built on or providing laborers for various unfree labor systems in the Americas, the Caribbean, Africa, and Eastern Europe.

Spain's rise had been spectacular, but its empire was vulnerable. Although silver from the Americas vastly enhanced the Crown's ability to wage war, the costs of continuous conflict, the inflation generated by a steady influx of silver, and the need to defend a much greater perimeter absorbed Spain's new resources and a great deal more. Between 1492 and 1580, Spain's population grew from 4.9 million to 8 million, but over the course of the following century, it fell by 20 percent, mostly because of the escalating costs, both financial and human, of Spain's wars. As population declined, taxes rose. Castile grew poorer, not richer, in its century and a half of imperial glory. Most of the wealth of the Indies went elsewhere to pay for goods or services that Spain failed to provide for itself—to merchants in Genoa, to manufacturers in Lombardy and the Low Countries, and to bankers in Augsburg.

Explanations: Patterns of Conquest, Submission, and Resistance

By the middle of the 18th century, Europeans who thought seriously about the discovery of America and its global implications generally agreed that the whole process had been a moral outrage, possibly the worst in history. Conquest and settlement had killed millions of Indians, had enslaved millions of Africans, and had degraded Europeans. The benefits seemed small by comparison, even though economic gains were undeniably large by 1750. If the cruelest of the conquerors had been able to foresee the results of this process, asked the Abbé Raynal, would he have proceeded? "Is it to be imagined that there exists a being infernal enough to answer this question in the affirmative!" The success of the American Revolution, with its message of freedom and human rights, quieted such thinking for a time, but the critique has revived in recent years, especially in the developing world.

Modern historians, less moralistic than Raynal, also realize that he considerably underestimated the death toll. Even so, they are more interested in asking how and why these things happened. One major reason is geographical. The Eurasian land mass, the world's largest, follows an east-west axis that permits life forms and human inventions to travel immense distances without going through forbidding changes of climate. Chinese inventions eventually reached Europe. By contrast, the Americas, and sub-Saharan Africa, lie along north-south axes that do impose such barriers. Another compelling explanation for European success focuses on the prolonged isolation of the Americas from the rest of the world. If two communities of equal ability are kept apart, that with the larger and more varied population will be more inventive than the other, and its people will learn more rapidly from one another over time. For example, the use of iron spread gradually throughout nearly all of Asia, Africa, and Europe. And even though Europeans knew little about China, they slowly acquired Chinese inventions such as paper, the compass, and gunpowder. More than any other technological edge, far more than firearms or even horses, steel made military conquest possible. European armor stopped enemy spears and arrows, and European swords killed opponents swiftly without any need to reload.

The biological consequences of isolation were even more momentous than the technological barriers. The devastation European microbes inflicted upon the Indian population is the greatest tragedy in the history of humankind. The Indians' genetic makeup was more uniform than that of Europeans, Africans, or Asians. Indians were descended from a rather small sample of the total gene pool of Eurasia. Centuries spent in frigid Beringia had weeded out weaker people and killed the microbes that produce most diseases. The Indians first encountered by Europeans were bigger, stronger, and—at first contact—healthier than the newcomers, but they died in appalling numbers because they had almost no resistance to European diseases.

European plants also thrived at the expense of native vegetation. For example, when British settlers first crossed the Appalachian mountains, they marveled at the lush Kentucky bluegrass. They did not realize that they were looking at an accidental European import that had conquered the landscape even faster than they had. European animals also prevailed over potential American rivals. Horses multiplied at an astonishing rate in America, and wild herds moved north from Mexico faster than the Spaniards, transforming the way of life of the Apaches and the Sioux. The lowly sparrow never had it so good until someone turned a few loose in North America. But some life forms also moved from the Americas to Europe, Asia, and Africa. Indians probably gave syphilis to the first Europeans they met. Other American exports, such as corn, potatoes, and tomatoes, were far more benign and have enriched the diet of the rest of the world. Historian Alfred W. Crosby has called this larger process "the Columbian exchange." It ranks as one of the most important events of all time.

Conclusion

Americans like to believe that their history is a story of progress. They are right about its European phase. After its tragic beginnings in conquest, depopulation, and enslavement, things had to improve.

For thousands of years, the Americas had been cut off from the rest of the world. The major cultures of Eurasia and Africa had existed in relative isolation, engaging in direct contact with only their immediate neighbors. Islamic societies that shared borders with India, the East Indies, black Africa, and Europe had been the principal mediators among these cultures and, in that era, were more tolerant than most Christian societies.

In just 40 years, daring European navigators, supported by the Crowns of Portugal and Spain, joined the world together and challenged Islam's mediating role. Between 1492 and 1532, Europe, Africa, Asia, the Spice Islands, the Philippines, the Caribbean, Aztec Mexico, Inca Peru, and other parts of the Americas came into intense and often violent contact with one another. A few individuals gained much, and Spain acquired a military advantage within Europe that endured into the 1640s. Nearly everybody else suffered, millions horribly, especially in the Americas and Africa. And Spain spent the rest of the 16th century trying to create an imperial system that could impose order on this turbulent reality.

But Spain had many enemies. They too would find the lure of wealth and land overseas irresistible.

SUGGESTED READINGS

Two recent general surveys of early American history provide excellent coverage up to Independence: **Alan Taylor, *American Colonies*** (2001); and **Richard Middleton, *Colonial America: A History, 1565–1776,*** 3rd ed. (2002). For a useful collection of essays, see **Stanley N. Katz, John M. Murrin, and Douglas Greenberg, eds., *Colonial America: Essays in Politics and Social Development,*** 5th ed. (2001).

Brian M. Fagan, *The Great Journey: The Peopling of Ancient America* (1987) is a fine introduction to pre-Columbian America. See also **David Webster, *The Fall of the Ancient Maya: Solving the Mystery of the Maya Collapse*** (2002). **Jared Diamond, *Guns, Germs, and Steel: The Fates of Human Societies*** (1997) is provocative and challenging in its global perspective. For the age of explorations, see **Peter Russell, *Prince Henry 'the Navigator': A Life*** (2000); **G. V. Scammell, *The First Imperial Age: European Overseas Expansion c. 1400–1715*** (1989); and **Alfred W. Crosby's** classic synthesis, ***The Columbian Exchange: Biological and Cultural Consequences of 1492*** (1972). For the slave trade, see **John Thornton, *Africa and Africans in the Making of the Modern World, 1400–1800,*** 2nd ed. (1998), which insists that Africans retained control of their affairs, including the slave trade, through the 17th century; and **Patrick Manning, *Slavery and African Life: Occidental, Oriental, and African Slave Trades*** (1990), which emphasizes the devastating impact of the slave trade in the 18th and 19th centuries. **Ira Berlin's *Many Thousands Gone: The First Two Centuries of Slavery in North America*** (1998) is an effective and comprehensive synthesis of a huge subject.

James Lockhart and Stuart B. Schwartz, *Early Latin America: A History of Colonial Latin America and Brazil* (1983) is an outstanding introduction to the Iberian empires. **J. H. Parry's *The Spanish Seaborne Empire*** (1966) retains great value. **David J. Weber's *The Spanish Frontier in North America*** (1992) is easily the best introduction to its subject. For Brazil, see **John Hemming, *Red Gold: The Conquest of the Brazilian Indians, 1500–1760*** (1978).

 AMERICAN JOURNEY ONLINE

AND

INFOTRAC® COLLEGE EDITION

Visit the source collections at www.ajaccess.wadsworth.com and infotrac.thomsonlearning.com and use the Search function with the following key terms to explore documents, images, audio and video clips, articles, and commentary related to the material in this chapter.

Inca	Hernán Cortés
Maya	Tenochtitlán
Olmec	Anasazi
Mesoamerica	Cahokia
Aztecs	Christopher Columbus

GRADE AIDS

Visit the Liberty Equality Power Companion Web Site for resources specific to this textbook: http://history.wadsworth.com/murrin_LEP4e

The CD in the back of this book and the U.S. History Resource Center at http://history.wadsworth.com/u.s./ offer a variety of tools to help you succeed in this course, including access to quizzes; images; documents; interactive simulations, maps, and timelines; movie explorations; and a wealth of other sources.

Chapter 2

The Challenge to Spain and the Settlement of North America

MODERN VIEW OF MEXICO CITY
The conquest of Mexico made Spain the richest European empire and prompted it to think in grandiose terms. This view juxtaposes the Aztec ruins of Tlateloco in the foreground against a Spanish church that is far more imposing than anything built in the English or French colonies before 1776, but their people were eager to challenge Spanish power. In the background are modern high-rise apartments.

CHAPTER OUTLINE

Catholic France and two Protestant countries, the Dutch Republic and England, challenged Spanish power in Europe and overseas. None of them planted a permanent settlement in North America before 1600. In the quarter-century after 1600, they all did. The French converted thousands of Indians. The French and Dutch brought Indian hunters into the world market by trading European goods for their furs. By 1700, the English, who coveted the land itself, had founded 12 permanent colonies in North America and others in the West Indies.

These American colonies differed as much from one another as they did from their parent cultures in Europe. Europeans, Indians, and Africans interacted in contrasting ways in this strange "New World." In Mexico and Peru, the Spaniards had set themselves up as a European ruling class over a much larger Indian population of farmers, artisans, and miners. Spain's rivals created colonies of different kinds. Some, such as Virginia and Barbados, grew staple crops with indentured servants and African slaves. New France and New Netherland developed a prosperous trade with the Indians without trying to rule them. In New England, the Puritans relied on free labor provided by hardworking family members. After 1660, the English state conquered New Netherland, and English Quakers created another free-labor society in the Delaware valley, dedicated, more than any of the others, to human equality and complete religious liberty.

C H A P T E R   F O C U S

♦ Why did more Indians choose to become Catholics rather than Protestants?

♦ Why did Englishmen, crossing the Atlantic at nearly the same time, create such radically different societies in the Chesapeake colonies, the West Indies, and New England?

♦ How did England's Restoration colonies differ from those founded before 1660?

♦ If Pennsylvania really was the political failure described by many contemporaries, how could it have become such a spectacular economic success?

● The Protestant Reformation and the Challenge to Spain

Spain, the most militantly Catholic society in Europe, did its best to crush the Protestant Reformation. Many of Spain's European enemies became Protestants during the 16th century and had strong religious motives for exposing Spanish "cruelties" in the Americas. Most Protestants, however, proved no more humane than the Spaniards in their own dealings with Indians.

By the time Spain's enemies felt strong enough to challenge Spain overseas, the Protestant Reformation had shattered the religious unity of Europe. In November 1517, not long before Cortés landed in Mexico, Martin Luther nailed his 95 Theses to the cathedral door at Wittenberg in the German electorate of Saxony and touched off the Reformation. No human act, or "good work," Luther insisted, can be meritorious in the sight of God. Salvation comes through faith alone, and God grants saving faith only to those who hear his Word preached to them, struggle to understand it, and admit that, without God's grace, they are damned. Within a generation, the states of northern Germany and Scandinavia had embraced Lutheranism, but the Lutheran Church never played a major role in founding colonies overseas. Calvinism did.

John Calvin, a French Protestant, also embraced justification by faith alone and put his own militant principles into practice in the Swiss canton of Geneva. The Huguenot movement in France, the Dutch Reformed Church in the Netherlands, and the Presbyterian Kirk (or Church) of Scotland all embraced Calvin's principles, as set forth in *The Institutes of the Christian Religion* (1536). In England, the Anglican Church adopted Calvinist doctrines but not forms of worship, a compromise that prompted the Puri-

C H R O N O L O G Y

1517	Luther begins the Protestant Reformation
1577–80	Drake circumnavigates the globe
1580s	Gilbert claims Newfoundland for England (1583) • Ralegh twice fails to colonize Roanoke Island (1585–87) • England repels attack by the Spanish Armada (1588)
1607	English settlement established at Jamestown
1608	Champlain founds Quebec
1609	Virginia receives sea-to-sea charter
1613–14	Rolfe grows tobacco, marries Pocahontas
1618	Sandys implements London Company reforms
1619	First Africans arrive in Virginia • House of Burgesses and Headright system created
1620s	Pilgrims adopt Mayflower Compact, land at Plymouth (1620) • Dutch West India Company chartered (1621) • Opechancanough launches war of extermination in Virginia (1622) • King assumes direct control of Virginia (1624) • Minuit founds New Amsterdam (1626)
1630s	Puritans settle Massachusetts Bay (1630) • Maryland chartered (1632) • Williams founds Providence; Hooker founds Hartford (1636) • Anne Hutchinson banished to Rhode Island; Minuit founds New Sweden (1638) • New Haven Colony founded (1639)
1640s	Massachusetts "Body of Liberties" passed (1641) • English civil wars begin (1642) • Pavonia Massacre in New Netherland (1643) • Charles I beheaded (1649)
1655	New Netherland conquers New Sweden • Quakers invade New England
1660s	Charles II restored to English throne (1660) • Puritans institute Half-Way Covenant (1662) • First Carolina charter granted (1663) • New Netherland surrenders to the English (1664) • New Jersey becomes a separate colony (1665) • Carolina's Fundamental Constitutions proposed (1669)
1670s	First permanent English settlement established in South Carolina (1670) • Dutch retake New York (1673–74) • West New Jersey approves Concessions and Agreements (1677)
1680s	Charleston founded (1680) • Pennsylvania charter granted (1681) • New York and Pennsylvania each adopt a Charter of Liberties (1683)
1705	Virginia adopts comprehensive slave code

tan reform movement toward a more thoroughly Calvinist Church of England. Calvinists won major victories over Catholics in Europe in the last half of the 16th century. After 1620, Puritans carried their religious vision across the Atlantic to New England.

Calvinists rejected papal supremacy, the seven sacraments (they kept only baptism and the Lord's Supper),

Theodore de Bry.

SPANIARDS TORTURING INDIANS, AS DEPICTED BY THEODORE de BRY, LATE 16TH CENTURY

Among Protestants in northern Europe, images such as this one merged into a "black legend" of Spanish cruelty, which in turn helped justify their own challenge to Spanish power overseas. But in practice, the behavior of Protestant settlers toward Indians was often as harsh as anything the Spaniards had done.

clerical celibacy, veneration of the saints, and the acts of charity and the penitential rituals by which Catholics tried to earn grace and store up merits. They denounced these rites as "work righteousness." Calvin gave central importance to predestination. According to that doctrine, God decreed, even before creating the world, who will be saved and who will be damned. Christ died, Calvin insisted, not for all humankind, but only for God's elect. Calvinists kept the Lord's Supper, but in denying that Christ is actually present in the bread and wine, they broke with Luther as well as with Rome. Because salvation and damnation were beyond human power to alter, Calvinists—especially English Puritans—felt a compelling inner need to find out whether they were saved. They struggled to recognize in themselves a conversion experience, the process by which God's elect discovered that they were among the chosen.

France, the Netherlands, and England, all with powerful Protestant movements, challenged Spanish power in Europe. Until 1559, France was the main threat, with Italy as the battleground, but Spain won that phase. In the 1560s, with France embroiled in its own Wars of Religion, a new challenge came from the 17 provinces of the Netherlands, which Spain ruled. The Dutch rebelled against the heavy taxes and severe Catholic orthodoxy imposed by Philip II. As Spanish armies put down the rebellion in

the 10 southern provinces (modern Belgium), merchants and Protestants fled north. Many went to Amsterdam, which replaced Spanish-controlled Antwerp as the economic center of northern Europe. The seven northern provinces gradually took shape as the Dutch Republic, or the United Provinces of the Netherlands. The Dutch turned their resistance into a war for independence from Catholic Spain. The conflict lasted 80 years until 1648, drained Spanish resources, and spread to Asia, Africa, and America. England long remained on the edges of this European struggle, only to emerge in the end as the biggest winner overseas.

New France

About 16 million people lived in France in 1500, more than three times the population of Spain. The French made a few stabs at overseas expansion before 1600, but with little success. "The sun shines for me as for the others," growled King Francis I (1515–47) when reminded that the pope had divided all non-Christian lands between Spain and Portugal. "I should like to see the clause of Adam's will which excludes me from a share of the world."

Early French Explorers

In 1524, Francis sent Giovanni da Verrazano, an Italian, to America in search of a northwest passage to Asia. (Magellan's voyage had shown how difficult it was to sail around South America and across the Pacific.) Verrazano explored the North American coast from the Carolinas to Nova Scotia and noted Manhattan's superb potential as a harbor but found no passage to Asia. Between 1534 and 1543, Jacques Cartier made three voyages to North America. He sailed up the St. Lawrence River in search of Saguenay, a wealthy kingdom rumored to be in the interior. Instead, he discovered the severity of a Canadian winter and gave up. For the rest of the century, the French ignored Canada, except for a few fur traders and for fishermen who descended on Newfoundland each year in growing numbers. By the 1580s, the Canadian fisheries rivaled New Spain in the volume of shipping they employed.

After 1550, the French turned to warmer climates. Some Huguenots briefly challenged the Portuguese in Brazil. Others sacked Havana, prompting Spain to turn it into a fortified, year-round naval base under the command of Admiral Pedro Menéndez de Avilés. Still others planted a settlement on the Atlantic coast of Florida. Menéndez attacked them in 1565, talked them into surrendering, and then executed every man who refused to accept the Catholic faith. He did spare some women and children.

In France, the Wars of Religion blocked further efforts at expansion for the rest of the 16th century. King Henry IV (1589–1610), a Protestant, converted to Catholicism and granted limited toleration to Huguenots through the Edict of Nantes in 1598, thus ending the civil wars for the rest of his reign. Henry was a *politique;* he insisted that the survival of the state take precedence over religious differences. Moreover, he believed in toleration for its own sake. Another *politique* was the Catholic soldier and explorer Samuel de Champlain.

Missions and Furs

Champlain, whose mother may have been a Huguenot, believed that Catholics and Huguenots could work together, Europeanize the Indians, convert them, and even marry them. Before his death in 1635, he made 11 voyages to Canada. During his second trip (1604–06), he planted a predominantly Huguenot settlement in Acadia (Nova Scotia). In 1608, he sailed up the St. Lawrence River, established friendly relations with the Montagnais, Algonquin, and Huron Indians, and founded Quebec. "Our sons shall wed your daughters," he told them, "and we shall be one people." Many Frenchmen cohabited with Indian women, but only 15 formal marriages took place between them in the 17th century. Champlain's friendliness toward the Indians of the St. Lawrence valley also had some unpleasant consequences: It drew him into their wars against the Iroquois Five Nations farther south. At times, Iroquois hostility almost destroyed New France.

Champlain failed to unite Catholics and Protestants in mutual harmony. Huguenots in France were eager to trade with Canada, but few settled there. Their ministers showed no interest in converting the Indians, whereas Catholic priests became zealous missionaries. In 1625, the French Crown declared that only the Catholic faith could

---

H I S T O R Y   T H R O U G H   F I L M

Black Robe (1991)

Directed by Bruce Beresford. Starring Lothaire Bluteau (Father Laforgue), Aden Young (Daniel), Jean Brusseau (Samuel de Champlain), and Sandrine Holt (Annuka).

In *Black Robe,* director Bruce Beresford has given us the most believable film portrayal of 17th-century North America—both the landscape and its peoples—yet produced. This Canada–Australia co-production won six Genie Awards (Canada's equivalent of the Oscar), including best picture, best director, and best cinematography.

The film is based on Brian Moore's novel of the same title, and Moore wrote the screenplay. It was filmed on location amid the spectacular scenery in the Lac St. Jean/ Saguenay region of Quebec.

In New France in the 1630s, Father Laforgue (Lothaire Bluteau), a young Jesuit, and Daniel (Aden Young), his teen-aged assistant and translator, leave on Laforgue's first mission assignment. Samuel de Champlain (Jean Brusseau), the governor of the colony, has persuaded the Algonquin tribe to convey the two to their mission site among the Hurons, far in the interior.

Before long, Daniel falls in love with Annuka (Sandrine Holt), the beautiful daughter of Algonquin chief Chomina (August Schellenberg). When the priest inadvertently watches the young couple make love, he knows that, according to his faith, he has committed a mortal sin. From that point, his journey into the North American heartland threatens to become a descent into hell.

The Algonquins, guided by a dream quest, pursue a logic that makes no sense to the priest. Conversely, his religious message baffles them. Even so, when Chomina is wounded and Laforgue and Daniel are captured by the Iroquois, Annuka seduces their lone guard, kills him, and enables all four of them to escape. Chomina dies of his wounds, politely but firmly rejecting baptism until the end. What Indian, he asks, would want to go to the Christian heaven, populated by many black robes but none of his ancestors?

With the priest's approval, Daniel and Annuka go off by themselves. Laforgue reaches the mission, only to find many of the Indians dead or dying from some European disease. As the film closes, we learn that smallpox would

be practiced in New France, thus ending Champlain's dream of a colony that was more tolerant than France. Acadia soon became Catholic as well.

Early New France is a tale of missionaries and furs, of attempts to convert the Indians and of efforts to trade with them. The career of Etienne Brûlé, the first French *coureur de bois* (roamer of the woods), illustrates how incompatible these goals could be. Champlain left this teenage lad with the Indians in the winter of 1610 to learn their languages and customs. Brûlé absorbed more than that. He enjoyed hunting, the sexual permissiveness of Indian culture, and the chance to go where no European had ever been. He soon forgot most of his Christian training. Once, when he was about to be tortured to death by Indians, he tried to cry out to God, but the only prayer he could recall was, ominously, grace before meals. Desperate, he flashed a religious medal, and, when a thunderclap signaled divine approval, the Indians released him. Brûlé

apparently learned little from that experience. In 1632, he was caught robbing an Indian grave and was executed and eaten by the offended tribe. *Coureurs de bois,* such as Brûlé, did much for the fur trade but made life difficult for the missionaries.

After 1630, Jesuit missionaries made heroic efforts to bring Christian salvation to the wilderness. The Society of Jesus, or Jesuits, emerged in the 16th century as the Catholic Church's best-educated and most militant religious order. Uncompromising in their opposition to Protestants, Jesuits proved remarkably flexible in dealing with non-Christian peoples, from China to North America. Other missionaries insisted that Indians must be Europeanized before they could be converted, but the Jesuits disagreed. They saw nothing contradictory about a nation of Christians that retained its Indian culture. The Jesuits also tried to protect their converts from contamination by the *coureurs de bois.*

Black Robe, based on Brian Moore's novel of the same title, is set in 17th-century North America.

Kobal Collection/Alliance/Goldwyn.

devastate the mission in the following decade, and the Jesuits would abandon it in 1649.

Brian Moore's realism romanticizes nobody but treats both the Jesuits and the Algonquins with great respect. The screenplay drew criticism for its harsh depiction of the Iroquois, but it portrayed them through the eyes of the people they planned to torture. A smaller criticism is that Laforgue

is the lone priest on the journey during which he commits the sin of watching Daniel and Annuka make love. Jesuits, however, traveled in pairs precisely so they would always be accompanied by someone who could hear their confessions. Bruce Beresford, an Australian, directed *Breaker Morant* (1979), a highly acclaimed film set in the Boer War a century ago, and also *Driving Miss Daisy* (1989).

SOUTHEASTERN INDIANS AT WORK

Jacques Le Moyne, an artist who accompanied the French Huguenot expedition to Florida in 1564, painted this scene of Indians in a canoe loaded with produce. They are rowing past one of their capacious storehouses. Engraving by Theodore de Bry.

Theodore de Bry.

After learning to speak several Algonquian and Iroquoian dialects, the Jesuits began to convert the five confederated Huron nations and baptized several thousand of their members. The Jesuits mastered Indian languages, lived in Indian villages, accepted most Indian customs, and converted 10,000 Indians in 40 years, but this success antagonized Indians who were still attached to their own rituals. When smallpox devastated the Hurons in the 1640s, Jesuits baptized hundreds of dying victims to ensure their salvation. Many of the Indian survivors noticed that death usually followed this mysterious rite. Suspecting witchcraft, their resistance grew stronger. A second disaster occurred when the Iroquois attacked, defeated, and scattered the Hurons. Despite these setbacks, the Jesuits' courage remained strong. They were the only Europeans who measured up to Indian standards of bravery under torture. Some of them, such as Isaac Jogues and Jean de Brebeuf, died as martyrs. Even so, their efforts slowly lost ground to the fur trade, especially after the Crown assumed control of New France in 1663.

New France under Louis XIV

Royal intervention transformed Canada after 1663 when Louis XIV and his minister, Jean-Baptiste Colbert, took charge of the colony and tried to turn it into a model absolutist society—peaceful, orderly, deferential. Government was in the hands of two appointive officials: a governor-general responsible for military and diplomatic affairs, and an *intendant* who administered justice. Justice was made affordable to everyone, partly by banning lawyers. The people paid few taxes, and the church tithe was set at half its rate in France.

The governor appointed all militia officers and granted promotion through merit, not by selling commissions. When the Crown sent professional soldiers to New France after 1660, the governor put them under the command of Canadian officers, who knew the woodlands—a decision that had no parallel in the English colonies. Colbert also sent 774 young women to the St. Lawrence, to provide brides for settlers and soldiers. He offered bonuses to couples who produced large families and fined fathers whose children failed to marry while still in their teens. Between 1663 and 1700, the population of New France increased from 3,000 to about 14,000, even though close to 70 percent of 10,000 immigrants throughout the colonial era went back to France, usually to claim a tiny inheritance. About one-fourth of the population concentrated in three cities—Quebec, Three Rivers, and Montreal. Montreal, the largest, became the center of the fur trade.

Farming took hold in the St. Lawrence valley, and by the 1690s, Canada was growing enough wheat to feed itself and to give its *habitants*, or settlers, a level of comfort about equal to that of contemporary New Englanders. A new class of *seigneurs*, or gentry, claimed most of the land between Quebec and Montreal, but they had few feudal privileges and never exercised the kind of power wielded by aristocrats in France. Few of them even became militia captains, an office open to *habitants*. Yet when the Church was also the *seigneur*, as often happened near Quebec and

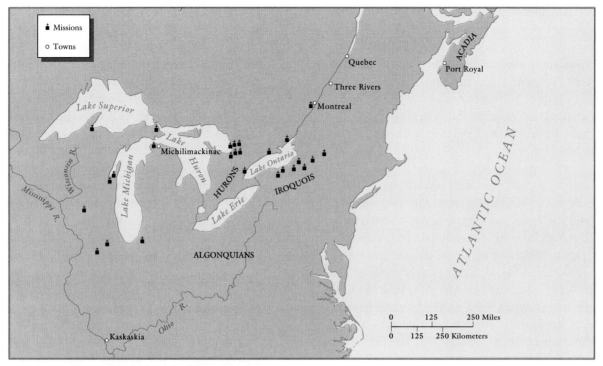

MAP 2.1 NEW FRANCE AND THE JESUIT MISSIONS

The Jesuits established Indian missions near Montreal and far into the interior of North America, most of them well beyond the range of French military aid in any emergency.

Montreal, the obligations imposed on farmers could be heavy.

Colbert even tried to ban Frenchmen from Indian territory by limiting the fur trade to annual fairs at Montreal and Quebec, thus bringing the Indians to the settlers, not the settlers to the Indians. Still, he failed to rein in the *coureurs de bois,* although a stint in the forests was becoming something a man did just once or twice in his youth, before settling down. Colbert's policy failed and, by 1700, even led to a quiet rebellion in the west. Hundreds of Frenchmen settled in the Mississippi River valley between the missions of Cahokia and Kaskaskia in what became the Illinois country. By 1750, these communities contained 3,000 residents. The settlers rejected *seigneurs,* feudal dues, tithes, and compulsory militia service. They did, however, import African slaves from Louisiana. Most settlers prospered as wheat farmers, and many married Christian Indian women from the missions.

But Canada did not long remain the center of French overseas activity. Like other Europeans, most of the French who crossed the Atlantic preferred the warmer climes of the Caribbean. At first, the French in the West Indies joined with other enemies of Spain to prey upon Spanish colonies and ships, contributing the word "buccaneer" *(boucanier)* to the English language. Then they trans-

formed the island colonies of Saint-Domingue (modern Haiti), Guadeloupe, and Martinique into centers of sugar or coffee production, where a small planter class prospered from the labor of thousands of slaves. The sugar islands were worth far more than Canada. By the late 18th century, Saint-Domingue was generating more wealth than any other colony in the world.

The Dutch and Swedish Settlements

For most of the 17th century, the Dutch were more active overseas than the French. In alliance with France during Europe's Thirty Years' War (1618–48), the Dutch wore down and finally destroyed Spain's bid for "universal monarchy" in Europe. The Netherlands, the most densely populated part of Europe, surpassed northern Italy in manufacturing and moved ahead of all competitors in finance, shipping, and trade. The Dutch Republic, with a population of 2 million by 1600, offered an ideological as well as a political challenge to Spanish absolutism.

In contrast to Spain, which stood for Catholic orthodoxy and the centralizing tendencies of Europe's "new monarchies," Dutch republicanism emphasized local liberties,

prosperity, and, in major centers such as Amsterdam, informal religious toleration. Political power was decentralized to the cities and their wealthy merchants, who favored religious toleration, tried to keep trade as free as possible, and resisted the monarchical ambitions of the House of Orange. The prince of Orange usually served as *stadholder* (captain general) of Holland, the richest province, and commanded its armies, and sometimes those of other Dutch provinces as well.

The Dutch Republic—with Protestant dissenters from many countries, a sizable Jewish community, and a Catholic minority that exceeded 30 percent of the population—was actually a polyglot confederation. Amsterdam's merchant republicanism competed with the Dutch Reformed Church for the allegiance of the people. Only during a military crisis could the prince of Orange mobilize the Dutch Reformed clergy and impose something like Calvinist orthodoxy, even on the cities. The States General, to which each province sent representatives, became a weak central government for the republic. The broader public did not vote or participate actively in public life. The tension between tolerant merchant republicanism and Calvinist orthodoxy carried over into New Netherland.

Profit was the dominant motive in Dutch expansion overseas. By 1600, Dutch commercial assets were already enormous. The Bank of Amsterdam, founded in 1609, was the most important financial institution in Europe for the next century. By 1620, Dutch foreign trade probably exceeded that of the rest of Europe combined. Even during the long war with Spain, the Dutch traded with Lisbon and Seville for products from the East Indies and America. This effrontery so annoyed Philip II that he twice committed a grave blunder in the 1590s, when he confiscated all of the Dutch ships crowding his ports. The Dutch retaliated by sailing into the Atlantic and Indian Oceans to acquire colonial goods at the source. Spanish power finally crumbled. The Dutch threat forced Spain to use expensive convoys to protect the silver fleets crossing the Atlantic. Spain's supply of precious metals, after peaking in the 1590s, fell sharply in the 1630s, as the rapidly declining Indian population reduced the labor supply for the silver mines.

The East and West India Companies

In 1602, the States General chartered the Dutch East India Company, the richest corporation the world had yet seen. It pressured Spain where it was weakest, in the Portuguese East Indies. Elbowing the Portuguese out of the Spice Islands and even out of Nagasaki in Japan, the Dutch set up their own capital at Batavia (now Jakarta) on the island of Java.

The Atlantic and North America also attracted the Dutch, although never as strongly as did the East Indies. In 1609, during a 12-year truce between Spain and the Netherlands, Henry Hudson, an Englishman in Dutch service, sailed up what the Dutch called the North River (the English later renamed it the Hudson) and claimed the whole area for the Netherlands. In 1614, some Lutheran refugees from Amsterdam built a fort near modern Albany to trade with the Mahicans and Iroquois for furs, but they did not occupy the site on a year-round basis.

In 1621, when the truce expired between the Netherlands and Spain, the States General chartered the Dutch West India Company and gave it jurisdiction over the African slave trade, Brazil, the Caribbean, and North America. The West India Company harbored strong Orangist sympathies and even some Calvinist fervor, sustained by refugees fleeing from the Spanish army. Within the company, other activities—such as Piet Heyns's capture of the entire Spanish treasure fleet in 1627—were more attractive than opportunities in North America. The company took over Portugal's slave-trading posts in West Africa and for a while even dominated Angola. It also occupied the richest sugar-producing region of Brazil until the Portuguese took it back, as well as Angola, in the 1640s.

In North America, the Dutch claimed the Delaware, the Hudson, and the Connecticut river valleys. The company put most of its effort, and some of its religious fervor, into the Hudson valley. The first permanent settlers arrived in 1624. Two years later, Deacon Pierre Minuit, leading 30 Walloon (French-speaking) Protestant refugee families, bought Manhattan Island from the Indians and founded the port of New Amsterdam. The Dutch established Fort Orange (modern Albany) 150 miles upriver for trade with the Iroquois. Much like New France, New Netherland depended on the goodwill of nearby Indians, and the fur trade gave the colony a similar urban flavor. But unlike the settlers of New France, few Dutchmen ventured into the deep woods. There were no *coureurs de bois* and hardly any missionaries. The Indians brought their furs to Fort Orange and exchanged them for firearms and other goods that the Dutch sold more cheaply than anyone else.

In other ways, New Netherland resembled New France. In the 1630s, decades before the French created *seigneuries* in the St. Lawrence valley, the Dutch established "patroonships," vast estates under a single landlord, mostly along the Hudson. But patroonships never thrived, largely because few Dutch settlers had much interest in becoming peasants. The one exception was Rensselaerswyck, a gigantic estate on both banks of the Hudson above and below Fort Orange, which exported wheat and flour to the Caribbean.

New Netherland as a Pluralistic Society

New Netherland became North America's first experiment in ethnic and religious pluralism. The Dutch were a mixed people with a Flemish majority and a Walloon minority. Both came to the colony. So did Danes, Norwegians, Swedes, Finns, Germans, and Scots. One observer in the 1640s counted 18 languages spoken by the 450 inhabitants of New Amsterdam.

The government of the colony tried to utilize this diversity by drawing on two conflicting precedents from the Netherlands. On the one hand, it appealed to religious refugees by emphasizing the company's Protestant role in the struggle against Spain. This policy, roughly speaking, reflected the Orangist position in the Netherlands. On the other hand, the West India Company sometimes recognized that acceptance of religious diversity might stimulate trade. The pursuit of prosperity through toleration was the normal role of the city of Amsterdam in Dutch politics. Minuit and Pieter Stuyvesant represented the religious formula for unity, and they resisted toleration even in the name of commerce.

After Minuit returned to Europe in 1631, the emphasis shifted rapidly from piety to trade. The Dutch sold muskets to the Iroquois to expand their own access to the fur trade. They began to export grain to the Caribbean, a more elusive goal in which the patroonships were supposed to give the colony a strong agricultural base. In 1643, however, Willem Kieft, a stubborn and quarrelsome governor, slaughtered a tribe of Indian refugees to whom he had granted asylum from other Indians. This Pavonia Massacre, which took place across the Hudson from Manhattan, set off a war with nearby Algonquian nations that nearly destroyed New Netherland. By the time Stuyvesant replaced Kieft in 1647, the colony's population had fallen to about 700 people. An autocrat, Stuyvesant made peace and then strengthened town governments and the Dutch Reformed Church. During his administration, the population rose to more than 6,000 by 1664, twice that of New France. Most newcomers arrived as members of healthy families who reproduced readily, enabling the population to double once every generation.

Swedish and English Encroachments

Back in Europe, Minuit organized another refugee project, this one for Flemings who had been uprooted by the Spanish war. When Dutch authorities refused to back him, he turned for support to the Protestant kingdom of Swe-

den. Financed by private Dutch capital, he returned to America in 1638 with Flemish and Swedish settlers to found New Sweden, with its capital at Fort Christina (modern Wilmington) near the mouth of the Delaware River, on land claimed by New Netherland. After Minuit died on his return trip to Europe, the colony became less Flemish and Calvinist and more Swedish and Lutheran, at a time when Stuyvesant was trying to make New Netherland an orthodox Calvinist society. The Swedes and Dutch lost another common bond in 1648 when their long war with Spain finally ended. In 1654, the Swedes seized Fort Casimir, a Dutch post that provided access to the Delaware. In response, Stuyvesant took over all of New Sweden the next year, and Amsterdam sent over settlers to guarantee Dutch control. Stuyvesant actively persecuted Lutherans in New Amsterdam but had to tolerate them in the Delaware Valley settlements. Orthodoxy and harmony were not easily reconciled.

The English, already entrenched around Chesapeake Bay to the south and New England to the east (discussed in the next section), threatened to overwhelm the Dutch as they moved from New England onto Long Island and into what is now Westchester County, New York. Kieft welcomed them in the 1640s and gave them local privileges greater than those enjoyed by the Dutch, in the hope that their farms and herds would give the colony valuable exports to the Caribbean. Stuyvesant regarded these "Yankees" (a Dutch word that probably meant "land pirates") as good Calvinists, English-speaking equivalents of his Dutch Reformed settlers. They agitated for a more active role in government, but their loyalty was questionable. If England attacked the colony, would these Puritans side with the Dutch Calvinists or the Anglican invaders? Which ran deeper, their religious or their ethnic loyalties? Stuyvesant learned the unpleasant answer when England attacked him in 1664.

☙ The Challenge from Elizabethan England

England's interest in America emerged slowly, even though ships from Bristol may have reached North America several years before Columbus's first voyage. If so, the English did nothing about it. In 1497, Henry VII (1485–1509) sent Giovanni Cabato (John Cabot), an Italian mariner who had moved to Bristol, to search for a northwest passage to Asia. Cabot probably reached Newfoundland, which he took to be part of Asia. He sailed again in 1498 with five ships but was lost at sea. Only one vessel returned, but Cabot's voyages gave England a vague claim to portions of the North American coast.

The English Reformation

When interest in America revived during the reign of Elizabeth I (1558–1603), England was rapidly becoming a Protestant kingdom. Elizabeth's father, Henry VIII (1509–47), desperate for a male heir, had broken with the pope to divorce his queen and had remarried. He proclaimed himself the "Only Supreme Head" of the Church of England, confiscated monastic lands, and opened the way for serious Protestant reformers. Under Elizabeth's younger brother, Edward VI (1547–53), the government embraced Protestantism. When Edward died, Elizabeth's older sister, Mary I (1553–58), reimposed Catholicism, burned hundreds of Protestants at the stake, and drove thousands into exile, where many of them became Calvinists. Elizabeth, however, accepted Protestantism, and in her reign the exiles returned. The Church of England, as reconstituted under Elizabeth, became an odd compromise—Calvinist in doctrine and theology, but still largely Catholic in structure, liturgy, and ritual. By the time of Elizabeth's death, England's Catholics were a tiny, fitfully persecuted minority, but one with powerful allies abroad, especially in Spain.

Some Protestants demanded a more complete reformation—the eradication of Catholic vestiges and the replacement of the Anglican Book of Common Prayer with sermons and psalms as the dominant mode of worship. These "Puritans," also called Non-Separatists, insisted they were loyal to the true Church of England and resisted any relaxation of Calvinist rigor. They would play a major role in English expansion overseas. More extreme Protestants, called Separatists, denied that the Church of England was a true church and began to set up independent congregations of their own. Some of them would found the small colony of Plymouth.

Hawkins and Drake

In 1560, England was a rather backward country of 3 million people. Its chief export was woolen cloth, most of which was shipped to the Netherlands, where the Dutch turned it into finished textiles. During the 16th century, the numbers of both people and sheep grew rapidly, and they sometimes competed for the same land. When farms were enclosed for sheep pasture, laborers were set adrift and often faced bleak prospects, creating the impression that England was overpopulated. Even without the enclosures, internal migration was becoming routine for a great many people. Thousands headed for London. Although deaths greatly outnumbered births in London, new arrivals lifted the city's population from 50,000 in 1500 to 200,000 in 1600 and, including the suburbs, to 575,000 by 1700. By then London was the largest city in Western Europe, containing more than 10 percent of England's population of 5 million. After 1600, internal migration fueled overseas settlement. Before then, interest in America centered not in London, but in the southwestern ports already involved in the Newfoundland fisheries.

Taking advantage of friendly relations that still prevailed between England and Spain, John Hawkins of Plymouth made three voyages to New Spain between 1562 and 1569. On his first trip, he bought slaves from the Portuguese in West Africa and sold them to the Spaniards in Hispaniola where, by paying all legal duties, he tried to set himself up as a legitimate trader. Spanish authorities disapproved, and on his second voyage he had to trade at gunpoint. On his third trip, the Spanish viceroy, in command of a much larger fleet, trapped his six vessels in a Mexican port. After promising Hawkins quarter, the viceroy sank four of his ships. Hawkins and his young kinsman Francis Drake escaped, both vowing vengeance.

Drake even began to talk of freeing slaves from Spanish tyranny. His most dramatic exploit came between 1577 and 1580, when he rounded Cape Horn and plundered Spanish possessions along the undefended Pacific coast of Peru. Knowing that the Spaniards would be waiting for him if he returned by the same route, he sailed north, explored San Francisco Bay, and continued west around the world to England—the first circumnavigation since Magellan's voyage more than half a century earlier. Elizabeth rewarded him with a knighthood.

Gilbert, Ireland, and America

By the 1560s, the idea of permanent colonization intrigued several Englishmen. England had a model close at hand in Ireland, which the English Crown had claimed for centuries. As of 1560, however, England had achieved little direct control over Ireland, except around Dublin. After 1560, the English tried to impose their agriculture, language, local government, legal system, aristocracy, and religion on the clan-based, mostly pastoral and Gaelic-speaking Irish. The Irish responded by becoming more intensely Roman Catholic than ever.

The English formed their preconceptions about American Indians largely from contact with the Irish who, claimed one Elizabethan, "live like beasts, void of law and all good order" and are "more uncivil, more uncleanly, more barbarous and more brutish in their customs and demeanors, than in any part of the world that is known." The English tried to conquer Ulster in the northeast and Munster in the southwest, the most Gaelic provinces.

In Ulster, the Protestant invaders drove out most of the residents and took over the land. In Munster, they ejected the Catholic leaders and tried to force the remaining Catholic Irish to become tenants under Protestant land-lords. Terror became an acceptable tactic, as when the English slaughtered 200 Irish at a Christmas feast in 1574.

Sir Humphrey Gilbert, a well-educated humanist, was one of the most brutal of Elizabeth's captains in the Irish wars of the 1560s. "He thought his dogs' ears too good to hear the speech of the greatest nobleman amongst them," one admirer noted. In subduing Munster in 1569, Gilbert killed nearly everyone in his path and destroyed all of the crops, a strategy that the English later employed against Indians. Massacring women and children "was the way to kill the men of war by famine," explained one apologist. For 80 years after 1560, Ireland attracted more English settlers than all American and Caribbean colonies combined. Only after 1641, when the Irish rose and killed thousands of English settlers, did the Western Hemisphere replace Ireland as a preferred site for English colonization.

Fresh from his Irish exploits, Gilbert began to think about colonizing America. In an essay titled "A Discourse How Her Majesty May Annoy the King of Spain" (1577), he proposed that England grab control of the Newfoundland fisheries, a nursery of seamen and naval power. He urged the founding of settlements close enough to New Spain to provide bases for plundering. He obtained a royal patent in 1578 and sent out a fleet, but his ships got into a fight somewhere short of America and limped back to England. He tried again in 1583. This time his fleet sailed north to claim Newfoundland. The crews of 22 Spanish and Portuguese fishing vessels and 18 French and English ships listened in astonishment as he read his royal patent to them, divided up the land among them, assigned them rents, and established the Church of England among this mostly Catholic group. He then sailed away to explore more of the American coast. His own ship went under during a storm.

Ralegh, Roanoke, and War with Spain

Gilbert's half-brother, Sir Walter Ralegh (or Raleigh), obtained his own patent from the queen and tried twice to plant a colony in North America. In 1585, he sent a large expedition to Roanoke Island in Pamlico Sound, but the settlers planted no crops and exasperated the Indians with demands for food during a time of drought. In June 1586, the English killed the local chief, Wingina, whose main offense was apparently a threat to resettle his people on the mainland and leave the colonists to starve—or work. Days later, when the expected supply vessels failed to arrive on schedule, the colonists sailed back to England on the ships of Sir Francis Drake, who had just burned the Spanish city of St. Augustine with the support of Florida Indians, whom he freed from service to the Spanish. The supply ships reached Roanoke a little later, only to find the site abandoned. They left a small garrison there and sailed off in quest of Spanish plunder. The garrison was never heard from again.

Ralegh sent a second expedition to Roanoke in 1587, one that included some women—an indication that he envisioned a permanent colony, not just an outpost for raiding New Spain. When Governor John White went back to England for more supplies, his return to Roanoke was delayed by the assault of the Spanish Armada on England in 1588. By the time he reached Roanoke in 1590, the settlers had vanished, leaving a cryptic message—"CROATOAN"—carved on a tree. The colonists may have settled among the Chesapeake nation of Indians near the entrance to Chesapeake Bay. Sketchy evidence suggests that the Powhatans, the most powerful Indians in the area, wiped out the Chesapeakes, along with any English living with them, in spring 1607, just as an English fleet arrived in the bay.

The Spanish Armada touched off a war that lasted until 1604. The exploits of Hawkins, Drake, and Ralegh helped provoke this conflict, as did Elizabeth's intervention in the Dutch war against Spain. The loss of the Armada, first to nimbler English ships in the English Channel and then to fierce storms off the Irish coast, crippled Spain. The war also strained England's resources.

By 1600, Richard Hakluyt the elder and his cousin Richard Hakluyt the younger were publishing accounts of English exploits overseas and offering advice on how to make future colonization efforts more successful. The Hakluyts celebrated the deeds of Hawkins, Drake, Gilbert, and Ralegh, who were all West Country men with large ambitions and limited financial resources. Although their plundering exploits continued to pay, they could not afford to sustain a colony such as Roanoke until it could return a profit. But beginning in the 1590s, London became intensely involved in American affairs by launching privateering fleets against Spain. Even though London merchants remained more interested in trade with India, the Mediterranean, and Muscovy than in North American projects, the city's growing involvement with Atlantic privateering marked a significant shift. The marriage of London capital to West Country experience would permit Virginia to succeed where earlier settlements had failed.

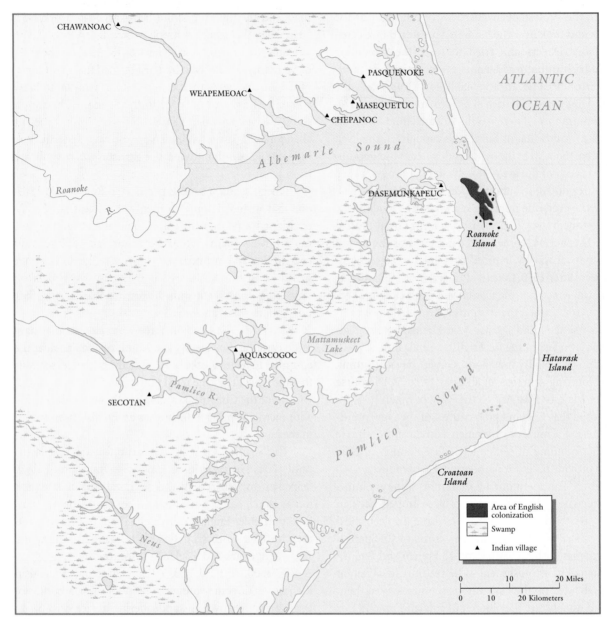

MAP 2.2 ROANOKE COLONY, 1584–1590
Roanoke marked the first English attempt to plant a permanent colony in North America.

The Swarming of the English

In the 17th century, more than 700,000 people sailed from Europe or Africa to the English colonies in North America and the Caribbean. Most of the European migrants were unmarried younger sons. With no inheritance at home, they hoped to improve their lot in a warmer climate. Instead, most spent their time trying to stay alive under the threat of malaria, typhoid fever, and other lethal maladies. Most of the Europeans arrived as servants. At first, at least some of the Africans were regarded as servants rather than slaves. Most of the men, whether Europeans or Africans, never fathered children.

The Europeans who settled in New England or the Hudson and Delaware valleys were the most fortunate. Because Puritans and Quakers migrated as families into wholesome and healthy regions, their population expanded at a rate far beyond anything known in Europe. The descendants of this small, idealistic minority soon became a substantial part of the total population, and they played a role in American history far out of proportion to their original numbers. As the accompanying table shows, the New England and Middle Atlantic colonies together attracted only 5.4 percent of the immigrants, but by 1700, they contained 37 percent of all the people in the English colonies and 55 percent of the Europeans.

THE PATTERN OF SETTLEMENT IN THE ENGLISH COLONIES UP TO 1700

Region	Who Came (in thousands)		Population in 1700 (in thousands)	
	Europeans	Africans	Europeans	Africans
West Indies	220 (29.6%)	316 (42.5%)	33 (8.3%)	115 (28.8%)
South	135 (18.1%)	30 (4.0%)	82 (20.5%)	22 (5.5%)
Mid-Atlantic	20 (2.7%)	2 (0.3%)	51 (12.8%)	3 (0.8%)
New England	20 (2.7%)	1 (0.1%)	91 (22.8%)	2 (0.5%)
Total	395 (53.1%)	349 (46.9%)	257 (64.4%)	142 (35.6%)

☙ The Chesapeake and West Indian Colonies

In 1606, King James I of England (1603–25) chartered the Virginia Company with authority to colonize North America between the 34th and 45th parallels. The company had two headquarters. One, in the English city of Plymouth, raised only a small amount of capital but won jurisdiction over the northern portion of the grant. Known as the Plymouth Company, it carried on the West Country expansionist traditions of Gilbert and Ralegh. In 1607, it planted a colony at Sagadahoc on the coast of Maine. But the colonists found the cold winter intimidating, and when the Abenaki Indians refused to trade with them, they abandoned the site in September 1608. The Plymouth Company ran out of money and gave up.

The other branch, which had its offices in London, decided to colonize the Chesapeake Bay area. In 1607, the London Company sent out three ships carrying 100 men and 4 boys. They sailed up the Powhatan River (which they renamed the James), landed at a defensible peninsula, built a fort and other crude buildings, and called the place Jamestown. The investors hoped to find gold or silver, a northwest passage to Asia, a cure for syphilis, or other valuable products for sale in Europe. The settlers expected to persuade or compel local Indians to work for them, much as the Spanish had done. If the Indians proved hostile, the settlers were told to form alliances with more distant Indians and subdue those who resisted. Company officials did not realize that a war chief named Powhatan ruled virtually all of the Indians below the fall line.[1] He

had no rival within striking distance. The company's other expectations proved equally skewed.

The Jamestown Disaster

Jamestown was a deathtrap. Every summer, the James River became contaminated around Jamestown and sent out killing waves of dysentery and typhoid fever. Before long, malaria also set in. Only 38 of the original 104 colonists survived the first year. Of the 325 who came before 1609, fewer than 100 remained alive in the spring of that year.

The survivors owed their good fortune to the resourcefulness of Captain John Smith, a soldier and adventurer who outmaneuvered other members of the colony's ruling council and took charge. When his explorations uncovered neither gold or silver nor any quick route across the continent to Asia, he concentrated instead on sheer survival. He tried to awe Powhatan, maintain friendly relations with him, and buy corn. Powhatan captured Smith in December 1607, and they worked out an uneasy truce, but Powhatan was deeply suspicious. "Some doubt I have of your coming hither, that makes me not so kindly seeke to relieve you," he declared, ". . . for many do informe me, your coming is not for trade, but to invade my people and possesse my Country." But food remained scarce among the English. The colony had too many gentlemen and specialized craftsmen (including a perfumer) who considered farming beneath their dignity. Over their protests, Smith set them to work raising grain for four hours a day.

In 1609, the London Company sent out 600 more settlers under Lieutenant Governor Thomas Gates, but his ship ran aground on Bermuda, and the crew spent a year building another vessel. About 400 new settlers reached Virginia before Gates arrived. After suffering a severe injury in an explosion, Smith was shipped back to England, and the colony lacked firm leadership for the next year. Wearying Powhatan with their endless demands for corn at a time of severe drought, the settlers provoked the

---

[1] The *fall line*, defined by the first waterfall encountered on each river by a vessel sailing inland from the sea, marked a significant barrier to penetration of the continent. In the South, the area below the falls is called the *tidewater*. The land between the falls and the Appalachians is called the *piedmont*.

The Toast of London: Pocahontas

By all accounts, Pocahontas was the favorite daughter of her father, Powhatan, the most powerful Indian chief between the fall line and Chesapeake Bay south of the Potomac River as of 1607. After Indians captured Captain John Smith in December 1607, the 11- or 12-year-old girl may have saved his life and impelled Smith and Powhatan toward a mutual understanding, but if so Smith never mentioned the incident until 1624, years after her death. She clearly grew fond of Smith and visited him often in Jamestown.

After Smith returned to England, war broke out between Powhatan's people and the settlers in 1609 and lasted intermittently until 1614. Probably to protect Pocahontas, Powhatan placed her with the distant Potomac Indians, but they were eager to trade with the English and betrayed her to them. Carried as a prisoner to Jamestown, she charmed the widower John Rolfe so completely that he fell in love with her and, after she promised to become a Christian, he married her with the governor's permission. She took Rebecca as her Christian name. The wedding improved relations between the settlers and Powhatan, and they made peace.

Rolfe also developed a strain of tobacco milder than the local variety, shipped it to England, and got an excellent price for it. In effect, he started Virginia's first export boom, for the whole colony soon took to raising tobacco.

In 1616, Rolfe and Pocahontas sailed for England. For nearly a year they became one of London's top sensations, welcome at court, moving in the most prestigious social circles, and attending the theater. The couple also had a son whom they named Thomas. After nearly a year in the capital, the two decided to return to Virginia, but Pocahontas became seriously ill before the ship could reach the English Channel. She was taken ashore at Gravesend, where she died on March 21, 1617. By then she was already the best known Indian in the English-speaking world. Rolfe left Thomas with an uncle in England and returned to Virginia. Thomas, in turn, fathered numerous descendants.

The inscription around the portrait says "Matoaka [one of her Indian names] alias Rebecca [her baptismal name] daughter of the powerful Prince Powhatan, Emperor of Virginia."

Indian war that Smith had avoided. They almost starved during winter 1610. One settler was executed for cannibalizing his wife. Two were tied to posts and left to starve to death for raiding company stores. Some escaped to the Indians, but those who were caught fleeing were executed.

When Gates finally reached Jamestown with 175 colonists in June 1610, he found only 60 settlers alive (plus a garrison at Point Comfort) and the food supply nearly exhausted. Gates despaired, packed everyone aboard ship, and started downriver. Virginia was going the way of Roanoke and Sagadahoc, despite its greater resources. Instead, the small fleet came abreast of the new governor, Thomas West, baron de la Warr, sailing up the James with 300 new colonists. They all went back to Jamestown, and the colony managed to survive.

De la Warr and Gates found themselves in the middle of the colony's first Indian war, which lasted from 1609 to 1614. Powhatan's warriors picked off any settlers who strayed far from Jamestown. The English retaliated by slaughtering whole villages and destroying crops, as they had in Ireland. In August 1610, for example, Commander George Percy attacked the Paspahegh Indians, who had

CAPTAIN JOHN SMITH SUBDUING OPECHANCANOUGH, THE WARRIOR CHIEF OF THE PAMUNKEY INDIANS, 1608
Note the difference in height between Opechancanough and Smith, even as depicted by a European artist.

refused to give the colonists more corn and had sheltered runaways. He burned the Paspahegh's crops, massacred most of them, captured the "queen" and her children, and started back to Jamestown by boat. When the soldiers murmured because "the queen and her children were spared," Percy had the children thrown overboard and let his men shoot "out their brains in the water." At Jamestown, a settler suggested burning the queen alive. Percy, feeling merciful, had her put to the sword instead. Percy's strategy was terroristic. The slaughter of one tribe might intimidate others. The war finally ended after the English captured Pocahontas, Powhatan's favorite daughter, and used her as a hostage to negotiate peace.

Despite the Indian war, the colony's prospects improved after 1610. The governors imposed martial law on the settlers and sent some of them to healthier locations, such as Henrico, 50 miles upstream. Through the efforts of John Rolfe, the colony began to produce a cash crop. In 1613, Rolfe imported a mild strain of tobacco from the West Indies. It brought such a good price in England that the king—who had insisted no one could build a colony

"upon smoke"—was proved wrong. Soon, settlers were even growing tobacco in the streets of Jamestown.

Reorganization, Reform, and Crisis

In 1609, a new royal charter extended Virginia's boundaries to the Pacific, although no one yet knew how far away that was. A third charter in 1612 made the London Company a joint-stock company. It resembled a modern corporation except that each stockholder had only one vote regardless of how many shares he owned. The stockholders met quarterly in the company's General Court but entrusted everyday management to the company's treasurer, who until 1618 was Sir Thomas Smyth, a wealthy London merchant. The lack of profits led to turmoil among the stockholders, who replaced Smyth in 1618 with Sir Edwin Sandys, the Puritan son of the archbishop of York.

In 1618, the company adopted an ambitious reform program for Virginia. It encouraged economic diversification, such as glassblowing, planting grape vines, and raising silkworms. English common law replaced martial law. The settlers were allowed to elect their own assembly, the House of Burgesses, to meet with the governor and his council and make local laws. Finally—the most popular reform—settlers were permitted to own land. Under this "headright" system, a colonist received 50 acres for each person whose passage to Virginia he financed. By 1623, Sandys had shipped 4,000 settlers to Virginia, but the economic diversification program failed. Only tobacco found a market. Corn still provided most of the food. Instead of growing silkworms and grapes, Virginians raised Indian crops with Indian methods, which meant using hoes instead of plows.

The flood of newcomers strained the food supply and soured relations with the Indians, especially after Powhatan died and was succeeded by his militant brother, Opechancanough. On Good Friday in March 1622, the new chief launched an attack that was intended to wipe out the whole colony. Without a last-minute warning from a friendly Indian, Jamestown might not have survived. As it turned out, 347 settlers were killed that day, and most of the outlying settlements were destroyed. Newcomers who arrived in subsequent months had nowhere to go and, with food again scarce, hundreds died over the winter. "Oh, that you did see my daily and hourly sighs, groans, and tears, and thumps that I afford my own breast, and rue and curse the time of my birth, with holy Job," complained Richard Frethorne, a servant, to his parents a year after the massacre. "I thought no head had been able to hold so much water as hath and doth daily flow from mine eyes."

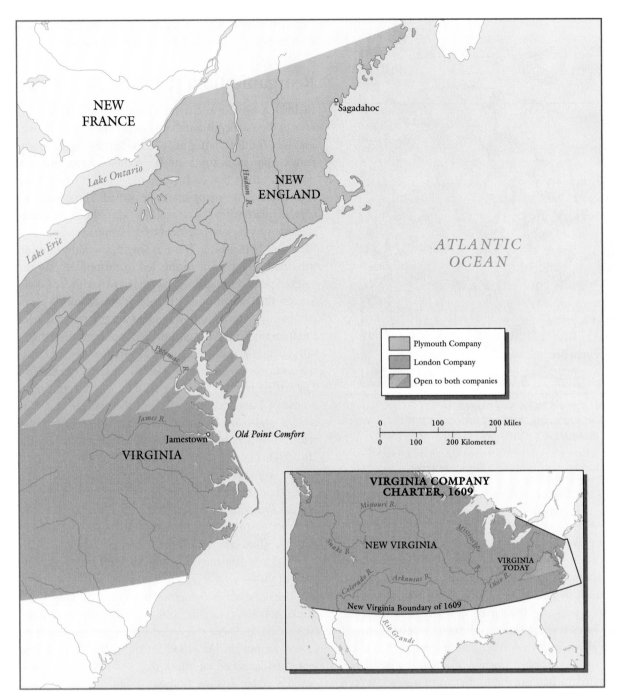

MAP 2.3   VIRGINIA COMPANY CHARTER, 1606
This charter gave the Plymouth Company jurisdiction over what would become New England and New York, and the London Company jurisdiction over most of what became Virginia and North Carolina. They shared jurisdiction over the intervening area. The insert map shows Virginia's revised sea-to-sea boundaries laid out in the 1609 charter.

Back in London, Smyth and his allies turned against Sandys, withdrew their capital, and asked the king to intervene. A royal commission visited the colony and found only 1,200 settlers alive out of the 6,000 sent over since 1607. In 1624, the king declared the London Company bankrupt and assumed direct control of Virginia, making it the first royal colony, with a governor and council appointed by the Crown. The London Company had invested some £200,000 in the enterprise, equal to £1,400 or £1,500 for every surviving settler, at a time when skilled English craftsmen were lucky to earn £50 per year. Such extravagance guaranteed that future colonies would be organized in different ways.

Tobacco, Servants, and Survival

Between Opechancanough's 1622 attack and the 1640s, Virginia proved that it could survive. Despite an appalling death rate, about a thousand new settlers came each year, and population grew slowly, to 5,200 by 1634 and 8,100 by 1640. For 10 years, the settlers warred against Opechancanough. In 1623, they poisoned 200 Indians they had invited to a peace conference. In most years, they attacked the Indians just before harvest time, destroying their crops and villages. By the time both sides made peace in 1632, all Indians had been expelled from the peninsula between the James and York rivers below Jamestown.

That area became secure for tobacco, and the export of tobacco financed the importation of indentured servants, even after the price of tobacco fell sharply in the 1630s. Most servants were young men, often desperate, who agreed to work for a term of years in exchange for the cost of passage, for bed and board during their years of service, and for modest freedom dues when their term expired. Those signing indentures in England usually had valuable skills and negotiated terms of four or five years. Those arriving without an indenture, most of whom were younger and less skilled, were sold by the ship captain to a planter. Those older than age 19 served five years, whereas those younger than 19 served until age 24. The system turned servants into freemen who hoped to prosper on their own. Most former servants became tenants for several years while they tried to save enough to buy their own land. Better tobacco prices enabled many to succeed between 1640 and 1660, but those who imported the servants were always in a stronger economic position, collecting the headright of 50 acres for each one. Because deaths still outnumbered births, the colony needed a steady flow of newcomers to survive.

In 1634, Virginia was divided into counties, each with its own justices of the peace, who sat together as the county court and, by filling their own vacancies, soon became a self-perpetuating oligarchy. Most counties also became Anglican parishes, with a church and a vestry of prominent laymen, usually the justices. The vestry managed temporal affairs for the church, including the choice of the minister. Although the king did not recognize the House of Burgesses until 1639, it met almost every year

THE OPECHANCANOUGH MASSACRE OF 1622

This famous event, as portrayed in an engraving from the workshop of Theodore de Bry, depicts the warriors as treacherous, bloodthirsty savages and the settlers as innocent victims.

Courtesy of the John Carter Brown Library at Brown University.

after 1619 and was well established by 1640. Before long, only a justice could hope to be elected as a burgess.

Until 1660, many former servants managed to acquire land, and some even served on the county courts and in the House of Burgesses. As tobacco prices fell after 1660, however, upward mobility became more difficult. Political offices usually went to the richest 15 percent of the settlers, those able to pay their own way across the Atlantic. They, and eventually their descendants, monopolized the posts of justice of the peace and vestryman, the pool from which burgesses and councillors were normally chosen. Virginia was becoming an oligarchy, and after 1660, resentments became increasingly acute among those shut off from power and unable to prosper.

Maryland

Maryland had different origins but became much the same kind of society as Virginia. It grew out of the social and religious vision of Sir George Calvert and his son Cecilius, both of whom became Catholics and looked to America as a refuge for persecuted English and Irish people of that faith. Sir George, a prominent officeholder, had invested in the London Company. When he resigned his royal office because of his Catholicism, King James I made him baron Baltimore in the Irish peerage. Both James and Charles I (1625–49) encouraged his colonial projects.

TOBACCO LABORER, ST. MARY'S CITY, MARYLAND

St. Mary's City has been reconstructing the 17th-century Chesapeake world through archaeology and other modern scholarship. This scene illustrates labor patterns during the era of indentured servitude.

Image courtesy of Historic St. Mary's City.

The Maryland charter of 1632 made Baltimore "lord proprietor" of the colony. It came close to making Baltimore king within Maryland, the most sweeping delegation of power that the Crown could grant. After 1630, most new colonies were proprietary projects, often with the Maryland charter as a model. Many of them embodied the distinctive social ideals of their founders.

George Calvert died as the Maryland patent was being issued, and Cecilius inherited Maryland and the peerage. Like Champlain, he believed that Catholics and Protestants could live in peace in the same colony, but he expected the servants, most of whom were Protestants, to continue to serve the Catholic gentlemen of the colony after their indentures expired. Baltimore made the gentlemen manor lords, with the power to preside over courts leet and courts baron, feudal tribunals that were nearly obsolete in England.

Those plans were never fulfilled. The condition of English Catholics improved under Charles I and his queen, Henrietta Maria, a French Catholic for whom the province was named. Because few Catholics emigrated, most settlers were Protestants. The civil war that erupted in England in 1642 (see following discussion) soon spread to Maryland. Protestants overthrew Lord Baltimore's regime several times between 1642 and 1660, but the English state always sided with him, even when the Puritans were in power there. During these struggles, Baltimore conceded a bicameral legislature to the colony, knowing that Protestants would dominate the elective assembly and that Catholics would control the appointive council. He also approved the Toleration Act of 1649, which granted freedom of worship to Christians (but not to Maryland's tiny Jewish minority).

The manorial system did not survive these upheavals. Protestant servants, after their indentures expired, acquired their own land rather than become tenants under Catholic manor lords, most of whom died or returned to England. When Maryland's unrest ended around 1660, the colony was raising tobacco, corn, and livestock and was governed by county courts similar to those in Virginia. If anything, the proprietary family's Catholicism and its claims to special privileges made the Maryland assembly more articulate than the Virginia House of Burgesses in demanding the liberties of Englishmen. Otherwise, religion provided the biggest difference between the two colonies. Virginia was Anglican, but Maryland had no established church and no vestries. Most Maryland Protestants had to make do without ministers until the 1690s.

Chesapeake Family Life

In the 1620s, European men outnumbered women in Virginia by at least 5 to 1. Among new immigrant servants as late as the 1690s, the ratio was still 5 to 2. Population became self-sustaining about 1680, when live births finally began to outnumber deaths. Among adults, this transition made little difference before 1700. Until then, most prominent people were immigrants.

Life expectancy slowly improved as the colonists planted orchards to provide wholesome cider to drink, but it still remained much lower than in England, where those who survived childhood could expect to live into their

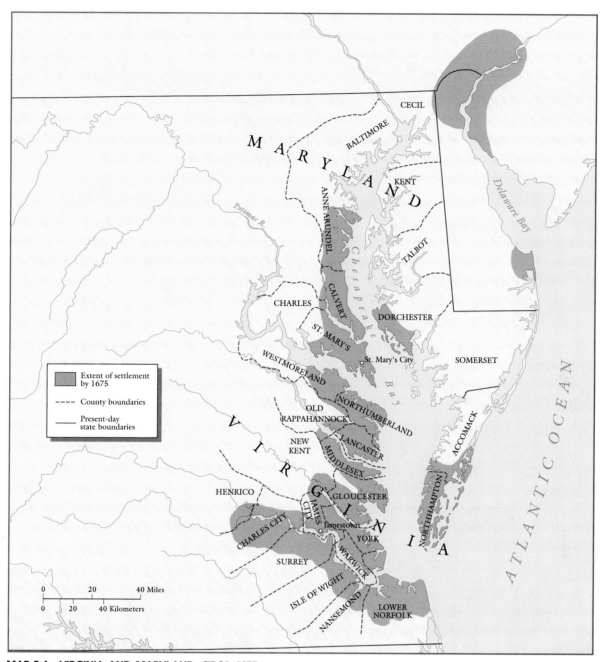

MAP 2.4 VIRGINIA AND MARYLAND, CIRCA 1675
Nearly 70 years after the founding of Jamestown, settlement remained confined to the tidewater and the eastern shore.

fifties. The Chesapeake immigrants had survived childhood diseases in Europe, but men at age 20 could expect to live only to about 45, with 70 percent dead by age 50. Women died at even younger ages, especially in areas ravaged by malaria, a dangerous disease for pregnant women. In those places, women rarely lived to age 40. England's patriarchal families found it hard to survive in the Chesapeake. About 70 percent of the men never married or, if they did, produced no children. Most men waited years after completing their service before they could marry.

Because women could not marry until they had finished their indentures, most spent a good part of their childbearing years unwed. About one-fifth had illegitimate children, despite severe legal penalties, and roughly one-third were pregnant on their wedding day. Virtually all women married, most as soon as they could.

In a typical Chesapeake marriage, the groom was in his thirties and the bride eight or ten years younger. Although men outlived women, this age gap meant that the husband usually died before his wife, who then quickly

remarried. In one Virginia county, three-fourths of all children lost a parent, and one-third lost both. Native-born settlers married at a much earlier age than immigrants; women were often in their middle to late teens when they wed. Orphans were a major community problem. Stepparents were common because surviving spouses with property usually remarried. Few lived long enough to become grandparents. By the time the oldest child in a household was 20, the husband and wife, because of successive remarriages, might not even be that child's blood relatives.

Under these circumstances, family loyalties tended to focus on other kin—on uncles, aunts, cousins, older stepbrothers or stepsisters—thus contributing to the value that Virginia and Maryland placed on hospitality. Patriarchalism remained weak. Because fathers died young, even members of the officeholding elite that took shape after 1650 had difficulty passing on their status to their sons. Only toward the end of the 17th century were the men holding office likely to be descended from fathers of comparable distinction.

The West Indies and the Transition to Slavery

Before 1700, far more Englishmen went to the West Indies than to the Chesapeake. Between 1624 and 1640, they settled the Leeward Islands (St. Christopher, Nevis, Montserrat, and Antigua) and Barbados, tiny islands covering a little more than 400 square miles. In the 1650s, England seized Jamaica from Spain, increasing this total by a factor of 10. At first, English planters grew tobacco, using the labor of indentured servants. Then, beginning around 1645 in Barbados, sugar replaced tobacco, with dramatic social consequences. The Dutch, who were then being driven from Brazil by the Portuguese, provided some of the capital for this transition, showed the English how to raise sugar, introduced them to slave labor on a massive scale, and for a time dominated the exportation and marketing of the crop.

Sugar became so valuable that planters imported most of their food from North America rather than divert land and labor from the cash crop. Sugar required a heavy investment in slaves and mills, and large planters with many slaves soon dominated the islands. Ex-servants found little employment, and most of them left after their terms expired. Many joined the buccaneers or moved to the mainland. Their exodus hastened the transition to slavery. In 1660, Europeans out-

numbered slaves in the islands by 33,000 to 22,000. By 1700, the white population had stagnated, but the number of slaves had increased sixfold. By 1775, they would triple again. Planters appropriated about 80 percent of their slaves' labor for their own profit, a rate of exploitation that had probably never been reached anywhere else. They often worked their slaves to death and then bought others to replace them. Of the 316,000 Africans imported before 1700, only 115,000 remained alive in that year.

Observers were depressed by the moral climate on the islands, where underworked and overfed planters arrogantly dominated their overworked and underfed slaves. Some of the islands were "of no advantage," remarked one governor, who thought they were "better under water than above." In 1671, another governor canvassed 40 parishes in the Leeward Islands and found just "one drunken orthodox [Anglican] priest, one drunken sectary priest, and one drunken parson." Yet the islands generated enormous wealth for the English empire, far more than the mainland colonies well into the 18th century. Around 1700, the islands sent sugar worth £710,000 per year to England at a time when Chesapeake planters were getting only £230,000 for their tobacco.

The Rise of Slavery in North America

Africans first came to Virginia in 1619 when, John Rolfe reported, a Dutch ship "sold us twenty Negars." Their status remained ambiguous for decades, even after slavery had been sharply defined in the West Indies. In Virginia

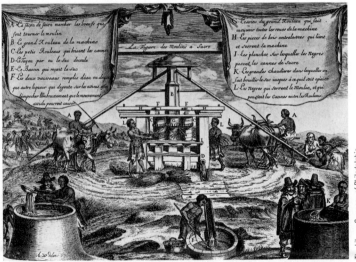

The Library Company of Philadelphia.

SUGAR MILL

This 1665 engraving shows an animal-powered sugar mill, worked by African slaves, in one of the French West Indian islands.

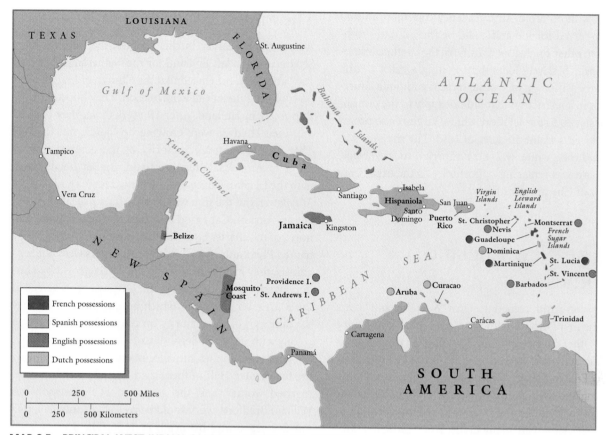

MAP 2.5 PRINCIPAL WEST INDIAN COLONIES IN THE 17TH CENTURY

Spain retained control of the large islands of Cuba, Hispaniola, and Puerto Rico while its English, French, and Dutch rivals settled the smaller but fertile islands east of Puerto Rico or south of Cuba.

and Maryland, many of the first Africans had Hispanic names. They were Creoles who had acquired a great deal of intercultural experience around the Atlantic world and were in a stronger position to negotiate with their masters than those who came later would be. Some Africans were treated as servants and won their freedom after several years. On Virginia's eastern shore, where as late as the 1660s perhaps 30 percent of African people were free, one "Anthony Johnson Negro" even became the master of other Africans, one of whom complained that Johnson held him beyond the term of his indenture. (The court backed Johnson.) But other Africans in the early years were already serving for life, and this pattern prevailed by the end of the 17th century.

This uncertainty about status is understandable. Because the English had no experience with slavery at home, a rigid caste system took time to crystallize. When Hugh Davis was whipped in 1630 "for abusing himself to the dishonor of God and shame of Christians, by defiling his body in lying with a negro," his offense may have been sodomy rather than miscegenation. The record is unclear.

Fifty years later, when Katherine Watkins, a white woman, accused John Long, a mulatto, of raping her, the neighbors (both men and women) blamed her, not him, for engaging in seductive behavior, which they described in lurid detail. The case of Elizabeth Key, a mulatto, a Christian, and the bastard daughter of Thomas Key, shows similar ambiguity. In 1655, when she claimed her freedom, her new owner fought to keep her enslaved. William Greensted, who had fathered two children by her, sued on her behalf, won, and then married her. One settler had no qualms about keeping her in bondage because of her dark skin, despite the known wishes of her deceased father. Another—Greensted—fell in love with her.

In the generation after 1680, the caste structure of the Chesapeake colonies became firmly set. Fewer indentured servants reached the Chesapeake from England, as the Delaware valley and the expanding English army and navy competed more successfully for the same young men. Slaves took their place. Some of the emerging great planters, such as William Byrd I and William Fitzhugh, made a deliberate choice after 1680 to replace indentured

servants with enslaved Africans. They cost more to buy, but they served for life and could be treated more ruthlessly than other Englishmen. In 1705, the Virginia legislature, in which slaveholders were gaining greater weight, forbade the whipping of a white servant without a court's permission, a restriction that did not apply to the punishment of slaves. To attract more whites, Virginia also promised every ex-servant 50 acres of land. The message was obvious: Every white was now superior to any black. Racial caste was replacing opportunity as the organizing principle of Chesapeake society.

☛ The New England Colonies

Captain John Smith coined the term "New England" years before the first Puritans left for America. It became an apt phrase. Other Europeans founded colonies to engage in economic activities they could not pursue at home, but the New England settlers reproduced the mixed economy of old England, with minor variations. Their family farms raised livestock and European grains, as well as corn. Their artisans specialized in many crafts, from carpentry and shipbuilding to printing. Their quarrel with England was over religion, not economics. They came to America, they insisted, to worship as God commanded, not as the Church of England required. That imperative made them critical of other English practices as well. Driven by a radical communitarian vision, the first settlers created towns, congregations, and law courts well suited to Puritan purposes while changing the English models on which they drew. Later generations were less certain of their place in the world, less eager to question English ways, and more inclined to drift back toward English models. They wanted to preserve what had already been accomplished. They became conservative communitarians.

The Pilgrims and Plymouth

As mentioned earlier in this chapter, the Pilgrims were Separatists who left England for the Netherlands between 1607 and 1609, convinced that the Church of England was no true daughter of the Reformation. They hoped to worship freely in Holland. After 10 years there, they realized that their children were growing up Dutch, not English. That fear prompted a minority of the congregation to move to America. After negotiating rather harsh terms with the London Company, they sailed for Virginia on the *Mayflower*. But the ship was blown off course late in 1620, landing first on Cape Cod and then on the mainland well north of the charter boundaries of Virginia, at a place they named Plymouth. Two-thirds of the settlers were not Separatists; they had been added to the passenger list by London investors. Before landing, the 100 passengers agreed to the Mayflower Compact, which bound them all to obey the decisions of the majority, an essential precaution in a colony with uncertain legal status.

Short on supplies, the colonists suffered keenly during the first winter. Half of them died, including all but three married women and the governor. His successor was William Bradford, who would be reelected annually for all but five years until his death in 1656. The settlers fared much better when spring came. The Patuxet Indians of the area had been wiped out by disease in 1617, but their fields were ready for planting. Squanto, the only Patuxet to survive, had been kidnapped in 1614 by coastal traders and carried to England. He had just made his way home and showed up at Plymouth one day in March 1621. He taught the settlers Indian methods of fishing and growing corn. He also introduced them to Massasoit, the powerful Wampanoag sachem (or chief), whose people celebrated the first thanksgiving feast with the settlers after the 1621 harvest. After a decade, the settlers numbered about 300. By paying off their London creditors, they gained political autonomy and private ownership of their flourishing

MASSASOIT'S PIPE

This rather whimsical artifact, popularly known as Massasoit's pipe, comes from an elite Indian grave in the Narragansett-Wampanoag country, mid-17th century, about the time that Massasoit died. He celebrated the first thanksgiving with the Pilgrims.

farms. During the 1630s, they founded several new towns and sold their surplus crops to the colonists flooding into Massachusetts.

Covenant Theology

A much larger Puritan exodus settled Massachusetts Bay between 1630 and 1641. The best-educated English group yet to cross the Atlantic, 130 of them had attended a university, most often Cambridge, a Puritan center. Puritans distrusted Charles I and his courtiers, especially William Laud, bishop of London and then archbishop of Canterbury, whom they accused of Catholic sympathies and of Arminianism, a heresy named for a Dutch theologian who had challenged strict Calvinists a generation earlier. To Puritans, the stakes were high indeed by the late 1620s. During that early phase of the Thirty Years' War (1618–48), Catholic armies seemed about to crush the German Reformation. Charles I blundered into a brief war against both Spain and France, raised money for the war by dubious methods, and dissolved Parliament when it protested. Puritans complained that Laud punished them for their piety but left blatant sinners alone. God's wrath would descend on England, they warned.

These matters were of genuine urgency to Puritans, who embraced what they called "covenant theology." According to this system, God had made two personal covenants with humans: the covenant of works and the covenant of grace. In the covenant of works, God had promised Adam that if he kept God's law he would never die—but Adam ate of the forbidden fruit, was expelled from the Garden of Eden, and died. All of Adam's descendants remained under the same covenant, but because of his Fall would never be capable of keeping the law. All humans deserved damnation, but God was merciful and answered sin with the covenant of grace. God would save his chosen people: "I will be their God, and they shall be my people" (Jeremiah 31:34). Everyone else would be damned: "Saith the Lord: yet I loved Jacob, and I hated Esau" (Malachi 1:3). Even though the covenant of works could no longer bring eternal life, it remained in force and established the strict moral standards that every Christian must strive to follow, before and after conversion. A Christian's inability to keep the law usually triggered the conversion experience by demonstrating that only faith, not works, could save.

At this level, covenant theology merely restated Calvinist orthodoxy, but the Puritans gave it a novel social

LINK TO THE PAST

A City upon a Hill

Governor John Winthrop preached a lay sermon entitled "A Model of Christian Charity" to his fellow passengers aboard the Arbella as they sailed to New England in 1630. The following passage has become the most famous part of any sermon by a New Englander in the 17th century.

For we must consider that we shall be as a City upon a Hill, the eyes of all people are upon us; so that if we shall deal falsely with our God in this work we have undertaken, and so cause Him to withdraw His present help from us, we shall be made a story and a by-word through the world. We shall open the mouths of enemies to speak evil of the ways of God and all professors [i.e., professing Christians] for God's sake; we shall shame the faces of many of God's worthy servants, and cause their prayers to be turned into Curses upon us till we be consumed out of the good land where we are going. . . . Beloved, there is now set before us life and good, death

and evil, in that we are commanded this day to love the Lord our God, and to love one another, to walk in His ways and to keep His Commandments and His Ordinances and His Laws, and the Articles of our Covenant with Him that we may live and be multiplied, and that the Lord our God may bless us in the land where we go. . . .

1. American popular culture regards this sermon as a celebration of the Puritan sense of mission, but why did Winthrop issue such a stark warning about the consequences of failure?

For additional sources related to this feature, visit the *Liberty, Equality, Power* Web site at:

http://history.wadsworth.com/murrin_LEP4e

dimension by pairing each personal covenant with a communal counterpart. The social equivalent of the covenant of grace was the church covenant. Each congregation organized itself into a church, a community of the elect. The founders, or "pillars," of each church, after satisfying one another of their own conversions, agreed that within their church the Gospel would be properly preached and discipline would be strictly maintained. God, in turn, promised to bestow saving grace within that church—not to everyone, of course, but presumably to most of the children of the elect. The communal counterpart of the covenant of works was the key to secular history. Puritans called it the "national" covenant. It determined not who was saved or damned, but the rise and fall of nations or peoples. As a people, New Englanders agreed to obey the law, and God promised to prosper them. They, in turn, covenanted with their magistrates to punish sinners. If magistrates enforced God's law and the people supported these efforts, God would not punish the whole community for the misdeeds of individuals. But if sinners escaped public account, God's anger would be terrible toward his chosen people of New England. God gave them much and demanded much in return.

For New Englanders, the idea of the covenant became a powerful social metaphor, explaining everything from crop failures and untimely deaths to Indian wars and political contention. Towns and militia companies used covenants to organize themselves. If only because a minister could always think of something that had missed proper correction, the covenant generated an almost automatic sense of moral crisis. It had a built-in dynamic of moral reform that was becoming obvious even before the migrants crossed the ocean.

In England, the government had refused to assume a godly role. Puritans fleeing to America hoped to escape the divine wrath that threatened England and to create in America the kind of churches that God demanded. A few hoped to erect a model "city upon a hill" to inspire all humankind. Governor John Winthrop developed this idea in a famous sermon of 1630, but this theme seldom appeared in the writings of other founders. It became more common a generation later when, ironically, any neutral observer could see that the rest of the world no longer cared what New Englanders were doing.

Massachusetts Bay

In 1629, several English Puritans obtained a charter for the Massachusetts Bay Company, a typical joint-stock corporation except for one feature: The charter did not specify where the company was to be located. Puritan investors going to New England bought out the other stockholders. Led by Winthrop, they carried the charter to America, beyond the gaze of Charles I. They used it not to organize a business corporation, but as the constitution for the colony. In the 1630s, the General Court created by the charter became the Massachusetts legislature. New England settlers came from the broad middle range of English society—few rich, few very poor. Most had owned property in England. When they sold it to go to America, they probably liquidated far more capital than the London Company had invested in Virginia. A godly haven was expensive to build.

An advance party that sailed in 1629 took over a fishing village on the coast and renamed it Salem. The Winthrop fleet brought 1,000 settlers in 1630. In small groups, they scattered around the bay, founding Dorchester, Roxbury, Boston, Charlestown, and Cambridge. Each town formed around a minister and a magistrate. The local congregation was the first institution to take shape. From it evolved the town meeting, as the settlers began to distinguish more sharply between religious and secular affairs. Soon the colonists were raising European livestock and growing English wheat and other grains, along with corn. Perhaps 30 percent of them perished during the first winter. A few hundred others grew discouraged and returned to England. Conditions after that rapidly improved, as they had at Plymouth a decade earlier. About 13,000 settlers came to Massachusetts by 1641, most as families—a unique event in Atlantic empires to that time.

Settlers did a brisk business selling grain to the newcomers arriving each year. When the flow of immigrants ceased in 1641, that trade collapsed, creating a crisis that lessened as towns improved their economic infrastructure by increasing their capacity to build ships or to raise sheep and produce woolen textiles. Towns also adopted the "warning out" system. It prohibited newcomers from settling in a town without the permission of the authorities. By limiting the mobility of labor, it kept wages below their market value. Ironically, Europe's first overseas free-labor society needed this coercive mechanism to get itself started. The region began to prosper after 1650 as Boston merchants opened up West Indian markets for New England grain, lumber, and fish. The economic success of the region depended on its ability to ship food and lumber products to colonies that grew staple crops. The very existence of colonies committed to free labor was an oddity. To prosper, they had to trade with more typical colonies, the societies elsewhere in the hemisphere that raised tobacco and sugar with unfree labor.

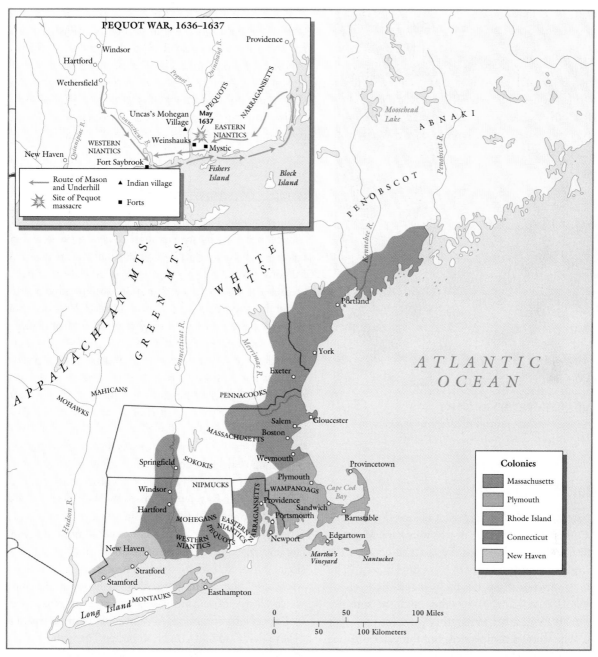

MAP 2.6   NEW ENGLAND IN THE 1640S

The five Puritan colonies spread over the Atlantic coast and nearby islands, the shores and islands of Narragansett Bay, both sides of Long Island Sound, and much of the Connecticut Valley. Although New Hampshire and Maine (not named as such on this map) were not founded by Puritans, Massachusetts extended its government over their settlers during the English civil wars. The insert map shows the principal military campaign of the Pequot War.

The region's economy imperiled Puritan orthodoxy. Few Boston merchants and almost no fishermen could meet the religious standards of a Puritan society. Although few of these men became church members in the first generation, the colony needed their services and had to put up with them. The fishing towns of Marblehead and Glouces- ter did little to implement Puritan values or even to found churches in the early decades, while Boston merchants increasingly favored toleration of Protestant dissenters because it would be good for business. Although these contrasts softened with time, Puritan orthodoxy was mostly a rural phenomenon.

Photograph © 2003 Museum of Fine Arts, Boston.

PORTRAIT OF ROBERT GIBBS (1670)
New Englanders did not provide distinctive garments for small boys and girls. They wore the same clothes.

Puritan Family Life

In rural areas, New Englanders soon observed a remarkable fact. After the first winter, deaths were rare. Mariners sailing to the Chesapeake noted the contrast between the sickly Virginians and the robust New Englanders. "The air of the country is sharp, the rocks many, the trees innumerable, the grass little, the winter cold, the summer hot, the gnats in summer biting, the wolves at midnight howling," one woman complained. But the place was undeniably healthy, and families grew rapidly as 6 or even 10 children reached maturity. The settlers had left most European diseases behind and had encountered no new ones in the bracing climate. For the founders and their children, life expectancy far exceeded the European norm. More than one-fifth of the men who founded Andover lived past age 80. Infant mortality fell, and few mothers died in childbirth. Because people lived so long, New England families became intensely patriarchal. Many fathers refused to grant land titles to their sons before their own deaths. In the early years, settlers often moved, looking for the richest soil, the best neighbors, and the most inspiring minister. By about 1645, most of them had found what they wanted. Migration into or out of country towns be-

came much lower than in England, and the New England town settled into a tight community that slowly became an intricate web of cousins. Once the settlers had formed a typical farming town, they grew reluctant to admit "strangers" to their midst. New Englanders largely avoided slavery, not out of sympathy for Africans or hatred of the institution, but to keep outsiders from contaminating their religion.

Conversion, Dissent, and Expansion

Among serious Puritans, competing visions of the godly society became divisive enough to spawn several new colonies. The vital force behind Puritanism was the quest for conversion. Probably because of John Cotton's stirring sermons in Boston, the settlers crossed an invisible boundary in the mid-1630s. As Cotton's converts described their religious experiences, their neighbors turned from analyzing the legitimacy of their own conversions to assessing the validity of someone else's. Afraid that Cotton's ecstatic converts had not scrutinized their own hearts with sufficient rigor, Thomas Shepard and other nearby ministers began to impose tests for regeneracy, and the standards of acceptance escalated rapidly.

The conversion experience was deeply ambiguous to a Puritan. Anyone who found no inner trace of saving grace was damned. Anyone who was absolutely certain of salvation had to be relying on personal merit and was also damned. Conversion took months, even years to achieve. It began with the discovery that one could not keep God's law and that one *deserved* damnation, not for an occasional misdeed, but for what one was at one's best—a wretched sinner. It progressed through despair to hope, which always arose from passages of scripture that spoke to that person's condition. A "saint" at last found reason to believe that God had saved him or her. The whole process involved a painful balance between assurance and doubt. A saint was sure of salvation, but never too sure.

This quest for conversion generated dissent and new colonies. The founders of Connecticut feared that Massachusetts was becoming too severe in certifying church members. The founders of the New Haven Colony worried that the Bay Colony was too lenient. The first Rhode Islanders disagreed with all of them.

In the mid-1630s, Reverend Thomas Hooker, alarmed by Cotton's preaching, led his people west to the Connecticut River, where they founded Hartford and other towns south of the charter boundary of Massachusetts. John Winthrop, Jr., built Saybrook Fort at the mouth of the river, and it soon merged with Hooker's towns into

the colony of Connecticut. In 1639, an affluent group planted the New Haven Colony on Long Island Sound. The leaders were Theophilus Eaton, a wealthy London merchant, and Reverend John Davenport, who imposed the strictest requirements for church membership in New England.

The residents of most towns agreed on the kind of worship they preferred, but some settlers, such as Roger Williams and Anne Hutchinson, made greater demands. Williams, who served briefly as Salem's minister, was a Separatist who refused to worship with anyone who did not explicitly repudiate the Church of England. Nearly all Massachusetts Puritans were Non-Separatists who claimed only to be reforming the Anglican Church. In 1636, after Williams challenged the king's right as a Christian to grant Indian lands to anyone at all, the colony banished him. He fled to Narragansett Bay with a few disciples and founded Providence. He developed eloquent arguments for religious liberty and the complete separation of church and state.

Anne Hutchinson, a merchant's wife and an admirer of John Cotton, claimed that virtually all other ministers were preaching only the covenant of works, not the covenant of grace, and were leading people to hell. She won a large following in Boston. At her trial there, she claimed to have received direct messages from God (the Antinomian heresy). Banished in 1638, she and her followers also fled to Narragansett Bay, where they founded Newport and Portsmouth. These towns united with Providence to form the colony of Rhode Island and accepted both the religious liberty and the separation of church and state that Williams advocated.

Much of this territorial expansion reflected not just religious idealism, but also a quest for more land that threatened the neighboring Indians. Connecticut and Massachusetts waged a war of terror and annihilation against the Pequot Indians, who controlled the fertile Thames River valley in Connecticut. In May 1637, New England soldiers debated with their chaplain which of two Pequot forts to attack, the one held by warriors or the one with women, children, and the elderly. He probably told them to remember Saul and the Amalekites because, with horrified Narragansett Indians looking on as nominal allies of the settlers, the Puritan army chose the second fort, set fire to all the wigwams, and shot everyone who tried to flee. The godly had their own uses for terrorism.

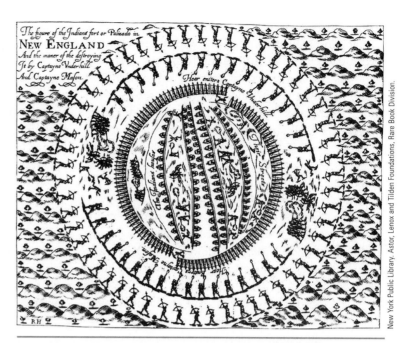

THE PURITAN MASSACRE OF THE PEQUOT INDIANS, 1637
The massacre took place at what is now Mystic, Connecticut. Most of the victims were women and children. The Indians shown in the outer circle were Narragansett allies of the settlers and were appalled by the carnage.

New York Public Library, Astor, Lenox and Tilden Foundations, Rare Book Division.

Congregations, Towns, and Colony Governments

These struggles helped shape New England's basic institutions. Congregations abolished the distinctive rites of Anglicanism—vestments, incense, the Book of Common Prayer, church courts, bishops. The sermon became the center of worship, and each congregation chose and ordained its own minister. No singing was permitted, except of psalms, with each worshiper warbling in his or her own key. Congregations sometimes sent ministers and laymen to a synod, but its decisions were advisory, not binding. A 1648 synod issued the Cambridge Platform, which defined Congregationalist worship and church organization.

By then the town had become something distinct from the congregation. Some towns chose independent farms at the outset, but many adopted a medieval system that appeared nowhere else in colonial America: open-field agriculture. In that system, farmers owned scattered strips of land within a common field, and the town decided what crops to grow. Although this emphasis on communal cooperation may have appealed to the founders, who were also short of oxen and plows at first and had to share them, the open-field system did not survive the first generation.

Town meetings decided who got how much land. It was distributed broadly but never equally. In Springfield,

at one extreme, the Pynchon family controlled most of the land and most of the labor as well. In other towns, such as Dedham, the distribution was much more equitable. In some villages, town meetings occurred often, made most of the decisions, and left only the details to a board of elected "selectmen." In others, the selectmen did most of the governing. All adult males usually participated in local decisions, but Massachusetts and New Haven restricted the vote for colonywide offices to men who were full church members, a decision that greatly narrowed the electorate by the 1660s.

Massachusetts had a bicameral legislature by the 1640s. Voters in each town chose representatives who met as the Chamber of Deputies, or lower house. Voters also elected the governor and the magistrates, or upper house (the Council or, in its judicial capacity, the Court of Assistants). The magistrates also staffed the county courts. The Court of Assistants heard major criminal cases and appeals from the counties. Final appeals were heard by the General Court, with both houses sitting together to decide judicial questions.

Massachusetts defined its legal system in the "Body of Liberties" of 1641 (which may actually be history's first bill of rights) and in a comprehensive law code of 1648 that was widely imitated in other colonies. Massachusetts sharply reduced the number of capital offenses under English law and listed them in the order of the Ten Commandments. Unlike England, Massachusetts seldom executed anyone for a crime against property. Other distinctive features of the legal system included an explicit recognition of the liberties of women, children, servants,

foreigners, and even "the Bruite Creature," or animals; a serious effort to ban professional lawyers; and the swift punishment of crime.

New England also transformed the traditional English jury system. New Haven abolished juries altogether because the Bible does not mention them. But the other colonies vastly expanded the role of civil (noncriminal) juries, using them even to decide appeals, something that never happened in England. Except in capital trials, however, the criminal jury—a fixture of English justice—almost disappeared in New England. The punishment of sin involved fidelity to the covenant and was too important to leave to 12 ordinary men. This system worked well because even sinners shared its values. Most offenders appeared in court and accepted their punishments. Acquittals were rare, almost unheard of in New Haven. Yet hardly anyone ran away to avoid trial or punishment.

Infant Baptism and New Dissent

Although most of the founders of the New England colonies became church members during the fervor of the 1630s, their children had trouble achieving conversion. They had never lived as part of a beleaguered minority in England, nor had they experienced the joy of joining with other holy refugees in founding their own church. They had to find God on their own and then persuade their elders—who were on guard because leniency had let Williams, Hutchinson, and other deviants through—that their conversions were authentic. Most failed. They grew up, married, and requested baptism for their children. The

BOSTON TOWN HOUSE

Erected in 1657, the Town House was probably the most imposing European structure in the region at the time.

© Bettmann/Corbis.

Cambridge Platform declared that only "saints" (the converted) and their children could be baptized. But what about the grandchildren of the saints if their own parents had not yet experienced conversion? By 1660, this problem was becoming acute.

Dissenters offered two answers, and the ministers a third. In the 1640s, some settlers became Baptists. Noting that scripture contains no mandate to baptize infants, they argued that only converted adults should receive that rite. Their position challenged the logic of a covenanted community by implying that New England was no different from Europe. The community was a mass of sinners from whom God would randomly choose a few saints. Samuel Gorton, a Baptist expelled from Massachusetts and Plymouth (he denounced the magistrates as "just asses"), founded Warwick, Rhode Island, in the 1640s. When Massachusetts arrested him, accused him of blasphemy, and put him on trial for his life, the legislature banished him instead, but Gorton appealed to Parliament in England, and Massachusetts backed down. Baptist principles also attracted Henry Dunster, the able president of Harvard College, which had been founded in 1636 to educate ministers and magistrates for a Puritan society. When the courts began to harass Baptists, Dunster left for more tolerant Plymouth.

Even more alarming to the Puritan establishment were the Quakers, who invaded the region from England in the 1650s (to be discussed later in the chapter). Quakers found salvation within themselves—through God, the Inner Light present in all people if they will only let it shine forth. To Puritans, the Quaker answer to the conversion dilemma seemed blasphemous and Antinomian. Massachusetts hanged four Quakers who refused to stop preaching, including Mary Dyer, who was once a disciple of Anne Hutchinson.

The clergy's answer to the lack of conversions, worked out at a synod in 1662, became known as the Half-Way Covenant. Parents who had been baptized but had not yet experienced conversion could bring their children before the church, "own the covenant" (that is, subject themselves and their offspring to the doctrine and discipline of the church), and have their children baptized. In practice, women often experienced conversion before age 30, men closer to 40, but many never did. In most churches, women also began to outnumber men as full members. For 15 or 20 years after 1662, most churches were still dominated by the lay members of the founding generation. Despite the urging of the clergy (by then most ministers were young Harvard graduates, not venerable saints), aging church members resisted implementation of the Half-Way Covenant. But as the founders died off in the 1670s and 1680s, the covenant took hold and soon led to

something like universal baptism. Almost every child had an ancestor who had been a full church member.

Dissent persisted anyhow. The orthodox colonies were divided over whether to persecute or to ignore their Baptist and Quaker minorities. Ministers preached "jeremiads," shrill warnings against any backsliding from the standards of the founding generation, but many laypeople disliked the persecution of conscientious Protestants. By the 1670s, innovation seemed dangerous and divisive, but the past was also becoming a burden that no one could shoulder.

The English Civil Wars

The 1640s were a critical decade in England and the colonies. From 1629 to 1640, Charles I governed without Parliament, but when he tried to impose the Anglican Book of Common Prayer on Presbyterian Scotland, his Scottish subjects rebelled and even invaded England. Needing revenue, Charles summoned two Parliaments in 1640 only to find that many of its members, especially the Puritans, sympathized with the Scots. In 1641, Irish Catholics launched a massive revolt against the Protestant colonizers of their land. King and Parliament agreed that the Irish must be crushed, but neither dared trust the other with the men and resources to do the job. Instead, they began to fight each other.

In 1642, the king and Parliament raised separate armies and went to war. Parliament gradually won the military struggle and then had to govern most of England without a king. In January 1649, after its moderate members had been purged by its own New Model Army, Parliament beheaded Charles, abolished the House of Lords, and proclaimed England a Commonwealth (or republic). Within a few years, Oliver Cromwell, Parliament's most successful general, dismissed Parliament, and the army proclaimed him "Lord Protector" of England. He convened several of his own Parliaments, including one that consisted entirely of godly men, but these experiments failed. The army, even when it drafted a written constitution for England, could not win legitimacy for a government that ruled without the ancient trinity of "King, Lords, and Commons." Cromwell also faced a challenge outside Parliament from "levelers," "diggers," and "ranters" who claimed to speak for "the people" while demanding sweeping social reforms.

Cromwell died in September 1658, and his regime collapsed. Part of the army invited Charles II (1660–85) back from exile to claim his throne. After 20 years of turmoil, this Restoration government did its best to restore the old order. It brought back the House of Lords. The Church of England was reestablished under its episcopal

form of government. The English state, denying any right of dissent, persecuted both Catholics and Protestant dissenters: Presbyterians, Congregationalists, Baptists, and Quakers. This persecution drove thousands of Quakers to the Delaware valley after 1675.

The First Restoration Colonies

England had founded 6 of the original 13 colonies before 1640. Six others were founded or came under English rule during the Restoration era (1660–88). The last, Georgia, was settled in the 1730s (see chapter 4). Most of the new colonies shared certain common features and also differed in some respects from earlier settlements. All were proprietary in form. As with Maryland earlier, a proprietary charter enabled the organizers to pursue daring social experiments. Except for Pennsylvania, the Restoration colonies were all founded by men with big ideas and small purses. The proprietors tried to attract settlers from the older colonies because importing them from Europe was too expensive.

The most readily available prospects were servants completing their indentures in the West Indies and being driven out by the sugar revolution. The most prized settlers, however, were New Englanders. Although the proprietors distrusted both their piety and their politics, New Englanders had built the most thriving colonies in North America. Cromwell had tried but failed to attract New Haven settlers to Jamaica. Few New Englanders would go farther south than New York or New Jersey. Settlers from the West Indies would populate South Carolina.

The Restoration colonies made it easy for settlers to acquire land, and they competed with one another by offering newcomers strong guarantees of civil and political liberties. They all promised either toleration or full religious liberty, at least for Christians. Whereas Virginia and New England (except Rhode Island) were still homogeneous societies, the Restoration colonies all attracted a mix of religious and ethnic groups. None of them found it easy to translate this human diversity into political stability.

Most of the new proprietors were "cavaliers" who had supported Charles II and his brother James, duke of York, during their long exile. Charles owed them something, and a colonial charter cost nothing to grant. Many proprietors took part in more than one project. The eight who obtained charters for Carolina in 1663 and 1665 were also prominent in organizing the Royal African Company, which soon made England a major participant in the African slave trade. Two of the Carolina proprietors obtained a charter from the duke of York for New Jersey as

well. William Penn, although the son of a Commonwealth admiral, became a friend of James and invested in West New Jersey before acquiring Pennsylvania from the king.

Far more than New England or Virginia, the Restoration colonies foreshadowed the diversity that would characterize the United States after 1790. South Carolina became the first home of the cotton kingdom. The Middle Atlantic provinces set much of the tone for the Midwest.

Carolina, Harrington, and the Aristocratic Ideal

In 1663, eight courtiers obtained a charter by which they became the board of proprietors for a colony to be founded south of Virginia. Calling their province Carolina in honor of the king, they tried to colonize the region in the 1660s but achieved little success until the following decade. Most of the settlers came from two sources. Former servants from Virginia and Maryland, many in debt, hoped that they would be left alone if they claimed land around Albemarle Sound in what eventually became North Carolina. Another wave of former servants came from Barbados. They settled the area that became South Carolina, 300 miles south of Albemarle, and began to export grain and meat to the West Indies.

To the proprietors in England, these scattered settlements made up a single colony called Carolina. Led by Anthony Ashley-Cooper, later the first earl of Shaftesbury and the principal organizer of England's Whig Party, the proprietors drafted the Fundamental Constitutions of Carolina in 1669, an incredibly complex plan for organizing the new colony. Philosopher John Locke, Shaftesbury's young secretary, helped write the document.

The Fundamental Constitutions drew on the work of Commonwealth England's most prominent republican thinker, James Harrington, author of *Oceana* (1656). He tried to design a republic that could endure—unlike ancient Athens or Rome, which had finally become despotic states. Harrington argued that how land was distributed ought to determine whether power should be lodged in one man (monarchy), a few men (aristocracy), or many (a republic). Where ownership of land was widespread, he insisted, absolute government could not prevail. He proposed several other devices to prevent one man, or a few, from undermining a republic, such as frequent rotation of officeholders (called "term limits" today), the secret ballot, and a bicameral legislature in which the smaller house would propose laws and the larger house approve or reject them. Harrington had greater impact on colonial governments than any other thinker of his time.

Shaftesbury believed that Harrington had uncovered the laws of history. By emphasizing Henry VIII's confisca-

tion of monastic lands and their sale to an emerging gentry, Harrington seemed to have an explanation for the decline of the monarchy, England's civil wars, and the execution of Charles I—an explanation that was anathema to the king because, if Harrington was correct, the monarchy was still in trouble. English writers dared not discuss these ideas openly in the 1660s, but by applying Harrington's principles at a safe distance of 3,000 miles, the Carolina proprietors could choose the kind of society they desired and devise institutions to ensure its success. Well aware that the House of Lords had been abolished for 11 years after 1649, they were not yet certain whether the English aristocracy could survive at home. In Carolina, they hoped to create a thriving aristocratic society.

The Fundamental Constitutions proposed a government that was far more complex than any colony could sustain. England had three supreme courts; Carolina would have eight. A Grand Council of proprietors and councillors would exercise executive power and propose all laws. Their bills would have to pass a Parliament of commoners and nobles (called "landgraves" and "casiques"). The nobles would control 40 percent of the land. In a later version of the text, a noble who lost his land or permanently left the colony would forfeit his title, an application of Harrington's warning not to divorce power from land. A distinct group of manor lords would also have large estates. The document guaranteed religious toleration to all who believed in God, but everyone had to join a church or lose his citizenship. The document also envisioned a class of lowly whites, "leetmen," who would live on small tracts and serve the great landlords—and it accepted slavery. "Every Freeman of Carolina shall have absolute Power and Authority over his Negro Slaves," declared Article 110.

Conditions were bleak on Barbados for ex-servants, but not bleak enough to make the Fundamental Constitutions attractive to the Barbadians who settled in Carolina. Between 1670 and 1700, the proprietors tried several times, without success, to win their approval of the document. In the 1680s, weary of resistance from the predominantly Anglican Barbadians, the proprietors shipped 1,000 dissenters from England and Scotland to South Carolina. These newcomers formed the nucleus of a proprietary party in South Carolina politics and made religious diversity a social fact, but their influence was never strong enough to win approval for the Fundamental Constitutions. The Barbadians remained in control.

Carolina presented its organizers with other unanticipated obstacles to these aristocratic goals. The proprietors assumed that land ownership would be the key to everything else, including wealth and status, but many settlers prospered in other ways. Some of them, especially in Albe-

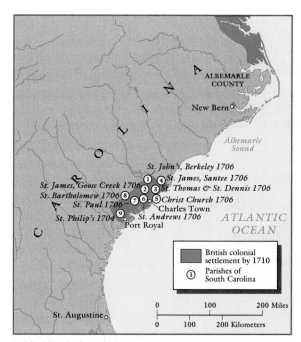

MAP 2.7 EARLY CAROLINA, CIRCA 1710
The first nine parishes of South Carolina and the English settlements along Albemarle Sound that became North Carolina.

marle, exploited the virgin forests all around them to produce masts, turpentine, tar, and pitch for sale to English shipbuilders. Other settlers raised cattle and hogs by letting them run free on open land. Some of South Carolina's African slaves were probably America's first cowboys. The settlers also traded with the Indians, usually for deerskins, often acquired west of the Appalachians. As in New France and New Netherland, the Indian trade sustained a genuine city, Charleston, the first in the American South, founded in 1680 at the confluence of the Ashley and Cooper rivers. The Indian trade also became something more dangerous than hunting or trapping animals. Carolina traders allied themselves with some Indians to attack others and drag the captives, mostly women and children, to Charleston for sale as slaves. Until 1715, the Indian slave trade was the colony's biggest business. South Carolina exported more enslaved Indians to other colonies than it imported Africans for its emerging plantations.

In the early 18th century, South Carolina and North Carolina became separate colonies, and South Carolina's economy began to move in a new direction. For two decades, until the mid-1720s, a parliamentary subsidy sustained a boom in the naval stores industry, which in turn stimulated a large demand for slaves, but Charleston merchants increasingly invested their capital, acquired in the Indian trade, in rice plantations. In the 1690s, planters learned how to grow rice from slaves who had cultivated it

in West Africa. It gradually became the staple export of South Carolina and triggered a sharp growth of African slavery. In 1700, more than 40 percent of the colony's population of 5,700 were African or Indian slaves engaged in a wide variety of activities. The Indian slave trade collapsed after 1715. By 1730, two-thirds of the colony's 30,000 people were African slaves, most of whom toiled on rice plantations.

New York: An Experiment in Absolutism

In 1664, James, duke of York, obtained a charter from his royal brother for a colony between the Delaware and Connecticut rivers. Charles II claimed that the territory of New Netherland was rightfully England's because it was included in the Virginia charter of 1606. James sent a fleet to Manhattan, and the English settlers on Long Island rose to support his claim. Reluctantly, Stuyvesant surrendered without resistance. The English renamed the province New York. New Amsterdam became New York City, and Fort Orange became Albany. The Dutch ceded New Netherland with few regrets. It had never been profitable anyway. New York took over all of Long Island, most of which had been ruled by Connecticut, but never made good on its claim to the Connecticut River as its eastern boundary. New York also inherited New Netherland's role as mediator between the settlers and the Iroquois Five Nations. In effect, the duke of York's autocratic colony assumed most of the burdens of this relationship while unintentionally conferring most of the benefits on the Quakers who would begin to settle the Delaware valley a decade later. The shield provided by New York and the Iroquois would make the Quaker experiment in pacifism a viable option.

Richard Nicolls, the first English governor of New York, planned to lure Yankees to the Jersey coast as a way of offsetting the preponderance of Dutch settlers in the Hudson valley. Although English soldiers abused many Dutch civilians, official policy toward the Dutch was conciliatory. Those who chose to leave could take their property with them. Those who stayed retained their property and were assured of religious toleration. Most stayed. Except in New York City and the small Dutch portion of Long Island, Dutch settlers still lived under Dutch law. Dutch inheritance practices, which were far more generous to women than English law, survived in New York well into the 18th century. England also expected to take over the colony's trade with Europe, but New York's early governors realized that a total ban on commerce with Amsterdam could ruin the colony. Under various legal subterfuges, they allowed this trade to continue.

The duke boldly tried to do in New York what he and the king did not dare attempt in England—to govern without an elective assembly. This policy upset English settlers on Long Island far more than the Dutch, who had no experience with representative government. Governor Nicolls compiled a code of laws (the Duke's Laws) that were culled mostly from New England statutes. With difficulty, he secured the consent of English settlers to this code in 1665, but thereafter he taxed and governed on his own, seeking only the advice and consent of his appointed council and of a court of assize, also appointive, that dispensed justice, mostly to the English settlers.

This policy made it difficult to attract English colonists to New York, especially after New Jersey became a separate proprietary colony in 1665. The two proprietors, Sir George Carteret and John, baron Berkeley, granted settlers the right to elect an assembly, which made New Jersey far more attractive to English settlers than New York. The creation of New Jersey also slowed the flow of Dutch settlers across the Hudson and thus helped to keep New York Dutch.

The transition from a Dutch to an English colony did not go smoothly. James expected his English invaders to assimilate the conquered Dutch, but the reverse was more common for two or three decades. Most Englishmen who settled in New York after the conquest married Dutch women (few unmarried English women were available) and sent their children to the Dutch Reformed Church. In effect, the Dutch were assimilating the English. Nor did the Dutch give up their loyalty to the Netherlands. In 1673, when a Dutch fleet threatened the colony, the Dutch refused to assist the English garrison of Fort James at the southern tip of Manhattan. Eastern Long Island showed more interest in reuniting with Connecticut than in fighting the Dutch. Much like Stuyvesant nine years earlier, the English garrison gave up without resistance. New York City now became New Orange and Fort James was renamed Fort William, both in honor of young William III of Nassau, Prince of Orange, the new *stadholder* (military leader) of the Dutch Republic in its struggle with France. Thus James and William became antagonists in New York 15 years before the Glorious Revolution, in which William would drive James from the English throne (see chapter 3).

New Orange survived for 15 months, until the Dutch Republic again concluded that the colony was not worth what it cost and gave it back to England at the end of the war. The new governor, Major Edmund Andros, arrested seven prominent Dutch merchants and tried them as aliens after they refused to swear an oath of loyalty to England that might oblige them to fight other Dutchmen. Faced with the confiscation of their property, they gave in. Andros also helped secure bilingual ministers for Dutch

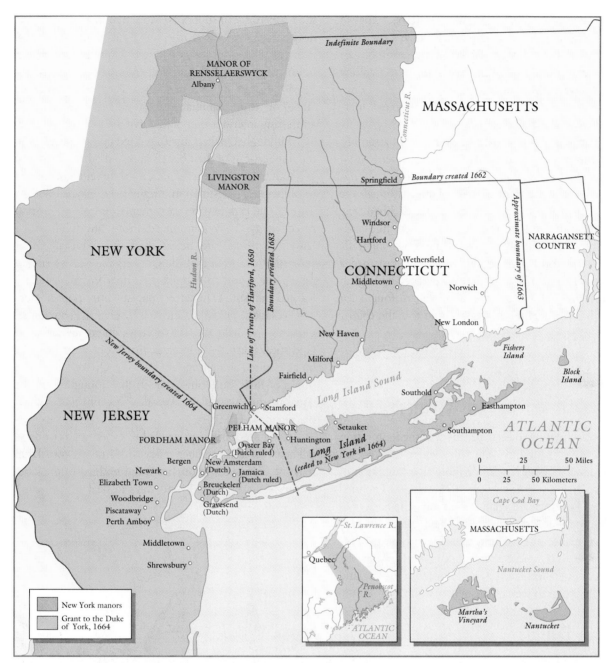

MAP 2.8 THE DUKE OF YORK'S COLONIAL CHARTER

This map shows the boundary of New York as set forth in the charter of 1664, the compromise boundary the first English governor negotiated with Connecticut, and the principal manors created in the 17th century.

Reformed pulpits. These preachers made a great show of their loyalty to the duke, a delicate matter now that James, in England, had openly embraced the Catholic faith. Ordinary Dutch settlers looked with suspicion on the new ministers and on wealthier Dutch families who socialized with the governor or sent their sons to New England to learn English.

English merchants in New York City resented the continuing Amsterdam trade and the staying power of the Dutch elite. They believed the colony had to become more English to attract newcomers. When Andros failed to renew the colony's basic revenue act before returning to England in 1680, the merchants refused to pay any duties not voted by an elective assembly. The court of assize, supposedly a bastion of absolutism, supported the tax strike, convicted the duke's customs collector of usurping authority, and sent him to England for punishment where, of course, James exonerated him. The justices also fined

several Dutch officeholders for failing to respect English liberties. The English (but not Dutch) towns on Long Island joined in the demand for an elective assembly, an urgent matter now that William Penn's much freer colony on the Delaware threatened to drain away the small English population of New York. Several prominent merchants did move to Philadelphia.

The duke finally relented and conceded an assembly. When it met in 1683, it adopted a Charter of Liberties that proclaimed government by consent. It also imposed English law on the Dutch parts of the province. Although the drain of English settlers to Pennsylvania declined, few immigrants came to New York at a time when thousands were landing in Philadelphia. Philadelphia's thriving trade cut into New York City's profits. New York remained a Dutch society with a Yankee enclave, governed by English intruders. In 1689, when James and William fought for the English throne, their struggle would tear the colony apart.

☙ Brotherly Love: The Quakers and America

The most fascinating social experiment of the Restoration era took place in the Delaware valley where Quakers led another family-based, religiously motivated migration of more than 10,000 people between 1675 and 1690. Founded by George Fox during England's civil wars, the Society of Friends expanded dramatically in the 1650s as it went through a heroic phase of missionaries and martyrs, including the four executed in Massachusetts. After the Restoration, Quakers faced harsh persecution in England and finally began to seek refuge in America.

Quaker Beliefs

Quakers infuriated other Christians. They insisted that God, in the form of the Inner Light, is present in all people, who can become good—even perfect—if only they will let that light shine forth. They took literally Jesus's advice to "Turn the other cheek." They became pacifists, enraging Catholics and most other Protestants, all of whom had found ways to justify war. Quakers also obeyed Jesus's command to "swear not." They denounced oathtaking as sinful. Again, other Christians reacted with horror because their judicial systems rested on oaths.

Although orderly and peaceful, Quakers struck others as dangerous radicals whose beliefs would bring anarchy. For instance, slavery made them uncomfortable, although the Friends did not embrace abolitionism until a century later (see chapter 5). Furthermore, in what they called "the Lamb's war" against human pride, Quakers refused to doff their hats to social superiors. More than any other simple device, hats symbolized the social hierarchy of Europe. Every man knew his place so long as he understood whom to doff to, and who should doff to him. Quakers also refused to accept or to confer titles. They called everyone "thee" or "thou," familiar terms used by superiors when addressing inferiors, especially servants.

Although Quakers disliked theological speculation, the implications of their beliefs appalled other Christians. Without the bother of a refutation, the Inner Light seemed to obliterate predestination, original sin, maybe even the Trinity. Quakers had no sacraments, not even an organized clergy. They denounced Protestant ministers as "hireling priests," no better than the "papists." Other Protestants retorted that the Quakers were conspiring to return the world to "popish darkness" by abolishing a learned ministry. (The terms "papists" and "popish" were abusive labels applied to Catholics by English Protestants.) Quakers also held distinctive views about revelation. If God speaks directly to Friends, that Word must be every bit as inspired as anything in the Bible. Quakers compiled books of their "sufferings," which they thought were the equal of the "Acts of the Apostles," a claim that seemed blasphemous to others.

Contemporaries expected the Society of Friends to fall apart as each member followed his or her own Light in some unique direction, but it did nothing of the kind. In the 1660s, Quakers found ways to deal with discord.

North Wind Picture Archives.

HEXAGONAL QUAKER MEETING HOUSE
This unique design emphasizes the Quaker belief in the fundamental equality of all souls under God. The interior has no altar or pulpit, no front or back. All worshippers are equally close to God.

The heart of Quaker worship was the "weekly meeting" of the local congregation. There was no sermon or liturgy. People spoke whenever the Light inspired them. But because a few men and women spoke often and with great effect, they became recognized as "public friends," the closest the Quakers came to having a clergy. Public friends occupied special, elevated seats in some meetinghouses, and many went on missionary tours in Europe or America. The weekly meetings within a region sent representatives to a "monthly meeting," which resolved questions of policy and discipline. The monthly meetings sent delegates to the "yearly meeting" in London. At every level, decisions had to be unanimous. There is only one Inner Light, and it must convey the same message to every believer. This insistence on unanimity provided strong safeguards against schism.

Quaker Families

Quakers transformed the traditional family as well. Women enjoyed almost full equality, and some of them, such as Mary Dyer, became exceptional preachers, even martyrs. Women held their own formal meetings and made important decisions about discipline and betrothals. Quaker reforms also affected children, whom most Protestants saw as tiny sinners whose wills must be broken by severe discipline. But once Quakers stopped worrying about original sin, their children became innocents in whom the Light would shine if only they could be protected from worldly corruption. In America, Quakers created affectionate families, built larger houses than non-Quakers with equivalent resources, and worked hard to acquire land for all their children. Earlier than other Christians, they began to limit family size to give more love to the children they did have. After the missionary impulse declined, Quakers seldom associated with non-Quakers, and the needs of their own children became paramount. To marry an outsider meant expulsion from the Society, a fate more likely to befall poor Friends than rich ones. Poor Quakers had difficulty finding spouses precisely because their children might never receive the advantages that most Friends had come to expect.

Persecution in England helped drive Quakers across the ocean, but the need to provide for their children was another powerful motive for emigration. By 1700, about half of the Quakers in England and Wales had moved to America.

West New Jersey

In 1674, the New Jersey proprietors split their holding into two colonies. Sir George Carteret claimed what he now called East New Jersey, a province near New York City with half a dozen towns populated by Baptist, Quaker, Puritan, and Dutch Reformed settlers. Lord Berkeley claimed West New Jersey and promptly sold it to the Quakers, who then founded two colonies in America: West New Jersey and Pennsylvania. In the 1680s, when Quakers bought out the proprietor of East New Jersey and also gained power in Delaware (formerly New Sweden), they seemed poised to dominate the entire region between Maryland and New York. The West Jersey purchasers divided their proprietary into 100 shares. Two of the organizers were Edward Byllinge, a former "leveler," and William Penn, an admirer of Harrington. They revived in West Jersey many radical ideals of the English Commonwealth era.

In 1676, Byllinge drafted a document, the West New Jersey Concessions and Agreements, which was approved by the first settlers in 1677. It lodged legislative power in a unicameral assembly, elected by secret ballot, and it empowered voters to instruct their representatives. In the court system, juries would decide both fact and law. Judges would merely preside over the court and, if asked by a juror, offer advice. Although the document was never fully implemented, it made West Jersey the most radical political experiment attempted in America before the Revolution. West Jersey Quakers believed that godly people could live together in love—without war, lawyers, or internal conflict. They kept government close to the people, made land easy to acquire, and promised freedom of worship to everyone. In the 1680s, lawsuits often ended with one litigant forgiving the other, and criminal trials sometimes closed with the victim embracing the perpetrator. But as social and religious diversity grew, the system broke down. Non-Quakers increasingly refused to cooperate. In the 1690s, the courts became impotent, and Quaker rule collapsed some years before the Crown took over the colony in 1702.

Pennsylvania

By 1681, Quaker attention was already shifting to the west bank of the Delaware River. There, William Penn launched a much larger, if rather more cautious, "holy experiment" in brotherly love. The son of a Commonwealth admiral, Penn grew up surrounded by privilege. He knew well both Charles II and the duke of York, attended Oxford and the Inns of Court (England's law schools), went on the grand tour of Europe, and began to manage his father's Irish estates. Then something happened that embarrassed his family. "Mr. William Pen," reported a neighbor in December 1667, ". . . is a Quaker again, or some very melancholy thing." Penn often traveled to the continent on behalf of the Society of Friends, winning converts and recruiting settlers in the Netherlands and Germany. In England he was jailed several times for his beliefs, and in the so-called

***PENN'S TREATY WITH THE INDIANS,* BY BENJAMIN WEST**

This 1771 painting celebrates William Penn's efforts, nearly a century earlier, to establish peaceful relations with the Delaware Indians.

Penn-Meade trial of 1670, he challenged a judge's right to compel a jury to reconsider its verdict. In a landmark decision, a higher court vindicated him.

A gentleman and a Quaker, Penn was no ordinary colonizer. Using his contacts at court, he converted an old debt (owed to his father by the king) into a charter for a proprietary colony that Charles named Pennsylvania in honor of the deceased admiral. The emerging imperial bureaucracy disliked the whole project and, after failing to block it, inserted several restrictions into the charter. Penn agreed to enforce the Navigation Acts (see chapter 3), to let the Crown approve his choice of governor, to submit all legislation to the English Privy Council for approval, and to allow appeals from Pennsylvania courts to the Privy Council in England.

Contemporaries said little about the most striking innovation attempted by the Quaker colonists. They entered America unarmed. Pennsylvanians did not even organize a militia until the 1740s. Friendly relations with Indians were essential to the project's success, and Penn was careful to deal fairly with the Lenni Lenape, or Delaware Indians. They liked him and called him "Miquon," their word for "quill" and thus a pun on "Penn."

More thought went into planning Pennsylvania than into the creation of any other colony. Twenty drafts survive of Penn's First Frame of Government, his 1682 constitution for the province. It evolved from what was a larger version of the West Jersey Concessions and Agreements into something more Harringtonian but still quite

MAP 2.9   EARLY PENNSYLVANIA AND NEW JERSEY, CIRCA 1700

This map shows the first three counties of Pennsylvania and its capital of Philadelphia, the three counties of what would soon become Delaware, the colony of West New Jersey and its capital of Burlington, and the early towns of East New Jersey including its capital of Perth Amboy.

WILLIAM PENN IN ARMOR AND PENN'S CELL IN THE TOWER OF LONDON

The son of an English admiral, William Penn was not always a pacifist. In the 1660s, an unknown artist painted him in this military pose. After his conversion to the Society of Friends, Penn paid a steep price for his religious convictions. Accused of blasphemy, he was imprisoned in this bleak cell from December 1668 to July 1669.

liberating. The settlers would elect a council of 72 men to staggered three-year terms. The council would draft all legislation and submit copies to the voters. In the early years, the voters would meet to approve or reject these bills in person. Penn anticipated that as the province expanded, such meetings would become impractical. Voters would then elect an assembly of 200, which would increase gradually to 500, about the size of the House of Commons, although for a much smaller population. Government would still remain close to the people. Penn gave up the power to veto bills but retained control of the distribution of land. Capital punishment was abolished for crimes against property and most other offenses, except murder. Religious liberty, trial by jury, and habeas corpus all received strong guarantees.

Settlers had been arriving in Pennsylvania for a year when Penn landed in 1682 with his First Frame of Government. Some lived in caves along the river. Others, imitating the nearby Swedes, built log cabins. The colonists persuaded Penn that the First Frame was too cumbersome for a small colony, and the first legislature worked with

him to devise a simpler government. In what became known as the Second Frame, or the Pennsylvania Charter of Liberties of 1683, the council was reduced to 18 men and the assembly to 36. The assembly's inability to initiate legislation soon became a major grievance.

Penn laid out Philadelphia as "a green country town" and organized other settlements. Although an idealist, he hoped that land sales and other revenues would provide a handsome support for his family. Then, in 1684, he returned to England to answer Lord Baltimore's complaint that Philadelphia fell within the charter boundaries of Maryland, a claim that was soon verified. This dispute troubled the Penn family until the 1760s, when the Mason-Dixon line finally established the modern boundary.

In England, persecution had kept Quaker antiauthoritarianism in check, at least in relations with other Friends. In the colony, these attitudes soon became public. Penn expected his settlers to defer to the leaders among them. He created the Free Society of Traders to control commerce with England and gave high offices to its members.

From the start, however, wealth in Pennsylvania rested on trade not with England, but with other colonies, especially in the Caribbean. That trade was dominated by Quakers from Barbados, Jamaica, New York, and Boston. These men owed little to Penn and became an opposition faction in the colony. They and others demanded more land, especially in Philadelphia. They claimed that they could not afford to pay Penn's quitrents,[2] and they quarreled more often than was seemly for men of brotherly love.

In exasperation, Penn finally appointed John Blackwell, an old Cromwellian soldier, as governor in 1688, ordering him to end the quarrels and collect quitrents but to rule "tenderly." Boys jeered Blackwell as he tried to enter Penn's Philadelphia house, and the council refused to let him use the colony's great seal. Debate in the legislature became angrier than ever. After 13 months, Blackwell resigned. Each Quaker, he complained, "prayed for the rest on the First Day [of the week], and preyed on them the other six." The local mosquitoes, he added, "were worse than armed men but not nearly so nettlesome as the men without Armes." Because Penn had supported James II in England, he lost control of the colony between 1691 and 1693.

In 1691, the Society of Friends suffered a brief schism in the Delaware valley. A Quaker schoolteacher, George Keith, urged all Quakers to systematize their beliefs and even wrote his own catechism, only to encounter the opposition of the public friends, who included the colony's major officeholders. When he attacked them directly, he was convicted and fined for abusing civil officers. He claimed that he was being persecuted for his religious beliefs, but the courts insisted that his only crime was his attack on public authority. In contrast to Massachusetts in the 1630s, no one was banished, and Pennsylvania remained a haven for all religions. The colony's government

changed several more times before 1701, when Penn and the assembly finally agreed on the Fourth Frame, or Charter of Privileges, which gave Pennsylvania a unicameral legislature, but its politics remained turbulent and unstable into the 1720s.

Despite these controversies, Pennsylvania quickly became an economic success, well established in the Caribbean trade as an exporter of wheat and flour. Quaker families were thriving, and the colony's policy of religious liberty attracted thousands of outsiders. Some were German pacifists who shared the major goals of the Society of Friends. Others were Anglicans and Presbyterians who warned London that Quakers were unfit to rule—anywhere.

Conclusion

In the 16th century, France, the Netherlands, and England all challenged Spanish power in Europe and across the ocean. After 1600, all three founded their own colonies in North America and the Caribbean. New France became a land of missionaries and traders and developed close ties of cooperation with most nearby Indians. New Netherland also was founded to participate in the fur trade. Both colonies slowly acquired an agricultural base.

The English, by contrast, desired the land itself. They founded colonies of settlement that threatened nearby Indians, except in the Delaware valley, where Quakers insisted on peaceful relations. The southern mainland and Caribbean colonies produced staple crops for sale in Europe, first with the labor of indentured servants and then with enslaved Africans. The Puritan and Quaker colonies became smaller versions of England's mixed economy, with an emphasis on family farms. Maintaining the fervor of the founders was a problem for both. After conquering New Netherland, England controlled the Atlantic seaboard from Maine to South Carolina, and by 1700 the population of England's mainland colonies was doubling every 25 years. England was beginning to emerge as the biggest winner in the competition for empire.

---

[2] A feudal relic, a *quitrent* was an annual fee, usually small, required by the patent that gave title to a piece of land. It differed from ordinary rents in that nonpayment led to a suit for debt, not ejection from the property.

SUGGESTED READINGS

W. J. Eccles, *The French in North America, 1500–1783,* rev. ed. (1998) is a concise and authoritative survey. **C. R. Boxer,** *The Dutch Seaborne Empire, 1600–1800* (1965) is still the best synthesis of Dutch activity overseas. **Joyce E. Chaplin's** *Subject Matter: Technology, the Body, and Science on the Anglo-American Frontier, 1500–1676* (2001), and **Karen O. Kupperman,** *Indians and English: Facing Off in Early America* (2000) are efforts to keep Indians and the settlers of early Virginia and New England within a common focus. **Edmund S. Morgan's** *American Slavery, American Freedom: The Ordeal of Colonial Virginia* (1975) has become a classic, but **Thad W. Tate and David L. Ammerman, eds.,** *The Chesapeake in the Seventeenth-Century: Essays on Anglo-American Society* (1979) is also indispensable. For the West Indies, see **Richard S. Dunn,** *Sugar and Slaves: The Rise of the Planter Class in the English West Indies, 1624–1713* (1972). **Winthrop Jordan's** *White over Black: American Attitudes toward the Negro, 1550–1812* (1968) retains its freshness and acuity.

Edmund S. Morgan's *Visible Saints: The History of a Puritan Idea* (1963) is a brief and accessible introduction to Puritan values in New England's first century. **Carla G. Pestana's** *Quakers and Baptists in Colonial Massachusetts* (1991) deals with the principal dissenters from the New England Way. **Daniel Vickers,** *Farmers and Fishermen: Two Centuries of Work in Essex County, Massachusetts, 1630–1850* (1994) is an outstanding introduction to the New England economy.

For the Restoration colonies, see especially **Robert C. Ritchie,** *The Duke's Province: A Study of New York Politics and Society, 1664–1691* (1977); **Gary B. Nash,** *Quakers and Politics: Pennsylvania Politics, 1681–1726* (1968); **Barry J. Levy,** *Quakers and the American Family: British Settlement in the Delaware Valley* (1988); **Peter H. Wood,** *Black Majority: Negroes in Colonial South Carolina from 1670 through the Stono Rebellion* (1974); and **Alan Gallay,** *The Indian Slave Trade: The Rise of the English Empire in the American South, 1670–1717* (2002).

 AMERICAN JOURNEY ONLINE
A N D
INFOTRAC COLLEGE EDITION

Visit the source collections at www.ajaccess.wadsworth.com and infotrac.thomsonlearning.com and use the Search function with the following key terms to explore documents, images, audio and video clips, articles, and commentary related to the material in this chapter.

Protestant Reformation	Massachusetts Bay Company
Sir Walter Ralegh	Quaker
Jamestown	Anne Hutchinson
John Smith	New York
Pilgrims	William Penn
Plymouth	

GRADE AIDS

Visit the Liberty Equality Power Companion Web Site for resources specific to this textbook: http://history.wadsworth.com/murrin_LEP4e

The CD in the back of this book and the U.S. History Resource Center at http://history.wadsworth.com/u.s./ offer a variety of tools to help you succeed in this course, including access to quizzes; images; documents; interactive simulations, maps, and timelines; movie explorations; and a wealth of other sources.

Chapter **3**

England Discovers
Its Colonies: Empire,
Liberty, and Expansion

THE KINGFISHER ENGAGING THE BARBARY PIRATES ON 22 MAY, 1681,
BY WILLEM VAN DE VELDE THE YOUNGER
By the end of the 17th century, England had become the greatest naval power in the world,
a position that Great Britain would maintain until overtaken by the United States in the
Second World War.

CHAPTER OUTLINE

I n 1603, when James VI of Scotland ascended the throne of England as King James I (1603–25), England was still a weak power on the fringes of Europe with no colonies except in Ireland. By 1700, England was a global giant, able to tip Europe's balance of power. It possessed 20 colonies in North America and the Caribbean, controlled much of the African slave trade, and had muscled its way into distant India. Commerce and colonies had vastly magnified England's power in Europe.

This transformation occurred during a century of political and religious upheaval at home. King and Parliament fought over their respective powers—a long struggle that led to civil war and the execution of one king in 1649 and to the overthrow of another in 1688. The result was a unique constitution that rested on parliamentary supremacy and responsible government under the Crown.

This upheaval produced competing visions of politics and the good society. At one extreme, the ruling Stuart dynasty often seemed to be trying to create an absolute monarchy, similar to that of Spain or France. Opponents of absolutism groped for ways to guarantee government by consent without undermining public order. England's colonies shared in the turmoil. Yet by 1700, all of them had begun to converge around the newly defined principles of English constitutionalism. All adopted representative government at some point during the century. All affirmed the values of liberty and property under the English Crown.

England also quarreled with the colonies, whose sheer diversity daunted anyone who hoped to govern them. The colonies formed not a single type, but a spectrum of settlement with contrasting economies, social relationships, and institutions. Yet by 1700, England had created a system of regulation that respected colonial liberties while asserting imperial power.

CHAPTER FOCUS

♦ What were the major colonial goals of English mercantilists, and how close to success did they come?

♦ What enabled the Middle Colonies to avoid the Indian wars that engulfed New England and Virginia in the mid-1670s?

♦ On what common principles did English political culture begin to converge in both the mother country and the colonies after the Glorious Revolution?

♦ What enabled sparsely settled New France to resist British expansion with great success for more than half a century, whereas Spanish Florida seemed almost helpless against the same threat?

The Atlantic Prism and the Spectrum of Settlement

Over thousands of years, the Indians of the Americas, at first a fairly homogeneous people, had become diversified into hundreds of distinct cultures and languages. The colonists of 17th-century North America and the Caribbean were following much the same course. America divided them. The Atlantic united them. Their connection with England gave them what unity they could sustain.

As long as population remained small, no colony could duplicate the complexity of England. The settlers had to choose what to bring with them and what to leave behind, what they could provide for themselves and what they would have to import—choices dictated both by their motives for crossing the ocean and by what the new environment would permit. The colonists sorted themselves out along a vast arc from the cold North to the subtropical Caribbean. If we can imagine England as a source of white light and the Atlantic as a prism refracting that light, 17th-century America becomes a spectrum of settlement, with each color merging imperceptibly into the shade next to it. Each province had much in common with its neighbors but shared few traits with more distant colonies. At the extremes, the sugar and slave society of Barbados had almost nothing in common with Puritan Massachusetts. Nor did Canada share many characteristics with the French West Indies.

CHRONOLOGY

1642	Civil war erupts in England • Miantonomo abandons planned war of extermination
1643	New England Confederation created
1644	Opechancanough's second massacre in Virginia
1649	England becomes a commonwealth
1651	Parliament passes first Navigation Act
1652–54	First Anglo-Dutch War
1660	Charles II restored to English throne • Parliament passes new Navigation Act
1662	Charles II grants Rhode Island Charter
1663	Staple Act passed • Charles II grants Connecticut Charter
1664	English conquest of New Netherland
1670	First permanent English settlement established in South Carolina
1673	Plantation Duty Act passed • Dutch retake New York for 15 months
1675	Lords of Trade established • Metacom's War breaks out in New England
1676	Bacon's Rebellion breaks out in Virginia
1678	Popish Plot crisis begins in England
1680	Pueblos revolt in New Mexico
1684	Massachusetts Charter revoked
1685	Louis XIV revokes Edict of Nantes
1686	Dominion of New England established
1688–89	Glorious Revolution occurs in England
1689	Anglo-French wars begin • Glorious Revolution spreads to Massachusetts, New York, and Maryland
1691	Leisler executed in New York
1692	19 people hanged for witchcraft in Salem
1696	Parliament passes comprehensive Navigation Act • Board of Trade replaces Lords of Trade
1699	French establish Louisiana • Woolens Act passed
1701	Iroquois make peace with New France
1702–04	Carolina slavers destroy Florida missions
1707	Anglo-Scottish union creates kingdom of Great Britain
1713	Britain and France make peace
1714	George I ascends British throne
1715	Yamasee War devastates South Carolina

Demographic Differences

The most pronounced differences involved life expectancy, the sex ratio (the ratio of men to women in any society), and family structure. At one extreme were the all-male, multiethnic buccaneering societies in the Caribbean that lived only for plunder. In the sugar colonies, Euro-

pean men often died by age 40, and slaves even sooner. Because women settlers were scarce at first, the family itself seemed an endangered institution. Even when the sex ratio evened out and families began to emerge, couples had few children. Life expectancy in early South Carolina was slightly better than in the islands, slightly lower than in the Chesapeake Bay area. In the Chesapeake colonies, men who survived childhood diseases lived to an average age of about 45 years during the last half of the 17th century, still less than in England, where life expectancy exceeded 50. In Virginia and Maryland, as natural increase replaced immigration as the main source of population growth after 1680, women became more numerous, married much earlier, and raised larger families.

The northern colonies were much healthier. In the Delaware valley, a man who reached adulthood could expect to live past 60. In New Netherland, life expectancy and family size exceeded Europe's by 1660, and men outnumbered women among the newcomers by only 2 to 1. On Long Island in the 1680s, one woman claimed that she had more than 300 living descendants. New England was one of the healthiest places in the world. Because the sex ratio rapidly approached equality and because the thriving economy permitted couples to marry perhaps two years earlier than in England, population growth exploded. Canada followed a similar pattern. In the late 17th century, the birthrate in New France caught up with New England's, and population grew at a comparable pace.

These demographic differences had significant consequences. For example, the Caribbean and southern colonies were youthful societies in which men with good connections could expect to achieve high office while in their thirties, or even their twenties. By contrast, the New England colonies gradually became dominated by grandfathers. A man rarely became even a selectman before his forties. Magistrates were even older. Simon Bradstreet was almost 90 when he completed his last term as governor of Massachusetts in 1692. Despite the appalling death rate in the sugar and tobacco colonies, young men remained optimistic and upbeat, as they looked forward to challenging the world and making their fortunes. But in New England, people grew more despondent as the century progressed,

THE SPECTRUM OF SETTLEMENT: DEMOGRAPHY, ETHNICITY, ECONOMY, 1650–1700

Category	West Indies	Lower South	Chesapeake	Mid-Atlantic	New England	New France
Life expectancy for men, age 20	40	42	45	60+	Late 60s	60s
Family size	Below replacement rate	About two children	Rising after 1680	Very large	Very large	Very large
Race and ethnicity	Black majority by circa 1670s	Black majority by circa 1710	Growing black minority	Ethnic mix, N.W. Europe, English a minority	Almost all English	Almost all French
Economy	Sugar	Rice, 1690s ff	Tobacco	Furs, farms	Farms, fishing, shipbuilding	Furs, farms

THE SPECTRUM OF SETTLEMENT: RELIGION AND GOVERNMENT, CIRCA 1675–1700

Category	West Indies	Lower South	Chesapeake	Mid-Atlantic	New England	New France
Formal religion	Anglican Church establishment	Anglican Church establishment by circa 1710	Anglican Church establishment (after 1692 in Md.)	Competing sects, no established church	Congregational Church established	Catholic Church established
Religious tone	Irreverent	Contentious	Low-church Anglican	Family-based piety, sectarian competition	Family-based piety, intensity declining	Intensely Catholic
Local government	Parish	Parish and phantom counties (i.e., no court)	County and parish	County and township	Towns and counties; parishes after 1700	Cities
Provincial government	Royal	Proprietary	Royal (Va.), proprietary (Md.)	From proprietary to royal, except in Pa.	Corporate, with Mass. and N.H. becoming royal	Royal absolutism

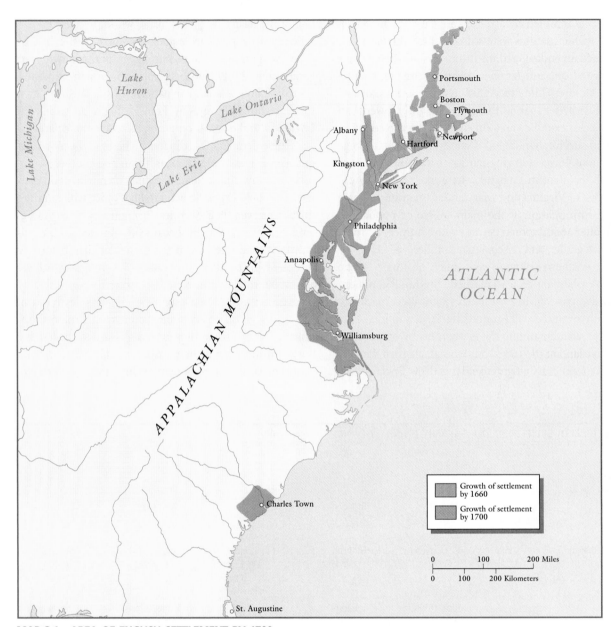

MAP 3.1   AREA OF ENGLISH SETTLEMENT BY 1700

This map differentiates the areas settled before 1660 from those settled between 1660 and 1700, or roughly the Restoration era.

even though they lived much longer. The typical sermon was a gloomy jeremiad that deplored the failings of the rising generation.

Race, Ethnicity, and Economy

The degree of racial and ethnic mixture also varied from region to region, along with economic priorities. The West Indies already had a large slave majority by 1700 and were well on their way to becoming a New Africa, except that the European minority had a firm grip on wealth and power. In 1700, English settlers were still a clear majority in the southern mainland colonies, but African slaves became a majority in South Carolina around 1710 and were increasing rapidly. They would comprise 40 percent of Virginia's population by the 1730s. Africans were less numerous in the Delaware and Hudson valleys, although slavery became deeply entrenched in New York City and parts of New Jersey.

In the Middle Atlantic region, settlers from all over northwestern Europe were creating a new ethnic mosaic, especially in New Jersey and Pennsylvania. English colo-

nists were probably always a minority, outnumbered at first by the Dutch, and later by Germans, Scots, and Irish. But New England was in every sense the most English of the colonies. In ethnic composition, it may have been more English than England, which by 1700 had sizable Dutch Reformed, French Huguenot, and Scottish Presbyterian minorities. New France was as French as New England was English. The farther south one went, the more diverse the population; the farther north, the more uniform.

Slavery and staple crops went together. The slave societies raised sugar, rice, or tobacco for sale in Europe. General farming and family labor also went together. By 1700, the Middle Atlantic was the wheat belt of North America. The New Englanders farmed and exported fish and lumber to the West Indies.

Religion and Education

With the exception of Spanish Florida, the intensity of religious observance varied immensely across the spectrum of settlement, ranging from irreverence and indifference in the West Indies to intense piety in New England and New France. Because formal education in the 17th century nearly always had a religious base, literacy followed a similar pattern. Colonists everywhere tried to prevent slaves from learning to read, and low literacy prevailed wherever slavery predominated. Chesapeake settlers provided almost no formal schooling for their children before the founding of the College of William and Mary in 1693 and of a Latin grammar school in Annapolis at about the same time. Even some of the justices of the peace in Maryland and Virginia were unable to write. By contrast, the Dutch maintained several good schools in New Netherland. Massachusetts founded Harvard College in 1636 and in 1642 required every town to have a writing school, and larger towns to support a Latin grammar school, in order to frustrate "ye old deluder Satan," as a 1647 school law phrased it. The Jesuits founded a college (actually more akin to a secondary school) in Quebec a few years before Harvard opened. France sent a bishop to Quebec in 1659, and he established a seminary (now Laval University) in the 1660s. Along the spectrum, piety, literacy, and education all grew stronger from south to north, although laymen in New France never became as literate as in New England.

Public support for the clergy followed the same pattern. By 1710, the established church of the mother country was the legally established church in the West Indies and in the southern mainland colonies. Establishment and dissent fought to a standstill in the Middle Atlantic, with toleration claiming the real victory in New York and full religious liberty in Pennsylvania. In New England, Old World dissent became the New World establishment. Public support for the clergy was much greater in the north than in the south. The sugar islands had the most wealth, but they maintained only one clergyman for every 3,000 to 9,000 people, depending on the island. In the Chesapeake, the comparable ratio was about one for every 1,500 people by 1700. It was perhaps one for every 1,000 in New York, one for every 600 in New England, and still lower in New France.

Moral standards also rose from south to north. New Englanders boasted that they were far more godly than all other colonists. The Puritans "give out that they are Israelites," reported a Dutch visitor to Connecticut, "and that we in our colony are Egyptians, and that the English in the Virginias are also Egyptians." As early as 1638, one Marylander quipped that a neighbor deserved to be "whippt at virginea" or "hanged in new England."

Local and Provincial Governments

Forms of government also varied. Drawing on their English experience, settlers could choose from among parishes, boroughs (towns), and counties. A colony's choices depended on its location along the spectrum of settlement.

The only important local institution in the sugar islands and in South Carolina was the parish, which took on many secular functions, such as poor relief. The Chesapeake colonies relied primarily on the county but also made increasing use of the parish. Few parishes were ever organized in the Middle Atlantic colonies, but the county as a form of government arrived with the English conquest of New Netherland in 1664 and became a powerful institution. Townships also appeared. New England's most basic local institution was the town. Massachusetts created counties in the 1640s, followed 20 years later by Connecticut and in the 1680s by Plymouth. Rhode Island and New Hampshire waited until the 18th century before creating counties. After 1700, towns large enough to support more than one church also adopted the parish system. In local government as in its economy, New England's use of the full range of parishes, towns, and counties made the region more fully English than other colonies.

The West Indian colonies all had royal governments by the 1660s (see the subsection "The Lords of Trade and Imperial Reform" later in this chapter). Proprietary forms dominated the mainland south of New England, except for royal Virginia. Until the 1680s, New England relied on corporate forms of government in which all officials,

even governors, were elected. This system survived in Connecticut and Rhode Island until independence and beyond.

Unifying Trends: Language, War, Law, and Inheritance

Despite all this diversity, the 17th century produced a few trends toward greater homogeneity. For instance, language became more uniform in America than in England. True, the New England dialect derived mostly from East Anglia, the southern accent from southern and western England, and Middle Atlantic speech from north-central England. But Londoners went to all of the colonies (in England, people went to London), and London English affected every colony and softened the contrasts among the emerging regional dialects.

Another area of uniformity was the manner in which the settlers waged war: They did it in their own way, not with the professional armies that were just taking hold in Europe, but with short-term volunteers for whom terror against Indian women and children was often the tactic of choice. Europe was moving toward limited wars; the colonists demanded quick and total victories.

In the colonies, law became a simpler version of England's complex legal system. Justice was local and uncomplicated—in fact, an organized legal profession did not emerge until the 18th century. The absence of lawyers pleased most settlers.

Finally, no mainland American colony rigidly followed English patterns of inheritance. Instead, the colonies were developing their own practices. Some women had a chance to acquire property, usually by inheritance from a deceased husband, particularly in the Chesapeake colonies during the long period when men greatly outnumbered women. The single women who crossed the Atlantic as servants were desperate people who had hit bottom in England. Those who survived enjoyed a fantastic chance at upward mobility. Many won a respectability never available to them in England. In every colony, younger sons also found their situation improved. They played a huge role in settling the colonies, especially among the Chesapeake elite, and they showed little inclination to preserve institutions that had offered them no landed inheritance in England. Most families made no distinction between the eldest and other sons, except in New England. The Puritan colonies honored a biblical mandate to give the eldest son a double share. That practice strengthened patriarchy in the region, but it was much less discriminatory than primogeniture, which in England gave all land to the eldest son.

The Beginnings of Empire

In the chaotic 1640s, the English realized that their colonies overseas were bringing them few benefits. England had no coherent colonial policy.

Upheaval in America: The Critical 1640s

England's civil wars rocked its emerging empire, politically and economically. As royal power collapsed in the 1640s, the West Indian colonies demanded and received elective assemblies. The Dutch, taking advantage of the chaos in England, helped finance the sugar revolution in Barbados and seized control of trade in and out of England's West Indian and Chesapeake colonies. By 1650, most sugar and tobacco exports were going to Amsterdam, not London.

During the civil wars, nobody in England exercised effective control over the colonies. The king had declared that their trade was to remain in English hands, but no agency existed to enforce that claim. The new elective assemblies of Barbados and the Leeward Islands preferred to trade with the Dutch, even after the English Crown took over those colonies in 1660. The mainland colonies had been organized by joint-stock companies or proprietary lords under royal charters, but there the colonists governed themselves. As the New England settlements expanded, the new colonies of Connecticut, Rhode Island, and New Haven did not even bother to obtain royal charters. On the mainland, only Virginia had a royal governor.

The chaos of the 1640s gave Indians a unique opportunity to resist the settlers. As civil war disrupted trade with England and threatened to cut off regular supplies of muskets and gunpowder, the Indians gained a powerful advantage over the settlements. That danger seemed so ominous that Rhode Island ordered young men to learn how to use bows and arrows. Although the Indians of the eastern woodlands never united into an effective league, many of them, such as Miantonomo in New England and Opechancanough in Virginia, began to think of driving the Europeans out altogether.

Indians greatly outnumbered settlers, except in eastern New England and the Virginia tidewater. Between 1643 and 1647, the Iroquois nearly wiped out New France, and the Hudson valley Algonquians almost destroyed New Netherland. Maryland, beset by conflicts with Susquehannock Indians and by civil war among its colonists, nearly ceased to exist. The number of settlers there may have fallen to 300 by 1648. In Virginia, the aging warrior

Opechancanough staged another massacre, killing 500 settlers without warning on a holy day in 1644. This time the settlers recovered more quickly, took Opechancanough prisoner in 1646, and murdered him. They broke up his chiefdom and made its member tribes accept treaties of dependency.

Only New England avoided war with the Indians—just barely. Miantonomo, sachem of the Narragansetts, called for a war of extermination against the settlers, to be launched by a surprise attack in 1642. He abandoned the plan when settlers got wind of it. The colonists created their own defensive alliance in 1643, the New England Confederation, which united the four orthodox colonies of Massachusetts, Plymouth, Connecticut, and New Haven. Rhode Island was not invited to join. The confederation persuaded the Mohegans to kill Miantonomo, and tensions with the Narragansett Indians remained high. The Narragansetts controlled some of the finest land in New England. Massachusetts, Plymouth, and Connecticut all wanted that land, but the Narragansetts were still too powerful to intimidate. When threatened, they withdrew into inaccessible places that terrified most of the settlers. After the Narragansetts made it clear that they would fight if they had to, the Puritans backed down.

What happened in the colonies seemed of little interest to the English people in the turbulent 1640s. Later, as the debris of civil war was cleared away and the extent of Dutch commercial domination became obvious, the English turned their eyes westward once again. In a sense, England first discovered its colonies and their importance around 1650.

Mercantilism as a Moral Revolution

During the 17th century, most of the European powers adopted a set of policies now usually called mercantilism. The decline of the Spanish Empire persuaded many observers that the power of a state depended more on its underlying economy than on armies or the silver that paid for them. Mercantilists argued that power derived ultimately from the wealth of a country, that the increase of wealth required vigorous trade, and that colonies had become essential to that growth. Clearly, a state had to control the commerce of its colonies. Mercantilists, however, disagreed over the best ways to promote economic growth. The Dutch favored virtual free trade within Europe. England preferred some kind of state regulation of the domestic and imperial economy.

After a century of religious wars, neither Catholics nor Protestants had won a decisive victory in Europe. To European statesmen of the time, these conflicts merely confirmed their belief that governments reflected the passions of men. Philosophers agreed that the major passions are glory, love, and greed. Glory seemed nobler than carnal love, and love more inspiring than greed, which in any case was beneath the dignity of a gentleman. Still, the endless wars, driven by the quest for glory and the love of holy

LINK TO THE PAST

A Desperate Strategy

During the slaughter of the Pequots at Mystic Fort in 1637, the Narragansett Indians had been allies of the Puritans, and they witnessed the massacre. By 1642, their principal sachem, Miantonomo, had reached a grim conclusion about the only proper way to deal with the settlers encroaching upon their lands:

O*ur fathers had plenty of deer and skins, our plains were full of deer, as also our woods, and of turkies, and our coves full of fish and fowl. But these English have gotten our land, they with scythes cut down the grass, and with axes fell the trees; their cows and horses eat the grass, and their hogs spoil our clam banks, and we shall be starved; therefore . . . When you see the three fires that* will be made forty days hence, in a clear night, then do as we, and the next day fall on and kill men, women, and children, but no cows, for they will serve to eat till our deer be increased again.

1. Why did both Opechancanough and Miantonomo decide that their best chance of survival lay in annihilating all Europeans?

For additional sources related to this feature, visit the *Liberty, Equality, Power* Web site at:

http://history.wadsworth.com/murrin_LEP4e

causes, had crippled Spain, killed one-third of the German people, and nearly destroyed the English state.

As time passed, statesmen began to look more favorably upon greed, a passion in which they found interesting properties. The pursuit of glory or love inspires intense but unpredictable activity, followed by relaxation or even exhaustion. Greed, because it is insatiable, fosters *predictable* behavior—namely, the pursuit of self-interest, a softer term than greed and one that most people preferred to use. By creating economic incentives, then, a state could induce its people to work to increase not only their own wealth and power but also that of the whole country. Likewise, by imposing import duties and other disincentives, the state could discourage actions detrimental to its power.

At first these ideas were as gloomy as the world in which they arose. Early mercantilists assumed that the world contained a fixed supply of wealth. A state, to augment its own power, would have to expropriate the wealth of a rival. Trade wars would replace religious wars, although presumably they would be less destructive, which they usually were. Gradually, however, a more radical idea took hold: The growth of trade might multiply the wealth of the whole world, with all nations benefiting and becoming so interdependent that war between them would be recognized as suicidal. That vision of peace and unending growth has never been realized, but it still inspires people today.

Mercantilism marked a major breakthrough toward modernity. It gradually became associated with the emerging idea of unending progress, and it made statesmen rethink the role of legislation in their societies.

Europeans were already familiar with two kinds of progress, one associated with Renaissance humanism, the other explicitly Christian. The opening of the Americas had already reinforced both visions. Humanists knew that the distant ancestors of Europeans had all been "barbarians" who had advanced over the centuries toward "civility." Their own encounters with the indigenous peoples of Africa, Ireland, and America underscored this dualistic view by revealing new "savages" who seemed morally and culturally inferior to the "civilized" colonists. Most Christians shared these convictions, but they also believed that human society was progressing toward a future Millennium in which Christ will return to earth and reign with his saints in perfect harmony for 1,000 years. To missionaries, both Catholic and Protestant, the discovery of millions of "heathens" in the Americas stimulated millennial thinking. God had chosen this moment to open a new hemisphere to Christians, they explained, because the Millennium was near. Both the humanist and the Christian notions of progress were static concepts, however.

© The British Museum.

A PICTISH MAN HOLDING A HUMAN HEAD,
BY JOHN WHITE, LATE 16TH CENTURY

In the ancient world, the Picts were among the ancestors of the English and the Scots. John White, who painted many Indian scenes on Roanoke Island in the 1580s, believed that the English had been "savages" not all that long ago and that American Indians, like the English, could progress to "civility." America made him think of "progress."

Humanity would advance to a certain level, and progress would cease. Mercantilism, by contrast, marked a revolution of the human imagination precisely because it could arouse visions of endless progress.

Mercantilism also promoted a more modern concept of law. In the past, most jurists believed that legislation merely restated natural laws or immemorial customs in written form. Mercantilists, on the other hand, saw law as an agent of change. They intended to modify behavior, perhaps even transform society. They had no illusions about achieving perfection, however. At first, they probably considered anything that made their exhausted world less terrible to be a triumph. But as the decades passed, mercantilists became more confident of their ability to improve society.

The First Navigation Act

English merchants began debating trade policy during a severe depression in the 1620s. They agreed that a nation's wealth depended on its balance of trade, that a healthy nation ought to export more than it imports, and that the difference—or balance—could be converted into military strength. They also believed that a state needed colonies to produce essential commodities that were unavailable at home. And they argued that a society ought to export luxuries, not import them. English merchants observed Dutch commercial success and determined that it rested on a mastery of these principles. For England to catch up, Parliament would have to intervene.

With the close of the Thirty Years' War in Europe in 1648, the three major Protestant powers—Sweden, the Netherlands, and England—no longer had reason to avoid fighting one another. England reacted quickly after the execution of Charles I. London merchants clamored for measures to stifle Dutch competition. Parliament listened to them, not to Oliver Cromwell and other Puritans who regarded war between two Protestant republics as an abomination. The merchants got their Navigation Act—and their naval war.

In 1650, Parliament banned foreign ships from English colonies. A year later, it passed the first comprehensive Navigation Act, aimed at Dutch competition. Under this act, Asian and African goods could be imported into the British Isles or the colonies only in English-owned ships, and the master and at least half of each crew had to be Englishmen. European goods could be imported into Britain or the colonies in either English ships or the ships of the producing country, but foreigners could not trade between one English port and another.

This new attention from the English government angered the colonists in the West Indies and North America. Mercantilists assumed that the colonies existed only to enrich the mother country. Why else had England permitted them to be founded? But the young men growing sugar in Barbados or tobacco in Virginia hoped to prosper on their own. Selling their crops to the Dutch, who offered the lowest freight rates, added to their profits. Although New England produced no staple that Europeans wanted except fish, Yankee skippers cheerfully swapped their fish or forest products in the Chesapeake for tobacco, which they then carried directly to Europe, usually to Amsterdam.

Barbados greeted the Navigation Act by proclaiming virtual independence. Virginia recognized Charles II as king and continued to welcome Dutch and Yankee traders. In 1651, Parliament dispatched a naval force to America. It compelled Barbados to submit to Parliament and then sailed to the Chesapeake, where Virginia and Maryland capitulated in 1652. In return, the Virginians received the right to elect their own governor, a privilege that the restored Crown revoked in 1660. Without resident officials to enforce English policy, however, trade with the Dutch continued.

By 1652, England and the Netherlands were at war. For two years, the English navy—trim and efficient after a decade of struggle against the king—dealt heavy blows to the Dutch. Finally, in 1654, Cromwell sent Parliament home and made peace. A militant Protestant, he preferred to fight Catholic Spain rather than the Netherlands. In the tradition of Drake, Gilbert, and Ralegh, he sent a fleet to take Hispaniola. It failed in that mission, but it seized Jamaica in 1655.

Restoration Navigation Acts

By the Restoration era, mercantilist thinking had become widespread. Although the new royalist Parliament invalidated all legislation passed during the Commonwealth period, these Cavaliers promptly reenacted and extended the original Navigation Act in a series of new measures. The Navigation Act of 1660 required that all colonial trade be carried on English ships (a category that included colonial vessels but now excluded the Scots), but the master and *three-fourths* of the crew had to be English. The act also created a category of "enumerated commodities," of which sugar and tobacco were the most important, permitting these products to be shipped from the colony of origin *only* to England or to another English colony—the intent being to give England a monopoly over the export of major staples from every English colony to Europe and to the rest of the world. The colonists could still export nonenumerated commodities elsewhere. New England could send fish to a French sugar island, for example, and Virginia could export wheat to Cuba, provided the French and the Spanish would let them.

In a second measure, the Staple Act of 1663, Parliament regulated goods going to the colonies. With few exceptions, products from Europe, Asia, or Africa had to land in England before they could be delivered to the settlements.

A third measure, the Plantation Duty Act of 1673, required captains of colonial ships to post bond in the colonies that they would deliver all enumerated commodities to England, or else pay on the spot the duties that would be owed in England (the "plantation duty"). England hoped that this measure would eliminate all incentives to smuggle. To make it effective, England sent customs officers to the colonies for the first time to collect the duty and prosecute all violators. Because the only income

Houghton Library, Harvard University, Cambridge, MA.

MIRROR OF THE FRENCH TYRANNY (1673)

When Louis XIV sent the French army into the Netherlands, France replaced Spain as Europe's most militant Catholic power, as this Protestant view suggests.

of these officials came from fees and from their share of condemned vessels, their livelihood was precarious. At first, colonial governments regarded customs collectors as parasites. Maryland officials even murdered one of them in the 1680s.

Parliament intended nothing less than a revolution in Atlantic trade. Properly enforced, the Navigation Acts would dislodge the Dutch and establish English hegemony over Atlantic trade, and that is what happened in the next half-century. In 1600, about 90 percent of England's exports consisted of woolen cloth. By 1700, colonial and Asian commerce accounted for 30 to 40 percent of England's overseas trade, and London had become the largest city in Western Europe. As the center of England's colonial trade, its population tripled during the 17th century.

Enforcement long remained uneven, but in the 1670s, a war between France and the Netherlands diverted critical Dutch resources from trade to defense, thus helping England catch up with the Dutch. By 1700, Brit-

ain had the most powerful navy in the world. By 1710 or so, virtually all British colonial trade was carried on British ships. Sugar, tobacco, and other staple crops all passed through Britain on their way to their ultimate destination. Nearly all of the manufactured goods consumed in the colonies were made in Britain. Most products from Europe or Asia destined for the colonies passed through Britain first, although some smuggling of these goods continued.

Few government policies have ever been as successful as England's Navigation Acts, but England achieved these results without pursuing a steady course toward increased imperial control. For example, in granting charters to Rhode Island in 1662 and to Connecticut in 1663, Charles II approved elective governors and legislatures in both colonies. (The Connecticut charter also absorbed the New Haven Colony into the Hartford government.) These elective officials could not be dismissed or punished for failure to enforce the Navigation Acts. Moreover, the Crown also

chartered several new Restoration colonies (see chapter 2), whose organizers had few incentives to obey the new laws. Making the empire work would take time.

● Indians, Settlers, Upheaval

As time passed, the commercial possibilities and limitations of North America were becoming much clearer. The French and Dutch mastered the fur trade because they controlled the two all-water routes to the interior, via the St. Lawrence system and the Hudson and Mohawk valleys. South Carolinians could go around the southern extreme of the Appalachians. They all needed Indian trading partners.

As of 1670, no sharp boundaries yet existed between Indian lands and colonial settlements. Boston, the largest city north of Mexico, was only 15 miles from an Indian village. Connecticut valley towns were surrounded by Indians. The outposts on the Delaware River were islands in a sea of Indians. In the event of war, nearly every European settlement was vulnerable to attack.

Indian Strategies of Survival

By the 1670s, most of the coastal tribes in regular contact with Europeans had already been devastated by disease or soon would be. European diseases, by magnifying the depleted tribes' need for captives, also increased the intensity of wars among Indian peoples, probably to their highest point ever. The Iroquois, for example, although hard hit by smallpox and other ailments, acquired muskets from the Dutch and used them, first to attack other Iroquoian peoples and then Algonquians. These "mourning wars" were often initiated by the widow or bereaved mother or sister of a deceased loved one. She insisted that her male relatives repair the loss. Her warrior relatives then launched a raid and brought back captives. Adult male prisoners, who might take revenge if allowed to live, were usually tortured to death. Most women and children were adopted and assimilated. Adoption worked because the captives shared the cultural values of their captors. They became Iroquois. As early as the 1660s, most Indians in the Five Nations were adoptees, not native-born Iroquois. In this way, the confederacy remained strong while its rivals declined. In the southern piedmont, the warlike, Sioux-speaking Catawba Indians also assimilated thousands from other tribes. Further into the southern interior, the nations that were becoming Creeks assimilated adoptees from a wide variety of ethnic backgrounds. They and other southern

nations also became adept at playing off the Spaniards against the English (and later the French).

In some ways, America became as much a new world for the Indians as it did for the colonists. European cloth, muskets, hatchets, knives, and pots were welcomed among the Indians and spread far into the interior, but they came at a price. Indians who learned to use them gradually abandoned traditional skills and became increasingly dependent on trade with Europeans, a process that was not complete until the 19th century. Alcohol, the one item always in demand, was also dangerous. Indian men drank to alter their mood and achieve visions, not for sociability. Drunkenness became a major, if intermittent, social problem.

Settlers who understood that their future depended on the fur trade, as in New France, tried to stay on good terms with the Indians. Pieter Stuyvesant put New Netherland on such a course, and the English governors of New York followed his lead after 1664. Edmund Andros, governor from 1674 to 1680, cultivated the friendship of the Iroquois League, in which the five member nations had promised not to wage war against one another. In 1677, Andros and the Five Nations agreed to make New York the easternmost link in what the English called the Covenant Chain of peace, a huge defensive advantage for a lightly populated colony. Thus, while New England and Virginia fought bitter Indian wars in the 1670s, New York avoided conflict. The Covenant Chain later proved flexible enough to incorporate other Indians and colonies as well.

Where the Indian trade was slight, war became more likely. In 1675, it erupted in both New England and the Chesapeake. In the 1640s, Virginia had negotiated treaties of dependency with the member nations of the Powhatan chiefdom, in the hope of keeping them loyal in the event of war with other Indians. The New England colonies had similar understandings with the large non-Christian nations of the region, but the Puritan governments placed even greater reliance on a growing number of Christianized Indians.

Puritan Indian Missions

Serious efforts to convert Indians to Protestantism began in the 1640s on the island of Martha's Vineyard under Thomas Mayhew, Sr., and Thomas Mayhew, Jr., and in Massachusetts under John Eliot, pastor of the Roxbury church. Eliot tried to make the nearby Indian town of Natick into a model mission community.

The Mayhews were more successful than Eliot, although he received most of the publicity. They worked with local sachems and challenged only the tribal powwows

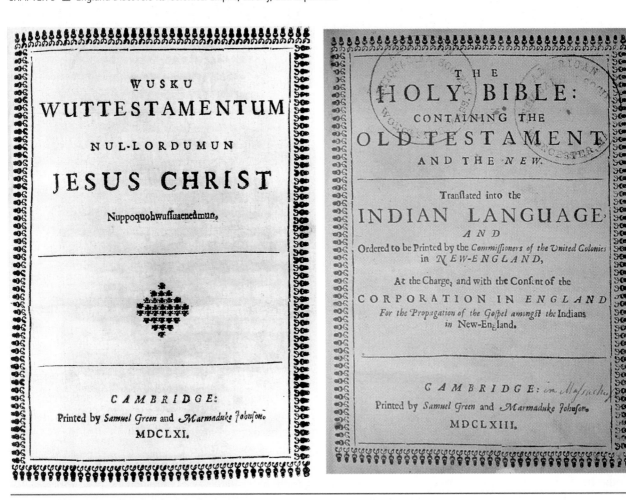

TITLE PAGES OF JOHN ELIOT'S INDIAN BIBLE

On the left is the New Testament (1661); on the right is the complete Bible (1663). Eliot's translation took many years to complete. Most copies of the Indian Bible were destroyed in Metacom's War of 1675–76.

(prophets or medicine men) and even converted some of them when they proved unable to cure smallpox. The Mayhews encouraged Indian men to teach the settlers of Martha's Vineyard and Nantucket how to catch whales, an activity that made them a vital part of the settlers' economy without threatening their identity as men. Eliot, by contrast, attacked the authority of the sachems as well as the powwows, challenged the traditional tribal structure, and insisted on turning Indian men into farmers, a female role in Indian society. Yet he did translate the Bible and a few other religious works into the Massachuset language.

By the early 1670s, more than 1,000 Indians, nearly all of them survivors of coastal tribes that had been decimated by disease, lived in a string of seven "praying towns," and Eliot was busy organizing five more, mostly among the Nipmucks of the interior. By 1675, about 2,300 Indians, perhaps one-quarter of all those living in southeastern New England, were in various stages of conversion to Christianity. But only 160 of them had achieved the kind of conversion experience that Puritans required for full membership in a church. Indians did not share the Puritan sense of sin. They could not easily grasp why their best deeds should stink in the nostrils of the Lord. The more powerful nations felt threatened by this pressure to convert, and resistance to Christianity became one cause of the war that broke out in 1675. Other causes were the settlers' lust for Indian lands, the intrusion of their livestock onto Indian cornfields, and the fear, especially among younger warrior-hunters, that their whole way of life was in danger of extinction.

Metacom (whom the English called King Philip) was one of those Indians. He was sachem of the Wampanoags and the son of Massasoit, who had celebrated the first thanksgiving feast with the Pilgrims. Metacom once remarked that if he became "a praying sachem, I shall be a poor and weak one, and easily be trod upon."

Metacom's (or King Philip's) War

War broke out shortly after Plymouth executed three Wampanoags accused of murdering John Sassamon, a Harvard-educated Indian preacher who may have been spying on Metacom. The fighting began in the frontier town of Swansea in June 1675, after settlers killed an Indian they found looting an abandoned house. When the Indians demanded satisfaction the next day, the settlers laughed in their faces. The Indians took revenge, and the violence escalated into war.

The settlers, remembering their easy triumph over the Pequots a generation earlier (see chapter 2), were confident of victory. But, since the 1630s, the Indians had acquired firearms. They had built forges to make musket balls and repair their weapons. They had even become marksmen with the smoothbore musket by firing several smaller bullets, instead of a single musketball, with each charge. The settlers, who had usually paid Indians to do their hunting for them, were terrible shots. In the tradition of European armies, they discharged volleys without aiming. To the shock of the colonists, Metacom won several engagements against Plymouth militia, usually by ambushing the noisy intruders. He then escaped from Plymouth Colony and headed toward the upper Connecticut valley, where he burned five Massachusetts towns in three months.

Massachusetts and Connecticut joined the fray. Rather than attack Metacom's Wampanoags, they went after the Narragansetts, who had accepted some Wampanoag refugees but were trying to remain neutral. Many prominent settlers dreamed of acquiring their fertile lands. In the Great Swamp Fight of December 1675, a Puritan army, with the aid of Indian guides, attacked an unfinished Narragansett fort and massacred hundreds of Indians, most of them women and children, but not before the Indians had picked off a high percentage of the officers. The surviving warriors joined Metacom and showed that they too could use terror. They torched more frontier settlements. Altogether, about 800 settlers were killed, and two dozen towns were destroyed or badly damaged in the war.

Atrocities were common on both sides. When one settler boasted that his Bible would save him from harm, the Indians disemboweled him and stuffed the sacred book in his belly. At least 17 friendly Indians were murdered by settlers, some in cold blood before dozens of witnesses, but for more than a year New England juries refused to convict anyone. On one occasion, when some Maine Indians were brought to Marblehead as prisoners, the women of that fishing village literally tore them to pieces with their bare hands.

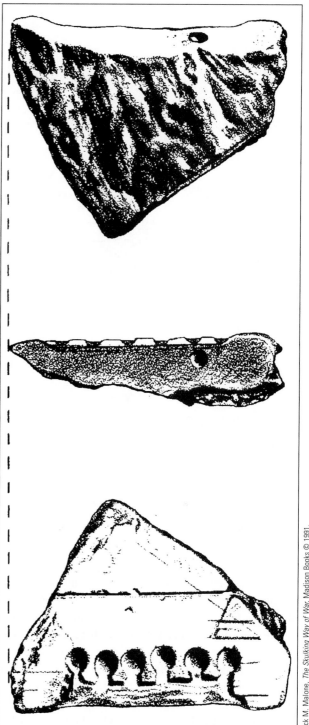

Patrick M. Malone, *The Skulking Way of War*, Madison Books © 1991.

BULLET MOLD IN USE AMONG NEW ENGLAND INDIANS, CIRCA 1675

Indians could make bullets and repair muskets, but they remained dependent on Europeans for their supply of gunpowder. In early 1676, the Indian leader Metacom ran low on gunpowder after failing to acquire more from New France. Over the next several months, he lost the war.

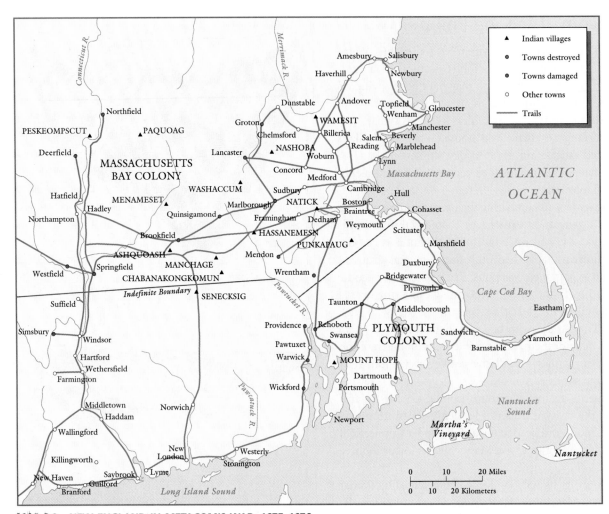

MAP 3.2 NEW ENGLAND IN METACOM'S WAR, 1675–1676
This map locates Indian villages and New England towns, and it indicates which towns were destroyed, damaged, or unscathed during the war.

Frontier settlers demanded the annihilation of all nearby Indians, even the Christian converts. The Massachusetts government, shocked to realize that it could not win the war without Indian allies, did what it could to protect the "praying" Indians. The magistrates evacuated them to a bleak island in Boston harbor, where they spent a miserable winter of privation but then enlisted to fight against Metacom in the spring campaign. Some settlers may even have tried to assassinate Eliot by ramming his boat in Boston harbor. The accused men, who insisted that the collision was accidental, were acquitted.

The war nearly tore New England apart, and it did split the clergy. Increase Mather, a prominent Boston minister, saw the conflict as God's judgment on a sinful people and warned that no victory would come until New England repented and reformed. At first, the Massachusetts General Court agreed. It blamed the war on young men who wore their hair too long, on boys and girls who took leisurely horse rides together, on people who dressed above their station in life, and on blaspheming Quakers. Quakers, in turn, saw the war as divine punishment for their persecution by the Puritans. In Connecticut, which stopped hounding Quakers during the war, only one town was destroyed. Another Boston minister, William Hubbard, insisted that the war was only a brief testing time, after which the Lord would lead his saints to victory over the heathen. To Daniel Gookin, a magistrate committed to Eliot's mission work, the war was an unspeakable tragedy for both settlers and Indians.

Despite their disagreements, the settlers pulled together and won the war in 1676. Governor Andros of New York persuaded the Mohawks to attack Metacom's winter camp and disperse his people, who by then were short of gunpowder. The New Englanders, working closely with Mohegan and Christian Indian allies, then hunted down Metacom's war parties, killed hundreds of Indians, including Metacom, and sold hundreds more into West Indian slavery. Some of those enslaved had not even been party to

the conflict and had actually requested asylum from it. As the tide turned, the Massachusetts government sided with Hubbard by ordering a day of thanksgiving, but Increase Mather's church observed a fast day instead. The colony had not reformed adequately, he explained.

Virginia's Indian War

In Virginia, Governor Sir William Berkeley, who had led the colony to victory over Opechancanough 30 years earlier, rejoiced in the New Englanders' woes. Metacom's War was the least they deserved for the way the Puritans had ripped England apart and executed Charles I during the civil wars. Then Virginia began to have troubles of its own.

In 1675, the Doegs, a dependent Indian nation in the Potomac valley, demanded payment of an old debt from a local planter. When he refused, they ran off some of his livestock. After his overseer killed one of them, the others fled but later returned to ambush and kill the man. The county militia mustered and followed the Doegs across the Potomac into Maryland. At a fork in the trail, the militia split into two parties. Each found a group of Indians in a shack a few hundred yards up the path it was following. Both parties fired at point-blank range, killing 11 at one cabin and 14 at the other. One of the bands was indeed Doeg; the other was not: "Susquehannock friends," blurted one Indian as he fled.

The Susquehannocks were a strong Iroquoian-speaking people with firearms; they had moved south to escape Iroquois attacks. At Maryland's invitation, they had recently occupied land north of the Potomac. Berkeley, still hoping to avoid war, sent John Washington (ancestor of George) with some Virginia militia to investigate the killings and, if possible, to set matters right.

Washington preferred vengeance. His Virginia militia joined with a Maryland force, and together they besieged a formidable Susquehannock fort on the north bank of the Potomac. The fort was too strong to take without artillery even though the attackers had a huge edge in numbers. When the Indians sent out five or six sachems to negotiate, the militia murdered them and then laid siege to the fort for the next six weeks. The Indians, short of provisions, finally broke out one night with all their people, killing several militiamen. After hurling taunts of defiance and promises of vengeance, they disappeared into the forest. Apparently

blaming Virginia more than Maryland, they killed more than 30 Virginia settlers in January 1676. The colonists began to panic.

Berkeley favored a defensive strategy against the Indians; most settlers wanted to attack. In March 1676, the governor summoned a special session of the Virginia legislature to approve the creation of a string of forts above the fall line of the major rivers, with companies of "rangers" to patrol the stretches between them. Berkeley also hoped to maintain a distinction between the clearly hostile Susquehannocks and other Indians who might still be neutral or friendly. Frontier settlers, mostly former servants frustrated by low tobacco prices and unable to acquire tidewater lands because established planters had bought them up, demanded war against all Indians. Finally, to avoid further provocation, Berkeley restricted the fur trade to a few of his close associates. To the men excluded from that circle, his actions looked like favoritism. To settlers in frontier counties, whose access to new lands was blocked by the Indians and who now had to pay higher taxes, Berkeley's strategy seemed intolerable, ineffective, and needlessly expensive.

In both the Second (1665–67) and Third (1672–74) Anglo-Dutch Wars, Berkeley had built costly forts to protect the colony from the Dutch navy, but Dutch warships had sailed around the forts and mauled the tobacco fleet anyway. Accordingly, colonists denounced the building of any more forts and demanded an offensive campaign waged by unpaid volunteers, who would take their rewards by plundering and enslaving Indians. In April, the frontier

© Wendell Metzen/Bruce Coleman Inc.

CRUDE HOUSING FOR SETTLERS IN NORTH AMERICA
When the first settlers came to North America, their living quarters were anything but luxurious. The crude housing shown in this modern reconstruction of Jamestown remained typical of Virginia and Maryland through the 17th century.

settlers found a reckless leader in Nathaniel Bacon, a young newcomer to the colony with a scandalous past and £1,800 to invest. Using his political connections (he was the governor's cousin by marriage), he managed an appointment to the council soon after his arrival in the colony in 1674. Bacon, the owner of a plantation and trading post in Henrico County at the falls of the James River (now Richmond), was one of the men excluded from the Indian trade under Berkeley's new rules.

Bacon's Rebellion

Ignoring Berkeley's orders, Bacon marched his frontiersmen south in search of the elusive Susquehannocks. After several days, his weary men reached a village of hospitable Occaneechees, who offered them shelter, announced that they knew where to find a Susquehannock camp, and even offered to attack it. The Occaneechees surprised and defeated the Susquehannocks and returned with their captives to celebrate the victory with Bacon. But after the Occaneechees had fallen asleep, Bacon's men massacred them and seized their furs and prisoners. On their return to Henrico in May, the Baconians boasted of their prowess as Indian killers.

By then, Berkeley had outlawed Bacon, dissolved the legislature, and called the first general election since 1661. The 1661 assembly had recently imposed a property requirement for voting, but Berkeley suspended it and asked the burgesses to bring their grievances to Jamestown for redress at the June assembly. "How miserable that man is,"

he complained, "that Governes a People where six parts of seaven at least are Poore Endebted Discontented and Armed."

As one measure of their resentment against elite planters, voters elected a fair number of burgesses who were not JPs, almost unheard of since mid-century. Henrico's voters elected Bacon to the assembly. Berkeley had him arrested when he reached Jamestown and made him go down on his knees before the governor and council and apologize for his disobedience. Berkeley then forgave him and restored him to his seat in the council. By then, even the governor had abandoned his effort to distinguish between hostile and friendly Indians, but he still favored a defensive war. While the burgesses were passing laws to reform the county courts, the vestries, and the tax system, Bacon slipped away to Henrico, summoned his followers again, and marched on Jamestown. At gunpoint, he forced Berkeley to commission him as general of volunteers and compelled the legislature to authorize another expedition against the Indians.

Berkeley retreated downriver to Gloucester County and mustered its militia, but they refused to follow him against Bacon. They would fight only Indians. Mortified, Berkeley fled to the eastern shore, the only part of the colony that was safe from Indian attack and thus still loyal to him. Bacon hastened to Jamestown, summoned a meeting of planters at the governor's Green Spring mansion, made them swear an oath of loyalty to him, and ordered the confiscation of the estates of Berkeley's supporters, who were men in the process of becoming great planters.

HENRY LATROBE'S SKETCH OF GREEN SPRING, THE HOME OF GOVERNOR SIR WILLIAM BERKELEY, AT THE TIME OF BACON'S REBELLION

Green Spring was one of the first great houses built in Virginia. Latrobe made this drawing in the 1790s.

Meanwhile, Berkeley raised his own force on the eastern shore by promising the men an exemption from taxes for 21 years and the right to plunder the rebels.

Royal government collapsed. During summer 1676, hundreds of settlers set out to make their fortunes by plundering Indians, other colonists, or both. Bacon's Rebellion was the largest upheaval in the American colonies before 1775. Later legends to the contrary, it had little to do with liberty but a lot to do with class resentments.

Bacon never did kill a hostile Indian. While he was slaughtering and enslaving the unresisting Pamunkeys along the frontier, Berkeley assembled a small fleet and retook Jamestown in August. Bacon rushed east, exhibiting his Indian captives along the way, and laid siege to James-

town. He captured the wives of prominent Berkeley supporters and forced them to stand in the line of fire as he dug his trenches closer to the capital. After suffering only a few casualties, the governor's men grew discouraged, and in early September the whole force returned to the eastern shore. Bacon then burned Jamestown to the ground. He also boasted of his ability to hold off an English army, unite Virginia with Maryland and North Carolina, and win Dutch support for setting up an independent Chesapeake republic. Instead he died of dysentery in October.

Berkeley soon regained control of Virginia. Using the ships of the London tobacco fleet, he overpowered the plantations that Bacon had fortified. Then, in January 1677, a force of 1,000 redcoats arrived, too late to help but

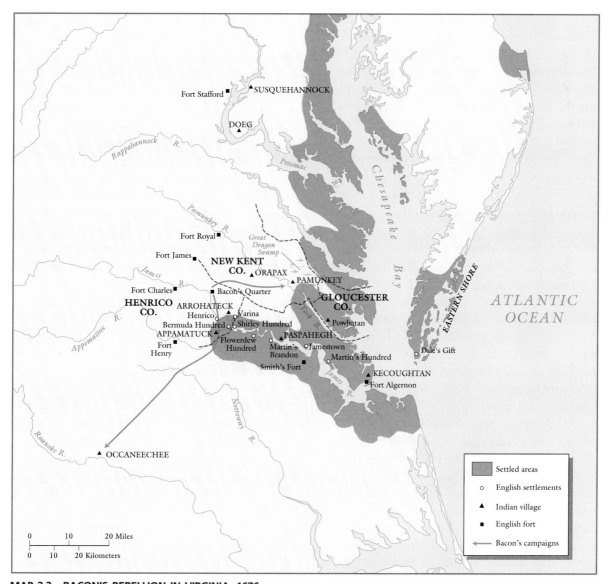

MAP 3.3 BACON'S REBELLION IN VIRGINIA, 1676

Settlement had just reached the fall line by the 1670s. The map also shows Bacon's two military campaigns, against the Occaneechees and the Pamunkeys.

in time to strain the colony's depleted resources. Ignoring royal orders to show clemency, Berkeley hanged 23 of the rebels. A new assembly repudiated the reforms of 1676, and in many counties the governor's men used their control of the courts to continue plundering the Baconians through confiscations and fines. Summoned to England to defend himself, Berkeley died there in 1677 before he could present his case.

Crisis in England and the Redefinition of Empire

Bacon's Rebellion helped trigger a political crisis in England. Because Virginia produced little tobacco in 1676 during the uprising, English customs revenues fell sharply, and the king was obliged to ask Parliament for more money. Parliament's response was tempered by the much deeper problem of the royal succession. Charles II had fathered many bastards, but his royal marriage was childless. After the queen reached menopause in the mid-1670s, his brother James, duke of York, became his heir. By then, James had become a Catholic. When Charles dissolved the Parliament that had sat from 1661 until 1678, he knew he would have to deal with a new House of Commons terrified by the prospect of a Catholic king.

The Popish Plot, the Exclusion Crisis, and the Rise of Party

In this atmosphere of distrust, a cynical adventurer, Titus Oates, fabricated the sensational story that he had uncovered a sinister "Popish Plot" to kill Charles and bring James to the throne. In the wake of these accusations, the king's ministry fell, and the parliamentary opposition won majorities in three successive elections between 1678 and 1681. Organized by Lord Shaftesbury (the Carolina proprietor), the opposition demanded that James, a Catholic, be excluded from the throne in favor of his Protestant daughters by his first marriage, Mary and Anne. It also called for a guarantee of frequent elections and for an independent electorate not under the influence of wealthy patrons. The king's men began castigating Shaftesbury's followers as Whigs, the name of an obscure sect of Scottish religious extremists who favored the assassination of both Charles and James. Whigs in turn denounced Charles's courtiers as Tories, a term for Irish Catholics who murdered Protestant landlords. Like Puritan, Quaker, Papist, and other terms of abuse, both words stuck.

England's party struggle reflected a deep rift between Court and Country forces. As of 1681, Tories were a Court party. They favored the legitimate succession, a standing army with adequate revenues to maintain it, the Anglican Church without toleration for Protestant dissenters, and a powerful monarchy. The Whigs were a Country opposition that stood for the exclusion of James from the throne, a decentralized militia rather than a standing army, toleration of Protestant dissenters but not of Catholics, and an active role in government for a reformed Parliament. During this struggle, James fled to Scotland in virtual exile. But Charles, after getting secret financial support from King Louis XIV of France, dissolved Parliament in 1681 and ruled without one for the last four years of his reign.

The Lords of Trade and Imperial Reform

English politics of the 1670s and 1680s had a profound impact on the colonies. The duke of York emerged from the Third Anglo-Dutch War as the most powerful shaper of imperial policy. At his urging, the government created a new agency in 1675, the Lords Committee of Trade and Plantations, or more simply, the Lords of Trade. This agency, a permanent committee of the Privy Council, enforced the Navigation Acts and administered the colonies. Although Virginia was the oldest royal colony, the West Indies became the object of most of the new policies, simply because the Caribbean remained a much more important theater of international competition and wealth. The instruments of royal government first took shape in the islands and were then extended to the mainland.

In the 1660s, the Crown took control of the governments of Barbados, Jamaica, and the Leeward Islands. The king appointed the governor and upper house of each colony; the settlers elected an assembly. The Privy Council in England reserved to itself the power to hear appeals from colonial courts and to disallow colonial legislation after the governor had approved it. The Privy Council also issued a formal commission and a lengthy set of instructions to each royal governor. In the two or three decades after 1660, these documents became standardized, especially after the Lords of Trade began to apply the lessons learned in one colony to problems anticipated in others.

The king's commission defined a governor's powers. From the Crown's point of view, the commission *created* the constitutional structure of each colony, a claim that few settlers accepted. The colonists believed they had an inherent right to constitutional rule even without the king's explicit warrant.

Written instructions told each royal governor how to use his broad powers. They laid out what he must do, such as command the militia, and what he must avoid, such as approving laws detrimental to English trade. Despite some confusion at first, Crown lawyers eventually agreed that

these instructions were binding only on the governor, not on the colony as a whole. In other words, royal instructions never acquired the force of law.

London also insisted that each colony pay the cost of its own government. Ironically, this requirement strengthened colonial claims to self-rule. After a long struggle in Jamaica, the Crown imposed a compromise in 1681 that had broad significance for all of the colonies. The Lords of Trade threatened to make the Jamaica assembly as weak as the Irish Parliament, which could debate and approve only those bills that had first been adopted by the English Privy Council. Under the compromise, the Jamaica assembly retained its power to initiate and amend legislation, in return for agreeing to a permanent revenue act, a measure that freed the governor from financial dependence on the assembly.

Metacom's War and Bacon's Rebellion lent urgency to these reforms and speeded up their use in the mainland colonies. The Lords of Trade ordered soldiers to Virginia, along with a royal commission to investigate grievances there. In 1676, they also sent an aggressive customs officer, Edward Randolph, to Massachusetts. His lengthy reports recommended that the colony's charter be revoked. The Lords of Trade viewed New England and all proprietary colonies with deep suspicion, although they failed to block the founding of Pennsylvania as a new proprietary venture. They had reason for concern. As late as 1678, Virginia remained the only royal colony on the mainland. The Lords of Trade might enforce compliance with the Navigation Acts elsewhere, but they possessed no effective instruments for punishing violators in North America. The king could demand and reprimand, but not command.

The Jamaica model assumed that each royal governor would summon an assembly on occasion, although not often. In the 1680s, the Crown imposed a similar settlement on Virginia—an occasional assembly with full powers of legislation in exchange for a permanent revenue act. Although New York had been an experiment in autocracy since the English conquest of 1664, James conceded an assembly to that colony, too, in exchange for a permanent revenue act in 1683. The Jamaica model was becoming the norm for the Lords of Trade. James's real preference emerged after the English Court of Chancery revoked the Massachusetts Charter in 1684. Charles II died and his brother became King James II in early 1685. The possibility of a vigorous autocracy in America suddenly reappeared.

The Dominion of New England

Absolutist New York now became the king's model for reorganizing New England. James disallowed the New York Charter of Liberties of 1683 (see chapter 2) and abolished the colony's assembly but kept the permanent revenue act in force. In 1686, he sent Sir Edmund Andros, the autocratic governor of New York from 1674 to 1680, to Massachusetts to take over a new government called the Dominion of New England. James added New Hampshire, Plymouth, Rhode Island, Connecticut, New York, and both Jerseys to the Dominion. Andros governed this vast domain through an appointive council and a superior court that rode circuit dispensing justice. There was no elective assembly. Andros also imposed religious toleration on the Puritans, even forcing one Boston church to let Anglicans use its meetinghouse for public worship for part of each Sunday.

At first, Andros won support from merchants who had been excluded from politics by the Puritan requirement that they be full church members, but his rigorous enforcement of the Navigation Acts soon alienated them too. When he tried to compel New England farmers to take out new land titles that included annual quitrents, he enraged the whole countryside. His suppression of a tax revolt in Essex County, Massachusetts, started many people thinking more highly of their rights as Englishmen than of their peculiar liberties as Puritans. By 1688, government by consent probably seemed more valuable than ever.

The Glorious Revolution

Events in England and France undermined the Dominion of New England. James II proclaimed toleration for Protestants and Catholics and began to name Catholics to high office, in violation of recent laws. In 1685, Louis XIV revoked the 1598 Edict of Nantes that had granted toleration to Protestants, and he launched a vicious persecution of the Huguenots. About 160,000 fled the kingdom, the largest forced migration of Europe's early modern era. Many went to England; several thousand settled in the English mainland colonies. James II tried to suppress the news of Louis's persecution, which made his own professions of toleration seem hypocritical, even though his commitment was probably genuine. In 1688, his queen gave birth to a son who would clearly be raised Catholic, thus imposing a Catholic *dynasty* on England. Several Whig and Tory leaders swallowed their mutual hatred and invited William of Orange, the *stadholder* of the Netherlands, to England. The husband of the king's older Protestant daughter Mary, William had become the most prominent Protestant soldier in Europe during a long war against Louis XIV.

William landed in England in November 1688. Most of the English army sided with him, and James fled to France in late December. Parliament declared that James

Thomas B. Macaulay, *History of England from the Accession of James II*, ed. by Charles H. Firth (London: Macmillan, 1914).

Thomas B. Macaulay, *History of England from the Accession of James II*, ed. by Charles H. Firth (London: Macmillan, 1914).

CALVINISM ON ITS DEATHBED AND LE ROY DE FRANCE

Louis XIV's persecution of the Huguenots led his supporters to hope that France would soon be rid of all Protestants. In *Le Roy de France*, the Dutch Protestant response to the persecution depicts Louis, the sun king, as death.

had abdicated the throne and named William III (1689–1702) and Mary II (1689–94) as joint sovereigns. It also passed a Toleration Act that gave Protestant dissenters (but not Catholics) the right to worship publicly and a Declaration of Rights that guaranteed a Protestant succession and condemned as illegal many of the acts of James II. This Glorious Revolution also brought England and the Netherlands into war against Louis XIV, who supported James.

The Glorious Revolution in America

The Boston militia overthrew Andros on April 18 and 19, 1689, even before they knew whether William had succeeded James. Andros's attempt to suppress the news that William had landed in England convinced the Puritans that he was part of a global Popish Plot to undermine Protestant societies everywhere. After some hesitation, Massachusetts resumed the forms of its old charter government. The other New England colonies followed its example. In May and June, the New York City militia took over Fort James at the southern tip of Manhattan and renamed it Fort William. To hostile observers, this action seemed almost a replay of the events of 1673, when the Dutch had reconquered New York and renamed the fort

for William. Francis Nicholson, lieutenant governor in New York under Andros, refused to proclaim William and Mary as sovereigns without direct orders from England and soon sailed for home. The active rebels in New York City were nearly all Dutch who had little experience with traditional English liberties. Few had held high office. Their leader, Jacob Leisler, dreaded conquest by Catholics from New France and began to act like a Dutch *stadholder* in a nominally English colony.

Military defense became Leisler's highest priority, but his demands for supplies soon alienated even his Yankee supporters on Long Island. Although he summoned an elective assembly, he made no effort to revive the Charter of Liberties of 1683 while continuing to collect duties under the permanent revenue act of that year. He showed little respect for the legal rights of his opponents, most of whom were English or were Dutch merchants who had served the Dominion of New England. He jailed several Anti-Leislerians for months without bringing them to trial, and when his own assembly raised questions about their legal rights, he sent it home. Loud complaints against his administration reached the Crown in London.

In Maryland, Protestants overthrew Lord Baltimore's Catholic government in 1689. The governor of Maryland had refused to proclaim William and Mary, even after all of the other colonies had done so. To Lord Baltimore's dis-

may, the messenger he sent from London to Maryland with orders to accept the new monarchs died en route. Had he arrived, the government probably would have survived the crisis.

The English Response

England responded in different ways to each of these upheavals. The Maryland rebels won the royal government they requested from England and soon established the Anglican Church in the colony. Catholics could no longer worship in public, hold office, or even expect toleration. Most prominent Catholic families, however, braced themselves against the Protestant storm and remained loyal to their faith.

In New York, the Leislerians suffered a deadly defeat. Leisler and his Dutch followers, who had no significant contacts at the English court, watched helplessly as their enemies, working through the imperial bureaucracy that William inherited from James, manipulated the Dutch king of England into undermining his loyal Dutch supporters in New York. The new governor, Henry Sloughter, named prominent Anti-Leislerians to his council, arrested Leisler and his son-in-law in 1691, tried both for treason, and had them hanged, drawn, and quartered. The assembly elected that year was controlled by Anti-Leislerians, most of whom were English. It passed a modified version of the Charter of Liberties of 1683, this time denying toleration to Catholics. Like its predecessor, this charter was later disallowed. Bitter struggles between Leislerians and Anti-Leislerians would characterize New York politics until after 1700.

Another complex struggle involved Massachusetts. In 1689, Increase Mather, acting as the colony's agent in London, failed to persuade Parliament to restore the charter of 1629. Over the next two years, he negotiated a new charter, which gave the Crown what it had been demanding since 1664—the power to appoint governors, justices, and militia officers, and the power to veto laws and to hear judicial appeals. The 1691 charter also granted toleration to all Protestants and based voting rights on property qualifications, not church membership. In effect, liberty and property had triumphed over godliness.

While insisting on these concessions, William also accepted much of the previous history of the colony, even if it did not augur well for the emerging model of royal government. The General Court, not the governor as in other

THE FORT PROTECTING NEW YORK CITY, AS SEEN FROM BROOKLYN HEIGHTS, 1679

This sketch, probably by Jasper Danckaerts or Peter Sluyter, two Dutch visitors, shows the fort at the southern tip of Manhattan Island. When the English conquered New Netherland in 1664, the fort was renamed for James, the lord proprietor of what now became New York. When the Dutch retook the fort in 1673, they changed its name to Fort William (for William of Orange). When the English regained control in 1674, they again renamed it Fort James, but when James II was overthrown in the Glorious Revolution of 1688–89, the settlers named it for William once again. Thereafter, the fort took the name of the reigning British monarch.

royal colonies, retained control over the distribution of land. The council remained an elective body, although it was chosen annually by the full legislature, not directly by the voters. The governor could veto any councillor. Massachusetts also absorbed the colonies of Plymouth and Maine. New Hampshire regained its autonomy, but until 1741 it usually shared the same royal governor with Massachusetts. Rhode Island and Connecticut resumed their charter governments.

The Salem Witch Trials

When Mather sailed into Boston harbor with the new charter in May 1692, he found the province besieged by witches. The accusations arose in Salem Village (modern Danvers) among a group of girls that included a young daughter and a niece of the local minister, Samuel Parris, and then spread to older girls, some of whom had been orphaned during the Indian wars. The girls howled, barked, and stretched themselves into frightful contortions. At first, Parris treated the outbursts as cases of demonic possession, but after weeks of prayer sessions brought no improvement, he accepted a diagnosis of witchcraft. With adult encouragement, the girls accused many village residents of witchcraft. The accusers came from families that

HISTORY THROUGH FILM

Three Sovereigns for Sarah (1986)

Directed by Philip Leacock. Starring Vanessa Redgrave (Sarah Cloyse), Phyllis Thaxter (Rebecca Nurse), and Kim Hunter (Mary Easty).

This film, originally a PBS American Playhouse miniseries, is the most powerful and effective dramatization ever made of the Salem witch trials of 1692. The three principal actresses were all previous Academy Award winners. When this series appeared, British director Philip Leacock was perhaps best known in the United States for *The War Lover* (1962) and *The Daughters of Joshua Cabe* (1972).

The screenplay by Victor Pisano, who also produced the film, concentrates on the three Towne sisters: Sarah Cloyse (Vanessa Redgrave), Rebecca Nurse (Phyllis Thaxter), and Mary Easty (Kim Hunter). Rebecca Nurse's ordeal became a major turning point in the Salem tragedy. Hers was one of the early trials, and at first the jury acquitted her, only to be urged by the judges to reconsider the verdict. They did, and she was hanged. After this reversal, no one else was acquitted. Mary Easty, after she too had been convicted, sent a petition to the magistrates, one of the most eloquent documents ever written in colonial America. As a committed Christian, she accepted her own death, but she urged the judges to reconsider their procedures because she knew that she was innocent, and so must be many of the other condemned witches. She was hanged.

Of the three sisters, only Sarah Cloyse survived the trials. The film focuses on Cloyse's lifelong efforts to vindicate the reputations of her two sisters. Vanessa Redgrave's portrayal of her suffering and her resistance to the whole appalling affair is one of the most compelling performances of her long and distinguished career.

The screenplay, by concentrating on the three sisters and their families, brings home the human tragedy that the trials became. This emphasis forced Pisano to leave out other important victims. For example, the Reverend George Burroughs, the only minister executed in the trials (or in any New England colony in the 17th century, for that matter), is not even mentioned. In addition, Pisano never explains that Sarah Cloyse survived because the grand jury refused to indict her. Grand juries were exempt from explaining their decisions to anyone else, and so we do not know why she became an exception, but evidently the jurors believed that she was too dedicated a Christian woman to sell her soul to the devil. Finally, the screenplay attributes the onset of the crisis to fortune telling in the Samuel Parris household by Tituba, an Indian slave from South America who reached the village via Barbados. Guilt for indulging in this occult activity presumably triggered the seizures of the afflicted girls. Several historians have demolished this interpretation since the film appeared. We simply do not know what set off the girls' fits.

Three Sovereigns for Sarah is a grim, compelling, relentless drama. It romanticizes nothing and makes clear, unlike some Hollywood depictions of these events, that nothing about the trials was sexy. The accusation scenes, dominated by girls, convey the madness of the whole affair. Most of those accused and executed were grandmothers. When they are turned off the ladder, their bodies bounce as the nooses take hold. This film is a cinematic triumph.

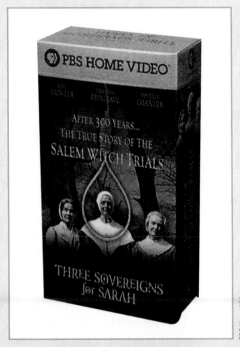

PBS Home Video.

Three Sovereigns for Sarah **brings home the human tragedy of the Salem witch trials of 1692.**

strongly supported Parris. Most of the accused were old women in families that had opposed his appointment as village minister. The number of the accused escalated sharply, and the crisis spread far beyond the village after 14-year-old Abigail Hobbs confessed in April that she had made a compact with the devil in Maine at age 10 just before the Indian war broke out. New England seemed on the edge of a calamity—an external enemy of Indians, ruled by Satan and supported by missionaries and gunpowder from Catholic New France, had joined with an internal enemy of numerous witches to destroy Massachusetts. By 1692, the Abenakis Indians had devastated the northern frontier, and Massachusetts had not found any effective way to strike back.

In June, the trials began in Salem Town. The court, composed mostly of judges who had compromised their Puritanism through willing service to the Dominion of New England, hanged 19 people, pressed one man to death because he refused to stand trial, and allowed several other people to die in jail. All of those executed insisted on their innocence. Nobody who confessed was hanged. Many of the victims were grandmothers, several quite conspicuous for their piety. One was a former minister at Salem Village who had become a Baptist. The governor finally halted the trials after the girls accused his wife of witchcraft. By then, public support for the trials was collapsing. The trials, along with the new charter, brought the Puritan era to a close.

The Completion of Empire

The Glorious Revolution killed absolutism in English America and guaranteed that royal government would be representative government in the colonies. Both Crown and colonists took it for granted that any colony settled by the English would elect an assembly to vote on all taxes and consent to all local laws. Governors would be appointed by the Crown or a lord proprietor. (Governors were elected in Connecticut and Rhode Island.) But royal government soon became the norm, especially after the New Jersey proprietors surrendered their powers of government in 1702, and the Carolina proprietors followed suit after their last governor was deposed by the settlers in 1719. On the other hand, the Crown restored proprietary rule in Maryland in 1716, after the fifth Lord Baltimore converted to the Church of England. By the 1720s, however, Maryland and Pennsylvania (along with Delaware, which became a separate colony under the Penn proprietorship in 1704) were the only surviving proprietary provinces on the mainland, and their proprietors were usually careful to abide by the rules of imperial administration.

This transition to royal government seems smoother in retrospect than it did at the time. London almost lost control of the empire in the 1690s. Overwhelmed by the pressures of the French war, the Lords of Trade could not keep pace with events in the colonies. When French

MATTHEW HOPKINS, *DISCOVERIE OF WITCHES* (1647)

This woodcut depicts activities that New Englanders associated with the behavior of witches, including flying through the air on poles or brooms.

© Hulton Archive/Getty Images.

privateers disrupted the tobacco trade, Scottish smugglers stepped in and began to divert it to Glasgow in defiance of the Navigation Acts. New York became a haven for pirates. The northern colonies could not cooperate effectively in the war against New France. Parliament, suspecting William of favoring Dutch interests over English, even threatened to take control of the colonies away from the king.

William took action in 1696. With his approval, Parliament passed a new, comprehensive Navigation Act that plugged several loopholes in earlier laws and extended to America the English system of vice admiralty courts, which dispensed quick justice without juries. When the new courts settled routine maritime disputes or condemned enemy merchant ships captured by colonial privateers, their services were highly regarded by the settlers.

MAP 3.4   GOVERNMENT AND RELIGION IN THE BRITISH COLONIES, 1720

This map shows which colonies were royal, proprietary, or corporate in structure and whether Anglican or Congregational churches were established by law or whether, instead, the Quakers or the Dutch Reformed church predominated or numerous sects competed for the loyalties of the settlers.

But when the courts tried to assume jurisdiction over the Navigation Acts, they aroused controversy.

William also replaced the Lords of Trade in 1696 with a new agency, the Board of Trade. Its powers were almost purely advisory. It corresponded with governors and other officials in the colonies, listened to lobbyists in England, and made policy recommendations to appropriate governmental bodies, whether Parliament, the Treasury, or a secretary of state. The board tried to collect information on complex questions and to offer helpful advice. It was, in short, an early attempt at government by experts. John Locke, England's foremost philosopher and an able economist, was one of the board's first members.

Another difficult problem was resolved in 1707 when England and Scotland agreed to merge their separate parliaments and become the single kingdom of Great Britain. At a stroke, the Act of Union placed Scotland inside the Navigation Act system, legalized Scottish participation in the tobacco trade, and opened numerous colonial offices to ambitious Scots. By the middle of the 18th century, most of Scotland's growing prosperity derived from its trade with the colonies. In a very real sense, the tobacco trade built Glasgow.

Imperial Federalism

The transformations that took place between 1689 and 1707 defined the structure of the British Empire until the American Revolution. Although Parliament claimed full power over the colonies, in practice it seldom regulated anything colonial except Atlantic commerce. Even the Woolens Act of 1699, designed to protect the English woolens industry from Irish and colonial competition, did not prohibit the manufacture of woolen textiles in the colonies. It simply prohibited their export. The Hat Act of 1732 was similarly designed, except for a clause limiting the number of apprentices or slaves a colonial hatter could maintain. Nobody enforced that provision.

When Parliament regulated oceanic trade, its measures were usually enforceable. But compliance was minimal to nonexistent when Parliament tried to regulate inland affairs through statutes protecting white pines (needed as masts for the navy) or through the Iron Act of 1750, which prohibited the erection of certain types of new iron mills. To get things done within the colonies, the Crown had to win the settlers' agreement through their lawful assemblies and unsalaried local officials. In effect, the empire had stumbled into a system of de facto federalism, an arrangement that no one could quite explain or justify. Parliament exercised only limited powers, and the colonies controlled the rest. What seemed an arrangement of convenience in London soon acquired overtones of right in America, the right to consent to all taxes and local laws.

The Mixed and Balanced Constitution

The Glorious Revolution transformed British politics in a way that profoundly affected the colonies after 1700. To Europe's surprise, Britain, whose government had seemed wildly unstable for half a century, quickly became a far more powerful state under its limited government after 1689 than the Stuart kings had been able to sustain with their pretensions to absolute monarchy. The British constitution, which made ministers legally responsible for their public actions, proved remarkably stable. Before long, many Englishmen were celebrating this achievement as the wonder of the age. In the ancient world, as had been pointed out by republican thinker James Harrington (see chapter 2), free societies had degenerated into tyrannies. Liberty had always been fragile and was easily lost. Yet England had retained its liberty and grown stronger in the process. England had defied history.

The explanation, nearly everyone agreed, lay in England's "mixed and balanced" constitution, which embraced Harrington's ideas about republican liberty but absorbed them into a monarchical framework. Government by King, Lords, and Commons mirrored society itself—the monarchy, aristocracy, and commonality—and literally embodied all three in its structure. As long as each freely consented to government measures, English liberty would be secure because each had voluntarily placed the public good ahead of its own interests. But if either the Crown, the Lords, or the Commons acquired the power to dominate or manipulate the other two, English liberty would be in peril. That danger fueled an unending dialogue in 18th-century Britain. The underlying drama was always the struggle of power, especially royal patronage, against liberty, and liberty usually meant a limitation of governmental power.

Power had to be controlled, or liberty would be lost. Nearly everyone agreed that a direct assault on Parliament through a military coup was highly unlikely. The real danger lay in corruption, in the ability of Crown ministers to undermine the independence and integrity of the House of Commons.

The wars with France made Britain a great power, but they also aroused acute constitutional anxieties. After 1689, England raised larger fleets and armies than it had ever mobilized before. To support them, the kingdom created for the first time a funded national debt, in which the state agreed to pay the interest due to its creditors

In London, Harvard's Best Undermines Yale's Orthodoxy

Jeremiah Dummer, colonial agent, was the son of Jeremiah and Ann, or Hannah, Atwater Dummer. His father, a Boston silversmith and engraver, became the first native-born painter of significant ability. The son was born in 1681 and, according to President Increase Mather, became the ablest student at Harvard College in his generation. After graduating in 1699, he sailed for the Netherlands, where he arrived in 1702. He studied at the University of Leyden and the University of Utrecht, which awarded him both an A.M. and a Ph.D. degree in 1703. He was the first native-born American to receive a doctorate of philosophy. He returned to Boston a year later but was unable to get an appointment either to the Harvard faculty or to a conventional pulpit. His exceptional learning evidently intimidated others.

Dummer returned to London in 1708 and stayed in Europe for the rest of his life. He soon ingratiated himself with the Tory Party, which remained in power until the death of Queen Anne in 1714. When the Board of Trade contemplated the revocation of all colonial charters in 1715, Dummer wrote *The Defence of the New England Charters,* which he finally published in London in 1721. It was promptly reprinted in Boston and again in 1745 and 1765. It was also reprinted twice in London during the decade before the Revolutionary War broke out. New England patriots held that pamphlet in high regard.

Dummer secured an appointment as the colonial agent for both Massachusetts and Connecticut, a position that he filled quite ably for two decades. His most significant accomplishment came when he persuaded an English gentleman, Elihu Yale, to donate his large personal library to the Connecticut college that had

JEREMIAH DUMMER

This portrait by Sir Godfrey Kneller reveals the extent to which Dummer had become an English gentleman during his long residence in London. His periwig would have scandalized pious New Englanders.

been founded in 1701 and, two decades later, was in the process of moving to New Haven. In gratitude, the institution changed its name to Yale College, but because nearly all of the religious volumes were Anglican, the Yale faculty read them and, except for Tutor Jonathan Edwards, converted to the Church of England in 1722.

Although Dummer earned fame on a visit to Paris by openly challenging a Jesuit over the propriety of invoking the saints, his puritan convictions grew more relaxed in Europe, and rumors reached Boston that he might even have his own harem. He died in 1739. "He had an elegant Taste both in Men and Books," reported the *Gentleman's Magazine,* "and was a Person of excellent Learning, solid Judgment, and polite Conversation, without the least Tincture of Political or Religious Bigotry."

ahead of all other obligations. This simple device gave Britain enormous borrowing power. In 1694, the government created the Bank of England to facilitate its own finances; the London Stock Exchange also emerged in the 1690s. Parliament levied a heavy land tax on the gentry and excises on ordinary people to meet wartime expenses. Together, debt, bank, stock market, and new sources of revenue added up to a financial revolution that enabled England to outspend France, despite having only one-fourth of France's population. These resources and a sharp expansion of offices during the wars vastly increased patronage. By giving offices to members of Parliament, Crown ministers were almost assured of majority support for their measures.

VIEW OF THE HARVESTING FIELD OF JAMES HIGFORD'S MANOR, DIXTON, GLOUCESTERSHIRE (CIRCA 1725–35)

The Country wing of British politics was dominated by landed gentlemen who owned great estates. The men who actually worked their fields seldom had a voice in politics.

HAMPTON COURT PALACE

This elegant palace near London was one of Queen Anne's residences. Court architecture and protocol were hierarchical and designed to be awesome.

As during the controversy over the Popish Plot, public debates still pitted Court against Country. The Court favored policies that strengthened its war-making capabilities. The Country stood for liberty. Each of the parties, Whig and Tory, had Court and Country wings. Between 1680 and 1720, however, they reversed their polarities. Although the Tories had begun as Charles II's Court party, by 1720 most of them were a Country opposition. Whigs had defended Country positions in 1680, but by 1720 most of them were strong advocates for the Court policies of George I (1714–27). Court spokesmen defended the military buildup, the financial revolution, and the new patronage as essential to victory over France. Their Country opponents denounced standing armies, attacked the financial revolution as an engine of corruption, favored an early peace with France, demanded more frequent elections, and tried to ban placemen (officeholders who sat in Parliament) from the House of Commons.

Court Whigs emerged victorious during the long ministry of Sir Robert Walpole (1721–42), but their opponents were more eloquent and controlled more presses. By the 1720s, the opposition claimed many of the kingdom's best writers, especially Tories Alexander Pope, Jonathan Swift, John Gay, and Henry St. John, viscount Bolingbroke. Their detestation of Walpole was shared by a smaller band of radical Whigs, including John Trenchard and Thomas Gordon, who wrote *Cato's Letters*, four volumes of collected newspaper essays. The central theme of the opposition was corruption—the indirect and insidious means by which ministers threatened the independence of Parliament and thus English liberty. This debate over liberty soon reached America. *Cato's Letters* were especially popular in the northern colonies, while Bolingbroke won numerous admirers among the gentry in the southern colonies.

Contrasting Empires: Spain and France in North America

After 1689, Britain's enemies were France and Spain, Catholic powers with their own American empires. Until 1689, the three empires had coexisted in America without much contact among them, but Europe's wars soon engulfed them all. Spain and France shared a zeal for converting Indians that exceeded anything displayed by English Protestants, but their American empires had little else in common.

The Pueblo Revolt

In the late 17th century, the Spanish missions of North America entered a period of crisis. Franciscan zeal began to slacken, and fewer priests took the trouble to master Indian languages, insisting instead that the Indians learn Spanish. For all of their good intentions, the missionaries regarded Indians as children and often whipped or even shackled them for minor infractions. They refused to trust them with firearms. Disease also took a heavy toll. A declining Indian population led to more pressing labor demands by missionaries, and despite strong prohibitions, some Spaniards enslaved some Indians in Florida and New Mexico. After 1670, Florida also feared encroachments by English Protestants out of South Carolina, who were eager to enslave unarmed Indians, whether or not they had embraced Christianity. By 1700, the European refusal to enslave other Christians protected only white people.

The greatest challenge to the Spanish arose in New Mexico, where the Pueblo population had fallen from 80,000 to 17,000 since 1598. A prolonged drought, together with Apache and Navajo attacks, prompted many Pueblos to abandon the Christian God and resume their old forms of worship. Missionaries responded with whippings and even several executions in 1675. Popé, a San Juan Pueblo medicine man who had been whipped for his beliefs, moved north to Taos Pueblo, where he organized the most successful Indian revolt in American history. In 1680, in a carefully timed uprising, the Pueblos killed 400 of the 2,300 Spaniards in New Mexico and destroyed or plundered every Spanish building in the province (see the chapter 1 map, "Spanish Missions in Florida and New Mexico, circa 1675"). They desecrated every church and killed 21 of New Mexico's 33 missionaries. "Now," they exulted, "the God of the Spaniards, who was their father, is dead," but the Pueblos' own god, whom they obeyed, "[had] never died." Spanish survivors fled from Santa Fe down the Rio Grande to El Paso.

Popé lost his influence when the traditional Pueblo rites failed to end the drought or stop the attacks of hostile Indians. When the Spanish returned in the 1690s, this time as conquerors, the Pueblos were badly divided. Most villages yielded without much resistance, and Spain accepted their submission, but Santa Fe held out until December 1693. When it fell, the Spanish executed 70 men and gave 400 women and children to the returning settlers as their slaves. The Hopi Indians to the west, however, never again submitted to Spanish rule.

Before these crises, missionaries in both Florida and New Mexico had often resisted the demands of Spanish governors. By 1700, the state ruled and missionaries obeyed. Spain's daring attempt to create a demilitarized Christian frontier was proving to be a tragic failure for both Indians and Franciscans.

New France and the Middle Ground

A different story unfolded along the western frontier of New France over the same decades. There the Iroquois menace made possible an unusual accommodation between the colony and the Indians of the Great Lakes region. The survival of the Iroquois Five Nations depended on their ability to assimilate captives seized from other nations through incessant warfare. Their raiders, armed with muskets, terrorized western Indians, carried away thousands of captives, and left behind grisly trophies of their cruelty to discourage revenge. The Iroquois wars depopulated nearly all of what is now the state of Ohio and much of the Ontario peninsula. The Indians around Lakes Erie and Huron either fled west to escape these horrors or were absorbed by the Iroquois. The refugees, mostly Algonquian-speaking peoples, founded new communities farther west. Most of these villages contained families from several different tribes, and village loyalties gradually supplanted older tribal (or ethnic) loyalties, which often broke down under Iroquois pressure. When the refugees disagreed with one another or came into conflict with the Sioux to their west, the absence of traditional tribal structures made it difficult to resolve their differences. Over time, French soldiers, trappers, and missionaries stepped in as mediators.

The French were not always welcome. In 1684, the only year for which we have a precise count, the Algonquians killed 39 French traders. Yet the leaders of thinly populated New France were eager to erect an Algonquian shield against the Iroquois and, in later decades, against the British. They began by easing tensions among the Algonquians while supplying them with firearms, brandy, and other European goods. In fact, to the exasperation of missionaries, brandy became the lubricant of the fur trade by keeping the warriors hunting for pelts and dependent on French traders. New France, in turn, provided the resources that the Algonquians needed to strike back against the Iroquois. By 1701, Iroquois losses had become so heavy that the Five Nations negotiated a peace treaty with the French and the western Indians. The Iroquois agreed to remain neutral in any war between France and England. France's Indian allies, supported by a new French fort erected at Detroit in 1701, began returning to the fertile lands around Lakes Erie and Huron. That region became the Great Lakes Middle Ground, over which no one could

IROQUOIS WARRIORS LEADING AN INDIAN PRISONER INTO CAPTIVITY, 1660s

Because Indian populations had been depleted by war and disease, a tribe's survival became dependent on its ability to assimilate captives. This is a French copy of an Iroquois pictograph.

Archives Nationales.

wield sovereign power, although New France exercised great influence within it. France always ran a deficit in supporting the fur trade but kept the trade going mostly to block British expansion.

France's success in the interior rested more on intelligent negotiation than on force. Officials who gave orders instead of fostering negotiations merely alienated France's Indian allies. Blind obedience to commands, grumbled the warriors, was slavery. Hugely outnumbered, the French knew that they could not impose their will on the Indians. Indians respected those Frenchmen who honored their ways. The French conducted diplomacy according to Indian, not European rules. The governor of New France became a somewhat grander version of a traditional Indian chief. Algonquians called him Onontio ("Great Mountain"), the supreme alliance chief who won cooperation through persuasion and who had learned that, among the Indians, persuasion was always accompanied by gifts. The respect accorded to peacetime chiefs was roughly proportionate to how much they gave away, not to how much they accumulated. The English, by contrast, tried to "buy" land from the Indians and regarded the sale of both the land and of the Indians' right to use it as irrevocable. The French understood that this idea had no place in Indian culture. Agreements were not final contracts but required regular renewal, always with an exchange of gifts. The strongest party had to be more generous than all others.

Middle Ground diplomacy came at a price. It involved New France in the Indian slave trade even though Louis XIV expressly forbade the enslavement of Indians, a command finally rescinded in 1709. Because Indians fought wars mostly to acquire captives, Onontio's western allies frequently presented captives to French traders who realized that to refuse the gift would be an insult and could jeopardize New France's alliances with the western nations.

By the 1720s, up to 5 percent of the colony's population consisted of enslaved Indians. In the most commercial neighborhood of Montreal, every other household owned one or two slaves.

French Louisiana and Spanish Texas

The pattern worked out by the French and the Indians on the Great Lakes Middle Ground also took hold, although in a more fragile form, in the lower Mississippi valley. In quest of a passage to Asia, Father Jacques Marquette and trader Louis Joliet paddled down the Mississippi to its juncture with the Arkansas River in 1673. But once they became convinced that the Mississippi flowed into the Gulf of Mexico and not the Pacific, they turned back. Then, in 1682, René-Robert Cavelier, *sieur* de La Salle traveled down the Mississippi to its mouth, claiming possession of the entire area for France and calling it Louisiana (for Louis XIV). But when La Salle returned in 1684 by way of the Gulf of Mexico to plant a colony there, he overshot the mouth of the Mississippi, landed in Texas, and wandered around for three years in search of the great river until his exasperated men murdered him.

In 1699, during a brief lull in the wars between France and England, the French returned to the Gulf of Mexico. Pierre le Moyne d'Iberville, a Canadian, landed with 80 men at Biloxi, built a fort, and began trading with the Indians. In 1702, he moved his headquarters to Mobile, closer to the more populous nations of the interior, especially the Choctaws, who were looking for allies against the English. The Choctaws could still field 5,000 warriors but had suffered heavy losses from slaving raids organized by South Carolinians and carried out mostly by that colony's

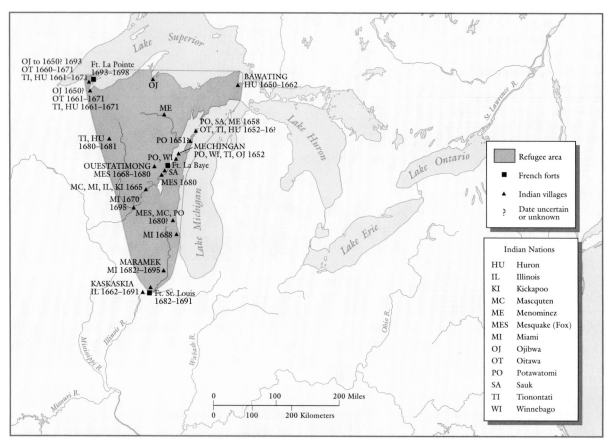

MAP 3.5   FRENCH MIDDLE GROUND IN NORTH AMERICA CIRCA 1700

French power in North America rested mostly on the arrangements French governors worked out with refugee Algonquian Indians trying to resist Iroquois raids in the Great Lakes region.

Chickasaw and Creek allies. About 1,800 Choctaws had been killed and 500 enslaved during the preceding decade. Using the Choctaws to anchor their trading system, the French created a weaker, southern version of the Great Lakes Middle Ground, acting as mediators and trading brandy, firearms, and other European products for furs and food. Often, during the War of the Spanish Succession (1702–13), the French received no European supplies, and they remained heavily outnumbered by the Indians. Although European diseases had been ravaging the area since the 1540s, the Indians of the lower Mississippi valley still numbered about 70,000. In 1708, the French numbered fewer than 300, including 80 Indian slaves. The French were lucky to survive at all. They did so, in large part, by trying to protect their allies from South Carolina slavers and by refusing to enslave other Indians.

Spain, alarmed at any challenge to its monopoly on the Gulf of Mexico, founded Pensacola in 1698, more to counter the English than the French. Competition from France prompted the Spanish to move into Texas in 1690, where they established missions near the modern Texas–Louisiana border. At first, the missionaries were cordially received by the Tejas (Texas) Indians, but they brought smallpox with them. The Indians rejected their explanation that the epidemic was God's "holy will" and told the missionaries to get out or be killed. They departed in 1693, leaving Texas to the Indians for another 20 years.

An Empire of Settlement: The British Colonies

By 1700, 250,000 settlers and slaves were already living in England's mainland colonies, and the population was doubling every 25 years. New France matched that pace, but with only 14,000 people in 1700, it could not close the gap. By contrast, the population of the Spanish missions continued to decline. In the struggle for empire, a growing population became Britain's greatest advantage.

The Engine of British Expansion: The Colonial Household

Virginia's Robert "King" Carter, who died in 1730, became the first settler to acquire a thousand slaves and several hundred thousand acres of land. His household differed strikingly from that of an ordinary Pennsylvania or New England farmer, but both had something in common that distinguished them from households in England. With few exceptions, colonial families rejected the English customs of entail and primogeniture. *Entail* prohibited a landowner, or his heir, from dividing up his landed estate (that is, selling part of it) during his lifetime. *Primogeniture* obliged him to leave all of his land to his eldest surviving son. Under this system, younger sons clearly ranked below the oldest son, and daughters usually ranked behind both unless one of them could marry a man who would bring new resources into the family. Primogeniture and entail became more common in the 18th-century colonies than they had been before, but until the late colonial period they failed to structure social relations the way they did in England. A Virginia planter, for example, might entail his home plantation (the one on which he had erected his big house) and bequeath it to his oldest son, but he would also leave land and slaves, sometimes whole plantations, to his other sons. The primacy of the eldest son was far more sentimental than structural. By contrast, the patriarchs of colonial households tried to pass on their status to all of their sons and to provide dowries that would enable all of their daughters to marry men of equal status. Until 1750 or so, these goals were usually realistic.

For younger sons, then, the colonies presented a unique opportunity. Benjamin Franklin began his *Autobiography,* colonial America's greatest success story, by boasting that he was "the youngest Son of the youngest Son for 5 Generations back." Despite those odds, Franklin became a gentleman with an international reputation. He made enough money to retire as a printer, commissioned a genteel portrait of himself, engaged in scientific experiments, and entered public life. He no longer worked with his hands.

English households had become Americanized in the colonies during the earliest years of settlement, as soon as Virginia and Plymouth made land available to nearly all male settlers. By the mid-18th century, the question was whether that system could survive the pressures of a rising population. Social change began to drive American households back toward English practices. Only continual expansion onto new lands would allow the colonial household to provide equal opportunity for all sons, much less for all daughters.

Colonial households were patriarchal. The father expected to be loved and revered by his wife and children but insisted on being obeyed. A man's standing in the community depended on his success as a master at home. A mature male was expected to be the master of others. In New England and Pennsylvania, typical householders probably thought they were the rough equals of most other householders. Above all, a patriarch strove to perpetuate his household into the next generation and to preserve his own economic independence, or autonomy. Of course, complete independence was impossible. Every household owed small debts or favors to its neighbors, but these obligations seldom compromised the family's standing in the community.

Although farmers rarely set out to maximize profits, they did try to grow an agricultural surplus, if only as a hedge against drought, storms, and other unpredictable events. For rural Pennsylvanians, this surplus averaged about 40 percent of the total crop. With the harvest in, farmers marketed their produce, often selling it to merchants in Boston, New York, or Philadelphia for local consumption or for export to the West Indies or Europe. Farmers used the proceeds to pay taxes or their ministers' salaries and to buy British imports. Although these arrangements sometimes placed families in short-term debt to merchants, most farmers and artisans managed to avoid long-term debt. Settlers accepted temporary dependency among freemen—of sons on their parents, indentured servants on their masters, or apprentices and journeymen on master craftsmen. Sons often worked as laborers on neighboring farms, as sailors, or as journeymen craftsmen, provided that such dependence was temporary. A man who became permanently dependent on others lost the respect of his community.

The Voluntaristic Ethic and Public Life

Householders carried their quest for independence into public life. In entering politics and in waging war, their autonomy became an ethic of voluntarism. Few freemen could be coerced into doing something of which they disapproved. They had to be persuaded or induced to volunteer. "Obedience by compulsion is the Obedience of Vassals, who without compulsion would disobey," explained one essayist. "The Affection of the People is the only Source of a Cheerful and rational Obedience." Local officials serving without pay frequently ignored orders contrary to their own interests or the interests of their community.

Most young men accepted military service only if it suited their future plans. They would serve only under officers they knew, and then for only a single campaign. Few reenlisted. To the exasperation of professional British soldiers, provincials, like Indians, regarded blind obedience to commands as slavery. They did not enlist in order to become soldiers for life. After serving, they used their bonus and their pay, and often the promise of a land grant, to speed their way to becoming masters of their own households. Military service, for those who survived, could lead to land ownership and an earlier marriage. For New England women, however, war reduced the supply of eligible males and raised the median age of marriage by about two years, which meant, in effect, one fewer pregnancy per marriage.

Three Warring Empires, 1689–1716

When the three empires went to war after 1689, the Spanish and French fought mostly to survive. The British fought to expand their holdings. None of them won a decisive advantage in the first two wars, which ended with the Treaty of Utrecht in 1713.

Smart diplomacy with the Indians protected the western flank of New France, but the eastern parts of the colony were vulnerable to English invasion. The governors of New France knew that Indian attacks against English towns would keep the English colonies disorganized and

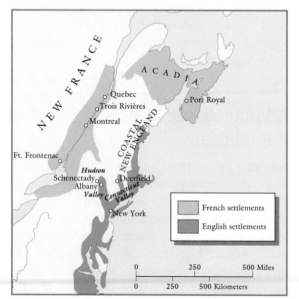

MAP 3.6 NORTHEASTERN THEATER OF WAR, 1689–1713

For a quarter of a century, the colonies north of the Quaker settlements in the Delaware Valley were locked in a brutal and costly struggle against the French and Indians to their north and west.

make them disperse their forces. Within a year after the outbreak of war between France and England in 1689, Indians had devastated most of coastal Maine and parts of New Hampshire and had burned the Mohawk valley town of Schenectady, killing 60 and taking 27 captives.

In each of the four colonial wars between Britain and France, New Englanders called for the conquest of New France, usually through a naval expedition against Quebec, combined with an overland attack on Montreal. In King William's War (1689–97), Sir William Phips of Massachusetts forced Acadia to surrender in 1690 (although the French soon regained it) and then sailed up the St. Lawrence, where his force proved inadequate to take the heavily fortified city of Quebec. The overland attack on Montreal had already collapsed amid intercolonial bickering and an outbreak of smallpox. French attacks, with Indians providing most of the fighters, continued to ravage the frontier.

In 1704, during Queen Anne's War (1702–13), the French and Indians destroyed Deerfield, Massachusetts, in a winter attack and marched most of its people off to captivity in Canada. Hundreds of New Englanders from Deerfield and other towns spent months or even years as captives. One of them was Eunice Williams, young daughter of John Williams, the pastor of Deerfield. Refusing to return to New England when the town's captives were released, she remained in Canada, became a Catholic, and married an Indian. Another New England woman who refused to return was Esther Wheelwright, daughter of a prominent Maine family. Captured by the Abenakis, she was taken to New France, where she also refused repatriation, converted to Catholicism, became a nun (Esther Marie Joseph de L'Enfant Jésus), and finally emerged as mother superior of the Ursuline Order in Canada—surely an unlikely career for a Puritan girl!

As the war dragged on, New Englanders twice failed to take Port Royal in Acadia, but a combined British and colonial force finally succeeded in 1710, renaming the colony Nova Scotia. An effort to subdue Quebec the following year met with disaster when many of the British ships ran aground in a treacherous stretch of the St. Lawrence River.

Farther south, the imperial struggle was grimmer and even more tragic. The Franciscan missions of Florida were already in decline, but mission Indians still attracted Carolina slavers, who invaded Florida between 1702 and 1704 with a large force of Indian allies, wrecked the missions, dragged off 4,000 women and children as slaves, and drove 9,000 Indians from their homes, some of whom then joined their attackers and got firearms. The invaders failed to take the Spanish fortress of St. Augustine, but slaving raids spread devastation as far west as the lands of the Choctaws and far south along the Florida peninsula.

PORTRAIT OF ESTHER WHEELWRIGHT

Esther Wheelwright (1696–1780), an English Puritan who was captured by the French and Indians during Queen Anne's War, converted to Catholicism and became Sister Esther Marie Joseph de L'Enfant Jésus and eventually Mother Superior of the Ursuline nuns in New France.

SOUTH CAROLINA COLONISTS ENSLAVING AN INDIAN

The colony enslaved thousands of Indians from 1680 through 1715, a practice that was finally abandoned after the Yamasee War nearly destroyed the colony.

South Carolina's greed for Indian slaves and other abuses finally alienated the colony's strongest Indian allies, the Yamasees. Traders frequently abused Indian women, including some of high status, an offense almost unknown within Indian communities. In addition, faltering Atlantic markets during wartime compelled Indian hunters to bring in more deerskins for smaller returns, and many hunters fell deeply in debt, a process that could lead to enslavement. In 1707, to resolve disputes between traders and Indians, South Carolina created the office of Indian agent, which was held first by John Wright and then Thomas Nairne. They belonged to rival factions of Indian traders, and their controversies paralyzed the colony's gov-

ernment. In late 1714, Wright's bloc filed so many lawsuits against Nairne that for six months he could not leave Charleston to address Yamasee grievances. When the exasperated Indians threatened war, the government sent both Nairne and Wright to resolve the crisis in April 1715. Nairne brought a message of peace; Wright privately threatened war, which would most likely lead to enslavement. Taking no chances, the Yamasees killed both men and all the other traders who had just arrived to collect their debts. Throughout the Southeast, all other Indian nations trading with South Carolina, except the Chickasaws, followed the Yamasees' example, wiping out nearly all of the colony's experienced traders and launching a war

BRITISH WARS AGAINST FRANCE (AND USUALLY SPAIN), 1689–1763

European Name	American Name	Years	Peace
War of the League of Augsburg	King William's War	1689–1697	Ryswick
War of the Spanish Succession	Queen Anne's War	1702–1713	Utrecht
War of Jenkins' Ear, merging with		1739–1748	
War of the Austrian Succession	King George's War	1744–1748	Aix-la-Chapelle
Seven Years' War	French and Indian War	1754–1763*	Paris

*The French and Indian War began in America in 1754 and then merged with the Seven Years' War in Europe, which began in 1756.

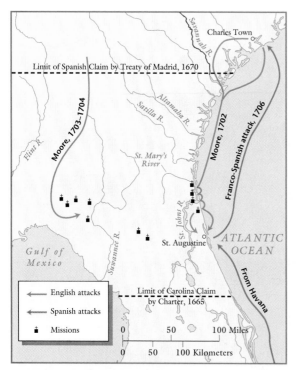

MAP 3.7 SOUTHEASTERN THEATER OF WAR, 1702–13
In this theater, the English and their Indian allies did most of the attacking, destroyed Spain's Florida missions, and enslaved thousands. Spain and France tried to attack Charleston, South Carolina, but their 1706 expedition failed after it was ravaged by disease.

that almost destroyed the colony before the Yamasees were thrust back and nearly exterminated. Some Yamasees and some escaped African slaves fled as refugees to Spanish Florida.

The wars of 1689–1716 halted the movement of British settlers onto new lands in New England and the Carolinas. Only four Maine towns survived the wars; by 1720, after half a century, South Carolina still had only 5,200 settlers (and 11,800 enslaved Africans and Indians). In Pennsylvania, Maryland, and Virginia—colonies that had not been deeply involved in the wars—the expansive thrust continued.

Conclusion

The variety and diversity of the colonies posed a huge challenge to the English government. After 1650, it found ways to regulate colonial trade, mostly for the mutual ben-

efit of both England and the colonies. The colonies, often beset by hostile Indians and internal discord, began to recognize that they needed protection that only England could provide. Once the Crown gave up its claims to absolute power, the two sides discovered much on which they could agree.

Political values in England and the colonies began to converge during the Glorious Revolution and its aftermath. Englishmen throughout the empire insisted that the right to property was sacred, that without it liberty could never be secure. They celebrated liberty under law, government by consent, and the toleration of all Protestants. They barred Catholics from succession to the throne and loaded them with severe disabilities of other kinds. In an empire dedicated to "liberty, property, and no popery," Catholics became big losers.

So did Indians and Africans. Racism directed against Indians mostly welled up from below, taking root among ordinary settlers who competed with Indians for many of the same resources, especially land, and then bore the brunt of Indian reprisals. Colonial elites tried, often ineffectually, to contain this popular rage that nearly tore apart both New England and Virginia in 1675–76. By contrast, racism directed against enslaved Africans was typically imposed from above and increasingly enforced by law. Ordinary settlers and Africans knew one another by name, made love, sometimes even married, stole hogs together, ran away together, and even fought together under Nathaniel Bacon's leadership. The men in the process of becoming great planters used their power in the legislature to criminalize all of these activities because they were terrified by the upheaval that ex-servants could create and hoped for greater stability from a labor force serving for life. They rewarded small planters and servants with white supremacy.

By the 18th century, the British colonists, despite or perhaps even because of their growing racism, had come to believe they were the freest people on earth. They attributed this fortune to their widespread ownership of land and to the English constitutional principles they had incorporated into their own governments. When George I became king in 1714, they proudly proclaimed their loyalty to the Hanoverian dynasty that guaranteed a Protestant succession to the British throne. In their minds, the British empire had become the world's last bastion of liberty.

SUGGESTED READINGS

The most comprehensive account of the Navigation Acts and England's instruments of enforcement is still **Charles M. Andrews, *The Colonial Period of American History,* vol. 4** (1938). **Ian K. Steele's *The English Atlantic, 1675–1740: An Exploration of Communication and Community*** (1986) is careful and original.

Daniel K. Richter's *The Ordeal of the Longhouse: The People of the Iroquois League in the Era of European Colonization* (1992); **Richard W. Cogley's *John Eliot's Mission to the Indians before King Philip's War*** (1999); **Jill Lepore's *The Name of War: King Philip's War and the Origins of American Identity*** (1998); and **Wilcomb Washburn, *The Governor and the Rebel: A History of Bacon's Rebellion in Virginia*** (1957) are all essential to understanding the crisis of the 1670s. For the transition to slavery after Bacon's Rebellion, see **Anthony S. Parent, Jr., *Foul Means: The Formation of a Slave Society in Virginia, 1660–1740*** (2003).

For the Dominion of New England and the Glorious Revolution in the colonies, see **Richard R. Johnson, *Adjustment to Empire: The New England Colonies, 1675–1715*** (1981); **John M. Murrin, "The Menacing Shadow of Louis XIV and the Rage of Jacob Leisler: The Constitutional Ordeal of Seventeenth-Century New York,"** in **Stephen L. Schechter and Richard B. Bernstein, eds., *New York and the Union: Contributions to the American Constitutional Experience*** (1990), pp. 29–71; and **Lois G. Carr and David W. Jordan, *Maryland's Revolution of Government, 1689–1692*** (1974). The best study of Salem witchcraft, which is also a superb introduction to the Indian wars in northern New England, is **Mary Beth Norton, *In the Devil's Snare: The Salem Witchcraft Crisis of 1692*** (2002).

For the French and Spanish colonies in these critical decades, see especially **Richard White, *The Middle Ground: Indians, Empires, and Republics in the Great Lakes Region, 1650–1815*** (1991); **Ramón Gutiérrez, *When Jesus Came, the Corn Mothers Went Away: Marriage, Sexuality, and Power in New Mexico, 1500–1846*** (1992), particularly on the Pueblo revolt; and **Daniel H. Usner, Jr., *Indians, Settlers, & Slaves in a Frontier Exchange Economy: The Lower Mississippi Valley before 1783*** (1992).

On the householder economy in English North America, see **Laurel Thatcher Ulrich's *Good Wives: Images and Reality in the Lives of Women in Northern New England*** (1982), and **Mary M. Schweitzer, *Custom and Contract: Household, Government, and the Economy in Colonial Pennsylvania*** (1987).

 AMERICAN JOURNEY ONLINE AND INFOTRAC COLLEGE EDITION

Visit the source collections at www.ajaccess.wadsworth.com and infotrac.thomsonlearning.com and use the Search function with the following key terms to explore documents, images, audio and video clips, articles, and commentary related to the material in this chapter.

Iroquois
Algonquians
Navigation Act
Metacom's War
(or King Philip's War)

Bacon's Rebellion
Glorious Revolution
Salem witch trials
Pueblo Revolt

GRADE AIDS

Visit the Liberty Equality Power Companion Web Site for resources specific to this textbook: http://history.wadsworth.com/murrin_LEP4e

The CD in the back of this book and the U.S. History Resource Center at http://history.wadsworth.com/u.s./ offer a variety of tools to help you succeed in this course, including access to quizzes; images; documents; interactive simulations, maps, and timelines; movie explorations; and a wealth of other sources.

Chapter 4

Provincial America and the Struggle for a Continent

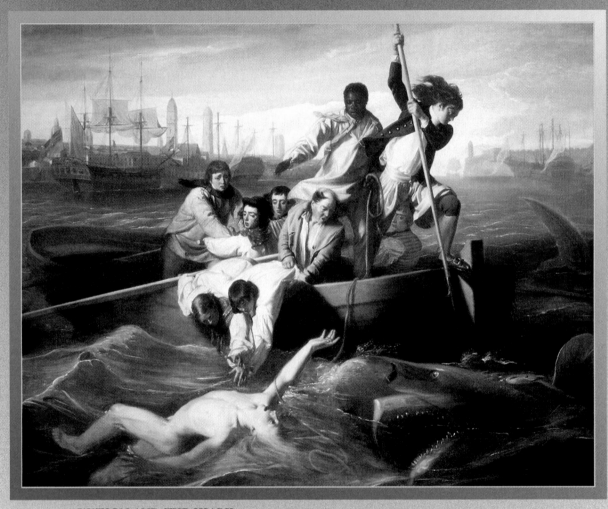

1963.6.1 (1904)/PA: Copley, John Singelton, "Watson and the Shark," Ferdinand Lammot Belin Fund
© 1998 Board of Trustees, National Gallery of Art, Washington, 1778, oil on canvas, 1.82 x 2.297
(71 3/4 x 90 1/2); framed: 2.413 x 2.642 x .101 (95 x 104 x 4).

WATSON AND THE SHARK
John Singleton Copley's 1778 painting, dramatically depicting a young man's rescue from shark attack, began the democratization of heroism. Note that a black man holds the traditional central and elevated place of honor in the painting, and that only one person on the rescue boat is a "gentleman." In this work, Copley announced that ordinary men can be heroes.

CHAPTER OUTLINE

The British colonists believed they were the freest people on earth. Yet during the 18th century they faced a dilemma peculiarly their own. To maintain the opportunity that settlers had come to expect, the colonies had to expand onto new lands. But provincial society also increasingly emulated the cultural values of Great Britain—its architecture, polite learning, evangelical religion, and politics. Relentless expansion made this emulation difficult because the two often worked at cross purposes: An anglicized province would become far more hierarchical than the colonies had so far been and might not even try to provide a rough equality of opportunity. The settlers tried to sustain both, an effort that brought brutal conflict with their neighbors—the Indians, the Spanish, and the French.

When the British again went to war against Spain and France after 1739, the settlers joined in the struggle and declared that liberty itself was at stake. Less fortunate people among them disagreed. Slaves in the southern colonies saw Spain, not Britain, as a beacon of liberty. In the eastern woodlands, most Indians identified France, not Britain, as the one ally genuinely committed to their survival and independence.

CHAPTER FOCUS

- ◆ Why was it difficult to sustain both continual expansion and the anglicization of the colonies in the 18th century?
- ◆ How were the colonists able to embrace both the enlightenment and evangelical religion at the same time?

♦ How could both the royal governors and the colonial assemblies grow stronger at the same time?

♦ What made the War for North America (1754–63) so much more decisive than the three earlier Anglo-French conflicts?

Expansion versus Anglicization

In the 18th century, as the British colonists sought to emulate their homeland, many of the institutions and material goods they had left behind in the 17th century began to reappear. After 1740, for example, imports of British goods grew spectacularly, even faster than population. The gentry dressed in the latest London fashions and embraced that city's standards of taste and elegance. Between 1720 and 1750, wealthy settlers built handsome mansions in the older portions of the colonies. Virginia planters erected "big houses," such as Mount Vernon, built by Lawrence Washington and bequeathed to his half-brother George. In Boston, on Beacon Hill, the merchant Thomas Hancock built a stylish residence that later passed to his nephew John. Newspapers and learned professions based on English models proliferated after 1700, and colonial seaports began to resemble Bristol and other provincial cities in England.

But the population of British North America doubled every 25 years. Each new generation required twice as many colleges, ministers, lawyers, physicians, craftsmen, printers, sailors, and unskilled laborers as the preceding generation. Without them, standards of "civility" would decline. None of these institutions could meet colonial needs unless it continued to grow. As the 18th century progressed, the colonies became the scene of a contest between the unrelenting pace of raw expansion and these newer, anglicizing tendencies.

Colonies that looked only to England, or even Europe, to satisfy their needs for skilled talent could no longer attract as many people as they needed. In 1700, for example, Oxford and Cambridge universities in England had managed to fill the colonies' needs for Anglican clergymen by sending over those graduates who were unable to find parishes at home. Most of them went to the southern colonies. By 1750, the colonial demand far exceeded what stagnant Oxford and Cambridge could supply, and the colonies were also importing Scottish and Irish clergymen. Before long, those sources also proved inadequate. By contrast, northern colonies trained their own ministers, lawyers, and doctors in their own colleges, as well as their own printers, shipwrights, and other skilled craftsmen. Although still colonies, they were becoming Amer-

C H R O N O L O G Y	
1690	Massachusetts invents fiat money
1704	*Boston News-Letter* founded
1712	Slaves revolt in New York City
1716	Spanish begin to settle Texas
1718	Beginning of Scots-Irish emigration to North America
1721	Boylston introduces smallpox inoculation in Boston
1730	300 slaves revolt in Virginia, and 29 are hanged
1732	Georgia charter granted by Parliament
1733	Molasses Act passed
1734	Edwards launches massive religious revival in the Connecticut valley
1735	Zenger acquitted of seditious libel in New York
1738	Spanish found Mose in Florida
1739	Slaves revolt in Stono, South Carolina
1739–41	Whitefield launches Great Awakening
1741	New York slave conspiracy trials lead to 35 executions
1745	New England volunteers take Louisbourg
1747	Ohio Company of Virginia founded • Anti-impressment rioters in Boston resist Royal Navy
1750	Massachusetts converts from paper money to silver
1754	Washington attacks French patrol near the forks of the Ohio River • Albany Congress proposes plan for colonial union
1755	Braddock suffers disaster near Fort Duquesne • British expel Acadians from Nova Scotia
1756–57	Loudoun antagonizes the colonies as commander-in-chief
1756	French take Oswego
1757	French take Fort William Henry • Pitt becomes Britain's war minister
1758	British take Fort Duquesne • British take Fortress Louisbourg and Fort Frontenac • French repel British attack at Ticonderoga
1759	British take Ticonderoga and Crown Point • Wolfe dies taking Quebec; Montcalm also killed
1760	Montreal falls; Canada surrenders to the British
1760–61	Cherokee War devastates South Carolina backcountry
1762	Spain enters war, loses Havana and Manila
1763	Peace of Paris ends Seven Years' War

ica's first modernizing societies. They learned to do for themselves what Britain had to do for the southern colonies.

Much of this change occurred during prolonged periods of warfare. War interrupted expansion, which then resumed at an even more frantic pace with the return of

peace. By midcentury, the wars were becoming a titanic struggle for control of the North American continent. Gradually, Indians realized that they would be the ultimate victims of British victory. Constant expansion for British settlers meant unending retreat for them.

Threats to Householder Autonomy

As population rose, some families acquired more prestige than others. Although the status of "gentleman" was less rigid in the colonies than in Britain, it usually implied a man who performed no manual labor, and such men began to dominate public life. Before 1700, ordinary farmers and small planters had often sat in colonial assemblies. In the 18th century, the assemblies grew much more slowly than the overall population. In the five colonies from New York to Maryland, they remained almost unchanged in size despite enormous population growth. The men who took part in public life above the local level came, more and more, from a higher social status. They had greater wealth, a more impressive lineage, and a better education than ordinary farmers or craftsmen. Unlike their counterparts in England, however, few colonial gentlemen enjoyed a patron–client relationship with the voters. In England, one or two families dominated each of the "pocket boroughs" that elected most members of Parliament. In the colonies, most voters remained independent.

By midcentury, despite the high value that colonists placed on householder autonomy, patterns of dependency were beginning to emerge. In tidewater Virginia by 1760, about 80 percent of the land was entailed. Younger sons had to look west for an inheritance. In one Maryland county, 27 percent of the householders were tenants who worked small tracts of land without slaves, or were men who owned a slave or two but had no claim to land. Such families could not satisfy the ambitions of all their children. In Pennsylvania's Chester County, a new class of married farm laborers arose. Their employers, without granting them title or lease, would let them use a small patch of land on which they could build a cottage and raise some food. Called "inmates" in Chester County records (or "cottagers" in England), such people made up 25 percent of the county population. Tenants on New York manors had to accept higher rents and shorter leases after 1750. In Chebacco Parish in Ipswich, Massachusetts, half of the farmers had land enough for only some of their sons by 1760.

Families that could not provide for all of their children reverted to English social norms. A father favored his sons over his daughters, unless he could marry a daughter to a wealthy suitor. In Connecticut, from the 1750s to the 1770s, about 75 percent of eligible sons inherited some

land, but for daughters the rate fell from 44 to 34 percent. When a father could not support all his sons, he favored the eldest over the younger sons. The younger sons, in turn, took up a trade or headed for the frontier. To increase their resources, many New England farmers added a craft or two to the household. The 300 families of Haverhill, Massachusetts, supported 44 workshops and 19 mills by 1767. In Northampton, more than one-third of all the farming families also practiced a craft. Families in the town of Lynn began making shoes in quantity, many for export. Most families added a craft in order to sustain household autonomy. The goal of independence continued to exercise great power, but it was under siege. The fear of imperiled autonomy energized the whole westward movement (see chapter 7).

Anglicizing the Role of Women

The changing role of women provides a dramatic example of the anglicizing tendencies of the 18th century. When they married, most women received a dowry from their father, usually in cash or goods, not land. Under the common law doctrine of coverture, married women could not make a contract. The legal personality of the husband "covered" the wife, and he made all legally binding decisions. If he died first, his widow was entitled to dower rights, usually one-third of the estate, which passed, after her death, to the couple's surviving children.

Women in many, perhaps most, households had to work harder to maintain the family status—at the spinning wheel, for example. New England women did virtually all of the region's weaving, a male occupation in other colonies. In a sense, women were becoming more English, thus reversing some earlier trends. Until 1700, many Chesapeake widows inherited all of their husbands' property and administered their own estates. After 1700, such arrangements were rare. In the Hudson valley, Dutch law had been much more generous than English common law in bestowing property rights on women, but during the 18th century, English law gradually prevailed. In New England, too, as Puritan intensity waned, women suffered losses. Before 1700, courts had routinely punished men for sexual offenses, such as fornication, and many men had pleaded guilty and accepted their sentence. After 1700, almost no man would plead guilty to a sexual offense, except perhaps that of making love to his wife before their wedding day. However, to avoid a small fine, some husbands humiliated their wives by denying that charge, even if their wives had already pleaded guilty after giving birth to a child that had obviously been conceived before marriage. Courts rarely convicted men of sex offenses, not even serious crimes such as rape. The European double standard of

sexual behavior, which punished women for their indiscretions while tolerating male infractions, had been in some jeopardy under the Puritan regime. It now revived.

🌐 Expansion, Immigration, and Regional Differentiation

The end of the wars encouraged renewed expansion. After 1715, the settled portions of North America enjoyed their longest era of peace since the arrival of Europeans. The wars had emptied the borderlands of most of their inhabitants. Until midcentury, people poured into these areas without provoking the strong Indian nations of the interior. As the colonies expanded, they fitted, more or less snugly, into distinct regions, although only New Englanders had acquired a self-conscious sense of regional identity before independence.

Emergence of the Old South

Renewed immigration, free and unfree, drove much of the postwar expansion. After 1730, the flow became enormous. In that year, about 630,000 settlers and slaves lived in the mainland colonies. By 1775, another 248,000 Africans and 284,000 Europeans had landed, including 50,000 British convicts, shipped mostly to Maryland and Virginia, where they served long indentures. During this period, the African slave trade to North America reached its peak. Most of the 210,000 voluntary immigrants settled in the middle or southern colonies. Free migration decisively outweighed the influx of slaves only after 1763.

Almost 90 percent of the slaves went to the southern colonies. At least 84,000 slaves went to Charleston, 70,000 to Virginia, and 25,000 to Maryland. One-eighth of the slaves went to northern colonies. New England had 15,000 blacks by 1770, New York had 19,000, and New Jersey, Pennsylvania, and Delaware had a combined total of 16,000. About 80 percent of the slaves arrived from Africa on overcrowded, stinking, British-owned vessels. Most of the rest came, a few at a time, from the West Indies on smaller New England ships.

This massive influx of slaves created the Old South, a society consisting of wealthy slaveholding planters, a much larger class of small planters, and thousands of slaves. By 1720, slaves made up 70 percent of South Carolina's population. By 1740, they made up 40 percent of Virginia's and 30 percent of Maryland's. Slaves performed most of the manual labor in the southern colonies.

Their arrival transformed the social structure of the southern colonies. In 1700, most members of Virginia's House of Burgesses were small planters who raised tobacco with a few indentured servants and perhaps a slave or two. After 1730, the typical burgess was a great planter who owned at least 20 slaves. And by 1750, the rice planters of South Carolina were richer than any other group in British North America. Tobacco and rice planters had few contacts with each other, except in North Carolina, where they seldom got along well. They did not yet think of themselves as southerners.

The life of slaves in the upper South (Maryland, Virginia, and the Albemarle region of North Carolina) differed considerably from the life of slaves in the lower South (from Cape Fear in North Carolina through South Carolina and

CONTRACT FOR THE CONVICT TRADE

The convict trade, which provided long-term servants for American colonists, became quite well organized in the 18th century.

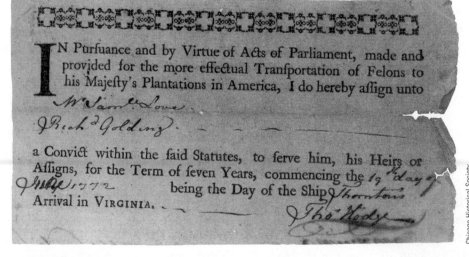

Chicago Historical Society.

After John Barbot, from Churchill's Voyages.

THE GOLD COAST OF AFRICA AT THE HEIGHT OF THE SLAVE TRADE
This 18th-century view of the Gold Coast shows five European slaving posts, including "Mina" or Elmina, the Portuguese fortress built in 1481 and captured by the Dutch in the 17th century.

eventually Georgia). The Chesapeake tobacco planters organized their slaves into gangs, supervised them closely, and kept them in the fields all day, weather permitting. To make their plantations more self-sufficient, they also trained perhaps 10 percent of their slaves as blacksmiths, carpenters, coopers, or other skilled artisans. The planters, who saw themselves as benevolent paternalists, encouraged family life among their workers, who by the 1720s were beginning to achieve a rate of reproduction that almost equaled that of the settlers. Slaveholders even explained brutal whippings as fatherly efforts to correct the behavior of members of their household.

Paternalism soon extended to religion. In the 1720s, for the first time on any significant scale, many Virginia planters began to urge their slaves to convert to Christianity. At first, only adults who had a good command of the catechism, which they had to learn orally because they were not allowed to become literate, were accepted into the church, but by the 1730s, growing numbers of infants were also baptized. These efforts continued to expand despite a massive slave uprising. A rumor spread that the British government had promised emancipation to any slave who converted but that the colony was suppressing the news. On a Sunday in September 1730, about 300 slaves, mostly from Norfolk and Princess Anne counties, tried to escape through the Great Dismal Swamp. The planters hired Indians to track them, crushed the rebels, and hanged 29 of them. Yet the conversion effort continued to gain momentum mostly, it seems, because planters

hoped that Christian slaves would be more docile and dutiful.

South Carolina planters began with similar paternalistic inclinations, but the rice swamps and mosquitoes defeated them. "Carolina is in the spring a paradise, in the summer a hell, and in the autumn a hospital," claimed one visitor. Whites who supervised slave gangs in the rice fields quickly caught malaria. Although malaria was seldom fatal, it left its victims vulnerable to other diseases that often killed them. Many rice planters relocated their big houses to higher ground, at a safe distance from their rice fields. With only a few exceptions, they showed no inclination to Christianize their laborers.

Africans fared much better than whites in the marshy rice fields. (Modern medicine has shown that many Africans possess a "sickle cell" in the blood that grants them protection against malaria but can also expose their children to a deadly form of inherited anemia.) As the ability of Africans to resist malaria became evident, Carolina planters seldom ventured into the rice fields and became less paternalistic than their Virginia counterparts except toward their household servants. After midcentury, many of them chose to spend their summers in Charleston or else found summer homes on high ground in the interior. Others vacationed in Newport, Rhode Island.

This situation altered work patterns. To produce a crop of rice, planters devised the task system, in which the slaves had to complete certain chores each day, after which their time was their own. Slaves used their free time to raise

crops, hunt, or fish, activities that enabled them to create a largely invisible economy of their own. The South Carolina planters relied on a large class of white artisans in Charleston for local manufacturing such as blacksmithing, coopering, and carpentry.

Thus, while many Chesapeake slaves were acquiring the skills of artisans, Carolina slaves were heading in the other direction. Before rice became the colony's staple, they had performed a wide variety of tasks. But the huge profits from rice now condemned nearly all of them to monotonous, unpleasant labor in the marshes, even though they were freed from the direct oversight of their masters. Rice culture also left Africans with low rates of reproduction. Yet because the task system gave them more control over their own lives, slaves preferred it to gang labor.

This freedom meant slower assimilation into the British world. African words and customs survived longer in South Carolina than in the Chesapeake colonies. Newly imported slaves spoke Gullah, originally a pidgin language (that is, a simple second language for everyone who spoke it). Gullah began with a few phrases common to many West African languages, gradually added English words, and became the natural language of subsequent generations. Modern black English, which developed from Gullah, was born in the Carolina rice fields.

The South Carolina slave population failed to grow by natural increase until perhaps the 1770s, a half-century later than in the tobacco colonies. Even South Carolina planters had difficulty replacing themselves before 1760. But by the Revolution, the American South was becoming the world's only self-sustaining slave society. Nowhere else could staple colonies reproduce their enslaved labor force without continuous imports from Africa.

Everywhere that slavery took hold, the system required a great deal of brute force to maintain it. Slaves convicted of arson were often burned at the stake, an unthinkable punishment to inflict on a white person. Whippings were frequent, and the master or overseer determined the number of stripes. In South Carolina, one overseer killed five slaves in two or three years before 1712. When one slave fell asleep and lost a parcel of rice in the

A TOBACCO PLANTATION

This illustration shows the owner and perhaps his overseer or factor supervising the completion of wooden hogsheads to hold the year's tobacco crop. The white men are dressed as gentlemen. The African laborers wear hardly any clothing at all. Note the ships off in the distance.

river, he chained him, whipped him twice a day, refused to give him food, and confined him at night in a "hellish Machine contrived by him into the Shape of a Coffin where [he] could not stir." The victim finally obtained a knife from one of his children and committed suicide.

If extreme cruelty of this sort was rare, random acts of violence were common and, from a slave's perspective, unpredictable. In Virginia, William Byrd II was one of the most refined settlers in the colony and owned its largest library. His diary reveals that when he and his wife, Lucy, disagreed, the slaves could suffer. "My wife and I had a terrible quarrel about whipping Eugene while Mr. Mumford was there but she had a mind to show her authority before company but I would not suffer it, which she took very ill." On that occasion, Eugene was spared, but slaves were not always so lucky. On another occasion, "My wife caused Prue to be whipped violently notwithstanding I desired not, which provoked me to have Anaka whipped likewise who had deserved it much more, on which my wife flew into such a passion she hoped she would be revenged of me." This time both slaves were whipped, apparently for minor infractions. The Byrds also quarreled about whether Lucy could beat Jenny with the fire tongs. House servants must have dreaded the days that Byrd spent in Williamsburg, leaving Lucy in charge of the plantation.

The southern colonies prospered in the 18th century by exchanging their staple crops for British imports. By midcentury, much of this trade had been taken over by Scots. Glasgow became the leading tobacco port of the Atlantic. Although tobacco profits remained precarious before 1730, they improved in later decades, partly because Virginia guaranteed a high-quality leaf by passing an inspection law in 1730 (Maryland followed suit in 1747), and partly because a tobacco contract between Britain and France brought lucrative revenues to both governments and opened up a vast continental market for Chesapeake planters. By 1775, more than 90 percent of their tobacco was reexported to Europe from Britain.

Other exports and new crafts also contributed to rising prosperity. South Carolina continued to export provisions to the sugar islands and deerskins to Britain. Indigo, used as a dye by the British textile industry, received a cash bounty from Parliament and emerged at midcentury as a second staple crop, pioneered by a woman planter, Eliza Lucas Pinckney. North Carolina, where the population increased fivefold between 1720 and 1760 and more than doubled again by 1775, sold naval stores (pitch, resin, turpentine) to British shipbuilders. Many Chesapeake planters turned to wheat as a second cash crop. It required mills to grind it into flour, barrels in which to pack it, and ships to carry it away. It did for the Chesapeake what tobacco had failed to do: It created cities. Norfolk and Baltimore had nearly 10,000 people by 1775, and smaller cities, such as Alexandria and Georgetown, were also thriving. Shipbuilding, closely tied to the export of wheat, became an important Chesapeake industry.

The Mid-Atlantic Colonies: The "Best Poor Man's Country"

The mid-Atlantic colonies had been pluralistic societies from the start. Immigration added to this ethnic and religious complexity after 1700. The region had the most prosperous family farms in America and, by 1760, the two largest cities, Philadelphia and New York. Pennsylvania outpaced New York in the competition for immigrants. Mostly in the 1680s and 1690s, New York governors had granted their political supporters enormous manorial estates that dominated the Hudson valley and discouraged immigration. As late as 1750, the small colony of New Jersey had as many settlers as New York but fewer slaves. Pennsylvania's growth exploded, driven by both natural increase and a huge surge of immigration. The 12th colony to be founded out of the original 13, Pennsylvania was the second most populous by 1770, surpassed only by Virginia.

After 1720, Ireland and Germany replaced England as the source of most voluntary immigrants. About 70 percent of Ireland's emigrants came from Ulster. They were Presbyterians whose forebears had come to Ireland from Scotland in the 17th century. (Historians now call them the Scots-Irish, a term that was seldom used at the time.) Most of them left for America to avoid an increase in rents and to enjoy greater trading privileges than the British Parliament allowed Ireland. The first Ulsterites sailed for New England in 1718. They expected a friendly reception from fellow Calvinists, but the Yankees treated them with suspicion. Some of them stayed and introduced linen

JOHN HANCOCK'S BOSTON MANSION

Located on Beacon Hill, the mansion was an excellent example of the elegant houses that wealthy Americans aspired to own.

North Wind Picture Archives.

manufacturing in New Hampshire, but after 1718, most immigrants from Ulster headed for the Delaware valley. About 30 percent of Irish immigrants came from southern Ireland. Most of these were Catholics, but perhaps one-quarter were Anglicans. They too headed for the mid-Atlantic colonies. Altogether, some 80,000 Irish reached the Delaware valley before 1776.

Perhaps 70,000 of the free immigrants were Germans. Most of them arrived as families, often as "redemptioners," a new form of indentured service that was attractive to married couples because it allowed them to find and bind themselves to their own masters. Families could stay together. After redemptioners completed their service, most of them streamed into the interior of Pennsylvania, where Germans outnumbered the original English and Welsh settlers by 1750. In an outburst that he later regretted, Benjamin Franklin complained that German "boors" were taking over the colony. Other Germans moved to the southern backcountry with the Irish. The mid-Atlantic colonies, already North America's breadbasket, were the favored destination of free immigrants because the expanding economies of the region offered many opportunities.

These colonies grew excellent wheat and built their own ships to carry it abroad. At first, New York flour outsold Pennsylvania's, but Pennsylvania gained the edge in the 1720s after it instituted a new system of public inspection and quality control. When Europe's population started to surge after 1740, the middle colonies began to ship flour across the Atlantic. Before 1760, both Philadelphia and New York City overtook Boston's stagnant population of 15,000. Philadelphia, with 32,000 people, was the largest city in British North America by 1775.

The Backcountry

Many of the Scots-Irish, together with some of the Germans, pushed west into the mountains and up the river valleys into the interior parts of Virginia and the Carolinas. In South Carolina, about 100 miles of pine barrens stood between these backcountry settlements and the rice plantations along the coast. Most of the English-speaking colonists were immigrants from Ulster, northern England, or lowland Scotland who brought their folkways with them and soon gave the region its own distinctive culture. Although most of them farmed, many turned to hunting or raising cattle. Unlike the coastal settlements, the backcountry showed few signs of anglicizing. It had no newspapers, few clergymen or other professionals, and little elegance. Some parts, especially in South Carolina, had almost no government. A visiting Anglican clergyman bemoaned "the abandon'd Morals and profligate Principles" of the settlers. In 1768, he preached to a gathering who had never before heard a minister, or even the Lord's Prayer. "After the Service," he wrote, "they went out to Revell[in]g, Drinking, Singing, Dancing and Whoring, and most . . . were drunk before I quitted the Spott." Refined easterners found the backcountry more than a little frightening.

Backcountry settlers were clannish and violent. They drank heavily and hated Indians. After 1750, the situation became quite tense in Pennsylvania, where the Quaker legislature insisted on handling differences with the Indians through peaceful negotiation, even though few Quakers lived on the frontier. (The Moravian Brethren, a pacifist German sect, maintained Indian missions in Pennsylvania and North Carolina but had little impact on other colonists.) Once fighting broke out against the Indians, most backcountry residents demanded their extermination. Virginia and South Carolina faced the same problem.

MORAVIAN BETHLEM

The Moravian Brethren made Bethlehem, Pennsylvania, their main settlement in the northern colonies. They erected some of the largest structures in the mainland colonies. This engraving is from a painting by Thomas Pownall, royal governor of New Jersey and Massachusetts in the 1750s.

New England: A Faltering Economy and Paper Money

New England was a land of farmers, fishermen, lumberjacks, shipwrights, and merchants and still considered itself more pious than the rest of the British Empire, but the region faced serious new problems. Few immigrants, either slave or free, went there. In fact, since about 1660, more people had been leaving the region, mostly for New York and New Jersey, than had been arriving.

New England's relative isolation in the 17th century began to have negative social and economic effects after 1700. Life expectancy declined as diseases from Europe, especially smallpox and diphtheria, invaded the region by way of Atlantic commerce. The first settlers had left these diseases behind in Europe, but lack of exposure in childhood made later generations vulnerable. When smallpox threatened to devastate Boston in 1721, Zabdiel Boylston, a self-taught doctor, began inoculating people with the disease on the theory that healthy people would survive the injection and become immune. Although the city's leading physicians opposed the experiment as too risky, it worked and soon became a regular feature of public health in many colonies. Even so, a diphtheria epidemic in the 1730s and high military losses after 1740 reduced population growth. New England's rate of growth fell behind that of other regions.

After the earlier wars ended in 1713, New England's economy began to weaken. The region had prospered in the 17th century, mostly by exporting cod, grain, and barrel staves to the West Indies. After 1700, however, Yankees had trouble feeding themselves, much less others. A blight called the "wheat blast" first appeared in the 1660s and slowly spread until cultivation of wheat nearly ceased. Because Yankees preferred wheat bread to cornbread, they had to import flour from New York and Pennsylvania and, eventually, wheat from the Chesapeake colonies. Poverty became a huge social problem in Boston, where by the 1740s about one-third of all adult women were widows, mostly poor. Poor relief became a major public expense.

After grain exports declined, the once-profitable West Indian trade barely broke even. Yet its volume remained large, especially when enterprising Yankees opened up new markets in the lucrative French sugar islands. Within the West Indian market, competition from New York and Philadelphia grew almost too severe for New Englanders to meet, because those cities had flour to export and shorter distances over which to ship it. Mostly, the Yankees shipped fish and forest products to the islands in exchange for molasses, which they used as a sweetener (cheaper than sugar) or distilled into rum. Rum joined cod and lumber as a major export. British West Indian planters, alarmed

by the flood of cheap French molasses, urged Parliament to stamp out New England's trade with the French West Indies. Parliament passed the Molasses Act of 1733, which placed a prohibitive duty of six pence per gallon on all foreign molasses. Strictly enforced, the act would have strangled New England trade; instead, it gave rise to bribery and smuggling, and the molasses continued to flow.

Shipbuilding gave New England most of its leverage in the Atlantic economy. Yankees made more ships than all of the other colonies combined, although the Chesapeake colonies and the Delaware valley were closing the gap by the 1760s. New England ships earned enough from freight in most years to offset losses elsewhere, but Boston merchants often had to scramble to pay for their imports. New England ran unfavorable balances with nearly every trading partner, especially England. Yankees imported many British products but produced little that anybody in Britain wanted to buy. Whale oil, used in lamps, was an exception. A prosperous whaling industry emerged on the island of Nantucket, where surviving Indians taught settlers how to use harpoons and actively participated in the trade until they were decimated by disease. But the grain trade with the mid-Atlantic and Chesapeake colonies was not profitable. Settlers there eagerly bought rum and a few slaves from Yankee vessels that stopped on their way back from the West Indies. Newport even became deeply involved in slave trading along the African coast. Although that traffic never supplied a large percentage of North America's slaves, it contributed to the city's growth.

New England's experience with paper money illustrates these economic difficulties. In response to a military emergency in 1690, Massachusetts invented fiat money—that is, paper money backed, not by silver or gold, but only by the government's promise to accept it in payment of taxes. This system worked well enough until serious depreciation set in after the Treaty of Utrecht. The return of peace in 1713 meant that nearly all paper money would be retired within a few years through taxes already pledged for that purpose. To sustain its paper currency, the Massachusetts legislature created four land banks between 1714 and 1728. Settlers could borrow paper money using their land as security and pay off the debt over 10 years at 5 percent interest. But when the value of New England's currency declined steadily in relation to the British pound, most Boston merchants turned against paper money. They sold many of their wares on credit only to be repaid in depreciated paper. Farmers, who had originally been suspicious of land banks, became strong advocates after they discovered that they could benefit as debtors. When Britain forbade the governor to consent to any new public land banks, the countryside organized a private land bank that issued huge amounts of paper in 1741, provoking a

major crisis. Parliament intervened to crush the bank. But as the bank's supporters pointed out, land banks worked quite well in colonies outside New England, such as Pennsylvania, where Franklin became an eloquent supporter.

The declining value of money touched off a fierce debate that raged from 1714 until 1750. Creditors attacked paper money as fraudulent: Only gold and silver, they claimed, had real value. Defenders retorted that, in most other colonies, paper was holding its value. The problem, they insisted, lay with the New England economy, which could not generate enough exports to pay for the region's imports. The elimination of paper, they warned, would only deepen New England's problems. War disrupted shipping in the 1740s, and military expenditures sent New England currency to a new low. Then, in 1748, Parliament agreed to reimburse Massachusetts for these expenses at the 1745 exchange rate. Governor William Shirley and House Speaker Thomas Hutchinson, an outspoken opponent of paper money, barely persuaded the legislature to use the grant to retire all paper and convert to silver money. That decision was a drastic example of anglicization. Although fiat money was the colony's own invention, Massachusetts repudiated its own offspring in 1750 in favor of orthodox methods of British public finance. As Hutchinson's critics had warned, however, silver gravitated to Boston and back to London to pay for imports. New England's economy entered a deep depression in the early 1750s, from which it did not revive until after 1755, when the wars resumed.

☛ Anglicizing Provincial America

Forms of production made these regions diverse. What made them more alike was what they retained or acquired from Britain, not what they found in America. Although each region exported its own distinctive products, patterns of consumption became quite similar throughout the colonies. In the mid-1740s, the mainland colonies and the West Indies consumed almost identical amounts of British imports. Just 10 years later, the mainland provinces had forged ahead by a margin of two to one. Their ability to consume ever larger quantities of British goods was making the mainland colonies more valuable to the empire than the sugar islands.

In the 18th century, printing and newspapers, the learned professions, and the intellectual movement known as the Enlightenment all made their mark on British North America. The new colony of Georgia was in many ways a by-product of the English Enlightenment. A powerful transatlantic religious revival, the Great Awakening, swept across Britain and the colonies in the 1730s and 1740s. And colonial political systems tried to recast themselves in the image of Britain's mixed and balanced constitution.

The World of Print

Few 17th-century American settlers owned books, and except in New England, even fewer engaged in the intellectual debates of the day. For most of the century, only Massachusetts had printing presses, first in Cambridge to serve Harvard College, the clergy, and the government, and then in Boston beginning in 1674. For the next century, Boston remained the printing capital of North America. In the 1680s, William Bradford became Philadelphia's first printer, but after a Quaker controversy drove him from the colony, he moved to New York. By 1740, Boston had eight printers; New York and Philadelphia each had two. No other community had more than one.

WOODEN PRESS IN A COLONIAL PRINT SHOP
Modern drawing by Edwin Tunis.

The American Power of an English Education

The son of Stephen DeLancey, a Huguenot refugee who fled the persecution of Louis XIV and became a prominent New York City merchant in the 1690s, James DeLancey was born in 1703 and was sent by his parents to England for his education. At Cambridge University, his tutor was Thomas Herring, who rose in the hierarchy of the Church of England until he became Archbishop of Canterbury. After leaving Cambridge, DeLancey studied law at Lincoln's Inn and established contacts with several prominent London merchants. His English friends gave him a degree of influence with the British government that probably no other American-born public official could match. DeLancey's life became a study in the use of power.

Back in New York, James completed the anglicization of his family by marrying the wealthy heiress of Caleb Heathcote, whose brother had been one of the founders of the Bank of England. At age 26, he was appointed to the New York Council. In 1732, a new governor, William Cosby, insisted that his predecessor, Lieutenant Governor Rip Van Dam, turn over half of his salary from the time of Cosby's appointment until his arrival in New York. When Van Dam refused, Cosby sued him in equity before the New York Supreme Court to avoid a jury trial. After Chief Justice Lewis Morris sided with Van Dam, Cosby dismissed him, appointed DeLancey chief justice, and won a favorable judgment. Morris retaliated by establishing *The New York Weekly Journal* as an opposition newspaper with John Peter Zenger as printer. Using materials supplied by two lawyers, James Alexander and William Smith, Jr., the *Journal* attacked the governor and his inner circle as corrupt.

Chief Justice DeLancey twice asked a grand jury to indict Zenger for "seditious libel," the crime of criticizing the government, but it refused. The attorney general then filed an "information" against Zenger to bring him to trial. DeLancey set his bail at £400, a gigantic sum, and then disbarred Alexander and Smith, Zenger's attorneys, when they objected to two of the judges. The Morrisites brought Andrew Hamilton, Philadelphia's most prominent lawyer and the speaker of the Pennsylvania assembly, to New York to defend Zenger. He persuaded the jury to decide the general issue, guilty or not guilty, instead of a narrow verdict on whether Zenger had published the objectionable issues, which would have allowed the judges to determine whether they were seditious. Zenger was acquitted in August 1735.

Despite this setback, DeLancey's power continued to grow. His supporters dominated the assembly and made life so miserable for Governor George Clinton in the 1740s that he resolved to sail for Britain and make his case to London in person. Instead, he learned that DeLancey's friends had won him a commission as lieutenant governor. If Clinton left the colony, DeLancey would take over. And indeed, after Clinton's successor as governor committed suicide shortly after arriving in New York, Lieutenant Governor DeLancey finally took charge in 1753. He summoned the Albany Congress that met a year later and became a major force in organizing New York's war effort against New France. He served as acting governor from 1753–55 and again from 1757–60. He died in office.

A BRIEF

NARRATIVE

OF THE

CASE *and* TRYAL *of* JOHN PETER ZENGER, *Printer of the* NEW-YORK *Weekly Journal.*

A BRIEF NARRATIVE OF THE CASE AND TRYAL OF JOHN PETER ZENGER (NY, 1736)

James DeLancey presided over this famous trial and did everything in his power to secure Zenger's conviction for seditious libel, but the jury acquitted him. The narrative was written by James Alexander, one of Zenger's lawyers.

Not surprisingly, Boston also led the way in newspaper publishing. John Campbell, the city's postmaster, established the *Boston News-Letter* in 1704, only a few years after provincial newspapers had begun to appear in England. By the early 1720s, two more papers had opened in Boston, and Philadelphia and New York City had each acquired one. The *South Carolina Gazette* was founded in Charleston in 1732 and the *Virginia Gazette* at Williamsburg in 1736. By then, Boston had added several more. Benjamin Franklin took charge of the *Pennsylvania Gazette* in 1729, and John Peter Zenger launched the controversial *New York Weekly Journal* in 1733 and won a major victory for freedom of the press when a jury acquitted him of "seditious libel," the crime of criticizing government officials.

These papers were weeklies that devoted nearly all of their space to European affairs. Before midcentury, they rarely reported local news because they assumed their readers already knew it. At first, they merely reprinted items from the *London Gazette.* Beginning in the 1720s, however, the *New England Courant,* under James Franklin, also began to reprint Richard Steele's essays from the *Spectator,* Joseph Addison's pieces from the *Tatler,* and the angry, polemical writings, mostly aimed at religious bigotry and political and financial corruption, of "Cato," a pen name used jointly by John Trenchard and Thomas Gordon. *Cato's Letters,* which Gordon later published in four volumes, became immensely popular among colonial printers and readers. In short, newspapers began to spread the English Enlightenment throughout the North American colonies.

Benjamin Franklin personified the Enlightenment values that the newspapers were spreading. As a boy, although raised in Puritan Boston, he skipped church on Sundays to read Addison and Steele and to perfect his prose style. As a young printer with the *New England Courant* in the 1720s, he helped publish the writings of John Checkley, an Anglican whom the courts twice prosecuted in a vain attempt to silence him. Franklin joined the Church of England after moving to Philadelphia. After 1729, he made his *Pennsylvania Gazette* the best-edited paper in America. It reached 2,000 subscribers, four times the circulation of a Boston weekly.

Franklin was always looking for ways to improve society. In 1727, he and some friends founded the Junto, a debating society that met Friday evenings to discuss literary and philosophical questions. It later evolved into the American Philosophical Society, which still thrives near Independence Hall. Franklin was a founder of North America's first Masonic lodge in 1730, the Library Company of Philadelphia a year later, the Union Fire Company in 1736, the Philadelphia Hospital in 1751, and an academy that became the College of Philadelphia (now the University of Pennsylvania) in the 1750s. Besides his famous electrical experiments, he invented the Franklin stove (much more efficient than a fireplace) and the lightning rod. By the 1760s, he had become the most celebrated North American in the world and was thinking of retiring to England.

The Enlightenment in America

The English Enlightenment, which rejected a vengeful God and exalted man's capacity for knowledge and social improvement, grew out of the rational and benevolent piety favored by Low Church (latitudinarian) Anglicans in Restoration England. These Anglicans disliked rigid doctrine, scoffed at conversion experiences, attacked superstition, and rejected all "fanaticism," whether that of High Church Laudians, who had brought on England's great crisis of 1640–42, or that of the Puritans, who had dismantled the monarchy. High Church men, a small group after 1689, stood for orthodoxy, ritual, and liturgy.

SEA CAPTAINS CAROUSING IN SURINAM

This painting by John Greenwood (ca. 1750) suggests the condescension that refined people could bestow on those who did the basic work of the empire. Although the captains are well dressed, they all seem determined to get as drunk as possible when not at sea.

Enlightened writers greeted Sir Isaac Newton's laws of motion as one of the greatest intellectual achievements of all time, joined the philosopher John Locke in looking for ways to improve society, and began to suspect that moderns had surpassed the ancients in learning and wisdom. John Tillotson, archbishop of Canterbury until his death in 1694, embodied this "polite and Catholick [that is, universal] spirit." He preached morality rather than dogma and had a way of defending the doctrine of eternal damnation that left his listeners wondering how a merciful God could possibly have ordained such a cruel punishment.

Enlightened ideas won an elite constituency in the mainland colonies even before newspapers began publishing and circulating these new views. Tillotson had a huge impact on America. His sermons appeared in numerous southern libraries and made a deep impression at Harvard College, beginning with two young tutors, William Brattle and John Leverett, Jr. After Leverett replaced Samuel Willard as college president in 1708, Tillotson's ideas became entrenched in the curriculum. For the rest of the century, most Harvard-trained ministers, although still claiming to be Calvinists, embraced Tillotson's latitudinarian piety. They stressed the similarities, not the differences, between Congregationalists and Anglicans and favored broad religious toleration. After 1800, most Harvard-educated ministers became Unitarians who no longer believed in hell or the divinity of Jesus.

In 1701, largely in reaction against this trend at Harvard, a new college was founded as a bastion of orthodoxy in Connecticut, becoming Yale College when it finally settled in New Haven. Sadly for orthodox Congregationalists, most of the faculty converted to the Church of England in 1722 and sailed for England to be ordained by the bishop of London. Their leader, Timothy Cutler, became the principal Anglican spokesman in Boston. Samuel Johnson, another defector, became the first president of King's College (now Columbia University) in New York City in the 1750s and won a considerable reputation as a moral philosopher.

Lawyers and Doctors

The rise of the legal profession helped spread Enlightenment ideas. Before 1700, most colonists despised lawyers as men who took advantage of the misery of others and who deliberately stirred up discord. Virginia and Massachusetts briefly abolished the legal profession. Only in Maryland did it take firm hold before 1700, but then it began to spread everywhere. In 1692, three English lawyers handled nearly all of the cases in the province of New York; by 1704, there were eight. In Boston, the legal profession seemed disreputable as late as 1720. Three British immigrants, all of them Anglicans, handled most cases. When a Congregational clergyman resigned his Connecticut pulpit and moved to Boston to practice law, he too joined Anglican King's Chapel. Benjamin Gridley, a Harvard man famous for his impiety, took up law and wrote enlightened essays for Boston newspapers in the 1730s, turned his office into an informal law school, and set up a debating society, the Sodalitas, in which students disputed legal questions within the context of contemporary oratory and philosophy. By then, a college education was almost a prerequisite to a legal career in New England.

Most Massachusetts lawyers before 1760 were either Anglicans or young men who had rejected the Congregational ministry as a career. Some were scoffers and skeptics, and most probably thought of themselves as a new learned elite. By the 1790s, lawyers saw themselves as the cultural vanguard of the new republic. Poet John Trumbull, playwright Royall Tyler, and novelist Hugh Henry Brackenridge all continued to practice law while writing on the side. Poet William Cullen Bryant, writer Washington Irving, and novelist Charles Brockden Brown turned from the law to full-time writing. Clearly, law and the Enlightenment rode together in 18th-century America.

Medicine also became an enlightened profession, with Philadelphia setting the pace. William Shippen earned degrees at Princeton and Edinburgh, the best medical school in the world at the time, before returning to Philadelphia in 1762, where he became the first American to lecture on medicine, publish a treatise on chemistry, and dissect human cadavers—a practice that shocked the unenlightened. His student John Morgan became the first professor of medicine in North America when the College of Philadelphia established a medical faculty a few years later.

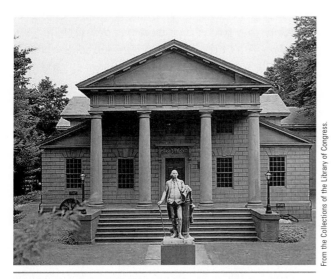

From the Collections of the Library of Congress.

THE REDWOOD LIBRARY, NEWPORT, RHODE ISLAND
Designed by architect Peter Harrison and erected between 1748 and 1750, this elegant building was named for Abraham Redwood, who donated £500 for the purchase of books in 1747.

Benjamin Rush, who also studied at Princeton and Edinburgh, brought the latest Scottish techniques to the newly founded Philadelphia Hospital. He too became an enlightened reformer. He attacked slavery and alcohol and supported the Revolution. Many colonial physicians embraced radical politics.

Georgia: The Failure of an Enlightenment Utopia

In the 1730s, Anglican humanitarianism and the Enlightenment belief in the possibility of social improvement converged in Britain to provide support for the founding of Georgia, named for King George II (1727–60). The sponsors of this project had several goals. They hoped to create a society that could make productive use of England's "worthy" poor (but not the lazy or criminal poor). Believing that South Carolina might well be helpless if attacked by Spain, they also intended—with no sense of irony—to shield that colony's slave society from Spanish Florida by populating Georgia with disciplined, armed free men. The founders of Georgia were appalled by what cheap English gin was doing to the sobriety and industry of the working people of England. They hoped to produce silk and wine, items that no other British colony had yet succeeded in making. They prohibited hard liquor and slavery. Slaves would make Georgia a simple extension of South Carolina, with all of its vulnerabilities.

A group of distinguished trustees, including members of both houses of Parliament, set themselves up as a nonprofit corporation and announced that they would give land away, not sell it. Led by James Oglethorpe, the

---

M U S I C A L   L I N K   T O   T H E   P A S T

He Could Make a Lass Weep

**Composers: Francis Hopkinson (music),
                     Thomas Parnell (lyrics)**

**Title: "My Days Have Been So Wondrous
              Free" (1759)**

Until almost the American Revolution, American music was European music, especially English music, and most of it was church music. Thomas Hopkinson was America's earliest secular songwriter, and "My Days Have Been so Wondrous Free" was probably the first American secular song. Although the title and the song's rhythm suggest a jaunty mood, the song is not as upbeat as a superficial listen might indicate. Francis Hopkinson's music complimented and added depth to the lyrics written decades earlier by Thomas Parcell. A romantic and bittersweet yearning permeates the song, although whether such yearning is directed toward communing with nature or with a romantic companion is uncertain.

Hopkinson worked in an environment where no American song tradition, no American publishing companies, and no consumer demand for American secular songs existed. He was a multitalented Renaissance man in the style of his contemporaries and friends Thomas Jefferson and Benjamin Franklin, exhibiting expertise in the fields of music, painting, inventing, writing, the law, and politics (he was a delegate to the Continental Congress and signed the Declaration of Independence).

"My Days" also represented an early example of two important traditions in American songwriting. First, Hopkinson purposely crafted compositions that untrained amateurs could perform and enjoy. "The best of [my songs] is that they are so easy that any Person who can play at all may perform them without much Trouble, & I have endeavour'd to make the melodies pleasing to the untutored Ear," he explained. Second, his songs meant to provoke emotion and emanated from "the Imagination of an Author who composes from his Heart, rather than his Head."

Although Hopkinson's songs did not attain large popularity, they did fulfill his elevated purposes in at least one family. After Hopkinson sent Jefferson some of his songs, Jefferson replied: "Accept my thanks . . . and my daughter's . . . I will not tell you how much they have pleased us, nor how well the last of them merits praise for its pathos, but relate a fact only, which is that while my elder daughter was playing it on the harpsichord, I happened to look toward the fire, & saw the younger one in tears. I asked her if she was sick? She said 'no; but the tune was so mournful.'"

1. Why do you think the colonists took more than a hundred years to develop their own popular songs, relying instead on material imported from England and the rest of Europe?

Listen to an audio recording of this music on the Musical Links to the Past CD.

trustees obtained a 20-year charter from Parliament in 1732, raised money from Anglican friends, and launched the colony on land claimed by both Spain and Britain. The trustees recruited foreign Protestants, including some Germans who had just been driven out of Salzburg by its Catholic bishop, a small number of Moravian Brethren (a German pacifist sect, led by Count Nicholas von Zinzendorf), and French Huguenots. In England, they interviewed many prospective settlers to distinguish the worthy poor from the unworthy. They engaged silk and wine experts and recruited Scottish Highlanders as soldiers.

But the trustees refused to consult the settlers on what might be good for them or for Georgia. As refined men of the Enlightenment, they believed they knew what the colony needed. They created no elective assembly, nor did they give the British government much chance to supervise them. Under their charter, Georgia laws had to be approved by the British Privy Council. Therefore the trustees passed only three laws during their 20 years of rule. One laid out the land system, and the others prohibited slavery and hard liquor. The trustees governed through regulations instead of laws. An elective assembly, the trustees promised, would come later, after Georgia's character had been firmly set.

In 1733, the first settlers laid out Savannah, a town with spacious streets. Within 10 years, 1,800 charity cases and just over 1,000 self-supporting colonists reached Georgia. The most successful were the Salzburgers, who agreed with the prohibitions on slavery and alcohol and built a thriving settlement at Ebenezer, farther up the Savannah River. The Moravian Brethren left for North Carolina after five years rather than bear arms. A group of Lowland Scots known as the Malcontents grew disgruntled and, after Oglethorpe ignored their complaints, left for South Carolina.

The land system never worked as planned. The trustees gave 50 acres to every male settler whose passage was paid for out of charitable funds. Those who paid their own way could claim up to 500 acres. Ordinary farmers did poorly; they could not support a family on 50 acres of the sandy soil around Savannah. Because the trustees envisioned every landowner as a soldier, women could not inherit land, nor could landowners sell their plots.

The settlers were unable to grow grapes or to persuade the sickly worms that survived the Atlantic crossing to make silk out of mulberry leaves. They clamored for rum, smuggled it into the colony when they could, and insisted that Georgia would never thrive until it had slaves. By the mid-1740s, enough people had died or left to reduce the population by more than half, and by 1752, the population had dropped below the 2,800 who had first settled the colony.

Between 1750 and 1752, the trustees gave up. They dropped their ban on alcohol, allowed the importation of slaves, summoned an elective assembly (but only to consult, not legislate), and finally surrendered their charter to Parliament. The establishment of royal government in 1752 at last gave Georgia an elective assembly with full powers of legislation, and Georgia became what it was never meant to be, a smaller version of South Carolina, producing rice and indigo with slave labor. By then, however, in one of the supreme ironies of the age, the colony had done more to spread religious revivalism than to vindicate Enlightenment ideals. Georgia helped turn both

A VIEW OF SAVANNAH ON MARCH 29, 1734

This painting by Peter Gordon emphasizes the wide streets and spacious atmosphere of this planned city.

John Wesley and George Whitefield into the greatest revivalists of the 18th century.

The Great Awakening

Between the mid-1730s and the early 1740s, an immense religious revival, the Great Awakening, swept across the Protestant world. Within the British Empire, it affected some areas more intensely than others. England, Scotland, Ulster, New England, the mid-Atlantic colonies, and for a time South Carolina responded warmly to emotional calls for a spiritual rebirth. Southern Ireland, the West Indies, and the Chesapeake colonies remained on the margins until Virginia and Maryland were drawn into a later phase of revivalism in the 1760s and 1770s. The Great Awakening shattered some denominational loyalties in the colonies and enabled the Methodists and the Baptists to surge ahead of all Protestant rivals in the generation after 1780.

Origins of the Revivals

Some of the earliest revivals arose among the Dutch in New Jersey. Guiliam Bertholf, a farmer and cooper (barrel maker), was a lay reader who had been ordained in an obscure corner of the Netherlands in 1694 (Amsterdam did not approve) and returned to preach to his former neighbors in Hackensack and Passaic. His emotional piety won many adherents. After 1720, Theodorus Jacobus Frelinghuysen sparked several revivals in his congregation in New Brunswick, New Jersey. The local Presbyterian pastor, Gilbert Tennent, watched and learned.

Tennent was a younger son of William Tennent, Sr., an Anglican-turned-Presbyterian minister who had moved from Ulster to America. At Neshaminy, Pennsylvania, he set up the Log College, where he trained his sons and other young men as evangelical preachers. The Tennent family dominated the Presbytery of New Brunswick, used it to ordain ministers, and sent them off to any congregation that requested one, even in other presbyteries. That practice angered the Philadelphia Synod, the governing body of the Presbyterian church in the colonies. Most of its ministers emphasized orthodoxy over a personal conversion experience. In a 1740 sermon, *The Dangers of an Unconverted Ministry,* Gilbert Tennent denounced those preachers for leading their people to hell. His attack split the church. In 1741, the outnumbered revivalists withdrew and founded their own Synod of New York.

In New England, Solomon Stoddard of Northampton presided over six revivals, which he called "harvests of souls," between the 1670s and his death in 1729. Jonathan Edwards, his grandson and successor—the only member of the Yale faculty who had not defected to the Anglicans in 1722—touched off a revival in 1734 and 1735 that rocked dozens of Connecticut valley towns. The revival ended suddenly when a prominent man, overwhelmed by the burden of his sins, slit his own throat. Edwards's *A Faithful Narrative of the Surprising Work of God* (1737) explained what a revival was—an emotional response to God's Word that brought sudden conversions to scores of people. He described these conversions in acute detail and won admirers in Britain as well as in New England.

In England, John Wesley and George Whitefield set the pace. At worldly Oxford University, Wesley and his brother

In actuality, some presbyteries had more churches than others. Arrows indicate descending lines of authority.

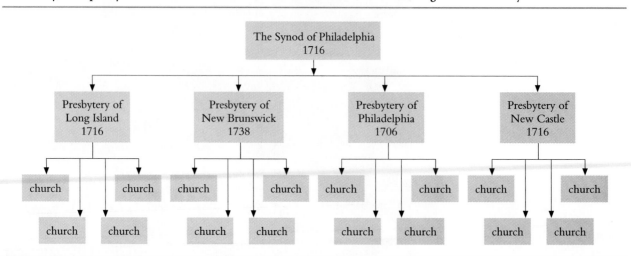

THE SYNOD OF PHILADELPHIA BY 1738

Charles founded the Holy Club, a High Church society whose members fasted until they could barely walk. One even lay prostrate for hours on the frigid earth, lost in prayer while his hands turned black. These methodical practices prompted scoffers to call them Methodists. Still dissatisfied with the state of his soul, Wesley went to Georgia as a missionary in 1735, an unhappy experience for him. He fell in love with a woman who did not return his affection, and the settlers rejected his ascetic piety. In 1737, on the return voyage to England, some Moravians convinced him that, for all his zeal, he had never grasped the central Protestant message, justification by faith alone. Some months later, he was deeply moved by Edwards's *Faithful Narrative.* Soon, Wesley found his life's mission, the conversion of sinners, and it launched him on an extraordinary preaching career of more than 40 years.

George Whitefield, who had been a talented amateur actor in his youth, joined the Holy Club at Oxford and became an Anglican minister. He followed Wesley to Georgia, founded an orphanage, then returned to England and preached all over the kingdom to raise money for it. He had the power to move masses of people through a single sermon, and he too began to preach the "new birth"—the necessity of a conversion experience. When many pastors banned him from their pulpits, he responded by preaching in open fields to anyone who would listen. Newspapers reported the controversy, and soon Whitefield's admirers began to notify the press where he would be on any given day. Colonial newspapers, keenly sensitive to the English press, also reported his movements.

Whitefield Launches the Transatlantic Revival

In 1739, Whitefield made his second trip to America, ostensibly to raise funds for his orphanage at Bethesda, Georgia. Everyone knew who he was from newspaper accounts, and thousands flocked to hear him preach. After landing in Delaware, he preached his way northward through Philadelphia, New Jersey, and New York City, and then headed south through the Chesapeake colonies and into South Carolina. In September 1740, he sailed to Newport and for two months toured New England. During his travels, he met Benjamin Franklin, Gilbert Tennent, and Jonathan Edwards. In the cities he sometimes attracted as many as 30,000 people, or twice the population of Boston. His voice was so musical, claimed one observer, that he could seduce a crowd just by the way he said "Mesopotamia." Using his acting skills, he imitated Christ on the cross, shedding "pious tears" for poor sinners. Or he became God at the Last Judgment, thundering: "Depart from me ye accursed into everlasting fire!" When he wept,

his audience wept with him. When he condemned them, they fell to the ground in agony.

Although Whitefield wore the surplice of an Anglican minister and carried the *Book of Common Prayer* when he preached, Anglicans treated him with reserve or hostility. In Charleston and New York City, the official spokesmen for the bishop of London denounced him, but Presbyterians, Congregationalists, and Baptists embraced him, at least until some of them began to fear that he was doing more harm than good. To many he embodied the old Non-Separatist ideal that all English Protestants were really members of the same church.

Disruptions

When other preachers tried to take up Whitefield's role after he moved on, they aroused fierce controversy. In South Carolina, Hugh Bryan, a Savannah River planter, began preaching the evangelical message to his slaves. In 1742, not long after a major slave revolt had rocked the colony, he denounced slavery as a sin and warned that God would pour out his wrath on the planters unless they rejected it. Proclaiming himself an American Moses, he attempted to part the waters of the Savannah River and lead the slaves to freedom in Georgia. Instead, he almost drowned. He then confessed publicly that he had been deluded. This fiasco discredited evangelicalism among the planters of the lower South for another generation, but Bryan and his family continued to convert their own slaves. African American evangelical piety, including some of the first black preachers, took root from these efforts.

Whitefield's successors caused severe disturbances in New England. Gilbert Tennent preached there for months. Lacking Whitefield's musical voice and Oxford diction, Tennent spoke with a Scottish burr and specialized in Holy Laughter, the scornful peals of a triumphant God as sinners tumble into hell. He abandoned the usual garb of a minister for a robe and sandals and let his hair grow long, thereby proclaiming himself a new John the Baptist heralding the Second Coming of Christ. Many ecstatic followers believed that the biblical Millennium was at hand.

James Davenport, who succeeded Tennent, denounced unregenerate ministers by name. He liked to preach by eerie candlelight, roaring damnation at his listeners, even grabbing Satan and wrestling him back to hell. He advised his admirers to drink rat poison rather than listen to another lifeless sermon. In 1743, he established the Shepherd's Tent in New London to train awakened preachers. This outdoor school abandoned the classical curriculum of colleges and insisted only on a valid conversion experience. He organized a book-burning, in which titles by Increase Mather and other New England dignitaries went

up in flames, and he threw his britches on the fire, declaring them a mark of human vanity. A New England grand jury, asked to indict him, proclaimed him mad instead. Like Bryan in South Carolina, he repented and claimed that he had been deluded. The Shepherd's Tent collapsed.

Long-Term Consequences of the Revivals

The revivals had dramatic consequences. As time passed, they feminized evangelical churches. Amid the enthusiasm of Whitefield's tour, more men than usual had joined a church, but after another year or two, men became difficult to convert. The number of women church members began to soar, however, until by 1800 they often formed a majority of 3 or 4 to 1, and in some congregations acquired an informal veto over the choice of the minister.

Partly in reaction to the revivals, thousands of men became Freemasons, often instead of joining a church. After 1730, the Masons made some headway among the merchants and professionals of Philadelphia and Boston, but during and after the Revolution, their membership grew spectacularly. They appealed to men of all denominations, accepting even a few Catholics, Jews, and Indians. Artisans began to dominate city lodges, and the Masons penetrated deeply into the countryside as well. They very nearly turned their order into a religion of manliness, complete with secret and mysterious rituals. They extolled sobriety, industry, brotherhood, benevolence, and citizenship. At first, most clergymen saw Masons as a force for good, but by the 1820s, the order would be drawing angry criticism.

The revivals shattered the unity of New England's Congregational Church. Evangelicals seceded from dozens of congregations to form their own "Separate" churches. Many of those that survived went Baptist by the 1760s, thereby gaining protection under the toleration statutes of the New England colonies. In the middle colonies, the revivals strengthened denominational loyalties and energized the clergy. In the 1730s, most people in the region, particularly in New Jersey and Pennsylvania, had never joined a church. The revivals prompted many of them to become New Side (evangelical) Presbyterians, Old Side (antirevival) Presbyterians, or nonevangelical Anglicans. Similar cleavages ran through the German population. The southern colonies were less affected, although evangelical Presbyterians made modest gains in the Virginia backcountry after 1740. Finally, in the 1760s, the Baptists began to win thousands of converts, as did the Methodists after 1776, whose numbers surpassed the Baptists a few decades later.

The revivals broke down localism by creating new cosmopolitan links with Britain and between colonies. Whitefield ran the most efficient publicity machine in the Atlantic world. In London, Glasgow, and Boston, periodicals called the *Christian History* carried news of revivals occurring anywhere in the empire. For years, London evangelicals held regular Letter Days, at which they read accounts of revivals in progress. Revivalists wrote often to one another. When fervor declined in New England, Jonathan Edwards organized a Concert of Prayer with his Scottish correspondents, setting regular times for them all to beseech the Lord to pour out his grace once more. As Anglicans split into Methodists and Latitudinarians, Congregationalists into New Lights (prorevival) and Old Lights (antirevival), and Presbyterians into comparable New Side and Old Side synods, evangelicals discovered that they had more in common with revivalists in other denominations than with antirevivalists in their own. When New Side Presbyterians chose a new president of the College of New Jersey in 1757, they saw nothing strange in naming a Congregationalist, Jonathan Edwards.

Edwards was the most able apologist for revivals in Britain or America and probably the most profound theologian that North America has yet produced. When Boston's Charles Chauncy (very much a man of the Enlightenment) attacked the revivals as frauds because of their emotional excesses, Edwards replied with *A Treatise concerning Religious Affections* (1746), which displayed his own mastery of Enlightenment sources, including Newton and Locke. Although admitting that no emotional response, however intense, was proof by itself of the presence of God in a person's soul, he insisted that intense feeling must always accompany the reception of divine grace. That view upset people who believed that a rational God must have established a polite and genteel religion. For Edwards, an unemotional piety could never be the work of God. In effect, Edwards countered Chauncy's emotional defense of reason with his own rational defense of emotion.

New Colleges

The Great Awakening also created several new colleges. Each was set up primarily by a single denomination, but all admitted other Protestants. In 1740, North America had only three colleges: Harvard, William and Mary, and Yale. Although Yale eventually embraced the revivals, all three opposed them at first. In 1746, middle colony evangelicals, eager to show their commitment to classical learning after the fiasco of the Shepherd's Tent, founded the College of New Jersey. It graduated its first class in

1748 and settled in Princeton in 1756. Unlike the older colleges, it drew students from all 13 colonies and sent its graduates throughout America, especially to the middle and southern colonies. It also reshaped the Presbyterian Church. When Presbyterians healed their schism and reunited in 1758, the New Siders set the terms. Outnumbered in 1741, they held a large majority of ministers by 1758. Through control of Princeton, their numbers had increased rapidly. The Old Side, still dependent on the University of Glasgow in Scotland, could barely replace those who died.

New Light Baptists founded the College of Rhode Island (now Brown University) in the 1760s. Dutch Reformed revivalists established Queens College (now Rutgers University) in New Jersey, mostly to train evangelical ministers who could preach in English. Eleazer Wheelock opened an evangelical school for Indians in Lebanon, Connecticut. After his first graduate, Samson Occum, raised £12,000 in England for the school, Wheelock moved to New Hampshire and used most of the money to found Dartmouth College instead. By 1790, Dartmouth was turning out more graduates, and far more ministers, than any other American college.

In the 1750s, Anglicans countered with two new colleges of their own: the College of Philadelphia (now the University of Pennsylvania), which also had Old Side Presbyterian support, and King's College (now Columbia University) in New York. Their undergraduate programs remained small, however, and few of their students chose a ministerial career. In the competition for student loyalties, nonevangelicals could not yet compete effectively with revivalists.

The Denominational Realignment

The revivals transformed American religious life. In 1700, the three strongest denominations had been the Congregationalists in New England, the Quakers in the Delaware valley, and the Anglicans in the South. By 1800, all three had lost ground to newcomers: the Methodists, who grew at an astonishing rate as the Church of England collapsed during the Revolution; the Baptists, who leaped into second place; and the Presbyterians. Methodists and Baptists did not expect their preachers to attend college, and they recruited ministers from a much broader segment of the population than their rivals could tap. Although they never organized their own Shepherd's Tent, they embraced similar principles, demanding only personal conversion, integrity, knowledge of the Bible, and a talent for preaching.

Antirevivalist denominations, especially Anglicans and Quakers, lost heavily. New Light Congregationalists made only slight gains because, when their people left behind the established churches of New England and moved west, they usually joined a Presbyterian church, which provided a structure and network of support that isolated congregations in a pluralistic society could not sustain.

☙ Political Culture in the Colonies

In politics as in other activities, the colonies became more like Britain during the 18th century. A quarter-century of warfare after 1689 convinced the settlers that they needed the protection of the British state and strengthened their admiration for its parliamentary system. Most colonial voters and assemblymen were more "independent" than their British counterparts, who lived in a hierarchical world of patrons and clients. Still, provincial politics began to absorb many of the values and practices that had taken hold in Britain after the Glorious Revolution. Colonists agreed that they were free because they were British, because they too had mixed constitutions that united monarchy, aristocracy, and democracy in almost perfect balance.

By the 1720s, every colony except Connecticut and Rhode Island had an appointive governor, either royal or proprietary, plus a council and an elective assembly. The governor stood for monarchy and the council for aristocracy. In Massachusetts, Rhode Island, and Connecticut, the council or upper house was elected (indirectly in Massachusetts). In all other colonies except Pennsylvania, an appointive council played an active legislative role. The office of councillor was not hereditary, but many councillors served for life, especially in Virginia, and some were succeeded by their sons.

THE SPECTRUM OF COLONIAL POLITICS		
Constitutional Type	Successful	Unsuccessful
Northern "Court"	New York, circa 1710–28 New Hampshire after 1741 Massachusetts after 1741 New Jersey after 1750	New York after 1728 Pennsylvania (successful in peace, ineffective in war)
Southern "Country"	Virginia after 1720 South Carolina after 1730 Georgia after 1752	Maryland North Carolina

Connecticut and Rhode Island never really belonged to this system.

The Rise of the Assembly and the Governor

In all 13 colonies, once the Crown took over Georgia, the settlers elected the assembly, which embodied a colony's "democratic" elements. The right to vote in the colonies, although narrowing as population rose, was more widely shared than in England, where two-thirds of adult males were disenfranchised, a ratio that continued to rise. By contrast, something like three-fourths of free adult white men could vote in the colonies, and a fair number of those who were ineligible at any given time would win that right by acquiring property as they grew older. The frequency of elections varied—from every seven years in New York (from the 1740s on) and Virginia, as well as in Britain, to at least once a year in five colonies. As the century advanced, legislatures sat longer and passed more laws. The lower house—the assembly—usually initiated major bills. The rise of the assembly was a major political fact of the era. It made most of its gains at the expense of the council.

Every royal colony except New York and Georgia already had an assembly with a strong sense of its own privileges when the first royal governor arrived, but the governors in most colonies also grew more effective as time passed. Because the governor's instructions usually challenged some existing practices, clashes often occurred in which the first royal governors never got all of their demands. Nevertheless, they did win concessions and became much more effective over the years. In almost every colony, the most successful governors were men who

served between 1730 and 1765. Most of them had learned by then that their success depended less on their prerogatives (specific royal powers embodied in their commissions) than on their ability to win over the assembly through persuasion or patronage.

Early in the century, conflicts between the governor and an assembly majority tended to be legalistic. Each side cited technical precedents to justify the governor's prerogatives or the assembly's traditional privileges. Later on, when conflict spilled over into pamphlets and newspapers, it often pitted an aggrieved minority (unable to win a majority in the assembly) against both governor and assembly. These contests were ideological. The opposition accused the governor of corruption, of threatening the colonists' liberties, and he denounced the opposition as a "faction." Everyone condemned factions, or political parties, as self-interested and destructive. "Party is the madness of many for the gain of a few," declared poet Alexander Pope. Hardly anyone claimed to be a party leader; the other side was the faction.

"Country" Constitutions: The Southern Colonies

Although the colonies were all aware of the ideological currents in British politics, they reacted to them in different ways. In most southern colonies, the Country principles of the British opposition (see chapter 3) became the common assumptions of public life, acceptable to both governor and assembly, typically after a failed attempt to impose the Court alternative. When a governor, such as

THE GOVERNOR'S PALACE AT WILLIAMSBURG, VIRGINIA

The governor's palace was built during the term of Governor Alexander Spotswood (1710–22) and restored in the 20th century. For Spotswood, the palace was an extension of royal might and splendor across the ocean. He set a standard of elegance that many planters imitated when they built their own great houses in the second quarter of the 18th century.

Colonial Williamsburg Foundation.

Virginia's Alexander Spotswood (1710–22), used his patronage to fill the assembly with his own "placemen," the voters turned them out at the next election. Just as Spotswood learned that he could not manipulate the house through patronage, the assembly discovered that it could not coerce a governor who had a permanent salary. Accordingly, Virginia and South Carolina cultivated a "politics of harmony," a system of ritualized mutual flattery. Governors found that they could accomplish more through persuasion than through patronage, and the assemblies responded by showing their appreciation. The planters of Virginia and South Carolina concluded that their societies embodied almost exactly what British opposition writers had been demanding. Factions disappeared, allowing the governor and the assembly to pursue the "common good" in an atmosphere free of rancor or corruption. Georgia adopted similar practices in the 1750s.

This system worked well because the planters were doing what Britain wanted them to do: shipping staple crops to Britain. Both sides could agree on measures that would make this process more efficient, such as the Virginia Tobacco Inspection Act of 1730. In Virginia, public controversy actually ceased. Between 1720 and 1765, particularly during the able administration of Sir William Gooch (1727–49), the governor and House of Burgesses engaged in only one public quarrel, an unparalleled record of political harmony. South Carolina's politics became almost as placid from the 1730s into the 1760s, but harmony there masked serious social problems that were beginning to emerge in the unrepresented backcountry. By contrast, the politics of harmony never took hold in Maryland, where the lord proprietor always tried to seduce assemblymen with his lavish patronage, nor in factional North Carolina, where the tobacco and rice planters continually wrangled, and the growing backcountry distrusted both sides.

"Court" Constitutions: The Northern Colonies

With many economic interests and ethnic groups to satisfy, the northern colonies often produced political factions. Governors with a large vision of the public welfare could win support by using patronage to reward some groups and to discipline others. William Shirley, governor of Massachusetts from 1741 to 1756, used judicial and militia appointments and war contracts to build a majority in the assembly. Like Sir Robert Walpole in Britain, he was a master of Court politics. In New Hampshire, Benning Wentworth created a political machine that rewarded just about every assemblyman between 1741 and 1767. An ineffective opposition in both colonies accused the governors of corrupting the assembly, but Shirley and Wentworth each claimed that his actions were essential to his colony's needs. Both governors remained in tight control.

The opposition, although seldom able to implement its demands at the provincial level, was important nonetheless. It kept settlers alert to any infringements on their liberties. It dominated the town of Boston from 1720 on, and it reminded people that resistance to authority might be the only means to preserve liberty. Boston artisans engaged in ritualized mob activities that had a sharp political edge. Every year on Guy Fawkes Day (November 5), a North End mob and a South End mob bloodied each other for the privilege of burning effigies of the pope, the devil, and the Stuart pretender to the British throne. These men were raucously celebrating liberty, property, and no popery—the British constitution as they understood it. The violence made many wealthy merchants nervous, and by 1765 some of them would become its targets.

New York's governors, particularly Robert Hunter (1710–19), achieved great success even before 1720, mostly by playing off one faction against another in a colony that had been fiercely divided since Leisler's rebellion of 1689. Hunter's salary and perquisites became more lucrative than those attached to any other royal office in North America, and after 1716 he and his successor were so satisfied with their control of the assembly that they let 10 years pass without calling a general election. During the 25 years after 1730, later governors lost these advantages, primarily because London gave the governorship to a series of men who were eager to rebuild their tattered fortunes at New York's expense. This combination of greed and need gave new leverage to the assembly, and it attacked many royal prerogatives during the 1740s. Of the mainland colonies, only the governor of New York emerged weaker by 1760 than he had been in 1730.

Pennsylvania, by contrast, kept its proprietary governor weak well into the 1750s. After three decades of factionalism, a unified Quaker Party won undisputed control of the assembly during the 1730s. The governor, who by this time was never a Quaker, had a lot of patronage to dispense. He found it useless in controlling the Quaker assemblymen, who had lost interest in becoming judges if that meant administering oaths. Nor could he win these pacifists over with military commissions or war contracts, no matter how lucrative. The colonists, both north and south, absorbed the ideology of the British opposition, which warned that those in power were always trying to destroy liberty and that corruption was power's most dangerous weapon. By 1776, that view would justify independence and the repudiation of a "corrupt" king and Parliament. Before the 1760s, however, it served different purposes. In the south, this ideology celebrated both the

political success of Virginia and South Carolina and Anglo-American harmony. In the north, it replicated its role in Britain and became the language of frustrated minorities unable to defeat the governor or control the assembly.

◈ The Renewal of Imperial Conflict

A new era of imperial war began in 1739 and continued, with only a brief interruption, until 1763. The British colonies, New Spain, and New France all became involved, and eventually so did all the Indians of the eastern woodlands. By 1763, France had been expelled from North America. Britain controlled the continent east of the Mississippi, and Spain claimed the land west of it.

Challenges to French Power

In the decades of peace after 1713, the French tried, with mixed results, to strengthen their position in North America. At great cost, they erected the continent's most formidable fortress, Louisbourg, on Cape Breton Island. A naval force stationed there could protect the French fishery and guard the approaches to the St. Lawrence River. The French also built Fort St. Frédéric (the British called it Crown Point) on Lake Champlain and maintained their Great Lakes posts at Forts Frontenac, Michilimackinac, and Detroit. To bolster its weak hold on the Gulf of Mexico, France created the Company of the Indies, which shipped 7,000 settlers and 2,000 slaves to Louisiana between 1717 and 1721 but then failed to supply them. By 1726, half had starved to death or had fled. Another 5,000 slaves, but few settlers, reached the colony by 1730. The French founded New Orleans, which became the capital of Louisiana in 1722.

Despite these efforts, the French hold on the interior began to weaken, both north and south. From all points of the compass, Indians returned to the Ohio valley, mostly to trade with pacifist Pennsylvania or with Fort Oswego, a new British post on Lake Ontario. Compared with the French, the British were often clumsy in their dealings with Indians, but they had one advantage: British trade goods were cheaper than French goods, although no better in quality. Many of the Indians founded what the French disparagingly called "republics," villages outside

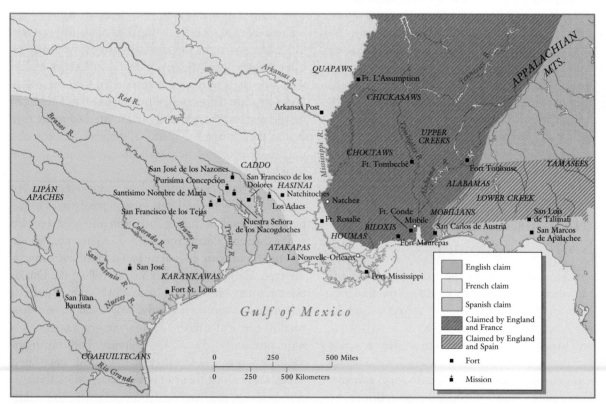

MAP 4.1   FRENCH LOUISIANA AND SPANISH TEXAS, CIRCA 1730

In this part of North America, French and Spanish settlers and missionaries were spread quite thinly over a vast area and surrounded by much larger numbers of Indian peoples.

◈ View an animated version of this map or related maps at http://history.wadsworth.com/murrin_LEP4e.

the French alliance system that were willing to trade with the British. The chiefs at Venango, Logstown, and other republics accepted people from all tribes—Delawares from the east, Shawnees from the south and east, Mingoes (Iroquois who had left their homeland) from the north, and other Algonquians of the Great Lakes region to the west. Because the inhabitants of each new village had blood relatives living among all of the nearby nations, the chiefs welcomed Pennsylvania traders and hoped that none of their neighbors would endanger their own relatives by attacking them.

Sometimes even the French system of mediation broke down. In the northwest from 1712 to 1737, the French and their Algonquian allies fought a long, intermittent war with the Fox nation. In the southwest, an arrogant French officer decided to take over the lands of the Natchez Indians (the last of the Mississippian mound builders) and ordered them to move. While pretending to comply, the Natchez planned a counterstroke and, on November 28, 1729, killed every French male in the vicinity. In the war that followed, the French and their Choctaw allies destroyed the Natchez as a distinct people, although some Natchez refugees found homes among the Chickasaws or the Creeks.

During the war, in 1730, the French barely averted a massive slave uprising in New Orleans. To stir up hatred between Indians and Africans, the French turned over some of the African leaders of the revolt to the Choctaws to be burned alive. They also encouraged hostilities between the Choctaws and the Chickasaws, largely because they could not afford enough gifts to hold an alliance with both nations. This policy did serious damage to the French. Instead of weakening the pro-British Chickasaws, it touched off a civil war among the Choctaws, and France lost both influence and prestige.

The Danger of Slave Revolts and War with Spain

To counter the French, Spain sent missionaries and soldiers into Texas between 1716 and 1720 and founded a capital at Los Adaes, a few miles from the French trading post at Natchitoches. To prevent smuggling, Spain refused to open a seaport on the Gulf Coast. As a result, its tiny outposts had to depend on French trade goods for supplies, sometimes even for food. The Texas missions won few converts and suffered frequent depredations by Indians carrying French muskets. In 1719, the survivors of these attacks abandoned their missions in eastern Texas and fled west to San Antonio, which eventually became the capital.

The Spanish presence in Florida proved troublesome to the British, especially in South Carolina. In the 16th century, Francis Drake had proclaimed himself a liberator when he attacked St. Augustine and promised freedom to Indians and Africans groaning under Spanish tyranny (see chapter 2). By the 1730s, the roles had been reversed. On several occasions after 1680, Spanish Florida had promised freedom to any slaves who escaped from Carolina and were willing to accept Catholicism. In 1738, the governor established, just north of St. Augustine, a new town, Gracia Real de Santa Teresa de Mose (or Mose for short, pronounced Moe-shah). He put a remarkable African in charge, a man who took the name Francisco Menéndez at baptism. He had escaped from slavery, had fought with the Yamasees against South Carolina in 1715, and had fled to Florida, only to be enslaved again. Yet he became literate in Spanish and, while still a slave, rose to the rank of militia captain. After winning his freedom, he took charge of Mose in 1738 and made it the first community of free blacks in what is now the United States. The very existence of Mose acted as a magnet for Carolina slaves.

In 1739, the governor of Spanish Florida offered liberty to any slaves from the British colonies who could make their way to Florida. This manifesto, and rumors about Mose, touched off the Stono Rebellion in South Carolina, the most violent slave revolt in the history of the 13 colonies. Some of the rebellion's leaders were Catholics from the African Kingdom of the Kongo, which Portuguese missionaries had converted in the 16th century.

On Sunday morning, September 9, 1739, a force of 20 slaves attacked a store at Stono (south of Charleston), killed the owner, seized weapons, and moved on to assault other houses and to attract new recruits. Heading toward Florida, they killed about 25 settlers that day and nearly captured Lieutenant Governor William Bull, who happened to be riding by and just managed to gallop away. When the rebels reached the Edisto River, they stopped, raised banners, and shouted "Liberty," hoping to begin a general uprising. There the militia caught them and killed about two-thirds of the growing force. In the weeks that followed, the settlers killed another 60. None of the rebels reached Florida, but, as the founders of Georgia had foreseen, South Carolina was indeed vulnerable in any dispute with Spain.

In 1739, at almost the same moment, the War of Jenkins's Ear, derisively named for a ship captain who displayed his severed ear to Parliament as proof of Spanish cruelty, broke out between Britain and Spain. The war cost Britain dearly because Spanish defenses held everywhere. Some 3,000 men from the 13 colonies, eager for plunder, joined expeditions in 1741 and 1742 against the seaport of Cartagena, New Granada (now Colombia), and against Cuba and Panama. All were disasters (see map on p. 143).

CHRISTIAN BURIAL IN THE KONGO, 18TH CENTURY

At least some of the Africans who organized the Stono rebellion in South Carolina in 1739 were Catholics from the kingdom of the Kongo.

Most of the men died of disease; only 10 percent of the volunteers returned home. But one of the survivors, Lawrence Washington, so admired the British naval commander, Edward Vernon, that he named his Virginia plantation Mount Vernon. Britain also experienced a surge of patriotic fervor from the war. Both "God Save the King" and "Rule Britannia" were written during the struggle.

Georgia was supposed to protect South Carolina. General Oglethorpe, its governor, retaliated against the Spanish by invading Florida in 1740. He dispersed the black residents of Mose and occupied the site, but the Spaniards mauled his garrison in a surprise counterattack. Oglethorpe retreated without taking St. Augustine and returned to Georgia with disturbing reports. Spain, he said, was sending blacks into the British colonies to start slave uprisings. And Spanish priests in disguise were intermingled with the black conspirators and would try to destroy British fortifications. This news set off panics in the rice and tobacco colonies, but it had its biggest impact in New York City.

Back in 1712, a slave revolt had shaken the city. After setting fire to a barn one night, slaves had shot 15 settlers who rushed to put out the blaze, killing nine. Twenty-one slaves were executed, some after gruesome tortures.

By 1741, New York City's 2,000 slaves were the largest concentration of blacks in British North America outside of Charleston. On March 18, Fort George burned down in what was probably an accident, but when a series of suspicious fires broke out, the settlers grew nervous. Some of the fires probably provided cover for an interracial larceny ring that operated out of the tavern of John Hughson, a white man. When the New York Supreme Court offered freedom to Mary Burton, a 16-year-old Irish servant girl at the tavern, in exchange for her testimony, she swore that the tavern was the center of a hellish "popish plot" to murder the city's whites, free the slaves, and make Hughson king of the Africans. Several free black Spanish sailors, who had been captured and enslaved by privateers, also were accused, although apparently their only crime was to insist that they were free men. After Oglethorpe's warning reached New York in June, the number of the accused escalated, and John Ury, a recently arrived High Churchman and a Latin teacher, was hanged as the likely Spanish priest.

The New York conspiracy trials, which continued from May into August of 1741, reminded one observer of the Salem witch frenzy of 1692, in which the testimony of several girls had led to 19 hangings. The toll in New York was worse. Four whites and 18 slaves were hanged, 13

SAVAGES OF SEVERAL NATIONS, NEW ORLEANS, 1735

This painting by Alexandre de Batz depicts a multiethnic Indian village near New Orleans. The woman at lower left was a Fox Indian who had been captured and enslaved. The African boy was an adoptee.

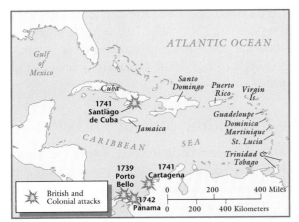

MAP 4.2 CARIBBEAN THEATER OF WAR, 1739–1742
Spanish defenses held up remarkably well against repeated and very costly British attacks.

slaves were burned alive, and 70 were banished to the West Indies. The judges spoke pompously about the sacred rights of Englishmen, again in danger from popish conspirators, and grew enraged at any African who dared to imperil what the colony would not let him share.

In 1742, King Philip V of Spain nearly accomplished what Oglethorpe and the New York judges dreaded. He sent 36 ships and 2,000 soldiers from Cuba with orders to devastate Georgia and South Carolina, "sacking and burning all the towns, posts, plantations, and settlements" and freeing the slaves. Although the invaders probably outnumbered the entire population of Georgia, Oglethorpe raised 900 men and met them on St. Simons Island in July. After he ambushed two patrols, Spanish morale collapsed. When a British soldier deserted to the Spanish with word of how weak Georgia really was, Oglethorpe arranged to have the Spanish intercept a letter that implicated the deserter as a spy sent to lure them to their destruction. They departed in haste, leaving British North America as a safe haven once more for liberty, property, no popery—and slavery.

Britain did achieve one other success against Spain. Between 1740 and 1744, Commodore George Anson rounded Cape Horn, plundered and burned a small port in Peru, captured several prizes, and then sailed across the Pacific, where he captured the Manila galleon, the world's richest ship, loaded with silver that sailed annually

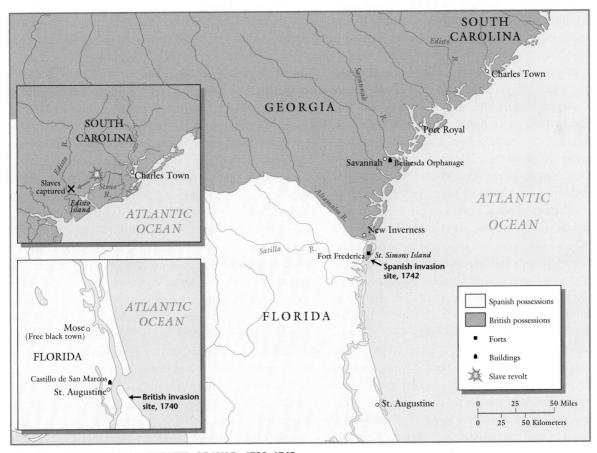

MAP 4.3 SOUTHEASTERN THEATER OF WAR, 1739–1742
Florida's defenders repelled a British attack led by James Oglethorpe, and then Oglethorpe turned back a much larger Spanish invasion of Georgia.

from Mexico to the Philippines. Anson completed his circumnavigation of the globe and returned to England with 1.3 million Spanish silver dollars and more than 35,000 ounces of unminted silver. Even though only one of Anson's six ships completed the voyage, his success alarmed the Spanish about the security of their lightly defended Pacific possessions. Spain would be reluctant to challenge Britain in the next war.

France versus Britain: King George's War

In 1744, France joined Spain in the war against Britain. The main action then shifted to the north. When the French laid siege to Annapolis Royal, the capital of Nova Scotia, Governor William Shirley of Massachusetts intervened just in time to save the small garrison, and the French withdrew. Shirley then planned his own offensive, a rash attack on Fortress Louisbourg on Cape Breton Island. With only a few lightly armed Yankee vessels at his disposal, he asked the commander of the British West Indian squadron, Sir Peter Warren, for assistance. But Shirley's expedition, which included about one-sixth of all the adult males of Massachusetts, set out before Warren could respond. With no heavy artillery of his own, Shirley ordered the expedition to take the outer batteries of the fortress, capture their guns, and use them to knock down its walls. Had the Yankees met a French fleet instead of the Royal Navy, which arrived in the nick of time, nearly every family in New England might have lost a close relative. The most amazing thing about this venture is that it worked. The British navy drove off the French, and untrained Yankee volunteers subdued the mightiest fortress in America with its own guns. Louisbourg fell on June 16, 1745.

After that, however, nothing went right. Hundreds of volunteers died of various afflictions before regular troops arrived to take over. Elaborate plans to attack Quebec by sea in 1746 and 1747 came to nothing because no British fleet appeared. French and Indian raiders devastated the weakly defended frontier, while Shirley held back most of his men for a Canada offensive that never took place. Bristol County farmers rioted against high taxes. When the Royal Navy finally docked at Boston in late 1747, its commander sent gangs of sailors ashore to compel anyone they could seize into serving with the fleet. An angry crowd descended on the sailors, took some officers hostage, and controlled the streets of Boston for three days before the naval commander relented and released all of the Massachusetts men he had impressed. (The rioters let him keep outsiders.) Finally, to offset losses in Europe, Britain had to return Louisbourg to France under the Treaty of Aix-la-Chapelle, which ended the war in 1748. New England had suffered enormous losses and had gained nothing except pride. Yet well into 1747, public opinion had strongly supported the war. The clergy, in particular, saw it as an apocalyptic struggle of free British Protestants against popish tyranny.

The Impending Storm

The war had driven back the frontiers of British settlement in North America, but the colonies had promised land grants to many volunteers. Thus peace touched off a frenzy of expansion that alarmed Indians and French alike. The British, aware that their hold on Nova Scotia was feeble, recruited 2,500 Protestants from the continent of Europe to populate the colony and sent four regiments of redcoats to accompany them. In 1749, they founded the town of Halifax, which became the new capital of Nova Scotia. The governor also emphasized that his colony would be European, not Indian, by offering bounties for Indian scalps even though the war had ended. When the Micmac Indians, who had lived in peace with French settlers for more than a century, turned to the Acadians for support, the British relented. The Acadians were still too numerous to challenge.

In the 13 colonies, settlers eagerly pressed on to new lands. Yankees swarmed north into Maine and New Hampshire and west into the middle colonies, creating serious tensions. By refusing to pay rent to the manor lords of the Hudson valley, they sparked a tenant revolt in 1753 that the wealthy Livingston family had difficulty subduing. A year later, Connecticut's delegation to the Albany Congress (discussed in the next section) used bribes to acquire an Indian title to all of northern Pennsylvania, which Connecticut claimed on the basis of its sea-to-sea charter of 1663. The blatant encroachments of New York speculators and settlers on Mohawk lands west of Albany so infuriated the Mohawks' Chief Hendrik that he bluntly told the governor of New York in 1753, "the Covenant Chain is broken between you and us [the Iroquois League]. So brother you are not to hear of me any more, and Brother we desire to hear no more of you." New York, Pennsylvania, and Virginia competed for trade with the new Indian republics between Lake Erie and the Ohio River. The expansionist thrust pitted colony against colony, as well as settler against Indian, and British against French.

Virginians, whom the Indians called "long knives," were particularly aggressive. Citing their own 1609 sea-to-sea charter (see the chapter 2 map, "Virginia Company Charter, 1606"), they organized the Ohio Company of Virginia in 1747 to settle the Ohio valley and established their first outpost at the place where the Monongahela and Allegheny rivers converge to form the Ohio River (the site

PORTRAIT OF CHIEF HENDRIK OF THE MOHAWKS
Hendrik's ultimatum to New York in 1753 precipitated the
summoning of the Albany Congress a year later.

of modern Pittsburgh). The company hired George Washington as a surveyor. Farther south, encroachments upon the Cherokees almost provoked war with South Carolina in 1750.

The French response to these intrusions verged on panic. The fall of Louisbourg had interrupted the flow of French trade goods to the Ohio country for several years, and the men who had long been conducting Indian diplomacy had either died or left office by the late 1740s. Authoritarian newcomers from France replaced them and began giving orders to Indians instead of negotiating with them. The French did, however, make some constructive moves. They rebuilt Louisbourg and erected Fort Beauséjour on the neck that connects mainland Canada to Nova Scotia. In 1755, they erected Fort Carillon (Ticonderoga to the British) on Lake Champlain to protect Crown Point.

Far more controversial was the new French policy in the area between the Great Lakes and the Ohio. Without trying to explain themselves to the Indians, they launched two expeditions into the area. In 1749, Pierre-Joseph Céloron de Blainville led several hundred men down the Allegheny and the Ohio, then up the Miami and back to Canada. He ordered western Indians to join him, but most of them refused. To the Indians, the French were acting like British settlers, intruding on their lands. Along the

way, Blainville buried plaques, claiming the area for France. The Indians removed them. Marquis Duquesne sent 2,000 Canadians, with almost no Indian support, to erect a line of posts from Fort Presque Isle (now Erie, Pennsylvania) to Fort Duquesne (now Pittsburgh).

The French clearly intended to prevent British settlement west of the Alleghenies. Duquesne thought this policy so obviously beneficial to the Indians that it needed no explanation. Yet the Mingoes warned him not to build a fort in their territory, and a delegation of Delawares and Shawnees asked the Virginians if they would be willing to expel the French from the Ohio country and then go back home. The Indians did not like Virginia's response. In 1753, Virginia sent Washington to the Ohio country to warn Duquesne to withdraw, and a small Virginia force began building its own fort at the forks of the Ohio. Washington was not the man to win over the Indians, who, he declared, had "nothing human except the shape." Duquesne ignored Washington, advanced toward the Ohio, expelled the Virginians, took over their site, and finished building the fort. Virginia sent Washington back to the Ohio in 1754. On May 28, after discovering a French patrol nearby, Washington launched an attack. That order set off a world war.

The War for North America

Beginning in 1755, the modernizing British state with its professional army came into direct contact with the householder society and the voluntaristic ethic of the colonists. The encounter was often unpleasant, but the gap between the two sides lessened as each became more familiar with the other. At first, the war with France generated fierce tensions between Britain and the colonies, but both sides learned to cooperate effectively until together they achieved victory.

Of the four wars fought between Britain and France from 1689 to 1763, only the last began in America. That conflict, popularly known as the French and Indian War, was also the biggest and produced the most sweeping results. Among all of America's wars from 1750 to the present, according to unpublished calculations by Thomas L. Purvis, it achieved the fourth highest rate of mobilization and, measured by casualties per capita (excluding Indians), it was the third bloodiest contest Americans have ever fought. Only World War II, the Civil War, and the Revolution put a higher percentage of men under arms. Only the Civil War and the Revolution killed a higher percentage of those mobilized.

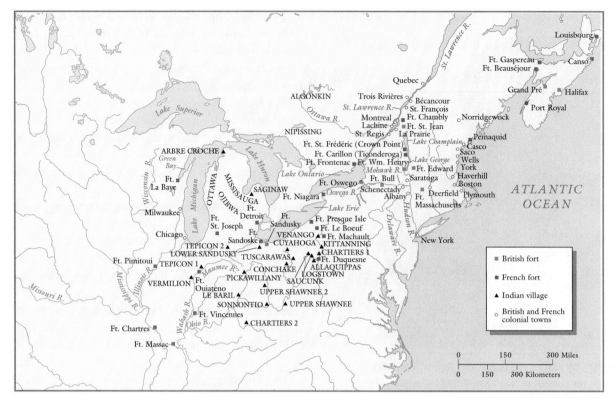

MAP 4.4 FRANCE VERSUS BRITAIN IN NORTH AMERICA BY 1755
North of the Ohio River, much of North America was becoming a series of fortresses along the frontiers separating New France from the British colonies.

The Albany Congress and the Onset of War

In spring 1754, both New France and Virginia were expecting a limited clash at the forks of the Ohio River. Neither anticipated the titanic struggle that encounter would set off, nor did the French and British governments, which hoped to limit any conflict to a few strategic points in North America. New Englanders, however, saw an apocalyptic struggle in the making between "Protestant freedom" and "popish slavery," with the North American continent as the battleground. "The continent is not wide enough for us both," declared one preacher, "and they [the French] intend to have the whole."

Britain, fearful that the Six Nations (the Tuscaroras had joined the original Five Nations by the 1720s) might side with New France, ordered New York to host an intercolonial congress at Albany to meet with the Iroquois and redress their grievances. The governor invited every colony as far south as Virginia, except nonroyal Connecticut and Rhode Island. Virginia and New Jersey declined to attend. Governor Shirley of Massachusetts, on his own initiative, invited Connecticut and Rhode Island to participate, and the Massachusetts legislature instructed its delegates to work for a plan of intercolonial union.

In Philadelphia, Benjamin Franklin too was thinking about colonial union. On May 9, 1754, his *Pennsylvania Gazette* printed the first political cartoon in American history, with the caption "Unite or die." A month later, he drafted his "Short Hints towards a Scheme for Uniting the Northern Colonies," which he presented to the Albany Congress in June. His plan called for a "President General" to be appointed by the Crown as commander-in-chief and to administer the laws of the union, and for a "Grand Council" to be elected for three-year terms by the lower houses of each colony. Deputies would be apportioned according to tax receipts. The union would have the power to raise soldiers, build forts, levy taxes, regulate the Indian trade when it touched the welfare of more than a single colony, purchase land from the Indians, and supervise western settlements until the Crown organized them as new colonies. To take effect, the plan would require ap-

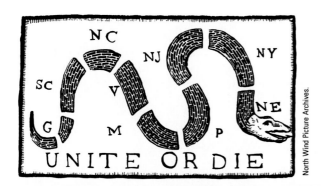

BENJAMIN FRANKLIN'S SNAKE CARTOON

The first newspaper cartoon in colonial America, this device appeared in the *Pennsylvania Gazette* in spring 1754. The cartoon called for colonial union on the eve of the Albany Congress and drew on the folk legend that a snake, cut into pieces, could revive and live if it somehow joined its severed parts together before sundown.

proval by the Crown and by each colonial legislature and presentation to Parliament for its consent. The Albany Congress adopted an amended version of Franklin's proposal.

Both Shirley and Franklin were far ahead of public opinion. Newspapers did not even discuss the Albany Plan. Every colony rejected it, most with little debate, some unanimously. The voting was close only in Massachusetts, which had borne the heaviest burden in the three earlier wars with New France. As Franklin later explained, the colonies feared that the president general might become too powerful, but they also distrusted one another. Despite the French threat, they were not ready to patch up their differences and unite. They did not yet see themselves as "Americans."

The Board of Trade responded by drafting its own plan of union. Its plan resembled Franklin's, except that the Grand Council could only requisition—instead of tax—and colonial union would not require Parliament's approval. After news arrived that Washington had surrendered his small force to the French at Great Meadows in July 1754, Britain decided that the colonies were incapable of uniting in their own defense. Even if they could, the precedent would be dangerous. London sent redcoats to Virginia instead—two regiments, commanded by General Edward Braddock. For Britain, colonial union and direct military aid were policy *alternatives*. Although military aid would cost the British government more than the proposed union, it seemed the safer choice. By winter of 1754–55, colonial union was a dead issue on both sides of the ocean.

Yet the Albany Congress achieved one major objective. Addressing Iroquois grievances against New York, it urged the Crown to take charge of relations with all western Indians. London created two Indian superintendencies—one south of the Ohio, which went first to Edmund Atkin and then John Stuart; and one north of the Ohio, which went to William Johnson, an Irish immigrant to New York who had influence with the Mohawks. These offices would survive the war.

Britain's Years of Defeat

In 1755, London hoped that a quick victory by Braddock at the forks of the Ohio River would keep the war from spreading. Braddock's regiments landed in Virginia, a signal that London probably intended to let Virginia, rather than Quaker Pennsylvania, control the upper Ohio valley, including what is now Pittsburgh. At a council of high officials called by Braddock at Alexandria, Virginia, Governor Shirley persuaded him to accept New England's much broader war objectives. Instead of a single expedition aimed at one fort, to be followed by others if time permitted, the campaign of 1755 became four distinct offensives designed to crush the outer defenses of New France and leave it open to British invasion. Braddock was so impressed with Shirley that he named him second in command of the British army in North America, not bad for an English lawyer with no military training who had arrived almost penniless in Boston 25 years earlier.

Braddock and Shirley tried to make maximum use of both redcoats and provincials. The redcoats were highly disciplined professional soldiers who served long terms and had been trained to fight other professional armies. Irregular war in the forests of North America made them uneasy. Provincials, by contrast, were recruited by individual colonies. They were volunteers, often quite young, who usually enlisted only for a single campaign. They knew little about military drill, expected to serve under the officers who had recruited them, and sometimes refused to obey orders that they disliked. Provincials admired the courage of the redcoats but were shocked by their irreverence and by the brutal discipline imposed on them by their officers. Nevertheless, thousands of colonists also enlisted in the British army, providing up to 40 percent of its strength in North America by 1760.

Under the enlarged plan for 1755, the redcoats in Nova Scotia together with New England provincials would assault Fort Beauséjour, where the Acadian peninsula joins mainland Canada. New England and New York provincials would attack Crown Point, and Shirley, commissioned as a British colonel, would lead two regiments of redcoats (recently recruited in New England) to Niagara and cut off New France from the western Indians. Braddock, with the strongest force, would attack Fort Duquesne.

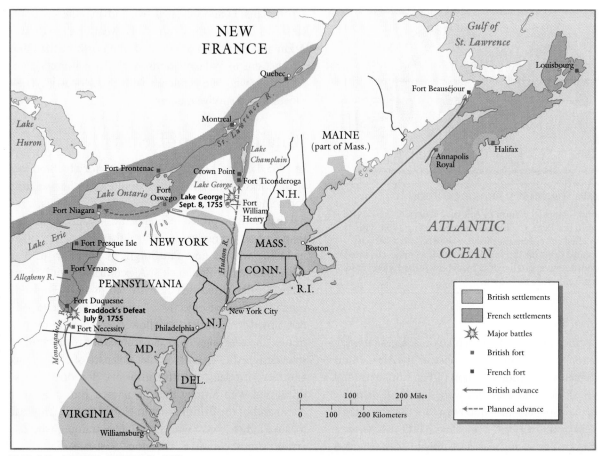

MAP 4.5   BRITISH OFFENSES, 1755

The British launched four major offenses against the French: in Nova Scotia, at Lake George, at Fort Oswego, and at the Forks of the Ohio River, where Edward Braddock led his men to disaster.

Instead, Braddock alienated the Indians and marched to disaster on the Monongahela. The western Delawares asked him whether their villages and hunting rights would be secure under the British. He replied, "No Savage Should Inherit the Land." The chiefs retorted that "if they might not have Liberty To Live on the Land they would not Fight for it." Braddock declared that he "did not need their Help." It took Braddock several months to hack a road through the wilderness wide enough for his artillery. He took care to prevent ambushes at two fords of the Monongahela, and as he crossed that stream on July 9, he pushed on, confident that he had overcome all obstacles.

At Fort Duquesne, the French commander, Liénard, *sieur* de Beaujeu, could muster only 72 French, 146 Canadians, and 637 Indians against the 1,400 regulars under Braddock and 450 Virginia provincials. Beaujeu had planned to attack the British at the fords of the Monongahela, but the Indians thought such an assault would be suicidal and refused. "Will you allow your father to act

alone?" he finally asked melodramatically. "I am sure to defeat them." As Beaujeu marched out, the reluctant Indians followed. Too late to attack at the fords, the French ran into the British vanguard a few miles southeast of the fort. They clashed along a narrow path with thick forest and brush on either side. Beaujeu was killed at once, and his men almost broke, but they rallied and took cover on the British flanks. Braddock's rear elements rushed toward the sound of the guns and there, massed together, the redcoats formed a gigantic bull's-eye. The Indians and the French poured round after round into them, while the British fired wild volleys at the invisible enemy. The British lost 977 killed or wounded, along with their artillery. Braddock was killed. Only 39 French and Indians were killed or wounded. The redcoats finally broke and ran. Washington, who had fought as a Virginia volunteer, reported that offensive operations would be impossible for the rest of the year. Braddock's road through the wilderness now became a highway for the enemy. For the first time in the his-

tory of Quaker Pennsylvania, its settlers faced the horrors of a frontier war.

In Nova Scotia, Fort Beauséjour fell on June 17, 1755. Then the commanders did something to indicate that this war would not be a conventional, limited struggle. When the Acadians refused to take an oath that might have obliged them to bear arms against other Frenchmen, the British and Yankees responded with an 18th-century version of ethnic cleansing. They rounded up between 6,000 and 7,000 Acadians, forced them aboard ships, and expelled them from the province, to be scattered among the 13 colonies, none of which was prepared for the influx. A second roundup in 1759 caught most of the families that had evaded the first one. The British also resumed their merciless war against the Micmac Indians.

The officers who organized these expulsions insisted that they had found a humane way of compelling French Catholics to assimilate with the Protestant majority. Reasoning also that the Acadians were not British subjects because they had not taken the oath, and that only British subjects could own land in a British colony, the government of Nova Scotia confiscated the land the Acadians had farmed for generations and redistributed it to Protestant settlers, mostly from New England. About 3,000 of the Acadian refugees, after spending miserable years as unwanted Catholic exiles in a Protestant world, finally made it to French Louisiana, where their descendants became known as Cajuns. Others went to France, and some even made their way back to Nova Scotia or what later became New Brunswick. Few remained in the 13 colonies.

In the principal northern theater of war in 1755, William Johnson led his provincials against Crown Point. The French commander, Jean-Armand, baron Dieskau, hoping to repeat the French success against Braddock, attacked a body of provincials on September 8 and drove it back in panic to its base camp, the improvised Fort William Henry near Lake George. French regulars assailed the fort but were driven off with heavy losses in a six-hour struggle. Colonial newspapers proclaimed the battle a great victory because the provincials had not only held the field but had also wounded

and captured Dieskau. Johnson probably could have taken poorly defended Crown Point, but he too had been wounded and was content to hold Fort William Henry and nearby Fort Edward at the headwaters of the Hudson. It took a more professional eye than his to distinguish the carnage of victory from the carnage of defeat.

Farther west, Shirley's Niagara campaign reached Oswego on Lake Ontario and then stopped for the winter, held in check by the French at Fort Frontenac on the lake's northern shore. Oswego was soon cut off by heavy snows. Malnutrition and disease ravaged the garrison.

A World War

With the death of Braddock and the capture of Dieskau, military amateurs took over both armies: Shirley in the British colonies and Governor-General Pierre de Rigaud de Vaudreuil in New France. Vaudreuil, a Canadian, understood his colony's weakness without Indian support. First, the white population of the 13 colonies outnumbered that of New France by 13 to 1; Massachusetts alone had nearly three times as many settlers as New France. Second, Vaudreuil knew that if the redcoats and the British colonies could concentrate their resources in a few critical places, they had a good chance of overwhelming New France. Therefore, a frontier war that pitted New France primarily against ordinary settlers—horrible though it was—remained the most effective way to force the British colonies to scatter their resources over a vast area.

© Hulton Archive/Getty Images.

THE ENGLISH LION DISMEMBER'D (1756)
This striking cartoon reflects British consternation during the first half of the Seven Years' War. France had just taken the Mediterranean island of Minorca from the British.

As long as Vaudreuil was in charge, New France kept winning. Indian attacks devastated frontier settlements, especially in Pennsylvania, a pacifist colony without even a militia when the war began. Even so, the French government decided that New France needed a professional general and sent Louis-Joseph, marquis de Montcalm, in 1756. Shocked and repelled by the brutality of frontier warfare, Montcalm tried to turn the conflict into a traditional European struggle of sieges and battles in which the advantage (as Vaudreuil well understood) would pass to the British. Nevertheless, Montcalm won several major successes. Oswego fell in summer 1756. When Fort William Henry surrendered to him a year later, he promised the garrison the honors of war, which meant that it could keep its property and march unmolested to Fort Edward. But France's Indian allies considered this agreement a betrayal of their customs. They killed or carried off 308 of the 2,300 prisoners, an event that colonial newspapers called the Fort William Massacre. Most of those killed were trying to save their property, which the Indians considered their rightful plunder. Montcalm lost heavily at Fort William Henry. He never again managed to raise sizable bodies of Indian allies, and because the British blamed him for the "massacre," they refused to grant the honors of war to any French force for the rest of the conflict.

HISTORY THROUGH FILM

The Last of the Mohicans (1992)

This movie, the most recent and most effective film version of James Fenimore Cooper's immensely successful 1826 novel of the same title, centers on the siege and capture of Fort William Henry in 1757, an event that had enormous consequences for everyone involved. During the Seven Years' (or French and Indian) War, the French, accompanied by a huge contingent of Indian allies, besiege this British fort at the northern tip of Lake George in New York. Hawkeye (Daniel Day-Lewis) is a frontiersman reared among Indians, who include his two closest friends, Chingachgook (Russell Means) and Chingachgook's son, Uncas (Eric Schweig). The trio are escorting to the fort a party that includes British Major Heyward (Steven Waddington) and Cora (Madeleine Stowe) and Alice (Jodhi May), the two daughters of Colonel Munro (Maurice Reyes), the commander of the fort. Heyward plans to marry Cora. Through the treachery of another Indian, Magua (Wes Studi), the party is ambushed, but the trio of escorts rescues the major and the two women and leads them safely to the fort just as the siege begins.

Fort William Henry soon falls to the French. General Montcalm (Patrick Chereau) accepts the formal surrender

Directed by Michael Mann. Starring Daniel Day-Lewis (Hawkeye), Russell Means (Chingachgook), Eric Schweig (Uncas), Steven Waddington (Major Heyward), Madeleine Stowe (Cora), Jodhi May (Alice), and Wes Studi (Magua).

of the British garrison and promises them the "honors of war," the right to march away with their unloaded muskets and their personal possessions. Instead, Magua defies Montcalm and leads a murderous assault against the column as it tries to retreat to Fort Edward at the head of the Hudson River. In a climactic action sequence, Heyward is captured and is being tortured to death when Hawkeye shoots him to end his misery. Alice leaps off a cliff rather than submit to Magua, who has already killed Uncas. Chingachgook then kills Magua. Along with Hawkeye and Cora, Chingachgook survives, thus becoming the last of the Mohicans.

Cooper gave the Iroquois the role of the attacking Indians, probably because most of them did side with the British during the American Revolution. But in the Seven Years' War, most of those who fought were on the British side. The film version addresses this problem by making the Hurons, by then a minor nation, into the pro-French Indians, thereby providing a rare example of a movie being more historically accurate than the novel on which it rests. The film, like Cooper, makes the massacre far more destructive than it actually was. Most of the settlers killed or captured that day were trying to protect their personal

Meanwhile, Braddock's defeat, combined with the British loss of Minorca in the Mediterranean, convinced the British government that the struggle with France could not be limited to a few outposts. Britain declared war on France in 1756, and the French and Indian War in the colonies merged with a general European struggle—the Seven Years' War (1756–63)—involving France, Austria, and Russia against Prussia, which was heavily subsidized by Britain. Although religion had little to do with the war in Europe, the Seven Years' War aligned coalitions of Protestant states against Catholic states in a way not seen there for a century. To many North American clergymen, a Protestant victory might herald the onset of the Millen-

nium. The conflict spread even to India, where British forces expelled the French from nearly all of that vast subcontinent.

Reluctant to antagonize Britain, Spain remained neutral for most of the war, a choice that had huge implications within North America. In the previous war, Spain had been able to turn the slaves of South Carolina against their masters and to create unrest even in New York. At a minimum, Spanish hostilities early in the war would have forced the British to fight in another theater of conflict. Instead, Spain's neutrality permitted Britain to concentrate its resources against New France. By 1762, when Spain finally entered the war in a vain effort to prevent a total

The Last of the Mohicans tells of the siege and capture of Britain's Fort William Henry in 1757, during the French and Indian War.

property, which the Indians regarded as their rightful plunder. The French had traditionally raised Indian forces with the promise of loot and captives. Montcalm's attempt to impose European standards of war by intervening on the British soldiers' and settlers' behalf meant that he broke faith with his Indian allies and was never again able to raise a force of comparable size. That the massacre occurred at

all meant that he lost credibility with the British and their settlers. For the rest of the conflict, the British never again granted a French force the honors of war. Montcalm's great victory became, in the long run, a severe defeat for France.

In 1979, director Michael Mann won an award as best director from the Directors' Guild of America for *The Jericho Mile*.

British victory, the French had already surrendered Canada, and Britain's seasoned army and navy easily rolled over Spain's less experienced forces.

Imperial Tensions: From Loudoun to Pitt

In 1755, London, to its dismay, realized that Shirley, an amateur, had taken command of the British army in North America. The government dispatched an irascible Scot, John Campbell, earl of Loudoun, to replace him and began pouring in reinforcements. Loudoun had a special talent for alienating provincials. Colonial units did not care to serve under his command and sometimes bluntly rejected his orders. Provincials believed they had a contractual relationship with *their* officers; they had never agreed to serve under Loudoun's professionals. They refused to serve beyond their term of enlistment, most of which expired on November 1 or December 1 of each year. Even when the British ordered them to stay longer, many of them defiantly marched home.

In fact, many British officers despised the provincials, especially their officers. "The Americans are in general the dirtiest most contemptible cowardly dogs that you can conceive," snarled General James Wolfe; "They fall down dead in their own dirt and desert by battalions, officers and all." General John Forbes was usually more positive, but he too once suggested "shooting dead a Dozen of their cowardly Officers at the Head of the Line." Other British officers held more favorable opinions. Horatio Gates, Richard Montgomery, Hugh Mercer, and Arthur St. Clair all remained in America after the war and became generals in the American army during the Revolution. Colonel Isaac Barré praised American courage in the House of Commons in 1765 and even coined the phrase "Sons of Liberty" to describe them—a label instantly adopted by men who resisted Britain's postwar policies.

As the new commander-in-chief, Loudoun faced other problems—the quartering (or housing) of British soldiers, the relative rank of British and provincial officers, military discipline, revenue, and smuggling. He tried to impose authoritarian solutions on them all. When he sent redcoats into a city, he demanded that the assembly pay to quarter them or else he would take over buildings by force. He tried to make any British captain superior in rank to any provincial officer, a rule that antagonized such experienced New England officers as General John Winslow and his six colonels. Loudoun ordered New England troops to serve directly under British officers and to accept the harsh discipline of the British army, an arrangement that New Englanders thought violated the terms of their enlistment. They refused to cooperate. When some colonial assemblies refused to vote adequate supplies, Loudoun urged

Parliament to tax the colonies directly. Shocked that the molasses trade with the French West Indies was proceeding as usual, he urged the navy to stamp it out or imposed embargoes on colonial shipping, an action that punished fair traders as well as smugglers. Loudoun built up his forces but otherwise achieved little.

In 1757, William Pitt came to power as Britain's war minister and found workable voluntaristic solutions to the problems that had defeated Loudoun's authoritarian methods. Pitt understood that consent worked better than coercion in the colonies. Colonial assemblies built barracks to house British soldiers. Pitt declared that every provincial officer would rank immediately behind the equivalent British rank but above all lesser officers, British or provincial. He then promoted every British lieutenant colonel to the rank of "colonel in America only." That decision left only about 30 British majors vulnerable to being ordered about by a provincial colonel, but few of them had independent commands anyway. Provincial units under the command of their own officers cooperated with the British army, and the officers began to impose something close to British discipline on them, including hundreds of lashes for routine offenses.

Rather than impose a parliamentary tax, Pitt set aside £200,000 beginning in 1758 (later reduced to £133,000) and told the colonies that they could claim a share of it in proportion to their contribution to the war effort. In effect, he persuaded the colonies to compete voluntarily in support of his stupendous war effort. The subsidies covered something less than half of the cost of fielding 20,000 provincials each year from 1758 to 1760, and rather smaller numbers in 1761 and 1762 as operations shifted to the Caribbean. Smuggling angered Pitt as much as it did anyone else, but British conquests soon reduced that problem. By 1762, Canada, Martinique, and Guadeloupe, as well as Spanish Havana, were all in British hands. Few places were any longer worth smuggling to, except Saint-Domingue.

Pitt had no patience with military failure. After Loudoun called off his attack on Louisbourg in 1757, Pitt replaced him with James Abercrombie. He also put Jeffrey Amherst in charge of a new Louisbourg expedition, with James Wolfe as one of his brigadiers. By 1758, the British Empire had finally put together a military force capable of overwhelming New France and had learned how to use it. In the last years of the war, cooperation between redcoats and provincials became routine and devastatingly effective.

The Years of British Victory

By 1758, the Royal Navy had cut off Canada from reinforcements and even from routine supplies. Britain had sent more than 30 regiments to North America. Combined with 20,000 provincials, thousands of bateau men

rowing supplies into the interior, and swarms of privateers preying on French commerce, Britain had mustered perhaps 60,000 men in North America and in nearby waters. Most of them now closed in on the 75,000 people of New France. Montcalm, who in any case was running out of goods for use in the Indian trade, refused to encourage more Indian attacks on the frontier and prepared to defend the approaches to Canada at Forts Duquesne, Niagara, Frontenac, Ticonderoga, Crown Point, and Louisbourg.

Spurred on by Quaker mediators, the British and colonial governments came to terms with the western Indians in 1758, promising not to seize their lands after the war and arranging an uneasy peace. Few settlers or officials had yet noticed a new trend that was emerging dur-ing the conflict: Before the 1750s, Indian nations had often waged terrible wars against one another. Now, however, few Indians in the northeastern woodlands were willing to attack others. In 1755, for example, some Senecas fought with New France and some Mohawks with the British, but they maneuvered carefully to avoid confronting each other. This Iroquois sense of solidarity was beginning to spread. Iroquois and western Algonquians, once deadly enemies, saw real advantages in cooperation. A sense of pan-Indian identity was beginning to emerge. Although most Indians regarded the French as far less dangerous than the British and even fought alongside the French, they were never French puppets. They fought, negotiated, and made peace in 1758 to preserve their own hold on the land.

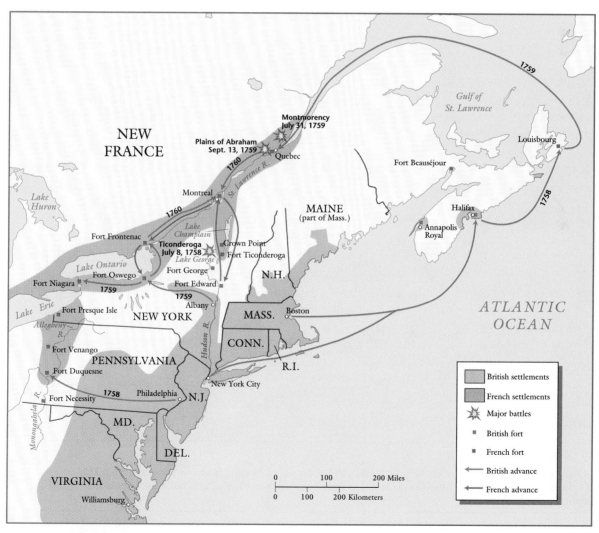

MAP 4.6 CONQUEST OF CANADA, 1758–1760

In three campaigns, the British with strong colonial support first subdued the outer defenses of New France, then took Quebec in 1759 and Montreal in 1760.

 View an animated version of this map or related maps at http://history.wadsworth.com/murrin_LEP4e.

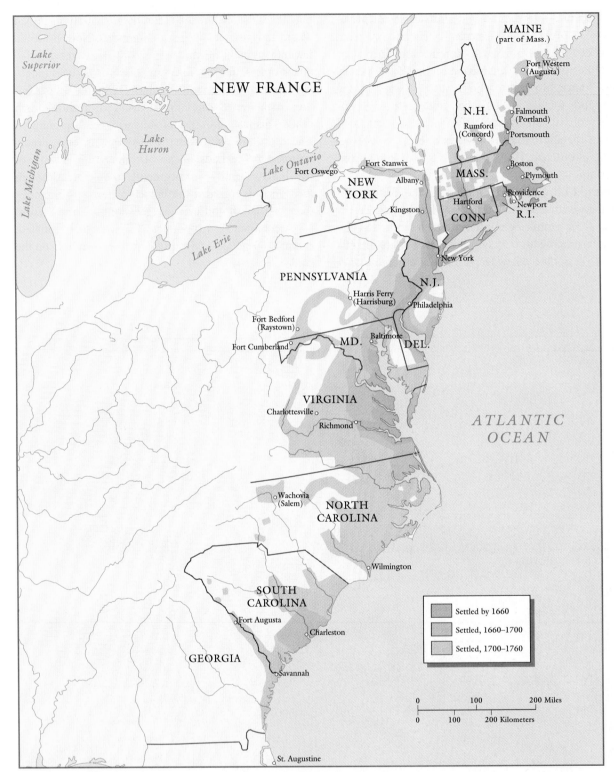

MAP 4.7 GROWTH OF POPULATION TO 1760

Between 1700 and 1760, the population of the British colonies had increased by more than a factor of six, from 250,000 to almost 1.6 million. Settlement had filled the piedmont in most areas and was beginning to cross the Appalachian watershed into the Ohio Valley.

Peace with the western Indians in 1758 permitted the British to revive the grand military plan of 1755, except that this time the overall goal was clear—the conquest of New France. Amherst and Wolfe, with 9,000 regulars and 500 provincials, besieged Louisbourg for 60 days. It fell in September, thus adding Cape Breton Island to the British province of Nova Scotia. A force of 3,000 provincials under Colonel John Bradstreet advanced to Lake Ontario, took Fort Frontenac, and began building a fleet. This victory cut off the French in the Ohio valley from their supplies. A powerful force of regulars under John Forbes and provincials under Washington marched west, this time through Pennsylvania, to attack Fort Duquesne, but the French blew up the fort and retreated north just before they arrived. The British erected Fort Pitt on the ruins.

The only British defeat in 1758 occurred in northern New York when Abercrombie sent 6,000 regulars and 9,000 provincials against Ticonderoga (Carillon), defended by Montcalm and 3,500 troops. Instead of waiting for his artillery to arrive or trying to outflank the French, Aber-crombie ordered a frontal assault against a heavily fortified position. His regulars were butchered by the withering fire, and after witnessing the carnage for several hours, the horrified provincials fled. Like Indians, they regarded such attacks as sheer madness. When Pitt heard the news, he sacked Abercrombie, put Amherst in charge of the New York theater of war, and left Wolfe at Louisbourg to plan an attack up the St. Lawrence River against Quebec.

In 1759, while the provincials on Lake Ontario moved west and took Niagara, Amherst spent the summer cautiously reducing Ticonderoga and Crown Point. (Pitt expected him to reach Montreal.) The most dramatic campaign occurred farther east. In June, Wolfe ascended the St. Lawrence River with 8,000 redcoats and colonial rangers and laid siege to Quebec, defended by Montcalm with 16,000 regulars, Canadian militia, and Indians. When an attack below the city failed, Wolfe mounted howitzers on high ground across the river from Quebec and began reducing most of the city to rubble. Frustrated by the French refusal to come out and fight, he turned loose his

Clements Library, University of Michigan, Ann Arbor.

DEATH OF GENERAL WOLFE (1771)

Benjamin West, who was born in Pennsylvania, taught himself to paint, opened a studio in Philadelphia, and then went to Europe. He studied the great Italian masters for several years and then settled in London, where he became the first American artist to have an enormous impact. Contemporary heroes were displayed in classical attire, but West used their actual uniforms. George III was so impressed that he made West the history painter to the royal court.

American rangers ("the worst soldiers in the universe," he boasted), who ravaged and burned more than 1,400 farms. Anyone who resisted was shot and scalped. Still the French held out.

By September, both Wolfe and Montcalm realized that the British fleet would soon have to depart or risk being frozen in during the long winter. Wolfe made a last desperate effort, preferring to die rather than fail. His men silently sailed up the river, climbed a formidable cliff above the city in darkness, and on the morning of September 13, 1759, deployed on the Plains of Abraham behind Quebec. Montcalm panicked. Instead of using his artillery to defend the walls from inside (Wolfe's force had been able to drag only two guns with them), he marched out of Quebec onto the plains. Both generals now had what they craved most, a set-piece European battle that lasted about 15 minutes. Wolfe and Montcalm were both mortally wounded, but the British drove the French from the field and took Quebec. After the fall of Montreal in 1760, Canada surrendered.

The Cherokee War and Spanish Intervention

In December 1759, as the British were completing their triumph over France, the Cherokees, who had been allies and trading partners of South Carolina, reacted to a long string of violent incidents by attacking backcountry settlers. Within a year, they drove the frontier back 100 miles. South Carolina appealed to Amherst for help, and he sent regular soldiers who laid waste to the Cherokee Lower Towns in the Appalachian foothills. When that expedition failed to bring peace, another one the next year devastated the Middle Towns farther west, while Virginia threatened the Overhill Towns. The Cherokees made peace in December 1761, but the backcountry settlers, left brutalized and lawless, soon became severe political problems for South Carolina's government.

Only then, in January 1762, after the French and the Cherokees had been defeated, did Spain finally enter the war. British forces quickly took Havana and even Manila in the distant Philippines. France and Spain sued for peace.

The Peace of Paris

In 1763, the Peace of Paris ended the war. Britain returned Martinique and Guadeloupe to France. France surrendered to Great Britain several minor West Indian islands and all of North America east of the Mississippi, except New Orleans. In exchange for Havana, Spain ceded Florida to the British and also promised to pay a large ransom for the return of Manila. To compensate its Spanish ally, France gave all of Louisiana west of the Mississippi and New Orleans to Spain. Most of the Spanish and African occupants of Florida withdrew to other parts of the Spanish empire, but nearly all French settlers remained behind in Canada, the Illinois country, and what was now Spanish Louisiana.

The British colonists were jubilant. The age of warfare and frontier carnage seemed over at last. Britain and the colonies could now develop their vast resources in an imperial partnership and would share unprecedented prosperity. But the western Indians angrily rejected the peace settlement. No one had conquered them, and they denied the right or the power of France to surrender their lands to Great Britain. They began to plan their own war of liberation.

Conclusion

Between 1713 and 1754, expansion and renewed immigration pushed North American settlement ever farther into the interior. With a population that doubled every 25 years, many householders no longer enjoyed the opportunity to give all of their sons and daughters the level of economic success that they were enjoying. By midcentury, many families took up a trade or looked westward for what their old community could not provide. Women worked harder just to sustain levels of opportunity for their households. Many families had to favor sons over daughters and the eldest son over his younger brothers, reluctantly following practices used in England.

The colonies anglicized in other ways as well. Newspapers and the learned professions spread the English Enlightenment to the colonies. English revivalists, especially George Whitefield, had a tremendous impact in North America. The northern colonies borrowed Court politics from Walpole's Britain, while most southern colonies favored politics as envisioned by the Country opposition in Britain. Both considered themselves the freest people on earth. When expansion and imperial rivalries again led to war after 1739, the colonists discovered that enslaved Africans associated Spain with liberty, whereas most eastern woodland Indians looked to New France for support. The threat of internal upheaval kept King George's War indecisive in the 1740s. Taking advantage of Spain's neutral position when Britain and France went to war after 1754, the British Empire mobilized its full resources and conquered New France.

The French and Indian War left behind vivid memories. Provincials admired the courage of the redcoats and the victories they won but hated their brutal discipline and arrogant officers. British officials greatly exaggerated what military force alone could accomplish and underestimated colonial contributions to the imperial cause. The concord and prosperity that were supposed to follow Britain's great triumph yielded instead to bitter strife.

SUGGESTED READINGS

The best study of 18th-century immigration is **Bernard Bailyn, *Voyagers to the West: A Passage in the Peopling of America on the Eve of the Revolution*** (1986). **A. Roger Ekirch, *Bound for America: The Transportation of British Convicts to the Colonies*** (1987) is also important. For gentility and the Enlightenment, excellent studies include **Richard L. Bushman, *The Refinement of America: Persons, Houses, Cities*** (1992); **Ned Landsman, *From Colonials to Provincials: Thought and Culture in America, 1680–1760*** (1998); **David S. Shields, *Civil Tongues & Polite Letters in British America*** (1997); and **Charles E. Clark, *The Public Prints: The Newspaper in Anglo-American Culture, 1665–1740*** (1994). For early Georgia, see **Harold E. Davis, *The Fledgling Province: Social and Cultural Life in Colonial Georgia, 1773–1776*** (1976); and **Larry E. Ivers, *British Drums on the Southern Frontier: The Military Colonization of Georgia, 1733–1749*** (1974). **Frank J. Lambert's *"Pedlar in Divinity": George Whitefield and the Transatlantic Revivals*** (1994) provides a strong introduction to the Great Awakening. **Bernard Bailyn's *The Origins of American Politics*** (1968) touched off a considerable debate. See especially **Jack P. Greene, "Political Mimesis: A Consideration of the Historical and Cultural Roots of Legislative Behavior in the British Colonies in the Eighteenth Century,"** with a comment by Bailyn and a reply by Greene, in ***American Historical Review,*** 75 (1969), 333–367.

For the renewal of imperial conflict after 1739, see **T. J. Davis, *A Rumor of Revolt: The "Great Negro Plot" in Colonial New York*** (1985); **Fred Anderson, *Crucible of War: The Seven Years War and the Fate of Empire in British North America, 1754–1766*** (2000); **Timothy J. Shannon, *Indians and Colonists at the Crossroads of Empire: The Albany Congress of 1754*** (2000); and **Ian K. Steele, *Betrayals: Fort William Henry and the "Massacre"*** (1990).

 ## AMERICAN JOURNEY ONLINE
AND
 ## INFOTRAC COLLEGE EDITION

Visit the source collections at www.ajaccess.wadsworth.com and infotrac.thomsonlearning.com and use the Search function with the following key terms to explore documents, images, audio and video clips, articles, and commentary related to the material in this chapter.

John Peter Zenger	Great Awakening
Francisco Menéndez	King George's War
Albany Congress	Cherokee War
French and Indian War	Peace of Paris
Enlightenment	

GRADE AIDS

Visit the Liberty Equality Power Companion Web Site for resources specific to this textbook: http://history.wadsworth.com/murrin_LEP4e

  The CD in the back of this book and the U.S. History Resource Center at http://history.wadsworth.com/u.s./ offer a variety of tools to help you succeed in this course, including access to quizzes; images; documents; interactive simulations, maps, and timelines; movie explorations; and a wealth of other sources.

Reform, Resistance, Revolution

ENGAGEMENT AT THE NORTH BRIDGE IN CONCORD, APRIL 19, 1775
This 1775 painting by Ralph Earl is quite accurate in its details. It shows the first American military victory in the war when the militia drove the British back from Concord Bridge and eventually through Lexington and all the way to Boston.

CHAPTER OUTLINE

B ritain left an army in North America after 1763 and taxed the colonies to pay part of its cost. The colonists agreed that they should contribute to their own defense but insisted that taxation without representation violated their rights as Englishmen. Three successive crises shattered Britain's North American empire by 1776.

In the first, the Stamp Act crisis, the colonists began by petitioning for a redress of grievances. When that effort failed, they nullified the Stamp Act and continued their resistance until Parliament repealed the tax in 1766. The jubilant colonists celebrated their victory. In the second, the Townshend crisis of 1767–70, Parliament imposed new taxes on certain imported goods. The colonists petitioned and resisted simultaneously, mostly through an intercolonial nonimportation movement. The British sent troops to Boston. After several violent confrontations, the soldiers withdrew, and Parliament modified but did not repeal the Townshend Revenue Act. The duty on tea remained. Repeal of the other duties broke the back of the nonimportation movement. This time nobody celebrated. The Tea Act of 1773 launched the third crisis, and it quickly escalated. Boston destroyed British tea without bothering to petition first. When Parliament responded with the Coercive Acts of 1774, the colonists created the Continental Congress to organize further resistance. Neither side dared back down, and the confrontation careened toward military violence. The war broke out in April 1775. Fifteen months later, the colonies declared their independence.

CHAPTER FOCUS

♦ Why, in 1766, did the colonists stop resisting and rejoice over the repeal of the Stamp Act, even though the Revenue Act of 1766 continued to tax molasses?

♦ Why did the colonists start a revolution after the government lowered the price of tea through the Tea Act of 1773?

♦ In 1775, Lord North promised that Parliament would not tax any colony that paid its share of the costs of imperial defense and gave adequate salaries to its civil officers, but the Second Continental Congress rejected the proposal out of hand. Had George Grenville offered something of the kind between 1763 and 1765, could Britain have averted the Revolution?

♦ How and why did a resistance movement, dedicated to protecting the colonists' rights as Englishmen, end by proclaiming American independence instead?

🌎 Imperial Reform

In 1760, George III (1760–1820) inherited the British throne at the age of 22. The king's pronouncements on behalf of religion and virtue at first won him many admirers in North America, but the political coalition leading Britain to victory over France fell apart. The king's new ministers set out to reform the empire.

From Pitt to Grenville

The king, along with his tutor and principal adviser, John Stuart, earl of Bute, feared that the Seven Years' War would bankrupt Britain. From 1758 on, despite one victory after another, George and Bute grew increasingly despondent. When William Pitt, the king's war minister, urged a preemptive strike on Spain before Spain could attack Britain, Bute forced him to resign in October 1761, even though Pitt had become the most popular official of the century. Bute soon learned that Pitt had been right. Spain entered the war in January 1762. In May, Bute replaced Thomas Pelham-Holles, duke of Newcastle and the most powerful politician of the previous 25 years, as first lord of the treasury. To economize, Bute next reduced Britain's subsidies to Prussia, its only major ally in Europe. So eager were the king and Bute to end the war that they gave back to France the wealthy West Indian islands of Guadeloupe and Martinique.

The British press harshly denounced Bute. As soon as Parliament approved the Treaty of Paris, Bute dismayed the king by resigning. He had had enough. In April 1763, George Grenville (Pitt's brother-in-law) became first lord of the treasury, although the king distrusted him and found him only marginally acceptable. Pitt and Newcastle, who blamed Grenville for having sided with Bute against them, would have nothing at all to do with him.

The Grenville Ministry

Grenville spent most of his first year coping with a crisis at home that later dovetailed with events in the colonies. John Wilkes, a radical journalist, questioned the king's

---

C H R O N O L O G Y

1745–55	Land riots rock New Jersey
1760–61	Cherokee War devastates South Carolina backcountry
1760	George III becomes king of Great Britain
1761	Pitt resigns as war minister
1763	Grenville ministry takes power • Wilkes publishes *North Briton* No. 45 • Pontiac's War begins • King issues Proclamation of 1763
1764	Parliament passes Currency and Sugar Acts
1765	Parliament passes Quartering Act • Stamp Act passed and nullified • Rockingham replaces Grenville as prime minister
1766	Parliament repeals Stamp Act, passes Declaratory Act and Revenue Act of 1766 • Chatham (Pitt) ministry takes power
1767	Parliament passes New York Restraining Act and Townshend Revenue Act
1768	Massachusetts assembly dispatches Circular Letter • Wilkes elected to Parliament • Massacre of St. George's Fields occurs in England • Massachusetts refuses to rescind Circular Letter • *Liberty* riot occurs in Boston • Governors dissolve assemblies that support Circular Letter • Redcoats sent to Boston
1769	Nonimportation becomes effective • Regulators achieve major goals in South Carolina
1770	North becomes prime minister • Boston Massacre • Townshend Revenue Act partially repealed • Nonimportation collapses
1771	North Carolina regulators defeated at Alamance Creek
1772	*Gaspée* affair in Rhode Island increases tensions
1772–73	Twelve colonies create committees of correspondence
1773	Tea Act passed • Boston Tea Party protests tea duty • Wheatley's poetry published in London
1774	American Quakers prohibit slaveholding • Parliament passes Coercive Acts and Quebec Act • First Continental Congress convenes in Philadelphia
1775	Revolutionary War begins at Lexington and Concord • Second Continental Congress creates Continental Army • Olive Branch Petition fails • George III issues Proclamation of Rebellion
1775–76	Americans invade Canada
1776	Paine publishes *Common Sense* • British evacuate Boston • Continental Congress approves Declaration of Independence

---

integrity in the 45th number of the *North Briton,* a newspaper founded to vilify Bute, a Scot (or "North Briton"). The government used a general warrant (one that specified neither the person nor place to be searched) to invade the newspaper's offices and arrest Wilkes, a member of Parliament as well as a journalist. He was charged with

publishing a seditious libel. But Chief Justice Charles Pratt, an admirer of Pitt, declared general warrants illegal and freed Wilkes. The government promptly arrested Wilkes on a special warrant, but Pratt again freed him, declaring that parliamentary privilege extended to seditious libels. London artisans shouted lustily for "Wilkes and Liberty!" Grenville had given the opposition two popular issues, and its leaders expected to overturn him during the winter session of Parliament. Grenville triumphed, however. A reading of Wilkes's pornographic *Essay on Woman* to a shocked and amused House of Lords got Grenville enough votes in the Commons for an unexpectedly huge victory on parliamentary privilege. Months later, after the shock had faded, Grenville also managed a narrow win on general warrants. Wilkes fled to France and was outlawed in Britain, but "45" became a symbol of liberty on both sides of the ocean.

As the Wilkes affair subsided, Grenville turned his attention to the colonies. Britain's national debt had nearly doubled during the last war with France and stood at £130 million. Interest on the debt absorbed more than half of annual revenues, and Britain was already one of the most heavily taxed societies in the world. The sheer scale of Britain's victory required more revenue just to police the conquered colonies. In 1762 and 1763, Bute and Grenville decided to leave 20 battalions with about 7,000 men in America, mostly in Canada and Florida, with smaller garrisons scattered throughout Indian territory. Because the colonists would receive the benefit of this protection, Grenville argued, they ought to pay a reasonable portion of the cost, and eventually all of it. He never asked the settlers to contribute anything to Britain's national debt or to Britain's heavy domestic needs, but he did insist that the colonies begin to pay toward their own defense.

Instead of building on the voluntaristic measures that Pitt had used to win the war, Grenville reverted to the demands for coercive reforms that had crisscrossed the Atlantic during Britain's years of defeat from 1755 to 1757. London, he believed, must gain effective centralized control over the colonies. To the settlers, victory over France would mean new burdens, not relief. To Grenville, the willing cooperation of the colonies after 1758 reflected the empire's weakness, not its strength. He thought Britain had won the war, not with the cooperation of the colonies, but despite their obstruction. He believed that the British government had to act quickly to establish its authority before the colonies, with their astonishing rate of growth, slipped completely out of control. In effect, he set in motion a self-fulfilling prophecy in which the British government brought about precisely what it was trying to prevent. Nearly every step it took undermined the colonies' loyalty to Britain.

Indian Policy and Pontiac's War

The king's Proclamation of 1763 set up governments in Canada, Florida, and other conquered colonies, and it honored wartime commitments to the western Indians. It tried to regulate the pace of western settlement by laying out the so-called Proclamation Line along the Appalachian watershed. No settlements could be planted west of that line unless Britain first purchased the land by treaty from the Indians. Settlers would be encouraged to move instead to Nova Scotia, northern New England, Georgia, or Florida. Because most Iroquois land lay east of the line, the Six Nations felt threatened by the new policy, even though Sir William Johnson, the northern superintendent, upheld their claims. General Amherst's decision in 1760 to cut back sharply on gifts to Indians angered many of them. His contempt for Indian customs deprived the government of its major leverage with Indians, at a time when their ability to unite had become stronger than ever.

In 1761, Neolin, a western Delaware, reported a vision in which God commanded Indians to return to their ancestral ways. Neolin called for an end to Indian dependence on the Anglo-Americans, although he did accept Christian ideas of heaven and hell. European vices, he said, especially drinking rum, blocked the path to heaven. "Can ye not live without them?" he asked. God was punishing Indians for accepting European ways: "If you suffer the English among you, you are dead men. Sickness, smallpox, and their poison will destroy you entirely." Neolin stopped short of condemning the French, who were still living in the Great Lakes region. Many of his followers even hoped that their display of unity would attract the support of King Louis XV of France (1715–74), restore the friendly relations of the past, and halt British expansion.

With a unity never seen before, the Indians struck in 1763. The conflict became known as Pontiac's War, named for an Ottawa chief. Senecas, Mingoes, Delawares, Shawnees, Wyandots, Miamis, Ottawas, and other nations attacked 13 British posts in the West. Between May 16 and June 20, all of the forts fell except Niagara, Pitt, Detroit, and a tiny outpost on Green Bay that the Indians did not bother to attack. For months, the Indians kept Forts Detroit and Pitt under close siege, something Indians were supposed to be incapable of doing. They hoped to drive British settlers back to the Eastern seaboard.

Enraged by these successes, Amherst ordered Colonel Henry Bouquet, commander at Fort Pitt, to distribute smallpox-infested blankets among the western nations, touching off a lethal epidemic in 1763 and 1764. "You will do well to try to Inoculate the Indians by means of Blankets," he wrote to Bouquet, "as well as to Try Every other Method that can serve to Extirpate this Execrable

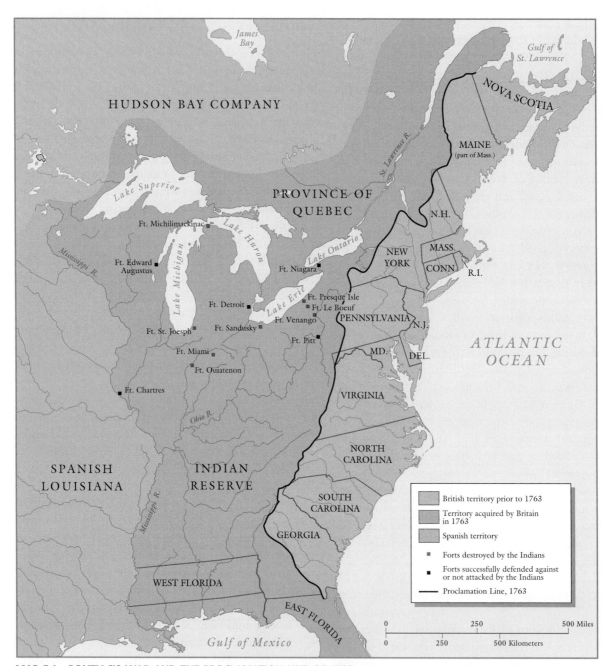

MAP 5.1 PONTIAC'S WAR AND THE PROCLAMATION LINE OF 1763

Britain claimed possession of North America east of the Mississippi only to face an extraordinary challenge from the Indians of the interior, who wiped out eight garrisons but could not take Detroit, Niagara, or Fort Pitt.

 View an animated version of this map or related maps at http://history.wadsworth.com/murrin_LEP4e.

Race." In 1764, British and provincial forces ended resistance and restored peace. The British then reluctantly accepted the role that the French had played in the Great Lakes region by distributing gifts and mediating differences.

But 10 years of conflict had brutalized the frontiersmen. Perhaps sensing the Indians' growing revulsion against warring with one another, many settlers began to assume that all Indians must be the enemies of all whites.

In December 1763, the Scots-Irish of Paxton Township, Pennsylvania, murdered six unarmed Christian Indians—two old men, three women, and a child—at nearby Conestoga. Two weeks later, the "Paxton Boys" slaughtered 14 more Christian Indians who had been brought to Lancaster for protection. After Governor John Penn removed 140 Moravian mission Indians to Philadelphia for safety, the Paxton Boys marched on the capital determined to kill them all.

Denouncing the Paxton Boys as "Christian white Savages," Benjamin Franklin led a delegation from the assembly that met the marchers at Germantown and persuaded them to go home after they presented a list of their grievances. The Moravian Indians had been spared. All efforts to bring the murderers to justice failed, however, and the frontiersmen of Pennsylvania and Virginia virtually declared an open season on Indians that continued for years. Settlers in Augusta County, Virginia, slaughtered nine Shawnees in 1765. Frederick Stump, a Pennsylvanian, murdered 10 more in 1768 but could not be convicted in his frontier county. Such atrocities kept western Indians smoldering. London had hoped that its officials would bring even-handed justice to the frontier. Indians had won real benefits from the superintendents, such as protection from land speculators, but otherwise they found little to choose between Amherst's smallpox blankets and the murderous rage of the Paxton Boys and their imitators.

ANTI-FRANKLIN CARTOON

Pontiac's War and the Paxton riots inspired this anti-Franklin cartoon in which Quakers and Franklin protect Indians from settlers instead of settlers from Indians.

The Sugar Act

In a step that settlers found ominous, Grenville's Sugar Act of 1764 proclaimed it "just and necessary, that a revenue be raised . . . in America for defraying the expenses of defending, protecting, and securing" the colonies. The act placed duties on Madeira wine, coffee, and other products, but Grenville expected the greatest revenue to come from the molasses duty of three pence per gallon. The Molasses Act of 1733 had been designed to keep French molasses out of North America by imposing a prohibitive duty of six pence per gallon. Instead, by paying a bribe of about a penny per gallon, merchants got French molasses certified as British. By 1760, more than 90 percent of all molasses imported into New England came from the French islands. Planters in the British islands gave up, lost interest in New England markets, and turned their molasses into quality rum for sale in Britain and Ireland. Nobody, in short, had any interest in stopping the trade in French molasses. New England merchants said they were willing to pay a duty of one pence (the current cost of bribes), but Grenville insisted on three. He hoped to raise £100,000 per year from the molasses duty, although in public he seldom put the figure above £40,000.

The Sugar Act also launched Grenville's war against smugglers. It vastly increased the amount of paperwork required of ship captains and permitted seizures of ships for what owners considered mere technicalities. In effect, Grenville tried to make it more profitable for customs officers to hound the merchants than to accept bribes from them. The Sugar Act encouraged them to prosecute violators in vice admiralty courts, which did not use juries, rather than in common law courts, which did. Prosecutors were virtually immune from any suit for damages, even when the merchant won an acquittal, so long as the judge certified "probable cause" for the seizure.

The Currency Act and the Quartering Act

Grenville passed several other imperial measures. The Currency Act of 1764 responded to wartime protests of London merchants against Virginia's paper money, which had been issued for the colony's defense. (That money had lost almost 15 percent of its value between 1759 and 1764.) The act forbade the colonies to issue any paper money as legal tender. The money question had become urgent because the Sugar Act (and, later, the Stamp Act) required that all duties be paid in specie (silver or gold). Supporters of those taxes argued that the new duties would keep the specie in America to pay the army, but the colonists replied that the drain of specie from some colonies would put impossible constraints on trade. Boston and Newport, for instance, would pay most of the molasses tax, but the specie collected there would follow the army to Quebec,

New York, the Great Lakes, and Florida. Grenville saw "America" as a single region in which specie would circulate to the benefit of all. The colonists knew better. As of 1765, "America" existed only in British minds, not yet in colonial hearts.

Another reform measure was the Quartering Act of 1765, requested by Sir Thomas Gage, Amherst's successor as army commander. Gage asked for parliamentary authority to quarter soldiers in private homes, if necessary, when on the march and away from their barracks. Parliament ordered colonial assemblies to vote specific supplies, such as beer and candles, for the troops, which the assemblies were willingly doing already. It also required the army to quarter its soldiers only in public buildings, such as taverns, which existed in large numbers only in cities. The Quartering Act solved no problems, but it created several new ones.

The Stamp Act

In early 1764, when Parliament passed the Sugar Act, Grenville announced that a stamp tax on legal documents and on publications might also be needed. The army in North America was costing Britain £225,000 per year. Other expenses, including the navy, transport, and Indian gifts, brought the annual total closer to £400,000. Grenville needed more revenue, and a stamp tax seemed the best way to raise it. No one in the House of Commons, he declared, doubted Parliament's right to impose such a tax. Because Parliament had never levied a direct tax on the colonies, however, he also knew that he must persuade the settlers that a stamp tax would not be a constitutional innovation. His supporters insisted that the measure did not violate the principle of no taxation without representation. Each member of Parliament, they argued, represented the entire empire, not just a local constituency. The colonists were no different from the large nonvoting majority of subjects within Great Britain. All were "virtually" represented in Parliament. Grenville also denied that there was any legal difference between external taxes (port duties, such as that on molasses) and internal (or inland) taxes, such as the proposed stamp tax.

Grenville put off passage of the Stamp Act while he collected more complete information about legal forms in the colonies. He also indicated that, if the colonies could devise a revenue plan better than a stamp tax, he would listen. His offer created confusion and became a public relations disaster for the government. All 13 colonial assemblies drafted petitions objecting to the Stamp Act as a form of taxation without representation. Most of them also attacked the duties imposed by the Sugar Act. They too rejected the distinction between internal and external taxes

(for revenue, as against for the regulation of trade). Both kinds, they declared, violated the British constitution. While agreeing that they ought to contribute to their own defense, they urged the government to return to the traditional method of requisitions, in which the Crown asked a colony for a specific sum, and the assembly decided how (or whether) to raise it. Colonists feared that taxation by Parliament might tempt Britain to rule them without consulting their assemblies.

When these petitions began to reach London, Parliament refused to receive them, citing a standing rule that prohibited petitions against money bills and declaring that any petition challenging the right of Parliament to pass such a tax was simply inadmissible. To Grenville, requisitions were not a better idea. They had often been tried, had never worked efficiently, and never would. He rejected the petitions with a clear conscience. But to the colonists, he seemed to have acted in bad faith all along. He had asked their advice and had then refused even to consider it.

The Stamp Act passed in February 1765, to go into effect on November 1. All contracts, licenses, commissions, and most other legal documents would be void unless they were executed on officially stamped paper. Law courts would not recognize any document that lacked the proper stamp, and the colonists would quietly if grudgingly accept Parliament's power to tax them. The act would almost enforce itself. A stamp duty was also put on all newspapers and pamphlets, a requirement likely to anger every printer in the colonies. Playing cards and dice were also taxed.

When the Stamp Act became law, most colonial leaders resigned themselves to a situation that seemed beyond their power to change. Daniel Dulany, a Maryland lawyer who did more than any other colonist to refute the argument for virtual representation, drew a line short of overt resistance. "I am upon a Question of *Propriety,* not of Power," he wrote; ". . . at the same Time that I invalidate the Claim upon which [the Stamp Act] is founded, I may very consistently recommend a Submission to the Law, whilst it endures." Instead, ordinary settlers decided to take direct action to prevent implementation of the act.

❧ The Stamp Act Crisis

Resistance to the Stamp Act began in spring 1765 and continued for nearly a year, until it was repealed. Patrick Henry, a newcomer to the Virginia House of Burgesses, launched the first wave by introducing five resolutions on May 30 and 31. His resolves passed by margins ranging between 22 to 17 and 20 to 19; one was rescinded and expunged from the record the next day. Henry had two more

in his pocket that he decided not to introduce. Over the summer, the *Newport Mercury* printed six of Henry's seven resolutions, and the *Maryland Gazette* printed all of them. Neither paper reported that some of the seven had not passed. To other colonies, Virginia seemed to have taken a far more radical position than it actually had. The last resolve printed in the *Maryland Gazette* claimed that anyone defending Parliament's right to tax Virginia "shall be Deemed, an Enemy to this his Majesty's Colony."

In their fall or winter sessions, eight colonial legislatures passed new resolutions condemning the Stamp Act. Nine colonies sent delegates to the Stamp Act Congress, which met in New York in October. It passed resolutions affirming colonial loyalty to the king and "all due subordination" to Parliament but condemned the Stamp and Sugar Acts. By 1765, nearly all colonial spokesmen agreed that the Stamp Act was unconstitutional, that colonial representation in Parliament (urged by a few writers) was impractical because of the distance and the huge expense, and that therefore the Stamp Act had to be repealed. They accepted the idea of virtual representation *within* the colonies—their assemblies, they said, represented both voters and nonvoters—but the colonists ridiculed the argument when it was applied across the Atlantic. A disenfranchised Englishman who acquired sufficient property could become a voter, pointed out Daniel Dulany, in a pamphlet that was widely admired, even in Britain. But, Dulany explained, no colonist, no matter how wealthy he became, could vote for a member of Parliament. Members of Parliament paid the taxes that they levied on others within Britain, but they would never pay any tax imposed on the colonies.

Nullification

No matter how eloquent, resolutions and pamphlets alone could not defeat the Stamp Act. Street violence might, however, and Boston showed the way, led by men calling themselves Sons of Liberty. On August 14, the town awoke to find an effigy of Andrew Oliver, the stamp distributor, hanging on what became the town's Liberty Tree (the gallows on which enemies of the people deserved to be hanged). The sheriff admitted that he dared not remove the effigy. After dark, a crowd of men roamed the streets, shouted defiance at the governor and council, and demolished a new building Oliver was erecting that "they called the Stamp Office," beheaded and burned Oliver's effigy, and finally invaded Oliver's home, "declaring they would kill Him." He had already fled to a neighbor's home. Thoroughly cowed, he resigned.

On August 26, an even angrier crowd all but demolished the elegant mansion of Lt. Governor Thomas Hutchinson. Most Bostonians believed that, in letters to British friends, Hutchinson had defended and even helped to draft the Stamp Act. In fact, he had quietly opposed it. Shocked by the destruction of property, the militia finally appeared to police the streets, but when Governor Sir Francis Bernard tried to arrest those responsible for the first riot, he got nowhere. Bostonians deplored the events of August 26 but approved those of August 14. No one was punished for either event, although the whole city knew that Ebenezer McIntosh, a poor shoemaker and a leader of the annual Pope's Day (Guy Fawkes Day) processions, had organized both riots.

Everywhere except Georgia, the stamp master was forced to resign before the law took effect on November 1. With no one to distribute the stamps, the act could not be

New York Public Library.

LORD BUTE AND GEORGE GRENVILLE HANGED IN EFFIGY, 1765 OR 1766

Bute and Grenville were always unpopular in the colonies, but even more so after passage of Grenville's Stamp Act. This image, which shows both men (Bute wears a kilt) chained to the devil, borrowed from the popular rites of Pope's Day (Guy Fawkes Day), November 5. Especially in Boston, images of the pope, the Stuart pretender to the British throne, and the devil were destroyed each year on this day. Bute was especially vulnerable because his family name was Stuart.

implemented. Merchants adopted nonimportation agreements to pressure the British into repeal. Following Boston's lead, the Sons of Liberty took control of the streets in other cities. After November 1, they agitated to open the ports and courts, which had closed down rather than operate without stamps. Neither the courts nor the customs officers had any stamps to use because nobody dared distribute them. As winter gave way to spring, most ports and some courts resumed business. Only Newport matched Boston's level of violence, but in New York City a clash between the Sons of Liberty and the British garrison grew ugly and almost escalated into an armed encounter. Violent resistance worked. The Stamp Act was nullified—even in Georgia, eventually.

Repeal

The next move was up to Britain. For reasons that had nothing to do with the colonies, the king dismissed Grenville in summer 1765 and replaced his ministry with a narrow coalition organized primarily by William Augustus, duke of Cumberland, the king's uncle. An untested young nobleman, Charles Watson-Wentworth, marquess of Rockingham, took over the treasury. This Old Whig ministry had to deal with the riots in America, and Cumberland—the man who had sent Braddock to America in winter 1754–55—may have favored a similar use of force in late 1765. If so, he never had a chance to issue the order. On October 31, minutes before an emergency cabinet meeting on the American crisis, he died of a heart attack, leaving Rockingham in charge of the government. At first, Rockingham favored amending the Stamp Act, but by December he had decided on repeal. To win over the other ministers, the king, and Parliament, he would need great skill.

To Rockingham, the only alternative to repeal seemed to be a ruinous civil war in America, but as the king's chief minister, he could hardly tell Parliament that the world's greatest empire must yield to unruly mobs. He needed a better reason for repeal. Even before the first American nonimportation agreements reached London on December 12 (New York City's) and December 26 (Philadelphia's), he began to mobilize the British merchants and manufacturers who traded with America. They petitioned Parliament to repeal the Stamp Act. They condemned the Grenville program as an economic disaster, and their arguments gave Rockingham the leverage he needed.

Rockingham won the concurrence of the other ministers by promising to support a Declaratory Act affirming Parliament's sovereignty over the colonies. When William Pitt eloquently demanded repeal in the House of Commons on January 14, 1766, Rockingham gained a powerful, although temporary, ally. "I rejoice that America has resisted," declared Pitt. "Three millions of people, so dead to all the feelings of liberty, as voluntarily to submit to be slaves, would have been fit instruments to make slaves of the rest." Parliament "may bind [the colonists'] trade, confine their manufactures, and exercise every power whatsoever," Pitt declared, "except that of taking their money out of their pockets without their consent."

Rockingham still faced resistance from the king, who hinted that he favored "modification" rather than repeal. George III appeared willing to repeal all the stamp duties except those on dice and playing cards, the two levies most difficult to enforce. Only Grenville, however, was ready to use the army to enforce even an amended Stamp Act. Rockingham brought the king around by threatening to resign, which would have forced the king to bring back Grenville, whom he hated. Many pro-American witnesses appeared before Parliament to urge repeal, including Benjamin Franklin, who gave a masterful performance. Slowly, Rockingham put together his majority.

Three pieces of legislation ended the crisis. The first, the Declaratory Act, affirmed that Parliament had "full power and authority to make laws and statutes of sufficient force and validity to bind the colonies and people of America . . . in all cases whatsoever." Rockingham resisted pressure to insert the word "taxes" along with "laws and statutes." That omission permitted the colonists, who drew a sharp distinction between legislation (which, they conceded, Parliament had a right to pass) and taxation (which it could not), to interpret the act as an affirmation of their position, while nearly everyone in Britain read precisely the opposite meaning into the phrase "laws and statutes." Old Whigs hoped that Parliament would never again have to proclaim its sovereign power over America. Like the royal veto of an act of Parliament, that power existed, explained Edmund Burke; and like the veto, which had not been used for 60 years, it should never again be invoked. The colonists agreed. They read the Declaratory Act as a face-saving gesture that made repeal of the Stamp Act possible.

The second measure repealed the Stamp Act because it had been "greatly detrimental to the commercial interests" of the empire. The third, which modern historians call the Revenue Act of 1766, even though its preamble described it as a regulation of trade, reduced the duty on molasses from three pence per gallon to one penny, but imposed the duty on all molasses, British or foreign, imported into the mainland colonies. Although the act was more favorable to the molasses trade than any other measure yet passed by Parliament, it was also, beyond any doubt, a revenue measure, and it generated more income for the empire than any other colonial tax. Few colonists

The European Power
of a Self-Taught American

The youngest son of a youngest son for five consecutive generations, Benjamin Franklin was born into a tradesman's family in Boston in 1706. His father apprenticed him to his older brother, James, a printer who founded *The New England Courant* in 1721. Benjamin even took over briefly as publisher and editor of the paper after James was jailed for criticizing the government. But Benjamin considered James a harsh master, and in 1723, he fled from his brother and made his way to Philadelphia, where he became a journeyman printer. In 1724, he sailed to London, where he read widely and improved his writing and printing skills. Back in Philadelphia by 1726, he set up his own press and founded *The Pennsylvania Gazette,* which soon became the best-edited newspaper in British North America. He did his best to support causes that would improve the city. Having earned enough to live comfortably, he retired in 1747. Only then did he begin the active pursuit of science and public service.

Franklin's electrical experiments earned him a towering reputation throughout the Atlantic world. He also won election to the Pennsylvania assembly, where he soon emerged as the leader of the moderate wing of the Quaker Party by urging it to organize the province for defensive war against the French and Indians, who began devastating Pennsylvania's frontier settlements in 1755. These commitments made him a dangerous opponent of the Penn family, who angrily resisted all attempts to tax their extensive lands and help pay for the war. Franklin grew so exasperated with the Penns that he carried the struggle against them to London in 1757.

He spent 24 of the last 33 years of his life abroad—in London from 1757–62 and again from 1765–75, and in Paris from 1776–85. Those cities and Philadelphia sustained the most vigorous attacks on slavery in the north Atlantic world, and by 1776, Franklin had embraced the cause. In Britain he was quite well received most of the time. Oxford University and the St. Andrews University in Scotland granted him honorary doctorates, and he was a welcome guest in many of Britain's finest country houses. In both 1757 and 1765, he arrived in London as an outspoken defender of the British empire and looked as though he would become an overt loyalist, but the Townshend Crisis (1767–70) changed his mind. He concluded that the men administering the colonies could not be trusted, and he did his best to warn them through satirical publications, such as *Rules by Which a Great Empire May Be Reduced to a Small One* (1773).

After returning to Philadelphia in 1775, Franklin served in the Second Continental Congress, including the committee that drafted the Declaration of Independence. He then became the United States' first minister to France, took Paris by storm, negotiated the treaty of alliance in 1778, and played a major role in drafting the Peace of Paris that ended the war in 1783. Back in America, he served as a delegate to the Philadelphia Convention in 1787 and, in his last composition, one that appeared shortly before his death in 1790, he published an eloquent protest against slavery. His service abroad was probably indispensable to the success of the new nation.

Benjamin West's *Benjamin Franklin Drawing Electricity from the Sky* (ca. 1817).

"THE REPEAL OR THE FUNERAL OF MISS AMERIC-STAMP"

This London cartoon of 1766 shows George Grenville carrying the coffin of the Stamp Act with Lord Bute behind him. Contemporaries would easily have identified the other personalities.

Courtesy of the John Carter Brown Library at Brown University.

attacked it for violating the principle of no taxation without representation. In Britain, it seemed that the colonists objected to internal taxes but would accept external duties.

Against the advice of British friends, the colonists greeted repeal with wild celebrations. Over the next decade, many communities observed March 18 as the anniversary of the Stamp Act's repeal. Neither side fully appreciated the misunderstandings that had made repeal possible or their significance. In the course of the struggle, both sides, British and colonial, had rejected the distinction between external and internal taxes. They could find no legal or philosophical basis for condemning the one while approving the other. Hardly anyone except Franklin noticed in 1766 that the difference was quite real and that the crisis had in fact been resolved according to that distinction. Parliament had tried to extend its authority over the internal affairs of the colonies and had failed, but it continued to collect port duties in the colonies, some to regulate trade, others for revenue. No one knew how to justify this division of authority, but the external–internal cleavage marked, even defined, the power axis of the empire, the boundary between what Parliament could do on its own and what, internally, only the Crown could do, and then only with the consent of the colonists.

Another misunderstanding was equally grave. Only the riots had created a crisis severe enough to push Parliament into repeal. Both sides, however, preferred to believe that economic pressure had been decisive. For the colonies, this conviction set the pattern of resistance for the next two imperial crises.

The Townshend Crisis

The goodwill created by repeal did not last. In 1766, the king again replaced his ministry. This time he persuaded William Pitt to form a government. He and Pitt shared a contempt for the aristocratic families that had governed Britain since 1714, most of whom were now Rockingham Whigs. Both the king and Pitt considered factions immoral and put their faith in a government of "measures, not men." Pitt appealed to men of goodwill from all parties, but few responded. His ministry, which included many supporters of the Grenville program, faced serious opposition within Parliament. Pitt compounded that problem by accepting a peerage as earl of Chatham, a decision that removed his compelling oratory from the House of Commons and left Charles Townshend as his spokesman in that chamber. A witty, extemporaneous speaker, Townshend had betrayed every leader he ever served. The only point of real consistency in his political career had been his hard-line attitude toward the colonies.

The Townshend Program

New York had already created a small crisis for the new earl of Chatham by objecting to the Quartering Act as a disguised form of taxation without consent. Under the old rules, the army asked for quarters and supplies and the assembly voted them. Consent was an integral part of the process. Now one legislature (Parliament) was telling others (the colonial assemblies) what they must do. New York refused. In 1767, Parliament passed the New York Restraining Act, which forbade New York's governor to sign any law until the assembly complied with the Quartering Act. The crisis fizzled out when the governor bent the rules and announced that the assembly had already complied with the substance (if not all the specifics) of the Quartering Act before the Restraining Act went into effect. In the end, instead of helping the army, the Quartering Act weakened colonial loyalty to Britain.

Chatham soon learned that he could not control the House of Commons from his position in the House of

Lords. During the Christmas recess of 1766–67, he saw the extent of his failure and began to slip into an acute depression that lasted more than two years. He refused to communicate with other ministers or even with the king. The colonists, who admired him more than any other Englishman of the day, expected sympathy from his administration. Instead, they got Townshend, who took charge of colonial policy in spring 1767.

As chancellor of the exchequer, Townshend presented the annual budget to the House of Commons. A central aspect of that year's budget, the Townshend Revenue Act of 1767, imposed new duties in colonial ports on certain imports that the colonies could legally buy only from Britain: tea, paper, glass, red and white lead, and painter's colors. But Townshend also removed more duties on tea within Britain than he could offset with the new revenue collected in the colonies. Revenue, clearly, was not his object. The statute's preamble stated his real goal: To use the new American revenues to pay the salaries of governors

and judges in the colonies, thereby freeing them from dependence on the assemblies. This devious strategy aroused suspicions of conspiracy in the colonies. Many sober provincials began to believe that, deep in the recesses of the British government, men really were plotting to deprive them of their liberties.

Other measures gave appellate powers to the vice admiralty courts in Boston, Philadelphia, and Charleston and created a separate American Board of Customs Commissioners to enforce the trade and revenue laws in the colonies. The board was placed in Boston, where resistance to the Stamp Act had been fiercest, rather than in Philadelphia, which had been rather quiet in 1765 and would have been a much more convenient location. Townshend was eager for confrontation.

The British army also began to withdraw from nearly all frontier posts and concentrate near the coast. Although the primary motive was to save money, the implications were striking. It was one thing to keep an army in

---

M U S I C A L   L I N K   T O   T H E   P A S T

An American Heart of Oak

Composers: William Boyce (music),
John Dickinson (lyrics)
Title: "Liberty Song" (1768)

Within weeks of publication, this sprightly tune spread throughout the colonies, along with the political message embedded in its lyrics. It formed part of the attack by John Dickinson against the Townshend Revenue Act. Dickinson's pamphlet *Letters from a Farmer in Pennsylvania* argued that the Act went against traditional English philosophies of government because "no tax designed to produce revenue can be considered constitutional unless a people's elected representatives voted for it." But to reach those colonists who did not read pamphlets or newspapers, Dickinson also used popular song.

"Liberty Song" repeats Dickinson's written sentiments in a more rousing manner, and one can imagine the lyrics sung loudly by carousers in a public tavern or meeting place: "This bumper I crown for our Sov'reign's health / and this for Britannia's glory and wealth / That wealth, and that glory immortal may be / If she is but just, and if we are but free." These lines demonstrate that, like most colonists, Dickinson viewed himself as a loyal and patriotic British subject. In his song and pamphlet, he made no arguments for independence. He

claimed that if Britain treated her subjects in a "just" manner, they would continue to loyally serve the government. But this relatively new and controversial insistence on a more equal two-way relationship between Britain and its American colonies, instead of a paternalistic relationship, provoked increasing friction with the mother country, presaging more open oppositions such as the Boston Tea Party and, eventually, the Revolution.

Dickinson penned his "Liberty Song" lyrics to fit a popular 1750s British patriotic stage tune entitled "Heart of Oak" that celebrated the navy's victories in the Seven Years' War, and they helped the song achieve quick popularity. It was also telling that "Liberty Song" was based on music from Europe. European music enjoyed a pervasive and dominating influence in the colonies. A distinctly American music would not make a significant appearance for at least another half-century.

1. Do you think that the medium of popular song is effective for spreading political messages?
2. Why do so few popular songs on today's best-selling charts feature political content?

Listen to an audio recording of this music on the Musical Links to the Past CD.

America to guard the frontier and then ask the colonists to pay part of its cost, but an army far distant from the frontier presumably existed only to police the colonists. Why should they pay any part of its cost if its role was to enforce policies that would deprive them of their liberties?

Townshend ridiculed the distinction between internal and external taxes, a distinction that he attributed to Chatham and the colonists, but he declared that he would honor it anyway. After winning approval for his program, he died suddenly in September 1767 and passed on to others the dilemmas he had created. Frederick, Lord North, became chancellor of the exchequer. Chatham resigned, and Augustus Henry Fitzroy, duke of Grafton, became prime minister.

Resistance: The Politics of Escalation

The external–internal distinction was troublesome for the colonists. Since 1765, they had objected to all taxes for revenue, but in 1766, they had accepted the penny duty on molasses with few complaints. Defeating the Townshend Revenue Act would prove tougher than nullifying the Stamp Act. Parliament had never been able to impose its will on the internal affairs of the colonies, as the Stamp Act fiasco demonstrated, but it did control the seas. Goods subject to duties might arrive aboard any of hundreds of ships from Britain each year, but screening the cargo of every vessel threatened to impose an enormous, perhaps impossible burden on the Sons of Liberty. A policy of general nonimportation would be easier to implement, but British trade played a bigger role in the colonial economy than North American trade did in the British economy. To hurt Britain a little, the colonies would have to harm themselves a lot.

The colonists divided over strategies of resistance. The radical *Boston Gazette* called for complete nonimportation of all British goods. The merchants' paper, the *Boston Evening Post*, disagreed. In October, the Boston town meeting encouraged greater use of home manufactures and authorized voluntary nonconsumption of British goods. But there was no organized resistance against the new measures, and the Townshend duties became operative in November 1767 with little opposition. A month later, John Dickinson, a Philadelphia lawyer, tried to rouse his fellow colonists to action through 12 urgent letters printed in nearly every colonial newspaper. These *Letters from a Farmer in Pennsylvania* denied the distinction between internal and external taxes, insisted that all parliamentary taxes for revenue violated the colonists' rights, and speculated darkly about Townshend's real motives.

Massachusetts again set the pace of resistance. In February 1768, its assembly petitioned the king, not Parliament, against the new measures. Without waiting for a reply, it also sent a Circular Letter to the other assemblies, urging them to pursue "constitutional measures" of resistance against the Quartering Act, the new taxes, and the use of Townshend revenues to pay the salaries of governors and judges. The implication was that, because Britain responded only to resistance, the colonies had better work together.

The British ministry got the point and did not like it. Wills Hill, earl of Hillsborough and secretary of state for the American colonies (an office created in 1768), responded so sharply that he turned tepid opposition into serious resistance. He ordered the Massachusetts assembly to rescind the Circular Letter and instructed all governors to dissolve any assembly that dared to accept it. In June 1768, the Massachusetts House voted 92 to 17 not to rescind. Most other assemblies had shown little interest in the Townshend program, particularly in the southern colonies where governors already had fixed salaries. Even so, they bristled at being told what they could or could not debate. All of them took up the Circular Letter or began to draft their own. One by one, the governors dissolved their assemblies until government by consent really seemed in peril.

The next escalation again came from Boston. On March 18, 1768, the town's celebration of the anniversary of the Stamp Act's repeal grew so raucous that the governor and the new American Board of Customs Commissioners asked Hillsborough for troops. He ordered General Gage, based in New York, to send two regiments from Nova Scotia to Boston. On June 10, before Gage could respond, a riot broke out in Boston after customs collectors seized John Hancock's sloop *Liberty* for having smuggled Madeira wine (taxed under the Sugar Act) on its *previous* voyage. By waiting until the ship had a new cargo, informers and customs officials could split larger shares when the sloop was condemned. Terrified by the fury of the popular response, the commissioners fled to Castle William in Boston harbor and again petitioned Hillsborough for troops. He sent two more regiments from Ireland.

At about this time, nonimportation at last began to take hold. Two dozen Massachusetts towns adopted pacts in which they agreed not to consume British goods. Boston merchants drafted a nonimportation agreement on March 1, 1768, conditional on its acceptance by New York and Philadelphia. New York agreed, but Philadelphia balked, preferring to wait and see whether Parliament would make any effort to redress colonial grievances. There the matter rested until the *Liberty* riot prompted most Boston merchants to agree to nonimportation,

effective January 1. New York again concurred, but Philadelphia held out until early 1769, when it became obvious that Parliament would make no concessions.

Spurred on by the popular but mistaken belief that the nonimportation agreements of 1765 had forced Parliament to repeal the Stamp Act, the colonists again turned to a strategy of economic sanctions. Nonimportation affected only imports from Britain. Tea, consumed mostly by women, was the most objectionable import of all. No one tried to block the importation of West Indian molasses, which was essential to the rum industry of Boston and Newport and which brought in about £30,000 a year under the Revenue Act of 1766. Rum was consumed mostly by men. Some women resented the disproportionate sacrifices they were asked to make. On the other hand, the Sons of Liberty knew that virtually all molasses came from the French islands, and that nonimportation would injure only French planters and American manufacturers and consumers and put no pressure on Parliament or British merchants. The only proven way to resist the penny duty was through smuggling.

Believing that he held the edge with the army on its way, Governor Bernard leaked this news in late August 1768. The public response stunned him. The Boston town meeting asked him to summon the legislature, which Bernard had dissolved in June after it stood by its Circular Letter. When Bernard refused, the Sons of Liberty asked the other towns to elect delegates to a "convention" in Boston. The convention contained most of the radical members of the House of Representatives but not the conservatives. It had no legal standing in the colony's royal government. Boston, professing alarm over the possibility of a French invasion, urged its citizens to arm themselves. When the convention met, it accepted Boston's definition of colonial grievances but refused to sanction violence. Boston had no choice but to go along. It could not call the shots for the whole colony. Instead, the *Boston Gazette* portrayed the city as an orderly community (which it usually was) that had no need of British troops.

An Experiment in Military Coercion

The British fleet entered Boston harbor in battle array by October 2, 1768, and landed 1,000 soldiers, sent by General Gage from Nova Scotia. They soon discovered that

The Granger Collection, New York.

PAUL REVERE'S ENGRAVING OF THE BRITISH ARMY LANDING IN BOSTON, 1768

The navy approached the city in battle array, a sight familiar to veterans of the French wars. To emphasize the peaceful, Christian character of Boston, Revere exaggerated the height of the church steeples.

their most troublesome enemy was not the Sons of Liberty but the Quartering Act, which required that British soldiers be lodged in public barracks where available. Massachusetts had built such barracks—in Castle William, miles away on an island in Boston harbor, where the soldiers could hardly function as a police force. According to the act, any attempt to quarter soldiers on private property would expose the officer responsible to being cashiered from the army, after conviction before any two justices of the peace. And several prominent patriots, such as John Adams and James Otis, Jr., were justices. The soldiers pitched their tents on Boston Common. Seventy men deserted in the first week, about 7 percent of the force. Eventually, the soldiers took over a building that had been the Boston poorhouse. The regiments from Ireland joined them later.

To warn the public against the dangers posed by a standing army in time of peace, the patriots compiled a "Journal of the Times" describing how British soldiers were undermining public order in Boston—clashing with the town watch, endangering the virtue of young women, disturbing church services, and picking fights. The "journal" always appeared first as a newspaper column in some other city, usually New York. Only later was it reprinted in Boston, after memories of any specific incident had grown hazy. Yet violence against customs officers ceased for many months. John Mein (pronounced "mean"), loyalist editor of the *Boston Chronicle,* caricatured leading patriots (John Hancock's generosity, for example, made him "the milch-cow of the disaffected") and began to publish customs records that exposed merchants who were violating the nonimportation agreement. This information

After obtaining commissions from Charleston as militia officers and justices of the peace, the regulators chased the outlaws out of the colony, many of them into North Carolina. They then imposed order on what they called the "little people," poor settlers who often made a living as hunters, many of whom may have aided the outlaws. The discipline imposed by the regulators, typically whippings and forced labor, outraged their victims, who organized as "moderators" and got their own commissions from the governor. With both sides claiming legality, about 600 armed regulators confronted an equal force of moderators at the Saluda River in 1769. Civil war was avoided only by the timely arrival of an emissary from the governor bearing a striking message: South Carolina would finally bring government to the backcountry by providing a circuit court system for the entire colony. Violence ebbed, but tensions remained severe.

In North Carolina, the backcountry's problem was corruption, not the absence of government. The settlers, mostly immigrants pushing south from Pennsylvania, found the county courts under the control of men with strong blood or business ties to powerful families in the eastern counties. Because county officials were appointed by the governor, political success required gaining access to his circle. These justices, lawyers, and merchants seemed to regard county government as an engine for fleecing farmers through regressive poll taxes, fees, and court costs, and through suits for debt. North Carolina's regulator movement arose to reform these abuses. The backcountry counties contained more than half the colony's population, but they elected only 17 of the 78 assemblymen.

In 1768, the regulators refused to pay taxes in Orange County, which was part of the Granville District. Governor William Tryon mustered 1,300 eastern militiamen, one-sixth of whom were officers, including more than half of the assemblymen from the eastern counties. With 8 generals and 14 colonels, and led by an elite unit of Gentlemen Volunteer Light Dragoons, this force overawed the regulators for a time. Then, in a bid for a voice in the 1769 assembly, the regulators managed to capture six seats. These new assemblymen called for the secret ballot, fixed salaries (instead of fees) for justices and other officials, and a land tax rather than poll taxes. But they were outvoted by the eastern majority. After losing ground in the 1770 election, they stormed into Hillsborough, closed the Orange County Court, and whipped Edmund Fanning, a Yale graduate whose lust for fees had made him the most detested official in the backcountry. They also seized the court docket and scribbled unflattering comments next to many of the names of their creditors. Tryon responded by marching 1,000 militiamen westward, who defeated a force of more than 2,000 poorly armed regulators in early 1771

at the battle of Alamance Creek. Seven regulators were hanged, and many fled the colony. North Carolina entered the struggle for independence as a bitterly divided society.

Slaves and Women

In Charleston, South Carolina, in 1765, the Sons of Liberty marched through the streets chanting "Liberty and No Stamps." To their amazement, slaves organized a parade of their own, shouting, "Liberty! Liberty!" Merchant Henry Laurens tried to convince himself that they probably did not know the meaning of the word.

About the middle of the 18th century, slavery came under serious attack for the first time. An antislavery movement arose on both sides of the Atlantic and attracted both patriots and loyalists. In the 1740s and 1750s, Benjamin Lay, John Woolman, and Anthony Benezet urged fellow Quakers to free their slaves. In the 1750s, the Quaker Yearly Meeting placed the slave trade off limits and finally, in 1774, forbade slaveholding altogether. Any Friend who failed to comply by 1779 was disowned. Britain's Methodist leader John Wesley, in almost every other respect a social conservative, also attacked slavery, as did several colonial disciples of Jonathan Edwards. Two and three decades after the Great Awakening, many evangelicals began to agree with the message of South Carolina's Hugh Bryan in 1742, that slavery was a sin.

By the 1760s, supporters of slavery found that they now had to defend the institution. Hardly anyone had bothered to do so earlier, because a social hierarchy seemed necessary and inevitable, and slavery simply marked one extreme of that hierarchy. As equal rights became a popular topic, however, some began to suggest that *all* people could claim these rights, and slavery came under attack. In Scotland, Adam Smith, the most original economist of the age, praised African slaves for their "magnanimity," which, he claimed, "the soul of the sordid master is scarce capable of conceiving." Arthur Lee, a Virginian, defended the character of his fellow planters against Smith's charge but discovered that he could not justify slavery, "always the deadly enemy to virtue and science." Patrick Henry agreed. Slavery, he wrote, "is as repugnant to humanity as it is inconsistent with the Bible and destructive of liberty." He himself kept slaves, but only because of "the general inconvenience of living without them. I will not, I cannot justify it." In England, Granville Sharp, an early abolitionist, brought the Somerset case before the Court of King's Bench in 1771 and compelled a reluctant Chief Justice William Murray, baron Mansfield, to declare slavery incompatible with the "free air" of England. That decision gave England's 10,000 or 15,000 blacks a chance to claim their freedom.

From the Collections of the Library of Congress.

"A SOCIETY OF PATRIOTIC LADIES AT EDENTON IN NORTH CAROLINA"

This 1775 London cartoon satirized the active role of women in resisting British policies.

New Englanders began to head in similar directions. Two women, Sarah Osborn and Phillis Wheatley, played leading roles in the movement. Osborn, an English immigrant to Newport, Rhode Island, and a widow, opened a school in 1744 to support her family. A friend of revivalist George Whitefield, she also taught women and blacks and began holding evening religious meetings, which turned into a big local revival. At one point in the 1760s, about one-sixth of Newport's Africans were attending her school. That made them the most literate African population in the colonies, although they were living in the city most deeply involved in the African slave trade. Osborn's students supported abolition of the slave trade and, later, of slavery itself.

In 1761, an eight-year-old girl who would become known as Phillis Wheatley arrived in Boston from Africa and was purchased by wealthy John Wheatley as a servant for his wife, Susannah, who treated her more like a daughter than a slave, taught her to read and write, and emancipated her when she came of age. In 1767, Phillis published her first poem in Boston, and in 1773, a volume of her poetry was printed in London, making her a transatlantic celebrity by age 20. Her poems deplored slavery but rejoiced in the Christianization of Africans. Some of them supported the patriot cause, but she withheld those from the London edition.

Soon many of Boston's blacks sensed an opportunity for emancipation. On several occasions in 1773 and 1774, they petitioned the legislature or the governor for freedom,

PHILLIS WHEATLEY

Engraving of Phillis Wheatley opposite the title page of her collected poems, published in 1773.

American Antiquarian Society.

pointing out that, although they had never forfeited their natural rights, they were being "held in slavery in the bowels of a free and Christian Country." When the legislature passed a bill on their behalf, Governor Hutchinson vetoed it. Boston slaves made it clear to General Gage, Hutchinson's successor, that they would serve him as a loyal militia in exchange for their freedom. In short, they offered allegiance to whichever side supported their emancipation. Many patriots began to rally to their cause. "If we would look for Liberty ourselves," the town of Medfield declared in 1773, ". . . we ought not to continue to enslave others but immediately set about some effectual method to prevent it for the future."

The patriots could look to another group of allies as well. Many women became indispensable to the broader resistance movement. They could not vote or hold office, but without their willing support, nonimportation would have been not just a failure, but a fiasco. In thousands of households, women joined the intense discussions about liberty and agreed to make homespun clothing to take the place of imported British textiles.

Freedom's ferment made a heady wine. After 1773, any direct challenge to British power would trigger enormous social changes within the colonies.

The Last Imperial Crisis

The surface calm between 1770 and 1773 ended when Lord North moved to save the East India Company, Britain's largest corporation, from bankruptcy. The company was being undersold in southeastern England and the colonies by low-priced, smuggled Dutch tea, which left the East India Company's warehouses bulging with millions of unsold pounds of tea. North's main concern was the company, not colonial resistance to Townshend's tea duty. Without solving the company's problems, he created a colonial crisis too big for Britain to handle.

The Tea Crisis

North decided to rescue the East India Company by empowering it to undersell its rivals, the smugglers of Dutch tea. Benjamin Franklin, who was still in London as a colonial agent, reminded North that he could achieve that goal in the colonies by repealing the Townshend duty for sound economic reasons. North rejected that idea. The settlers, he thought, would hardly revolt if he somehow managed to give them cheap tea. His Tea Act of 1773 repealed import duties on tea in England but retained the Townshend duty in the colonies. In both places, North estimated, legal tea would be cheaper than anyone else's. The company would be saved, and the settlers, by willingly buying legal tea, would accept Parliament's right to tax them.

Another aspect of the Tea Act antagonized most merchants in the colonies. The company had been selling tea to all comers at public auctions in London, but the Tea Act gave it a monopoly on the shipping and distribution of tea in the colonies. Only company ships could carry it, and a few consignees in each port would have the exclusive right to sell it. The combined dangers of taxation and monopoly again forged the coalition of artisans and merchants that had helped defeat the Stamp Act by 1766 and resist the Townshend Act by 1769. Patriots saw the Tea Act as a Trojan horse that would destroy liberty by seducing the settlers into accepting parliamentary sovereignty. Unintentionally, North gave a tremendous advantage to those determined to resist the Tea Act. He had devised an oceanic, or external, measure that the colonists could actually nullify despite British control of the seas. No one would have to police the entire waterfront looking for tea importers. The patriots had only to wait for the specially chartered tea ships and prevent them from landing their cargoes.

"THE BOSTONIANS PAYING THE EXCISE-MAN, OR TARRING AND FEATHERING"
This London cartoon of 1774 satirizes the Sons of Liberty.

Courtesy of the John Carter Brown Library at Brown University.

Direct threats usually did the job. As the first tea ship approached Philadelphia, the Sons of Liberty greeted the skipper with a rude welcome: "What think you Captain, of a halter around your neck—ten gallons of liquid tar decanted on your pate—with the feathers of a dozen wild geese laid over that to enliven your appearance? Only think seriously of this—and fly to the place from whence you came—fly without hesitation—without the formality of a protest—and above all, . . . let us advise you to fly without the wild geese feathers." The ship quickly departed.

Similar scenes took place in every port except Boston. There, Governor Hutchinson, whose sons were the local tea consignees, decided to face down the radicals. He refused to grant clearance papers to three tea ships that, under the law, had to pay the Townshend duty within 21 days of arrival or face seizure. Hutchinson meant to force them to land the tea and pay the duty. This timetable led to urgent mass meetings for several weeks and generated a major crisis. Finally, convinced that they had no other way to block the landing of the tea, Boston radicals disguised themselves as Indians and threw 342 chests of tea, worth about £11,000 sterling (more than $700,000 in 2004 dollars), into Boston harbor on the night of December 16, 1773.

Britain's Response: The Coercive Acts

This willful destruction of private property shocked both Britain and America. Convinced that severe punishment was essential to British credibility, Parliament passed four Coercive Acts during spring 1774. The Boston Port Act closed the port of Boston until Bostonians paid for the tea. A new Quartering Act allowed the army to quarter soldiers on civilian property if necessary. The Administration of Justice Act (a response to the Boston Massacre trials) permitted a British soldier or official who was charged with a crime while carrying out his duties to be tried either in another colony or in England. Most controversial of all was the Massachusetts Government Act. It overturned the Massachusetts Charter of 1691, made the council appointive, and restricted town meetings. In effect, it made Massachusetts like other royal colonies. Before it passed, the king named General Gage, already the commander of the British army in North America, as the new governor of Massachusetts, with the clear implication that he could use military force against civilians.

THE MASSACHUSETTS CALENDAR; OR AN ALMANACK (1774)

In the era of witch trials, engravings of devils were meant to be taken literally. By the Revolution, they had become symbolic. The cover of this almanac castigates Governor Thomas Hutchinson of Massachusetts who, it suggests, deserves damnation.

Parliament also passed a fifth law, unrelated to the Coercive Acts but significant nonetheless. The Quebec Act established French civil law and the Roman Catholic Church in the Province of Quebec, provided for trial by jury in criminal but not in civil cases, gave legislative power (but not the power to tax) to an appointive governor and council, and extended the administrative boundaries of Quebec to the area between the Great Lakes and the Ohio River, saving only the legitimate charter claims of other colonies. Historians now regard the act as

a farsighted measure that gave French Catholics the toleration that the empire had denied to Acadians 20 years earlier, but settlers from New England to Georgia were appalled. Instead of conciliation and toleration, they saw a deliberate revival of the power of New France and the Catholic Church on their northern border, this time bolstered by Britain's naval and military might. The Quebec Act added credibility to the fear that evil ministers in London were conspiring to destroy British and colonial liberties. Many British colonists suspected that the autocratic government of Quebec might become a model for restructuring their own provinces. The settlers lumped the Quebec Act together with the Coercive Acts and coined their own name for all of them: the Intolerable Acts.

The Radical Explosion

The interval between passage of the Boston Port Act in March 1774 and the Massachusetts Government Act in May permits us to compare the response that each provoked. The Port Act was quite enforceable and immune to nullification by the colonists. It led to another round of nonimportation and to the summoning of the First Continental Congress. But the Government Act *was* nullified by the colonists. It led to war. The soldiers marching to Concord on April 19, 1775, were trying to enforce that act against settlers who absolutely refused to obey it.

Gage took over as governor of Massachusetts in May 1774, before Parliament passed the Massachusetts Government Act. In June, he closed the ports of Boston and Charlestown, just north of Boston. The navy gave him more than enough power to do so. At first, Boston split over the Port Act. Many merchants wanted to abolish the Boston Committee of Correspondence and pay for the tea

to avoid an economic catastrophe, but they were badly outvoted in a huge town meeting. Boston then called for a colonial union and for immediate nonimportation and nonconsumption of British goods. By then, some radicals were losing patience with nonimportation as a tactic. Parliament had already shut Boston down.

Discouraging news arrived from elsewhere. A mass meeting in New York City rejected immediate nonimportation in favor of an intercolonial congress. Philadelphia followed New York's lead. In both cities, cautious merchants hoped that a congress might postpone or prevent radical measures of resistance.

This was only a momentary success. North assumed that the Coercive Acts would isolate Boston from the rest of the province, Massachusetts from the rest of New England, and New England from the other colonies, a goal that Britain would pursue through 1777. Instead, contributions began pouring in from all of the colonies to help Boston survive. The Stamp Act crisis and the Townshend crisis had been largely urban affairs. The Intolerable Acts politicized the countryside on a scale never seen before. When royal governors outside Massachusetts dismissed their assemblies to prevent them from joining the resistance movement, colonists there did what Massachusetts had done in 1768: They elected "provincial congresses," or conventions, to organize resistance. These bodies were much larger than the legal assemblies they displaced, and they mobilized far more people. As the congresses took hold, royal government began to collapse almost everywhere.

Numerous calls for a continental congress made the movement irresistible. By June, it was also obvious that any congress would adopt nonimportation. Except for some details, that issue had been settled, even before the

"THE ABLE DOCTOR, OR AMERICA SWALLOWING THE BITTER DRAUGHT"
This 1774 engraving by Paul Revere used "The Bostonians Paying the Excise-Man" as a model but turned it into a patriot statement. In Revere's version, the British are forcing tea down the throat of America (represented by a ravished lady, Liberty). The British are also imposing martial law in Boston.

© Bettmann/Corbis.

congress met, by mandates that the delegates brought with them.

Despite these signs of disaffection, Gage remained optimistic through most of the summer. Then news of the Massachusetts Government Act arrived on August 6. Gage's authority disintegrated when he tried to enforce the act, which marked the most dramatic attempt yet made by Parliament to control the internal affairs of the colonies. The "mandamus councillors," whom Gage appointed to the new upper house under the act, either resigned their seats or fled to Boston to seek protection from the army. The Superior Court could not hold its sessions, even in Boston under the guns of the army, because jurors refused to take an oath under the new act. At the county level (the real center of royal power in the colony), popular conventions closed the courts and took charge in August and September. Gage was beginning to realize that none of his major objectives was achievable.

Before this explosion of radical activity, Gage had called for a new General Court to meet in Salem in October. Many towns sent representatives, but others followed

A POLITICAL LESSON (1774)

When General Sir Thomas Gage replaced Thomas Hutchinson as royal governor of Massachusetts in 1774, he closed the port of Boston and moved the capital to Salem. This cartoon shows him thrown from his horse, presumably representing the people.

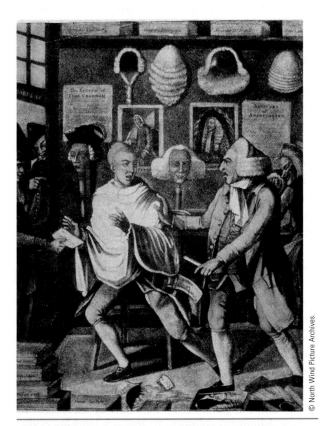

THE PATRIOTICK BARBER OF NEW YORK (1775)

British army and navy officers who came to New York often disguised themselves as civilians when dealing with tradesmen. This cartoon shows what happened when one officer was outed while dealing with a barber who was also a Son of Liberty.

the lead of the Worcester County Convention, which in August urged all towns to elect delegates to a provincial congress in Concord, 17 miles inland, out of range of the navy. Although Gage revoked his call for a General Court, about 90 representatives met at Salem anyway. When Gage refused to recognize them, they adjourned to Concord in early October and joined the 200 delegates already gathered there as the Massachusetts Provincial Congress. That body became the de facto government of the colony and implemented the radical demands of the Suffolk County Convention (representing Boston and its hinterland), which included a purge of unreliable militia officers, the creation of a special force of armed "minutemen" able to respond rapidly to any emergency, and the payment of taxes to the congress in Concord, not to Gage in Boston. The Provincial Congress also collected military stores at Concord and created an executive arm, the Committee of Public Safety. North assumed that Gage's army would uphold the new Massachusetts government. Instead, Gage's government survived only where the army could protect it.

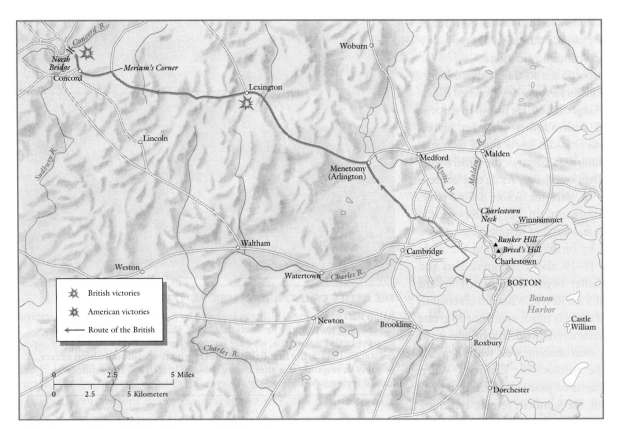

MAP 5.3 LEXINGTON, CONCORD, AND BOSTON, 1775
The British march to Lexington and Concord on April 19, 1775, touched off the Revolutionary War. The colonists drove the redcoats back to Boston and then besieged the city for 11 months until the British withdrew.

all of their forces in Boston, the British were too weak to defend other positions or to intervene in the short Indian conflict, Lord Dunmore's War, that broke out in the upper Ohio valley in 1774. The collapse of royal government meant that the rebels now controlled the militia and most of the royal powderhouses.

The militia became the key to political allegiance. Compulsory service with the militia politicized many waverers, who decided that they really were patriots when a redcoat shot at them or when they drove a loyalist into exile. The militia kept the countryside committed to the Revolution wherever the British army was too weak to overwhelm them.

The Second Continental Congress

When the Second Continental Congress met in May 1775, it inherited the war. For months it pursued the conflicting strategies of resistance and conciliation. It voted to turn the undisciplined men besieging Boston into a Continental Army. As in earlier wars, the soldiers were volunteers who expected to serve for only a few months, or a single

campaign. In the absence of royal authority, they elected their officers, who tried to win their obedience through persuasion, not command. Supplying the soldiers with food and munitions became a huge problem.

Most of the men were Yankees who would have preferred to serve under their own officers, but Congress realized that a successful war effort would have to engage the other colonies as well. On June 15, at the urging of John Adams of Massachusetts, Congress made George Washington of Virginia commanding general. When Washington took charge of the Continental Army, he was appalled at the poor discipline among the soldiers and their casual familiarity with their officers. He insisted that officers behave with a dignity that would instill obedience, and as the months passed, most of them won his respect. As the year ended, however, nearly all of the men went home, and Washington had to train a new army for 1776. But enthusiasm for the cause remained strong, and fresh volunteers soon filled his camp.

In June 1775, fearing that the British might recruit French Canadians to attack New York or New England, Congress authorized an invasion of Canada, designed to

win over the French before they could side with the British. Two forces of 1,000 men each moved northward. One, under General Richard Montgomery, took Montreal in November. The other, commanded by Colonel Benedict Arnold, advanced on Quebec through the Maine wilderness and laid siege to the city, where Montgomery joined Arnold in December. With enlistments due to expire at year's end, they decided to assault the city, partly to get maximum service out of their men and partly to inspire some of them to reenlist. Their attack on December 31 was a disaster. Nearly half of the 900 men still with them were killed, wounded, or captured. Montgomery was killed and Arnold wounded. Both were hailed as American heroes.

The colonial objective in this fighting was still to restore government by consent under the Crown. After rejecting Lord North's Conciliatory Proposition out of hand, Congress approved an Olive Branch Petition to George III on July 5, 1775, in the hope of ending the bloodshed. Moderates, led by John Dickinson, strongly favored the measure. The petition affirmed the colonists' loyalty to the Crown, did not even mention "rights," and implored the king to take the initiative in devising "a happy and permanent reconciliation." Another document written mostly by Thomas Jefferson, "The Declaration of the Causes and Necessities of Taking Up Arms," set forth the colonies' grievances and justified their armed resistance. "We have counted the cost of this contest," Jefferson proclaimed, "and find nothing so dreadful as voluntary slavery." Like the Olive Branch Petition, the declaration assured the British people "that we mean not to dissolve that Union which has so long and so happily subsisted between us." The king's refusal even to receive this moderate petition strengthened colonial radicals. It reached London along with news of Bunker (Breeds) Hill. George III replied with a formal proclamation of rebellion on August 23.

Congress began to function more and more like a government, but with few exceptions, it assumed royal rather than parliamentary powers, which were taken over by the individual colonies. Congress did not tax or regulate trade, beyond encouraging nonimportation. It passed no laws. It took command of the Continental Army, printed paper money, opened diplomatic relations with Indian nations, took over the postal service, and decided which government was legitimate in individual colonies—all functions previously performed by the Crown. In short, Congress thought of itself as a temporary plural executive for the continent, not as a legislature.

War and Legitimacy, 1775–1776

Throughout 1775, the British reacted with fitful displays of violence and grim threats of turning slaves and Indians against the settlers. When the weak British forces could neither restore order nor make good on their threats, they conciliated no one, enraged thousands, and undermined British claims to legitimacy. The navy burned Falmouth (now Portland), Maine, in October. On November 7, John Murray, earl of Dunmore and governor of Virginia, offered freedom to any slaves of rebel planters who would join his 200 redcoats. About 800 slaves mustered under his banner only to fall victim to smallpox after the Virginia militia defeated them in a single action. On January 1, Dunmore bombarded Norfolk in retaliation, setting several buildings ablaze. The patriot militia, who considered Norfolk a loyalist bastion, burned the rest of the city and then blamed Dunmore for its destruction. Overall, his campaign undermined whatever loyalist sentiment survived among Virginia planters beyond Norfolk.

British efforts suffered other disasters in Boston and the Carolinas. The greatest colonial victory came at Boston, where most of the British army lay virtually imprisoned. On March 17, 1776, after Washington fortified Dorchester Heights south of the city and brought heavy artillery (from Ticonderoga) to bear on it, the British pulled out and sailed for Nova Scotia. A loyalist uprising by Highland Scots in North Carolina was crushed at Moore's Creek Bridge on February 27, and a British naval expedition sent to take Charleston was repulsed with heavy losses in June. Cherokee attacks against Virginia failed in 1776 because they occurred after Dunmore had left and did not fit into any larger general strategy. Before spring turned to summer, patriot forces had won control of the territory of all 13 colonies. Except in East and West Florida, Quebec, and Nova Scotia, the British had been driven from the continent.

Independence

George III's dismissal of the Olive Branch Petition left moderates no option but to yield or fight. In late 1775, Congress created a committee to correspond with foreign powers. By early 1776, the delegates from New England, Virginia, and Georgia already favored independence, but they knew that unless they won over all 13 colonies, the British would have the leverage to divide them. The British attack on Charleston in June nudged the Carolinas toward independence.

Resistance to independence came mostly from the mid-Atlantic colonies, from New York through Maryland. Elsewhere, provincial congresses had supplanted the colonial assemblies in 1774 and 1775. In the middle colonies, however, both assemblies and congresses met and competed for the loyalties of the people. None of the five legal assemblies in the mid-Atlantic region ever repudiated the Crown. All of them had to be overthrown along with royal

Congress finally broke the mid-Atlantic stalemate. On May 15, 1776, it voted to suppress "every kind of authority" under the British Crown, thus giving radicals an opportunity to seize power in Pennsylvania and New Jersey. Moderates remained in control in New York, Delaware, and Maryland, but they reluctantly accepted independence as inevitable. In early June, Congress postponed a vote on independence but named a committee of five, including Jefferson, John Adams, and Franklin, to prepare a declaration that would vindicate America's decision to the whole world.

On July 2, with the necessary votes in place, Congress passed Richard Henry Lee's resolution "that these United colonies are, and of right, ought to be, Free and Independent States; . . . and that all political connexion between them, and the state of Great Britain, is, and ought to be, totally dissolved." Two days later, 12 colonies, with New York abstaining for the time being, unanimously approved Jefferson's Declaration of Independence, as amended by Congress.

"We hold these truths to be self-evident, that all men are created equal, that they are endowed by their Creator with certain unalienable Rights, that among these are Life, Liberty, and the pursuit of Happiness," Congress proclaimed in what is perhaps the most famous statement ever made in American public life. Whenever "any Form of Government becomes destructive of these ends, it is the Right of the People to alter or to abolish it, and to institute new Government, laying its foundation on such principles . . . as to them shall seem most likely to effect their Safety and Happiness." The longest section of the Declaration indicted George III as a tyrant.

During the three days that Congress was proclaiming American independence, the first ships of the largest armada yet sent across the Atlantic by any European state began landing British soldiers on Staten Island. Americans celebrated the creation of their new republic at the very moment that they faced a military challenge more ominous than any they had ever confronted before.

Conclusion

Between 1763 and 1776, Britain and the colonies became trapped in a series of self-fulfilling prophecies. The British feared that without major reforms to guarantee Parliament's control of the empire, the colonies would drift toward independence. Colonial resistance to the new policies convinced the British that a movement for independence really was under way, a perception that led to even sterner measures. Until a few months before it happened, nearly all colonists denied that they desired independence, but they began to fear that the British government was determined to deprive them of their rights as Englishmen. Britain's policy drove them toward a closer union with one another and finally provoked armed resistance. With the onset of war, both sides felt vindicated. The thousands of redcoats heading toward America did not bode well for colonial liberties. When the colonists finally did leave the empire, British ministers believed that their predictions had finally come true.

Both sides were wrong. The British had no systematic plan to destroy liberty in North America, and until winter 1775–76, hardly any colonists favored independence. But the three imperial crises undermined mutual confidence and brought about what no one had desired in 1765, or even 1774—an independent American nation. Unable to govern North America, Britain now faced the grim task of conquering it instead.

SUGGESTED READINGS

The best one-volume narrative history of the coming of the Revolution remains **Merrill Jensen's** *The Founding of a Nation: A History of the American Revolution, 1763–1776* (1968). **Bernard Bailyn's** *The Ideological Origins of the American Revolution* (1967) has had an enormous impact. **Gregory Evans Dowd** provides a fresh perspective in *War under Heaven: Pontiac, the Indian Nations, and the British Empire* (2002). On the three imperial crises, **Edmund S. and Helen M. Morgan's** *The Stamp Act Crisis, Prologue to Revolution,* 3rd ed. (1953, 1995) has lost none of its saliency. Nor has **John Shy's** *Toward Lexington: The Role of the British Army in the Coming of the American Revolution* (1965). **Pauline Maier's** *From Resistance to Revolution: Colonial Radicals and the Development of American Opposition to Britain, 1765–1776* (1972) and **Richard D. Brown's** *Revolutionary Politics in Massachusetts: The Boston Committee of Correspondence and the Towns* (1970) are both excellent on the process of disaffection. **David Ammerman's** *In the Common Cause: American Response to the Coercive Acts of 1774* (1974) is especially strong on the First Continental Congress and its aftermath. **David Hackett Fischer's** *Paul Revere's Ride* (1994) is a rare combination of exhaustive research and stirring prose. **Pauline Maier's**

American Scripture: Making the Declaration of Independence (1997) uses 90 local declarations of independence issued in spring 1776 to give context to Jefferson's famous text.

Important studies of internal tensions include **Gary B. Nash,** *The Urban Crucible: Social Change, Political Consciousness, and the Origins of the American Revolution* (1979); **Woody Holton's** imaginative *Forced Founders: Indians, Debtors, Slaves, and the Making of the American Revolution in Virginia* (1999); **James P. Whittenburg's "Planters, Merchants, and Lawyers: Social Change and the Origins of the North Carolina Regulation,"** *William and Mary Quarterly,* 3d ser., 34 (1977): 214–38; and **Richard M. Brown,** *The South Carolina Regulators* (1963). **David Grimsted's "Anglo-American Racism and Phillis Wheatley's 'Sable Veil,' 'Length'ned Chain,' and 'Knitted Heart,'"** in **Ronald Hoffman and Peter J. Albert, eds.,** *Women in the Age of the American Revolution* (1989) is a superb study of the emerging antislavery movement and the role of women in it.

 AMERICAN JOURNEY ONLINE
AND
INFOTRAC COLLEGE EDITION

Visit the source collections at www.ajaccess.wadsworth.com and infotrac.thomsonlearning.com and use the Search function with the following key terms to explore documents, images, audio and video clips, articles, and commentary related to the material in this chapter.

Stamp Act	Battle of Lexington
Proclamation of 1763	Battle of Concord
Pontiac	Phillis Wheatley
William Pitt	First Continental Congress
George Grenville	Second Continental Congress
Boston Massacre	Declaration of Independence
Boston Tea Party	

GRADE AIDS

Visit the Liberty Equality Power Companion Web Site for resources specific to this textbook: http://history.wadsworth.com/murrin_LEP4e

The CD in the back of this book and the U.S. History Resource Center at http://history.wadsworth.com/u.s./ offer a variety of tools to help you succeed in this course, including access to quizzes; images; documents; interactive simulations, maps, and timelines; movie explorations; and a wealth of other sources.

Chapter 6

The Revolutionary Republic

THE PASSAGE OF THE DELAWARE
This painting by Thomas Sully, completed in 1818, celebrates George Washington's attack on the Hessian garrison of Trenton, New Jersey, on December 26, 1776, as a turning point of the Revolutionary War.

CHAPTER OUTLINE

The Revolutionary War killed a higher percentage of Americans who fought in it than any other American conflict except the Civil War. It was a civil war in its own right. Neighbors were more likely to shoot at neighbors during the Revolution than they were between 1861 and 1865, when the geographical line separating the two sides would be much sharper. Twice, in 1776 and 1780, the British had a chance to win a decisive victory, but in both campaigns the Americans somehow rallied. The Americans won only by bringing in France as an ally, and France brought in Spain.

During the war, ever more Americans began to think in crude racial categories. Ideas about racial inferiority clashed sharply with claims of universal rights and human equality. As settlers and Indians, whites and blacks redefined their differences, they often resorted to racial stereotypes. Most Indians and enslaved Africans hoped that Britain would win the war.

Even as the war raged and the economy disintegrated, Americans drafted state constitutions and eloquent bills of rights that reached far beyond the racism many of them felt. They knew they were attempting something daring—the creation of a stable, enduring republic. Some European monarchies were 1,000 years old. No republic had ever lasted that long. Educated people knew a great deal about the city-states of classical Greece and about republican Rome—how they had called forth the noblest sentiments of patriotism for a time and then decayed into despotisms. Still, once Americans broke with Britain, they warmly embraced republicanism and never looked back. They were able to build viable republican governments because they grasped the voluntaristic dynamics of their society. They knew they had to restructure their governments through persuasive means. The use of force against armed fellow citizens would be self-defeating.

The war also demonstrated how weak Congress was, even after ratification of the Articles of Confederation in 1781. Congress could not pay its debts. It could not expel the British from their western military posts or defeat the Indians of the Ohio country. In the Northwest Ordinance of 1787, Congress nevertheless announced plans to create new western states and to admit them to the Union as full equals of the original 13. During that same summer, the Philadelphia Convention drafted a new Constitution for the United States. After ratification by 11 states in 1787 and 1788, it went into effect in April 1789. The federal system it created was the most distinctive achievement of the Revolutionary generation.

CHAPTER FOCUS

♦ How did American constitutionalism after 1776 differ from the British constitutional principles that the colonists had accepted and revered before 1776?

♦ Why, given that the Declaration of Independence proclaimed that all men are created equal, did most Indians and blacks, when given the chance, side with Britain?

♦ In what ways did the values shared by independent householders limit the reforms that the Revolution could offer to other Americans?

♦ The Articles of Confederation generally favored small states, especially in giving all states one vote in Congress. Why then did large states ratify quickly while three small states held up final ratification for years? The Constitution shifted power to large states. Why then did most small states ratify quickly while every large state except Pennsylvania came close to rejecting the new government?

Hearts and Minds: The Northern War, 1776–1777

Because the men who ruled Britain believed that the loss of the colonies would be a fatal blow to British power, the price of patriotism escalated once independence became the goal. Britain raised more soldiers and larger fleets than ever before and more than doubled its national debt. Americans, too confident after their early successes, staggered under the onslaught.

The British Offensive

The first setback came in Canada. The Americans, devastated by smallpox, had to retreat from Quebec when a

CHRONOLOGY

1769	Spanish found San Diego
1775	Settlement of Kentucky begins
1776	Virginia becomes first state to adopt a permanent constitution and bill of rights • British forces land on Staten Island • Declaration of Independence adopted • Pennsylvania constitution creates unicameral legislature • British win battle of Long Island; New York City falls • Washington wins at Trenton
1777	Washington wins at Princeton • Howe takes Philadelphia • Burgoyne surrenders at Saratoga • Congress completes the Articles of Confederation
1778	Franco-American alliance negotiated
1779	Indians form confederation from the Gulf to the Great Lakes • Spain declares war on Britain • Continental dollar collapses
1780	Massachusetts constitution approved • Pennsylvania adopts gradual emancipation • British take Charleston and overrun South Carolina • Gordon riots in London discredit other reformers • Arnold's treason uncovered • Americans win at King's Mountain
1781	Continental Army mutinies • Americans win at Cowpens • Congress creates executive departments • Articles of Confederation ratified • Cornwallis surrenders at Yorktown
1782	Gnadenhutten massacre leaves 100 unarmed Indians dead
1783	Peace of Paris recognizes American independence
1785	Congress passes Land Ordinance
1786	Virginia passes Statute for Religious Freedom • Annapolis convention meets
1786–87	Shays's Rebellion in Massachusetts protests taxes and economic woes
1787	Congress passes the Northwest Ordinance • Philadelphia Convention drafts a new federal Constitution
1787–88	Eleven states ratify the Constitution
1789	First federal Congress sends Bill of Rights to the states
1799	New York adopts gradual emancipation
1804	New Jersey adopts gradual emancipation

fresh British force sailed up the St. Lawrence River in May 1776. By July, Sir Guy Carleton drove them back into northern New York, to Fort Ticonderoga on Lake Champlain. Both sides built ships to control that strategic waterway. Largely through Benedict Arnold's efforts, the Americans held, and Carleton returned to Canada for the winter.

Farther south, Richard, viscount Howe, admiral of the British fleet, and his brother General William Howe prepared an awesome striking force on Staten Island. They

also acted as peace commissioners, with power to restore whole colonies to the king's peace and to pardon individual rebels. They hoped to avoid using their huge army, but when they wrote George Washington to open negotiations, he refused to accept the letter because it did not address him as "General." To do so would have recognized the legitimacy of his appointment. Benjamin Franklin, an old friend of the Howes, wrote that "it must give your lordship pain to be sent so far on so hopeless a business." Unable to negotiate, the Howes had to fight.

Since spring, Washington had moved his army from Boston to New York City, where he had about 19,000 men to face more than 30,000 redcoats and Hessians. Early successes had kept morale high among American forces and helped to sustain the *rage militaire* (warlike enthusiasm) that had prompted thousands to volunteer in 1775 and 1776, including 4,000 veterans of 1775 who reenlisted for 1776. Although some served in the Continental Army and others with state militia units, the difference between the two forces was still minimal. Neither of them gave formal military training, and the men in both served only for short terms.

Washington, who knew that civilian morale could be decisive, was reluctant to abandon any large city. Against conventional military wisdom, he divided his inferior force and sent half of it from Manhattan to Long Island. Most of the men dug in on Brooklyn Heights, just two miles from lower Manhattan, and waited for a frontal attack. The British invaded Long Island, a loyalist stronghold, and on August 27, 1776, sent a force around the American left flank through unguarded Jamaica Pass. While Hessians feinted a frontal assault, the flanking force crushed the American left and rear and sent the survivors reeling.

The Howes did nothing to prevent the evacuation of the rest of the American army to Manhattan, even though the navy could have cut them off. Instead, the British opened informal talks with several members of Congress on Staten Island on September 11, without acknowledging Congress's legality. The talks collapsed when the Americans insisted that the British recognize their independence before discussing substantive issues. Washington evacuated lower Manhattan. The British took New York City, much of which was destroyed by an accidental fire on September 21. The Howes then appealed directly to the people to lay down their arms and return to British allegiance within 60 days in exchange for a full pardon. In southern New York state, thousands complied.

In October, the Howes drove Washington out of Manhattan and Westchester and then turned on two garrisons he had left behind. On November 16, at a cost of 460 casualties, the British forced 3,000 men to surrender at Fort Washington on the Manhattan side of the Hudson River. General Nathanael Greene, a lame Rhode Island Quaker who had given up pacifism for soldiering, saved his men on the New Jersey side by abandoning Fort Lee, including all of his supplies.

The Howes probably could have destroyed Washington's army on Long Island or Manhattan, but they knew what they were doing. British victories and the American reliance on short-term volunteers were destroying Washington's army. British success seemed to prove that no American force could stand before a properly organized British army. But to capture Washington's entire army would have been a political embarrassment, leading to massive treason trials, executions, and great bitterness. Instead, Britain's impressive victories demoralized Americans and encouraged them to go home, many with their muskets. In September, 27,000 Americans stood fit for duty in the northern theater (including the Canadian border); by December, only 6,000 remained, most of whom intended to leave when their enlistments expired on December 31.

The Howes' strategy nearly worked. In December, British forces swept across New Jersey as far south as Burlington. They captured Charles Lee, next in command after Washington, and Richard Stockton, a signer of the Declaration of Independence. Several thousand New Jersey residents, including Stockton, took the king's oath. To seal off Long Island Sound from both ends, the Howes also captured Newport, Rhode Island. Many observers thought the war was all but over as sad remnants of the Continental Army crossed the Delaware River into Pennsylvania, confiscating all boats along the way so that the British could not follow them. One general believed that the time had come to "bargain away the Bubble of Independency for British Liberty well secured." Charles Carroll, another signer of the Declaration, agreed. Even Jefferson began to think about the terms on which a restoration of the monarchy might be acceptable.

The Trenton-Princeton Campaign

Washington knew he had to do something dramatic to restore morale and encourage his soldiers to reenlist. On the night of December 25, 1776, he crossed the ice-choked Delaware and marched south, surprising the Trenton garrison at dawn. At almost no cost to the attackers, 1,000 Hessians, suffering from Christmas hangovers, surrendered. The British sent their most energetic general, Charles, earl Cornwallis, south with 8,000 men to "bag the fox"— Washington and the 5,000 Continentals and militia still with him. Cornwallis caught him at Trenton near sunset on January 2 but decided to wait until dawn before attacking. British patrols watched the Delaware to prevent another escape across the river, but Washington tried

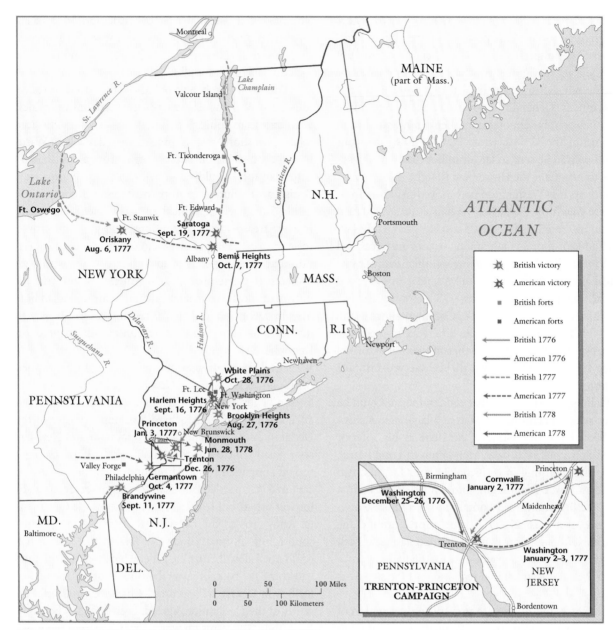

MAP 6.1   REVOLUTIONARY WAR IN THE NORTHERN STATES

This map shows the campaigns in New York and New Jersey in 1776–77, in northern New York and around Philadelphia in 1777, and at Monmouth, New Jersey, in 1778. The inset shows Washington's Trenton and Princeton campaigns after Christmas 1776.

 View an animated version of this map or related maps at http://history.wadsworth.com/murrin_LEP4e.

nothing of the kind. Leaving his campfires burning, he muffled the wheels of his wagons and guns and stole around the British left flank, heading north. At dawn, he met a British regiment just beginning its march from Princeton to Trenton. The Battle of Princeton amounted to a series of sharp clashes in which the Americans, with a 5-to-1 edge, mauled yet another outpost.

Washington's two quick victories had an enormous impact on the war, although they inspired few reenlistments. The Howes, who until January had shown a firm grasp of revolutionary warfare, blundered in not hounding Washington's remnant of an army to its destruction after Princeton. Instead, afraid that Washington might pick off their outposts one at a time, they called in their garrisons and concentrated the army along the Raritan River from New Brunswick to the sea. As the British departed, the militia returned, asking who had sworn oaths to the king. Those who had taken the oath now groveled, as the price of acceptance, or fled to British lines. The Howes had encouraged loyalists to come forward and then

abandoned them to the king's enemies. The Hessians had aroused fierce hatred by looting and raping their way across New Jersey. Together, the British and the Hessians had lost the hearts and minds of the settlers. In Howe's 1777 campaign, few would be willing to declare for the Crown. The Revolution survived.

The Campaigns of 1777 and Foreign Intervention

Britain's thoughtful strategy of 1776 gave way to incoherence in 1777. The Howes again had a plan for winning the war, but it required 20,000 reinforcements that did not exist. Instead, Lord George Germain, Britain's war minister, ordered the Howes to take Philadelphia. He also sent John Burgoyne, a poet and playwright as well as a general, to Canada with orders to march his army south and link up with the garrison of New York City, commanded by Sir Henry Clinton. A small force under Barry St. Leger was to march down the Mohawk valley and threaten Albany from the west. When few reinforcements reached the Howes, they rejected an overland march to Philadelphia as too risky and decided to invade by sea, a decision that allowed Washington to shift men north to oppose Burgoyne.

The British campaign made little sense. If the point of Burgoyne's march was to move his army to New York City, he should have gone by sea. If the point was to force a battle with New Englanders, his army should have been larger. And if Howe's army—Britain's largest—would not challenge Washington's, who would?

The Loss of Philadelphia

After Trenton and Princeton, Washington recruited a virtually new army in 1777. He demanded stricter discipline and longer terms of enlistment. Congress responded by raising the number of lashes a soldier could receive from 39 to 100 and by promising a cash bonus to anyone enlisting for three years and a land bounty to anyone serving for the duration. Congress never came close to raising the 75,000 men it hoped for, but these new policies did create a solid foundation for the Continental Line, or Army. Longer terms made military training a real possibility, which in turn made the Continentals much more professional than the militia. These improvements took time, however, and did not fully take hold until 1778 and later, after the first year of service.

The Continental Army acquired its own distinctive character. The men who signed up were often poor. About half of the New Jersey Line came from families that were not on the tax rolls. Some recruits were British deserters. Short-term militia, by contrast, usually held a secure place in their communities and were more likely than the Continentals to be church members. As the 1777 recruits came in, the two northern armies, swelled by militia, grew to about 28,000 men fit for duty—17,000 in northern New York and 11,000 under Washington.

The Howes sailed south from New York with 13,000 men. When river pilots could not guarantee a safe ascent up the Delaware against American fire, the fleet sailed on to Chesapeake Bay and landed the troops at Head of Elk, Maryland, on August 24. The British marched toward Philadelphia through southeastern Pennsylvania, a region thickly populated with loyalists and neutral Quakers. Few militia turned out to help Washington, but most residents, aware of the atrocities committed by the Hessians in New Jersey, fled rather than greet the British army as liberators. The British burned many of their abandoned farmhouses.

After his experience in New York, Washington was wary of being trapped in a city. Instead of trying to hold Philadelphia, he took up strong positions at Brandywine

Lewis Walpole Library, Yale University.

CONGRESS FLEEING PHILADELPHIA BY BALLOON, 1777

This British cartoon mocked Congress as it fled from the British army in the 1777 campaign. Hot air balloon flights, still experimental, were becoming a popular rage in France and Britain. The first flight across the English Channel would occur in 1783.

Creek along the British line of march. On September 11, Howe again outmaneuvered him, drove in his right flank, inflicted 1,000 casualties while suffering 500, and forced the Americans to retreat. Congress fled to Lancaster, and the British occupied Philadelphia on September 26. Eight days later, Washington surprised an outpost at Germantown, but the British rallied from early losses and drove him off.

Washington headed west to Valley Forge, where the army endured a miserable winter. There, Frederich Wilhelm, baron von Steuben, a Prussian serving with the Continental Army who would soon become a major general, devised a drill manual based on Prussian standards that he modified for use by the Americans. Through his efforts, the Continentals became far more soldierly. Other European volunteers also helped. From France came the marquis de Lafayette and Johann, baron de Kalb. The Poles sent Thaddeus Kosciuszko (a talented engineer) and Casimir, count Pulaski. De Kalb and Pulaski died in American service. By the last years of the war, perhaps one-fifth of all Continental officers were professional soldiers from Europe, who gave the American officer corps an aristocratic tone that alarmed civilians.

Saratoga

In northern New York, Fort Ticonderoga fell to Burgoyne on June 2, 1777, but little went right for the British after that. Colonel St. Leger, with 900 soldiers and an equal number of Indians, reached Fort Schuyler in the Mohawk valley in August and defeated 800 militia at Oriskany, but when Benedict Arnold approached with an additional

HISTORY THROUGH FILM

Mary Silliman's War (1993)

Directed by Stephen Surjik. Starring Nancy Palk (Mary Silliman), Richard Donat (Selleck Silliman), Paul Boretski (David Holly), Joanne Miller (Amelia), Elias Williams (Peter), and Allan Royal (Thomas Jones)

Strong movies about the Revolutionary War are hard to find. *Mary Silliman's War* is the rare exception. It rests on the outstanding research of Joy Day Buel and Richard Buel, Jr., on the life of an articulate woman, Mary Fish Noyes Silliman Dickinson, a woman who was widowed three times in the course of a long life (1736–1818). She left behind numerous letters and journals that make possible the reconstruction and dramatization of her life. Steven Schechter, who co-produced the film, also wrote most of the screenplay. It picks up Mary's story in 1779 when she was living in Fairfield, Connecticut, with her second husband, Gold Selleck Silliman, and their children. Selleck commanded the militia that had to respond to emergencies, and he also served as prosecuting attorney in his civilian capacity. In the northern states, the Revolutionary War had become mostly a series of destructive raids, with the British and loyalists based on Long Island and the patriots on the mainland. For good reason, both sides worried about traitors and spies in their midst.

As the film opens, Selleck is successfully prosecuting two loyalist townsmen. When they are sentenced to death, Mary objects that the war is turning neighbor against neighbor, but Selleck will not relent. In retaliation, the loyalists stage a night raid on the Silliman home, capture Selleck, and take him to New York City, which was the headquarters of the British army. The message seemed clear. If the Fairfield loyalists were to be executed, Selleck would also die. Thomas Jones, a magistrate and perhaps the most prominent loyalist living on Long Island, had known Selleck since their undergraduate days at Yale College. He acted as an intermediary. When George Washington refused to exchange a captured British officer for Selleck because he was not an officer in the Continental Army, Mary had to face an unpleasant dilemma. An American privateer, Capt. David Holly, offered to raid Long Island, capture Judge Jones, and force the British to negotiate an exchange. Mary disliked privateers and did not approve of Holly, but after the British raided Fairfield

1,000 men, the Indians fled and St. Leger withdrew to Oswego.

Burgoyne's army of 7,800, advancing from Ticonderoga toward Albany, was overwhelmed in the upper Hudson valley. As his supply line to Canada grew longer, American militia swarmed behind him to cut it. When he detached 700 Hessians to forage in the Green Mountains, they ran into 2,600 militia raised by John Stark of New Hampshire. On August 16 at Bennington, Vermont, Stark killed or captured nearly all of them. A relief force of 650 Hessians was also mauled. By the time Burgoyne's surviving sol-diers reached the Hudson and started toward Albany, the Americans under Horatio Gates outnumbered them 3 to 1. The British got as far as Bemis Heights, 30 miles north of Albany, but failed to break through in two costly battles on September 19 and Octo-

ber 7, with Arnold again distinguishing himself. Burgoyne retreated 10 miles to Saratoga, where he surrendered his entire army on October 17.

French Intervention

Colonial resistance delighted the French court, which was still recovering from its defeats in the Seven Years' War. In May 1776, Louis XVI authorized secret aid to the American rebels. A French dramatist, Pierre-Augustin Caron de Beaumarchais, author of *The Barber of Seville* (1775) and *The Marriage of Figaro* (1784), set up the firm of Roderique Hortalez et Compagnie to smuggle supplies through Britain's weak blockade of the American coast. (The British navy had deployed most of its ships to transport and supply the army and had few left for blockade duty.)

and burned most of the town, she consented. The rest of the story explores the consequences of this decision. Mary's deep religious convictions are emphasized throughout the film.

The screenplay telescopes the chronology of these events somewhat, invents a romance between Amelia (a servant in the Silliman household) and Captain Holly, and uses the slave Peter to illustrate the dilemmas that African Americans faced during the war. But the central plot line follows a drama that is well-documented in the historical record and exposes a side of the Revolutionary War that few Americans are even vaguely aware of. The struggle was a long, brutal conflict that brought liberty to many and equality to smaller numbers but also turned some neighbors against others.

Mary Fish Silliman at age 58, four years after the death of her second husband, Gold Selleck Silliman.

Fairfield Historical Society.

About 90 percent of the gunpowder used by Americans from 1775 to 1777 came either from captured British supplies or from abroad. Hortalez et Compagnie's 14 ships brought in most of what arrived from Europe. Without this aid, the Americans could not have continued the war.

In December 1776, Benjamin Franklin arrived in France as an agent of the American Congress. Although the French court could not officially receive him without risking a declaration of war by Britain, the 70-year-old Franklin took Parisian society by storm by adopting simple clothes, replacing his wig with a fur cap, and playing to perfection the role of an innocent man of nature. Through Beaumarchais, he kept the supplies flowing and organized privateering raids on British commerce, which the French court claimed it could not stop.

The fall of Philadelphia and Burgoyne's surrender at Saratoga persuaded the French to intervene openly. The loss of Philadelphia alarmed Foreign Minister Charles Gravier, comte de Vergennes. He feared that Congress might give up unless France entered the war. But Burgoyne's defeat convinced Louis that the Americans could win and that intervention was a good risk. Franklin and Vergennes signed two treaties in February 1778. One, a commercial agreement, granted Americans generous trading terms with France. In the other, France made a perpetual alliance with the United States, recognized American independence, agreed to fight until Britain conceded independence, and disavowed all territorial ambitions on the North American continent. Americans could not have hoped for more. Vergennes also brought Spain into the war a year later.

The Franco-American treaties stunned London. Lord North put together a plan of conciliation that conceded virtually everything but independence and sent a distinguished group of commissioners under Frederick Howard, earl of Carlisle, to present it to Congress and block the French alliance. In 1775, such terms would have resolved the imperial crisis, but in June 1778, Congress recognized them as a sign of British desperation and rejected them out of hand.

Americans now expected a quick victory, while the British regrouped. George III declared war on France, recalled the Howe brothers, and ordered General Clinton to abandon Philadelphia. Wary of being caught at sea by the French, Clinton marched overland to New York in June 1778. Washington's newly disciplined army attacked his rear at Monmouth, New Jersey, and almost drove the British from the field, but the redcoats rallied and won a draw. Fearing a French invasion of the British Isles while most of the Royal Navy was in American waters, the British redeployed their forces on a global scale. They stood on the defensive in America through most of 1778 and 1779 and even evacuated Newport, but loyalists often raided Connecticut and New Jersey from their bases in New York City, Staten Island, and Long Island.

Spanish Expansion and Intervention

Like France, Spain was eager to avenge old defeats against Britain. The Spanish king, Charles III (1759–88), had endured the loss of Florida shortly after ascending the throne but had received Louisiana from France in compensation. Spanish rule there did not begin smoothly. In 1769, Spain suppressed a small revolt against its restrictions on trade, but in later years, when its trade policy became more favorable, Louisiana enjoyed a level of prosperity it had never before known. The province attracted 2,000 immigrants from the Canary Islands, perhaps 3,000 Acadian refugees, and other French settlers from the Illinois country, some of whom founded St. Louis in 1764. Louisiana remained heavily French even under Spanish rule.

During this time, Spaniards also moved into California, partly in response to the migration of Russian hunters into Alaska. Spain founded San Diego in 1769. In the next few years, Spaniards explored the Pacific coastline as far north as southern Alaska, set up an outpost at San Francisco Bay, and built a series of Franciscan missions under Junípero Serra. With little danger from other Europeans, Spain sent relatively few soldiers to California. In fact, its

THE MISSION OF SAN CARLOS BORROMEO
The Spanish mission at Carmel, California, was founded in 1770.

© Alon Reininger/Woodfin Camp.

California frontier duplicated many aspects of the earlier Florida missions. For the last time in the history of North America, missionaries set the tone for a whole province. As in Florida, the Indians died in appalling numbers from European diseases, and many objected to the harsh discipline of the missions.

Charles III recognized the danger of one imperial power urging the subjects of another to revolt and never made a direct alliance with the United States, but in 1779, he joined France in its war against Britain, hoping to retake Gibraltar and to stabilize Spain's North American borders. Although Spain failed to take Gibraltar, it overran British West Florida. At the end of the war, Britain ceded East Florida as well. By 1783, for the first time in a century, Spain once again controlled the entire coastline of the Gulf of Mexico.

The Reconstitution of Authority

In 1776, the prospect of independence touched off an intense debate among Americans on constitutionalism. They agreed that every state needed a written constitution to limit the powers of government in terms more explicit than the precedents, statutes, and customs that made up Britain's unwritten constitution. They moved toward ever-fuller expressions of popular sovereignty—the theory that all power must be derived from the people. For four years, these lively debates sparked a learning process until, by 1780, Americans knew what they meant when they insisted that the people of a republic must be their own governors.

John Adams and the Separation of Powers

No one learned more from this process than John Adams. When Thomas Paine advocated a simple, unicameral legislature to carry out the people's will, Adams took alarm. He replied in *Thoughts on Government,* a tract that influenced the men drafting Virginia's constitution, which other states then imitated.

In 1776, Adams was already moving away from the British notion of a "mixed and balanced" constitution, in which government by King, Lords, and Commons embodied the distinct social orders of British society. He was groping toward quite a different notion, the separation of powers. Government, he affirmed, should be divided into three branches—an executive armed with veto power, a legislature, and a judiciary independent of both. The legislature, he insisted, must be bicameral, so that each house could expose the failings of the other. A free government need not embody distinct social orders to be stable. It could uphold republican values by being properly balanced within itself.

Governments exist to promote the happiness of the people, Adams declared, and happiness depends on "virtue," both public and private. Public virtue meant "patriotism," the willingness of independent householders to value the common good above their personal interests and even to die for their country. The form of government that rests entirely on virtue, Adams argued, is a republic. Americans must elect legislatures that would mirror the diversity of society. Britain had put the nobility in one house and the commoners in another, but in America, everyone was a commoner. America had no social orders. In what sense, then, could any government reflect American society? Adams came close to saying that the legislature should represent the "interests" of its citizens, but he did not face the implications of that argument. Should citizens enter politics to pursue selfish interests? What then of selfless patriotism?

In 1776, Adams knew only that the legislature should mirror society and that the structure of a republic should be more complex and balanced than what Paine advocated. Unicameral legislatures, which Georgia, Pennsylvania, and Vermont all adopted, horrified him: "A single assembly, possessed of all the powers of government, would make arbitrary laws for their own interest, execute all laws arbitrarily for their own interest, and adjudge all controversies in their own favor," he warned.

Adams had not yet found a way to distinguish between everyday legislation and the power to create a constitution, and neither had his admirers. While struggling to define what a republic ought to be, they could not escape two assumptions on which European politics rested—that government itself must be sovereign, and that it alone could define the rights of the people. A few ordinary settlers had already spotted the dangers of those assumptions. As the citizens of Concord, Massachusetts, warned in October 1776: "A Constitution alterable by the Supreme Legislative [Power] is no Security at all to the Subject against any Encroachment of the Governing part on . . . their Rights and Privileges."

This concern would eventually prompt Americans, including Adams, to invent the embodiment of popular sovereignty in its purest form, the constitutional convention. But meanwhile, in 1776, most Americans still assumed that governments must be sovereign. In the early state constitutions, every state lodged sovereign power in its legislature and let the legislature define the rights of citizens. In 1776, the American reply to Britain's sovereign Parliament was 13 sovereign state legislatures—14, with Vermont.

The Virginia Constitution

Only years of struggle exposed the inadequacy of the assumptions that the government possesses supreme authority and that the rights of the people must be defined by the government. In June 1776, Virginia became the first state to adopt a permanent, republican constitution. The provincial congress (called a "convention" in Virginia), which had assumed full legislative powers, affirmed "that the legislative and executive powers . . . should be separate and distinct from the judiciary"—but then wrote a constitution that made the legislature sovereign. The legislature chose the governor, the governor's council, and all judges above the level of justice of the peace. The governor had no veto and hardly any patronage. The lower house faced annual elections, but members of the upper house served four-year terms.

George Mason drafted a declaration of rights that the Virginia delegates passed before approving the constitution, on the theory that the people should define their rights before empowering the government. The amended text affirmed human equality but was carefully worded to exclude enslaved people. It upheld the right to life, liberty, property, and the pursuit of happiness. It condemned hereditary privilege, called for rotation in office, provided strong guarantees for trial by jury and due process, and extolled religious liberty. Legally, Virginia's bill of rights was merely a statute, with no more authority than any other law, but it was eloquent, and many states copied it.

Other states adopted variations of the Virginia model. Because America had no aristocracy, uncertainty about the proper makeup of the upper house was widespread. Some states imposed higher property qualifications on "senators" than on "representatives." In three states, the lower house elected the upper house. Maryland chose state senators through an electoral college, but most states created separate election districts for senators. Most states also increased the number of representatives in the lower house. Inland counties, which were underrepresented in most colonial assemblies, became better represented, and men of moderate wealth won a majority of seats in most states, displacing the rich, who had been winning most colonial elections. Most states also stripped the governor of patronage and of royal prerogatives, such as the power to dissolve the legislature. At this stage, only New York empowered the governor, in conjunction with a Council of Revision, to reject bills passed by the legislature.

The Pennsylvania Constitution

Many states disagreed sharply on constitutional issues. Pennsylvania learned how troubling these questions could become. Radicals there overthrew Crown, proprietor, and assembly in June 1776, rejected the leadership of both the old Quaker and Proprietary parties, and elected artisans to office in Philadelphia and ordinary farmers in rural areas. Until 1776, most officeholders had been either Quakers or Anglicans. Now, Scots-Irish Presbyterians and German Lutherans or Calvinists replaced most of them and drafted a new constitution in their own quest for legitimacy.

In 1776, Pennsylvania came closer than any other state to recognizing the constitutional dangers of resting sovereignty solely in the government—and government's arm, the legislature—rather than in the citizens. The radicals even summoned a special convention whose only task was to write a constitution. That document established a unicameral assembly and a plural executive of 12 men, one of whom would preside and thus be called "president." All freemen who paid taxes, and their adult sons living at home, could vote. Elections were annual, voting was by secret ballot, legislative sessions were open to the public, and no representative could serve for more than four years out of any seven. All bills were to be published before passage for public discussion throughout the state. Only at the next session of the legislature could they be passed into law, except in emergencies. Pennsylvania also created a Council of Censors to meet every seven years to determine whether the constitution had been violated. It could also recommend amendments.

The Pennsylvania constitution, however, never worked as planned and generated intense conflict in late 1776 as the British army drew near. In this emergency, the convention that drafted the constitution also began to pass laws, destroying any distinction between itself and the legislature it had created. Likewise, the convention and the legislatures that eventually succeeded it rarely delayed the enactment of a bill until after the voters had had time to discuss it. The war lent a sense of emergency to almost every measure. Even more alarming, many residents condemned the new constitution as illegitimate. The men driven from power in 1776 never consented to it and saw no good reason why they should accept it. The radicals, calling themselves Constitutionalists, imposed oaths on all citizens obliging them to uphold the constitution and then disenfranchised those who refused to support it, such as Quakers.

These illiberal measures gave radicals a majority in the legislature into the 1780s and kept voter turnout low in most elections, although some men (mostly leaders of the old Proprietary Party) took the oaths only to form an opposition party. Called Anticonstitutionalists at first (that is, opponents of the 1776 constitution), they soon took the name Republicans. After the war, as the disenfranchised regained the right to vote, Republicans won a solid majority in the legislature. In 1787, they won ratification of the federal Constitution, and then, in 1790, they replaced the

1776 state constitution with a new one that created a bicameral legislature and an elective governor with a veto that could be overridden. By then, Massachusetts had created the definitive model of constitution-making.

Massachusetts Redefines Constitutionalism

Another bitter struggle occurred in Massachusetts that finally generated a new consensus about what a constitution should be. After four years of intense debate, Massachusetts found a way to lodge sovereignty with the people and not with government—that is, a way to distinguish a constitution from simple laws.

In response to the Massachusetts Government Act passed by Parliament in 1774 (see chapter 5), the colonists had prevented the royal courts from sitting. In the three western counties of Worcester, Hampshire, and Berkshire, they had ousted from office a group of wealthy, intermarried families (called "river gods" in Connecticut valley towns), most of whom became loyalists. The courts remained closed until the British withdrew from Boston in March 1776, and the provincial congress moved into the city and reestablished itself as the General Court under the royal charter of 1691. The legislature then reapportioned itself. Under the old system, most towns elected a single representative. A few (such as Salem) chose two. Only Boston could elect four. The new system let towns choose representatives in proportion to population. It rewarded the older, populous eastern towns at the expense of the lightly settled western towns.

When the General Court also revived royal practice by appointing its own members as county judges and justices of the peace, the western counties exploded. Their hatred of the river gods extended to eastern gentlemen as well. Denouncing the "antient Mode of Government among us which we so much detest and abhor," they attacked the reapportionment act and refused to reopen the courts in Hampshire and Berkshire counties. Most of Berkshire's radicals were Baptists in religion and Lockeans in politics. They insisted on contracts or compacts as the basis of authority in both church and state and continued to use county conventions in place of the courts. To the Berkshire Constitutionalists, a "convention" was becoming the purest expression of the will of the people, superior to any legislature. These uneducated farmers set the pace in demanding a formal constitution for the state.

In fall 1776, the General Court asked the towns to authorize it to draft a constitution. By a 2-to-1 margin, the voters agreed, a result that reflected growing *distrust* of the legislature. Six months earlier, hardly anyone would have questioned such a procedure. The legislature drafted a constitution over the next year and then, in an unusual precaution, asked the towns to ratify it. The voters rejected it by the stunning margin of 5 to 1. Some towns objected to the lack of a bill of rights, and a few insisted that it should have been drafted by a separate convention. Several towns wanted the governor to be directly elected by the people, but most gave no reason for their disapproval. Voters angry with a particular clause were likely to condemn the whole document.

Chastened, the General Court urged the towns to postpone the question until after the war. Hampshire County reopened its courts in April 1778, but Berkshire County threatened to secede from the state unless the legislature summoned a constitutional convention. Drawing upon John Locke, these farmers insisted that they were now in a "state of nature," subject to no legitimate government. They might even join a neighboring state that had a proper constitution. At a time when Vermont was making good its secession from New York, theirs was no idle threat.

The General Court gave in, and a convention met in Boston in December 1779. John Adams drafted a constitution that the convention used as its starting point. A constitution now had to be drafted by a convention, elected for that specific purpose, and then ratified by the people. The people would then be the source of all legitimate authority.

In the four years since 1776, Adams's thoughts on the separation of powers and bicameralism had matured. Like the Virginia constitution, the Massachusetts constitution began with a bill of rights. Both houses would be elected annually. The House of Representatives would be chosen by the towns, as reapportioned in 1776. Senators would be elected by counties and apportioned according to property values, not population. The governor would be elected by the people and would have a veto that two-thirds of both houses could override. Property qualifications rose as a man's civic duties increased. Voters must own £50 of real property or £100 of personal property, representatives must have £100 in land or £200 in other property, senators must have £300 in land or £600 in total wealth, respectively, and the governor had to own £1,000 in landed property. He also had to be a Christian. For purposes of ratification only, all free adult males were eligible to vote. In accepting the basic social compact, everyone (that is, all free men) would have a chance to consent. Voters were asked to vote on each article separately, not on the document as a whole.

During spring 1780, town meetings began the ratification process. The convention tallied the results and declared that the constitution had received the required two-thirds majority, but it juggled the figures on two articles, both involving religion, to get this result. Those articles provided for the public support of ministers and required

the governor to be a Christian. Baptists objected to all taxes for the support of religion, and many Protestants wanted to exclude Catholics from the governorship. The new constitution promptly went into effect and, although it has often been amended, is still in force today, making it the world's oldest written constitution. Starting with New Hampshire in 1784, other states adopted the Massachusetts model.

Confederation

The states' creativity had no counterpart in the Continental Congress, which met almost continuously during the war. Before independence, hardly anyone had given serious thought to how an American nation ought to be governed. Dozens of colonists had drafted plans of conciliation with Britain, some quite innovative, but through 1775 only Benjamin Franklin and Connecticut's Silas Deane had presented plans for an American union. Franklin's was an updated version of the Albany Plan of 1754 (see chapter 4). Another anonymous proposal appeared in an American newspaper, but none of the three plans attracted public comment. Colonists passionately debated the empire and their state governments, but not America.

Congress began discussing the American union in summer 1776 but did not produce the final text of what became the "Articles of Confederation and perpetual Union" until a year and a half later. Congress had been voting by state since the First Continental Congress in 1774. Delegates from large states favored representation according to population, but no census existed to give precise numbers, and the small states insisted on being treated as equals. As long as Britain was ready to embrace any state that defected, small states had great leverage: The tail could wag the dog. In one early draft of the Articles of Confederation, John Dickinson rejected proportional representation in favor of state equality. He enumerated the powers of Congress, which did not include levying taxes or regulating trade. To raise money, Congress would have to print it or requisition specific amounts from the states. Congress then split over how to apportion these requisitions. Northern states wanted to count slaves in computing the ratios. Southern states wanted to apportion requisitions on the basis of each state's free population.

Western lands were another tough issue. States with fixed borders pressured states with boundary claims stretching into the Ohio or Mississippi valleys to surrender their claims to Congress. Many speculators favored the land cessions. Congress could not resolve these issues in 1776.

Debate resumed after Washington's victories at Trenton and Princeton. Thomas Burke of North Carolina introduced a resolution that eventually became part of the Articles of Confederation: "Each state retains its sovereignty, freedom and independence, and every power, jurisdiction, and right, which is not by this confederation expressly delegated to the United States in Congress assembled." The acceptance of Burke's resolution, with only Virginia dissenting, ensured that the Articles would contain a firm commitment to state sovereignty. Only after Saratoga, however, was Congress able to complete the Articles. In the final version, Congress was given no power over western land claims, and requisitions would be based on each state's free population. In 1781, Congress tried to change the formula so that each slave was counted as three-fifths of a person for the purpose of apportioning requisitions, but this amendment was never ratified.

In November 1777, Congress asked the states to ratify the Articles by March 10, 1778, but only Virginia met the deadline. Most states tried to attach conditions, which Congress rejected, but by midsummer 10 had ratified. The three dissenters were Delaware, New Jersey, and Maryland—all states without western land claims who feared their giant neighbors. Maryland held out for more than three years, until Virginia agreed to cede its land claims north of the Ohio River to Congress. The Articles finally went into force on March 1, 1781.

By then, the Continental Congress had lost most of its power. Some of its most talented members, including Jefferson and Samuel Adams, had returned home to help reshape their state governments. Others, such as Washington, had taken army commands, and some, including Benjamin Franklin, John Adams, and John Jay, had departed on diplomatic assignments. The congressional effort to manage everything through committees created impossible bottlenecks. In 1776, the states had looked to Congress to confer legitimacy on their new governments, especially in the middle colonies, but as the states adopted their own constitutions, their legitimacy became more obvious than that of Congress. Even more alarming, by the late 1770s, Congress simply could not pay its bills.

☭ The Crisis of the Revolution, 1779–1783

Americans expected a quick victory under the French alliance. Instead, the struggle turned into a grim war of attrition, testing which side would first exhaust its resources or lose the will to fight. Loyalists became much more important to the British war effort, both as a source of manpower and as the main justification for continuing the war. Most settlers, argued Lord North, were still loyal to Britain. They could turn the contest around. To abandon

them would be dishonorable and might lead to a bloodbath. The British began to look to the Deep South as the likeliest recruiting ground for armed loyalists. The Carolinas, bitterly divided by the regulator movements and vulnerable to massive slave defections, seemed a promising source.

The Loyalists

Most loyalists were committed to English ideas of liberty. Many of them had objected openly to the Stamp Act and other British measures but doubted that Parliament intended to undermine government by consent in the colonies. They also thought that creating a new American union was a far riskier venture than remaining part of the British empire. For many, the choice of loyalties was painful. Some waited until the fighting reached their neighborhood before deciding which soldiers to flee from and which to shoot at. The loyalists then learned a stark truth: They could not fire at their neighbors and expect to retain their homes except under the protection of the British army. The British, in turn, were slow to take advantage of the loyalists. In the early years of the war, British officers regarded the loyalists' military potential with the same disdain that they bestowed on the patriots. As the war continued, however, the loyalists, who stood to lose everything in an American victory, showed that they could be fierce soldiers.

About one-sixth of the white population chose the British side in the war, and 19,000 men joined more than 40 loyalist military units, mostly after 1778 when Britain grew desperate for soldiers. Unlike most patriots, loyalists served long terms, even for the duration, because they could not go home unless they won. By 1780, the number of loyalists under arms exceeded the number of Continentals by almost two to one. State governments retaliated by banishing prominent loyalists under pain of death and by confiscating their property.

Loyalist Refugees, Black and White

When given the choice, most slaves south of New England sided with Britain. In New England, where they sensed that they could gain freedom by joining the rebels, many volunteered for military service. Elsewhere, although some fought for the Revolution, they realized that their best chance of emancipation lay with the British army. During the war, more than 50,000 slaves (about 10 percent) fled their owners; of that total, about 20,000 were evacuated by the British. The decision to flee carried risks. In South Carolina, hundreds reached the sea islands in an effort to join the British during Clinton's 1776 invasion, only to face their owners' wrath when the British failed to rescue them. Others approached British units only to be treated as contraband (property) and to face possible resale. Most slaves who reached British lines won their freedom, however, even though the British army never became an instrument of systematic emancipation.

When the British withdrew after the war, blacks went with them, many to Jamaica, some to Nova Scotia, others to London. In the 1780s, the British even created a colony for former slaves at Sierra Leone in West Africa.

The war, in short, created an enormous stream of refugees, black and white. In addition to 20,000 former slaves, some 60,000 to 70,000 colonists left the states for other parts of the British empire. The American Revolution created 30 refugees for every 1,000 people, compared with 5 per 1,000 created by the French Revolution in the 1790s. About 35,000 settlers found their way to Nova Scotia, the western part of which became the province of New Brunswick in the 1780s. Another 6,000 to 10,000 fled to Quebec, settled upriver from the older French population,

AN OFFER OF FREEDOM

An American newspaper reported on British efforts to gain the support of slaves by offering them freedom.

Extract of a letter from Monmouth county, June 12.
" Ty, with his party of about 20 blacks and whites, laſt Friday afternoon took and carried off priſoners, Capt. Barns Smock and Gilbert Vanmater; at the ſame time ſpiked up the iron four pounder at Capt. Smock's houſe, but took no ammunition: Two of the artillery horſes, and two of Capt. Smock' horſes, were likewiſe taken off."
The above-mentioned Ty is a Negroe, who bears the title of Colonel, and commands a motly crew at Sandy-Hook.

Courtesy, American Antiquarian Society.

National Archives of Canada/C-002001.

ENCAMPMENT OF LOYALISTS AT JOHNSTON, ONTARIO, JUNE 6, 1784
This painting by James Peachey depicts the arrival of loyalist exiles in Upper Canada.

and in 1791 became the new province of Upper Canada (later Ontario). A generous land policy, which required an oath of allegiance to George III, attracted thousands of new immigrants to Canada from the United States in the 1780s and 1790s. By the War of 1812, four-fifths of Upper Canada's 100,000 people were American-born. Although only one-fifth of them could be traced to loyalist resettlement, the settlers supported Britain in that war. In a real sense, the American Revolution laid the foundation for two new nations—the United States and Canada—and competition between them for settlers and loyalties continued long after the fighting stopped.

The Indian Struggle for Unity and Survival

Indians of the eastern woodlands also began to play a more active role in the war. For them the stakes were immense. Most of them saw that an American victory would threaten their survival as a people on their ancestral lands. Nearly all of them sided with Britain in the hope that a British victory might stem the flood of western expansion. In the final years of the war, they achieved a level of unity without precedent in their history.

At first, most Indians tried to remain neutral. The British were rebuffed when they asked the Iroquois to fight against the colonists. The Delawares and the Shawnees, defeated in Lord Dunmore's War in 1774, also stood neutral. Only the Cherokees took up arms in 1776. Short on ammunition and other British supplies, they took heavy losses before making peace and accepting neutrality. The

Chickamaugas, a splinter group, continued to resist. In the Deep South, only the Catawbas—by now much reduced in number—fought on the American side.

Burgoyne's invasion brought the Iroquois into the war in 1777. The Mohawks in the east and the Senecas in the west sided with Britain under the leadership of Joseph Brant, a literate and educated Mohawk and a Freemason. His sister, Mary Brant, emerged as a skillful diplomat in the alliance between the Iroquois and the loyalists. A minority of Oneidas and some Tuscaroras fought with the Americans. Most of them were becoming Christians under a patriot Presbyterian missionary, Samuel Kirkland. Despite severe strains during the Revolution, the Iroquois League was not shattered until after the war, when those who fought for Britain migrated to Canada.

A minority of Shawnees, led by Cornplanter, and of Delawares, led by White Eyes and Killbuck, also pursued friendly relations with the Americans. They provided intelligence to American forces and served as wilderness guides, but they refused to fight other Indians and did their best to preserve peace along the frontier. Christian Moravian Indians in the Ohio country took a similar stance. The reluctance of Indians to kill other Indians, already evident during the Seven Years' War, became even more obvious during the Revolution. Loyalists and patriots were far more willing than Indians to kill one another.

Frontier racism, already conspicuous in Pontiac's War, became more vicious than ever and made Indian neutrality all but impossible. Backcountry settlers from Carolina through New York refused to accept the neutrals on their own terms. Indian warriors, especially young men

New York State Historical Association, Cooperstown, New York.

JOSEPH BRANT, PORTRAIT BY GILBERT STUART (1786)

Brant, a Mohawk and a Freemason, was one of Britain's most effective commanders of loyalist and Indian forces. After the war, he led most of the Six Nations to Canada for resettlement.

Chicago Historical Society.

AMERICAN FLAGS, 1779

Even three years after independence, no standardized version of the flag had yet taken hold. People were still experimenting with their own patterns.

strongly influenced by nativist prophets, increasingly believed that the Great Spirit had created whites, Indians, and blacks as separate peoples who ought to remain apart. Their militancy further enraged the settlers. Young white hunters, disdained by many easterners as "near savages," proved their worth as "whites" by killing Indians.

The hatred of Indians grew so extreme that it threatened to undercut the American war effort. In 1777, a Continental officer had Cornplanter murdered. In 1778, American militia killed White Eyes. Four years later, Americans massacred 100 unarmed Moravian mission Indians at Gnadenhutten, Ohio. Nearly all of them were women and children, who knelt in prayer as, one by one, their skulls were crushed with mallets. This atrocity brutalized Indians as well as settlers. Until then, most Indians had refrained from the ritual torture of prisoners, but after Gnadenhutten they resumed the custom, not as a general practice, but to punish atrocities. When they captured known leaders of the massacre, they burned them alive.

Faced with hatred, Indians united to protect their lands. They won the frontier war north of the Ohio River. The Iroquois ravaged the Wyoming valley of Pennsylvania in 1778. When an American army devastated Iroquoia in

1779 and committed many atrocities along the way, the Indians fell back on the British post at Niagara and continued the struggle. In 1779, nearly all Indians, from the Creeks on the Gulf Coast to the nations of the Great Lakes, exchanged emissaries and planned an all-out war along the frontier. George Rogers Clark of Virginia thwarted their offensive with a daring winter raid in which he captured Vincennes and cut off the western nations from British supplies. But the Indians regrouped and by 1782 drove the Virginia "long knives" out of the Ohio country.

Attrition

After 1778, George III's determination to continue the war bitterly divided his kingdom. Much of the British public doubted that the war could be won. Trade was disrupted,

MAP 6.2 WAR ON THE FRONTIER, 1777–82
Indian unity during the Revolution exceeded even what had been achieved in Pontiac's War.

thousands of ships were lost to privateers, taxes and the national debt soared, military recruits became harder to find, and a French invasion became a serious threat. Political dissent rose and included widespread demand for the reduction of royal patronage and for electoral reforms. A proposal to abolish Lord George Germain's office, clearly an attack on the American war, failed in the House of Commons by only 208 votes to 201 in March 1780. A resolve condemning the influence of the Crown carried in April, 233 to 215. The king had great difficulty persuading North not to resign.

Desperate for men, the British army had been quietly recruiting Irish Catholics, and North supported a modest degree of toleration for English and Scottish Catholics. This leniency produced a surge of Protestant violence culminating in the Gordon riots, named for an eccentric agitator, Lord George Gordon. For a week in June 1780, crowds roared through the streets of London, smashing

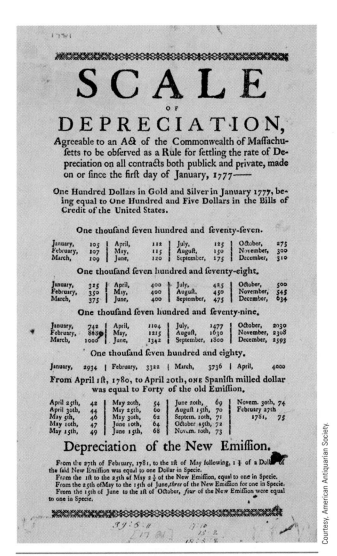

SCALE
OF
DEPRECIATION,

Agreeable to an Act of the Commonwealth of Massachusetts to be observed as a Rule for settling the rate of Depreciation on all contracts both publick and private, made on or since the first day of January, 1777——

One Hundred Dollars in Gold and Silver in January 1777, being equal to One Hundred and Five Dollars in the Bills of Credit of the United States.

One thousand seven hundred and seventy-seven.

January,	105	April,	112	July,	125	October,	275
February,	107	May,	115	August,	150	November,	300
March,	109	June,	120	September,	175	December,	310

One thousand seven hundred and seventy-eight.

January,	325	April,	400	July,	425	October,	500
February,	350	May,	400	August,	450	November,	545
March,	375	June,	400	September,	475	December,	634

One thousand seven hundred and seventy-nine.

January,	742	April,	1104	July,	1477	October,	2030
February,	868	May,	1215	August,	1630	November,	2308
March,	1000	June,	1342	September,	1800	December,	2593

One thousand seven hundred and eighty.

January,	2934	February,	3322	March,	3736	April,	4000

From April 1st, 1780, to April 20th, ONE Spanish milled dollar was equal to Forty of the old Emission.

Depreciation of the New Emission.

April 25th,	42	May 20th,	54	June 20th,	69	Novem. 30th,	74
April 30th,	44	May 25th,	60	August 15th,	70	February 27th	
May 5th,	46	May 30th,	62	Septem. 10th,	71	1781,	75
May 10th,	47	June 10th,	64	October 15th,	72		
May 15th,	49	June 15th,	68	Novem. 10th,	73		

From the 27th of February, 1781, to the 1st of May following, 1½ of a Dollar of the said New Emission was equal to one Dollar in Specie.
From the 1st to the 25th of May 2½ of the New Emission, equal to one in Specie.
From the 25th of May to the 15th of June, three of the New Emission for one in Specie.
From the 15th of June to the 1st of October, four of the New Emission were equal to one in Specie.

Courtesy, American Antiquarian Society.

DEPRECIATION OF THE DOLLAR

By 1779, the dollar had become all but worthless.

Catholic chapels attached to foreign embassies, liberating prisoners from city jails, and finally attacking the Bank of England. The army, supported by Lord Mayor John Wilkes, put down the rioters. This spectacular violence discredited the demands for reform that had seemed on the verge of toppling North. The riots gave him one more chance to win the war.

Attrition also weakened the United States. Indian raids reduced harvests, and military levies kept thousands of men away from productive work. Loyalist raids into Connecticut and New Jersey wore down the defenders and destroyed a great deal of property. A 1779 raid on Virginia carried off or destroyed property worth £2 million. Merchants lost most of their European and West Indian markets, although a few of them made huge profits through blockade running or privateering. Average household income plunged by more than 40 percent. Even some American triumphs came at a high price. Burgoyne's surrender left Americans with the burden of feeding his army for the rest of the war. When a French fleet called at Boston, the crews devoured an alarming share of available provisions, as did the French army that landed at Newport in 1780.

These heavy demands led to the collapse of the Continental dollar in 1779–80. Congress had been printing money to pay its bills, using the Spanish dollar as its basic monetary unit. With the French alliance bolstering American credit, this practice worked reasonably well into 1778. The money depreciated but without causing widespread dissatisfaction. As the war ground on, though, the value of Continental money fell to less than a penny on the dollar in 1779. Congress agreed to stop the printing presses and to rely instead on requisitions from the states and on foreign and domestic loans, but without paper it could not even pay the army. Congress and the army had to

THE PRESENT STATE OF GREAT BRITAIN (1779?), PROBABLY BY JAMES GILLRAY

The war is going badly for weary John Bull (England). America, the Indian, is stealing liberty, the Dutch are lifting Britain's purse, and the French are attacking. Only a surly Scot is defending John Bull, and he may lose his dagger.

Colonial Williamsburg.

requisition supplies directly from farmers in exchange for certificates geared to an inflation rate of 40 to 1, well below its true rate. Many farmers, rather than lose money on their crops, simply cut back production. William Beadle, a Connecticut shopkeeper, tried to fight inflation by accepting Continental money at face value until he saw the consequences. Rather than leave his wife and children impoverished, he slit their throats and shot himself.

Continental soldiers—unpaid, ill-clothed, and often poorly fed—grew mutinous. As they became more professional through frequent drill, they also became contemptuous of civilians. The winter of 1779–80, the worst of the century, marked a low point in morale among the main force of Continentals snowed in with Washington at Morristown, New Jersey. Many deserted. In May 1780, two Connecticut regiments of the Continental Line, without food for three days, threatened to go home, raising the danger that the whole army might dissolve. Their officers barely managed to restore control. On paper, Washington had 16,000 men. His real strength was 3,600 men and not even enough horses to move his artillery.

☛ The British Offensive in the South

Sensing a unique opportunity in 1780, the British attacked in the Deep South with great success. The Revolution entered its most critical phase and nearly collapsed. "I have almost ceased to hope," Washington confessed at one point. In December 1778, a small British amphibious force had taken Savannah and had held it through 1779 against an American and French counterthrust. The British even restored royal government with an elective assembly in Georgia between 1780 and 1782. By early 1780, they were ready to move from this enclave and launch a general offensive. Their commander, General Clinton, was a cautious man who had been in charge of Britain's war effort since 1778. He had exasperated loyalist supporters by remaining on the defensive in New York City. By the time he took command in Georgia in January 1780, he had finally devised a strategy for winning the war, but he revealed its details to no one.

Clinton's New York army would invade South Carolina, take Charleston, and unleash armed loyalists to pacify the countryside. Part of the regular forces would remain in the Carolinas to deal with any other army the Americans might field. Clinton would sail with the rest back to New York and land on the Jersey coast with a force three times larger than Washington's at Morristown. By dividing this army into two columns, Clinton could break through both passes of the Watchung Mountains leading to Morristown. Washington must either hold fast and

be overwhelmed or else abandon his artillery for lack of horses and attack one of the invading columns on unfavorable terms. Either way, Clinton reasoned, the Continental Army would be destroyed. He was also negotiating secretly with Benedict Arnold for the surrender of West Point, which would open the Hudson River to British ships as far north as Albany. Arnold, who thought that Congress had never adequately rewarded his heroism, had begun trading intelligence for cash in 1779. Finally, if the French landed in Newport, as everyone expected, Clinton would then move against them with nearly his entire New York fleet and garrison. If he succeeded there too, he would have smashed every professional force in North America within a year's time. His remaining task would then be pacification, which he could pretty much leave to loyalists.

Clinton's invasion of South Carolina began with awesome successes. While the British navy sealed off Charleston from the sea, an army of 10,000 closed off the land approaches to the city and trapped Benjamin Lincoln and 5,000 defenders. Their surrender on May 12 gave Britain its largest haul of prisoners in the entire war. Clinton had already turned loose his angry, well-trained loyalists under Banastre Tarleton and Patrick Ferguson. Tarleton caught the 350 remaining Continentals at the Waxhaws near the North Carolina border on May 29 and, in what became infamous as "Tarleton's quarter," killed them all.

The calculated brutality of Britain's pacification policy was designed to terrorize civilians into submission. It succeeded for a time, but Thomas Sumter began to fight back after loyalists burned his plantation. His mounted raiders attacked British outposts and terrorized loyalists. At Hanging Rock on August 6, Sumter's 800 men scattered 500 loyalists, killing or wounding nearly half of them before Sumter's own men embarked on an orgy of looting and drinking. All participants on both sides were colonists.

Leaving Cornwallis in command of 8,300 men in South Carolina, Clinton sailed north with one-third of his Carolina army, only to learn that his plans for New Jersey had gone awry. During his absence, the leading loyalists, fearing that he would never take the initiative in the north, had persuaded Wilhelm, baron von Knyphausen, the temporary commander, to land in New Jersey with 6,000 men on the night of June 6–7, 1780. Even a force that small would pose a grave threat to Washington unless the militia came to his aid. Most loyalists hoped that the militia was so weary from the harsh winter and numerous raids that they would not turn out. Some companies had even begun to muster women. To the dismay of the British, however, the militia appeared in force on June 7.

Only then, after an inconclusive engagement, did Knyphausen learn that Clinton was on his way with his own plan of attack. The British pulled back to the coast and waited, but they had lost the element of surprise.

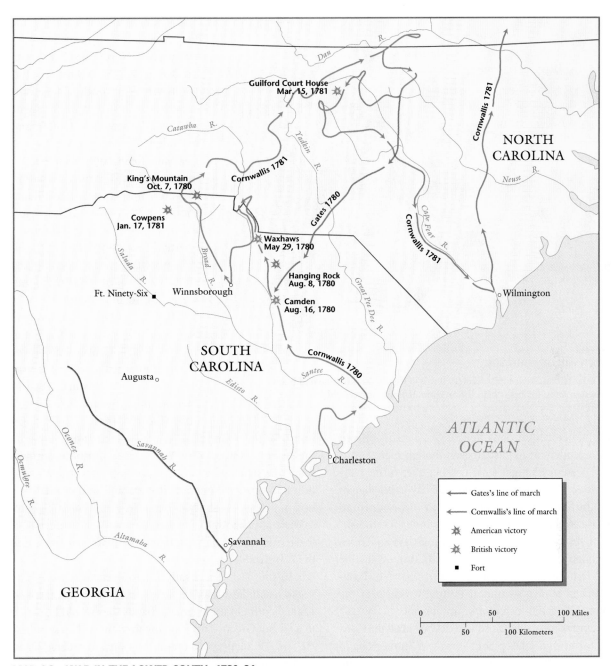

MAP 6.3 WAR IN THE LOWER SOUTH, 1780–81
British victories in 1780 nearly restored Georgia and South Carolina to the Crown, but after Guilford Court House in March 1781, the Americans regained the advantage throughout the region.

 View an animated version of this map or related maps at http://history.wadsworth.com/murrin_LEP4e.

Clinton attacked at Springfield on June 23 while loyalists set fire to the village. The battle became America's civil war in miniature. New Jersey loyalist regiments attacked the New Jersey regiments of the Continental Line, who were assisted by New Jersey militia. The defense was stout enough to persuade Clinton to withdraw to New York.

With Washington's army still intact, Clinton ignored the French when they landed at Newport. After June 1780, the British put all of their hopes on the southern cam-

paign. Even Arnold's attempt to betray West Point was thwarted in September. Clinton's agent, John André, was caught and hanged, but Arnold escaped to British lines and became a general in the British army.

Despite Sumter's harassment, Cornwallis's conquest of the Carolinas proceeded rapidly. Congress scraped together 900 tough Maryland and Delaware Continentals, put Horatio Gates, the hero of Saratoga, in command, and sent them south against Cornwallis. Bolstered by 2,000

SELF-PORTRAIT OF JOHN ANDRÉ

André, a talented amateur artist, sketched this self-portrait after he had been condemned to hang for his role in the treason of Benedict Arnold.

1,800 strong to challenge Patrick Ferguson's loyalists at King's Mountain near the North Carolina border on October 7, 1780. Nearly all of the combatants on both sides were Americans. Losing only 88 men, rebel marksmen picked off many defenders, advanced from tree to tree, and finally overwhelmed the loyalists, killing 160 men, including Ferguson, and capturing 860. They shot many prisoners and hanged a dozen, their answer to "Tarleton's quarter." This victory, the first major British setback in the Deep South, stung Cornwallis, who halted his drive into North Carolina.

In October 1780, Congress sent Nathanael Greene to the Carolinas with a small Continental force. When Sumter withdrew for several months to nurse a wound, Francis Marion took his place. A much abler leader, Marion (who became known as the Swamp Fox) operated from remote bases in the swampy low country. Yet Greene's prospects seemed desperate. The ugliness of the partisan war—the mutilation of corpses, killing of prisoners, and wanton destruction of property—shocked him. The condition of his own soldiers appalled him. Yet Greene and Marion devised a masterful strategy of partisan warfare that finally wore out the British.

In the face of a greatly superior enemy, Greene ignored a standard maxim of war and split up his force of 1,800 Continentals. In smaller bands they would be easier to feed, but Greene's decision involved more than supplies. He sent 300 men east to bolster Marion and ordered Daniel Morgan and 300 riflemen west to threaten the British outpost of Ninety-Six. Tarleton urged Cornwallis to turn and crush the 1,000 men still with Greene, but Greene had no intention of engaging a superior force. Cornwallis worried that after Morgan's King's Mountain victory, he might raise the entire backcountry against the British, and so he divided his own army. He sent Tarleton with a mixed force of 1,100 British and loyalists after Morgan, who decided to stand with his back to a river at a place called Cowpens, where a loyalist kept cattle. Including militia, Morgan had 1,040 men.

Tarleton attacked on January 17, 1781. In another unorthodox move, Morgan sent his militia out front as skirmishers. He ordered them to fire two rounds and then redeploy in his rear as a reserve. Relieved of their fear of

Virginia and North Carolina militia, Gates rashly offered battle at Camden on August 16 even though many of his men had been up all night with diarrhea after eating half-baked bread. The militia, who lacked bayonets, fled in panic at the first British charge. The exposed Continentals fought bravely but were crushed. Gates rode an astonishing 240 miles away from the scene in three days and, from Hillsborough, North Carolina, informed Congress that he had suffered "total Defeat." Two days after Camden, Tarleton surprised Sumter's camp at Fishing Creek, near the Waxhaws, killing 150 men and wounding 300.

In four months, the British had destroyed all the Continental forces in the Deep South, mauled Sumter's band of partisans, and left North Carolina open to invasion. These victories seemed to fulfill Clinton's boast that he would strip "three stripes . . . from the detestable thirteen." When the French foreign minister heard the news, he quietly inquired whether Britain would make peace, with each side keeping what it currently possessed. Cornwallis turned the pacification of South Carolina over to his loyalists, many of whom were exiles from other states, and marched confidently on to "liberate" North Carolina.

The Partisan War

Yet resistance continued. Tarleton and Sumter fought one battle to a draw. Farther west, frontier riflemen, angered by Britain's alliance with the Indians, crossed the Blue Ridge

Yale University Art Gallery, Gift of Ebenezer Baldwin, B.A. 1808.

a bayonet charge, they obeyed. As they pulled back, the British rushed forward into the Continentals, who also retreated at first, then wheeled and discharged a lethal volley. After Morgan's cavalry charged into the British left flank, the militia returned to the fray. Although Tarleton escaped, Morgan annihilated his army. For the first time in the war, an American force had clearly outfought a British army without an advantage of numbers or terrain.

As Morgan rejoined Greene, Cornwallis staked everything on his ability to find Greene and crush him, precisely what he had failed to do to Washington after Trenton and Princeton four years earlier. But Greene outthought him. He placed flatboats in his rear at major river crossings and then lured Cornwallis into a march of exhaustion. In a race to the Dan River, Cornwallis burned his baggage in order to travel lightly. Greene escaped on his flatboats across the Yadkin River, flooded with spring rains, just ahead of Cornwallis—who had to march to a ford 10 miles upstream, cross the river, and then march back while Greene rested. Greene repeated this stratagem all the way to the Dan until he judged that Cornwallis was so weak that the Americans could offer battle at Guilford Court House on March 15, 1781. With militia, he outnumbered Cornwallis 4,400 to 1,900. Although the British retained possession of the battlefield, they lost one-quarter of their force and the strategic initiative. Cornwallis retreated to Wilmington to refit. He then marched north into Virginia—the seat of southern resistance, he told Clinton, the one place where Britain could achieve decisive results. Instead of following him, Greene returned to South Carolina, where he and Marion took the surviving British outposts one by one. After the British evacuated Ninety-Six on July 1, 1781, they held only Savannah and Charleston in the Deep South. Against heavy odds, Greene had reclaimed the region for the Revolution.

Mutiny and Reform

After the Camden disaster, army officers and state politicians demanded reforms to strengthen Congress and win the war. State legislatures sent their ablest men to Congress. Maryland, the last state to hold out, finally completed the American union by ratifying the Articles of Confederation.

Before any reforms could take effect, discontent again erupted in the army. Insisting that their three-year enlistments had expired, 1,500 men of the Pennsylvania Line got drunk on New Year's Day 1781, killed three officers, and marched out of their winter quarters at Morristown. General Clinton sent agents from New York to promise them a pardon and their back pay if they defected to the British, but instead the mutineers marched south toward

Princeton and turned Clinton's agents over to Pennsylvania authorities, who executed them. Congress, reassured, negotiated with the soldiers. More than half of them accepted discharges, and those who remained in service got furloughs and bonuses for reenlistment. Encouraged by this treatment, 200 New Jersey soldiers at Pompton also mutinied, but Washington used New England units to disarm them and had two of the leaders executed. The army held together, but well into 1781 more loyalists were still serving with the British than Continentals with Washington.

Civilian violence, such as the "Fort Wilson" riot in Philadelphia, also prompted Congress to change policies. Radical artisans blamed the city's rich merchants for the rampant inflation of 1779 and demanded price controls as a remedy. The merchants blamed paper money. In October, several men were killed when the antagonists exchanged shots near the fortified home of James Wilson, a wealthy lawyer. Spokesmen for the radicals deplored the violence and abandoned the quest for price controls. For city dwellers rich and poor, sound money was becoming the only solution to the devastating inflation.

Congress interpreted these disturbances as a call for reform at the national level. While armed partisans were making the war more radical, politics veered in a conservative direction, toward the creation of European state forms, such as executive departments and a bank. Patriot leaders gave up efforts at price control and allowed the market to set prices and the value of money. Congress stopped printing money, abandoned its cumbersome committee system, and created separate executive departments of foreign affairs, finance, war, and marine. Robert Morris, a Philadelphia merchant, became the first secretary of finance, helped organize the Bank of North America (America's first), and made certain that the Continental Army was clothed and well fed, although it still was not paid. Congress began to requisition revenue from the states. The states began to impose heavy taxes but could never collect enough to meet both their own and national needs. Congress tried to amend the Articles of Confederation in 1781 and asked the states to accept a 5 percent duty on all imports. Most states quickly ratified the "impost" amendment, but Rhode Island rejected it in 1783. Amendments to the Articles needed unanimous approval by the states, and this opposition killed the impost. A new impost proposal in 1783 was defeated by New York in 1786.

The reforms of 1781 just barely kept a smaller army in the field for the rest of the war, but the new executive departments had an unforeseen effect. Congress had been a plural executive, America's answer to the imperial Crown. But once Congress created its own departments, it looked more like a national legislature, and a feeble one at that,

because it still had no power to compel obedience. It began to pass, not just "orders" and "resolves," but also "ordinances," which were intended to be permanent and binding. It still could not punish anyone for noncompliance, which may be why it never called any of its measures "laws."

From the Ravaging of Virginia to Yorktown and Peace

Both Cornwallis and Washington believed that events in Virginia would decide the war. When a large British force raided the state in late 1780, Governor Thomas Jefferson called up enough militia to keep the British bottled up in Portsmouth, while he continued to ship men and supplies to Greene in the Carolinas. Thereafter, the state's ability to raise men and supplies almost collapsed.

In January 1781, Clinton sent Arnold by sea from New York with 1,600 men, mostly loyalists. They sailed up the James, took the new capital of Richmond almost without resistance, and gutted it. When Jefferson called out the militia, few responded. Virginia had not experienced the partisan struggles that drew men to both sides in New Jersey and the Carolinas. The state provided a different kind of test for American values under stress. The voluntaristic ethic nearly failed to get the state through a long war. Most Virginia freemen had already done service, if only as short-term militia, thousands of them in response to the 1780 raid. In 1781, they thought it was now someone else's turn. For months, there was no one else. Cornwallis took command in April, and Arnold departed for New York. But the raids continued into summer, sweeping as far west as Charlottesville, where Tarleton, who had recruited a new legion since Cowpens, scattered the Virginia legislature and came within minutes of capturing Jefferson on June 3. Many of Jefferson's slaves greeted the British as liberators. Washington sent Lafayette with 1,200 New England and New Jersey Continentals to contain the damage, while Cornwallis, on Clinton's orders, withdrew to Yorktown.

At last, Washington saw an opportunity to launch a major strike. He learned that a powerful French fleet under François, comte de Grasse, would sail with 3,000 soldiers from Saint-Domingue on August 13 for Chesapeake Bay. Cooperating closely with the French army commander, Jean Baptiste Donatien, comte de Rochambeau, Washington sprang his trap. Rochambeau led his 5,000 soldiers from Newport to the outskirts of New York, where they joined Washington's 5,000 Continentals. After feinting an attack to freeze Clinton in place, Washington led the combined French and American armies 400 miles south to tidewater Virginia, where they linked up with Lafayette's Americans and the other French army brought by de Grasse. After de Grasse's fleet beat off a British relief force at the Battle of the Capes on September 5, Washington cut off all retreat routes and besieged Cornwallis in Yorktown. On October 19, 1781, Cornwallis surrendered his entire army of 8,000 men. Many escaped slaves had died during the siege, most from smallpox, but Virginia planters hovered nearby to reclaim the survivors.

Yorktown brought down the British government in March 1782. Lord North resigned, and George III even drafted an abdication message, although he never released it. The new ministry, committed to American independence as the price of peace, continued to fight the French

"THE AMERICAN RATTLE SNAKE"
This 1782 cartoon celebrated the victory of Yorktown, the second time in the war that an entire British army had surrendered to the United States.

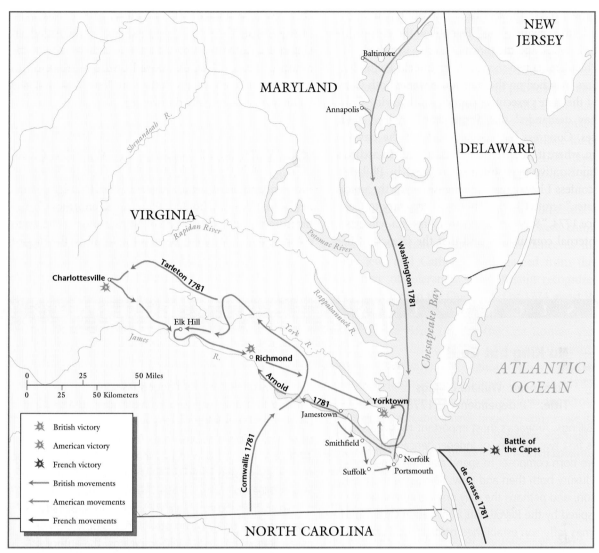

MAP 6.4 VIRGINIA AND THE YORKTOWN CAMPAIGN

After the British ravaged much of Virginia, Washington and a French fleet and army were able to trap Lord Cornwallis at Yorktown, force his surrender, and guarantee American independence.

in the Caribbean and the Spanish at Gibraltar, but the British evacuated Savannah and Charleston and concentrated their remaining forces in New York City.

Contrary to the French Treaty of 1778, and against Franklin's advice, John Jay and John Adams opened secret peace negotiations in Paris with the British. They won British recognition of the Mississippi, but without New Orleans, as the western boundary of the new republic. New Englanders retained the right to fish off Newfoundland. The treaty recognized the validity of prewar transatlantic debts, and Congress promised to urge the states to restore confiscated loyalist property. These terms gave American diplomats almost everything they could have desired. After the negotiations were far advanced, the Americans told Vergennes, the French foreign minister,

what they were doing. He feigned indignation, but the threat of a separate peace gave him the leverage he needed with Spain. Spain stopped demanding that France keep fighting until Gibraltar surrendered. The Treaty of Paris, although not ratified for months, ended the war in February 1783.

Western Indians were appalled to learn that the treaty gave their lands to the United States. They had not been conquered, whatever European diplomats might say. Their war for survival continued with few breaks into 1795.

Congress still faced ominous problems. In March 1783, many Continental officers threatened a coup d'état unless Congress granted them generous pensions. Washington, confronting them at their encampment at Newburgh, New York, fumbled for his glasses and remarked,

Elsewhere, legislative action was necessary. Pennsylvania led the way in 1780 with the modern world's first gradual emancipation statute. It declared that all children born to Pennsylvania slaves after a given date would become free at age 28. In other words, slaves, not masters or taxpayers, had to pay the costs of their own emancipation. This requirement left them unable to compete on equal terms with free whites, who usually entered adult life with inherited property. Some masters shipped their slaves south before the moment of emancipation, and some whites kidnapped freedmen and sent them south. The Pennsylvania Abolition Society was organized largely to fight these abuses. By 1800, Philadelphia had the largest community of free blacks in America, with their own churches and other voluntary societies.

The Pennsylvania pattern took hold, with variations, in most other northern states until all of them had made provision for emancipation. Where slaves constituted more than 10 percent of the population, as in southern New York and northeastern New Jersey, slaveholders' resistance delayed legislation for years. New York yielded in 1799, and finally so did New Jersey in 1804.

In the upper South, many Methodists and Baptists supported emancipation in the 1780s, only to retreat in later years. Maryland and Virginia authorized the manumission of individual slaves. By 1810, more than one-fifth of Maryland's slaves had been freed, as had 10,000 of Virginia's 300,000 slaves, including more than 300 freed under Washington's will after he died in 1799. But slaves were essential to the plantation economy and were usually their masters' most valuable asset. In the South, emancipation would have amounted to a social revolution and the impoverishment of the planter class. Planters supported the Christianization of their slaves and other humane reforms, but they resisted emancipation, especially with the rise of cotton as a new cash crop after the war. Tragically, the slaves contributed a great deal to the acceptance of cotton as a new staple, which in turn guaranteed that their children and grandchildren would remain in bondage. Cut off from British textiles during the war, South Carolina slaves insisted on growing cotton as a substitute. Their owners quickly recognized the enormous potential of that crop.

Maryland and Virginia, where population growth among the slaves exceeded what the tobacco economy could absorb, banned the Atlantic slave trade, as had all states outside the Deep South. Georgia and South Carolina, to make good their losses during the war and to meet the demand for cotton after 1790, reopened the Atlantic slave trade. South Carolina imported almost 60,000 more Africans before Congress prohibited that traffic in 1808.

The Challenge to Patriarchy

Nothing as dramatic as emancipation altered relations between the sexes, although subtle changes did occur. With the men away fighting, many women were left in charge of the household, sometimes with interesting consequences. "I hope you will not consider yourself as commander in chief of your own house," Lucy Knox warned her soldier husband, Henry, in 1777, "but be convinced . . . that there is such a thing as equal command." Although some women acquired new authority, nearly all of them had to work harder to keep their households functioning. The war cut them off from most European consumer goods. Household manufactures, mostly the task of women, filled the gap. Women accepted these duties without insisting on broader legal or political rights, but soaring food prices made many women assertive. In numerous food riots through 1779, women tried to force merchants to lower prices or stop hoarding grain.

Attitudes toward marriage were also changing. The common-law rule of coverture (see chapter 4) still denied wives any legal personality, but some of them, citing their own support of the Revolution, persuaded state governments not to impoverish them by confiscating the property of their loyalist husbands. Many writers insisted that good marriages rested on mutual affection, not on property settlements. In portraits of wealthy northeastern families, husbands and wives were beginning to appear as equals. Parents were urged to respect the personalities of their children and to avoid severe discipline. Traditional reverence for the elderly was giving way to an idealization of youth and energy.

In 1780, to relieve the sufferings of Continental soldiers, Esther de Berdt Reed organized the Philadelphia Ladies Association, the first women's society in American history to take on a public role. Although few women yet demanded equal political rights, the New Jersey Constitution of 1776 let them vote if they headed a household (usually as a widow) and paid taxes. This right was revoked in 1807.

Especially in the Northeast, more women learned to read and write. Philosophers, clergymen, and even popular writers were beginning to treat women as morally superior to men, a sharp reversal of earlier teachings. The first female academies were founded in the 1790s. By 1830, nearly all native-born women in the Northeast had become literate. The ideal of the "republican wife" and the "republican mother" took hold, giving wives and mothers an expanding educational role within the family. They encouraged diligence in their husbands and patriotism in their sons. The novel became a major cultural form in the United States. Its main audience was female, as were many

WOMEN VOTING IN LATE 18TH-CENTURY NEW JERSEY

Alone among the 13 states, the New Jersey constitution of 1776 permitted women to vote if they were the heads of their households, a category that included mostly widows. This privilege was revoked in 1807.

of the authors. Novels cast women as central characters and warned young women to beware of suitors motivated only by greed or lust.

Western Expansion, Discontent, and Conflict with Indians

Westward expansion continued during the Revolutionary War. With 30 axmen, Daniel Boone, a North Carolina hunter, hacked out the Wilderness Road from Cumberland Gap to the Kentucky bluegrass country in early 1775. The first settlers called Kentucky "the best poor man's country" and challenged the speculative Transylvania Company, which claimed title to the land. They insisted that the land should belong to those who tilled its soil, not to nonresidents with paper titles from governments far to the east in Virginia or London.

Although few Indians lived in Kentucky, it was the favorite hunting ground of the Shawnees and other nations. Their raids often prevented the settlers from planting crops. The settlers hunted and put up log cabins against the inside walls of large rectangular stockades, 10 feet high and built from oak logs. At each corner, a blockhouse with a protruding second story permitted the defenders to fire along the outside walls. Three of these Kentucky stations were built—at Boonesborough, St.

Asaph, and Harrodsburg. They withstood Indian attacks until late in the war.

Because of the constant danger, settlement grew slowly at first. In 1779, when George Rogers Clark's victory at Vincennes provided a brief period of security, thousands of settlers moved in. After 1780, however, the Indians renewed their attacks, this time with British allies who could smash the stockades with artillery. Kentucky lived up to its old Indian reputation as the "dark and bloody ground." Only a few thousand settlers stuck it out until the war ended, when they were joined by swarms of newcomers. Speculators and absentees were already trying to claim the best bluegrass land. The Federal Census of 1790 listed 74,000 settlers and slaves in Kentucky and about half that many in Tennessee, where the Cherokees had ceded a large tract after their defeat in 1776. These settlers thrived both because few Indians lived there and because British and Spanish raiders found it hard to reach them.

To the south and north of this bulge, settlement was much riskier. After the war, Spain supplied arms and trade goods to Creeks, Cherokees, Choctaws, and Chickasaws who were willing to resist Georgia's attempt to settle its western lands. North of the Ohio River, where confederated Indians had won their military struggle, Britain refused to withdraw its garrisons and traders from Niagara,

Missouri Historical Society.

DANIEL BOONE PROTECTS HIS FAMILY

During and after the Revolution, family portraits in the Northeast began to place husband and wife on an equal level and to emphasize their role in nurturing children. But in the West, the husband and father remained the protector of his family. This 1874 lithograph was copied from an 1852 statue by Horatio Greenough that was meant to demonstrate, in the artist's words, "the superiority of the white man" over all other races. Contemporaries assumed that the central figure was Boone, who performs heroic deeds while his wife and child cower in fear.

Detroit, and a few other posts, even though, according to the Treaty of Paris, those forts now lay within the boundaries of the United States. To justify their refusal, the British pointed to Congress's failure to honor America's obligations to loyalists and British creditors under the treaty. When small groups of Indians sold large tracts of land to Georgia, Pennsylvania, and New York, as well as to Congress, the Indian nations repudiated those sales and, supported by either Spain or Britain, continued to resist into the 1790s.

During the Revolutionary War, many states and Congress had recruited soldiers with promises of land after the war ended, and now they needed Indian lands to fulfill these pledges. The few Indian nations that had supported the United States suffered the most. In the 1780s, after Joseph Brant led most of the Iroquois north to Canada, New York confiscated much of the land of the friendly Iroquois who stayed. South Carolina dispossessed the Catawbas of most of their ancestral lands. The states had a harder time seizing the land of hostile Indians, who usually had Spanish or British allies.

Secessionist movements arose in the 1780s when neither Congress nor eastern state governments seemed able to solve western problems. Some Tennessee settlers seceded from North Carolina and for a time maintained a separate state called Franklin. Separatist sentiment also ran strong in Kentucky. Even the settlers of western Pennsylvania thought of setting up on their own after Spain closed the Mississippi to American traffic in 1784. James Wilkinson explored the possibility of creating an independent republic west of the Appalachians under Spanish protection. When Congress refused to recognize Vermont's independence from New York, even the radical Green Mountain Boys sounded out Canadian officials about readmission to the British empire as a separate province.

The Northwest Ordinance

After Virginia ceded its land claims north of the Ohio River to Congress in 1781, other states followed suit. Jefferson offered a resolution in 1784 that would have created 10 or more new states in this Northwest Territory. Each state could adopt the constitution and laws of any of the older states and, when its population reached 20,000, could be admitted to the Union on equal terms with the original 13. The possibility that the northwestern states, plus Kentucky, Tennessee, and Vermont, might outvote the old 13 made Congress hesitate, and Jefferson's resolution was never implemented. In the Land Ordinance of 1785, however, Congress authorized the survey of the Northwest Territory and its division into townships six miles square,

each composed of 36 "sections" of 640 acres. Surveyed land would be sold at auction starting at a dollar an acre. Alternate townships would be sold in sections or as a whole, to satisfy settlers and speculators, respectively.

In July 1787, while the Constitutional Convention met in Philadelphia, Congress (sitting in New York) returned to the problem of governing the Northwest Territory. By then, Massachusetts veterans were organizing the Ohio Company under Manassah Cutler to obtain a huge land grant from Congress. Cutler joined forces with William Duer, a New York speculator who was organizing the Scioto Company. Together they pried from Congress 1.5 million acres for the Ohio Company veterans and an option on 5 million more acres, which the Ohio Company assigned to the Scioto Company. The Ohio Company agreed to pay Congress two installments of $500,000 in depreciated securities. To meet the first payment, Duer's backers lent Cutler's $200,000. Once again, speculators, rather than settlers, seemed to be winning the West.

In July, Congress passed the Northwest Ordinance of 1787 to provide government for the region. Rejecting Jefferson's earlier goal of 10 or more states, the ordinance authorized the creation of from 3 to 5 states, to be admitted to the Union as full equals of the original 13. The ordinance thus rejected colonialism among white people except as a temporary phase through which a "territory" would pass on its way to statehood. Congress would appoint a governor and a council to rule until population reached 5,000. At that point, the settlers could elect an assembly empowered to pass laws, although the governor (obviously modeled on earlier royal governors) had an absolute veto. When population reached 60,000, the settlers could adopt their own constitution and petition Congress for statehood. The ordinance protected civil liberties, made provision for public education, and prohibited slavery within the region.

Southern delegates all voted for the Northwest Ordinance despite its antislavery clause. They probably hoped that Ohio would become what Georgia had been in the 1730s, a society of armed free men able to protect vulnerable slave states, such as Kentucky, from hostile invaders. The Ohio valley was the republic's most dangerous frontier. Southern delegates also thought that most settlers would come from Maryland, Virginia, and Kentucky. Even if they could not bring slaves with them, they would have southern loyalties. New Englanders, by contrast, were counting on the Ohio Company to lure their own veterans to the region.

Finally, the antislavery clause may have been part of a larger Compromise of 1787, involving both the ordinance and the clauses on slavery in the federal Constitution. The

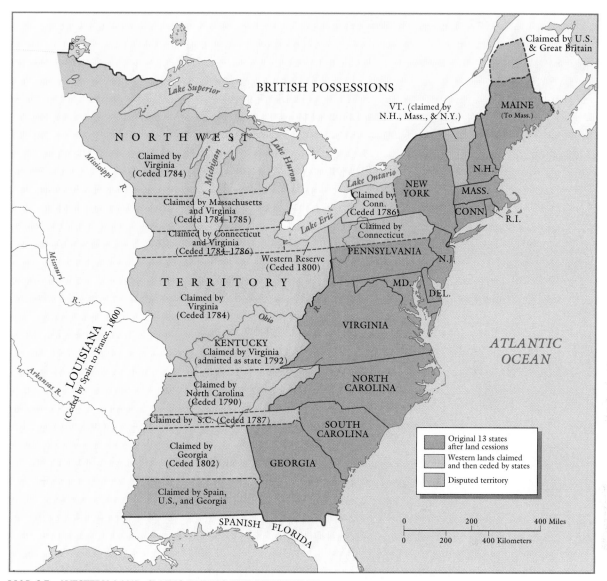

MAP 6.5 WESTERN LAND CLAIMS DURING THE REVOLUTION
One of the most difficult questions that Congress faced was the competing western land claims of several states.
After Virginia ceded its claims north of the Ohio to Congress, other states followed suit, creating the national domain
and what soon became the Northwest Territory.

 View an animated version of this map or related maps at http://history.wadsworth.com/murrin_LEP4e.

Philadelphia Convention permitted states to count three-fifths of their slaves for purposes of representation and direct taxation. The antislavery concession to northerners in the ordinance was made at the same time that southern states won this concession in Philadelphia. Several congressmen were also delegates to the Constitutional Convention and traveled back and forth between the two cities while these decisions were being made. They may have struck a deal.

Congress had developed a coherent western policy. After 1787, only the Indians, who drove away hundreds

of squatters, stood in the way. Federal surveyors risked their lives in Ohio, and few buyers stepped forward when the first townships were offered for sale in late 1787. Yet by 1789, the Ohio Company had established the town of Marietta, Kentuckians had founded a town that would soon be called Cincinnati, and tiny outposts had been set up at Columbia and Gallipolis. But without massive help from the new federal government, the settlers had little chance of overcoming stout Indian resistance.

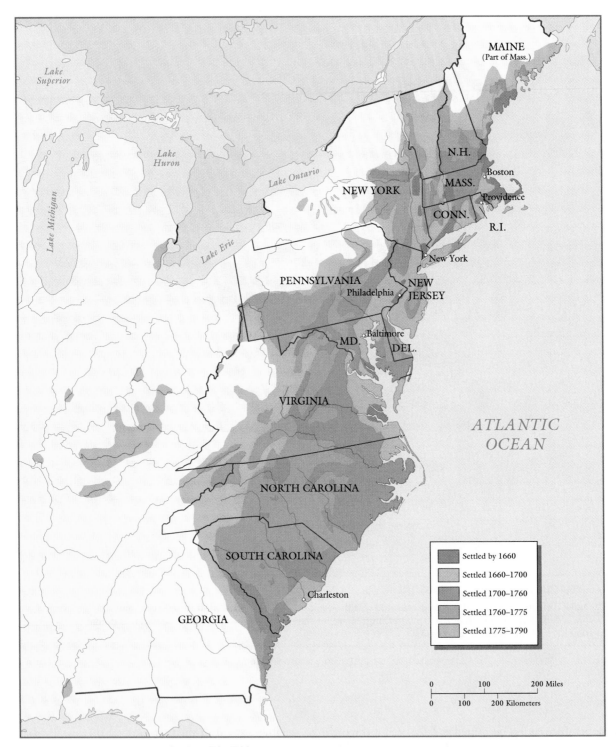

MAP 6.6   ADVANCE OF SETTLEMENT TO 1790

Between 1760 and 1790, America's population grew from nearly 1.6 million to almost 4 million. The area of settlement was spreading west of Pittsburgh and into much of Kentucky and parts of Tennessee.

 View an animated version of this map or related maps at http://history.wadsworth.com/murrin_LEP4e.

🔊 A More Perfect Union

The 1780s were difficult times. The economy failed to rebound, debtors fought creditors, and state politics became bitter and contentious. Out of this ferment arose the demand to amend or even replace the Articles of Confederation.

Commerce, Debt, and Shays's Rebellion

In 1784, British merchants flooded American markets with exports worth £3.7 million, the greatest volume since 1771. But Americans could not pay for them. Exports to Britain that year were £750,000—less than 40 percent of the £1.9 million of 1774, the last year of peace. When Britain invoked the Navigation Acts to close the British West Indies to American ships (but not to American goods), indirect returns through this once profitable channel also faltered. Trade with France closed some of the gap, but because the French could not offer the long-term credit that the British had provided, it remained disappointing. The American economy entered a depression that lifted only slightly in 1787 and 1788 before the strong recovery of the 1790s. British imports fell by 40 percent in 1785. Exports rose to almost £900,000 but remained far below prewar levels. Private debts became a huge social problem that the states, buried under their own war debts, could not easily mitigate. Merchants, dunned by British creditors, sued their customers, many of whom could not even pay their taxes. Farmers, faced with the loss of their crops, livestock, and even their farms, resisted foreclosures and looked to their state governments for relief.

About half of the states issued paper money in the 1780s, and many passed stay laws to postpone the date on which a debt would come due. Massachusetts, which remembered its fierce conflicts over paper money before 1750 (see chapter 4), rejected both options and raised taxes to new highs. In 1786, many farmers in Hampshire County took matters into their own hands. Crowds gathered to prevent the courts from conducting business, much as patriots had done against the British in 1774. Governor James Bowdoin insisted that acts of resistance that had been appropriate against a tyrannical monarch were unacceptable in a government elected by the people. But in early 1787, the protestors, loosely organized under a Continental Army veteran, Captain Daniel Shays, attacked the federal arsenal at Springfield. An army of volunteers under Benjamin Lincoln marched west with artillery and scattered the Shaysites. Even so, Shaysites won enough seats in the May assembly elections to pass a stay law. In Massachusetts, Shays's Rebellion converted into nationalists many gentlemen and artisans who until then had opposed strengthening the central government.

Cosmopolitans versus Localists

The tensions racking Massachusetts surfaced elsewhere as well. Crowds of debtors in other states closed law courts or even besieged the legislature. State politics reflected a persistent cleavage between "cosmopolitan" and "localist" coalitions. Merchants, professional men, urban artisans, commercial farmers, southern planters, and former Continental Army officers made up the cosmopolitan bloc. They looked to energetic government, both state and continental, to solve their problems. They favored aggressive trade policies, hard money, payment of public debts, good salaries for executive officials and judges, and leniency to returning loyalists. The localists were farmers, rural artisans, and militia veterans who distrusted those policies. They demanded paper money and debtor relief. They supported generous salaries for representatives, so that ordinary men could serve, which cosmopolitans resisted.

In most states, localists defeated their opponents most of the time. They destroyed the feudal revival (see chapter 5) by confiscating the gigantic land claims of the Granville District, the Fairfax estate, the Calvert and Penn proprietaries, and the manorial estates of New York loyalists. (Because their owners were patriots, Rensselaerswyck and Livingston Manor survived to become the site of agrarian violence into the 1840s, when the manors were finally abolished.) Except in Vermont, localists were much less adept at blocking the claims of land speculators, some of whom put together enormous tracts. Yet cosmopolitans lost so often that many of them despaired of state politics and looked to a strengthened central government for relief.

Congress faced its own fiscal problems. Between October 1781 and February 1786, it requisitioned $15.7 million from the states but received only $2.4 million. Its annual income had fallen to $400,000 at a time when interest on its debt approached $2.5 million and when the principal on the foreign debt was about to come due. Requisitions were beginning to seem as inefficient as George Grenville had proclaimed them to be when he proposed the Stamp Act.

Foreign relations also took an ominous turn. Without British protection, American ships that entered the Mediterranean risked capture by Barbary pirates and the enslavement of their crews. In 1786, Foreign Secretary John Jay

An American Views
the French Revolution

Gouverneur Morris, the youngest son in one of provincial New York's most prominent families, was born in 1752 at the manor of Morrisania in what is now the Bronx. He attended the Academy of Philadelphia and then King's College (now Columbia University), studied law, and soon prospered in his profession. As the revolutionary crisis unfolded, he stood for conciliation until the fighting began and then sided with the patriots. During the drafting of New York's 1777 constitution, he advocated the abolition of slavery and toleration of Roman Catholics, but on other issues he was quite conservative. He favored a strong executive with an absolute veto, for example. In 1780, he broke his ankle, and his leg was amputated below the knee. Thereafter, he was as famous for his oaken stump as for his oratory. In 1787, just before departing for the Philadelphia Convention, he purchased Morrisania from an older brother.

At the Convention, he opposed the three-fifths clause, warned against what a later generation would call the "slave power," supported the creation of a powerful executive, and became perhaps the strongest advocate of the electoral college. But his most significant contribution came when the Committee on Style asked him to take the resolves that had been approved by the delegates and turn them into a single document, a constitution. He compressed the delegates' 23 articles into seven and wrote nearly all of the preamble, including "We the people of the United States," rather than enumerate the separate states as in the Articles of Confederation.

In December 1788, he sailed for France on business and landed in a kingdom that was about to explode in the most momentous revolution that Europe had ever seen. He became prominent enough to correspond directly with Louis XVI, and he sympathized deeply with Queen Marie Antoinette. He backed those who favored a moderate constitutional monarchy, and in 1792,

President George Washington secured his appointment as minister plenipotentiary to France. He kept a diary in these years and filled it with pungent comments about people and events. In the polemical debate between Edmund Burke and Thomas Paine, he sided with Burke, the conservative. He also used his diplomatic immunity to shield royalist refugees until the French republic asked for his recall in 1794. He crossed the Channel and for four years gave the British government advice on how to defeat revolutionary France.

After returning to the United States, he became a prominent Federalist who opposed Thomas Jefferson's Embargo and James Madison's drift into war with Britain by 1812. By 1814, although he had been one of America's foremost nationalists in the 1780s, he became so exasperated with Democratic-Republican policies that he urged the secession of New York and New England from the Union. With peace restored, however, he joined Governor DeWitt Clinton in urging New York State to build the Erie Canal. He died in 1816.

© Bettmann/Corbis.

**GOUVERNEUR MORRIS IN A LITHOGRAPH
ENGRAVED BY ALONZO CHAPPEL**

The man who gave the federal Constitution its final stylistic form then went to Paris, where he witnessed the most radical phase of the French Revolution.

negotiated a treaty with Don Diego de Gardoqui, the Spanish minister to the United States. It offered northern merchants trading privileges with Spanish colonies in exchange for the closure of the Mississippi River to American traffic for 25 years. Seven northern states voted for the treaty, but all five southern states in Congress rejected these terms, thus defeating the treaty, which needed nine votes for ratification under the Articles of Confederation. Angry talk of disbanding the Union soon filled Congress. Delegates began haggling over which state would join what union if the breakup occurred. The quarrel became public in February 1787 when a Boston newspaper called for a dissolution of the Union.

By the mid-1780s, many cosmopolitans were becoming nationalists eager to strengthen the Union. Many of them had served long, frustrating years in the army or in Congress, unable to carry out measures that they considered vital to the Confederation. In 1785, some of them tried to see what could be done outside Congress. To resolve disputes about navigation rights on the Potomac River, George Washington invited Virginia and Maryland delegates to a conference at Mount Vernon, where they drafted an agreement that was acceptable to both states and to Congress. Prompted by James Madison, a former congressman, the Virginia legislature then urged all of the states to participate in a convention at Annapolis to explore ways to improve American trade.

Four states, including Maryland, ignored the call, and the New Englanders had not yet arrived when, in September 1786, the delegates from the four middle states and Virginia accepted a report drafted by Alexander Hamilton of New York. It asked all of the states to send delegates to a convention at Philadelphia the next May "to devise such further provisions as shall appear to them necessary to render the constitution of the Federal Government adequate to the exigencies of the Union." Seven states responded positively before Congress endorsed the convention on February 21, 1787, and five accepted later. Rhode Island refused to participate. Madison used the winter months to study the defects of classical and European confederacies and to draft a plan for a stronger American union.

The Philadelphia Convention

The convention opened in May 1787 with a plan similar to the Virginia constitution of 1776. It proposed an almost sovereign Parliament for the United States. By September, the delegates had produced a document that was much closer to the Massachusetts constitution of 1780, with a clear separation of powers. The delegates, in four months of secret sessions, repeated the constitutional learning process that had taken four years at the state level after 1776.

With Washington presiding, Governor Edmund Randolph proposed the Virginia, or "large state," plan. Drafted by Madison, it proposed a bicameral legislature, with representation in both houses apportioned according to

"THE HERO WHO DEFENDED THE MOTHERS WILL PROTECT THE DAUGHTERS"

Washington is hailed by young women near the bridge at Trenton on the way to his inauguration as first President of the United States, 1789.

population. The legislature would choose the executive and the judiciary. It would possess all powers currently lodged in Congress and the power "to legislate in all cases to which the separate States are incompetent." It could "negative all laws passed by the several States, contravening in [its] opinion . . . the articles of Union." Remarkably, the plan did not include specific powers to tax or regulate trade. Madison apparently believed it wiser to be vague and sweeping, rather than explicit. His plan also required ratification by state conventions, not by state legislatures. Within two weeks, the delegates agreed on three-year terms for members of the lower house and seven-year terms for the upper house. The legislature would choose the executive for a single term of seven years.

In mid-June, delegates from the small states struck back. William Paterson proposed the New Jersey Plan, which gave the existing Congress the power to levy import duties and a stamp tax (as in Grenville's imperial reforms of 1764 and 1765), to regulate trade, and to use force to collect delinquent requisitions from the states (as in North's Conciliatory Proposition of 1775). Each state would have one vote. As another alternative, perhaps designed to terrify the small states into accepting the Virginia Plan, Hamilton suggested a government in which both the senate and the executive would serve "on good behavior"—that is, for life! To him, the British constitution still seemed the best in the world, but he never formally proposed his plan.

All of the options before the convention at that point seemed counterrevolutionary. Madison's Parliament for America, Paterson's emulation of Grenville and North, and Hamilton's enthusiasm for the British empire all challenged in major ways the principles of 1776. As the summer progressed, however, the delegates asked themselves what the voters would or would not accept and relearned the hard lessons of popular sovereignty that the state constitutions had taught. The result was a federal Constitution that was truly revolutionary.

Before the Constitution took its final shape, however, the debate grew as hot as the summer weather. The small states warned that their voters would never accept a constitution that let the large states swallow them. The large states insisted on proportional representation in both houses. "The Large States dare not dissolve the Confederation," retorted Delaware's Gunning Bedford in the most inflammatory outburst of the convention. "If they do, the small ones will find some foreign ally of more honor and good faith, who will take them by the hand and do them justice." Then the Connecticut delegates announced that

they would be happy with proportional representation in one house and state equality in the other.

In mid-July, the delegates accepted this Connecticut Compromise and then completed the document by September. They finally realized that they were creating a government of laws, to be enforced on individuals through federal courts, and were not propping up a system of congressional resolutions to be carried out (or ignored) by the states. Terms for representatives were reduced to two years, and terms for senators to six, with each state legislature choosing two senators. The president would serve four years, could be reelected, and would be chosen by an Electoral College. Each state received as many electors as it had congressmen and senators combined, and the states were free to decide how to choose their electors. Each elector had to vote for two candidates, one of whom had to be from another state. This provision reflected the fear that localist impulses might prevent a majority vote for anyone. The delegates knew that Washington would be the first president, but there was no obvious choice after him.

In other provisions, free and slave states agreed to count only three-fifths of the slaves in apportioning both representation and direct taxes. The enumeration of congressional powers became lengthy and explicit and included taxation, the regulation of foreign and interstate commerce, and the catchall "necessary and proper" clause. Madison's negative on state laws was replaced by the gentler "supreme law of the land" clause. Over George Mason's last-minute objection, the delegates voted not to include a bill of rights.

With little debate, the convention approved a revolutionary proposal for ratifying the Constitution. This clause called for special conventions in each state and declared that the Constitution would go into force as soon as any nine states had accepted it, even though the Articles of Confederation required unanimous approval for all amendments. The delegates understood that they were proposing an illegal but peaceful overthrow of the existing legal order—that is, a revolution. They hoped that once nine or more states accepted the Constitution, the others would follow their example after the new government got under way and would make ratification unanimous. At that point, their revolution would become both peaceful and legal. The Constitution would then rest on popular sovereignty in a way that the Articles never had. The Federalists, as supporters of the Constitution now called themselves, were willing to risk destroying the Union in order to save and strengthen it. But they knew that they would have to use persuasion, not force, to win approval.

Ratification

When the Federalist delegates returned home, they made a powerful case for the Constitution in newspapers, most of which favored a stronger central government. Most Anti-Federalists, or opponents of the Constitution, were localists with few interstate contacts and only limited access to the press. The Federalists gave them little time to organize. The first ratifying conventions met in December. Delaware ratified unanimously on December 7, Pennsylvania by a 46-to-23 vote five days later, and New Jersey unanimously on December 18. Georgia ratified unanimously on January 2, and Connecticut soon approved, also by a lopsided margin.

Except in Pennsylvania, these victories were in small states. Ironically, although the Constitution was mostly a "large state" document, small states embraced it while large states hesitated. Small states, once they had equality in the senate, saw many advantages in a strong central government. Under the Articles, for example, New Jersey residents had to pay duties to neighboring states on foreign goods imported through New York City or Philadelphia. Under the new Constitution, import duties would go to the federal government, a clear gain for every small state but Rhode Island, which stood to lose import duties at both Providence and Newport.

By contrast, Pennsylvania was the only large state with a solid majority for ratification. But Anti-Federalists there eloquently demanded a federal bill of rights and major changes in the structure of the new government. Large states could think of going it alone. Small states could not—except for Rhode Island with its two cities and its long history of defying its neighbors.

The first hotly contested state was Massachusetts, which set a pattern for struggles in other divided states. Federalists there won by a slim margin (187 to 168) in February 1788. They blocked Anti-Federalist attempts to make ratification conditional on the adoption of specific amendments. Instead, the Federalists promised to support a bill of rights by constitutional amendment after ratification. But the Rhode Island legislature voted overwhelmingly not even to summon a ratifying convention. Maryland and South Carolina ratified easily in April and May, bringing the total to eight of the nine states required. Then conventions met almost simultaneously in New Hampshire, Virginia, New York, and North Carolina. In each, a majority at first opposed ratification.

As resistance stiffened, the ratification controversy turned into the first great debate about the American Union, over what kind of nation the United States should be. By summer 1788, Anti-Federalists were eloquent and well organized. They argued that the new government would be too remote from the people to be trusted with the broad powers specified in the Constitution. They warned that in a House of Representatives divided into districts of 30,000 people (twice the size of Boston), only prominent and wealthy men would be elected. The new government would become an aristocracy or oligarchy that would impose heavy taxes and other burdens on the people. The absence of a bill of rights also troubled them.

During the struggle over ratification, Hamilton, Madison, and Jay wrote a series of 85 essays, published first in New York newspapers and widely reprinted elsewhere, in which they defended the Constitution almost clause by clause. Signing themselves "Publius," they later published the collected essays as *The Federalist Papers,* the most comprehensive body of political thought produced by the Revolutionary generation. In *Federalist, no. 10,* Madison argued that a large republic would be far more stable than a small one. He challenged 2,000 years of accepted wisdom, which insisted that only small republics could survive. Small republics were inherently unstable, Madison insisted, because majority factions could easily gain power within them, trample on the rights of minorities, and ignore the common good. In a republic as huge and diverse as the United States, however, factions would seldom be able to forge a majority. "Publius" hoped that the new government would draw on the talents of the wisest and best-educated citizens. To those who accused him of trying to erect an American aristocracy, he pointed out that the Constitution forbade titles and hereditary rule.

Federalists won a narrow majority (57 to 46) in New Hampshire on June 21, and Madison guided Virginia to ratification (89 to 79) five days later. New York approved, by 30 votes to 27, one month later, bringing 11 states into the Union, enough to launch the new government. North Carolina rejected the Constitution in July 1788 but finally ratified in November 1789 after the first Congress had drafted the Bill of Rights and sent it to the states. Rhode Island, after voting seven times not to call a ratifying convention, finally summoned one that ratified by a vote of only 34 to 32 in May 1790.

Conclusion

Americans survived the most devastating war they had yet fought and won their independence, but only with massive aid from France. Most Indians and blacks who could do so sided with Britain. During the struggle, white

Americans affirmed liberty and equality for themselves in their new state constitutions and bills of rights, but they rarely applied these values to blacks and Indians, even though every northern state adopted either immediate or gradual emancipation. The discontent of the postwar years created the Federalist coalition, which drafted and ratified a new national Constitution to replace the Articles of Confederation. Federalists endowed the new central government with more power than Parliament had ever successfully exercised over the colonies but insisted that the Constitution was fully compatible with the liberty and equality proclaimed during the Revolution. Nothing resembling the American federal system had ever been tried before. Under this new system, sovereignty was removed from government and bestowed on the people, who then empowered separate levels of government through their state and federal constitutions. As the Great Seal of the United States proclaimed, it was a *novus ordo seclorum*, a new order for the ages.

SUGGESTED READINGS

Stephen Conway's *The War of American Independence, 1775–1783* (1995) is a recent history that is strong and accessible. **Charles Royster's** *A Revolutionary People at War: The Continental Army and American Character, 1775–1783* (1979) is the best study of its kind. The essays in **John Shy's** *A People Numerous and Armed: Reflections on the Military Struggle for American Independence,* rev. ed. (1990) have had a tremendous influence on other historians. For the critical 1776 and 1777 campaigns, see **Ira D. Gruber, *The Howe Brothers and the American Revolution*** (1972). **Judith L. Van Buskirk, *Generous Enemies: Patriots and Loyalists in Revolutionary New York*** (2002) analyzes patterns in America's most fiercely contested state and is quite insightful about Arnold's treason and André's execution. **Walter Edgar's** *Partisans and Redcoats: The Southern Conflict That Turned the Tide of the American Revolution* (2001) is a fresh study of the bitter partisan war in the Lower South. For the war's impact on slavery, see **Sylvia R. Frey, *Water from the Rock: Black Resistance in a Revolutionary Age*** (1991) and **Arthur Zilversmit, *The First Emancipation:*** *The Abolition of Slavery in the North* (1967). Of the numerous studies of loyalism, **Paul H. Smith's** *Loyalists and Redcoats: A Study in British Revolutionary Policy* (1964) remains one of the best.

The single most important book on emerging American constitutionalism remains **Gordon S. Wood, *The Creation of the American Republic, 1776–1787*** (1969). **H. James Henderson's** *Party Politics in the Continental Congress* (1974) is a major contribution. **Jackson Turner Main's** *Political Parties before the Constitution* (1973) carefully investigates postwar divisions within the states. **Jack N. Rakove** won a Pulitzer Prize for *Original Meanings: Politics and Ideas in the Making of the Constitution* (1996). **Saul Cornell** provides a thoughtful approach to *The Other Founders: Anti-Federalism and the Dissenting Tradition in America* (1999). **Stuart Leibiger, *Founding Friendship: George Washington, James Madison, and the Creation of the American Republic*** (1999) is insightful and original.

AMERICAN JOURNEY ONLINE
AND
INFOTRAC COLLEGE EDITION

Visit the source collections at www.ajaccess.wadsworth.com and
infotrac.thomsonlearning.com and use the Search function with
the following key terms to explore documents, images, audio
and video clips, articles, and commentary related to the material
in this chapter.

George Washington	Daniel Boone
Yorktown	Northwest Ordinance
Saratoga	Shays's Rebellion
General William Howe	

GRADE AIDS

**Visit the Liberty Equality Power Companion Web Site for resources specific to
this textbook:** http://history.wadsworth.com/murrin_LEP4e

 The CD in the back of this book and the U.S. History Resource Center at
http://history.wadsworth.com/u.s./ offer a variety of tools to help you succeed in
this course, including access to quizzes; images; documents; interactive simulations,
maps, and timelines; movie explorations; and a wealth of other sources.

In the first 30 years of government under the Constitution, the Americans consolidated their republic and expanded their commerce with a war-torn Europe. In these years their population shot from 4 million to 10 million persons; their agrarian republic spilled across the Appalachians and reached the Mississippi River; their exports rose; and their seaport towns became cities. In the midst of this rapid change, the revolutionary republic drifted from its moorings in the patriarchal household. Increasing thousands of white men found it hard to maintain their status as propertied citizens or to pass that status on to new generations; others simply grew impatient with the responsibilities and constraints of rural patriarchy. The resultant erosion of authority, along with the increasingly equalitarian implications of revolutionary republicanism, encouraged women, slaves, and the growing ranks of propertyless white men to imagine that the revolutionary birthrights of liberty and equality—perhaps even power—might also belong to them. By 1820, the Founders' republic, which depended on widespread proprietorship and well-ordered paternal authority, was expanding, prosperous, and in deep trouble. An individualistic, democratic, and insecure order was taking its place.

CHAPTER FOCUS

♦ What was the nature of the American agricultural economy and of agricultural society in the years 1790 through 1815?

♦ What was the history of slavery in these years? In what areas (and in what ways) did it expand? In what areas (and, again, in what ways) was the slave system called into question?

♦ In what ways was the spread of evangelical Protestantism in these years beginning to shape American society and culture?

♦ Which Americans benefited from economic and social change between 1790 and 1815? Which did not?

The Farmer's Republic

In 1782, J. Hector St. John de Crèvecoeur, a French soldier who had settled in rural New York, explained American agrarianism through the words of a fictionalized farmer. First of all, he said, the American farmer owns his own land and bases his claim to dignity and citizenship on that fact. He spoke of "the bright idea of property," and went on: "This formerly rude soil has been converted by my father into a pleasant farm, and in return, it has established all our rights; on it is founded our rank, our freedom, our power as citizens, our importance as inhabitants of [a

CHRONOLOGY

1789	National government under the Constitution begins
1791	Vermont enters the union as the 14th state
1792	Kentucky enters the union as the 15th state
1793	Beginning of Anglo-French War • Eli Whitney invents the cotton gin
1794	Anthony Wayne defeats the northwestern Indians at Fallen Timbers • British abandon their forts in the Old Northwest
1795	Northwestern Indians cede most of Ohio at Treaty of Greenville
1796	Tennessee enters the union as the 16th state
1799	Successful slave revolution in Haiti
1800	Gabriel's Rebellion in Virginia
1801	First camp meeting at Cane Ridge, Kentucky
1803	Jefferson purchases the Louisiana Territory from France • Ohio enters the union as the 17th state
1805	Tenskwatawa's first vision
1810	Nationalist Cherokee chiefs depose old local leaders
1811	Battle of Tippecanoe
1812	Second war with Britain begins

rural neighborhood]." Second, farm ownership endows the American farmer with the powers and responsibilities of fatherhood. "Often when I plant my low ground," he said, "I place my little boy on a chair which screws to the beam of the plough—its motion and that of the horses please him; he is perfectly happy and begins to chat. As I lean over the handle, various are the thoughts which crowd into my mind. I am now doing for him, I say, what my father did for me; may God enable him to live that he may perform the same operations for the same purposes when I am worn out and old!"

Crèvecoeur's farmer, musing on liberty and property, working the ancestral fields with his male heir strapped to the plough, evokes a proud citizen of America's revolutionary republic. Few of Crèvecoeur's fellow citizens were as poetic as he, but they shared his concern with propertied independence and its social and political consequences. From New England through the mid-Atlantic and on into the southern Piedmont and backcountry, few farmers in 1790 thought of farming as a business. Their first concern was to provide subsistence for their households. Their second was to achieve long-term security and the ability to pass their farm on to their sons. The goal was to create what rural folks called a "competence": the ability to live up to neighborhood standards of material decency while protecting the long-term independence of

their household—and thus the dignity and political rights of its head. Most of these farmers raised a variety of animals and plants, ate most of what they grew, traded much of the rest within their neighborhoods, and sent small surpluses into outside markets.

The world's hunger for American food, however, was growing. West Indian and European markets for American meat and grain had grown since the mid-18th century. They expanded dramatically between 1793 and 1815, when war disrupted farming in Europe. American farmers took advantage of these markets, but few gambled with local food supplies or neighborly relations. They continued to rely on family and neighbors for subsistence and risked little by sending increased surpluses overseas. Thus they profited from world markets without becoming dependent on them.

Households

Production for overseas markets after 1790 did, however, alter relationships within rural households. Farm labor in postrevolutionary America was carefully divided by sex.

Men worked in the fields, and production for markets both intensified that labor and made it more exclusively male. In the grain fields, for instance, the long-handled scythe was replacing the sickle as the principal harvest tool. Women could use the sickle efficiently, but the long, heavy scythe was designed to be wielded by men. At the same time, farmers completed the substitution of ploughs for hoes as the principal cultivating tools—not only because ploughs worked better but also because rural Americans had developed a prejudice against women working in the fields. By the early 19th century, visitors to the long-settled farming areas (with the exception of some mid-Atlantic German communities) seldom saw women in the fields. In his travels through France, Thomas Jefferson spoke harshly of peasant communities where he saw women doing field labor.

At the same time, household responsibilities multiplied and fell more exclusively to women. It was farm women's labor and ingenuity that helped create a more varied and nutritious rural diet in these years. Bread and salted meat remained staples. The bread was the old mix of Indian corn and coarse wheat ("rye and Injun," the

---

LINK TO THE PAST

Jefferson's Farmer-Patriots

In 1781, a French friend asked Thomas Jefferson 23 questions about Virginia. To a query about commerce and manufacturing, Jefferson answered that Virginians were farmers with little need for domestic manufactures or trade with each other, and explained why that was a good system for a republic:

*T*hose who labour in the earth are the chosen people of God, if ever he had a chosen people, whose breasts he has made his peculiar deposit for substantial and genuine virtue. It is the focus in which he keeps alive that sacred fire, which otherwise might escape from the face of the earth. Corruption of morals in the mass of cultivators is a phaenomenon of which no age nor nation has furnished an example. It is the mark set on those, who not looking up to heaven, to their own soil and industry, as does the husbandman, for their subsistence, depend for it on the casualties and caprice of customers. Dependence begets subservience and venality, suffocates the germ of virtue, and prepares fit tools for the designs of ambition. This, the natural progress and consequence of the arts, has sometimes perhaps been retarded by accidental circumstances:

but, generally speaking, the proportion which the aggregate of the other classes of citizens bears in any state to that of its husbandmen, is the proportion of its unsound to its healthy parts, and is a good-enough barometer whereby to measure its degree of corruption.

THOMAS JEFFERSON

From *Notes on the State of Virginia*

1. Jefferson insists that land-owning farmers are ideal citizens of a republic. Why was that so? And why were persons engaged in nonfarming occupations less suited to citizenship?
2. How does this statement reconcile with Jefferson's discussion of slavery and its cultural results in Queries XIV and XVIII?
3. What is the assumed role of international commerce in Jefferson's sociopolitical formulation?

For additional sources related to this feature, visit the *Liberty, Equality, Power* Web site at:

http://history.wadsworth.com/murrin_LEP4e

farmers called it), with crust so thick that it was used as a scoop for soups and stews. Although improved brines and pickling techniques augmented the supply of salt meat that could be laid by, farmers' palates doubtless told them that it was the same old salt meat. By the 1790s, however, other foods were becoming available. Improved winter feeding for cattle and better techniques for making and storing butter and cheese kept dairy products on the tables of the more prosperous farm families throughout the year. Chickens became more common, and farm women began to fence and manure their kitchen gardens, planting them with potatoes, turnips, cabbages, squashes, beans, and other vegetables that could be stored in the root cellars that were becoming standard features of farmhouses. By the 1830s, a resident of Weymouth, Massachusetts, claimed that "a man who did not have a large garden of potatoes, crooked-necked squashes, and other vegetables . . . was regarded [as] improvident." He might have added poultry and dairy cattle to the list, and he might have noted that all were more likely to result from the labor of women than from the labor of men.

Rural Industry

Industrial outwork provided many farmers with another means of protecting their independence by working their wives and children harder. From the 1790s onward, city merchants provided country workers with raw materials

HISTORY THROUGH FILM

A Midwife's Tale

Directed by Richard D. Rodgers (PBS).

The historian Laurel Thatcher Ulrich's *A Midwife's Tale* won the Pulitzer Prize for history and biography in 1991. Shortly thereafter, the Public Broadcasting System (PBS) turned the book into a documentary movie—a close and imaginative analysis of the diary of Martha Ballard, a Maine farm woman and midwife of the late 18th and early 19th centuries. Events are acted out on screen, and period modes of dress, housing, gardening, washing, coffin-making, spinning and weaving, and other details are reconstructed with labored accuracy.

The viewer hears the sounds of footfalls, horses, hand-looms, and dishes, but the only human sounds are an occasional cough, exclamation, or drinking song. The principal narrative is carried by an actress who reads passages from the diary, and Thatcher occasionally breaks in to explain her own experiences with the diary and its interpretation. The result is a documentary film that knows the difference between dramatizing history and making it up. It also dramatizes the ways in which a skilled and sensitive historian goes about her work.

Martha Ballard was a midwife in a town on the Kennebec River. She began keeping a daily diary at the age of 50 in 1785, and continued until 1812. Most of the film is about her daily life: delivering babies, nursing the sick, helping neighbors, keeping house, raising and supervising the labor of her daughters and niece, gardening and tending cattle and turkeys. In both the book and the film, the busyness of an ordinary woman's days—and a sense of her possibilities and limits—in the early republic comes through in exhausting detail. The dailiness of her life is interrupted only occasionally by an event: a fire at her husband's sawmill, an epidemic of scarlet fever, a parade organized to honor the death of George Washington, the rape of a minister's wife by his enemies (including the local judge, who is set free), and a neighbor's inexplicable murder of his wife and six children.

There is also the process of getting old. At the beginning, Martha Ballard is the busy wife in a well-run household. As she ages and her children leave to set up households of their own, Ballard hires local girls who—perhaps

and paid them for finished shoes, furniture, cloth, brooms, and other handmade goods. In Marple, Pennsylvania, a farming town near Philadelphia, fully one-third of households were engaged in weaving, furniture making, and other household industry in the 1790s. As late as the 1830s, when the rise of the factory system had reduced the demand for household manufactures, 33,000 New England women were still weaving palm leaf hats at home. Most of the outwork was taken on by large, relatively poor families, with the work organized in ways that shored up the authority of fathers. When young Caleb Jackson and his brother began making shoes for a Massachusetts merchant in 1803, the account was carried in their father's name. When New Hampshire women and girls fashioned

hats, the accounts were kept in the name of the husband or father. In general, household industry was part-time work performed only by the dependent women and children of the household. Even when it was the family's principal means of support, the work was arranged in ways that supported traditional notions of fatherhood and proprietorship.

In eastern Massachusetts in the 1790s, for instance, when thousands of farmers on small plots of worn-out land became household shoemakers, skilled men cut the leather and shaped the uppers, while the more menial tasks of sewing and binding were left to the women. In the town of North Reading, the family of Mayo Greenleaf Patch made shoes throughout the 1790s. Patch was a poor

because an increasingly democratic culture has made them less subservient than Ballard would like, perhaps because Ballard is growing old and impatient, perhaps both—tend to be surly. Her husband, a surveyor who works for merchants speculating in local land, is attacked twice in the woods by squatters and spends a year and a half in debtor's jail—not for his own debts but because, as tax collector, he failed to collect enough. While the husband is in jail and his aging wife struggles to keep the house going, their son moves his own family into the house and Martha is moved into a single room and is made to feel unwanted—a poignant and unsentimental case of the strained relations between generations that historians have discovered in the early republic.

A Midwife's Tale is a modest film that comes as close as a thorough and imaginative historian and a good filmmaker can to recreating the texture of lived experience in the northeastern countryside at the beginning of the 19th century. Students who enjoy the movie should go immediately to the book.

"...a film of almost tactile pleasure and keen intelligence." — *The Boston Globe*

PBS Home Video.

The PBS documentary movie *A Midwife's Tale* is based on the Pulitzer Prize–winning book of the same name by historian Laurel Thatcher Ulrich.

man who drank too much and lived on a small plot of land owned by his father-in-law; the family income came largely from shoemaking. Yet Patch, when asked to name his occupation, described himself as a "yeoman"—a fiction subsidized by the labor of Patch's wife and children.

Neighbors

The struggle to maintain household independence involved most farmers in elaborate networks of neighborly cooperation. Few farmers possessed the tools, labor, and food they would have needed to be truly independent. They regularly worked for one another, borrowed oxen and plows, and swapped surpluses of one kind of food for another. Women frequently traded ashes, herbs, butter and eggs, vegetables, seedlings, baby chicks, goose feathers, and the products of their spinning wheels and looms. Such exchanges of goods and services were crucial to the workings of a rural neighborhood, and the feminine character of those exchanges may have increased the authority of women within households and neighborhoods. Some cooperative undertakings—house and barn-raisings and husking bees, for example—brought the whole neighborhood together, transforming a chore into a pleasant social event. The gossip, drinking, and dancing that took place on such occasions were welcome rewards for neighborly cooperation.

Few neighborhood transactions involved money. In 1790, the states and federal government had not yet issued paper money, and the widespread use of Spanish, English,

Lewis Miller (1796–1882). The Historical Society of York County, PA.

OLD MRS. HANSMAN KILLING A HOG

This Pennsylvania farm wife seldom if ever worked in the fields, but her daily round of work was no dainty business. Along with other arduous and dirty labors, she killed and butchered hogs not only for her family but for some of her neighbors as well.

and French coins testified to the shortage of specie. In New England, farmers kept careful accounts of neighborhood debts. In the South and West, on the other hand, farmers used a "changing system" in which they simply remembered what they owed; they regarded the New England practice as a sign of Yankee greed and lack of character. Yet farmers everywhere relied more on barter than on cash: "Instead of money going incessantly backwards and forwards into the same hands," observed a French traveler in Massachusetts in 1790, "[Americans] supply their needs in the countryside by direct reciprocal exchanges. The tailor and the bootmaker go and do their work at the home of the farmer . . . who most frequently provides the raw material for it and pays for the work in goods. They write down what they give and receive on both sides, and at the end of the year they settle a large variety of exchanges with a very small quantity of coin." Such a system created an elaborate network of neighborhood debt. In Kent, Connecticut, for instance, the average farmer left 20 creditors when he died. The debts were indicators not of exploitation and class division, however, but of a highly structured and absolutely necessary system of neighborly cooperation.

Inheritance

The rural republicanism envisioned by men such as Jefferson and Crèvecoeur rested on widespread farm ownership and on a rough equality among adult male householders. Even as they were formulating that vision, however, its social base was disintegrating. Overcrowding and the growth of markets caused the price of good farmland to rise sharply throughout the older settlements. Young people could expect to inherit only a few acres of exhausted land or to move to wilderness land in the backcountry. Failing those options, they would quit farming altogether. Crèvecoeur's baby boy—who in fact ended up living in Boston—was in a more precarious position than his seat on his father's plough might have indicated.

In Revolutionary America, fathers had been judged by their ability to support and govern their households, to serve as good neighbors, and to pass land on to their sons and substantial dowries on to their daughters. After the war, fewer farm fathers could meet those expectations. Those in the old settlements had small farms and large families, which made it impossible for them to provide competence for all their offspring. Fathers felt that they had failed as fathers, and their daughters and sons, with no prospect of an adequate inheritance, were obliged to leave home. Most fathers tried valiantly to provide for all of their heirs (generally by leaving land to their sons and personal property to their daughters). Few left all of their land

to one son, and many stated in their wills that the sons to whom they left the land must share barns and cider mills—even the house—on farms that could be subdivided no further. Such provisions suited a social system that guaranteed the independence of the household head through complex relations with kin and neighbors. They also indicated that the system had reached the end of the line.

Outside New England, farm tenancy was on the increase. In parts of Pennsylvania and in other areas as well, farmers often bought farms when they became available in the neighborhood, rented them to tenants to augment the household income, and then gave them to their sons when they reached adulthood. The sons of poorer farmers often rented a farm in the hope of saving enough money to buy it. Some fathers bought tracts of unimproved land in the backcountry—sometimes on speculation, more often to provide their sons with land they could make into a farm. Others paid for their sons' educations or arranged apprenticeships to provide them with an avenue of escape from a declining countryside. As a result, more and more young men left home. The populations of the old farming communities grew older and more female, while the populations of the rising frontier settlements and seaport cities became younger and more male. The young men who stayed home often had nothing to look forward to but a lifetime as tenants or hired hands.

Standards of Living

The rise of markets in the late 18th and early 19th centuries improved living standards for some families but widened the disparity between prosperous farmers and their marginal and disinherited neighbors. Most farmhouses in the older rural areas were small, one-story structures. Few farmers, especially in the South and West, bothered to keep their surroundings clean or attractive. They repaired their fences only when they became too dilapidated to function. They rarely planted trees or shrubs, and housewives threw out garbage to feed the chickens and pigs that foraged near the house.

Inside, homes had few rooms and many people. Beds stood in every room, and few family members slept alone.

Old Dartmouth Historical Society/New Bedford Whaling Museum.

THE DINING ROOM OF DR. WHITBRIDGE, A RHODE ISLAND COUNTRY DOCTOR, CIRCA 1815

It is a comfortable, neatly furnished room, but with little decoration, and the doctor must sit near the fire in layered clothing to ward off the morning chill.

Growing up in Bethel, Connecticut, future show business entrepreneur P. T. Barnum shared a bed with his brother and an Irish servant; guests shared beds in New England taverns until the 1820s. The hearth remained the source of heat and light in most farmhouses. In the period from 1790 to 1810, more than half the households in central Massachusetts—an old and relatively prosperous area—owned only one or two candlesticks. One of the great disparities between wealthy families and their less affluent neighbors was that wealthy families could light their houses at night. Another disparity was in the outward appearance of houses. The wealthier families painted their houses white as a token of pristine republicanism, which stood in stark and unrepublican contrast to the weathered gray-brown clapboard siding of their neighbors.

Some improvements emerged in personal comfort. Beds in most houses may have been shared, but as time passed more of them had mattresses stuffed with feathers. At mealtimes, only the poorest families continued to eat with their fingers or with spoons from a common bowl. By 1800, individual place settings with knives and forks and china plates, along with chairs instead of benches, had become common in rural America. Although only the wealthiest families had upholstered furniture, ready-made chairs were widely available; the number of chairs per household in Massachusetts, for instance, doubled in the first third of the 19th century. Clocks, one of the first items to be mass produced in the United States, appeared in the more prosperous rural households: As early as the 1790s,

fully 35 percent of the families in Chester County, Pennsylvania, owned at least one clock.

🌎 From Backcountry to Frontier

The United States was a huge country in 1790, at least on paper. In the treaty that ended the War of Independence in 1783, the British ignored Indian claims and ceded all of the land from the Atlantic Ocean to the Mississippi River to the new republic, with the exceptions of Spanish Florida and New Orleans. The states then surrendered their individual claims to the federal government, and in 1790, George Washington became president of a nation that stretched nearly 1,500 miles inland. Still, most white Americans lived on thin strips of settlement along the Atlantic coast and along the few navigable rivers that emptied into the Atlantic. Some were pushing their way into the wilds of Maine and northern Vermont, and in New York others set up communities as far west as the Mohawk Valley. Pittsburgh was a struggling new settlement, and two outposts had been established on the Ohio River: at Marietta and at what would become Cincinnati.

Farther south, farmers had occupied the Piedmont lands up to the eastern slope of the Appalachians and were spilling through the Cumberland Gap into the new lands of Kentucky and Tennessee. North of the Ohio River, however, the Shawnee, Miami, Delaware, and Potawatomie nations, along with smaller tribes, controlled nearly all of the land shown on the Northwest Ordinance's neatly gridded and largely fictitious map. To the south, Indians whom the whites called the "Five Civilized Tribes" still occupied much of their ancestral land: the Cherokees in the Carolinas and northern Georgia, the Creeks in Georgia and Alabama, the Choctaws and Chickasaws in Mississippi, and the Seminoles in southern Georgia and Spanish Florida. Taken together, Indian peoples occupied most of the land that treaties and maps showed as the interior of the United States.

The Destruction of the Woodland Indians

Although many of the woodland tribes were still intact and still living on their ancestral lands in 1790, they were in serious trouble. The members of the old Iroquois Federation had been restricted to reservations in New York and Pennsylvania; many had fled to Canada. The once-powerful Cherokees had been severely punished for fighting on the side of the British during the Revolution and by 1790 had ceded three-fourths of their territory to the Americans. Like the Iroquois, by this time they were nearly surrounded by white settlements.

In the Old Northwest, the Shawnee, Miami, and other tribes—with the help of the British, who still occupied seven forts within what was formally the United States—continued to trade furs and to impede white settlement. Skirmishes with settlers, however, brought reprisals, and the Indians faced not only hostile pioneers but the U.S. Army as well. In the Ohio country, punitive expeditions led by General Josiah Harmar and General Arthur St. Clair failed in 1790 and 1791—the second ending in an Indian victory in which 630 soldiers died. In 1794, President Washington sent a third army, under General "Mad Anthony" Wayne, which defeated the Indians at Fallen Timbers, near present-day Toledo. The Treaty of Greenville forced the Native Americans to cede two-thirds of what are now Ohio and southeastern Indiana. At this point, the British decided to abandon their forts in the Old Northwest. Following their victory at Fallen Timbers, whites filtered into what remained of Indian lands. In 1796, President Washington threw up his hands and announced that "I believe scarcely any thing, short of a Chinese Wall, or a line of troops, will restrain Land Jobbers and the encroachment of settlers upon the Indian Territory." Five years later, Governor William Henry Harrison of Indiana Territory admitted that frontier whites "consider the murdering of the Indians in the highest degree meritorious."

Relegated to smaller territory but still dependent on the European fur trade, the natives of the Northwest now fell into competition with settlers and other Indians for the diminishing supply of game. The Creeks, Choctaws, and other tribes of the Old Southwest faced the same problem: Even when they chased settlers out of their territory, the settlers managed to kill or scare off the deer and other wildlife, thus ruining the old hunting grounds. When the Shawnee sent hunting parties farther west, they met irate western Indians. The Choctaws also sent hunters across the Mississippi, where they found both new sources of furs and angry warriors of the Osage and other peoples of Louisiana and Arkansas. The Indians of the interior now realized that the days of the fur trade, on which they depended for survival, were numbered.

Faced with shrinking territories, the disappearance of wildlife, and diminished opportunities to be traditional hunters and warriors, many Indian societies sank into despair. Epidemics of European diseases (smallpox, influenza, measles) attacked peoples who were increasingly sedentary and vulnerable. Old internal frictions grew nastier. In the Old Southwest, full-blooded Indians came into conflict with mixed-blood Indians, who often no longer spoke the native language and who wanted their people to

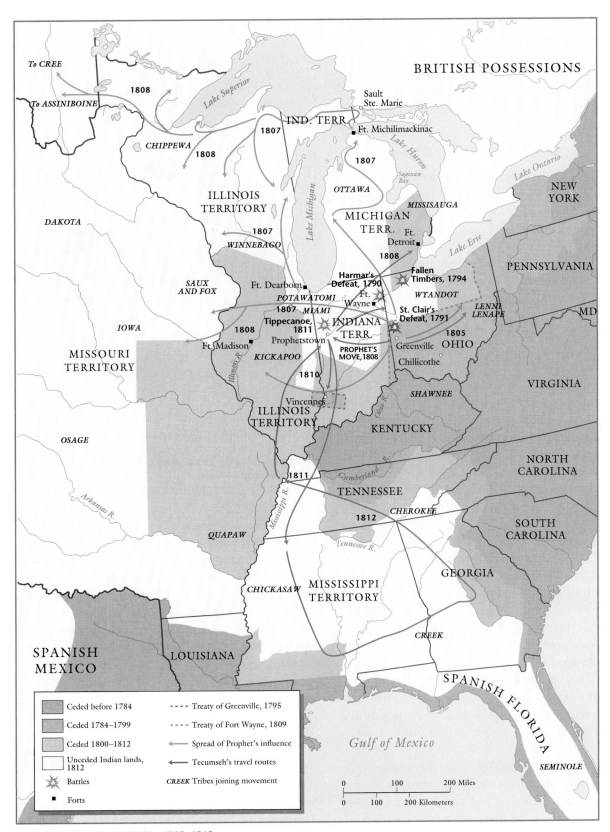

MAP 7.1 NATIVE AMERICA, 1783–1812

Native Americans had lost a lot before the American Revolution, but the losses grew worse as British, French, and Spanish traders, missionaries, and soldiers were replaced by a democratic republic of farmers who wanted Indian land. By 1812, Indian peoples in the Northwest were battered and increasingly threatened by settlement; Indians of the Southwest continued to occupy most of their old lands, but they would lose everything within the next generation.

adopt white ways. Murder and clan revenge plagued the tribes, and depression and suicide became more common. The use of alcohol, which had been a scourge on Indian societies for two centuries, increased. Indian males spent more time in their villages and less on the hunt, and by most accounts they drank more and grew more violent.

The Failure of Cultural Renewal

Out of this cultural wreckage emerged visionary leaders who spoke of a regenerated native society and the expulsion of all whites from the old tribal lands. One of the first was Chief Alexander McGillivray, a mixed-blood Creek who had sided with the British during the Revolution. Between 1783 and 1793, McGillivray tried to unite the Creeks under a national council that could override local chiefs and to form alliances with other tribes and with Spanish Florida. McGillivray's premature death in 1793, coupled with the mistrust with which many traditionalist Creeks viewed his schemes, prevented the realization of his vision.

The Cherokees north and east of the Creeks did succeed in making a unified state. Angered by the willingness of village chiefs to be bribed and flattered into selling land, and by the departure of tribe members to remote locations in the Appalachians or to government land in Arkansas, a group of young chiefs staged a revolt between 1808 and 1810. Previously, being a Cherokee had meant loyalty to one's clan and kin group and adherence to the tribe's ancient customs. Now it meant remaining on the tribe's ancestral land (migration across the Mississippi was regarded as treason) and unquestioning acceptance of the laws, courts, and police controlled by the national council. By 1810, the Cherokee had transformed themselves from a defeated and divided tribe into a nation within a nation.

Among the many prophets who emerged during these years, the one who came closest to military success was Tenskwatawa, a fat, one-eyed, alcoholic Shawnee who had failed as a warrior and medicine man. He went into a deep trance in 1805, and the people thought he was dead. During preparations for his funeral, he awoke and told them he had visited heaven and hell and had received a prophetic vision. First, all Indians must stop drinking and fighting among themselves. They must also return to their traditional food, clothing, tools, and hairstyles, and must extinguish all of their fires and start new ones without using European tools. All who opposed the new order (including local chiefs, medicine men, shamans, and witches) must be put down by force. When all of that had been done, God (a monotheistic, punishing God borrowed from the Christians) would restore the world that Indians had known before the whites came over the mountains.

TENSKWATAWA

The Shawnee prophet Tenskwatawa ("The Open Door"), brother of Tecumseh, was painted by George Catlin in 1836—long after the defeat of his prophetic attempt to unify American Indians.

Tenskwatawa's message soon found its way to the Delawares (who attacked the Christians among their people as witches) and other native peoples of the Northwest. When converts flooded into the prophet's home village, he moved to Prophetstown (Tippecanoe) in what is now Indiana. There, with the help of his brother Tecumseh, he created an army estimated by the whites at anywhere between 650 and 3,000 warriors and pledged to end further encroachment by whites. Tecumseh, who took control of the movement, announced to the whites that he was the sole chief of all the Indians north of the Ohio River; land cessions by anyone else would be invalid. Tenskwatawa's prophecy and Tecumseh's leadership had united the Indians of the Old Northwest in an unprecedented stand against white encroachment.

Tecumseh's confederacy posed a threat to the United States. A second war with England was looming, and Tecumseh was receiving supplies and encouragement from the British in Canada. He was also planning to visit the southern tribes in an attempt to bring them into his confederacy. The prospect of unified resistance by the western tribes in league with the British jeopardized every settler west of the Appalachians. In 1811, William Henry

Harrison led an army toward Prophetstown. With Tecumseh away, Tenskwatawa ordered an unwise attack on Harrison's army and was beaten at the Battle of Tippecanoe.

Tecumseh's still-formidable confederacy, joined by the traditionalist wing of the southern Creeks, fought alongside the British in the War of 1812 and lost (see chapter 8). The loss destroyed the military power of the Indians east of the Mississippi River. General Andrew Jackson forced the Creeks (including those who had served as his allies) to cede millions of acres of land in Georgia and Alabama. The other southern tribes, along with the members of Tecumseh's northern confederacy, watched helplessly as new settlers took over their hunting lands. Some of the Indians moved west, and others tried to farm what was left of their old land. All of them had to deal with settlers and government officials who neither feared them nor took their sovereignty seriously. By this time, most whites simply assumed that the Indians would have to move on to the barren land west of the Mississippi (see chapter 12).

The Backcountry, 1790–1815

To easterners, the backcountry whites who were displacing the Indians seemed no different from the defeated aborigines. In fact, in accommodating themselves to a borderless forest used by both Indians and whites, many settlers—like many Indians—had melded Indian and white ways. To clear the land, backcountry farmers simply girdled the trees and left them to die and fall down by themselves. They plowed the land by navigating between the stumps. To easterners' minds, the worst offense was that women often worked the fields, particularly while their men, as did Indians, spent long periods away on hunting trips for food game and animal skins for trade. The arch-pioneer Daniel Boone, for instance, braided his hair, dressed himself in Indian leggings, and, with only his dogs for company, disappeared for months at a time on "long hunts." When easterners began to "civilize" his neighborhood, Boone moved farther west.

Eastern visitors were appalled not only by the poverty, lice, and filth of frontier life but also by the drunkenness and violence of the frontiersmen. Americans everywhere drank heavily in the early years of the 19th century, but everyone agreed that frontiersmen drank more and were more violent when drunk

than men anywhere else. Travelers told of no-holds-barred fights in which frontiersmen gouged the eyes and bit off the noses and ears of their opponents. No account was complete without a reckoning of the number of one-eyed, one-eared men the traveler had met on the frontier. Stories arose of half-legendary heroes such as Davy Crockett of Tennessee, who wrestled bears and alligators and had a recipe for Indian stew, and Mike Fink, a Pennsylvania boatman who brawled and drank his way along the rivers of the interior until he was shot and killed in a drunken episode that none of the participants could clearly remember. Samuel Holden Parsons, a New Englander serving as a judge in the Northwest Territory, called the frontiersmen "our white savages." Massachusetts conservative Timothy Pickering branded them "the least worthy subjects of the United States. They are little less savage than the Indians."

After 1789, settlers of the western backcountry made two demands of the new national government: protection from the Indians and a guarantee of the right to navigate the Ohio and Mississippi rivers. The Indians were pushed back in the 1790s and finished off in the War of 1812, and in 1803, Jefferson's Louisiana Purchase (see chapter 8) ended the European presence on the rivers and at the crucial chokepoint at New Orleans. Over these years, the pace of settlement quickened. In 1790, only 10,000 settlers lived west of the Appalachians—about 1 American in 40. By 1800, the number of settlers had risen to nearly 1 million. By 1820, 2 million Americans were westerners—one in five.

The new settlers bought land from speculators who had acquired tracts under the Northwest Ordinance in the

A NORTHWESTERN FARM

A settler, R. H. Constant, built this farm in pioneer Sangamon County, Illinois. The original house was a log cabin; a separate kitchen was added at a later date. Sangamon County was settled largely from the upper South, and Constant's farm, like most farms in the neighborhood, was surrounded by a traditional Virginia split-rail or "worm" fence—like those that Constant's younger neighbor, the rail-splitter Abraham Lincoln, helped to build.

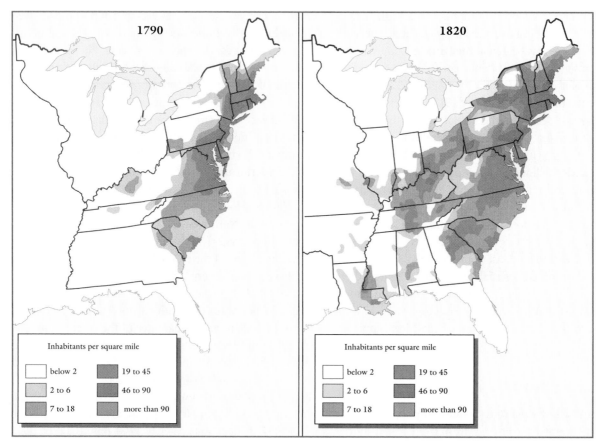

MAP 7.2   POPULATION DENSITY, 1790–1820

The population of the United States nearly doubled between 1790 and 1820, growing from 5.2 million to 9.6 million persons. In the South, an overwhelmingly rural population spread rapidly across space. The population of the Northeast and mid-Atlantic also occupied new territory over these years, but the rise of seaport towns and intensely commercialized (and often overcrowded) farming areas were turning the North into a much more densely settled region.

Northwest; from English, Dutch, and American land companies in western New York; and from land dealers in the Southwest and in northern New England. They built frame houses surrounded by cleared fields, planted marketable crops, and settled into the struggle to make farms out of the wilderness and to meet mortgage payments along the way. By 1803, four frontier states had entered the union: Vermont (1791), Kentucky (1792), Tennessee (1796), and Ohio (1803). Louisiana soon followed (1812), and when war ended in 1815, one frontier state after another gained admission: Indiana (1816), Mississippi (1817), Illinois (1818), Alabama (1818), Maine (1820), and Missouri (1821).

As time passed, the term *backcountry,* which easterners had used to refer to the wilderness and the dangerous misfits who lived in it, fell into disuse. By 1820, the term *frontier* had replaced it. The new settlements no longer represented the backwash of American civilization. They were its cutting edge.

The Plantation South, 1790–1820

In 1790, the future of slavery was uncertain in the Chesapeake (the states of Virginia, Maryland, and Delaware, where the institution first took root in North America). The tobacco market had been precarious since before the Revolution, and it continued to decline after 1790. Tobacco depleted the soil, and by the late 18th century, tidewater farms and plantations were giving out. As lands west of the Appalachians opened to settlement, white tenants, laborers, and small farmers left the Chesapeake in droves. Many of them moved to Kentucky, Tennessee, or the western reaches of Virginia. Many others found new homes in nonslave states north of the Ohio River. Faced with declining opportunities within the slave societies of the Chesapeake, thousands of the poorer whites had voted with their feet.

Slavery and the Republic

With slave labor becoming less necessary, Chesapeake planters continued to switch to grain and livestock—crops that required less labor than tobacco—and tried to think up new uses for slaves. Some planters divided their land into small plots and rented both the plots and their slaves to white tenant farmers. Others, particularly in Maryland, recruited tenants from the growing ranks of free blacks. Still others hired out their slaves as artisans and urban laborers. None of these solutions, however, could employ the great mass of slaves or repay the planters' huge investment in slave labor.

In this situation, many Chesapeake planters (who had, after all, fought a revolution in the name of natural rights) began to manumit their slaves. The farmers of Maryland and Delaware in particular set their slaves free; by the time those states sided with the North in 1861, more than half the blacks in Maryland and nine-tenths of those in Delaware were free. Virginia's economic and cultural commitment to the plantation was stronger, but even the Old Dominion showed a strong movement toward manumitting slaves. George Washington stated that he wished "to liberate a certain species of property," and manumitted his slaves by will. (The manumissions were to take place at the death of his widow—thus, as one wag declared, surrounding Mrs. Washington with 100 people who wanted her dead.) Robert Carter, reputedly the largest slaveholder in Virginia, also freed his slaves, as did many others. The free black population of Virginia stood at 2,000 in 1782, when the state passed a law permitting manumission. The number of free blacks rose to 12,766 in 1790, to 20,124 in 1800, and to 30,570 in 1810. In all, the proportion of Virginia blacks who were free increased from 4 percent in 1790 to 7 percent in 1810.

There were, however, limits on the manumission of Virginia slaves. First, few planters could afford to free their slaves without compensation. Second, white Virginians feared the social consequences of black freedom. Thomas Jefferson, for instance, owned 175 slaves when he penned the phrase that "all men are created equal." He lived off their labor, sold them to pay his debts, gave them as gifts, and sometimes sold them away from their families as a punishment. Through it all, he insisted that slavery was wrong. He could imagine emancipation; however, only if freed slaves would be colonized far from Virginia. A society of free blacks and whites, Jefferson insisted, would end in disaster: "Deep rooted prejudices entertained by the whites; ten thousand recollections, by the blacks, of the injuries they have sustained; new provocations; the real distinctions which nature has made ... [will] produce convulsions which will probably never end but in the extermination of the one or the other race." Near the end of an adult lifetime of condemning slavery but doing nothing to end it, Jefferson cried out that white Virginians held "a wolf by the ears": They could not hold onto slavery forever, and they could never let it go.

The Recommitment to Slavery

Jefferson's dilemma eased as cotton cultivation increased farther south. British industrialization created a demand for cotton from the 1790s onward, and planters knew they could sell all the cotton they could grow. But long-staple

GOING TO TENNESSEE

The Pennsylvanian Lewis Miller met with this group of slaves near Staunton, Virginia, in 1853. They were being sent from their old farms in Virginia to the slave markets of Tennessee and from there to the cotton fields of the newer southern states. In the years after 1820, hundreds of thousands of upper South slaves suffered this migration.

Arise! Arise! and weep no more dry up your tears, we Shall part no more. Come rose we go to Tennessee, that happy Shore To old virginia never – never – return. —

Abby Aldrich Rockefeller Folk Art Center, Williamsburg, VA.

cotton, the only profitable variety, was a delicate plant that thrived only on the Sea Islands off Georgia and South Carolina. The short-staple variety was hardier, but its sticky seeds had to be removed by hand before the cotton could be milled. One adult slave would work an entire day to clean a single pound of short-staple cotton—a profit-killing expenditure of labor. In 1790, the United States produced only 3,000 bales of cotton, nearly all of it on the plantations of the Sea Islands.

In 1793, Eli Whitney, a Connecticut Yankee who had come south to work as a tutor, set his mind to the problem. Within a few days, he had made a model of a cotton "gin" (a southern contraction of "engine") that combed the seeds from the fiber with metal pins fitted into rollers. Working with Whitney's machine, a slave could clean 50 pounds of short-staple cotton in a day. At a stroke, cotton became the great American cash crop and plantation agriculture was rejuvenated. Cotton production grew to 73,000 bales in 1800, to 178,000 bales in 1810, and to 334,000 bales in 1820. By 1820, cotton accounted for more than half the value of all agricultural exports.

Short-staple cotton grew well in the hot, humid climate and long growing season of the Lower South (roughly, the land below the southern borders of Virginia and Kentucky), and it grew almost anywhere: in the rolling Piedmont country east of the Appalachians, in the coastal lowlands, and—especially—in the virgin lands of the Old Southwest. It was also a labor-intensive crop that could be grown in either small or large quantities; farmers with few or no slaves could make a decent profit, and planters with extensive land and many slaves could make enormous amounts of money. Best of all, the factories of England and, eventually, of the American Northeast, had a seemingly insatiable appetite for southern cotton.

Plantation slavery, now rejuvenated, spread rapidly into the new cotton-growing regions of the South. Meanwhile, Chesapeake planters, who lived too far north to grow cotton, continued to diversify. To finance the transition to mixed agriculture, they sold their excess slaves at high prices to planters in the cotton frontier. Up until about 1810, most of the slaves who left Virginia had traveled to Kentucky or Tennessee with their masters. There-

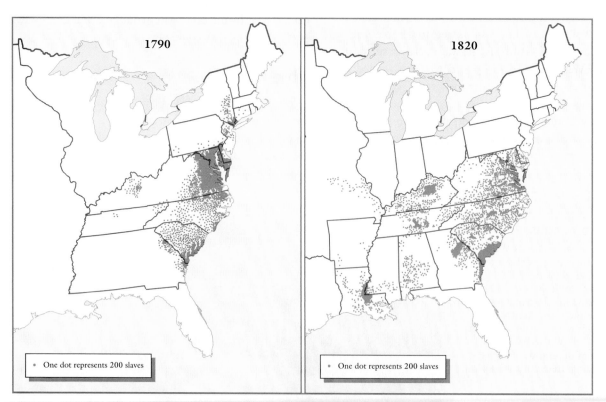

MAP 7.3   DISTRIBUTION OF SLAVE POPULATION, 1790–1820

In 1790, slaves were concentrated in the Chesapeake and in the South Carolina and Georgia low-country. Over the next 30 years, as a result of the decline of slave-based agriculture in Virginia and the beginnings of the cotton boom further south, Chesapeake planters were selling or freeing their slaves, whereas cotton farmers, through both the internal and international slave trade, were beginning to build a Black Belt that stretched through the interior of the Carolinas and on through the Southwest.

View an animated version of this map or related maps at http://history.wadsworth.com/murrin_LEP4e.

after, most of them left Virginia as commodities in the burgeoning interstate slave trade, headed for the new plantations of Georgia, Alabama, and Mississippi.

The movement of slaves out of the Chesapeake was immense. In the 1790s, about 1 in 12 Virginia and Maryland slaves was taken south and west. The figure rose to 1 in 10 between 1800 and 1810, and to 1 in 5 between 1810 and 1820. In 1790, planters in Virginia and Maryland had owned 56 percent of all American slaves; by 1860, they owned only 15 percent. The demand for slaves in the new cotton lands had thus provided many Chesapeake planters with a means of disposing of an endangered investment and with cash to pay for their transition to new crops.

The other center of slavery during the 18th century—coastal South Carolina and Georgia—made a massive recommitment to slave labor in the years after the Revolution. There, the principal crop, rice, along with other American foodstuffs, was experiencing a sharp rise in international demand. Most planters in this region were switching from indigo (a source of blue dye) to cotton as a secondary crop, creating an increase in the demand for slaves. Thousands of slaves in this region had either run away or been carried off by the British in the Revolution, and planters knew that the African slave trade was scheduled to end in 1808. With slave prices rising and slave-produced crops becoming steadily more profitable, they rushed to import as many African slaves as they could in the time remaining. Between 1788 and 1808, some 250,000 slaves were brought directly from Africa to the United States—nearly all of them to Charleston and Savannah. That figure equaled the number of Africans who had been brought to North America during the whole colonial period.

Race, Gender, and Chesapeake Labor

The transition to grain and livestock agriculture in the Chesapeake and the rise of the cotton belt in the Lower South imposed new kinds of labor on the slaves. The switch to mixed farming in Maryland and Virginia brought about a shift in the chores assigned to male and female slaves. Wheat cultivation, for example, meant a

Collection of the Maryland Historical Society, Baltimore.

AN OVERSEER DOING HIS DUTY

In 1798, the architect and engineer Benjamin Latrobe sketched a white overseer smoking a cigar and supervising slave women as they hoed newly cleared farmland near Fredericksburg, Virginia. A critic of slavery, Latrobe sarcastically entitled the sketch *An Overseer Doing His Duty*.

switch from the hoes used for tobacco to the plow and grain cradle—both of which called for the upper-body strength of adult men. The grain economy also required carts, wagons, mills, and good roads, and thus created a need for more slave artisans, nearly all of whom were men. Many of these slave artisans were hired out to urban employers and lived as a semifree caste in cities and towns. In the diversifying economy of the Chesapeake, male slaves did the plowing, mowing, sowing, ditching, and carting and performed most of the tasks requiring artisan skills. All of this work demanded high levels of training and could be performed by someone working either by himself or in a small group with little need for supervision.

Slave women were left with all of the lesser tasks. Contrary to legend, few slave women in the Chesapeake worked as domestic servants in the planter's house. A few of them worked at cloth manufacture, sewing, candle molding, and meat salting, but most female slaves still did farm work—hoeing, weeding, spreading manure, cleaning stables—monotonous work that called for little skill and was closely supervised. This new division of labor was clearly evident during the wheat harvest. On George Washington's farm, for example, male slaves, often working alongside temporary white laborers, moved in a broad line as they mowed the grain. Following them came a gang of children and women bent over and moving along on their hands and knees as they bound wheat into shocks. Similarly, Thomas Jefferson, who had been appalled to see

RICE FIELDS OF THE SOUTH

The rice fields of coastal South Carolina, with their complex systems of irrigation, were often created by Africans who had done similar work in West Africa before their enslavement.

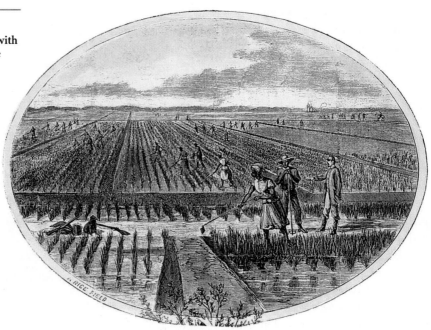

French women working in the fields, abandoned his concern for female delicacy when his own slaves were involved. At the grain harvest, he instructed his overseers to organize "gangs of half men and half women."

The Lowland Task System

On the rice and cotton plantations of South Carolina and Georgia, planters faced different labor problems. Slaves made up 80 percent of the population in this region, more than 90 percent in many parishes. Farms were large, and the two principal crops demanded skilled, intensive labor. The environment encouraged deadly summer diseases and kept white owners and overseers out of the fields. Planters solved these problems by organizing slaves according to the so-called task system. Each morning the owner or overseer assigned a specific task to each slave and allowed him to work at his own pace. When the task was done, the rest of the day belonged to the slave. Slaves who failed to finish their task were punished, and when too many slaves finished early, the owners assigned heavier tasks. In the 18th century, each slave had been expected to tend three to four acres of rice per day. In the early 19th century, with the growth of the rice market, the assignment was raised to five acres.

The task system encouraged slaves to work hard without supervision, and they turned the system to their own uses. Several slaves would often work together until all of their tasks were completed. Strong, young slaves would sometimes help older and weaker slaves after they had finished their own tasks. Once the day's work was done, the slaves would share their hard-earned leisure out of sight of the owner. A Jamaican visitor remarked that South Carolina and Georgia planters were "very particular in employing a negro, without his consent, after his task is finished, and agreeing with him for the payment which he is to receive." Farther west, low-country slaves who were moved onto the cotton frontier often imposed the task system on new plantations, sometimes against the resistance of masters.

Slaves under the task system won the right to cultivate land as "private fields"—not the little garden plots common in the Chesapeake, but farms of up to five acres on which they grew produce and raised livestock for market. A lively trade developed in slave-produced goods, and by the late 1850s, slaves in the low-country not only produced and exchanged property but also passed it on to their children. The owners tolerated such activity because slaves on the task system worked hard, required minimal supervision, and made money for their owners. The rice and cotton planters in South Carolina and Georgia were among the richest men in the country.

The Seaport Cities, 1790–1815

When the first federal census takers made their rounds in 1790, they found 94 percent of the population living on farms and in rural villages. The remaining 6 percent lived in the 24 towns that had populations of more than 2,500 (a census definition of "urban" that included many com-

munities that were, by modern standards, tiny). Only five communities had populations larger than 10,000: Baltimore (13,503), Charleston (16,359), Boston (18,038), New York (33,131), and Philadelphia (42,444). All five were seaport cities—testimony to the key role of international commerce in the economy of the early republic.

Commerce

These cities had grown steadily during the 18th century, handling imports from Europe and farm exports from America. With the outbreak of war between Britain and France in 1793—a world war that lasted until 1814—the overseas demand for American foodstuffs and for shipping to carry products from the Caribbean islands to Europe further strengthened the seaport cities. Foreign trade during these years was risky and uneven, subject to the tides of war and the strategies of the belligerents. French seizures of American shipping and the resulting undeclared war of 1798–1800, the 1805 British ban on America's reexport trade (the carrying of goods from French islands in the Caribbean), Jefferson's importation ban of 1806 and his trade embargo of 1807, and America's entry into the war in 1812 all disrupted the maritime economy and threw the seaports into periods of economic collapse (see chapter 8). But by 1815, wartime commerce had transformed the seaports and the institutions of American business. New York City had become the nation's largest city, with a population that had grown from 33,131 in 1790 to 96,373 in 1810. Philadelphia's population had risen to 53,722 by 1810, Boston's to 34,322, and Baltimore's to 46,555. Between 1800 and 1810, for the first time in American history, the growth of the urban population exceeded that of the rural population.

Seaport merchants in these years amassed the private fortunes and built the financial infrastructure that would soon take up the task of commercializing and industrializing the northern United States. Old merchants such as the Brown brothers of Providence and Elias Hasket Darby of Salem grew richer, and newcomers such as immigrant John Jacob Astor of New York City built huge personal fortunes. To manage those fortunes, new institutions emerged. Docking and warehousing facilities expanded dramatically. Bookkeepers were replaced by accountants who were familiar with the new double-entry system of accounting, and insurance and banking companies were formed to handle the risks and rewards of wartime commerce.

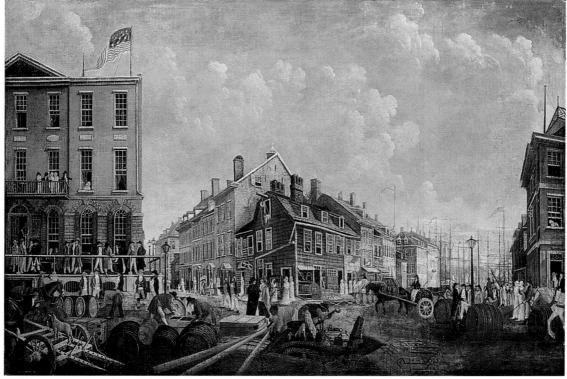

From the Collection of the New-York Historical Society.

A SCENE NEAR THE NEW YORK CITY DOCKS IN 1798 OR 1799

The large building on the left is the Tontine Coffee House, which housed the Stock Exchange and the principal insurance offices, at the corner of Water and Wall streets.

household that included four or more dependents. In short, they had become wage earners for life. In the seaport cities between 1790 and 1820, the world of artisans such as Paul Revere, Benjamin Franklin, and Thomas Paine was passing out of existence and was being replaced by wage labor.

The loss of independence undermined the paternal status of artisan husbands and fathers. As wage earners, few could support their family unless the wife and children earned money to augment family income. Working-class women took in boarders and did laundry and found work as domestic servants or as peddlers of fruit, candy, vegetables, cakes, or hot corn. They sent their children out to scavenge in the streets. The descent into wage labor and the reliance on the earnings of women and children clashed sharply with the republican, patriarchal assumptions of fathers.

The Historical Society of Pennsylvania, Procession of the Victuallers, by John Lewis Krimmel (Bc85 K89).

PROCESSION OF VICTUALLERS, 1815

The frequent and festive parades in the seaport cities included militia companies, political officials, clergymen, and artisans organized by trade. In this Philadelphia parade celebrating the end of the War of 1812, the victuallers, preceded by militia cavalrymen, carry a penned steer and a craft flag high atop a wagon, while butchers in top hats and clean aprons ride below. Behind them, shipbuilders drag a ship through the streets. Such parades were vivid displays of the system of interlocking labors that made up the city and of the value of artisans within that system.

The Withering of Patriarchal Authority

In the 50 years following the Declaration of Independence, the patriarchal republic created by the Founding Fathers became a democracy. The decline of authority and deference and the rise of individualistic, democratic social and political forms had many roots—most obviously in rural overcrowding, the movement of young people west and into the towns, and, more happily, in the increasingly democratic implications of American Revolutionary ideology. Most Americans witnessed the initial stirrings of change as a withering of paternal authority in their own households. Some—slaves and many women in particular—welcomed the decline of patriarchy. Others (the fathers themselves, disinherited sons, and women who looked to the security of old ways) considered it a disaster of unmeasured proportions. Whether they experienced the transformation as a personal rise or fall, Americans by the early 19th century had entered a world where received authority and past experience had lost their power. A new democratic faith emerged, grounded in the experience, intellect, and intuition of ordinary people.

Paternal Power in Decline

The philosopher Ralph Waldo Emerson, who reached adulthood in the 1830s, later mused that he had had the misfortune to be young when age was respected and to have grown old when youth counted for everything. Arriving in America at about the time Emerson came of age, the French visitor Alexis de Tocqueville observed that paternal power was largely absent in American families. "All that remains of it," he said, "are a few vestiges in the first years of childhood. . . . But as soon as the young American approaches manhood, the ties of filial obedience are relaxed day by day; master of his thoughts, he is soon master of his conduct. . . . At the close of boyhood the man appears and begins to trace out his own path."

From the mid-18th century onward, especially after the Revolution, many young people grew up knowing that their fathers would be unable to help them and that they would have to make their own way in the world. The consequent decline of parental power became evident in many ways—perhaps most poignantly in changing patterns of courtship and marriage. In the countryside, young men knew that they would not inherit the family farm, and young women knew that their father would be able to provide only a small dowry. As a result, fathers exerted less control over marriage choices than when marriage

entailed a significant transfer of property. Young people now courted away from parental scrutiny and made choices based on affection and personal attraction rather than on property or parental pressure. In 18th-century America, rural marriages had united families; now they united individuals. One sign of youthful independence (and of young people's lack of faith in their future) was the high number of pregnancies outside of marriage. Such incidents had been few in the 17th-century North, but in the second half of the 18th century and in the first decades of the 19th, the number of first births that occurred within eight months of marriage averaged between 25 and 30 percent, with the rates running much higher among poor couples. Apparently, fathers who could not provide for their children could not control them either.

The Alcoholic Republic

The erosion of the old family economy was paralleled by a dramatic rise in alcohol consumption. Americans had been drinking alcohol since the time of the first settle-

ments. (The Puritan flagship *Arabella* had carried three times as much beer as water.) But drinking, like all other "normal" behaviors, took place within a structure of paternal authority. Americans tippled every day in the course of their ordinary activities: at family meals and around the fireside, at work, and at barn-raisings, militia musters, dances, court days (even judges and juries passed the bottle), weddings, funerals, corn-huskings—even at the ordination of ministers. Under such circumstances, drinking—even drunkenness—seldom posed a threat to authority or to the social order.

That old pattern of communal drinking persisted into the 19th century, but during the 50 years following the Revolution, it gradually gave way to a new pattern. Farmers, particularly those in newly settled areas, regularly produced a surplus of grain that they turned into whiskey. In Washington County in western Pennsylvania, for example, 1 family in 10 operated a distillery in the 1790s. Whiskey was safer than water and milk, which were often tainted, and it was cheaper than coffee or tea. It was also cheaper than imported rum, so Americans embraced

John Lewis Krimmel, American, 1786–1821 Village Tavern, 1813–14, oil on canvas, 16-7/8 x 22-1/2 in. (42.8 x 56.9 cm), The Toledo Museum of Art, Toledo, Ohio. Purchased with funds from the Florence Scott Libbey Bequest in Memory of her Father, Maurice A. Scott.

INTERIOR OF AN AMERICAN INN, 1813

In this democratic, neighborly scene in a country inn in the early republic, men of varying degrees of wealth, status, and inebriety are drinking and talking freely with each other. One man's wife and daughter have invaded this male domain, perhaps to question the time and money spent at the inn.

farmers in that state wanted to retain power in a society made up more of urban, immigrant wage earners. (When Rhode Island finally reformed the franchise in 1843, the new law included a freehold requirement that applied only to the foreign-born.) With that exception, the white men of every state held the vote.

Early 19th-century suffrage reform gave political rights to propertyless men, and thus took a long step away from the Founding Fathers' republic and toward mass democracy. At the same time, however, reformers explicitly limited the democratic franchise to those who were white and male. New Jersey's revolutionary constitution, for instance, had granted the vote to "persons" who met a freehold qualification. This loophole enfranchised property-holding widows, many of whom exercised their rights. A law of 1807 abolished property restrictions and gave the vote to all white men; the same law closed the loophole that had allowed propertied women to vote. The question of woman suffrage would not be raised again until women raised it in 1848 (see chapter 11); it would not be settled until well into the 20th century.

New restrictions also applied to African Americans. The revolutionary constitutions of Massachusetts, New Hampshire, Vermont, and Maine—northeastern states with tiny black minorities—granted the vote to free blacks. New York and North Carolina laws gave the vote to "all men" who met the qualifications, and propertied African Americans in many states (a tiny but symbolically crucial minority) routinely exercised the vote. Postrevolutionary laws that extended voting rights to all white men often specifically excluded or severely restricted votes for blacks. Free blacks lost the suffrage in New York, New Jersey, Pennsylvania, Connecticut, Maryland, Tennessee, and North Carolina—all states in which they had previously voted. By 1840, fully 93 percent of blacks in the North lived in states that either banned or severely restricted their right to vote. And the restrictions were explicitly about race. A delegate to the New York constitutional convention of 1821, noting the movement of freed slaves into New York City, argued against allowing them to vote: "The whole host of Africans that now deluge our city (already too impertinent to be borne), would be placed upon an equal with the citizens." A Michigan legislator later confirmed the distinction between "Africans" and "citizens" when he insisted that neither blacks nor Indians belonged to the "great North American Family," and thus could never be citizens of the republic.

Thus the "universal" suffrage of which many Americans boasted was far from universal: New laws dissolved the old republican connections between political rights and property, and thus saved the citizenship of thousands who were becoming propertyless tenants and wage earners; the same laws that gave the vote to all white men, however, explicitly barred other Americans from political participation. Faced with the disintegration of Jefferson's republic of proprietors, the wielders of power had chosen to blur the emerging distinctions of social class while they hardened the boundaries of sex and race. The "democracy" of white men would return to this formula repeatedly as the 19th century unfolded.

☙ Republican Religion

The Founding Fathers had been largely indifferent to organized religion, although a few were pious men. Some, like George Washington, a nominal Episcopalian, attended church out of a sense of obligation. Many of the better educated, including Thomas Jefferson, subscribed to deism, the belief that God had created the universe but did not intervene in its affairs. Many simply did not bother themselves with thoughts about religion. When asked why the Constitution mentioned neither God nor religion, Alexander Hamilton is reported to have smiled and answered, "We forgot."

The Decline of the Established Churches

In state after state, postrevolutionary constitutions withdrew government support from religion, and the First Amendment to the U.S. Constitution clearly prescribed the national separation of church and state. Reduced to their own sources of support, the established churches went into decline. The Episcopal Church, which had been the established Church of England in the southern colonies until the Revolution, went into decline. In Virginia, only 40 of the 107 Episcopal parishes supported ministers in the early 19th century. Nor did the Episcopal Church travel west with southern settlers. Of the 408 Episcopal congregations in the South in 1850, 315 were in the old seaboard states.

In New England, the old churches fared little better. The Connecticut Congregationalist Ezra Stiles reported in 1780 that 60 parishes in Vermont and an equal number in New Hampshire were without a minister. In Massachusetts, according to Stiles's reports, 80 parishes lacked a minister. In all, about one-third of New England's Congregational pulpits were vacant in 1780, and the situation was worse to the north and west. In Vermont between 1763 and 1820, the founding of churches followed the incorporation of towns by an average of 15 years, an indi-

cation that frontier settlement in that state proceeded almost entirely without the benefit of organized religion. In 1780, nearly all of the 750 Congregational churches in the United States were in New England. In the next 40 years, although the nation's population rose from 4 to 10 million, the number of Congregational churches rose by only 350. Ordinary women and men were leaving the churches that had dominated the religious life of colonial America, sometimes ridiculing the learned clergy as they departed. To Ezra Stiles and other conservatives, it seemed that the republic was plunging into atheism.

The Rise of the Democratic Sects

The collapse of the established churches, the social dislocations of the postrevolutionary years, and the increasingly antiauthoritarian, democratic sensibilities of ordinary Americans provided fertile ground for the growth of new democratic sects. These were the years of camp-meeting revivalism, years in which Methodists and Baptists grew from small, half-organized sects into the great popular denominations they have been ever since. They were also years in which fiercely independent dropouts from older churches were putting together a loosely organized movement that would become the Disciples of Christ. At the same time, ragged, half-educated preachers were spreading the Universalist and Freewill Baptist messages in upcountry New England, while in western New York young Joseph Smith was receiving the visions that would lead to Mormonism (see chapter 10).

The result was, first of all, a vast increase in the variety of choices on the American religious landscape. Within that welter of new churches was a roughly uniform democratic style shared by the fastest-growing sects. First, they renounced the need for an educated, formally authorized clergy. Religion was now a matter of the heart and not the head; crisis conversion (understood in most churches as personal transformation that resulted from direct experience of the Holy Spirit) was a necessary credential for preachers; a college degree was not. The new preachers substituted emotionalism and storytelling for Episcopal ritual and Congregational theological lectures; stories attracted listeners, and they were harder for the learned clergy to refute. The new churches also held up the Bible as the one source of religious knowledge, thus undercutting all theological knowledge and placing every literate Christian on a level with the best-educated minister. These tendencies often ended in Restorationism—the belief that all theological and institutional changes since the end of biblical times were manmade mistakes, and that religious

organizations must restore themselves to the purity and simplicity of the church of the Apostles. In sum, this loose democratic creed rejected learning and tradition and raised up the priesthood of all believers.

Baptists and Methodists were by far the most successful at preaching to the new populist audience. The United States had only 50 Methodist churches in 1783; by 1820 it had 2,700. Over those same years, the number of Baptist churches rose from 400 to 2,700. Together, in 1820, these two denominations outnumbered Episcopalians and Congregationalists by 3 to 1, almost a reversal of their relative standings 40 years earlier. Baptists based much of their appeal in localism and congregational democracy. Methodist success, on the other hand, entailed skillful national organization. Bishop Francis Asbury, the head of the church in its fastest-growing years, built an episcopal bureaucracy that seeded churches throughout the republic and sent circuit-riding preachers to places that had none. These early Methodist missions were grounded in self-sacrifice to the point of martyrdom. Asbury demanded much of his itinerant preachers, and until 1810, he strongly suggested that they remain celibate. "To marry," he said, "is to locate." Asbury also knew that married circuit riders would leave many widows and orphans behind, for hundreds of them worked themselves to death. Of the men who served as Methodist itinerants before 1819, at least 60 percent died before the age of 40.

From seaport cities to frontier settlements, few Americans escaped the sound of Methodist preaching in the early 19th century. The Methodist preachers were common men who spoke plainly, listened carefully to others, and carried hymnbooks with simple tunes that anyone could sing. They also, particularly in the early years, shared traditional folk beliefs with their humble flocks. Some of the early circuit riders relied heavily on dreams; some could predict the future; many visited heaven and hell and returned with full descriptions. In the end, however, the hopefulness and simplicity of the Methodist message attracted ordinary Americans. The Methodists rejected the old terrors of Calvinist determinism and taught that although salvation comes only through God, men and women can decide to open themselves to divine grace and thus play a decisive role in their own salvation. They also taught that a godly life is a gradual, lifetime growth in grace—thus allowing for repentance for minor, and sometimes even major, lapses of faith and behavior. By granting responsibility (one might say sovereignty) to the individual believer, the Methodists established their democratic credentials and drew hundreds of thousands of Americans into their fold.

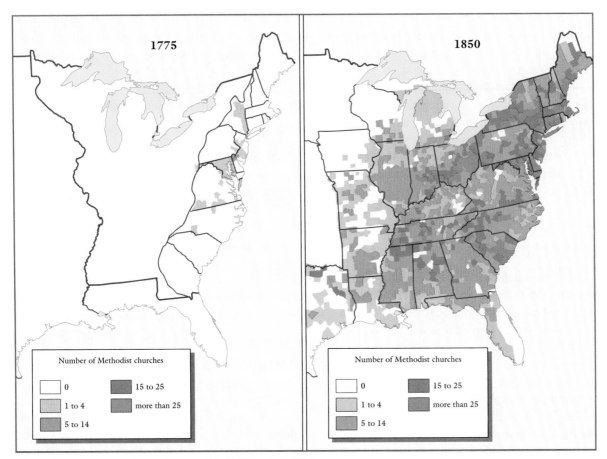

MAP 7.4 GROWTH OF AMERICAN METHODISM, 1775–1850

This is a county-by-county map of the rise of American Methodism from the Revolution through the eve of the Civil War. In 1775, Methodism was almost nonexistent in British North America. By 1850, the Methodists were the largest Protestant denomination in the United States, and they were truly a national faith: There were Methodist churches in almost every county in the country.

The Christianization of the White South

During these same years, evangelical Protestantism became the dominant religion of the white South. That triumph constituted a powerful assault on the prerevolutionary structure of authority, because the Baptists, Methodists, and evangelical Presbyterians who achieved it saw it as a revolt of poor and middling folk against the cultural dominance of the gentry. The essence of southern evangelicalism was a violent conversion experience followed by a life of piety and a rejection of what evangelicals called "the world." To no small degree, "the world" was the economic, cultural, and political world controlled by the planters. James McGready, who preached in rural North Carolina, openly condemned the gentry: "The world is in all their thoughts day and night. All their talk is of corn and tobacco, of land and stock. The price of merchandise and negroes are inexhaustible themes of conversation. But

for them, the name of Jesus has no charms; it is rarely mentioned unless to be profaned." In the 1790s, this was dangerous talk, as McGready learned when young rakes rode their horses through one of his outdoor meetings, tipped over the benches, set the altar on fire, and threatened to kill McGready himself.

Southern Baptists, Methodists, and Presbyterians spread their democratic message in the early 19th century through the camp meeting. Although its origins stretched back to the 18th century, the first full-blown camp meeting took place at Cane Ridge, Kentucky, in 1801. Here the annual "Holy Feast," a three-day communion service of Scotch-Irish Presbyterians, was transformed into an outdoor, interdenominational revival at which hundreds experienced conversion under Presbyterian, Methodist, and Baptist preaching. Estimates of the crowd at Cane Ridge ranged from 10,000 to 20,000 persons, and by all accounts the enthusiasm was nearly unprecedented. Some converts fainted; others succumbed to uncontrolled bod-

Lewis Miller (1796–1882). The Historical Society of York County, PA.

CAMP MEETING NEAR YORK, PENNSYLVANIA, 1808

Painting from memory, the local artist Lewis Miller portrayed a Methodist camp meeting at Codorus Creek in 1808, catching the evangelicals in their powerful combination of individual piety and public, democratic display. Miller remembered their tent city and the shanty from which the evangelists preached. In the center of the sketch, male and female converts revel together in public humiliation and spiritual triumph. A crowd in which men and women stand separately looks on.

ily jerkings, while a few barked like dogs—all of them visibly taken by the Holy Spirit. Such exercises fell upon women and men, whites and blacks, rich and poor, momentarily erasing southern social distinctions in moments of profound and very public religious ecstasy. A witness to a later camp meeting recounted that "to see a bold and courageous Kentuckian (undaunted by the horrors of war) turn pale and tremble at the reproof of a weak woman, a little boy, or a poor African; to see him sink down in deep remorse, roll and toss, and gnash his teeth, till black in the face, entreat the prayers of those he came to devour ... who can say the change was not supernatural?"

Evangelicals and Slavery

Southern evangelicalism was a subversive movement from its origins before the Revolution into the early 19th century. Although it reviled worldliness, southern evangelicalism was at bottom conservative because it seldom questioned the need for social hierarchy. As the 19th century progressed, the Baptists, Methodists, and Presbyterians of the South, although they never stopped railing against greed and pride, learned to live comfortably within a system of fixed hierarchy and God-given social roles.

Slavery became the major case in point. For a brief period after the Revolution, evangelicals included slavery on their list of worldly sins. Methodists and Baptists preached to slaves as well as to whites, and Bishop Francis Asbury,

principal architect of American Methodism, was familiar with John Wesley's statement that slavery was against "all the laws of Justice, Mercy, and Truth." In 1780, a conference of Methodist preachers ordered circuit riders to free their slaves and advised all Methodists to do the same. In 1784, the Methodists declared that they would excommunicate members who failed to free their slaves within two years. Lay Methodists took the order seriously: On the Delmarva Peninsula (Delaware and the Eastern Shore of Maryland and Virginia), for instance, Methodist converts freed thousands of slaves in the late 18th century. Other evangelicals shared their views. As early as 1787, southern Presbyterians prayed for "final abolition," and two years later, Baptists condemned slavery as "a violent deprivation of the rights of nature and inconsistent with a republican government."

The period of greatest evangelical growth, however, came during the years in which the South was committing irrevocably to plantation slavery. As increasing numbers of both slaves and slave owners came within the evangelical fold, the southern churches had to rethink their position on slavery. The Methodists never carried out their threat to excommunicate slaveholders, confessing in 1816 that southerners were so committed to slavery that "little can be done to abolish the practice so contrary to moral justice." Similarly, the Baptists and Presbyterians never translated their antislavery rhetoric into action. By 1820, evangelicals were coming to terms with slavery. Instead of demanding freedom for slaves, they suggested, as the

Methodist James O'Kelly put it, that slave owners remember that slaves were "dear brethren in Christ" who should not be treated cruelly and who should be allowed to attend religious services. By the 1830s, with large numbers of the planter elite converted to the evangelical fold, this evolved into a full-scale effort to Christianize the institution of slavery (see chapter 10).

After 1820, few southern evangelicals spoke out against slavery. Those who held to their antislavery views were concentrated in the upcountry, where few whites owned slaves. Many of these were joining the stream of poor and middling whites who were moving to free states north of the Ohio River. A Kentucky farmer and carpenter named Thomas Lincoln, for instance, belonged to a Baptist congregation that had separated from its parent church over the question of slavery. When he moved his family to a site near Pidgeon Creek, Indiana, Lincoln helped build an antislavery Baptist church and served it as trustee. He also arranged a job as church sexton for his young son Abraham.

The Beginnings of African American Christianity

Slaves in America who were Christian in the 17th and 18th centuries mostly were converted by Anglican missions. Blacks participated in the revivals of the southern Great Awakening, and the number of Christian slaves increased steadily in the second half of the 18th century. In the slave communities of the Upper South, as well as the burgeoning free and semifree urban black populations of both the North and South, the evangelical revivals of the late 18th and early 19th centuries appealed powerfully to African Americans who sensed that the bonds of slavery were loosening. By 1820, most blacks outside the Deep South considered themselves Christians. In the South Carolina and Georgia low-country, however, few slaves were Christians before 1830.

From 1780 to 1820, for the first time, thousands of slaves embraced Christianity and began to turn it into a religion of their own. Slaves attended camp meetings (the Cane Ridge revival included a black preacher, probably from the independent church in Lexington), listened to itinerant preachers, and joined the Baptist and Methodist congregations of the southern revival.

Blacks were drawn to revival religion for many of the same reasons as whites. They found the informal, storytelling evangelical preachers more attractive than the old Anglican missionaries. The revivalists, in turn, welcomed slaves and free blacks to their meetings and sometimes recruited them as preachers. Evangelical, emotional preaching; the falling, jerking, and other camp-meeting "exercises"; and the revivalists' emphasis on singing and other forms of audience participation were much more attractive than the cold, high-toned preaching of the Anglicans. So were the humility and suffering of the evangelical whites. Slaves respected Methodist missionaries who entered their cabins and talked with them on their own terms; they listened more closely to men such as James McGready than to the slaveholders who rode horses through McGready's meetings. Finally, the slaves gloried in the evangelicals' assault on the slaveholders' culture and in the antislavery sentiments of many white evangelicals.

BETHEL AME CHURCH
Founded in 1794 by the Reverend Richard Allen and nine other blacks who resented discrimination at the hands of white Methodists, Philadelphia's Bethel African Methodist Episcopal Church became a cornerstone of the city's free black community.

The result was a huge increase in the number of African American Christians. Methodists, who counted converts more carefully than some others, claimed 20,000 black members in 1800—one in three American Methodists.

Neither antislavery beliefs nor openness to black participation, however, persisted long among white evangelicals. Although exceptions existed, most "integrated" congregations in both the North and South were in fact internally segregated, with blacks sitting in the back of the church or upstairs in the gallery, and with only whites serving in positions of authority. Blacks began organizing independent churches. In Philadelphia, black preachers Richard Allen and Absalom Jones rebelled against segregated seating in St. George's Methodist Church and, in 1794, founded two separate black congregations; by 1800, about 40 percent of Philadelphia's blacks belonged to one of those two churches. Similar secessions resulted in new churches farther south: in Baltimore; in Wilmington, Delaware; in Richmond; in Norfolk; and in the cluster of villages that had risen to serve the Chesapeake's new mixed economy. Even Charleston boasted an independent Methodist conference made up of 4,000 slaves and free blacks in 1815.

By 1820, roughly 700 independent black churches operated in the United States where there had been none at all 30 years earlier. Only after 1830 did an independent Christian tradition exist among the majority of blacks who remained plantation slaves (see chapter 10). The democratic message of the early southern revival, the brief attempt of white and black Christians to live out the implications of that message, and the independent black churches that rose from the failure of that attempt all left a permanent stamp on southern Protestantism, black and white.

Black Republicanism: Gabriel's Rebellion

Masters who talked of liberty and natural rights sometimes worried that slaves might imagine that such language could apply to themselves. The Age of Democratic Revolution took a huge step in that direction in 1789, when the French Revolution—fought in the name of "Liberty, Equality, and Fraternity"—went beyond American notions of restored English liberties and into the heady regions of universal natural rights. Among the first repercussions outside of France was a revolution on the Caribbean island of Hispaniola in the French colony of Saint-Domingue. That island's half-million slaves fought out a complicated political and military revolt that began with the events in Paris in 1789 and resulted—after the

defeats of Spanish, English, and French armies—with the creation of the independent black republic of Haiti on the western one-third of the island. Slave societies throughout the hemisphere heard tales of terror from refugee French planters and stories of hope from the slaves they brought with them (12,000 of these entered South Carolina and Louisiana alone). In 1800, a conservative Virginia white complained that "Liberty and Equality has been infused into the minds of the negroes." A South Carolina congressman agreed that "this newfangled French philosophy of liberty and equality" was stirring up the slaves. Even Thomas Jefferson, who applauded the spread of French republicanism, conceded that "the West Indies appears to have given considerable impulse to the minds of the slaves . . . in the United States."

Slaves from the 1790s onward whispered of natural rights and imagined themselves as part of the Democratic Revolution. This covert republic of the slaves sometimes came into the open, most ominously in Richmond in 1800, where a slave blacksmith named Gabriel hatched a well-planned conspiracy to overthrow Virginia's slave regime. Gabriel had been hired out to Richmond employers for most of his adult life; he was shaped less by plantation slavery than by the democratic, loosely interracial underworld of urban artisans. In the late 1790s, the repressive acts of the Federalist national government and the angry responses of the Jeffersonian opposition (see chapter 8), along with the news from Saint-Domingue (present-day Haiti), drove the democratic sensibilities of that world to new heights. Gabriel's plans took shape within that heated ideological environment.

Gabriel, working with his brother and other hired-out slave artisans, planned his revolt with military precision. Working at religious meetings, barbecues, and the grog shops of Richmond, they recruited soldiers among slave artisans, adding plantation slaves only at the last moment. Gabriel planned to march an army of 1,000 men on Richmond in three columns. The outside columns would set diversionary fires in the warehouse district and prevent the militia from entering the town. The center would seize Capitol Square, including the treasury, the arsenal, and Governor James Monroe.

Although his army would be made up of slaves, and although his victory would end slavery in Virginia, Gabriel hoped to make a republican revolution, not a slave revolt. His chosen enemies were the Richmond "merchants" who had controlled his labor. Later, a co-conspirator divulged the plan: The rebels would hold Governor Monroe hostage and split the state treasury among themselves, and "if the white people agreed to their freedom they would then hoist a white flag, and [Gabriel] would dine and drink with the merchants of the city on the day when it would

be agreed to." Gabriel expected what he called "the poor white people" and "the most redoubtable republicans" to join him. He in fact had the shadowy support of two Frenchmen, and rumors indicated that other whites were involved, although never at levels that matched the delusions of the conspirators. Gabriel planned to kill anyone who opposed him, but he would spare Quakers, Methodists, and Frenchmen, for they were "friendly to liberty." Unlike those of earlier slave insurgents, Gabriel's dreams did not center on violent retribution or a return to or reconstruction of West Africa. He was an American revolutionary, and he dreamed of a truly democratic republic for Virginia. His army would march into Richmond under the banner "Death or Liberty."

Gabriel and his co-conspirators recruited at least 150 soldiers who agreed to gather near Richmond on August 30, 1800. The leaders expected to be joined by 500 to 600 more rebels as they marched upon the town. On the appointed day, however, it rained heavily. Rebels could not reach the meeting point, and amid white terror and black betrayals, Gabriel and his henchmen were hunted down, tried, and sentenced to death. In all, the state hanged 27 supposed conspirators, while others were sold and transported out of Virginia. The condemned carried their radical republican dreams to their graves. A white Virginian marveled that the rebels on the gallows displayed a "sense of their [natural] rights, [and] a contempt of danger." When asked to explain the revolt, one condemned man replied in terms that could only have disturbed the white republicans of Virginia: "I have nothing more to offer than what General Washington would have had to offer, had he been taken by the British and put to trial by them. I have

adventured my life in endeavoring to obtain the liberty of my countrymen, and am a willing sacrifice in their cause."

Conclusion

Between 1790 and 1820, Americans had transformed their new republic—with paradoxical results. The United States more than doubled in both size and population during these years. American trade with Britain, continental Europe, and the Caribbean skyrocketed. Some Americans amassed fortunes, others made more modest gains, while still others saw their positions deteriorate. Nonwhite Americans experienced the expansion of the republic and the growth of commerce as unmixed catastrophes: Indians between the Appalachians and the Mississippi River lost everything; their hunting grounds became American farmland, much of it worked by slaves who now knew that their masters would never voluntarily free them.

The transformation stemmed both from American independence and from the expansion of agriculture and increased exports of American farm products. When Americans traded plantation staples and surplus food for European (largely British) manufactured goods and financial services, however, they deepened their colonial dependence on the old centers of the world economy—even as they insisted on their independence with a bellicose republican nationalism. This formed the cluttered backdrop of social change, economic and geographic growth, and continuing vulnerability to the whims and needs of the Old World powers against which Federalists and Jeffersonian Republicans fought each other to determine the ultimate outcome of the American Revolution.

SUGGESTED READINGS

Douglas C. North, *The Economic Growth of the United States, 1790–1860* (1961) is an economic overview of these years. On rural society in the North, see **Christopher Clark,** *The Roots of Rural Capitalism: Western Massachusetts, 1780–1860* (1990); **Laurel Thatcher Ulrich,** *A Midwife's Tale: The Life of Martha Ballard, Based on Her Diary, 1785–1812* (1990); **Martin Bruegel,** *Farm, Shop, Landing: The Rise of a Market Society in the Hudson Valley, 1780–1860;* and **Jack Larkin,** *The Reshaping of Everyday Life, 1790–1840* (1988). Good accounts of Native Americans in these years include **Anthony F. C. Wallace,** *The Death and Rebirth of the Seneca* (1969); and **Gregory Evans Dowd,** *A Spirited Resistance: The North American Indian Struggle for a New World* (1992). **Stephen Aron,** *How the West was Lost: The Transformation of Kentucky from Daniel Boone to Henry Clay* (1996), treats white settler societies. Economic change in the South is traced in **Robert William Fogel and Stanley L. Engerman,** *Time on the Cross: The Economics of American Negro Slavery* (1974). The social history of colonial and early national slavery is ably covered in **Ira Berlin,** *Many Thousands Gone: The First Two Centuries of Slavery in North America* (1998). On urban labor, see the early chapters of **Sean Wilentz,** *Chants Democratic: New York City and the Rise of the American Working Class* (1984). The study of religion in the postrevolutionary years begins with two books: **Nathan O. Hatch,** *The Democratization of American Christianity* (1989); and **Jon Butler,** *Awash in a Sea of Faith: Christianizing the American People* (1990). The concluding section of **Gordon Wood,** *The Radicalism of the American Revolution* (1992) discusses the "democratization of mind" during these years. Other important books on these topics are listed in the Suggested Readings for chapter 10.

AMERICAN JOURNEY ONLINE
AND
 INFOTRAC COLLEGE EDITION

Visit the source collections at www.ajaccess.wadsworth.com and
infotrac.thomsonlearning.com and use the Search function with
the following key terms to explore documents, images, audio
and video clips, articles, and commentary related to the material
in this chapter.

Eli Whitney	Tenskwatawa
Cotton	James Monroe
Tecumseh	Gabriel's Rebellion

GRADE AIDS

**Visit the Liberty Equality Power Companion Web Site for resources specific to
this textbook:** http://history.wadsworth.com/murrin_LEP4e

The CD in the back of this book and the U.S. History Resource Center at
http://history.wadsworth.com/u.s./ offer a variety of tools to help you succeed in
this course, including access to quizzes; images; documents; interactive simulations,
maps, and timelines; movie explorations; and a wealth of other sources.

U.S. government. National politics was now caught up and subsumed within the struggle over international republicanism.

As Britain and France went to war in 1793, President Washington declared American neutrality, thereby abrogating obligations made in the 1778 treaties with the French. Washington and most of his advisers realized that the United States was in no condition to fight a war. They also wanted to stay on good terms with Great Britain. Ninety percent of American imports came from Britain, and 90 percent of the federal revenue came from customs duties on those imports. Thus both the nation's commerce and the financial health of the government depended on good relations with Great Britain. Moreover, Federalists genuinely sympathized with the British in the war with France. They regarded the United States as a "perfected" England and viewed Britain as the defender of hierarchical society and ordered liberty against the homicidal anarchy of the French.

Jefferson and his friends saw things differently. They applauded the French for carrying on the republican revolution Americans had begun in 1776, and they had no affection for the "monarchical" politics of the Federalists or for Americans' continued neocolonial dependence on British trade. The faction led by Jefferson and Madison wanted to abandon the English mercantile system and trade freely with all nations. They did not care if that course of action hurt commercial interests (most of which supported the Federalists) or impaired the government's ability to centralize power in itself. Although they agreed that the United States should stay out of the war, the Jeffersonians sympathized as openly with the French as the Federalists did with the British.

Citizen Genêt

Throughout the war years from 1793 to 1815, both Great Britain and France, by intervening freely in the internal affairs of the United States, made American isolationism impossible.

In April 1793, the French sent Citizen Edmond Genêt as minister to the United States. Genêt's ruling Girondists were the revolutionary faction that had declared the war on all monarchies; they ordered Genêt to enlist American aid with or without the Washington administration's consent. After the president's proclamation of neutrality, Genêt openly commissioned American privateers to harass British shipping and enlisted Americans in intrigues against the Spanish outpost of New Orleans. Genêt then opened France's Caribbean colonies to American shipping, providing American shippers a choice between French free trade and British mercantilism. Genêt's mission came to an abrupt end in summer 1793, when Robespierre and the

infamous Terror drove the Girondists from power. Learning that he would be guillotined if he returned to France, Genêt accepted the hospitality of Americans, married a daughter of George Clinton, the old anti-Federalist governor of New York, and lived out the rest of his life as an American country gentleman.

The British responded to Genêt's free-trade declaration with a promise to seize any ship trading with French colonies in the Caribbean. Word of these Orders in Council—almost certainly by design—reached the Royal Navy before American merchant seamen had learned of them, with the result that 250 American ships fell into British hands. The Royal Navy also began searching American ships for English sailors who had deserted or who had switched to safer, better-paying work in the American merchant marine. Inevitably, some American sailors were kidnapped into the British navy in a contemptuous and infuriating assault on American sovereignty. Meanwhile the British, operating from Canada and from their still-garrisoned forts in the Northwest, began promising military aid to the Indians north of the Ohio River. Thus, while the French ignored the neutrality of the United States, the English engaged in both overt and covert acts of war.

Western Troubles

The problems with France and on the high seas were accompanied by an intensified threat from British and Indian forces in the Northwest Territory, as well as from settlers in that region. The situation came to a head in summer and fall 1794. The Shawnee and allied tribes, emboldened by two victories over American armies, plotted with the British and talked of driving all settlers out of their territory. At the same time, frontier whites, sometimes with the encouragement of English and Spanish officials, grew increasingly contemptuous of a national government that could neither pacify the Indians nor guarantee their free use of the Mississippi River. President Washington heard that 2,000 Kentuckians were armed and ready to attack New Orleans—a move that would have started a war between the United States and Spain. Settlers in Georgia were making unauthorized forays against the Creeks. Worst of all, settlers up and down the frontier refused to pay the Federalists' excise tax on whiskey—a direct challenge to federal authority. In western Pennsylvania, mobs tarred and feathered excise officers and burned the property of distillers who paid the tax. In July 1794, near Pittsburgh, 500 militiamen marched on the house of General John Neville, one of the most hated of the federal excise collectors. Neville, his family, and a few federal soldiers fought the militiamen, killing two and wounding six before they abandoned the house to be looted and

MAP 8.1 THE WEST, 1790–1796

In 1790, the United States "owned" nearly all of its present territory east of the Mississippi River, but white Americans remained concentrated east of the Appalachians (see the map on population density, p. 242), and independent Indian peoples controlled most of the map of the United States. The Battle of Fallen Timbers and the resultant Treaty of Greenville pushed white settlement across Ohio and into Indiana, but the Indians of the Norwest remained intact, determined, and in touch with the British in Canada. Native Americans also controlled nearly all of the Southwest, and Florida and the Gulf Coast—including all outlets from the interior to the Caribbean—remained in Spanish hands. The American west was very far from secure in the 1790s.

burned. Two weeks later, 6,000 "Whiskey Rebels" met at Braddock's Field near Pittsburgh, threatening to attack the town.

Faced with serious international and domestic threats to his new government, Washington determined to defeat the Indians and the Whiskey Rebels by force, thus securing American control of the Northwest. He sent General "Mad"

Anthony Wayne against the northwestern tribes. Wayne's decisive victory at Fallen Timbers in August 1794—fought almost in the shadow of a British fort—ended the Indian-British challenge in the Northwest for many years (see chapter 7).

In September, Washington ordered 12,000 federalized militiamen from eastern Pennsylvania, Maryland, Virginia,

minister and refused to carry on relations with the United States until it addressed French grievances.

The French ordered that American ships carrying "so much as a handkerchief" made in England be confiscated without compensation and announced that American seamen serving in the British navy would be summarily hanged if captured.

President Adams wanted to protect American commerce from French depredations, but he knew that the United States might not survive a war with France. He also knew that French grievances (including Jay's Treaty and the abrogation of the French-American treaties of 1778) were legitimate. He decided to send a mission to France, made up of three respected statesmen: Charles Cotesworth Pinckney of South Carolina, John Marshall of Virginia, and Elbridge Gerry of Massachusetts. When these prestigious delegates reached Paris, however, they were left cooling their heels in the outer offices of the Directory—the revolutionary committee of five that had replaced France's beheaded king. At last, three French officials (the correspondence identified them only as "X, Y, and Z"—and the incident later became known as the XYZ affair) discreetly hinted that France would receive them if they paid a bribe of $250,000, arranged for the United States to loan $12 million to the French government, and apologized for unpleasant remarks that John Adams had made about France. The delegates refused, saying "No, not a sixpence," and returned home. There a journalist transformed their remark into "Millions for defense, but not one cent for tribute."

President Adams asked Congress to prepare for war, and the French responded by seizing more American ships. Thus began, in April 1798, an undeclared war between France and the United States in the Caribbean. While the French navy dealt with the British in the North Atlantic, French privateers inflicted costly blows on American shipping. After nearly a year of fighting, with the British providing powder and shot for American guns, the U.S. Navy chased the French privateers out of the Caribbean.

The Crisis at Home, 1798–1800

The troubles with France precipitated a crisis at home. Disclosure of the XYZ correspondence, together with the quasi-war in the Caribbean, produced a surge of public hostility toward the French and, to some extent, toward their Republican friends in the United States. Many Federalists, led by Alexander Hamilton, wanted to use the crisis to destroy their political opponents. Without consulting President Adams, the Federalist-dominated Congress passed several wartime measures. The first was a federal property tax—graduated, spread equally between sections of the country, and justified by military necessity—nonetheless a direct federal tax. Congress then passed four laws known as the Alien and Sedition Acts. The first three were directed at immigrants: They extended the naturalization period from 5 to 14 years and empowered the president to detain enemy aliens during wartime and to deport those he deemed dangerous to the United States. The fourth law—the Sedition Act—set jail terms and fines for persons who advocated disobedience to federal law or who wrote, printed, or spoke "false, scandalous, and malicious" statements against "the government of the United States, or the President of the United States [note that Vice President Jefferson was not included], with intent to defame . . . or to bring them or either of them, into contempt or disrepute."

President Adams never used the powers granted under the Alien Acts, but the Sedition Act resulted in the prosecution of 14 Republicans, most of them journalists. William Duane, editor of the *Philadelphia Aurora,* was indicted when he and two Irish friends circulated a petition against the Alien Act on the grounds of a Catholic church. James Callendar, editor of a Jeffersonian newspaper in Richmond, was arrested, while another prominent Republican went to jail for statements made in a private letter. Jedediah Peck, a former Federalist from upstate New York, was arrested when he petitioned Congress to repeal the Alien and Sedition Acts. Matthew Lyon, a scurrilous and uncouth Republican congressman from Vermont, had brawled with a Federalist representative in the House chamber; he went to jail for his criticisms of President Adams, Federalist militarism, and what he called the "ridiculous pomp" of the national administration.

Republicans, charging that the Alien and Sedition Acts violated the First Amendment, turned to the states for help. Southern states, which had provided only 4 of the 44 congressional votes for the Sedition Act, took the lead. Jefferson provided the Kentucky legislature with draft resolutions, and Madison did the same for the Virginia legislature. These so-called Virginia and Kentucky Resolves restated the constitutional fundamentalism that had guided Republican opposition to the Federalists through the 1790s. Jefferson's Kentucky Resolves reminded Congress that the Alien and Sedition Acts gave the national government powers not mentioned in the Constitution and that the 10th Amendment reserved such powers to the states. He also argued that the Constitution was a "compact" between sovereign states and that state legislatures could "nullify" federal laws they deemed unconstitutional, thus anticipating constitutional theories that states'-rights southerners would use after 1830.

The Virginia and Kentucky Resolves demonstrated the extremes to which Jefferson and Madison might go. Beyond that, however, they had few immediate effects. Opposition to the Sedition Act ranged from popular attempts to obstruct the law to fistfights in Congress, and Virginia began calling up its militia. No other states followed the lead of Virginia and Kentucky, however, and talk of armed opposition to Federalist policies was limited to a few areas in the South.

The Politicians and the Army

Federalists took another ominous step by implementing President Adams's request that Congress create a military prepared for war. Adams wanted a stronger navy, both because the undeclared war with France was being fought on the ocean and because he agreed with other Federalists that America's future as a commercial nation required a respectable navy. Hamilton and others (who were becoming known as "High Federalists") preferred a standing army. At the urging of Washington and against his own judgment, Adams had appointed Hamilton inspector general. As such, Hamilton would be the de facto commander of the U.S. Army. Congress authorized a 20,000-man army, and Hamilton proceeded to raise it. Congress also provided for a much larger army to be called up in the event of a declaration of war. When Hamilton expanded the officer corps in anticipation of such an army, he excluded Republicans and commissioned only his political friends. High Federalists wanted a standing army to enforce the Alien and Sedition Acts and to put down an impending rebellion in the South. Beyond that, there was little need for such a force. The war was being fought at sea, and most Americans believed that the citizen militia could hold off any land invasion until an army was raised. The Republicans, President Adams, and many other Federalists now became convinced that Hamilton and his High Federalists were determined to destroy their political opponents, enter into an alliance with Great Britain, and impose Hamilton's statist designs on the nation by force. By 1799, Adams and many of his Federalist friends had come to see Hamilton and his supporters as dangerous, antirepublican militarists.

Adams was both fearful and angry. First the Hamiltonians had tried to rob him of the presidency, then they had passed the Alien and Sedition Acts, the direct tax, and plans for a standing army without consulting him. None of this would have been possible if not for the crisis with France.

Adams, who had resisted calls for a declaration of war, began looking for ways to declare peace. In a move that he knew would split his party and probably cost him reelection in 1800, he opened negotiations with France and stalled the creation of Hamilton's army while the talks took place. At first the Senate refused to send an envoy to France. The senators relented when Adams threatened to resign and leave the presidency to Vice President Jefferson. In the agreement that followed, the French canceled the obligations that the United States had assumed under the treaties of 1778. But they refused to pay reparations for attacks on American shipping since 1793—the very point over which many Federalists had wanted to declare war. Peace with France cut the ground from under the more militaristic and repressive Federalists and intensified discord among the Federalists in general. (Hamilton would campaign against Adams in 1800.) It also damaged Adams's chances for reelection.

The Election of 1800

Thomas Jefferson and his Democratic Republicans approached the election of 1800 better organized and more determined than they had been four years earlier. Moreover, events in the months preceding the election worked in their favor. The Alien and Sedition Acts, the direct tax of 1798, and the Federalist military buildup were never popular. The army suppressed a minor tax rebellion led by Jacob Fries in Pennsylvania; prosecutions under the Sedition Act revealed its partisan origins; and the Federalists showed no sign of repealing the tax or abandoning the Alien and Sedition Acts and the new military even when peace seemed certain. Taken together, these events gave credence to the Republicans' allegation that the Federalists were using the crisis with France to increase their power, destroy their opposition, and overthrow the American republic. The Federalists' actions, charged the Republicans, were expensive, repressive, unwise, and unconstitutional; they also constituted the classic means by which despots destroyed liberty. The Federalists countered by warning that the election of Jefferson and his radical allies would release the worst horrors of the French Revolution onto the streets of American towns. Each side believed that its defeat in the election would mean the end of the republic.

The Democratic Republicans were strong in the South and weak in the Northeast; North Carolina was the one southern state in which Adams had significant support. Jefferson knew that in order to achieve a majority in the electoral college, he had to win New York, the state that had cost him the 1796 election. Jefferson's running mate, Aaron Burr, arranged a truce in New York between Republican factions led by the Clinton and Livingston families and chose candidates for the state legislature who were likely to win. In New York City, Burr played skillfully

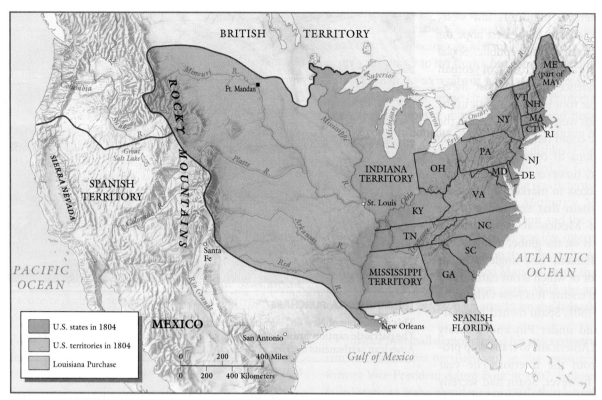

MAP 8.3 LOUISIANA PURCHASE

Jefferson's Louisiana Purchase nearly doubled the geographic size of the United States. It ended European competition for control of the North American interior and granted the United States the mouth of the Mississippi River, thus strengthening white settlements between the Appalachians and the Mississippi and increasing American control over those settlements.

with it. Jefferson was more certain than ever that the republic could preserve itself through peaceful expansion. The "wise and frugal" government he had promised in 1801 was becoming a reality.

The combination of international peace, territorial expansion, and inexpensive, unobtrusive government left the Federalists without an issue in the 1804 election. They went through the motions of nominating Charles Pinckney of South Carolina as their presidential candidate and then watched Jefferson capture the electoral votes of every state but Delaware and Connecticut. As he began his second term in 1805, Jefferson could assume that he had ended the Federalist threat to the republic.

The Republic and the Napoleonic Wars, 1804–1815

In spring 1803, a few weeks after closing the deal for Louisiana, Napoleon Bonaparte declared war on Great Britain. This 11-year war, like the wars of the 1790s, domi-

nated the national politics of the United States. Most Americans wanted to remain neutral. Few Republicans supported Bonaparte as they had supported the French revolutionaries of 1789, and none but the most rabid Federalists wanted to intervene on the side of Great Britain, but neither France nor Britain would permit American neutrality.

The Dilemmas of Neutrality

At the beginning, both Britain and France, whose rural economies were disrupted by war, encouraged the Americans to resume their role as neutral carriers and suppliers of food. For a time, Americans made huge profits. Between 1803 and 1807, U.S. exports—mostly foodstuffs and plantation staples—rose from $66.5 million to $102.2 million. Reexports—goods produced in the British, Spanish, and French islands of the Caribbean, picked up by American vessels, and then reloaded in American ports onto American ships bound for Europe—rose even faster, from $13.5 million to $58.4 million.

In 1805, France and Great Britain began systematically to interfere with that trade. Also in 1805, the Royal Navy under Lord Nelson destroyed the French and Spanish fleets at the Battle of Trafalgar. Later that year, Napoleon's armies won a decisive victory over Austria and Russia at the Battle of Austerlitz and won effective control of Europe. The war reached a stalemate: Napoleon's army occupied Europe, and the British navy controlled the seas.

Britain decided to use its naval supremacy to blockade Europe and starve the French into submission. In the Essex Decision of 1805, the British ministry dusted off what was known as the Rule of 1756, which stated that a European country could not use a neutral merchant marine to conduct wartime trade with its colonies if its mercantile laws forbade such use during peacetime. Translated into the realities of 1805, the Essex Decision meant that the Royal Navy could seize American ships engaged in the reexport trade with France. In spring 1806, Congress, angered by British seizures of American ships, passed the Non-Importation Act forbidding the importation of British goods that could be bought elsewhere or that could be manufactured in the United States. A month after that, Britain blockaded long stretches of the European coast. Napoleon responded with the Berlin Decree, which outlawed all trade with the British Isles. The British answered with an Order in Council that demanded that neutral ships trading with Europe stop first for inspection and licensing in a British port. Napoleon responded with the Milan Decree, which stated that any vessel that obeyed the British decrees or allowed itself to be searched by the Royal Navy was subject to seizure by France. Beginning in 1805 and ending with the Milan Decree in December 1807, the barrage of European decrees and counterdecrees meant that virtually all American commerce with Europe had been outlawed by one or the other of the warring powers.

Trouble on the High Seas

Given British naval supremacy, French decrees were effective only against American ships that entered ports controlled by France. The Royal Navy, on the other hand, maintained a loose blockade of the North American coast and stopped and searched American ships as they left the major seaports. Hundreds of ships were seized, along with their cargoes and crews. Under British law, the Royal Navy could impress any British subject into service during wartime. The British were certain that many British subjects, including legions of deserters from the Royal Navy, were hiding in the American merchant marine, and they were right. The danger, low pay, bad food, and draconian discipline on British warships encouraged many British sailors to jump ship and take jobs as American merchantmen.

Many of the British warships that stopped American merchant ships on the high seas were undermanned; the sailors their officers commandeered often included Englishmen who had taken out U.S. citizenship (an act the British did not recognize) and, inevitably, native-born Americans. An estimated 6,000 American citizens were impressed into the Royal Navy between 1803 and 1812.

The kidnapping of American sailors, even more than maritime seizures of American property and other violations of American neutral rights, enraged the citizens of the United States and brought the country close to war in summer 1807. In June, the American naval frigate Chesapeake, which was outfitting in Norfolk, Virginia, signed on four English deserters from the British navy, along with some Americans who had joined the British navy and then deserted. The British warship H.M.S. Leopard was also docked at Norfolk, and some of the deserters spotted their old officers and taunted them on the streets. The Leopard left port and resumed its patrol of the American coast. Then, on June 21, its officers caught the Chesapeake off Hampton Roads and demanded the return of the British deserters. When the captain refused, the British fired on the Chesapeake, killing 3 Americans and wounding 18. The British then boarded the Chesapeake, seized the four deserters, and later hanged one of them. The Chesapeake limped back into port.

The Chesapeake affair set off huge anti-British demonstrations in the seaport towns and angry cries for war throughout the country. President Jefferson responded by barring British ships from American ports and American territorial waters and by ordering state governors to prepare to call up as many as 100,000 militiamen. The United States in 1807 stood at the brink of full-scale war with the most powerful nation in the world.

Embargo

Jefferson wanted to avoid war, which would inevitably bring high taxes, government debt, a bloated military and civil service, and the repression of dissent—precisely the evils that Jefferson had vowed to eliminate. Worse, war carried the danger of defeat and thus the possible failure of America's republican experiment.

Jefferson had one more card to play: He could suspend trade with Europe altogether and thus keep American ships out of harm's way. For many years, Jefferson had assumed that U.S. farm products and the U.S. market for imported goods had become crucial to the European economies. He could use trade as a means of "peaceable coercion" that would both ensure respect for American neutral rights and keep the country out of war. "Our commerce," he wrote just before taking office, "is so valuable to

the damage had been done: The British and their Indian allies occupied many of the remaining American garrisons in the Northwest and transformed the U.S. invasion of Upper Canada into a British occupation of much of the Northwest.

The invasion of Canada from the east went no better. In October a U.S. force of 6,000 faced 2,000 British and Indians across the Niagara River separating Ontario from western New York. The U.S. regular army crossed the river, surprised the British, and established a toehold at Queenston Heights. While the British were preparing a counterattack, New York militiamen refused to cross the river to reinforce the regular troops. Ohio militiamen had behaved the same way when Hull invaded Canada, and similar problems had arisen with the New York militia near Lake Champlain. Throughout the war, citizen-soldiers proved that Jefferson's confidence in the militia could not be extended to the invasion of other countries. The British regrouped and slaughtered the outnumbered, exhausted U.S. regulars at Queenston Heights.

As winter set in, it was clear that Canada would not fall as easily as the Americans had assumed. The invasion, which U.S. commanders had thought would knife through an apathetic Canadian population, had the opposite effect: The attacks by the United States turned the ragtag assortment of American loyalist émigrés, discharged British soldiers, and American-born settlers into a self-consciously British Canadian people. Years later, an Englishwoman touring Niagara Falls asked a Canadian ferryman if it was true that Canadians had thrown Americans off Queenston Heights to their death on the rocky banks of the Niagara River. "Why yes," he replied, "there was a good many of them; but it was right to show them that there was water between us, and you know it might help to keep the rest of them from coming to trouble us on our own ground."

Tecumseh's Last Stand

Tecumseh's Indian confederacy, bruised but not broken in the Battle of Tippecanoe (see chapter 7), allied itself with the British in 1812. On a trip to the southern tribes, Tecumseh found the traditionalist wing of the Creeks—led by prophets who called themselves Red Sticks—willing to join him. The augmented confederacy provided stiff resistance to the United States throughout the war. The Red Sticks chased settlers from much of Tennessee. They then attacked a group of settlers who had taken refuge in a stockade surrounding the house of an Alabama trader named George Mims. In what whites called the Massacre at Fort Mims, the Red Sticks (reputedly with the collusion of black slaves within the fort) killed at least 247 men, women, and children. In the Northwest, Tecumseh's warriors, fighting alongside the British, spread terror throughout the white settlements.

A wiser U.S. army returned to Canada in 1813. They raided and burned the Canadian capital at York (Toronto) in April, and then fought inconclusively throughout the summer. An autumn offensive toward Montreal failed, but the Americans had better luck on Lake Erie. The barrier of Niagara Falls kept Britain's saltwater navy out of the upper Great Lakes, and on Lake Erie the British and Americans engaged in a frenzied shipbuilding contest throughout the first year of the war. The Americans won. In September 1813, Commodore Oliver Hazard Perry cornered

BATTLE OF THE THAMES

The Battle of the Thames relieved the Northwest of the British and Indian threat. It became most memorable to Americans, however, as the battle in which Tecumseh was finally killed.

From the Collections of the Library of Congress.

and destroyed the British fleet at Put-in-Bay. Control of Lake Erie enabled the United States to cut off supplies to the British in the Northwest, and a U.S. army under William Henry Harrison retook the area and continued on into Canada. On October 5, Harrison caught up with a force of British and Indians at the Thames River and beat them badly. In the course of that battle, Richard M. Johnson, a War Hawk congressman acting as commander of the Kentucky militia, killed Tecumseh. Proud militiamen returned to Kentucky with pieces of hair and clothing and even swatches of skin torn from Tecumseh's corpse. Their officers reaped huge political rewards: The Battle of the Thames would eventually produce a president of the United States (Harrison), a vice president (Johnson), 3 governors of Kentucky, 3 lieutenant governors, 4 U.S. senators, and about 20 congressmen—telling evidence of how seriously the settlers of the interior had taken Tecumseh.

The following spring, General Andrew Jackson's Tennessee militia, aided by Choctaw, Creek, and Cherokee allies, attacked and slaughtered the Red Sticks, who had fortified themselves at Horseshoe Bend in Alabama. With the Battle of the Thames and the Battle of Horse Shoe Bend, the military power of the Indian peoples east of the Mississippi River was broken.

The British Offensive, 1814

The British defeated Napoleon in April 1814, thus ending the larger war from which the War of 1812 erupted. With both sides thinking about peace, the British decided to concentrate their resources on the American war and in 1814 went on the offensive. The British had already blockaded much of the American coast and had shut down ports from Georgia to Maine. During summer 1814, they began to raid the shores of Chesapeake Bay and marched on Washington, D.C. As retribution for the torching of the Canadian capital at York, they chased the army and politicians out of town and burned down the capitol building and the president's mansion. In September the British attacked the much larger city of Baltimore, but they could not blast their way past the determined garrison that commanded the harbor from Fort McHenry. This was the battle that inspired Francis Scott Key to write "The Star-Spangled Banner,"

a doggerel poem that was later set to music and chosen as the national anthem in the 1930s. When a British offensive on Lake Champlain stalled during the autumn, the war reached a stalemate: Britain had prevented the invasion of Canada and had blockaded the American coast, but neither side could take and hold the other's territory.

The British now shifted their attention to the Gulf Coast, particularly to New Orleans, a city of vital importance to U.S. trans-Appalachian trade and communications. Peace negotiations had begun in August, and the British wanted to capture and hold New Orleans as a bargaining chip. A large British amphibious force landed and camped eight miles south of New Orleans. There they met an American army made up of U.S. regulars, Kentucky and Tennessee militiamen, clerks, workingmen, free blacks from the city, and about a thousand French pirates—all under the command of Andrew Jackson of Tennessee. Throughout late December and early January, unaware that a peace treaty had been signed on December 24, the armies exchanged artillery barrages and the British probed and attacked American lines. On January 8, the British launched a frontal assault. A formation of 6,000 British soldiers marched across open ground toward 4,000 Americans concealed behind breastworks. With the first American volley, it was clear that the British had made a

Allyn Cox, 19741 Architect of the Capitol.

THE BURNING OF THE CAPITOL

The United States suffered one of its greatest military embarrassments ever when British troops burned the Capitol in 1814. This 1974 painting is on an archway in the present-day Capitol building.

CHAPTER FOCUS

♦ What was the nationalizing dream of the American System, and how did improvements in transportation actually channel commerce within and between regions?

♦ How did northern farm families experience the transition into commercial agriculture between 1815 and 1850?

♦ What was the relationship between urban industrial growth and the commercialization of the northern countryside?

♦ What were the nature and limits of the Market Revolution in the South? Why?

CHRONOLOGY

1790 Samuel Slater builds his first Arkwright spinning mill at Pawtucket, Rhode Island

1801 John Marshall appointed chief justice of the Supreme Court

1807 Robert Fulton launches first steamboat

1813 Boston Associates erect their first textile mill at Waltham, Massachusetts

1815 War of 1812 ends

1816 Congress charters Second Bank of the United States • Congress passes protective tariff • *Dartmouth College* v. *Woodward* defines a private charter as a contract that cannot be altered by a state legislature • *McCulloch* v. *Maryland* affirms Congress's "implied powers" under the Constitution

1818 National Road completed to Ohio River at Wheeling, Virginia

1822 President Monroe vetoes National Road reparations bill

1824 *Gibbons* v. *Ogden* extends power of national government

1825 New York completes the Erie Canal between Buffalo and Albany

1828 Baltimore and Ohio Railroad (America's first) completed

1835 Main Line Canal connects Philadelphia and Pittsburgh

Government and Markets

The 14th Congress met in the last days of 1815. Made up overwhelmingly of Jeffersonian Republicans, this Congress nevertheless would reverse many of the positions taken by Jefferson's old party. It would charter a national bank, enact a protective tariff, and debate whether to build a national system of roads and canals at federal expense. As late as 1811, the Republicans viewed such programs as heresy, but by 1815, the Republican majority in Congress had come to accept it as orthodox. The War of 1812 had demonstrated that the United States was unable to coordinate a fiscal and military effort. It had also convinced many Republicans that reliance on foreign trade rendered the United States dependent on Europe. The nation, they said, must abandon Jefferson's export-oriented agrarianism and encourage national independence through subsidies to commerce and manufactures.

The American System: The Bank of the United States

Nationalist Henry Clay retained his power in the postwar Congress and headed the drive for a neo-Federalist program of protective tariffs, internal improvements, and a national bank. He called his program the American System, arguing that it would foster national economic growth and a salutary interdependence between geographical sections, thus a happy and healthy republic.

In 1816, Congress chartered a Second Bank of the United States, headquartered in Philadelphia and empowered to establish branches wherever it saw fit. The government agreed to deposit its funds in the Bank, to accept the Bank's notes as payment for government land, taxes, and other transactions, and to buy one-fifth of the Bank's stock. The Bank of the United States was more powerful than the one a Republican Congress had rejected as unconstitutional in 1811. The fiscal horrors of the War of 1812, however, had left most representatives in favor of moving toward a national currency and centralized control of money and credit. The alternative was to allow state banks—which had increased in number from 88 to 208 between 1813 and 1815—to issue unregulated and grossly inflated notes that might throw the anticipated postwar boom into chaos.

With no discussion of the constitutionality of what it was doing, Congress chartered the Bank of the United States as the sole banking institution empowered to do business throughout the country. Notes issued by the Bank would be the first semblance of a national currency (they would soon constitute from one-tenth to one-third of the value of notes in circulation). Moreover, the Bank could regulate the currency by demanding that state bank-notes used in transactions with the federal government be redeemable in gold. In 1816, the Bank set up shop in Philadelphia's Carpenter's Hall, and, in 1824, moved around the corner to a Greek Revival edifice modeled after the Parthenon—a marble embodiment of the conservatism

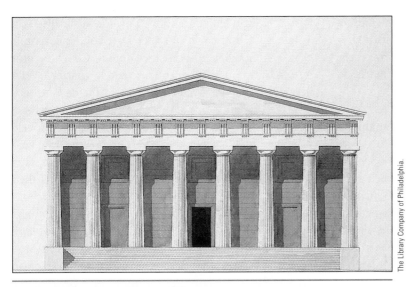

THE BANK OF THE UNITED STATES
The classical Greek façade of the Bank of the United States reinforced its image as a conservative, centralizing—but still republican—financial force.

that directors of the Bank of the United States adopted as their fiscal stance. From that vantage point they would fight a running battle with state banks and local interests in an effort to impose direction on the transition to a market society.

The American System: Tariffs and Internal Improvements

In 1816, Congress drew up the first overtly protective tariff in U.S. history. Shepherded through the House by Clay and his fellow nationalist Calhoun, the Tariff of 1816 raised tariffs an average of 25 percent, extending protection to the nation's infant industries at the expense of foreign trade and American consumers. Again, wartime difficulties had paved the way: Because Americans could not depend on imported manufactures, Congress considered the encouragement of domestic manufactures a patriotic necessity. The tariff had strong support in the Northeast and the West and enough southern support to ensure its passage by Congress. Tariffs would rise and fall between 1816 and the Civil War, but the principle of protectionism would persist.

Bills to provide federal money for roads, canals, and other "internal improvements" had a harder time winning approval. The British wartime blockade had hampered coastal shipping and had made Americans dependent on the wretched roads of the interior. Many members of the 14th Congress, after spending days of bruising travel on their way to Washington, were determined to give the United States an efficient transportation network. Consensus was hard to reach. Some urged completion of the National Road linking the Chesapeake with the trans-Appalachian West. Some talked of an inland canal system to link the northern and southern coastal states. Others wanted a federally subsidized turnpike from Maine to Georgia.

Internal improvements, however, were subject to local ambitions and were of doubtful constitutionality as well. Congress agreed to complete the National Road, but President Madison and his Republican successor James Monroe both refused to support further internal improvements without a constitutional amendment. In 1822, Monroe even vetoed a bill authorizing repairs on the National Road, stating once again that the Constitution did not empower the federal government to build roads within the sovereign states.

With a national government squeamish about internal improvements, state governments took up the cause. The resulting transportation network after 1815 reflected the designs of the most ambitious states rather than the nationalizing dreams of men such as Henry Clay. New York's Erie Canal was the most spectacular accomplishment, but the canal systems of Pennsylvania and Ohio were almost as impressive. Before 1830, most toll roads were built and owned by corporations chartered by state governments, with the governments providing $5 million of the $30 million that it cost to build the roads. State expenditures on canals and railroads were even greater. Fully $41.2 million of the $58.6 million spent on the canals before 1834 came from state governments, as did more than one-third of the $137 million spend on railroads before 1843. Much of the rest came from foreign investors. Private entrepreneurs could not have built the transportation network that produced the market economy without the active support of state governments. States provided direct funding, bond issues, and corporate charters that gave the turnpike, canal, and railroad companies the privileges and immunities that made them attractive to private investors.

Markets and the Law

The Revolution replaced British courts with national and state legal systems based in English common law—systems that made legal action accessible to most white males. Thus many of the disputes generated in the transition to a market society ended up in court. The courts removed social conflicts from the public arena and brought them into a peaceful courtroom. There they dealt with the

conflicts in language that only lawyers understood and resolved them in ways that tended to promote the entrepreneurial use of private property, the sanctity of contracts, and the right to do business shielded from neighborhood restraints and the tumult of democratic politics.

John Marshall, who presided over the Supreme Court from 1801 to 1835, took the lead. From the beginning, he saw the Court as a conservative hedge against the excesses of democratically elected legislatures. His early decisions protected the independence of the courts and their right to review legislation (see chapter 8). From 1816 onward, his decisions encouraged business and strengthened the national government at the expense of the states. Marshall's most important decisions protected the sanctity of contracts and corporate charters against state legislatures. For example, in *Dartmouth College* v. *Woodward* (1816), Dartmouth was defending a royal charter granted in the 1760s against changes introduced by a Republican legislature determined to transform Dartmouth from a privileged bastion of Federalism into a state college. Daniel Webster, who was both a Dartmouth alumnus and the school's highly paid lawyer, finished his argument before the Supreme Court on an emotional note: "It is, sir, as I have said, a small college. And yet there are those who love it—." Reputedly moved to tears, Marshall ruled that a state legislature could not alter Dartmouth's corporate charter. Although in this case the Supreme Court was protecting Dartmouth's independence and its chartered privileges, Marshall and Webster knew that the decision also protected the hundreds of turnpike and canal companies, manufacturing corporations, and other ventures that held privileges under corporate charters granted by state governments. Once the charters had been granted, the states could neither regulate the corporations nor cancel their privileges. Thus corporate charters acquired the legal status of contracts, beyond the reach of democratic politics.

Two weeks after the *Dartmouth* decision, Marshall handed down the majority opinion in *McCulloch* v. *Maryland*. The Maryland legislature, nurturing old Jeffersonian doubts about the constitutionality of the Bank of the United States, had attempted to tax the Bank's Baltimore branch, and the Bank had challenged the legislature's right to do so. Marshall decided in favor of the Bank. He stated, first, that the Constitution granted the federal government "implied powers" that included chartering the Bank, and he denied Maryland's right to tax the Bank or any other federal agency: "The power to tax," he said, "involves the power to destroy." It was Marshall's most explicit blow

---

LINK TO THE PAST

Charles Brockden Brown's American System

In 1809, Charles Brockden Brown, America's first professional literary man and a dedicated Jeffersonian, urged Congress to help create a national market society. The old Jeffersonian combination of agriculture and foreign trade, he said, kept Americans dependent on Europe and drew them into wars. As an alternative, he proposed a vision of national wealth and self-sufficiency:

W*hen we think on our helpless dependence, for the comforts and decencies of life, upon nations three thousand miles off, we may, without a crime, be disposed to wish that all intercourse of this kind, were at an end; that we should sit, quiet spectators of the storms that shake the rest of the world—employing all our vigor in building up an empire here in the West; and in cementing the members of our vast and growing nation, into one body.*

There is something charming too in the picture of a world within ourselves. . . . We should go on multiplying persons and towns and cottages faster; and thus become much greater and more wealthy, if all our surplus products were consumed by mouths at home, and not abroad. If the millions who now weave and sow and hammer and file for us, were members of our own body, swelling by their gains and their experiences, the tide of circulation in our own community.

1. Here, in the words of a northern Jeffersonian, were the seeds of the American System. As of 1809, what were the motives for proposing that system?
2. How did arguments for that system grow and change over succeeding years? For clues, link to the works of Henry Clay (1810), Henry Niles (1823), Edward Everett (1830), and Daniel Webster (1836).

For additional sources related to this feature, visit the *Liberty, Equality, Power* Web site at:

http://history.wadsworth.com/murrin_LEP4e

against Jeffersonian strict constructionism. Americans, he said, "did not design to make their government dependent on the states." And yet many, particularly in Marshall's native South, remained certain that that was precisely what the founders had intended.

In *Gibbons* v. *Ogden* (1824) the Marshall Court broke a state-granted steamship monopoly in New York. The monopoly, Marshall argued, interfered with federal jurisdiction over interstate commerce. Like *Dartmouth College* v. *Woodward* and *McCulloch* v. *Maryland,* this decision empowered the national government in relation to the states. And like them, it encouraged private entrepreneurialism. Agreeing with congressmen who supported the American System, John Marshall's Supreme Court assumed that a natural and beneficial link existed between federal power and market society.

Meanwhile, the state courts were working quieter but equally profound transformations of American law. In the early republic, state courts had often viewed property not only as a private possession but as part of a neighborhood. Thus when a miller built a dam that flooded upriver farms or impaired the fishery, the courts might make him take those interests into account, often in ways that reduced the business uses of his property. By the 1830s, New England courts were routinely granting the owners of industrial mill sites unrestricted water rights, even when the exercise of those rights inflicted damage on their neighbors. As early as 1805, the New York Supreme Court in *Palmer* v. *Mulligan* had asserted that the right to develop property for business purposes was inherent in the ownership of property. A Kentucky court, asked to decide whether a railroad could come into downtown Louisville despite the protests of residents over the noise and the showers of sparks, decided that the public need for transportation outweighed the danger and annoyance to nearby residents. Railroads were necessary, and "private injury and personal damage . . . must be expected." "The onward spirit of the age," concluded the Kentucky court, "must, to a reasonable extent, have its way." In the courts of northern and western states, that "onward spirit" demanded legal protection for the business uses of private property, even when such uses conflicted with old common law restraints.

The Transportation Revolution

After 1815, dramatic improvements in transportation—more and better roads, steamboats, canals, and finally railroads—tied old communities together and penetrated previously isolated neighborhoods. These improvements made the transition to a market society physically possible.

Transportation in 1815

In 1815, the United States was a rural nation stretching from the old settlements on the Atlantic coast to the trans-Appalachian frontier, with transportation facilities that ranged from primitive to nonexistent. Americans despaired of communicating, to say nothing of doing business on a national scale. In 1816, a Senate committee reported that $9 would move a ton of goods across the 3,000-mile expanse of the North Atlantic from Britain to the United States; the same $9 would move the same ton of goods only 30 miles inland. A year later, the cost of transporting wheat from the new settlement of Buffalo to New York City was three times greater than the selling price of wheat in New York. Farming for profit made sense only for farmers near urban markets or with easy river access to the coast.

West of the Appalachians, transportation was almost entirely undeveloped. Until about 1830, most westerners were southern yeomen who settled near tributaries of the Ohio-Mississippi River system—a network of navigable streams that reached the sea at New Orleans. Frontier farmers floated their produce downriver on jerry-built flatboats; at New Orleans it was trans-shipped to New York and other eastern ports. Most boatmen knocked down their flatboats, sold the lumber, and walked home to Kentucky or Ohio over the dangerous path known as the Natchez Trace.

Transporting goods to the western settlements was even more difficult. Keelboatmen such as the legendary Mike Fink could navigate upstream, using eddies and back currents, sailing when the wind was right, but usually poling their boat against the current. Skilled crews averaged only 15 miles per day, and the trip from New Orleans to Louisville took three to four months. (The downstream trip took a month.) Looking for better routes, some merchants dragged finished goods across Pennsylvania and into the West at Pittsburgh, but transport costs made these goods prohibitively expensive. Consequently, the trans-Appalachian settlements—home to one in five Americans by 1820—remained marginal to the market economy. By 1815, New Orleans was shipping about $5 million of western produce annually—an average of only $15 per farm family in the interior.

Improvements: Roads and Rivers

In 1816, Congress resumed construction of the National Road (first authorized in 1802) that linked the Potomac River with the Ohio River at Wheeling, Virginia. The smooth, crushed-rock thoroughfare reached Wheeling in 1818. At about the same time, Pennsylvania extended the

A RIVER STEAMBOAT IN 1826

By the mid-1820s, steamboats regularly plied the river systems of the United States. Businessmen and elite travelers rented nicely appointed cabins on the steamer and viewed the scenery as they strolled the comfortable (and usually uncrowded) passenger deck. Poorer passengers bought passage on the "Safety Barge" that was dragged behind the steamer.

Thomas L. McKenney, Sketches of a Tour to the Lakes (1827).

Lancaster Turnpike to make it run from Philadelphia to the Ohio River at Pittsburgh. These ambitious roads into the West, however, had few effects. The National Road made it easier for settlers and a few merchants' wagons to reach the West, but the cost of moving bulky farm produce over the road remained high. Eastbound traffic on the National Road consisted largely of cattle and pigs, which carried themselves to market. Farmers continued to float their corn, cotton, wheat, salt pork, and whiskey south by riverboat and thence to eastern markets.

The steamboat opened the West to commercial agriculture. Tinkerers and mechanics had been experimenting with steam-powered boats for a generation or more when an entrepreneur named Robert Fulton launched the *Clermont* on an upriver trip from New York City to Albany in 1807. Over the next few years, Americans developed flat-bottomed steamboats that could navigate rivers even at low water. The first steamboat reached Louisville from New Orleans in 1815. Two years later, with 17 steamboats already working western rivers, the *Washington* made the New Orleans–Louisville run in 25 days, a feat that convinced westerners that two-way river trade was possible. By 1820, 69 steamboats were operating on western rivers. The 60,000 tons of produce that farmers and planters had shipped out of the interior in 1810 grew to 500,000 tons in 1840. By the eve of the Civil War, two million tons of western produce—most of it southwestern cotton—reached the docks at New Orleans. The steamboat had transformed the interior from an isolated frontier into a busy commercial region that traded farm and plantation products for manufactured goods.

Improvements: Canals and Railroads

In the East, state governments created rivers where nature had made none. In 1817, Governor DeWitt Clinton talked the New York legislature into building a canal linking the Hudson River with Lake Erie, thus opening a continuous water route between the Northwest and New York City. The Erie Canal was a near-visionary feat of engineering: Designed by self-taught engineers and built by gangs of Irish immigrants, local farm boys, and convict laborers, it stretched 364 miles from Albany to Buffalo. Although "Clinton's Ditch" passed through carefully chosen level ground, it required a complex system of 83 locks, and it passed over 18 rivers on stone aqueducts. Construction began in 1819, and the canal reached Buffalo in 1825. It was clear even before then that the canal would repay New York state's investment of $7.5 million many times over, and that it would transform the territory it served.

The Erie Canal had its first and most powerful effects on western New York, which had been a raw frontier accessible to the East only over a notoriously bad state road. By 1830, the New York corridor of the Erie Canal, settled largely from hill-country New England, was one of the world's great grain-growing regions, dotted with market towns and new cities such as Syracuse, Rochester, and Buffalo.

The Erie Canal was an immense success, and legislators and entrepreneurs in other states joined a canal boom that lasted for 20 years. When construction began on the Erie Canal, there were fewer than 100 miles of canal in the

NEAR LOCKPORT ON THE ERIE CANAL

This engraving of the Deep Cut through hills near Lockport, New York, was commissioned for the official volume celebrating completion of the Erie Canal in 1825. It gives the canal a scale and an awesome beauty meant to rival and perhaps surpass the works of nature.

The Granger Collection.

United States. By 1840, there were 3,300 miles, nearly all of them in the Northeast and Northwest. Northwestern states, Ohio in particular, built ambitious canal systems that linked isolated areas to the Great Lakes and thus to the Erie Canal. Northeastern states followed suit: A canal between Worcester and Providence linked the farms of central Massachusetts with Narragansett Bay. Another canal linked the coal mines of northeastern Pennsylvania with the Hudson River at Kingston, New York. In 1835, Pennsylvania completed a canal from Philadelphia to Pittsburgh, although at one point goods were shifted onto an unwieldy railroad that crossed a mountain.

The first American railroads connected burgeoning cities to rivers and canals. The Baltimore and Ohio Railroad, for example, linked Baltimore to the rivers of the West. Although the approximately 3,000 miles of railroads built between the late 1820s and 1840 helped the market positions of some cities, they did not constitute a national or even a regional rail network. A national system developed with the 5,000 miles of track laid in the 1840s and with the flurry of railroad building that gave the United States a rail network of 30,000 miles by 1860—a continuous, integrated system that created massive links between the East and the Northwest and that threatened to put canals out of business. In fact, the New York Central, which paralleled the Erie Canal, rendered that canal obsolete. Other railroads, particularly in the northwestern states, replaced canal and river transport almost completely, even though water transport remained cheaper. By 1860, few farmers in the North and West lived more than 20 road miles from railroads, canals, or rivers that could deliver their produce to regional, national, and international markets.

Time and Money

The transportation revolution brought a dramatic reduction in the time and money it took to move heavy goods. Turnpikes cut the cost of wagon transport in half between 1816 and 1860—from 30 cents per ton-mile to 15 cents. In 1816, freight rates on the Ohio-Mississippi system had been 1.3 cents per ton-mile for downriver travel and 5.8 cents for upriver travel; steamboats cut both costs to a bit more than a third of a cent. The Erie Canal and the Ohio canals reduced the distance between East and West and carried goods at about a cent per ton-mile; the railroads of the 1850s carried freight much faster, although at two to three times the cost. And the longer the haul, the greater the per-mile savings: Overall, the cost of moving goods across long distances dropped 95 percent between 1815 and 1860.

Improvements in speed were nearly as dramatic. The overland route from Cincinnati to New York in 1815 (by keelboat upriver to Pittsburgh, then by wagon the rest of the way) had taken a minimum of 52 days. Steamboats traveled from Cincinnati to New Orleans, then passed goods on to coasting ships that finished the trip to New York City in a total of 28 days. By the 1840s, upriver steamboats carried goods to the terminus of the Main Line Canal at Pittsburgh, which delivered them to Philadelphia, which sent them by train to New York City for a total transit time of 18 to 20 days. At about the same time, the Ohio

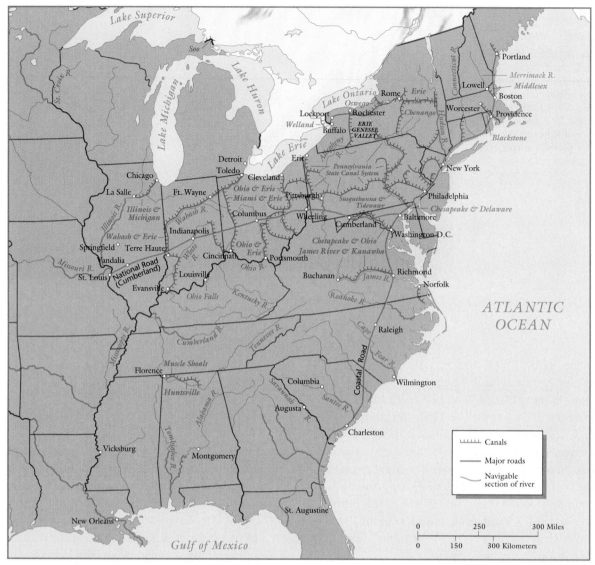

MAP 9.1 RIVERS, ROADS, AND CANALS, 1825–1860

In the second quarter of the 19th century, transportation projects linked the North and Northwest into an integrated economic and social system. There were fewer improvements in the South: farm produce traveled down navigable rivers from bottomland plantations to river and seaport towns, thence to New York for shipment overseas; southern legislatures and entrepreneurs saw little use for further improvements.

canal system enabled Cincinnati to send goods north through Ohio, across Lake Erie, over the Erie Canal, and down the Hudson to New York City—an all-water route that reduced costs and made the trip in 18 days. By 1852, the Erie Railroad and its connectors could make the Cincinnati–New York City run—although at a higher cost than water routes—in six to eight days. Similar improvements occurred in the densely settled and increasingly urbanized Northeast. By 1840, travel time between the big northeastern cities had been reduced to from one-fourth to one-eleventh of what it had been in 1790, with people, goods, and information traveling at an average of 15 miles

per hour. Such improvements in speed and economy made a national market economy possible.

By 1840, improved transportation had made a Market Revolution. Foreign trade, which had driven American economic growth up to 1815, continued to expand. In 1815, American exports totaled $52.6 million; imports totaled $113 million. Both rose dramatically in the years of the Market Revolution: Exports (now consisting more of southern cotton than of northern food crops) increased sixfold to $333.6 million by 1860; imports (mostly European manufactured goods) tripled to $353.6 million. Yet the increases in foreign trade represented vast reductions

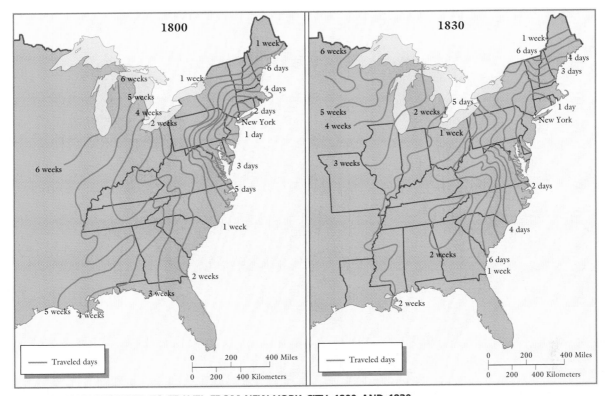

MAP 9.2   TIME REQUIRED TO TRAVEL FROM NEW YORK CITY, 1800 AND 1830
These maps illustrate the increasing ease of travel in the first third of the 19th century. In general, travelers could cover nearly twice as much territory in a day in 1830 than in 1800, although in both cases travel became more difficult as one left the densely settled east.

in the proportion of American market activity that involved other countries. Before 1815, Americans had exported about 15 percent of their total national product; by 1830, exports accounted for only 6 percent of total production. The reason for this shift was that after 1815, the United States developed self-sustaining domestic markets for farm produce and manufactured goods. The great engine of economic growth—particularly in the North and West—was not the old colonial relationship with Europe but a burgeoning internal market.

Markets and Regions

Henry Clay and other proponents of the American System dreamed of a market-driven economy that would transcend sectionalism and create a unified United States. Instead, until at least 1840, the Market Revolution produced greater results within regions than between them. The farmers of New England traded food for finished goods from Boston, Lynn, Lowell, and other towns in what was becoming an urban, industrial region. Philadelphia sold its manufactures to and bought its food from the farmers of the Delaware valley. Although the Erie Canal created a

huge potential for interregional trade, until 1839, most of its eastbound tonnage originated in western New York. In the West, market-oriented farmers fed such rapidly growing cities as Rochester, Cleveland, Chicago, and Cincinnati, which in turn supplied the farmers with locally manufactured farm tools, furniture, shoes, and other goods. Farther south, the few plantations that did not produce their own food bought surpluses from farmers in their own region. Thus until about 1840, the Market Revolution was more a regional than an interregional phenomenon.

In the 1840s and 1850s, however, the new transport networks turned the increasingly industrial Northeast and mid-Atlantic and the commercial farms of the Old Northwest into a unified market society. The earliest settlers in the Northwest were southerners who had carried on a limited trade through the river system that led to New Orleans. From the 1840s onward, produce left the Northwest less often by the old Ohio River route than by canal and railroad directly to the Northeast. Of the total produce exported from the Old Northwest in 1853, only 29 percent went by way of the river system, whereas 60 percent went by way of the Erie Canal alone. At the same time, canals and roads from New York, Philadelphia, and Baltimore

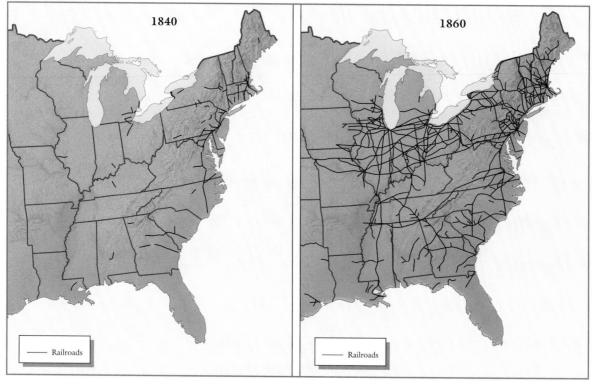

MAP 9.3   RAILROADS IN THE UNITED STATES, 1840 AND 1860

In these 20 years, both the North and South built railway systems. Northerners built rail lines that integrated the market economies of the Midwest and the East—both within sections and between them. For the most part, Southern railroads linked the plantation belt with the ocean. Revealingly, only a few lines connected the North and South.

became the favored passageways for commodities entering the West. As early as 1835, some 55 percent of the West's imported sugar, salt, iron, and coffee entered the region by the Great Lakes, Pennsylvania, or Wheeling routes. By 1853, that figure stood at 71 percent. In those years, the Ohio-Mississippi River system carried vastly increased amounts of goods, but that increase, particularly after 1840, added up to a shrinking share of the expanded total. In short, western farmers and northeastern businessmen and manufacturers were building a national market from which the South was largely excluded.

From Yeoman to Businessman: The Rural North and West

In the old communities of the Northeast, the Market Revolution sent some of the young people off to cities and factory towns and others to the West. Those who remained at home engaged in new forms of agriculture on a transformed rural landscape, while their cousins in the Northwest transformed a wilderness into cash-producing farms.

Shaping the Northern Landscape

An early 19th-century New England farm geared toward family subsistence required only 3 acres of cultivated land, 12 acres of pasture and meadow, another acre for the house, outbuildings, and vegetable garden, and a 30-acre woodlot to stoke the hearth that cooked the food and heated the house. Visitors to even the oldest towns found farmsteads, tilled fields, and pastures scattered across a heavily wooded landscape. In the 18th century, overcrowding had encouraged some farmers to turn woodlots into poor farmland. In the 19th century, however, millions of trees were stripped from the New England countryside and livestock raising replaced mixed farming. New Englanders who tried to grow grain on their rocky, worn-out soil could not compete with the farmers of western New York and the Old Northwest, who possessed fertile lands and ready access to markets. At the same time, however, the factories and cities of the Northeast provided Yankee farmers with a market for meat and other perishables. Beef became the great New England cash crop. Dairy products were not far behind, and the proximity to city markets encouraged the spread of poultry and egg farms, fruit orchards, and truck gardens. The burgeoning shoe indus-

try bought leather from the farmers, and woolen mills created a demand for wool. In 1840, Vermont held 5.75 times more sheep than people.

The rise of livestock specialization reduced the amount of land under cultivation. Early in the century, New Englanders still tilled their few acres in the old three-year rotation: corn the first year, rye the second, fallow the third. By the 1820s and 1830s, as farmers raised more livestock and less grain, the land that remained in cultivation was farmed more intensively. Farmers saved manure and ashes for fertilizer, plowed more deeply and systematically, and tended their crops more carefully. These improved techniques, along with cash from the sale of their livestock and the availability of food at stores, encouraged Yankee farmers to allocate less land to growing food crops. In Concord, Massachusetts—the hometown of the agrarian republic—the portion of town land in tillage dropped from 20 percent to 7 percent between 1771 and 1850.

The transition to livestock raising transformed woodlands into open pastures. As farmers leveled the forests, they sold the wood to fuel-hungry cities. In 1829, a cord of wood sold for $1.50 in Maine and for $7 in Boston. Over the next decade, manufacturers began marketing cast-iron stoves that heated houses less expensively and more efficiently than open hearths, and canals brought cheap Pennsylvania anthracite to the Northeast. Farmers who needed pastureland could gain substantial one-time profits from the sale of cut wood. The result was massive deforestation. In 1790, in the central Massachusetts town of Petersham, forest covered 85 percent of the town lands. By 1830, the creation of pastureland through commercial woodcutting had reduced the forested area to 30 percent. By 1850, woods covered only 10 percent of the town, the pasturelands were overgrazed and ruined, and the landscape was dotted with abandoned farms. The pattern was the same throughout New England. At the beginning of European settlement, 95 percent of the region had been covered by forest. By 1850, forest covered only 30 percent of Connecticut, 32 percent of Rhode Island, 40 percent of Massachusetts, 45 percent of Vermont, and 50 percent of New Hampshire.

The Transformation of Rural Outwork

On that denuded landscape, poor families with many children continued to supplement their income with industrial outwork (see chapter 7). But the quickening of market activity brought new kinds of dependence. Before the 1820s, outworkers had used local raw materials such as wool, leather, and flax and had spent only their spare time on such work. Merchants who bought their finished products often complained that outworkers kept their best work for themselves and for exchange with their neighbors. In the 1820s, the manufacture of shoes and textiles began to be concentrated in factories, and outworkers who remained were reduced to dependence. Merchants now provided them with raw materials with which to make such items as cloth-covered buttons and palm-leaf hats (imported materials that only merchants could supply), and set the pace of labor and the quality of the finished goods. In the 1830s, fully 33,000 New England women were fashioning palm-leaf hats in their homes, far more than the 20,000 who worked in New England's much-publicized cotton mills. Although outwork still helped poor families to maintain their independence, control of their labor had passed to merchants and other agents of the regional economy.

Farmers as Consumers

With the shift to specialized market agriculture, New England farmers became customers for necessities that their forebears had produced themselves or had acquired through barter. They heated their houses with coal dug by Pennsylvania miners. They wore cotton cloth made by the factory women at Lowell. New Hampshire farm girls made straw hats for them, and the craftsmen of Lynn made their shoes. By 1830 or so, many farmers were even buying food. The Erie Canal and the western grain belt sent flour from Rochester into eastern neighborhoods where grain no longer grew. Many farmers found it easier to produce specialized crops for market, and to buy flour, butter, cheese, eggs, and vegetables at country stores—some of it from distant places, some of it produced by farm women in their own neighborhoods.

The turning point came in the 1820s. The storekeepers of Northampton, Massachusetts, for instance, had been increasing their stock in trade by about 7 percent per decade since the late 18th century. In the 1820s, they increased it 45 percent and now carried not only local farm products and sugar, salt, and coffee, but also bolts of New England cloth, sacks of western flour, a variety of necessities and little luxuries from the wholesale houses of New York City and Boston, and pattern samples from which to order silverware, dishes, wallpaper, and other household goods. Those goods were better than what could be made at home and were for the most part cheaper. The price of finished cloth, for instance, declined sixfold between 1815 and 1830; as a result, spinning wheels and handlooms disappeared from the farmhouses of New England. Farm families preferred pies and bread made from western white flour to the old "Rye and Injun" (see chapter 7), and gladly turned their woodlands and unproductive grain

Old Sturbridge Village. Photo by: Thomas Neill, #25.K74f.1994.2.1.

A NEW ENGLAND COUNTRY STORE

An 1830s Massachusetts country store was a community gathering place, a market for farm produce, and the source of a growing variety of commodities from the outside world.

fields into cash-producing pastures. Coal and cast-iron stoves replaced the family hearth. These consumer goods passed increased authority over the interior of rural households to women.

Material standards of living rose, but more families felt poor, and many more were incapable of feeding, clothing, and warming themselves in years when the market failed. By the 1820s and 1830s, northeastern farmers depended on markets in ways that their fathers and grandfathers would have considered dangerous not only to family welfare but also to the welfare of the republic.

The Northwest: Southern Migrants

One reason the Market Revolution in the Northeast went as smoothly as it did was that young people with little hope of inheriting land in the old settlements moved away to towns and cities or to the new farmlands of the Northwest. Between 1815 and 1840—precisely the years in which northeastern agriculture became a cash-crop business—migrants from the older areas transformed the Northwest Territory into a working agricultural landscape. In 1789, no Americans lived there. When the Treaty of Greenville made southern and eastern Ohio safe, settlers poured into the area. By 1800, the white population of Ohio numbered 45,365. In 1810, the population of Ohio, Indiana, and Illinois numbered 267,562, and settlement skyrocketed after the peace of 1815. By 1830, 1,438,379 whites lived in Ohio, Indiana, and Illinois. By 1860, the population of those three states, along with that of the new states of Wisconsin and

Michigan, numbered 6,926,884—22 percent of the nation's total population. (With the inclusion of the Old Southwest, nearly half of the population was west of the Appalachians; the geographic center of population was near Chillicothe, Ohio.)

In the Northwest until about 1830, most settlers were yeomen from Kentucky and Tennessee, usually a generation removed from Virginia, the Carolinas, and western Maryland. They moved along the Ohio and up the Muskingum, Miami, Scioto, Wabash, and Illinois rivers to set up farms in the southern and central counties of Ohio, Indiana, and Illinois. When southerners moved north of the Ohio River into territory that banned slavery, they often did so saying that slavery blocked opportunities for poor whites. The Methodist preacher Peter Cartwright left Kentucky with this thought: "I would get entirely clear of the evil of slavery," and "could raise my children to work where work was not thought a degradation." Similar hopes drew thousands of other southern yeomen north of the Ohio.

But even those who rejected slavery seldom rejected southern folkways. Like their kinfolk in Kentucky and Tennessee, the farmers of southern and central Ohio, Indiana, and Illinois remained tied to the river trade and to a mode of agriculture that favored free-ranging livestock over cultivated fields. The typical farmer fenced in a few acres of corn and left the rest of his land in woods to be roamed by southern hogs known as "razorbacks" and "land sharks." As late as 1860, southern-born farmers in the Northwest averaged 20 hogs apiece. These animals were thin and tough (they seldom grew to more than 200 pounds), and they could run long distances, leap fences, fend for themselves in the woods, and walk to distant markets. They were notoriously fierce; many more settlers were injured by their own hogs than by wild animals. When it was time to gather the hogs for slaughter, settlers often played it safe and hunted them with guns.

The southern-born pioneers of the Northwest, like their cousins across the Ohio River, depended more on their families and neighbors than on distant markets. Newcomers found that they could neither rent tools from their southern neighbors nor present them with "gifts" during hard times. Southerners insisted on repaying debts in kind and on lending tools rather than renting them, thus engaging outsiders in the elaborate network of

"neighboring" through which transplanted southerners made their livings. As late as the 1840s, in the bustling town of Springfield, Illinois, barter was the preferred system of exchange. "In no part of the world," said a Scotsman in southern Illinois, "is good neighborship found in greater perfection than in the western territory."

The Northwest: Northern Migrants

Around 1830, a stream of northeasterners migrated to the Northwest via the Erie Canal and on Great Lakes steamboats. They filled the new lands of Wisconsin and Michigan and the northern counties of the older northwestern states. Most of them were New Englanders who had spent a generation in western New York (such settlers accounted for three-fourths of the early population of Michigan). The rest came directly from New England or—from the 1840s onward—from Germany and Scandinavia. Arriving in the Northwest along the market's busiest arteries, they duplicated the intensive, market-oriented farming they had known at home. They penned their cattle and hogs and fattened them up, making them bigger and worth more than those farther south. They planted their land in grain and transformed the region—beginning with western New York's Genesee Country in the 1820s and rolling through the Northwest—into one of the world's great wheat-producing regions. In 1820, the Northwest had exported only 12 percent of its agricultural produce. By 1840, that figure had risen to 27 percent, and it stood even higher among northern-born grain farmers. By 1860, the Northwest, intensively commercialized and tied by canals

and railways to eastern markets, was exporting 70 percent of its wheat. In that year it produced 46 percent of the nation's wheat crop, nearly all north of the line of southern settlement.

The new settlers were notably receptive to improvements in farming techniques. Even with plenty of southern proponents of "progress" and plenty of "backward" northerners, the line between new and old agricultural ways tended to separate northern grain farmers from corn, hogs, and southern settlers. In breaking new land, for instance, southerners still used the old shovel plow, which dug a shallow furrow and skipped over roots. Northerners preferred newer, more expensive cast-iron plows, which cut cleanly through oak roots 4 inches thick. By the 1830s, the efficient, expensive grain cradle had become the standard harvest tool in northwestern wheat fields. From the 1840s onward, even this advanced hand tool was replaced by mass-produced machinery such as the McCormick reaper. Instead of threshing their grain by driving cattle and horses over it, farmers bought new horse-powered and treadmill threshers and used hand-cranked fanning mills to speed the process of cleaning the grain.

Most agricultural improvements were tailored to grain and dairy farming and were taken up most avidly by the northern farmers. Others rejected them as expensive and "unnatural." They thought that cast-iron plows poisoned the soil and that fanning mills made a "wind contrary to nater," and thus offended God. John Chapman, an eccentric Yankee who earned the nickname "Johnny Appleseed" by planting apple tree cuttings in southern Ohio and Indiana before the settlers arrived, planted only

THE McCORMICK REAPER

The boy Abraham Lincoln grew up on Indiana and Illinois farms on which cultivation was haphazard and tools were simple. Later, as a Whig and Republican politician, he rejected that world for the belief that intensive, mechanized farming improved not only crop yields but also intellectual, moral, and political standards, "whose course shall be onward and upward, and which, while the earth endures, shall not pass away." As he spoke, this factory in his hometown of Springfield, Illinois, churned out the implements that were bringing that new world into being.

Chicago Historical Society.

low-yield, common trees; he regarded grafting, which farmers farther north and east were using to improve the quality of their apples, as "against nature." Southerners scoffed at the Yankee fondness for mechanical improvements, the systematic breeding of animals and plants, careful bookkeeping, and farm techniques learned from magazines and books. "I reckon," said one, "I know as much about farming as the printers do."

Conflict between intensive agriculture and older, less market-oriented ways reached comic proportions when the Illinois legislature imposed stiff penalties on farmers who allowed their small, poorly bred bulls to run loose and impregnate cows with questionable sperm, thereby depriving the owners of high-bred bulls of their breeding fees and rendering the systematic breeding of cattle impossible. When the poorer farmers refused to pen their bulls, the law was rescinded. A local historian explained that "there was a generous feeling in the hearts of the people in favor of an equality of privileges, even among bulls."

Households

The Market Revolution transformed 18th-century households into 19th-century homes. For one thing, Americans began to limit the size of their families. White women who married in 1800 gave birth to an average of 6.4 children. Those who married between 1800 and 1849 averaged 4.9 children. The decline was most pronounced in the North, particularly in commercialized areas. Rural birth rates remained at 18th-century levels in the southern uplands, in the poorest and most isolated communities of the North, and on the frontier. (As the New Yorker Washington Irving passed through the Northwest in the 1830s, he noted in his journal: "Illinois—famous for children and dogs—in house with nineteen children and thirty-seven dogs.") These communities practiced the old labor-intensive agriculture and relied on the labor of large families. For farmers who used newer techniques or switched to livestock, large families made less sense. Moreover, large broods hampered the ability of future-minded parents to provide for their children and conflicted with new notions of privacy and domesticity that were taking shape among an emerging rural middle class.

The commercialization of agriculture was closely associated with the emergence of the concept of housework. Before 1815, farm wives had labored in the house, the barnyard, and the garden while their husbands and sons worked in the fields. With the Market Revolution came a sharper distinction between "male work" that was part of the cash economy and "female work" that was not. Even such traditional women's tasks as dairying, vegetable gardening, and poultry raising became men's work once they became cash-producing specialties. (A Pennsylvanian who lived among market-oriented New Englanders in the Northwest was appalled at such tampering with hallowed gender roles and wrote the Yankees off as "a shrewd, selfish, enterprising, cow-milking set of men.")

At the same time, new kinds of women's work emerged within households. Although women had fewer children to care for, the culture began to demand forms of childrearing that were more intensive, individualized, and mother-centered. Store-bought white flour, butter, and eggs and the new iron stoves eased the burdens of food preparation, but they also created demands for pies, cakes, and other fancy foods that earlier generations had only imagined. Although farm women no longer spun and wove their own cloth, the availability of manufactured cloth created the expectation that their families would dress more neatly and with greater variety than they had in the past—at the cost of far more time spent by women on sewing, washing, and ironing. Similar expectations demanded greater personal and domestic cleanliness,

A SOAP ADVERTISEMENT FROM THE 1850S
The rigors of "Old Washing Day" lead the mother in this advertisement to abuse the children and house pets, while her husband leaves the house. With American Cream Soap, domestic bliss returns: The children and cats are happy, the husband returns, and the wife has time to sew.

and farm women from the 1830s onward spent time planting flower beds, cleaning and maintaining prized furniture, mirrors, rugs, and ceramics, and scrubbing floors and children. The market and housework grew hand in hand: Among the first mass-produced commodities in the United States was the household broom.

Housework was tied to new notions of privacy, decency, and domestic comfort. Before 1820, farmers cared little about how their houses looked, often tossing trash and garbage out the door for the pigs and chickens that foraged near the house. In the 1820s and 1830s, as farmers began to grow cash crops and adopt middle-class ways, they began to plant shade trees and keep their yards free of trash. They painted their houses and sometimes their fences and outbuildings, arranged their woodpiles into neat stacks, surrounded their houses with flowers and ornamental shrubs, and tried to hide their privies from view. The new sense of refinement and decorum extended into other aspects of country life. The practice of chewing (and spitting) tobacco was gradually banned in churches and meeting halls, and in 1823, the minister in Shrewsbury, Massachusetts, ordered dogs out of the meetinghouse.

Inside, prosperous farmhouses took on an air of privacy and comfort. Separate kitchens and iron stoves replaced open hearths. Many families used a set of matched dishes for individual place settings, and the availability of finished cloth permitted the regular use of tablecloths, napkins, doilies, curtains, bedspreads, and quilts. Oil lamps replaced homemade candles, and the more comfortable families began to decorate their homes with wallpaper and upholstered furniture. Farm couples moved their beds away from the hearth and (along with the children's beds that had been scattered throughout the house) put them into spaces designated as bedrooms. They took the washstands and basins, which were coming into more common use, out of the kitchen and put them into the bedroom, thus making sleeping, bathing, and sex more private than they had been in the past. At the center of this new house stood the farm wife—apart from the bustling world of commerce, but decorating and caring for the amenities that commerce bought, and demanding that men respect the new domestic world that commerce had made possible.

Smithsonian Institution.

A WESTERN NEW YORK FARM

Here is a developer's rendition of a farm in western New York in the second quarter of the 19th century. The frame house (built onto the pioneer settler's log cabin) is fronted with a lawn, decorative shrubs, a shade tree, and dry walkways. Flanking the house are a vegetable garden and a well-tended orchard. Cash-crop fields stretch out behind the farmstead. A well-constructed fence marks off the home property and separates it from the road (another sign of progress) and the farm fields. The fence, the house, and a substantial barn are painted white. This was the rural comfort and respectability that northern farm families made for themselves from the 1820s onward.

Neighborhoods: The Landscape of Privacy

By the 1830s and 1840s, the Market Revolution had transformed the rural landscape of the Northeast. The forests had been reduced, the swamps had been drained, and most of the streams and rivers were interrupted by mill dams. Bears, panthers, and wolves had disappeared, along with the beaver and many of the fish. Now English cattle and sheep browsed on extensive pastures of English grasses dotted with English wildflowers such as buttercups, daisies, and dandelions. Next to the pastures lay neatly cultivated croplands that were regularly fertilized and seldom allowed to lie fallow. And at the center stood brightly painted houses and outbuildings surrounded by flowers and shrubs and vegetable gardens. Many towns, particularly in New England, had planted shade trees along the country roads, completing a rural landscape of straight lines and human cultivation—a landscape that made it easy to think of nature as a commodity to be altered and controlled.

Within that landscape, old practices and old forms of neighborliness fell into disuse. Neighbors continued to exchange goods and labor and to contract debts that might be left unpaid for years, but debts were more likely to be owed to profit-minded storekeepers and creditors, and even debts between neighbors often were paid in cash.

Traditionally, storekeepers had allowed farmers to bring in produce and have it credited to a neighbor/creditor's account—a practice that made the storekeeper an agent of neighborhood bartering. In 1830, half of the stores in rural Massachusetts carried accounts of this sort; by 1850, that figure had dropped to one in four. Storekeepers began to demand cash payment or to charge lower prices to those who paid cash.

The farm newspapers that appeared in these years urged farmers to keep careful records of the amount of fertilizer used, labor costs, and per-acre yields and discouraged them from relying on the old system of neighboring. Neighborly rituals such as parties, husking bees, barn-raisings—with their drinking and socializing—were scorned as an inefficient and morally suspect waste of time. The *Farmer's Almanac* of 1833 warned New England farmers: "If you love fun, frolic, and waste and slovenliness more than economy and profit, then make a husking."

Thus the efficient farmer after the 1820s concentrated on producing commodities that could be marketed outside the neighborhood and used his cash income to buy material comforts for his family and to pay debts and provide a cash inheritance for his children. Although much of the old world of household and neighborhood survived, farmers subsisted and maintained the independence of their households not through those spheres but through unprecedented levels of dependence on the outside world.

🌐 The Industrial Revolution

In the 50 years following 1820, American cities grew faster than ever before or since. The old seaports—New York City in particular—grew rapidly in these years, but the fastest growth was in new cities that served commercial agriculture and in factory towns that produced for a largely rural domestic market. Even in the seaports, growth derived more from commerce with the hinterland than from international trade. Paradoxically, the Market Revolution and improved transportation in the countryside had produced the beginnings of industry and the greatest period of urban growth in U.S. history.

Factory Towns: The Rhode Island System

Jeffersonians held that the United States must always remain rural. Americans, they insisted, could expand into the rich new agricultural lands of the West, trade their farm surpluses for European finished goods, and thus avoid creating cities with their dependent social classes. Federalists

SAMUEL SLATER'S MILL AT PAWTUCKET, RHODE ISLAND

The first mill was small, painted white, and topped with a cupola. Set among craftsmen's workshops and houses, it looked more like a Baptist meetinghouse than a first step into industrialization.

The Granger Collection, New York.

argued that Americans, in order to retain their independence, must produce their own manufactured goods. Neo-Federalists combined those arguments after the War of 1812. Along with other advocates of industrial expansion, they argued that America's abundant water power—particularly the fast-running streams of the Northeast—would enable Americans to build their factories across the countryside instead of creating great industrial cities. Such a decentralized factory system would provide employment for country women and children and thus subsidize the independence of struggling farmers. The first American factories were built on those premises.

The American textile industry originated in industrial espionage. The key to mass-produced cotton and woolen textiles was a water-powered machine that spun yarn and thread. The machine had been invented and patented by the Englishman Richard Arkwright in 1769. The British government, to protect its lead in industrialization, forbade the machinery or the people who operated it to leave the country. Scores of textile workers, however, defied the law and made their way to North America. One of them was Samuel Slater, who had served an apprenticeship under Jedediah Strutt, a partner of Arkwright who had improved on the original machine. Working from memory while employed by Moses Brown, a Providence merchant, Slater built the first Arkwright spinning mill in America at Pawtucket, Rhode Island, in 1790.

Slater's first mill was a small frame building tucked among the town's houses and craftsmen's shops. It spun only cotton yarn, providing work for children in the mill and for women who wove yarn into cloth in their homes. Thus this first mill satisfied the neo-Federalists' requirements: It required no factory town, and it supplemented the household incomes of farmers and artisans. As his business grew and he advertised for widows with children, however, Slater encountered families headed by landless, impoverished men. Slater's use of children from these families prompted "respectable" farmers and craftsmen to pull their children out of Slater's growing complex of mills. More poor families arrived to take their places, and during the first years of the 19th century, Pawtucket grew rapidly into a disorderly mill town.

Soon Slater and other mill owners built factory villages in the countryside, where they could exert better control over their operations and their workers. The practice became known as the Rhode Island (or "family") system. At Slatersville, Rhode Island, at Oxford, Massachusetts, and at other locations in southern New England, mill owners built whole villages surrounded by company-owned farmland that they rented to the husbands and fathers of their mill workers. The workplace was closely supervised, and drinking and other troublesome prac-tices were forbidden in the villages. Fathers and older sons either worked on rented farms or as laborers at the mills.

By the late 1820s, Slater and most of the other owners were eliminating outworkers and were buying power looms, thus transforming the villages into disciplined, self-contained factory towns that turned raw cotton into finished cloth, but at great cost to old forms of household independence. When President Andrew Jackson visited Pawtucket in 1829, he remarked to Samuel Slater, "I understand you taught us how to spin, so as to rival Great Britain in her manufactures; you set all these thousands of spindles to work, which I have been delighted in viewing, and which have made so many happy, by a lucrative employment." "Yes sir," replied Slater, "I suppose that I gave out the psalm and they have been singing to the tune ever since."

Factory Towns: The Waltham System

A second act of industrial espionage was committed by a wealthy, cultivated Bostonian named Francis Cabot Lowell. Touring English factory districts in 1811, Lowell asked the plant managers questions and made secret drawings of the machines he saw. He also experienced a genteel distaste for the squalor of the English textile towns. Returning home, Lowell joined with wealthy friends to form the

Boston Manufacturing Company—soon known as the Boston Associates. In 1813, they built their first mill at Waltham, Massachusetts, and then expanded into Lowell, Lawrence, and other new towns near Boston during the 1820s. The company, operating under what became known as the Waltham system, built mills that differed from the early Rhode Island mills in two ways: First, they were heavily capitalized and as fully mechanized as possible; they turned raw cotton into finished cloth with little need for skilled workers. Second, the operatives who tended their machines were young, single women recruited from the farms of northern New England, which were switching to livestock raising, and thus had little need for the labor of daughters. The company housed the young women in carefully supervised boardinghouses and enforced rules of conduct both on and off the job. The young women worked steadily, never drank, seldom stayed out late, and attended church faithfully. They dressed neatly—often stylishly—and read newspapers and

American Textile History Museum. Lowell, Mass.

WOMEN IN THE MILLS

Two female weavers from a Massachusetts textile mill proudly display the tools of their trade. This tintype was made in about 1860, when New England farm women such as these were being replaced by Irish immigrant labor.

made the consumer goods were growing more numerous and at the same time disappearing from view. With the exception of textiles and a few other commodities, few goods were made in mechanized factories before the 1850s. Most of the clothes and shoes, brooms, hats, books, furniture, candy, and other goods available in country stores and city shops were made by hand. City merchants and master craftsmen met the growing demand by hiring more workers. The largest handicrafts—shoemaking, tailoring, and the building trades—were divided into skilled and semiskilled segments and farmed out to subcontractors, who could turn a profit only by cutting labor costs. The result was the creation of an urban working class, not only in the big seaports and factory towns but also in scores of milling and manufacturing towns throughout the North and the West.

The rise of New York City's ready-made clothing trade provides an example. In 1815, wealthy Americans wore tailor-made clothing; everyone else wore clothes sewn by women at home. In the 1820s, the availability of cheap manufactured cloth and an expanding pool of cheap—largely female—labor, along with the creation of the southern and western markets, transformed New York City into the center of a national market in ready-made clothes. The first big market was in "Negro cottons"—graceless, hastily assembled shirts, pants, and sack dresses with which southern planters clothed their slaves. Within a few years, New York manufacturers were sending dungarees and hickory shirts to western farmers and supplying shoddy, inexpensive clothing to the growing ranks of urban workers. By the 1830s, many New York tailoring houses, including the storied Brooks Brothers, were offer-

HISTORY THROUGH FILM

Gangs of New York (2002)

Directed by Martin Scorsese. Starring Leonardo DiCaprio (Amsterdam Vallon), Daniel Day-Lewis (Bill "The Butcher" Cutting), and Cameron Diaz (Jenny Everdeane).

This is Martin Scorsese's movie about the Five Points of New York—the most dangerous neighborhood in mid-19th-century North America. It is an operatic tragedy: An Irish boy (Leonardo DiCaprio) whose father, the leader of a gang called the Dead Rabbits, is killed by a nativist chieftain (Daniel Day-Lewis) in a gang fight spends his childhood in an orphanage, and then returns to the neighborhood to take revenge. He becomes part of the criminal entourage of his father's killer, falls in love with a beautiful and talented female thief (Cameron Diaz) who had been raised (and used) by the same gang boss, and bides his time—tortured all the while by the prospect of killing a second father figure. In the end, the Irish boy resurrects his father's gang and challenges the nativists to a battle for control of the Five Points. The battle coincides with the Draft Riots of 1863, and the film ends (as it had begun) in a horrendous bloodbath. The Irish thug kills the nativist thug, and the film ends with U2 singing about "We Who Built America."

For those who can stomach close-up fights with clubs and hatchets, it is a good enough melodrama. Unhappily, Scorsese casts his story against real history and gets most of it wrong. The film takes pains to "reconstruct" Manhat-

tan's Five Points, but our first view of the neighborhood is taken from a painting of a Brooklyn street. The oppressive noise and overcrowding that contemporary visitors describe are obliterated by a large public space at the center of the Points—historically nonexistent, but a fine field for the gang fights that begin and end the movie. Historically, the gangs were headquartered at saloons and firehouses, but Scorsese's operatic sensibilities move the Dead Rabbits into catacombs beneath the Old Brewery—complete with torchlight, a crude armory, and an untidy pyramid of skulls. The nativists, on the other hand, prefer an Asian motif, holding their get-togethers in an ornate Chinese theater and social house that lends an air of orientalist extravaganza to a neighborhood that knew nothing of such things. The catalogue of crimes against history could go on and on: The Dead Rabbits did not follow the cross into battle (Irish street gangs were not particularly religious), Irish priests did not look like Peter the Hermit, and Leonardo DiCaprio does not have a convincing Irish accent.

The "reformers" who minister to the Five Points receive equally silly treatment. The chief of the reformers are the aristocratic Schermerhorns. In fact, most Five Points

ing fancier ready-made clothes to members of the new middle class.

High rents and costly real estate, together with the absence of water power, made it impossible to set up large factories in cities. The nature of the clothing trade and the availability of cheap labor created a system of subcontracting that transformed needlework into the first "sweated" trade in America. Merchants kept a few skilled male tailors to take care of the custom trade and to cut cloth into patterned pieces for ready-made clothing. The pieces were sent out, often by way of subcontractors, to needleworkers, who sewed them together in their homes. Male tailors continued to do the finishing work on men's suits, but most of the work—on cheap goods destined for the South and West—fell to women, who worked long hours for piece rates that ranged from 75 cents to $1.50 per week. In 1860,

Brooks Brothers, which concentrated on the high end of the trade, kept 70 workers in its shops and used 2,000 to 3,000 outworkers, most of them women. Along with clothing, women in garrets and tenements manufactured the items with which the middle class decorated itself and its homes: embroidery, doilies, artificial flowers, fringe, tassels, fancy-bound books, and parasols. All provided work for ill-paid legions of female workers. In 1860, 25,000 women (about one-fourth of the total workforce) worked in manufacturing jobs in New York City; fully two-thirds of them were in the clothing trades.

Other trades followed similar patterns. For example, northeastern shoes were made in uniform sizes and sent in barrels all over the country. Like tailoring, shoemaking was divided into skilled operations and time-consuming unskilled tasks. The relatively skilled and highly paid work

Daniel Day-Lewis and his Five Points gang.

© Kobal/Picture Desk.

missionaries were middle-class evangelicals who had little to do with the Schermerhorns or the other old families of New York. The movie reformers hold a dance for the neighborhood; in fact, the evangelicals hated dancing and parties. The reformers also attend a public hanging, cheering as four innocent men are put to death. But New York had outlawed public executions a generation earlier; felons were now hanged within prison walls before small invited audiences. Even if public hangings had persisted, reformers would not have attended them (they had stopped going to such spectacles soon after 1815), and had they been dragged out of their parlors to witness an execution, they would not

have cheered. There is also an appearance by P. T. Barnum. Barnum had made his museum the premier middle-class entertainment spot in New York by eschewing low theater, cockfights, and other raucous and violent shows. Yet the movie has Barnum sponsoring a bare-knuckle prizefight—an act that would have cost him his reputation and his livelihood. The climactic riot includes another Barnum fabrication: Barnum's museum is set on fire; his menagerie escapes, and a terrified elephant romps through the burning streets. It almost certainly did not happen, but even the most fact-bound historian must bow to Scorsese's artistic license on that one.

CHARLES OAKFORD'S HAT STORE IN PHILADELPHIA, CIRCA 1855

Such specialized retail establishments (unlike the craftsmen's shops that preceded them) hid the process of manufacturing from customers' view.

The Library Company of Philadelphia.

of cutting and shaping the uppers was performed by men; the drudgery of sewing the pieces together went to low-paid women. In the shops of Lynn, Massachusetts, in the shoemakers' boardinghouses in Rochester and other new manufacturing cities of the interior, and in the cellars and garrets of New York City, skilled shoemakers performed the most difficult work for taskmasters, who passed the work along to subcontractors who controlled poorly paid, unskilled workers. Skilled craftsmen could earn as much as $2 per day making custom boots and shoes. Men shaping uppers in boardinghouses earned a little more than half of that; women binders could work a full week and earn as little as 50 cents. In this, as in other trades, wage rates and gendered tasks reflected the old family division of labor, which was based on the assumption that female workers lived with an income-earning husband or father. In fact, increasing numbers of them were young women living alone or older women who had been widowed, divorced, or abandoned—often with small children.

In their offices, counting rooms, and shops, members of the new middle class entertained notions of gentility based on the distinction between manual and nonmanual work. Lowly clerks and wealthy merchants prided themselves on the fact that they worked with their heads and not their hands. They fancied that their entrepreneurial and managerial skills were making the Market Revolution happen, while manual workers simply performed tasks thought up by the middle class. The old distinction between proprietorship and dependence—a distinction that had placed master craftsmen and independent tradesmen, along with farm-owning yeomen, among the respectable "middling sort"—disappeared. The men and women of

an emerging working class struggled to create dignity and a sense of public worth in a society that hid them from view and defined them as "hands."

The Market Revolution in the South

With the end of war in 1815, the cotton belt of the South expanded dramatically. The resumption of international trade, the revival of textile production in Britain and on the continent, and the emergence of factory production in the northeastern United States encouraged southern planters to extend the short-staple cotton lands of South Carolina and Georgia into a belt that would stretch—on Indian land from which the defeated natives were evicted—across the Old Southwest and beyond the Mississippi into Texas and Arkansas. The speed with which that happened startled contemporaries: By 1834, the new southwestern states of Alabama, Mississippi, and Louisiana grew more than half the U.S. cotton crop. By 1859, these states, along with Georgia, produced fully 79 percent of American cotton.

The southwestern plantation belt produced stupendous amounts of cotton. In 1810, the South produced 178,000 bales of ginned cotton—more than 59 times the 3,000 bales it had produced in 1790. By 1820, production stood at 334,000 bales. As southwestern cotton lands opened, production jumped to 1.35 million bales in 1840 and to 4.8 million on the eve of the Civil War. Over these years, cotton accounted for one-half to two-thirds of the value of all U.S. exports. The South produced three-fourths of the world supply of cotton—a commodity that, more than any other, was the raw material of industrialization in Britain and Europe and, increasingly, in the northeastern United States.

The Organization of Slave Labor

The plantations of the cotton belt were among the most intensely commercialized farms in the world. Although some plantations grew supplementary cash crops and produced their own food, many grew nothing but cotton—a practice that produced huge profits in good years but sent planters into debt and forced them to sell slaves and land in bad years. Nearly all of the plantation owners, from the proudest grandee to the ambitious farmer with a few slaves, organized their labor in ways that maximized production and reinforced the dominance of the white men who owned the farms.

Cotton, which requires a long growing season and a lot of attention, was well suited to slave labor and to the

climate of the Deep South. After the land was cleared and plowed, it was set out in individual plants. Laborers weeded the fields with hoes throughout the hot, humid growing season. In the fall, the cotton ripened unevenly. In a harvest season that lasted up to two months, pickers swept through the fields repeatedly, selecting only the ripe bolls. Plantations that grew their own food cultivated large cornfields and vegetable gardens and kept large numbers of hogs. To cope with diverse growing seasons and killing times that overlapped with the cotton cycle, planters created complex labor systems.

On a large plantation in Louisiana in the 1850s, Frederick Law Olmstead, a New York landscape architect, watched a parade of slaves going into the fields. First came the hoe gang: "forty of the largest and strongest women I ever saw together: they were all in a single uniform dress of bluish check stuff, and skirts reaching little below the knee; their legs and feet were bare; they carried themselves loftily, each with a hoe sloping over the shoulder and walking with a free powerful swing, like Zouaves on the march." Following the hoe gang came the "cavalry, thirty strong, mostly men, but some women, two of whom rode astride, on the plow mules."

Although this slave force was larger than most, its organization was familiar to every southerner: Gangs of women wielded the hoes, and men did the plowing, accompanied, especially during the busiest times, by strong women who rode "astride" (and not, like white ladies, sidesaddle). The division of labor by sex was standard: Even at harvest festivals, teams of men shucked the corn while women prepared the meal and the after-supper dance. During the harvest, when every slave was in the fields, men tended to work beside men, women beside women. Most of the house slaves were women, and female slaves often worked under the direction of the plantation mistress—planters' wives, who were assuming greater control over their own domestic settings. Under the supervision of the mistress, female house slaves cared not only for the house, but for dairy cattle, chickens and geese, and vegetable gardens and orchards as well.

Although black women routinely worked in southern fields, white women did so only on the poorest farms and only at the busiest times of the year. Like their northern cousins, they took care of the poultry and cattle and the vegetable gardens—and not the profit-oriented fields. As the larger farms grew into plantations, white women took on the task of supervising the household slaves instead of doing the work. According to northern visitors, this association of labor with slavery encouraged laziness among southern whites and robbed work of the dignity it enjoyed in other parts of the country.

Paternalism

On the whole, the exploitation of slave labor after 1820 became both more systematic and more humane. An estimated 55 percent of southern slaves spent all of their time cultivating cotton, and it was brutal work by any standard. The arduous chore of transforming wilderness into cotton land demanded steady work in gangs, as did the yearly cotton cycle. Planters paid close attention to labor discipline: They supervised the work more closely than in the past, tried (often unsuccessfully) to substitute gang labor for the task system, and forcibly "corrected" slaves whose work

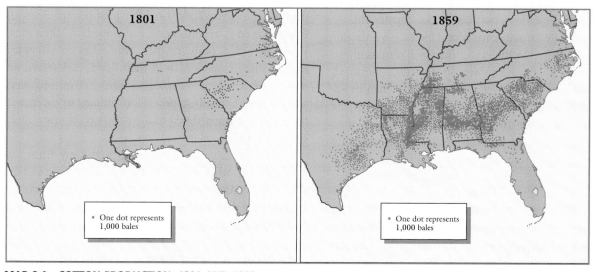

MAP 9.4 COTTON PRODUCTION, 1801 AND 1859
Short-staple cotton thrived wherever there was fertile soil, heat and humidity, low altitude, and a long growing season. As a result, a great belt of cotton and slavery took shape in the Lower South, from the midlands of South Carolina through East Texas.

HAULING THE WHOLE WEEK'S PICKING

William Henry Brown made this collage of a slave harvest crew near Vicksburg, Mississippi, in 1842. The rigors of the harvest put everyone, including small children, into the fields.

was slow or sloppy. At the same time, planters clothed the new discipline within a larger attempt to make North American slavery into a system that was both paternalistic and humane. Food and clothing seem to have improved, and individual cabins for slave families became standard. State laws often forbade the more brutal forms of discipline, and they uniformly demanded that slaves have Sundays off. More and more, the slaves spent that day listening to Christian missionaries provided by the planters.

The systematic paternalism on 19th-century farms and plantations sprang from both planter self-interest and a genuine attempt to exert a kindly, paternal control over slaves that planters uniformly called "our people" or "our family, black and white." The Louisiana planter Bennet H. Barrow insisted that the master must make the slave "as comfortable at home as possible, affording him what is essentially necessary for his happiness—you must provide for him your self and by that means creat[e] in him a habit of perfect dependence on you." On the whole, slaves endured the discipline and accepted the food, clothing, time off, and religious instruction—but used all of them to serve themselves and not the masters (see chapter 10).

Slaves' material standards rose. One rough indicator is physical height. On the eve of the Civil War, southern slaves averaged about an inch shorter than northern whites, but they were fully three inches taller than newly imported Africans, two inches taller than slaves on the Caribbean island of Trinidad, and one inch taller than British Marines. Slaves suffered greater infant mortality than whites, but those who survived infancy lived out "normal" life spans. The most telling evidence is that although Brazil, Cuba, and other slave societies had to import Africans to make up for the deaths of slaves, the slave population of the United States increased threefold—from 1,191,354 to 3,953,760—between 1810 and 1860. Imports of new Africans were banned after 1808 (and runaways outnumbered new Africans who were smuggled into the country); the increase reflected that—alone among slave populations of the Western Hemisphere—births outnumbered deaths among North American slaves.

Yeomen and Planters

Cotton brought economies of scale: Planters with big farms and many slaves operated more efficiently and more profitably than farmers with fewer resources. As the price of slaves and good land rose, fewer and fewer owners shared in the profits of the cotton economy, and wealth became more concentrated. Good farmland with ready access to markets was dominated by large plantations. By 1861, only one in four southern white households owned slaves. The Market Revolution had commercialized southern agriculture, but a shrinking proportion of the region's white population shared in the benefits. The result was not simply an unequal distribution of wealth, but the creation of a dual economy: plantations at the commercial center and a white yeomanry on the fringes.

Some small farmers remained in the plantation counties—most of them on poor, hilly land far from navigable rivers. They tended to be commercial farmers, growing a few bales of cotton with family labor and perhaps a slave or two. Many of them were poor relatives of prosperous plantation owners. They voted the great planters into office, and used their cotton gins and tapped into their marketing networks. Some of them worked as overseers for their wealthy neighbors, sold them food, and served on local slave patrols. Economic disparities between planters and farmers in the plantation belt continued to widen, but the farmers remained tied to the cotton economy and its economic and social imperatives.

Most small farmers, however, lived away from the plantations in what was called the upcountry: the eastern slopes of the Appalachians from the Chesapeake through Georgia, the western slopes of the mountains in Kentucky and Tennessee, the pine-covered hill country of northern Mississippi and Alabama, parts of Texas and Louisiana, and most of the Ozark Plateau in Missouri and Arkansas. All of these lands were too high, cold, isolated, and heavily wooded to support plantation crops. Here the farmers built a yeoman society that shared many of the characteristics of the 18th-century countryside, North and South

(see chapter 7). While northern farmers commercialized, their southern cousins continued in a household- and neighborhood-centered agriculture until the Civil War and beyond.

Many southern farmers stayed outside the market almost entirely. The mountaineers of the southern Appalachians sent a trickle of livestock and timber out of their neighborhoods, but the mountains remained largely outside the market until the coming of big-business coal mines in the late 19th century. Moreover, farmers in large parts of the upcountry South preferred to raise livestock instead of growing cotton or tobacco. They planted cornfields and let their pigs run loose in the woods and on unfenced private land. In late summer and fall, they rounded up the animals and sold them to drovers, who conducted cross-country drives and sold the animals to flatland merchants and planters. These hill-country yeomen lived off a market with which they had little firsthand experience. It was a way of life that sustained some of the most fiercely independent neighborhoods in the country.

Yeomen and the Market

A larger group of southern yeomen practiced mixed farming for household subsistence and neighborhood exchange, with the surplus sent to market. Most of these farmers owned their own land. The settlement of new lands in the old backcountry and the southwestern states reversed the 18th-century growth of white tenancy (see chapter 7). Few of these farmers kept slaves. In the counties of upland Georgia, for instance, only 10 to 30 percent of households had slaves.

These farmers practiced a complicated system of "subsistence plus" agriculture. Northern yeomen before 1815 had grown grain and livestock with which they fed their families and traded with neighbors. Whatever was left over they sent to market, but cotton, like tobacco and other southern cash crops, was not a food; it contributed nothing to family subsistence. Most middling and poor farmers played it safe: They put most of their land into subsistence crops and livestock, cultivating only a few acres of cotton. They devoted more acreage to cotton as transportation made markets more accessible—particularly when railroads penetrated upland neighborhoods in the 1850s—but few southern yeomen allowed themselves to become wholly dependent on the market. The income from a few bales of cotton paid their debts and taxes and bought coffee, tea, sugar, tobacco, cloth, and shoes, but they continued to enter and leave the market at will, for their own purposes. The market served their interests; it seldom dominated them.

This way of life discouraged acquisitiveness and ambition. Because few farms were self-sufficient, the yeomen

farmers routinely traded labor and goods with each other. In the plantation counties, such cooperation tended to reinforce the power of planters who put some of their resources at the disposal of their poorer neighbors. In the upcountry, cooperation reinforced neighborliness. As one upland Georgian remarked, "Borrowing . . . was neighboring." Debts contracted within the network of kin and neighbors were generally paid in kind or in labor, and creditors often allowed their neighbors' debts to go unpaid for years.

Among southern neighborly restraints on entrepreneurialism, none was more distinctive than the region's attitude toward fences. Northerners never tired of comparing their neatly fenced farms with the dilapidated or absent fences of the South. In the bourgeois North, well-maintained fences were considered a sign of ambitious, hardworking farmers and the poor fences of the South were considered a sign of laziness. Actually, the scarcity of fences in most southern neighborhoods reflected local custom and state law. Georgia, for instance, required farmers to fence their planted fields but not the rest of their land. In country neighborhoods, where families fished and hunted for food, and where livestock roamed freely, fences conflicted with a local economy that required neighborhood use of privately owned land. In this sense, the northerners were right: The lack of fences in the South reflected neighborhood constraints on the private use of private property, and thus on individual acquisitiveness and ambition. Such constraints, however, were necessary to the subsistence of families and neighborhoods as they were organized in the upland South.

A Balance Sheet: The Plantation and Southern Development

The owners of the South's large farms were among the richest men in the Western Hemisphere. In 1860, the 12 wealthiest counties in the United States were in the South; the wealthiest of all was Adams County, Mississippi, on the Mississippi River. Southern wealth, however, was concentrating in fewer hands. The slaves whose labor created the wealth owned nothing. As much as one-third of southern white families lived in poverty, and a declining proportion of the others owned slaves. In 1830, some 36 percent of southern white households had owned at least one slave. By 1850, the percentage had dropped to 31 percent; by 1860, to 26 percent. And huge disparities existed even among the slaveholding minority; in 1860, only one-fifth of the slaveholders (1 in 20 white families) owned 20 or more slaves, thus crossing the generally acknowledged line that separated farmers from planters. At the apex of southern society were a few great planters: Between 2 and 3 percent of southern white men owned half of all the southern slaves.

The widening gap between planters and yeomen created a dangerous fault line in southern politics (see chapter 11). In economic terms, the concentration of wealth in the hands of a few planters had profound effects on how the Market Revolution affected the region. Much of the white population remained marginal to the market economy. A South Carolina yeoman who raised cattle claimed, "I never spent more than ten dollars a year, which was for salt, nails, and the like. Nothing to wear, eat or drink was purchased, as my farm provided all." Whereas in the North, the rural demand for credit, banking facilities, farm tools, clothing, and other consumer goods fueled a revolution in commerce, finance, and industry, the South remained a poor market for manufactured goods. The slaves wore cheap cloth made in the Northeast, and the planters furnished themselves and their homes with finery from Europe. In the North, the exchange of farm produce for finished goods was creating self-sustaining economic growth by the 1840s, but the South continued to export its plantation staples and to build only those factories, commercial institutions, and cities that served the plantation. In the North, the Market Revolution produced commercial agriculture, a specialized labor force, and technological innovation. In the South, it simply produced more slavery.

Not that the South neglected technological innovation and agricultural improvement. Southerners developed Eli Whitney's hand-operated cotton gin into equipment capable of performing complex milling operations; they made many significant improvements in steamboat design as well. They also developed—among other things—the cotton press, a machine with a huge wooden screw powered by horses or mules, used to compress ginned cotton into tight bales for shipping. Jordan Goree, a slave craftsman in Huntsville, Texas, won a reputation for being able to carve whole trees into perfect screws for these machines. Yet the few such innovations had to do with the processing and shipping of cotton rather than with its production. The truth is that cotton was a labor-intensive crop that discouraged innovation. Moreover, plantation slaves often resisted their enslavement by sabotaging expensive tools and draft animals, scattering manure in haphazard ways, and passively resisting innovations that would have added to their drudgery. Cotton fields continued to be cultivated by clumsy, mule-drawn plows that barely scratched the soil, by women wielding hoes, and by gangs who harvested the crop by hand.

Southern state governments spent little on internal improvements. A Virginia canal linked the flour mills at Richmond with inland grain fields, and another connected the Chesapeake Bay with the National Road, but planters in the cotton belt had ready access to the South's magnificent system of navigable rivers, while upland whites saw little need for expensive, state-supported internal improvements. Nor did the South build cities. In 1800, about 82 percent of the southern workforce and about 70 percent of the northern workforce were employed in agriculture. By 1860, only 40 percent of the northern workforce was so employed, but in the South the proportion had risen to 84 percent. The South used its canals and railroads mainly to move plantation staples to towns that trans-shipped them out of the region. Southern cities were located on the periphery of the region and served as transportation depots for plantation crops. River cities such as Louisville, Memphis, and St. Louis were little more than stopping places for steamboats. The great seaports of New Orleans, Charleston, and Baltimore sometimes shipped cotton directly to British and European markets. More often, however, they sent it by coasting vessel to New York City, where it was trans-shipped to foreign ports.

Thus while the North and the Northwest developed towns and cities throughout their regions, southern cities continued to be few and to perform the colonial functions of 18th-century seaport towns. Southern businessmen turned to New York City for credit, insurance, and coastal and export shipping. From New York they ordered finished goods for the southern market. *DeBow's Review,* the principal business journal of the South, reported that South Carolina storekeepers who bought goods from Charleston wholesalers concealed that fact and claimed they had bought them directly from New York City. For it was well known that New York provided better goods at lower prices than any supplier in the South. DeBow testified to the superior skill and diversification of the North when, after trying several New Orleans sources, he awarded the contract for his *Review* to a northern printer.

A COTTON PRESS

Mule-driven presses such as the one shown here packed southern cotton into bales for easier transport to market. The cotton was pressed into a frame by a wooden screw carved from a whole tree.

That was not surprising in any case, because DeBow received three-fourths of his income from northern advertisers. In all, southerners estimated that 40 cents of every dollar produced by cotton remained in the Northeast.

Conclusion

In 1858, James H. Hammond, a slaveholding senator from South Carolina, asked:

> What would happen if no cotton was furnished for three years? . . . England would topple headlong and carry the whole civilized world with her save the South. No, you dare not make war on cotton. No power on earth dares to make war on cotton. Cotton is king.

Along with other planter-politicians, Hammond argued, as Jefferson had argued in 1807, that farmers at the fringes of the world market economy could coerce the commercial-industrial core. He was wrong. The commitment to cotton and slavery had not only isolated the South politically, but it had also deepened the South's dependence on the world's financial and industrial centers.

The North and West underwent a qualitative Market Revolution after 1815—a revolution that enriched both and that moved the Northeast from the old colonial periphery (the suppliers of food and raw materials) into the core (the suppliers of manufactured goods and financing) of the world market economy. In contrast, the South, by exporting plantation staples in exchange for imported goods, worked itself deeper and deeper into dependence—now as much on the American Northeast as on the old colonial rulers in London.

SUGGESTED READINGS

Works on the earlier phases of questions covered in this chapter are listed in the Suggested Readings for chapter 7. For a broad economic, cultural, and political synthesis, see **Charles G. Sellers, *The Market Revolution: Jacksonian America, 1815–1848*** (1991). **George Rogers Taylor, *The Transportation Revolution, 1815–1860*** (1951) remains the best single book on its subject. On legal and constitutional issues, see **R. Kent Newmeyer, *The Supreme Court under Marshall and Taney*** (1968); and **Morton J. Horwitz, *The Transformation of American Law, 1780–1860*** (1977). Changes in northern rural society are treated in **Christopher Clark, *The Roots of Rural Capitalism: Western Massachusetts, 1780–1860*** (1990); **Carolyn Merchant, *Ecological Revolutions: Nature, Gender, and Science in New England*** (1989); **Martin Bruegel, *Farm, Shop, Landing: The Rise of a Market Society in the Hudson Valley, 1780–1860*** (2002); and **John Mack Faragher, *Sugar Creek: Life on the Illinois Prairie*** (1986). Solid studies of industrial communities include **Thomas Dublin, *Women at Work: The Transformation of Work and Community in Lowell, Massachusetts, 1810–1860*** (1979); and **Anthony F. C. Wallace, *Rockdale: The Growth of an American Village in the Early Industrial Revolution*** (1978). On the plantation, see ***Southern Honor: Ethics & Behavior in the Old South*** (1982); and **Christine Leigh Heyerman, *Southern Cross: The Beginnings of the Bible Belt*** (1997). On the economics of slavery, see **Eugene D. Genovese, *The Political Economy of Slavery: Studies in the Economy and Society of the Slave South*,** 2d ed. (1989) and **R. W. Fogel, *Without Consent or Contract: The Rise and Fall of American Slavery*** (1989). On the southern yeomanry, see **Stephanie McCurry, *Masters of Small Worlds: Yeoman Households, Gender Relations, & the Political Culture of the South Carolina Lowcountry*** (1995); and **Steven Hahn, *The Roots of Southern Populism: Yeoman Farmers and the Transformation of the Georgia Upcountry, 1850–1890*** (1983).

AMERICAN JOURNEY ONLINE
AND
INFOTRAC COLLEGE EDITION

Visit the source collections at www.ajaccess.wadsworth.com and infotrac.thomsonlearning.com and use the Search function with the following key terms to explore documents, images, audio and video clips, articles, and commentary related to the material in this chapter.

Erie Canal	Robert Fulton
Francis Cabot Lowell	Cyrus McCormick
Henry Clay	John Marshall

GRADE AIDS

Visit the Liberty Equality Power Companion Web Site for resources specific to this textbook: http://history.wadsworth.com/murrin_LEP4e

The CD in the back of this book and the U.S. History Resource Center at http://history.wadsworth.com/u.s./ offer a variety of tools to help you succeed in this course, including access to quizzes; images; documents; interactive simulations, maps, and timelines; movie explorations; and a wealth of other sources.

govern themselves and seldom experienced the rigors of patriarchal family government. Thus mothers assumed responsibility for nurturing the children who would be carriers of the new middle-class culture—and fathers, ministers, and other authorities recognized the importance of that job. Edward Kirk, a minister in Albany, insisted that "the hopes of human society are to be found in the character, in the views, and in the conduct of mothers."

The new ethos of moral free agency was mirrored in the Sunday schools. When Sunday schools first appeared in the 1790s, their purpose was to teach working-class children to read and write by having them copy long passages from the Bible. Their most heavily publicized accomplishments were feats of memory: In 1823, Jane Wilson, a 13-year-old in Rochester, memorized 1,650 verses of scripture; Pawtucket, Rhode Island, claimed a mill girl who could recite the entire New Testament.

After the revivals of the 1820s and 1830s, the emphasis shifted from promoting feats of memory to preparing children's souls for conversion. Middle-class children were now included in the schools, corporal punishment was forbidden, and Sunday school teachers now tried to develop the moral sensibilities of their charges. They had the children read a few Bible verses each week and led them in a discussion of the moral lessons conveyed by the text. The proudest achievements of the new schools were children who made good moral choices. Thus Sunday schools became training grounds in free agency and moral accountability—a transformation that made sense only in a sentimental world where children could be trusted to make moral choices.

Sentimentality

Improvements in the printing, distribution, and marketing of books led to an outpouring of popular literature, much of it directed at the middle class. There were cookbooks, etiquette books, manuals on housekeeping, sermons, and sentimental novels—many of them written, and most of them read, by women. The works of popular religious writers such as Lydia Sigourney, Lydia Maria Child, and Timothy Shay Arthur found their way into thousands of middle-class homes. Sarah Josepha Hale, whose *Godey's Lady's Book* was the first mass-circulation

A MIDDLE-CLASS NEW ENGLAND FAMILY AT HOME, 1837
The room is carpeted and comfortably furnished. Father reads his newspaper; books rest on the table. Mother entertains their only child, and a kitten joins the family circle. This is the domestic foundation of sentimental culture on display.

Abby Aldrich Rockefeller Folk Art Center, Williamsburg, VA.

magazine for women, acted as an arbiter of taste not only in furniture, clothing, and food but also in sentiments and ideas. Upon reviewing the cloying, sentimental literature read in middle-class homes, Nathaniel Hawthorne was not the only "serious" writer to deplore a literary marketplace dominated by "a damned mob of scribbling women."

Hawthorne certainly had economic reason for complaint. Sentimental novels written by women outsold by wide margins his *Scarlet Letter* and *House of Seven Gables*, Ralph Waldo Emerson's essays, Henry David Thoreau's *Walden*, Herman Melville's *Moby Dick*, Walt Whitman's *Leaves of Grass*, and other works of the American Renaissance of the 1850s. Susan Warner's *The Wide, Wide World* broke all sales records when it appeared in 1850. Harriet Beecher Stowe's *Uncle Tom's Cabin* (1852) broke the records set by Warner. In 1854, Maria Cummin's *The Lamplighter* (the direct target of Hawthorne's lament about scribbling women) took its place as the third of the monster best sellers of the early 1850s.

These sentimental novels upheld the new middle-class domesticity. They sacralized the middle-class home and the trials and triumphs of Christian women. The action in each takes place indoors, usually in the kitchen or parlor, and the heroines are women (in Stowe's book, docile slave Christians are included) who live under worldly patriarchy but who triumph through submission to God. The stories embody spiritual struggle, the renunciation of greed and desire, and mother love. The home is a shrine (and keeping it clean is a sacrament) that is juxtaposed to the marketplace and the world of competition,

brutality, and power. Unlike the female characters in British and European novels of the time, the women in these American novels are intelligent, generous persons who grow in strength and independence. (The French visitor Alexis de Tocqueville commented that European women "almost think it a privilege to appear futile, weak, and timid. The women of America never lay claim to rights of that sort.")

In sentimental domestic fiction, women assume the role of evangelical ministers, demonstrating Christian living by precept, example, and moral persuasion. Female moral influence, wielded by women who had given themselves to God, is at war with the male world of politics and the marketplace—areas of power, greed, and moral compromise. Although few sentimental writers shared the views of the feminist Margaret Fuller, they would have agreed with her on the place of religion in women's lives. "I wish women to live first for God's sake," she wrote. "Then she will not make an imperfect man her God, and thus sink to idolatry."

The most successful sentimental novel of the 1850s was Harriet Beecher Stowe's *Uncle Tom's Cabin.* Stowe's book was also the most powerful antislavery tract of these years—in part because it successfully dramatized the moral and political imperatives of the northern middle class. At its core, *Uncle Tom's Cabin* indicts slavery as a system of absolute power at odds with domesticity and Christian love. The novel reverses the power relations of this world: In it, the home, and particularly the kitchen, is the ultimate locus of good, whereas law, politics, and the marketplace—the whole realm of men—are moved to the periphery and defined as unfeeling destroyers. Based solidly in revival Christianity, the novel lambastes the rational calculation, greed, and power hunger of the "real world" that was made and governed by white men and upholds domestic space filled with women, slaves, and children who gain spiritual power through submission to Christ. The two most telling scenes—the deaths of the Christian slave Uncle Tom and the perfect child Eva St. Claire—reenact the crucifixion of Jesus. Uncle Tom prays for his tormentors as he is beaten to death, and little Eva extracts promises of Christian behavior from her deathbed. Both are powerless, submissive characters who die in order to redeem a fallen humankind. Their deaths are thus Christian triumphs that convert the powerful and hasten the millennial day when the world will be governed by a feminized Christian love and not by male power.

Thus *Uncle Tom's Cabin* and other popular sentimental novels were not, as Hawthorne and his friends believed, frivolous fairytales into which housewives retreated from the real world. They were subversive depictions of a higher spiritual reality that would move the feminine ethos of the Christian home to the center of civilization. That vision drove an organized public assault on irreligion, drunkenness, prostitution, slavery, and other practices and institutions that substituted passion and force for Christian love (see chapter 11), an assault that tried to "domesticate" the world and shape it in the image of the middle-class evangelical home.

Fine Arts

Educated Americans of the postrevolutionary generation associated the fine arts with the sensuality, extravagance, and artificiality of European courts and European Catholicism. To them, the fine arts were the products of despotism and had nothing to offer the republicans of America. In making government buildings and monuments, building expensive homes, and painting portraits of wealthy and powerful men, American artists copied the classic simplicity of ancient Greece and Rome—republican styles tested by time and free of any hint of sensuality or luxury.

In the 1820s and 1830s, however, educated Americans began to view literature and the arts more favorably. American nationalists began to demand an American art that could compete with the arts of the despotic Old World. At the same time, evangelical Christianity and sentimental culture glorified a romantic cult of feeling that was, within its limits, far more receptive to aesthetic experience than Calvinism and the more spartan forms of republicanism had been. Finally, the more comfortable and educated Americans fell into a relationship with nature that called out for aesthetic expression. From the beginnings of English settlement, Americans had known that their civilization would be made in a contest with wilderness—wilderness they saw as dark, filled with demons, and implacably hostile to civilization. After 1815, with the Indians finally broken and scattered, with the agricultural frontier penetrating deep into the interior, and with improvements in transportation and communications annihilating distance, educated northeasterners became certain that Americans would win their age-old contest with nature—that civilization would supplant wilderness on the North American continent. The result was a multivoiced conversation about the relations between nature and civilization—a conversation that occupied a large portion of the new American art and literature that rose between 1830 and the Civil War.

Nature and Art

Much of the new American art was practical, to be lived in and used. Andrew Jackson Downing and other landscape designers and architects created beautiful country cottages

had a strict Calvinist upbringing in a family in which his father, an uncle, and his grandfather were all Baptist ministers. As a young man he rejected his family, set about making money, and became a deist—actions that deeply wounded his parents. When his father died, Miller was stricken with guilt. He moved back to his hometown, took up his family duties, became a leader of the Baptist church, and (after reading a sermon entitled "Parental Duties") began the years of Bible study that resulted in his world-ending prophecies. Alexander Campbell, one of the founders of the Disciples of Christ, dramatized his filial piety when he debated the free-thinking socialist Robert Owen before a large audience in the Methodist meetinghouse in Cincinnati in 1828. He insisted that his white-haired father (himself a Scots Presbyterian minister) stand in the pulpit above the debaters.

The Prophet Joseph Smith

The weakening patriarchal family and attempts to shore it up were central to the life and work of one of the most unique and successful religious leaders of the period: the Mormon prophet Joseph Smith (see also chapter 13). Smith's father was a landless Vermont Baptist who moved his wife and nine children to seven rented farms within 20 years. Around 1820, when young Joseph was approaching manhood, the family was struggling to make mortgage payments on a small farm outside Palmyra, New York. That farm—Joseph referred to it as "my father's house"—was a desperate token of the Smith family's commitment to yeoman independence and an endangered rural patriarchy. Despite the efforts of Joseph and his brothers, a merchant cheated the Smith family out of the farm. With that, both generations of the Smiths faced lifetimes as propertyless workers. To make matters worse, Joseph's mother and some of his siblings began to attend an evangelical Presbyterian church in Palmyra, apparently against the father's wishes.

Before the loss of the farm, Joseph had received two visions warning him away from existing churches and telling him to wait for further instructions. In 1827, the Angel Moroni appeared to him and led him to golden plates that translated into *The Book of Mormon*. It told of a light-skinned people, descendants of the Hebrews, who had sailed to North America long before Columbus. They had had an epic, violent history, a covenanted relationship with God, and had been visited and evangelized by Jesus following his crucifixion and resurrection.

Joseph Smith later declared that his discovery of *The Book of Mormon* had "brought salvation to my father's house" by unifying the family. It eventually unified thousands of others under a patriarchal faith based on restored theocratic government, male dominance, and a democracy among fathers. The good priests and secular leaders of *The Book of Mormon* are farmers who labor alongside their neighbors; the villains are self-seeking merchants, lawyers, and bad priests. The account alternates between periods when the people obey God's laws and periods when they do not, each period accompanied by the blessings or punishments of a wrathful God. Smith carried that model of brotherly cooperation and patriarchal authority into the Church of Jesus Christ of Latter-Day Saints, which he founded in 1830.

The new church was ruled, not by professional clergy, but by an elaborate lay hierarchy of adult males. On top sat the father of Joseph Smith, rescued from destitution and shame, who was appointed Patriarch of the Church. Below him were Joseph Smith and his brother Hyrum, who were called First and Second Elders. The hierarchy descended through a succession of male authorities that finally reached the fathers of households. Smith claimed that this hierarchy restored the ancient priesthood that had disappeared over the 18 centuries of greed and error that he labeled the Great Apostasy of the Christian churches. Americans who knew the history of the Market Revolution and the Smith family's travails within it, however, might have noted similarities between the restored ancient order and a poor man's visionary retrieval of the social order of the 18th-century North.

⬤ The Rise of Popular Culture

Of course, not all of the northern plain folk spent their time in church. Particularly in cities and towns, they became both producers and consumers of a nonreligious (sometimes irreligious) commercial popular culture. The sports and shows attended by northern plain folk, like the churches that they attended, were often grounded in an antisentimental view of the world and in traditional forms of patriarchy and masculinity.

Blood Sports

Urban working-class neighborhoods were particularly fertile ground for popular amusements. Young working men formed a bachelor subculture that contrasted with the piety and self-restraint of the middle class. They organized volunteer fire companies and militia units that spent more time drinking and fighting rival groups than drilling or putting out fires. Gathering at firehouses, saloons, and street corners, they drank, joked, and boasted, and nur-

tured notions of manliness based on physical prowess and coolness under pressure.

They also engaged in such "blood sports" as cock fighting, ratting, and dog fighting, even though many states had laws forbidding such activities. In 1823, an English tourist in New York City noted that "it is perfectly common for two or three cockfights to regularly take place every week." Such contests grew increasingly popular during the 1850s and often were staged by saloonkeepers doubling as sports impresarios. One of the best known was Kit Burns of New York City, who ran Sportsman Hall, a saloon frequented by prizefighters, criminals, and their hangers-on. Behind the saloon, however, was a space—reached through a narrow doorway that could be defended against the police—with animal pits and a small amphitheater that seated 250 but that regularly held 400 yelling spectators.

Although most of the spectators were working men, a few members of the old aristocracy who rejected middle-class ways also attended these events. In 1861, for instance, 250 spectators paid as much as $3 each to witness a fight between roosters belonging to the prizefighter John Morrissey and Mr. Genet, president of the New York City board of aldermen. A newspaper estimated bets on the event at $50,000. Frederick Van Wyck, scion of a wealthy old New York family, remembered an evening he had spent at Tommy Norris's livery stable, where he witnessed a fight between billy goats, a rat baiting, a cockfight, and a boxing match between bare-breasted women. "Certainly for a lad of 17, such as I," he recalled, "a night with Tommy Norris and his attraction was quite a night."

Boxing

Prizefighting emerged from the same subterranean culture that sustained cockfights and other blood sports. This sport, imported from Britain, called for an enclosed ring, clear rules, cornermen, a referee, and a paying audience. The early fighters were Irish or English immigrants, as were many of the promoters and spectators. Boxing's popularity rose during the 1840s and 1850s, a time of increasing immigration and violence in poor city neighborhoods. Many of the fighters had close ties with ethnic-based saloons, militia units, fire companies, and street gangs such as New York's (Irish) Dead Rabbits and (native) Bowery B'hoys, and many labored at occupations with a peculiarly ethnic base. Some of the best American-born fighters were New York City butchers—a licensed, privileged trade from which cheap immigrant labor was systematically excluded. Butchers usually finished work by 10 A.M. They could then spend the rest of the day idling at a firehouse or a bar and often were prominent figures in neighborhood gangs.

PRIZEFIGHTERS
The Irishman James "Yankee" Sullivan and the native-born Tom Hyer were immensely popular heroes of native and Irish workingmen, as well as of the street gangs and political factions of their respective ethnic groups.

acknowledged evil in themselves while claiming moral superiority over the hypocrites and frauds who governed the world. A murderer in Ned Buntline's *G'hals of New York* (1850) remarks, "There isn't no *real* witue [virtue] and honesty nowhere, 'cept among the perfessional *dishonest.*" By contrast, in middle-class sentimental novels, the universe was benign; good could be nurtured, and evil could be defeated and transformed. Harriet Beecher Stowe's slave driver Simon Legree—the best-known villain in American literature—is evil not because of a natural disposition toward evil, but because he had been deprived of a mother's love during childhood.

Family, Church, and Neighborhood: The White South

Antebellum white southerners remained localistic and culturally conservative. Farm and plantation labor and the routines of family life still centered in the household, and prospects for most whites remained rooted in inherited land and family help. While the new northern middle class nourished a cosmopolitan culture and a domestic sentimentalism that subverted traditional authority, southerners—planters and yeomen alike—distrusted outsiders and defended rural neighborhoods grounded in the authority of fathers and the integrity of families.

Southern Families

Most southern whites regarded themselves less as individuals than as representatives of families that extended through time from the distant past to unborn generations. Southern boys often received the family names of heroes as their first names: Jefferson Davis, for example, or Thomas Jefferson (later, "Stonewall") Jackson. More often, however, they took the name of a related family—Peyton Randolph, Preston Brooks, Langdon Cheves—and carried them as proud and often burdensome badges of who they were. Children learned early on that their first duty was to their family's reputation. When young Benjamin Tillman of South Carolina was away at school, his sister wrote, "Don't relax in your efforts to gain a good education. . . .

I want you to be an ornament to your family." Two years later, another sister wrote, "Do, Bud, study hard and make good use of your time. . . . I want you to do something for the Tillman name."

In the white South, reputation and the defense of family honor were everything. Boys and girls were taught to act as though everyone were watching them, ready to note any hint of inadequacy. A boy with a reputation for cowardice, for ineptness at riding or fighting, or for failure to control his emotions or hold his liquor was an embarrassment to his family. Membership in the South's democracy of white men depended less on wealth than on the maintenance of personal and family integrity.

An "unsullied reputation," insisted Albert Gallatin Brown of Mississippi, placed a man "on a social level with all his fellows." As John Horry Dent, an Alabama slaveholder and bad amateur poet, put it:

> Honor and shame from all conditions rise;
> Act well your part and there the honor lies.

Among southern white men, wealth generally counted for less than did maintaining one's personal and family honor and thus winning membership in the democracy of honorable males.

The code of honor, although it forged ties of equality and respect among white men, made rigid distinctions between men and women and whites and blacks. Women and girls who misbehaved—with transgressions ranging

COLONEL AND MRS. WHITESIDE

Colonel and Mrs. James Whiteside are pictured at home in their mansion on the heights above Chattanooga, Tennessee. The Colonel, Bible in hand, looks directly at his wife, while she looks shyly and indirectly back at him. Their infant son wears the traditional small child's dress, and the slaves are pictured as both subservient and comfortable. Here is southern patriarchy at its most genteel.

Hunter Museum of American Art, Chattanooga, Tennessee, Gift of Mr. and Mrs. Thomas B. Whiteside.

from simple gossip to poor housekeeping to adultery—damaged not only their own reputation but also the honor of the fathers, brothers, or husbands who could not control them. Such a charge could mean social death in a rural community made up of patriarchal households and watchful neighbors. In 1813, Bolling Hall of Alabama advised his daughter, "If you learn to restrain every thought, action, and word by virtue and religion, you will become an ornament." A "good man" or a "good woman" was someone who upheld the family by acting within a prescribed social role ("Act well your part. . . ."), and not, as the children of the northern middle class were being taught, by acting as an autonomous, self-governing individual.

The southern code of honor blunted attacks on social hierarchy and inherited status. When sentimental northerners attacked slavery because it denied the freedom of the individual, one southerner responded in a way that was meant to end the argument: "Do you say that the slave is held to involuntary service? So is the wife, [whose] relation to her husband, in the great majority of cases, is made for her and not by her." Few white southerners would have questioned the good sense of that response. Southern life was not about freedom, individual fulfillment, or social progress; it was about honoring the obligations to which one was born.

Southern Entertainments

Southerners of all classes and races were leisure-loving people, but the rural character of the South threw them upon their own resources rather than on commercial entertainments. They drank, told stories, engaged in wrestling and boxing matches, and danced. For evangelicals who withdrew from such entertainments, church socials and camp meetings filled the gap. Rural southerners both in and out of the churches engaged in corn-huskings, birthday celebrations, berry-picking expeditions, and so forth. Books were not as readily available as they were in the North. Whereas the big publishing houses produced many titles aimed at northern and western readers and at such specialized constituencies as commercial farmers or middle-class housewives, the southern literary market was too small to justify such special attention. Most southern families owned a Bible, and wealthier families often read histories, religious and political tracts, and English (seldom American) literature, with Shakespeare leading the way and Sir Walter Scott's tales of medieval chivalry not far behind. (Such stories exercised a strong fascination on some southerners; in the last years before the Civil War, jousting tournaments were held in which southern gentlemen clad in armor fought from horseback with lances and broadswords.) Hunting and fishing were passionate pursuits among southern men. Fox and deer hunts provided the gentry with an opportunity to display their skill with horses and guns, while the hunts of poorer whites and slaves both provided sport and enhanced their threatened roles as providers. Although state laws forbade slaves to own guns or dogs, thousands of slave owners found it wise to overlook the laws and to allow slaves to hunt as a favorite recreation.

The commercial entertainments in the South were concentrated in the larger towns and along the major rivers. Showboats brought theatrical troupes, minstrel shows, animal acts, and other entertainment to the river towns. The gentry's love of horses and competition made New Orleans the horse racing capital of the country; New Orleans also was the only southern city where one could watch a professional prizefight. Various violent contests appealed to New Orleans audiences. In 1819, a New Orleans impresario advertised a program that offered a bull versus six "of the strongest dogs in the country"; six bulldogs versus a Canadian bear; a "beautiful Tiger" versus a black bear; and 12 dogs versus a "strong and furious Opeloussas Bull." The advertisement further promised: "If the tiger is not vanquished in his fight with the Bear, he will be sent alone against the last Bull; and if the latter conquers all his enemies, several pieces of fireworks will be placed on his back, which will produce a very entertaining amusement." The impresario also stated that the premises had been inspected by the mayor of New Orleans, and that children would be admitted at half price. Although such events were outlawed in later years, they continued to be held on the sly. In 1852, a crowd of 5,000 gathered outside New Orleans to watch a bull and a grizzly bear fight to the death.

The Camp Meeting Becomes Respectable

The camp-meeting revivals of the early 19th century had transformed the South into an evangelical Bible belt (see chapter 7), although that label wouldn't be applied for another century. By 1860, 88 percent of southern church members were Methodist, Baptist, Presbyterian, or Disciples of Christ. Revival religion had spread from the frontier and upcountry yeomanry into both slave cabins and plantation mansions. Some evangelicals had risen into the slaveholding class, and many of the old families had been converted. As a result, the deist or indifferently Anglican gentry of the 18th century became outnumbered by earnest Baptist and Methodist planters who considered themselves the fathers of an inclusive southern Christian community.

Southern camp meetings continued throughout the antebellum years, but they were no longer the inclusive, ecstatic camp meetings of the past. They were often limited to a single denomination—usually Methodist—and were held on permanent campgrounds maintained by the churches. Conducted with more decorum than in the past, they were routine community events: Women began baking a week ahead of time and looked forward to visiting with neighbors and relatives as much as they did to getting right with God.

The goal of camp meetings was still to induce spiritual crisis and conversion, and sinners still wept and fell on their way to being saved, but such manifestations as the barking exercise and the jerks (see chapter 7) disappeared. Unfriendly observers after the 1820s could find nothing more offensive than simple breaches of decorum among the women. For instance, in 1828 an Englishwoman attended a meeting near Cincinnati at which nearly 100 women came forward to fall at the feet of Christ until "they were soon all lying on the ground in an indescribable confusion of heads and legs." The southern humorist George W. Harris described a fictional camp meeting at which his comic character Sut Lovingood put lizards up the preacher's pant leg. A fat woman fainted in the confusion, rolled down a hill, "tangled her laig an' garters in the top of a huckilberry bush, wif her head in the branch and jis' lay still."

The churches that grew out of southern revivals reinforced localistic neighborhoods and the patriarchal family. Some southern communities began when a whole congregation moved onto new land; others were settled by the chain migration of brothers and cousins, and subsequent revivals spread through family networks. Rural isolation limited most households to their own company during the week, but on Sundays, church meetings united the neighborhood's cluster of extended families into a community of believers. In most neighborhoods, social connections seldom extended beyond that. The word *church* referred ultimately to the worldwide community of Christians, and the war between the "church" and the "world" referred to a cosmic history that would end in millennial fire. In the day-to-day understandings of southern evangelicals, however, the church was the local congregation and the world was local sins and local sinners, many of whom were related to members of the church. Churches disciplined members for such worldly practices as drinking, gambling, dancing, swearing, fornication, and adultery, and even for giving the *impression* of sinful behavior. Mount Olive Baptist Church in North Carolina, for example, expelled Mary Bivens because she was "too thick with young men."

Religious Conservatism

Southern evangelicalism based itself, like religious conservatism in the North, on the sovereignty of God, a conviction of human sinfulness, and an acceptance of disappointment and pain as part of God's grand and unknowable design. "Oh man," lamented one slaveholder, "when will thou meekly submit to God without a murmur. . . . His will be done should be your constant prayer." Southern church people continued to interpret misfortune as divine punishment. When yellow fever was killing 1,000 people every week in New Orleans in 1853, the Episcopal bishop (and soon to be Confederate general) Leonidas Polk asked God to "turn us from the ravages of the pestilence, wherewith for our iniquities, thou are visiting us."

The same view held at home. When the young son of a planter family died, the mother was certain that God had killed the child because the parents had loved him more than God: "But God took him for he saw he was our idol." A grieving South Carolinian received this consolation from a relative: "Hope you are quite reconciled to the loss of your darling babe. As it was the will of God to take him, we must obey, and He will be angry at us if we go past moderate grief." Francis Pickens, another South Carolinian, wrote after losing his wife and child, "I had almost forgot there was a God, and now I stand the scattered . . . and blasted monument of his just wrath." It was a far cry from the middle-class North's garden cemeteries and the romantic, redemptive deaths of children in sentimental fiction.

Southern cultural conservatism was rooted in religion, in the family, and in a system of fixed social roles. Southern preachers assumed that patriarchal social relations were crucial to Christian living within an irredeemably imperfect and often brutal world. Southerners revered the patriarch and slaveholder Abraham more than any other figure in the Bible, and John C. Calhoun proclaimed "Hebrew Theocracy" the best government ever experienced by humankind. The father must—like Abraham—govern and protect his household; the mother must assist the father; and the women, children, and slaves must faithfully act out the duties of their stations. That meant a Christian must strive to be a good mother, a good father, a good slave; by the same token, a Christian never questioned his or her God-given social role.

Pro-slavery Christianity

In revolutionary and early national America, white southerners had been the most radical of republicans. Jefferson-

ian planter-politicians led the fights for equal rights and the absolute separation of church and state, and southern evangelicals were the early republic's staunchest opponents of slavery. By 1830, however, the South was an increasingly conscious minority within a democratic and capitalist nation. The northern middle classes proclaimed a link between material and moral progress, identifying both with individual autonomy and universal rights. A radical northern minority was agitating for the immediate abolition of slavery.

Southerners met this challenge with an "intellectual blockade" against outside publications and ideas and with a moral and religious defense of slavery. The Bible provided plenty of ammunition. Pro-slavery clergymen constantly stated that the Chosen People of the Old Testament had been patriarchs and slaveholders, and that Jesus had lived in a society that sanctioned slavery and never criticized the institution. Some ministers claimed that blacks were the descendants of Ham and thus deserved enslavement. The most common religious argument, however, was that slavery had given millions of heathen Africans the priceless opportunity to become Christians and to live in a Christian society. Thornton Stringfellow, a Virginia Baptist minister, insisted that "their condition . . . is now better than that of any equal number of laborers on earth, and is daily improving."

Like their northern counterparts, southern clergymen applauded the material improvements of the age, but they insisted that moral improvement occurred only when people embraced the timeless truths of the Bible. The South Carolinian William F. Hutson put it simply: "In religion and morals, we doubt all improvements, not known to certain fishermen who lived eighteen hundred years ago." Northern notions of progress through individual liberation, equal rights, and universal Christian love were wrong-headed and dangerous. The Presbyterian John Adger asserted that relations of dominance and submission (and not "barbarism and personal savage independence") were utterly necessary to both social and individual fulfillment, and that the distribution of rights and responsibilities was unequal and God-given. "The rights of the father are natural, but they belong only to the fathers. Rights of property are natural, but they belong only to those who have property," and such natural rights were coupled with the awesome duties of fatherhood and proprietorship. In the end, southern pro-slavery intellectuals rejected Jefferson's "self-evident" equality of man; Edmund Ruffin, for instance, branded that passage of the

Declaration of Independence as "indefensible" as well as "false and foolish."

The Private Lives of Slaves

Some southern blacks, particularly in cities and town, were free. But the overwhelming majority were slaves. In law, in the census, and in the minds of planters, slaves were members of a plantation household over which the owner exercised absolute authority, not only as owner but also as paternal protector and lawgiver. Yet both slaveholders and slaves knew that slaves could not be treated like farm animals or little children. Wise slaveholders learned that the success of a plantation depended less on terror and draconian discipline (although whippings—and worse—were common) than on the accommodations by which slaves traded labor and obedience for some measure of privilege and autonomy within the bounds of slavery. After achieving privileges, the slaves called them their own: holidays, garden plots, friendships, and social gatherings both on and off the plantation; hunting and fishing rights; and so on. Together, these privileges provided some of the ground on which they made their own lives within slavery.

The Slave Family

The most precious privilege was the right to make and maintain families. As early as the Revolutionary War era, most Chesapeake slaves lived in units consisting of mother, father, and small children. On Charles Carroll's Maryland

SLAVE CABINS ON A PLANTATION IN NORTHERN FLORIDA
Consisting of one room and set exactly 12 feet apart, this was minimal housing indeed. Yet it provided slaves with a place to live in families and the rudimentary sense of proprietorship exercised by these black workers sitting in front of their "own" houses.

farms in 1773, for example, 325 of the 400 slaves lived in such families. At Thomas Jefferson's Monticello, most slave marriages were for life, and small children almost always lived with both parents. The most common exceptions to this practice were fathers who had married away from their own plantations and who visited "broad wives" and children during their off hours. In Louisiana between 1810 and 1864, half the slaves lived in families headed by both parents; another one-fourth lived in single-parent families. Owners encouraged stable marriages because they made farms more peaceful and productive and because they flattered the owners' religious and paternalistic sensibilities. For their part, slaves demanded families as part of the price of their labor.

Yet slave families were highly vulnerable. Many slaveholders assumed that they had the right to coerce sex from female slaves; some kept slaves as concubines, and a few even moved them into the main house. They tended, however, to stay away from married women. While the slave community—in contrast to the whites—seldom punished sex before marriage, it took adultery seriously. Slaveholders knew that violations of married slave women could be enormously disruptive and strongly discouraged them. A far more serious threat to slave marriages was the death, bankruptcy, or departure of the slaveholders. Between one-fifth and one-third of slave marriages were broken by such events.

Slaveholders who encouraged slave marriages—even perhaps solemnizing them with a religious ceremony—

knew that marriage implied a form of self-ownership that conflicted with the slaves' status as property. Some conducted ceremonies in which couples "married" by jumping over a broomstick; others had the preacher omit the phrases "let no man put asunder" and "till death do you part" from the ceremony. Slaves knew that such ceremonies had no legal force. A Virginia slave remarked, "We slaves knowed that them words wasn't bindin'. Don't mean nothin' lessen you say, 'What God has jined, caint no man pull asunder.' But dey never would say dat. Jus' say 'Now you married.'" A black South Carolina preacher routinely ended the ceremony with "Till death or buckra [whites] part you."

Slaves modified their sense of family and kinship to accommodate such uncertainties. Because separation from father or mother was common, children spread their affection among their adult relatives, treating grandparents, aunts, and uncles almost as though they were parents. In fact, slaves often referred to all their adult relatives as parents. They also called nonrelatives "brother," "sister," "aunt," and "uncle," thus extending a sense of kinship to the slave community at large. Slaves chose as surnames for themselves the names of former owners, Anglicized versions of African names, or names that simply sounded good. They rarely chose the name of their current owner, however. Families tended to use the same given names from one generation to the next, naming boys after their father or grandfather, perhaps to preserve the memory of fathers who might be taken away. They seldom named

---

L I N K   T O   T H E   P A S T

A Slave Mother and the Slave Trade

In 1852, a slave mother from Virginia was caught up in the domestic slave trade. She wrote this to her husband:

*D*ear Husband I write you a letter to let you know of my distress my master has sold Albert to a trader on Monday court day and myself and other child is for sale also and I want you to let [me] hear from you very soon before next cort if you can I don't know when I don't want you to wait till Christmas I want you to tell Dr. Hamilton your master if either will buy me then can attend to it know and then I can go afterwards

I don't want a trader to get me they asked me if I had got any person to buy me and I told them no they told me to the court house too they never put me up A man buy the name of brady bought albert and is gone I don't know

whare they say he lives in scottsville my things is in several places some is in stanton and if I would be sold I don't know what will become of them I don't expect to meet with the luck to get that way till I am quite heart sick nothing more I am and ever will be your kind wife Marie Perkins.

---

1. Slaves uniformly feared the unpredictability and destructiveness of the domestic slave trade. Within this simple letter, how many social and personal injuries can you count?

For additional sources related to this feature, visit the *Liberty, Equality, Power* Web site at:

http://history.wadsworth.com/murrin_LEP4e

FIVE GENERATIONS OF A SLAVE FAMILY ON A SOUTH CAROLINA SEA ISLAND PLANTATION, 1862

Complex family ties such as those of the family shown here were among the most hard-won and vulnerable cultural accomplishments of enslaved blacks.

girls after their mother, however. Unlike Southern whites, slaves never married a first cousin, even though many members of their community were close relatives. The origins and functions of some of these customs are unknown. We know only that slaves practiced them consistently, usually without the knowledge of the slaveholders.

White Missions

A powerful aspect of planter paternalism was a widespread Christian mission to the slaves. By the 1820s, southern evangelicalism had long since abandoned its hostility toward slavery, and slaveholders commonly attended camp meetings and revivals. These prosperous converts faced conflicting duties. Their churches taught them that slaves had immortal souls and that planters were as responsible for the spiritual welfare of their slaves as they were for the spiritual welfare of their own children. One preacher remarked that it was difficult "to treat them as property, and at the same time render to them that which is just and equal as immortal and accountable beings, and as heirs of the grace of life, equally with ourselves." A planter on his deathbed told his children that humane treatment and religious instruction for slaves was the duty of slave owners; if these were neglected, "we will have to answer for the loss of their souls." After Nat Turner's bloody slave revolt in 1831 (to be discussed later in this chapter), missions to the slaves took on new urgency: If the churches were to help create a family-centered, Christian society in the South, that society would have to include the slaves. The

result after 1830 was a concerted attempt to Christianize the slaves.

To this end, Charles Colcock Jones, a Presbyterian minister from Georgia, spent much of his career writing manuals on how to preach to slaves. He taught that no necessary connection linked social position and spiritual worth—that there were good and bad slaveholders and good and bad slaves. He also taught, preaching from the Epistles of Paul ("Servants, obey your masters"), that slaves must accept the master's authority as God's, and that obedience was their prime religious virtue. Jones warned white preachers never to become personally involved with their slave listeners—to pay no attention to their quarrels, their complaints about their master or about their fellow slaves, or about working conditions on the plantation. "We separate entirely their religious from their civil condition," he said, "and contend that one may be attended to without interfering with the other." The catechism Jones prepared for slaves included the question, "What did God make you for?" The answer was, "To make a crop."

The evangelical mission to the slaves was not as completely self-serving as it may seem. For to accept one's worldly station, to be obedient and dutiful within that station, and to seek salvation outside of this world were precisely what the planters demanded of themselves and their own families. An important goal of plantation missions was, of course, to create safe and profitable plantations. Yet that goal was to be achieved by Christianizing both slaveholders and slaves—a lesson that some slaveholders

sense of themselves as a historical people with a role to play in God's cosmic drama. In slave Christianity, Moses the liberator (and not the slaveholders' Abraham) stood beside Jesus. The slaves' appropriation of the book of Exodus denied the smug assumption of the whites that they were God's chosen people who had escaped the bondage of despotic Europe to enter the promised land of America. To the slaves, America was Egypt, they were the chosen people, and the slaveholders were Pharaoh. Thomas Wentworth Higginson, a Boston abolitionist who went south during the Civil War to lead a Union regiment of freed South Carolina slaves, wrote that his men knew the Old Testament books of Moses and the New Testament book of Revelation. "All that lies between," he said, "even the life of Jesus, they hardly cared to read or to hear." He found their minds "a vast bewildered chaos of Jewish history and biography; and most of the events of the past, down to the period of the American Revolution, they instinctively attribute to Moses."

The slaves' religious songs, which became known as "spirituals," told of God's people, their travails, and their ultimate deliverance. In songs and sermons, the figures of Jesus and Moses were often blurred, and it was not always clear whether deliverance—accompanied by divine retribution—would take place in this world or the next. In any case, deliverance always meant an end to slavery, with the possibility that it might bring a reversal of relations between slaves and masters. "The idea of a revolution in the conditions of the whites and blacks," said the escaped slave Charles Ball, "is the corner-stone of the religion of the latter."

Religion and Revolt

Unlike slaves in Cuba, Jamaica, Brazil, and other New World plantation societies, North American slaves seldom went into organized, armed revolt. The environment of the United States was unfriendly to such events. American plantations were relatively small and dispersed, and the southern white population was large, vigilant, and well armed. Whites also enjoyed—until the cataclysm of the Civil War—internal political stability. The slaves encountered few promising opportunities to win their freedom by violent means. Thousands of slaves demonstrated their hatred of the system by running away. Others fought slave owners or overseers, sabotaged equipment and animals, stole from planters, and found other ways to oppose slavery, but most knew that open revolt was suicide.

Christianity convinced slaves that history was headed toward an apocalypse that would result in divine justice and their own deliverance, and thus held out the possibility of revolt. Slave preachers seldom indulged in prophecy and almost never told their congregations to become actively engaged in God's divine plan because they knew that open resistance was hopeless. Slave Christians believed that God hated slavery and would end it, but that their role was to have faith in God, take care of one another, preserve their identity as a people, and await deliverance. Only occasionally did slaves take retribution and deliverance into their own hands.

The most ambitious conspiracy was hatched by Denmark Vesey, a free black of Charleston, South Carolina. Vesey was a leading member of an African Methodist congregation that had seceded from the white Methodists and had been independent from 1817 to 1821. At its height, the church had 6,000 members, most of them slaves. Vesey and some of the other members read widely in political tracts, including the antislavery arguments in the Missouri debates (see chapter 12) and in the Bible. They talked about their delivery out of Egypt, with all white men, women, and children being cut off. They identified Charleston as Jericho and planned its destruction in 1822: A few dozen Charleston blacks would take the state armory, then arm rural slaves who would rise up to help them. They would kill the whites, take control of the city, commandeer ships in the harbor, and make their getaway, presumably to black-controlled Haiti. Word of the conspiracy spread secretly into the countryside, largely through the efforts of Gullah Jack, who was both a Methodist and an African conjurer. Jack recruited African-born slaves as soldiers, provided them with charms as protection against whites, and used his spiritual powers to terrify others into keeping silent.

In the end, the Vesey plot was betrayed by slaves. As one coerced confession followed another, white authorities hanged Vesey, Gullah Jack, and 34 other accused conspirators, 22 of them in one day. Even so, frightened whites knew that most of the conspirators (estimates ranged from 600 to 9,000) remained at large and unidentified.

Nat Turner

In August 1831, in a revolt in Southampton County, Virginia, some 60 slaves shot and hacked to death 55 white men, women, and children. Their leader was Nat Turner, a Baptist lay preacher. Turner was neither a conjurer like Gullah Jack (he violently opposed plantation conjurers) nor a republican revolutionary like Denmark Vesey or the Richmond slave Gabriel (see chapter 7). He was, he told his captors, an Old Testament prophet and an instrument of God's wrath. As a child, he had prayed and fasted often, and the spirit—the same spirit who had spoken to the

NAT TURNER

This contemporary woodcut depicts scenes from Nat Turner's rebellion. In this bloodiest of all North American slave revolts, 55 whites, most of them women and children, were shot and hacked to death.

prophets of the Bible—had spoken directly to him. When he was a young man, he had run away to escape a cruel overseer, but when God told him that he had not chosen Nat merely to have him run away, Nat returned. He justified his return by quoting one of the slave owners' favorite verses of scripture: "He who knoweth his master's will and doeth it not, shall be beaten with many stripes." But Turner made it clear that his Master was God, not a slave owner.

Around 1830, Turner received visions of the final battle in Revelation, recast as a fight between white and black spirits. He saw Christ crucified against the night sky, and the next morning he saw Christ's blood in a cornfield. Convinced by a solar eclipse in February 1831 that the time had come, Turner began telling other slaves about his visions, recruited his force, and launched a bloody and hopeless revolt that ended in mass murder, failure, and the execution of Turner and his followers.

The Vesey and Turner revolts, along with scores of more limited conspiracies, deeply troubled southern whites. Paternalistic slaveholders were increasingly committed to making slavery both domestic and Christian. For their part, slaves recognized that they could receive decent treatment and pockets of autonomy in return for outward docility. Vesey and Turner opened wide cracks

in that mutual charade. During the Turner revolt, slaves whose masters had been murdered joined the rebels without a second thought. A plantation mistress who survived by hiding in a closet listened to the murders of her husband and children and heard her house servants arguing over possession of her clothes. A Charleston grandee named Elias Horry, upon finding that his coachman was among the Vesey conspirators, asked him, "What were your intentions?" The formerly submissive slave replied that he had intended "to kill you, rip open your belly, and throw your guts in your face."

Such stories sent a chill through the white South—a suspicion that despite the appearance of peace, they were surrounded by people who would kill them in an instant. While northerners patronized plays and cheap fiction that dramatized the trickery and horror beneath placid appearances, the nightmares of slaveholding paternalists were both more savage and closer to home.

Conclusion

By the second quarter of the 19th century, Americans had made a patchwork of regional, class, and ethnic cultures. The new middle classes of the North and West compounded their Protestant and republican inheritance with

a new entrepreneurial faith in progress. The result was a way of life grounded in the self-made and morally accountable individual and the sentimentalized (often feminized) domestic unit.

Their means of proposing that way of life as a national culture for the United States often offended others. The middle class met resistance, first of all, from poorer urban dwellers and the less prosperous farmers in their own sections—a northern and western majority that remained grimly loyal to the unsentimental, male-dominated families of their fathers and grandfathers, to new and old religious sects that continued to believe in human depravity and the mysterious workings of providence, and to the suspicion that perfidy and disorder lurked behind the smiling moral order of market economics and sentimental culture. They were also people who enjoyed dark and playful popular entertainments that often mocked middle-class sentimentalism. In the South, most white farmers persisted in a neighborhood-based, intensely evangelical, and socially conservative way of life; when asked their opinions, they often talked like classic Jeffersonian yeomen. Southern planters, although they shared in the northern elite's belief in material progress and the magic of the market, were bound by family values, a system of slave labor, and a code of honor that was strikingly at variance with middle-class faith in an orderly universe and perfectible individuals. Slaves in these years continued to make cultural forms of their own; and despite their exclusion from the white world of liberty and equality, they tied their aspirations to the family (although in broader and more flexible ways than most whites), to an evangelical Protestant God, and to the individual and collective dignity that republics promise to their citizens.

SUGGESTED READINGS

Stuart M. Blumin, *The Emergence of the Middle Class: Social Experience in the American City, 1760–1900* (1989) is a thorough study of work and material life among the urban middle class. Studies that treat religion, family, and sentimental culture include **Paul E. Johnson,** *A Shopkeeper's Millennium: Society and Revivals in Rochester New York, 1815–1837* (1978); **Mary P. Ryan,** *Cradle of the Middle Class: The Family in Oneida County, New York, 1790–1865* (1981); and **Jane Tompkins,** *Sensational Designs: The Cultural Work of American Fiction, 1790–1860* (1985). The works of **Jon Butler** and **Nathan Hatch** listed in the Suggested Readings for chapter 7 are the best overviews of religion in these years. Studies of popular literature and entertainments include **Elliott J. Gorn,** *The Manly Art: Bare-Knuckle Prize Fighting in America* (1986); **Eric Lott,** *Love & Theft: Blackface Minstrelsy and the American Working Class* (1993); **David S. Reynolds,** *Beneath the American Renaissance: The Subversive Imagination in the Age of Emerson and Melville* (1988); and **Paul E. Johnson,** *Sam Patch, the Famous Jumper* (2003). **Peter Kolchin,** *American Slavery, 1619–1877* (1993) is a good synthesis of the literature. Now-classic treatments of slave culture are **Eugene D. Genovese,** *Roll, Jordan, Roll: The World the Slaves Made* (1974); and **Lawrence W. Levine,** *Black Culture and Black Consciousness: Afro-American Folk Thought from Slavery to Freedom* (1977). Two essential books on the culture of southern whites are **Bertram Wyatt-Brown,** *Southern Honor: Ethics & Behavior in the Old South* (1982); and **Christine Leigh Heyerman,** *Southern Cross: The Beginnings of the Bible Belt* (1997). An enlightening counterpoint between black and white understandings of the slave trade (and, by extension, of the slave South generally) is presented in **Walter Johnson,** *Soul by Soul: Life Inside the Antebellum Slave Market* (1999).

AMERICAN JOURNEY ONLINE
AND
INFOTRAC COLLEGE EDITION

Visit the source collections at www.ajaccess.wadsworth.com and
infotrac.thomsonlearning.com and use the Search function with
the following key terms to explore documents, images, audio
and video clips, articles, and commentary related to the material
in this chapter.

Uncle Tom's Cabin	Nat Turner
Harriet Beecher Stowe	*The Book of Mormon*
Denmark Vesey	Joseph Smith
Sarah Josepha Hale	

GRADE AIDS

**Visit the Liberty Equality Power Companion Web Site for resources specific to
this textbook:** http://history.wadsworth.com/murrin_LEP4e

 The CD in the back of this book and the U.S. History Resource Center at
http://history.wadsworth.com/u.s./ offer a variety of tools to help you succeed in
 this course, including access to quizzes; images; documents; interactive simulations,
maps, and timelines; movie explorations; and a wealth of other sources.

strongest in plantation counties, where they commanded the votes not only of wealthy planters but also of smaller farmers, and of lawyers, storekeepers, and craftsmen in county-seat towns. Upland, nonplantation neighborhoods in which Whigs ran well (eastern Tennessee, western North Carolina, and parts of Virginia are examples) were places where Whigs promised state-sponsored internal improvements that would link ambitious but isolated farmers to outside markets. On the other hand, some plantation districts with easy access to markets, such as the South Carolina low-country, opposed expensive Whig projects that would benefit other areas.

Many other southern exceptions to the link between commerce and the Whig Party were grounded in the prestige and power of local leaders. Southern statesmen who broke with the Jacksonians in the 1830s—John C. Calhoun in South Carolina, Hugh Lawson White in Tennessee, and others—took personal and regional followings with them (see chapter 12). Political campaigners also had to contend with southerners such as George Reynolds of Pickens County, Alabama. Reynolds was a half-literate yeoman who fathered 17 children and had 234 direct descendants living in his neighborhood, which he delivered as a bloc to politicians who pleased him. Despite the vagaries of southern kinship and community, Whigs knew that their core constituency in the South was in communities that were or wanted to be linked to commercial society.

In sharp contrast with the North and West, southern political divisions had little to do with religion. The South was thoroughly evangelized by 1830, but southern Baptists, Methodists, and Presbyterians seldom combined religion and politics. The southern evangelical churches had begun as marginal movements that opposed the Anglican establishment; they continued to distrust ties between church and state. Although they enforced morality within their own households and congregations, southern evangelicals seldom asked state legislatures to pass moral legislation. In extreme cases, southern premillennialists rejected politics altogether, insisting that Jesus would soon return to take the reins of government. (One political canvasser faced with that argument responded, "I will bet one hundred dollars he can't carry Kentucky.") Southern evangelicals who embraced the world of the market assumed, along with their northern Whig counterparts, that the new economy encouraged a Christian, civilized life. Other southern churchgoers responded to the Jacksonians' denunciations of greed and the spirit of speculation. Thus, even though many southern communities were bitterly divided over religion, the divisions seldom shaped party politics.

The social, religious, cultural, and economic bases of party divisions formed coherent Whig and Democratic political cultures. Whig voters in the North and South either were or hoped to become beneficiaries of the Market Revolution and wanted government to subsidize economic development. In the North, they also demanded that government help shape market society into a prosperous, orderly, and homogeneous Christian republic. Democrats, North and South, demanded a minimal government that kept taxes low and that left citizens, their families, and their neighborhoods alone.

The Politics of Economic Development

Both Whigs and Democrats accepted the transition to market society, but they wanted to direct it into different channels. Whigs wanted to use government and the market to make an economically and morally progressive—albeit hierarchical—republic. Democrats viewed both government and the new institutions of market society with suspicion and vowed to allow neither to subvert the equal rights and rough equality of condition that were, in their view, the preconditions of republican citizenship. In language that echoed their Jeffersonian forebears, Jacksonian Democrats demanded that the market remain subservient to the republic.

Government and Its Limits

"The government," remarked a New York City Whig in 1848, "is not merely a machine for making wars and punishing felons, but is bound to do all that is within its power to promote the welfare of the People—its legitimate scope is not merely negative, representative, defensive, but also affirmative, creative, constructive, beneficent." *The American Review,* a Whig periodical, agreed: "Forms of government are instituted for the protection and fostering of virtue, and are valuable only as they accomplish this."

The Whigs insisted that economic development, moral progress, and social harmony were linked and that government should foster them. Market society, they argued, opened up opportunities for individual Americans. As long as people developed the work habits and moral discipline required for success, they would be rewarded. To poor farmers and city workers who believed that the Market Revolution undermined their independence, Whigs promised social mobility within a new system of interdependence—but only to deserving individuals. According to the New York *Herald* in 1836, "The mechanic who attends quietly to his business—is industrious and attentive—belongs to no club—never visits the porter-house—is always at work or with his family—such a man gradu-

ally rises in society and becomes an honor to himself, his friends, and to human nature." The *Herald* editor continued, "On the contrary, look at the Trade Unionist—the pot-house agitator—the stirrer-up of sedition—the clamorer for higher wages—After a short time, he ends his career in the Pen or State Prison." Whigs believed that the United States exhibited a harmony of class interests and an equality of opportunity that every virtuous person would recognize and that only resentful, mean-spirited, unworthy people would doubt. Pointing to self-made Whigs such as Daniel Webster and Abraham Lincoln, they demanded activist government that nurtured the economic, cultural, and moral opportunities provided by market society.

Democrats seldom praised or condemned market society per se. Instead, they argued for the primacy of citizenship: Neither government nor the market, they said, should be allowed to subvert the civil and legal equality among independent men on which the republic rested. Often sharing a view of human nature that was (in contrast to the Whigs' more optimistic views) a grim combination of classical republicanism and gothic romance, Democrats saw government not as a tool of progress but as a dangerous—although regrettably necessary—concentration of power in the hands of imperfect, self-interested men. The only safe course was to limit its power. In 1837, the *United States Magazine and Democratic Review* declared: "The best government is that which governs least," and went on to denounce the "natural imperfection, both in wisdom and judgment and purity of purpose, of all human legislation, exposed constantly to the pressure of partial interest; interests which, at the same time that they are essentially selfish and tyrannical, are ever vigilant, persevering, and subtle in all the arts of deception and corruption."

Democrats argued that the Whig belief in benign government and social harmony was absurd. Corporate charters, privileged banks, and subsidies to turnpike, canal, and railroad companies, they said, benefited privileged insiders and transformed republican government into an engine of inequality. Granting such privileges, warned one Democrat, was sure "to break up that social equality which is the legitimate foundation of our institutions, and the destruction of which would render our boasted freedom a mere phantom." George Bancroft, a radical Democrat from Massachusetts, concurred: "A republican people," he said, "should be in an equality in their social and political condition; . . . pure democracy inculcates equal rights—equal laws—equal means of education—and *equal means* of wealth also." By contrast, the government favored by the Whigs would enrich a favored few. Bancroft and other Democrats demanded limited government that was deaf to the demands of special interests.

Banks

Andrew Jackson's national administration destroyed the Bank of the United States (see chapter 12). As a result, regulation of banking, credit, and currency fell to the state governments. The proper role of banks emerged as a central political issue in nearly every state, particularly after the widespread bank failures following the crash of 1837. Whigs defended banks as agents of economic progress, arguing that they provided credit for roads and canals, loans to businessmen and commercial farmers, and the banknotes that served as the chief medium of exchange. Democrats, on the other hand, branded banks as agents of inequality dominated by insiders who controlled artificial concentrations of money, who enjoyed chartered privileges, and who issued banknotes and expanded or contracted credit to their own advantage. In short, they regarded banks as government-protected institutions that enabled a privileged few to make themselves rich at the public's expense.

The economic boom of the 1830s and the destruction of the national bank created a dramatic expansion in the number of state-chartered banks—from 329 in 1830 to 788 in 1837. Systems varied from state to state. South Carolina, Georgia, Tennessee, Kentucky, and Arkansas had state-owned banks. Many new banks in the Old Northwest were also partially state-owned. Such banks often operated as public-service institutions. Georgia's Central Bank, for example, served farmers who could not qualify for private loans, as did other state-owned banks in the South. The charter of the Agricultural Bank of Mississippi (1833) stipulated that at least half of the bank's capital be in long-term loans (farm mortgages) rather than in short-term loans to merchants.

Beginning in the 1820s, many states had introduced uniform banking laws to replace the unique charters previously granted to individual banks. The new laws tried to stabilize currency and credit. In New York, the Safety-Fund Law of 1829 required banks to pool a fraction of their resources to protect both bankers and small noteholders in the case of bank failures. The result was a self-regulating and conservative community of state banks. Laws in other states required that banks maintain a high ratio of specie (precious metals) to notes in circulation. Such laws, however, were often evaded. Michigan's bank inspectors, for instance, complained that the same cache of silver and gold was taken from bank to bank one step ahead of them. At one bank, an inspector encountered a bank teller who had 10 metal boxes behind his counter. The teller opened one of the boxes and showed that it was full of federal silver dollars. The wary inspector picked up another one and found that it was full of nails covered

THE EUREKA SCHOOLHOUSE IN SPRINGFIELD, VERMONT

Mandated by state law and supported by local taxes, such one-room schools taught generations of American children the three R's.

North Wind Picture Archives.

tends to produce equality, not by leveling all to the condition of the base, but by elevating all to the association of the wise and good."

The schools taught a basic Whig axiom: that social questions could be reduced to questions of individual character. A textbook entitled *The Thinker, A Moral Reader* (1855) told children to "remember that all the ignorance, degradation, and misery in the world, is the result of indolence and vice." To teach that lesson, the schools had children read from the King James Bible and recite prayers acceptable to all of the Protestant sects. Such texts reaffirmed a common Protestant morality while avoiding divisive doctrinal matters. Until the arrival of significant numbers of Catholic immigrants in the 1840s and 1850s, few parents complained about Protestant religious instruction in the public schools.

Political differences centered less on curriculum than on organization. Whigs wanted state-level centralization and proposed state superintendents and state boards of education, normal schools (state teachers' colleges), texts chosen at the state level and used throughout the state, and uniform school terms. They also (often with the help of economy-minded Democrats) recruited young women as teachers. In addition to fostering Protestant morality in the schools, these women were a source of cheap labor: Salaries for female teachers in the northern states ranged from 40 to 60 percent lower than the salaries of their male coworkers. Largely as a result, the proportion of women among Massachusetts teachers rose from 56 percent in 1834 to 78 percent in 1860.

Democrats objected to the Whigs' insistence on centralization as elitist, intrusive, and expensive. They preferred to give power to individual school districts, thus enabling local school committees to tailor the curriculum, the length of the school year, and the choice of teachers and texts to local needs. Centralization, they argued, would create a metropolitan educational culture that served the purposes of the rich but ignored the preferences of farmers and working people. It was standard Democratic social policy: inexpensive government and local control. Henry Barnard, Connecticut's superintendent of schools, called his Democratic opponents "ignorant demagogues" and "a set of blockheads." Horace Mann denounced them as "political madmen." As early as 1826, Thaddeus Stevens, who would become a prominent Pennsylvania Whig, argued that voters must "learn to dread ignorance more than taxation."

Ethnicity, Religion, and the Schools

The argument between Whig centralism and Democratic parsimony dominated the debate over public education until the children of Irish and German immigrants began to enter schools by the thousands in the mid-1840s. Most immigrant families were poor and relied on their children to work and supplement the family income. Consequently, the children's attendance at school was irregular at best. Moreover, most immigrants were Catholics. The Irish regarded Protestant prayers and the King James Bible as heresies and as hated tools of British oppression. Some of the textbooks were worse. Olney's *Practical System of Modern Geography*, a standard textbook, declared that "the Irish in general are quick of apprehension, active, brave and hospitable; but passionate, ignorant, vain, and superstitious." A nun in Connecticut complained that Irish chil-

dren in the public schools "see their parents looked upon as an inferior race."

Many Catholic parents simply refused to send their children to school. Others demanded changes in textbooks, the elimination of the King James Bible (perhaps to be replaced by the Douay Bible), tax-supported Catholic schools, or at least tax relief for parents who sent their children to parish schools. Whigs, joined by many native-born Democrats, saw Catholic complaints as popish assaults on the Protestantism that they insisted was at the heart of American republicanism.

Many school districts, particularly in the rural areas to which many Scandinavian and German immigrants found their way, created foreign-language schools and provided bilingual instruction. In other places, state support for church-run charity schools persisted. For example, both Catholic and Protestant schools received such assistance in New York City until 1825, and in Lowell, Massachusetts; Hartford and Middletown, Connecticut; and Milwaukee, Wisconsin, at various times from the 1830s through the 1860s. New Jersey extended state support to Catholic as well as other church schools until 1866. In northeastern cities, however, where immigrant Catholics often formed militant local majorities, such demands led to violence and to organized nativist (anti-immigrant) politics. In 1844, the Native American Party, with the endorsement of the Whigs, won the New York City elections. That same year in Philadelphia, riots that pitted avowedly Whig Protestants against Catholic immigrants, ostensibly over the issue of Bible reading in schools, killed 13 people. Such conflicts would severely damage the northern Democratic coalition in the 1850s (see chapter 13).

Prisons

From the 1820s onward, state governments built institutions to house orphans, the dependent poor, the insane, and criminals. The Market Revolution increased the numbers of such persons and made them more visible, more anonymous, and more separated from family and community resources. Americans in the 18th century (and many in the 19th century as well) had assumed that poverty, crime, insanity, and other social ills were among God's ways of punishing sin and testing the human capacity for both suffering and charity. By the 1820s,

however, reformers were arguing that deviance was the result of childhood deprivation. "Normal" people, they suggested, learned discipline and respect for work, property, laws, and other people from their parents. Deviants were the products of brutal, often drunken households devoid of parental love and discipline. The cure was to place them in a controlled setting, teach them work and discipline, and turn them into useful citizens.

In state legislatures, Whigs favored putting deviants in institutions for rehabilitation. Democrats, although they agreed that the states should care for criminals and dependents, regarded attempts at rehabilitation as wrongheaded and expensive; they favored institutions that isolated the insane, warehoused the dependent poor, and punished criminals. Most state systems were a compromise between the two positions.

Pennsylvania built prisons at Pittsburgh (1826) and Philadelphia (1829) that put solitary prisoners into cells to contemplate their misdeeds and to plot a new life. The results of such solitary confinement included few reformations and numerous attempts at suicide. Only New Jersey imitated the Pennsylvania system. Far more common were institutions based on the model developed in New York at Auburn (1819) and Sing Sing (1825). In the Auburn system, prisoners slept in solitary cells and marched in military formation to meals and workshops; they were forbidden to speak to one another at any time. The rule of silence, it was believed, encouraged both discipline and contemplation. The French writer Alexis de Tocqueville, visiting a New York prison in 1830, remarked that "the silence within these vast walls . . . is that of death. . . . There

Prisoners at the State Prison at Auburn.

The Granger Collection, New York.

AUBURN PRISON
Inmates at New York's Auburn Prison were forbidden to speak and were marched in lockstep between workshops, dining halls, and their cells.

were a thousand living beings, and yet it was a vast desert solitude."

The Auburn system was designed both to reform criminals and to reduce expenses, for the prisons sold workshop products to the outside. Between these two goals, Whigs favored rehabilitation. Democrats favored profit-making workshops, and thus lower operating costs and lower taxes. Robert Wiltse, named by the Democrats to run Sing Sing prison in the 1830s, used harsh punishments (including flogging and starving), sparse meals, and forced labor to punish criminals and make the prison pay for itself. In 1839, William Seward, as the newly elected Whig governor of New York, fired Wiltse and appointed administrators who substituted privileges and rewards for punishment and emphasized rehabilitation over profit making. They provided religious instruction; they improved food and working conditions; and they cut back on the use of flogging. When Democrats took back the statehouse in the 1842 elections, they discovered that the Whigs' brief experiment in kindness had produced a $50,000 deficit, so they swiftly reinstated the old regime.

Asylums

The leading advocate of humane treatment for people deemed to be insane was Dorothea Dix, a Boston humanitarian who was shocked by the incarceration and abuse of the insane in common jails. She traveled throughout the country urging citizens to pressure their state legislatures into building asylums committed to what reformers called "moral treatment." The asylums were to be clean and pleasant places, preferably outside the cities, and the inmates were to be treated humanely. Attendants were not to beat inmates or tie them up, although they could use cold showers as a form of discipline. Dix and other reformers wanted the asylums to be safe, nurturing environments in which people with mental illness could be made well.

By 1860, the legislatures of 28 of the 33 states had established state-run insane asylums. Whig legislators, with minimal support from Democrats, approved appropriations for the more expensive and humane moral treatment facilities. Occasionally, however, Dorothea Dix won Democratic support as well. In North Carolina, she befriended the wife of a powerful Democratic legislator as the woman lay on her deathbed; the dying woman convinced her husband to support building an asylum. His impassioned speech won the approval of the lower house for a state asylum to be named Dix Hill. In the North Carolina senate, however, the proposal was supported by 91 percent of the Whigs and only 14 percent of the Democrats—a partisan division that was repeated in state after state.

THE WHIPPING POST AND PILLORY AT NEW CASTLE, DELAWARE
Delaware was a slave state that continued to inflict public, corporal punishment on lawbreakers. Many of the witnesses to the whipping depicted here are small children, who are supposedly learning a lesson.

The South and Social Reform

On most economic issues, southern state legislatures divided along the same lines as northern legislatures: Whigs wanted government participation in the economy, Democrats did not. On social questions, however, southern Whigs and Democrats responded in distinctly southern ways. The South was a rural, culturally conservative region of patriarchal households that viewed every attempt at government intervention as a threat to independence. Most southern voters, Whigs as well as Democrats, perceived attempts at "social improvement" as expensive and wrong-headed.

The southern states enacted school laws and drew up blueprints for state school systems, but the culturally homogeneous white South had little need for schools to enforce a common culture. Moreover, the South had less money and less faith in government. Consequently, southern schools tended to be locally controlled, to be infused with southern evangelical culture, and to have a limited curriculum and a short school year. In 1860, northern children attended school for an average of more than 50 days a year; white children in the South attended school for an average of 10 days annually.

By 1860, every slave state except Florida (which had a tiny population) and the Carolinas operated prisons modeled on the Auburn system. Here, however, prisons stressed punishment and profits over rehabilitation. Although some southerners favored northern-style reforms, they knew that southern voters would reject them. Popular votes in Alabama in 1834 and in North Carolina in 1846 brought in resounding defeats for proposals to build or reform penitentiaries in those states. While northern evangelicals were preaching that criminals could be rescued, southern preachers demanded Old Testament vengeance, arguing that hanging, whipping, and branding were sanctioned by the Bible, inexpensive, and more effective than mere incarceration. Other southerners, defending the code of honor, charged that victims and their relatives would be denied vengeance if criminals were tucked away in prisons. Some southern prisons leased prison labor (and sometimes whole prisons) to private entrepreneurs, and dreams of reforming southern criminals were forgotten.

The South did participate in temperance—the all-consuming reform that is discussed in the next section. By the 1820s, Baptists and Methodists had made deep inroads into southern society. Southern ministers preached against dueling, fighting, dancing, gambling, and drinking, while churchgoing women discouraged their husbands, sons, and suitors from drinking. Many southern men either stopped drinking altogether or sharply reduced their consumption. Accordingly, the South contributed its share to the national drop in alcohol consumption. During the 1840s, the Washington Temperance Society and other voluntary temperance groups won a solid footing in southern towns, but southern religious and temperance organizations were based on individual decisions to abstain. Legal prohibition, which became dominant in the North, got nowhere in the South. In the 1850s, when one northern legislature after another passed statewide prohibition, the only slave state to follow was tiny, northern-oriented Delaware.

At bottom, southern resistance to social reform stemmed from a conservative, Bible-based acceptance of suffering and human imperfection and a commitment to the power and independence of white men who headed families. Any proposal that sounded like social tinkering or the invasion of paternal rights was doomed to failure. To make matters worse, many reforms—public schools, Sunday schools, prohibitionism, humane asylums—were seen as the work of well-funded and well-organized missionaries from the Northeast who wanted to fashion society in their own self-righteous image. The southern distrust of reform was powerfully reinforced after 1830, when northern reformers began to call for abolition of slavery and equality of the sexes—reforms most white southerners found unthinkable.

Excursus: The Politics of Alcohol

Central to party formation in the North was the fight between evangelical Whigs who demanded that government regulate public (and often private) morality and Democrats who feared both big government and the Whig cultural agenda. The most persistent issue in the argument was the question of alcohol—so much so that in many places the temperance question defined the differences between Democrats and Whigs.

Ardent Spirits

Drinking had been a part of social life since the beginning of English settlement, but the withering of authority and the disruptions of the Market Revolution led to increased consumption, increased public drunkenness, and a perceived increase in alcohol-led violence and social problems (see chapter 7). Beginning in the 1790s, physicians and a few clergymen attacked not only habitual drunkenness but also alcohol itself. And for a short time after 1812, Federalist politicians and Congregational clergymen formed "moral societies" in New England that discouraged strong drink. Their imperious tone and their association with the old seats of authority, however, doomed them to failure.

The temperance crusade began in earnest in 1826, when northeastern evangelicals founded the American Society for the Promotion of Temperance (soon renamed the American Temperance Society). The movement's manifesto was Lyman Beecher's *Six Sermons on the Nature, Occasions, Signs, Evils, and Remedy of Intemperance* (1826). Addressing the churchgoing middle class, Beecher declared alcohol an addictive drug and warned that even moderate drinkers risked becoming hopeless drunkards. Thus temperance, like other evangelical reforms, was presented as a contest between self-control and slavery to one's appetites. By encouraging total abstinence, reformers hoped to halt the creation of new drunkards while the old ones died out. Even though Beecher pinned his hopes on self-discipline, he wanted middle-class abstainers to spread reform through both example and coercion. As middle-class evangelicals eliminated alcohol from their own lives, they would cease to offer it to their guests, buy or sell it, or provide it to their employees, and they would encourage their friends to do the same.

THE DRUNKARD'S PROGRESS

This popular print describes the drunkard's progression from social drinking to alcoholism, isolation, crime, and death by suicide. His desolate wife and daughter and his burning house are at bottom.

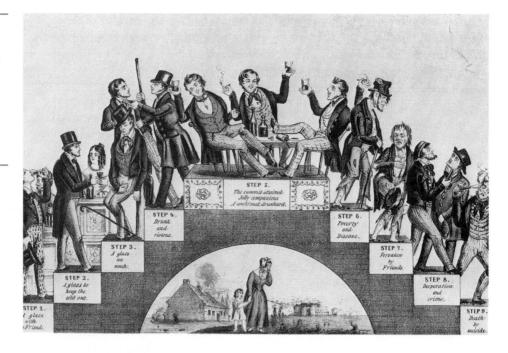

In the atmosphere surrounding the middle-class revivals of the 1820s and 1830s, Beecher's crusade gathered strength. Charles Grandison Finney (see chapter 10), in his revival at Rochester, made total abstinence a condition of conversion. Many other ministers and churches followed suit, and by the mid-1830s, members of the middle class had largely disengaged themselves from alcohol and from the people who drank it. Following a temperance lecture by Finney's coworker Theodore Dwight Weld, for instance, Rochester grocers Elijah and Albert Smith rolled their stock of whiskey out on the sidewalk, smashed the barrels, and let the liquor spill into the street. Other merchants threw their liquor into the Erie Canal or sold it off at cost. Hundreds of evangelical businessmen pledged that they would refuse to rent to merchants who sold liquor, sell grain to distillers, or enter a store that sold alcohol. Many of them made abstinence a condition of employment, placing ads that carried the line "None But Temperate Men Need Apply." Abstinence and opposition to the use of distilled spirits (people continued to argue about wine and beer) had become a badge of middle-class respectability.

Among themselves, the reformers achieved considerable success. By 1835, the American Temperance Society claimed 1.5 million members and estimated that 2 million Americans had renounced ardent spirits (whiskey, rum, and other distilled liquors); 250,000 had formally pledged to completely abstain from alcohol. The society further estimated that 4,000 distilleries had gone out of business, and that many of the survivors had cut back their production. Many politicians no longer bought drinks to win vot-

ers to their cause. The Kentucky Whig Henry Clay, once known for keeping late hours, began to serve only cold water when he entertained at dinner. And in 1833, members of Congress formed the American Congressional Temperance Society. The U.S. Army put an end to the age-old liquor ration in 1832, and increasing numbers of militia officers stopped supplying their men with whiskey. The annual consumption of alcohol, which had reached an all-time high in the 1820s, dropped by more than half in the 1830s (from 3.9 gallons of pure alcohol per adult in 1830 to 1.8 gallons in 1840).

The Origins of Prohibition

In the middle 1830s, Whigs made temperance a political issue. Realizing that voluntary abstinence would not put an end to drunkenness, Whig evangelicals drafted coercive, prohibitionist legislation. First, they attacked the licenses granting grocery stores and taverns the right to sell liquor by the drink and to permit it to be consumed on the premises. The licenses were important sources of revenue for local governments. They also gave local authorities the power to cancel the licenses of troublesome establishments. Militant temperance advocates, usually in association with local Whigs, demanded that the authorities use that power to outlaw all public drinking places. In communities throughout the North, the licensing issue, always freighted with angry divisions over religion and social class, became the issue around which local parties organized. The question first reached the state level in Massachusetts, when in 1838 a Whig legislature passed the

Fifteen-Gallon Law, which decreed that merchants could sell ardent spirits only in quantities of 15 gallons or more, thus outlawing every public drinking place in the state. In 1839, Massachusetts voters sent enough Democrats to the legislature to rescind the law.

The Whig attempt to cancel tavern licenses proved unenforceable because proprietors simply operated without licenses or found ways to get around the laws. While the Massachusetts Fifteen-Gallon Law was in effect, one Boston tavern keeper painted stripes on a pig and charged patrons an admission fee of six cents (the old price of a drink) to view the "exhibition." He then provided customers—who paid over and over to see the pig—with a "complimentary" glass of whiskey.

Leading Democrats agreed with Whigs that Americans drank too much, but whereas Whigs insisted that regulating morality was a proper function of government, Democrats warned that government intrusion into areas of private choice would violate republican liberties. The Democrats of Rochester, New York, responding to the license issue, made the following declaration:

> Anything which savours of restraint in what men deem their natural rights is sure to meet with opposition, and men convinced of error by force will most likely continue all their lives unconvinced in their reason. Whatever shall be done to stay the tide of intemperance, and roll back its destroying wave, must be done by suasive appeals to the reason, the interest, or the pride of men; but not by force.

In many communities, alcohol became the defining difference between Democrats and Whigs. In 1834, for instance, a Whig campaign worker ventured into a poor neighborhood in Rochester and asked a woman how her husband planned to vote. "Why, he has always been Jackson," she said, "and I don't think he's joined the Cold Water."

The Democratization of Temperance

Democratic voters held ambiguous attitudes toward temperance. Many of them continued to drink, while many others voluntarily abstained or cut down. Yet almost without exception they resented the coercive tactics of the Whigs and supported their party's pledge to protect them from evangelical meddling in their private lives. In 1830, when Lyman Beecher's Hanover Street Church in Boston caught fire, the volunteer fire companies (which doubled as working-class drinking clubs) arrived, noted that it was the hated Beecher's church, and made no effort to put out the fire. Unbeknownst to the Reverend Beecher, the church had rented basement space to a merchant who used it to store barrels of rum. According to a contemporary report,

the crowd that gathered to watch the church burn to the ground cheered as the barrels exploded one by one.

Democrats, despite their opposition to prohibition, often spoke out against drunkenness. Many craft unions denied membership to heavy drinkers, and hundreds of thousands of rural and urban Democrats quietly stopped drinking. (The sharp drop in alcohol consumption in the 1830s can be explained in no other way.) In the late 1830s, former antiprohibitionists launched a temperance movement of their own.

One evening in 1840—in the depths of a devastating economic depression—six craftsmen were drinking at Chase's Tavern in Baltimore. More or less as a joke, they sent one of their number to a nearby temperance lecture; he came back a teetotaler and converted the others. They then drew up a total abstinence pledge and promised to devote themselves to the reform of other drinkers. Within months, from this beginning a national movement had emerged, called the Washington Temperance Society. With a core membership of men who had opposed temperance in the 1830s, the Washingtonians differed from older temperance societies in several ways. First, they identified themselves as members of the laboring classes. Second, they were avowedly nonreligious: Although many of them were churchgoers (usually Methodist or Baptist), many were not, and the Washingtonians avoided religious controversy by avoiding religion. Third, the Washingtonians—at least those who called themselves True Washingtonians—rejected recourse to politics and legislation and concentrated instead on the conversion of drinkers through compassion and persuasion. Finally, they welcomed "hopeless" drunkards—who accounted for about 10 percent of the membership—and hailed them as heroes when they sobered up.

Temperance Schisms

Even though Whig reformers welcomed the Washingtonians at first, they soon had second thoughts. The nonreligious character of the movement disturbed those who saw temperance as an arm of evangelical reform. Previous advocates of temperance had assumed that sobriety would be accompanied by evangelical decorum. Instead, the meetings, picnics, and parades held by the Washingtonians were continuous with a popular culture that Whig evangelicals opposed. While the temperance regulars read pamphlets and listened to lectures by clergymen, lawyers, and doctors, the Washingtonians enjoyed raucous sing-alongs, comedy routines, barnyard imitations, dramatic skits, and even full-dress minstrel shows geared to temperance themes. Meetings featured experience speeches by reformed drunkards. Speaking extemporaneously, they

THE ATTACK ON THE CALIFORNIA HOUSE

In the big antebellum cities, volunteer fire companies were often ethnic clubs, and many were tied to street gangs. In 1849, a Philadelphia Irish gang called the Killers, some of them wearing their fire hats and carrying their fire horns, attacked a black-owned gambling and drinking establishment called the California House. The blacks (and apparently some of their white patrons) fought back with guns.

won the first round, the whites refused to accept defeat. Over the next few nights, they wrecked a black-owned tavern; broke into black households to terrorize families and steal property; attacked whites who lived with, socialized with, or operated businesses catering to blacks; wrecked the African Presbyterian Church; and destroyed a black church on Wharton Street by sawing through its timbers and pulling it down. Sporadic racial violence wracked the city throughout the 1830s and 1840s, reaching its height in 1849. That summer a firehouse gang of Irish immigrants calling themselves "the Killers" attacked the California House, a black-owned tavern and gambling hall. The black patrons had anticipated the attack and had armed themselves, and in the melee five Killers were shot. For two months, tempers simmered. Finally, the Killers set a fire at the California House that spread to nearby houses. They fought off neighborhood blacks, rival firemen, and the police. The riot ended only when the city sent in four companies of militia.

Conceptions of Racial Difference

Meanwhile, educated whites were being taught to think in racist terms. Among most scientists, biological determinism replaced historical and environmental explanations of racial differences; many argued that whites and blacks were separate species. Democrats welcomed that "discovery." John Van Evrie, a New York doctor and Democratic pamphleteer, declared that "it is a palpable and unavoidable fact that Negroes are a different species," and that the story of Adam and Eve referred only to the origin of white people. In 1850, the *Democratic Review* confided, "Few or none now seriously adhere to the theory of the unity of the races. The whole state of the science at this moment seems to indicate that there are several distinct races of men on the earth, with entirely different capacities, physical and mental."

As whites came to perceive racial differences as God-given and immutable, they changed the nature of those

differences as well. In the 18th and early 19th centuries, whites had stereotyped blacks as ignorant and prone to drunkenness and thievery, but they had also maintained a parallel stereotype of blacks as loyal and self-sacrificing servants. From the 1820s onward, racists continued to regard blacks as incompetent, but they found it harder to distinguish mere carelessness from dishonesty. Now they saw all blacks as treacherous, shrewd, and secretive—individuals who only *pretended* to feel loyalty to white families and affection for the white children they took care of, while awaiting the chance to steal from them or poison them. The writer Herman Melville, a lifelong Democrat who shared little of his compatriots' racism but who helped codify their fascination with duplicity and deceit, dramatized these fears in *Benito Cereno,* a novel about slaves who commandeered a sailing ship and its captain and crew, then (with knives secretly at the throats of their captives) acted out a servile charade for unsuspecting visitors who came aboard.

Above all, Democratic ideologues pronounced blacks unfit to be citizens of the white man's republic. Whigs often supported various forms of black suffrage; Democrats uniformly opposed it. Their insistence that blacks were incapable of citizenship reinforced their concept of an equally natural white male political capacity. This exclusion of blacks (by Democrats whose own political competence was often doubted by wealthier and better-educated Whigs) was designed to protect the republic while extending citizenship to all white men. The most vicious racist assaults were often carried out beneath symbols of the revolutionary republic. Antiblack mobs in Baltimore, Cincinnati, and Toledo called themselves Minute Men and Sons of Liberty. Philadelphia blacks who gathered to hear the Declaration of Independence read on the Fourth of July were attacked for "defiling the government." The antiabolitionist mob that sacked Lewis Tappan's house rescued a portrait of George Washington and carried it as a banner during their later attacks on Finneyite evangelicals and English actors.

The Beginnings of Antislavery

Before 1830, only a few whites considered slavery a moral issue. Quakers, at their annual meeting in 1758, had condemned both the slave trade and slavery, and Methodists and some Baptists had done the same late in the century. Washington, Jefferson, and other Chesapeake gentlemen doubted the wisdom if not the morality of holding slaves; New England Federalists had condemned slavery in the course of condemning Jeffersonian masters. But there were too few Quakers to make a difference, and the movement to free slaves in the Upper South and the antislavery

sentiments of southern evangelicals both died out early in the 19th century. Southerners and most northerners—when they bothered to think about it at all—tended to accept slavery as the result of human (read "black") depravity and God's unknowable plan.

Organized opposition to slavery before 1831 was pretty much limited to the American Colonization Society, founded in 1816. Led by wealthy, generally conservative northern churchmen and a contingent of Chesapeake gentlemen, the society proposed the voluntary, gradual, and compensated emancipation of slaves and the "repatriation" of free blacks to West Africa. Although the society transported a few thousand blacks to Liberia, it never posed a serious threat to slavery. Southerners, who owned 2 million slaves by 1830, opposed emancipation whether compensated or not, and few free blacks were interested in moving to Africa. The society's campaign to deport them so disturbed many free blacks that they substituted "Colored" for "African" in naming their institutions. One black churchman explained that references to Africa provided "an available excuse for a powerful enemy, the American Colonization Society, to use . . . as a weapon of our own make, to expel ourselves from our beloved country."

Although few white Americans actively opposed slavery before 1830, the writing was on the wall. Emancipation in the North, although it came about quietly, constituted an implicit condemnation of slavery in the South. So did events outside the United States. Toussaint L'Ouverture's successful slave revolution in Haiti in 1804 threatened slavery everywhere (see chapter 7). The British, whose navy could enforce their dictates on the seas, outlawed the Atlantic slave trade in 1808. Mexico, Peru, Chile, Gran Colombia (present-day Colombia, Venezuela, Ecuador, and Panama), and other new republics carved out of the Spanish empire emancipated their slaves. The most powerful blow came in 1830 when the British Parliament emancipated the slaves of Jamaica, Bermuda, and other Caribbean islands ruled by Britain.

Abolitionists

Religious revivals during the late 1820s and early 1830s created a reform-minded evangelical culture in the northern United States. Radical abolitionism dates from 1831, when William Lloyd Garrison published the first issue of the *Liberator.* Already a veteran reformer, Garrison condemned slavery as a national sin and demanded immediate emancipation—or at least an immediate start toward emancipation. "I am in earnest," he declared in his first editorial; "I will not equivocate—I will not excuse—I will not retreat a single inch—and I will be heard!"

In these ways, a radical minority forced politicians to demonstrate the complicity of the party system (and the Democrats in particular) in the institution of slavery, brought the slavery question to public attention, and tied it to questions of civil liberties in the North and political power in the South. They were a dangerous minority indeed.

🌐 The Politics of Gender and Sex

Whigs valued a reformed masculinity that was lived out in the sentimentalized homes of the northern business classes or in the Christian gentility of the Whig plantation and farm. Jacksonian voters, on the other hand, often defended domestic patriarchy. Whereas most were unimaginative paternalists, Democrats often made heroes of men whose flamboyant, rakish lives directly challenged Whig domesticity. Whigs denounced Andrew Jackson for allegedly stealing his wife from her lawful husband; Democrats often admired him for the same reason. Richard M. Johnson of Kentucky, who was vice president under Martin Van Buren, openly kept a mulatto mistress and had two daughters by her; with his pistols always at hand, he accompanied her openly around Washington, D.C. "Prince" John Van Buren, the president's son and himself a prominent New York Democrat, met a "dark-eyed, well-formed Italian lady" who called herself Amerigo Vespucci and claimed to be a direct descendant of the man for whom America was named. She became young Van Buren's "fancy lady," remaining with him until he lost her in a high-stakes card game.

Whigs made Democratic contempt for sentimental domesticity a political issue. William Crane, a Michigan Whig, claimed that Democrats "despised no man for his sins," and went on to say that "brothel-haunters flocked to this party, because here in all political circles, and political movements, they were treated as nobility." Much of the Whig cultural agenda (and much of Democratic hatred of that agenda) was rooted in contests between Whig and Democratic masculine styles.

Appetites

Many of the reforms urged by Whig evangelicals had to do with domestic and personal life rather than with politics. Their hopes for the perfection of the world hinged more on the character of individuals than on the role of institutions. Calvinism had taught that because human beings were innately selfish and subject to animal appetites, they must submit to godly authority. Evangelicals, on the other hand, defined original sin as a *tendency* toward selfishness and sin that could be fought off—with God's help—through prayer and personal discipline. They hoped to perfect the world by filling it with godly, self-governing individuals.

It was not an easy task, for opportunities to indulge in vanity, luxury, and sensuality were on the rise. Charles Finney, for instance, preached long and hard against vanity. "A self-indulgent Christian," he said, "is a contradiction. You might as well write on your clothes 'NO TRUTH IN RELIGION,'" he told fashionably dressed women, for their dress proclaimed "GIVE ME DRESS, GIVE ME FASHION, GIVE ME FLATTERY, AND I AM HAPPY." Finney also worried about the effect of money, leisure time, and cheap novels on middle-class homes. He could not, he said, "believe that a person who has ever known the love of God can relish a secular novel" or open his or her home to "Byron, Scott, Shakespeare, and a host of triflers and blasphemers of God." Evangelicals also disdained luxury in home furnishings; they discouraged the use of silks and velvets and questioned the propriety of decorating the home with mahogany, mirrors, brass furnishings, and upholstered chairs and sofas.

Members of the evangelical middle class tried to define levels of material comfort that would separate them from the indulgences of those above and below them. They made similar attempts in the areas of food and sex. Sylvester Graham (now remembered for the wheat cracker that bears his name) gave up the ministry in 1830 to become a full-time temperance lecturer. Before long, he was lecturing on the dangers of excess in diet and sex. He claimed that the consumption of red meat, spiced foods, and alcohol produced bodily excitement that resulted in weakness and disease. Sex—including fornication, fantasizing, masturbation, and bestiality—affected the body in even more destructive ways, and the two appetites reinforced each other. (Graham admitted that marital sex, although it was physiologically no different from other forms of sex, was preferable, for it was the least exciting.)

Acting on Graham's concerns, reformers established a system of Grahamite boardinghouses in which young men who were living away from home were provided with diets that helped them control their other appetites. Oberlin College, when it was founded by evangelicals in 1832, banned "tea and coffee, highly seasoned meats, rich pastries, and all unholsome [sic] and expensive foods." Among others who heeded Graham's advice were such future feminists as Lucy Stone, Susan B. Anthony, and Amelia Bloomer. Reformers who did not actually adopt Graham's system shared his concern over the twin evils of rich food and sexual excess. John R. McDowall, a divinity student who headed a mission to New York City prosti-

tutes, admitted, "Having eaten until I am full, lust gets the control of me." John Humphrey Noyes (another divinity student who turned to reform) set up a community in Oneida, New York, that indulged in plural marriage but at the same time urged sexual self-control; he also believed that a perfect Christian world would not allow meat-eating.

Moral Reform

Although most middle-class households failed to embrace Grahamism, simple food and sexual control became badges of class status. Men supposedly had the greatest difficulty taming their appetites. The old image—beginning with Eve and including Delilah and Jezebel and other dangerous women of the Old Testament—of woman as seductress persisted in the more traditionalist churches and in the pulp fiction from which middle-class mothers tried to protect their sons (see chapter 10). Whig evangelicals, on the other hand, had made the discovery that women were naturally free of desire and that only men were subject to the animal passions. "What terrible temptations lie in the way of your sex," wrote Harriet Beecher Stowe to her husband. "Tho I did love you with an almost insane love before I married you, I never knew yet or felt the pulsation which showed me that I could be tempted in that way. I loved you as I now love God." The middle-class ideal combined female purity and male self-control. For the most part it was a private reform, contained within the home. Sometimes, however, evangelical domesticity produced moral crusades to impose that ethos on the world at large. Many of these crusades were led by women.

In 1828, a band of Sunday school teachers—most of them women—initiated an informal mission to prostitutes that grew into the New York Magdalen Society. Taking a novel approach to an age-old question, the society argued that prostitution was created by brutal fathers and husbands who abandoned their young daughters or wives, by dandies who seduced them and turned them into prostitutes, and by lustful men who bought their services. Prostitution, in other words, was not the result of the innate sinfulness of prostitutes; it was the result of the brutality and lust of men. The solution was to remove young prostitutes from their environment, pray with them, and convert them to middle-class morality.

The Magdalen Society's *First Annual Report* (1831) inveighed against male lust and printed shocking life histories of prostitutes. Some men, however, read it as pornography; others used it as a guidebook to the seamier side of New York City. The wealthy male evangelicals who had bankrolled the Magdalen Society withdrew their support, and the organization fell apart. Thereupon many of the women reformers set up the Female Moral Reform Society, with a House of Industry in which prostitutes were taught morality and household skills to prepare them for new lives as domestic servants in pious middle-class homes. This effort also failed, largely because few prostitutes were interested in domestic service or evangelical religion. That fact became distressingly clear when in 1836 the society was obliged to close its House of Industry after the residents had taken it over during the caretaker's absence.

The Female Moral Reform Society was more successful with members of its own class. Its newspaper, the *Advocate of Moral Reform,* circulated throughout the evangelical North, eventually reaching 555 auxiliary societies with 20,000 readers. Now evangelical women fought prostitution by publishing the names of customers. They campaigned against pornography, obscenity, lewdness, and seduction and accepted the responsibility of rearing their sons to be pure, even when it meant dragging them out of brothels. Occasionally, they prosecuted men who took advantage of servant girls. They also publicized the names of adulterers, and they had seducers brought into court. In the process, women reformers fought the sexual double standard and assumed the power to define what was respectable and what was not.

Women's Rights

From the late 1820s onward, middle-class women in the North assumed roles that would have been unthinkable to their mothers and grandmothers. Evangelical domesticity made loving mothers (and not stern fathers) the principal rearers of children. Housewives saw themselves as missionaries to their families, responsible for the choices their children and husbands made between salvation or sin. In that role, women became arbiters of fashion, diet, and sexual behavior. Many joined the temperance movement and moral reform societies, where they became public reformers while posing as mothers protecting their sons from rum sellers and seducers. Such experiences gave them a sense of spiritual empowerment that led some to question their own subordinate status within a system of gendered social roles. Lydia Maria Child, a writer of sentimental fiction and manuals on household economy as well as a leading abolitionist and moral reformer, proclaimed, "Those who urged women to become missionaries and form tract societies . . . have changed the household utensil to a living, energetic being, and they have no spell to turn it into a broom again."

The antislavery movement turned many women into advocates of women's rights. Abolitionists, following the perfectionist implications of Whig evangelicalism to their

an indicator of personal history and cultural loyalties. In the states and neighborhoods, Whigs embraced commerce and activist government, arguing that both would foster prosperity, social harmony, and moral progress. Faith in progress and improvement led Northern and western Whigs—primarily the more radical evangelicals among them—to entertain the hope that liberty and equality might apply to women and blacks. Democrats, on the other hand, were generally more localistic and culturally conservative. Like the Whigs, they seldom doubted the value of commerce, but they worried that the Market Revolution and its organization of banking, credit, and monetary supply was creating unprecedented levels of inequality and personal dependence among the republic's white male citizenry; they were certain that Whig public works projects and Whig taxation increased inequality and corrupted the republic. Democrats also looked with angry disbelief at attempts of Whigs (and rebellious members of Whig families) to govern the private and public behavior of their neighbors, and sometimes even to tinker with ancient distinctions of gender and race.

In sum, Whigs reformulated the revolutionary legacy of liberty and equality, moving away from classical notions of citizenship and toward liberty of conscience and equality of opportunity within a market-driven democracy. They often attempted to civilize that new world by using government power to encourage commerce, social interdependence, and cultural homogeneity. When Democrats argued that Whig "interdependence" in fact meant dependence and inequality, Whigs countered with promises of individual success for those who were morally worthy of it. Democrats trusted none of that. Theirs was a Jeffersonian formulation grounded in a fierce defense of the liberty and equality of white men, and in a minimal, inexpensive, decentralized government that protected the liberties of those men without threatening their independence or their power over their households and within their neighborhoods.

SUGGESTED READINGS

On party ideologies, see **John Ashworth, 'Agrarians & Aristocrats': Party Political Ideology in the United States, 1837–1846** (1983), and **Daniel Walker Howe, The Political Culture of the American Whigs** (1979). Constituencies and state-level issues are addressed in **Lee Benson, The Concept of Jacksonian Democracy: New York as a Test Case** (1961); **Ronald P. Formisano, The Transformation of Political Culture: Massachusetts Parties, 1790s–1840s** (1983); and **Lacy K. Ford, Jr., Origins of Southern Radicalism: The South Carolina Upcountry, 1800–1860** (1988). **Richard J. Carwardine, Evangelicals and Politics in Antebellum America** (1993) is an insightful study of religion and politics in these years. On the politics of schools, see **Carl F. Kaestle, Pillars of the Republic: Common Schools and American Society, 1780–1860** (1983). Influential studies of prisons and asylums include **David J. Rothman, The Discovery of the Asylum: Social Order and Disorder in the New Republic** (1971) and **Michael Meranze, Laboratories of Virtue: Punishment, Revolution, and Authority in Philadelphia, 1760–1835** (1996).

Drinking and temperance are the subjects of **W. J. Rorabaugh, The Alcoholic Republic: An American Tradition** (1979). The standard study of free blacks is **Leon F. Litwack, North of Slavery: The Negro in the Free States, 1790–1860** (1960), which can be supplemented with **Gary B. Nash, Forging Freedom: The Formation of Philadelphia's Black Community, 1720–1840** (1988) and **Shane White, Stories of Freedom in Black New York** (2002). The literature on reform movements is synthesized in **Steven Mintz, Moralists & Modernizers: America's Pre–Civil War Reformers** (1995). Students might also consult **Robert H. Abzug, Cosmos Crumbling: American Reform and the Religious Imagination** (1994); **Jean Fagan Yellin, Women & Sisters: The Antislavery Feminists in American Culture** (1989); and **Lori D. Ginzberg, Women and the Work of Benevolence: Morality, Politics, and Class in the 19th-Century United States** (1990). The cultural and moral underpinnings of reform are a subtext of **Karen Halttunen's** subtle and important **Murder Most Foul: The Killer and the American Gothic Imagination** (1998).

AMERICAN JOURNEY ONLINE
AND
 INFOTRAC COLLEGE EDITION

Visit the source collections at www.ajaccess.wadsworth.com and
infotrac.thomsonlearning.com and use the Search function with
the following key terms to explore documents, images, audio
and video clips, articles, and commentary related to the material
in this chapter.

Dorothea Dix

Free Blacks

Abolitionism

Herman Melville

William H. Seward

American Colonization Society

American Anti-Slavery Society

Seneca Falls

Women's Rights

Sarah Grimke

GRADE AIDS

**Visit the Liberty Equality Power Companion Web Site for resources specific to
this textbook:** http://history.wadsworth.com/murrin_LEP4e

 The CD in the back of this book and the U.S. History Resource Center at
http://history.wadsworth.com/u.s./ offer a variety of tools to help you succeed in
this course, including access to quizzes; images; documents; interactive simulations,
maps, and timelines; movie explorations; and a wealth of other sources.

Chapter 12

Jacksonian Democracy

JACKSON AS DEMOCRACY INCARNATE
Andrew Jackson struck a romantic military pose for this portrait painted in 1820.
Posing as the embodiment of democracy and as an extravagantly melodramatic hero,
Jackson imposed himself on his times as few Americans have done.

C H A P T E R   O U T L I N E

N ational political leaders from the 1820s until the outbreak of the Civil War faced two persistent questions. First, a deepening rift between slave and free states threatened the very existence of the nation. Second, explosive economic development and territorial expansion made new demands on the political system—demands that raised the question of government participation in economic life.

The Whig Party proposed the American System as the answer to both questions. The national government, said the Whigs, should subsidize roads and canals, foster industry with protective tariffs, and maintain a national bank capable of exercising centralized control over credit and currency. The result would be a peaceful, prosperous, and truly national market society. If the South, the West, and the Northeast were profiting by doing business with each other, the argument went, sectional fears and jealousies would quiet down. Jacksonian Democrats, on the other hand, argued that the American System was unconstitutional, that it violated the rights of states and localities, and that it would tax honest citizens in order to benefit corrupt and wealthy insiders. Most dangerous of all, argued the Democrats, Whig economic nationalism would create an activist, interventionist national government that would anger and frighten the slaveholding South. To counter both threats, the Jacksonians resurrected Jefferson's agrarian republic of states' rights and inactive, inexpensive government—all of it deeply inflected in the code of white male equality, domestic patriarchy, and racial slavery that was being acted out in families, neighborhoods, and state legislatures.

C H A P T E R   F O C U S

- ◆ In terms of party development, what were the long-term results of the Missouri controversy and the Panic of 1819? Why?
- ◆ At the national level, how did Jacksonian Democrats and their opponents deal with widening differences between the northern and southern states during these years?

♦ How did they address issues raised by economic development?

♦ What was peculiarly "national" about the Second Party System?

🌐 Prologue: 1819

Jacksonian Democracy was rooted in two events that occurred in 1819. First, the angry debate that surrounded Missouri's admission as a slave state revealed the centrality and vulnerability of slavery within the Union. Second, a severe financial collapse led many Americans to doubt the Market Revolution's compatibility with the Jeffersonian republic. By 1820, politicians were determined to reconstruct the limited-government, states'-rights coalition that had elected Thomas Jefferson. By 1828, they had formed the Democratic Party, with Andrew Jackson at its head.

The West, 1803–1840s

When Jefferson bought the Louisiana Territory in 1803, he knew that he was giving future generations of Americans a huge "Empire for Liberty." He knew almost nothing, however, about the new land itself. Only a few French trappers and traders had traveled the plains between the Mississippi and the Rocky Mountains, and no white person had seen the territory drained by the Columbia River. In 1804, Jefferson sent an expedition under Meriwether Lewis, his private secretary, and William Clark, brother of the Indian fighter George Rogers Clark, to explore the land he had bought. To prepare for the expedition, Lewis studied astronomy, zoology, and botany; Clark was already an accomplished mapmaker. The two kept meticulous journals of one of the epic adventures in American history.

In May 1804, Lewis and Clark and 41 companions boarded a keelboat and two large canoes at the village of St. Louis. That spring and summer they poled and paddled 1,600 miles up the Missouri River, passing through rolling plains dotted by the farm villages of the Pawnee, Oto, Missouri, Crow, Omaha, Hidatsa, and Mandan peoples. The villages of the lower Missouri had been cut off from the western buffalo herds and reduced to dependence by mounted Sioux warriors, who had begun to establish their hegemony over the northern plains.

Lewis and Clark traveled through Sioux territory and stopped for the winter at the prosperous, heavily fortified Mandan villages at the big bend of the Missouri River in Dakota country. In the spring they hired Toussaint Charbonneau, a French fur trader, to guide them to the Pacific. Although Charbonneau turned out to be useless, his wife,

---

C H R O N O L O G Y

1804–06 Lewis and Clark explore the northern regions of the Louisiana Purchase

1819 Controversy arises over Missouri's admission to the Union as a slave state • Panic of 1819 marks the first failure of the national market economy

1820 Missouri Compromise adopted

1823 Monroe Doctrine written by Secretary of State John Quincy Adams

1824–25 Adams wins the presidency over Andrew Jackson • Adams appoints Henry Clay as secretary of state • Jacksonians charge a "Corrupt Bargain" between Adams and Clay

1827 Cherokees in Georgia declare themselves a republic

1828 Jackson defeats Adams for the presidency • "Tariff of Abominations" passed by Congress • John C. Calhoun's *Exposition and Protest* presents doctrine of nullification

1830 Congress passes the Indian Removal Act

1832 Jackson reelected over Henry Clay • *Worcester* v. *Georgia* exempts the Cherokee from Georgia law • Jackson vetoes recharter of the Bank of the United States

1833 Force Bill and Tariff of 1833 end the nullification crisis

1834 Whig Party formed in opposition to Jacksonians

1836 Congress adopts "gag rule" to table antislavery petitions • Van Buren elected president

1837 Financial panic ushers in a severe economic depression

1838 U.S. Army marches the remaining Cherokee to Indian Territory

1840 Whig William Henry Harrison defeats Van Buren for presidency

---

a teenaged Shoshone girl named Sacajawea, was an indispensable guide, interpreter, and diplomat. With her help, Lewis and Clark navigated the upper Missouri, crossed the Rockies to the Snake River, and followed that stream to the Columbia River. They reached the Pacific in November 1805 and spent the winter at what is now Astoria, Oregon. Retracing their steps the following spring and summer, they returned to St. Louis in September 1806. They brought with them many volumes of drawings and notes, along with assurances that the Louisiana Purchase had been worth many, many times its price.

As time passed, Americans began to settle the southern portions of the Louisiana Purchase. Louisiana itself, strategically crucial and already the site of sugar plantations and the town of New Orleans, entered the Union in 1812. Settlers were also filtering into northern Louisiana and the Arkansas and Missouri territories. Farther north

and west, the Sioux extended their control over the northern reaches of the land that Jefferson had bought.

The Sioux were aided in their conquest by the spread of smallpox. The disease moved up the Missouri River periodically from the 1790s onward; by the 1830s, epidemics were ravaging the sedentary peoples of the Missouri. The Mandans, who had been so hospitable to Lewis and Clark, got the worst of it: They were almost completely wiped out. The Sioux and their Cheyenne allies, who lived in small bands and were constantly on the move, fared better. Their horse-raiding parties now grew into armies of mounted invaders numbering as many as 2,000, and they extended their hunting lands south into what is now southern Nebraska and as far west as the Yellowstone River. In the 1840s, white settlers began crossing the southern plains, while white politicians entered into a fateful debate on whether these lands would become the site of northern farms or southern plantations. At the same time, the newly victorious Sioux never doubted that the northern plains would be theirs forever.

The Argument over Missouri

Early in 1819, slaveholding Missouri applied for admission to the Union as the first new state to be carved out of the Louisiana Purchase. New York Congressman James Tallmadge, Jr., quickly proposed two amendments to the Missouri statehood bill. The first would bar additional slaves from being brought into Missouri (16 percent of Missouri's people were already slaves). The second would emancipate Missouri slaves born after admission when they reached their 25th birthday. Put simply, the Tallmadge amendments would admit Missouri only if Missouri agreed to become a free state.

The congressional debates on the Missouri question had nothing to do with humanitarian objections to slavery and everything to do with political power. Rufus King of New York, an old Federalist who led the northerners in the Senate, insisted that he opposed the admission of a new slave state "solely in its bearing and effects upon great political interests, and upon the just and equal rights of the freemen of the nation." Northerners had long chafed at the added representation in Congress and in the electoral college that the "three-fifths" rule granted to the slave states (see chapter 6). The rule had, in fact, added significantly to southern power: In 1790, the South, with 40 percent of the white population, controlled 47 percent of the votes in Congress—enough to decide close votes both in Congress and in presidential elections. Federalists pointed out that of the 12 additional electoral votes the three-fifths rule gave to the South, 10 had gone to Thomas Jefferson in 1800 and had given him the election. Without the bogus votes provided by slavery, they argued, Virginia's stranglehold on the presidency would have been broken with Washington's departure in 1796.

In 1819, the North held a majority in the House of Representatives. The South, thanks to the recent admissions of Alabama and southern-oriented Illinois, controlled a bare majority in the Senate. Voting on the Tallmadge amendments was starkly sectional: Northern congressmen voted 86 to 10 for the first amendment, 80 to 14 for the second; southerners rejected both, 66 to 1 and 64 to 2. In the Senate, a unanimous South defeated the Tallmadge amendments with the help of the two Illinois senators and three northerners. Deadlocked between a Senate in favor of admitting Missouri as a slave state and a House dead set against it, Congress broke off one of the angriest sessions in its history and went home.

The Missouri Compromise

The new Congress that convened in the winter of 1819–20 passed the legislative package that became known as the Missouri Compromise. Massachusetts offered its northern counties as the new free state of Maine, thus neutralizing fears that the South would gain votes in the Senate with the admission of Missouri. Senator Jesse Thomas of Illinois proposed the so-called Thomas Proviso: If the North would admit Missouri as a slave state, the South would agree to outlaw slavery in territories above 36°30′ N latitude—a line extending from the southern border of Missouri to Spanish (within a year, Mexican) territory. That line would open Arkansas Territory (present-day Arkansas and Oklahoma) to slavery and would close to slavery the remainder of the Louisiana Territory—land that would subsequently become all or part of nine states.

Congress admitted Maine with little debate, but the terms of the Thomas Proviso met northern opposition. A joint Senate-House committee finally decided to separate the two bills. With half of the southern representatives and nearly all of the northerners supporting it, the Thomas Proviso passed. Congress next took up the admission of Missouri. With the votes of a solid South and 14 compromise-minded northerners, Missouri entered the Union as a slave state. President James Monroe applauded the "patriotic devotion" of the northern representatives "who preferr'd the sacrifice of themselves at home" to endangering the Union. His words were prophetic: Nearly all of the 14 were voted out of office when they faced angry northern voters in the next election.

The Missouri crisis brought the South's commitment to slavery and the North's resentment of southern political power into collision, revealing an uncompromisable gulf between slave and free states. While northerners vowed

to relinquish no more territory to slavery, southerners talked openly of disunion and civil war. A Georgia politician announced that the Missouri debates had lit a fire that "seas of blood can only extinguish." President Monroe's secretary of state, John Quincy Adams, saw the debates as an omen: Northerners would unanimously oppose the extension of slavery whenever the question came to a vote. Adams confided in his diary:

> Here was a new party ready formed, . . . terrible to the whole Union, but portentiously terrible to the South—threatening in its progress the emancipation of all their slaves, threatening in its immediate effect that Southern domination which has swayed the Union for the last twenty years.

Viewing the crisis from Monticello, the aging Thomas Jefferson was distraught:

> A geographical line, coinciding with a marked principle, moral and political, once conceived and held up to the angry passions of men, will never be obliterated; every new irritation will mark it deeper and deeper. . . . This momentous question, like a fire-bell in the night, awakened and filled me with terror. I considered it at once the knell of the Union.

The Panic of 1819

Politicians debated the Missouri question against a darkening backdrop of economic depression—a downturn that would shape political alignments as much as the slavery question. The origins of the Panic of 1819 were international and numerous: European agriculture was recovering from the Napoleonic wars, thereby reducing the demand for American foodstuffs; war and revolution in the New World had cut off the supply of precious metals (the base of the international money supply) from the mines of Mexico and Peru; debt-ridden European governments hoarded the available specie; and American bankers and businessmen met the situation by expanding credit and issuing banknotes that were mere dreams of real money. Coming in the first years of the Market Revolution, this speculative boom was encouraged by American bankers who had little experience with corporate charters, promissory notes, bills of exchange, or stocks and bonds.

Congress had in part chartered the Second Bank of the United States in 1816 (see chapter 9) to impose order on this situation, but the Bank itself under the presidency of the genial Republican politician William Jones became part of the problem. The western branch offices in Cincinnati and Lexington became embroiled in the speculative boom, and insiders at the Baltimore branch hatched criminal schemes to enrich themselves. With matters spinning out

of control, Jones resigned early in 1819. The new president, Langdon Cheves of South Carolina, curtailed credit and demanded that state banknotes received by the Bank of the United States be redeemed in specie (precious metals). By doing so, Cheves rescued the Bank from the paper economy created by state-chartered banks, but at huge expense: When the state banks were forced to redeem their notes in specie, they demanded payment from their own borrowers, and the national money and credit system collapsed.

The depression that followed the Panic of 1819 was the first failure of the market economy. Local ups and downs had occurred since the 1790s, but this collapse was nationwide. Employers who could not meet their debts went out of business, and hundreds of thousands of wage workers lost their jobs. In Philadelphia, unemployment reached 75 percent; 1,800 workers in that city were imprisoned for debt. A tent city of the unemployed sprang up on the outskirts of Baltimore. Other cities and towns were hit as hard, and the situation was no better in the countryside. Thomas Jefferson reported that farms in his neighborhood were selling for what had earlier been a year's rent, and a single session of the county court at Nashville handled more than 500 lawsuits for debt.

Faced with a disastrous downturn that none could control and that few understood, many Americans directed their resentment onto the banks, particularly on the Bank of the United States. John Jacob Astor, a New York merchant and possibly the richest man in America at that time, admitted that "there has been too much Speculation and too much assumption of Power on the Part of the Bank Directors which has caused [sic] the institution to become unpopular." William Gouge, who would become the Jacksonian Democrats' favorite economist, put it more bluntly: When the Bank demanded that state banknotes be redeemed in specie, he said, "the Bank was saved and the people were ruined." By the end of 1819, the Bank of the United States had won the name that it would carry to its death in the 1830s: the Monster.

Republican Revival

The crises during 1819 and 1820 prompted demands for a return to Jeffersonian principles. President Monroe's happily proclaimed Era of Good Feelings—a new era of partyless politics created by the collapse of Federalism—was, according to worried Republicans, a disaster. Without opposition, Jefferson's dominant Republican Party had lost its way. The nationalist Congress of 1816 had enacted much of the Federalist program under the name of Republicanism;

the result, said the old Republicans, was an aggressive government that helped bring on the Panic of 1819. At the same time, the collapse of Republican Party discipline in Congress had allowed the Missouri question to degenerate into a sectional free-for-all. By 1820, many Republicans were calling for a Jeffersonian revival that would limit government power and guarantee southern rights within the Union.

Martin Van Buren Leads the Way

The busiest and the most astute of those Republicans was Martin Van Buren, leader of New York's Bucktail Republican faction, who took his seat in the Senate in 1821. An immensely talented man with no influential family connections (his father was a Hudson valley tavern keeper) and little formal education, Van Buren had built his political career out of a commitment to Jeffersonian principles, personal charm, and party discipline. He and his colleagues in New York, deploying group discipline oiled by the partisan use of government patronage, had begun to invent the modern political party—arguing that it was a necessary weapon in democracy's contests with the well-placed, well-educated gentlemen who had monopolized public office. Arriving in Washington in the aftermath of the Missouri debates and the Panic of 1819, he hoped to apply his new politics to what he perceived as a dangerous turning point in national public life.

Van Buren's New York experience, along with his reading of national politics, told him that disciplined political parties were necessary democratic tools. The Founding Fathers—including Jefferson—had denounced parties, claiming that republics rested on civic virtue, not competition. Van Buren, on the other hand, claimed that the Era of Good Feelings had turned public attention away from politics, allowing privileged insiders—many of them unreconstructed Federalists—to create a big national state and to reorganize politics along sectional lines. Van Buren insisted that competition and party divisions were inevitable and good, but that they must be made to serve the republic. He wrote:

> We must always have party distinctions, and the old ones are the best. . . . If the old ones are suppressed, geographical differences founded on local instincts or what is worse, prejudices between free & slave holding states will inevitably take their place.

Working with like-minded politicians, Van Buren reconstructed the coalition of northern and southern agrarians that had elected Thomas Jefferson. The result was the Democratic Party and, ultimately, a national two-party system that persisted until the eve of the Civil War.

The Election of 1824

With the approach of the 1824 presidential election, Van Buren and his friends supported William H. Crawford, Monroe's secretary of war and a staunch Georgia Republican. The Van Burenites controlled the Republican congressional caucus, the body that traditionally chose the party's presidential candidates. The public distrusted the caucus as undemocratic because it represented the only party in government and thus could dictate the choice of a president. Van Buren, however, continued to regard it as a necessary tool of party discipline. With most congressmen fearing their constituents, only a minority showed up for the caucus vote. They dutifully nominated Crawford.

With Republican Party unity broken, the list of sectional candidates grew. John Quincy Adams was the son of a Federalist president, successful secretary of state under Monroe, and one of the northeastern Federalist converts to Republicanism who, according to people like Van Buren and Crawford, had blunted the republican thrust of Jefferson's old party. He entered the contest as New England's favorite son. Henry Clay of Kentucky, a nationalist who claimed as his own the American System of protective tariffs, centralized banking, and government-sponsored internal improvements, expected to carry the West. John C. Calhoun of South Carolina announced his candidacy, but when he saw the swarm of candidates, he dropped out and put himself forth as the sole candidate for vice president.

The wild card was Andrew Jackson of Tennessee, who in 1824 was known only as a military hero—scourge of the southern Indians and victor over the British at New Orleans (see chapter 8). He was also a frontier nabob with a reputation for violence: He had killed a rival in a duel, had engaged in a shoot-out in a Nashville tavern, and had reputedly stolen his wife from her estranged husband. According to Jackson's detractors, such impetuosity marked his public life as well. As commander of U.S. military forces in the South in 1818, Jackson had led an unauthorized invasion of Spanish Florida, claiming that it was a hideout for Seminole warriors who raided into the United States and a sanctuary for runaway Georgia slaves. During the action, he had occupied Spanish forts, summarily executed Seminoles, and hanged two British subjects. Secretary of State John Quincy Adams had belatedly approved the raid, knowing that the show of American force would encourage the Spanish to sell Florida to the United States. Secretary of War Crawford, on the other hand, as an "economy" measure, had reduced the number of major generals in the U.S. Army from two to one, thus eliminating Jackson's job. After being appointed governor of newly acquired Florida in 1821, Jackson retired from public life

The Granger Collection.

JOHN QUINCY ADAMS

The politician enjoyed a remarkably productive career as Monroe's Secretary of State, then rode into the presidency in the conflicted and controversial election of 1824. The intelligence and erudition that the picture projects had served him well as a diplomat. As president, it marked him as aloof, aristocratic, and incapable of governing a democratic nation.

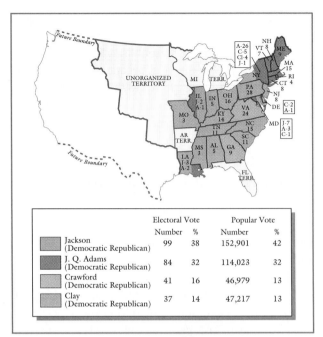

	Electoral Vote		Popular Vote	
	Number	%	Number	%
Jackson (Democratic Republican)	99	38	152,901	42
J. Q. Adams (Democratic Republican)	84	32	114,023	32
Crawford (Democratic Republican)	41	16	46,979	13
Clay (Democratic Republican)	37	14	47,217	13

MAP 12.1   PRESIDENTIAL ELECTION, 1824

Voting in the four-cornered contest of 1824 was starkly sectional. John Quincy Adams carried his native New England, while Crawford and Clay carried only a few states in their own sections. Only Andrew Jackson enjoyed national support: He carried states in every section but New England, and he ran a strong second in many of the states that were awarded to other candidates.

"A Corrupt Bargain"

Jackson assumed that he had won the election: He had received 42 percent of the popular vote to his nearest rival's 33 percent, and he was clearly the nation's choice, but his 99 electoral votes were 32 shy of the plurality demanded by the Constitution. And so, acting under the 12th Amendment, the House of Representatives would select a president from among the top three candidates. As the candidate with the fewest electoral votes, Henry Clay was eliminated, but he remained Speaker of the House and had enough support to throw the election to either Jackson or Adams. Years later, Jackson told a dinner guest that Clay had offered to support him in exchange for Clay's appointment as secretary of state—an office that traditionally led to the presidency. When Jackson turned him down, according to Jacksonian legend, Clay went to Adams and made the same offer. Adams accepted what became known as the "Corrupt Bargain" in January 1825. A month later, the House of Representatives voted: Clay's supporters, joined by several old Federalists, switched to Adams, giving him a one-vote victory. Soon after becoming president, Adams appointed Henry Clay as his secretary of state.

later that year. In 1824, eastern politicians knew Jackson only as a "military chieftain," "the Napoleon of the woods," a frontier hothead, and, possibly, a robber-bridegroom.

Jackson may have been all of those things, but the easterners failed to recognize his immense popularity, particularly in the new states of the South and the West. Thus, in the election of 1824, in the 16 states that chose presidential electors by popular vote (six states still left the choice to their legislatures), Jackson polled 152,901 votes to Adams's 114,023 and Clay's 47,217. Crawford, who suffered a crippling stroke during the campaign, won 46,979 votes. Jackson's support was not only larger but also more nearly national than that of his opponents. Adams carried only his native New England and a portion of New York. Clay's meager support was limited to the Northwest, and Crawford's to the Southeast and to the portions of New York that Van Buren was able to deliver. Jackson carried 84 percent of the votes of his own Southwest, and won victories in Pennsylvania, New Jersey, North Carolina, Indiana, and Illinois, and ran a close second in several other states.

From the Collections of the Library of Congress.

"THE SYMPTOMS OF A LOCKED JAW"

In 1827, Henry Clay published a rebuttal of Jacksonian charges that he had participated in a Corrupt Bargain to deliver the presidency to John Quincy Adams. Here, a pro-Clay cartoonist displays Clay as a tailor in the act of sewing Andrew Jackson's mouth shut. Neither the rebuttal nor the cartoon worked: the long-term suspicions of the bargain with Adams ruined Clay's chances to become president.

Reaction to the alleged Corrupt Bargain between John Quincy Adams and Henry Clay dominated the Adams administration and gave rise to a rhetoric of intrigue and betrayal that nourished a rising democratic movement. Before the vote took place in the House of Representatives, Andrew Jackson remarked, "Rumors say that deep intrigue is on foot," and predicted a "bargain & sale" of the presidency. After the election, Jackson declared that the "gamester" Henry Clay has subverted the democratic will to his own purposes and that "the rights of the people have been bartered for promises of office." "So you see," Jackson said, "The *Judas* of the West has closed the contract and will receive the thirty pieces of silver. His end will be the same." Others in Washington were equally appalled. Robert Y. Hayne of South Carolina denounced the "monstrous union between Clay & Adams," and Louis McLane of Delaware declared the coalition of Clay and Adams utterly "unnatural & preposterous." (Eventually, Clay challenged Virginia Senator John Randolph, one of his nastiest critics, to a duel. Clay's shot passed harmlessly through Randolph's flowing coat, and Randolph fired a gentlemanly shot into the air, but the charge of corruption would follow Clay for the rest of his political life.)

Jacksonian Melodrama

Andrew Jackson regarded the intrigues that robbed him of the presidency in 1825 as the culmination of a long train of corruption that the nation had suffered over the previous 10 years. Although in the campaign he had made only vague policy statements, he had firm ideas of what had gone wrong with the republic. In 1821, after having been "betrayed" by members of Monroe's cabinet over his raid into Florida, Jackson had retired to his plantation near Nashville to ponder the state of the nation and fill page after page with what he called "memorandums." (This was the kind of gaffe that appalled his educated eastern opponents and pleased nearly everyone else.)

A frontier planter with a deep distrust of banks, Jackson claimed that the Panic of 1819 had been brought on by self-serving miscreants in the Bank of the United States. He insisted that the national debt was another source of corruption; it must be paid off and never allowed to recur. The federal government under James Monroe was filled with swindlers, and in the name of a vague nationalism they were taking power for themselves and scheming against the liberties of the people. The politicians had been bought off, said Jackson, and had attempted—through "King Caucus"—to select a president by backstairs deals rather than by popular election. Finally, in 1825, they had stolen the presidency outright.

Like hundreds of thousands of other Americans, Jackson sensed that something had gone wrong with the republic—that selfishness and intrigue had corrupted the government. In the language of revolutionary republicanism, which Jackson had learned as a boy in the Carolina backwoods and would speak throughout his life, a corrupt power once again threatened to snuff out liberty.

In his "memorandums," Jackson set against the designs of that power the classic republican safeguard: a virtuous citizenry. Unlike most of his revolutionary forebears, however, he believed that government should follow the will of popular majorities. An aroused public, he said, was the republic's best hope: "My fervent prayers are that our republican government may be perpetual, and the people alone by their virtue, and independent exercise of their free suffrage can make it perpetual."

More completely than any of his rivals, Jackson had captured the rhetoric of the revolutionary republic. And, with his fixation on secrecy, corruption, and intrigues, he transformed both that rhetoric and his own biography into popular melodrama. Finally, with a political alchemy that his rivals never understood, Jackson submerged old notions of republican citizenship into a firm faith in majoritarian democracy: Individuals might become selfish and corrupt, he believed, but a democratic majority

was, by its very nature, opposed to corruption and governmental excess. Thus the republic was safe only when governed by the will of the majority. The Corrupt Bargain of 1825 had made that clear: Either the people or political schemers would rule.

Adams versus Jackson

While Jackson plotted revenge, John Quincy Adams assumed the duties of the presidency. He was well prepared. The son of a Federalist president, he had been an extraordinarily successful secretary of state under Monroe, guiding American diplomacy in the postwar world.

Nationalism in an International Arena

In the Rush-Bagot Treaty of 1817 and the British-American Convention of 1818, Secretary of State John Quincy Adams helped pacify the Great Lakes, restore American fishing rights off the coast of Canada, and draw the U.S.– Canadian boundary west to the Rocky Mountains—actions that transformed the Canadian–American frontier from a battleground into the peaceful border that it has been ever since. He pacified the southern border as well. In 1819, following Jackson's raid into Florida, the Adams-Onis Treaty procured Florida for the United States and defined the U.S.–Spanish border west of the Mississippi in ways that gave the Americans claims to the Pacific Coast in the Northwest.

Trickier problems had arisen when Spanish colonies in the Americas declared their independence. Spain could not prevent this, and the powers of Europe, victorious over Napoleon and determined to roll back the republican revolution, talked openly of helping Spain or of annexing South American territory for themselves. Both the Americans and the British opposed such a move, and the British proposed a joint statement outlawing the interference of any outside power (including themselves) in Latin America. Adams had thought it better for the United States to make its own policy than to "come in as cock-boat in the wake of the British man-of-war." In 1823, he wrote what became known as the Monroe Doctrine. Propounded at the same time that the United States recognized the new Latin American republics, it declared American opposition to any European attempt at colonization in the New World without (as the British had wanted) denying the right of the United States to annex new territory. Although the international community knew that the British navy, and not the Monroe Doctrine, kept the European powers out of the Americas, Adams had announced that the

United States was determined to become the preeminent power in the Western Hemisphere.

Nationalism at Home

As president, Adams tried to translate his fervent nationalism into domestic policy. Although the brilliant, genteel Adams had dealt smoothly with European diplomats, as president of a democratic republic he went out of his way to isolate himself and to offend popular democracy. In his first annual message to Congress, Adams outlined an ambitious program for national development under the auspices of the federal government: roads, canals, a national university, a national astronomical observatory ("lighthouses of the skies"), and other costly initiatives:

> The spirit of improvement is abroad upon the earth.... While foreign nations less blessed with ... freedom ... than ourselves are advancing with gigantic strides in the career of public improvement, were we to slumber in indolence or fold up our arms and proclaim to the world that we are palsied by the will of our constituents, would it not ... doom ourselves to perpetual inferiority?

Congressmen could not believe their ears as they listened to Adams's extravagant proposals. Here was a president who had received only one in three votes and who had entered office accused of intrigues against the democratic will. And yet at the first opportunity he was telling Congress to pass an ambitious program and not to be "palsied" by the will of the electorate. Even the many members of Congress who favored Adams's program were afraid to vote for it.

Adding to his reputation as an enemy of democracy whenever opportunity presented itself, Adams heaped popular suspicions not only on himself but also on his program. Hostile politicians and journalists never tired of joking about Adams's "lighthouses to the skies." More lasting, however, was the connection they drew between federal public works projects and high taxes, intrusive government, the denial of democratic majorities, and expanded opportunities for corruption, secret deals, and special favors. Congress never acted on the president's proposals, and the Adams administration emerged as little more than a long prelude to the election of 1828.

The Birth of the Democratic Party

As early as 1825, it was clear that the election of 1828 would pit Adams against Andrew Jackson. To the consternation of his chief supporters, Adams did nothing to prepare for the contest. He refused to remove even his noisiest enemies from appointive office, and he built no political organization for what promised to be a stiff contest for reelection.

Commodore David Porter, Commander of the Mexican Navy

Imperial wars and republican revolutions transformed the politics of the world in the late 18th and early 19th centuries. They also provided opportunities for international adventurers. Experienced naval officers were in particular demand, and some of them ended up in odd places: The Irishman William ("Admiral Guillermo") Brown sailed for revolutionary Buenos Aires; Thomas Cochrane, dismissed from the Royal Navy, became an admiral in the navies of Chile and Brazil; Admiral Murad Reis (a Scotsman named Lysle) sailed for the Tripoli pirates; and the American Commodore David Porter, for two tumultuous years beginning in 1826, commanded the naval forces of the Republic of Mexico.

David Porter was a brave and headstrong officer. He had spent two years in a Tripolitan prison; had pestered British commerce, the British whaling fleet, and the Royal Navy itself in the War of 1812; and was chasing pirates in the Caribbean when he launched an unauthorized raid into Puerto Rico (a Spanish possession) in 1824. (Porter did such things repeatedly: 10 years earlier, he had claimed the Marquesas Islands for an American government that had not authorized his action and did not want the islands.) John Quincy Adams, as secretary of state and then as president, was managing delicate relations with Spain, Spain's former mainland colonies, and the Spanish Caribbean. He encouraged the Navy as it court-martialed and suspended Porter for his Puerto Rican foray. Feeling betrayed, Porter offered his services to Mexico.

Mexico, along with Colombia and the Confederation of Central America, envisioned a grand republican fleet that would keep Spain off the mainland, destroy the Spanish fleet, and liberate Cuba. David Porter liked the idea. He went to Mexico City, agreed on a salary and a grant of land, set up headquarters in Veracruz, and began building the Mexican navy.

Nothing went right. The alliance of Latin American republics collapsed, and the Mexican government, embroiled in bankruptcy and intrigue, lost interest in its navy. Porter's officers were freebooters from England and Spain, and his sailors—many of whom were convicted felons—did not know how to sail. Still, he procured ships and trained crews, and in 1826 he sailed to the northern coast of Cuba to harass Spanish shipping. After a short, successful cruise, he took refuge in Key West (yet another flaunting of international boundaries) for much of 1827 and left only when the Mexican government, under subtle threats from Secretary of State Henry Clay, ordered him back to Veracruz.

Throughout 1828, he lobbied Mexico City (unsuccessfully) for his back pay and his land grant, and watched his ships rot and his sailors turn into vagrants on the streets of Veracruz. Worse, he ran afoul of General Antonio López de Santa Anna, who was emerging as the postrevolutionary strongman of Mexico. On one of Porter's trips to Mexico City, four assassins attacked him. He killed two and chased off the others, and was always certain that Santa Anna had sent them. Later, two more killers entered his bedroom in Veracruz, and Porter ran one of them through with his sword. It was time to leave Mexico.

President Andrew Jackson rescued him. Jackson did not value the niceties of diplomacy as did Adams and Clay; indeed, his own experience with military freelancing was similar to David Porter's. Porter sneaked out of Mexico and accepted appointment as Consul-General at Algiers, then as head of the American diplomatic mission to the Ottoman Empire. He built a grand orientalist mansion outside of Constantinople and died there in 1843.

U.S. Naval Historical Center Photograph.

COMMODORE DAVID PORTER

The opposition was much more active. Van Buren and like-minded Republicans (with their candidate Crawford hopelessly incapacitated) switched their allegiance to Jackson. They wanted Jackson elected, however, not only as a popular hero but as head of a disciplined and committed Democratic Party that would continue the states'-rights, limited-government positions of the old Jeffersonian Republicans.

The new Democratic Party Richmond *Enquirer* linked popular democracy with the defense of southern slavery. Van Buren began preparations for 1828 with a visit to John C. Calhoun of South Carolina. Calhoun was moving along the road from postwar nationalism to states'-rights conservatism; he also wanted to stay on as vice president and thus keep his presidential hopes alive. After convincing Calhoun to support Jackson and to endorse limited government, Van Buren wrote to Thomas Ritchie, editor of the *Enquirer* and leader of Virginia's Republicans, who could deliver Crawford's southern supporters to Jackson. In his letter, Van Buren proposed to revive the alliance of "the planters of the South and the plain Republicans of the North" that had won Jefferson the presidency. Reminding Ritchie of how one-party government had allowed the Missouri question to get out of hand, Van Buren insisted that "if the old [party loyalties] are suppressed, prejudices between free and slave holding states will inevitably take their place."

Thus a new Democratic Party, committed to an agrarian program of states' rights and minimal government and dependent on the votes of both slaveholding and non-slaveholding states (beginning, much like Jefferson's old party, with Van Buren's New York and Ritchie's Virginia), would ensure democracy, the continuation of slavery, and the preservation of the Union. The alternative, Van Buren firmly believed, was an expensive and invasive national state (Adams's "lighthouses to the skies"), the isolation of the slaveholding South, and thus mortal danger to the republic.

The Election of 1828

The presidential campaign of 1828 was an exercise in slander rather than a debate on public issues. Adhering to custom, neither Adams nor Jackson campaigned directly, but their henchmen viciously personalized the campaign. Jacksonians hammered away at the Corrupt Bargain of 1825 and at the dishonesty and weakness that Adams had supposedly displayed in that affair. The Adams forces attacked Jackson's character. They reminded voters of his duels and tavern brawls and circulated a "coffin handbill" describing Jackson's execution of militiamen during the Creek War. One of Henry Clay's newspaper friends circu-

lated the rumor that Jackson was a bastard and that his mother was a prostitute, but the most egregious slander of the campaign centered on Andrew Jackson's marriage. In 1790, Jackson had married Rachel Donelson, probably aware that she was estranged but not formally divorced from a man named Robards. Branding the marriage an "abduction," the Adams team screamed that Jackson had "torn from a husband the wife of his bosom," and had lived with her in a state of "open and notorious lewdness." They branded Rachel Jackson (now a deeply pious plantation housewife) an "American Jezebel," a "profligate woman," and a "convicted adulteress" whose ungoverned passions made her unfit to be First Lady of a "Christian nation."

The Adams strategy ultimately backfired. Many voters did agree that only a man who strictly obeyed the law was fit to be president and that Jackson's "passionate" and "lawless" nature disqualified him, but many others criticized Adams for making Jackson's private life a public issue. Some claimed that Adams's rigid legalism left no room for privacy or for local notions of justice. Whatever the legality of their marriage, Andrew and Rachel Jackson had lived as models of marital fidelity and romantic love for nearly 40 years; their neighbors had long ago forgiven whatever transgressions they may have committed. Thus,

The Hermitage: Home of President Andrew Jackson, Nashville, TN.

RACHEL DONELSON JACKSON AS A MATURE PLANTATION MISTRESS

Andrew Jackson supposedly wore this miniature portrait of his beloved Rachel over his heart after her death in 1828.

on the one hand, Jackson's supporters accused the Adams campaign of a gross violation of privacy and honor. On the other, they defended Jackson's marriage—and his duels, brawls, executions, and unauthorized military ventures—as a triumph of what was right and just over what was narrowly legal. The attempt to brand Jackson as a lawless man, in fact, enhanced his image as a melodramatic hero who battled shrewd, unscrupulous, legalistic enemies by drawing on his natural nobility and force of will.

The campaign caught the public imagination. Voter turnout was double what it had been in 1824, totaling 56.3 percent. Jackson won the election with 56 percent of the popular vote (a landslide unmatched until the 20th century) and with a margin of 178 to 83 in electoral votes. Adams carried New England, Delaware, and most of Maryland and took 16 of New York's 36 electoral votes. Jackson carried every other state. It was a clear triumph of democracy over genteel statesmanship, of limited government over expansive nationalism, and of the South and the West over New England. Just as clearly, it was a victory of popular melodrama over old forms of cultural gentility.

A People's Inauguration

Newspapers estimated that from 15,000 to 20,000 citizens (Duff Green's *United States Telegraph,* a Jackson paper, claimed 30,000) came to Washington to witness Jackson's

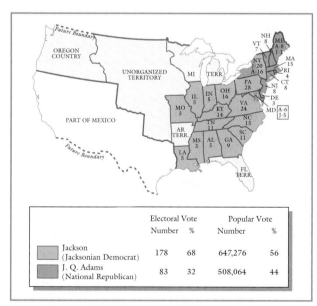

MAP 12.2   PRESIDENTIAL ELECTION, 1828

The 1828 presidential contest was a clear result of the organizing efforts that were building a national Democratic party under the name of Andrew Jackson. Jackson picked up all of the states that had gone for Crawford or Clay in 1824, leaving only New England and small portions of the mid-Atlantic for John Quincy Adams.

inauguration on March 4, 1829. They were "like the inundation of the northern barbarians into Rome," remarked Senator Daniel Webster. Many had traveled as much as 500 miles, and "they really seem to think that the country is rescued from some dreadful danger." As members of the Washington establishment watched uneasily, the crowd filled the open spaces and the streets near the east portico of the Capitol Building, where Jackson was to deliver his inaugural address.

Jackson arrived at the Capitol in deep mourning. In December, his wife Rachel had gone to Nashville to shop and had stopped to rest in a newspaper office. There, for the first time, she read the accusations that had been made against her. She fainted on the spot. Although she had been in poor health, no one would ever convince Jackson that her death in January had not been caused by his political enemies. As he arrived to assume the presidency, he wore a black suit and black tie, a black armband, and a black hatband that trailed down his neck in what was called a weeper.

Jackson's inaugural address was vague. He promised "proper respect" for states' rights and a "spirit of equity, caution, and compromise" on the question of the tariff, which was beginning to cause sectional controversy. He promised to reform the civil service by replacing "unfaithful or incompetent" officers, and he vowed to retire the national debt through "a strict and faithful economy." Beyond that, he said little, although he took every opportunity to flatter the popular majority. He had been elected "by the choice of a free people" (and not by King Caucus or Corrupt Bargains), and he pledged "the zealous dedication of my humble abilities to their service and their good." He finished—as he often finished an important statement—by reminding Americans that a benign providence looked over them. He then looked up to a roar of applause.

The new president traveled slowly from the Capitol to the White House, with the throng following and growing noisier along the way. The crowd followed him into the White House, where refreshments had been provided. Soon Jackson's well-wishers were ranging through the mansion, muddying the carpets, tipping things over, breaking dishes, and standing in dirty boots on upholstered chairs. Jackson had to retreat to avoid being crushed. The White House staff lured much of the crowd outside by moving the punch bowls and liquor to the lawn. A wealthy Washington matron who had admired the well-behaved crowd at the inaugural address exclaimed, "What a scene did we witness! *The Majesty of the People* had disappeared, and a rabble, a mob, of boys, negros, women, children, scrambling, fighting, romping. What a pity, what a pity." Another guest pronounced the occasion a "Saturnalia . . . of mud

THE PRESIDENT'S LEVEE

Robert Cruikshank drew Jackson's inaugural reception with men and women of all classes, children, dogs, and bucking horses celebrating the Old General's victory. Cruikshank subtitled his lithograph *All Creation Going to the White House.*

and filth." A Democratic newspaper reported more favorably: "General Jackson is *their own* President. . . . He was greeted by them with an enthusiasm which bespoke him the Hero of a popular triumph."

The Spoils System

Jackson had begun to assemble his administration months before he took office. Martin Van Buren, who had mobilized much of the support Jackson gained between 1824 and 1828, was the new secretary of state—positioned to succeed Jackson as president. Van Buren quit his newly won post as governor of New York and came to Washington, where he became Jackson's most valued adviser. Other appointments were less promising, for Jackson filled the remaining cabinet posts with old friends and political supporters who in many cases proved unfit for their jobs. A critic looked at Jackson's cabinet and pronounced it—with the exception of Van Buren—"the Millennium of the Minnows."

Others were more concerned about what Jackson would do to the civil service than about whom he named to his cabinet. During the campaign, Jackson had vowed to fire corrupt officeholders—a term he applied to grafters, incompetents, long-term officeholders who considered their jobs personal property, and those who supported John Quincy Adams. Early in the administration, opponents complained that Jackson was replacing able, educated, patriotic public servants with some dubious appointments. They soon had convincing evidence: Samuel Swarthout, whom Jackson had appointed collector of the Port of New York (an office that handled $15 million dollars in tariff revenue annually), stole $1.2 million and took off for Europe.

Actually, much of the furor over Jackson's "spoils system" was overwrought and misdirected. He aimed, Jackson claimed, only to institute "rotation in office" and to eject officeholders who expected to hold lifetime appointments. Arguing that most government jobs could be performed by any honest, reasonably intelligent citizen, Jackson proposed ending the long tenures that, he said, turned the civil service into "support of the few at the expense of the many." Jackson removed about 1 in 10 executive appointees during his eight years in office, and his replacements (at least at the level of ambassadors, federal judges and attorneys, and cabinet members) were as wealthy and well-educated as their predecessors. They were, however, most decidedly *political* appointees. Acting out of his own need for personal loyalty and on the advice of Van Buren and other architects of the Democratic Party, Jackson filled vacancies—down to postmasters in the smallest towns—with Democrats who had worked for his election.

Jackson sought Van Buren's advice on appointments. Van Buren knew the political value of dispensing government jobs; one of his henchmen coined the phrase "To the victor belongs the spoils." In resorting to patronage to build the party, however, Jackson gave his opponents an important issue. Revolutionary republicans feared a government of lackeys dependent on a powerful executive, and congressional opponents argued that Jackson was using appointments to "convert the entire body of those in office into corrupt and supple instruments of power."

"A standing army," railed Henry Clay in the Senate, "has been, in all free countries, a just object of jealousy and suspicion. But is not a corps of one hundred thousand dependents upon government, actuated by one spirit, obeying one will, and aiming at one end, more dangerous than a standing army?" It became an anti-Jacksonian axiom that Jackson had made the federal civil service an arm of the Democratic Party and of despotic executive power.

Jacksonian Democracy and the South

In the 1828 election, even though Jackson ran strongly in every region but New England, the base of his support was in the South, where he won 8 of every 10 votes. Southerners had grown wary of an activist government in which they were in the minority. They looked to Jackson not only as a military hero but also as a Tennessee planter who talked about returning to republican fundamentals. Although southerners expected Jackson to look after southern interests, disagreement arose within the administration about how those interests should be protected. Some sided with Vice President Calhoun, who believed that any state had the right to veto federal legislation and even in extreme cases to secede from the Union. Others agreed with Secretary of State Van Buren that the Union was inviolable and that the South's best safeguard was in a political party committed to states' rights within the Union. The differences were fought out in the contest between Calhoun and Van Buren for the right to succeed Jackson as president, a contest that shaped every major issue of Jackson's first term.

Southerners and Indians

When Jackson entered office, a final crisis between frontier whites and the native peoples of the eastern woodlands was under way. By the 1820s, few Native Americans were left east of the Appalachians. The Iroquois of New York were penned into tiny reservations, and the tribes of the Old Northwest were broken and scattered. But in the Old Southwest, 60,000 Cherokees, Creeks, Choctaws, Chickasaws, and Seminoles were still living on their ancestral lands, with tenure guaranteed by federal treaties that (at least implicitly) recognized them as sovereign peoples. Congress had appropriated funds for schools, tools, seeds, and training to help these Civilized Tribes make the transition to farming. Most government officials assumed that the tribes would eventually trade their old lands and use their farming skills on new land west of the Mississippi.

Southwestern whites resented federal Indian policy as an affront to both white democracy and states' rights. The poorer farmers coveted the Indians' land, and states'-rights southerners denied that the federal government had the authority to make treaties or to recognize sovereign peoples within their states. Resistance centered in Georgia, where Governor George Troup brought native lands under the state's jurisdiction and then turned them over to poor whites by way of lotteries—thus tying states' rights to white hunger for Indian land. At one point, Troup sent state surveyors onto Creek territory before federal purchase from the Indians was complete, telling President Adams that if he resisted state authority he would be considered a "public enemy." The Cherokees in Georgia pressed the issue in 1827 by declaring themselves a republic with its own constitution, government, courts, and police, but at almost the same time, a gold discovery on their land made it even more attractive to whites. The Georgia legislature promptly declared Cherokee law null and void, extended Georgia's authority into Cherokee country, and began surveying the lands for sale. Hinting at the old connection between state sovereignty and the protection of slavery, Governor Troup warned that the federal "jurisdiction claimed over one portion of our population may very soon be asserted over *another*." Alabama and Mississippi quickly followed Georgia's lead by extending state authority over Indian lands and denying federal jurisdiction.

Indian Removal

President Jackson agreed that the federal government lacked the authority to recognize native sovereignty within a state and declared that he could not protect the Cherokees and the other Civilized Tribes from state governments. Instead, he offered to remove them to federal land west of the Mississippi, where they would be under the authority of the benevolent federal government. Congress made that offer official in the Indian Removal Act of 1830.

The Cherokees, with the help of New England missionaries, had taken their claims of sovereignty to court in the late 1820s. In 1830, John Marshall's Supreme Court ruled in *Cherokee Nation* v. *Georgia* that the Cherokees could not sue Georgia because they were not a sovereign people but "domestic dependent nations," thus dependents of the federal government, and not of the state of Georgia, although somehow "nations" as well. The Court's decision in *Worcester* v. *Georgia* (1832) declared that Georgia's extension of state law over Cherokee land was unconstitutional. President Jackson ignored the decision, however, reportedly telling a congressman, "John Marshall has made his decision: *now let him enforce it!*" In the end, Jackson sat back as the southwestern states encroached on

Woolaroc Museum.

TRAIL OF TEARS

In 1838, the U.S. Army marched 18,000 Cherokee men, women, and children, along with their animals and whatever they could carry, out of their home territory and into Oklahoma. At least 4,000—most of them old or very young—died on the march.

System, but the Missouri debates had sent Carolinians looking for ways to safeguard slavery. The Denmark Vesey slave conspiracy of 1822 (see chapter 10) had stirred fears among the outnumbered whites of coastal South Carolina. Their fears grew more intense when federal courts shot down a state law forbidding black merchant seamen from moving about freely while their ships were docked at Charleston. Carolinians were disturbed too by persistent talk of gradual emancipation—at a time when their own commitment to slavery was growing stronger. Finally, southerners noted that in the congressional logrolling that made the Tariff of 1828, many western representatives had abandoned their old Jeffersonian alliance with the South to trade favors with the Northeast.

With the growth in the Northeast of urban markets for western produce, the American System's promise of interdependence among regions was beginning to work—but in ways that united the Northwest and Northeast against the export-oriented South. The Tariff of 1828 was the last straw: It benefited the city and commercial food producers at the expense of the plantation, and it demon-strated that the South could do nothing to block the passage of such laws.

Nullification

As early as 1827, Calhoun concluded that southern states could protect themselves from national majorities only if they possessed the power to veto federal legislation within their boundaries. In 1828, in his anonymously published essay *Exposition and Protest,* he argued that the Constitution was a compact between sovereign states and that the states (not the federal courts) could decide the constitutionality of federal laws. A state convention (like the conventions that had ratified the Constitution) could nullify any federal law within state borders. "Constitutional government and the government of a majority," Calhoun argued, "are utterly incompatible." *Exposition and Protest* echoed the Virginia and Kentucky Resolves of 1798 and 1799 and anticipated the secessionist arguments of 1861: The Union was a voluntary compact between sovereign states, states were the ultimate judges of the validity of

federal law, and states could break the compact if they wished.

Nullification was a dangerous measure, and Calhoun and his friends tried to avoid it. They knew that President Jackson was a states'-rights slaveholder who disliked the Tariff of 1828, and they assumed that Vice President Calhoun would succeed to the presidency in time and would protect southern interests. They were wrong on both counts. Jackson favored states' rights, but only within a perpetual and inviolable Union. His Indian policy, which had emboldened some southerners, was simply an acknowledgment of state jurisdiction over institutions within state boundaries. A tariff, on the other hand, was ultimately a matter of foreign policy, clearly within the jurisdiction of the federal government. To allow a state to veto a tariff would be to deny the legal existence of the United States.

Jackson revealed his views at a program celebrating Jefferson's birthday on April 13, 1830. Calhoun's southern friends dominated the speechmaking, and Jackson listened quietly as speaker after speaker defended the extreme states'-rights position. After the formal speeches were over, the president rose to propose an after-dinner toast. It was a powerful denunciation of what he had just heard: "Our Federal Union," he said in measured tones, *"It must be preserved."* Isaac Hill, a New Hampshire Democrat and a supporter of Van Buren, reported that "an order to arrest Calhoun where he sat would not have come with more blinding, staggering force." Dumb-struck, the southerners looked to Calhoun, who as vice president was to propose the second toast. Obviously shaken by Jackson's unqualified defense of the Union, Calhoun offered this toast: "The Union. Next to our liberties the most dear." They were strong words, but they had little meaning after Jackson's affirmation of the Union. A few days later, a South Carolina congressman on his way home asked the president if he had any message for him to take back. "Yes, I have," replied Jackson. "Please give my compliments to my friends in your state, and say to them, that if a single drop of blood shall be shed there in opposition to the laws of the United States, I will hang the first man I can lay my hand on engaged in such treasonable conduct, upon the first tree I can reach."

Having reaffirmed the Union and rejected nullification, Jackson asked Congress to reduce the tariff rates in the hope that he could isolate the nullifiers from southerners who simply hated the tariff. The resulting Tariff of 1832 lowered the rates on many items but still affirmed the principle of protectionism. That, along with the Boston abolitionist William Lloyd Garrison's declaration of war on slavery in 1831, followed by Nat Turner's bloody slave uprising in Virginia that same year (see chapter 10), led the whites of South Carolina and Georgia to intensify their distrust of outside authority and their insistence on the right to govern their own neighborhoods. South Carolina, now with Calhoun's open leadership and support, called a state convention that nullified the Tariffs of 1828 and 1832.

In Washington, President Jackson raged that nullification (not to mention the right of secession that followed logically from it) was illegal. Insisting that "Disunion . . . is *treason,*" he asked Congress for a Force Bill empowering him to personally lead a federal army into South Carolina. At the same time, however, he supported the rapid reduction of tariffs. When Democratic attempts at reduction bogged down, Henry Clay, who was now back in the Senate, took on the tricky legislative task of rescuing his beloved protective tariff while quieting southern fears. The result was the Compromise Tariff of 1833, which by lowering tariffs over the course of several years, gave southern planters the relief they demanded while maintaining moderate protectionism and allowing northern manufacturers time to adjust to the lower rates. Congress also passed the Force Bill. Jackson signed both into law on March 2, 1833.

With that, the nullification crisis came to a quiet end. No other southern state had joined South Carolina in nullifying the tariff, although some states had made vague pledges of support in the event that Jackson led his army to Charleston. The Compromise Tariff of 1833 isolated the South Carolina nullifiers. Deprived of their issue and most of their support, they declared victory and disbanded their convention—but not before nullifying the Force Bill. Jackson chose to overlook that last defiant gesture because he had accomplished what he wanted: He had asserted a perpetual Union, and he had protected southern interests within it.

The "Petticoat Wars"

The spoils system, Indian removal, nullification, and other heated questions of Jackson's first term were fought out against a backdrop of gossip, intrigue, and angry division within the inner circles of Jackson's government. The talk centered on Peggy O'Neal Timberlake, a Washington tavern keeper's daughter who, in January 1829, had married John Henry Eaton, Jackson's old friend and soon to be his secretary of war. Timberlake's former husband, a navy purser, had recently committed suicide; it was rumored that her affair with Eaton was the cause. Eaton was middle-aged; his bride was 29, pretty, flirtatious, and, according to Washington gossip, "frivolous, wayward, [and] passionate." Knowing that his marriage might cause trouble for the new administration, Eaton had asked for

and received Jackson's blessings—and, by strong implication, his protection.

The marriage of John and Peggy Eaton came at a turning point in the history of both Washington society and elite sexual mores. Until the 1820s, most officeholders had left their families at home. They took lodgings at taverns and boardinghouses and lived in a bachelor world of shirtsleeves, tobacco, card-playing, and occasional liaisons with local women, but in the 1820s, the boardinghouse world was giving way to high society. Cabinet members, senators, congressmen, and other officials moved into Washington houses, and their wives presided over the round of dinner parties through which much of the government's business was done. As in other wealthy families, political wives imposed new forms of gentility and politeness on these affairs, and they assumed the responsibility of drawing up the guest lists. Many of them determined to exclude Peggy Eaton from polite society.

The exclusion of Peggy Eaton split the Jackson administration in half. Jackson was committed to protect her. He had met his own beloved Rachel while boarding at her father's Nashville tavern, and their grand romance (as well as the gossip that surrounded it) was a striking parallel to the affair of John and Peggy Eaton. That, coupled with Jackson's honor-bound agreement to the Eaton marriage, ensured that he would protect the Eatons to the bitter end. Always suspicious of intrigues, Jackson labeled the "dark and sly insinuations" about Peggy Eaton part of a "conspiracy" against his presidency. Motivated by chivalry, personal loyalty, grief and rage over Rachel's death, and angry disbelief that political intrigue could sully the private life of a valued friend, Jackson insisted to his cabinet that Peggy Eaton was "as chaste as a virgin!" Jackson noted that the rumor spreaders were not only politicians' wives but also prominent clergymen. Most prominent among the latter was Ezra Styles Ely of Philadelphia, who had recently called for an evangelical "Christian Party in politics." Jackson blamed the conspiracy on "females with clergymen at their head."

In fact, Mrs. Eaton's tormentors included most of the cabinet members as well as Jackson's own White House "family." Widowed and without children, Jackson had invited his nephew and private secretary, Andrew Jackson Donelson, along with his wife and her sister, to live in the White House. Donelson's wife, serving as official hostess, resolutely shunned Peggy Eaton. Jackson, who valued domestic harmony and personal loyalty, assumed that schemers had invaded and subverted his own household. Before long, his suspicions centered on Vice President Calhoun, whose wife, Floride Bonneau Calhoun, a haughty and powerful Washington matron, was a leader of the assault on Peggy Eaton. Only Secretary of State Van Buren,

a widower and an eminently decent man, included the Eatons in official functions. Sensing that Jackson was losing his patience with Calhoun, Van Buren's friends, soon after the Jefferson birthday banquet in spring 1830, showed Jackson a letter from William H. Crawford revealing that while serving in Monroe's cabinet Calhoun, contrary to his protestations, had favored censuring Jackson for his unauthorized invasion of Florida in 1818. An open break with Calhoun became inevitable.

The Fall of Calhoun

Jackson resolved the Peggy Eaton controversy, as he would resolve nullification, in ways that favored Van Buren in his contest with Calhoun. He sent Donelson, his wife, and his sister-in-law back to Tennessee and invited his friend W. B. Lewis and his daughter to take their place, but he pointedly made Peggy Eaton the official hostess at the

The Rats leaving a Falling House.

AN OPPOSITION CARTOON ON THE CABINET SHUFFLE OF 1831

The cabinet rats run from the falling house of government, while a bewildered Jackson retains Van Buren by standing on his tail.

White House. In spring 1831, Van Buren gave Jackson a free hand to reconstruct his tangled administration. He offered to resign his cabinet post and engineered the resignations of nearly all other members of the cabinet, thus allowing Jackson to remake his administration without firing anyone. Many of those who left were southern supporters of Calhoun. Jackson replaced them with a mixed cabinet that included political allies of Van Buren. Also at this time, President Jackson began to consult with an informal Kitchen Cabinet that included journalists Amos Kendall and Francis Preston Blair, along with Van Buren and a few others. The Peggy Eaton controversy and the resulting shakeup in the administration were contributing mightily to the success of Van Buren's southern strategy.

Van Buren's victory over Calhoun came to a quick conclusion. As part of his cabinet reorganization, Jackson appointed Van Buren minister to Great Britain—an important post that would remove him from the heat of Washington politics. Vice President Calhoun, sitting as president of the Senate, rigged the confirmation so that he cast the deciding vote against Van Buren's appointment— a petty act that turned out to be his last exercise of national power. Jackson replaced Calhoun with Van Buren as the vice presidential candidate in 1832 and let it be known that he wanted Van Buren to succeed him as president.

Petitions, the Gag Rule, and the Southern Mails

Van Buren and other architects of the Democratic Party promised to protect slavery with a disciplined national coalition committed to states' rights within an inviolable Union. The rise of a northern antislavery movement (see chapter 11) posed a direct challenge to that formulation. Middle-class evangelicals, who were emerging as the reformist core of the northern Whig Party, had learned early on that Jacksonian Democrats wanted to keep moral issues out of politics. In 1828 and 1829, when they petitioned the government to stop movement of the mail on Sundays, Jackson had turned them down. They next petitioned the government for humane treatment of the Civilized Tribes, whose conversion to Christianity had been accomplished largely by New England missionaries; again, the Jackson administration had refused. The evangelicals suspected Jackson of immorality, and they were appalled by his defense of Peggy Eaton and his attack on gentlewomen and preachers. Most of all, reformist evangelicals disliked the Democrats' rigid party discipline, which in each case had kept questions of morality from shaping politics.

In the early 1830s, a radical minority of evangelicals formed societies that were committed to the immediate abolition of slavery, and they devised ways of making the national government confront the slavery question. In 1835, abolitionists launched a "postal campaign," flooding the mail—both North and South—with antislavery tracts that southerners and most northerners considered incendiary. From 1836 onward, they bombarded Congress with petitions, most of them for the abolition of slavery and the slave trade in the District of Columbia (where Congress had undisputed jurisdiction), others against the interstate slave trade, slavery in the federal territories, and the admission of new slave states.

Some Jacksonians, including Jackson himself, wanted to stop the postal campaign with a federal censorship law. Calhoun and other southerners, however, argued that the states had the right to censor mail crossing their borders. Knowing that state censorship of the mail was unconstitutional and that federal censorship of the mail would be a political disaster, Amos Kendall, a Van Burenite who had become postmaster general in the cabinet shuffle, proposed an informal solution. Without changing the law, he would simply look the other way as local postmasters violated postal regulations and removed abolitionist materials from the mail. Almost all such materials were published in New York City and mailed from there. The New York postmaster, a loyal appointee, proceeded to sift them out of the mail and thus cut off the postal campaign at its source. The few tracts that made it to the South were destroyed by local postmasters. Calhoun and his supporters continued to demand that the states be given the power to deal with the mailings, but the Democrats had no intention of relinquishing federal control over the federal mail. They made it clear, however, that no abolitionist literature would reach the South as long as Democrats controlled the U.S. Post Office.

The Democrats dealt in a similar manner with antislavery petitions to Congress. Southern extremists demanded that Congress disavow its power to legislate on slavery in the District of Columbia, but Van Buren, who was preparing to run for president, declared that Congress did have that power but should never use it. In dealing with the petitions, Congress simply voted at each session from 1836 to 1844 to table them without reading them, thus acknowledging that they had been received but sidestepping any debate on them. This procedure, which became known as the "gag rule," was passed by southern Whigs and southern Democrats with the help of most (usually 80 percent or more) of the northern Democrats. Increasingly, abolitionists sent their petitions to ex-President John Quincy Adams, who had returned to Washington as a Whig congressman from Massachusetts. Like other northern Whigs, Adams openly opposed both slavery and the gag rule in Congress. Northern Whigs began calling him

Old Man Eloquent, while Calhoun dubbed him "a mischievous, bad old man." But most southerners saw what the Democrats wanted them to see: that their surest guarantee of safety within the Union was a disciplined Democratic Party determined to avoid sectional arguments.

Thus the Jacksonians answered the question that had arisen with the Missouri debates: how to protect the slave-holding South within the federal Union. Whereas Calhoun and other southern radicals found the answer in nullification and other forms of state sovereignty, Jackson and the Democratic coalition insisted that the Union was inviolable and that any attempt to dissolve it would be met with force. At the same time, a Democratic Party uniting northern and southern agrarians into a states'-rights, limited-government majority could guarantee southern rights within the Union. This answer to the southern question stayed in place until the breakup of the Democratic Party on the eve of the Civil War.

Jacksonian Democracy and the Market Revolution

Jacksonian Democrats cherished a nostalgic loyalty to the simplicity and naturalness of Jefferson's agrarian republic. They assumed power at the height of the Market Revolution, and they spent much of the 1830s and 1840s trying to reconcile the market and the republic. Like the Jeffersonians before them, Jacksonian Democrats welcomed commerce as long as it served the independence and rough equality of white men on which republican citizenship rested, but paper currency and the dependence on credit that came with the Market Revolution posed problems. The so-called paper economy separated wealth from "real work" and encouraged an unrepublican spirit of luxury and greed. Worst of all, the new paper economy required government-granted privileges that the Jacksonians, still speaking the language of revolutionary republicanism, branded "corruption." For the same reasons, the protective tariffs and government-sponsored roads and canals of the American System were antirepublican and unacceptable. The Jackson presidency aimed to curtail government involvement in the economy, to end special privilege, and thus to rescue the republic from the Money Power.

Jacksonians were opposed by those who favored an activist central government (by the mid-1830s they called themselves Whigs) that would encourage orderly economic development through the American System of protective tariffs, a federally subsidized transportation network, and a national bank. This system, they argued, would encourage national prosperity. At the same time, it

would create a truly national market economy that would soften sectional divisions. Jacksonian rhetoric about the Money Power and the Old Republic, they argued, was little more than the demagoguery of unqualified, self-seeking politicians.

The Second Bank of the United States

The argument between Jacksonians and their detractors came to focus on the Second Bank of the United States, a mixed public-private corporation chartered by Congress in 1816 (see chapter 9). The national government deposited its revenue in the bank, thus giving it an enormous capital base. The government deposits also included state banknotes that had been used to pay customs duties or to buy public land; the Bank of the United States had the power to demand redemption of these notes in specie (gold and silver), thus discouraging state banks from issuing inflationary notes that they could not back up. The bank also issued notes of its own, and these served as the beginnings of a national paper currency. Thus with powers granted under its federal charter, the Bank of the United States exercised central control over the nation's monetary and credit systems.

Most members of the business community valued the Bank of the United States because it promised a stable, uniform paper currency and competent, centralized control over the banking system. But millions of Americans resented and distrusted the national bank, citing its role in the Panic of 1819 as evidence of the dangers posed by privileged, powerful institutions. President Jackson agreed with the latter. A southwestern agrarian who had lost money in an early speculation, he was leery of paper money, banks, and the credit system. He insisted that both the bank and paper money were unconstitutional and that the only safe, natural, republican currencies were gold and silver. Above all, Jackson saw the Bank of the United States as a government-sponsored concentration of power that threatened the republic.

The Bank War

The charter of the Bank of the United States ran through 1836, but Senators Henry Clay and Daniel Webster encouraged Nicholas Biddle, the Bank's brilliant, aristocratic president, to apply for recharter in 1832. Clay planned to oppose Jackson in the presidential election later that year, and he knew that Jackson hated the bank. He and his friends hoped to provoke the hot-tempered and supposedly erratic Jackson into a response they could use against him in the election.

Biddle applied to Congress for a recharter of the Bank of the United States in January 1832. Congress passed the recharter bill in early July and sent it on to the president. Jackson understood the early request for recharter as a political ploy. On July 4, Van Buren visited the White House and found Jackson sick in bed; Jackson took Van Buren's hand and said, "The bank, Mr. Van Buren, is trying to kill me, *but I will kill it!*" Jackson vetoed the bill.

Jackson's Bank Veto Message, sent to Congress on July 10, was a manifesto of Jacksonian Democracy. Written by Amos Kendall, Francis Preston Blair, and Roger B. Taney—republican fundamentalists who both hated the bank and understood the popular culture that shared their hatred—the message combined Jeffersonian verities with appeals to the public's prejudice. Jackson declared that the bank was "unauthorized by the Constitution, subversive of the rights of the states, and dangerous to the liberties of the people." Its charter, Jackson complained, bestowed special privilege on the bank and its stockholders, almost all of whom were northeastern businessmen or, worse, British investors. Having made most of its loans to southerners and westerners, the bank was a huge monster that sucked resources out of the agrarian South and West and poured them into the pockets of wealthy, well-connected northeastern gentlemen and their English friends. The granting of special privilege to such people (or to any others) threatened the system of equal rights that was essential in a republic. Jackson granted that differences in talents and resources inevitably created social distinctions, but he stood firm against "any prostitution of our Government to the advancement of the few at the expense of the many." He concluded with a call to the civic virtue and the conservative, God-centered Protestantism in which he and most of his agrarian constituency had been raised: "Let us firmly rely on that kind Providence which I am sure watches with peculiar care over the destinies of our Republic, and on the intelligence and wisdom of our countrymen. Through *His* abundant goodness and *their* patriotic devotion our liberty and Union will be preserved."

Henry Clay, Nicholas Biddle, and other anti-Jacksonians had expected the veto. And the Bank Veto Message was a long, rambling attack that, in their opinion, demonstrated Jackson's unfitness for office. "It has all the fury of a chained panther biting the bars of its cage," said Biddle, concluding that "it really is a manifesto of anarchy." So certain were they that the public shared their views that Clay's supporters distributed Jackson's Bank Veto Message as *anti*-Jackson propaganda during the 1832 campaign. They were wrong: A majority of the voters shared Jackson's attachment to a society of virtuous, independent producers and to republican government in its pristine form; they also agreed that the republic was in danger of subversion

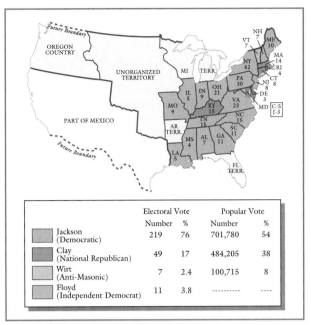

		Electoral Vote		Popular Vote	
		Number	%	Number	%
	Jackson (Democratic)	219	76	701,780	54
	Clay (National Republican)	49	17	484,205	38
	Wirt (Anti-Masonic)	7	2.4	100,715	8
	Floyd (Independent Democrat)	11	3.8	----------	----

MAP 12.3 PRESIDENTIAL ELECTION, 1832

The election of 1832 was a landslide victory for Andrew Jackson. The National Republican Henry Clay carried only his native Kentucky, along with Delaware and southern New England. A defeated and resentful South Carolina ran its own candidate. Jackson, on the other hand, won in the regions in which he had been strong in 1828 and added support in New York and northern New England.

by parasites who grew rich by manipulating credit, prices, paper money, and government-bestowed privileges. Jackson portrayed himself as both the protector of the Old Republic and a melodramatic hero contending with illegitimate, aristocratic, privileged, secretive powers. With the bank and Jackson's veto as the principal issues, Jackson won reelection by a landslide in 1832.

Jackson began his second term determined to kill the Bank of the United States before Congress could reverse his veto. The bank would be able to operate under its old charter until 1836, but Jackson was determined to speed its death by withdrawing government deposits as they were needed and by depositing new government revenues in carefully selected state banks—soon to be called Pet Banks by the opposition. By law, the decision to remove the deposits had to be made by the secretary of the treasury, and Treasury Secretary Louis McLane, along with most of the cabinet, doubted the wisdom if not the legality of withdrawing these funds. Jackson in response transferred McLane to the vacant post of secretary of state and named William J. Duane as treasury secretary. Duane, too, refused to withdraw the deposits. Jackson fired him and appointed Roger B. Taney, the attorney general and a close adviser who had helped write the Bank Veto Message. A loyal Democrat who hated banks as much as Jackson did,

Taney withdrew the deposits. In 1835, when the old Federalist John Marshall died, Jackson rewarded Taney by making him Chief Justice of the Supreme Court—a post from which he continued to serve the Democratic Party.

The Beginnings of the Whig Party

Conflict over deposit removal and related questions of presidential power united opposers to the Jacksonian Democrats—most of them committed advocates of the American System—into the Whig Party in 1834. The name of the party, as everyone who knew the language of the republic immediately recognized, stood for legislative opposition to a power-mad executive. Jackson, argued the Whigs, had transformed himself from the limited executive described in the Constitution into King Andrew I. This had begun with Jackson's arbitrary uses of the executive patronage. It had become worse when Jackson began to veto congressional legislation. Earlier presidents had exercised the veto only nine times, usually on unimportant bills and always on the grounds that the proposed legislation was unconstitutional. Jackson used the veto often—too often, said the Whigs, when a key component of the American System was at stake. In May 1830, for instance, Jackson vetoed an attempt by Congress to buy stock in a turnpike to run from the terminus of the National Road at Louisville to Maysville, Kentucky. Jackson argued that because the road would be entirely in Kentucky, it was "partial" legislation that would take money from the whole people to benefit just one locality. He also questioned whether such federal subsidies were constitutional. Most important, however, Jackson announced that he was determined to reduce federal expenditures in order to retire the national debt—hinting strongly that he would oppose all federal public works.

The bank veto conveyed the same message even more strongly, and the withdrawal of the government deposits brought the question of "executive usurpation" to a head in 1834. Withdrawal of the deposits, together with Jackson's high-handed treatment of his treasury secretaries, caused uneasiness even among the president's supporters, and his enemies took extreme measures. Nicholas Biddle, announcing that he must clean up the affairs of the Bank of the United States before closing its doors, demanded that all its loans be repaid—a demand that undermined the credit system and produced a sharp financial panic. No doubt one reason for Biddle's action was to punish Andrew Jackson. While Congress received a well-orchestrated petition campaign to restore the deposits, Henry Clay led an effort in the Senate to censure the president, which it did in March 1834. Daniel Webster, the Bank's best friend

KING ANDREW

In this widely distributed opposition cartoon, King Andrew, with a scepter in one hand and a vetoed bill in the other, tramples on internal improvements, the Bank of the United States, and the Constitution.

in government, and Clay, who had watched as Jackson denied one component after another of his American System, led the old National Republican coalition (the name that anti-Jacksonians had assumed since 1824) into the new Whig Party. They were joined by southerners (including Calhoun) who resented Jackson's treatment of the South Carolina nullifiers and Biddle's bank, and who distrusted his assurances on slavery. In any case, Jackson's war on the Bank of the United States did the most to separate parties. His withdrawal of the deposits chased lukewarm supporters into the opposition, while Democrats who closed ranks behind him could point to an increasingly sharp division between the Money Power and the Old Republic. Referring to Biddle's panic of 1834, James K. Polk of Tennessee, who led the Democrats in the House of Representatives, declared that "the question is in fact whether we shall have the Republic without the Bank or the Bank without the Republic."

A Balanced Budget

In part, Jackson removed the deposits because he anticipated a federal surplus revenue that, if handed over to Biddle's Bank of the United States, would have made it stronger than ever. The Tariffs of 1828 and 1832 produced substantial government revenue, and Jackson's frugal administration spent little of it. Even the Compromise Tariff of 1833 left rates temporarily high, and the brisk sale of

public lands was adding to the surplus. In 1833, for the only time in history, the United States paid off its national debt. Without Jackson's removal of the deposits, a growing federal treasury would have gone into the bank and would have found its way into the hated paper economy.

Early in his administration, Jackson had favored distributing surplus revenue to the states to be used for internal improvements, but he came to distrust even that minimal federal intervention in the economy, fearing that redistribution would encourage Congress to keep land prices and tariff rates high. Whigs, who by now despaired of ever creating a federally subsidized, coordinated transportation system, picked up the idea of redistribution. With some help from the Democrats, they passed the Deposit Act of 1836, which increased the number of banks receiving federal deposits (thus removing power from Jackson's Pet Banks) and distributed any federal surplus to the states to be spent on roads, canals, and schools. Jackson, who distrusted state-chartered banks as much as he distrusted the Bank of the United States, feared that the new deposit banks would use their power to issue mountains of new banknotes. He demanded a provision limiting their right to print banknotes. With that provision, he reluctantly signed the Deposit Act.

Jackson and many members of his administration had deep fiscal and moral concerns about the inflationary boom that accompanied the rapid growth of commerce, credit, roads, canals, new farms, and the other manifestations of

North Wind Picture Archives.

A MOCK BANKNOTE DECRYING THE DEMOCRATS' DESTRUCTION OF THE BANK OF THE UNITED STATES
A gang of officeholders pull Van Buren into perdition over the prostrate bodies of honest citizens. At right, Jackson, dressed as an old woman, watches.

the Market Revolution in the 1830s. After insisting that his hard-money, anti-inflationary provision be added to the Deposit Act, Jackson issued a Specie Circular in 1836, which provided that speculators could buy large parcels of public land only with silver and gold coins, and settlers could continue to buy farm-sized plots with banknotes. Henceforth, speculators would have to bring wagonloads of coins from eastern banks to frontier land offices. With this provision, Jackson hoped to curtail speculation and to reverse the flow of specie out of the South and West and into the Northeast. The Specie Circular was Jackson's final assault on the paper economy. It repeated familiar themes: It favored hard currency over paper, settlers over speculators, and the South and West over the Northeast.

The Second American Party System

In his farewell address in 1837, Jackson spoke once again of the incompatibility between the republic and the Money Power. He warned against a revival of the Bank of the United States and against all banks, paper money, the spirit of speculation, and every aspect of the "paper system." That system encouraged greed and luxury, which were at odds with republican virtue, he said. Worse, it thrived on special privilege, creating a world in which insiders meeting in "secret conclaves" could buy and sell elections. The solution, as always, was an arcadian society of small producers, a vigilant democratic electorate, and a chaste republican government that granted no special privileges.

"Martin Van Ruin"

Sitting beside Jackson as he delivered his farewell address was his chosen successor, Martin Van Buren. In the election of 1836, the Whigs had acknowledged that Henry Clay, the leader of their party, could not win a national election. Instead, they ran three sectional candidates— Daniel Webster in the Northeast, the old Indian fighter William Henry Harrison in the West, and Hugh Lawson White of Tennessee, a turncoat Jacksonian, in the South. With this ploy, the Whigs hoped to deprive Van Buren of a majority and throw the election into the Whig-controlled House of Representatives.

The strategy failed. Van Buren had engineered a national Democratic Party that could avert the dangers of sectionalism, and he questioned the patriotism of the Whigs and their sectional candidates, asserting that "true republicans can never lend their aid and influence in creating geographical parties." That, along with his associa-

tion with Jackson's popular presidency, won him the election. Van Buren carried 15 of the 26 states and received 170 electoral votes against 124 for his combined opposition. His popular plurality, however, was less than 51 percent.

Van Buren had barely taken office when the inflationary boom of the mid-1830s collapsed. Economic historians ascribe the Panic of 1837 and the ensuing depression largely to events outside the country. The Bank of England, concerned over the flow of British gold to American speculators, cut off credit to firms that did business in the United States. As a result, British demand for American cotton fell sharply, and the price of cotton dropped by half. With much of the speculative boom tied to cotton grown in the Southwest, the collapse of the economy was inevitable. The first business failures came in March 1837, just as Van Buren took office. By May, New York banks, unable to accommodate people who were demanding hard coin for their notes, suspended specie payments. Other banks followed suit, and soon banks all over the country— including Nicholas Biddle's newly renamed Bank of the United States of Pennsylvania—went out of business. Although few American communities escaped the economic downturn, the commercial and export sectors of

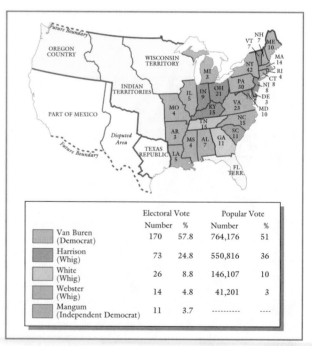

		Electoral Vote		Popular Vote	
		Number	%	Number	%
	Van Buren (Democrat)	170	57.8	764,176	51
	Harrison (Whig)	73	24.8	550,816	36
	White (Whig)	26	8.8	146,107	10
	Webster (Whig)	14	4.8	41,201	3
	Mangum (Independent Democrat)	11	3.7	----------	----

MAP 12.4 PRESIDENTIAL ELECTION, 1836

In 1836, the Whigs tried to beat the Democrats' national organization with an array of sectional candidates, hoping to throw the election into the House of Representatives. The strategy failed. Martin Van Buren, with significant support in every section of the country, defeated the three Whig candidates combined.

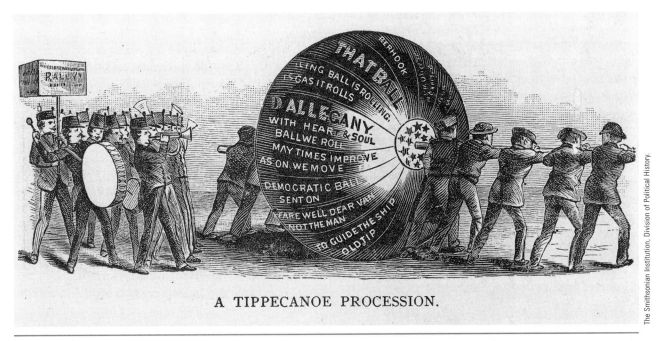

A TIPPECANOE PROCESSION.

"A TIPPECANOE PROCESSION"

In 1840, the Whigs, who had earlier been repelled by the boisterous electioneering techniques of the Democrats, filled the campaign with humor and noise, beating the Democrats at their own game. Among many other things, the Whigs covered a great paper ball with slogans (none of which had anything to do with national issues) and rolled it across the midwestern and northeastern states—accompanied by brass bands and shouts of "Keep the ball rolling!"

the economy suffered most. In the seaport cities, one firm after another closed its doors, and about one-third of the workforce was unemployed. Wages for those who kept their jobs declined by some 30 to 50 percent. It was the deepest, most widespread, and longest economic depression Americans had ever faced.

Whigs blamed the depression on Jackson's hard-money policies, particularly his destruction of the Bank of the United States and his Specie Circular. With economic distress the main issue, Whigs scored huge gains in the midterm elections of 1838, even winning control of Van Buren's New York with a campaign that castigated the president as "Martin Van Ruin." Democrats blamed the crash on speculation, luxury, and Whig paper money. Whigs demanded a new national bank, but Van Buren proposed the complete divorce of government from the banking system through what was known as the Sub-Treasury, or Independent Treasury. Under this plan, the federal government would simply hold and dispense its money without depositing it in banks; it would also require that tariffs and land purchases be paid in gold and silver coins or in notes from specie-paying banks, a provision that allowed government to regulate state banknotes without resorting to a central bank. Van Buren asked Congress to set up the Independent Treasury in 1837, and Congress spent the rest of Van Buren's time in office arguing about it. The Indepen-

dent Treasury Bill finally passed in 1840, completing the Jacksonian separation of bank and state.

The Election of 1840

Whigs were confident that they could blame Van Buren for the country's economic troubles and take the presidency away from him in the election of 1840. Trying to offend as few voters as possible, they passed over their best-known leaders, Senators Henry Clay and Daniel Webster, and nominated William Henry Harrison of Ohio as their presidential candidate. Harrison was the hero of the Battle of Tippecanoe (see chapter 7) and a westerner whose Virginia origins made him palatable in the South. He was also a proven vote-getter: As the Whigs' "western" candidate in 1836, he had carried seven states scattered across the Northwest, the Middle Atlantic, New England, and the Upper South. Best of all, he was a military hero who had expressed few opinions on national issues and who had no political record to defend. As his running mate, the Whigs chose John Tyler, a states'-rights Virginian who had joined the Whigs out of hatred for Jackson. To promote this baldly pragmatic ticket, the Whigs came up with a catchy slogan: "Tippecanoe and Tyler Too." Philip Hone, a wealthy New York City Whig, admitted that the slogan (and the ticket) had "rhyme, but no reason in it."

Early in the campaign, a Democratic journalist, commenting on Harrison's political inexperience and alleged unfitness for the presidency, wrote, "Give [Harrison] a barrel of hard cider, and settle a pension of two thousand a year on him, and my word for it, he will sit out the remainder of his days in his log cabin." Whigs who had been trying to shake their elitist image seized on the statement and launched what was known as the Log Cabin Campaign. The log cabin, the cider barrel, and Harrison's folksiness and heroism constituted the entire Whig campaign, while Van Buren was pictured as living in luxury at the public's expense. The Whigs conjured up an image of a nattily dressed President "Van Ruin" sitting on silk chairs and dining on gold and silver dishes while farmers and workingmen struggled to make ends meet. Whig doggerel contrasted Harrison the hero with Van Buren the professional politician:

> The knapsack pillow'd Harry's head
> The hard ground eas'd his toils;
> While Martin on his downy bed
> Could dream of naught but spoils.

Democrats howled that Whigs were peddling lies and refusing to discuss issues, but they knew they had been beaten at their own game. Harrison won only a narrow majority of the popular vote, but a landslide of 234 to 60 votes in the electoral college.

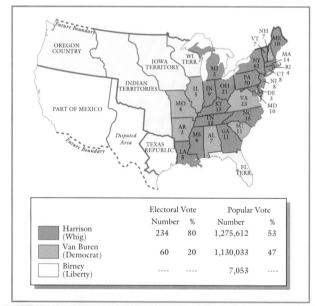

	Electoral Vote		Popular Vote	
	Number	%	Number	%
Harrison (Whig)	234	80	1,275,612	53
Van Buren (Democrat)	60	20	1,130,033	47
Birney (Liberty)	----	----	7,053	----

MAP 12.5 PRESIDENTIAL ELECTION, 1840

In 1840, the Whigs united under William Henry Harrison, the one Whig candidate who had won national support four years earlier. Borrowing campaign tactics from the Democrats and inventing many of their own, Whigs campaigned hard in every state. The result was a Whig victory and a truly national two-party system.

Two Parties

The election of 1840 signaled the completion of the second party system—the most fully national alignment of parties in U.S. history. Andrew Jackson had won in 1828 with Jefferson's old southern and western agrarian constituency; in 1832, he had carried his old voters and had won added support in the Middle Atlantic states and in northern New England. In 1836, Whigs capitalized on southern resentment of Jackson's defeat of Calhoun and nullification and on southern mistrust of the New Yorker Van Buren to break the Democratic hold on the South. Whigs came out of their old northeastern strongholds to carry Ohio, Illinois, Kentucky, Georgia, South Carolina, and even Jackson's Tennessee. Jackson had won 8 in 10 southern votes; Van Buren carried barely half but won majorities in old anti-Jackson neighborhoods in New England. The election of 1840 completed the transition: Harrison and Van Buren contested the election in nearly every state; perhaps most significantly, they received nearly equal levels of support in the slave and free states. Van Buren's dream of a national party system was realized. Ironically, the final pieces fell into place in an election that cost him the presidency.

The election of 1840 also witnessed the high-water mark of voter turnout. Whig and Democratic organizations focused on presidential elections, and prospective voters met a quadrennial avalanche of oratory, door-to-door canvassing, torchlight parades, and party propaganda. As the contests became national, Democrats or Whigs could take no state in the Union for granted. (In 1828, winning candidates carried individual states by an average of 36 percent; by 1840, that figure had dropped to 11 percent.) Both Whigs and Democrats maintained organizations and contested elections in nearly every neighborhood in the country, and the result was increased popular interest in politics. In 1824, about one in four adult white men had voted in the presidential election. Jackson's vengeful campaign of 1828 lifted the turnout to 56.3 percent, and it stayed at about that level in 1832 and 1836. The campaign of 1840 brought out 78 percent of the eligible voters, and the turnout remained at that high level throughout the 1840s and 1850s.

Conclusion

By 1840, American politics operated within a stable, national system of two parties, both of which depended on support in every section of the country. Whigs argued for the economic nationalism of the American System. Democrats argued for the limited, inexpensive govern-

ment that since Jefferson's day had been a bulwark of both republicanism and slavery. The party system provided answers to the questions of sectionalism and economic development that had helped bring it into being. Democrats successfully fought off the American System: They dismantled the Bank of the United States, refused federal support for roads and canals, and revised the tariff in ways that mollified the export-oriented South. The result, however, was not the return to Jeffersonian agrarianism that many Democrats had wanted but an inadvertent experiment in laissez-faire capitalism. The stupendous growth of the American economy between 1830 and 1860 became a question of state and local—not national—government action. On the growing political problems surrounding slavery, the two-party system did what Van Buren had hoped it would do: Because the Whig and (especially) Democratic Parties needed both northern and southern support, they were careful to focus national political debates on economic development, avoiding any discussion of sectional questions. It worked that way until the party system disintegrated on the eve of the Civil War.

SUGGESTED READINGS

Arthur M. Schlesinger, Jr., *The Age of Jackson* (1945) is a classic treatment of politics from the 1820s through the 1840s, whereas **Harry L. Watson,** *Liberty and Power: The Politics of Jacksonian America* (1990) is an excellent modern synthesis. On presidential elections, the best place to start is the essays in **Arthur M. Schlesinger, Jr., and Fred J. Israels, eds.,** *History of American Presidential Elections, 1789–1968,* 3 vols. (1971). **George Dangerfield,** *The Era of Good Feelings* (1953) and **Glover Moore,** *The Missouri Controversy, 1819–1821* (1953) are standard treatments of their subjects. On nullification, see **William W. Freehling,** *Prelude to Civil War: The Nullification Controversy in South Carolina, 1816–1836* (1965) and **Richard E. Ellis,** *The Union at Risk: Jacksonian Democracy, States' Rights and the Nullification Crisis* (1987). Two important accounts of slavery in national politics are **William Lee Miller,** *Arguing About Slavery: The Great Battle in the United States Congress* (1996) and **Don E. Fehrenbacher,** *The Slaveholding Republic: An Account of the United States Government's Relations to Slavery* (2001). On Jackson and Indian Removal, a good introduction is **Robert V. Remini,** *Andrew Jackson and His Indian Wars* (2001). On the Bank War, see **Bray Hammond,** *Banks*

and Politics in America from the Revolution to the Civil War (1957) and **Peter Temin,** *The Jacksonian Economy* (1967). The making of the party system is the subject of **Richard Hofstadter,** *The Idea of a Party System: The Rise of Legitimate Opposition in the United States, 1780–1840* (1969) and **Richard P. McCormick,** *The Second American Party System: Party Formation in the Jacksonian Era* (1966).

  AMERICAN JOURNEY ONLINE AND INFOTRAC COLLEGE EDITION

Visit the source collections at www.ajaccess.wadsworth.com and infotrac.thomsonlearning.com and use the Search function with the following key terms to explore documents, images, audio and video clips, articles, and commentary related to the material in this chapter.

Lewis and Clark	Missouri Compromise
Monroe Doctrine	Andrew Jackson
Henry Clay	Indian Removal Act

GRADE AIDS

Visit the Liberty Equality Power Companion Web Site for resources specific to this textbook: http://history.wadsworth.com/murrin_LEP4e

The CD in the back of this book and the U.S. History Resource Center at http://history.wadsworth.com/u.s./ offer a variety of tools to help you succeed in this course, including access to quizzes; images; documents; interactive simulations, maps, and timelines; movie explorations; and a wealth of other sources.

Chapter 13

Manifest Destiny: An Empire for Liberty—or Slavery?

MANIFEST DESTINY
This painting portrays the self-serving symbolism of America's westward expansion in the mid-19th century. White pioneers on foot, on horseback, and in oxen-drawn wagons cross the plains, driving the Indians and buffalo before them while a farmer breaks the sod on the farming frontier. A stagecoach and puffing locomotives follow an ethereal Columbia in flowing raiment bearing a schoolbook and stringing telegraph wire across the continent.

CHAPTER OUTLINE

When William Henry Harrison took the oath as the first Whig president on March 4, 1841, the stage seemed set for the enactment of Henry Clay's American System. Instead, Harrison contracted pneumonia after he delivered an interminable inaugural address outdoors in a sleet and snow storm. He died a month later, and John Tyler, a states-rights Virginian, became president. Tyler had become a nominal Whig only because of his hatred of Andrew Jackson. He proceeded to read himself out of the Whig Party by vetoing two bills to create a new national bank. Their domestic program a shambles, the Whigs lost control of the House in the 1842 midterm elections. Thereafter, the political agenda shifted to the Democratic program of territorial expansion. Through annexation, negotiation, and war, the United States increased its size by 50 percent in the years between 1845 and 1848, but this achievement reopened the issue of slavery's expansion and planted the bitter seeds of civil war.

CHAPTER FOCUS

♦ What impulses lay behind the Manifest Destiny of America's westward expansion?

♦ How did westward expansion relate to the issue of slavery?

♦ What were the causes and consequences of the Mexican-American War?

♦ What issues were at stake in the congressional debates that led to the Compromise of 1850?

♦ How successfully did the compromise resolve these issues?

☙ Growth as the American Way

By 1850, older Americans had seen the area of the United States quadruple in their lifetime. During the 47 years since the Louisiana Purchase of 1803, the American population had also quadrupled. If those rates of growth had continued after 1850, the United States would have contained 1.8 *billion* people at the end of the 20th century and would have occupied every square foot of land on the globe. If the sevenfold increase in the gross national product that Americans enjoyed from 1800 to 1850 had persisted, today's U.S. economy would be larger than that of today's entire world economy.

Many Americans in 1850 took this prodigious growth for granted. They considered it evidence of God's beneficence to this virtuous republic. During the 1840s, a group of expansionists affiliated with the Democratic Party began to call themselves the Young America movement. They proclaimed that it was the Manifest Destiny of the United States "to overspread and to possess the whole of the continent which Providence has given us for the development of the great experiment of liberty," wrote John L. O'Sullivan, editor of the *Democratic Review,* in 1845.

Not all Americans considered this unbridled expansion good. For the earliest Americans, whose ancestors had arrived on the continent thousands of years before the Europeans, it was a story of defeat and contraction rather than of conquest and growth. By 1850, the white man's diseases and guns had reduced the Indian population north of the Rio Grande to fewer than half a million, a fraction of the population of two or three centuries earlier. The relentless westward march of white settlements had pushed all but a few thousand Indians beyond the Mississippi. In the 1840s, the U.S. government decided to create a "permanent Indian frontier" at about the 95th meridian (roughly the western borders of Iowa, Missouri, and Arkansas). But white emigrants were already violating that frontier on the overland trails to the Pacific, and settlers were pressing against the borders of Indian territory. In little more than a decade, the idea of "one big reservation" in the West would give way to the policy of forcing Indians onto small reservations. The government "negotiated" with Indian chiefs for vast cessions of land in return for annuity payments that were soon spent on the white man's firewater and other purchases from shrewd or corrupt traders. Required to learn the white man's ways or perish, many Indians perished—of disease, malnutrition, and alcohol, and in futile efforts to break out of the reservations and regain their land.

C H R O N O L O G Y

1844	Senate rejects Texas annexation • James K. Polk elected president
1845	Congress annexes Texas • Mexico spurns U.S. bid to buy California and New Mexico
1846	U.S. declares war on Mexico • U.S. forces under Zachary Taylor win battles of Palo Alto and Resaca de la Palma • U.S. and Britain settle Oregon boundary dispute • U.S. occupies California and New Mexico • House passes Wilmot Proviso • U.S. forces capture Monterrey, Mexico
1847	Americans win battle of Buena Vista • U.S. Army under Winfield Scott lands at Veracruz • Americans win battles of Contreras, Churubusco, Molino del Rey, and Chapultepec • Mexico City falls
1848	Treaty of Guadalupe Hidalgo ends Mexican War, fixes Rio Grande as border, cedes New Mexico and California to U.S. • Gold discovered in California • Spain spurns Polk's offer of $100 million for Cuba • Zachary Taylor elected president
1849	John C. Calhoun pens "Address of the Southern Delegates" • California seeks admission as a free state
1850	Taylor dies, Millard Fillmore becomes president • Bitter sectional debate culminates in Compromise of 1850 • Fugitive Slave Law empowers federal commissioners to recover escaped slaves
1851	Fugitive Slave Law provokes rescues and violent conflict in North • American filibusters executed in Cuba
1852	Uncle Tom's Cabin becomes best seller • Franklin Pierce elected president
1854	Anthony Burns returned from Boston to slavery • William Walker's filibusters invade Nicaragua • Pierce tries to buy Cuba • Ostend Manifesto issued
1856	William Walker legalizes slavery in Nicaragua
1860	William Walker executed in Honduras

Manifest Destiny and Slavery

If the Manifest Destiny of white Americans spelled doom for red Americans, it also presaged a crisis in the history of black Americans. By 1846, the Empire for Liberty that Thomas Jefferson had envisioned for the Louisiana Purchase seemed more an empire for slavery: Territorial acquisitions since 1803 had brought into the republic the slave states of Louisiana, Missouri, Arkansas, Florida, Texas, and parts of Alabama and Mississippi. Only Iowa, admitted in 1846, joined the ranks of the free states.

The division between slavery and freedom in the rest of the Louisiana Purchase had supposedly been settled by the Compromise of 1820. Although the issue frequently disturbed public tranquility for a quarter-century there-

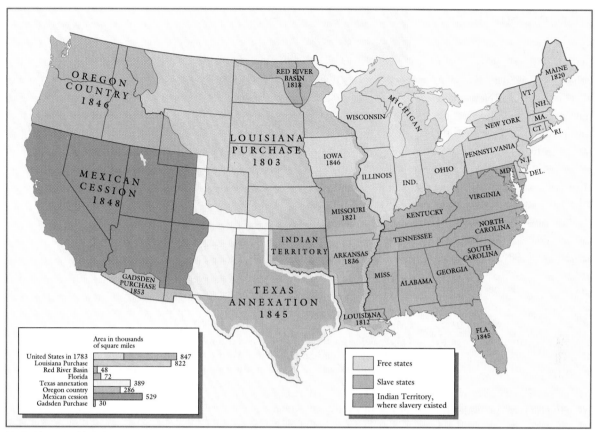

MAP 13.1   FREE AND SLAVE STATES AND TERRITORIES, 1848

Two developments of critical importance to the controversy over the expansion of slavery in the 1840s and 1850s are illustrated by this map: the larger number of slave than free states entering the Union from the territories acquired from France (Louisiana Purchase) and Spain (Florida) and the huge amount of new territory added by the acquisition of Texas and the Southwest from Mexico and the settlement of the Oregon boundary in the 1840s.

 View an animated version of this map or related maps at http://history.wadsworth.com/murrin_LEP4e.

after, as long as the controversy focused on the morality of slavery where it already existed, the two-party system—in which both major parties did their best to evade the issue—managed to contain its explosive potential. When the issue became the expansion of slavery into new territories, however, evasion and containment no longer sufficed. The issue first arose with the annexation of Texas, which helped provoke war with Mexico in 1846—a war that many antislavery northerners considered an ugly effort to expand slavery.

The Westering Impulse

Many Americans of European descent saw their future in the West. In the 1840s, Horace Greeley urged, "Go west, young man." And to the West they went in unprecedented numbers, driven in part by the depression of 1837–43 that prompted thousands to search for cheap land and better opportunity. "The West is our object, there is no other

hope left for us," declared one farmer as he and his family set out on the Oregon Trail. "There is nothing like a new country for poor folks."

An earlier wave of migration had populated the region between the Appalachians and the Missouri River, bringing a new state into the Union on an average of every three years. During those years, reports from explorers, fur traders, missionaries, and sailors filtered back from California and the Pacific Northwest, describing the bounteous resources and benign climates of those wondrous regions. Richard Henry Dana's *Two Years before the Mast* (1840), the story of his experience in the cowhide and tallow trade between California and Boston, alerted thousands of Americans to this new Eden on the Pacific. Guidebooks rolled off the presses describing the boundless prospects that awaited settlers who would turn "those wild forests, trackless plains, untrodden valleys" into "one grand scene of continuous improvements, universal enterprise, and unparalleled commerce."

The Hispanic Southwest

Of course, another people of partial European descent already lived in portions of the region west of the 98th meridian. The frontier of New Spain had pushed north of the Rio Grande early in the 17th century. By the time Mexico won its independence from Spain in 1821, some 80,000 Mexicans lived in this region. Three-fourths of them had settled in the Rio Grande Valley of New Mexico, and most of the rest in California. Centuries earlier, the Spaniards had introduced horses, cattle, and sheep to the New World. These animals became the economic mainstay of Hispanic society along New Spain's northern frontier. Later, Anglo-Americans would adopt Hispanic ranching methods to invade and subdue the lands of the arid western plains. Spanish words still describe the tools of the trade and the very land itself: *bronco, mustang, lasso, rodeo, stampede, canyon, arroyo, mesa.*

Colonial society on New Spain's northern frontier had centered on the missions and the presidios. Intended to Christianize Indians, the missions also became an instrument to exploit their labor, while the presidios (military posts) protected the settlers from hostile Indians. By the late 18th century, the mission system had fallen into decline, and a decade and a half after Mexican independence in 1821, it collapsed entirely. The presidios, underfunded and understaffed, also declined after Mexican independence, so that the defense of Mexico's far northern provinces increasingly fell to the residents. But by the 1830s, many residents of New Mexico and California were more interested in bringing American traders in than in keeping American settlers out. A flourishing trade over the Santa Fe Trail from Independence, Missouri, brought American manufactured goods to Santa Fe, New Mexico (and points south), in exchange for Mexican horses, mules, beaver pelts, and silver. New England ships carried American goods all the way around the horn of South America to San Francisco and other California ports in exchange for tallow and hides produced by *californio* ranchers. This trade linked the economies of New Mexico and California more closely to the United States than to the Mexican heartland. The trickle of Americans into California and New Mexico in the 1820s foreshadowed the flood that would engulf these regions two decades later.

North Wind Picture Archives.

EMIGRANTS MAKING CAMP IN THE SNOW

This drawing portrays the harsh conditions and dangers faced by many pioneers who crossed plains and mountains. Women often had to do a man's work as well as to cook and take care of children. One can only hope that this family did not suffer the fate of the Donner party, trapped by an early snowfall in the Sierra Nevada Mountains in October 1846. Nearly half of the 87 people in the Donner party died during the subsequent winter.

The Oregon and California Trails

In 1842 and 1843, Oregon fever swept the Mississippi Valley. Thousands of farm families sold their land, packed their worldly goods in covered wagons along with supplies for five or six months on the trail, hitched up their oxen, and headed out from Independence or St. Joseph, Missouri, for the trek of almost 2,000 miles to the river valleys of Oregon or California. On the way, they passed through regions claimed by three nations—the United States, Mexico, and Britain—and they settled on land owned by Mexico (California) or claimed jointly by the United States and Britain (Oregon, which then stretched north to the border of Russian Alaska). But no matter who claimed it, the land was occupied mostly by Indians, who viewed this latest intrusion with wary eyes. Few of the emigrants thought about settling down along the way, for this vast reach of arid plains, forbidding mountains, and burning wastelands was then known as the Great American Desert. White men considered it suitable only for Indians and the disappearing breed of mountain men who had roamed the region trapping beaver.

During the next quarter-century, half a million men, women, and children crossed a half continent in one of the great sagas of American history. After the migration of farm families to Oregon and California came the 1847

exodus of the Mormons to a new Zion in the basin of the Great Salt Lake and the 1849 gold rush to California. The stories of these migrants were of triumph and tragedy, survival and death, courage and despair, success and failure. Most of them reached their destinations; some died on the way—victims of disease, exposure, starvation, suicide, or homicide by Indians or by fellow emigrants. Of those who arrived safely, a few struck it rich, most carved out a modest although hard living, and some drifted on, still looking for the pot of gold that had thus far eluded them. Together, they generated pressures that helped bring a vast new empire—more than a million square miles—into the United States by 1848.

Migration was mostly a male enterprise. Adult men outnumbered women on the Oregon Trail and on the California Trail before the gold rush by more than 2 to 1, and in the gold rush by more than 10 to 1. The quest for new land, a new start, and a chance to make a big strike repre-

sented primarily masculine ideals. Women felt more rooted in family, home, and community, and less willing to pull up stakes to march into the wilderness. Yet even on the rough mining frontier of the West, men sought to replicate as soon as possible the homes and communities they had left behind. "We want families," wrote a Californian in 1858, "because their homes and hearth stones everywhere, are the only true and reliable basis of any nation." Except during the gold rush, and the figures for the absolute numbers of men and women notwithstanding, family groups predominated on the overland trails. Half of the emigrants were mothers and children, and some of the single men had relatives among the travelers.

Many of the women were reluctant migrants. Although middle-class urban families had made some small beginnings toward equal partnership in marriage, men still ruled the family on the midwestern farms from which most of the migrants came. Men made the decision to go;

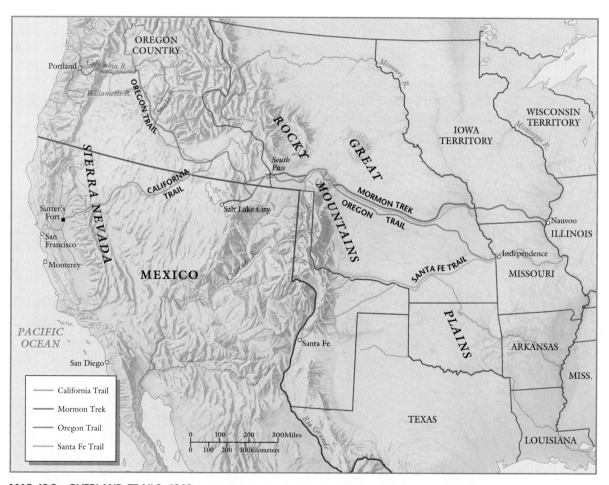

MAP 13.2   OVERLAND TRAILS, 1846

The Santa Fe Trail was mainly a route for trade between the United States and the Mexican province (before 1848) of New Mexico. The other three trails carried hundreds of thousands of Americans to new homes in the West.

women obeyed. Diaries kept by women on the trail testify to their unhappiness:

> What had possessed my husband, anyway, that he should have thought of bringing us away out through this God-forsaken country? . . . Oh, how I wish we never had started for the Golden Land. . . . I would make a brave effort to be cheerful and patient until the camp work was done. Then . . . I would throw myself down on the ground and shed tears, wishing myself back home with my friends and chiding myself for consenting to take this wild goose chase.

For some families it did turn out to be a wild goose chase, but for many of those who stayed the course and settled in the far West, it was a success story, made so in great measure by the women. They turned houses into homes, settlements into communities. The frontier did not break down the separate spheres of men and women. Woman's sphere in the West was still the home and the family, the bearing and nurturing of children, the management of the household economy. Man's sphere remained the world of public events and economic production.

The Mormon Migration

Patriarchal rule was strongest among those migrants with the most nearly equal sex ratio—the Mormons. Subjected to persecution that drove them from their original home in western New York to Ohio, Missouri, and eventually to Illinois, the Mormons established Nauvoo, Illinois, a thriving community of 15,000 souls, based on collective economic effort and theocratic discipline imposed by their founder and prophet, Joseph Smith. But the people of Illinois proved no more hospitable to the Mormons than the sect's previous neighbors had been. Smith did not make matters any easier. His insistence that God spoke through him, his autocratic suppression of dissent, and his assertion that the Mormons were the only true Christians and would inherit the earth provoked hostility. When a dissident faction of Mormons published Smith's latest revelation, which sanctioned polygamy, he ordered their printing press destroyed. The county sheriff arrested him, and in June 1844, a mob broke into the jail and killed him.

Smith's martyrdom prompted yet another exodus. Under the leadership of Smith's successor, Brigham Young, the Mormons began the long trek westward that would eventually lead them to the Great Salt Lake basin in a part of Mexican territory that soon was ceded to the United States in the wake of the Mexican War. A man of iron will and administrative genius, Young organized the migration down to the last detail. Arriving with the advance guard of Mormon pioneers at a pass overlooking the Great Basin on July 24, 1847, Young, who was ill with tick fever, struggled from his wagon and stared at the barren desert and mountains surrounding the lake. "This is the right place," he declared. Here the Mormons could build their Zion undisturbed.

JOSEPH MUSTERING THE NAUVOO LEGION

This painting depicts a self-defense force organized by Mormons in Nauvoo, Illinois, in the early 1840s. Beleaguered by neighbors, the Mormons decided to emigrate to Mexican territory in the West after Joseph Smith was murdered in 1844.

Joseph Mustering the Nauvoo Legion, C.C.A. Christensen.

They built a flourishing community, making the desert bloom with grain and vegetables irrigated by water they ingeniously diverted from mountain streams. Organizing the economy and the civil society as he had organized the exodus, Young reigned as leader of the church, and from 1850 to 1857 as governor of the newly created Utah Territory.

Zion, however, did not remain undisturbed. Relations with the government in Washington, D.C., and with those sent out as territorial officials were never smooth, especially after Young's proclamation in 1852 that authorized polygamy. (Although Young married a total of 55 women, most Mormon men could afford to support no more than one wife and her children; only about one-sixth of Mormon marriages were polygamous.) When conflict between the Mormons and the U.S. Army broke out in 1857, Young surrendered his civil authority and made an uneasy peace with the government.

The Republic of Texas

As the Mormons were starting west, a crisis between Mexico and the United States was coming to a boil. Although the United States had renounced any claim to Texas in a treaty with Spain negotiated in 1819, many Americans believed that Texas had been part of the Louisiana Purchase. By the time the treaty was ratified in 1821, Mexico had won its independence from Spain. The new Republic of Mexico wanted to develop its northern borderlands in Texas by encouraging immigration and settlement there. Thus, Stephen F. Austin, a Missouri businessman, secured a large land grant from Mexico to settle 300 families from the United States. Despite their pledge to become Roman Catholics and Mexican citizens, these immigrants and many who followed remained Protestants and Americans at heart. They also brought in slaves, in defiance of a recent Mexican law abolishing slavery. Despite Mexican efforts to ban any further immigration, 30,000 Americans lived in Texas by 1835, outnumbering Mexicans 6 to 1.

American settlers, concentrated in east Texas, initially had little contact with Mexican *tejanos* (Texans), whose settlements were farther south and west, but political events in Mexico City in 1835 had repercussions on the northern frontier. A new conservative national government seemed intent on consolidating its authority over the northern territories, including Coahuila-Texas. In response, the Anglo-American settlers and the *tejanos* forged a political alliance to protest any further loss of autonomy in their province. When the Mexican government responded militarily, many Texans—both Anglo and Mexican—fought back. Then, in March 1836, delegates from across Texas met at a village appropriately called Washington. They declared Texas an independent republic and adopted a constitution based on the U.S. model.

The American Revolution had lasted seven years; it took the Texans less than seven months to win and consolidate their independence. Mexican General Antonio López de Santa Anna led the Mexican army that captured the Alamo (a former mission converted to a fort) in San Antonio on March 6, 1836, killing all 187 of its defenders, including the legendary Americans Davy Crockett and Jim Bowie. Rallying to the cry "Remember the Alamo!" Texans swarmed to the revolutionary army commanded by Sam Houston. When the Mexican army slaughtered another force of more than 300 men after they had surrendered at Goliad on March 19, the Texans were further inflamed. A month later, Houston's army, aided by volunteers from southern U.S. states, routed a larger Mexican force on the San Jacinto River (near present-day Houston) and captured Santa Anna himself. Under duress, he signed a treaty granting Texas its independence. The Mexican congress later repudiated the treaty but could not muster enough strength to reestablish its authority north of the Nueces River. The victorious Texans elected Sam Houston president of their new republic and petitioned for annexation to the United States.

The Annexation Controversy

President Andrew Jackson, wary of provoking war with Mexico or quarrels with antislavery northerners who charged that the annexation of Texas was a plot to expand slavery, rebuffed the annexationists. So did his successor, Martin Van Buren. Although disappointed, the Texans turned their energies to building their republic. The British government encouraged the Texans, in the hope that they would stand as a buffer against further U.S. expansion. Abolitionists in England even cherished the notion that Britain might persuade the Texans to abolish slavery. Texas leaders made friendly responses to some of the British overtures, probably in the hope of provoking American annexationists to take action. They did.

Soon after Vice President John Tyler became president on the death of William Henry Harrison in 1841, he broke with the Whig Party that had elected him. Seeking to create a new coalition to reelect him in 1844, Tyler seized on the annexation of Texas as "the only matter that will take sufficient hold of the feelings of the South to rally it on a southern candidate."

Tyler named John C. Calhoun of South Carolina as secretary of state to negotiate a treaty of annexation. The southern press ran scare stories about a British plot to use Texas as a beachhead for an assault on slavery, and

annexation became a popular issue in the South. Calhoun concluded a treaty with the eager Texans, but then he made a mistake: He released to the press a letter he had written to the British minister to the United States, informing him that, together with other reasons, Americans wanted to annex Texas in order to protect slavery, an institution "essential to the peace, safety, and prosperity" of the United States. This seemed to confirm abolitionist charges that annexation was a pro-slavery plot. Northern senators of both parties provided more than enough votes to defeat the treaty in June 1844.

By then, Texas had become the main issue in the forthcoming presidential election. Whig candidate Henry Clay had come out against annexation, as had the leading contender for the Democratic nomination, former president Martin Van Buren. Van Buren's stand ran counter to the rising tide of Manifest Destiny sentiment within the Democratic Party. It also angered southern Democrats, who were determined to have Texas. Through eight ballots at the Democratic national convention, they blocked Van Buren's nomination; on the ninth, the southerners broke the stalemate by nominating one of their own, James K. Polk of Tennessee. Polk, a staunch Jacksonian who had served as Speaker of the House of Representatives during Jackson's presidency, was the first "dark horse" candidate (not having been a contender before the convention).

HISTORY THROUGH FILM

The Alamo (1960)

Directed by John Wayne. Starring John Wayne (Davy Crockett), Richard Widmark (Jim Bowie), Laurence Harvey (William Travis).

The legendary actor John Wayne worked a decade to obtain backing for an epic film about the heroic but doomed defense of the Alamo. When the movie was finally released in 1960, Wayne not only played the lead role as Davy Crockett, but he was also the producer and director. Out of his depth in this last role, he received advice from the director of Wayne's best movies, John Ford, which helped overcome some but not all of the awkward, sentimental scenes in the film.

Three hours long, *The Alamo* begins with General Sam Houston, commander of the Texas revolutionary army, ordering Colonel William Travis to delay the Mexican regulars commanded by Santa Anna at the Alamo long enough for Houston to organize his ragtag volunteers in east Texas into an effective fighting force. Colonel Jim Bowie, a rival of Travis for command of the garrison, considers the Alamo (a mission converted into a fort) a trap and wants to pull out, because the Mexican army outnumbers the Texans 20 to 1.

Right away, Hollywood departs from historical reality. Houston had actually ordered Bowie to blow up the Alamo and retreat to join him. But Bowie and Travis agreed to stay and fight, supported by Davy Crockett and his fellow Tennessee volunteers who had come to Texas looking for excitement. The tension between Travis and Bowie (with Crockett as a mediator) was real and is vividly portrayed if sometimes overdramatized in the film, but the tension concerned their relative authority, not strategy.

In wide-screen splendor, the film depicts the approach of the Mexican army, the artillery duels between the garrison and the Mexicans, and the infantry assaults that finally overpower the garrison after 13 days of resistance, killing them to the last man, sparing only the wife and child of a Texas lieutenant. The combat footage in the final attack is spectacular. Mexican artillery bombard the Alamo, infantry move forward taking heavy casualties, swarm over the wall, and overwhelm the doomed defenders. Bowie is wounded early in the fight and sent to an improvised hospital in the chapel, where he dies fighting from his bed. Travis is killed at the gate after dispatching several Mexicans with his sword. Crockett fights with fury until he is impaled by a Mexican lancer, but lives long enough to throw a torch into the powder magazine, blowing up the fort and hundreds of Mexicans.

In reality, none of it happened this way. Bowie had gone to bed with typhoid fever early in the siege; Travis was killed early in the final assault with a bullet through his

Southerners exulted in their victory. "We have triumphed," wrote one of Calhoun's lieutenants. "Polk is nearer to *us* than any public man who was named. He is a large Slave holder and [is for] Texas—States rights *out & out*." Polk's nomination undercut President Tyler's forlorn hope of being reelected on the Texas issue, so he bowed out of the race.

Polk ran on a platform that called not only for the annexation of Texas but also the acquisition of all of Oregon up to 54°40′ (the Alaskan border). That demand was aimed at voters in the western free states, who believed that bringing Oregon into the Union would balance the expansion of slavery into Texas with the expansion of free territory in the Northwest. Polk was more than comfortable with this platform. In fact, he wanted not only Texas and Oregon, but California and New Mexico as well.

Texas fever swept the South during the campaign. So powerful was the issue that Clay began to waver, stating that he would support annexation if it could be done without starting a war with Mexico. This concession won him a few southern votes but angered northern antislavery Whigs. Many of them voted for James G. Birney, candidate of the Liberty Party, which opposed any more slave territory. Birney probably took enough Whig votes from Clay in New York to give Polk victory there and in the electoral college.

John Wayne and Linda Cristal in an advertising poster for *The Alamo*.

head; and Crockett along with a few others surrendered but were executed on Santa Anna's orders. For Hollywood, and perhaps for most Americans, however, history is less important than legend. The Alamo became a heroic legend, a rallying cry for Texans in 1836, and a powerful symbol ever since. The film version dramatizes the legend better than an accurate version could have done.

The movie also reflects the cold-war mentality of the 1950s and Wayne's own full-blooded anti-Communism stance. Crockett's windy speeches about freedom and individual rights evoke the 1950s rhetoric of "better dead than red." Ironically, the Texans were fighting for an independent republic with slavery, in defiance of Mexico's recent abolition of the institution—an issue that the film virtually ignores.

Although The Alamo might have carried more punch if edited down to two hours, it nevertheless is visually powerful. It received seven Academy Award nominations, including one for Best Picture, but received only one Oscar—for sound.

Acquisition of Texas and Oregon

Although the election was extremely close (Polk won only a plurality of 49.5 percent of the popular vote), Democrats regarded it as a mandate for annexation. Eager to leave office in triumph, lame-duck President Tyler submitted to Congress a joint resolution of annexation, which required only a simple majority in both houses instead of the two-thirds majority in the Senate that a treaty would have required. Congress passed the resolution in March 1845. Texas thus bypassed the territorial stage and came in as the 15th slave state in December 1845. Backed now by the United States, Texans claimed a southern and western border beyond the Nueces River all the way to the Rio Grande, which nearly tripled the area that Mexico had formerly defined as Texas. Mexico responded by breaking off diplomatic relations with the United States. The stage was set for five years of bitter controversy that included a shooting war with Mexico and political warfare in the United States over the issue of slavery expansion.

Meanwhile, Polk lost no time in addressing his promise to annex Oregon. "Our title to the country of the Oregon is 'clear and unquestionable,'" he said in his inaugural address. "Already our people are preparing to perfect that title by occupying it with their wives and children." The problem was to persuade Britain to recognize the title. Both countries had jointly "occupied" Oregon since 1818, overseeing the fur trade carried on by British and American companies. Chanting the slogan "Fifty-four forty or fight!" many Americans in 1845 demanded all of Oregon, as pledged in the Democratic platform. But Polk proved unwilling to fight for 54°40′. So far, Americans had settled only in the region south of the Columbia River, at roughly the 46th parallel. In June 1846, Polk accepted a compromise treaty that split the Oregon country between the United States and Britain at the 49th parallel. Several Democratic senators from the Old Northwest (states north of the Ohio River and west of Pennsylvania) accused Polk of betrayal and voted against the treaty. They had supported Texas to the Rio Grande, and they had expected Polk to support Oregon to 54°40′. A sectional breach had opened in the Democratic Party that would soon grow wider.

🌎 The Mexican War

Having finessed a war with Britain, Polk provoked one with Mexico in order to gain California and New Mexico. In 1845, he sent a special envoy to Mexico City with an offer to buy California and New Mexico for $30 million. To help Mexico make the right response, he ordered federal troops to the disputed border area between Mexico and Texas, dispatched a naval squadron to patrol the Gulf Coast of Mexico, and instructed the American consul at Monterrey (the Mexican capital of California) to stir up annexation sentiment among settlers there. These strong-arm tactics provoked a political revolt in Mexico City that brought a militant anti-American regime to power.

Polk responded in January 1846 by ordering 4,000 soldiers under General Zachary Taylor to advance all the way to the Rio Grande. Recognizing that he could achieve his goals only through armed conflict, Polk waited for news from Texas that would justify a declaration of war, but none came. His patience having run out, on May 9, 1846, he began to draft a message to Congress asking for a declaration of war on general grounds of Mexican defiance. That evening, word finally arrived that two weeks earlier Mexican troops had crossed the Rio Grande and attacked an American patrol, killing 11 soldiers. Polk had what he wanted. He quickly revised his message and sent it to Congress on May 11.

Most Whigs opposed war with Mexico. But in the end, not wanting to be branded unpatriotic, all but a handful of them voted for the final declaration of war,

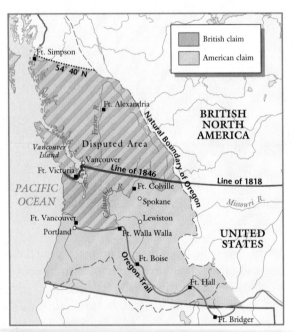

MAP 13.3   SETTLEMENT OF THE OREGON BOUNDARY DISPUTE, 1846

Before the 1840s, the only white residents of the Oregon country were fur traders and missionaries. Migration of Americans over the Oregon Trail created pressures to make all of Oregon part of the United States, but President Polk was not willing to go to war for the boundary of 54°40′.

which passed the House by 174 to 14 and the Senate by 40 to 2. Despite their continuing opposition to what they called "Mr. Polk's War," most Whigs voted supplies for the army. Having witnessed the demise of the Federalist Party after it had opposed the war in 1812, one Whig congressman said sarcastically that from then on he had decided to vote for "war, pestilence, and famine."

The United States went to war with a tiny regular army of fewer than 8,000 men, supplemented by 60,000 volunteers in state regiments, and an efficient navy that quickly established domination of the sea lanes. Mexican soldiers outnumbered American in most of the battles, but the Americans had higher morale, better leadership, and better weapons (especially artillery). They also enjoyed the backing of a more determined, stable government and a far richer, stronger economy. The U.S. forces won every battle—and the war—in a fashion that humiliated the proud Mexicans and left a legacy of national hostility and border violence. Especially remarkable was the prominent role played by junior American officers trained at West Point, for whom the Mexican War was a rehearsal for a larger conflict that would take place 15 years later: Robert E. Lee, Ulysses S. Grant, Pierre G. T. Beauregard, George B. McClellan, Braxton Bragg, George H. Thomas, Thomas J. Jackson, George G. Meade, Jefferson Davis, and others, whose names would become household words during the Civil War.

Military Campaigns of 1846

The Mexican War proceeded through three phases. The first phase was carried out by Zachary Taylor's 4,000 regulars on the Rio Grande. In two small battles on May 8 and 9, at Palo Alto and Resaca de la Palma, they routed numerically superior Mexican forces even before Congress had declared war. Those victories made "Old Rough and Ready" Taylor a hero, a reputation he rode to the presidency two years later. Reinforced by several thousand volunteers, Taylor pursued the retreating Mexicans 100 miles south of the Rio Grande to the heavily fortified Mexican city of Monterrey, and took the city after four days of fighting in September 1846. Mexican resistance in the area crumbled, and Taylor's force settled down as an army of occupation.

Meanwhile, the second phase of American strategy had gone forward in New Mexico and California. In June 1846, General Stephen Watts Kearny led an army of 1,500 tough frontiersmen and regulars west from Fort Leavenworth toward Santa Fe. Kearny bluffed and intimidated the New Mexico governor, who fled southward without ever ordering the local 3,000-man militia into action. Kearny's army occupied Santa Fe on August 18 without

AMERICAN FORCES IN SALTILLO, MEXICO

This posed photograph of General John E. Wool and his staff of Zachary Taylor's army on its march southward from Monterrey through Saltillo in November 1846 is the earliest known photograph of an American military force. Photography had recently been invented, and pictures such as this one were extremely rare before the 1850s.

firing a shot. With closer economic ties to the United States than to their own country, which taxed them well but governed them poorly, many New Mexicans seemed willing to accept American rule.

After receiving reinforcements, Kearny left a small occupation force and divided his remaining troops into two contingents, one of which he sent under Colonel Alexander Doniphan into the Mexican province of Chihuahua. In the most extraordinary campaign of the war, these 800 Missourians marched 1,500 miles, foraging supplies along the way; fought and beat two much larger enemy forces; and finally linked up with Zachary Taylor's army near Monterrey in spring 1847.

Kearny led the other contingent across deserts and mountains to California. Events there had anticipated his arrival. In June 1846, a group of American settlers backed by Captain John C. Frémont, a renowned western explorer with the army topographical corps, captured Sonoma and raised the flag of an independent California, displaying the silhouette of a grizzly bear. Marked by exploits both courageous and comic, this "bear-flag revolt" paved the way for the conquest of California by the *americanos*. The U.S. Pacific Fleet seized California's ports and the capital at Monterrey; sailors from the fleet and volunteer soldiers under Frémont subdued Mexican resistance. Kearny's weary and battered force arrived in December 1846, barely in time to help with the mopping up.

Military Campaigns of 1847

New Mexico and California had fallen into American hands, and Mexican armies had experienced nothing but defeat, but the Mexican government refused to admit that the war was over. A political maneuver by President Polk to secure a more tractable government in Mexico had backfired. In one of Mexico's many palace revolts, Santa Anna had been overthrown and forced into exile in Cuba in 1844. A shadowy intermediary convinced Polk in July 1846 that if Santa Anna returned to power, he would make peace on American terms in return for $30 million. Polk instructed the navy to pass Santa Anna through its blockade of Mexican ports. The wily Mexican general then rode in triumph to Mexico City, where yet another new government named him supreme commander of the army and president of the republic. Breathing fire, Santa Anna spoke no more of peace. Instead, he raised new levies and marched north early in 1847 to attack Taylor's army near Monterrey.

Taylor, 62 years old, was still rough but not as ready to withstand a counteroffensive as he had been a few weeks earlier. After capturing Monterrey in September 1846, he had let the defeated Mexican army go and had granted an eight-week armistice in the hope that it would allow time for peace negotiations. Angry at Taylor's presumption in making such a decision and suspicious of the general's political ambitions, Polk canceled the armistice and named General-in-Chief Winfield Scott to command the third phase of the war, a campaign against Mexico City. A large, punctilious man, Scott acquired the nickname "Old Fuss and Feathers" for a military professionalism that contrasted with the homespun manner of "Rough and Ready" Zach Taylor. Scott decided to lead an invasion of Mexico's heartland from a beachhead at Veracruz, and in January 1847 ordered the transfer of more than half of Taylor's troops to his own expeditionary force.

Left with fewer than 5,000 men, most of them untried volunteers, Taylor complained bitterly of political intrigue and military favoritism. Nevertheless, he marched out to meet Santa Anna's army of 18,000. In a two-day battle on February 22 and 23 at Buena Vista, Taylor's little force bent but never broke. They inflicted twice as many casualties as they suffered in a fierce struggle highlighted by the brilliant counterattack of a Mississippi regiment commanded by Jefferson Davis. The bloodied Mexican army retreated toward the capital. When news of the victory reached the East, Taylor's popularity soared to new heights. If Polk had wanted to quash a political rival by taking away most of his troops—as Taylor believed—he had achieved just the opposite.

But it was General Scott who actually won the war. With a combined army-navy force, he took the coastal fortress at Veracruz in March 1847. Over the next five months, his army, which never totaled more than 14,000 men (with considerable turnover because of expiring one-year enlistments), marched and fought its way over more than 200 miles of mountains and plains to Mexico City. It was a bold, high-risk action. When Scott's forces reached the fortifications of Mexico City, held by three times their numbers, the Duke of Wellington, who was following the campaign closely, predicted, "Scott is lost—he cannot capture the city, and he cannot fall back upon his base." But capture it he did, on September 14, after fierce hand-to-hand combat in the battles of Contreras, Churubusco, Molino del Rey, and Chapultepec. It was a brilliant success, even though it owed much to wrangling among Mexican leaders that forced Santa Anna to spend almost as much time facing down his internal enemies as fighting the Americans.

Antiwar Sentiment

The string of military victories prevented the significant U.S. antiwar sentiment from winning even wider support. The war had enthusiastic support in the South and West and among Democrats, but the Whigs and many people in the Northeast, especially in New England, considered it "a wicked and disgraceful war." Democrats and Whigs had different notions of progress. Democrats believed in expanding American institutions over *space*—in particular, the space occupied by Mexicans and Indians. Whigs, on the other hand, believed in improving American institutions over *time*. "Opposed to the instinct of boundless acquisition stands that of Internal Improvement," said Horace Greeley. "A nation cannot simultaneously devote its energies to the absorption of others' territories and the improvement of its own."

Antislavery people raised their eyebrows when they heard Manifest Destiny rhetoric about "extending the blessings of American liberty" to benighted regions. They suspected that the real reason was the desire to extend slavery. Hosea Biglow, the rustic Yankee philosopher created by the abolitionist poet James Russell Lowell, observed:

> They jest want this Californy
> So's to lug new slave-states in
> To abuse ye an' to scorn ye,
> And to plunder ye like sin.

The Wilmot Proviso

The slavery issue overshadowed all others in the debate over the Mexican War. President Polk could not understand the reason for the fuss. "There is no probability,"

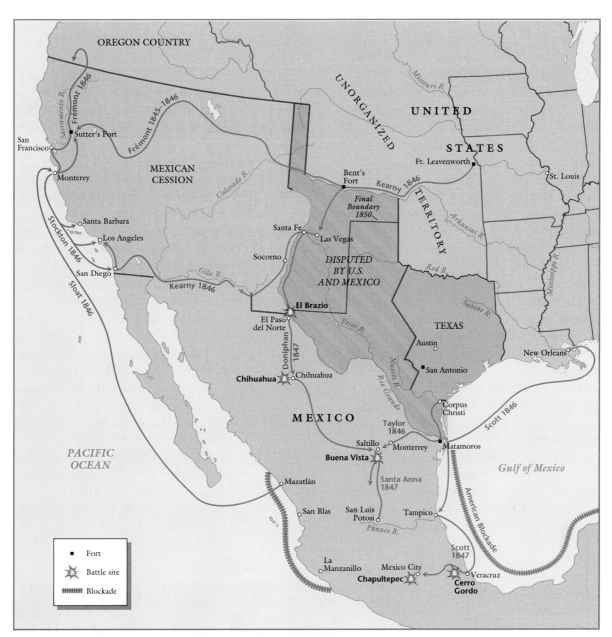

MAP 13.4 PRINCIPAL CAMPAIGNS OF THE MEXICAN WAR, 1846–1847

This map provides a graphic illustration of the vast territory over which the Mexican War was fought; the distance from Veracruz to San Francisco is 2,500 miles.

 View an animated version of this map or related maps at http://history.wadsworth.com/murrin_LEP4e.

he wrote in his diary, "that any territory will ever be acquired from Mexico in which slavery would ever exist." But other Americans were less sure. Many southerners hoped that slavery would spread into the fertile lowlands of Mexican territory. Many northerners feared that it might. Their fear was strengthened by an editorial in a Charleston newspaper: "California is peculiarly adapted for slave labor. The right to have [slave] property protected

there is not a mere abstraction." The issue came to a head early in the war. On August 8, 1846, Pennsylvania Democratic Congressman David Wilmot offered an amendment to an army appropriations bill: "... that, as an express and fundamental condition of the acquisition of any territory from the Republic of Mexico ... neither slavery nor involuntary servitude shall ever exist in any part of said territory."

This famous Wilmot Proviso framed the national debate over slavery for the next 15 years. The House passed the amendment. Nearly all northern Democrats joined all northern Whigs in the majority, while southern Democrats and southern Whigs voted almost unanimously against it. (In the Senate, greater southern strength defeated the proviso.) This outcome marked an ominous wrenching of the party division between Whigs and Democrats into a *sectional* division between free and slave states. It was a sign that the two-party system might not successfully contain the convulsive question of slavery expansion.

Several factors underlay the split of northern Democrats from their own president on this issue. Ever since southern Democrats had blocked Van Buren's nomination in 1844, resentment had been growing in the party's northern wing. Polk's acceptance of 49° latitude for Oregon's northern boundary exacerbated this feeling. "Our rights to Oregon have been shamefully compromised," fumed an Ohio Democrat. "The administration is Southern, Southern, Southern! ... Since the South have fixed boundaries for free territory, let the North fix boundaries for slave territories." The reduced rates of the Walker tariff in 1846 (sponsored by Robert J. Walker of Mississippi, Polk's secretary of the treasury) annoyed Democrats from Pennsylvania's industrial districts. Polk further angered Democrats from the Old Northwest by vetoing a rivers and harbors bill that would have provided federal aid for transportation improvements in their districts. The Wilmot Proviso was in part the product of these pent-up frustrations over what northerners were increasingly calling "the slave power." "The time has come," said a Democratic congressman in 1846, "when the Northern Democracy should make a stand. Every thing has taken a Southern shape and been controlled by Southern caprice for years. ... We must satisfy the Northern people ... that we are not to extend the institution of slavery as a result of this war."

The slavery issue hung like the sword of Damocles over Polk's efforts to negotiate peace with Mexico. Polk also came under pressure from expansionist Democrats who, excited by military victory, wanted more Mexican territory, perhaps even "all Mexico." Polk had sent diplomat Nicholas Trist with Scott's army to negotiate the terms of Mexican surrender. Authorized to pay Mexico $15 million for California, New Mexico, and a Texas border on the Rio Grande, Trist worked out such a treaty. In the meantime, though, Polk had succumbed to the "all Mexico" clamor. He ordered Trist back to Washington, intending to replace him with someone who would exact greater concessions from Mexico. Trist ignored the recall, signed the treaty of Guadalupe Hidalgo on February 2, 1848, and sent it to Washington. Although angered by Trist's defiance, Polk nonetheless decided to end the controversy by submitting the treaty to the Senate, which approved it on March 10 by a vote of 38 to 14. Half the opposition came from Democrats who wanted more Mexican territory and half from Whigs who wanted none. As it was, the treaty sheared off half of Mexico and increased the size of the United States by one-fourth.

SLAVE AUCTION IN ST. LOUIS

The public buying and selling of human beings in cities such as St. Louis made a mockery of American boasts of liberty and gave a powerful impetus to the drive to prohibit the expansion of slavery into the territories acquired from Mexico. This painting hints at the ugliest dimension of the slave trade, the sale of mothers and children apart from fathers and sometimes apart from each other.

Margaret Fuller Fights for a Roman Republic

Margaret Fuller's father, a Massachusetts lawyer and congressman, taught her to read English at age three and Latin at age six. By the time she reached her twenties she was mixing with the New England Unitarian elite and Transcendentalist philosophers such as Ralph Waldo Emerson, to whom she taught German pronunciation. As a prolific essayist and editor of the Transcendentalist magazine *The Dial,* Fuller (1810–1850) urged the opening of wider intellectual and professional opportunities for women. In 1844, she became literary editor of Horace Greeley's *New York Tribune,* the first woman to hold such a position. In 1846, she went to Europe as foreign correspondent for the *Tribune*—also a first for a woman. She traveled from England through the continent to Italy, where she fell in love with Giovanni Angelo, the Marchese d'Ossoli, with whom she had a son in 1848. Whether they ever married officially is unclear; as a Catholic (albeit a liberal one), Ossoli technically could not marry a Protestant, but Margaret began calling herself Marchioness Ossoli.

She and the Marchese threw themselves into the fight for a Roman republic that was part of the revolutionary fervor sweeping across Europe in 1848–49. Fuller worked with Giuseppe Mazzini, Giuseppe Garibaldi, and other Italian liberals seeking to overthrow the old order. Her reports to the *Tribune* were infused with the ideals of liberty and equality she had carried from the New World to the Old. When the Roman republic was overthrown in July 1849, she fled with Ossoli and their son to Florence, where she began writing a history of the republic. A year later they were on a ship to the United States, which struck a sandbar in a storm off Fire Island, New York, and sank with the loss of all on board.

Fuller's formidable body of writings inspired women and men in both America and Europe with a vision of emancipation from repressive conventions of religion, thought, and gender.

James Smith Noel Collection, Noel Memorial Library. Louisiana State University in Shreveport.

MARGARET FULLER

The Election of 1848

The treaty did nothing to settle the question of slavery in the new territory, however. Mexico had abolished the institution two decades earlier; would the United States reintroduce it? Many Americans looked to the election of 1848 to decide the matter. Four positions on the issue emerged, each identified with a candidate for the presidential nomination.

The Wilmot Proviso represented the position of those determined to bar slavery from all territories. The Liberty Party endorsed the proviso and nominated Senator John P. Hale of New Hampshire for president.

Southern Democrat John C. Calhoun formulated the "southern-rights" position. Directly challenging the Wilmot Proviso, Calhoun introduced resolutions in the Senate in February 1847 affirming the right of slave owners to take their human property into any territory. The Constitution protected the right of property, Calhoun pointed out; Congress could no more prevent a settler from taking his slaves to California than it could prevent him from taking his horses there.

Although most southerners agreed with Calhoun, the Democratic Party sought a middle ground. The Polk administration endorsed the idea of extending the old Missouri Compromise line of 36°30′ to the Pacific. This

would have excluded slavery from present-day Washington, Oregon, Idaho, Utah, Nevada, and the northern half of California, but would have allowed it in present-day New Mexico, Arizona, and southern California. Secretary of State James Buchanan, also a candidate for the Democratic presidential nomination (Polk did not seek renomination), embraced this position.

Another compromise position became known as "popular sovereignty." Identified with Senator Lewis Cass of Michigan, yet another contender for the Democratic nomination, this concept proposed to let the settlers of each territory decide for themselves whether to permit slavery. This solution contained a crucial ambiguity: It did not specify *at what stage* the settlers of a territory could decide on slavery. Most northern Democrats assumed that a territorial legislature would make that decision as soon as it was organized. Most southerners assumed that it would not be made until the settlers had drawn up a state constitution. That would normally happen only after several years as a territory, during which time slavery might well have taken deep enough root to be implanted in the state constitution. So long as neither assumption was tested, each faction could support popular sovereignty.

The Democratic convention nominated Cass for president, thereby seeming to endorse popular sovereignty. In an attempt to maintain party unity, however, the platform made no mention of the matter. The attempt was not entirely successful: Two Alabama delegates walked out when the convention refused to endorse Calhoun's southern-rights position, and an antislavery faction from New York walked out when it failed to win a credentials fight.

The Whig convention tried to avoid a similar schism by adopting no platform at all, but the slavery issue would not die. In the eyes of many antislavery delegates who styled themselves Conscience Whigs, the party made itself ridiculous by nominating Zachary Taylor for president. Desperate for victory, the Whigs chose a hero from a war that most of them had opposed. But the fact that Taylor was also a large slaveholder who owned several plantations in Louisiana and Mississippi was too much for the Conscience Whigs. They bolted from the party and formed a coalition with the Liberty Party and antislavery Democrats.

The Free Soil Party

The Free-Soilers met in convention in August 1848. The meeting resembled a religious camp meeting more than a political gathering. Speakers proclaimed slavery "a great moral, social, and political evil—a relic of barbarism which must necessarily be swept away in the progress of Christian civilization." The convention did not say how

that would be done, but it did adopt a platform calling for "no more Slave States and no more Slave Territories." The Free Soil Party nominated former president Martin Van Buren, with Charles Francis Adams, the son and grandson of presidents, as his running mate.

The campaign was marked by the futile efforts of both major parties to bury the slavery issue. Free Soil pressure compelled both northern Democrats and Whigs to take a stand against slavery in the territories. Whigs pointed to their earlier support of the Wilmot Proviso, while Democrats said popular sovereignty would keep the territories free. In the South, though, the two parties presented other faces. There, the Democrats pointed with pride to their expansionist record that had brought to the nation hundreds of thousands of square miles of territory—territory into which slavery might expand. But Taylor proved the strongest candidate in the South because he was a southerner and a slaveholder. "Will the people of [the South] vote for a Southern President or a Northern one?" asked southern newspapers. "We prefer Old Zack with his sugar and cotton plantations and four hundred negroes to all their compromises."

Taylor carried 8 of the 15 slave states and increased the Whig vote in the South by 10 percent over 1844, while the Democratic vote declined by 4 percent. Although he did less well in the north, he carried New York and enough other states to win the election. The Free-Soilers won no electoral votes but polled 14 percent of the popular vote in the north. They also elected nine congressmen along with two senators who would be heard from in the future: Salmon P. Chase of Ohio, architect of the Free Soil coalition in 1848, and Charles Sumner of Massachusetts, leader of the Conscience Whigs.

The Gold Rush and California Statehood

About the time Nicholas Trist was putting the finishing touches on the treaty to make California part of the United States, workers building a sawmill on the American River near Sacramento discovered flecks of gold in the riverbed. The word gradually leaked out, reaching the East in August 1848, where a public surfeited with tall tales out of the West greeted this news with skepticism. But in December, Polk's final message to Congress confirmed the "extraordinary" discoveries of gold. Two days later, a tea caddy containing 320 ounces of pure gold from California arrived in Washington. Now all doubts disappeared. By spring 1849, 100,000 gold-seekers were poised to take off by foot on the overland trail or by ship—either around Cape Horn or to the isthmus of Central America, where

Courtesy of the California History Room, California State Library, Sacramento, California.

THE CALIFORNIA GOLD RUSH

Prospectors for gold in the foothills of California's Sierra Nevada came from all over the world, including China. This photograph shows American-born and Chinese miners near Auburn, California, a year or two after the initial gold rush of 1849. It illustrates the original technology of separating gravel from gold by panning or by washing the gravel away in a sluice box, leaving the heavier gold flakes behind.

after a land crossing, they could board another ship to take them up the Pacific Coast to the new boomtown of San Francisco. Eighty thousand actually made it that first year (5,000 succumbed to a cholera epidemic). Some of them struck it rich, most kept hoping to, and more came by the scores of thousands every year from all over the world, including China.

Political organization of California could not be postponed. The mining camps needed law and order; the settlers needed courts, land and water laws, mail service, and other amenities of established government. In New Mexico, the 60,000 former Mexican citizens, now Americans, also needed a governmental structure for their new allegiance. Nor could the growing Mormon community at Salt Lake be ignored.

Still, the slavery question paralyzed Congress. In December 1848, lame-duck president Polk recommended extension of the Missouri Compromise 36°30′ line to the Pacific. The Whig-controlled House defied him, reaffirmed the Wilmot Proviso, drafted a bill to organize California as a free territory, and debated abolishing the slave trade and even slavery itself in the District of Columbia. Fistfights flared in Congress; southerners declared that they would secede if any of those measures became law; the Democratic Senate quashed all the bills. A southern caucus asked Calhoun to draft an address set-

ting forth its position. He eagerly complied, producing in January 1849 a document that breathed fire against "unconstitutional" northern efforts to keep slavery out of the territories. Calhoun reminded southerners that their "property, prosperity, equality, liberty, and safety" were at stake and prophesied secession if the South did not prevail.

But Calhoun's firebomb fizzled. Only two-fifths of the southern congressmen and senators signed it. The Whigs wanted nothing to do with it. They looked forward to good times in the Taylor administration and opposed rocking the boat. "We do not expect an administration which we have brought into power [to] do any act or permit any act to be done [against] our safety," said Robert Toombs of Georgia, a leading Whig congressman. "We feel *secure* under General Taylor," added his fellow Georgian Alexander H. Stephens.

They were in for a rude shock. Taylor viewed matters as a nationalist, not as a southerner. New York's antislavery Senator William H. Seward became one of his principal advisers. A novice in politics, Taylor was willing to be guided by Seward. As a military man, he was attracted to the idea of vanquishing the territorial problem by outflanking it. He proposed to admit California and New Mexico (the latter comprising present-day New Mexico, Arizona, Nevada, Utah, and part of Colorado) immediately as *states*, skipping the territorial stage.

From the South came cries of outrage. Immediate admission would bring in two more free states because slavery had not existed under Mexican law, and most of the 49ers were Free Soil in sentiment. With the administration's support, Californians held a convention in October 1849, drew up a constitution excluding slavery, and applied to Congress for admission as a state. Taylor's end run would tip the existing balance of 15 slave and 15 free states in favor of the North, probably forever. The South would lose its de facto veto in the Senate. "For the first time," said freshman Senator Jefferson Davis of Mississippi, "we are about permanently to destroy the balance of power between the sections." Davis insisted that slave labor was suitable to mining and that slavery should be permitted in California. Southerners vowed never to "consent to be

KIDNAPPING AGAIN!

This is a typical poster printed by abolitionist opponents of the Fugitive Slave Law. It was intended to rally the citizens of Boston against the recapture and reenslavement of Anthony Burns, a fugitive slave from Virginia seized in Boston in May 1854.

but a real human being whose plight invited sympathy and help. Consequently, many northerners who were not necessarily opposed to slavery in the South nonetheless felt outrage at the idea of fugitives being seized in a land of freedom and returned to slavery. The "underground railroad" that helped spirit slaves out of bondage took on legendary status. Stories of secret chambers where fugitives were hidden, dramatic trips in the dark of the moon between stations on the underground, and clever or heroic measures to foil pursuing bloodhounds exaggerated the legend.

Probably fewer than 1,000 of a total 3 million slaves actually escaped to freedom each year. But to southerners the return of those fugitives, like the question of the legality of slavery in California or New Mexico, was a matter of *honor* and *rights*. "Although the loss of property is felt," said Senator James Mason of Virginia, sponsor of the Fugitive Slave Act, "the loss of honor is felt still more." The fugitive slave law, said another southern politician, was "the only measure of the Compromise [of 1850] calculated to secure the rights of the South." Southerners therefore regarded obedience to the law as a test of the North's good faith in carrying out the compromise.

The law's provisions were extraordinary. It created federal commissioners who could issue warrants for arrests of fugitives and before whom a slaveholder would bring a captured fugitive to prove ownership. All the slaveholder needed for proof was an affidavit from a slave-state court or the testimony of white witnesses. The fugitive had no right to testify on his or her own behalf. The commis-

sioner received a fee of $10 if he found the owner's claim valid, but only $5 if he let the fugitive go. (The difference was supposedly justified by the larger amount of paperwork required to return the fugitive to slavery.) The federal treasury would pay all costs of enforcement. The commissioner could call on federal marshals to apprehend fugitives, and the marshals in turn could deputize any citizen to help. A citizen who refused could be fined up to $1,000, and anyone who harbored a fugitive or obstructed his or her capture would be subject to imprisonment. Northern senators had tried in vain to weaken some of these provisions and to amend the law to give alleged fugitives the rights to testify, to habeas corpus, and to a jury trial.

Abolitionists denounced the law as draconian, immoral, and unconstitutional. They vowed to resist it. Opportunities soon came, as slave owners sent agents north to recapture fugitives, some of whom had escaped years earlier (the act set no statute of limitations). In February 1851, slave-catchers arrested a black man living with his family in Indiana and returned him to an owner who said he had run away 19 years before. A Maryland man tried to claim ownership of a Philadelphia woman who he said had escaped 22 years earlier; he also wanted her six children, all of whom were born in Philadelphia. In this case, the commissioner disallowed his claim to both mother and children. But statistics show that the law was rigged in favor of the claimants. In the first 15 months of its operation, 84 fugitives were returned to slavery and only 5 were released. (For the entire decade of the 1850s, the ratio was 332 to 11.)

The Slave-Catchers

Unable to protect their freedom through legal means, many blacks, with the support of white allies, resorted to flight and resistance. Thousands of northern blacks fled to Canada—3,000 in the last three months of 1850 alone. In February 1851, slave-catchers arrested a fugitive who had taken the name Shadrach when he escaped from Virginia a year earlier. They rushed him to the federal courthouse, where a few deputy marshals held him, pending a hearing. But a group of black men broke into the courtroom, overpowered the deputies, and spirited Shadrach out of the country to Canada. This was too much for the Fillmore administration. In April 1851, another fugitive, Thomas Sims, was arrested in Boston, and the president sent 250 soldiers to help 300 armed deputies enforce the law and return Sims to slavery.

Continued rescues and escapes kept matters at fever pitch for the rest of the decade. In the fall of 1851, a Maryland slave owner and his son accompanied federal mar-

THE UNDERGROUND RAILROAD

The Quaker merchant Levi Coffin was one of the principal "conductors" on the underground railroad. He is shown in this painting standing on the wagon wearing a broad-brimmed hat. His home in central Indiana (depicted here) and, after 1847, his home in Cincinnati were stations on the road for fugitive slaves escaping north to freedom.

"The Underground Railroad" painting by Charles T. Webber (1893) from the Cincinnati Art Museum (#1927.26).

shals to Christiana, Pennsylvania, a Quaker village, where two of the man's slaves had taken refuge. The hunters ran into a fusillade of gunfire from a house where a dozen black men were protecting the fugitives. When the shooting stopped, the slave owner was dead and his son was seriously wounded. Three of the blacks fled to Canada. This time Fillmore sent in the marines. They helped marshals arrest 30 black men and a half-dozen whites, who were indicted for treason. But the government's case fell apart, and the U.S. attorney dropped charges after a jury acquitted the first defendant, a Quaker.

Another white man who aided slaves was not so lucky. Sherman Booth was an abolitionist editor in Wisconsin who led a raid in 1854 to free a fugitive from custody. Convicted in a federal court, Booth appealed for a writ of habeas corpus from the Wisconsin Supreme Court. The court freed him and declared the Fugitive Slave Law unconstitutional. That assertion of states' rights prompted the southern majority on the U.S. Supreme Court to overrule the Wisconsin court, assert the supremacy of federal law, and order Booth back to prison.

Two of the most famous fugitive slave cases of the 1850s ended in deeper tragedy. In spring 1854, federal marshals in Boston arrested a Virginia fugitive, Anthony Burns. Angry abolitionists poured into Boston to save him. Some of them tried to attack the federal courthouse, where a deputy was killed in an exchange of gunfire. But the new president, Franklin Pierce, was determined not to back down. "Incur any expense," he wired the district attorney in Boston, "to enforce the law." After every legal move to free Burns had failed, Pierce sent a U.S. revenue cutter to carry Burns back to Virginia. While thousands of angry Yankees lined the streets under American flags hanging upside down to signify the loss of liberty in

the cradle of the Revolution, 200 marines and soldiers marched this lone black man back into bondage.

Two years later Margaret Garner escaped from Kentucky to Ohio with her husband and four children. When a posse of marshals and deputies caught up with them, Margaret seized a kitchen knife and tried to kill her children and herself rather than return to slavery. She managed to cut her three-year-old daughter's throat before she was overpowered. After complicated legal maneuvers, the federal commissioner remanded the fugitives to their Kentucky owner. He promptly sold them down the river to Arkansas, and, in a steamboat accident along the way, one of Margaret Garner's sons drowned in the Mississippi.

Such events had a profound impact on public emotions. Most northerners were not abolitionists, and few of them regarded black people as equals. But millions of them moved closer to an antislavery—or perhaps it would be more accurate to say anti-Southern—position in response to the shock of seeing armed slave-catchers on their streets. "When it was all over," agreed two theretofore conservative Whigs in Boston after the Anthony Burns affair, "I put my face in my hands and wept. I could do nothing less. . . . We went to bed one night old-fashioned, conservative, compromise Union Whigs and waked up stark mad Abolitionists."

Several northern states passed new personal liberty laws in defiance of the South. Although those laws did not make it impossible to recover fugitives, they made it so difficult, expensive, and time consuming that many slave owners gave up trying. The failure of the North to honor the Fugitive Slave Law, part of the Compromise of 1850, was one of the South's bitter grievances in the 1850s. Several southern states cited it as one of their reasons for seceding in 1861.

Uncle Tom's Cabin

A novel inspired by the plight of fugitive slaves further intensified public sentiment. Harriet Beecher Stowe, author of *Uncle Tom's Cabin,* was the daughter of Lyman Beecher, the most famous clergyman-theologian of his generation, and the sister of Henry Ward Beecher, the foremost preacher of the next generation. Writing this book made her more famous than either of them. Having grown up in the doctrinal air of New England Calvinist notions of sin, guilt, and atonement, Harriet lived for 18 years in Cincinnati, where she became acquainted with fugitive slaves who had escaped across the Ohio River. During the 1840s, in spare moments that she carved out from the duties of bearing and nurturing seven children, Stowe wrote numerous short stories. Outraged by the Fugitive Slave Law in 1850, she responded to her sister-in-law's suggestion: "Hattie, if I could use a pen as you can, I would write something that will make this nation feel what an accursed thing slavery is."

In 1851, writing by candlelight after putting the children to bed, Stowe turned out a chapter a week for serial publication in an antislavery newspaper. When the installments were published as a book in spring 1852, *Uncle Tom's Cabin* became a runaway best seller and was eventually translated into 20 languages. Contrived in plot, didactic in style, steeped in sentiment, *Uncle Tom's Cabin* is nevertheless a powerful novel with unforgettable characters. Uncle Tom is not the fawning, servile Sambo of later caricature, but a Christlike figure who bears the sins of white people and carries the salvation of black people on his shoulders. The novel's central theme is the tragedy of the breakup of families by slavery—the theme most likely to pluck at the heartstrings of middle-class Americans of that generation. Few eyes remained dry as they read about Eliza fleeing across the ice-choked Ohio River to save her son from the slave trader, or about Tom grieving for the wife and children he had left behind in Kentucky when he was sold.

Although banned in some parts of the South, *Uncle Tom's Cabin* found a wide but hostile readership there. A measure of the defensiveness of southerners toward the book is the tone of the reviews that appeared in southern journals. The editor of the South's leading literary periodical instructed the reviewer: "I would have the review as hot as hellfire, blasting and searing the reputation of [this] vile wretch in petticoats." Pro-slavery authors rushed into print with more than a dozen novels challenging Stowe's themes, but all of them together made nothing like the impact of *Uncle Tom's Cabin.* The book helped shape a whole generation's view of slavery.

The Granger Collection, New York.

HARRIET BEECHER STOWE

A portrait of Harriet Beecher Stowe painted shortly after the publication of *Uncle Tom's Cabin* made her world famous.

Filibustering

If the prospects for slavery in New Mexico appeared unpromising, southerners could contemplate a closer region where slavery already existed—Cuba. Enjoying an economic boom based on slave-grown sugar, this Spanish colony only 90 miles from American shores had nearly 400,000 slaves in 1850—more than any American state except Virginia. President Polk, his appetite for territory not yet sated by the acquisition of Texas, Oregon, and half of Mexico, offered Spain $100 million for Cuba in 1848. The Spanish foreign minister spurned the offer, stating that he would rather see the island sunk in the sea than sold.

If money did not work, revolution might. Cuban planters, restive under Spanish rule, intrigued with American expansionists in the hope of fomenting an uprising on the island. Their leader was Narciso López, a Venezuelan-born Cuban soldier of fortune. In 1849, López recruited several hundred American adventurers for the first "filibustering" expedition against Cuba (from the Spanish *filibustero,* a freebooter or pirate). When President Taylor ordered the navy to prevent López's ships from leaving New York, López shifted his operations to the friendlier environs of New Orleans, where he raised a new force of

filibusters, many of them Mexican War veterans. Port officials in New Orleans looked the other way when the expedition sailed in May 1850, but Spanish troops drove the filibusters into the sea after they had established a beachhead in Cuba.

Undaunted, López escaped and returned to a hero's welcome in the South, where he raised men and money for a third try in 1851. This time, William Crittenden of Kentucky, nephew of the U.S. attorney general, commanded the 420 Americans in the expedition. But the invasion ended in fiasco and tragedy. Spanish soldiers suppressed a local uprising timed to coincide with the invasion and then defeated the filibusters, killing 200 and capturing the rest. López was garroted in the public square of Havana, after which 50 American prisoners, including Crittenden, were lined up and executed by firing squad.

These events dampened southerners' enthusiasm for Cuba, but only for a time. "Cuba must be ours," declared Jefferson Davis, in order to "increase the number of slaveholding constituencies." In 1852, the Democrats nominated Franklin Pierce of New Hampshire for president. Although a Yankee, Pierce had a reputation as a "doughface"—a northern man with southern principles. Southern Democrats were delighted with his nomination. Pierce was "as reliable as Calhoun himself," wrote one, while another said that "a nomination so favorable to the South had not been anticipated." Especially gratifying was Pierce's support for annexing Cuba, which he made one of the top priorities of his new administration after winning a landslide victory over a demoralized Whig Party weakened by schism between its northern and southern wings.

Pierce covertly encouraged a new filibustering expedition to Cuba. This one was to be led by former Governor John Quitman of Mississippi. While Quitman was recruiting hundreds of volunteers, southerners in Congress introduced a resolution to suspend the neutrality law that prohibited American interference in the internal affairs of other countries. But, at the last moment, Pierce backed off, fearful of political damage in the North if his administration became openly identified with filibustering. The Quitman expedition never sailed.

Pierce again tried to buy Cuba, instructing the American minister in Madrid to offer Spain $130 million. The minister was Pierre Soulé, a flamboyant Louisianian who managed to alienate most Spaniards by his clumsy intriguing. Soulé's crowning act came in October 1854 at a meeting with the American ministers to Britain and France in Ostend, Belgium. He persuaded them to sign what came to be known as the Ostend Manifesto. "Cuba is as necessary to the North American republic as any of its present . . . family of states," declared this document. If Spain persisted in refusing to sell, then "by every law, human and divine, we shall be justified in wresting it from Spain."

LINK TO THE PAST

Demands for the Expansion of Slavery

Albert Gallatin Brown was a true fire-eater—a Southern-rights radical whose fiery secessionist rhetoric resonated through the 1850s. He had resisted the Compromise of 1850 because it admitted California as a free state: "We ask you to give us our rights" in California, he thundered in the House of Representatives; "if you refuse, I am for taking them by armed occupation." In 1851, he urged Mississippi's secession; when that did not happen, he threw his energy into the efforts to acquire Cuba and other tropical regions suitable for slavery. In 1858, as a United States senator, he spelled out his demands for Cuba and several additional Central American provinces in a speech to his Mississippi constituents.

I want Cuba, and I know that sooner or later we must have it. . . . I want Tamaulipas, Potosi, and one or two other Mexican States; and I want them all for the same reason—for the planting or spreading of slavery. And a foothold in Central America will powerfully aid us in acquiring those other States. . . . Yes, I want these Countries for the spread of slavery.

1. Do you think the South would have been well served if Brown's demands had been met?
2. Would the Civil War have been avoided?

For additional sources related to this feature, visit the CD accompanying this text or the *Liberty, Equality, Power* Web site at:

http://history.wadsworth.com/murrin_LEP4e

This "manifesto of the brigands," as antislavery Americans called it, caused an international uproar. The administration repudiated the Ostend Manifesto and recalled Soulé. Nevertheless, acquisition of Cuba remained an objective of the Democratic Party. The issue played a role in both the 1860 presidential election and the secession controversy during 1860 and 1861. Meanwhile, American filibustering shifted its focus 750 miles south of Havana to Nicaragua. There, the most remarkable of the *filibusteros*, William Walker, had proclaimed himself president and restored the institution of slavery.

The Gray-Eyed Man of Destiny

A native of Tennessee and a brilliant, restless man, Walker had earned a medical degree from the University of Pennsylvania and studied and practiced law in New Orleans before joining the 1849 rush to California. Weighing less than 120 pounds, Walker seemed an unlikely fighter or leader of men. But he fought three duels, and his luminous eyes, which seemed to transfix his fellows, won him the sobriquet "gray-eyed man of destiny."

Walker found his true calling in filibustering. At the time, numerous raids were taking place back and forth across the border with Mexico, some of them staged to seize more of that country for the United States. In 1853, Walker led a ragged "army" of footloose 49ers into Baja California and Sonora and declared the region an independent republic. Exhaustion and desertion depleted his troops, however, and the Mexicans drove the survivors back to California.

Walker decided to try again, with another goal. Many southerners eyed Nicaragua's potential for growing cotton, sugar, coffee, and other crops. The unstable Nicaraguan government offered a tempting target. In 1854, Walker signed a contract with rebel leaders in the civil war of the moment. The following spring, he led an advance guard of filibusters to Nicaragua and proclaimed himself commander-in-chief of the rebel forces. At the head of 2,000 American soldiers, he gained control of the country and named himself president in 1856. The Pierce administration extended diplomatic recognition to Walker's regime.

But things soon turned sour. The other Central American republics formed an alliance to invade Nicaragua and overthrow Walker. To win greater support from the southern states, Walker issued a decree in September 1856 reinstituting slavery in Nicaragua. A convention of southern economic promoters meeting in Savannah praised Walker's efforts "to introduce civilization in the States of Central America, and to develop these rich and productive regions by slave labor." Boatloads of new recruits arrived in Nicaragua from New Orleans. But in spring 1857, they succumbed to disease and to the Central American armies.

Walker escaped to New Orleans, where he was welcomed as a hero. He had no trouble recruiting men for another attempt, but the navy stopped him in November 1857. Southern congressmen condemned the naval commander and encouraged Walker to try again. He did, in December 1858, after a New Orleans jury refused to convict him of violating the neutrality law. On this third expedition, Walker's ship struck a reef and sank. Undaunted, he tried yet again. He wrote a book to raise funds for another invasion of Nicaragua, urging "the hearts of Southern youth to answer the call of honor. . . . The true field for the expansion of slavery is in tropical America." A few more southern youths answered the call, but they were stopped in Honduras. There, on September 12, 1860, the gray-eyed man met his destiny before a firing squad.

Conclusion

Within the three-year period from 1845 to 1848, the annexation of Texas, the settlement of the Oregon boundary dispute with Britain, and the acquisition by force of New Mexico and California from Mexico added 1,150,000 square miles to the United States. This expansion was America's "manifest destiny," according to Senator Stephen A. Douglas of Illinois. He further proclaimed:

> Increase, and multiply, and expand, is the law of this nation's existence. You cannot limit this great republic by mere boundary lines. Any one of you gentlemen might as well say to a son twelve years old that he is big enough, and must not grow any larger, and in order to prevent his growth put a hoop around him and keep him to his present size. Either the hoop must burst and be rent asunder, or the child must die. So it would be with this great nation.

But other Americans feared that the country could not absorb such rapid growth without strains that might break it apart. At the outbreak of the war with Mexico, Ralph Waldo Emerson predicted that "the United States will conquer Mexico, but it will be as the man swallows the arsenic, which brings him down in turn. Mexico will poison us." Emerson proved correct. The poison was the reopening of the question of slavery's expansion, which had supposedly been settled by the Missouri Compromise in 1820. The admission of Texas as a huge new slave state and the possibility that more slave states might be carved out of the territory acquired from Mexico provoked northern congressmen to pass the Wilmot Proviso. Southerners bristled at this attempt to prevent the further expansion of slavery. Threats of secession and civil war poisoned the atmosphere in 1849 and 1850.

The Compromise of 1850 defused the crisis and appeared to settle the issue once again, but events would soon prove that this compromise had merely postponed the crisis. The fugitive slave issue and filibustering expeditions to acquire more slave territory kept sectional controversies smoldering. In 1854, the Kansas-Nebraska Act would cause them to burst into a hotter flame than ever.

SUGGESTED READINGS

For the theme of Manifest Destiny, the best introduction is **Frederick Merk, *Manifest Destiny and Mission in American History*** (1963). See also the essays in **Samuel W. Haynes and Christopher Morris, eds., *Manifest Destiny and Empire*** (1997). Two good studies of the overland trails to California and Oregon and other points West are **John D. Unruh, Jr., *The Plains Across: The Overland Emigrants and the Trans-Mississippi West, 1840–1860*** (1979), and **John Mack Faragher, *Women and Men on the Overland Trail*** (1978). A fine introduction to the impact of American expansion on the Indians of the West is **Philip Weeks, *Farewell, My Nation: The American Indian and the United States 1820–1890*** (rev. ed., 2000). A good study of the relationship between American expansion and the coming of war with Mexico is **David Pletcher, *The Diplomacy of Annexation: Texas, Oregon, and the Mexican War*** (1973). For the Mexican War, a good narrative is **John S. D. Eisenhower, *So Far from God: The U.S. War with Mexico 1846–1848*** (1989). Opposition to and support for the war by different elements of the public are chronicled in **John H. Schroeder, *Mr. Polk's War: American Opposition and Dissent, 1846–1848*** (1973), and **Robert W. Johannsen, *To the Halls of the Montezumas: The Mexican War in the American Imagination*** (1985). For the conflict provoked by the issue of slavery's expansion into territory acquired from Mexico, see **David M. Potter, *The Impending Crisis 1848–1861*** (1976); **Richard H. Sewell, *Ballots for Freedom: Antislavery Politics in the United States 1837–1860*** (1976); **Michael A. Morrison, *Slavery and the American West: The Eclipse of Manifest Destiny and the Coming of the Civil War*** (1997); and **Leonard D. Richards, *The Slave Power: The Free North and Southern Domination, 1780–1860*** (2000). The best study of the Compromise of 1850 is **Holman Hamilton, *Prologue to Conflict: The Crisis and Compromise of 1850*** (1964). The passage and enforcement of the Fugitive Slave Act is the subject of **Stanley W. Campbell, *The Slave Catchers*** (1970). Still the best book on filibustering is **Robert E. May, *The Southern Dream of a Caribbean Empire 1854–1861*** (1971).

 AMERICAN JOURNEY ONLINE
AND
INFOTRAC COLLEGE EDITION

Visit the source collections at www.ajaccess.wadsworth.com and infotrac.thomsonlearning.com and use the Search function with the following key terms to explore documents, images, audio and video clips, articles, and commentary related to the material in this chapter.

Uncle Tom's Cabin	Mormons
Harriet Beecher Stowe	Manifest Destiny
Henry Clay	Texas Republic
Martin Van Buren	Battle of the Alamo
fugitive slave	Compromise of 1850
The Book of Mormon	Stephen Douglas

GRADE AIDS

Visit the Liberty Equality Power Companion Web Site for resources specific to this textbook: http://history.wadsworth.com/murrin_LEP4e

The CD in the back of this book and the U.S. History Resource Center at http://history.wadsworth.com/u.s./ offer a variety of tools to help you succeed in this course, including access to quizzes; images; documents; interactive simulations; maps, and timelines; movie explorations; and a wealth of other sources.

future. "The admission of Kansas into the Union as a slave state is now a point of honor," wrote Congressman Preston Brooks of South Carolina. "The fate of the South is to be decided with the Kansas issue." On the other side, Charles Sumner of Massachusetts gave a well-publicized speech in the Senate on May 19 and 20 entitled "The Crime against Kansas." "Murderous robbers from Missouri," charged Sumner, "from the drunken spew and vomit of an uneasy civilization" had committed the "rape of a virgin territory, compelling it to the hateful embrace of slavery." Among the southern senators whom Sumner singled out for special condemnation and ridicule was Andrew Butler of South Carolina, a cousin of Congressman Brooks. Butler was a "Don Quixote," said Sumner, "who had chosen a mistress to whom he has made his vows . . . the harlot, Slavery."

The Caning of Sumner

Sumner's speech incensed southerners, none more than Preston Brooks, who decided to avenge his cousin. He knew that Sumner would never accept a challenge to a duel. Anyway, dueling was for gentlemen, and even horsewhipping was too good for this Yankee blackguard. Two days after the speech, Brooks walked into the Senate chamber and began beating Sumner with a heavy cane. His legs trapped beneath the desk bolted to the floor, Sumner wrenched it loose as he stood up to try to defend himself, whereupon Brooks clubbed him so ferociously that Sumner slumped forward, bloody and unconscious.

News of the incident sent a thrill of pride through the South and a rush of rage through the North. Charleston newspapers praised Brooks for "standing forth so nobly in defense of . . . the honor of South Carolinians." Brooks resigned from Congress after censure by the House and was unanimously reelected. From all over the South came gifts of new canes, some inscribed with such mottoes as "Hit Him Again" and "Use Knock-Down Arguments." But, in the North, the Republicans gained thousands of voters as a result of the affair. It seemed to prove their contentions about "the barbarism of slavery." "Has it come to this," asked the poet William Cullen Bryant, editor of the *New York Evening Post*, "that we must speak with bated breath in the presence of our Southern masters? . . . Are we to be chastised as they chastise their slaves?" A veteran New York politician reported that he had "never before seen anything at all like the present state of deep, determined, & desperate feelings of hatred, & hostility to the further extension of slavery, & its political power."

Republicans were soon able to add "Bleeding Kansas" to "Bleeding Sumner" in their repertoire of winning issues. Even as Sumner was delivering his speech in Washington,

SOUTHERN CHIVALRY — ARGUMENT versus CLUB'S.

Prints Division, The New York Public Library, Astor, Lenox and Tilden Foundations.

THE CANING OF SUMNER

This drawing by an antislavery Northerner shows pro-slavery Congressman Preston Brooks of South Carolina beating Senator Charles Sumner of Massachusetts with a heavy cane on the floor of the Senate on May 22, 1856. It portrays the inability of the South to respond to the power of Northern arguments, symbolized by the pen in Sumner's right hand and a speech in his left hand, except with the unthinking power of the club. Note other Southern senators in the background smiling on the scene or preventing Northern senators from coming to Sumner's aid. The caning of Sumner was the worst of several instances of North-South violence or threatened violence on the floor of Congress in the 1850s, presaging the violence on the battlefields of the 1860s.

an "army" of pro-slavery Missourians, complete with artillery, marched on the free-state capital of Lawrence, Kansas. On May 21, they shelled and sacked the town, burning several buildings. A rival force of free-state men arrived too late to intercept them. One of the free-state "captains" was John Brown, an abolitionist zealot who considered himself anointed by the Lord to avenge the sins of slaveholders. When he learned of the murder of several free-state settlers and the sack of Lawrence, he "went crazy—crazy," according to one of his followers. We must "fight fire with fire," Brown declared. "Something must be done to show these barbarians that we, too, have rights." Leading four of his sons and three other men to a proslavery settlement at Pottawatomie Creek on the night of May 24–25, 1856, Brown dragged five men from their cabins and split open their heads with broadswords.

Here was the Old Testament retribution of an eye for an eye. Brown's murderous act set off a veritable civil war in Kansas. One of Brown's sons was among the estimated 200 men killed in the bushwhackings and raids. Not until President Pierce sent a tough new territorial governor and 1,300 federal troops to Kansas in September 1856 did the violence subside—just in time to save the Democrats from possible defeat in the presidential election.

⊕ The Election of 1856

By 1856, the Republicans had become the largest party in the North. With the old Free-Soilers as their radical core, they had recruited about three-fourths of the former Whigs and one-fifth of the Democrats. They were also the first truly sectional party in American history because they had little prospect of carrying a single county in the slave states. At their first national convention, the Republicans wrote a platform that focused mainly on that "relic of barbarism," slavery. The platform also incorporated the old Whig program of federal aid to internal improvements, including a railroad to California. For its presidential nominee, the party steered away from its most prominent leaders, who were identified with the old parties, and turned instead to John C. Frémont. This "Pathfinder of the West" had a dashing image as an explorer and for his role in the acquisition of California. With little political experience, he had few political enemies and his antislavery credentials were satisfactory.

The Democrats chose as their candidate James Buchanan, a veteran of 30 years in various public offices. He had been minister to Britain during the Kansas-Nebraska controversy and so was not tainted with its unpopularity in the North, as were Pierce and Douglas, the other aspirants for nomination. The Democratic platform endorsed popular sovereignty and condemned the Republicans as a "sectional party" that incited "treason and armed resistance in the Territories."

This would be a three-party election because the American Party was still in the field. Having become mainly a waystation for former southern Whigs, the party nominated ex-Whig Millard Fillmore. The three-party campaign sifted out into a pair of two-party contests: Democrats versus Americans in the South; Democrats versus Republicans in the North. Fillmore, despite a good showing of 44 percent of the popular vote in the South, carried only Maryland. Considering Buchanan colorless but safe, the rest of the South gave him three-fourths of the electoral votes he needed for victory.

The real excitement in this election showed itself in the North. For many Republicans, the campaign was a moral cause, an evangelical crusade against the sin of slavery. Republican "Wide Awake" clubs marched in torchlight parades chanting "Free Soil, Free Speech, Free Men, Frémont!" A veteran politician in Indiana marveled: "Men, Women & Children all seemed to be out, with a kind of fervor I have never witnessed before in six Pres. Elections in which I have taken an active part." The turnout of eligible voters in the North was a remarkable 83 percent. One awestruck journalist, anticipating a Republican victory, wrote that "the process now going on in the United States is a *Revolution.*"

Not quite. Although the Republicans swept New England and the upper parts of New York state and the Old Northwest—both settled by New Englanders, where evangelical and antislavery reform movements had taken hold—the contest in the lower North was close. Buchanan needed only to carry Pennsylvania and either Indiana or Illinois to win the presidency, and the campaign focused on those states. The immigrant and working-class voters of the eastern cities and the rural voters of the lower Midwest, descendants of upland southerners who had settled there, were antiblack and antiabolitionist in sentiment. They were ripe for Democratic propaganda that accused Republicans of favoring racial equality. "Black Republicans," declared an Ohio Democratic newspaper, intended to "turn loose . . . millions of negroes, to elbow you in the workshops, and compete with you in fields of honest labor." A Democrat in Pennsylvania told voters that "the one aim" of the Republicans was "to elevate the African race in this country to complete equality of political and economic condition with the white man." Indiana Democrats organized parades, with young girls in white dresses carrying banners inscribed "Fathers, save us from nigger husbands."

The Republicans in these areas denied that they favored racial equality. They insisted that the main reason for keeping slavery out of the territories was to enable white farmers and workers to make a living there without competition from black labor. But their denials were in vain. Support for the Republican Party by prominent black leaders, including Frederick Douglass, convinced hundreds of thousands of voters that the Black Republicans were racial egalitarians. For the next two decades, that sentiment

POPULAR AND ELECTORAL VOTES IN THE 1856 PRESIDENTIAL ELECTION

Candidate	Free States		Slave States		Total	
	Popular	Electoral	Popular	Electoral	Popular	Electoral
Buchanan (Democrat)	1,227,000	62	607,000	112	1,833,000	174
Frémont (Republican)	1,338,000	114	0	0	1,338,000	114
Fillmore (American)	396,000	0	476,000	8	872,000	8

concurrence, Chief Justice Taney issued the Court's ruling stating that Congress lacked the power to keep slavery out of a territory, because slaves were property and the Constitution protects the right of property. For good measure, Taney also wrote that the circuit court should not have accepted the Scott case in the first place because black men were not citizens of the United States and therefore had no standing in its courts. Five other justices wrote concurring opinions. The two non-Democratic northern justices (both former Whigs, one of them now a Republican) dissented vigorously. They stated that blacks were legal citizens in several northern states and were therefore citizens of the United States. To buttress their opinion that Congress could prohibit slavery in the territories, they cited Congress's Constitutional power to make "all needful rules and regulations" for the territories.

Modern scholars agree with the dissenters. In 1857, however, Taney had a majority, and his ruling became law. Modern scholars have also demonstrated that Taney was motivated by his passionate commitment "to southern life and values" and by his determination to stop "northern aggression" by cutting the ground out from under the hated Republicans. His ruling that their program to exclude slavery from the territories was unconstitutional was designed to do just that.

Republicans denounced Taney's "jesuitical decision" as based on "gross perversion" of the Constitution. The *New York Tribune* sneered that the Dred Scott decision was "entitled to just as much moral weight as would be the judgment of a majority of those congregated in any Washington bar-room." Several Republican state legislatures resolved that the ruling was "not binding in law and conscience." They looked forward to the election of a Republican president who could "reconstitute" the Court and secure a reversal of the decision. "The remedy," said the *Chicago Tribune,* "is the ballot box. . . . Let the next President be Republican, and 1860 will mark an era kindred with that of 1776."

The Lecompton Constitution

Instead of settling the slavery controversy, the Dred Scott decision intensified it. Meanwhile, pro-slavery advocates, having won legalization of slavery in the territories, moved to ensure that it would remain legal when Kansas became a state. That required deft maneuvering, because legitimate antislavery settlers outnumbered pro-slavery settlers by more than two to one. In 1857, the pro-slavery legislature (elected by the fraudulent votes of border ruffians two years earlier) called for a constitutional convention at Lecompton to prepare Kansas for statehood. Because the election for delegates was rigged, Free Soil voters refused

to participate. One-fifth of the registered voters thereupon elected convention delegates, who met at Lecompton and wrote a state constitution that made slavery legal.

Then a nagging problem arose. Buchanan had promised that the Lecompton constitution would be presented to voters in a fair referendum. The problem was how to pass the pro-slavery constitution given the antislavery majority of voters. The convention came up with an ingenious solution. Instead of a referendum on the whole constitution, it would allow the voters to choose between a constitution "with slavery" and one "with no slavery." The catch was that the constitution "with no slavery" guaranteed slave owners' "inviolable" right of property in the 200 slaves already in Kansas and their progeny. It also did nothing to prevent future smuggling of slaves across the 200-mile border with Missouri. Once in Kansas, they, too, would become "inviolable" property.

Free-state voters branded the referendum a farce and boycotted it. One-quarter of the eligible voters went to the polls in December 1857 and approved the constitution "with slavery." Meanwhile, in a fair election policed by federal troops, the antislavery party won control of the new territorial legislature and promptly submitted both constitutions to a referendum that was boycotted by pro-slavery voters. This time, 70 percent of the eligible voters went to the polls and overwhelmingly rejected both constitutions.

Which referendum would the federal government recognize? That question proved even more divisive than the Kansas-Nebraska debate four years earlier. President Buchanan faced a dilemma. He had promised a fair referendum. But southerners, who dominated both the Democratic Party and the administration (the vice president and four of the seven cabinet members were from slave states), threatened secession if Kansas was not admitted to statehood under the Lecompton constitution "with slavery." "If Kansas is *driven out of the Union for being a Slave State,*" thundered Senator James Hammond of South Carolina, "can any Slave State remain in it with honor?" Buchanan caved in. He explained to a shocked northern Democrat that if he did not accept the Lecompton constitution, southern states would "secede from the Union or take up arms against us." Buchanan sent the Lecompton constitution to Congress with a message recommending statehood. Kansas, said the president, "is at this moment as much a slave state as Georgia or South Carolina."

What would Stephen Douglas do? If he endorsed the Lecompton constitution, he would undoubtedly be defeated in his bid for reelection to the Senate in 1858. And he regarded the Lecompton constitution as a travesty of popular sovereignty. He broke with the administration on the issue. He could not vote to "force this constitution down the throats of the people of Kansas," he told the

Senate, "in opposition to their wishes and in violation of our pledges."

The fight in Congress was long and bitter. The South and the administration had the votes they needed in the Senate and won handily there, but the Democratic majority in the House was so small that the defection of even a few northern Democrats would defeat the Lecompton constitution. The House debate at one point got out of hand and a wild fistfight erupted between Republicans and southern Democrats. "There were some fifty middle-aged and elderly gentlemen pitching into each other like so many Tipperary savages," wrote a bemused reporter, "most of them incapable, from want of wind and muscle, from doing each other any serious harm."

When the vote was finally taken, two dozen northern Democrats defected, providing enough votes to defeat Lecompton. Both sides then accepted a compromise proposal to resubmit the constitution to Kansas voters, who decisively rejected it. This meant that while Kansas would not come in as a slave state, neither would it come in as a free state for some time yet. Nevertheless, the Lecompton debate had split the Democratic Party, leaving a legacy of undying enmity between southerners and Douglas. The election of a Republican president in 1860 was now all but assured.

The Economy in the 1850s

Beginning in the mid-1840s, the American economy enjoyed a dozen years of unprecedented growth and prosperity, particularly for the railroads. The number of miles in operation quintupled during those years. Railroad construction provided employment for many immigrants and spurred growth in industries that produced rails, rolling stock, and other railroad equipment. Most railroad construction took place in the Old Northwest, linking the region more closely to the Northeast and continuing the reorientation of transportation networks from a north-south river pattern to an east-west canal and rail pattern. By the mid-1850s, the east-west rail and water routes carried more than twice as much freight tonnage as the north-south river routes. This closer binding of the western and eastern states reinforced the effect of slavery in creating a self-conscious "North" and "South."

Although the Old Northwest remained predominantly agricultural, rapid expansion of railroads there laid the basis for its industrialization. During the 1850s, industrial output in the free states west of Pennsylvania grew at twice the rate of Northeast industrial output and three times as great as the rate in the South. The Northwest urban growth rate tripled that of the Northeast and quadrupled that of the South. Chicago became the terminus for 15 rail lines in the 1850s, during which its population grew by 375 percent. In 1847, two companies that contributed to the rapid growth of agriculture during this era built their plants in Illinois: the McCormick reaper works at Chicago and the John Deere steel-plow works at Moline.

According to almost every statistical index available from that period, economic expansion considerably outstripped even the prodigious pace of population increase. While the number of Americans grew by 44 percent during these 12 years (1844–56), the value of both exports and imports increased by 200 percent; mined coal tonnage by 270 percent; banking capital, industrial capital, and

BRIDGE OF THE MILWAUKIE AND CHICAGO RAILROAD AT RACINE, WISCONSIN

By the 1850s, Chicago had become the hub for a dozen or more railroads that tied the fast-growing Midwest to the older South and East. This illustration shows the railroad bridge over the Root River between Chicago and Milwaukee.

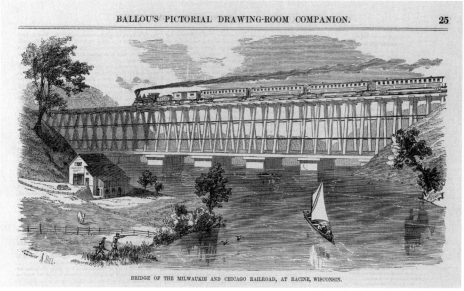

BALLOU'S PICTORIAL DRAWING-ROOM COMPANION.   25

BRIDGE OF THE MILWAUKIE AND CHICAGO RAILROAD, AT RACINE, WISCONSIN.

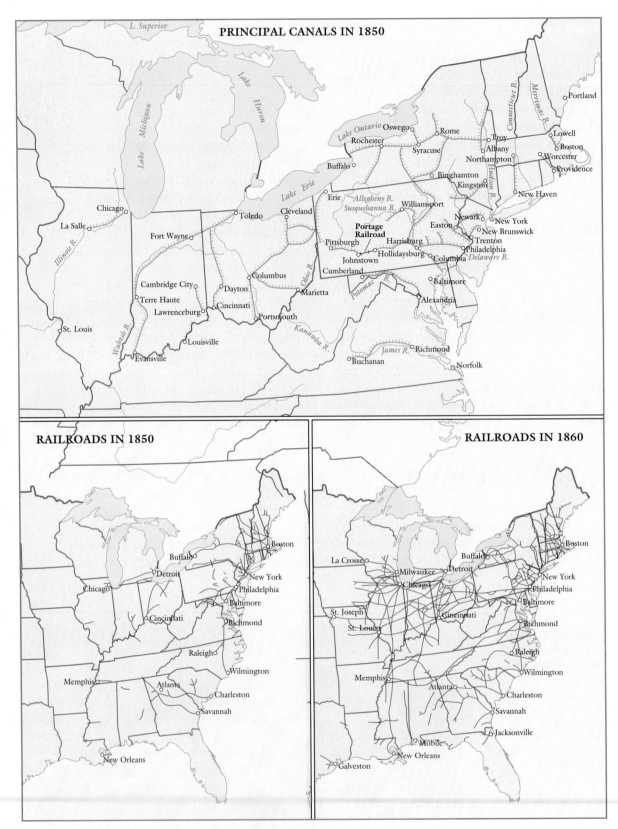

MAP 14.3 MAIN TRANSPORTATION ROUTES IN THE 1850S

These maps illustrate how the transportation networks by natural waterways (rivers and the Atlantic coastal waters) oriented commerce north and south while the canals and railroads linked east and west. By 1860, railroads tied the Midwestern states economically to the Northeast.

industrial output by approximately 100 percent; farmland value by 100 percent; and cotton, wheat, and corn harvests by about 70 percent. These advances meant a significant increase of per capita production and income, although the distance between rich and poor was widening—a phenomenon that has characterized all capitalist economies during stages of rapid industrial growth.

By the later 1850s, the United States had forged ahead of most other countries to become the second-leading industrial producer in the world, behind only Britain. But the country was still in the early stages of industrial development. Agricultural product processing and raw materials still played the dominant role. By 1860, the four leading industries, measured by value added in manufacturing, were cotton textiles, lumber products, boots and shoes, and flour milling. Iron and machinery, industries typical of a more mature manufacturing economy, ranked sixth and seventh.

"The American System of Manufactures"

The United States had pioneered in one crucial feature of modern industry: the mass production of interchangeable parts. This revolutionary concept had begun with the manufacture of firearms earlier in the 19th century and had spread to many products by the 1850s. High wages and a shortage of the skilled craftsmen who had traditionally fashioned guns, furniture, locks, watches, and other products had compelled American entrepreneurs to seek alternative methods. "Yankee ingenuity," already world-famous, came up with an answer: special-purpose machine tools that would cut and shape an endless number of parts that could be fitted together with other similarly produced parts to make whole guns, locks, clocks, and sewing machines in mass quantities.

These products were less elegant and less durable than products made by skilled craftsmen, but they were also less expensive and thus more widely available to the "middling classes" of a society that pro-

fessed to be more democratic than Europe in its consumer economy as well as in its politics.

Such American-made products were the hit of the first World's Fair, the Crystal Palace Exhibition at London in 1851. British manufacturers were so impressed by Yankee techniques, which they dubbed "the American system of manufactures," that they sent two commissions to the United States to study them. "The labouring classes are comparatively few," reported one commission in 1854, "and to this very want . . . may be attributed the extraordinary ingenuity displayed in many of these labour-saving machines." The British firearms industry imported American experts to help set up the Enfield Armoury in London to manufacture the new British army rifle.

The British also invited Samuel Colt of Connecticut, inventor of the famous six-shooting revolver, to set up a factory in England stocked with machinery from Connecticut. In testimony before a parliamentary committee in 1854, Colt summed up the American system of manufactures in a single sentence: "There is nothing that cannot be produced by machinery." Although the British had a half-century head start over Americans in the Industrial Revolution, Colt's testimony expressed a philosophy that would enable the United States to surpass Britain as the leading industrial nation by 1880.

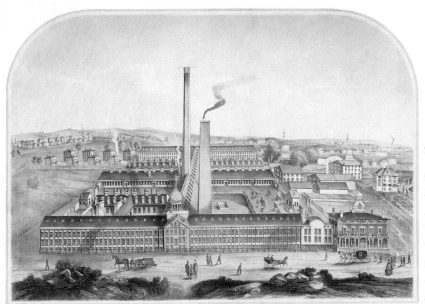

COLT ARMS PLANT IN HARTFORD, CONNECTICUT

Samuel Colt's factory for manufacturing firearms was a showpiece for the American system of manufactures in the 1850s. All of the processes for production of the famous Colt revolver were housed under one roof, with power-driven machinery cutting the metal and shaping the interchangeable parts. Hand filing was necessary, however, for a perfect fit of the parts because the tolerances of machine tools were not yet as finely calibrated as they later became.

The British industrial commissions also cited the American educational system as an important reason for the country's technological proficiency. "Educated up to a far higher standard than those of a much superior grade in the Old World," reported the 1854 commission, "every [American] workman seems to be continually devising some new thing to assist him in his work, and there is a strong desire . . . to be 'posted up' in every new improvement." By contrast, the British workman, trained by long apprenticeship "in the trade," rather than in school, lacked "the ductility of mind and the readiness of apprehension for a new thing" and was therefore "unwilling to change the methods he has been used to."

Whether this British commission was right in its belief that American schooling encouraged the "adaptative versatility" of Yankee workers, it was certainly true that public education and literacy were more widespread in the United States than in Europe. Almost 95 percent of adults in the free states were literate in 1860, compared with 65 percent in England and 55 percent in France. The standardization and expansion of public school systems that had begun earlier in New England had spread to the mid-Atlantic states and into the Old Northwest by the 1850s. Nearly all children received a few years of schooling, and most completed at least six or seven years.

This improvement in education coincided with the feminization of the teaching profession, which opened up new career opportunities for young women. The notion that the "woman's sphere" was in the home, rearing and nurturing children, ironically projected that sphere outside the home into the schoolroom when schools took over part of the responsibility of socializing and educating children. By the 1850s, nearly three-quarters of the public school teachers in New England were women (who worked for lower salaries than male teachers), a trend that was spreading to the mid-Atlantic states and the Old Northwest as well.

The Southern Economy

The feminization of teaching had not yet reached the South. Nor had the idea of universal public education taken deep root in the slave states. In contrast to the North, where 94 percent of the entire population could read and write, 80 percent of the free population and only 10 percent of the slaves in the South were literate. This was one of several differences between North and South that antislavery people pointed to as evidence of the backward, repressive, and pernicious nature of a slave society.

© Bettmann/Corbis.

THE COUNTRY SCHOOL
This famous painting by Winslow Homer portrays the typical one-room rural schoolhouse in which millions of American children learned the "three R's" (reading, writing, and arithmetic) in the 19th century. By the 1850s, teaching elementary school was a profession increasingly dominated by women, an important change from earlier generations.

Still, the South shared in the economy's rapid growth following recovery from the depression of 1837–43. Cotton prices and production both doubled between 1845 and 1855. Similar increases in price and output emerged in tobacco and sugar. The price of slaves, a significant index of prosperity in the southern economy, also doubled during this decade. Southern crops provided three-fifths of all U.S. exports, with cotton alone supplying more than half.

But a growing number of southerners deplored the fact that the "colonial" economy of the South was so dependent on the export of agricultural products and the import of manufactured goods. The ships that carried southern cotton were owned by northern or British firms; financial and commercial services were provided mostly by Yankees or Englishmen. In the years of rising sectional tensions around 1850, many southerners began calling for economic independence from the North. How could they obtain their rights, they asked, if they were "financially more enslaved than our negroes?" Yankees "abuse and denounce slavery and slaveholders," declared a southern newspaper in 1851, yet "we purchase all our luxuries and necessaries from the North. . . . Our slaves are clothed with Northern manufactured goods and work with Northern hoes, ploughs, and other implements. . . . The slaveholder dresses in Northern goods . . . and on Northern-made paper, with a Northern pen, with Northern ink, he resolves and re-resolves in regard to his rights."

Southerners must "throw off this humiliating dependence," declared James D. B. De Bow, the young champion of economic diversification in the South. In 1846, De Bow had founded in New Orleans a periodical eventually known as *De Bow's Review*. Proclaiming on its cover that "Commerce is King," the *Review* set out to make this slogan a southern reality. De Bow took the lead in organizing annual commercial conventions that met in various southern cities during the 1850s. In its early years, this movement encouraged southerners to invest in shipping lines, railroads, textile mills ("bring the spindles to the cotton"), and other enterprises. "Give us factories, machine shops, work shops," declared southern proponents of King Commerce, "and we shall be able ere long to assert our rights."

Economic diversification in the South did make headway during the 1850s. The slave states quadrupled their railroad mileage, increased the amount of capital invested in manufacturing by 77 percent, and boosted their output of cotton textiles by 44 percent. But like Alice in Wonderland, the faster the South ran, the farther behind it seemed to fall—for northern industry was growing even faster. The slave states' share of the nation's manufacturing capacity actually dropped from 18 to 16 percent during the decade. In 1860, the North had five times more industrial

output per capita than the South, and it had three times the railroad capital and mileage per capita and per thousand square miles. Southerners had a larger percentage of their capital invested in land and slaves in 1860 than they had had 10 years earlier. Some 80 percent of the South's labor force worked in agriculture—the same as 60 years earlier. By contrast, while farming remained, at 40 percent, the largest single occupation in the North, the northern economy developed a strong manufacturing and commercial sector whose combined labor force almost equaled that of agriculture by 1860.

The Sovereignty of King Cotton

A good many southerners preferred to keep it that way. "That the North does our trading and manufacturing mostly is true," wrote an Alabama planter in 1858. "We are willing that they should. Ours is an agricultural people, and God grant that we may continue so. It is the freest, happiest, most independent, and with us, the most powerful condition on earth." In the later 1850s, the drive for economic diversification in the South lost steam. King Cotton reasserted its primacy over King Commerce as cotton output *and* prices continued to rise, suffusing the South in a glow of prosperity. "Our Cotton is the most wonderful talisman on earth," declared a planter. "By its power we are transmuting whatever we choose into whatever we want." In a speech that became famous, James Hammond of South Carolina told his fellow senators in 1858 that "the slaveholding South is now the controlling power of the world. . . . No power on earth dares to make war on cotton. Cotton *is* king."

Even the commercial conventions in the South seemed to have embraced this gospel. In 1854, they merged with a parallel series of planters' conventions, and thereafter the delegates heard as much about cotton as they did about commerce. By the later 1850s, one of the main goals of these conventions was to reopen the African slave trade, prohibited by law since 1808. Many southerners rejected that goal, however, partly on moral grounds and partly on economic grounds. Older slave states such as Virginia, which profited from the sale of slaves to the booming cotton frontier of the Deep South, objected to any goal that would lower the price of their largest export. The conventions also lobbied for the annexation of Cuba, which would bring a productive agricultural economy and 400,000 more slaves into the United States.

Nowhere in the South, said defenders of slavery, did one see such "scenes of beggary, squalid poverty, and wretchedness" as one could find in any northern city. Black slaves, they insisted, enjoyed a higher standard of living than white "wage slaves" in northern factories.

whether they work or not. . . . What a glorious thing is slavery, when want, misfortune, old age, debility, and sickness overtake [the slave]."

Labor Conditions in the North

How true was this portrait of poverty and starvation among northern workers? Some northern labor leaders did complain that the "slavery" of the wage system gave "bosses" control over the hours, conditions, and compensation of labor. Use of this wage-slavery theme in labor rhetoric declined during the prosperous years of the 1850s, and no evidence indicates that a northern working man ever offered to change places with a southern slave. Average per capita income was about 40 percent higher in the North than in the South. Although that average masked large disparities between rich and poor—even between the middle class and the poor—those disparities

were no greater, and probably less, in the North than in the South.

To be sure, substantial numbers of recent immigrants, day laborers, and young single women in large northern cities lived on the edge of poverty—or slipped over the edge. Many women seamstresses, shoe binders, milliners, and the like, who worked 60 or 70 hours per week in the outwork system earned less than a living wage. Some of them resorted to prostitution in order to survive. The widespread adoption of the newly invented sewing machine in the 1850s did nothing to make life easier for seamstresses; it only lowered their per-unit piecework wages and forced them to turn out more shirts and trousers than before. Many urban working-class families could not survive on the wages of an unskilled or semi-skilled father. The mother had to take in laundry, boarders, or outwork, and one or more children had to work. Much employment was seasonal or intermittent, leaving

---

M U S I C A L   L I N K   T O   T H E   P A S T

The Waltz—An Immoral Dance?

Composer: G. Jullien

Title: "Prima Donna Waltz" (c. late 1850s)

As tame and old-fashioned as the waltz may sound to modern ears, for many 19th-century observers, its arrival represented an alarming and morally dangerous development in American life. It did away with the niceties and social introductions of country dances, minuets, gavottes, and other dances championed previously in the American past. Those dances kept young people at a socially acceptable distance, constantly switching partners, never allowing a couple to concentrate on each other for an extended time. But couples who engaged in waltzing gripped each other in close embrace, intently gazed in each other's eyes at shockingly close range, and refused to share their partners or acknowledge other dancers on the floor. Worse yet, as reported by music historian Thornton Hagert, "The hypnotic effect of the unrelenting and mechanical turning, turning of the early waltz was thought to summon up uncontrollable passions that would surely lead to ridicule or even dishonor, disease and pregnancy." Despite numerous warnings of pernicious influence, waltz tempos steadily increased as the 19th century ambled forward, which presumably made dancers even dizzier and further clouded their personal judgment and morality. In addition, waltz steps were simplified as time went on, allowing more young people

to participate in the waltz fad with little training.

The torrent of controversy surrounding the waltz presaged similar outcries against future American dance crazes such as the ragtime-influenced turkey trot of the 1910s, the jazz-inflected Charleston of the 1920s, the acrobatic lindy hop of the big band era, and the anarchic mosh pit chaos of the 1970s punk rock scene. American youth have often seized music as an outlet and excuse to exhibit and play out emotions and feelings normally excluded from public view, to the chagrin of some of their elders. Musical expression by the American youth of the mid-20th century often featured distorted and screeching electric guitars, but such contraptions and the music they accompanied were probably no more threatening to American parents of the 1950s than the graceful bugle-led strains of the "Prima Donna Waltz" were for American parents of the 1850s.

1. Why do you think popular dances became simpler and less formal as the 19th century unfolded?
2. What do you think such cultural changes said about the character of the maturing United States?

Listen to an audio recording of this music on the Musical Links to the Past CD.

workers without wages for long periods, especially during winter. The poverty, overcrowding, and disease in the tenement districts of a few large cities—especially New York City—seemed to lend substance to pro-slavery claims that slaves were better off.

But they were not—even apart from the psychological contrast between being free and being a slave. New York City's poverty, although highly concentrated and visible, was exceptional. In the North, only one-fourth of the people lived in cities or towns of more than 2,500 people. Wages and opportunities for workers were greater in the North than anywhere else in the world, including the South. That was why 4 million immigrants came to the United States from 1845 to 1860 and why seven-eighths of

© Bettmann/Corbis.

THE PANIC ON WALL STREET
This cartoon satirizes the consternation among New York investors and financiers when banks and businesses crashed in autumn 1857. Notice the smirk on the faces of two men in the foreground, who undoubtedly stood to benefit from foreclosures on defaulted property. The panic was no laughing matter, though, because it led to a short but sharp recession in 1857 and 1858.

them settled in free states. It was also why twice as many white residents of slave states migrated to free states than vice versa. And it was one reason why northern farmers and workers wanted to keep slaves *and* free blacks out of the territories, where their cheaper labor would lower wages.

The Panic of 1857

In fall 1857, the relative prosperity of the North was interrupted by a financial panic that caused a short-lived but intense depression. When the Crimean War in Europe (1854–56) cut off Russian grain from the European market, U.S. exports had mushroomed to meet the deficiency.

After the Crimean War ended, U.S. grain exports slumped. The sharp rise in interest rates in Britain and France, caused by the war, spread to U.S. financial markets in 1857 and dried up sources of credit. Meanwhile, the economic boom of the preceding years had caused the American economy to overheat: Land prices had soared, railroads had built beyond the capacity of earnings to service their debts, and banks had made too many risky loans.

This speculative house of cards came crashing down in September 1857. The failure of one banking house sent a wave of panic through the financial community. Banks

suspended specie payments, businesses failed, railroads went bankrupt, construction halted, and factories shut down. Hundreds of thousands of workers were laid off, and others went on part-time schedules or took wage cuts, just as the cold winter months were arriving. The specter of class conflict such as had occurred during the European revolutions of 1848 haunted the public. Unemployed workers in several northern cities marched in parades carrying banners demanding work or bread. A mob broke into the shops of flour merchants in New York City. On November 10, a crowd gathered on Wall Street and threatened to break into the U.S. customs house and subtreasury vaults, where $20 million was stored. Soldiers and marines had to be called out to disperse the mob.

But the country got through the winter with little violence. No one was killed in the demonstrations—in contrast to the dozens who had been killed in ethnic riots a few years earlier and the hundreds killed in the guerrilla war in Kansas. Class conflict turned out to be the least threatening of the various discords that endangered society in the 1850s. Charity and public works helped tide the poor over the winter, and the panic inspired a vigorous religious revival. Spontaneous prayer meetings arose in many northern cities, bringing together bankers and seamstresses, brokers and streetsweepers. They asked God's forgiveness for the greed and materialism that,

in a self-flagellating mood, they believed had caused the panic.

Perhaps God heeded their prayers. In any event, the depression was short-lived. By early 1858, banks had resumed specie payments; the stock market rebounded in the spring; factories reopened; railroad construction resumed; and by spring 1859, recovery was complete. The modest labor union activities of the 1850s revived after the depression, as workers in some industries went on strike to bring wages back to prepanic levels. In February 1860, the shoemakers of Lynn, Massachusetts, began the largest strike in U.S. history up to that time, eventually involving 20,000 workers in the New England shoe industry. Despite the organization of several national unions of skilled workers during the 1850s, less than 1 percent of the labor force was unionized in 1860.

Sectionalism and the Panic

The Panic of 1857 probably intensified sectional hostility more than it did class conflict. The South largely escaped the depression. Its export-driven economy seemed insulated from domestic downturns. After a brief dip, cotton and tobacco prices returned to high levels and production continued to increase: The cotton crop set new records in 1858 and 1859. Southern boasts about the superiority of the region's economic and labor systems took on added bravado. "Who can doubt, that has looked at recent events, that cotton is supreme?" asked Senator James Hammond in March 1858. "When thousands of the strongest commercial houses in the world were coming down," he told Yankees, "what brought you up? . . . We have poured in upon you one million six hundred thousand bales of cotton. . . . We have sold it for $65,000,000, and saved you."

Northerners were not grateful for their rescue. In fact, many of them actually blamed the South for causing the depression or for blocking measures to ease its effects in the North. Southern congressmen had provided most of the votes for a new tariff in 1857 that brought duties to their lowest levels in 40 years. Some northern Republicans blamed the tariff for causing the panic and wanted to revise certain duties upward to help hard-hit industries, especially Pennsylvania iron, which were being undercut by cheaper imports. They directed their arguments to workers as much as to manufacturers. "We demand that American laborers shall be protected against the pauper labor of Europe," they declared. Tariff revision would "give employment to thousands of mechanics, artisans, laborers, who have languished for months in unwilling idleness." In each session of Congress from 1858 through 1860, however, a combination of southerners and about half of the northern Democrats blocked Republican efforts to raise tariffs. In the words of one bitter Pennsylvania Republican, this was proof that Congress remained "shamelessly prostituted, in a base subserviency to the Slave Power." Republicans made important gains in the Pennsylvania congressional elections of 1858, setting the stage for a strong bid in a state that they had to carry if they were to win the presidency in 1860.

Three other measures acquired additional significance after the Panic of 1857. Republicans supported each of them as a means to promote economic health and to aid farmers and workers. But southerners perceived all of them as aimed at helping *northern* farmers and workers and used their power to defeat them. One was a homestead act to grant 160 acres of public land to each farmer who settled and worked the land. Believing that this bill "would prove a most efficient ally for Abolition by encouraging and stimulating the settlement of free farms with Yankees," southern senators defeated it after the House had passed it in 1859. The following year both houses passed the homestead act, but Buchanan vetoed it and southern senators blocked an effort to pass it over his veto. A similar fate befell bills for land grants to a transcontinental railroad and for building agricultural and mechanical colleges to educate farmers and workers. In the Old Northwest, where these measures were popular, Republican prospects for 1860 were enhanced by southern and Democratic opposition to them.

The Free-Labor Ideology

By the later 1850s, the Republican antislavery argument had become a finely honed philosophy that historians have labeled a "free-labor ideology." It held that all work in a free society was honorable, but that slavery degraded the calling of manual labor by equating it with bondage. Slaves worked inefficiently, by compulsion; free men were stimulated to work hard and efficiently by the desire to get ahead. Social mobility was central to the free-labor ideology. Free workers who practiced the virtues of industry, thrift, self-discipline, and sobriety could move up the ladder of success. "I am not ashamed to confess," Abraham Lincoln told a working-class audience in 1860, "that twenty-five years ago I was a hired laborer, mauling rails, at work on a flat-boat—just what might happen to any poor man's son!" But in the free states, said Lincoln, a man knows that

> he can better his condition. . . . There is no such thing as a freeman being fatally fixed for life, in the condition of a hired laborer. . . . The man who labored for another last year, this year labors for himself, and next year will hire others to labor for him. . . . The free labor system opens the way for all—gives hope to all, and energy, and progress, and improvement of condition to all.

Lincoln drew too rosy a picture of northern reality, for large numbers of wage laborers in the North had little hope of advancing beyond that status. Still, he expressed a belief that was widely shared in the antebellum North. "There is not a working boy of average ability in the New England states, at least," observed a visiting British industrialist in 1854, "who has not an idea of some mechanical invention or improvement in manufactures, by which, in good time, he hopes to better his condition, or rise to fortune and social distinction." Americans could point to numerous examples of men who had achieved dramatic upward mobility. Belief in this "American dream" was most strongly held by Protestant farmers, skilled workers, and white-collar workers who had some real hope of getting ahead. These men tended to support the Republican Party and its goal of excluding slavery from the territories.

Slavery was the antithesis of upward mobility. Bondsmen were "fatally fixed in that condition for life," as Lincoln noted. Slaves could not hope to move up the ladder of success, nor could free men who lived in a society where they had to compete with slave labor. "Slavery withers and blights all it touches," declared an Iowa Republican. "It is a curse upon the poor, free, laboring white men." In the United States, social mobility often depended on geographic mobility. The main reason so many families moved into new territories was to make a new start, move ahead. But, declared a Republican editor, if slavery goes into the territories, "the free labor of all the states will not. If the free labor of the states goes there, the slave labor of the southern states will not, and in a few years the country will teem with an active and energetic population."

Southerners contended that free labor was prone to unrest and strikes. Of course it was, said Lincoln in a speech to a New England audience during the shoemakers' strike of 1860. "I am glad to see that a system prevails in New England under which laborers *can* strike when they want to (Cheers). . . . I like the system which lets a man quit when he wants to, and wish it might prevail everywhere (Tremendous applause)." Strikes were one of the ways in which free workers could try to improve their prospects. "I want every man," said Lincoln, "to have the chance—and I believe a black man is entitled to it—in which he can better his condition." That was why Republicans were determined to contain the expansion of slavery because if the South got its way in the territories, "free labor that can strike will give way to slave labor that cannot!"

The Impending Crisis

From the South came a maverick voice that echoed the Republicans. Hinton Rowan Helper considered himself a spokesman for the nonslaveholding whites of the South.

Living in upcountry North Carolina, a region of small farms and few slaves, he had brooded for years over slavery's retarding influence on southern development. In 1857, he poured out his bitterness in a book entitled *The Impending Crisis of the South*. Using selective statistics from the 1850 census, he pictured a South mired in economic backwardness, widespread illiteracy, poverty for the masses, and great wealth for the elite. He contrasted this dismal situation with the bustling, prosperous northern economy and its near-universal literacy, neat farms, and progressive institutions. What was the cause of this startling contrast? "Slavery lies at the root of all the shame, poverty, ignorance, tyranny, and imbecility of the South," he wrote. Slavery monopolized the best land, degraded all labor to the level of bond labor, denied schools to the poor, and impoverished all but "the lords of the lash [who] are not only absolute masters of the blacks [but] of all nonslaveholding whites, whose freedom is merely nominal, and whose unparalleled illiteracy and degradation is purposely and fiendishly perpetrated." The remedy? Nonslaveholding whites must organize and use their votes to overthrow "this entire system of oligarchical despotism."

No southern publisher dared touch this book. Helper lugged his bulky manuscript to New York City, where a printer brought it out in summer 1857. *The Impending Crisis* was virtually banned in the South, and few southern whites read it, but it made a huge impact in the North. Republicans welcomed it as confirmation of all they had been saying about the evils of slavery and the virtues of free labor. The Republican Party subsidized an abridged edition and distributed thousands of copies as campaign documents. During the late 1850s, a war of books (Helper's *Impending Crisis* versus Fitzhugh's *Cannibals All*) exacerbated sectional tensions. Fitzhugh's book circulated freely in the North, whereas the sale or possession of Helper's book was a criminal offense in many parts of the South. The New England Antislavery Society even invited Fitzhugh to New Haven to debate the abolitionist Wendell Phillips. Fitzhugh expressed surprise at his courteous reception in the North, aware that Phillips and other abolitionists could not set foot in the South without peril to their life. Northern spokesmen did not hesitate to point out the moral: A free society could tolerate free speech and a free press, but a slave society could not.

Southern Nonslaveholders

How accurate was Helper's portrayal of southern poor whites degraded by slavery and ready to revolt against it? The touchy response of many southern leaders suggested that the planters felt uneasy about that question. After all, slaveholding families constituted less than one-third of the

North Wind Picture Archives.

A SOUTHERN YEOMAN FARMER'S HOME

This modest log cabin on the edge of a small clearing, with the farmer's wife drawing water from a well in the foreground, was typical of nonslaveholders' farms in the backcountry of the South. Often stigmatized as poor whites, many of these families were in fact comfortable by the standards of the day. They did not feel the sense of oppression by the planter class that Hinton Rowan Helper believed they should feel.

white population in slave states, and the proportion was declining as the price of slaves continued to rise. Open hostility to the planters' domination of society and politics was evident in the mountainous and upcountry regions of the South. These would become areas of Unionist sentiment during the Civil War and of Republican strength after it.

But Helper surely exaggerated the disaffection of most nonslaveholders in the South. Three bonds held them to the system: kinship, economic interest, and race. In the Piedmont and the low-country regions of the South, nearly half of the whites were in slaveholding families. Many of the rest were cousins or nephews or in-laws of slaveholders in the South's extensive and tightly knit kinship network. Moreover, many young, ambitious nonslaveholders hoped to buy slaves eventually. Some of them *rented* slaves. And because slaves could be made to do the menial, unskilled labor in the South—the "mudsill" tasks, in Senator Hammond's language—white workers monopolized the more skilled, higher-paying jobs.

Most important, even if they did not own slaves, white people owned the most important asset of all—white skin. White supremacy was an article of faith in the South (and in most of the North, for that matter). Race

was a more important social distinction than class. The southern legal system, politics, and social ideology were based on the concept of "*herrenvolk* democracy" (the equality of all who belonged to the "master race"). Subordination was the Negro's fate, and slavery was the best means of subordination. Emancipation would loose a flood of free blacks on society and would undermine the foundations of white supremacy. Thus many of the poor whites in the South and immigrant workers or poorer farmers in the North supported slavery.

The *herrenvolk* theme permeated pro-slavery rhetoric. "With us," said John C. Calhoun in 1848, "the two great divisions of society are not the rich and the poor, but white and black; and all the former, the poor as well as the rich, belong to the upper class, and are respected and treated as equals." True freedom as Americans understood it required equality of rights and status (although not of wealth or income). Slavery ensured such freedom for all whites by putting a floor under them, a mudsill of black slaves that kept whites from falling into the mud of inequality. "Break down slavery," said a Virginia congressman, "and you would with the same blow destroy the great Democratic principle of equality among men."

The Lincoln-Douglas Debates

Abraham Lincoln believed the opposite. For him, slavery and freedom were incompatible; the one must die that the other might live. This became the central theme of a memorable series of debates between Lincoln and Douglas in 1858, which turned out to be a dress rehearsal for the presidential election of 1860.

The debates were arranged after Lincoln was nominated to oppose Douglas's reelection to the Senate. State legislatures elected U.S. senators at that time, so the campaign was technically for the election of the Illinois legislature. The real issue, however, was the senatorship, and Douglas's prominence gave the contest national significance. Lincoln launched his bid with one of his most notable speeches. "'A house divided against itself cannot stand,'" he said, quoting the words of Jesus recorded in the Gospel of Mark (3:25). "I believe this government cannot endure, permanently half slave and half free. . . . It will become all one thing, or all the other." Under the Dred Scott decision, which Douglas had endorsed, slavery was legal in all of the territories. And what, asked Lincoln, would prevent the Supreme Court, using the same reasoning that had led it to interpret the Constitution as protecting property in slaves, from legalizing slavery in free states? (A case based on this question was then before the New York

HISTORY THROUGH FILM

Abe Lincoln in Illinois (1940)

Directed by John Cromwell. Starring Raymond Massey (Abraham Lincoln), Gene Lockhard (Stephen Douglas), Ruth Gordon (Mary Todd Lincoln).

Raymond Massey's portrayal of Abraham Lincoln in Robert Sherwood's Broadway play, which opened in 1938 and was made into a movie in 1940, launched this Canadian-born actor as the image and voice of Lincoln on stage, screen, and radio for a generation. More people saw or heard Massey as Lincoln than ever saw or heard the real Lincoln. Perhaps that was appropriate because Sherwood's Lincoln spoke more to the generation of the Second World War than to the generation of the Civil War.

In one of the film's most dramatic scenes of the Lincoln-Douglas debates, Massey/Lincoln delivers a speech against slavery that applied equally to Fascist totalitarianism and defended democracy in language resonant with the four freedoms that the Allies fought for in the Second World War. In an interview, Massey said that "If you substitute the word *dictatorship* for the word *slavery* throughout Sherwood's script, it becomes electric for our time." In the final scene, as Lincoln departs from Springfield to take up the burdens of the presidency, Massey's Lincoln sees beyond the challenge of disunion to the challenge to democracy in a world at war.

Sherwood skillfully wove together Lincoln's words with his own script to portray Lincoln's growth from the gawky youth of 1831 to the champion of freedom and democracy in 1861. Sherwood took many liberties, but what scriptwriter does not? He combined bits and pieces of several Lincoln speeches into one; he invented incidents and wrenched chronology in some of the 12 scenes from these 30 years of Lincoln's life.

Perhaps the film's sharpest departure from reality is the tension it depicts between "politics," which is bad, and "democracy," which is good. Sherwood's Lincoln doesn't want to play the dirty game of politics; early in the film, the homespun youth declares: "I don't want to be no politi-

cian." It is Mary Todd Lincoln who is ambitious for her husband and pushes a reluctant Abraham toward his destiny. The real Lincoln, of course, loved the game of politics and played it masterfully. He was also as ambitious in his own right as Mary was for him; Lincoln's law partner William Herndon said that Abraham's ambition was "a little engine that knew no rest." Sherwood's Lincoln who transcends politics to become a great statesman could not have existed without the real Lincoln, the ambitious politician.

© Bettmann/Corbis.

Raymond Massey as the 23-year-old Abraham Lincoln just elected captain of a New Salem militia company in the Black Hawk War of 1832.

Courtesy of the Illinois State Historical Library.

THE LINCOLN-DOUGLAS DEBATES

The Lincoln-Douglas contest for the Senate in 1858 produced the most famous—and fateful—political debates in American history. At stake was nothing less than the future of the nation. Thousands of people crowded into seven towns to listen to these three-hour debates that took place outdoors from August to October in weather ranging from stifling heat to cold rain. Audiences were most friendly to Lincoln in antislavery northern Illinois, as portrayed in this illustration of the debate in Galesburg, home of Knox College and a hotbed of abolitionism.

courts.) The advocates of slavery, charged Lincoln, were trying to "push it forward, till it shall become lawful in all the States." But Republicans intended to keep slavery out of the territories, thus stopping its growth and placing it "where the public mind shall rest in the belief that it is in the course of ultimate extinction."

The seven open-air debates between Douglas and Lincoln focused almost entirely on the issue of slavery. Douglas asked: Why could the country not continue to exist half slave and half free as it had for 70 years? Lincoln's talk about the "ultimate extinction" of slavery would provoke the South to secession. Douglas professed himself no friend of slavery, but if people in the southern states or in the territories wanted it, they had the right to have it. Douglas did not want black people—either slave or free—in

Illinois. Lincoln's policy would not only free the slaves but would also grant them equality. "Are you in favor of conferring upon the negro the rights and privileges of citizenship?" Douglas called out to supporters in the crowd. "No, no!" they shouted back. He continued:

> Do you desire to strike out of our State Constitution that clause which keeps slaves and free negroes out of the State . . . in order that when Missouri abolishes slavery she can send one hundred thousand emancipated slaves into Illinois, to become citizens and voters on an equality with yourselves? ("Never," "no.") . . . If you desire to allow them to come into the State and settle with the white man, if you desire them to vote . . . then support Mr. Lincoln and the Black Republican party, who are in favor of the citizenship of the negro. ("Never, never.")

Douglas's demagoguery put Lincoln on the defensive. He responded with cautious denials that he favored "social and political equality" of the races. The "ultimate extinction" of slavery might take a century. It would require the voluntary cooperation of the South and would perhaps be contingent on the emigration of some freed slaves from the country. But come what may, freedom must prevail. Americans must reaffirm the principles of the founding fathers. In Lincoln's words, a black person was

> entitled to all the natural rights enumerated in the Declaration of Independence, the right to life, liberty and the pursuit of happiness. (Loud cheers.) I hold that he is as much entitled to these as the white man. I agree with Judge Douglas he is not my equal in many respects. . . . But in the right to eat the bread, without leave of anybody else, which his own hand earns, *he is my equal and the equal of Judge Douglas, and the equal of every living man.*
>
> (Great applause.)

Lincoln deplored Douglas's "care not" attitude whether slavery was voted up or down. He "looks to no end of the institution of slavery," said Lincoln. By endorsing the Dred Scott decision, Lincoln claimed, Douglas looks to its "perpetuity and nationalization." Douglas was thus "eradicating the light of reason and liberty in this American people." That was the real issue in the election, insisted Lincoln.

> That is the issue that will continue in this country when these poor tongues of Judge Douglas and myself shall be silent. It is the eternal struggle between these two principles—right and wrong—throughout the world. . . . The one is the common right of humanity and the other the divine right of kings. . . . No matter in what shape it comes, whether from a king who seeks to bestride the people of his own nation and live by the fruit of their labor, or from one race of men as an apology for enslaving another race, it is the same tyrannical principle.

The Freeport Doctrine

The popular vote for Republican and Democratic state legislators in Illinois was virtually even in 1858, but because apportionment favored the Democrats, they won a majority of seats and reelected Douglas. Lincoln, however, was the ultimate victor; his performance in the debates lifted him from political obscurity, while Douglas further alienated southern Democrats. In the Freeport debate, Lincoln had asked Douglas how he reconciled his support for the Dred Scott decision with his policy of popular sovereignty, which supposedly gave residents of a territory the power to vote slavery down. Douglas replied that even though the Court had legalized slavery in the territories, the enforcement of that right would depend on the people who lived there. This was a popular answer in the North, but it gave added impetus to southern demands for congressional passage of a federal slave code in territories such as Kansas, where the Free Soil majority had by 1859 made slavery virtually null. In the next two sessions of Congress after the 1858 elections, southern Democrats, led by Jefferson Davis, tried to pass a federal slave code for all territories. Douglas and northern Democrats joined with Republicans to defeat it. Consequently, southern hostility toward Douglas mounted as the presidential election of 1860 approached.

The 1859–60 session of Congress was particularly contentious. Once again a fight over the speakership of the House set the tone. Republicans had won a plurality of House seats, but lacking a majority could not elect a Speaker without the support of a few border-state representatives from the American (Know-Nothing) Party. The problem was that the Republican candidate for Speaker was John Sherman, who, along with 67 other congressmen, had signed an endorsement of Hinton Rowan Helper's *The Impending Crisis of the South* (without, Sherman later admitted, having read it). This was a red flag to southerners, even to ex-Whigs from the border states, who refused to vote for Sherman. Through 43 ballots and two months, the House remained deadlocked. Tensions escalated, and members came armed to the floor. One observer commented that "the only persons who do not have a revolver and knife are those who have two revolvers."

As usual, southerners threatened to secede if a Black Republican became Speaker. Several of them wanted a shootout on the floor of Congress. We "are willing to fight the question out," wrote one, "and to settle it right there." The governor of South Carolina told one of his state's congressmen: "If . . . you upon consultation decide to make the issue of force in Washington, write or telegraph me, and I will have a regiment in or near Washington in the shortest possible time." To avert a crisis, Sherman withdrew his candidacy and the House finally elected a conservative ex-Whig as Speaker on the 44th ballot.

John Brown at Harpers Ferry

Southern tempers were frayed even at the start of this session of Congress because of what had happened at Harpers Ferry, Virginia, the previous October. After his exploits in Kansas, John Brown had disappeared from public view but had not been idle. Like the Old Testament warriors he admired and resembled, Brown intended to carry his war against slavery into Babylon—the South. His favorite New Testament passage was Hebrews 9:22: "Without shedding of blood there is no remission of sin." Brown worked up a plan to capture the federal arsenal at Harpers Ferry, arm slaves with the muskets he seized there, and move southward along the Appalachian Mountains attracting more slaves to his army along the way until the "whole accursed system of bondage" collapsed.

Brown recruited five black men and seventeen whites, including three of his sons, for this reckless scheme. He also had the secret support of a half-dozen Massachusetts and New York abolitionists, who had helped him raise funds. On the night of October 16, 1859, Brown led his men across the Potomac River and occupied the sleeping town of Harpers Ferry without resistance. Few slaves flocked to his banner, but the next day state militia units poured into town and drove Brown's band into the fire-engine house. At dawn on October 18, a company of U.S. marines commanded by Colonel Robert E. Lee and Lieutenant J. E. B. Stuart stormed the engine house and captured the surviving members of Brown's party. Four townsmen, one marine, and 10 of Brown's men (including two of his sons) were killed; not a single slave was liberated.

John Brown's raid lasted 36 hours, but its repercussions resounded for years. Brown and six of his followers were promptly tried by the state of Virginia, convicted, and hanged. This scarcely ended matters. The raid sent a wave of revulsion and alarm through the South. Although no slaves had risen in revolt, it revived fears of slave insurrection that were never far beneath the surface of southern consciousness. Exaggerated reports of Brown's network of abolitionist supporters confirmed southern suspicions that a widespread northern conspiracy was afoot, determined to destroy their society. Although Republican leaders denied any connection with Brown and disavowed his actions, few southerners believed them. Had not Lincoln talked of the extinction of slavery? And had not William H. Seward, who was expected to be the next Republican presidential nominee, given a campaign speech in 1858 in

Kansas State Historical Society.

JOHN BROWN

This modern mural of John Brown is full of symbolism. Holding an open Bible, Brown bestrides the earth like an Old Testament prophet while dead Union and Confederate soldiers lie at his feet. Other soldiers clash behind him, slaves struggle to break free, and God's wrath at a sinful nation sends a destructive tornado to earth in the background.

which he predicted an irrepressible conflict between the free and slave societies?

Many northerners, impressed by Brown's dignified bearing and eloquence during his trial, considered him a martyr to freedom. In his final statement to the court, Brown said:

> I see a book kissed, which I suppose to be the Bible, which teaches me that all things whatsoever I would that men should do to me, I should do even so to them. It teaches me, further, to remember them that are in bonds as bound with them. I endeavored to act up to that instruction. . . . Now, if it is deemed necessary that I should forfeit my life for the furtherance of the ends of justice, and mingle my blood further with the blood of my children and with the blood of millions in this slave country whose rights are disregarded by wicked, cruel, and unjust enactments, I say, let it be done.

On the day of Brown's execution, bells tolled in hundreds of northern towns, guns fired salutes, and ministers preached sermons of commemoration. "The death of no man in America has ever produced so profound a sensation," commented one northerner. Ralph Waldo Emerson declared that Brown had made "the gallows as glorious as the cross."

This outpouring of northern sympathy for Brown shocked and enraged southerners and weakened the already frayed threads of the Union. "The Harper's Ferry invasion has advanced the cause of disunion more than any event that has happened since the formation of the

government," observed a Richmond, Virginia, newspaper. "I have always been a fervid Union man," wrote a North Carolinian, but "the endorsement of the Harper's Ferry outrage . . . has shaken my fidelity. . . . I am willing to take the chances of every possible evil that may arise from disunion, sooner than submit any longer to Northern insolence."

Something approaching a reign of terror now descended on the South. Every Yankee seemed to be another John Brown; every slave who acted suspiciously seemed to be an insurrectionist. Hundreds of northerners were run out of the South in 1860, some wearing a coat of tar and feathers. Several "incendiaries," both white and black, were lynched. "Defend yourselves!" Senator Robert Toombs cried out to the southern people. "The enemy is at your door . . . meet him at the doorsill, and drive him from the temple of liberty, or pull down its pillars and involve him in a common ruin."

Conclusion

Few decades in American history witnessed a greater disjunction between economic well-being and political upheaval than the 1850s. Despite the recession following the Panic of 1857, the total output of the American economy grew by 62 percent during the decade. Railroad mileage more than tripled, value added by manufacturing nearly doubled, and gross farm product grew by 40 percent. Americans were more prosperous than ever before.

Yet a profound malaise gripped the country. Riots between immigrants and nativists in the mid-1850s left more than 50 people dead. Fighting in Kansas between pro-slavery and antislavery forces killed at least 200. Fistfights broke out on the floor of Congress. A South Carolina congressman bludgeoned a Massachusetts senator to unconsciousness with a heavy cane. Representatives and senators came to congressional sessions armed with weapons as well as with violent words.

The nation proved capable of absorbing the large influx of immigrants despite the tensions and turmoil of the mid-1850s. It might also have been able to absorb the huge territorial expansion of the late 1840s had not the slavery issue been reopened in an earlier territorial acquisition, the Louisiana Purchase, by the Kansas-Nebraska Act of 1854. This legislation, followed by the Dred Scott decision

in 1857, seemed to authorize the unlimited expansion of slavery. Within two years of its founding in 1854, however, the Republican Party emerged as the largest party in the North on a platform of preventing all future expansion of slavery. By 1860, the United States had reached a fateful crossroads. As Lincoln had said, it could not endure permanently half slave and half free. The presidential election of 1860 would decide which road America would take into the future.

SUGGESTED READINGS

For a detailed and readable treatment of the mounting sectional conflict in the 1850s, see **Allan Nevins, *Ordeal of the Union,*** 2 vols. (1947), and ***The Emergence of Lincoln,*** 2 vols. (1950). The Kansas-Nebraska Act and its political consequences are treated in **Gerald W. Wolff, *The Kansas-Nebraska Bill: Party, Section, and the Coming of the Civil War*** (1977). The conflict in Kansas itself is treated in **Nicole Etcheson, *Bleeding Kansas: Contested Liberty in the Civil War Era*** (2004). For the cross-cutting issue of nativism and the Know-Nothings, see **William E. Gienapp, *The Origins of the Republican Party, 1852–1856*** (1987), and **Tyler Anbinder, *Nativism and Politics: The Know Nothing Party in the Northern United States*** (1992). Two excellent studies of the role of Abraham Lincoln in the rise of the Republican Party are **Don E. Fehrenbacher, *Prelude to Greatness: Lincoln in the 1850s*** (1962), and **Kenneth Winkle, *The Young Eagle: The Rise of Abraham Lincoln*** (2003). The southern response to the growth of antislavery political sentiment in the North is the theme of **William J. Cooper, Jr., *The South and the Politics of Slavery 1828–1856*** (1978).

The year 1857 witnessed a convergence of many crucial events; for a stimulating book that pulls together the threads of that year of crisis, see **Kenneth M. Stampp, *America in 1857: A Nation on the Brink*** (1990). For economic developments during the era, an older classic is still the best introduction: **George Rogers Taylor, *The Transportation Revolution, 1815–1860*** (1951). An important dimension of the southern economy is elucidated in **Fred Bateman and Thomas Weiss, *A Deplorable Scarcity: The Failure of Industrialization in the Slave Economy*** (1981). Still the best study of the Republican free-labor ideology is **Eric Foner, *Free Soil, Free Labor, Free Men: The Ideology of the Republican Party before the Civil War*** (2nd ed., 1995). For southern yeoman farmers, a good study is **Stephanie McCurry, *Masters of Small Worlds: Yeoman Households, Gender Relations, and the Political Culture of the Antebellum South Carolina Low Country*** (1995). The best single study of the Dred Scott case is **Don E. Fehrenbacher, *The Dred Scott Case: Its Significance in American Law and Politics*** (1978), which was published in an abridged version with the title ***Slavery, Law, and Politics: The Dred Scott Case in Historical Perspective*** (1981).

 ## AMERICAN JOURNEY ONLINE AND INFOTRAC COLLEGE EDITION

Visit the source collections at www.ajaccess.wadsworth.com and infotrac.thomsonlearning.com and use the Search function with the following key terms to explore documents, images, audio and video clips, articles, and commentary related to the material in this chapter.

Dred Scott
Lincoln-Douglas debates
Abraham Lincoln
Jefferson Davis

Harpers Ferry
John Brown
Kansas-Nebraska Act
Know-Nothings

GRADE AIDS

Visit the Liberty Equality Power Companion Web Site for resources specific to this textbook: http://history.wadsworth.com/murrin_LEP4e

The CD in the back of this book and the U.S. History Resource Center at http://history.wadsworth.com/u.s./ offer a variety of tools to help you succeed in this course, including access to quizzes; images; documents; interactive simulations, maps, and timelines; movie explorations; and a wealth of other sources.

The Election of 1860

A hotbed of Southern-rights radicalism, Charleston, South Carolina, turned out to be the worst possible place for the Democrats to hold their national convention. Sectional confrontations took place inside the convention hall and on the streets. Since 1836, the Democratic Party had required a two-thirds majority of delegates for a presidential nomination, a rule that in effect gave Southerners veto power if they voted together. Although Stephen A. Douglas had the backing of a simple majority of the delegates, southern Democrats were determined to deny him the nomination. His opposition to the Lecompton constitution in Kansas and to a federal slave code for the territories had convinced pro-slavery Southerners that they would be unable to control a Douglas administration.

The first test came in the debate on the platform. Southern delegates insisted on a plank favoring a federal slave code for the territories. Douglas could not run on a platform that contained such a plank, and if the party adopted it, Democrats were sure to lose every state in the North. By a slim majority, the convention rejected the plank and reaffirmed the 1856 platform endorsing popular sovereignty. Fifty Southern delegates thereupon walked out of the convention. Even after they left, Douglas could not muster a two-thirds majority, nor could any other candidate. After 57 futile ballots, the convention adjourned to meet in Baltimore six weeks later to try again.

CHRONOLOGY

1860 Lincoln elected president (November 6) • South Carolina secedes (December 20) • Federal troops transfer from Fort Moultrie to Fort Sumter (December 26)

1861 Rest of lower South secedes (January–February) • Crittenden Compromise rejected (February) • Jefferson Davis inaugurated as provisional president of new Confederate States of America (February 18) • Abraham Lincoln inaugurated as president of the United States (March 4) • Fort Sumter falls; Lincoln calls out troops, proclaims blockade (April) • Four more states secede to join Confederacy (April–May) • Battle of Bull Run (Manassas) (July 21) • Battle of Wilson's Creek (August 10) • The *Trent* affair (November–December)

1862 Union captures Forts Henry and Donelson (February 6 and 16) • Congress passes Legal Tender Act (February 25) • Battle of Pea Ridge (March 7–8) • Battle of the *Monitor* and *Merrimac* (*Virginia*) (March 9) • Battle of Glorieta Pass (March 26–28) • Battle of Shiloh (April 6–7) • Union Navy captures New Orleans (April 25) • Stonewall Jackson's Shenandoah Valley campaign (May–June) • Seven Days' battles (June 25–July 1) • Second Battle of Manassas (Bull Run) (August 29–30) • Lee invades Maryland (September) • Battle of Corinth (October 3–4) • Battle of Perryville (October 8)

1863 Congress passes National Banking Act (February 25)

THE POLITICAL QUADRILLE

This cartoon depicts the four presidential candidates in 1860. Clockwise from the upper left are John C. Breckinridge, Southern Rights Democrat; Abraham Lincoln, Republican; John Bell, Constitutional Union; and Stephen A. Douglas, Democrat. All are dancing to the tune played by Dred Scott, symbolizing the importance of the slavery issue in this campaign. Each candidate's partner represents a political liability: for example, Breckinridge's partner is the disunionist William L. Yancey wearing a devil's horns, while Lincoln's partner is a black woman who supposedly gives color to Democratic accusations that Republicans believed in miscegenation.

THE POLITICAL QUADRILLE
Music by Dred Scott

By then the party was too badly shattered to be put back together. That pleased some pro-slavery radicals, who were convinced that the South would never be secure in a nation dominated by a Northern majority. The election of a Black Republican president, they believed, would provide the shock necessary to mobilize a Southern majority for secession. Two of the most prominent secessionists were William L. Yancey and Edmund Ruffin. In 1858, they founded the League of United Southerners to "fire the Southern heart . . . and at the proper moment, by one organized, concerted action, we can precipitate the Cotton States into a revolution." After walking out of the Democratic convention, the eloquent Yancey inspired a huge crowd in Charleston's moonlit courthouse square to give three cheers "for an Independent Southern Republic" with his concluding words: "Perhaps even now, the pen of the historian is nibbed to write the story of a new revolution."

The second convention in Baltimore reprised the first at Charleston. This time, an even larger number of delegates from Southern states walked out. They formed their own Southern Rights Democratic Party and nominated John C. Breckinridge of Kentucky (the incumbent vice president) for president on a slave-code platform. When regular Democrats nominated Douglas, the stage was set for what would become a four-party election. A coalition of former southern Whigs, who could not bring themselves to vote Democratic, and northern Whigs, who considered the Republican Party too radical, formed the Constitutional Union Party, which nominated John Bell of Tennessee for president. Bell had no chance of winning; the party's purpose was to exercise a conservative influence on a campaign that threatened to polarize the country.

The Republicans Nominate Lincoln

From the moment the Democratic Party broke apart, it became clear that 1860 could be the year when the dynamic young Republican Party elected its first president. The Republicans could expect no electoral votes from the 15 slave states. In 1856, however, they had won all but five northern states, and with only two or three of those five they could win the presidency. The crucial states were Pennsylvania, Illinois, and Indiana. Douglas might still carry them and throw the presidential election into the House, where anything could happen. Thus the Republicans had to carry at least two of the swing states to win.

As the Republican delegates poured into Chicago for their convention—held in a huge building nicknamed the Wigwam because of its shape—their leading presidential prospect was William H. Seward of New York. An experienced politician who had served as governor and senator, Seward was by all odds the most prominent Republican, but in his long career he had made many enemies. His antinativist policies had alienated some former members of the American Party, whose support he would need to carry Pennsylvania. His "Higher Law" speech against the Compromise of 1850 and his "Irrepressible Conflict" speech in 1858, predicting the ultimate overthrow of slavery, had given him a reputation for radicalism that might drive away voters in the vital swing states of the lower North.

Several of the delegates, uneasy about that reputation, staged a stop-Seward movement. The next candidate to the fore was Abraham Lincoln. Although he too had opposed nativism, he had done so less noisily than Seward. His "House Divided" speech had made essentially the same point as Seward's "Irrepressible Conflict" speech, but his reputation was still that of a more moderate man. He was from one of the lower-North states where the election would be close, and his rise from a poor farm boy and rail-splitter to successful lawyer and political leader perfectly reflected the free-labor theme of social mobility extolled by the Republican Party. By picking up second-choice votes from states that switched from their favorite sons, Lincoln overtook Seward and won the nomination on the third ballot. Seward accepted the outcome gracefully, and the Republicans headed into the campaign as a united, confident party.

Their confidence stemmed in part from their platform, which appealed to many groups in the North. Its main plank pledged exclusion of slavery from the territories. Other planks called for a higher tariff (especially popular in Pennsylvania), a homestead act (popular in the Northwest), and federal aid for construction of a transcontinental railroad and for improvement of river navigation. This program was designed for a future in which the "house divided" would become a free-labor society modeled on Northern capitalism. Its blend of idealism and materialism proved especially attractive to young people; a large majority of first-time voters in the North voted Republican in 1860. Thousands of them joined Wide-Awake clubs and marched in huge torchlight parades through the cities of the North.

Southern Fears

Militant enthusiasm in the North was matched by fear and rage in the South. Few people there could see any difference between Lincoln and Seward—or for that matter

the South." If Georgia remained in a Union "ruled by Lincoln and his crew," a secessionist in that state told non-slaveholders, "in TEN years or less our CHILDREN will be the *slaves* of negroes."

Most whites in the South voted for Breckinridge, who carried 11 slave states. Bell won the upper-South states of Virginia, Kentucky, and Tennessee. Missouri went to Douglas—the only state he carried, although he came in second in the popular vote. Although Lincoln received less than 40 percent of the popular vote, he won every free state and swept the presidency by a substantial margin in the electoral college (three of New Jersey's seven electoral votes went to Douglas).

The Lower South Secedes

Lincoln's victory provided the shock that Southern fire-eaters had craved. The tension that had been building up for years suddenly exploded like a string of firecrackers, as seven states seceded one after another. According to the theory of secession, when each state ratified the Constitution and joined the Union, it authorized the national government to act as its agent in the exercise of certain functions of sovereignty—but the states had never given away their fundamental underlying sovereignty. Any state, then, by the act of its own convention, could withdraw from its "compact" with the other states and reassert its individual sovereignty. Therefore, the South Carolina legislature called for such a convention and ordered an election of delegates to consider withdrawing from the United States. On December 20, 1860, the South Carolina convention did withdraw, by a vote of 169 to 0.

The outcome was closer in other lower-South states. Unconditional unionism was rare, but many conservatives and former Whigs, including Alexander H. Stephens of Georgia, shrank from the drastic step of secession. At the conventions in each of the next six states to secede, some delegates tried to delay matters with vague proposals for "cooperation" among all Southern states, or even with proposals to wait until after Lincoln's inauguration on March 4, 1861, to see what course he would pursue. Those minority factions were overridden by proponents of immediate secession. The conventions followed the example of South Carolina and voted to take their states out of the Union: Mississippi on January 9, 1861, Florida on the 10th, Alabama on the 11th, Georgia on the 19th, Louisiana on the 26th, and Texas on February 1. In those six states as a whole, 20 percent of the delegates voted against secession, but most of these, including Stephens, "went with their states" after the final votes had been tallied. Delegates from the seven seceding states met in Montgomery,

BANNER OF THE SOUTH CAROLINA SECESSION CONVENTION

With its banner featuring a palmetto tree and a snake reminiscent of the American Revolution's "Don't Tread on Me" slogan, the South Carolina secession convention in 1860 looked forward to a grand new Southern republic composed of all 15 slave states and built on the ruins of the old Union. Note the large South Carolina keystone of the arch and the stones of free states lying cracked and broken on the ground.

Courtesy of The South Carolina Historical Society.

Alabama, in February to create a new nation to be called the Confederate States of America.

Northerners Affirm the Union

Most people in the North considered secession unconstitutional and treasonable. In his final annual message to Congress, on December 3, 1860, President Buchanan insisted that the Union was not "a mere voluntary association of States, to be dissolved at pleasure by any one of the contracting parties." If secession was consummated, Buchanan warned, it would create a disastrous precedent that would make the United States government "a rope of sand." He continued:

> Our thirty-three States may resolve themselves into as many petty, jarring, and hostile republics. . . . By such a dread catastrophe the hopes of the friends of freedom throughout the world would be destroyed. . . . Our example for more than eighty years would not only be lost, but it would be quoted as proof that man is unfit for self-government.

European monarchists and conservatives were already expressing smug satisfaction at "the great smashup" of the republic in North America. They predicted that other disaffected minorities would also secede and that the United States would ultimately collapse into anarchy and revolution. That was precisely what Northerners and even some upper-South Unionists feared. "The doctrine of secession is anarchy," declared a Cincinnati newspaper. "If any minority have the right to break up the Government at pleasure, because they have not had their way, there is an end of all government." Lincoln denied that the states had ever possessed independent sovereignty before becoming part of the United States. Rather, they had been colonies or territories that never would have become part of the United States had they not accepted unconditional sovereignty of the national government. No government, said Lincoln, "ever had provision in its organic law for its own termination. . . . No State, upon its own mere motion, can lawfully get out of the Union. . . . They can only do so against law, and by revolution."

In that case, answered many Southerners, we invoke the right of revolution to justify secession. After all, the United States was born of revolution. The secessionists maintained that they were merely following the example of their forefathers in declaring independence from a government that threatened their rights and liberties. An Alabaman asked rhetorically: "[Were not] the men of 1776, who withdrew their allegiance from George III and set up for themselves . . . Secessionists?"

Northerners could scarcely deny the right of revolution: They too were heirs of 1776. But "the right of revolution, is never a legal right," said Lincoln. "At most, it is but a moral right, when exercised for a morally justifiable cause. When exercised without such a cause revolution is no right, but simply a wicked exercise of physical power." The South, in Lincoln's view, had no morally justifiable cause. In fact, the event that had precipitated secession was his own election by a constitutional majority. For Southerners to cast themselves in the mold of 1776 was "a libel upon the whole character and conduct" of the Founding Fathers, said the antislavery poet and journalist William Cullen Bryant. They rebelled "to establish the rights of man . . . and principles of universal liberty," whereas Southerners in 1861 were rebelling to protect "a domestic despotism. . . . Their motto is not liberty, but slavery."

Compromise Proposals

Bryant conveniently overlooked the fact that slavery had existed in most parts of the republic founded by the revolutionaries of 1776. In any event, most people in the North agreed with Lincoln that secession was a "wicked exercise

of physical power." The question was what to do about it. All kinds of compromise proposals came before Congress when it met in December 1860. To sort them out, the Senate and the House each set up a special committee. The Senate committee came up with a package of compromises sponsored by Senator John J. Crittenden of Kentucky. The Crittenden Compromise consisted of a series of proposed constitutional amendments: to guarantee slavery in the states perpetually against federal interference; to prohibit Congress from abolishing slavery in the District of Columbia or on any federal property (forts, arsenals, naval bases, and so on); to deny Congress the power to interfere with the interstate slave trade; to compensate slaveholders who were prevented from recovering fugitive slaves who had escaped to the North; and, most important, to protect slavery south of latitude 36°30′ in all territories "now held *or hereafter acquired.*"

Given the appetite of the South for more slave territory in the Caribbean and Central America, that italicized phrase, in the view of most Republicans, might turn the United States into "a great slavebreeding and slavetrading empire." But even though endorsement of the territorial clause in the Crittenden Compromise would require Republicans to repudiate the platform on which they had just won the election, some conservatives in the party were willing to accept it in the interest of peace and conciliation. Their votes, together with those of Democrats and upper-South Unionists whose states had not seceded, might have gotten the compromise through Congress. It is doubtful, however, that the approval of three-quarters of the states required for ratification would have been forthcoming. In any case, word came from Springfield, Illinois, where President-elect Lincoln was preparing for his inaugural trip to Washington, telling key Republican senators and congressmen to stand firm against compromise on the territorial issue. "Entertain no proposition for a compromise in regard to the *extension* of slavery," wrote Lincoln.

> Filibustering for all South of us, and making slave states would follow . . . to put us again on the high-road to a slave empire. . . . We have just carried an election on principles fairly stated to the people. Now we are told in advance, the government shall be broken up, unless we surrender to those we have beaten. . . . If we surrender, it is the end of us. They will repeat the experiment upon us *ad libitum.* A year will not pass, till we shall have to take Cuba as a condition upon which they will stay in the Union.

Lincoln's advice was decisive. The Republicans voted against the Crittenden Compromise, which therefore failed in Congress. Most Republicans, though, went along with a proposal by Virginia for a "peace convention" of all the states to be held in Washington in February 1861. Although the seven seceded states sent no delegates, hopes that

THE BOMBARDMENT OF FORT SUMTER, APRIL 12, 1861
This drawing shows the incoming shells from Confederate batteries at Fort Moultrie and Cummings Point, and Fort Sumter's return fire. Note that Confederate shells have set the fort's interior on fire, but the American flag is still flying. It would soon be lowered in surrender as the fire crept toward the powder magazine.

heart and hearthstone all over this broad land, will yet swell the chorus of the Union when again touched, as surely they will be, by the better angels of our nature.

Lincoln hoped to buy time with his inaugural address—time to demonstrate his peaceful intentions and to enable southern Unionists (whose numbers Republicans overestimated) to regain the upper hand. But the day after his inauguration, Lincoln learned that time was running out. A dispatch from Major Anderson informed him that provisions for the soldiers at Fort Sumter would soon be exhausted. The garrison must either be resupplied or evacuated. Any attempt to send in supplies by force would undoubtedly provoke a response from Confederate guns at Charleston. And by putting the onus of starting a war on Lincoln's shoulders, such an action would undoubtedly divide the North and unite the South, driving at least four more states into the Confederacy. Thus, most members of Lincoln's cabinet, along with the army's General-in-Chief Winfield Scott, advised Lincoln to withdraw the troops from Sumter. That, however, would bestow a great moral victory on the Confederacy. It would confer legitimacy on the Confederate government and would probably lead to

diplomatic recognition by foreign powers. Having pledged to "hold, occupy, and possess" national property, could Lincoln afford to abandon that policy during his first month in office? If he did, he would go down in history as the president who consented to the dissolution of the United States.

The pressures from all sides caused Lincoln many sleepless nights; one morning he rose from bed and keeled over in a dead faint. Finally he hit upon a solution that evidenced the mastery that would mark his presidency. He decided to send in unarmed ships with supplies but to hold troops and warships outside the harbor with authorization to go into action only if the Confederates used force to stop the supply ships. And he would give South Carolina officials advance notice of his intention. This stroke of genius shifted the decision for war or peace to Jefferson Davis. In effect, Lincoln flipped a coin and said to Davis, "Heads I win; tails you lose." If Confederate troops fired on the supply ships, the South would stand convicted of starting a war by attacking "a mission of humanity" bringing "food for hungry men." If Davis allowed the supplies to go in peacefully, the U.S. flag would continue to fly

over Fort Sumter. The Confederacy would lose face at home and abroad, and southern Unionists would take courage.

Davis did not hesitate. He ordered General Beauregard to compel Sumter's surrender before the supply ships got there. At 4:30 A.M. on April 12, 1861, Confederate guns set off the Civil War by firing on Fort Sumter. After a 33-hour bombardment in which the rebels fired 4,000 rounds and the skeleton gun crews in the garrison replied with 1,000—with no one killed on either side—the burning fort lowered the U.S. flag in surrender.

Choosing Sides

News of the attack triggered an outburst of anger and war fever in the North. "The town is in a wild state of excitement," wrote a Philadelphia diarist. "The American flag is to be seen everywhere. . . . Men are enlisting as fast as possible." A Harvard professor born during George Washington's presidency was astounded by the public response. "The heather is on fire," he wrote. "I never knew what a popular excitement can be." A New York woman wrote that the "time before Sumter" seemed like another century. "It seems as if we were never alive till now; never had a country till now."

Because the tiny U.S. Army—most of whose 16,000 soldiers were stationed at remote frontier posts—was inadequate to quell the "insurrection," Lincoln called on the states for 75,000 militia. The free states filled their quotas immediately. More than twice as many men volunteered as Lincoln had requested. Recognizing that the 90 days' service to which the militia were limited by law would be too short a time, on May 3, Lincoln issued a call for three-year volunteers. Before the war was over, more than 2 million men would serve in the Union army and navy.

The eight slave states still in the Union rejected Lincoln's call for troops. Four of them—Virginia, Arkansas, Tennessee, and North Carolina—soon seceded and joined the Confederacy. Forced by the outbreak of actual war to choose between the Union and the Confederacy, most residents of those four states chose the Confederacy. As a former Unionist in North Carolina remarked, "The division must be made on the line of slavery. The South must go with the South. . . . Blood is thicker than Water."

Few found the choice harder to make than Robert E. Lee of Virginia. One of the most promising officers in the U.S. Army, Lee believed that Southern states had no legal right to secede. General-in-Chief Winfield Scott wanted Lee to become field commander of the Union army. Instead, Lee sadly resigned from the army after the Virginia convention passed an ordinance of secession on April 17. "I must side either with or against my section," Lee told a Northern friend. "I cannot raise my hand against my birthplace, my home, my children." Along with three sons and a nephew, Lee joined the Confederate army. "I foresee that the country will have to pass through a terrible ordeal," he wrote, "a necessary expiation perhaps for our national sins."

Most Southern whites embraced war against the Yankees with less foreboding and more enthusiasm. When news of Sumter's surrender reached Richmond, a huge crowd poured into the state capitol square and ran up the Confederate flag. "Everyone is in favor of secession [and] perfectly frantic with delight," wrote a participant. "I never in all my life witnessed such excitement." The London *Times* correspondent described crowds in North Carolina with "flushed faces, wild eyes, screaming mouths, hurrahing for 'Jeff Davis' and 'the Southern Confederacy.'" No one in those cheering crowds could know that before the war ended, at least 260,000 Confederate soldiers would lose their lives (along with 365,000 Union soldiers) and that the slave South they fought to defend would be utterly destroyed.

The Border States

Except for Delaware, which remained firmly in the Union, the slave states that bordered free states were sharply divided by the outbreak of war. Leaders in these states talked vaguely of neutrality, but they were to be denied that luxury—Maryland and Missouri immediately, and Kentucky in September 1861 when first Confederate and then Union troops crossed their borders.

SLAVERY AND SECESSION

The higher the proportion of slaves and slaveholders in the population of a southern state, the greater the intensity of secessionist sentiment.

	Percentage of Population Who Were Slaves	Percentage of White Population in Slaveholding Families
Seven states that seceded December 1860–February 1861 (South Carolina, Mississippi, Florida, Alabama, Georgia, Louisiana, Texas)	47%	38%
Four states that seceded after the firing on Fort Sumter (Virginia, Arkansas, Tennessee, North Carolina)	32	24
Four border slave states remaining in Union (Maryland, Delaware, Kentucky, Missouri)	14	15

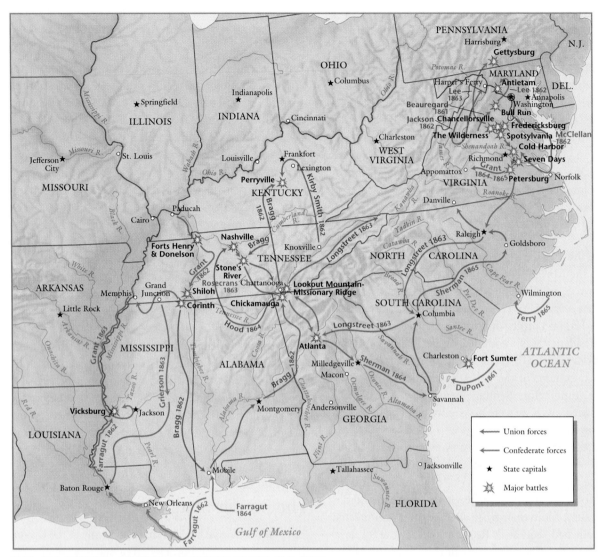

MAP 15.2 PRINCIPAL MILITARY CAMPAIGNS OF THE CIVIL WAR

This map vividly illustrates the contrast between the vast distances over which the armies fought in the western theater of the war and the concentrated campaigns of the Army of the Potomac and the Army of Northern Virginia in the East.

 View an animated version of this map or related maps at http://history.wadsworth.com/murrin_LEP4e.

The first blood was shed in Maryland on April 19, 1861, when a mob attacked Massachusetts troops traveling through Baltimore to Washington. The soldiers fired back, and, in the end, 12 Baltimoreans and 4 soldiers were dead. Confederate partisans burned bridges and tore down telegraph wires, cutting Washington off from the North for nearly a week until additional troops from Massachusetts and New York reopened communications and seized key points in Maryland. The troops also arrested many Confederate sympathizers, including the mayor and police chief of Baltimore, a judge, and two dozen state legislators. To prevent Washington from becoming surrounded by enemy territory, federal forces turned Maryland into an occupied state. Although thousands of Marylanders slipped into Virginia to join the Confederate army, a sub-

stantial majority of Maryland residents remained loyal to the Union.

The same was true of Missouri. Aggressive action by Union commander Nathaniel Lyon provoked a showdown between Unionist and pro-Confederate militia that turned into a riot in St. Louis on May 10 and 11, 1861, in which 36 people died. Lyon then led his troops in a summer campaign that drove the Confederate militia, along with the governor and pro-Southern legislators, into Arkansas, where they formed a Missouri Confederate government in exile. Reinforced by Arkansas regiments, these rebel Missourians invaded their home state, and on August 10 defeated Lyon (who was killed) in the bloody battle of Wilson's Creek in the southwest corner of Missouri. The victorious Confederates marched northward all the way to

the Missouri River, capturing a Union garrison at Lexington 40 miles east of Kansas City on September 20. By then, Union forces made up of regiments from Iowa, Illinois, and Kansas as well as Missouri had regrouped and drove the ragged Missouri Confederates back into Arkansas.

From then until the war's end, Unionists maintained political control of Missouri through military power. Even so, continued guerrilla attacks by Confederate "bushwhackers" and counterinsurgency tactics by Unionist "jayhawkers" turned large areas of the state into a no-man's-land of hit-and-run raids, arson, ambush, and murder. During these years, the famous postwar outlaws Jesse and Frank James and Cole and Jim Younger rode with the notorious rebel guerrilla chieftains William Quantrill and "Bloody Bill" Anderson. More than any other state, Missouri suffered from a civil war within the Civil War, and its bitter legacy persisted for generations.

In elections held during summer and fall 1861, Unionists gained firm control of the Kentucky and Maryland legislatures. Kentucky Confederates, like those of Missouri, formed a state government in exile. When the Confederate Congress admitted both Kentucky and Missouri to full representation, the Confederate flag acquired its 13 stars. Nevertheless, two-thirds of the white population in the four border slave states favored the Union, although some of that support was undoubtedly induced by the presence of Union troops.

The Creation of West Virginia

The war produced a fifth Union border state: West Virginia. Most of the delegates from the portion of Virginia west of the Shenandoah Valley had voted against secession. A region of mountains, small farms, and few slaves, western Virginia's economy was linked more closely to nearby Ohio and Pennsylvania than to the South. Its largest city, Wheeling, was 330 miles from Richmond but only 60 miles from Pittsburgh. Delegates who had opposed Virginia's secession from the Union returned home determined to secede from Virginia. With the help of Union troops, who crossed the Ohio River and won a few small battles against Confederate forces in the area during summer 1861, they accomplished their goal. Through a complicated process of conventions and referendums—carried out in the midst of raids and skirmishes—they created the new state of West Virginia, which entered the Union in 1863.

Indian Territory and the Southwest

To the south and west of Missouri, civil war raged along a different border—between Southern states and territories—for control of the resources of that vast region. In the Indian Territory (present-day Oklahoma), the Native Americans, who had been resettled there from Eastern states in the generation before the war, chose sides and carried on bloody guerrilla warfare against each other as ferocious as the bushwhacking in Missouri. The more prosperous Indians of the five "civilized tribes" (Cherokees, Creeks, Seminoles, Chickasaws, and Choctaws), many of them of mixed blood and some of them slaveholders, tended to side with the Confederacy. Some tribes signed treaties of alliance with the Confederate government. Aided by white and black Union regiments operating out of Kansas and Missouri, the pro-Union Indians gradually gained control of most of the Indian Territory.

In the meantime, Confederates had made their boldest bid to fulfill antebellum Southern ambitions to win the Southwest. A small army composed mostly of Texans pushed up the Rio Grande valley into New Mexico in 1861. The following February, they launched a deeper strike to capture Santa Fe. With luck, they hoped to push even farther westward and northward to gain the mineral wealth of California and Colorado gold mines, whose millions were already helping to finance the Union war effort and could do wonders for Confederate finances. A good many Southerners lived in these Western territories and in California.

At first, the Confederate drive up the Rio Grande went well. The Texans won a victory over the Unionist New Mexico militia and a handful of regulars at the battle of Valverde, 100 miles south of Albuquerque, on February 21, 1862. They continued up the valley, occupied Albuquerque and Santa Fe, and pushed on toward Fort Union near Santa Fe. But Colorado miners who had organized themselves into Union regiments and had carried out the greatest march of the war, over the rugged Rockies in winter, met the Texans in the battle of Glorieta Pass on March 26–28. The battle was a tactical draw, but a unit of Coloradans destroyed the Confederate wagon train, forcing the Southerners into a disastrous retreat back to Texas. Of the 3,700 who had started out to win the West for the Confederacy, only 2,000 made it back. The Confederates had shot their bolt in this region; the West and Southwest remained safe for the Union.

The Balance Sheet of War

If one counts three-quarters of the border state population (including free blacks) as pro-Union, the total number of people in Union states in 1861 was 22.5 million, compared with 9 million in the Confederate states. The North's military manpower advantage was even greater because the Confederate population total included 3.7 million slaves compared with 300,000 slaves in Union

areas. At first, neither side expected to recruit blacks as soldiers. Eventually, the Union did enlist 180,000 black soldiers and at least 10,000 black sailors; the Confederacy held out against that drastic step until the war was virtually over. Altogether, about 2.1 million men fought for the Union and 850,000 for the Confederacy. That was close to half of the North's male population of military age (18 to 40) and three-quarters of the comparable Confederate white population. Because the labor force of the South consisted mainly of slaves, the Confederacy was able to enlist a larger proportion of its white population.

The North's economic superiority was even greater. The Union states possessed nine-tenths of the country's industrial capacity and registered shipping, four-fifths of its bank capital, three-fourths of its railroad mileage and rolling stock, and three-fourths of its taxable wealth.

These statistics gave pause to some Southerners. In a long war that mobilized the total resources of both sides,

the North's advantages might prove decisive. But in 1861, few anticipated how long and intense the war would be. Both sides expected a short and victorious conflict. Confederates seemed especially confident, partly because of their vaunted sense of martial superiority over the "blue-bellied" Yankee nation of shopkeepers. Many Southerners really did believe that one of their own could lick three Yankees. "Let brave men advance with flintlocks and old-fashioned bayonets, on the popinjays of Northern cities," said ex-Governor Henry Wise of Virginia, now a Confederate general, and "the Yankees would break and run."

Although this turned out to be a grievous miscalculation, the South did have some reason to believe that its martial qualities were superior. A higher proportion of Southerners than Northerners had attended West Point and other military schools, had fought in the Mexican War, or had served as officers in the regular army. Volunteer military companies were more prevalent in the ante-

HISTORY THROUGH FILM

The Red Badge of Courage (1951)

Directed by John Huston. Starring Audie Murphy (The Youth) and Bill Mauldin (The Loud Soldier).

Stephen Crane's short novel *The Red Badge of Courage* became an instant classic when it was published in 1895. Civil War veterans praised its realistic descriptions of the confusion, terror, chaos, courage, despair, and adrenaline-driven rage of men in battle. A story of young Henry Fleming (The Youth) and his buddy Wilson (The Loud Soldier) in their first battle (Chancellorsville), the novel traces Henry's transition from boyhood to manhood, from raw recruit to veteran, over two days of violent combat. Intended by Crane as a portrait of soldiers facing the ultimate moment of truth in combat, the novel strives for universality rather than specificity as a Civil War story. Thus the battle is not actually named (although circumstances make clear that it is Chancellorsville, despite the film misleadingly dating it in 1862). The 304th New York regiment is fictional, and even the fact that it is a Civil War battle is scarcely mentioned. Crane did achieve a sort of universality; the novel is a story of men at war—not simply a story of the Civil War.

The film remains more faithful to the book than most movies based on novels. Most of the dialogue is taken directly from Crane. Henry Fleming's self-doubts, fears, and eventual heroism after he first runs away are brilliantly portrayed on the screen by action and dialogue against a background of a narrator's words. Fleming is played by Audie Murphy, America's most decorated soldier in the Second World War, and Wilson by Bill Mauldin, whose Willie and Joe cartoons provided the most enduring images of the American infantryman in that war. Virtually unknown as actors before this film, they make the characters come alive with moving performances.

Much of the credit for this success belongs to director John Huston, who brought out the best in his inexperienced actors. One of Hollywood's most prominent directors, Huston had lobbied Louis Mayer of MGM to produce the film. Believing that "Nobody wants to see a Civil War movie," Mayer finally gave in but provided Huston with a skimpy budget. When Huston flew to Africa immediately

bellum South than in the North. As a rural people, Southerners were proficient in hunting, riding, and other outdoor skills useful in military operations. Moreover, the South had begun to prepare for war earlier than the North. As each state seceded, it mobilized militia and volunteer military companies. On March 6, 1861, the Confederate Congress had authorized an army of 100,000 men. By the time Lincoln called for 75,000 militia after the fall of Fort Sumter, the Confederacy already had 60,000 men under arms. Not until summer 1861 would the North's greater manpower begin to make itself felt in the form of a larger army.

Strategy and Morale

Even when fully mobilized, the North's superior resources did not guarantee success. Its military task was much more difficult than that of the South. The Confederacy had come into being in firm control of 750,000 square miles—a vast territory larger than all of Western Europe and twice as large as the 13 colonies in 1776. To win the war, Union forces would have to invade, conquer, and occupy much of that territory, cripple its people's ability to sustain a war of independence, and destroy its armies. Britain had been unable to accomplish a similar task in the war for independence, even though it enjoyed a far greater superiority of resources over the United States in 1776 than the Union enjoyed over the Confederacy in 1861. Victory does not always ride with the heaviest battalions.

To "win" the war, the Confederacy did not need to invade or conquer the Union or even to destroy its armies; it needed only to stand on the defensive and prevent the North from destroying Southern armies—to hold out long enough to convince Northerners that the cost of victory was too high. Most Confederates were confident in 1861 that they were more than equal to the task. Most

Audie Murphy (Henry Fleming), Bill Mauldin (The Loud Soldier), and their comrades in *The Red Badge of Courage.*

© Springer/Corbis.

after the filming was completed to begin directing *The African Queen,* studio executives cut several of Huston's scenes and reduced the movie's length to 69 minutes. The studio also did little to promote the film, and because audiences failed to identify with its grim realism and mostly unknown cast, *The Red Badge of Courage* was a box-office failure. Like the novel, however, it has become a classic that is still, a half-century after it was filmed, one of the best cinematic portrayals of the psychology of men in combat.

European military experts agreed. The military analyst of the London *Times* wrote:

> It is one thing to drive the rebels from the south bank of the Potomac, or even to occupy Richmond, but another to reduce and hold in permanent subjection a tract of country nearly as large as Russia in Europe. . . . No war of independence ever terminated unsuccessfully except where the disparity of force was far greater than it is in this case. . . . Just as England during the revolution had to give up conquering the colonies so the North will have to give up conquering the South.

The important factor of morale also seemed to favor the Confederacy. To be sure, Union soldiers fought for powerful symbols: nation, flag, constitution. "We are fighting to maintain the best government on earth" was a common phrase in their letters and diaries. It is a "grate [sic] struggle for Union, Constitution, and law," wrote a New Jersey soldier. A Chicago newspaper declared that the South had "outraged the Constitution, set at defiance all law, and trampled under foot that flag which has been the glorious and consecrated symbol of American Liberty."

But Confederates, too, fought for nation, flag, constitution, and liberty—of whites. In addition, they fought to defend their land, homes, and families against invading "Yankee vandals" who many Southern whites quite literally believed were coming to "free the negroes and force amalgamation between them and the children of the poor men of the South." An army fighting in defense of its homeland generally has the edge in morale. "We shall have the enormous advantage of fighting on our own territory and for our very existence," wrote a Confederate leader. "All the world over, are not one million of men defending themselves at home against invasion stronger in a mere military point of view, than five millions [invading] a foreign country?"

Mobilizing for War

More than four-fifths of the soldiers on both sides were volunteers; in the first two years of the war, nearly all of them were. The Confederacy passed a conscription law in April 1862, and the Union followed suit in March 1863, but even afterward, most recruits were volunteers. In both North and South, patriotic rallies with martial music and speeches motivated local men to enlist in a company (100 men) organized by the area's leading citizens. The recruits elected their own company officers (a captain and two lieutenants), who received their commissions from the state governor. A regiment consisted of 10 infantry companies, and each regiment was commanded by a colonel, with a lieutenant colonel and a major as second and third in command—all of them appointed by the governor.

Cook Collection, Valentine Museum, Richmond, Virginia.

THE RICHMOND GRAYS

This photograph depicts a typical volunteer military unit that joined the Confederate army in 1861. Note the determined and confident appearance of these young men. By 1865, one-third of them would be dead and several others maimed for life.

Cavalry regiments were organized in a similar manner. Field artillery units were known as batteries, a grouping of four or six cannon with their caissons and limber chests (two-wheeled, horse-drawn vehicles) to carry ammunition; the full complement of a six-gun battery was 155 men and 72 horses.

Volunteer units received a state designation and number in the order of their completion—the 2nd Massachusetts Volunteer Infantry, the 5th Virginia Cavalry, and so on. In most regiments, the men in each company generally came from the same town or locality. Some Union regiments were composed of men of a particular ethnic group. By the end of the war, the Union army had raised about 2,000 infantry and cavalry regiments and 700 batteries; the Confederates had organized just under half as many. As the war went on, the original thousand-man complement of a regiment was usually whittled down to

half or less by disease, casualties, desertions, and detachments. The states generally preferred to organize new regiments rather than keep the old ones up to full strength.

These were citizen soldiers, not professionals. They carried their peacetime notions of democracy and discipline into the army. That is why, in the tradition of the citizen militia, the men elected their company officers and sometimes their field officers (colonel, lieutenant colonel, and major) as well. Professional military men deplored the egalitarianism and slack discipline that resulted. Political influence often counted for more than military training in the election and appointment of officers. These civilians in uniform were extremely awkward and unmilitary at first, and some regiments suffered battlefield disasters because of inadequate training, discipline, and leadership. Yet this was the price that a democratic society with a tiny professional army had to pay to mobilize large armies almost overnight to meet a crisis. In time, these raw recruits became battle-hardened veterans commanded by experienced officers who had survived the weeding-out process of combat or of examination boards or who had been promoted from the ranks.

As the two sides organized their field armies, both grouped four or more regiments into brigades and three or more brigades into divisions. By 1862, they began grouping two or more divisions into corps and two or more corps into armies. Each of these larger units was commanded by a general appointed by the president. Most of the higher-ranking generals on both sides were West Point graduates, but others were appointed because they represented an important political, regional, or (in the North) ethnic constituency whose support Lincoln or Davis wished to solidify. Some of these "political" generals, like elected regimental officers, were incompetent, but as the war went on, they too either learned their trade or were weeded out. Some outstanding generals emerged from civilian life and were promoted up the ranks during the war. In both the Union and the Confederate armies, the best officers (including generals) *led* their men by example as much as by precept; they commanded from the front, not the rear. Combat casualties were higher among officers than among privates, and highest of all among generals, who died in action at a rate 50 percent higher than enlisted men.

Weapons and Tactics

In Civil War battles, the infantry rifle was the most lethal weapon. Muskets and rifles caused 80 to 90 percent of the combat casualties. From 1862 on, most of these weapons were "rifled"—that is, they had spiral grooves cut in the barrel to impart a spin to the bullet. This innovation was only a decade old, dating to the perfection in the 1850s of the "minié ball" (named after French army Captain Claude Minié, its principal inventor), a cone-shaped lead bullet with a base that expanded on firing to "take" the rifling of the barrel. This made it possible to load and fire a muzzle-loading rifle as rapidly (two or three times per minute) as the old smoothbore musket. Moreover, the rifle had greater accuracy and at least four times the effective range (400 yards or more) of the smoothbore.

Civil War infantry tactics adjusted only gradually to the greater lethal range and accuracy of the new rifle, however, for the prescribed massed formations had emerged from experience with the smoothbore musket. Close-order assaults against defenders equipped with rifles resulted in enormous casualties. The defensive power of the rifle became even greater when troops began digging into trenches. Massed frontal assaults became almost suicidal. Soldiers and their officers learned the hard way to adopt skirmishing tactics, taking advantage of cover and working around the enemy flank.

Logistics

Wars are fought not only by men and weapons but also by the logistical apparatus that supports and supplies them. The Civil War is often called the world's first modern war because of the role played by railroads, steam-powered ships, and the telegraph, which did not exist in earlier wars fought on a similar scale (those of the French Revolution and Napoleon). Railroads and steamboats transported supplies and soldiers with unprecedented speed and efficiency; the telegraph provided instantaneous communication between army headquarters and field commanders.

Yet these modern forms of transport and communications were extremely vulnerable. Cavalry raiders and guerrillas could cut telegraph wires, burn railroad bridges, and tear up the tracks. Confederate cavalry became particularly skillful at sundering the supply lines of invading Union armies and thereby neutralizing forces several times larger than their own. The more deeply the Union armies penetrated into the South, the more men they had to detach to guard bridges, depots, and supply dumps.

Once the campaigning armies had moved away from their railhead or wharfside supply base, they returned to dependence on animal-powered transport. Depending on terrain, road conditions, length of supply line, and proportion of artillery and cavalry, Union armies required one horse or mule for every two or three men. Thus a large invading Union army of 100,000 men (the approximate number in Virginia from 1862 to 1865 and in Georgia in 1864) would need about 40,000 draft animals. Confederate armies, operating mostly in friendly territory closer to

fast commerce raiders built in Liverpool made their way into Confederate hands in 1862. Named the *Florida* and the *Alabama*, they roamed the seas for the next two years, capturing or sinking Union merchant ships and whalers. The *Alabama* was the most feared raider. Commanded by the leading Confederate sea dog, Raphael Semmes, she sank 62 merchant vessels plus a Union warship before another warship, the U.S.S. *Kearsarge* (whose captain, John A. Winslow, had once been Semmes's messmate in the old navy), sank the *Alabama* off Cherbourg, France, on June 19, 1864. Altogether, Confederate privateers and commerce raiders destroyed or captured 257 Union merchant vessels and drove at least 700 others to foreign registry. This Confederate achievement, although spectacular,

made only a tiny dent in the Union war effort, especially when compared with the 1,500 blockade runners captured or destroyed by the Union navy, not to mention the thousands of others that decided not to even try to beat the blockade.

The *Monitor* and the *Virginia*

Its inadequate shipbuilding facilities prevented the Confederate navy from challenging Union seapower where it counted most—along the coasts and rivers of the South. Still, though plagued by shortages on every hand, the Confederate navy department demonstrated great skill at innovation. Southern engineers developed "torpedoes"

THE MONITOR AND MERRIMAC

This black-and-white photograph shows the crew of the Union ironclad *Monitor* standing in front of its revolving two-gun turret. In action, the sun canopy above the turret would be taken down, and all sailors would be at their stations inside the turret or the hull, as shown in the color painting of the famed battle, on March 9, 1862, between the *Monitor* and the Confederate *Virginia* (informally called the *Merrimac* because it had been converted from the captured U.S. frigate *Merrimack*). There is no photograph of the *Virginia*, which was blown up by its crew two months later when the Confederates retreated toward Richmond because its draft was too deep to go up the James River.

From the Collections of the Library of Congress.

© Bettmann/Corbis.

(mines) that sank or damaged 43 Union warships in southern bays and rivers. The South also constructed the world's first combat submarine, the *H. L. Hunley*, which sank a blockade ship off Charleston in 1864 but then went down herself before she could return to shore. Another important innovation was the building of ironclad "rams" to sink the blockade ships. The idea of iron armor for warships was not new—the British and French navies had prototype ironclads in 1861—but the Confederacy built the first one to see action. It was the C.S.S. *Virginia*, commonly called (even in the South) the *Merrimac* because it was rebuilt from the steam frigate U.S.S. *Merrimack*, which had been burned to the waterline by the Union navy at Norfolk when the Confederates seized the naval base there in April 1861. Ready for its trial-by-combat on March 8, 1862, the *Virginia* steamed out to attack the blockade squadron at Hampton Roads. She sank one warship with her iron ram and another with her 10 guns. Other Union ships ran aground trying to escape, to be finished off (Confederates expected) the next day. Union shot and shells bounced off the *Virginia's* armor plate. It was the worst day the U.S. Navy would have until December 7, 1941.

Panic seized Washington and the whole northeastern seaboard. In almost Hollywood fashion, however, the Union's own ironclad sailed into Hampton Roads in the nick of time and saved the rest of the fleet. This was the U.S.S. *Monitor*, completed just days earlier at the Brooklyn navy yard. Much smaller than the *Virginia*, with two 11-inch guns in a revolving turret (an innovation) set on a deck almost flush with the water, the *Monitor* looked like a "tin can on a shingle." It presented a small target and was capable of concentrating considerable firepower in a given direction with its revolving turret. The next day, the *Monitor* fought the *Virginia* in history's first battle between ironclads. It was a draw, but the *Virginia* limped home to Norfolk never again to menace the Union fleet. Although the Confederacy built other ironclad rams, some never saw action and none achieved the initial success of the *Virginia*. By the war's end, the Union navy had built or started 58 ships of the *Monitor* class (some of them double-turreted), launching a new age in naval history that ended the classic "heart of oak" era of warships.

☛ Campaigns and Battles, 1861–1862

Wars can be won only by hard fighting. This was a truth that some leaders on both sides overlooked. One of them was Winfield Scott, General-in-Chief of the U.S. Army. Scott, a Virginian who had remained loyal to the Union,

evolved a military strategy based on his conviction that a great many Southerners were eager to be won back to the Union. The main elements of his strategy were a naval blockade and a combined army-navy expedition to take control of the Mississippi, thus sealing off the Confederacy on all sides and enabling the Union to "bring them to terms with less bloodshed than by any other plan." The Northern press ridiculed Scott's strategy as the Anaconda Plan, after the South American snake that squeezes its prey to death.

The Battle of Bull Run

Most Northerners believed that the South could be overcome only by victory in battle. Virginia emerged as the most likely battleground, especially after the Confederate government moved its capital to Richmond in May 1861. "Forward to Richmond," clamored Northern newspapers, and forward toward Richmond moved a Union army of 35,000 men in July, despite Scott's misgivings and those of the army's field commander, Irvin McDowell. McDowell believed his raw, 90-day Union militia were not ready to fight a real battle. They got no farther than Bull Run, a sluggish stream 25 miles southwest of Washington, where a Confederate army commanded by Beauregard had been deployed to defend a key rail junction at Manassas.

Another small Confederate army in the Shenandoah Valley under General Joseph E. Johnston had given a Union force the slip and had traveled to Manassas by rail to reinforce Beauregard. On July 21, the attacking Federals forded Bull Run and hit the rebels on the left flank, driving them back. By early afternoon, the Federals seemed to be on the verge of victory, but a Virginia brigade commanded by Thomas J. Jackson stood "like a stone wall," earning Jackson the nickname he carried ever after. By midafternoon, Confederate reinforcements—including one brigade just off the train from the Shenandoah Valley—had grouped for a screaming counterattack (the famed "rebel yell" was first heard here). They drove the exhausted and disorganized Yankees back across Bull Run in a retreat that turned into a rout.

Although the Battle of Manassas (or Bull Run, as Northerners called it) was small by later Civil War standards, it made a profound impression on both sides. Of the 18,000 soldiers actually engaged on each side, Union casualties (killed, wounded, and captured) were about 2,800 and Confederate casualties 2,000. The victory exhilarated Confederates and confirmed their belief in their martial superiority. It also gave them a morale advantage in the Virginia theater that persisted for two years. And yet, Manassas also bred overconfidence. Some in the South thought the war was won. Northerners, by contrast, were

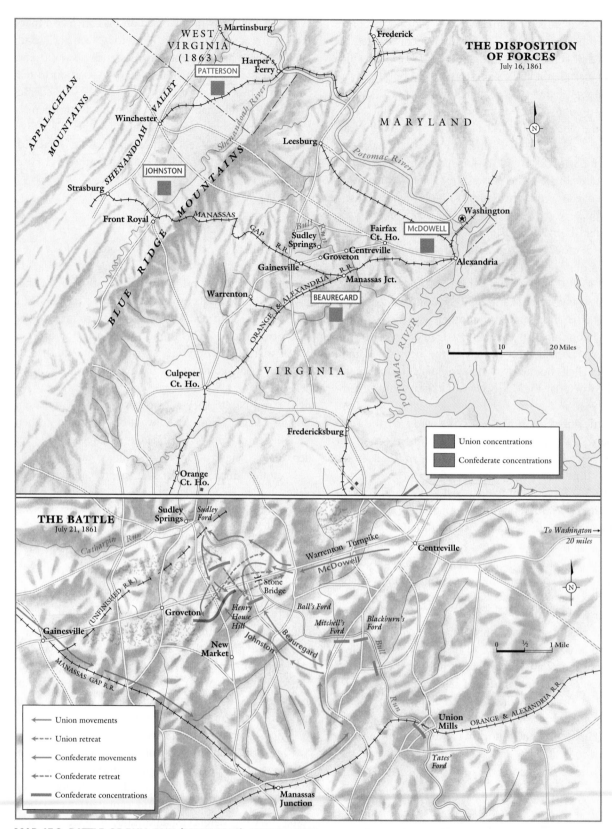

MAP 15.3 BATTLE OF BULL RUN (MANASSAS), JULY 21, 1861

The key to Confederate victory in the war's first major battle was the failure of Union General Robert Patterson to prevent the Confederate troops under General Joseph Johnston (upper map) from joining those under General Pierre G. T. Beauregard via the Manassas Gap Railroad (lower map) for a counterattack that won the battle.

jolted out of their expectations of a short war. A new mood of reality and grim determination gripped the North. Congress authorized the enlistment of up to 1 million three-year volunteers. Hundreds of thousands flocked to recruiting offices in the next few months. Lincoln called General George B. McClellan to Washington to organize the new troops into the Army of the Potomac.

An energetic, talented officer who was only 34 years old and small of stature but great with an aura of destiny, McClellan soon won the nickname "The Young Napoleon." He had commanded the Union forces that gained control of West Virginia, and he took firm control in Washington during summer and fall 1861. He organized and trained the Army of the Potomac into a large, well-disciplined, and well-equipped fighting force. He was just what the North needed after its dispiriting defeat at Bull Run. When Scott stepped down as General-in-Chief on November 1, McClellan took his place.

As winter approached, however, and McClellan did nothing to advance against the smaller Confederate army whose outposts stood only a few miles from Washington, his failings as a commander began to show. He was a perfectionist in a profession where nothing could ever be perfect. His army was perpetually *almost* ready to move. McClellan was afraid to take risks; he never learned the military lesson that no victory can be won without risking defeat. He consistently overestimated the strength of enemy forces facing him and used these faulty estimates as a reason for inaction until he could increase his own force. When newspapers began to publish criticism of McClellan from within the administration and among Republicans in Congress (he was a Democrat), he accused his critics of political motives. Having built a fine fighting machine, he was afraid to start it up for fear it might break. The caution that McClellan instilled in the Army of the Potomac's officer corps persisted for more than a year after Lincoln removed him from command in November 1862.

Naval Operations

Because of McClellan, no significant action occurred in the Virginia theater after the Battle of Bull Run until spring 1862. Meanwhile, the Union navy won a series of victories over Confederate coastal forts at Hatteras Inlet on the North Carolina coast, Port Royal Sound in South Carolina, and other points along the Atlantic and Gulf coasts. These successes provided new bases from which to expand and tighten the blockade. They also provided small Union armies with takeoff points for operations along the southern coast. In February and March 1862, an expeditionary force under General Ambrose Burnside

won a string of victories and occupied several crucial ports on the North Carolina sounds. Another Union force captured Fort Pulaski at the mouth of the Savannah River, cutting off that important Confederate port from the sea.

One of the Union navy's most impressive achievements was the capture in April 1862 of New Orleans, the Confederacy's largest city and principal port. Most Confederate troops in the area had been called up the Mississippi to confront a Union invasion of Tennessee, leaving only some militia, an assortment of steamboats converted into gunboats, and two strong forts flanking the river 70 miles below New Orleans. That was not enough to stop Union naval commander David G. Farragut, a native of Tennessee who was still loyal to the U.S. Navy in which he had served for a half century. In a daring action on April 24, 1862, Farragut led his fleet upriver past the forts, scattering the Confederate fleet and fending off fire rafts. He lost four ships, but the rest won through and compelled the surrender of New Orleans with nine-inch naval guns trained on its streets. Fifteen thousand Union soldiers marched in and occupied the city and its hinterland.

Fort Henry and Fort Donelson

These victories demonstrated the importance of seapower even in a civil war. Even more important were Union victories won by the combined efforts of the army and fleets of river gunboats on the Tennessee and Cumberland rivers, which flow through Tennessee and Kentucky and empty into the Ohio River just before it joins the Mississippi. The unlikely hero of these victories was Ulysses S. Grant, who had failed in several civilian occupations after resigning from the peacetime military in 1854. Grant rejoined when war broke out. His quiet efficiency and determined will won him promotion from Illinois colonel to brigadier general and the command of a small but growing force based at Cairo, Illinois, in fall 1861. When Confederate units entered Kentucky in September, Grant moved quickly to occupy the mouths of the Cumberland and Tennessee rivers. Unlike McClellan, who had known nothing but success in his career and was afraid to jeopardize that record, Grant's experience of failure made him willing to take risks. Having little to lose, he demonstrated that willingness dramatically in the early months of 1862.

Military strategists on both sides understood the importance of these navigable rivers as highways of invasion into the South's heartland. The Confederacy had built forts at strategic points along the rivers and had begun to convert a few steamboats into gunboats and rams to back up the forts. The Union also converted steamboats into "timberclad" gunboats—so called because they were

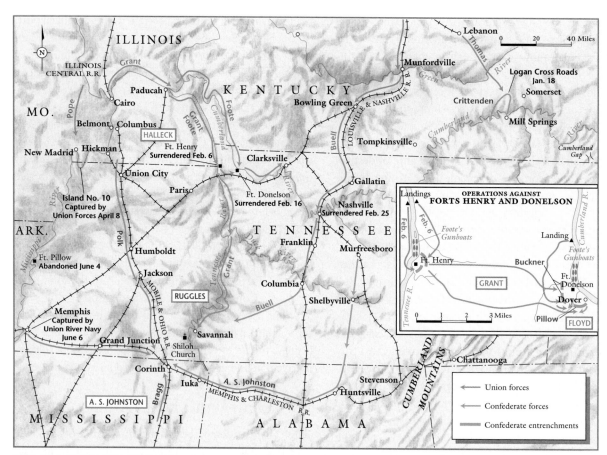

MAP 15.4 KENTUCKY–TENNESSEE THEATER, WINTER–SPRING 1862

This map illustrates the importance of rivers and railroads as lines of military operations and supply. Grant and Foote advanced up (southward) the Tennessee and Cumberland rivers while Buell moved along the Louisville and Nashville Railroad. Confederate divisions under the overall command of General Albert Sidney Johnston used railroads to concentrate at the key junction of Corinth.

armored just enough to protect the engine and the paddle wheels but not enough to impair speed and shallow draft for river operations. The Union also built a new class of ironclad gunboats designed for river warfare. Carrying 13 guns, these flat-bottomed, wide-beamed vessels drew only six feet of water. Their hulls and paddle wheels were protected by a sloping casemate sheathed in iron armor up to 2½ inches thick.

When the first of these strange-looking but formidable craft were ready in February 1862, Grant struck. His objectives were Forts Henry and Donelson on the Tennessee and Cumberland rivers just south of the Kentucky–Tennessee border. The gunboats knocked out Fort Henry on February 6. Fort Donelson proved a tougher nut to crack. Its guns repulsed a gunboat attack on February 14. The next day, the 17,000-man Confederate army attacked Grant's besieging army, which had been reinforced to 27,000 men. With the calm decisiveness that became his trademark, Grant directed a counterattack that penned the defenders back up in their fort. Cut off from support

by either land or river, the Confederate commander asked for surrender terms on February 16. Grant's reply made him instantly famous when it was published in the North: "No terms except an immediate and unconditional surrender can be accepted. I propose to move immediately upon your works." With no choice, the 13,000 surviving Confederates surrendered (some had escaped), giving Grant the most striking victory in the war thus far.

These victories had far-reaching strategic consequences. Union gunboats now ranged all the way up the Tennessee River to northern Alabama, enabling a Union division to occupy the region, and up the Cumberland to Nashville, which became the first Confederate state capital to surrender to Union forces on February 25. Confederate military units pulled out of Kentucky and most of Tennessee and reassembled at Corinth in northern Mississippi. Jubilation spread through the North and despair through the South. By the end of March 1862, however, the Confederate commander in the western theater, Albert Sidney Johnston (not to be confused with Joseph E. John-

ston in Virginia), had built up an army of 40,000 men at Corinth. His plan was to attack Grant's force of 35,000, which had established a base 20 miles away at Pittsburg Landing on the Tennessee River just north of the Mississippi–Tennessee border.

The Battle of Shiloh

On April 6, the Confederates attacked at dawn near a church called Shiloh, which gave its name to the battle. They caught Grant by surprise and drove his army toward the river. After a day's fighting of unprecedented intensity, with total casualties of 15,000, Grant's men brought the Confederate onslaught to a halt at dusk. One of the Confederate casualties was Johnston, who bled to death when a bullet severed an artery in his leg—the highest-ranking

general on either side to be killed in the war. Beauregard, who had been transferred from Virginia to the West, took command after Johnston's death.

Some of Grant's subordinates advised retreat during the dismal night of April 6–7, but Grant would have none of it. Reinforced by fresh troops from a Union army commanded by General Don Carlos Buell, the Union counterattacked the next morning (April 7) and, after 9,000 more casualties to the two sides, drove the Confederates back to Corinth. Although Grant had snatched victory from the jaws of defeat, his reputation suffered a decline for a time because of the heavy Union casualties (13,000) and the suspicion that he had been caught napping the first day.

Union triumphs in the western theater continued. The combined armies of Grant and Buell, under the overall command of the top-ranking Union general in the

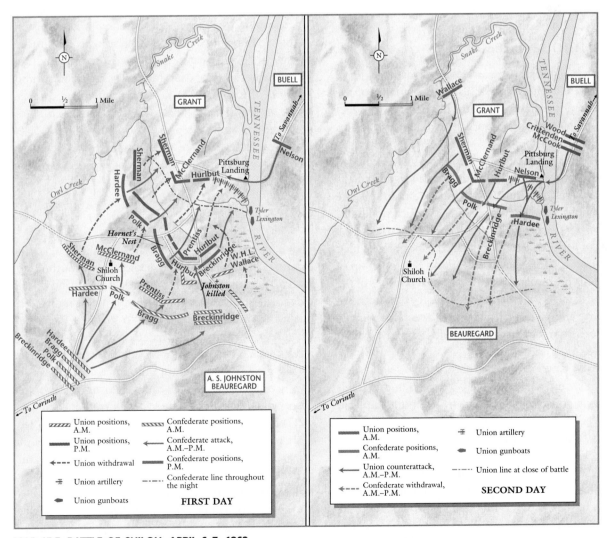

MAP 15.5 BATTLE OF SHILOH, APRIL 6–7, 1862

These two maps starkly illustrate the change of fortune from the first to the second day of the battle, with Confederates driving northward the first day and then being driven back over the same ground the second day.

West, Henry W. Halleck, drove the Confederates out of Corinth at the end of May. Meanwhile, the Union gunboat fleet fought its way down the Mississippi to Vicksburg, virtually wiping out the Confederate fleet in a spectacular battle at Memphis on June 6. At Vicksburg, the Union gunboats from the north connected with part of Farragut's fleet that had come up from New Orleans, taking Baton Rouge and Natchez along the way. The heavily fortified Confederate bastion at Vicksburg, however, proved too strong for Union naval firepower to subdue. Nevertheless, the dramatic succession of Union triumphs in the West from February to June—including a decisive victory at the battle of Pea Ridge in northwest Arkansas on March 7 and 8—convinced the North that the war was nearly won. "Every blow tells fearfully against the rebellion," boasted the leading Northern newspaper, the New York *Tribune*. "The rebels themselves are panic-stricken, or despondent. It now requires no very far reaching prophet to predict the end of this struggle."

The Virginia Theater

Even as the editorial writer wrote these words, affairs in Virginia were about to take a sharp turn in favor of the Confederacy. Within three months the Union, which had been so near a knockout victory that spring, was back on the defensive.

In the western theater, the broad rivers had facilitated the Union's invasion of the South, but in Virginia a half-dozen small rivers flowing west to east lay athwart the line of operations between Washington and Richmond and provided the Confederates with natural lines of defense. McClellan persuaded a reluctant Lincoln to approve a plan to transport his army down Chesapeake Bay to the tip of the Virginia peninsula, formed by the tidal portions of the York and James rivers. That would shorten the route to Richmond and give the Union army a seaborne supply line secure from harassment by Confederate cavalry and guerrillas.

This was a good plan—in theory. And the logistical achievement of transporting 110,000 men and all their equipment, animals, and supplies by sea to the jump-off point near Yorktown was impressive. But once again, McClellan's failings began to surface. A small Confederate blocking force at Yorktown held him for the entire month of April, as he cautiously dragged up siege guns to blast through defenses that his large army could have punched through in days on foot. McClellan slowly followed the retreating Confederate force up the peninsula to a new defensive line only a few miles east of Richmond, all the while bickering with Lincoln and Secretary of War

Edwin M. Stanton over the reinforcements they were withholding to protect Washington against a possible strike by Stonewall Jackson's small Confederate army in the Shenandoah Valley.

Jackson's month-long campaign in the Shenandoah (May 8–June 9), one of the most brilliant of the war, demonstrated what could be accomplished through deception, daring, and mobility. With only 17,000 men, Jackson moved by forced marches so swift that his infantry earned the nickname "Jackson's foot cavalry." Darting here and there through the valley, they marched 350 miles in the course of one month; won four battles against three separate Union armies, whose combined numbers surpassed Jackson's by more than 2 to 1 (but which Jackson's force always outnumbered at the point of contact); and compelled Lincoln to divert to the valley some of the reinforcements McClellan demanded.

Even without those reinforcements, McClellan's army substantially outnumbered the Confederate force defending Richmond, commanded by Joseph E. Johnston. As usual, though, McClellan overestimated Johnston's strength at double what it was and acted accordingly. Even so, by the last week of May, McClellan's army was within six miles of Richmond. A botched Confederate counterattack on May 31 and June 1 (the Battle of Seven Pines) produced no result except 6,000 Confederate and 5,000 Union casualties. One of those casualties was Johnston, who was wounded in the shoulder. Jefferson Davis named Robert E. Lee to replace him.

The Seven Days' Battles

That appointment marked a major turning point in the campaign. Lee had done little so far to earn a wartime reputation, having failed in his only field command to dislodge Union forces from control of West Virginia. His qualities as a commander began to manifest themselves when he took over what he renamed the Army of Northern Virginia. Those qualities were boldness, a willingness to take great risks, an almost uncanny ability to read the enemy commander's mind, and a charisma that won the devotion of his men. While McClellan continued to dawdle, Lee sent his dashing cavalry commander, J. E. B. "Jeb" Stuart, to lead a reconnaissance around the Union army to discover its weak points. Lee also brought Jackson's army in from the Shenandoah Valley and launched a June 26 attack on McClellan's right flank in what became known as the Seven Days' battles. Constantly attacking, Lee's army of 88,000 drove McClellan's 100,000 away from Richmond to a new fortified base on the James River. The offensive cost the Confederates 20,000 casualties (compared with 16,000

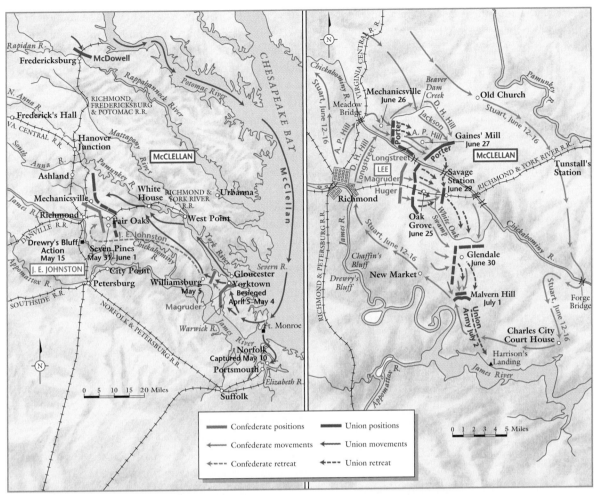

MAP 15.6 PENINSULA CAMPAIGN, APRIL–MAY 1862 [AND] SEVEN DAYS' BATTLES, JUNE 25–JULY 1, 1862
General McClellan used Union naval control of the York and James rivers to protect his flanks in his advance up the peninsula formed by these rivers (left map). When Robert E. Lee's Army of Northern Virginia counterattacked in the Seven Days' Battles (right map), McClellan was forced back to the James River at Harrison's Landing.

for the Union) and turned Richmond into one vast hospital. But it reversed the momentum of the war.

🌏 Confederate Counteroffensives

Northern sentiments plunged from the height of euphoria in May to the depths of despair in July. "The feeling of despondency here is very great," wrote a New Yorker, while a Southerner exulted that "Lee has turned the tide, and I shall not be surprised if we have a long career of successes." The tide turned in the western theater as well, where Union conquests in the spring had brought 50,000 square miles of Confederate territory under Union control. To occupy and administer this vast area, however, drew many thousands of soldiers from combat forces,

which were left depleted and deep in enemy territory and vulnerable to cavalry raids. During summer and fall 1862, the cavalry commands of Tennessean Nathan Bedford Forrest and Kentuckian John Hunt Morgan staged repeated raids in which they burned bridges, blew up tunnels, tore up tracks, and captured supply depots and the Union garrisons trying to defend them. By August the once-formidable Union war machine in the West seemed to have broken down.

These raids paved the way for infantry counteroffensives. After recapturing some territory, Earl Van Dorn's Army of West Tennessee got a bloody nose when it failed to retake Corinth on October 3 and 4. At the end of August, Braxton Bragg's Army of Tennessee launched a drive northward from Chattanooga through east Tennessee and Kentucky. It had almost reached the Ohio River in September but was turned back at the Battle of Perryville

on October 8. Even after these defeats, the Confederate forces in the western theater were in better shape than they had been four months earlier.

The Second Battle of Bull Run

Most attention, though, focused on Virginia. Lincoln reorganized the Union corps near Washington into the Army of Virginia under General John Pope, who had won minor successes as commander of a small army in Missouri and Tennessee. In August, Lincoln ordered the withdrawal of the Army of the Potomac from the peninsula to reinforce Pope for a drive southward from Washington. Lee quickly seized the opportunity provided by the separation of the two Union armies confronting him, by the ill will between McClellan and Pope and their subordinates, and by the bickering among various factions in Washington. To attack Pope before McClellan could reinforce him, Lee shifted most of his army to northern Virginia, sent Jackson's foot cavalry on a deep raid to destroy its supply base at Manassas Junction, and then brought his army back together to defeat Pope's army near Bull Run on August 29 and 30. The demoralized Union forces retreated into the Washington defenses, where Lincoln reluctantly gave McClellan command of the two armies and told him to reorganize them into one.

M U S I C A L   L I N K   T O   T H E   P A S T

Wartime Music as Inspiration and Catharsis

Composers: **Stephen C. Foster (music),**
 James Sloan Gibbons (lyrics)

Title: **"We Are Coming, Father Abraham, 300,000 More" (1862)**

Composers: **Stephen C. Foster (music), Cooper (lyrics)**

Title: **"Willie Has Gone to War" (1863)**

"We Are Coming, Father Abraham, 300,000 More," with its marchlike beat and patriotic lift, captures the optimism some in the North felt at the start of the war, when many estimated that the confrontation would be finished within half a year. The song probably was also used to shore up sagging spirits in some northern areas. Although the song, and others with similar sentiments, sold well with its message of eager voluntarism on the part of soldiers united for the Union, it did not produce a corresponding effect on sluggish troop recruitment efforts in the North.

"Willie Has Gone To War," released a year later and popular in the South as well as the North, presents the more gloomy and death-obsessed nature of Civil War music that surfaced in the second half of the conflict. For months, press dispatches reported the crushing defeats and mortal losses on both sides with violent and gory detail. The occasion of a soldier going to the front was no longer viewed as a celebratory occasion. In "Willie," the notion of oncoming tragedy and death is never stated, but it unmistakably lingers over the song, both in its bittersweet melody and in the Victorian images of nature that are cast as a poetic counterpoint to the fact of Willie going to war: "The bluebird is singing his lay, to all the sweet flowers in the dale / The wild bee is roaming at play, and soft is the sigh of the gale / I stray by the brookside alone, where oft we have wandered before / And weep for my lov'd one, my own, My Willie has gone to the war / . . . Willie has gone to the war, Willie, my loved one is gone!" The last line quoted, part of the chorus of the song, is especially haunting, as the song drops into a minor chord and features a melody that combines mournful and patriotic elements simultaneously.

Although some at the time argued that such sad music eroded morale, perhaps it would have been even more damaging to ignore the kinds of welling emotions that "Willie" and songs like it documented. The catharsis these songs provided helped Americans face the loss and sacrifice of the war, which saw over 1 million people killed and wounded. Confederate General Robert E. Lee maintained that he could not imagine fighting a war without music. George F. Root, one of the most successful songwriters and publishers of the Civil War period, insisted that, as a songwriter, he was patriotically serving his country through the medium of song and that such contributions were as important as the contributions of a general.

---

1. Why do you think Lee and Root attached such importance to the role of music in fighting a war?

Listen to an audio recording of this music on the Musical Links to the Past CD.

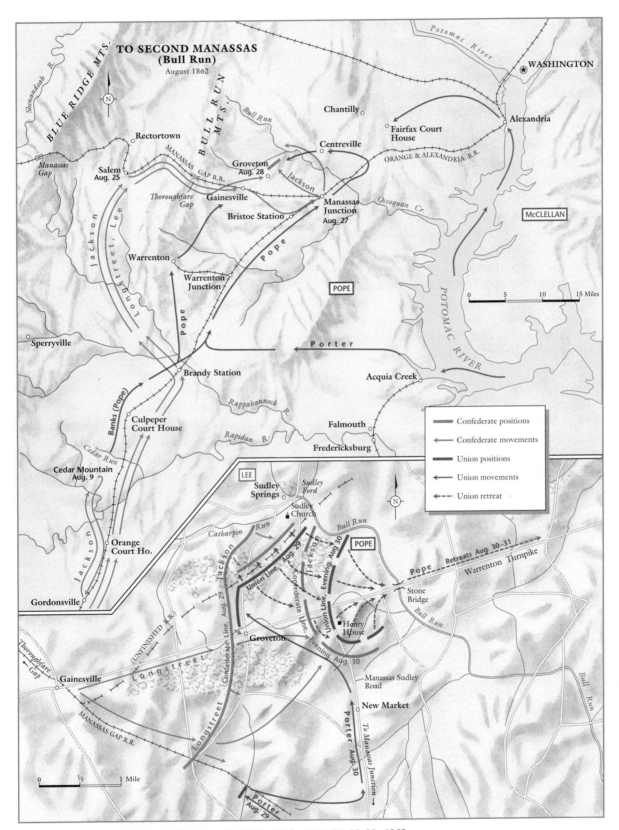

MAP 15.7 SECOND BATTLE OF MANASSAS (BULL RUN), AUGUST 29–30, 1862
Compare this map with the lower map on p. 488. Note that some of the heaviest fighting in both battles took place around the house owned by Judith Henry, which was destroyed and the elderly widow killed in her house in the first battle.

Lee decided to keep up the pressure by invading Maryland. On September 4, his weary troops began splashing across the Potomac 40 miles upriver from Washington. This move, which took place at the same time Braxton Bragg was invading Kentucky, presented several momentous possibilities: Maryland might be won for the Confederacy. Another victory by Lee might influence the U.S. congressional elections in November and help Democrats gain control of Congress, and might even force the Lincoln administration to negotiate peace with the Confederacy. Successful invasion of Maryland, coming on top of other Confederate successes, might even persuade Britain and France to recognize the Confederacy and offer mediation to end the war, especially since the long-expected cotton famine had finally materialized. In fact, in September 1862, the British and French governments were considering recognition and awaiting the outcome of Lee's invasion to decide whether to proceed. Great issues rode with the armies as Lee crossed the Potomac and McClellan cautiously moved north to meet him.

Conclusion

The election of 1860 had accomplished a national power shift of historic proportions. Through their domination of the Jeffersonian Republican coalition during the first quarter of the 19th century and of the Jacksonian Democrats thereafter, Southern political leaders had maintained effective control of the national government for most of the time before 1860. South Carolina's secession governor, Francis Pickens, described this leverage of power in a private letter to a fellow South Carolinian in 1857:

> We have the Executive [Buchanan] with us, and the Senate & in all probability the H[ouse of] R[epresentatives] too. Besides we have repealed the Missouri line & the Supreme Court in a decision of great power, has declared it . . . unconstitutional null and void. So, that before our enemies can reach us, they must first break down the Supreme Court—change the Senate & seize the Executive & . . . restore the Missouri line, repeal the Fugitive slave law &

change the whole govern[men]t. As long as the Govt. is on our side I am for sustaining it, & using its power for our benefit, & placing the screws upon the throats of our opponents.

In 1860, Pickens's worst-case scenario started to come true. With Lincoln's election as the first president of an antislavery party, the South lost control of the executive branch—and perhaps also of the House. They feared that the Senate and Supreme Court would soon follow. The Republicans, Southerners feared, would launch a "revolution" to cripple slavery and, as Lincoln had said in his "House Divided" speech two years earlier, place it "in course of ultimate extinction." The "revolutionary dogmas" of the Republicans, declared a South Carolina newspaper in 1860, were "active and bristling with terrible designs." Worst of all, the Northern Black Republicans would force racial equality on the South: "Abolition preachers will be on hand to consummate the marriage of your daughters to black husbands."

Thus the South launched a preemptive counterrevolution of secession to forestall a revolution of liberty and equality they feared would be their fate if they remained in the Union. As the Confederate secretary of state put it in 1861, the Southern states had formed a new nation "to preserve their old institutions [from] a revolution [that] threatened to destroy their social system."

Seldom has a preemptive counterrevolution so quickly brought on the very revolution it tried to prevent. If the Confederacy had lost the war in spring 1862, as appeared likely after Union victories from February to May of that year, the South might have returned to the Union with slavery intact. Instead, successful Confederate counteroffensives in summer 1862 convinced Lincoln that the North could not win the war without striking against slavery. Another issue that rode with Lee's troops as they crossed the Potomac into Maryland in September 1862 was the fate of an emancipation proclamation Lincoln had drafted two months earlier and then put aside to await a Union victory.

SUGGESTED READINGS

The most comprehensive one-volume study of the Civil War years is **James M. McPherson,** *Battle Cry of Freedom: The Civil War Era* (1988). The fullest and most readable narrative of the military campaigns and battles is **Shelby Foote,** *The Civil War: A Narrative,* 3 vols. (1958–1974). For the naval war, see **Ivan Musicant,** *Divided Waters: The Naval History of the Civil War* (1995). For the perspective of the soldiers and sailors who fought the battles, see **Bell I. Wiley's** two books: *The Life of Johnny Reb* (1943) and *The Life of Billy Yank* (1952). The motives of soldiers for enlisting and fighting are treated in **James M. McPherson,** *For Cause and Comrades: Why Men Fought in the Civil War* (1997).

For the home front in North and South, see **Phillip Shaw Paludan,** *"A People's Contest": The Union and Civil War, 1861–1865* (1988), and **Emory Thomas,** *The Confederate Nation, 1861–1865* (1979). For women and children, see **Elizabeth D. Leonard,** *Yankee Women: Gender Battles in the Civil War;* **George C. Rable,** *Civil Wards: Women and the Crisis of Southern Nationalism* (1989); and **James Marten,** *The Children's Civil War* (1998).

For biographical studies of leaders on both sides, consult the following: **Phillip S. Paludan,** *The Presidency of Abraham Lincoln* (1994); **William C. Cooper,** *Jefferson Davis, American* (2000); **Brooks D. Simpson,** *Ulysses S. Grant* (2000); and **Emory M. Thomas,** *Robert E. Lee* (1995). For a study of the Fort Sumter crisis and the outbreak of the war that sets these events in their long-term context, see **Maury Klein,** *Days of Defiance: Sumter, Secession, and The Coming of the Civil War* (1997). For the guerrilla war in Missouri, the most useful of several books is **Michael Fellman,** *Inside War: The Guerrilla Conflict in Missouri during the Civil War* (1989). Of the many studies of diplomacy during the war, the most useful is **David P. Crook,** *The North, The South, and the Powers 1861–1865* (1974), an abridged version of which was published with the title *Diplomacy during the Civil War* (1975).

 ## AMERICAN JOURNEY ONLINE
AND
INFOTRAC COLLEGE EDITION

Visit the source collections at www.ajaccess.wadsworth.com and infotrac.thomsonlearning.com and use the Search function with the following key terms to explore documents, images, audio and video clips, articles, and commentary related to the material in this chapter.

Fort Sumter	Stonewall Jackson
Abraham Lincoln	Battle of Bull Run (Manassas)
George B. McClellan	Battle of Shiloh
Robert E. Lee	

GRADE AIDS

Visit the Liberty Equality Power Companion Web Site for resources specific to this textbook: http://history.wadsworth.com/murrin_LEP4e

The CD in the back of this book and the U.S. History Resource Center at http://history.wadsworth.com/u.s./ offer a variety of tools to help you succeed in this course, including access to quizzes; images; documents; interactive simulations, maps, and timelines; movie explorations; and a wealth of other sources.

The Emancipation Proclamation exempted the border states, plus Tennessee and those portions of Louisiana and Virginia already under Union occupation because these areas were deemed not to be in rebellion, and Lincoln's constitutional authority for the proclamation derived from his power as commander-in-chief to confiscate enemy property. Although the proclamation could do nothing to liberate slaves in areas under Confederate control, it essentially made the Northern soldiers an army of liberation—however reluctant many of them were to risk their lives for that purpose. The North was now fighting for freedom as well as for Union. If the North won the war, slavery would die. But in the winter and spring of 1862–63, victory was far from assured.

A Winter of Discontent

Although Lee's retreat from Maryland and Braxton Bragg's retreat from Kentucky suggested that the Confederate tide might be ebbing, the tide soon turned. The Union could never win the war simply by turning back Confederate invasions. Northern armies would have to invade the South, defeat its armies, and destroy its ability to fight.

Displeased by McClellan's "slows" after Antietam, Lincoln replaced him on November 7 with General Ambrose E. Burnside. An imposing man whose muttonchop whiskers gave the anagram "sideburns" to the language, Burnside proposed to cross the Rappahannock River at Fredericksburg for a move on Richmond before bad weather forced both sides into winter quarters. Although Lee put his men into a strong defensive position on the heights behind Fredericksburg, Burnside nevertheless attacked on December 13. He was repulsed with heavy casualties that shook the morale of both the army and the public. When Lincoln heard the news, he said: "If there is a worse place than hell, I am in it."

News from the western theater did little to dispel the gloom in Washington. The Confederates had fortified Vicksburg on bluffs commanding the Mississippi River. This precaution gave them control of an important stretch of the river and preserved transportation links between the states to the east and west. Grant proposed to sever those links, and in November 1862, he launched a two-pronged drive against Vicksburg. With 40,000 men, he marched 50 miles southward from Memphis by land, while his principal subordinate William T. Sherman came down the river with 32,000 men accompanied by a gunboat fleet. Confederate cavalry raids destroyed the

---

L I N K   T O   T H E   P A S T

"We Cannot Escape History": Abraham Lincoln

In the closing passage of his annual message to Congress in December 1862, Lincoln soared to an eloquence that matched the later Gettysburg Address and Second Inaugural Address. In this passage, Lincoln was supporting a plan for gradual and compensated abolition of slavery everywhere by constitutional amendment. He did not expect Congress to pass such an amendment or the Confederate states to accept it even if Congress did pass it. The real reference point for this passage was the forthcoming Emancipation Proclamation, which Lincoln issued a month later.

The dogmas of the quiet past, are inadequate to the stormy present. The occasion is piled high with difficulty, and we must rise with the occasion. As our case is new, so we must think anew, and act anew. We must disenthrall our selves, and then, we shall save our country.

Fellow-citizens, we cannot escape history. We of this Congress and this administration, will be remembered in *spite of ourselves. No personal significance, or insignificance, can spare one or another of us. The fiery trial through which we pass, will light us down, in honor or dishonor, to the latest generation. . . . We—even we here— hold the power, and bear the responsibility. In giving freedom to the slave, we assure freedom to the free— honorable alike in what we give, and what we preserve. We shall nobly save, or meanly lose, the last best, hope of earth.*

1. Why did Lincoln say that in giving freedom to the slave we assure freedom to the free?
2. What did he mean by "the last best, hope of earth"?

For additional sources related to this feature, visit the *Liberty, Equality, Power* Web site at:

http://history.wadsworth.com/murrin_LEP4e

railroads and supply depots in Grant's rear, however, forcing him to retreat to Memphis. Meanwhile, Sherman attacked the Confederates at Chickasaw Bluffs on December 29 with no more success than Burnside had enjoyed at Fredericksburg.

The only bit of cheer for the North came in central Tennessee at the turn of the year. There, Lincoln had removed General Don Carlos Buell from command of the Army of the Cumberland for the same reason he had removed McClellan—lack of vigor and aggressiveness. Buell's successor, William S. Rosecrans, had proved a fighter in subordinate commands. On the Confederate side, Davis stuck with Braxton Bragg as commander of the Army of Tennessee, despite dissension from some subordinate officers within his ranks.

On the day after Christmas 1862, Rosecrans moved from his base at Nashville to attack Bragg's force 30 miles to the south at Murfreesboro. The ensuing three-day battle (called Stones River by the Union and Murfreesboro by the Confederacy) resulted in Confederate success on the first day (December 31) but defeat on the last. Both armies suffered devastating casualties. The Confederate retreat to a new base 40 miles farther south enabled the North to call Stones River a victory. Lincoln expressed his gratitude to Rosecrans: "I can never forget . . . that you gave us a hard-earned victory which, had there been a defeat instead, the nation could scarcely have lived over."

As it was, the nation scarcely lived over the winter of 1862–63. Morale declined, and desertions rose so sharply in the Army of the Potomac that Lincoln replaced Burnside with Joseph Hooker, a controversial general whose nickname "Fighting Joe" seemed to promise a vigorous offensive. Hooker did lift morale in the Army of the Potomac, but elsewhere matters went from bad to worse.

Renewing the campaign against Vicksburg, Grant bogged down in the swamps and rivers that protected that Confederate bastion on three sides. Only on the east, away from the river, did he find high ground suitable for an assault on Vicksburg's defenses. Grant's problem was to get his army across the Mississippi to that high ground, along with supplies and transportation to support an assault. For three months, he floundered in the Mississippi-Yazoo bottomlands, while disease and exposure depleted his troops. False rumors of excessive drinking that had dogged Grant for years broke out anew, but Lincoln resisted pressures to remove him from command. "What I want," Lincoln said, "is generals who will fight battles and win victories. Grant has done this, and I propose to stand by him." Lincoln reportedly added that he would like to know Grant's brand of whiskey so that he could send some to his other generals.

The Rise of the Copperheads

Lincoln's reputation reached a low point during this Northern winter of discontent. A visitor to Washington in February 1863 found that "the lack of respect for the President in all parties is unconcealed. . . . If a Republican convention were to be held tomorrow, he would not get the vote of a State." In this climate, the Copperhead faction of the Democratic Party found a ready audience for its message that the war was a failure and should be abandoned. Having won control of the Illinois and Indiana legislatures the preceding fall, Democrats there called for an armistice and a peace conference. They also demanded retraction of the "wicked, inhuman, and unholy" Emancipation Proclamation.

In Ohio, the foremost Peace Democrat, Congressman Clement L. Vallandigham, was planning to run for governor. What had this wicked war accomplished, Vallandigham asked Northern audiences: "Let the dead at Fredericksburg and Vicksburg answer." The Confederacy could never be conquered; the only trophies of the war were "debt, defeat, sepulchres." The solution was to "stop the fighting. Make an armistice. Withdraw your army from the seceded states." Above all, give up the unconstitutional effort to abolish slavery.

Vallandigham and other Copperhead spokesmen had a powerful effect on Northern morale. Alarmed by a wave of desertions, the army commander in Ohio had Vallandigham arrested in May 1863. A military court convicted him of treason for aiding and abetting the enemy. The court's action raised serious questions of civil liberties. Was the conviction a violation of Vallandigham's First Amendment right of free speech? Could a military court try a civilian under martial law in a state such as Ohio where civil courts were functioning?

Lincoln was embarrassed by the swift arrest and trial of Vallandigham, which he learned about from the newspapers. To keep Vallandigham from becoming a martyr, Lincoln commuted his sentence from imprisonment to banishment—to the Confederacy! On May 15, Union cavalry escorted Vallandigham under a flag of truce to Confederate lines in Tennessee, where the Southerners reluctantly accepted their uninvited guest. He soon escaped to Canada on a blockade runner. There, from exile, Vallandigham conducted his campaign for governor of Ohio—an election he lost in October 1863, after the military fortunes of the Union had improved.

Economic Problems in the South

Low morale in the North followed military defeat. By contrast, Southerners were buoyed by their military success

but were suffering from food shortages and hyperinflation. The tightening Union blockade, the weaknesses and imbalances of the Confederate economy, the escape of slaves to Union lines, and enemy occupation of some of the South's prime agricultural areas made it increasingly difficult to produce both guns and butter. Despite the conversion of hundreds of thousands of acres from cotton to food production, the deterioration of Southern railroads and the priority given to army shipments made food scarce in some areas. A drought in summer 1862 made matters worse. Prices rose much faster than wages. The price of salt, which was necessary to preserve meat in those days before refrigeration, shot out of sight. Even the middle class suffered, especially in Richmond, whose population had more than doubled since 1861. "The shadow of the gaunt form of famine is upon us," wrote a war department clerk in March 1863. "I have lost twenty pounds, and my wife and children are emaciated." The rats in his kitchen were so hungry that they nibbled bread crumbs from his daughter's hand "as tame as kittens. Perhaps we shall have to eat them!"

Poor people were worse off—especially the wives and children of nonslaveholders away in the army. By spring 1863, food supplies were virtually gone. Wrote a North Carolina farm woman to the governor in April 1863:

> A crowd of we Poor women went to Greenesborogh yesterday for something to eat as we had not a mouthful of meet nor bread in my house. What did they do but put us in gail in plase of giveing us aney thing to eat. . . . I have 6 little children and my husband in the armey and what am I to do?

Some women took matters into their own hands. Denouncing "speculators" who allegedly hoarded goods to drive up prices, they marched to stores, asked the price of bacon or cornmeal or salt, denounced such "extortion," and took what they wanted without paying. On April 2, 1863, a mob of more than 1,000 women and boys looted several shops in Richmond before the militia, under the personal command of Davis, forced them to disperse. The Confederate government subsequently released some emergency food stocks to civilians, and state and county governments aided the families of soldiers. Better crops in 1863 helped alleviate the worst shortages, but serious problems persisted.

The Wartime Draft and Class Tensions

In both South and North, the draft intensified social unrest and turned it in the direction of class conflict. The burst of patriotic enthusiasm that had prompted a million

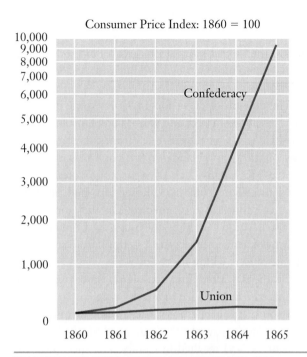

Consumer Price Index: 1860 = 100

WARTIME INFLATION IN THE CONFEDERACY AND THE UNION

men to join the colors in North and South during 1861 had waned by spring 1862. That April, the Confederacy enacted a draft that made all white men (with certain occupational exemptions) ages 18 to 35 liable to conscription. A drafted man could hire a substitute, but the price of substitutes soon rose beyond the means of the average Southern farmer or worker, giving rise to the bitter cry that it was "a rich man's war and a poor man's fight."

The cry grew louder in October 1862 when the Confederate Congress raised the draft age to 45 and added a clause exempting one white man from the draft on every plantation with 20 or more slaves. The purpose of this "overseer exemption" was to keep up production and prevent slave uprisings. It had been prompted by the complaints of planters' wives, who had been left alone to manage the slaves after the departure of husbands, sons, and overseers for the army. The so-called Twenty Negro Law was regarded as blatant discrimination by nonslaveholding farm families whose men were also at the front. In addition, raising the age limit to 45 took away many fathers of children too young to work the farm. The law provoked widespread draft-dodging and desertions.

Similar discontent greeted the enactment of a conscription law in the North. In summer 1863, some 30,000 Union soldiers—who had enlisted in 1861 for two years rather than the normal three—would be leaving military service, along with 80,000 of the nine-month militia called into service the preceding autumn. To meet the looming

THE RICHMOND BREAD RIOT

Illustrating the economic problems of the Confederacy and the suffering of poor civilians in overcrowded cities, the bread riot in Richmond involved 1,000 women and boys who broke into shops to take food and other goods on April 2, 1863. The rioters were white, although a few black children may have gotten into the act, as portrayed by the artist of this woodcut.

The Library of Virginia.

of paying a "commutation fee" of $300 that exempted him from the current draft call (but not necessarily from the next one). That provision raised the cry of "rich man's war, poor man's fight" in the North as well. The Democratic Party nurtured this sense of class resentment and racism intensified it. Democrats in Congress opposed conscription, just as they opposed emancipation. Democratic newspapers told white workers, especially the large Irish American population, that the draft would force them to fight a war to free the slaves, who would then come north to take their jobs. This volatile issue sparked widespread violence when the Northern draft got under way in summer 1863. The worst riot occurred in New York City July 13–16, where huge mobs consisting mostly of Irish Americans demolished draft offices, lynched several blacks, and destroyed huge areas of the city in four days of looting and burning.

NO. DRAFT

New York Historical Society.

THE NEW YORK CITY DRAFT RIOT

The worst urban violence in all of American history occurred in New York City July 13–16, 1863, when thousands of men and women, mostly poor Irish Americans, attacked draft offices, homes, businesses, and individuals. Black residents of the city were among the mob's victims because they symbolized labor competition to Irish Americans, who did not want to be drafted to fight a war to free the slaves. This illustration shows the burning of the Colored Orphan Asylum, a home for black orphans. More than 100 people were killed in the disturbance, most of them rioters shot down by police and soldiers.

shortfall of men, Congress decreed in March that all male citizens ages 20 to 45 must enroll for the draft. Not all of them would necessarily be called (administrative policy exempted married men over 35), but all would be liable.

The law was intended more to encourage volunteers to come forward than to draft men directly into the army. In the president's four calls for troops under this law, the War Department set a quota for every congressional district and allowed 50 days for the quota to be met with volunteers before resorting to a draft lottery. Some districts avoided drafting anyone by offering large bounties to volunteers. The bounty system produced glaring abuses, including "bounty jumpers" who enlisted and then deserted as soon as they got their money—often to enlist again under another name somewhere else.

The drafting process was also open to abuse. Like the Confederate law, the Union law permitted hiring substitutes. To keep the price from skyrocketing as it had in the Confederacy, the law allowed a drafted man the alternative

Draft riots in the North and bread riots in the South exposed alarming class fissures that deepened with the strains of full-scale war. Although inflation was much less serious in the North than in the South, Northern wages lagged behind price increases. Labor unions sprang up in several industries and struck for higher wages. In some areas, such as the anthracite coal fields of eastern Pennsylvania, labor organizations dominated by Irish Americans combined resistance to the draft and opposition to emancipation with violent strikes against industries owned by Protestant Republicans. Troops sent in to enforce the draft sometimes suppressed the strikes as well. These class, ethnic, and racial hostilities provided a volatile mixture in several Northern communities.

A Poor Man's Fight?

The grievance that it was a rich man's war and a poor man's fight was more apparent than real. Property, excise, and income taxes to sustain the war bore proportionately more heavily on the wealthy than on the poor. In the South, wealthy property owners suffered greater damage and confiscation losses than did nonslaveholders. The war liberated 4 million slaves, the poorest class in America. Both the Union and Confederate armies fielded men from all strata of society in proportion to their percentage of the population. If anything, among those who volunteered in 1861 and 1862, the planter class was overrepresented in the Confederate army and the middle class in the Union forces because those privileged groups believed they had more at stake in the war and joined up in larger numbers during the early months of enthusiasm. Those volunteers—especially the officers—suffered the highest percentage of combat casualties.

Nor did conscription fall much more heavily on the poor than on the rich. Those who escaped the draft by decamping to the woods, the territories, or Canada were mostly poor. The Confederacy abolished substitution in December 1863 and made men who had previously sent substitutes liable to the draft. In the North, several city councils, political machines, and businesses contributed funds to pay the commutation fees of drafted men who were too poor to pay out of their own pockets. In the end, it was neither a rich man's war nor a poor man's fight. It was an American war.

☙ Blueprint for Modern America

The 37th Congress (1861–63)—the Congress that enacted conscription, passed measures for confiscation and emancipation, and created the greenbacks and the national banking system (see chapter 15)—also enacted three laws that, together with the war legislation, provided what one historian has called "a blueprint for modern America": the Homestead Act, the Morrill Land-Grant College Act, and the Pacific Railroad Act. For several years before the war, Republicans and some northern Democrats had tried to pass these laws to provide social benefits and to promote economic growth, only to see them defeated by Southern opposition or by President Buchanan's veto. The secession of Southern states, ironically, enabled Congress to pass all three in 1862.

The Homestead Act granted a farmer 160 acres of land virtually free after he had lived on the land for five years and had made improvements on it. The Morrill Land-Grant College Act gave each state thousands of acres to fund the establishment of colleges to teach "agricultural and mechanical arts." The Pacific Railroad Act granted land and loans to railroad companies to spur building a transcontinental railroad from Omaha to Sacramento. Under these laws, the U.S. government ultimately granted 80 million acres to homesteaders, 25 million acres to states for land-grant colleges, and 120 million acres to several transcontinental railroads. Despite waste, corruption, and exploitation of the original Indian owners of this land, these laws helped farmers settle some of the most fertile land in the world, studded the land with state colleges, and spanned it with steel rails in a manner that altered the landscape of the western half of the country.

Women and the War

The war advanced many other social changes, particularly with respect to women. In factories and on farms, women replaced men who had gone off to war. Explosions in Confederate ordnance plants and arsenals killed at least 100 women, who were as surely war casualties as men killed in battle. The war accelerated the entry of women into the teaching profession, a trend that had already begun in the Northeast and now spread to other parts of the country. It also brought significant numbers of women into the civil service. During the 1850s, a few women had worked briefly in the U.S. Patent Office (including Clara Barton, who became a famous wartime nurse and founded the American Red Cross). The huge expansion of government bureaucracies after 1861 and the departure of male clerks to the army provided openings that were filled partly by women. After the war, the private sector began hiring women as clerks, bookkeepers, "typewriters" (the machine itself was invented in the 1870s), and telephone operators (the telephone was another postwar invention).

Women's most visible impact was in the field of medicine. The outbreak of war prompted the organization of soldiers' aid societies, hospital societies, and other volun-

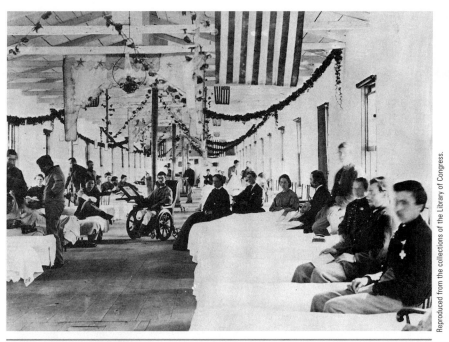

UNION ARMY HOSPITAL

The Armory Square military hospital in Washington, with its clean, cheerful wards apparently decorated for the Christmas holidays, showed Union medical care at its best.

tary associations to provide home front support for the soldiers, and women played a leading role. Their most important function was to help—and sometimes to prod— the medical branches of the Union and Confederate armies to provide more efficient, humane care for sick and wounded soldiers. Dr. Elizabeth Blackwell, the first American woman to earn an M.D. (1849), organized a meeting of 3,000 women in New York City on April 29, 1861. They put together the Women's Central Association for Relief, which became the nucleus for the most powerful voluntary association of the war, the U.S. Sanitary Commission.

Eventually embracing 7,000 local auxiliaries, the Sanitary Commission was an essential adjunct of the Union army's medical bureau. Most of its local volunteers were women, as were most of the nurses it provided to army hospitals. Nursing was not a new profession for women, but it lacked respect as a wartime profession, being classed only slightly above prostitution. The fame won by Florence Nightingale of Britain during the Crimean War a half-dozen years earlier had begun to change that perception. As thousands of middle- and even upper-class women volunteers flocked to army hospitals, nursing began its transformation from a menial occupation to a respected profession.

The nurses had to overcome the deep-grained suspicions of army surgeons and the opposition of husbands and fathers who shared the cultural sentiment that the shocking, embarrassingly physical atmosphere of an army hospital was no place for a respectable woman. Many

thousands of women went to work, winning grudging and then enthusiastic admiration. One Confederate surgeon praised women nurses as far superior to the convalescent soldiers who had formerly done that job, "rough country crackers" who did not "know castor oil from a gun rod nor laudanum from a hole in the ground." In the North, the treasurer of the Sanitary Commission, who at first had disliked the idea of his wife working as a nurse, was converted by her performance as a volunteer for the Sanitary Commission during summer 1862. "The little woman has come out amazingly strong during these past two months," he wrote. "Have never given her credit for a tithe of the enterprise, pluck, discretion, and force of character that she has shown."

The war also bolstered the fledgling women's rights movement. It was no coincidence that Elizabeth Cady Stanton and Susan B. Anthony founded the National Woman Suffrage Association in 1869, only four years after the war. Although a half century passed before women won the vote, this movement could not have achieved the momentum that made it a force in American life without the work of women in the Civil War.

The Confederate Tide Crests and Recedes

The Army of Northern Virginia and the Army of the Potomac spent the winter of 1862–63 on opposite banks of the Rappahannock River. With the coming of spring, Union commander Joe Hooker resumed the offensive with hopes of redeeming the December disaster at Fredericksburg. On April 30, instead of charging straight across the river, Hooker crossed his men several miles upriver and came in on Lee's rear. Lee quickly faced most of his troops about and confronted the enemy in dense woods, known locally as the Wilderness, near the crossroads hostelry of Chancellorsville. Nonplussed, Hooker lost the initiative.

The Battle of Chancellorsville

Even though the Union forces outnumbered the Confederates by almost two to one, Lee boldly went over to the

FEMALE SPIES AND SOLDIERS

In addition to working in war industries and serving as army nurses, some women pursued traditionally male wartime careers as spies and soldiers. One of the most famous Confederate spies was Rose O'Neal Greenhow, a Washington widow and socialite who fed information to officials in Richmond. Federal officers arrested her in August 1861 and deported her to Richmond in spring 1862. She was photographed with her daughter in the Old Capitol prison in Washington, D.C., while awaiting trial. In October 1864, she drowned in a lifeboat off Wilmington, North Carolina, after a blockade runner carrying her back from a European mission was run aground by a Union warship. The second photograph shows a Union soldier who enlisted in the 95th Illinois Infantry under the name of Albert Cashier and fought through the war. Not until a farm accident in 1911 revealed Albert Cashier to be a woman, whose real name was Jennie Hodgers, was her secret disclosed. Most of the other estimated 400 women who evaded the superficial physical exams and passed as men to enlist in the Union and Confederate armies were more quickly discovered and discharged—six of them after they had babies while in the army. A few, however, served long enough to be killed in action.

offensive. On May 2, Stonewall Jackson led 28,000 men on a stealthy march through the woods to attack the Union right flank late in the afternoon. As a result of the negligence of the Union commanders, the surprise was complete. Jackson's assault crumpled the Union flank as the sun dipped below the horizon. Jackson then rode out to scout the terrain for a moonlight attack but was wounded on his return by jittery Confederates who mistook him and his staff for Union cavalry. Nevertheless, Lee resumed the attack the next day. In three more days of fighting that caused 12,800 Confederate and 16,800 Union casualties (the largest number for a single battle in the war so far), Lee drove the Union troops back across the Rappahannock. It was a brilliant victory.

In the North, the gloom grew deeper. "My God!" exclaimed Lincoln when he heard the news of Chancellorsville. "What will the country say?" Copperhead opposition intensified. Southern sympathizers in Britain renewed efforts for diplomatic recognition of the Confederacy. Southern elation, however, was tempered by grief at the death on May 10 of Jackson, who had contracted pneumonia after amputation of his arm. Nevertheless, Lee decided to parlay his tactical victory at Chancellorsville into a strategic offensive by again invading the North. A victory on Union soil would convince Northerners and foreigners alike that the Confederacy was invincible. As his army moved north in June 1863, Lee was confident of success. "There never were such men in an army before," he

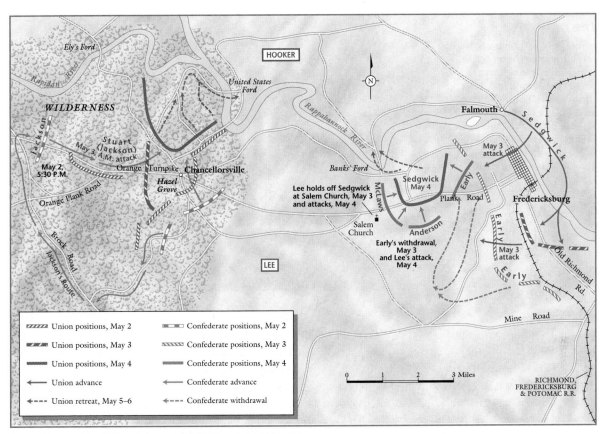

MAP 16.2 BATTLE OF CHANCELLORSVILLE, MAY 2–6, 1863
This map demonstrates the advantage of holding "interior lines," which enabled General Lee to shift troops back and forth to and from the Chancellorsville and Fredericksburg fronts over the course of three days while the two parts of the Union army remained separated.

wrote of his troops. "They will go anywhere and do anything if properly led."

The Gettysburg Campaign

At first, all went well. The Confederates brushed aside or captured Union forces in the northern Shenandoah Valley and in Pennsylvania. Stuart's cavalry threw a scare into Washington by raiding behind Union lines into Maryland and Pennsylvania. That very success led to trouble. With Stuart's cavalry separated from the rest of the army, Lee lost the vital intelligence that the cavalry garnered as the army's eyes. By June 28, several detachments of Lee's forces were scattered about Pennsylvania, far from their base and vulnerable.

At this point, Lee learned that the Army of the Potomac was moving toward him, now under the command of George Gordon Meade. Lee immediately ordered his own army to reassemble in the vicinity of Gettysburg, an agricultural and college town at the hub of a dozen roads leading in from all directions. There, on the morning of July 1,

the vanguard of the two armies met in a clash that grew into the greatest battle in American history.

As the fighting spread west and north of town, couriers pounded up the roads on lathered horses to summon reinforcements to both sides. The Confederates fielded more men and broke the Union lines late that afternoon, driving the survivors to a defensive position on Cemetery Hill south of town. General Richard Ewell, Jackson's successor as commander of the Confederate Second Corps, judging this position too strong to take with his own troops, chose not to press the attack as the sun went down on what he presumed would be another Confederate victory.

When the sun rose the next morning, however, the reinforced Union army was holding a superb defensive position from Culp's Hill and Cemetery Hill south to Little Round Top. Lee's principal subordinate, First Corps commander James Longstreet, advised against attack, urging instead a maneuver to the south, toward Washington, to force the Federals to attack Lee in a strong defensive position. But Lee believed his army invincible. After its victory on July 1, a move to the south might look like a retreat.

THE BATTLE OF GETTYSBURG

This is one of many paintings of Pickett's assault on the Union center on Cemetery Ridge at the climactic moment of the battle on July 3, 1863. The painting depicts "the high tide of the Confederacy" as Virginia and North Carolina troops pierce the Union line only to be shot down or captured— a fate suffered by half of the 13,000 Confederate soldiers who participated in Pickett's Charge.

National Park Service, Harpers Ferry Center.

Pointing to the Union lines, he said: "The enemy is there, and I am going to attack him there."

Longstreet reluctantly led the attack on the Union left. Once committed, his men fought with fury. The Union troops fought back with equal fury. As the afternoon passed, peaceful areas with names like Peach Orchard, Wheat Field, Devil's Den, and Little Round Top were turned into killing fields. By the end of the day, Confederate forces had made small gains at great cost, but the main Union line had held firm.

Lee was not yet ready to yield the offensive. Having attacked both Union flanks, he thought the center might be weak. On July 3, he ordered a frontal attack on Cemetery Ridge, led by a fresh division under George Pickett. After a two-hour artillery barrage, Pickett's 5,000 men and 8,000 additional troops moved forward on that sultry afternoon in a picture-book assault that forms our most enduring image of the Civil War. "Pickett's Charge" was shot to pieces; scarcely half of the men returned unwounded to their own lines. It was the final act in an awesome three-day drama that left some 50,000 men killed, wounded, or captured: 23,000 Federals and 25,000 to 28,000 Confederates.

Lee limped back to Virginia pursued by the Union troops. Lincoln was unhappy with Meade for not cutting off the Confederate retreat. Nevertheless, Gettysburg was a great Northern victory, and it came at the same time as other important Union successes in Mississippi, Louisiana, and Tennessee.

The Vicksburg Campaign

In mid-April, Grant had begun a move that would put Vicksburg in a vise. The Union ironclad fleet ran downriver past the big guns at Vicksburg with little dam-age. Grant's troops marched down the Mississippi's west bank and were ferried across the river 40 miles south of Vicksburg.

There they kept the Confederate defenders off balance by striking east toward Jackson instead of marching north to Vicksburg. Grant's purpose was to scatter the Confederate forces in central Mississippi and to destroy the rail network so that his rear would be secure when he turned toward Vicksburg. It was a brilliant strategy, flawlessly executed. During the first three weeks of May, Grant's troops marched 180 miles, won five battles, and trapped 32,000 Confederate troops and 3,000 civilians in Vicksburg between the Union army on land and the Union gunboats on the river.

But the Confederate army was still full of fight. Confederate soldiers threw back Union assaults against the Vicksburg trenches on May 19 and 22. Grant then settled down for a siege. By late June, he had built up his army to 70,000 men to ward off a Confederate army of 30,000 scraped together by Joseph Johnston to try to rescue Vicksburg. Running out of supplies, the Vicksburg garrison surrendered on July 4. Grant then turned east and drove off Johnston's force. On July 9, the Confederate garrison at Port Hudson, 200 river miles south of Vicksburg, surrendered to a besieging Union army. Northern forces now controlled the entire length of the Mississippi River. "The Father of Waters again goes unvexed to the sea," said Lincoln. The Confederacy had been torn in two, and Lincoln knew who deserved the credit. "Grant is my man," he said, "and I am his the rest of the war."

Chickamauga and Chattanooga

Northerners had scarcely finished celebrating the twin victories of Gettysburg and Vicksburg when they learned of

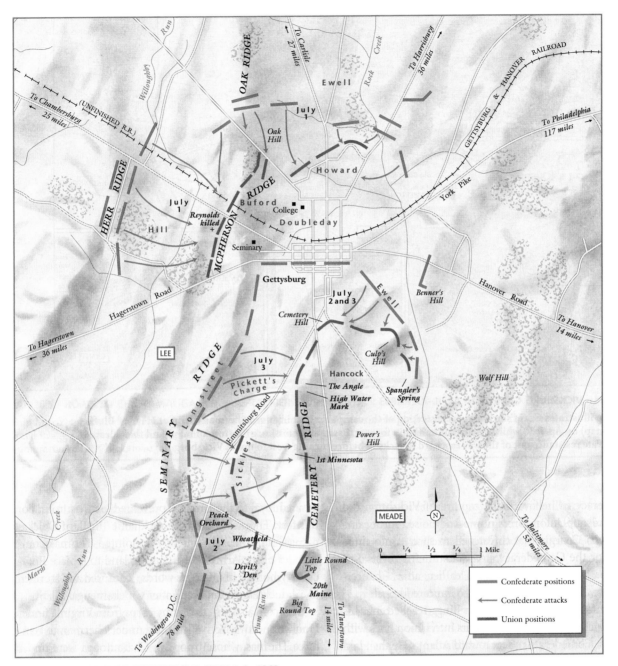

MAP 16.3 BATTLE OF GETTYSBURG, JULY 1–3, 1863
On July 2 and 3, the Union army had the advantage of interior lines at Gettysburg, which enabled General Meade to shift reinforcements from his right on Culp's Hill to his left near Little Round Top over a much shorter distance than Confederate reinforcements from one flank to the other would have to travel.

an important—and almost bloodless—triumph in Tennessee. After the traumatic Battle of Stones River at the end of 1862, the Union Army of the Cumberland and the Confederate Army of Tennessee had shadowboxed for nearly six months. On June 24, Union commander Rosecrans finally assaulted the Confederate defenses in the Cumberland foothills of east-central Tennessee. He used his cavalry and a mounted infantry brigade armed with new repeating rifles to get around the Confederate flanks while his infantry threatened the Confederate front. In the

first week of July, the Confederates retreated all the way to Chattanooga.

After a pause for resupply, Rosecrans's army advanced again in August, this time in tandem with a smaller Union army in eastern Tennessee commanded by Burnside, who had come to this theater after being removed from command in Virginia. Again the outnumbered Confederates fell back, evacuating Knoxville on September 2 and Chattanooga on September 9. This action severed the South's only direct east-west rail link. Having sliced the

Brown Brothers.

TRENCH WARFARE, 1864–1865

During the grueling campaigns of 1864 and 1865, the opposing armies entrenched wherever they paused. By the end of the war, hundreds of square miles in Virginia and Georgia looked like this, especially along a 35-mile line from a point east of Richmond to just southwest of Petersburg, where the armies confronted each other for more than nine months. Note not only the elaborate trench networks but also the absence of trees, cut down to provide firewood and to create open fields of fire for rifles and cannons.

length of time by the men in Pickett's Charge at Gettysburg exactly 11 months before.) "I regret this assault more than any other one I have ordered," said Grant.

Stalemate in Virginia

Now Grant moved all the way across the James River to strike at Petersburg, an industrial city and rail center 20 miles south of Richmond. If Petersburg fell, the Confederates could not hold Richmond. Once more Lee's troops raced southward on the inside track and blocked Grant's troops. Four days of Union assaults (June 15–18) produced another 11,000 Northern casualties but no breakthrough.

Such high Union losses in just six weeks—some 65,000 killed, wounded, and captured, compared with 37,000 Confederate casualties—cost the Army of the Potomac its offensive power. Grant reluctantly settled down for a siege along the Petersburg–Richmond front that would last more than nine grueling months.

Meanwhile, other Union operations in Virginia had achieved little success. Benjamin Butler bungled an attack up the James River against Richmond and was stopped by a scraped-together army under Beauregard. A Union thrust up the Shenandoah Valley was blocked at Lynchburg in June by Jubal Early, commanding Stonewall Jackson's old corps. Early then led a raid all the way to the out-

skirts of Washington on July 11 and 12 before being driven back to Virginia. Union cavalry under Philip Sheridan inflicted considerable damage on Confederate resources in Virginia—including the mortal wounding of Jeb Stuart in the battle of Yellow Tavern on May 11—but again failed to strike a crippling blow. In the North, frustration set in over failure to win the quick, decisive victory the public had expected in April.

The Atlanta Campaign

In Georgia, Sherman's army seemed to have accomplished more at less cost than Grant had in Virginia, but there too Union efforts had bogged down in apparent stalemate by August. The strategy and tactics of both Sherman and Johnston in Georgia contrasted with those of Grant and Lee in Virginia. Sherman forced Johnston south toward Atlanta by constantly flanking him to the Union right, generally without bloody battles. Grant constantly forced Lee back by flanking moves to the Union left, but only after bloody battles. By the end of June, Sherman had advanced 80 miles at the cost of 17,000 casualties to Johnston's 14,000—only one-third of the combined losses of Grant and Lee.

Davis grew alarmed by Johnston's apparent willingness to yield territory without a fight. Sherman again flanked the Confederate defenses (after a failed attack) at Kennesaw Mountain in early July. He crossed the Chattahoochee River and drove Johnston back to Peachtree Creek less than five miles from Atlanta. Fearing that Johnston would abandon the city, on July 17, Davis replaced him with John Bell Hood.

A fighting general from Lee's army who had lost a leg at Chickamauga, Hood immediately prepared to counterattack against the Yankees. He did so three times, in late July. Each time, the Confederates reeled back in defeat, suffering a total of 15,000 casualties to Sherman's 6,000. At last, Hood retreated into the formidable earthworks ringing Atlanta and launched no more attacks, although his army did manage to keep Sherman's cavalry and infantry from taking the two railroads leading into Atlanta from the south. Like Grant at Petersburg, Sherman seemed to settle down for a siege.

Peace Overtures

By August, the Confederate strategy of attrition seemed to be working. Union casualties on all fronts during the preceding three months totaled a staggering 110,000—double the number for any comparable period of the war. "Who shall revive the withered hopes that bloomed at the opening of Grant's campaign?" asked the leading Demo-

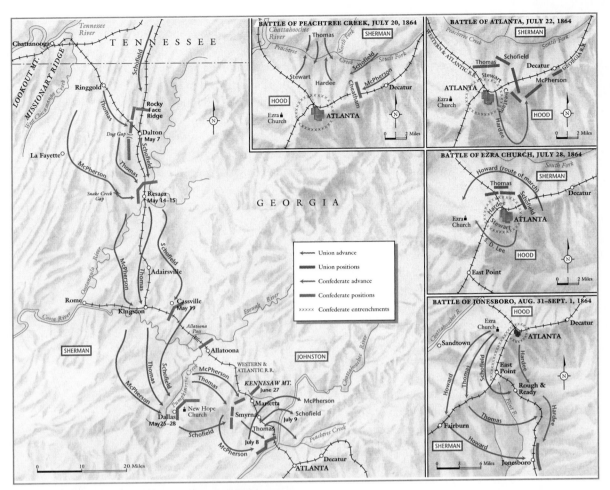

MAP 16.7   CAMPAIGN FOR ATLANTA, MAY–SEPTEMBER 1864

The main map illustrates Sherman's campaign of maneuver that forced Johnston back to Atlanta with relatively few battles. The first three inset maps show the Confederate counterattacks launched by Hood and the fourth shows how the Union army got astride the last two railroads entering Atlanta from the south and forced Hood to evacuate the city.

cratic newspaper, the *New York World*. "STOP THE WAR!" shouted Democratic headlines. "All are tired of this damnable tragedy."

Even Republicans joined the chorus of despair. "Our bleeding, bankrupt, almost dying country longs for peace," wrote Horace Greeley of the New York *Tribune*. Greeley became involved in abortive "peace negotiations" spawned by Confederate agents in Canada. Those agents convinced Greeley that they carried peace overtures from Davis, but Lincoln, aware that Davis's condition for peace was Confederate independence, was skeptical. Still, given the mood of the North in midsummer 1864, Lincoln could not reject any opportunity to stop the bloodshed. He deputized Greeley to meet with the Confederate agents in Niagara Falls on the Canadian side of the border. At almost the same time (mid-July), two other Northerners met under a flag of truce with Davis in Richmond. Lincoln had carefully instructed them—and Greeley—that his conditions

for peace were "restoration of the Union and abandonment of slavery."

Of course, Davis would no more accept those terms than Lincoln would accept his. Although neither of the peace contacts came to anything, the Confederates gained a propaganda victory by claiming that Lincoln's terms had been the only obstacle to peace. Northern Democrats ignored the Southern refusal to accept reunion as a condition of peace and focused on the slavery issue as the sole stumbling block. "Tens of thousands of white men must yet bite the dust to allay the negro mania of the President," ran a typical Democratic editorial. By August, even staunch Republicans such as national party chairman Henry Raymond and his associate Thurlow Weed were convinced that "the desire for peace" and the impression that Lincoln "is fighting not for the Union but for the abolition of slavery" made his reelection "an impossibility." Lincoln thought so, too. "I am going to be beaten," he told

John Bigelow Promotes the Union Cause in France

A founder of the Free Soil and Republican parties, a skillful writer and journalist, and a friend of Secretary of State William H. Seward, John Bigelow (1817–1911) went to Paris in 1861 as consul general of the American legation. His actual role in American foreign policy during the Civil War far exceeded the vague authority suggested by his official title. The American minister, William L. Dayton, was a political appointee who did not speak French and had no diplomatic experience. Fluent in French, Bigelow became an essential partner with Dayton. Bigelow's journalistic experience also enabled him to establish important contacts with Parisian reporters and editors. With Seward's encouragement and secret service funds from the U.S. government, Bigelow bribed members of the notoriously corrupt French press and planted pro-Union or anti-Confederate articles in key journals. He also purchased information about Confederate efforts to build iron-clad ships and commerce raiders in French shipyards. His exposure of these efforts caused the French government to clamp down on them as a violation of French neutrality.

When Dayton died suddenly in late 1864, Bigelow became minister in name as well as in fact. He devoted his efforts after Appomattox to pressing Emperor Napoleon to remove from Mexico the 35,000 French troops who were propping up Ferdi-nand Maximilian, whom Napoleon had established as Emperor of Mexico in 1864. The U.S. government sent 50,000 veteran troops

to Texas as a signal to France, which did withdraw the troops in 1866, whereupon the Mexican republicans captured Maximilian and executed him in 1867.

Bigelow returned to the United States in 1866, but during the rest of his long life he traveled abroad extensively, lived in Germany for several years, wrote several books about French history and about a famous predecessor in Paris, Benjamin Franklin, whose success in winning French support for the United States during the Revolution was brought full circle by Bigelow's role in preventing French support for the Confederacy during the Civil War.

From the Collections of the Library of Congress.

JOHN BIGELOW

a friend in August, "and unless some great change takes place, *badly* beaten."

Lincoln faced enormous pressure to drop emancipation as a condition of peace so the onus could be shifted to Jefferson Davis's insistence on Confederate independence. Lincoln refused to yield. He would rather lose the election than go back on the promise he had made in the Emancipation Proclamation. "No human power can subdue this rebellion without using the Emancipation lever as I have done," he told weak-kneed Republicans. Some 130,000 black soldiers and sailors were fighting for the Union.

They would not do so if they thought the North intended to forsake them:

> If they stake their lives for us they must be prompted by the strongest motive . . . the promise of freedom. And the promise being made, must be kept. . . . There have been men who proposed to me to return to slavery the[se] black warriors. . . . I should be damned in time & eternity for so doing. The world shall know that I will keep my faith to friends and enemies, come what will.

At the end of August, the Democrats nominated Mc-Clellan for president. The platform on which he ran de-

clared that "after four years of failure to restore the Union by the experiment of war . . . [we] demand that immediate efforts be made for a cessation of hostilities." Southerners were jubilant. Democratic victory on that platform, said the *Charleston Mercury,* "must lead to peace and our independence [if] for the next two months *we hold our own and prevent military success by our foes.*"

The Prisoner-Exchange Controversy

The Democratic platform also condemned the Lincoln administration's "shameful disregard" of prisoners of war in Confederate prison camps. This raised another contentious matter. By midsummer 1864, the plight of Union and Confederate captives had become one of the most bitter issues of the war. The upcoming presidential election and the generally worse conditions in Southern prisons made it mainly a Northern political issue.

In 1862, the Union and Confederate armed forces had signed a cartel for the exchange of prisoners captured in battle. The arrangement had worked reasonably well for a year, making large prison camps unnecessary. When the Union army began to organize regiments of former slaves, however, the Confederate government announced that if they were captured, they and their white officers would be put to death for the crime of fomenting slave insurrections. In practice, the Confederate government did not enforce this policy because Lincoln threatened retaliation on Confederate prisoners of war if it did so, but Confederate troops sometimes murdered black soldiers and their officers as they tried to surrender—most notably at Fort Pillow, a Union garrison on the Mississippi north of Memphis, where cavalry commanded by Nathan Bedford Forrest slaughtered scores of black (and some white) prisoners on April 12, 1864.

In most cases, Confederate officers returned captured black soldiers to slavery or put them to hard labor on Southern fortifications. Expressing outrage at this treatment of soldiers wearing the United States uniform, the Lincoln administration in 1863 suspended the exchange of prisoners until the Confederacy agreed to treat white and black prisoners alike. The Confederacy refused. The South would "die in the last ditch," said the Confederate exchange agent, before "giving up the right to send slaves back to slavery as property recaptured."

There matters stood as the heavy fighting of 1864 poured many thousands of captured soldiers into hastily contrived prison compounds that quickly became death camps. Prisoners were subjected to overcrowding, poor sanitation, contaminated water, scanty rations, inadequate medical facilities, and exposure to deep-South summer heat and northern winter cold. The suffering of Northern prisoners was especially acute, because the deterioration of the Southern economy made it hard to feed and clothe even Confederate soldiers and civilians, let alone Yankee prisoners. Nearly 16 percent of all Union soldiers held in Southern prison camps died, compared with 12 percent of Confederate soldiers in Northern camps. Andersonville was the most notorious hellhole. A stockade camp of 26 acres with neither huts nor tents, designed to accommodate 15,000 prisoners, it held 33,000 in August 1864. They died at the rate of more than 100 per day. Altogether, 13,000 Union soldiers died at Andersonville.

The suffering of Union prisoners brought heavy pressure on the Lincoln administration to renew exchanges, but the Confederates would not budge on the question of exchanging black soldiers. After a series of battles on the Richmond–Petersburg front in September 1864, Lee proposed an informal exchange of prisoners. Grant agreed, on condition that black soldiers captured in the fighting be included "the same as white soldiers." Lee replied that

BURIAL OF UNION POWS AT ANDERSONVILLE
On many days during summer 1864, at least 100 Union prisoners of war died of disease, malnutrition, or exposure at Andersonville Prison in Georgia. This scene of burial in long trenches became so commonplace as to dull the sense of horror.

"negroes belonging to our citizens are not considered subjects of exchange and were not included in my proposition." No exchange, then, responded Grant. The Union government was "bound to secure to all persons received into her armies the rights due to soldiers." Lincoln backed this policy. He would not sacrifice the principle of equal treatment of black prisoners, even though local Republican leaders warned that many in the North "will work and vote against the President, because they think sympathy with a few negroes, also captured, is the cause of a refusal" to exchange prisoners.

The Issue of Black Soldiers in the Confederate Army

During the winter of 1864–65, the Confederate government quietly abandoned its refusal to exchange black prisoners, and exchanges resumed. One reason for this reversal was a Confederate decision to recruit slaves to fight for the South. Two years earlier, Davis had denounced the North's arming of freed slaves as "the most execrable measure recorded in the history of guilty man." Ironically, a few black laborers and body servants with Southern armies had taken up arms in the heat of battle and had unofficially fought alongside their masters against the Yankees. By February 1865, Southern armies were desperate for manpower, and slaves constituted the only remaining reserve. Supported by Lee's powerful influence, Davis pressed the Confederate Congress to enact a bill for recruitment of black soldiers. The assumption that any slaves who fought for the South would have to be granted freedom generated bitter opposition to the measure. "What did we go to war for, if not to protect our property?" asked a Virginia senator. By three votes in the House and one in the Senate, the Confederate Congress finally passed the bill on March 13, 1865. Before any Southern black regiments could be organized, however, the war ended.

● Lincoln's Reelection and the End of the Confederacy

Despite Republican fears, battlefield events, rather than political controversies, had the strongest impact on U.S. voters in 1864. In effect, the election became a referendum on whether to continue fighting for unconditional victory. Within days after the Democratic national convention had declared the war a failure, the military situation changed dramatically.

The Capture of Atlanta

After a month of apparent stalemate on the Atlanta front, Sherman's army again made a large movement by the right flank to attack the last rail link into Atlanta from the south. At the battle of Jonesboro on August 31 and September 1, Sherman's men captured the railroad. Hood abandoned Atlanta to save his army. On September 3, Sherman sent a jaunty telegram to Washington: "Atlanta is ours, and fairly won."

This news had an enormous impact on the election. "VICTORY!" blazoned Republican headlines. "IS THE WAR A FAILURE? OLD ABE'S REPLY TO THE DEMOCRATIC CONVENTION." A New York Republican wrote that the capture of Atlanta, "coming at this political crisis, is the greatest event of the war." The *Richmond Examiner* glumly concurred. The fall of Atlanta, it declared, "came in the very nick of time [to] save the party of Lincoln from irretrievable ruin."

The Shenandoah Valley

If Atlanta was not enough to brighten the prospects for Lincoln's reelection, events in Virginia's Shenandoah Valley were. After Early's raid through the valley all the way to Washington in July, Grant put Philip Sheridan in charge of a reinforced Army of the Shenandoah and told him to "go after Early and follow him to the death." Sheridan infused the same spirit into the three infantry corps of the Army of the Shenandoah that he had previously imbued in his cavalry. On September 19, they attacked Early's force near Winchester, and after a day-long battle sent the Confederates flying to the south. Sheridan pursued them, attacking again on September 22 at Fisher's Hill 20 miles south of Winchester. Early's line collapsed, and his routed army fled 60 more miles southward.

Early's retreat enabled Sheridan to carry out the second part of his assignment in the Shenandoah Valley, which had twice served as a Confederate route of invasion and whose farms helped feed Confederate armies. Sheridan now set about destroying the valley's crops and mills so thoroughly that "crows flying over it for the balance of the season will have to carry their provender with them." Sheridan boasted that by the time he was through, "the Valley, from Winchester up to Staunton, ninety-two miles, will have little in it for man or beast."

But Jubal Early was not yet willing to give up. Reinforced by a division from Lee, on October 19, he launched a dawn attack across Cedar Creek, 15 miles south of Winchester. He caught the Yankees by surprise and drove them back in disorder. At the time of the attack, Sheridan was

at Winchester, returning to his army from Washington, where he had gone to confer on future strategy. He jumped onto his horse and sped to the battlefield in a ride that became celebrated in poetry and legend. By sundown, Sheridan's charisma and tactical leadership had turned the battle from a Union defeat into another Confederate rout. The battle of Cedar Creek ended Confederate power in the valley.

Sherman's and Sheridan's victories ensured Lincoln's reelection on November 8 by a majority of 212 to 21 in the electoral college. Soldiers played a notable role in the balloting. Every Northern state except three whose legislatures were controlled by Democrats had passed laws allowing absentee voting by soldiers. Seventy-eight percent of the military vote went to Lincoln—compared with 54 percent of the civilian vote. The men who were doing the fighting had sent a clear message that they meant to finish the job.

From Atlanta to the Sea

Many Southerners got the message, but not Davis. The Confederacy remained "as erect and defiant as ever," he told his Congress in November 1864. "Nothing has changed in the purpose of its Government, in the indomitable valor of its troops, or in the unquenchable spirit

Reproduced from the collections of the Library of Congress.

SHERMAN'S SOLDIERS TEARING UP THE RAILROAD IN ATLANTA

One of the objectives of Sherman's march from Atlanta to the sea was to demolish the railroads so they could not transport supplies to Confederate armies. The soldiers did a thorough job. They tore up the rails and ties, made a bonfire of the ties, heated the rails in the fire, and then wrapped them around trees, creating "Sherman neckties."

of its people." It was this last-ditch resistance that Sherman set out to break in his famous march from Atlanta to the sea.

Sherman had concluded that "We are not only fighting hostile armies, but a hostile people." Defeat of the Confederate armies was not enough to win the war; the railroads, factories, and farms that supported those armies must also be destroyed. The will of the civilians who sustained the war must be crushed. Sherman expressed more bluntly than anyone else the meaning of total war and was ahead of his time in his understanding of psychological warfare. "We cannot change the hearts of those people of the South," he said, "but we can make war so terrible and make them so sick of war that generations would pass away before they would again appeal to it."

In Tennessee and Mississippi, Sherman's troops had burned everything of military value within their reach. Now Sherman proposed to do the same in Georgia. He urged Grant to let him march through the heart of Georgia, living off the land and destroying all resources not needed by his army—the same policy Sheridan was carrying out in the Shenandoah Valley. Grant and Lincoln were reluctant to authorize such a risky move, especially with Hood's army of 40,000 men still intact in northern Alabama. Sherman assured them that he would send George Thomas to take command of a force of 60,000 men in Tennessee, who would be more than a match for Hood. With another 60,000, Sherman could "move through Georgia, smashing things to the sea. . . . I can make the march, and make Georgia howl!"

Lincoln and Grant finally consented. On November 16, Sherman's avengers marched out of Atlanta after burning a third of the city, including some nonmilitary property. Southward they marched 280 miles to Savannah, wrecking everything in their path that could by any stretch of the imagination be considered of military value.

The Battles of Franklin and Nashville

They encountered little resistance. Instead of chasing Sherman, Hood invaded Tennessee with the hope of recovering that state for the Confederacy, a disastrous campaign that virtually destroyed his army. On November 30, the Confederates attacked part of the Union force at Franklin, a town 20 miles south of Nashville. The slaughter claimed no fewer than 12 Confederate generals and 54 regimental commanders as casualties. Instead of retreating, Hood moved on to Nashville, where on December 15 and 16 Thomas launched an attack that almost wiped out the

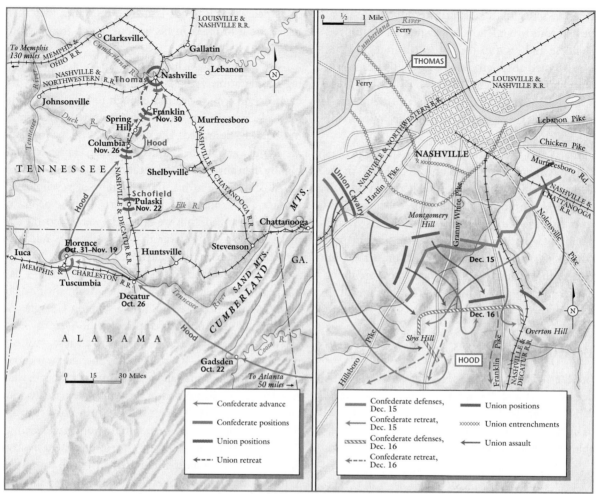

MAP 16.8 HOOD'S TENNESSEE CAMPAIGN, OCTOBER–NOVEMBER 1864 [AND] NASHVILLE, DECEMBER 15–16, 1864
The battle of Nashville on December 15–16, 1864, was the most carefully planned and decisive battle of the war. After Thomas's army drove the Confederates from their first line on December 15 (solid red line), they attacked again and overran the second position (striped red line) on the 16th. The Confederate army virtually disintegrated as it retreated.

Army of Tennessee. Its remnants retreated to Mississippi, where Hood resigned in January 1865.

Fort Fisher and Sherman's March through the Carolinas

News of Hood's defeat produced, in the words of a Southern diarist, "the darkest and most dismal day" of the Confederacy's short history, but worse was yet to come. Lee's army in Virginia drew its dwindling supplies overland from the Carolinas and through the port of Wilmington, North Carolina, the only city still accessible to blockade runners. Massive Fort Fisher guarded the mouth of the Cape Fear River below Wilmington, its big guns keeping blockade ships at bay and protecting the runners. The

Union navy had long wanted to attack Fort Fisher, but the diversion of ships and troops to the long, futile campaign against Charleston had delayed the effort. In January 1865, though, the largest armada of the war—58 ships with 627 guns—pounded Fort Fisher for two days, disabling most of its big guns. Army troops and marines landed and stormed the fort, capturing it on January 15. That ended the blockade running, and Sherman soon put an end to supplies from the Carolinas as well.

At the end of January, Sherman's soldiers headed north from Savannah, eager to take revenge on South Carolina, which to their mind had started the war. Here, they made even less distinction between civilian and military property than they had in Georgia and left even less of Columbia standing than they had of Atlanta. Seemingly invincible, Sherman's army pushed into North Carolina

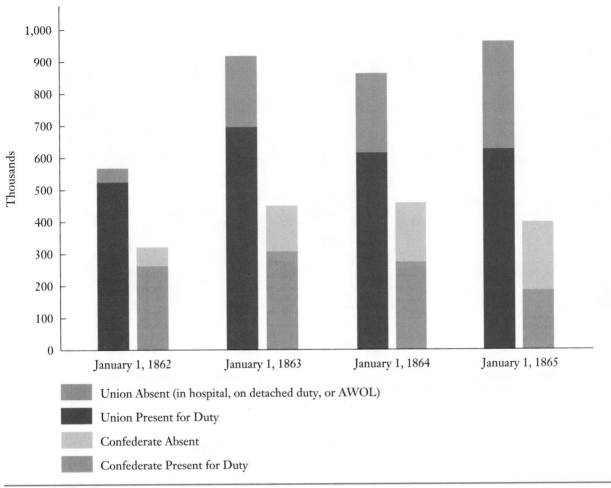

Union Absent (in hospital, on detached duty, or AWOL)

Union Present for Duty

Confederate Absent

Confederate Present for Duty

COMPARATIVE STRENGTH OF UNION AND CONFEDERATE ARMIES

and brushed aside the force that Joseph E. Johnston had assembled to stop them. The devastation left in their wake appalled Confederates. "All is gloom, despondency, and inactivity," wrote a South Carolinian. "Our army is demoralized and the people panic stricken. To fight longer seems to be madness."

But the war would not end until the Confederate armies surrendered, as Lincoln made clear in his second inaugural address on March 4, 1865. In the best-known words from that address, he urged a binding up of the nation's wounds "with malice toward none [and] charity for all." Even more significant, given that the conflict still raged, were these words:

> American Slavery is one of those offences which, in the providence of God . . . He now wills to remove [through] this terrible war, as the woe due to those by whom the offence came. . . . Fondly do we hope—fervently do we pray—that this mighty scourge of war may speedily pass away. Yet if God wills that it continue, until all the wealth piled by the bondman's two hundred and fifty years of

unrequited toil shall be sunk, and until every drop of blood drawn with the lash, shall be paid by another drawn with the sword, as was said three thousand years ago, so still it must be said "the judgments of the Lord, are true and righteous altogether."

The Road to Appomattox

The Army of Northern Virginia was now the only entity that kept the Confederacy alive, and it was on the verge of disintegration. Scores of its soldiers were deserting every day. On April 1, Sheridan's cavalry and an infantry corps smashed the right flank of Lee's line at Five Forks and cut off the last railroad into Petersburg. The next day, Grant attacked all along the line and forced Lee to abandon both Petersburg and Richmond. As the Confederate government fled its capital, its army set fire to all the military stores it could not carry. The fires spread and destroyed more of Richmond than the Northern troops had destroyed of Atlanta or Columbia.

THE FRUITS OF WAR

Several Southern cities suffered enormous damage in the Civil War from Union shelling and from the fires caused by Confederate soldiers when they destroyed everything of military value before evacuating the cities. Such was true of Charleston, where a Northern photographer who entered the city after it fell in February 1865 posed four black children amid the ruins to portray the symbolism of destruction and renewal.

Lee's starving men limped westward, hoping to turn south and join the remnants of Johnston's army in North Carolina. Sheridan's cavalry raced ahead and cut them off at Appomattox, 90 miles from Petersburg, on April 8. When the weary Confederates tried a breakout attack the next morning, their first probe revealed solid ranks of Union infantry arrayed behind the cavalry. It was the end. "There is nothing left for me to do," said Lee, "but to go and see General Grant, and I would rather die a thousand deaths." Lee met with Grant at the house of Wilmer

McLean, who in 1861 had lived near Manassas, where a shell had crashed through his kitchen roof during the first battle of Bull Run. McLean had moved to the remote village of Appomattox to escape the war, only to have its final drama played out in his parlor. There, the son of an Ohio tanner dictated surrender terms to a scion of one of Virginia's First Families.

The terms were generous. Thirty thousand captured Confederates were allowed to go home on condition that they promise never again to take up arms against the

CASUALTIES IN CIVIL WAR ARMIES AND NAVIES

Confederate records are incomplete; the Confederate data listed here are therefore estimates. The actual Confederate totals were probably higher.

	Killed and Mortally Wounded in Combat	Died of Disease	Died in Prison	Miscellaneous Deaths*	Total Deaths	Wounded, Not Mortally	Total Casualties
Union	111,904	197,388	30,192	24,881	364,345	277,401	641,766
Confederate (estimated)	94,000	140,000	26,000	No Estimates	260,000	195,000	455,000
Both Armies (estimated)	205,904	337,388	56,192	24,881	624,365	472,401	1,096,766

*Accidents, drownings, causes not stated, etc.

ABRAHAM LINCOLN IN 1865

This is the last photograph of Lincoln, taken on April 10, 1865, four days before his assassination. Four years of war had left their mark on the 56-year-old president; note the lines of strain, fatigue, and sadness in his face.

United States. After completing the surrender formalities on April 9, Grant introduced Lee to his staff, which included Colonel Ely Parker, a Seneca Indian. As Lee shook hands with Parker, he stared for a moment at Parker's dark features and said: "I am glad to see one real American here." Parker replied solemnly: "We are all Americans." And indeed they now were.

The Assassination of Lincoln

Wild celebrations broke out in the North at news of the fall of Richmond, followed soon by news of Appomattox. Almost overnight, the celebrations turned to mourning. On the evening of April 14, the care-worn Abraham Lincoln sought to relax by attending a comedy at Ford's

Theatre. In the middle of the play, John Wilkes Booth broke into Lincoln's box and shot the president fatally in the head. A prominent actor, Booth was a native of Maryland and a frustrated, unstable egotist who hated Lincoln for what he had done to Booth's beloved South. As he jumped from Lincoln's box to the stage and escaped out a back door, he shouted Virginia's state motto at the stunned audience: "Sic semper tyrannis" ("Thus always to tyrants").

Lincoln's death in the early morning of April 15 produced an outpouring of grief throughout the North and among newly freed slaves in the South. The martyred president did not live to see the culmination of his great achievement in leading the nation to a victory that preserved its existence and abolished slavery. Within 11 days after Lincoln's death, his assassin was trapped and killed in a burning barn in Virginia (April 26). The remaining Confederate armies surrendered one after another (April 26, May 4, May 26, June 23), and Union cavalry captured the fleeing Jefferson Davis in Georgia (May 10). The trauma of civil war was over, but the problems of peace and reconstruction had just begun.

Conclusion

Northern victory in the Civil War resolved two fundamental questions of liberty and power left unresolved by the Revolution of 1776 and the Constitution of 1789: (1) whether this fragile republican experiment in federalism called the United States would survive as one nation; and (2) whether that nation, founded on a charter of liberty, would continue to exist as the largest slaveholding country in the world. Before 1861, the question of whether a state could secede from the Union had remained open. Eleven states did secede, but their defeat in a war that cost 625,000 lives resolved the issue: Since 1865, no state has seriously threatened secession. And in 1865, the adoption of the 13th Amendment to the Constitution confirmed the supreme power of the national government to abolish slavery and ensure the liberty of all Americans.

The Civil War also accomplished a regional transfer of power from South to North. From 1800 to 1860, the slave states had used their leverage in the Jeffersonian Republican and Jacksonian Democratic parties to control national politics most of the time. A Southern slaveholder was president of the United States during two-thirds of the years from 1789 to 1861. Most congressional leaders and Supreme Court justices during that period were Southerners.

In the 50 years after 1861, no native of a Southern state was elected president, only one served as Speaker of the House and none as president pro tem of the Senate, and only 5 of the 26 Supreme Court justices appointed during that half-century were from the South. In 1860, the South's share of the national wealth was 30 percent; in 1870, it was 12 percent.

The institutions and ideology of a plantation society and a caste system that had dominated half the country before 1861 went down with a great crash in 1865—to be replaced by the institutions and ideology of free-labor capitalism. Once feared as the gravest threat to liberty, the power of the national government sustained by a large army had achieved the greatest triumph of liberty in American history. With victory and peace in 1865, the reunited nation turned its attention to the issue of equality.

SUGGESTED READINGS

Several studies offer important information and insights about questions of strategy and command in military operations: **Joseph G. Glatthaar,** *Partners in Command: The Relationships between Leaders in the Civil War* (1993); **Richard M. McMurry,** *Two Great Rebel Armies* (1989); **Michael C. Adams,** *Our Masters the Rebels: A Speculation on Union Military Defeat in the East, 1861–1865* (1978), reissued under the title *Fighting for Defeat* (1992); **Mark Grimsley,** *The Hard Hand of War: Union Military Policy toward Southern Civilians, 1861–1865* (1995); and **Gary W. Gallagher,** *The Confederate War* (1997). Of the many books about black soldiers in the Union army, the most useful is **Joseph T. Glatthaar,** *Forged in Battle: The Civil War Alliance of Black Soldiers and White Officers* (1990). The Confederate debate about enlisting and freeing slave soldiers is chronicled in **Robert Durden,** *The Gray and the Black: The Confederate Debate on Emancipation* (1972). Conscription in the Confederacy and Union is treated in **Albert B. Moore,** *Conscription and Conflict in the Confederacy* (1924), and **James W. Geary,** *We Need Men: The Union Draft in the Civil War* (1991).

For the draft riots in New York, see **Adrian Cook,** *The Armies of the Streets: The New York Draft Riots of 1863* (1974). The best study of the civil liberties issue in the North is **Mark E. Neely, Jr.,** *The Fate of Liberty: Abraham Lincoln and Civil Liberties* (1990), and the same author has covered the same issue in the Confederacy in *Southern Rights: Political Prisoners and the Myth of Confederate Constitutionalism* (1999). For Civil War medicine, **Alfred Jay Bollet,** *Civil War Medicine: Challenges and Triumphs* (2002) is indispensable. A succinct account of the emancipation issue is **Ira Berlin, et al.,** *Slaves No More: Three Essays on Emancipation and the Civil War* (1992).

The activities of women in the U.S. Sanitary Commission, as spies, and even as soldiers, are covered in **Jeanie Attie,** *Patriotic Toil: Northern Women and the Civil War* (1998); **Elizabeth D. Leonard,** *All the Daring of a Soldier: Women of the Civil War Armies* (1999); and **Deanne Blanton and Lauren M. Cook,** *They Fought Like Demons: Women Soldiers in the American Civil War* (2002).

AMERICAN JOURNEY ONLINE
AND
 INFOTRAC COLLEGE EDITION

Visit the source collections at www.ajaccess.wadsworth.com and
infotrac.thomsonlearning.com and use the Search function with
the following key terms to explore documents, images, audio
and video clips, articles, and commentary related to the material
in this chapter.

African American soldiers · Battle of Antietam
Civil War women · Battle of Chancellorsville
Abraham Lincoln · Battle of Gettysburg
George B. McClellan · Battle of Vicksburg
Horace Greeley

GRADE AIDS

**Visit the Liberty Equality Power Companion Web Site for resources specific to
this textbook:** http://history.wadsworth.com/murrin_LEP4e

The CD in the back of this book and the U.S. History Resource Center at
http://history.wadsworth.com/u.s./ offer a variety of tools to help you succeed in
this course, including access to quizzes; images; documents; interactive simulations,
maps, and timelines; movie explorations; and a wealth of other sources.

Chapter 17

Reconstruction, 1863–1877

SUNDAY MORNING IN VIRGINIA

This painting by Winslow Homer (1877) of four young black people and the grandmother of two of them is full of symbolism that illustrates important themes in both slavery and Reconstruction. The two lighter-skinned children, probably siblings, are reading the Bible while the dark-skinned children on either side—also probably brother and sister—follow along as they too learn to read. The grandmother listens with a wistful look into the distance, perhaps wishing that she was young enough to acquire the powerful tool of literacy denied to slaves. The religiosity of freedpeople, their humble homes, the partly white ancestry of some, and their thirst for education all are portrayed in this splendid painting.

CHAPTER OUTLINE

From the beginning of the Civil War, the North fought to "reconstruct" the Union. Lincoln first attempted to restore the Union as it had existed before 1861, but once the abolition of slavery became a Northern war aim, the Union could never be reconstructed on its old foundations. Instead, it must experience a "new birth of freedom," as Lincoln had said at the dedication of the military cemetery at Gettysburg.

But precisely what did "a new birth of freedom" mean? At the very least, it meant the end of slavery. The slave states would be reconstructed on a free-labor basis. But what would liberty look like for the 4 million freed slaves? Would they become citizens equal to their former masters in the eyes of the law? Would they have the right to vote? Should Confederate leaders and soldiers be punished for treason? On what terms should the Confederate states return to the Union? What would be the powers of the states and of the national government in a reconstructed Union?

CHAPTER FOCUS

♦ What were the positions of Presidents Abraham Lincoln and Andrew Johnson and of moderate and radical Republicans in Congress on the issues of restoring the South to the Union and protecting the rights of freed slaves?

♦ Why was Andrew Johnson impeached? Why was he acquitted?

♦ What were the achievements of Reconstruction? What were its failures?

♦ Why did a majority of the Northern people and their political leaders turn against continued federal involvement in Southern Reconstruction in the 1870s?

Wartime Reconstruction

Lincoln pondered the problems of Reconstruction long and hard. At first he feared that whites in the South would never extend equal rights to the freed slaves. After all, even most Northern states denied full civil equality to the few black people within their borders. In 1862 and 1863, Lincoln encouraged freedpeople to emigrate to all-black countries such as Haiti, where they would have a chance to get ahead without having to face the racism of whites. Black leaders, abolitionists, and many Republicans objected to that policy. Black people were Americans, they asserted. Why should they not have the rights of American citizens instead of being urged to leave the country?

Lincoln eventually acknowledged the logic and justice of that view, but in beginning the process of reconstruction, he first reached out to Southern *whites* whose allegiance to the Confederacy was lukewarm. On December 8, 1863, Lincoln issued his Proclamation of Amnesty and Reconstruction, which offered presidential pardon to Southern whites (with the exception of Confederate government officials and high-ranking military officers) who took an oath of allegiance to the United States and accepted the abolition of slavery. In any state where the number of white males aged 21 or older who took this oath equaled 10 percent of the number of voters in 1860, that nucleus could reestablish a state government to which Lincoln promised presidential recognition.

Because the war was still raging, this policy could be carried out only where Union troops controlled substantial portions of a Confederate state: Louisiana, Arkansas, and Tennessee in early 1864. Nevertheless, Lincoln hoped that once the process had begun in those areas, it might snowball as Union military victories convinced more and more Confederates that their cause was hopeless. In the end, those military victories were long delayed, and in most parts of the South, reconstruction did not begin until 1865.

Another problem that slowed the process was growing opposition within Lincoln's own party. Many Republicans believed that white men who had fought *against* the Union should not be rewarded with restoration of their political rights while black men who had fought *for* the Union were denied those rights. The Proclamation of Reconstruction had stated that

> any provision which may be adopted by [a reconstructed] State government in relation to the freed people of such State, which shall recognize and declare their permanent freedom, provide for their education, and which may yet be consistent, as a temporary arrangement, with their present condition as a laboring, landless, and homeless class, will not be objected to by the national Executive.

CHRONOLOGY

1863 Lincoln issues Proclamation of Amnesty and Reconstruction

1864 Congress passes Wade-Davis bill; Lincoln kills it by pocket veto

1865 Congress establishes Freedmen's Bureau • Andrew Johnson becomes president, announces his reconstruction plan • Southern states enact Black Codes • Congress refuses to seat Southern congressmen elected under Johnson's plan

1866 Congress passes civil rights bill and expands Freedmen's Bureau over Johnson's vetoes • Race riots in Memphis and New Orleans • Congress approves 14th Amendment • Republicans increase congressional majority in fall elections

1867 Congress passes Reconstruction acts over Johnson's vetoes • Congress passes Tenure of Office Act over Johnson's veto

1868 Most Southern senators and representatives readmitted to Congress under congressional plan of Reconstruction • Andrew Johnson impeached but not convicted • Ulysses S. Grant elected president • 14th Amendment is ratified

1870 15th Amendment is ratified

1871 Congress passes Ku Klux Klan Act

1872 Liberal Republicans defect from party • Grant wins reelection

1873 Economic depression begins with the Panic

1874 Democrats win control of House of Representatives

1875 Democrats implement Mississippi Plan • Congress passes civil rights act

1876 Centennial celebration in Philadelphia • Disputed presidential election causes constitutional crisis

1877 Compromise of 1877 installs Rutherford B. Hayes as president • Hayes withdraws troops from South

1883 Supreme Court declares civil rights act of 1875 unconstitutional

This seemed to mean that white landowners and former slaveholders could adopt labor regulations and other measures to control former slaves, so long as they recognized their freedom and made minimal provision for their education.

Radical Republicans and Reconstruction

These changes were radical advances over slavery, but for many Republicans they were not radical enough. Led by Thaddeus Stevens in the House and Charles Sumner in the Senate, the radical Republicans wanted to go much

LINCOLN'S FUNERAL PROCESSION IN CHICAGO, MAY 1, 1865

After a public funeral in Washington, D.C., on April 19, Lincoln's remains were transported by special train to New York City and then west to their final resting place in Springfield, Illinois, where Lincoln was buried on May 4, 1865. The funeral train stopped in major cities, where grieving citizens paid their last respects. An estimated 7 million people lined the tracks along the train's 1,000-mile journey, which reversed the route Lincoln had taken from Springfield to Washington, D.C., in February 1861.

further. If the freedpeople were landless, they said, provide them with land by confiscating the plantations of leading Confederates as punishment for treason. Radical Republicans also distrusted oaths of allegiance sworn by ex-Confederates. Rather than simply restoring the old ruling class to power, asked Charles Sumner, why not give freed slaves the vote, to provide a genuinely loyal nucleus of supporters in the South?

These radical positions did not command a majority of Congress in 1864. Yet the experience of Louisiana, the first state to reorganize under Lincoln's more moderate policy, convinced even nonradical Republicans to block Lincoln's program. With the protection of Union soldiers in the occupied portion of Louisiana (New Orleans and several parishes in the southern half of the state), enough white men took the oath of allegiance to satisfy Lincoln's

conditions. They adopted a new state constitution and formed a government that abolished slavery and provided a school system for blacks. But despite Lincoln's private appeal to the new government to grant literate blacks and black Union soldiers the right to vote, the reconstructed Louisiana legislature chose not to do so. It also authorized planters to enforce restrictive labor policies on black plantation workers. Louisiana's actions alienated a majority of congressional Republicans, who refused to admit representatives and senators from the "reconstructed" state.

At the same time, though, Congress failed to enact a reconstruction policy of its own. This was not for lack of trying. In fact, both houses passed the Wade-Davis reconstruction bill (named for Senator Benjamin Wade of Ohio and Representative Henry Winter Davis of Maryland) in July 1864. That bill did not enfranchise blacks, but it did

impose such stringent loyalty requirements on Southern whites that few of them could take the required oath. Lincoln therefore vetoed it.

Lincoln's action infuriated many Republicans. Wade and Davis published a blistering "manifesto" denouncing the president. This bitter squabble threatened for a time to destroy Lincoln's chances of being reelected. Union military success in fall 1864, however, combined with sober second thoughts about the consequences of a Democratic electoral victory, reunited the Republicans behind Lincoln. The collapse of Confederate military resistance the following spring set the stage for compromise between the president and Congress on a policy for the postwar South. Two days after Appomattox, Lincoln promised that he would soon announce such a policy, which probably would have included voting rights for some blacks and stronger measures to protect their civil rights. But three days later, Lincoln was assassinated.

🌐 Andrew Johnson and Reconstruction

In 1864, Republicans had adopted the name Union Party to attract the votes of War Democrats and border-state Unionists who could not bring themselves to vote Republican. For the same reason, they also nominated Andrew Johnson of Tennessee as Lincoln's running mate.

Of "poor white" heritage, Johnson had clawed his way up in the rough-and-tumble politics of east Tennessee. This region of small farms and few slaves held little love for the planters who controlled the state. Andrew Johnson denounced the planters as "stuck-up aristocrats" who had no empathy with the Southern yeomen for whom Johnson became a self-appointed spokesman. Johnson, although a Democrat, was the only senator from a seceding state who refused to support the Confederacy. For this stance, the Republicans rewarded him with the vice presidential nomination, hoping to attract the votes of pro-war Democrats and upper-South Unionists.

Booth's bullet therefore elevated to the presidency a man who still thought of himself as primarily a Democrat and a Southerner. The trouble this might cause in a party that was mostly Republican and Northern was not immediately apparent, however. In fact, Johnson's enmity toward the "stuck-up aristocrats" whom he blamed for leading the South into secession prompted him to utter dire threats against "traitors." "Treason is a crime and must be made odious," he said soon after becoming president. "Traitors must be impoverished. . . . They must not only be punished, but their social power must be destroyed."

Radical Republicans liked the sound of this pronouncement. It seemed to promise the type of reconstruction they favored—one that would deny political power to ex-Confederates and would enfranchise blacks. They envisioned a coalition between these new black voters and the small minority of Southern whites who had never supported the Confederacy. These men could be expected to vote Republican. Republican governments in Southern states would guarantee freedom and would pass laws to provide civil rights and economic opportunity for freed slaves. Not incidentally, they would also strengthen the Republican Party nationally.

Johnson's Policy

Radical Republicans, with a combination of pragmatic, partisan, and idealistic motives, prepared to implement a progressive reconstruction policy, but Johnson unexpectedly refused to cooperate. Instead of calling Congress into special session, he moved ahead on his own. On May 29, 1865, Johnson issued two proclamations. The first provided a blanket amnesty for all but the highest-ranking Confederate officials and military officers, and those ex-Confederates with taxable property worth $20,000 or more—the "stuck-up aristocrats." The second named a provisional governor for North Carolina and directed him to call an election of delegates to frame a new state constitution. Only white men who had received amnesty and taken an oath of allegiance could vote. Similar proclamations soon followed for other former Confederate states. Johnson's policy was clear: He would exclude both blacks and upper-class whites from the reconstruction process. The backbone of the new South would be yeomen whites who, like himself, had remained steadfastly loyal to the Union, along with those who now proclaimed themselves loyal.

Although at first many Republicans supported Johnson's policy, the radicals were dismayed. They feared that restricting the vote to whites would lead to oppression of the newly freed slaves and restoration of the old power structure in the South. They began to sense that Johnson (who had owned slaves) was as dedicated to white supremacy as any Confederate. "White men alone must govern the South," he told a Democratic senator. After a tense confrontation with a group of black men led by Frederick Douglass, who had visited the White House to urge black suffrage, Johnson told his private secretary: "Those damned sons of bitches thought they had me in a trap! I know that damned Douglass; he's just like any nigger, and he would sooner cut a white man's throat than not."

Moderate Republicans believed that black men should participate to some degree in the reconstruction process,

From the Collections of the Library of Congress.

ANDREW JOHNSON AND FREDERICK DOUGLASS

By 1866, the president and the leading black spokesman for equal rights represented opposite poles in the debate about Reconstruction. Johnson wanted to bring the South back into the Union on the basis of white suffrage; Douglass wanted black men to be granted the right to vote. Johnson's resistance to this policy as Republicans tried to enact it was a factor in his impeachment two years later.

but in 1865, they were not yet prepared to break with the president. They regarded his policy as an "experiment" that would be modified as time went on. "Loyal negroes must not be put down, while disloyal white men are put up," wrote a moderate Republican. "But I am quite willing to see what will come of Mr. Johnson's experiment." If the new Southern state constitutions failed to enfranchise at least literate blacks and those who had fought in the Union army, said another moderate, "the President then will be at liberty to pursue a sterner policy."

Southern Defiance

As it happened, none of the state conventions enfranchised a single black. Some of them even balked at ratifying the 13th Amendment (which abolished slavery). The rhetoric of some white Southerners began to take on a renewed anti-Yankee tone of defiance that sounded like 1861 all over again. Reports from Unionists and army officers in the South told of neo-Confederate violence against blacks and their white sympathizers. Johnson seemed to encourage such activities by his own rhetoric,

which sounded increasingly like that of a Southern Democrat, and by allowing the organization of white militia units in the South. "What can be hatched from such an egg," asked a Republican newspaper, "but another rebellion?"

Then there was the matter of presidential pardons. After talking fiercely about punishing traitors, and after excluding several classes of them from his amnesty proclamation, Johnson began to issue special pardons to many ex-Confederates, restoring to them all property and political rights. Moreover, under the new state constitutions, Southern voters were electing hundreds of ex-Confederates to state offices. Even more alarming to Northerners, who thought they had won the war, was the election to Congress of no fewer than nine ex-Confederate congressmen, seven ex-Confederate state officials, four generals, four colonels, and even the former Confederate vice president, Alexander H. Stephens. To apprehensive Republicans, it appeared that the rebels, unable to capture Washington in war, were about to do so in peace.

Somehow the aristocrats and traitors Johnson had denounced in April had taken over the reconstruction process.

Instead of weapons, they had resorted to flattering the presidential ego. Thousands of prominent ex-Confederates or their tearful female relatives applied for pardons confessing the error of their ways and appealing for presidential mercy. Reveling in his power over these once-haughty aristocrats who had disdained him as a humble tailor, Johnson waxed eloquent on his "love, respect, and confidence" toward Southern whites, for whom he now felt "forbearing and forgiving." More effective, perhaps, was the praise and support Johnson received from leading Northern Democrats. Although the Republicans had placed him on their presidential ticket in 1864, Johnson was after all a Democrat. That party's leaders enticed Johnson with visions of reelection as a Democrat in 1868 if he could manage to reconstruct the South in a manner that would preserve a Democratic majority there.

The Black Codes

That was just what the Republicans feared. Their concern that state governments devoted to white supremacy would reduce the freedpeople to a condition close to slavery was confirmed in fall 1865, when some of those governments enacted "Black Codes."

One of the first tasks of the legislatures of the reconstructed states was to define the rights of 4 million former slaves. The option of treating them exactly like white citizens was scarcely considered. Instead, the states excluded black people from juries and the ballot box, did not permit them to testify against whites in court, banned interracial marriage, and punished blacks more severely than whites for certain crimes. Some states defined any unemployed black person as a vagrant and hired him out to a planter, forbade blacks to lease land, and provided for the apprenticing to whites of black youths who did not have adequate parental support.

These Black Codes aroused anger among Northern Republicans, who saw them as a brazen attempt to reinstate a quasi-slavery. "We tell the white men of Mississippi," declared the *Chicago Tribune*, "that the men of the North will convert the State of Mississippi into a frog pond before they will allow such laws to disgrace one foot of the soil in which the bones of our soldiers sleep and over which the flag of freedom waves." And, in fact, the Union army's occupation forces did suspend the implementation of Black Codes that discriminated on racial grounds.

Land and Labor in the Postwar South

The Black Codes, although discriminatory, were designed to address a genuine problem. The end of the war had left black-white relations in the South in a state of limbo. The South's economy was in a shambles. Burned-out plantations, fields growing up in weeds, and railroads without tracks, bridges, or rolling stock marked the trail of war. Nearly half of the livestock in the former Confederacy and most other tangible assets except the land itself had been destroyed. Many people, white as well as black, lived from meal to meal. Law and order broke down in many areas. The war had ended early enough in the spring to allow the planting of at least some food crops, but who would plant and cultivate them? One-quarter of the South's white farmers had been killed in the war; the slaves were slaves no more. "We have nothing left to begin anew with," lamented a South Carolina planter. "I never did a day's work in my life, and I don't know how to begin."

Despite all of this trouble, life went on. Soldiers' widows and their children plowed and planted. Slaveless planters and their wives calloused their hands for the first time. Confederate veterans drifted home and went to work. Former slave owners asked their former slaves to work the land for wages or shares of the crop, and many did so. Others refused, because for them to leave the old place was an essential part of freedom. In slavery times, the only way to become free was to run away, and the impulse to leave the scene of bondage persisted. "You ain't, none o' you, gwinter feel rale free," said a black preacher to his congregation, "till you shakes de dus' ob de Ole Plantashun offen yore feet" (dialect in original source).

Thus the roads were alive with freedpeople who were on the move in summer 1865. Many of them signed on to work at farms just a few miles from their old homes. Others moved into town. Some looked for relatives who had been sold away during slavery or from whom they had been separated during the war. Some wandered aimlessly. Crime increased as people, both blacks and whites, stole food to survive—and as whites organized vigilante groups to discipline blacks and force them to work.

The Freedmen's Bureau

Into this vacuum stepped the U.S. Army and the Freedmen's Bureau. Tens of thousands of troops remained in the South as an occupation force until civil government could be restored. The Freedmen's Bureau (its official title was Bureau of Refugees, Freedmen, and Abandoned Lands), created by Congress in March 1865, became the principal agency for overseeing relations between former slaves and owners. Staffed by army officers, the bureau established posts throughout the South to supervise free-labor wage contracts between landowners and freedpeople. The Freedmen's Bureau also issued food rations to 150,000 people daily during 1865, one-third of them to whites.

Southern whites viewed the Freedmen's Bureau with hostility. Without it, however, the postwar chaos and devastation in the South would have been much greater—as some whites privately admitted. Bureau agents used their influence with black people to encourage them to sign free-labor contracts and return to work.

In negotiating labor contracts, the bureau tried to establish minimum wages. Lack of money in the South, however, caused many contracts to call for share wages—that is, paying workers with shares of the crop. At first, landowners worked their laborers in large groups (called gangs) under direct supervision, but many black workers resented this arrangement as reminiscent of slavery. Thus, a new system evolved, called sharecropping, whereby a black family worked a specific piece of land in return for a share of the crop produced on it.

THE FREEDMEN'S BUREAU

Created in 1865, the Freedmen's Bureau stood between freed slaves and their former masters in the postwar South, charged with the task of protecting freedpeople from injustice and repression. Staffed by officers of the Union army, the bureau symbolized the military power of the government in its efforts to keep peace in the South.

Land for the Landless

Freedpeople, of course, would have preferred to farm their own land. "What's de use of being free if you don't own land enough to be buried in?" asked one black sharecropper. "Might juss as well stay slave all yo' days" (dialect in original). Some black farmers did manage to save up enough money to buy small plots of land. Demobilized black soldiers purchased land with their bounty payments, sometimes pooling their money to buy an entire plantation on which several black families settled. Northern philanthropists helped some freedmen buy land. Most ex-slaves found the purchase of land impossible. Few of them had money, and even if they did, whites often refused to sell their land because it would mean losing a source of cheap labor and encouraging notions of black independence.

Several Northern radicals proposed legislation to confiscate ex-Confederate land and redistribute it to freedpeople, but those proposals went nowhere. The most promising effort to put thousands of slaves on land of their own also failed. In January 1865, after his march through Georgia, General William T. Sherman had issued a military order setting aside thousands of acres of abandoned plantation land in the Georgia and South Carolina low

SHARECROPPERS WORKING IN THE FIELDS

After the war, former planters tried to employ their former slaves in gang labor to grow cotton and tobacco, with the only difference from slavery being the grudging payment of wages. Freedpeople resisted this system as being too reminiscent of slavery. They compelled landowners to rent them plots of land on which these black families struggled to raise corn and cotton or tobacco, paying a share of the crop as rent—hence "sharecropping." This posed photograph was intended to depict the family labor of sharecroppers; in reality, most black farmers had a mule to pull their plow.

country for settlement by freed slaves. The army even turned over some of its surplus mules to black farmers. The expectation of "40 acres and a mule" excited freedpeople in 1865, but President Johnson's Amnesty Proclamation and his wholesale issuance of pardons restored most of this property to pardoned ex-Confederates. The same thing happened to white-owned land elsewhere in the South. Placed under the temporary care of the Freedmen's Bureau for subsequent possible distribution to freedpeople, by 1866 nearly all of this land had been restored to its former owners by order of President Johnson.

Education

Abolitionists were more successful in helping freedpeople obtain an education. During the war, freedmen's aid societies and missionary societies founded by abolitionists had sent teachers to Union-occupied areas of the South to set up schools for freed slaves. After the war, this effort was expanded with the aid of the Freedmen's Bureau. Two thousand Northern teachers, three-quarters of them women, fanned out into every part of the South. There they trained black teachers to staff first the mission schools and later the public schools established by Reconstruction state governments. After 1870, the missionary societies concentrated more heavily on making higher education available to African Americans. Many of the traditionally black colleges in the South today were founded and supported by their efforts. This education crusade, which the black leader W. E. B. Du Bois described as "the most wonderful peace-battle of the nineteenth century," reduced the Southern black illiteracy rate to 70 percent by 1880 and to 48 percent by 1900.

🌐 The Advent of Congressional Reconstruction

Political reconstruction shaped the civil and political rights of freedpeople. By the time Congress met in December 1865, the Republican majority was determined to control the process by which former Confederate states would regain full representation. Congress refused to admit the representatives and senators elected by the former Confederate states under Johnson's reconstruction policy and set up a special committee to formulate new

A BLACK SCHOOL DURING RECONSTRUCTION

In the antebellum South, teaching slaves to read and write was forbidden. Thus about 90 percent of the freedpeople were illiterate in 1865. One of their top priorities was education. At first, most of the teachers in the freedmen's schools established by Northern missionary societies were Northern white women. But as black teachers were trained, they took over the elementary schools, such as this one photographed in the 1870s.

terms. The committee held hearings at which Southern Unionists, freedpeople, and U.S. Army officers testified to abuse and terrorism in the South. Their testimony convinced Republicans of the need for stronger federal intervention to define and protect the civil rights of freedpeople. Many radicals wanted to go further and grant the ballot to black men, who would join with white Unionists and Northern settlers in the South to form a Southern Republican Party.

Most Republicans realized that Northern voters would not support such a radical policy, however. Racism was still strong in the North, where most states denied the right to vote to the few blacks living within their borders. Moderate Republicans feared that Democrats would exploit Northern racism in the congressional elections of 1866 if Congress made black suffrage a cornerstone of Reconstruction. Instead, the special committee decided to draft a constitutional amendment that would encour-

age Southern states to enfranchise blacks but would not require them to do so.

Schism between President and Congress

Meanwhile, Congress passed two laws to protect the economic and civil rights of freedpeople. The first extended the life of the Freedmen's Bureau and expanded its powers. The second defined freedpeople as citizens with equal legal rights and gave federal courts appellate jurisdiction to enforce those rights. To the dismay of moderates who were trying to heal the widening breach between the president and Congress, Johnson vetoed both measures. He followed this action with an intemperate speech to Democratic supporters in which he denounced Republican leaders as traitors who did not want to restore the Union

"PARDON, Columbia—'Shall I Trust These Men'?"

© Stock Montage, Inc.

"FRANCHISE—'And Not This Man'?"

© Stock Montage, Inc.

CARTOONS FOR FREEDOM

One of the best political cartoonists in American history, Thomas Nast drew scores of cartoons for *Harper's Weekly* in the 1860s and 1870s advocating the use of federal power to guarantee the liberty and enforce the equal rights of freed slaves. This illustration (1865) is an eloquent graphic expression of a powerful argument for giving freedmen the right to vote: black men who fought *for* the Union were more deserving of this privilege than white men who fought *against* it. Several of the kneeling figures are recognizable Confederate leaders: Alexander Stephens and Robert E. Lee in the foreground, Jefferson Davis to Lee's left, and John C. Breckinridge, Joseph E. Johnston, and Robert Toombs behind and to Davis's left.

except on terms that would degrade white Southerners. Democratic newspapers applauded the president for vetoing bills that would "compound our race with niggers, gypsies, and baboons."

The 14th Amendment

Johnson had thrown down the gauntlet to congressional Republicans, and they did not hesitate to take it up. With better than a two-thirds majority in both houses, they passed the Freedmen's Bureau and Civil Rights bills over the president's vetoes. Then on April 30, 1866, the special committee submitted to Congress its proposed 14th Amendment to the Constitution. After lengthy debate, the amendment received the required two-thirds majority in Congress on June 13 and went to the states for ratification. Section 1 defined all native-born or naturalized persons, including blacks, as American citizens and prohibited the states from abridging the "privileges and immunities" of citizens, from depriving "any person of life, liberty, or property without due process of law," and from denying to any person "the equal protection of the laws." Section 2 gave states the option of either enfranchising black males or losing a proportionate number of congressional seats and electoral votes. Section 3 disqualified a significant number of ex-Confederates from holding federal or state office. Section 4 guaranteed the national debt and repudiated the Confederate debt. Section 5 empowered Congress to enforce the 14th Amendment by "appropriate legislation." The 14th Amendment had far-reaching consequences. Section 1 has become the most important provision in the Constitution for defining and enforcing civil rights.

The 1866 Elections

Republicans entered the 1866 congressional elections campaign with the 14th Amendment as their platform. They made clear that any ex-Confederate state that ratified the amendment would be declared "reconstructed" and that its representatives and senators would be seated in Congress. Tennessee ratified the amendment, but Johnson counseled other Southern legislatures to reject the amendment, which they did. Johnson then prepared for an all-out campaign to gain a friendly Northern majority in the congressional elections.

Johnson began his campaign by creating a National Union Party made up of a few conservative Republicans who disagreed with their party, some border-state Unionists who supported the president, and Democrats. The inclusion of Democrats doomed the effort from the start. Many Northern Democrats still carried the taint of having opposed the war effort, and many Northern voters did not trust them. The National Union Party was further damaged by race riots in Memphis and New Orleans, where white mobs including former Confederate soldiers killed 80 blacks, among them several former Union soldiers. The riots bolstered Republican arguments that national power was necessary to protect "the fruits of victory" in the South. Perhaps the biggest liability of the National Union Party was Johnson himself. In a whistle-stop tour through the North, he traded insults with hecklers and embarrassed his supporters by comparing himself to Christ and his Republican adversaries to Judas.

Republicans swept the election: They gained a three-to-one majority in the next Congress. Having rejected the Reconstruction terms embodied in the 14th Amendment, Southern Democrats now faced far more stringent terms. "They would not cooperate in rebuilding what they destroyed," wrote an exasperated moderate Republican, so "we must remove the rubbish and rebuild from the bottom. Whether they are willing or not, we must compel obedience to the Union and demand protection for its humblest citizen."

The Reconstruction Acts of 1867

In March 1867, the new Congress enacted over Johnson's vetoes two laws prescribing new procedures for the full restoration of the former Confederate states (except Tennessee, which had already been readmitted) to the Union. These laws represented a complex compromise between radicals and moderates that had been hammered out in a confusing sequence of committee drafts, caucus decisions, all-night debates on the floor, and frayed tempers. The Reconstruction acts of 1867 divided the 10 Southern states into five military districts, directed army officers to register voters for the election of delegates to new constitutional conventions, and enfranchised males aged 21 and older (including blacks) to vote in those elections. The acts also disenfranchised (for these elections only) those ex-Confederates who were disqualified from holding office under the not-yet-ratified 14th Amendment—fewer than 10 percent of all white voters. When a state had adopted a new constitution that granted equal civil and political rights regardless of race and had ratified the 14th Amendment, it would be declared reconstructed and its newly elected congressmen would be seated.

These measures embodied a true revolution. Just a few years earlier, Southern whites had been masters of 4 million slaves and part of an independent Confederate nation. Now they were shorn of political power, with their former slaves not only freed but also politically empowered. To be sure, radical Republicans who warned that the

THE BURNING OF A FREEDMEN'S SCHOOL

Because freedpeople's education symbolized black progress, whites who resented and resisted this progress sometimes attacked and burned freedmen's schools, as in this dramatic illustration of a white mob burning a school during antiblack riots in Memphis in May 1866.

NEW YORK, SATURDAY, MAY 26, 1866.

revolution was incomplete as long as the old master class retained economic and social power turned out to be right in the end. In 1867, however, the emancipation and enfranchisement of black Americans seemed, as a sympathetic French journalist described it, "one of the most radical revolutions known in history."

Like most revolutions, the reconstruction process did not go smoothly. Many Southern Democrats breathed defiance and refused to cooperate. The presence of the army minimized antiblack violence, but thousands of white Southerners who were eligible to vote refused to do so, hoping that their nonparticipation would delay the process long enough for Northern voters to come to their senses and elect Democrats to Congress.

Blacks and their white allies organized Union leagues to inform and mobilize the new black voters into the Republican Party. Democrats branded Southern white Republicans as "scalawags" and Northern settlers as "carpetbaggers." By September 1867, the 10 states had 735,000 black voters and only 635,000 white voters registered. At least one-third of the registered white voters were Republicans.

President Johnson did everything he could to block Reconstruction. He replaced several Republican generals in command of Southern military districts with Democrats. He had his attorney general issue a ruling that interpreted the Reconstruction acts narrowly, thereby forcing a special session of Congress to pass a supplementary act

in July 1867. He encouraged Southern whites to obstruct the registration of voters and the election of convention delegates.

Johnson's purpose was to slow the process until 1868 in the hope that Northern voters would repudiate Reconstruction in the presidential election of that year, when Johnson planned to run as the Democratic candidate. Off-year state elections in fall 1867 encouraged that hope. Republicans suffered setbacks in several Northern states, especially where they endorsed referendum measures to enfranchise black men. "I almost pity the radicals," chortled one of President Johnson's aides after the 1867 elections. "After giving ten states to the negroes, to keep the Democrats from getting them, they will have lost the rest."

The Impeachment of Andrew Johnson

Johnson struck even more boldly against Reconstruction after the 1867 elections, despite warnings that he was risking impeachment. "What does Johnson mean to do?" an exasperated Republican asked another. "I am afraid his doings will make us all favor impeachment." In February 1868, Johnson took a fateful step. He removed from office Secretary of War Edwin M. Stanton, who had administered the War Department in support of the congressional Reconstruction policy. This appeared to violate the Tenure

of Office Act, passed the year before over Johnson's veto, which required Senate consent for such removals. By a vote of 126 to 47 along party lines, the House impeached Johnson on February 24. The official reason for impeachment was that he had violated the Tenure of Office Act (which Johnson considered unconstitutional). The real reason was Johnson's stubborn defiance of Congress on Reconstruction.

Under the U.S. Constitution, impeachment by the House does not remove an official from office. It is more like a grand jury indictment that must be tried by a petit jury—in this case, the Senate, which sat as a court to try Johnson on the impeachment charges brought by the House. If convicted by a two-thirds majority of the Senate, he would be removed from office.

The impeachment trial proved long and complicated, which worked in Johnson's favor by allowing passions to cool. The Constitution specifies the grounds on which a president can be impeached and removed: "Treason, Bribery, or other high Crimes and Misdemeanors." The issue was whether Johnson was guilty of any of these acts. His able defense counsel exposed technical ambiguities in the Tenure of Office Act that raised doubts about whether Johnson had actually violated it. Several moderate Republicans feared that the precedent of impeachment might upset the delicate balance of powers between the executive branch, Congress, and the judiciary that was an essential element of the Constitution. Behind the scenes, Johnson strengthened his case by promising to appoint the respected General John M. Schofield as secretary of war and to stop obstructing the Reconstruction acts. In the end, seven Republican senators voted for acquittal on May 16, and the final tally fell one vote short of the necessary two-thirds majority.

The Completion of Formal Reconstruction

The impeachment trial's end cleared the poisonous air in Washington, and Johnson quietly served out his term. Constitutional conventions met in the South during winter and spring 1867–68. Hostile whites described them as "Bones and Banjoes Conventions" and the Republican delegates as "ragamuffins and jailbirds." In sober fact, however, the delegates were earnest advocates of a new order, and the constitutions they wrote were among the

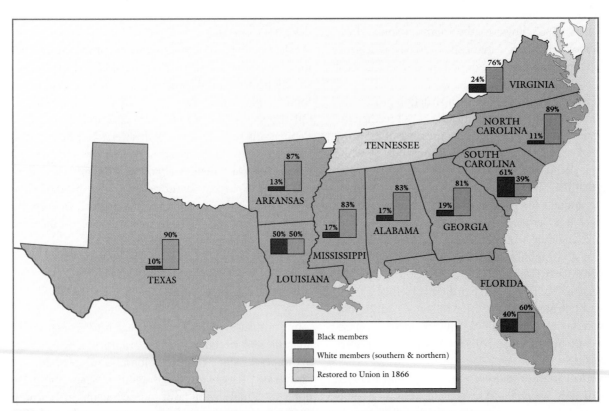

MAP 17.1 BLACK AND WHITE PARTICIPATION IN CONSTITUTIONAL CONVENTIONS, 1867–1868
Although black participation in these state constitutional conventions matched the African American percentage of the population only in South Carolina and Louisiana, the very presence of any black delegates in states where slavery had prevailed three years earlier was revolutionary.

most progressive in the nation. Three-quarters of the delegates to the 10 conventions were Republicans. About 25 percent of those Republicans were Northern whites who had relocated to the South after the war; 45 percent were native Southern whites who braved the social ostracism of the white majority to cast their lot with the despised Republicans; and 30 percent were blacks. Only in the South Carolina convention were blacks in the majority.

The new state constitutions enacted universal male suffrage, putting them ahead of most Northern states on that score. Some of the constitutions disenfranchised certain classes of ex-Confederates for several years, but by 1872, all such disqualifications had been removed. The constitutions mandated statewide public schools for both races for the first time in the South. Most states permitted segregated schools, but schools of any kind for blacks represented a great step forward. Most of the constitutions increased the state's responsibility for social welfare beyond anything previously known in the South.

Violence in some parts of the South marred the voting on ratification of these state constitutions. The Ku Klux Klan, a night-riding white terrorist organization, made its first appearance during the elections. Nevertheless, voters in seven states ratified their constitutions and elected new legislatures that ratified the 14th Amendment in spring 1868. That amendment became part of the U.S. Constitution the following summer, and the newly elected representatives and senators from those seven states, nearly all Republicans, took their seats in the House and Senate.

The 15th Amendment

The remaining three Southern states completed the reconstruction process in 1869 and 1870. Congress required them to ratify the 15th as well as the 14th Amendment. The 15th Amendment prohibited states from denying the right to vote on grounds of race, color, or previous condition of servitude. Its purpose was not only to prevent the reconstructed states from any future revocation of black suffrage, but also to extend equal suffrage to the border states and to the North. With final ratification of the 15th Amendment in 1870, the Constitution became truly color blind for the first time in U.S. history.

But the 15th Amendment still left half of the population disenfranchised. Many supporters of woman suffrage were embittered by its failure to ban discrimination on the grounds of gender as well as race. The radical wing of the suffragists, led by Elizabeth Cady Stanton and Susan B. Anthony, therefore opposed the 15th Amendment, causing a split in the woman suffrage movement.

This movement had shared the ideological egalitarianism of abolitionism since the Seneca Falls Convention of 1848. In 1866, male and female abolitionists formed the American Equal Rights Association (AERA) to work for both black and woman suffrage. Although some Republicans sympathized with the suffragists, they knew that no strong constituency among male voters favored granting the vote to women. A woman suffrage amendment to the state constitution of Kansas in 1867 suffered a lopsided defeat in a referendum. Most members of the AERA recognized that although Reconstruction politics made black enfranchisement possible, woman suffrage would have to wait until public opinion could be educated up to the standard of gender equality.

Stanton and Anthony refused to accept this reasoning. Why should illiterate Southern blacks have the right to vote, they asked, when educated Northern women remained shut out from the polls? It was "infinitely more important to secure the rights of 10 million women than to bring a million more men to the polls," declared Stanton. The 15th Amendment would establish "the most odious form of aristocracy the world has ever seen: an aristocracy of sex." When a majority of delegates at the 1869 convention of the AERA voted to endorse the 15th Amendment, several women led by Stanton and Anthony walked out and founded the National Woman Suffrage Association. The remainder reorganized themselves as the American Woman Suffrage Association. For the next two decades, these rival organizations, working for the same cause, remained at odds with each other.

The Election of 1868

Just as the presidential election of 1864 was a referendum on Lincoln's war policies, so the election of 1868 was a referendum on the Reconstruction policy of the Republicans. The Republican nominee was General Ulysses S. Grant. Although he had no political experience, Grant commanded greater authority and prestige than anyone else in the country. As general-in-chief of the army, he had opposed Johnson's Reconstruction policy in 1866 and had broken openly with the president in January 1868. That spring, Grant agreed to run for the presidency in order to preserve in peace the victory for Union and liberty he had won in war.

The Democrats turned away from Andrew Johnson, who carried too many political liabilities. They nominated Horatio Seymour, the wartime governor of New York, bestowing on him the dubious privilege of running against Grant. Hoping to put together a majority consisting of the South plus New York and two or three other Northern states, the Democrats adopted a militant platform denouncing the Reconstruction acts as "a flagrant usurpation of power . . . unconstitutional, revolutionary, and void."

The End of Reconstruction

Such promises were easier to make than to keep, as future years would reveal. In any case, the Democratic filibuster collapsed, and Hayes was inaugurated on March 4. He soon fulfilled his part of the Compromise of 1877: ex-Confederate Democrat David Key of Tennessee became postmaster general; in 1878, the South received more federal money for internal improvements than ever before; and federal troops left the capitals of Louisiana and South Carolina. The last two Republican state governments collapsed. The old abolitionist and radical Republican warhorses denounced Hayes's actions as a sellout of Southern blacks. His was a policy "of weakness, of subserviency, of surrender," in the words of the venerable crusader William Lloyd Garrison, a policy that sustained "might against right . . . the rich and powerful against the poor and unprotected."

Voices of protest could scarcely be heard above the sighs of relief that the crisis was over. Most Americans—including even most Republicans—wanted no more military intervention in state affairs. "I have no sort of faith in a local government which can only be propped up by foreign bayonets," wrote the editor of the New York *Tribune* in April 1877. "If negro suffrage means that as a permanency then negro suffrage is a failure."

Conclusion

Before the Civil War, most Americans had viewed a powerful government as a threat to individual liberties. That is why the first 10 amendments to the Constitution (the Bill of Rights) imposed strict limits on the powers of the federal government. During the Civil War and especially during Reconstruction, however, the national government had to exert an unprecedented amount of power to free the slaves and guarantee their equal rights as free citizens.

That is why the 13th, 14th, and 15th Amendments to the Constitution contained clauses stating that "Congress shall have power" to enforce these provisions for liberty and equal rights.

During the post–Civil War decade, Congress passed civil rights laws and enforcement legislation to accomplish this purpose. Federal marshals and troops patrolled the polls to protect black voters, arrested thousands of Klansmen and other violators of black civil rights, and even occupied state capitals to prevent Democratic paramilitary groups from overthrowing legitimately elected Republican state governments.

By 1875, many Northerners had grown tired of or alarmed by this continued use of military power to intervene in the internal affairs of states. The Supreme Court stripped the federal government of much of its authority to enforce certain provisions of the 14th and 15th Amendments. Traditional fears of military power as a threat to individual liberties came to the fore again.

The withdrawal of federal troops from the South in 1877 constituted both a symbolic and a substantive end of the 12-year postwar era known as Reconstruction. Reconstruction had achieved the two great objectives inherited from the Civil War: (1) to reincorporate the former Confederate states into the Union, and (2) to accomplish a transition from slavery to freedom in the South. That transition was marred by the economic inequity of sharecropping and the social injustice of white supremacy. A third goal of Reconstruction, enforcement of the equal civil and political rights promised in the 14th and 15th Amendments, was betrayed by the Compromise of 1877. In subsequent decades, the freed slaves and their descendants suffered repression into segregated, second-class citizenship. Not until another war hero-turned-president sent troops into Little Rock (chapter 28), 80 years after they had been withdrawn from New Orleans and Columbia, did the federal government launch a second Reconstruction to fulfill the promises of the first.

SUGGESTED READINGS

The most comprehensive and incisive history of Reconstruction is **Eric Foner,** *Reconstruction: America's Unfinished Revolution 1863–1872* (1988). For a skillful abridgement of this book, see **Foner,** *A Short History of Reconstruction* (1990). Also valuable is **Kenneth M. Stampp,** *The Era of Reconstruction, 1865–1877* (1965). Important for their insights on Lincoln and the reconstruction question are **Peyton McCrary,** *Abraham Lincoln and Reconstruction: The Louisiana Experiment* (1978) and **LaWanda Cox,** *Lincoln and Black Freedom: A Study in Presidential Leadership* (1981). A superb study of the South Carolina Sea Islands as a laboratory of Reconstruction is **Willie Lee Rose,** *Rehearsal for Reconstruction: The Port Royal Experiment* (1964).

Three important studies of Andrew Johnson and his conflict with Congress over Reconstruction are **Eric L. McKitrick,** *Andrew Johnson and Reconstruction* (1960); **Hans L. Trefousse,** *The Radical Republicans: Lincoln's Vanguard for Racial Justice* (1969); and **Michael Les Benedict,** *The Impeachment and Trial of Andrew Johnson* (1973). Two books by **Michael Perman** connect events in the South and in Washington during Reconstruction: *Reunion without Compromise: The South and Reconstruction, 1865–1868* (1973) and *The Road to Redemption: Southern Politics 1868–1879* (1984). For counter-Reconstruction violence in the South, see **George C. Rable,** *But There Was No Peace: The Role of Violence in the Politics of Reconstruction* (1984). The evolution of sharecropping and other aspects of the transition from slavery to freedom are treated in **Roger L. Ransom and Richard Sutch,** *One Kind of Freedom: The Economic Consequences of Emancipation* (1977).

Of the many books on African Americans in Reconstruction, the following are perhaps the most valuable: **Thomas Holt,** *Black over White: Negro Political Leadership in South Carolina during Reconstruction* (1977) and **Laura F. Edwards,** *Gendered Strife and Confusion: The Political Culture of Reconstruction*

(1997). An excellent collection of essays on the Freedmen's Bureau is **Paul A. Cimbala and Randall Miller, eds.,** *The Freedmen's Bureau and Reconstruction* (1999). Both black and white churches are the subject of **Daniel Stowell,** *Rebuilding Zion: The Religious Reconstruction of the South, 1863–1877* (1998).

AMERICAN JOURNEY ONLINE
AND
INFOTRAC COLLEGE EDITION

Visit the source collections at www.ajaccess.wadsworth.com and infotrac.thomsonlearning.com and use the Search function with the following key terms to explore documents, images, audio and video clips, articles, and commentary related to the material in this chapter.

Andrew Johnson	Transcontinental Railroad
Reconstruction	Ulysses S. Grant
Freedmen's Bureau	14th Amendment
Ku Klux Klan	15th Amendment

GRADE AIDS

Visit the Liberty Equality Power Companion Web site for resources specific to this textbook: http://history.wadsworth.com/murrin_LEP4e

The CD in the back of this book and the U.S. History Resource Center at http://history.wadsworth.com/u.s./ offer a variety of tools to help you succeed in this course, including access to quizzes; images; documents; interactive simulations, maps, and timelines; movie explorations; and a wealth of other sources.

reformers. In 1871, the century-long policy of negotiating treaties with Indian "nations" came to an end. From then on, Indians became "wards of the nation," to be civilized and prepared for citizenship, first on reservations and eventually on individually owned parcels of land that were carved out of the reservations.

With their military power broken and the buffalo gone, most Indians had acquiesced in the "reconstruction" that offered them citizenship by the 1880s. Also in the 1880s, the reformers found themselves in a strange alliance with land-hungry westerners, who greedily eyed the 155 million acres of land tied up in reservations. If part of that land could be allotted directly to individual ownership by Indian families, the remainder would become available for purchase by whites. The Dawes Severalty Act did just that in 1887. This landmark legislation called for the dissolution of Indian tribes as legal entities, offered Indians the opportunity to become citizens, and allotted each head of family 160 acres of farmland or 320 acres of grazing land.

For whites who were eager to seize reservation land, the Dawes Act brought a bonanza. At noon on April 22, 1889, the government threw open specified parts of the Indian Territory to "Boomers," who descended on the region like locusts and by nightfall had staked claim to nearly 2 million acres. In addition to the reservation lands legally opened for white settlement, many of the Indians who received individual land titles through the Dawes Act lost these lands to unscrupulous whites through fraud and misrepresentation. Eventually, whites gained title to 108 million acres of former reservation land.

For Indians, writes historian Philip Weeks, the Dawes Act "proved an unqualified failure." Private ownership of land was an alien concept to most tribes. And in many Indian cultures, farming was considered woman's work. To Americanize Indian males by compelling them to forsake hunting for farming was to strip them of their manhood. Some Indians were able to adapt to the new order, but many slipped further into depression, destitution, and alcoholism. Others worked to create a new culture out of the dust of the old.

Life went on for the Indians. They asserted their independence by subverting the power of governmental authorities whenever they could. Navajos forged ration coupons to obtain extra food from federal administrators. They refused to be herded into close living quarters as the administrators demanded. Instead, they followed traditional practices and built their homes far apart. Lakota Indians tricked census takers to obtain more provisions from reservation authorities. They would file past federal census counters giving their real names, then return to the line to be counted again. They would offer derisive fictitious names, such as the Lakota equivalent of "Dirty Prick."

Indians also found ways to reconstitute Native American cultures after the destruction of the buffalo. They created new rituals or borrowed rituals from other tribes to explain the changed world they had to negotiate. The Utes turned to the hallucinogenic drug peyote to commune with the spirit world and declare their difference from whites. The Navajo refused to accept white doctors' physical explanations for disease. They adapted the Apaches' ritual cures, the Chiricaha Windway and the Suckingway, to cure illnesses caused by winds, floods, snakes, and witches' darts. Some Indians found ways to use foreign practices to their own advantage. They turned to markets, selling their weaving and pottery, as a means for preserving traditional folkways.

Mexican Americans

Mexican Americans in the West were also forced to adjust to a new order. As with the Indians, some made this transition successfully, but many did not. At the hands of Anglo-American settlers, Mexican Americans lost their land, political influence, and much of their cultural identity. Even as early as 1849 in the northern California goldfields, resentment of "foreigners" provoked violence against Mexican American miners—and the Foreign Miners Tax of 1850 effectively forced Mexican Americans out of the goldfields (even though they were not "foreigners"). As the 19th century progressed, hordes of Anglo-American "squatters" invaded the expansive holdings of the Mexican American elite, who were forced to seek relief in the courts. Although their claims were generally upheld, these legal proceedings often stretched on for years. After exorbitant legal fees and other expenses were taken into account, a legal triumph was often a Pyrrhic victory. In the end, most Mexican American landholders in northern California had to sell the very lands they had fought to keep in order to pay their mounting debts. Similarly, ranchers in southern California had to sell their lands to pay outstanding debts after devastating droughts in the 1860s virtually destroyed the ranching industry. Forced off the land, California's Mexican Americans increasingly found themselves concentrated in segregated urban *barrios*.

The migration of Anglos into eastern Texas had played a role in fomenting the war for Texas independence and in bringing about the war with Mexico (see chapter 13). By the latter half of the 19th century, eastern Texas was overwhelmingly Anglo; most Mexican Americans were concentrated in the Rio Grande Valley of southern Texas. As in California, Anglos in Texas used force and intimidation, coupled with exploitative legal maneuvering, to disenfranchise the Mexican Americans. The vaunted Texas Rangers often acted as an Anglo vigilante force that exacted retribution for the real or imagined crimes of Mexican

Americans. Eventually, Mexican Americans in Texas were reduced to a state of peonage, dependent on their Anglo protectors for political and economic security.

Similar patterns prevailed in New Mexico, but the effects were mitigated somewhat because New Mexicans continued to outnumber Anglo-American settlers. Earlier in the 19th century, international trade along the Santa Fe Trail had strengthened the political and economic status of the New Mexican elites. Now these same elites consolidated their position by acting as power brokers between poorer New Mexicans and wealthy Anglos.

Despite all of these difficulties, Spanish-speaking peoples in the Southwest and California managed to preserve much of their distinctive culture. Moreover, Anglo-American immigrants adopted many Mexican American agricultural methods and mining techniques. Perhaps the most enduring legacy of the Spanish-speaking peoples is to be found in the areas of mining law, community property law, and—most important in the arid West—water law.

The New South

Southern whites began to rebuild their own culture in the decades following Reconstruction. Some refused to let go of the legacy of the defeated plantation South. They celebrated the Lost Cause by organizing fraternal and sororal organizations such as the United Daughters of the Confederacy (UDC). The UDC, like the Daughters of the American Revolution on which it was modeled, was open only to whites who could prove their relation to the "first families" of the South. Its members decorated the graves of Confederate soldiers, funded public statues of Confederate heroes, and sought to preserve a romanticized history of the slavery era. Several white Southern authors became famous writing stories about this fabled South. Thomas Nelson Page's story "Marse Chan" created a national craze for Southern literature in the 1880s. Published in a Northern magazine, the story was written in what Page claimed to be authentic black dialect. An aging freedman told of the glorious days "befo' de wah" when slaves "didn' hed nothin' 't all to do." Such stories made the romanticized Southern plantation, cleansed of the horrors of slavery, an appealing part of the national imagination.

Not all white Southerners revered the Lost Cause. Many looked to the future rather than the past. They attempted to modernize the South's economy and to diversify Southern agriculture. They encouraged Northern investment and the building of new railroads to tie the South into national and international markets. Rather than a Lost Cause, these Southerners looked to a New South.

The Republican Party did not disappear from the South after 1877. Nor was the black vote immediately and totally suppressed. Republican presidential candidates won about 40 percent of the votes in former slave states through the 1880s, and some blacks continued to win elections to state legislatures until the 1890s. Down to 1901, every U.S. Congress but one had at least one black representative from the South. Independent parties occasionally formed coalitions with Republicans to win local or state elections, especially in Virginia.

Even so, "bulldozing" of black voters (chapter 17) continued to keep the southern states solid for the Democrats. In 1880, the Democratic Party hoped to build on this foundation to win the presidency for the first time in a generation. Taking their cue from the Republicans, the Democrats nominated a Civil War hero, General Winfield Scott Hancock. His opponent was another Civil War general, James A. Garfield, who had served in Congress since the war. In an election with the closest popular vote in American history (Garfield had a plurality of only 10,000 votes out of 9 million cast), Hancock carried every southern state, while Garfield won all but three northern states—and the election.

According to legend, Hancock's defeat convinced forward-looking white Southerners that the way to salvation was not through politics. They rolled up their sleeves and went to work to build a New South of commerce, cotton mills, and steel. The legend embodies some truth. A new spirit of enterprise quickened Southern life in the 1880s. Some Southerners even went so far as to acknowledge that the Yankees had shown them the way, and they welcomed Northern investment. Henry Grady, editor of the Atlanta *Constitution,* was the leading spokesman for the New South ideology. In an 1886 speech to Northern businessmen, Grady boasted of the New South's achievements: "We have sown towns and cities in the place of theories, and put business above politics. . . . We have established thrift in city and country. We have fallen in love with work."

Southern Industry

Considerable reality underlay this rhetoric. The South's textile industry expanded rapidly during the 1880s. Along the piedmont from Virginia to Alabama, new cotton mills and company towns for their workers sprang up. The labor force was almost entirely white, drawn from farm families on the worn-out red clay soil of the piedmont. About 40 percent of the workers were women, and 25 percent were children aged 16 and younger. These "lintheads," as wealthier whites called them, labored long hours for wages about half the level prevailing in New England's mills. This cheap labor gave Southern mill owners a competitive advantage. In 1880, the South had only 5 percent of the country's textile-producing capacity; by 1900, it

had 23 percent and was well on its way to surpassing New England a generation later. At first, Southerners supplied most of the capital for this expansion. After 1893, an increasing amount came from the North, as New England mill owners came to recognize the benefits of relocating in the low-wage, nonunion South.

Tobacco was another Southern industry that developed from a regional crop. Most of the initial capital for this effort also came from the South, and unlike the textile industry, many of the workers in the tobacco factories were black. James B. Duke of North Carolina transformed the tobacco industry when he installed cigarette-making machines at Durham in 1885. In 1890, he created the American Tobacco Company, which controlled 90 percent of the market, with himself at its head. After Duke moved to New York in the 1880s, Northern capital played an important role in this regional industry as well.

Railroads and iron were two New South industries that depended even more on outside capital. During the 1880s, railroad construction in the South outpaced the national average. In 1886, Southern railroads shifted their 5-foot gauge to the national standard of 4 feet 8½ inches. This change integrated Southern lines into the national network and symbolized Northern domination of the region's railroads. During those same years, Northern capital helped fuel the growth of an iron and steel industry in the South. In 1880, the former slave states produced only 9 percent of the nation's pig iron; by 1890, after a decade of extraordinary expansion for the industry nationwide, that proportion had doubled. Most of the growth was concentrated in northern Alabama, where the proximity of coal, limestone, and ore made the new city of Birmingham the "Pittsburgh of the South."

The heavy Northern investment in these industries meant that the South had less control over economic decisions that affected its welfare. Some historians have referred to the South's "colonial" relationship to the North in the late 19th century. The low wages prevailing in the South made for inequitable distribution of the economic benefits of industrial growth. Average Southern per capita income remained only two-fifths of the average in the rest of the country well into the 20th century.

Southern Agriculture

The main reason for the South's relative poverty, however, was its weak agriculture. A crucial reason for this problem was low-level investment in farming. Although manufacturing capital increased by 300 percent per capita in the ex-Confederate states from 1880 to 1900, the amount invested in agriculture increased by only 29 percent per capita.

One-crop specialization, overproduction, declining prices, and an exploitative credit system all contributed to

the problem. The basic institution of the Southern rural economy was the crop lien system, which came into being because of the shortage of money and credit in the war-ravaged South. Few banks had survived the war, and land values had plummeted, which left farmers unable to secure a bank loan with their land as collateral. Instead, merchants in the crossroads country stores that sprang up across the South provided farmers with supplies and groceries in return for a lien on their next crop.

This system might have worked well if the merchants had charged reasonable interest rates and if cotton and tobacco prices had remained high enough for the farmer to pay off his debts after harvest with a little left over. But the country storekeeper charged a credit price 50 or 60 percent above the cash price, partly because he had no competition and partly because of the high risk of loss on his loans. And crop prices, especially for cotton, were dropping steadily. Cotton prices declined from an average of 12 cents per pound in the 1870s to 6 cents in the 1890s. As prices fell, many farmers went deeper and deeper into debt to the merchants. Sharecroppers and tenants incurred a double indebtedness: to the landowner whose land they sharecropped or rented, and to the merchant who furnished them supplies on credit. Because many landowners became merchants, and vice versa, that indebtedness was often to the same man. Many sharecroppers, particularly blacks, fell into virtual peonage.

One reason cotton prices fell was overproduction. Britain had encouraged the expansion of cotton growing in Egypt and India during the Civil War to make up for the loss of American cotton. After the war, Southern growers had to face international competition. By 1878, the Southern crop had reached the output of the best antebellum year, and during the next 20 years, output doubled. This overproduction drove prices ever lower. To obtain credit, farmers had to plant every acre with the most marketable cash crop—cotton. This practice exhausted the soil and required ever-increasing amounts of expensive fertilizer, which fed the cycle of overproduction and declining prices.

It also reduced the amount of land that could be used to grow food crops. Farmers who might otherwise have produced their own cornmeal and raised their own hogs for bacon became dependent on merchants for these supplies. Before the Civil War, the cotton states had been nearly self-sufficient in food; by the 1890s, they had to import nearly half their food at a price 50 percent higher than it would have cost to grow their own. Many Southerners recognized that only diversification could break this dependency, but the crop lien system locked them into it. "We ought to plant less [cotton and tobacco] and more of grain and grasses," said a North Carolina farmer in 1887, "but how are we to do it; the man who furnishes us rations

at 50 percent interest won't let us; he wants money crop planted. . . . It is cotton! cotton! cotton! Buy everything and make cotton pay for it."

Race Relations in the New South

The downward spiral of the rural Southern economy caused frustration and bitterness in which blacks became the scapegoats of white rage. Lynching rose to an all-time high in the 1890s, averaging 188 per year. The viciousness of racist propaganda reached an all-time low. Serious anti-black riots broke out at Wilmington, North Carolina, in 1898 and in Atlanta in 1906. Several states adopted new constitutions that disenfranchised most black voters by means of literacy or property qualifications (or both), poll taxes, and other clauses implicitly aimed at black voters. The new constitutions contained "understanding clauses" or "grandfather clauses" that enabled registrars to register white voters who were unable to meet the new requirements. In *Williams* v. *Mississippi* (1898), the U.S. Supreme Court upheld these disenfranchisement clauses on the grounds that they did not discriminate "on their face" against blacks. Most blacks lost the right to vote, and the Republican Party almost disappeared from most southern states. State Democratic parties then established primary elections in which only whites could vote. For the next 60 years, the primary was the only meaningful election in the South.

During these same years, most southern states passed "Jim Crow" laws, which mandated racial segregation in public facilities of all kinds. In the landmark case of *Plessy* v. *Ferguson* (1896), the Supreme Court sanctioned such laws so long as the separate facilities for blacks were equal to those for whites—which, in practice, they never were.

One of the worst features of race relations in the New South was the convict leasing system. Before 1865, most crimes by slaves were punished on the plantations. The Southern prison system was therefore inadequate to accommodate the increase in convicted criminals after emancipation. Most states began leasing convicts to private contractors—coal-mining firms, railroad construction companies, planters, and so on. The state not only saved the cost of housing and feeding the prisoners but also received an income for leasing them; the lessees obtained cheap labor whom they could work like slaves. The cruelty and exploitation suffered by the convicts became a national scandal. Ninety percent of the convicts were black, the result in part of discriminatory law enforcement practices. The convicts were ill fed, ill clothed, victimized by sadistic guards, and worked almost to death—sometimes literally to death. Annual mortality rates among convicts in several states ranged up to 25 percent.

Northern reformers condemned what they called "this newest and most revolting form of slavery." Thoughtful Southerners agreed; an official investigation in Georgia pronounced convict leasing "barbaric," "worse than slavery," and "a disgrace to civilized people." Reform groups, many of them led by white women, sprang up in the South to work for the abolition of convict leasing. They achieved some success after 1900, although leasing was replaced in some states or counties by the chain gang—a dubious improvement.

At this "nadir" of the black experience in freedom, as one historian has called the 1890s, a new black leader emerged as successor of the abolitionists and Reconstruction politicians who were fading from the scene. Frederick Douglass died in 1895; but in that same year, Booker T. Washington, a 39-year-old educator who had founded Tuskegee Institute in Alabama, gave a speech at the Atlanta Exposition that made him famous. In effect, Washington accepted segregation as a temporary accommodation between the races in return for white support of black efforts for education, social uplift, and economic progress. "In all things that are purely social we can be as separate as the fingers," said Washington, "yet one as the hand in all things essential to mutual progress."

BOOKER T. WASHINGTON IN HIS OFFICE AT TUSKEGEE

The most powerful black leader of his time, Washington built an excellent secondary school and industrial training institute at Tuskegee, Alabama, and gained great influence with philanthropists and political leaders. But many northern blacks accused him of acquiescing in segregation and second-class citizenship for blacks in return for the crumbs of philanthropy.

Washington's goal was not permanent second-class citizenship for blacks, but improvement through self-help and uplift until they earned white acceptance as equals. Yet to his black critics, Washington's strategy and rhetoric seemed to play into the hands of white supremacists. The Atlanta Exposition speech of 1895 launched a debate over means and ends in the black struggle for equality that, in one form or another, has continued for more than a century.

The Politics of Stalemate

During the 20 years between the Panic of 1873 and the Panic of 1893, serious economic and social issues beset the American polity. As described in the next chapter, the strains of rapid industrialization, an inadequate monetary system, agricultural distress, and labor protest built up to potentially explosive force. The two mainstream political parties, however, seemed indifferent to these problems. Paralysis gripped the national government as the Civil War continued to cast its shadow, preventing political leaders from grappling with new issues facing the country because they remained mired in the passionate partisanship of the past.

Knife-Edge Electoral Balance

The five presidential elections from 1876 through 1892, taken together, were the most closely contested elections in American history. No more than 1 percent separated the popular vote of the two major candidates in any of these contests except 1892, when the margin was 3 percent. The Democratic candidate won twice (Grover Cleveland in 1884 and 1892), and in two other elections carried a tiny plurality of popular votes (Tilden in 1876 and Cleveland in 1888) but lost narrowly in the Electoral College. During the 20 years covered by these five administrations, the Democrats controlled the House of Representatives in seven Congresses to the Republicans' three, while the Republicans controlled the Senate in eight Congresses to the Democrats' two. During only 6 of those 20 years did the same party control the presidency and both houses, and then by razor-thin margins.

The few pieces of major legislation during these years—the Pendleton Civil Service Act of 1883, the Interstate Commerce Act of 1887, and the Sherman Antitrust Act of 1890—could be enacted only by bipartisan majorities, and only after they had been watered down by numerous compromises. Politicians often debated the tariff, but the tariff laws they passed had little real impact on the economy. Tariffs were still the principal source of federal tax revenue, but because the federal budget amounted to less than 3 percent of the gross national product (compared with 20 percent today), federal fiscal policies played only a marginal role in the economy.

Divided government and the even balance between the two major parties accounted for the political stalemate. Neither party had the power to enact a bold legisla-

---

L I N K   T O   T H E   P A S T

Waving the Bloody Shirt

The Civil War cast a long shadow over the politics of the generation that had fought it. For decades after the war, political speakers in both North and South called on voters to "vote as you shot." In the North, this was called "waving the bloody shirt." Colonel Robert Ingersoll, who had commanded an Illinois cavalry regiment during the war, was a master of this genre; a speech he gave to Union veterans in 1876, urging them to vote Republican in the presidential election, is a classic example.

E*very state that seceded from the United States was a Democratic State. . . . Every man that tried to destroy this nation was a Democrat. Every man that loved slavery better than liberty was a Democrat.*

The man that assassinated Abraham Lincoln was a Democrat. . . . Every man that raised blood-hounds to pursue human beings was a Democrat. . . . Soldiers, every scar you have got on your heroic bodies was given to you by a Democrat.

1. Why did Ingersoll invoke the issues of the Civil War during an election that took place more than a decade after that war had ended?

For additional sources related to this feature, visit the *Liberty, Equality, Power* Web site at:

http://history.wadsworth.com/murrin_LEP4e

tive program; both parties avoided taking firm stands on controversial issues. Both parties practiced the politics of the past rather than the politics of the present. Individuals voted Republican or Democratic in the 1880s because they or their fathers had done so during the passionate years of the 1860s. Every Republican president from 1869 to 1901 had fought in the Union army; the one Democratic president, Grover Cleveland, had not. At election time, Republican candidates "waved the bloody shirt" to keep alive the memory of the Civil War. They castigated Democrats as former rebels or Copperheads who could not be trusted with the nation's destiny. Democrats, in turn, especially in the South, denounced racial equality and branded Republicans as the party of "Negro rule"—a charge that took on added intensity in 1890 when Republicans tried (and failed by one vote in the Senate) to enact a federal elections law to protect the voting rights of African Americans. From 1876 almost into the 20th century, scarcely anyone but a Confederate veteran could be elected governor or senator in the South.

Availability rather than ability or a strong stand on issues became the prime requisite for presidential and vice presidential nominees. Geographical availability was particularly important. The solid Democratic South and the rather less solid Republican North gave each party a firm bloc of electoral votes in every election. But in three large northern states—New York, Ohio, and Indiana—the two parties were so closely balanced that the shift of a few thousand votes would determine the margin of victory for one or the other party in the state's electoral votes. These three states alone represented 74 electoral votes, fully one-third of the total necessary for victory. The party that carried New York (36 electoral votes) and either of the other two won the presidency.

It is not surprising that of 20 nominees for president and vice president by the two parties in five elections, 16 were from these three states. Only once did each party nominate a presidential candidate from outside these three states: Democrat Winfield Scott Hancock of Pennsylvania in 1880 and Republican James G. Blaine of Maine in 1884—both lost.

Civil Service Reform

The most salient issue of national politics in the early 1880s was civil service reform. Old-guard factions in both parties opposed it. Republicans split into three factions known in the colorful parlance of the time as Mugwumps (the reformers), Stalwarts (who opposed reform), and Half-Breeds (who supported halfway reforms). Mugwumps and Half-Breeds combined to nominate James A. Garfield for president in 1880. Stalwarts received a consolation

prize with the nomination of Chester A. Arthur for vice president. Four months after Garfield took office, a man named Charles Guiteau approached the president at the railroad station in Washington and shot him. Garfield lingered for two months before dying on September 19, 1881.

Described by psychiatrists as a paranoid schizophrenic, Guiteau was viewed by the public as a symbol of the spoils system at its worst. He had been a government clerk and a supporter of the Stalwart faction of the Republican Party but had lost his job under the new administration. As he shot Garfield, he shouted, "I am a Stalwart and Arthur is president now!" This tragedy gave a final impetus to civil service reform. If the spoils system could cause the assassination of a president, it was time to get rid of it.

Although a Stalwart, President Arthur supported reform. In 1883, Congress passed the Pendleton Act, which established a category of civil service jobs that were to be filled by competitive examinations. At first, only one-tenth of government positions fell within that category, but a succession of presidential orders gradually expanded the list to about half by 1897. State and local governments began to emulate federal civil service reform in the 1880s and 1890s.

Like the other vice presidents who had succeeded presidents who died in office (John Tyler, Millard Fillmore, and Andrew Johnson), Arthur failed to achieve nomination for president in his own right. The Republicans turned in 1884 instead to their most charismatic figure, James G. Blaine of Maine. His 18 years in the House and Senate had included six years (1869–75) as Speaker of the House. He had made enemies over the years, however, especially among Mugwumps, who believed that his cozy relationship with railroad lobbyists while Speaker and rumors of other shady dealings disqualified him for the presidency.

The Mugwumps, heirs of the old Conscience Whig element of the Republican Party, had a tendency toward elitism and self-righteousness in their self-appointed role as spokesmen for political probity. They were small in number but large in influence. Many were editors, authors, lawyers, college professors, or clergymen. Concentrated in the Northeast, particularly in New York, they admired the Democratic governor of that state, Grover Cleveland, who had gained a reputation as an advocate of reform and "good government." When Blaine won the Republican nomination, the Mugwumps defected to Cleveland.

In such a closely balanced state as New York, that shift could make a decisive difference, but Blaine hoped to neutralize it by shaving a few percentage points from the normal Democratic majority of the Irish vote. He made the most of his Irish ancestry on the maternal side. But that

effort was rendered futile late in the campaign when a Protestant clergyman characterized the Democrats as the party of "Rum, Romanism, and Rebellion." Although Blaine was present when the Reverend Samuel Burchard made this remark, he failed to repudiate it. When the incident hit the newspapers, Blaine's hope for Irish support went glimmering. Cleveland carried New York State by 1,149 votes (a margin of one-tenth of 1 percent) and thus became the first Democrat to be elected president in 28 years.

The Tariff Issue

Ignoring a rising tide of farmer and labor discontent, Cleveland decided to make or break his presidency on the tariff issue. He devoted his annual State of the Union message in December 1887 entirely to the tariff, maintaining that lower duties would help all Americans by reducing the cost of consumer goods and by expanding American exports through reciprocal agreements with other nations. Republicans responded that low tariffs would flood the country with products from low-wage industries abroad, forcing American factories to close and throwing American workers out on the streets. The following year, the Republican nominee for president, Benjamin Harrison, pledged to retain the protective tariff. To reduce the budget surplus that had built up during the 1880s, the Republicans also promised more generous pensions for Union veterans.

The voters' response was ambiguous. Cleveland's popular-vote plurality actually increased from 29,000 in 1884 to 90,000 in 1888 (out of more than 10 million votes cast). Even so, a shift of six-tenths of 1 percent put New York in the Republican column and Harrison in the White House. Republicans also gained control of both houses of Congress. They promptly made good on their campaign pledges by passing legislation that almost doubled Union pensions and by enacting the McKinley Tariff of 1890. Named for Congressman William McKinley of Ohio, this law raised duties on a large range of products to an average of almost 50 percent, the highest since the infamous Tariff of Abominations in 1828.

The voters reacted convincingly—and negatively. They handed the Republicans a decisive defeat in midterm congressional elections, converting a House Republican majority of 6 to a Democratic majority of 147, and a Senate Republican majority of eight to a Democratic majority of six. Nominated for a third time in 1892, Cleveland built on this momentum to win the presidency by the largest margin in 20 years, but this outcome was deceptive. On March 4, 1893, when Cleveland took the oath of office for the second time, he stood atop a social and economic volcano that would soon erupt. When the ashes settled and the lava cooled, the political landscape would be forever altered.

Conclusion

In 1890, the superintendent of the U.S. Census made a sober announcement of dramatic import: "Up to and including 1880 the country had a frontier of settlement, but at present the unsettled area has been so broken into by isolated bodies of settlement that there can hardly be said to be a frontier line . . . any longer."

This statement prompted a young historian at the University of Wisconsin, Frederick Jackson Turner, to deliver a paper in 1893 that became the single most influential essay ever published by an American historian. For nearly 300 years, said Turner, the existence of a frontier of European-American settlement advancing relentlessly westward had shaped American character. To the frontier Americans owed their upward mobility, their high standard of living, and the rough equality of opportunity that made liberty and democracy possible. "American social development has been continually beginning over again on the frontier," declared Turner. He continued:

> This perennial rebirth, this fluidity of American life, this expansion westward with its new opportunities . . . furnish the forces dominating American character. . . . Frontier individualism has from the beginning promoted democracy [and] that restless, nervous energy, that dominant individualism . . . and withal that buoyancy and exuberance which comes with freedom—these are traits of the frontier, or traits called out elsewhere because of the existence of the frontier.

For many decades, Turner's insight dominated Americans' perceptions of themselves and their history. Today, however, the Turner thesis is largely discredited as failing to explain the experiences of the great majority of people throughout most of American history who lived and worked in older cities and towns or on farms or plantations hundreds of miles from any frontier, and whose culture and institutions were molded more by their place of origin than by a frontier. The whole concept of a frontier as a line of white settlement beyond which lay empty land has been discredited because other peoples had lived on that land for millennia.

The Turner thesis also ignored the environmental consequences of the westward movement. The virtual destruction of the bison, the hunting almost to extinction of other forms of wildlife, the ravaging of virgin forests by indiscriminate logging, and the plowing of semi-arid grasslands on the plains drastically changed the ecological balance in the West. They stored up trouble for the future in the form of soil erosion, dust bowls, and diminished biodiversity. Thoughtful Americans began to express concern about these problems in the 1890s, foreshadowing the launching of a conservation movement in the following decade.

The significance of the Turner thesis, however, is not whether he got everything right; in the 1890s, he expressed

a widely shared belief among white Americans. They believed that liberty and equality were at least partly the product of the frontier, of the chance to go west and start a new life. And now that opportunity seemed to be coming to an end at the same time that the Panic of 1893 was launching another depression, the worst that the American economy had yet experienced. This depression caused the social and economic tinder that had been accumulating during the two preceding decades to burst into flame.

SUGGESTED READINGS

Wallace Stegner, *Beyond the Hundredth Meridian* (1954) is a readable and evocative description of the West from the plains to the Pacific. The various western frontiers are described in the following books, whose subjects are indicated by their titles: **William Greever,** *The Bonanza West: The Story of the Western Mining Rushes* (1963); **Edward E. Dale,** *The Range Cattle Industry,* rev. ed. (1969); **William Savage,** *The Cowboy Hero: His Image in American History and Culture* (1979); **Gilbert C. Fite,** *The Farmer's Frontier, 1865–1900* (1966); **Sandra Myres,** *Western Women and the Frontier Experience, 1880–1915* (1982); and **Robert M. Utley,** *The Indian Frontier of the American West 1846–1890* (1984). On the 19th- and 20th-century myths of the frontier, see **Richard White and Patricia Nelson Limerick,** *The Frontier in American Culture* (1994). The Indians' response to the reservation system after the 1860s is discussed in **Frederick Hoxie, Peter C. Mancall, and James H. Merrill,** eds., *American Nations: Encounters in Indian Country, 1850 to the Present* (2001).

The classic study of the New South is **C. Vann Woodward,** *Origins of the New South, 1877–1913* (1951). It can be supplemented by **Edward L. Ayers,** *The Promise of the New South: Life After Reconstruction* (1992). The lost cause ideology is examined in **Gaines M. Foster,** *Ghosts of the Confederacy: Defeat, the Lost Cause, and the Emergence of the New South* (1987). Disenfranchisement of black voters is analyzed in **J. Morgan Kousser,** *The Shaping of Southern Politics: Suffrage Restriction and the Establishment of the One-Party South*

1880–1910 (1974). The rising tide of white racism is chronicled by **Joel Williamson,** *The Crucible of Race: Black-White Relations in the American South Since Emancipation* (1984), which was also published in an abridged edition with the title *A Rage for Order: Black-White Relations in the American South Since Emancipation* (1986). See also **Leon F. Litwack,** *Trouble in Mind: Black Southerners in the Age of Jim Crow* (1998). A readable narrative of political history in the Gilded Age is **H. Wayne Morgan,** *From Hayes to McKinley* (1969).

 AMERICAN JOURNEY ONLINE AND INFOTRAC COLLEGE EDITION

Visit the source collections at www.ajaccess.wadsworth.com and infotrac.thomsonlearning.com and use the Search function with the following key terms to explore documents, images, audio and video clips, articles, and commentary related to the material in this chapter.

Ghost Dance	Black cowboys
Dawes Severalty Act	Sitting Bull
Sand Creek Massacre	Crazy Horse
Jim Crow laws	George A. Custer
Plessy v. *Ferguson*	Battle of Little Big Horn
Wounded Knee	

GRADE AIDS

Visit the Liberty Equality Power Companion Web site for resources specific to this textbook: http://history.wadsworth.com/murrin_LEP4e

The CD in the back of this book and the U.S. History Resource Center at http://history.wadsworth.com/u.s./ offer a variety of tools to help you succeed in this course, including access to quizzes; images; documents; interactive simulations, maps, and timelines; movie explorations; and a wealth of other sources.

Economic Growth

During the 15 years between recovery from one depression in 1878 and the onset of another in 1893, the American economy grew at one of the fastest rates in its history. The gross national product (GNP) almost doubled, and per capita GNP increased by 35 percent. All sectors of the economy were expanding. The most spectacular growth was in manufacturing, which increased by 180 percent, whereas agriculture grew by 26 percent. Manufacturing passed agriculture in value added for the first time in the early 1880s, and by 1900 the value added of manufacturing was almost twice that of agriculture.

Railroads

The railroad was the single most important agent of economic growth during these years. Track mileage increased by 113 percent, from 103,649 to 221,864 miles; the number of locomotives and revenue cars (freight and passenger) increased by a similar amount. Railroads converted from iron to steel rails and wheels, boosting steel production from 732,000 tons in 1878 to 10,188,000 tons by 1900. Railroads were the largest consumers of coal, the largest carriers of goods and people, and the largest single employer of labor.

The power wielded by the railroad companies inevitably aroused hostility. Companies often charged less for long hauls than for short hauls in areas with little or no competition. The rapid proliferation of tracks produced overcapacity in some areas, which led to rate-cutting wars that benefited some shippers at the expense of others—usually large shippers at the expense of small ones. To avoid

"ruinous competition" (as the railroads viewed it), companies formed "pools" by which they divided traffic and fixed their rates. Some of these practices made sound economic sense; others appeared discriminatory and exploitative. Railroads gave credence to farmers' charges of monopoly exploitation by keeping rates higher in areas with no competition (most farmers lived in areas served by only one line) than in regions with competition. Grain elevators, many of which were owned by railroad companies, came under attack for cheating farmers by rigging the classification of their grain.

Farmers responded by organizing cooperatives to sell crops and buy supplies. The umbrella organization for many of these cooperatives was the Patrons of Husbandry, known as the Grange, founded in 1867. But because farmers could not build their own railroads, they organized "antimonopoly" parties and elected state legislators who enacted "Granger laws" in several states. These laws established railroad commissions that fixed maximum freight rates and warehouse charges. Railroads challenged the laws in court. Eight challenges made their way to the U.S. Supreme Court, which in *Munn* v. *Illinois* (1877) ruled that states could regulate businesses clothed with a "public

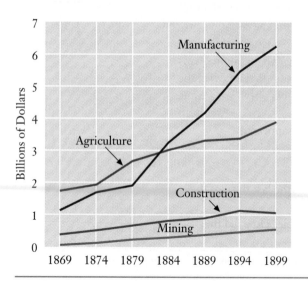

VALUE ADDED BY ECONOMIC SECTOR, 1869–1899 (IN 1879 PRICES)

interest"—railroads and other common carriers, millers, innkeepers, and the like. It was a landmark decision.

The welter of different and sometimes conflicting state laws, plus rulings by the U.S. Supreme Court in the 1880s that states could not regulate interstate railroad traffic, brought a drive for federal regulation. After years of discussion, Congress passed the Interstate Commerce Act in 1887. This law, like most such laws, reflected compromise between the varying viewpoints of shippers, railroads, and other pressure groups. It outlawed pools, discriminatory rates, long-haul versus short-haul differentials, and rebates to favored shippers. It required that freight and passenger rates must be "reasonable and just." What that meant was not entirely clear, but the law created the Interstate Commerce Commission (ICC) to define the requirement on a case-by-case basis. Because the ICC had minimal enforcement powers, however, federal courts frequently refused to issue the orders the ICC requested. Staffed by men who were knowledgeable about railroading, the ICC often sympathized with the viewpoint of the industry it was supposed to regulate. Nevertheless, its powers of publicity had some effect on railroad practices, and freight rates continued to decline during this period as railroad operating efficiency improved.

The outstanding example of the railroads' impact on everyday life was the creation of standard time zones. Before 1883, many localities and cities kept their own time, derived from the sun's meridian in each locality. When it was noon in Chicago, it was 11:27 A.M. in Omaha, 11:56 A.M. in St. Louis, 12:09 P.M. in Louisville, and 12:17 P.M. in Toledo. This situation played havoc with railroad timetables. In 1883, a consortium of railroads established four standard time zones—much the same as they exist in the 48 contiguous states today. They put new timetables into effect for these zones on November 18, 1883. Some grumbling followed about the arrogance of railroad presidents changing "God's time." The U.S. attorney general ruled that government agencies need not change their clocks until authorized to do so by Congress; the next day, he missed a train by eight minutes because he had not reset his watch to the new Eastern Standard Time. For the most part, however, the public accepted the change, and Congress finally sanctioned standard time zones in 1918.

Technology

Technological advances during this era had an enormous impact: the railroads gained automatic signals, air brakes, and knuckle couplers; steel mills added the Bessemer and then the open-hearth process. The 1870s produced the telephone, electric light, and typewriter; the elevator and structural steel made possible the first "skyscrapers" in the 1880s; and in the 1890s, the phonograph and motion pictures provided new forms of entertainment. This era also introduced the electric dynamo (generator), the basis for such household items as refrigerators and washing machines and a new source of industrial power that gradually replaced water power and the steam engine; and the internal combustion engine, which made possible the first automobiles (1890s) and the first airplane flight by the Wright brothers in 1903.

The American Middle Class

The American middle class became conscious of itself as a group situated between laborers and wealthy elites in the decades following the Civil War. New forms of corporate organization, growing per capita income, an increasingly complex social order, and ever faster national communications provided those Americans of moderate means with a set of common interests that distinguished them from other Americans. As they became more aware of these class interests, middle-class Americans attempted to re-create the nation in their own image. In the process, they changed American culture in profound ways.

The Philadelphia Centennial Exposition

The Philadelphia Centennial Exposition of 1876 became a defining moment for this middle class. Americans celebrated their 100th anniversary with an enormous economic fair. Its organizers wanted it to rival famous European fairs, which began with the 1851 Crystal Palace Exhibition in London. Organizers erected 249 temporary buildings, housing more than 30,000 exhibits, on 300 acres of land. Countries from all over the world displayed their economic and cultural products. Anxious to prove their economic might, these foreign countries spent extravagantly. British firms alone spent more than $4 million (in current U.S. dollars) on commercial displays, and Japan sent more than 7,000 packages of material to stock its exhibit. But the country most on display was the United States. Alexander Graham Bell and Christopher Sholes exhibited their new inventions: the telephone and the typewriter. Engineers unveiled the world's largest power generator, the Corliss Steam Engine, capable of driving more than 75 miles of belts and shafts running row after row of industrial machinery. Visitors were awed by recent industrial, agricultural, and cultural innovations, including elevators, monorails, streetcars, linoleum floor coverings, canned food, and

made headway in national periodicals. Paul Laurence Dunbar was a regular contributor to the *Century*, Charles Chesnutt published several stories in the prestigious *Atlantic Monthly*, and Booker T. Washington's *Up from Slavery* first appeared as a series of articles in the *Outlook*. W. E. B. Du Bois, a Harvard-educated and German-trained professor, published essays in the *Atlantic*, which he later collected in his forceful examination of African American life, *The Souls of Black Folk*.

The New Woman

The rise of the middle class changed women's lives. For most of the 19th century, the ideal of "separate spheres" had dominated relations between the sexes, especially among middle-class Americans. The male sphere was one of work, politics, and public events. The female sphere, by contrast, was one of domesticity, moral education, and child rearing. Men and women were not supposed to intrude into each other's spheres. It was "unnatural" for women to work outside the home, to enter the corrupting world of politics, or to engage in pleasurable sex. It was equally "unnatural" for men to devote themselves to child rearing, to "idle" themselves with domestic chores, or to live a life bereft of sexual passion. This doctrine of separate spheres frustrated increasingly educated women who wanted to work and play outside the home. It also meant that men and women spent substantial portions of their daily lives apart from each other. The ceremonial occasions, meals, and leisure activities that brought them together tended to be closely regulated. The lives of the young, in particular, were closely watched, guided, and supervised by parents, teachers, and ministers.

After the Civil War, women challenged the separate-sphere ideal in a variety of ways. Some women, ironically, transformed the ideal by trying to live it out in the rapidly changing world of consumerism. Books such as *The House Beautiful* instructed women on tasteful yet economical styles and methods for furnishing the middle-class home. To procure these furnishings, women had to leave their suburban houses to shop in downtown department stores. Old urban institutions evolved to meet women's new needs for public spaces for rest and amusement. Department stores and hotels added soda fountains to provide women with nonalcoholic drinks (including "tonics" such as the drug-laced Coca-Cola). Restaurants, once off-limits to women unaccompanied by men, began serving a female clientele.

The needs of corporate America for increasingly educated workers led to changes in American education that diminished the amount of time women devoted to child care. School enrollments went up in general. The education of children also expanded both up and down the age scale. The kindergarten movement brought thousands of American children to school at an earlier age than had been deemed advisable in previous decades. At the other end of the scale, the number of high schools grew rapidly in the late 1800s. Middle-class daughters benefited from this explosion of education. The number of female high school graduates rose steeply between 1870 and 1900 from 9,000 to 57,000. Some of the nation's most prestigious women's colleges were founded in the 1870s and 1880s, including Wellesley, Smith, Bryn Mawr, Radcliffe, and Barnard. The number of female college graduates increased in these same decades from 1,378 to 5,237.

Women's rising employment rates transformed the separate-spheres ideal. Women made up 20 percent of the nation's workforce in 1876. The total number of female workers doubled by 1900. Once limited chiefly to factory labor and domestic service, women increased their numbers in professional and white-collar occupations. Childhood education became even more of a female profession than it had been before the Civil War. Women replaced men as telephone operators because they purportedly did not talk back to callers and accepted lower wages. Women surged into new clerical jobs multiplying in corporate offices. At one office, the Metropolitan Life Insurance Company, more than half of the employees were women in the middle 1890s. By 1900, one-third of all clerical positions in the country were held by women. Department stores not only served increasing numbers of female customers, but they also hired women to work the counters that were once reserved for male clerks.

Work gave women a new sense of social independence. Their jobs were distant from their homes and from parental supervision. They received all of their pay in the form of wages, which, although low, heightened their sense of economic freedom. Working women came into close proximity both with one another and with men at work and in public, unsupervised places. To prevent male and female interaction at work, business managers often segregated functions according to sex. All stenographers were women, while men staffed the mailroom. Where men and women worked together, women were limited to strictly defined tasks that usually required little or no expert knowledge. Nonetheless, new forms of employment for working-class women propelled them into the lower middle classes. They, along with established middle-class women, found increased means and time for public amusement.

Women expressed their newfound sense of freedom in a variety of ways. They flocked out of doors. They took up physical exercise—many on a new invention, the modern two-wheeled bicycle. Croquet became a major fad

of the post–Civil War era. Other women pursued intellectual activities, forming book clubs to read the classics of Western literature as well as contemporary American works. Many women formed volunteer associations, from women's professional organizations to social reform efforts such as the Young Women's Christian Association and the settlement house movement.

The New Woman became a dominant figure of American popular culture in the 1890s. She replaced the earlier middle-class ideal of the voluptuous, plump, round-faced matron who wore richly adorned dresses. The New Woman, as drawn by artist Charles Dana Gibson in numerous magazine portraits, was tall, slender, and athletic. She rejected the ornate fashions of her mother's generation. Instead, she adopted a more practical style of clothing, wearing a simple skirt below a shirtwaist fashioned after men's clothing. The boundaries between the once separate spheres of men and women had begun to blur.

The World's Columbian Exhibition

The middle-class revolution culminated in 1893 at the Chicago World's Fair. Opened in the midst of an economic depression, the fair counted almost 30 million admissions at a time when the total U.S. population was 63 million. The Chicago fair, organized to celebrate the 400th anniversary of Columbus's discovery of America, dwarfed the Philadelphia exposition. Some 400 buildings spread across 700 acres housed 65,000 exhibits. The total cost of constructing and stocking the fair was more than $28 million ($550 million in current U.S. dollars). Size alone, however, was not what distinguished the fair.

The Chicago World's Fair was split into two distinct parts with strikingly different atmospheres. The first part, the White City, represented the middle-class ideal for the future of America. It was a majestic realm of neo-classical Beaux-Arts architecture, with broad, open courts, studded with statuary, and interspersed with lagoons, canals, fountains, and parks designed by the famous landscape architect Frederick Law Olmsted. The White City was a triumph of the City Beautiful movement, whose advocates called for urban planning and unity of style to combat the helter-skelter development of the modern city. The colossal white

buildings also had political motives. On the one hand, they stood as memorials to the expanding power of Chicago's corporate leaders over workers, blacks, and immigrants. On the other hand, by appropriating classical European styles, they announced the triumph of the United States as a world-class empire.

The majestic buildings housed miles of displays celebrating middle-class consumerism. Visitors were inundated with exhibits on housekeeping, home furnishings, and even model homes. One exhibit featured the furnished, two-story, wood-frame Workingman's Model Home that instructed young couples on how to achieve a middle-class lifestyle. Another model home displayed the electrified future house. It was stocked with electric stoves, washing machines, doorbells, fire alarms, and lighting fixtures. The Manufacturers and Liberal Arts Building, the largest building in the world in 1893, was one endless department store. Its 44-acre hall resembled an enormous railroad shed with exposed steel arches holding up a glass roof. Under the roof, hundreds of pavilions exhibited a myriad of manufactured consumer goods, all of which bore price tags to allow visitors to compare costs of similar items. Visitors could order for future purchase anything from firearms and Swiss clocks to garden furniture and baby carriages. The new communications technology on display included the phonograph and the kinetoscope (an early film projector). Visitors were awed by the power

From the Collections of the Library of Congress.

CHICAGO WORLD'S FAIR, 1893

A photograph of the canal and some of the exhibit buildings at the Chicago World's Fair in 1893. These structures have an air of permanence about them, but within a few years they were gone.

of electricity. Westinghouse's electric dynamos produced vastly greater amounts of power than the Corliss steam engines of the Philadelphia fair. A quarter of a million electric bulbs suffused the White City with white light after sunset.

The second part of the fair, the Midway Plaisance, was a mile-long collection of amusements, "ethnological" displays, cabarets, wild-animal acts, and exotic dancing. Anthropologists of the Smithsonian had originally planned the Midway as a living exhibition of the cultures of humankind. These displays were to be arranged hierarchically from lowest human civilizations at the west end progressing to the highest at the east end, where the midway abutted the White City. But the conception of the Midway changed several times. When the fair opened, Sol Bloom, an entrepreneur who specialized in popular culture, had transformed the Midway into what one observer called "a strange land, peopled with outlandish folk, echoing barbaric noises, and given over to strange customs, costumes, tongues, diets, dwellings and gods." The Midway, unlike the White City, gave visitors no sense of spatial arrangement or advance planning. The dominating feature, set at the center of the Midway, was the world's first Ferris Wheel. It stood 246 feet high and carried 36 cars, which could hold 60 passengers each. When fully loaded, the wheel spun more than 2,100 people around its axis.

The Chicago World's Fair was a phantasmagoria of the middle class's venerable dreams and repressed desires. While Frederick Jackson Turner gave his famous paper on the closing of the frontier at a conference of historians, Buffalo Bill ran his Wild West Show just beyond the Midway's western gates. Francis J. Bellamy, the editor of a popular magazine for youth, wrote and introduced the Pledge of Allegiance to the American flag at the fair. Numerous staples of the mass market debuted, including the stereotypical faces of Aunt Jemima and Cream of Wheat's Rastus and such goods as Juicy Fruit gum, Postum, and Shredded Wheat cereal. Historian Henry Adams, great-grandson of President John Adams and grandson of President John Quincy Adams, was overwhelmed by what he saw: "[S]ince Noah's ark, no such Babel of loose and ill-joined, such vague and ill-defined and unrelated thoughts and half-thoughts and experimental outcries as the Exposition, had ever ruffled the surface of the Lake [Michigan]."

No one knew what to do with the buildings when the fair closed in November 1893. Built to last only temporarily, none was suitable for any sort of permanent exhibition. A series of small fires and vandalism damaged much of the decorative work and some of the smaller buildings as tramps and transients moved into the remains of the White City. Finally, on the night of July 5, 1894, a massive fire destroyed the great buildings surrounding the central Court of Honor. The specific source of the fire was unclear, but it came in the midst of clashes between federal troops and railway workers striking against the Pullman Palace Car Company. In two hours, the buildings that once housed so many middle-class dreams went up in smoke.

Wealth and Inequality

All of the wonders of economic growth and technological change exhibited at the Chicago fair came at great human cost. One such cost was a widening gulf between rich and poor. Although the average per capita income of all Americans increased by 35 percent from 1878 to 1893, real wages advanced only 20 percent. That advance masked sharp inequalities of wages by skill, region, race, and gender. Many unskilled and semiskilled workers made barely enough to support themselves, much less a family; many families, especially recent immigrants (who formed a large part of the blue-collar workforce), needed two or three wage earners to survive.

The perception of class inequality was even greater than the reality. The estimated number of *millionaires* (a word that came into use during this era) was 300 in 1860; by 1892, the number was 4,000. Many of them practiced what the eccentric but brilliant economist Thorstein Veblen described in his book *The Theory of the Leisure Class* (1899) as "conspicuous consumption." They sent agents to Europe to buy paintings and tapestries from impoverished aristocrats. In their mansions on Fifth Avenue and their summer homes at Newport, they entertained lavishly, sometimes spending on a single party an amount that would have supported a tenement full of immigrant families for a year. These extravagant habits gave substance to the labeling of this era as the Gilded Age. Their well-publicized activities, while millions lived on the edge of poverty, sharpened the growing sense of class consciousness.

Some of the millionaires made their money by methods that critics considered predatory, providing another vivid epithet of the period: "robber barons." Some of the most conspicuous figures who bore this epithet, whether deserved or not, were William Vanderbilt (who once allegedly burst out in response to criticism: "The public be damned!"), Jay Gould, Jim Fisk, and Collis P. Huntington in railroading; John D. Rockefeller in oil; Andrew Carnegie and Henry Clay Frick in steel; James B. Duke in tobacco; and John Pierpont Morgan in banking.

Criticism of the robber barons sometimes focused more on the immense power commanded by their wealth than on the wealth itself. Fisk and Gould bribed legislators, manipulated the stock market, exploited workers,

The Molly Maguires (1970)

**Directed by Martin Ritt.
Starring Richard Harris (James McParlan), Sean Connery (Jack Kehoe), Samantha Eggar (Mary Raines).**

The gritty realism of *The Molly Maguires* offers a compelling portrait of labor conditions in 19th-century coal mines. Filmed on location in the anthracite region of eastern Pennsylvania, the film takes the viewer deep into the earth where Irish American miners labored long hours for a pittance at the dangerous, back-breaking, health-destroying job of bringing out the coal that heated American homes and fueled American industry.

These mining communities constituted a microcosm of ethnic and class tensions in American society. Most of the mine owners were Scots-Irish Presbyterians; many foremen, skilled workers, and police were English or Welsh Protestants; most of the unskilled workers were Irish Catholics. This was a volatile mixture, as vividly depicted in the movie. The skilled miners had formed the Workingmen's Benevolent Association, which had won modest gains for its members by 1873. Many Irish belonged to the Ancient Order of Hibernians, which aided sick miners and supported the widows and orphans of those who died—and there were many such. The inner circle of this order called itself the Molly Maguires, after an antilandlord organization in Ireland that resisted the eviction of tenants. In Pennsylvania, the Mollies retaliated against exploitative owners, unpopular foremen, and the police with acts of sabotage, violence, intimidation, and murder.

The economic depression following the Panic of 1873 exacerbated tensions and violence. The owners hired the Pinkerton detective agency to infiltrate and gather criminal evidence against the Mollies. Detective James McParlan went to work in the mines, gained the confidence of his fellow Irish Americans, and was eventually admitted to the Molly Maguires. For more than two years, he lived a dangerous double existence (foreshortened in the movie) that would have meant instant death if the Mollies had discovered his mole role. In a series of widely publicized trials from 1875 to 1877 in which McParlan was the main witness, dozens of Molly Maguires were convicted and 20 were hanged.

Richard Harris and Sean Connery are superb as McParlan and Jack Kehoe, the Mollies' leader. The real Jamie McParlan courted the sister-in-law of one of the Mollies; the film expands this into a poignant romance between McParlan and a retired miner's beautiful daughter. The love interest fits with the film's effective presentation of McParlan's conflicted conscience and the moral ambiguity of his role as the agent of justice (as defined by the ruling class), which requires him to betray the men with whom he had lived, sung, plotted, swapped stories, and carried out raids. What were McParlan's real motives? The film does not successfully answer that question, but neither does history. Most viewers, however, will take from this movie a feeling of empathy with the Mollies, whose protest against terrible conditions drove them to desperate acts of violence.

© Bettmann/Corbis.

Sean Connery (Jack Kehoe, right) and Art Lund (a fellow Molly Maguire) prepare to dynamite a coal train in *The Molly Maguires*.

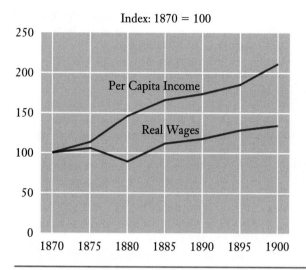

Index: 1870 = 100

REAL WAGES OF WORKERS AND PER CAPITA INCOME OF ALL AMERICANS, 1870–1900

and cheated stockholders in their various schemes to corner the gold market, milk the Erie Railroad for personal profit, and create a railroad empire in the Southwest. Rockefeller either bought out or ruined his competitors, obtained rebates and drawbacks on rail shipments of oil, and created a monopoly in his determined efforts to gain control of oil refining—efforts that culminated in the formation of the Standard Oil Trust in 1879. Carnegie and Frick pushed laborers to the limit in 72-hour workweeks, redefined skill levels and changed work rules, and sped up the pace in steel mills in a ceaseless quest for greater efficiency and lower labor costs. Morgan's banking firm built an empire of leveraged financing and interlocking corporate directorates, often using a New Jersey incorporation law passed in 1889 that permitted holding companies to gain control or dominant influence in several firms.

These activities could be—and were—defended on grounds of entrepreneurial innovation and efficiency, and the enterprises these men created did enable the United States to leap ahead of Britain as an industrial power. By 1913, American manufacturing output equaled that of the next three industrial nations combined—Germany, Britain, and France. The robber barons created wealth for all Americans—poorly distributed though it was—as well as for themselves, and not all of them practiced conspicuous consumption. Professing a gospel of stewardship, Carnegie, Rockefeller, and others gave away much of their wealth to educational and philanthropic institutions, establishing the basis for modern multibillion-dollar foundations.

The Antitrust Movement

Nevertheless, many Americans feared the power wielded by these tycoons. Their monopoly or near-monopoly share of the market in oil, steel, tobacco, sugar, transportation, and other products seemed to violate the ideal of fair competition. To curb that power, an "antitrust" movement emerged in the 1880s. The word *trust* derived from an investment strategy pioneered by Rockefeller, in which the stockholders of several refining companies turned over their shares to Standard Oil in return for so-called trust certificates. The term came to be applied to all large corporations that controlled a substantial share of any given market. In response to pressures to curb such trusts, several states passed antitrust laws in the 1880s.

Because the larger corporations operated across state lines, reformers turned to Congress, which responded in 1890 by passing the Sherman Antitrust Act (named for Senator John Sherman of Ohio, brother of the Civil War general). On the face of it, the Sherman Act seemed to mean business: "Every contract, combination in the form of trust or otherwise, or conspiracy, in restraint of trade or commerce among the several States is hereby declared to be illegal." But what constituted "restraint of trade"? For that matter, what constituted a trust? Did a holding company incorporated under New Jersey's 1889 law violate the Sherman Act? Of eight cases against corporations brought before federal courts from 1890 to 1893, the government lost seven. In 1895, the Supreme Court dealt the Sherman Act a crippling blow in *U.S. v. E. C. Knight Company.* In this case, which concerned a sugar-refining monopoly, the Court ruled that manufacturing was not commerce and therefore did not fall under jurisdiction of the law. For the time being, the Sherman Act was almost a dead letter.

🌐 Labor Strife

The drive for even greater speed and productivity on railroads and in factories gave the United States the unhappy distinction of having the world's highest rate of industrial accidents. Workmen's compensation was almost unknown; many families were impoverished by workplace accidents that killed or maimed their chief breadwinner. This was one source of a rising tide of labor discontent. Another was the erosion of worker autonomy in factories, where new machinery took over tasks once performed by skilled workers and where managers made decisions about the procedures and pace of operations once made by workers themselves. Many crafts that had once been a source of pride to those who practiced them became just a job that could be performed by anyone. Labor increasingly became a commodity bartered for wages rather than a craft whereby the worker sold the product of his labor rather than the labor itself. For the first time in American history, the census of 1870 reported that a majority of

employed persons worked for wages paid by others rather than working for themselves.

Skilled artisans considered this an alarming trend. Their efforts to preserve or recapture independence from bosses and robber barons fueled much of the labor unrest in the 1870s and 1880s. In 1866, the leaders of several craft unions had formed the National Labor Union. Labor parties sprang up in several states; the Labor Reform candidate for governor of Massachusetts in 1870 won 13 percent of the vote. In response to growing labor political activism, several states established bureaus or departments of labor that had little substantive power but that did begin to gather and report data for the first time. These pressures filtered up to Washington, where Congress created the Bureau of Labor in 1884 and elevated it to cabinet rank in 1903. In 1894, Congress also made the first Monday in September an official holiday—Labor Day—to honor working people.

THE RAILROAD STRIKES OF 1877
This illustration shows striking workers on the Baltimore and Ohio Railroad forcing the engineer and fireman from a train at Martinsburg, West Virginia, on July 17, 1877.

© Bettmann/Corbis.

The National Labor Union withered away in the depression of the 1870s, but industrial violence escalated. In the anthracite coal fields of eastern Pennsylvania, the Molly Maguires (an amalgam of a labor union and a secret order of Irish Americans) carried out guerrilla warfare against mine owners. In the later 1870s, the Greenbackers (a group that urged currency expansion to end deflation) and labor reformers formed a coalition that elected several local and state officials plus 14 congressmen in 1878. In 1880, the Greenback-Labor candidate for president won 3 percent of the popular vote.

The Great Railroad Strike of 1877

Railroads became an early focal point of labor strife. Citing declining revenues during the depression that followed the Panic of 1873, several railroads cut wages by as much as 35 percent between 1874 and 1877 (during that same period, the price index fell only 8 percent). When the Baltimore and Ohio Railroad announced its third 10 percent wage cut on July 16, 1877, workers struck. The strike spread rapidly to other lines. Traffic from St. Louis to the East Coast came to a halt. Ten states called out their militias. Strikers and militia fired on each other, and workers set fire to rolling stock and roundhouses. By the time federal troops gained control in the first week of August, at least 100 strikers, militiamen, and bystanders had been killed, hundreds more had been injured, and uncounted millions of dollars of property had gone up in smoke.

It was the worst labor violence in U.S. history to that time; the specter of class conflict frightened many Americans and generated a desperate view of the future.

The Knights of Labor

The principal labor organization that emerged in the 1880s was the Knights of Labor. Founded in Philadelphia in 1869, the Knights began as a secret fraternal society. Under the leadership of Terence V. Powderly, a machinist by trade, the Knights abandoned secrecy in 1879 and emerged as a potent national federation of unions—or "assemblies," as they were officially known. The Knights of Labor departed in several respects from the norm of labor organization at that time. Most of its assemblies were organized by industry rather than by craft, giving many unskilled and semiskilled workers union representation for the first time. Some assemblies admitted women; some also admitted blacks. Despite this inclusiveness, however, tendencies toward exclusivity of craft, gender, and race divided and weakened many assemblies.

A paradox of purpose also plagued the Knights. Most members wanted to improve their lot within the existing system through higher wages, shorter hours, better working conditions—the bread-and-butter goals of working people. This meant collective bargaining with employers; it also meant strikes. The assemblies won some strikes and lost some. Powderly and the Knights' national leadership discouraged strikes, however, partly out of practicality:

A losing strike often destroyed an assembly, as employers replaced strikes with strikebreakers, or "scabs."

Another reason for Powderly's antistrike stance was philosophical. Strikes constituted a tacit recognition of the legitimacy of the wage system. In Powderly's view, wages siphoned off to capital a part of the wealth created by labor. The Knights, he said, intended "to secure to the workers the full enjoyment of the wealth they create." This was a goal grounded both in the past independence of skilled workers and in a radical vision of the future—a vision in which workers' cooperatives would own the means of production. "There is no reason," said Powderly, "why labor cannot, through cooperation, own and operate mines, factories, and railroads."

The Knights did sponsor several modest workers' cooperatives. Their success was limited, partly from lack of capital and of management experience and partly because even the most skilled craftsmen found it difficult to compete with machines in a mass-production economy. Ironically, the Knights gained their greatest triumphs through strikes. In 1884 and 1885, successful strikes against the Union Pacific and Missouri Pacific railroads won enormous prestige and a rush of new members, which by 1886 totaled 700,000. But defeat in a second strike against the Missouri Pacific in spring 1886 was a serious blow. Then came the Haymarket bombing in Chicago.

Haymarket

Chicago was a hotbed of labor radicalism. In 1878, the newly formed Socialist Labor Party won 14 percent of the vote in the city, electing five aldermen and four members of the Illinois legislature. With recovery from the depression after 1878, the Socialist Labor Party fell onto lean times. Four-fifths of its members were foreign-born, mostly Germans. Internal squabbles generated several offshoots of the party in the 1880s. One of these embraced anarchism and called for the violent destruction of the capitalist system so that a new socialist order could be built on its ashes. Anarchists infiltrated some trade unions in Chicago and leaped aboard the bandwagon of a national movement centered in that city for a general strike on May 1, 1886, to achieve the eight-hour workday. Chicago police were notoriously hostile to labor organizers and strikers, so the scene was set for a violent confrontation.

The May 1 showdown coincided with a strike at the McCormick farm machinery plant in Chicago. A fight outside the gates on May 3 brought a police attack on the strikers in which four people were killed. Anarchists then organized a protest meeting at Haymarket Square on May 4. Toward the end of the meeting, when the rain-soaked crowd was already dispersing, the police suddenly arrived

in force. When someone threw a bomb into their midst, the police opened fire. When the wild melee was over, 50 people lay wounded and 10 dead, 6 of them policemen.

This affair set off a wave of hysteria against labor radicals. Police in Chicago rounded up hundreds of labor leaders. Eight anarchists (seven of them German-born) went on trial for conspiracy to commit murder, although no evidence turned up to prove that any of them had thrown the bomb. All eight were convicted; seven were sentenced to hang. One of the men committed suicide; the governor commuted the sentences of two others to life imprisonment; the remaining four were hanged on November 11, 1887. The case became a cause célèbre that bitterly divided the country. Many workers, civil libertarians, and middle-class citizens who were troubled by the events branded the verdicts judicial murder, but most Americans applauded the summary repression of un-American radicalism.

The Knights of Labor were caught in this antilabor backlash. Although the Knights had nothing to do with the Haymarket affair and Powderly had repeatedly denounced anarchism, his opposition to the wage system sounded suspiciously like socialism, perhaps even anarchism, to many Americans. Membership in the Knights plummeted from 700,000 in spring 1886 to fewer than 100,000 by 1890.

As the Knights of Labor waned, a new national labor organization waxed. Founded in 1886, the American Federation of Labor (AFL) was a loosely affiliated association of unions organized by trade or craft: cigar-makers, machinists, carpenters, and so on. Under the leadership of Samuel Gompers, an immigrant cigar-maker, the AFL accepted capitalism and the wage system, and worked for better conditions, higher wages, shorter hours, and occupational safety within the system—"pure and simple unionism," as Gompers called it. Most AFL members were skilled workers, and few were women or blacks—a strategy that enabled the AFL to survive and even to prosper in a difficult climate. Its membership grew from 140,000 in 1886 to nearly a million by 1900.

Labor militancy survived Haymarket, however. Two best-selling books helped keep alive the vision of a more equalitarian social order. Although their impact was less powerful than that of *Uncle Tom's Cabin* a generation earlier (see chapter 13), they nevertheless affected the millions who read them.

Henry George

The first, a book on economics titled *Progress and Poverty* (1879), seemed an unlikely candidate for best-seller status. Henry George, a self-educated author, had spent 15 years

working as a sailor, printer, and prospector before becoming a newspaper editor in California. In his travels, George had been struck by the appalling contrast between wealth and poverty. He fixed on "land monopoly" as the cause: the control of land and resources by the few at the expense of the many. His solution was 100 percent taxation on the "unearned increment" in the value of land—that is, on the difference between the initial purchase price and the eventual market value (minus improvements), or what today we would call capital gains. Such gains were created by society, he insisted, not by the landowner, and the total amount should be confiscated by taxation for the benefit of society. This would eliminate the need for all other taxes, George maintained; it would free productive capital and labor and would narrow the gulf between rich and poor.

Progress and Poverty achieved astonishing success. By 1905, it had sold 2 million copies and had been translated into several languages. But few economists endorsed the single tax, and the idea made little headway. The real impact of George's book came from its portrayal of the injustice of poverty in the midst of plenty. George became a hero to labor. He joined the Knights of Labor, moved to New York City, and ran for mayor as the candidate of the United Labor Party in 1886. He narrowly lost, but his campaign dramatized the grievances of labor and alerted the major parties to the power of that constituency. George's influence cast a long shadow into the next century; numerous Progressive leaders were first sensitized to social issues by their reading of *Progress and Poverty.*

Edward Bellamy

The other book that found a wide audience was a novel, *Looking Backward*, by Edward Bellamy. Like Harriet Beecher Stowe, Bellamy was a New England writer imbued with the tenets of Christian reform. *Looking Backward* is a utopian romance that takes place in the year 2000 and contrasts the America of that year with the America of 1887. In 2000, all industry is controlled by the national government, everyone works for equal pay, no one is rich and no one is poor, there are no strikes, no class conflict. Bellamy was not a Marxian socialist—he criticized the Marxian emphasis on class conflict—and he preferred to call his collectivist order Nationalism, not socialism. His vision of a world without social strife appealed to middle-class Americans, who bought a half million copies of *Looking Backward* every year for several years in the early 1890s. More than 160 Nationalist clubs sprang up to support the idea of public ownership, if not of all industries, then at least of public utilities.

Some of Bellamy's followers called themselves Christian Socialists. They formed the left wing of a broader movement, the Social Gospel, that deeply affected mainstream Protestant denominations (and many Catholic leaders as well) in the rapidly growing cities of the Gilded Age. Shocked by poverty and overcrowding in the sprawling tenement districts of urban America, clergymen and laypeople associated with the Social Gospel embraced a theology that considered aiding the poor as important as saving souls. They supported the settlement houses being established in many cities during the 1890s (see chapter 21) and pressed for legislation to curb the exploitation of the poor and provide them with opportunities for betterment. These efforts gathered strength during the 1890s and contributed to the rise of the Progressive movement after 1900.

The Homestead Strike

The 1890s provided plenty of evidence to feed middle-class fears that America was falling apart. Strikes occurred with a frequency and a fierceness that made 1877 and 1886 look like mere preludes to the main event. The most dramatic confrontation took place in 1892 at the Homestead plant (near Pittsburgh) of the Carnegie Steel Company. Carnegie and his plant manager, Henry Clay Frick, were determined to break the power of the country's strongest union, the Amalgamated Association of Iron, Steel, and Tin Workers. Frick used a dispute over wages and work rules as an opportunity to close the plant (a "lockout"), preparatory to reopening it with nonunion workers. When the union called a strike and refused to leave the plant (a "sitdown"), Frick called in 300 Pinkerton guards to oust them. (The Pinkerton detective agency had evolved since the Civil War era into a private security force that specialized in antiunion activities.) A full-scale gun battle between strikers and Pinkertons erupted on July 6, leaving nine strikers and seven Pinkertons dead and scores wounded. Frick persuaded the governor to send in 8,000 militia to protect the strikebreakers, and the plant reopened. Public sympathy, much of it pro-union at first, shifted when an anarchist tried to murder Frick on July 23. The failed Homestead strike crippled the Amalgamated Association; another strike against U.S. Steel (successor of Carnegie Steel) in 1901 destroyed it.

The Depression of 1893–1897

By the 1890s, the use of state militias to protect strikebreakers had become common. Events after 1893 brought an escalation of conflict. The most serious economic crisis since the 1873–78 depression was triggered by the Panic of

North Wind Picture Archives.

PENNSYLVANIA MILITIA AT CARNEGIE'S HOMESTEAD STEEL MILL, 1892
After the shoot-out between striking workers and Pinkerton guards, the Pennsylvania militia reopened the mills and protected strikebreakers from striking workers. This photograph shows the militia using steel beams manufactured by the mill as a makeshift barricade.

1893, a collapse of the stock market that plunged the economy into a severe four-year depression. Its complex origins included an economic slowdown abroad, which caused British banks to call some of their American loans, thereby draining gold from the United States at a time of political controversy about the American monetary system and nervousness in financial circles. Other causes included declining farm prices and attendant rural unrest and the overly rapid expansion of railroad construction and manufacturing capacity after 1885. The bankruptcy of the Reading Railroad and the National Cordage Company in early 1893 set off a process that by the end of the year had caused 491 banks and 15,000 other businesses to fail. By mid-1894, the unemployment rate had risen to more than 15 percent.

An Ohio reformer named Jacob Coxey conceived the idea of sending Congress a "living petition" of unemployed workers to press for appropriations to put them to work on road building and other public works. "Coxey's army," as the press dubbed it, inspired other groups to hit the road and ride the rails to Washington during 1894. This descent of the unemployed on the capital provoked arrests by federal marshals and troops, and ended in anticlimax when Coxey and others were arrested for trespass-

ing on the Capitol grounds. Coxey's idea for using public works to relieve unemployment turned out to be 40 years ahead of its time.

The Pullman Strike

Even more alarming to middle-class Americans than Coxey's army was the Pullman strike of 1894. George M. Pullman had made a fortune in the manufacture of sleeping cars and other rolling stock for railroads. Workers in his large factory complex lived in the company town of Pullman just south of Chicago, where they enjoyed paved streets, clean parks, and decent houses rented from the company. But Pullman controlled many aspects of their lives, including banning liquor from the town and punishing workers whose behavior did not suit his ideas of decorum. When the Panic of 1893 caused a sharp drop in orders for Pullman cars, the company laid off one-third of its workforce and cut wages for the rest by 30 percent, but did not reduce company house rents or company store prices. Pullman refused to negotiate with a workers' committee, which called a strike and appealed to the American Railway Union (ARU) for help.

Cleveland sent in federal troops. That action inflamed violence instead of containing it. The U.S. attorney general (a former railroad lawyer) obtained a federal injunction against Debs under the Sherman Antitrust Act on grounds that the boycott and the strike were a conspiracy in restraint of trade. This creative use of the Sherman Act, whose purpose had been to curb corporations, was upheld by the Supreme Court in 1895 and became a powerful weapon against labor unions in the hands of conservative judges.

For a week in July 1894, the Chicago railroad yards resembled a war zone. Millions of dollars of equipment went up in smoke. Thirty-four people, mostly workers, were killed. Finally, 14,000 state militia and federal troops restored order and broke the strike. Debs went to jail (for violation of the federal injunction) for six months. He emerged from prison a socialist.

To many Americans, 1894 was the worst year of crisis since the Civil War. The Pullman strike was only the most dramatic event of a year in which 750,000 workers went on strike and another 3 million were unemployed. But it was a surge of discontent from down on the farm that wrenched American politics off its foundations in the 1890s.

© Bettmann/Corbis.

COXEY'S ARMY ON THE MARCH

Reformer Jacob Coxey organized a group of unemployed workers, who traveled to Washington, D.C., as a "petition in boots" to lobby for a public works program to put them back to work in 1894. They failed on this occasion, but their efforts planted a seed that bore fruit during the Great Depression of the 1930s.

The Railway Union had been founded the year before by Eugene V. Debs. A native of Indiana, Debs had been elected secretary of the Brotherhood of Locomotive Firemen in 1875 at the age of 20. By 1893, he had become convinced that the conservative stance of the various craft unions in railroading (firemen, engineers, brakemen, and so forth) was divisive and contrary to the best interests of labor. He formed the ARU to include all railroad workers in one union. With 150,000 members, the union won a strike against the Great Northern Railroad in spring 1894. When George Pullman refused the ARU's offer to arbitrate the strike of Pullman workers, Debs launched a boycott by which ARU members would refuse to run any trains that included Pullman cars. When the railroads attempted to fire the ARU sympathizers, whole train crews went on strike and quickly paralyzed rail traffic.

Over the protests of Illinois Governor John P. Altgeld, who sympathized with the strikers, President Grover

Farmers' Movements

After the Civil War, farmers from the older states and immigrants from northern Europe poured into the territories and states of Dakota, Nebraska, Kansas, Texas, and—after 1889—Indian Territory. Some went on to the Pacific Coast states or stopped in the cattle-grazing and mining territories in between. This wave of settlement brought nine new states into the Union between 1867 and 1896 that almost equaled in total size all the states east of the Mississippi.

The vagaries of nature and weather were magnified in the West. Grasshopper plagues wiped out crops from Minnesota to Kansas several times in the 1870s. Dry, searing summer winds alternated with violent hailstorms to scorch or level whole fields of wheat and corn. Winter blizzards intensified the isolation of farm families and produced loneliness and depression, especially among women. Adding to these woes, the relatively wet years of the 1870s and early 1880s gave way to an abnormally dry cycle the following decade, causing many farmers who had moved beyond the zone of 20 inches of annual precipitation (roughly the 98th meridian) to give up and return east, sometimes with a sign painted on their wagon: "In God we trusted, in Kansas we busted."

RETURNING TO ILLINOIS, 1894

This photograph shows one of the thousands of farm families who had moved into Kansas, Nebraska, and other plains states in the wet years of the 1870s and 1880s, only to give up during the dry years of the 1890s. Their plight added fuel to the fire of rural unrest and protest during those years.

Despite these problems, America's soaring grain production increased three times as fast as the American population from 1870 to 1890. Only rising exports could sustain such expansion in farm production. But by the 1880s, the improved efficiency of large farms in eastern Europe brought intensifying competition and consequent price declines, especially for wheat, just as competition from Egypt and India had eroded prices for American cotton. Prices on the world market for these two staples of American agriculture—wheat and cotton—fell about 60 percent from 1870 to 1895, while the wholesale price index for all commodities (including other farm products) declined by 45 percent during the same period. Not surprisingly, distress was greatest and protest loudest in the wheat-producing West and the cotton-producing South.

Credit and Money

Victims of a world market largely beyond their control, farmers lashed out at targets nearer home: banks, commission merchants, railroads, and the monetary system. In truth, these institutions did victimize farmers, although not always intentionally. The long period of price deflation from 1865 to 1897, unique in American history, exacerbated the problem of credit. A price decline of 1 or 2 percent per year added that many points cumulatively to the nominal interest rate. If a farmer's main crop was wheat or cotton, whose prices declined even further, his real interest rate was that much greater. Thus it was not surprising that farmers who denounced banks or country-store merchants for gouging them also attacked a monetary system that brought deflation.

The federal government's monetary policies worsened deflation problems. The 1862 emergency wartime issuance of treasury "greenback" notes (see chapter 15) had created a dual currency—gold and greenbacks—with the greenback dollar's value relative to gold rising and falling according to Union military fortunes. After the war, the Treasury moved to bring the greenback dollar to par with gold by reducing the amount of greenbacks in circulation. This limitation of the money supply produced deflationary pressures. To complicate matters further, national banknotes backed by the banks' holding of government bonds continued to circulate as money. Because national banks were concentrated in the Northeast, the South and West suffered from downward pressures on prices they received for their crops because of money scarcity. Western farmers were particularly vociferous in their protests against this situation, which introduced a new sectional conflict into politics—not North against South, but East against West.

Because parity between greenbacks and gold would not be reached until 1879, a controversy arose in the postwar years over whether Union war bonds should be paid off in greenbacks or in gold. Congress resolved this issue in 1869 by passing the Public Credit Act, which required

Index: 1913 = 100

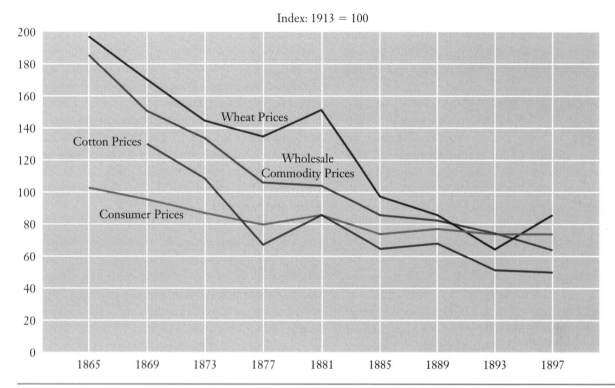

WHOLESALE AND CONSUMER PRICE INDEXES, 1865–1897

payment in gold. Because little silver had been coined into money for years, Congress enacted a law in 1873 that ended the coinage of silver dollars, thus putting the United States on the road to joining the international gold standard. In 1874, President Grant vetoed a bill sponsored by antideflation western congressmen to increase the number of greenbacks in circulation, setting the stage for enactment of the important Specie Resumption Act in 1875. When the provisions of this act went fully into effect on January 1, 1879, the U.S. dollar reached par with the gold dollar on the international market.

Grant's role in bringing about these steps toward "sound money" is more important than is generally recognized, but the benefits of his achievement were sharply debated then and remain controversial today. On the one hand, they strengthened the dollar, placed government credit on a firm footing, and helped create a financial structure for the remarkable economic growth that tripled the GNP during the last quarter of the 19th century. On the other hand, the restraints on money supply hurt the rural economy in the South and West; they hurt debtors who found that deflation enlarged their debts by increasing the value of greenbacks; and they probably worsened the two major depressions of the era (1873–78 and 1893–97) by constraining credit.

The Greenback and Silver Movements

Many farmers in 1876 and 1880 supported the Greenback Party, whose platform called for the issuance of more U.S. Treasury notes (greenbacks). Even more popular was the movement for "free silver." Until 1873, government mints had coined both silver and gold dollars at a ratio of 16 to 1—that is, 16 ounces of silver were equal in value to one ounce of gold. However, when new discoveries of gold in the West after 1848 placed more gold in circulation relative to silver, that ratio undervalued silver, so that little was being sold for coinage. This was the principal reason for the law of 1873 demonetizing silver, except for small coins. Antideflationists later branded this law as "the Crime of 1873"—a conspiracy to destroy silver, the people's money, in favor of gold, the bankers' money.

Ironically, just when the law of 1873 was enacted, the production of new silver mines began to increase dramatically, which soon brought the price of silver below the old ratio of 16 to 1. Silver miners joined with farmers to demand a return to silver dollars. In 1878, Congress responded by passing, over President Hayes's veto, the Bland-Allison Act requiring the Treasury to purchase and coin not less than $2 million nor more than $4 million of

silver monthly. Once again, silver dollars flowed from the mint, but those amounts failed to absorb the increasing production of silver and did little, if anything, to slow deflation. The market price of silver dropped to a ratio of 20 to 1.

Pressure for "free silver"—that is, for government purchase of all silver offered for sale at a price of 16 to 1 and its coinage into silver dollars—continued through the 1880s. The admission of five new western states in 1889 and 1890 contributed to the passage of the Sherman Silver Purchase Act in 1890. That act increased the amount of silver coinage, but not at the 16-to-1 ratio. Even so, it went too far to suit "gold bugs," who wanted to keep the United States on the international gold standard.

President Cleveland blamed the Panic of 1893 on the Sherman Silver Purchase Act, which caused a run on the Treasury's gold reserves triggered by uncertainty over the future of the gold standard. Cleveland called a special session of Congress in 1893 and persuaded it to repeal the Sherman Silver Purchase Act, setting the stage for the most bitter political contest in a generation.

The Farmers' Alliance

Agrarian reformers supported the free silver movement, but many had additional grievances concerning problems of credit, railroad rates, and the exploitation of workers and farmers by the "money power." A new farmers' organization emerged in the 1880s, starting in Texas as the Southern Farmers' Alliance and expanding into other southern states and the North. By 1890, it had evolved into the National Farmers' Alliance and Industrial Union, which was affiliated with the Colored Farmers' Alliance and also with the Knights of Labor.

Reaching out to 2 million farm families, the Alliance set up marketing cooperatives to eliminate the middlemen who profited as "parasites" on the backs of farmers. The Alliance served the social needs of farm families as well as their economic needs. Alliance farm families came together in what one historian has termed a "movement culture" that helped overcome their isolation, especially in the sparsely settled regions of the West. The Alliance also gave farmers a sense of pride and solidarity to counter the image of "hick" and "hayseed" being purveyed by an increasingly urban American culture.

The Farmers' Alliance developed a comprehensive political agenda. At a national convention in Ocala, Florida, in December 1890, it set forth these objectives: (1) a graduated income tax; (2) direct election of U.S. senators (instead of election by state legislatures); (3) free and unlimited coinage of silver at a ratio of 16 to 1; (4) effective government control and, if necessary, ownership of railroad, telegraph, and telephone companies; and (5) the establishment of "subtreasuries" (federal warehouses) for the storage of crops, with government loans at 2 percent interest on those crops. The most important of these goals, especially for southern farmers, was the subtreasuries. Government storage would allow farmers to hold their crops until market prices were more favorable. Low-interest government loans on the value of these crops would enable farmers to pay their annual debts and thus escape the ruinous interest rates of the crop lien system in the South and bank mortgages in the West.

These were radical demands for the time. Nevertheless, most of them eventually became law: the income tax and the direct election of senators by constitutional amendments in 1913; government control of transportation and communications by various laws in the 20th century; and the subtreasuries in the form of the Commodity Credit Corporation in the 1930s.

Anticipating that the Republicans and the Democrats would resist these demands, many Alliancemen were eager to form a third party. In Kansas they had already done so, launching the People's Party (whose members were known as Populists) in summer 1890. Southerners, mostly Democrats, opposed the idea of a third party for fear that it might open the way for the return of the Republican Party to power—with the Reconstruction bogey of "Negro rule." That this antiblack position could coexist alongside the Alliance's affiliation with black farmers suggests the schizophrenic nature of southern politics at the time.

In 1890, farmers helped elect numerous state legislators and congressmen who pledged to support their cause, but the legislative results were thin. By 1892, many Alliance members were ready to take the third-party plunge. The two-party system seemed fossilized and unable to respond to the explosive problems of the 1890s.

The Rise and Fall of the People's Party

Enthusiasm for a third party was particularly strong in the plains and mountain states, five of which had been admitted since the last presidential election: North and South Dakota, Montana, Wyoming, and Idaho. The most prominent leader of the Farmers' Alliance was Leonidas L. Polk of North Carolina. A Confederate veteran, Polk commanded support in the West as well as in the South. He undoubtedly would have been nominated for president by the newly organized People's Party had not death cut short his career at the age of 55 in June 1892.

The first nominating convention of the People's Party met at Omaha a month later. The preamble of their platform expressed the grim mood of delegates. "We meet in the midst of a nation brought to the verge of moral, political, and material ruin," it declared. "The fruits of the toil of millions are boldly stolen to build up colossal fortunes for a few. . . . From the same prolific womb of governmental injustice we breed the two great classes—tramps and millionaires." The platform called for unlimited coinage of silver at 16 to 1; creation of the subtreasury program for crop storage and farm loans; government ownership of railroad, telegraph, and telephone companies; a graduated income tax; direct election of senators; and laws to protect labor unions against prosecution for strikes and boycotts. To ease the lingering tension between southern and western farmers, the party nominated Union veteran James B. Weaver of Iowa for president and Confederate veteran James G. Field of Virginia for vice president.

Despite winning 9 percent of the popular vote and 22 electoral votes, Populist leaders were shaken by the outcome. In the South, most of the black farmers who were allowed to vote stayed with the Republicans. Democratic bosses in several southern states dusted off the racial demagoguery and intimidation machinery of Reconstruction days to keep white farmers in line for the party of white supremacy. Only in Alabama and Texas, among southern states, did the Populists get more than 20 percent of the vote. They did even worse in the older agricultural states of the Midwest, where their share of the vote ranged from 11 percent in Minnesota down to 2 percent in Ohio. Only in distressed wheat states such as Kansas, Nebraska, and the Dakotas and in the silver states of the West did the Populists do well, carrying Kansas, Colorado, Idaho, and Nevada.

The party remained alive, however, and the anguish caused by the Panic of 1893 seemed to boost its prospects. In several western states, Populists or a Populist-Democratic coalition controlled state governments for a time, and a Populist-Republican coalition won the state elections of 1894 in North Carolina.

President Cleveland's success in getting the Sherman Silver Purchase Act repealed in 1893 drove a wedge into the Democratic Party. Southern and western Democrats turned against Cleveland. In what was surely the most abusive attack on a president ever delivered by a member of his own party, Senator Benjamin Tillman of South Carolina told his constituents in 1894: "When Judas betrayed Christ, his heart was not blacker than this scoundrel, Cleveland, in deceiving the Democracy. He is an old bag of beef and I am going to Washington with a pitchfork and prod him in his fat ribs."

The Silver Issue

Democratic dissidents stood poised to take over the party in 1896. They adopted free silver as the centerpiece of their program. This stand raised possibilities for a fusion with the Populists, who hoped the Democrats would adopt other features of their platform as well. Meanwhile, out of the West came a new and charismatic figure, a silver-tongued orator named William Jennings Bryan, whose shadow would loom large across the political landscape for the next generation. A one-term congressman from Nebraska, Bryan had taken up the cause of free silver. He came to the Democratic convention in 1896 as a young delegate—only 36 years old. Given the opportunity to make the closing speech in the debate on the silver plank in the party's platform, Bryan brought the house to its feet in a frenzy of cheering with his peroration: "You shall not press down upon the brow of labor this crown of thorns, you shall not crucify mankind upon a cross of gold."

The Granger Collection, New York.

AN ANTI-BRYAN CARTOON, 1896

This cartoon in *Judge* magazine, entitled "The Sacrilegious Candidate," charged William Jennings Bryan with blasphemy in his "Cross of Gold" speech at the Democratic national convention. Bryan grinds his Bible into the dust with his boot while waving a crown of thorns and holding a cross of gold. In the background, a bearded caricature of an anarchist dances amid the ruins of a church and other buildings.

This speech catapulted Bryan into the presidential nomination. He ran on a platform that not only endorsed free silver but also embraced the idea of an income tax, condemned trusts, and opposed the use of injunctions against labor. Bryan's nomination created turmoil in the People's Party. Although some Populists wanted to continue as a third party, most of them saw fusion with silver Democrats as the road to victory. At the Populist convention, the fusionists got their way and endorsed Bryan's nomination. In effect, the Democratic whale swallowed the Populist fish in 1896.

The Election of 1896

The Republicans nominated William McKinley, who would have preferred to campaign on his specialty, the tariff. Bryan made that impossible. Crisscrossing the country in an unprecedented whistle-stop campaign covering 18,000 miles, Bryan gave as many as 30 speeches a day, focusing almost exclusively on the free silver issue. Republicans responded by denouncing the Democrats as irresponsible inflationists. Free silver, they said, would mean a 57-cent dollar and would demolish the workingman's gains in real wages achieved over the preceding 30 years.

Under the skillful leadership of Ohio businessman Mark Hanna, chairman of the Republican National Committee, McKinley waged a "front-porch campaign" in which various delegations visited his home in Canton, Ohio, to hear carefully crafted speeches that were widely publicized in the mostly Republican press. Hanna sent out an army of speakers and printed pamphlets in more than a dozen languages to reach immigrant voters. His propaganda portrayed Bryan as a wild man from the prairie whose monetary schemes would further wreck an economy that had been plunged into depression during a

---

L I N K   T O   T H E   P A S T

William Jennings Bryan's Cross of Gold Speech

William Jennings Bryan's famous "Cross of Gold" speech at the Democratic convention in 1896 made him the youngest presidential candidate in American history—at age 36, only a year older than the minimum stipulated by the Constitution. In that age before radio and television, Bryan's speech became the standard by which to measure political oratory, which had to move readers of cold print as well as listeners in a hot convention hall.

I f the gold standard advocates win, this country will be dominated by the financial harpies of Wall Street. I am trying to save the American people from that disaster—which will mean the enslavement of the farmers, merchants, manufacturers, and laboring classes to the most merciless and unscrupulous gang of speculators on earth—the money power. . . . We have petitioned, and our petitions have been scorned; we have entreated, and our entreaties have been disregarded; we have begged, and they have mocked when our calamity came. We beg no longer; we entreat no more; we petition no more. We defy them. . . . If they dare to come out in the open . . . we will fight them to the uttermost. Having behind us the producing masses of this nation and the world, supported by the commercial interests, the laboring interest, and the toilers everywhere, we will answer their demand for a gold standard by saying to them: You shall not press down upon the brow of labor this crown of thorns, you shall not crucify mankind upon a cross of gold.

1. What did Bryan mean by referring to the "enslavement" of farmers, merchants, manufacturers, and workers to the gold standard? Was he right?

For additional sources related to this feature, visit the *Liberty, Equality, Power* Web site at:

http://history.wadsworth.com/murrin_LEP4e

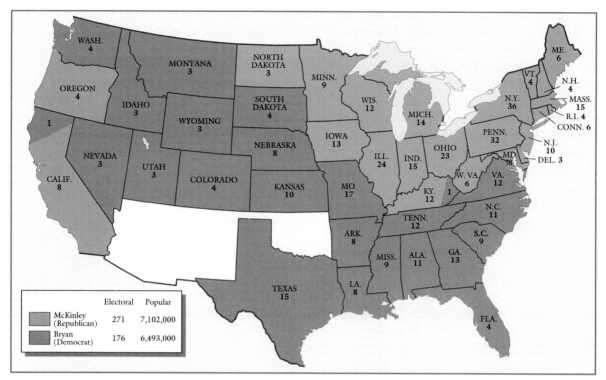

MAP 19.1 PRESIDENTIAL ELECTION OF 1896

Once again, note the continuity of voting patterns over the two generations from the 1850s to the 1890s by comparing this map with those on pages 444, 469, and 559.

Democratic administration. McKinley's election, by contrast, would maintain the gold standard, revive business confidence, and end the depression.

The 1896 election was the most impassioned and exciting in a generation. Many Americans believed that the fate of the nation hinged on the outcome. The number of voters jumped by 15 percent over the 1892 election. The sectional pattern of South and West versus Northeast and North Central was almost as pronounced as the North–South split of 1860. Republicans won a substantial share of the urban, immigrant, and labor vote by arousing fear about the Democratic 57-cent dollar and by inspiring hope with the slogan of McKinley as "the advance agent of prosperity." McKinley rode to a convincing victory by carrying every state in the northeast quadrant of the country. Bryan carried most of the rest. Republicans won decisive control of Congress as well as the presidency. They would maintain control for the next 14 years. The election of 1896 marked a crucial turning point in American political history away from the stalemate of the preceding two decades.

Whether by luck or by design, McKinley did prove to be the advance agent of prosperity. The economy pulled out of the depression during his first year in office and entered into a long period of growth—not because of anything the new administration did (except perhaps to encourage a revival of confidence) but because of the mysterious workings of the business cycle. With the discovery of rich new goldfields in the Yukon, in Alaska, and in South Africa, the silver issue lost potency, and a cascade of gold poured into the world economy. The long deflationary trend since 1865 reversed itself in 1897. Farmers entered a new—and unfamiliar—era of prosperity. Bryan ran against McKinley again in 1900 but lost even more emphatically. The nation seemed embarked on a placid sea of plenty. But below the surface, the currents of protest and reform that had boiled up in the 1890s still ran strong. They would soon surface again.

Conclusion

The 1890s were a major watershed in American history. On the past side of that divide lay a largely rural society and agricultural economy, and on the future side lay the cities and a commercial-industrial economy. Before the

1890s, most immigrants had come from northern and western Europe, and many became farmers. Later immigrants largely came from eastern and southern Europe, and nearly all settled in cities. Before the 1890s, the old sectional issues associated with slavery, the Civil War, and Reconstruction remained important forces in American politics; after 1900, racial issues would not play an important part in national politics for another 60 years. The election of 1896 ended 20 years of even balance between the two major parties and led to more than a generation of Republican dominance.

Most important, the social and political upheavals of the 1890s shocked many people into recognition that the liberty and equality they had taken for granted as part of the American dream was in danger of disappearing before the onslaught of wrenching economic changes that had widened and deepened the gulf between classes. The strikes and violence and third-party protests of the decade were a wake-up call. As the forces of urbanization and industrialism increased during the ensuing two decades, many middle-class Americans supported greater government power to carry out progressive reforms to cure the ills of an industrializing society.

SUGGESTED READINGS

For the impact of the railroad on the Gilded Age economy and culture, see **George R. Taylor and Irene D. Neu,** *The American Railroad Network, 1861–1890* (2003). For the rise of industry and "big business," the following are useful: **Glenn Porter,** *The Rise of Big Business, 1860–1910,* rev. ed. (1992), and **Harold G. Vatter,** *The Drive to Industrial Maturity: The U.S. Economy, 1865–1914* (1975). For the social and political response to these developments, see **Samuel P. Hay,** *The Response to Industrialism, 1885–1914* (1957).

The rise of the department store is examined in **William Leach,** *Land of Desire: Merchants, Power, and the Rise of a New American Culture* (1993). The effects of white-collar work on men and women are detailed in **Olivier Zunz,** *Making America Corporate, 1870–1920* (1990), and **Sue Porter Benson,** *Counter Cultures: Saleswomen, Managers, and Customers in American Department Stores, 1890–1940* (1986). The effects of the streetcar on suburbanization are covered in **Sam B. Warner, Jr.,** *Streetcar Suburbs: The Process of Growth in Boston, 1870–1900* (1962). The cultural development of American museums is the subject of **Steven Conn,** *Museums and American Intellectual Life, 1876–1926* (1998). Four conflicting visions of the Chicago World's Fair can be found in **Alan Trachtenberg,** *The Incorporation of America: Culture and Society in the Gilded Age* (1982); **Robert W. Rydell,** *All the World's a Fair: Visions of Empire at the American International Expositions,* *1876–1916* (1984); **James Gilbert,** *Perfect Cities: Chicago's Utopias of 1893* (1991); and **Christopher Robert Reed,** *"All the World Is Here": The Black Presence at the White City* (2000). Several interesting essays on late 19th-century middle-class culture appear in **Burton J. Bledstein and Robert D. Johnston, eds.,** *The Middling Sorts: Explorations in the History of the American Middle Class* (2001).

The labor movement is treated in **Melvin Dubofsky,** *Industrialism and The American Worker, 1865–1920,* rev. ed. (1985), and **Robert E. Weir,** *Beyond Labor's Veil: The Culture of the Knights of Labor* (1996). Two of the spectacular labor conflicts of the era are described in **Robert V. Bruce,** *1877: Year of Violence* (1959), and **Leon Wolff,** *Lockout, The Story of the Homestead Strike of 1892* (1965). The best modern survey of the Populist movement is **Lawrence Goodwyn,** *Democratic Promise: The Populist Moment in America* (1976), which was published in an abridged edition with the title *The Populist Moment* (1978). The politics of the 1890s culminating in the climactic election of 1896 are treated in **J. Rogers Hollingsworth,** *The Whirligig of Politics: The Democracy of Cleveland and Bryan* (1963), and **Paul W. Glad,** *McKinley, Bryan, and the People* (1964). For the beginnings of Progressive reform during this era, see the early chapters of **Michael McGerr,** *A Fierce Discontent: Rise and Fall of the Progressive Movement in America, 1870–1920* (2003).

AMERICAN JOURNEY ONLINE
 A N D
INFOTRAC COLLEGE EDITION

Visit the source collections at www.ajaccess.wadsworth.com and
infotrac.thomsonlearning.com and use the Search function with
the following key terms to explore documents, images, audio
and video clips, articles, and commentary related to the material
in this chapter.

John D. Rockefeller	Pullman strike
Andrew Carnegie	Farmers' Alliance
Homestead strike	William McKinley
Knights of Labor	William Jennings Bryan
Haymarket riots	Sherman Antitrust Act
Edward Bellamy	

GRADE AIDS

**Visit the Liberty Equality Power Companion Web site for resources specific to
this textbook:** http://history.wadsworth.com/murrin_LEP4e

The CD in the back of this book and the U.S. History Resource Center at
http://history.wadsworth.com/u.s./ offer a variety of tools to help you succeed in
this course, including access to quizzes; images; documents; interactive simulations,
maps, and timelines; movie explorations; and a wealth of other sources.

Chapter 20

An Industrial Society, 1890–1920

John Sloan, The City from Greenwich Village, 1922. National Gallery of Art. Gift of Helen Farr Sloan, 1970.1.1.

THE CITY FROM GREENWICH VILLAGE
This 1922 painting by John Sloan, one of America's foremost early-20th-century painters, captures both the expanse and night-time vitality of New York City. Cities such as New York were the most dynamic centers of business and culture during America's industrial age.

CHAPTER OUTLINE

With the collapse of populism in 1896 and the end of the depression in 1897, the American economy embarked on a remarkable stretch of growth. By 1910, America was unquestionably the world's greatest industrial power.

Corporations were changing the face of America. Their railroad and telegraph lines crisscrossed the country. Their factories employed millions. Their production and management techniques became the envy of the industrialized world. A new kind of building—the skyscraper—came to symbolize America's corporate power. These modern towers were made possible by the use of steel rather than stone framework and by the invention of electrically powered elevators.

Impelled upward by rising real estate values, they were intended to evoke the same sense of grandeur as Europe's medieval cathedrals. But these monuments celebrated man, not God; material wealth, not spiritual riches; science, not faith; corporations, not the commonweal. Reaching into the sky, dwarfing Europe's cathedrals, they were convincing embodiments of America's worldly might.

This chapter explores how the newly powerful corporations transformed America: how they revolutionized production and management; how the jobs they generated attracted millions of immigrants, southern blacks, and young single women to northern cities; and how they triggered an urban cultural revolution that made amusement parks, dance halls, vaudeville theater, and movies integral features of American life.

The power of the corporations dwarfed that of individual wage earners, but wage earners sought to limit the power of corporations through labor unions and strikes and by organizing institutions of collective self-help within their own ethnic or racial communities. Many found opportunities and liberties they had not known before. Immigrant entrepreneurs invented ways to make money through legal and illegal enterprise; young, single, working-class women pioneered a sexual revolution; and radicals dared to imagine building a new society where no one suffered from poverty, inequality, and powerlessness. The power of the new corporations, in other words, did not go unchallenged. Even so, a more egalitarian society would prove difficult to attain.

CHAPTER FOCUS

♦ How did corporations and workers respond to the social and economic turmoil of the late 19th century?

♦ Why did American elites become obsessed with physical and racial fitness? How did this obsession affect attitudes toward immigrants and blacks?

♦ What hardships and successes did immigrants experience in America? How does the immigrant experience compare to that of African Americans?

♦ What explains the new sexuality and the rise of feminism?

Sources of Economic Growth

A series of technological innovations in the late 19th century fired up the nation's economic engine, but technological breakthroughs alone do not fully explain the nation's spectacular economic boom. New corporate structures and new management techniques—in combination with the new technology—created the conditions that powered economic growth.

Technology

Two of the most important new technologies were the harnessing of electric power and the invention of the gasoline-powered internal combustion engine. Scientists had long been fascinated by electricity, but only in the late 19th century did they find ways to make it practically useful. The work of Thomas Edison, George Westinghouse, and Nikola Tesla produced the incandescent bulb that brought electric lighting into homes and offices and the alternating current (AC) that made electric transmission possible over long distances. From 1890 to 1920, the proportion of American industry powered by electricity rose from virtually nil to almost one-third. Older industries switched from expensive and cumbersome steam power to more efficient and cleaner electrical power. New sectors of the metalworking and machine-tool industries arose in response to the demand for electric generators and related equipment. Between 1900 and 1920, virtually every major city built electric-powered transit systems to replace horse-drawn trolleys and carriages. By 1912, some 40,000 miles of electric railway and trolley track had been laid. In New York City, electricity made possible the construction of the first subways. Electric lighting—on city streets, in department store windows, in brilliantly lit amusement parks such as New York's Coney Island—gave cities a new allure.

CHRONOLOGY

1897	Depression ends; prosperity returns
1899	Theodore Roosevelt urges Americans to live the "strenuous life"
1900–14	Immigration averages more than 1 million per year
1901	U.S. Steel is formed from 200 separate companies • Andrew Carnegie devotes himself to philanthropic pursuits • 1 of every 400 railroad workers dies on the job
1904	20 percent of the North's industrial population lives below poverty line
1905	*Lochner v. New York:* Supreme Court declares unconstitutional a New York state law limiting the workday of bakery employees • Industrial Workers of the World (IWW) founded
1907	Henry Ford unveils his Model T
1907–11	73 of every 100 Italian immigrants return to Italy
1909	Immigrants and their children constitute more than 96 percent of labor force building and maintaining railroads
1910	Black skilled tradesmen in northern cities reduced to 10 percent of total skilled trades workforce • 20,000 nickelodeons dot northern cities
1911	Triangle Shirtwaist Company fire kills 146 workers • Frederick Winslow Taylor publishes *The Principles of Scientific Management*
1913	Henry Ford introduces the first moving assembly line; employee turnover reaches 370 percent a year • 66 men, women, and children killed in "Ludlow massacre" • John D. Rockefeller establishes Rockefeller Foundation
1914	Henry Ford introduces the $5-per-day wage • Theda Bara, movies' first sex symbol, debuts • *The Masses,* a radical journal, begins publication
1919	Japanese farmers in California sell $67 million in agricultural goods, 10 percent of state's total
1920	Nation's urban population outstrips rural population for first time
1921	1,250,000 Model Ts sold, a 16-fold increase over 1912

The public also fell in love with the movies, which depended on electricity to project images onto a screen. Electric power, in short, stimulated capital investment and accelerated economic growth.

The first gasoline engine was patented in the United States in 1878, and the first "horseless carriages" began appearing on European and American roads in the 1890s, but few thought of them as serious rivals to trains and horses. Rather, they were seen as playthings for the wealthy, who liked to race them along country roads.

In 1900, Henry Ford was just an eccentric 37-year-old mechanic who built race cars in Michigan. In 1909, Ford

SURF AVENUE AND LUNA PARK, CONEY ISLAND, 1913

With its 1 million lights, Surf Avenue in Brooklyn, New York, advertised itself as the most brilliantly lit thoroughfare in the world. The avenue included the entrance to Luna Park, one of Coney Island's most popular attractions.

LUNA PARK. SURF AVENUE. BY NIGHT, CONEY ISLAND, N. Y.

© Lake County Museum/Corbis.

unveiled his Model T: an unadorned, even homely car, but reliable enough to travel hundreds of miles without servicing and cheap enough to be affordable to most working Americans. Ford had dreamed of creating an automobile civilization with his Model T, and Americans began buying his car by the millions. The stimulus this insatiable demand gave to the economy can scarcely be exaggerated. Millions of cars required millions of pounds of steel alloys, glass, rubber, petroleum, and other material. Millions of jobs in coal and iron-ore mining, oil refining and rubber manufacturing, steelmaking and machine tooling, road construction and service stations came to depend on automobile manufacturing.

Corporate Growth

Successful inventions such as the automobile required more than the mechanical ingenuity and social vision of inventors such as Henry Ford. They relied on corporations with sophisticated organizational and technical knowhow to mass-produce and mass-distribute the newly invented products. Corporations had played an important role in the nation's economic life since the 1840s, but in the late 19th and early 20th centuries, they underwent significant changes. The most obvious change was in their size. Employment in Chicago's International Harvester factory, where agricultural implements were built, nearly quadrupled from 4,000 in 1900 to 15,000 in 1916. Delaware's DuPont Corporation, a munitions and chemical manufacturer, employed 1,500 workers in 1902 and 31,000 workers in 1920. Founded with a few hundred employees

in 1903, the Ford Motor Company employed 33,000 at its Detroit Highland Park plant by 1916 and 42,000 by 1924. That same year, the 68,000 workers employed at Ford's River Rouge plant (just outside Detroit) made it the largest factory in the world.

This growth in scale was in part a response to the enormous domestic market. By 1900, railroads provided the country with an efficient transportation system that allowed corporations to ship goods virtually anywhere in the United States. A national network of telegraph lines allowed constant communication between buyers and sellers separated by thousands of miles. And the population, which was expanding rapidly, demonstrated an evergrowing appetite for goods and services.

Mass Production and Distribution

Manufacturers responded to this burgeoning domestic market by developing mass-production techniques that increased production speed and lowered unit costs. Mass production often meant replacing skilled workers with machines that were coordinated to permit high-speed, uninterrupted production at every stage of the manufacturing process. Mass-production techniques had become widespread in basic steel manufacturing and sugar refining by the 1890s, and they spread to the machine-tool industry and automobile manufacturing in the first two decades of the 20th century.

Such production techniques were profitable only if large quantities of output could be sold. Although the domestic market offered a vast potential for sales,

AN EARLY CIGARETTE ADVERTISEMENT (1885–1900)
This particular advertisement—including three trading cards, each featuring an attractive female stage star—was aimed at theatergoers, who were encouraged to "light up" between acts. Ads such as this one were part of an intensive promotional campaign to generate interest in smoking among a consuming public that was unaccustomed to the practice.

Morgan together fashioned the U.S. Steel Corporation from 200 separate iron and steel companies. U.S. Steel, with its 112 blast furnaces and 170,000 steelworkers, controlled 60 percent of the country's steelmaking capacity. Moreover, its 78 iron-ore boats and 1,000 miles of railroad gave it substantial control over procuring raw materials and distributing finished steel products.

Revolution in Management

The growth in the number and size of corporations revolutionized corporate management. The ranks of managers mushroomed, as elaborate corporate hierarchies defined both the status and the duties of individual managers. Increasingly, senior managers took over from owners the responsibility for long-term planning. Day-to-day operations fell to middle managers who oversaw particular departments (e.g., purchasing, research, production, labor) in corporate headquarters or who supervised regional sales offices or directed particular factories. Middle managers also managed the people—accountants, clerks, foremen, engineers, salesmen—in these departments, offices, or factories. The rapid expansion within corporate managerial ranks created a new middle class, whose members were intensely loyal to their employers but at odds both with blue-collar workers and with the older middle class of shopkeepers, small businessmen, and independent craftsmen.

As management techniques grew in importance, companies tried to make them more scientific. Firms introduced cost-accounting methods into purchasing and other departments charged with controlling the inflow of materials and the outflow of goods. Many corporations began requiring college or university training in science, engineering, or accounting for entry into middle management. Corporations that had built their success on a profitable invention or discovery sought to maintain their competitive edge by creating research departments and hiring professional scientists—those with doctorates from American or European universities—to come up with new technological and scientific breakthroughs. Such departments were modeled on the industrial research laboratory set up by the inventor-entrepreneur Thomas Edison in Menlo Park, New Jersey, in 1876.

Scientific Management on the Factory Floor

The most controversial and, in some respects, the most ambitious effort to introduce scientific practices into management occurred in production. Managers understood that improvements in factory organization as well as technological innovation could enhance the speed and efficiency of mass production. So, in league with engineers, they sought optimal arrangements of machines and deployments of workers that would achieve the highest speed in production with the fewest human or mechanical interruptions. Some of these managers, such as Frederick Winslow Taylor, the chief engineer at Philadelphia's Midvale Steel Company in the 1880s, styled themselves as the architects of scientific management. They examined every human task and mechanical movement involved in each production process. In "time-and-motion studies," they recorded every distinct movement a worker made in performing his or her job, how long it took, and how often it was performed. They hoped thereby to identify and eliminate wasted human energy. Eliminating waste might mean reorganizing a floor of machinery so as to reduce "down time" between production steps; it might mean instructing workers to perform their tasks differently; or it might mean replacing uncooperative skilled workers with machines tended by unskilled, low-wage laborers. Regardless of the method chosen, the goal was the same: to make human labor emulate the smooth and apparently effortless operation of an automatic, perfectly calibrated piece of machinery.

Taylor publicized his vision, first through speeches to fellow engineers and managers, and then through his writings. By the time he published *The Principles of Scientific Management* (1911), his ideas had already captivated countless corporate managers and engineers, many of whom sought to introduce "Taylorism" into their own production systems.

© Bettmann/Corbis.

Introducing scientific management practices rarely proceeded easily. Time-and-motion studies were costly, and Taylor's formulas for increasing efficiency and reducing waste often were less scientific than he claimed. Taylor also overestimated workers' willingness to play the mechanical role he assigned them; the skilled workers and general foremen, whom Taylor sought to eliminate, often resisted his schemes. In the end, managers and engineers who persisted in their efforts to apply scientific management usually modified Taylor's principles.

Henry Ford's engineers initially adopted Taylorism and with apparent success. By 1910, they had broken down automobile manufacturing into a series of simple, sequential tasks. Each worker performed only one task—adding a carburetor to an engine, inserting a windshield, mounting tires onto wheels. Then, in 1913, Ford's engineers introduced the first moving assembly line, a continuously moving conveyor belt that carried cars in production through each workstation. This innovation eliminated precious time previously wasted in transporting car parts (or partially built cars) by crane or truck from one work area to another. It also limited the time available to workers to perform their assigned tasks. Only the foreman, not the workers, could stop the line or change its speed.

By 1913, the continuous assembly line made Ford Motor Company's new Highland Park plant the most tightly integrated and continuously moving production system in American industry. The pace of production exceeded all expectations. Between 1910 and 1914, production time on Ford Model Ts dropped by 90 percent, from an average of more than 12 hours per car to 1.5 hours. A thousand Model Ts began rolling off the assembly line each day. This striking increase in the rate of production enabled Ford to slash the price of a Model T from $950 in 1909 to only $295 in 1923, a reduction of 70 percent. The number of Model Ts purchased by Americans increased 16-fold between 1912 and 1921, from 79,000 to 1,250,000. The assembly line quickly became the most admired—and most feared—symbol of American mass production.

Problems immediately beset the system, however. Repeating a single motion all day long induced mental stupor, and managerial efforts to speed up the line produced physical exhaustion—both of which increased the incidence of error and injury. Some workers tried to organize

© Bettmann/Corbis.

THE WORLD'S FIRST AUTOMOBILE ASSEMBLY LINE

Introduced by Henry Ford at his Highland Park plant in 1913, this innovation cut production time on Ford Model Ts by 90 percent, allowing Ford to reduce the price of his cars by more than half and to double the hourly wages of his workers.

education. By the time he died in 1919, he had given away or entrusted to several Carnegie foundations 90 percent of his fortune. Among the projects he funded were New York's Carnegie Hall, Pittsburgh's Carnegie Institute (now Carnegie-Mellon University), and 2,500 public libraries throughout the country.

Other industrialists, including John D. Rockefeller, soon followed Carnegie's lead. A devout Baptist with an ascetic bent, Rockefeller had never flaunted his wealth (unlike the Vanderbilts and others), but his ruthless business methods in assembling the Standard Oil Company and in crushing his competition made him one of the most reviled of the robber barons. In the wake of journalist Ida Tarbell's stinging 1904 exposé of Standard Oil's business practices, and of the federal government's subsequent prosecution of Standard Oil for monopolistic practices in 1906, Rockefeller transformed himself into a public-spirited philanthropist. Between 1913 and 1919, his Rockefeller Foundation dispersed an estimated $500 million. His most significant gifts included money to establish the University of Chicago and the Rockefeller Institute for Medical Research (later renamed Rockefeller University). His charitable efforts did not escape criticism, however; many Americans interpreted them as an attempt to establish control over American universities, scientific research, and public policy. Still, Rockefeller's largesse helped build for the Rockefeller family a reputation for public-spiritedness and good works, one that grew even stronger in the 1920s and 1930s. Many other business leaders, such as Julius Rosenwald of Sears Roebuck and Daniel and Simon Guggenheim of the American Smelting and Refining Company, also dedicated themselves to philanthropy during this time.

Obsession with Physical and Racial Fitness

The fractious events of the 1890s also induced many wealthy Americans to engage in what Theodore Roosevelt dubbed "the strenuous life." In an 1899 essay with that title, Roosevelt exhorted Americans to live vigorously, to test their physical strength and endurance in competitive athletics, and to experience nature through hiking, hunting, and mountain climbing. He articulated a way of life that influenced countless Americans from a variety of classes and cultures.

The 1890s were a time of heightened enthusiasm for competitive sports, physical fitness, and outdoor recreation. Millions of Americans began riding bicycles and eating healthier foods. A passion for athletic competition

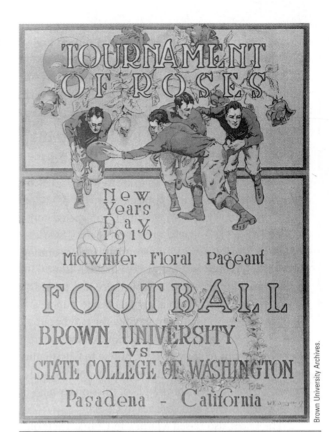

BROWN UNIVERSITY GOES TO THE ROSE BOWL

Seeking to demonstrate their physical prowess and racial fitness, the sons of the nation's elite took up the rough game of football. In the early years of the 20th century, Ivy League schools such as Brown fielded some of the country's best teams.

gripped American universities. The power and violence of football helped make it the sport of choice at the nation's elite campuses, and for 20 years Ivy League schools were the nation's football powerhouses. In athletic competition, as in nature, one could discover and recapture one's manhood, one's virility. The words "sissy" and "pussyfoot" entered common usage in the 1890s as insults hurled at men whose masculinity was found wanting.

Ironically, this quest for masculinity had a liberating effect on women, many of whom had internalized Victorian moral codes that frowned on strenuous outdoor activity for the "weaker" sex. In the vigorous new climate of the 1890s, young women began to engage in sports and other activities. They put away their corsets and long dresses and began wearing simple skirts, shirtwaists, and other clothing that gave them more comfort and freedom of movement. By the standards of the 1920s, these changes would seem mild, but in the 1890s, they were radical.

In the country at large, the new enthusiasm for athletics and the outdoor life reflected a widespread dissat-

isfaction with the growing regimentation of industrial society. Among wealthy Americans the quest for physical superiority reflected a deeper and more ambiguous anxiety: their *racial* fitness. Most of them were native-born Americans whose families had lived in the United States for several generations and whose ancestors had come from the British Isles, the Netherlands, or some other region of northwestern Europe. They liked to attribute their success and good fortune to their "racial superiority." They saw themselves as "natural" leaders, members of a noble Anglo-Saxon race endowed with uncommon intelligence, imagination, and discipline. But events of the 1890s had challenged the legitimacy of the elite's wealth and authority, and the ensuing depression mocked their ability to exert economic leadership. The immigrant masses laboring in factories, despite their poverty and alleged racial inferiority, seemed to possess a vitality that the "superior" Anglo-Saxons lacked. Immigrant families were overflowing with children. The city neighborhoods where these families lived exhibited social and cultural energy (especially apparent in popular entertainments—vaudeville, amusement parks, nickelodeons, and dance halls) that were missing in the sedate environs of the wealthy.

Some rich Americans, such as Henry Adams, Henry Cabot Lodge, and other members of Boston's declining political elite, reacted to the immigrants' vigor and industry by calling for a halt to further immigration, but not the ebullient Roosevelt; he argued instead for a return to fitness, superiority, and numerical predominance of the "English-speaking" races. He called on American men to live the strenuous life and on women to devote themselves to reproduction. The only way to avoid "race suicide," he declared, was for every American mother to have at least four children.

Such racialist thought was not limited to wealthy elites. Many other Americans, from a variety of classes and regions, also thought that all people demonstrated the characteristics of their race. Racial stereotypes served to describe not only blacks, Asians, and Hispanics, but also Italians ("violent"), Jews ("nervous"), and Slavs ("slow"). Such aspersions flowed as easily from the pens of compassionate reformers, such as Jacob Riis, who wanted to help the immigrants, as from the pens of bitter reactionaries, such as Madison Grant, who argued in *The Passing of the Great Race* (1916) that America should rid itself of "inferior" races.

Social Darwinism

Racialist thinking even received "scientific" sanction from distinguished biologists and anthropologists, who argued that racially inherited traits explained variations in the economic, social, and cultural lives of ethnic and racial groups. Many intellectuals believed that human society developed according to the "survival of the fittest" principle articulated by the English naturalist Charles Darwin to describe plant and animal evolution. Human history could be understood in terms of an ongoing struggle among races, with the strongest and the fittest invariably triumphing. The wealth and power of the Anglo-Saxon race was ample testimony, in this view, to its superior fitness.

This view, which would become known as Social Darwinism, was rooted in two developments of the late 19th century, one intellectual and one socioeconomic. Intellectually, it reflected a widely shared belief that human society operated according to principles that were every bit as scientific as those governing the natural world. The ability of 19th-century biologists, chemists, and physicists to penetrate the mysteries of the natural world generated confidence in science, in people's ability to know and control their physical environment. That confidence, in turn, prompted intellectuals to apply the scientific method to the human world. The social sciences—economics, political science, anthropology, sociology, psychology—took shape in the late 19th century, each trying to discover the scientific laws governing individual and group behavior. Awed by the accomplishments of natural scientists, social scientists were prone to exaggerate the degree to which social life mimicked natural life; hence the appeal of Social Darwinism, a philosophy that allegedly showed how closely the history of human beings resembled the history of animal evolution.

Social Darwinism was also rooted in the unprecedented interpenetration of the world's economies and peoples. Cheap and rapid ocean travel had bound together continents as never before. International trade, immigration, and imperial conquest made Americans more conscious of the variety of peoples inhabiting the earth. Although awareness of diversity sometimes encourages tolerance and cooperation, in the economically depressed years of the late 19th century, it encouraged intolerance and suspicion, fertile soil for the cultivation of Social Darwinism.

🌏 Immigration

Perhaps the most dramatic evidence of the nation's growing involvement in the international economy was the high rate of immigration. The United States had always been a nation of immigrants, but never had so many come in so short a time. Between 1880 and 1920, some

the new century when the U.S. economy experienced sustained growth broken only briefly by the Panic of 1907–08.

Chinese and Japanese Immigration

The relatively small numbers of Chinese and Japanese immigrants who came to the United States in the late 19th and early 20th centuries reflected the efforts of native-born Americans and their allies to keep them out. As many as 300,000 Chinese immigrants arrived in the United States between 1851 and 1882, and more than 200,000 Japanese immigrants journeyed to Hawaii and the western continental United States between 1891 and 1907. They contributed in major ways to the development of two of the West's major industries: railroad building and commercial agriculture. These two immigrant groups might have formed two of America's largest, each numbering in the millions, but the U.S. government began to exclude Chinese immigrant laborers in 1882 (The Chinese Exclusion Act) and Japanese immigrant laborers in 1907 (see chapter 22). The government also interpreted a 1790 law to mean that Chinese, Japanese, and other East Asian immigrants were ineligible for citizenship. These exclusions remained in force until the 1940s and 1950s. They expressed the racial prejudice felt by most native-born white Americans toward nonwhite Asian immigrants, and they also revealed how determined America was to remain a nation of European immigrants and their descendants.

The factors propelling Chinese and Japanese immigrants were similar to those motivating their European counterparts. The rural population in those countries was increasing at a rate faster than the labor requirements of the countryside's agricultural sector. Chinese and Japanese rural peasants were being integrated into an international market for agriculture, contributing to the global oversupply of agricultural goods and depressing prices. Many Chinese and Japanese immigrants, like their European counterparts, conceived of their movement beyond their countries' borders as temporary. They intended to move abroad just long enough to make enough money to establish themselves economically in their homelands. Thus the early streams of Chinese and Japanese migration to the United States were overwhelmingly composed of men looking for work. Similar to the European immigrants, the Chinese and Japanese sojourners tended to follow precise migratory paths—from one region or village in China or Japan to one city or region in the United States.

Conditions in China were more desperate than those in Japan, where industrialization had begun to generate new wealth and absorb some of the rural population. Chinese immigrants, as a result, often suffered greater hardship than did their Japanese counterparts. In the 19th century, many were forced to sign contracts with suppliers of overseas laborers that subjected them to slave-like conditions: They were herded onto boats for the transpacific voyage, bound to particular employers for years on end,

IMMIGRANT JAPANESE CHILDREN ARRIVE AT ANGEL ISLAND, SAN FRANCISCO HARBOR, 1905

Beginning in 1907, as a result of the "gentlemen's agreement" between the United States and Japanese governments, it would no longer be possible for Japanese immigrants such as these children to come to the United States.

© Bettmann/Corbis.

thrust into dangerous working conditions, and paid paltry wages. The conditions of their labor in the western states where they tended to settle inflamed the sentiments of white working men, who saw the Asian migration as a threat to their own wages and livelihoods. These white workers might have made common cause with Asian immigrant workers, but the racial prejudice they harbored toward the "yellow hordes" was simply too great. White workers became leaders of the movements in the western states to keep these immigrants out.

Significant numbers of Chinese and Japanese immigrants continued to try to enter the United States during the period of Asian immigrant exclusion—after 1882 in the case of the Chinese and 1907 in the case of the Japanese. Some were desperate to reunite themselves with family members already living in the United States, while others were driven by deteriorating economic circumstances in their homeland. Many attempted to enter the United States with forged papers declaring them to be merchants (a permitted class of Chinese and Japanese immigrants) when they were not, or to have been resident in the United States before the exclusion laws had gone into effect (and thus entitled to return). San Francisco was their principal port of entry, and Angel Island, in San Francisco harbor, became the counterpart of Ellis Island in New York harbor: the place where inspectors for the U.S. Bureau of Immigration interrogated them and scrutinized their documents and, more often than not, sent them back to Asia.

Others East Asian immigrants attempted to enter the United States through Canada or Mexico, hoping to find an unpatrolled part of the land border and to cross into the United States undetected. They became, in effect, America's first illegal aliens. That a certain percentage of East Asian immigrants were illegals subject to deportation generated considerable fear among the Asian immigrant populations resident in the United States, deepening tendencies within these communities to secrecy and to separation from mainstream American culture and society. Despite these considerable hardships, Asian immigrants would prove to be resourceful and to find ways to build homes and livelihoods in America.

Immigrant Labor

In the first decade of the 20th century, immigrant men and their male children constituted 70 percent of the workforce in 15 of the 19 leading U.S. industries. They concentrated in industries where work was the most backbreaking. Immigrants built the nation's railroads and tunnels; mined its coal, iron ore, and other minerals; stoked its hot and sometimes deadly steel furnaces; and slaughtered and packed its meat in Chicago's putrid packinghouses.

In 1909, first- and second-generation immigrants—especially Greeks, Italians, Japanese, and Mexicans—constituted more than 96 percent of the labor force that built and maintained the nation's railroads. Of the 750,000 Slovaks who arrived in America before 1913, at least 600,000 headed for the coal mines and steel mills of western Pennsylvania. The steel mills of Pittsburgh, Buffalo, Cleveland, and Chicago also attracted disproportionately large numbers of Poles and other Slavs.

Immigrants also performed "lighter" but no less arduous work. Jews and Italians predominated in the garment manufacturing shops of New York City, Chicago, Philadelphia, Baltimore, and Boston. In 1900, French-Canadian immigrants and their children held one of every two jobs in New England's cotton textile industry. By 1920, the prosperity of California's rapidly growing agricultural industry depended primarily on Mexican and Filipino labor. In these industries, immigrant women and children, who worked for lower wages than men, formed a large part of the labor force. Few states restricted child labor. More than 25 percent of boys and 10 percent of girls aged 10 to 15 were "gainfully employed."

Immigrants were as essential as fossil fuels to the smooth operation of the American economic machine. Sometimes, however, the machine consumed workers as well as coal and oil. Those who worked in heavy industry, mining, or railroading were especially vulnerable to accident and injury. In 1901, for instance, 1 in every 400 railroad workers died on the job and 1 in every 26 suffered injury. Between the years 1906 and 1911, almost one-quarter of the recent immigrants employed at the U.S. Steel Corporation's South Works (Pittsburgh) were injured or killed on the job. Lax attention to safety rendered even light industry hazardous and sometimes fatal. In 1911, a fire broke out on an upper floor of the Triangle Shirtwaist Company, a New York City garment factory. The building had no fire escapes. The owners of the factory, moreover, had locked the entrances to each floor as a way of keeping their employees at work. A total of 146 workers, mostly young Jewish and Italian women, perished in the fire or from desperate nine-story leaps to the pavement below.

Chronic fatigue and inadequate nourishment increased the risk of accident and injury. Workweeks averaged 60 hours—10 hours every day except Sunday. Workers who were granted Saturday afternoons off—thus reducing their workweek to a mere 55 hours—considered themselves fortunate. Steelworkers were not so lucky. They labored from 72 to 89 hours per week and were required to work one 24-hour shift every two weeks.

Most workers had to labor long hours simply to eke out a meager living. In 1900, the annual earnings of American manufacturing workers averaged only $400 to $500

farm acreage. Their specialization in fresh vegetables and fruits (particularly strawberries), combined with their family-labor-intensive agricultural methods, was yielding $67 million in annual revenues by 1919—one-tenth of the total California agriculture revenue that year. Japanese farmers sold their produce to Japanese fruit and vegetable wholesalers in Los Angeles, who had chosen a mercantile route to middle-class status. The success of Japanese farmers was all the more impressive given that the state of California had passed the Alien Land Law in 1913, prohibiting Japanese and other Asian aliens from owning property in the state. Japanese immigrant farmers thus depended on their native-born children or friendly whites to acquire land for them, arrangements that made them more vulnerable to losing the land—or control of it—than if they had been able to own it outright themselves.

Each ethnic group created its own history of economic success and social mobility. From the emerging middle classes came many leaders who would provide their ethnic groups with identity, legitimacy, and power and would lead the way toward Americanization and assimilation. Their children tended to do better in school than the children of working-class ethnics, and academic success served as a ticket to upward social mobility in a society that increasingly depended on university-trained engineers, managers, lawyers, doctors, and other professionals.

Political Machines and Organized Crime

The underside of this success story was the rise of government corruption and organized crime. Many ethnic entrepreneurs operated on the margins of economic failure and bankruptcy, and some accepted the help of those who promised financial assistance. Sometimes the help came from honest unions and upright government officials, but other times it did not. Unions were generally weak, and some government officials, lacking experience and economic security, were susceptible to bribery. Economic necessity became a breeding ground for government corruption and greed. A contractor who was eager to win a city contract—to build a trolley system, a sewer line, or a new city hall, for example—would find it necessary to pay off government officials who could throw the contract his way. By 1900, such payments, referred to as "graft," had become essential to the day-to-day operation of government in most large cities. The graft, in turn, made local officeholding a source of economic gain. Politicians began building political organizations called machines to guarantee their success in municipal elections. The machine "bosses" used a variety of legal and illegal means to bring victory on election day. They won the loyalty of urban

voters—especially immigrants—by providing poor neighborhoods with paved roads and sewer systems. They helped newly arrived immigrants find jobs (often on city payrolls) and occasionally provided food, fuel, or clothing to families in dire need. Many of their clients were grateful for these services in an age when government provided little public assistance.

The bosses who ran the political machines—including "King Richard" Croker in New York, James Michael Curley in Boston, Tom Pendergast in Kansas City, Martin Behrman in New Orleans, and Abe Ruef in San Francisco—served their own needs first. They saw to it that construction contracts went to those who offered the most graft, not to those who were likely to do the best job. They protected gamblers, pimps, and other purveyors of urban vice who contributed large amounts to their machine coffers. They often required city employees to contribute to their campaign chests, to solicit political contributions, and to get out the vote on election day. And they engaged in widespread election fraud by rounding up truckloads of newly arrived immigrants and paying them to vote a certain way; having their supporters vote two or three times; and stuffing ballot boxes with the votes of phantom citizens who had died, moved away, or never been born.

"KEEPING TAMMANY'S BOOTS SHINED"

This 1880s cartoon by Joseph Keppler declares that the real boss of New York City was not its elected mayor, Hugh Graham, here depicted as a lowly shoe-shiner, but the Tammany Hall political machine. The loose strap underneath the boot, used to control both City Hall and Tammany, belongs to Richard Croker, Tammany's leader from 1886 to 1901.

Big-city machines, then, were both positive and negative forces in urban life. Reformers despised them for disregarding election laws and encouraging vice, but many immigrants valued them for providing social welfare services and for creating opportunities for upward mobility.

The history of President John F. Kennedy's family offers one example of the economic and political opportunities opened up by machine politics. Both of Kennedy's grandfathers, John Francis ("Honey Fitz") Fitzgerald and Patrick Joseph Kennedy, were the children of penniless Irish immigrants who arrived in Boston in the 1840s. Fitzgerald excelled at academics and won a coveted place in Harvard's Medical School, but left Harvard that same year, choosing a career in politics instead. Between 1891 and 1905, Fitzgerald served as a Boston city councilor, Massachusetts state congressman and senator, U.S. congressman, and mayor of Boston. For much of this period, he derived considerable income and power from his position as the North End ward boss, where he supervised the trading of jobs for votes and favors for cash in his section of Boston's Democratic and Irish-dominated political machine.

Patrick Kennedy, an East Boston tavern owner and liquor merchant, became an equally important figure in Boston city politics. In addition to running the Democratic Party's affairs in Ward Two, he served on the Strategy Board, a secret council of Boston's machine politicians that met regularly to devise policies, settle disputes, and divide up the week's graft. Both Fitzgerald and Kennedy derived a substantial income from their political work and used it to lift their families into middle-class prosperity. Kennedy's son (and the future president's father), Joseph P. Kennedy, would go on to make a fortune as a Wall Street speculator and liquor distributor and to groom his sons for Harvard and the highest political offices in the land. But his rapid economic and social ascent had been made possible by his father's and father-in-law's earlier success in Boston machine politics.

Underworld figures, too, influenced urban life. In the early years of the 20th century, gangsterism was a scourge of Italian neighborhoods, where Sicilian immigrants had established outposts of the notorious Mafia, and in Irish, Jewish, Chinese, and other ethnic communities as well. Favorite targets of these gangsters were small-scale manufacturers and contractors, who were threatened with violence and economic ruin if they did not pay a gang for "protection." Gangsters enforced their demands with physical force, beating up or killing those who failed to abide by the "rules." In Chinese communities, secret societies originating in China, or *tongs,* and initially set up in America to strengthen communal life among the immigrants, occasionally crossed the line into crime. Some-

times this transition resulted from good intentions—for example, tong members might smuggle into the United States the wife and children of an immigrant Chinese man who had no legal way of reuniting his family—but other times, tongs enmeshed themselves in far more damaging criminal activities such as the opium trade, prostitution, and gambling.

Greedy for money, power, and fame, and willing to use any means necessary, many immigrant and ethnic criminals considered themselves authentic entrepreneurs cut from the American mold. By the 1920s, petty extortion had escalated in urban areas, and underworld crime had become big business. Al Capone, the ruthless Chicago mobster who made a fortune from gambling, prostitution, and bootleg liquor during Prohibition, once claimed: "Prohibition is a business. All I do is to supply a public demand. I do it in the best and least harmful way I can." New York City's Arnold Rothstein, whose financial sophistication won him a gambling empire and the power to fix the 1919 World Series, nurtured his reputation as "the J. P. Morgan of the underworld." Mobsters like Rothstein and Capone were charismatic figures, both in their ethnic communities and in the nation at large. Few immigrants, however, followed their criminal path to economic success.

African American Labor and Community

Unlike immigrants, African Americans remained a predominantly rural and southern people in the early 20th century. Most blacks were sharecroppers and tenant farmers. The markets for cotton and other southern crops had stabilized in the early 20th century, but black farmers remained vulnerable to exploitation. Landowners, most of whom were white, often forced sharecroppers to accept artificially low prices for their crops. At the same time, they charged high prices for seed, tools, and groceries at the local stores they controlled. Few rural areas generated enough business to support more than one store or to create a competitive climate that might force prices down. Those sharecroppers who traveled elsewhere to sell their crops or purchase their necessities risked retaliation—either physical assaults by white vigilantes or eviction from their land. Thus most remained beholden to their landowners, mired in poverty and debt.

Some African Americans sought a better life by migrating to industrial areas of the South and the North. In the South, they worked in iron and coal mines, in furniture and cigarette manufacture, as railroad track layers and longshoremen, and as laborers in the steel mills of

decades of the 20th century, few other manufacturers were prepared to follow Ford's lead, and most factory workers remained in a fragile economic state.

Samuel F. Gompers and the AFL

For those workers, the only hope for economic improvement lay in organizing unions powerful enough to wrest wage concessions from reluctant employers. This was not an easy task. The charged, often violent labor protests of the Gilded Age had been put down. Labor organizations, such as the Knights of Labor, that had unified workers had been defeated. Federal and state governments had shown themselves ready to use military force to break strikes. The

courts, following the lead of the U.S. Supreme Court, repeatedly found unions in violation of the Sherman Antitrust Act, even though that act had been intended to control corporations, not unions. Judges in most states usually granted employer requests for injunctions—court orders that barred striking workers from picketing their place of employment (and thus from obstructing employer efforts to hire replacement workers). Before 1916, no federal laws protected workers' right to organize or required employers to bargain with the unions to which their workers belonged.

This hostile legal environment retarded the growth of unions from the 1890s through the 1930s. It also made the major labor organization of those years, the American

---

MUSICAL LINK TO THE PAST

Before Jazz: An Early African American Orchestra

Composer: Wilbur C. Sweatman

Title: "Down Home Rag"

Performer: James Reese Europe's Society Orchestra (December 29, 1913)

The dense, smeared, and exciting sound of "Down Home Rag," with its frenetic tempo that approximates the speed of today's punk rock, represented one of the first attempts to define black musical identity before jazz became a commercial force. The band on this disc, the first black orchestra to secure a major recording contract, was led by James Reese Europe, the son of an Alabama slave.

Jim Crow segregation laws and practices extended into the world of professional music, limiting the opportunities and respect accorded to black musicians and composers. The strict color line in musicians' unions meant that blacks earned lesser wages and were often asked to wash dishes or work more hours than white musicians to keep their nonunion jobs. African Americans were also kept from performing and writing in the more high-brow world of classical music. To combat these problems, Europe became the leading force behind the Clef Club, a New York City trade union and booking agency created in 1910 for and by African American musicians. The Club's signature event was their May 2, 1912, staging of a "Concert of Negro Music" at Carnegie Hall, America's premiere venue for classical music, a place where no African American performers or compositions had previously been featured. Blacks and whites

sat in equal numbers in the capacity crowd, probably for the first time at an American concert. Following the show, more black composers and musicians received jobs, although the classical market was still heavily skewed toward whites.

Europe believed that African American orchestras needed to demonstrate their own character apart from white orchestral music. In "Down Home Rag," we hear a scaled-down 18-piece version of the 125-piece orchestra that showcased Europe's musical vision at Carnegie. The orchestra boasted a full-bodied, percussive, and singular sound, including 14 upright pianos and unorthodox instruments such as banjos, mandolins, and guitars combined with more traditional string instruments and percussion. Europe's mixing of violin-led melodies that sounded like 19th-century Virginia reels with an aggressive and layered rhythmic foundation provided an early preview of the mixing of black and white genres that characterized American music in the 20th century.

1. How would you describe the music that James Reese Europe created with his orchestra?
2. Why do you think Europe argued that African American orchestral music had to be different in character from that usually performed in America's classical concert halls?

For additional sources related to this feature, visit the *Liberty, Equality, Power* Web site at:

http://history.wadsworth.com/murrin_LEP4e

MEN AT WORK

This photo of male workers stoking a boiler conveys some of the grime and heat associated with much turn-of-the-20th-century blue-collar work as well as the strength and concentration required of workmen.

Underwood Photo Archives.

Federation of Labor (AFL), more timid and conservative than it had been before the depression of the 1890s. In the aftermath of that depression, the AFL focused on organizing craft, or skilled, workers such as carpenters, typographers, plumbers, painters, and machinists. Because of their skills, these workers commanded more respect from employers than did the unskilled laborers. Employers negotiated contracts, or trade agreements, with craft unions that stipulated the wages workers were to be paid, the hours they were to work, and the rules under which new workers would be accepted into the trade. These agreements were accorded the same legal protection that American law bestowed on other commercial contracts.

As the AFL emphasized these bread-and-butter issues, it withdrew from the political activism that had once occupied its attention. It no longer agitated for governmental regulation of the economy and the workplace. The AFL had concluded that labor's powerful opponents in the legislatures and the courts would find ways to undermine whatever governmental gains organized labor managed to achieve. That conclusion was reinforced by a 1905 ruling, *Lochner* v. *New York,* in which the U.S. Supreme Court declared unconstitutional a seemingly innocent New York state law limiting bakery employees to a 10-hour day.

The AFL's "business" unionism took its most forceful expression from its president, Samuel F. Gompers. A onetime Marxist and cigarmaker who had helped found the AFL in 1886, Gompers was reelected to the AFL presidency every year from 1896 until his death in 1924. The AFL showed considerable vitality under his leadership, especially in the early years when its membership quadrupled

from less than a half million in 1897 to more than 2 million in 1904. Aware of the AFL's growing significance and conservatism, the National Civic Federation, a newly formed council of corporate executives, agreed to meet periodically with the organization's leaders to discuss the nation's industrial and labor problems.

Nevertheless, the AFL had limited success. Its 2 million members represented only a small portion of the industrial workforce. Its concentration among craft workers, moreover, distanced it from most workers, who were not skilled. Unskilled and semiskilled workers could only be organized into an industrial union that offered membership to all workers in a particular industry. Gompers understood the importance of such unions and allowed several of them, including the United Mine Workers (UMW) and the International Ladies Garment Workers Union (ILGWU), to participate in the AFL. But AFL ranks remained dominated by skilled workers who looked down upon the unskilled. Ethnic background intensified these craftsmen's sense of superiority over the unskilled. Most skilled workers were from old immigrant stock—particularly English, Scottish, German, and Irish—and they shared the common prejudice against immigrants from Southern and Eastern Europe.

AFL members demonstrated even worse prejudice toward black workers. In the early 20th century, more than 10 AFL unions excluded African Americans from membership. The AFL's racist policies partially account for the shrinking numbers of black tradesmen between 1870 and 1910. White and black workers sometimes managed to set aside their suspicions of each other and cooperate. The

UMW allowed black workers to join and to rise to positions of leadership. In New Orleans, black and white dockworkers constructed a remarkable experiment in biracial unionism that flourished from the 1890s through the early 1920s. But these moments of cooperation were rare.

Although blacks made up too small a percentage of the working class to build alternative labor organizations that would counteract the influence of the AFL, the new immigrants from Eastern and Southern Europe were too numerous to be ignored. Their participation in the UMW enabled that union to grow from only 14,000 in 1897 to more than 300,000 in 1914. In 1909, a strike of 20,000 women workers against the owners of New York City's garment factories inspired tens of thousands of workers, male and female, to join the ILGWU.

"Big Bill" Haywood and the IWW

When the AFL failed to help them organize, immigrants turned to other unions. The most important was the Industrial Workers of the World (IWW), founded by western miners in 1905 and led by William "Big Bill" Haywood. The IWW rejected the AFL principle of craft organization, hoping instead to organize all workers into "one big union." It scorned the notion that only a conservative union could survive in American society, declaring its commitment to revolution instead.

The IWW refused to sign collective bargaining agreements with employers, arguing that such agreements only trapped workers in capitalist property relations. Capitalism had to be overthrown through struggles between workers and their employers at the point of production. Although hundreds of thousands of workers passed through its ranks or participated in its strikes, the IWW's membership rarely exceeded 20,000. Nevertheless, few labor organizations inspired as much fear. The IWW organized the poorest and most isolated workers—lumbermen, miners, and trackmen in the West, textile workers and longshoremen in the East. Emboldened by IWW leaders, these workers waged strikes against employers who were unaccustomed to having their authority challenged. Violence lurked beneath the surface of these strikes and occasionally erupted in bloody skirmishes between strikers and police, National Guardsmen, or the private security forces hired by employers. Some blamed the IWW for the violence, seeing it as a direct outgrowth of calls for a "class war." Others understood that the IWW was not solely responsible. Employers had shown themselves quite willing to resort to violence to enforce their will on employees. In 1913, for example, at Ludlow, Colorado, the Colorado Fuel and Iron Company, a subsidiary of Rockefeller's Standard Oil Company, brought in a private security force and the local

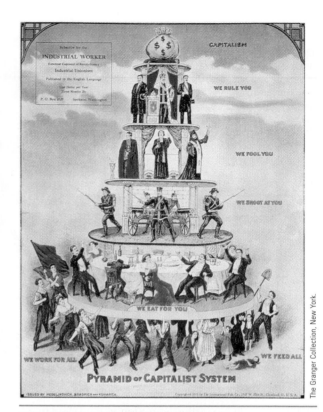

THE RADICAL CRITIQUE OF CAPITALISM

This "Pyramid of the Capitalist System" humorously illustrates how radicals analyzed capitalism—as an economic system that oppressed workers, rewarded the wealthy, and worshipped money. In this pyramid, the police, political leaders, and clerics are all depicted as the opponents of workers and the servants of capital.

militia (which it controlled) to break up a UMW strike. When the company evicted strikers and their families from their homes, the union set up 13 tent colonies to obstruct the entrances to the mines. The standoff came to a bloody conclusion in April 1914 when company police, firing into one colony of tents, killed 66 men, women, and children.

The "Ludlow massacre" outraged the nation. At hearings of the U.S. Commission on Industrial Relations, John D. Rockefeller, Jr., was humiliated by Commissioner Frank Walsh's disclosure that the industrialist had been complicit in the events leading up to the violence. The massacre revealed yet again what the IWW strikes had already demonstrated: that many American workers resented their low wages and poor working conditions; that neither the government nor employers offered workers a mechanism for airing and peacefully resolving their grievances; and that workers, as a result, felt compelled to protest through joining unions and waging strikes, even if it meant risking their lives. On the eve of the First World War, almost 40 years after the Great Railroad Strike of 1877 (chapter 19), industrial conflict still plagued the nation.

The Joys of the City

Industrial workers might be missing their fair share of the nation's prosperity, but they were crowding the dance halls, vaudeville theaters, amusement parks, and ballparks offered by the new world of commercial entertainment. Above all, they were embracing a new technological marvel, the movies.

Movies were well suited to poor city dwellers with little money, little free time, and little command of the English language. Initially, the movies cost only a nickel. The "nickelodeons" where they were shown were usually converted storefronts in working-class neighborhoods. Movies required little leisure time because at first they lasted only 15 minutes on average. Viewers with more time on their hands could stay for a cycle of two or three films (or for several cycles). And even non-English-speakers could understand what was happening on the "silent screen." By 1910, at least 20,000 nickelodeons dotted northern cities.

These early "moving pictures" were primitive by today's standards, but they were thrilling just the same. The figures appearing on the screen were "larger than life." Moviegoers could transport themselves to parts of the world they would otherwise never see, encounter people they would otherwise never meet, and watch boxing matches they could otherwise not afford to attend. The darkened theater provided a setting in which secret desires, especially sexual ones, could be explored. As one newspaper innocently commented in 1899: "For the first time in the history of the world it is possible to see what a kiss looks like."

No easy generalizations are possible about the content of these early films, more than half of which came from France, Germany, and Italy. American-made films tended toward slapstick comedies, adventure stories, and romances. Producers did not yet shy away, as they soon would, from the lustier or seedier sides of American life.

© Bettmann/Corbis.

THEDA BARA AS CLEOPATRA (1917)

Bara was the first movie actress to gain fame for her roles as a "vamp"—a woman whose irresistible sexual charm led men to ruin. Because little effort was made to censor movies before the early 1920s, movie directors were able to explore sexual themes and to film their female stars in erotic, and partially nude, poses.

The Hollywood formula of happy endings had yet to be worked out. In fact, the industry, centered in New York City and Fort Lee, New Jersey, had yet to locate itself in cheery southern California. In 1914, the movies' first sex symbol, Theda Bara, debuted in a movie that showed her tempting an upstanding American ambassador into infidelity and ruin. She would be the first of the big screen's

NICKELODEONS IN MAJOR AMERICAN CITIES, 1910				
Cities	Population	Nickelodeons (estimate)	Seating Capacity	Population per Seat
New York	4,338,322	450	150,000	29
Chicago	2,000,000	310	93,000	22
Philadelphia	1,491,082	160	57,000	26
St. Louis	824,000	142	50,410	16
Cleveland	600,000	75	22,500	27
Baltimore	600,000	83	24,900	24
San Francisco	400,000	68	32,400	12
Cincinnati	350,000	75	22,500	16
New Orleans	325,000	28	5,600	58

Source: Garth Jowett, *Film: The Democratic Art* (Boston: Little, Brown, 1976), p. 46.

many "vamps," so-called because the characters they portrayed, like vampires, thrived on the blood (and death) of men.

The New Sexuality and the Rise of Feminism

The appearance of the "vamp" was one sign of a growing popular dissatisfaction with the separate-sphere ideology that dominated American life in the 19th century (see chapter 19) and, in particular, of one notion central to it: that women were naturally chaste and passionless creatures. The leaders of this revolt against separate spheres included middle-class women who, after achieving first-rate educations at elite women's colleges, were told they could not participate in the nation's economic, governmental, or professional enterprises. Now they began to demand that they be allowed to enter what had been a man's world. The revolt drew as well on young, single, working-class women who were entering the workforce in large numbers and mixing at workplaces, in loosely supervised ways, with men their own age.

The associations between young men and women that sprang up at work carried over into their leisure. Young people of both sexes flocked to the dance halls that were opening in every major city. They rejected the stiff formality of earlier ballroom dances such as the cotillion or the waltz for the freedom and intimacy of newer forms, such as the fox trot, tango, and bunny-hug. They went to movies and to amusement parks together, and they engaged, far more than their parents had, in premarital sex. It is estimated that the proportion of women having sex before marriage rose from 10 percent to 25 percent in the generation that was coming of age between 1910 and 1920.

Feminism

This movement toward sexual freedom was one expression of women's dissatisfaction with the restrictions that had been imposed on them by earlier generations. By the

---

H I S T O R Y   T H R O U G H   F I L M

The Great White Hope (1970)

Directed by Martin Ritt. Starring James Earl Jones (Jack Jefferson) and Jane Alexander (Eleanor Backman).

This movie is a fictional retelling of the life of Jack Johnson, the first black world heavyweight boxing champion, and of the furor that his dominance over white boxers, his outspokenness, and his relationships with white women generated in early 20th-century America. The movie opens with white boxing promoters persuading a former white champion (James Bradley) to come out of retirement to battle the black champion, here called Jack Jefferson (rather than Johnson). In a subsequent scene, Jefferson destroys Bradley in the ring and reacts with defiant cheeriness to the boos and racial epithets that rain down upon him from the predominantly white crowd.

Jefferson refuses to accept any of the limitations that white society placed on black men at the time. He is neither submissive nor deferential toward whites, and he openly dates white women. One evening, federal agents burst in on Jefferson and his white lover, Eleanor Backman (Jane Alexander), and accuse Jefferson of violating the Mann Act, a 1910 law that made it illegal to transport women across state lines for sexual purposes (see page 635). At Jefferson's trial, prosecutors expected to convince a jury that Backman was coerced into sex, for no white woman, they intended to argue, would have freely chosen to consort with a black man in this way.

Jefferson manages to evade the authorities and flee to Europe, where Backman joins him. The early months abroad are invigorating for both, as Jefferson is celebrated for his fighting prowess and the couple's love for each other flourishes. Soon, however, the opponents dry up, money stops coming in, and a sense of despair grows between the two lovers. Their exile ends disastrously in Mexico, where Backman kills herself after an argument with Jefferson. Jefferson, his spirit finally broken, agrees to throw a fight against the newest Great White Hope, Jess Willard, in

second decade of the 20th century, eloquent spokeswomen had emerged to make the case for full female freedom and equality. The author Charlotte Perkins Gilman called for the release of women from domestic chores through the collectivization of housekeeping. Social activist Margaret Sanger insisted, in her lectures on birth control, that women should be free to enjoy sexual relations without having to worry about unwanted motherhood. The anarchist Emma Goldman denounced marriage as a kind of prostitution and embraced the ideal of "free love"—love unburdened by contractual commitment. Alice Paul, founder of the National Women's Party, brought a new militancy to the campaign for woman suffrage (see chapter 21).

These women were among the first to use the term *feminism* to describe their desire for complete equality with men. Some of them came together in Greenwich Village, a community of radical artists and writers in lower Manhattan, where they found a supportive environment in which to express and live by their feminist ideals. Crystal Eastman, a leader of the feminist Greenwich Village

group called Heterodoxy, defined the feminist challenge as "how to arrange the world so that women can be human beings, with a chance to exercise their infinitely varied gifts in infinitely varied ways, instead of being destined by the accident of their sex to one field of activity."

The movement for sexual and gender equality aroused considerable anxiety in the more conservative sectors of American society. Parents worried about the promiscuity of their children. Conservatives were certain that the "new women" would transform American cities into dens of iniquity. Vice commissions sprang up in every major city to clamp down on prostitution, drunkenness, and pornography. The campaign for prohibition—a ban on the sale of alcoholic beverages—gathered steam. Movie theater owners were pressured into excluding "indecent" films from their screens. Many believed the lurid tales of international vice lords scouring foreign lands for innocent girls who could be delivered to American brothel owners. This "white slave trade" inspired passage of the 1910 Mann Act, which made the transportation of women across state lines for immoral purposes a federal crime.

return for an opportunity to end his fugitive status and return to the United States.

Made in 1970, the *Great White Hope* was inspired by the brash heavyweight champion of the 1960s, Muhammad Ali. The film is quite faithful to the story of the real Jack Johnson, who dated white women, was arrested for "violating" the Mann Act, fled the country rather than submit to jail, and ultimately lost a heavyweight bout to Jess Willard. The film endows Backman, a fictional character, with more "class" and refinement than the real women who associated with Johnson usually possessed. The film also fictionalizes Johnson's fight against Willard by suggesting that Johnson could have won the fight had he not been required to throw it. Despite these changes, the film successfully re-creates the climate of the early years of the 20th century and the white hostility imperiling a black man who dared to assert his pride and independence.

James Earl Jones as Jack Jefferson.

MARGARET SANGER ON TRIAL, 1916

Feminist Margaret Sanger, left, was put on trial for using the U.S. mail service to circulate her book *The Woman Rebel*, which advocated birth control. A federal law barred the use of the mails to spread birth control advice or techniques.

© Bettmann/Corbis.

Nor did it escape the attention of conservatives that Greenwich Village was home not only to the dangerous exponents of "free love" but also to equally dangerous advocates of class warfare. Prominent IWW organizer Elizabeth Gurley Flynn was a member of Heterodoxy; her lover, Carlo Tresca, was an IWW theoretician. "Big Bill" Haywood also frequented Greenwich Village, where he was lionized as a working-class hero. When Greenwich Village radicals began publishing an avant-garde artistic journal in 1914, they called it *The Masses;* its editor was Max Eastman, the brother of Crystal. This convergence of labor and feminist militancy intensified conservative feeling that the nation had strayed too far from its roots.

Cultural conservatism was strongest in those areas of the country that were least involved in the ongoing industrial and sexual revolutions—in farming communities and small towns; in the South, where industrialization and urbanization were proceeding at a slower rate than elsewhere; and among old social elites, who felt pushed aside by the new corporate men of power.

Conservatives and radicals alike shared a conviction that the country could not afford to ignore its social problems—the power of the corporations; the poverty and powerlessness of wage earners; the role of women and African Americans. Conservatives were as determined to restore 19th-century moral standards as radicals were determined to achieve working-class emancipation and women's equality. But in politics, neither would become the dominant force. That role would fall to the so-called progressives, a diverse group of reformers who confidently and optimistically believed they could bring order and justice to the new society.

Conclusion

Between 1890 and 1920, corporate power, innovation, and demands had stimulated the growth of cities, attracted millions of immigrants, enhanced commercial opportunities, and created the conditions for a vibrant urban culture. Many Americans thrived in this new environment, taking advantage of business opportunities or, as in the case of women, discovering liberties in dress, employment, dating, and sex that they had not known. Millions of Americans, however, remained impoverished, unable to rise in the social order or to earn enough in wages to support their families. African Americans who had migrated to the North in search of economic opportunity suffered more than any other single group, as they found themselves shut out of most industrial and commercial employment.

Henry Ford, whose generous $5-per-day wage drew tens of thousands to his Detroit factories, was an exceptional employer. Although other employers had learned to restrain their crass displays of wealth and had turned toward philanthropy in search of a better public image, they remained reluctant to follow Ford's lead in improving the conditions in which their employees labored.

Working-class Americans proved resourceful in creating self-help institutions to serve their own and each other's needs. In some cities, they gained a measure of power through the establishment of political machines. Labor unions arose and fought for a variety of reforms, but their success was limited. How to inject greater equality and opportunity into an industrial society in which the gap between rich and poor had reached alarming proportions remained a daunting challenge.

SUGGESTED READINGS

For a general overview of the period, see **Alan Dawley, *Struggles for Justice: Social Responsibility and the Liberal State*** (1991), and **Nell Irvin Painter, *Standing at Armageddon: The United States, 1877–1919*** (1987). On economic growth and corporate development, see **Harold G. Vatter, *The Drive to Industrial Maturity: The United States Economy, 1860–1914*** (1975), **Glenn Porter, *The Rise of Big Business, 1860–1910*** (1973), and **Robert Kanigel, *The One Best Way: Frederick Winslow Taylor and the Enigma of Efficiency*** (1997). For a discussion of Ford's labor policies and their impact on immigrant workers, see **Stephen Meyer III, *The Five Dollar Day: Labor Management and Social Control in the Ford Motor Company, 1908–1921*** (1981). On the influence of Darwinist thinking on American culture, see **Robert Bannister, *Social Darwinism: Science and Myth in Anglo-American Social Thought*** (1970). For an excellent overview concerning immigration, consult **Roger Daniels, *Coming to America: A History of Immigration and Ethnicity in American Life*** (2002). The best single-volume history of European immigrants is **John Bodnar, *The Transplanted: A History of Immigration*** (1985). For an innovative account of European immigrants' encounters with racial patterns in the United States, see **Matthew Frye Jacobson, *Whiteness of a Different Color: European Americans and the Alchemy of Race*** (1998). The experience of Chinese immigrants during the period of American exclusion is discussed in **Erika Lee, *At America's Gates: Chinese Immigration During the Exclusion Era, 1882–1943*** (2003), while **Steven P. Erie, *Rainbow's End: Irish Americans and the Dilemmas of Urban Machine Politics, 1840–1945*** (1988), insightfully examines the benefits and costs of big city machines. **David Montgomery, *The Fall of the House of Labor, 1865–1925*** (1987), and **Herbert Gutman, *Work, Culture, and***

Society in Industrializing America (1976), are essential sources on both immigrant and nonimmigrant labor during this period. **John Hope Franklin and Alfred A. Moss Jr., *From Slavery to Freedom: A History of Negro Americans,*** 8th ed. (2000) offers a comprehensive account of African American life, while an important account of black female workers can be found in **Jacqueline Jones, *Labor of Love Labor of Sorrow: Black Women, Work and the Family from Slavery to the Present*** (1985). On the rise of mass culture, see **David Nasaw, *Going Out: The Rise and Fall of Public Amusements*** (1993), and **Warren I. Susman, *Culture as History: the Transformation of American Society in the Twentieth Century*** (1984). On the new woman and feminism, consult **Nancy F. Cott, *The Grounding of Modern Feminism*** (1987), and **Christine Stansell, *American Moderns: Bohemian New York and the Creation of a New Century*** (2000).

 AMERICAN JOURNEY ONLINE
AND
INFOTRAC COLLEGE EDITION

Visit the source collections at www.ajaccess.wadsworth.com and infotrac.thomsonlearning.com and use the Search function with the following key terms to explore documents, images, audio and video clips, articles, and commentary related to the material in this chapter.

Sherman Antitrust Act	Andrew Carnegie
Alice Paul	Frederick W. Taylor
"Big Bill" Haywood	doctrine of separate spheres
J. P. Morgan	Triangle Shirtwaist Company

GRADE AIDS

Visit the Liberty Equality Power Companion Web Site for resources specific to this textbook: http://history.wadsworth.com/murrin_LEP4e

 The CD in the back of this book and the U.S. History Resource Center at http://history.wadsworth.com/u.s./ offer a variety of tools to help you succeed in this course, including access to quizzes; images; documents; interactive simulations, maps, and timelines; movie explorations; and a wealth of other sources.

the 1880s and 1890s (see chapter 19) accelerated. Cheap, 10-cent periodicals such as *McClure's Magazine* and *Ladies Home Journal,* with circulations of 400,000 to 1 million, began to displace genteel and relatively expensive 35-cent publications such as *Harper's* and *The Atlantic Monthly.* The expanded readership brought journalists considerably more money and prestige and attracted many talented and ambitious men and women to the profession. Wider circulation also made magazine publishers more receptive to stories—particularly sensational ones about ill-gotten economic power, government corruption, and urban vice—that might appeal to their newly acquired millions of readers.

The Turn toward "Realism"

The American middle class's growing intellectual interest in "realism" also favored the muckrakers. "Realism" was a way of thinking that prized detachment, objectivity, and skepticism. Those who embraced it pointed out that constitutional theory, with its emphasis on citizenship, elections, and democratic procedures, had little to do with the

George Bellows, "Cliff Dwellers" 1913. Oil on canvas. Los Angeles County Museum of Art, Los Angeles County Fund.

CLIFF DWELLERS

George Bellows was a member of the Ashcan School, a group of painters who sought to create a distinctly American and "realist" style. Here Bellows portrays the urban masses sympathetically and in a way that evokes their connection to a group of quintessential Americans, the cliff-dwelling Pueblo Indians.

way government in the United States actually worked. What could one learn about bosses, machines, and graft from studying the Constitution? There was also a sense that the nation's glorification of the "self-made man" and of "individualism" was preventing Americans from coping effectively with large-scale organizations—corporations, banks, labor unions—and their sudden centrality to the nation's economy and to society. The realists, finally, criticized the tendency, which was prevalent among American writers and artists, to emulate European styles, and they called on them to pioneer new styles that would be better able to "capture" American life and thought.

By the first decade of the 20th century, intellectuals and artists of all sorts—philosophers John Dewey and William James; social scientists Thorstein Veblen and Charles Beard; novelists Frank Norris, Theodore Dreiser, and Upton Sinclair; painters John Sloan, George Bellows, and other members of the "Ashcan School"; photographers Jacob Riis and Lewis Hine; architects Louis Sullivan and Frank Lloyd Wright; jurists Oliver Wendell Holmes and Louis Brandeis—were attempting to create truer, more realistic

ways of representing and analyzing American society. Many of them were inspired by the work of investigative journalists, and some had been newspapermen. Years of firsthand observation enabled them to describe American society as it "truly was." They brought shadowy figures vividly to life. They pictured for Americans the captain of industry who ruthlessly destroyed his competitors; the con artist who tricked young people new to city life; the innocent immigrant girl who fell prey to the white slave traders; the corrupt policeman under whose protection urban vice flourished.

A large middle class, uneasy about the state of American society, applauded the muckrakers for telling these stories and became interested in reform. Members of this class put pressure on city and state governments to send crooked government officials to jail and to stamp out the sources of corruption and vice. Between 1902 and 1916, more than 100 cities launched investigations of the prostitution trade. At the federal level, all three branches of government felt compelled to address the question of "the trusts"—the concentration of power in the hands of a few

industrialists and financiers. Progressivism began to crystallize into a political movement centered on the abuses the muckrakers had exposed.

Settlement Houses and Women's Activism

Established by middle-class reformers, settlement houses were intended to help the largely immigrant urban poor cope with the harsh conditions of city life. Much of the inspiration for settlement houses came from young, college-educated, Protestant women from comfortable but not particularly wealthy backgrounds. Some had imbibed a commitment to social justice from parents and grandparents who had fought to abolish slavery. Highly educated, talented, and sensitive to social injustice, they rebelled against being relegated solely to the roles of wife and mother and sought to assert their independence in socially useful ways.

Hull House

Jane Addams and Ellen Gates Starr established the nation's first settlement house, in Chicago, in 1889. The two women had been inspired by a visit the year before to London's Toynbee Hall, where a small group of middle-class men had been living and working with that city's poor since 1884. Addams and Starr bought a decaying mansion that had once been the country home of a prominent Chicagoan, Charles J. Hull. By 1889, "Hull House" stood amidst factories, churches, saloons, and tenements inhabited by poor, largely foreign-born working-class families.

Addams quickly emerged as the guiding spirit of Hull House. She moved into the building and demanded that

Brown Brothers.

JANE ADDAMS

The founder of the settlement house movement, Addams was the most famous woman reformer of the progressive era. This photograph dates from the 1890s or 1900s, Hull House's formative period.

WOMEN ENROLLED IN INSTITUTIONS OF HIGHER EDUCATION, 1870–1930

Year	Women's Colleges (thousands of students)	Coed Institutions (thousands of students)	Total (thousands of students)	Percentage of All Students Enrolled
1870	6.5	4.6	11.1	21.0%
1880	15.7	23.9	39.6	33.4
1890	16.8	39.5	56.3	35.9
1900	24.4	61.0	85.4	36.8
1910	34.1	106.5	140.6	39.6
1920	52.9	230.0	282.9	47.3
1930	82.1	398.7	480.8	43.7

Source: From Mabel Newcomer, *A Century of Higher Education for American Women* (New York: Harper and Row, 1959), p. 46.

served traditional foods and drinks, provided meeting space for fraternal organizations, and offered camaraderie to men longing to speak in their native tongue. Saloonkeepers sometimes functioned as informal bankers, cashing checks and making small loans. Not surprisingly, many immigrants shunned the prohibition movement. They had no interest in being "uplifted" and "reformed" in this way. Here was a gulf separating the immigrant masses from the Protestant middle class that even compassionate reformers such as Jane Addams could not bridge.

A Nation of Clubwomen

Settlement house workers comprised only one part of a vast network of female reformers. Hundreds of thousands of women belonged to local women's clubs. Conceived as self-help organizations in which women would be encouraged to sharpen their minds, refine their domestic skills, and strengthen their moral faculties, these clubs began taking on tasks of social reform. Clubwomen typically focused their energies on improving schools, building libraries and playgrounds, expanding educational and vocational opportunities for girls, and securing fire and sanitation codes for tenement houses. In so doing, they made traditional female concerns—the nurturing and education of children, the care of the home—questions of public policy.

Clubwomen rose to prominence in black communities, too, and addressed similar sorts of issues; on matters of sexuality and alcohol, they often shared the conservative sentiments of their white counterparts. Some groups of black clubwomen ventured into community affairs more boldly than their white counterparts, however, especially in southern states, where black men were being stripped of the right to vote, to serve on juries, and to hold political office. Whites were prepared to punish any African American, male or female, who showed too much initiative or was thought to be challenging the principles of white supremacy. Even so, many black female activists persevered in the face of such threats, determined to provide leadership in their communities and voice their people's concerns.

☛ Socialism and Progressivism

Issues such as women's sexuality and men's alcoholism drew progressives in a conservative direction, but other issues drew them to socialism. In the early 20th century, socialism stood for the transfer of control over industry from a few industrialists to the laboring masses. Socialists believed that such a transfer, usually defined in terms of government ownership and operation of economic institutions, would make it impossible for wealthy elites to control society.

The Socialist Party of America, founded in 1901, became a political force during the first 16 years of the century, and socialist ideas influenced progressivism. In 1912, at the peak of its influence, the Socialist Party enrolled more than 115,000 members. Its presidential candidate, the charismatic Eugene Victor Debs of Terre Haute, Indiana, attracted almost a million votes—6 percent of the total votes cast that year. In that same year, 1,200 Socialists held elective office in 340 different municipalities. Of these, 79 were mayors of cities as geographically and demographically diverse as Schenectady, New York; Milwaukee, Wisconsin; Butte, Montana; and Berkeley, California. More than 300 newspapers and periodicals, with a combined circulation exceeding 2 million, spread the socialist gospel. The most important socialist publication was *Appeal to Reason,* published by Kansan Julius Wayland and sent out each week to 750,000 subscribers. In 1905, Wayland published, in serial form, a novel by an obscure muckraker named Upton Sinclair, which depicted the scandalous working conditions in Chicago's meatpacking industry. When it was later published in book form in 1906, *The Jungle* created such an outcry that the federal government was forced to regulate the meat industry.

The Many Faces of Socialism

Socialists came in many varieties. In Milwaukee, they consisted of predominantly German working-class immigrants and their descendants; in New York City, their numbers were strongest among Jewish immigrants from Eastern Europe. In the Southwest, tens of thousands of disgruntled native-born farmers who had been Populists in the 1890s now flocked to the socialist banner. In Oklahoma alone, these erstwhile Populists were numerous enough by 1912 to support 11 socialist weeklies. In that same year, Oklahoma voters gave a higher percentage of their votes, more than 16 percent, to the Socialist candidate Debs than did the voters of any other state. In the West, socialism was popular among miners, timber cutters, and others who labored in isolated areas where industrialists possessed extraordinary power over work and community matters. These radicals gravitated to the militant labor union, the Industrial Workers of the World (IWW) (see chapter 20), which found a home in the Socialist Party from 1905 to 1913.

Socialists differed from each other not only in their occupations and ethnic origins but also in their politics. The IWW was the most radical socialist group, with its

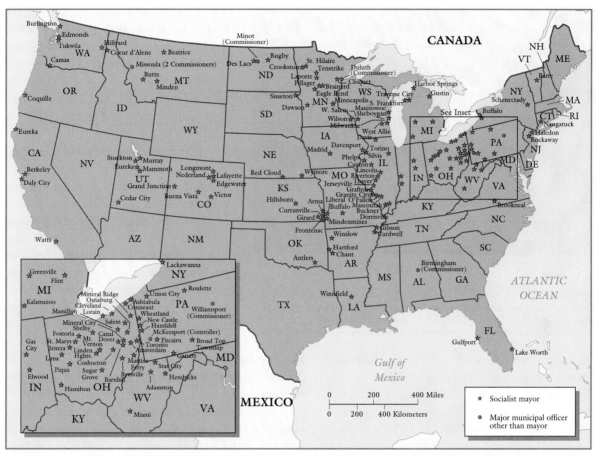

MAP 21.1 CITIES AND TOWNS ELECTING SOCIALIST MAYORS OR OTHER MAJOR MUNICIPAL OFFICERS, 1911–1920

This map reveals the strength of socialist electoral support in some unexpected areas: western Pennsylvania, Ohio, Illinois, Minnesota, a cluster of towns where Oklahoma, Missouri, and Kansas meet, Colorado, and Utah.

incessant calls for revolution. By contrast, mainstream socialism, as articulated by Debs, was more respectful of American political, cultural, and religious traditions. Mainstream socialists saw themselves as the saviors rather than the destroyers of the American republic—as the true heirs of Thomas Jefferson. Their confidence that the nation could be redeemed through conventional politics—through the election of Debs as president—is evidence of their affection for American democracy. And their faith in redemption reveals the degree to which Protestant religious beliefs underlay their quest for social justice and what they called a "cooperative commonwealth." Evolutionary socialists, led by Victor Berger of Milwaukee, abandoned talk of revolution altogether and chose instead an aggressive brand of reform politics. They were dubbed "gas and water socialists" because of their interest in improving city services.

These differences would, after 1912, fragment the socialist movement. For a decade or so, however, all of these divergent groups managed to coexist in a single political party thanks, largely, to the leadership of Debs.

When he was released from a Chicago jail in 1895 after serving time for his role in the strike against the Pullman Company (see chapter 19), Debs declared to a gathering of 100,000 admirers: "Manifestly the spirit of '76 still survives. The fires of liberty and noble aspirations are not yet extinguished. . . . The vindication and glorification of American principles of government, as proclaimed to the world in the Declaration of Independence, is the high purpose of this convocation."

Socialists and Progressives

Debs's speeches both attracted and disturbed progressives. On the one hand, he spoke compellingly about the dangers of unregulated capitalism and excessively concentrated wealth, both progressive concerns. His confidence that a strong state could bring the economic system under control mirrored the progressives' own faith in the positive uses of government. Progressives often worked hand-in-hand with socialists to win economic and political reforms, especially at the municipal and state levels, and

© Hulton Archive/Getty Images.

EUGENE V. DEBS

This photograph captures something of the energy and charisma of Debs as he addresses a working-class audience in New York during his 1912 presidential campaign.

many intellectuals and reformers easily moved back and forth between socialism and progressivism. Florence Kelley, Hull House reformer and Illinois factory inspector, was one such person; Clarence Darrow, a Chicago trial lawyer who successfully defended the IWW's William Haywood in 1907 against charges that he had murdered a former Idaho governor, was another. Walter Lippmann, who would become a close adviser to President Wilson during the First World War, began his political career in 1912 as an assistant to the Socialist mayor of Schenectady. Several of the era's most prominent intellectuals, including John Dewey, Richard Ely, and Thorstein Veblen, also traveled back and forth between the socialist and progressive camps. So did Helen Keller, the country's leading spokesperson for the disabled.

On the other hand, Debs's talk of revolution scared progressives, as did his efforts to organize a working-class political movement independent of middle-class involvement or control. Although progressives wanted to tame capitalism, they stopped short of wanting to eliminate it. They wanted to improve working and living conditions for the masses but not cede political control to them. The progressives hoped to offer a political program with enough socialist elements to counter the appeal of Debs's more radical movement. In this, they were successful.

Municipal Reform

Progressive-era reform battles first erupted over control of municipal transportation networks and utilities. Private corporations typically owned and operated street railways

and electrical and gas systems. Many of the corporations used their monopoly power to charge exorbitant fares and rates, and they often won that power by bribing city officials who belonged to one of the political machines. Corporations achieved generous reductions in real estate taxes in the same way.

The attack on private utilities and their protectors in city government gained momentum in the mid-1890s. In Detroit, reform-minded Mayor Hazen S. Pingree led successful fights to control the city's gas, telephone, and trolley companies. In Chicago in 1896 and 1897, a group of middle-class reformers ousted a corrupt city council and elected a mayor, Carter Harrison, Jr., who promised to protect Chicago's streetcar riders from exploitation. In Cleveland, the crusading reformer Tom Johnson won election as mayor in 1901, curbed the power of the streetcar interests, and brought honest and efficient government to the city.

Occasionally, a reform politician of Johnson's caliber would rise to power through one of the regular political parties. But this path to power was a difficult one, especially in cities where the political parties were controlled by machines. Consequently, progressives worked for reforms that would strip the parties of their power. Two of their favorite reforms were the city commission and the city manager forms of government.

The City Commission Plan

First introduced in Galveston, Texas, in 1900, in the wake of a devastating tidal wave, the city commission shifted municipal power from the mayor and his aldermen to five city commissioners, each responsible for a different department of city government. In Galveston and elsewhere, the impetus for this reform came from civic-minded businessmen who were determined to rebuild government on the same principles of efficient and scientific management that had energized the private sector. The results were often impressive. The Galveston commissioners restored the city's credit after a brush with bankruptcy, improved the city's harbor, and built a massive seawall to protect the city from future floods. They accomplished all of this on budgets that had been cut by one-third. In Houston, Texas; Des Moines, Iowa; Dayton, Ohio; Oakland, California; and elsewhere, city commissioners similarly improved urban infrastructures, expanded city ser-

vices, and strengthened the financial health of the cities. Many commissions established publicly owned utilities. By 1913, more than 300 cities, most of them small to middling in size, had adopted the city commission plan.

The City Manager Plan

The city commission system did not always work to perfection, however. Sometimes the commissioners used their position to reward electoral supporters with jobs and contracts; other times, they pursued power and prestige for their respective departments. The city manager plan was meant to overcome such problems. Under this plan, the commissioners continued to set policy, but policy implementation now rested with a "chief executive." This official, who was not elected but appointed by the commissioners, would curtail rivalries among commissioners and ensure that no outside influences interfered with the impartial, businesslike management of the city. The job of city manager was explicitly modeled after that of a corporation executive. First introduced in Sumter, South Carolina, in 1911 and then in Dayton, Ohio, in 1913, by 1919 the city manager plan had spread to 130 cities.

The Costs of Reform

Although these reforms limited corruption and improved services, they were not universally popular. Poor and minority voters, in particular, found that their influence in local affairs was weakened by the shift to city commissioners and city managers. Previously, candidates for municipal office (other than the mayor) competed in ward elections rather than in citywide elections. Voters in working-class wards commonly elected workingmen to represent them, and voters in immigrant wards made sure that fellow ethnics represented their interests on city councils. Citywide elections diluted the strength of these constituencies. Candidates from poor districts often lacked the money needed to mount a citywide campaign, and they were further hampered by the nonpartisan nature of such elections. Denied the support of a political party or platform, they had to make themselves personally known to voters throughout the city. That was a much easier task for the city's "leading citizens"—manufacturers, merchants, and lawyers—than it was for workingmen. In Dayton, the percentage of citizens voting Socialist rose from 25 to 44 percent in the years following the introduction of the commission manager system, while the number of Socialists elected to office declined from five to zero. Progressive political reforms thus frequently had the effect

of reducing the influence of radicals, minorities, and the poor in elections.

Political Reform in the States

As at the local level, political parties at the state level were often dominated by corrupt politicians who did the bidding of powerful private lobbies. In New Jersey in 1903, for example, industrial and financial interests, working through the Republican Party machine, controlled numerous appointments to state government, including the chief justice of the state supreme court, the attorney general, and the commissioner of banking and insurance. Such webs of influence ensured that New Jersey would provide large corporations such as the railroads with favorable political and economic legislation.

Restoring Sovereignty to "the People"

Progressives introduced reforms designed to undermine the power of party bosses, restore sovereignty to "the people," and encourage honest, talented individuals to enter politics. One such reform was the direct primary, a mechanism that enabled voters, rather than party bosses, to choose party candidates. Mississippi introduced this reform in 1902 and Wisconsin in 1903. By 1916, all but three states had adopted the direct primary. Closely related was a movement to strip state legislatures of their power to choose U.S. senators. State after state enacted legislation that permitted voters to choose Senate candidates in primary elections. In 1912, a reluctant U.S. Senate was obliged to approve the 17th Amendment to the Constitution, mandating the direct election of senators. The state legislatures ratified this amendment in 1913.

Populists had first proposed direct election of U.S. senators in the 1890s; they also proposed the initiative and the referendum, both of which were adopted first by Oregon in 1902 and then by 18 other states between 1902 and 1915. The initiative allowed reformers to put legislative proposals before voters in general elections without having to wait for state legislatures to act. The referendum gave voters the right in general elections to repeal an unpopular act that a state legislature had passed. Less widely adopted but important nevertheless was the recall, a device that allowed voters to remove from office any public servant who had betrayed his trust. As a further control over the behavior of elected officials, numerous states enacted laws that regulated corporate campaign contributions and restricted lobbying activities in state legislatures.

These laws neither eliminated corporate privilege nor destroyed the power of machine politicians. Nevertheless, they made politics more honest and strengthened the influence of ordinary voters.

Creating a Virtuous Electorate

Progressive reformers focused as well on creating a responsible electorate that understood the importance of the vote and that resisted efforts to manipulate elections. To create this ideal electorate, reformers had to see to it that all of those citizens who were deemed virtuous could cast their votes free of coercion and intimidation. At the same time, reformers sought to disenfranchise citizens who were considered irresponsible and corruptible. In pursuing these goals, progressives substantially altered the composition of the electorate and strengthened government regulation of voting. The results were contradictory. On the one hand, progressives enlarged the electorate by extending the right to vote to women; on the other hand, they either initiated or tolerated laws that barred large numbers of minority and poor voters from the polls.

The Australian Ballot

Government regulation of voting had begun in the 1890s when virtually every state adopted the Australian, or secret, ballot. This reform required voters to vote in private rather than in public. It also required the government, rather than political parties, to print the ballots and supervise the voting. Before this time, each political party had printed its own ballot with only its candidates listed. At election time, each party mobilized its loyal supporters. Party workers offered liquor, free meals, and other bribes to entice voters to the polls and to "persuade" them to cast the party ballot. Because the ballots were cast in public, few voters who had accepted gifts of liquor and food dared to cross watchful party officials. Critics argued that the system corrupted the electoral process. They also pointed out that it made "ticketsplitting"—dividing one's vote between candidates of two or more parties—virtually impossible.

The Australian ballot solved these problems. Although it predated progressivism, it embodied the progressives' determination to use government power to encourage citizens to cast their votes responsibly and wisely.

Personal Registration Laws

That same determination was apparent in the progressives' support for the personal registration laws that virtually every state passed between 1890 and 1920. These laws allowed prospective voters to register to vote only if they appeared at a designated government office with proper identification. Frequently, these laws also mandated a certain period of residence in the state before registration and a certain interval between registration and actual voting.

Personal registration laws were meant to disenfranchise citizens who showed no interest in voting until election day, when a party worker arrived with a few dollars and offered a free ride to the polls. However, they also excluded many hardworking, responsible, poor people who wanted to vote but had failed to register, either because their work schedules made it impossible or because they were intimidated by the complex regulations. The laws were particularly frustrating for immigrants with limited knowledge of American government and of the English language.

Disenfranchisement

Progressives also promoted election laws expressly designed to keep noncitizen immigrants from voting. In the 1880s, 18 states had passed laws allowing immigrants to vote without first becoming citizens. Progressives reversed this trend. At the same time, the newly formed Bureau of Immigration and Naturalization (1906) made it more difficult to become a citizen. Applicants for citizenship now had to appear before a judge who interrogated them, in the English language, on American history and civics. In addition, immigrants were required to provide two witnesses to vouch for their "moral character" and their "attachment to the principles of the Constitution." Finally, immigrants had to swear (and, if necessary, prove) that they were not anarchists or polygamists and that they had resided continuously in the United States for five years.

Most progressives defended the new rigor of the process. U.S. citizenship, they believed, carried responsibilities; it was not to be bestowed lightly. This position was understandable, given the electoral abuses progressives had exposed. Nevertheless, the reforms also had the effect of denying the vote to a large proportion of the population. In cities and towns where immigrants dominated the workforce, the numbers of registered voters fell steeply. Nowhere was exclusion more startling than in the South, where between 1890 and 1904 every ex-Confederate state passed laws designed to strip blacks of their right to vote. Because laws explicitly barring blacks from voting would have violated the Fifteenth Amendment, this exclusion had to be accomplished indirectly—through literacy tests, property qualifications, and poll taxes mandated by the legislatures of the ex-Confederate states. Any citizen who failed a reading test, or who could not sign his name, or

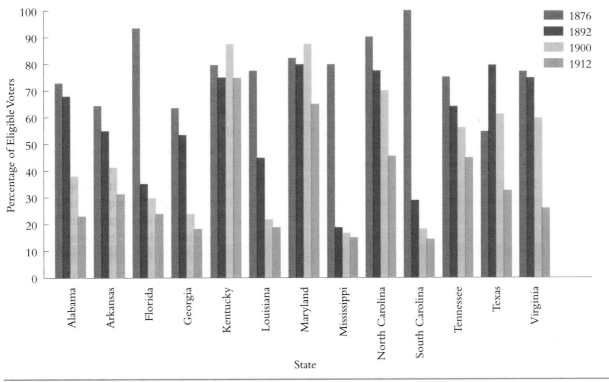

VOTER PARTICIPATION IN 13 SOUTHERN STATES, 1876, 1892, 1900, 1912

Source: Data from *Historical Statistics of the United States, Colonial Times to 1970* (White Plains, N.Y.: Kraus International, 1989).

who did not own a minimum amount of property, or who could not pay a poll tax, lost his right to vote. The citizens who failed these tests most frequently were blacks, who formed the poorest and least educated segment of the southern population, but a large portion of the region's poor whites also failed the tests. The effects of disenfranchisement were stark. In 1900 only 1,300 blacks voted in Mississippi elections, down from 130,000 in the 1870s. Virginia's voter turnout dropped from 60 percent of adult men (white and black) in 1900 to 28 percent in 1904.

Many progressives in the North, such as Governor Robert La Follette of Wisconsin, criticized southern disenfranchisement. Some, including Jane Addams and John Dewey, joined in 1910 with W. E. B. Du Bois and other black reformers to found the National Association for the Advancement of Colored People (NAACP), an interracial political organization that made black equality its primary goal. In the South, however, white progressives rarely challenged disenfranchisement, and most had little difficulty justifying it with progressive ideology. Because progressives everywhere considered the right to vote a precious gift granted only to those who could handle its responsibilities, they equally believed that it must be withheld from people deemed racially or culturally unfit. Progressives

in the North excluded many immigrants on just those grounds. Progressives in the South saw the disenfranchisement of African Americans in the same light.

Disillusionment with the Electorate

In the process of identifying those groups "unfit" to hold the franchise, some progressives soured on the electoral process altogether. The more they looked for rational and virtuous voters, the fewer they found. In *Drift and Mastery* (1914), Walter Lippmann developed a theory that ordinary people had been overwhelmed by industrial and social changes. Because these changes seemed beyond their comprehension or control, they "drifted," unable to "master" the circumstances of modern life or take charge of their own destiny. Lippmann did not suggest that such ordinary people should be barred from voting, but he did argue that more political responsibility should rest with appointed officials who possessed the training and knowledge necessary to make government effective and just. The growing disillusionment with the electorate, in combination with intensifying restrictions on the franchise, created an environment in which fewer and fewer Americans

© Bettmann/Corbis.

ANTIBLACK VIOLENCE

In 1913, a white mob destroyed a large part of the black section of Omaha, Nebraska. Race riots of this scale and devastation in early 20th-century America convinced many blacks that Booker T. Washington's message of accommodation was not working.

an 84-year-old man who had been married to a white woman for more than 30 years. There was a sad irony in the deaths of these African Americans. Murdered in Abraham Lincoln's hometown and within walking distance of his grave, they died just as black and white Americans everywhere were preparing to celebrate the centennial of the Great Emancipator's birth.

Booker T. Washington had long believed that blacks who educated themselves or who succeeded in business would be accepted as equals by whites. As Du Bois and other black militants observed, however, white rioters made no distinction between rich blacks and poor, or between solid citizens and petty criminals. All that had seemed to matter was the color of one's skin. Similarly, many black militants knew from personal experience that individual accomplishment was not enough to overcome racial prejudice. Du Bois was a brilliant scholar who became, in 1899, the first African American to receive a doctorate from Harvard University. Had he been white, Du Bois would have been asked to teach at Harvard or another elite academic institution, but no prestigious white university, in the South or North, ever made him an offer.

From the Niagara Movement to the NAACP

Seeing no future in accommodation, Du Bois and other young black activists came together at Niagara Falls in 1905 to fashion a new political agenda. They demanded that African Americans regain the right to vote in states that had taken it away; that segregation be abolished; and that the many discriminatory barriers to black advancement be removed. They declared their commitment to freedom of speech, the brotherhood of all men, and respect for the working man. Although their numbers were small, the members of the so-called Niagara movement were inspired by the example of the antebellum abolitionists. Meeting in Boston, Oberlin, and Harpers Ferry—all places of special significance to the abolitionist cause—they hoped to rekindle the militant, uncompromising spirit of that earlier crusade (see chapters 12 and 14).

The 1908 Springfield riot had shaken many whites. Some, especially those already working for social and economic reform, now joined in common cause with the Niagara movement. Together, black and white activists planned a conference for Lincoln's birthday in 1909 to revive, in the words of author William English Walling, "the spirit of the abolitionists" and to "treat the Negro on a plane of absolute political and social equality." Oswald Garrison Villard, the grandson of William Lloyd Garrison, called on "all believers in democracy to join in a National conference for the discussion of present evils, the voicing of protests, and the renewal of the struggle for civil and political liberty." The conference brought together distinguished progressives, white and black, including Mary White Ovington, Jane Addams, John Dewey, William Dean Howells, Ida B. Wells, and Du Bois. They drew up plans to establish an organization dedicated to fighting racial discrimination and prejudice. In May 1910, the National Association for the Advancement of Colored People (NAACP) was officially launched, with Moorfield Storey of Boston as president, Walling as chairman of the executive committee, and Du Bois as the director of publicity and research.

The formation of the NAACP marked the beginning of the modern civil-rights movement. The organization launched a magazine, the *Crisis*, edited by Du Bois, to publicize and protest the lynchings, riots, and other abuses directed against black citizens. Equally important was the Legal Redress Committee, which initiated lawsuits against city and state governments for violating the constitutional rights of African Americans. The committee scored its first major success in 1915, when the U.S. Supreme Court ruled that the so-called grandfather clauses of the Oklahoma and Maryland constitutions violated the 15th Amend-

© Bettmann/Corbis.

W. E. B. DU BOIS
Du Bois was one of the founders of the National Association for the Advancement of Colored People (NAACP), and the editor of its magazine, the *Crisis*. This photograph shows him in the offices of the *Crisis*. Du Bois would become one of the most important African American intellectuals and activists of the 20th century.

ment. (These clauses allowed poor, uneducated whites—but not poor, uneducated blacks—to vote, even if they failed to pay their state's poll tax or to pass its literacy test, by exempting the descendants of men who had voted before 1867.) NAACP lawyers won again in 1917 when the Supreme Court declared unconstitutional a Louisville, Kentucky, law that required all blacks to reside in predetermined parts of the city.

By 1914, the NAACP had enrolled thousands of members in scores of branches throughout the United States. The organization's success generated other civil-rights groups. The National Urban League, founded in 1911, worked to improve the economic and social conditions of blacks in cities. It pressured employers to hire blacks, distributed lists of available jobs and housing in African American communities, and developed social programs to ease the adjustment of rural black migrants to city life.

Progress toward racial equality was slow. Attacking segregation and discrimination through lawsuits was, by its nature, a slow strategy that would take decades to complete. The growing membership of the NAACP, although impressive, was not large enough to qualify it as a mass movement. And its interracial character made the organi-

zation seem dangerously radical to millions of whites. White NAACP leaders responded to this hostility by limiting the number and power of African Americans who worked for the organization. This policy, in turn, outraged black militants who argued that no civil-rights organization should be in the business of appeasing white racists.

Despite its limitations, the NAACP made significant strides. The NAACP gave Du Bois the security and visibility he needed to carry on his fight against Booker T. Washington's accommodationist philosophy. Even before his death in 1915, Washington's influence in black and white communities had begun to recede. The NAACP, more than any other organization, helped resurrect the issue of racial equality at a time when many white Americans had accepted as normal the practices of racial segregation and discrimination.

National Reform

The more progressives focused on economic and social matters, the more they sought to increase their influence in national politics. Certain problems demanded national solutions. No patchwork of state regulations, for example,

could curtail the power of the trusts, protect workers, or monitor the quality of consumer goods. Moreover, state and federal courts often were hostile toward progressive goals: They repeatedly struck down as unconstitutional reform laws regulating working hours or setting minimum wages, on the grounds that they impinged on the freedom of contract and trade. A national progressive movement could force passage of laws that were less vulnerable to judicial veto or elect a president who could overhaul the federal judiciary with progressive-minded judges.

National leadership would not emerge from Congress. The Democratic Party had been scarred by the Populist challenge of the 1890s. Divided between the radical Bryanites and the conservative followers of Grover Cleveland, and consequently unable to speak with one voice on questions of social and economic policy, after 1896 the Democrats seemed incapable of winning a national election or offering a national agenda. The Republican Party was more unified and popular, but it was controlled by a conservative Old Guard. Led by Senator Nelson Aldrich of Rhode Island and House Speaker Joseph G. Cannon of Illinois, the Republican Old Guard was pro-business and devoted to a 19th-century style of backroom patronage. When Robert La Follette arrived in the Senate from Wisconsin in 1907, the Old Guard ostracized him as a dangerous radical.

National progressive leadership came from the executive rather than the legislative branch, and from two presidents in particular, Republican Theodore Roosevelt and Democrat Woodrow Wilson. These two presidents sponsored reforms that profoundly affected the lives of Americans and altered the nature of the American presidency.

The Roosevelt Presidency

When the Republican bosses chose Theodore Roosevelt as William McKinley's running mate in 1900, their purpose was more to remove this headstrong, unpredictable character from New York state politics than to groom him for national leadership. As governor of New York, Roosevelt had been a moderate reformer, but even his modest efforts to rid the state's Republican Party of corruption and to institute civil service reform were too much for the state party machine, led by Thomas C. Platt. Consigning Roosevelt to the vice presidency seemed a safe solution. McKinley was a young, vigorous politician, fully in control of his party and his presidency.

Less than a year into his second term, in September 1901, McKinley was shot by an anarchist assassin. The president clung to life for nine days, and then died. Upon succeeding McKinley, Theodore Roosevelt, age 42, became the youngest chief executive in the nation's history.

Born to an aristocratic New York City family, Roosevelt nevertheless developed an uncommon affection for "the people." Asthmatic, sickly, and nearsighted as a boy, he remade himself into a vigorous adult. With an insatiable appetite for high-risk adventure—everything from "dude ranching" in the Dakota Territory, to big-game hunting in Africa, to wartime combat—he was also a voracious reader and an accomplished writer. Aggressive and swaggering in his public rhetoric, he was in private a skilled, patient negotiator. A believer in the superiority of the English-speaking peoples, he nevertheless appointed members of "inferior" races to important posts in his administration. Rarely has a president's personality so enthralled the American public. He is the only 20th-century president immortalized on Mount Rushmore.

Regulating the Trusts

Roosevelt quickly revealed his flair for the dramatic. In 1902, he ordered the Justice Department to prosecute the Northern Securities Company, a $400 million monopoly that controlled all railroad lines and traffic in the Northwest from Chicago to Washington state. Never before had an American president sought to use the Sherman Antitrust Act to break up a business monopoly. The news shocked J. P. Morgan, the banker who had brokered the Northern Securities deal. Morgan rushed to the White House, where he is said to have told Roosevelt, "If we have done anything wrong, send your man to my man and they can fix it up." Roosevelt would have none of this "fixing." In 1903, a federal court ordered Northern Securities dissolved, and the U.S. Supreme Court upheld the decision the next year. Roosevelt was hailed as the nation's "trust-buster."

Roosevelt, however, did not believe in breaking up all, or even most, large corporations. Industrial concentration, he believed, brought the United States wealth, productivity, and a rising standard of living. Rather than bust them up, Roosevelt argued, government should regulate the industrial giants and punish those that used their power improperly.

This new role would require the federal government to expand its powers. A newly fortified government—the centerpiece of a political program that Roosevelt would later call the New Nationalism—was to be led by a forceful president, who was willing to use all of the powers at his disposal to achieve prosperity and justice.

Toward a "Square Deal"

Roosevelt displayed his willingness to use government power to protect the economically weak in a 1902 coal

miners' strike. Miners in the anthracite fields of eastern Pennsylvania wanted recognition for their union, the United Mine Workers (UMW). They also wanted a 10 to 20 percent increase in wages and an eight-hour day. When their employers, led by George F. Baer of the Reading Railroad, refused to negotiate, they went on strike. In October, the fifth month of the strike, Roosevelt summoned the mine owners and John Mitchell, the UMW president, to the White House. Baer expected Roosevelt to threaten the striking workers with arrest by federal troops if they failed to return to work. Instead, Roosevelt supported Mitchell's request for arbitration and warned the mine owners that if they refused to go along, 10,000 federal troops would seize their property. Stunned, the mine owners agreed to submit the dispute to arbitrators, who awarded the unionists a 10 percent wage increase and a nine-hour day.

The mere fact that the federal government had ordered employers to compromise with their workers carried great symbolic weight. Roosevelt enjoyed a surge of support from Americans convinced that he shared their dislike for ill-gotten wealth and privilege. He also raised the hopes of African Americans when, only a month into his presidency, he dined with Booker T. Washington at the White House and then shrugged off the protests of white southerners who accused him of undermining segregation.

In his 1904 election campaign, Roosevelt promised that, if reelected, he would offer every American a "square deal." The slogan resonated with voters and helped carry Roosevelt to a victory (57 percent of the popular vote) over the conservative Democrat Alton B. Parker. To the surprise of many observers, Roosevelt had aligned the Republican Party with the cause of reform.

Expanding Government Power: The Economy

Emboldened by his victory, the president intensified his efforts to extend government regulation of economic affairs. His most important proposal was to give the government power to set railroad shipping rates and thereby to eliminate the industry's discriminatory marketing practices. The government, in theory, already possessed this power through the Interstate Commerce Commission (ICC), a regulatory body established by Congress in 1887, but the courts had so weakened the ICC's oversight and regulatory functions as to render it virtually powerless. Roosevelt achieved his goal in 1906, when Congress passed the Hepburn Act, which significantly increased the ICC's powers of rate review and enforcement. Roosevelt supported the Pure Food and Drug Act, passed by Congress that same year, which protected the public from fraudulently marketed and dangerous foods and medications. He also campaigned for the Meat Inspection Act (1906), which committed the government to monitoring the quality and safety of meat being sold to American consumers.

Expanding Government Power: The Environment

Roosevelt also did more than any previous president to extend federal control over the nation's physical environment. Roosevelt was not a "preservationist" in the manner of John Muir, founder of the Sierra Club, who insisted that the beauty of the land and the well-being of its wildlife should be protected from all human interference. Instead, Roosevelt viewed the wilderness as a place to live strenuously, to test oneself against the rough outdoors, and to match wits against strong and clever game. Roosevelt further believed that in the West—that land of ancient forests, lofty mountain peaks, and magnificent canyons—Americans could learn something important about their nation's roots and destiny. To preserve this West, Roosevelt oversaw the creation of 5 new national parks, 16 national monuments, and 53 wildlife reserves. The work of his administration led directly to the formation of the National Park Service in 1916.

From the Collections of the Library of Congress.

ENVIRONMENTALIST JOHN MUIR MEETS WITH THEODORE ROOSEVELT, 1903

This photo was taken on Glacier Point, Yosemite Park, where the two men were camping and discussing how best to preserve the U.S. wilderness.

GROWTH IN FEDERAL EMPLOYMENT, 1891–1917

Source: Reprinted by permission from *The Federal Government Service*, ed. W. S. Sayre (Englewood Cliffs, N.J.: Prentice-Hall, 1965), p. 41, The American Assembly.

the Democratic Party. It was a successful strategy that contributed to Wilson's reelection in 1916.

Conclusion

By 1916, the progressives had accomplished a great deal. They demonstrated that traditional American concerns with democracy and liberty could be adapted to an industrial age. They exposed and curbed some of the worst abuses of the American political system. They enfranchised women and took steps to protect the environment. They broke the hold of laissez-faire economic policies on national politics and replaced it with the idea of a strong federal government committed to economic regulation and social justice. They transformed the presidency into a post of legislative and popular leadership. They enlarged the executive branch by establishing new commissions and agencies charged with administering government policies.

The progressives, in short, had presided over the emergence of a new national government, one in which power increasingly flowed away from municipalities and states and toward Washington. This reorientation followed a compelling logic: A national government stood a better chance of solving the problems of growing economic inequality, mismanagement of natural resources, and consumer fraud than did local and state governments. The promise of effective remedies, however, brought new dangers. In particular, the new national government was creating a bureaucratic elite whose power rested on federal authority rather than private wealth or political machines. Progressives argued that the university-educated experts and scientific managers who staffed the new federal agencies would bring to the political process the very qualities that party politicians allegedly lacked: knowledge, dedication, and honesty. Few of these new public servants, however, were entirely disinterested. Some had close ties to the corporations and businesses that their agencies were expected to regulate. Others allowed their prejudices against women, immigrants, and minorities to shape social policy. Still others believed that "the people" could not be trusted to evaluate the government's work intelligently. For these reasons, the progressive approach to governance sometimes failed to enhance democracy and secure the people's sovereignty. America's imperial expansion and involvement in a world war would further demonstrate how a powerful state could serve illiberal ends.

SUGGESTED READINGS

No topic in 20th century American history has generated as large and rapidly changing a scholarship as has progressivism. Today, few scholars treat this political movement in the terms set forth by the progressives themselves: as a movement of "the people" against the "special interests." In *The Age of Reform: From Bryan to FDR* (1955), **Richard Hofstadter** argues that progressivism was the expression of a declining Protestant middle class at odds with the new industrial order. In *The Search for Order, 1877–1920* (1967), **Robert Wiebe** finds the movement's core in a rising middle class, closely allied to the corporations and bureaucratic imperatives that were defining this new order. **Gabriel Kolko**, *The Triumph of Conservatism: A Reinterpretation of American History* (1963), and **James**

Weinstein, *The Corporate Ideal in the Liberal State, 1900–1918* (1969), both argue that progressivism was the work of businessmen themselves, who were eager to ensure corporate stability and profitability in a dangerously unstable capitalist economy. Without denying the importance of this corporate search for order, **Nell Irvin Painter**, *Standing at Armageddon: The United States, 1877–1919* (1987), and **Alan Dawley**, *Struggles for Justice: Social Responsibility and the Liberal State* (1991), insist on the role of the working class, men and women, whites and blacks, in shaping the progressive agenda. **James T. Kloppenberg**, *Uncertain Victory: Social Democracy and Progressivism in European and American Thought, 1870–1920* (1986), and **Thomas J. Knock**, *To End All Wars: Woodrow Wilson and*

the Quest for a New World Order (1992), emphasize the influence of socialism on progressive thought, while **Martin J. Sklar, *The Corporate Reconstruction of American Capitalism, 1900–1916: The Market, the Law and Politics*** (1988), stresses the role of progressivism in "containing" or taming socialism. **Nick Salvatore** superbly captures the charisma and enigma of Debs in his ***Eugene V. Debs: Citizen and Socialist*** (1982). **Paul Boyer, *Urban Masses and Moral Order in America, 1820–1920*** (1978), treats progressivism as a cultural movement to enforce middle-class norms on an unruly urban and immigrant population. **Theda Skocpol, *Protecting Soldiers and Mothers: The Political Origins of Social Policy in the United States*** (1992), and **Robyn Muncy, *Creating a Female Dominion in American Reform, 1890–1935*** (1991), reconstruct the central role of middle-class Protestant women in shaping progressive social policy, while **Robert M. Crunden, *Ministers of Reform: The Progressives' Achievement in American Civilization, 1889–1920*** (1982), stresses the religious roots of progressive reform. **Alexander Keyssar, *The Right to Vote: The Contested History of Democracy in the United States*** (2000), is an indispensable guide to political reform during this period. An impressive recent attempt to synthesize the literature on progressivism is **Michael McGerr, *A Fierce Discontent: The Rise and Fall of the Progressive Movement in America, 1870–1920*** (2003).

 AMERICAN JOURNEY ONLINE AND INFOTRAC COLLEGE EDITION

Visit the source collections at www.ajaccess.wadsworth.com and infotrac.thomsonlearning.com and use the Search function with the following key terms to explore documents, images, audio and video clips, articles, and commentary related to the material in this chapter.

Eugene V. Debs
Helen Keller
Ida Tarbell
Jane Addams
John Muir
Robert La Follette
W. E. B. Du Bois

National Association for the
Advancement of Colored
People (NAACP)
Woman Suffrage
Theodore Roosevelt
Woodrow Wilson
Federal Reserve Act

Chapter 22

Becoming a World Power, 1898–1917

Culver Pictures.

UNCLE SAM GETS COCKY, 1901
From 1898 to 1917, the United States broadened its influence in world affairs and especially sought to establish its dominance in Latin America. This cartoon illustrates that dominance through the figure of a giant Uncle Sam rooster that dwarfs both the European chickens (gamely protesting, "you're not the only rooster in South America") and the diminutive Latin American republics.

CHAPTER OUTLINE

For much of the 19th century, most Americans were preoccupied by continental expansion. They treasured their distance from European societies, monarchs, and wars. Elections rarely turned on international events, and presidents rarely made their reputations as statesmen in the world arena. The diplomatic corps, like most agencies of the federal government, was small and inexperienced. The government projected its limited military power westward and possessed virtually no capacity or desire for involvement overseas.

The nation's rapid industrial growth in the late 19th century forced a turn away from such continentalism. Technological advances, especially the laying of transoceanic cables and the introduction of steamship travel, diminished America's physical isolation. The babel of languages one could hear in American cities testified to how much the Old World had penetrated the New. Then, too, Americans watched anxiously as England, Germany, Russia, Japan, and other industrial powers intensified their competition for overseas markets and colonies, and some believed America too needed to enter this contest. The voices making this argument grew more insistent and persuasive as the long economic depression of the 1890s stripped the United States of its prosperity and pride.

A war with Spain in 1898 gave the United States an opportunity to upgrade its military and acquire colonies and influence in the Western Hemisphere and Asia. Under Presidents William McKinley and Theodore Roosevelt, the United States pursued these initiatives and established a small but strategically important empire. Not all Americans supported this imperial project, and many protested the subjugation of the peoples of Cuba, Puerto Rico, and the Philippines that imperial expansion seemed to entail. In the eyes of anti-imperialists, the United States seemed to be becoming the kind of nation that many Americans had long despised—one that valued power more than liberty. Roosevelt brushed aside these objections and set about creating an international system in which a handful of industrial nations pursued their global economic interests, dominated world trade, and kept the world at peace. Woodrow Wilson, however, was more troubled by America's imperial turn. His doubts became apparent in his efforts to devise a policy toward postrevolutionary Mexico that restrained American might and respected Mexican desires for liberty. It was a worthy ambition but one that proved exceedingly difficult to achieve.

CHAPTER FOCUS

♦ What were the causes of the Spanish-American War?

♦ Over what countries did the United States exert control between 1898 and 1917, and what were the mechanisms of control? How did American expansion compare with that of other industrial powers?

♦ What were the similarities and differences in the foreign policies of Theodore Roosevelt, William Howard Taft, and Woodrow Wilson?

♦ What happened on Kettle and San Juan Hills, and why was the prominent role of one group in those battles excised from historical memory?

The United States Looks Abroad

By the late 19th century, sizable numbers of Americans had become interested in extending their country's influence abroad. The most important groups were Protestant missionaries, businessmen, and imperialists.

Protestant Missionaries

Protestant missionaries were among the most active promoters of American interests abroad. Overseas missionary activity grew quickly between 1870 and 1900, most of it directed toward China. Between 1880 and 1900, the number of women's missionary societies doubled, from 20 to 40; by 1915, these societies enrolled 3 million women. Convinced of the superiority of the Anglo-Saxon race, Protestant missionaries considered it their Christian duty to teach the Gospel to the "ignorant" Asian masses and save their souls. Missionaries also believed that their efforts would free those masses from their racial destiny, enabling them to become "civilized." In this "civilizing" effort, missionaries resembled progressive reformers who sought to uplift America's immigrant masses at home. (For the story of one missionary family in China, see the Americans Abroad feature in chapter 20, p. 617.)

Businessmen

For different reasons, industrialists, traders, and investors also began to look overseas, sensing that they could make fortunes in foreign lands. Exports of American manufactured goods rose substantially after 1880. By 1914, American foreign investment already equaled a sizable 7 percent of the nation's gross national product. Companies

CHRONOLOGY

1893	Frederick Jackson Turner publishes an essay announcing the end of the frontier
1898	Spanish-American War (April 14–August 12) • Treaty of Paris signed (December 10), giving U.S. control of Philippines, Guam, and Puerto Rico • U.S. annexes Hawaii
1899–1902	American-Filipino War
1899–1900	U.S. pursues Open Door policy toward China
1900	U.S. annexes Puerto Rico • U.S. and other imperial powers put down Chinese Boxer Rebellion
1901	U.S. forces Cuba to adopt constitution favorable to U.S. interests
1903	Hay–Bunau-Varilla Treaty signed, giving U.S. control of Panama Canal Zone
1904	"Roosevelt corollary" to Monroe Doctrine proclaimed
1905	Roosevelt negotiates end to Russo-Japanese War
1906–17	U.S. intervenes in Cuba, Nicaragua, Haiti, Dominican Republic, and Mexico
1907	Roosevelt and Japanese government reach a "gentlemen's agreement" restricting Japanese immigration to U.S. and ending discrimination against Japanese schoolchildren in California
1907–09	Great White Fleet circles the world
1909–13	William Howard Taft conducts "dollar diplomacy"
1910	Mexican Revolution
1914	Panama Canal opens
1914–17	Wilson struggles to develop a policy toward Mexico
1917	U.S. purchases Virgin Islands from Denmark

such as Eastman Kodak (film and cameras), Singer Sewing Machine Company, Standard Oil, American Tobacco, and International Harvester had become multinational corporations with overseas branch offices.

Some industrialists became entranced by the prospect of clothing, feeding, housing, and transporting the 400 million people of China. James B. Duke, who headed American Tobacco, was selling 1 billion cigarettes per year in East Asian markets. Looking for ways to fill empty boxcars heading west from Minnesota to Tacoma, Washington, the railroad tycoon James J. Hill imagined stuffing them with wheat and steel destined for China and Japan. He actually published and distributed wheat cookbooks throughout East Asia to convince Asians to shift from a rice-based to a bread-based diet (so that there would be a market for U.S. flour exports). Although export trade with East Asia during this period never fulfilled the expectations of Hill and other industrialists, their talk about the "wealth of

the Orient" impressed on politicians its importance to American economic health.

Events of the 1890s only intensified the appeal of foreign markets. First, the 1890 U.S. census announced that the frontier had disappeared and that America had completed the task of westward expansion. Then, in 1893, a young historian named Frederick Jackson Turner published an essay, "The Significance of the Frontier in American History," that articulated what many Americans feared: that the frontier had been essential to the growth of the economy and to the cultivation of democracy. Living in the wilderness, Turner argued, had transformed the Europeans who settled the New World into Americans. They shed their European clothing styles, social customs, and political beliefs, and acquired distinctively "American" characteristics—rugged individualism, egalitarianism, and a democratic faith. How, Turner wondered, could the nation continue to prosper now that the frontier had gone?

In recent years, historians of the American West have criticized Turner's "frontier thesis." They have argued that the very idea of the frontier as uninhabited wilderness overlooked the tens of thousands of Indians who occupied the region and that much else of what Americans believed about the West was based more on myth than on reality. They have also pointed out that it makes little sense to view the 1890s as a decade in which opportunities for economic gain disappeared in the West.

Even though these points are valid, they would have meant little to Americans living in Turner's time. For them, as for Turner, concern about the disappearing frontier expressed a fear that the increasingly urbanized and industrialized nation had lost its way. Turner's essay appeared just as the country was entering the deepest, longest, and most conflict-ridden depression in its history (see chapter 19). What could the republic do to regain its economic prosperity and political stability? Where would it find its new frontiers? One answer to these questions focused on the pursuit of overseas expansion. As Senator Albert J. Beveridge of Indiana declared in 1899: "We are raising more than we can consume. . . . We are making more than we can use. Therefore, we must find new markets for our produce, new occupation for our capital, new work for our labor."

Smithsonian Institution Photo No. 85-14366.

SINGER SEWING MACHINE ADVERTISEMENT

The Singer Sewing Machine Company was one of the first American multinational corporations. This advertisement, with its maps of the Western Hemisphere and its description of Singer as "the universal sewing machine," stresses Singer's global orientation.

Imperialists

Eager to assist in the drive for overseas expansion was a group of politicians, intellectuals, and military strategists who viewed such expansion as a key ingredient in the pursuit of world power. They wanted the United States to take its place alongside Britain, France, Germany, and Russia as a great imperial nation. They believed that the United States should build a strong navy, solidify a sphere of influence in the Caribbean, and extend markets into Asia. Their desire to control ports and territories beyond the continental borders of their own country made them imperialists. Many of them were also Social Darwinists (see chapter 20), who believed that America's destiny required that it prove itself the military equal of the strongest European nations and the master of the "lesser" peoples of the world.

One of the best-known imperialists of the period was Admiral Alfred Thayer Mahan. In an influential book, *The Influence of Sea Power upon History, 1660–1783* (1890), Mahan argued that all the world's great empires, beginning with Rome, had relied on their capacity to control the seas. Mahan called for the construction of a U.S. navy with enough ships and firepower to make its presence felt everywhere in the world. To be effective, that global fleet would require a canal across Central America through which U.S. warships could pass swiftly from the Atlantic to the Pacific Oceans. It would also require a string of far-flung service bases from the Caribbean to the southwestern Pacific. Mahan recommended that the U.S. government take possession of Hawaii and other strategically located Pacific islands with superior harbor facilities.

lease land to the United States for naval stations. The delegates to Cuba's constitutional convention were so outraged by these conditions that they refused even to vote on them. But the dependence of Cuba's vital sugar industry on the U.S. market and the continuing presence of a U.S. army on Cuban soil rendered resistance futile. In 1901, by a vote of 15 to 11, the delegates reluctantly wrote the Platt conditions into their constitution. "There is, of course, little or no independence left Cuba under the Platt Amendment," Wood candidly admitted to his friend Theodore Roosevelt, who had recently succeeded the assassinated McKinley as president.

Cuba's status, in truth, differed little from that of the Philippines. Both were colonies of the United States. In the case of Cuba, economic dependence closely followed political subjugation. Between 1898 and 1914, American trade with Cuba increased more than tenfold (from $27 million to $300 million), while investments more than quadrupled (from $50 million to $220 million). The United States intervened in Cuban political affairs five times between 1906 and 1921 to protect its economic interests and those of the indigenous ruling class with whom it had become closely allied. The economic, political, and military control that the United States imposed on Cuba would fuel anti-American sentiment there for years to come.

Puerto Rico received somewhat different treatment. The United States did not think independence appropriate, even though under Spanish rule the island had enjoyed a large measure of political autonomy and a parliamentary form of government. Nor did the United States follow its Cuban strategy by granting Puerto Rico nominal independence under informal economic and political controls. Instead, it annexed the island outright with the Foraker Act (1900). This act, unlike every previous annexation authorized by Congress since 1788, contained no provision for making the inhabitants of Puerto Rico citizens of the United States. Instead, Puerto Rico was designated an "unincorporated" territory, which meant that Congress would dictate the island's government and specify the rights of its inhabitants. Puerto Ricans were allowed no role in designing their government, nor was their consent to its establishment sought. With the Foraker Act, Congress had, in effect, invented a new, imperial mechanism for ensuring sovereignty over lands deemed vital to U.S. economic and military security. The U.S. Supreme Court upheld the constitutionality of this mechanism in a series of historic decisions, known as the Insular Cases, in the years from 1901 to 1904.

In some respects, Puerto Rico fared better than "independent" Cuba. Puerto Ricans were granted U.S. citizenship in 1917 and won the right to elect their own governor in 1947. Still, Puerto Ricans enjoyed fewer political rights than Americans in the 48 states. Moreover, throughout the 20th century, they endured a poverty rate far exceeding that of the mainland. As late as 1948, for example, three-fourths of Puerto Rican households subsisted on $1,000 or less annually, a figure below the U.S. poverty line. In its skewed distribution of wealth and its lack of industrial development, Puerto Rico resembled the poorly developed nations of Central and South America more than it did the affluent country that took over its government in 1900.

The subjugation of Cuba and the annexation of Puerto Rico troubled Americans far less than the U.S. takeover in the Philippines. Since the first articulation of the Monroe Doctrine in 1823, the United States had, in effect, claimed the Western Hemisphere as its sphere of influence. Within that sphere, many Americans believed, the United States possessed the right to act unilaterally to protect its interests. Before 1900, most of its actions (with

RECRUITING AMERICAN YOUTH FOR MILITARY SERVICE OVERSEAS

This U.S. Army advertisement portrays military duty in tropical areas under U.S. control as educational, leisurely, and exotic. The real work of such forces, maintaining social order and defeating anticolonial insurrections, is entirely effaced from this portrait, as are the native peoples who inhabited these lands.

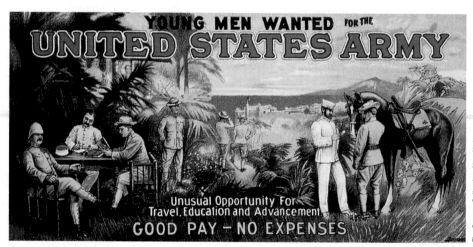

the exception of the Mexican War) had been designed to limit the influence of European powers—Britain, France, Russia and Spain—on the countries of the hemisphere. After 1900, however, the United States assumed a more aggressive role, seizing land, overturning governments it did not like, forcing its economic and political policies on weaker neighbors in order to turn the Caribbean Sea into what policy makers called an American Mediterranean.

China and the "Open Door"

Except for the Philippines and Guam, the United States made no effort to take control of Asian lands. Such a policy might well have triggered war with other world powers that were already well established in the area. Nor were Americans prepared to tolerate the financial and political costs Asian conquest would have entailed. The United States opted for a diplomatic rather than a military strategy to achieve its foreign policy objectives. For China, in 1899 and 1900, it proposed the policy of the "open door."

The United States was concerned that the actions of the other world powers in China would block its own efforts to open up China's markets to American goods. Britain, Germany, Japan, Russia, and France each coveted their own chunk of China, where they could monopolize trade, exploit cheap labor, and establish military bases. By the 1890s, each of these powers was building a sphere of influence, either by wringing economic and territorial concessions from the weak Chinese government or by seizing outright the land and trading privileges they desired.

To prevent China's breakup and to preserve American economic access to the whole of China, McKinley's secretary of state, John Hay, sent "open door" notes to the major world powers. The notes asked each power to open its Chinese sphere of influence to the merchants of other nations and to grant them reasonable harbor fees and railroad rates. Hay also asked each power to respect China's sovereignty by enforcing Chinese tariff duties in the territory it controlled.

None of the world powers embraced either of Hay's requests, although Britain and Japan gave provisional assent. France, Germany, Russia, and Italy responded evasively, indicating their support for the Open Door policy in theory but insisting that they could not implement it until all of the other powers had done so. Hay put the best face on their responses by declaring that all of the powers had agreed to observe his Open Door principles and that he regarded their assent as "final and definitive." Americans took Hay's bluff as evidence that the United States had triumphed diplomatically over its rivals. The rivals may have been impressed by Hay's diplomacy, but whether

IS THIS IMPERIALISM?

"NO BLOW HAS BEEN STRUCK EXCEPT FOR LIBERTY AND HUMANITY, AND NONE WILL BE."—WILLIAM McKINLEY

The Granger Collection, New York.

A DEFENSE OF AMERICA'S CHINA OPEN DOOR POLICY

This cartoon portrays a courageous William McKinley and standard bearer Uncle Sam engaging the vicious Chinese Boxers who had risen up to defeat the Western imperialists. "Is This Imperialism?" the cartoon asks, answering in McKinley's own words: "No blow has been struck except for liberty and humanity, and none will be."

they intended to uphold the United States' Open Door policy was not at all clear.

The first challenge to Hay's policy came from the Chinese. In May 1900, a Chinese organization, colloquially known as the "Boxers," sparked an uprising to rid China of all "foreign devils" and foreign influences. Hundreds of Europeans were killed, as were many Chinese men and women who had converted to Christianity. When the Boxers laid siege to the foreign legations in Beijing and cut off communication between that city and the outside world, the imperial powers raised an expeditionary force to rescue the diplomats and punish the Chinese rebels. The force, which included 5,000 U.S. soldiers, rushed over from the Philippines, broke the Beijing siege in August, and ended the Boxer Rebellion soon thereafter.

Hay feared that other major powers would use the rebellion as a reason to demand greater control over Chinese territory. He sent out a second round of Open Door notes, now asking each power to respect China's political independence and territorial integrity, in addition to guaranteeing unrestricted access to its markets. Impressed by America's show of military strength and worried that the

Chinese rebels might strike again, the imperialist rivals responded more favorably to this second round of notes. Britain, France, and Germany endorsed Hay's policy outright. With that support, Hay was able to check Russian and Japanese designs on Chinese territory. Significantly, when the powers decided that the Chinese government should pay them reparations for their property and personnel losses during the Boxer Rebellion, Hay convinced them to accept payment in cash rather than in territory. By keeping China intact and open to free trade, the United States had achieved a major foreign policy victory. Americans began to see themselves as China's savior as well.

✒ Theodore Roosevelt, Geopolitician

Roosevelt had been a driving force in the transformation of U.S. foreign policy during the McKinley administration. As assistant secretary of the navy, as a military hero, as a speaker and writer, and then as vice president, Roosevelt worked tirelessly to remake the country into one of the world's great powers. He believed that the Americans were a racially superior people destined for supremacy in

economic and political affairs. He did not assume, however, that international supremacy would automatically accrue to the United States. A nation, like an individual, had to strive for greatness and demand of its citizens physical and mental fitness. It had to build a military force that could convincingly project power overseas. And it had to be prepared to fight. All great nations, Roosevelt declared, ultimately depended on the skill and dedication of their warriors.

Roosevelt's appetite for a good fight caused many people to rue the ascension of this "cowboy" to the White House after McKinley's assassination in 1901. But behind his blustery exterior lay a shrewd analyst of international relations. As much as he craved power for himself and the nation, he understood that the United States could not rule every portion of the globe through military or economic means. Consequently, he sought a balance of power among the industrial nations through negotiation rather than war. Such a balance would enable each imperial power to safeguard its key interests and contribute to world peace and progress.

Absent from Roosevelt's geopolitical thinking was concern for the interests of less powerful nations. Roosevelt had little patience with the claims to sovereignty of small countries or the human rights of weak peoples.

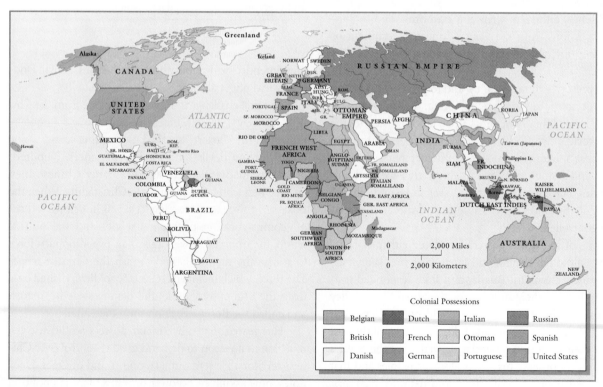

MAP 22.3   COLONIAL POSSESSIONS, 1900

In 1900, the British Empire was the largest in the world, followed by the French and Russian Empires. The U.S. Empire, if measured by the square miles of land held as colonial possessions, was small by comparison.

In his eyes, the peoples of Latin America, Asia (with the exception of Japan), and Africa were racially inferior and thus incapable of self-government or industrial progress. They were better suited to subservience and subsistence than to independence and affluence.

The Roosevelt Corollary

Ensuring U.S. dominance in the Western Hemisphere ranked high on Roosevelt's list of foreign policy objectives. In 1904, he issued a "corollary" to the Monroe Doctrine, which had asserted the right of the United States to keep European powers from meddling in hemispheric affairs. In his corollary, Roosevelt declared that the United States possessed a further right: the right to intervene in the domestic affairs of nations in the Western Hemisphere to quell disorder and forestall European intervention. The Roosevelt corollary formalized a policy that the United States had already deployed against Cuba and Puerto Rico in 1900 and 1901. Subsequent events in Venezuela and the Dominican Republic had further convinced Roosevelt of the need to expand the scope of U.S. intervention in hemispheric affairs.

Both Venezuela and the Dominican Republic were controlled by corrupt dictators. Both had defaulted on debts owed to European banks. Their delinquency prompted a German-led European naval blockade and bombardment

of Venezuela in 1902 and a threatened invasion of the Dominican Republic by Italy and France in 1903. The United States forced the German navy to retreat from the Venezuelan coast in 1903. In the Dominican Republic, after a revolution had chased the dictator from power, the United States assumed control of the nation's customs collections in 1905 and refinanced the Dominican national debt through U.S. bankers.

The willingness of European bankers to loan money to Latin America's corrupt regimes had created the possibility that the countries ruled by these regimes would suffer bankruptcy, social turmoil, and foreign intervention. The United States, under Roosevelt, did not hesitate to intervene to make sure that loans were repaid and social stability was restored. But rarely in Roosevelt's tenure did the United States show a willingness to help the people who had suffered under these regimes establish democratic institutions or achieve social justice. When Cubans seeking true national independence rebelled against their puppet government in 1906, the United States sent in the Marines to silence them.

The Panama Canal

Roosevelt's varied interests in Latin America embraced the building of a canal across Central America. The president had long believed, along with Admiral Mahan, that the

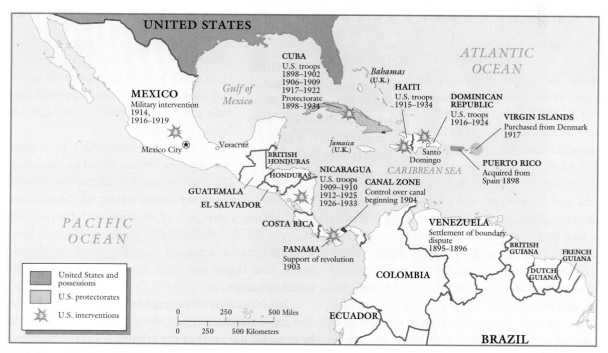

MAP 22.4 UNITED STATES PRESENCE IN LATIN AMERICA, 1895–1934

The United States possessed few colonies in Latin America but intervened (often repeatedly) in Mexico, Cuba, Nicaragua, Panama, Haiti, the Dominican Republic, and Venezuela to secure its economic and political interests.

Japanese government that he too was appalled by the Californians' behavior. In 1907, he reached a "gentlemen's agreement" with the Japanese, by which the Tokyo government promised to halt the immigration of Japanese adult male laborers to the United States in return for Roosevelt's pledge to end anti-Japanese discrimination. Roosevelt did his part by persuading the San Francisco school board to rescind its segregation ordinance.

At the same time, Roosevelt worried that the Tokyo government would interpret his sensitivity to Japanese honor as weakness. So he ordered the main part of the U.S. fleet, consisting of 16 battleships, to embark on a 45,000-mile world tour, including a splashy stop in Tokyo Bay. Many Americans deplored the cost of the tour and feared that the appearance of the U.S. Navy in a Japanese port would provoke military retaliation. Roosevelt brushed his critics aside, and, true to his prediction, the Japanese were impressed by the Great White Fleet's show of strength. Their response seemed to lend validity to the African proverb Roosevelt often invoked: "Speak softly and carry a big stick."

In fact, Roosevelt's handling of Japan was arguably the most impressive aspect of his foreign policy. Unlike many other Americans, he refused to let racist attitudes cloud his thinking. He knew when to make concessions and when to stand firm. His policies lessened the prospect of a war with Japan while preserving a strong U.S. presence in East Asia.

William Howard Taft, Dollar Diplomat

William Howard Taft brought impressive foreign policy credentials to the job of president. He had gained valuable experience in colonial administration as the first governor-general of the Philippines. As Roosevelt's secretary of war and chief negotiator for the Taft-Katsura agreement of 1905, he had learned a great deal about conducting diplomacy with imperialist rivals. Yet Taft lacked Roosevelt's grasp of balance-of-power politics and capacity for leadership in foreign affairs. Furthermore, Taft's secretary of state,

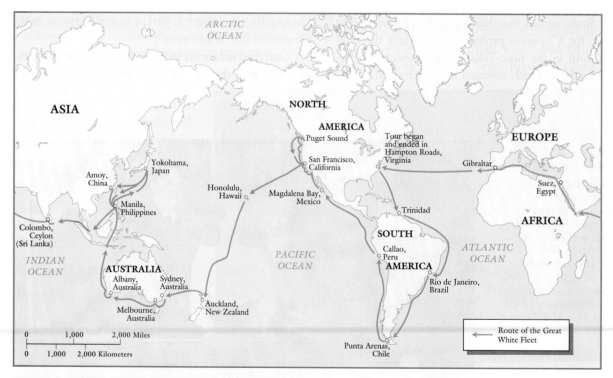

MAP 22.6 ROUTE OF THE GREAT WHITE FLEET, 1907–1909
A 16-battleship-strong U.S. fleet left Virginia in 1907 for a 45,000-mile world tour, whose most important stop was Japan. The map reveals the enormous distance ships had to travel to cross from the Atlantic to the Pacific in the days before the Panama Canal.

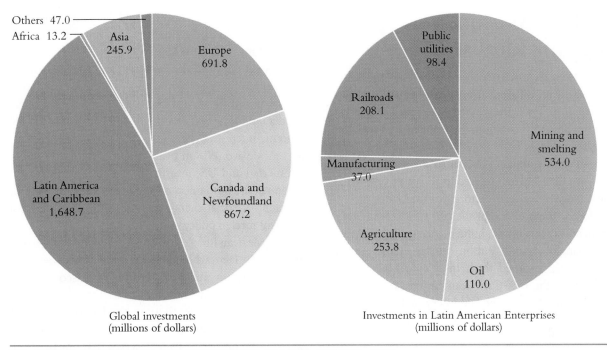

Global investments
(millions of dollars)

Investments in Latin American Enterprises
(millions of dollars)

U.S. GLOBAL INVESTMENTS AND INVESTMENTS IN LATIN AMERICA, 1914

Source: From Cleona Lewis, *America's Stake in International Investments* (Washington, D.C.: The Brookings Institute, 1938), pp. 576–606.

Philander C. Knox, a corporation lawyer from Pittsburgh, lacked diplomatic expertise. Knox's conduct of foreign policy seemed directed almost entirely toward expanding opportunities for corporate investment overseas, a disposition that prompted critics to deride his policies as "dollar diplomacy."

Taft and Knox believed that U.S. investments would effectively substitute "dollars for bullets," and thus offer a more peaceful and less coercive way of maintaining stability and order. Taking a swipe at Roosevelt's "big stick" policy, Taft announced that "modern diplomacy is commercial."

The inability of Taft and Knox to grasp the complexities of power politics, however, led to a diplomatic reversal in East Asia. Knox, prodded by banker associates, sought to expand American economic activities in China—even in Manchuria, where they encroached on the Japanese sphere of influence. In 1911, Knox proposed that a syndicate of European and American bankers buy the Japanese-controlled South Manchurian Railroad to open up North China to international trade. Japan reacted by signing a friendship treaty with Russia, its former enemy, which signaled their joint determination to exclude American, British, and French goods from Manchurian markets. Knox's plan to purchase the railroad collapsed, and the United States' Open Door policy suffered a serious blow.

Knox's further efforts to increase American trade with Central and South China triggered further hostile responses from the Japanese and the Russians and contributed to the collapse of the Chinese government and the onset of the Chinese Revolution in 1911.

Dollar diplomacy worked better in the Caribbean, where no major power contested U.S. policy. Knox encouraged American investment. Companies such as United Fruit of Boston, which established extensive banana plantations in Costa Rica and Honduras, grew powerful enough to influence both the economies and the governments of Central American countries. When political turmoil threatened their investments, the United States simply sent in its troops. Thus, when Nicaraguan dictator José Santos Zelaya reportedly began negotiating with a European country to build a second trans-Isthmian canal in 1910, a force of U.S. Marines toppled his regime. Marines landed again in 1912 when Zelaya's successor, Adolfo Diaz, angered Nicaraguans with his pro-American policies. This time the Marines were instructed to keep the Diaz regime in power. Except for a brief period in 1925, U.S. troops would remain in Nicaragua continuously from 1912 until 1933. Under Taft, the United States continued to do whatever American policy makers deemed necessary to bolster friendly governments and maintain order in Latin America.

Woodrow Wilson, Struggling Idealist

Woodrow Wilson's foreign policy in the Caribbean initially appeared no different from that of his Republican predecessors. In 1915, the United States sent troops to Haiti to put down a revolution; they remained as an army of occupation for 21 years. In 1916, when the people of the Dominican Republic (who shared the island of Hispaniola with the Haitians) refused to accept a treaty making them more or less a protectorate of the United States, Wilson forced them to accept the rule of a U.S. military government. When German influence in the Danish West Indies began to expand, Wilson purchased the islands from Denmark, renamed them the Virgin Islands, and added them to the U.S. Caribbean empire. By the time Wilson left office in 1921, he had intervened militarily in the Caribbean more often than any American president before him.

Wilson's relationship with Mexico in the wake of its revolution, however, reveals that he was troubled by a foreign policy that ignored a less powerful nation's right to determine its own future. He deemed the Mexicans capable of making democracy work and, in general, showed a concern for morality and justice in foreign affairs—matters to which Roosevelt and Taft had paid scant attention. Wilson wanted U.S. foreign policy to advance democratic ideals and institutions in Mexico.

Wilson's Mexican dealings were motivated by more than his fondness for democracy. He also feared that political unrest in Mexico could lead to violence, social disorder, and a revolutionary government hostile to U.S. economic interests. With a U.S.-style democratic government in Mexico, Wilson believed, property rights would be respected and U.S. investments would remain secure. Wilson's desire both to encourage democracy and to limit the extent of social change made it difficult to devise a consistent foreign policy toward Mexico.

The Mexican Revolution broke out in 1910 when dictator Porfirio Diaz, who had ruled for 34 years, was overthrown by democratic forces led by Francisco Madero. Madero's talk of democratic reform frightened many foreign investors, especially those in the United States and Great Britain, who owned more than half of all Mexican real estate, 90 percent of its oil reserves, and practically all of its railroads. Thus, when Madero himself was overthrown early in 1913 by Victoriano Huerta, a conservative general who promised to protect foreign investments, the dollar diplomatists in the Taft administration and in Great Britain breathed a sigh of relief. Henry Lane Wilson, the

Brown Brothers.

PANCHO VILLA

Francisco "Pancho" Villa was the charismatic commander of a rebel Mexican army during the years of the Mexican Revolution (1910–17). Failing to attract the support of President Wilson, Villa became a bitter enemy of the United States. After Villa's forces murdered more than 30 U.S. civilians, Wilson dispatched an army to Mexico to hunt him down. U.S. forces pursued him 300 miles into Mexico but never caught him.

U.S. ambassador to Mexico, had helped engineer Huerta's coup. Before close relations between the United States and Huerta could be worked out, however, Huerta's men murdered Madero.

Woodrow Wilson, who became president shortly after Madero's assassination in 1913, might have overlooked it (as did the European powers) and entered into close ties with Huerta on condition that he protect American property. Instead, Wilson refused to recognize Huerta's "government of butchers" and demanded that Mexico hold democratic elections. Wilson favored Venustiano Carranza and Francisco ("Pancho") Villa, two enemies of Huerta who commanded rebel armies and who claimed to be democrats. In April 1914, Wilson used the arrest of several U.S. sailors by Huerta's troops as a reason to send a fleet into Mexican waters. He ordered the U.S. Marines to occupy the Mexican port city of Veracruz and to prevent a German ship there from unloading munitions meant for Huerta's army. In the resulting battle between U.S. and Mexican forces, 19 Americans and 126 Mexicans were killed. The battle brought the two countries dangerously close to war. Eventually, however, American control over Veracruz weakened and embarrassed Huerta's regime to the point where Carranza was able to take power.

Carranza did not behave as Wilson had expected. Rejecting Wilson's efforts to shape a new Mexican government, he announced a bold land reform program. That program called for the distribution of some of Mexico's agricultural land to impoverished peasants and the transfer of developmental rights on oil lands from foreign corporations to the Mexican government. If the program went into effect, U.S. petroleum companies would lose control of their Mexican properties, a loss that Wilson deemed unacceptable. Wilson now threw his support to Pancho Villa, who seemed more willing than Carranza to protect U.S. oil interests. When Carranza's forces defeated Villa's forces in 1915, Wilson reluctantly withdrew his support of Villa and prepared to recognize the Carranza government.

Furious that Wilson had abandoned him, Villa and his soldiers pulled 18 U.S. citizens from a train in northern Mexico and murdered them, along with another 17 in an attack on Columbus, New Mexico. Determined to punish Villa, Wilson received permission from Carranza to send a U.S. expeditionary force under General John J. Pershing into Mexico to hunt down Villa's "bandits." Pershing's troops pursued Villa's forces 300 miles into Mexico but failed to catch them. The U.S. troops did, however, clash twice with Mexican troops under Carranza's command, once again bringing the countries to the brink of war. The United States, about to enter the First World War, could not afford a fight with Mexico; in 1917, Wilson quietly ordered Pershing's troops home and grudgingly recognized the Carranza government.

Wilson's policies toward Mexico in the years from 1913 to 1917 seemed to have produced few concrete results, except to reinforce an already deep antagonism among Mexicans toward the United States. His repeated changes in strategy, moreover, seemed to indicate a lack of skill and decisiveness in foreign affairs. Actually, however, Wilson recognized something that Roosevelt and Taft had not: that more and more peoples of the world were determined to control their own destinies. The United States, under Wilson, was looking for a way to support these peoples' democratic aspirations while also safeguarding its own economic interests. The First World War would make this quest for a balance between democratic principles and national self-interest all the more urgent.

Conclusion

We can assess the dramatic turn in U.S. foreign policy after 1898 either in relation to the foreign policies of rival world powers or against America's own democratic ideals. By the first standard, U.S. foreign policy looks impressive. The United States achieved its major objectives in world affairs: It tightened its control over the Western Hemisphere and projected its military and economic power into Asia. It did so while sacrificing relatively few American lives and while constraining the jingoistic appetite for truly extensive military adventure and conquest. The United States added only 125,000 square miles to its empire in the years from 1870 to 1900, while Great Britain, France, and Germany enlarged their empires by 4.7, 3.5, and 1.0 million square miles, respectively. Relatively few foreigners were subjected to American colonial rule. By contrast, in 1900, the British Empire extended more than 12 million square miles and embraced one-fourth of the world's population. At times, American rule could be brutal, as it was to Filipino soldiers and civilians alike, but on the whole it was no more severe than British rule and significantly less severe than that of the French, German, Belgian, or Japanese imperialists. McKinley, Roosevelt, Taft, and Wilson all placed limits on American expansion and avoided, until 1917, extensive foreign entanglements and wars.

If measured against the standard of America's own democratic ideals, however, U.S. foreign policy after 1898

must be judged more harshly. It demeaned the peoples of the Philippines, Puerto Rico, Guam, Cuba, and Colombia as inferior and primitive and denied them the right to govern themselves. In choosing to behave like the imperialist powers of Europe, the United States abandoned its long-standing claim to being a different kind of nation—one that valued liberty more than power.

Many Americans of the time judged their nation by both standards and thus faced a dilemma that would ex-tend throughout the 20th century. On the one hand, they believed with Roosevelt that the size, economic strength, and honor of the United States required it to accept the role of world power and policeman. On the other hand, they continued to believe with Wilson that they had a mission to spread the values of 1776 to the farthest reaches of the earth. The Mexico example demonstrates how hard it was for the United States to reconcile these two very different approaches to world affairs.

SUGGESTED READINGS

General works on America's imperialist turn in the 1890s and early years of the 20th century include **John Dobson,** *America's Ascent: The United States Becomes a Great Power, 1880–1914* (1978), **Walter LaFeber,** *The Cambridge History of Foreign Relations: The Search for Opportunity, 1865–1913* (1993), and **Emily Rosenberg,** *Spreading the American Dream: American Economic and Cultural Expansion, 1890–1945* (1982). **David F. Trask,** *The War with Spain in 1898* (1981), is a comprehensive study of the Spanish-American War, but it should be supplemented with **Philip S. Foner,** *The Spanish-Cuban-American War and the Birth of American Imperialism,* 2 vols. (1972). **Gerald F. Linderman,** *The Mirror of War: American Society and the Spanish-American War* (1974), brilliantly recaptures the shock that overtook Americans who discovered that their Cuban allies were black and the Spanish enemies were white. The role of gender in the Spanish-American War is explored in **Kristin L. Hoganson,** *Fighting for American Manhood: How Gender Politics Provoked the Spanish-American and Philippine-American Wars* (1998). **Stuart Creighton Miller,** *"Benevolent Assimilation": The American Conquest of the Philippines, 1899–1903* (1982), analyzes the Filipino-American war, **Louis A. Perez,** *Cuba under the Platt Amendment, 1902–1934* (1986), examines the extension of U.S. control over Cuba, while **Marilyn B. Young,** *The Rhetoric of Empire: American China Policy, 1895–1901* (1968), explores the unfolding Open Door policy. The acquisition of Guam and Samoa is examined in **Paul M. Kennedy,** *The Samoan Tangle* (1974), and the history of Puerto Rico following its annexation by the United States is explored in **Raymond Carr,** *Puerto Rico: A Colonial Experiment* (1984). The anti-imperialist movement is analyzed in **E. Berkeley Tompkins,** *Anti-Imperialism in the United States, 1890–1920: The Great Debate* (1970). **Howard K. Beale,** *Theodore Roosevelt and the Rise of America to World Power* (1956), is still a crucial work on Roosevelt's foreign policy, but it should be supplemented with **Richard H. Collin,** *Theodore Roosevelt's Caribbean: The Panama Canal, the Monroe Doctrine and the Latin American Context* (1990). Consult **Emily Rosenberg,** *Financial Missionaries to the World: The Politics and Culture of Dollar Diplomacy, 1900–1930* (1999), on the "dollar diplomacy" that emerged during the Taft Administration. On Wilson's foreign policy, consult **Thomas J. Knock,** *To End All Wars: Woodrow Wilson and the Quest for a New World Order* (1992), **Lloyd C. Gardner,** *Safe for Democracy: The Anglo-American Response to Revolution, 1913–1923* (1984), and **John S. D. Eisenhower,** *Intervention: The United States and the Mexican Revolution, 1913–1917* (1993).

AMERICAN JOURNEY ONLINE
AND
INFOTRAC COLLEGE EDITION

Visit the source collections at www.ajaccess.wadsworth.com and
infotrac.thomsonlearning.com and use the Search function with
the following key terms to explore documents, images, audio
and video clips, articles, and commentary related to the material
in this chapter.

William McKinley   American-Filipino War
Imperialism   Roosevelt Corollary
Spanish-American War   Panama Canal
Treaty of Paris   William Howard Taft
Theodore Roosevelt   Woodrow Wilson
Rough Riders

GRADE AIDS

**Visit the Liberty Equality Power Companion Web Site for resources specific to
this textbook:** http://history.wadsworth.com/murrin_LEP4e

The CD in the back of this book and the U.S. History Resource Center at
http://history.wadsworth.com/u.s./ offer a variety of tools to help you succeed in
this course, including access to quizzes; images; documents; interactive simulations,
maps, and timelines; movie explorations; and a wealth of other sources.

[Left column — partially visible map]

IC

*ATLANTIC
OCEAN*

PORTUGAL   SP

SPANISH
MOROCCO
(Sp.)

MOROCCO
(Fr.)

Allied pow
possession

Central po
Ottoman

Neutral co

MAP 23.1   EUR

**In the First Worl
Empire. Most of
Russia (red line).
colony) clashed**

 View an ani

ing tens of thou
bayonets, and
into enemy fir
progress, enabl
cut down appa

Europe's

Europe began it
Sarajevo, Bosnia
Archduke Franz
throne. This act v
imperial presenc
nians, Croatians,
in establishing ir
sponded to this p
Serbia, holding i

The conflict
series of treaties
camps. German
Triple Alliance, l
if attacked. Italy
be replaced by t
nations of the Tr
sia in the Triple
treaty to defend
sequently on Ju
to Serbia's aid. T
protect Austria-I
German troops
western ally. To i
through neutral
declaring war or
weeks, Europe v

Complicate
pean nations ur
But equally im
larger powers to
armies and navi
ain and Germa
struggle for Eu
peans had any
lead to a terribl
eration of your
in their civiliza

***GASSED*, BY JOHN SINGER SARGENT**

An artist renders the horror of a poison gas attack in the First World War. The Germans were the first to use this new and brutal weapon, which contributed greatly to the terror of war.

Imperial War Museum, London.

cold, wet, and rat-infested trenches. In Eastern Europe, the armies of Germany and Austria-Hungary squared off against those of Russia and Serbia. Although that front did not employ trench warfare, the combat was no less lethal. By the time the First World War ended, an estimated 8.5 million soldiers had died and more than twice that number had been wounded. Total casualties, both military and civilian, had reached 37 million. Europe had lost a generation of young men, as well as its confidence, stability, and global supremacy.

American Neutrality

Soon after the fighting began, Woodrow Wilson told Americans that this was a European war; neither side was threatening a vital American interest. The United States would therefore proclaim its neutrality and maintain normal relations with both sides while seeking to secure peace. Normal relations meant that the United States would continue trading with both camps. Wilson's neutrality policy met with lively opposition, especially from Theodore Roosevelt, who was convinced that the United States should join the Entente to check German power and expansionism. Most Americans, however, applauded Wilson's determination to keep the country out of war.

Neutrality was easier to proclaim than to achieve, however. Many Americans, especially those with economic and political power, identified culturally more with Britain than with Germany. They shared with the English a language, a common ancestry, and a commitment to liberty.

Wilson revered the British parliamentary system of government. His closest foreign policy adviser, Colonel Edward M. House, was pro-British, as was Robert Lansing, a trusted counselor in the State Department. William Jennings Bryan, Wilson's secretary of state, objected to this pro-British tilt, but he was a lone voice in Wilson's Cabinet.

Germany had no such attraction for U.S. policy makers. On the contrary, Germany's acceptance of monarchical rule, the prominence of militarists in German politics, and its lack of democratic traditions inclined U.S. officials to judge Germany harshly.

The United States had strong economic ties to Great Britain as well. In 1914, the United States exported more than $800 million in goods to Britain and its allies, compared with $170 million to Germany and Austria-Hungary (which came to be known as the Central Powers). As soon as the war began, the British and then the French turned to the United States for food, clothing, munitions, and other war supplies. The U.S. economy, which had been languishing in 1914, enjoyed a boom as a result. Bankers began to issue loans to the Allied Powers, further knitting together the American and British economies and giving American investors a direct stake in an Allied victory. Moreover, the British navy had blockaded German ports, which damaged the United States' already limited trade with Germany. By 1916, U.S. exports to the Central Powers had plummeted to barely 1 million dollars, a fall of more than 99 percent in two years.

The British blockade of German ports clearly violated American neutrality. The Wilson administration protested the British navy's search and occasional seizure of Ameri-

can merchant ships, but it never retaliated by suspending loans or exports to Great Britain. To do so would have plunged the U.S. economy into a severe recession. In failing to protect its right to trade with Germany, however, the United States compromised its neutrality and allowed itself to be drawn into war.

Submarine Warfare

To combat British control of the seas and to check the flow of U.S. goods to the Allies, Germany unveiled a terrifying new weapon, the *Unterseeboot,* or U-boat, the first militarily effective submarine. Early in 1915, Germany announced its intent to use its U-boats to sink on sight enemy ships en route to the British Isles. On May 7, 1915, without warning, a German U-boat torpedoed the British passenger liner *Lusitania,* en route from New York to London. The ship sank in 22 minutes, killing 1,198 men, women, and children, 128 of them U.S. citizens. Americans were shocked by the sinking. Innocent civilians who had been given no warning of attack and no chance to surrender had been murdered in cold blood. The attack appeared to confirm what anti-German agitators were saying: that the Germans were by nature barbaric and uncivilized. The circumstances surrounding the sinking of the *Lusitania,* however, were more complicated than most Americans realized.

Before its sailing, the Germans had alleged that the *Lusitania* was secretly carrying a large store of munitions to Great Britain (a charge later proved true) and that it therefore was subject to U-boat attack. Germany had warned American passengers not to travel on British passenger ships that carried munitions. Moreover, Germany claimed, with some justification, that the purpose of the U-boat attacks—the disruption of Allied supply lines—was no different from Britain's purpose in blockading German ports. Because its surface ships were outnumbered by the British navy, Germany claimed it had no alternative but to choose the underwater strategy. If a submarine attack seemed more reprehensible than a conventional sea battle, the Germans argued, it was no more so than the British attempt to starve the German people into submission with a blockade.

American political leaders might have used the *Lusitania* incident to denounce both Germany's U-boat strategy and Britain's blockade as actions that violated the rights of citizens of neutral nations. Only Secretary of State Bryan had the courage to say so, however, and his stand proved so unpopular in Washington that he resigned from office; Wilson chose the pro-British Lansing to take his place. Wilson denounced the sinking of the *Lusitania* and demanded that Germany pledge never to

launch another attack on the citizens of neutral nations, even when they were traveling in British or French ships. Germany acquiesced to Wilson's demand.

The resulting lull in submarine warfare was short-lived, however. In early 1916, the Allies began to arm their merchant vessels with guns and depth charges capable of destroying German U-boats. Considering this a provocation, Germany renewed its campaign of surprise submarine attacks. In March 1916, a German submarine torpedoed the French passenger liner *Sussex,* causing a heavy loss of life and injuring several Americans. Again Wilson demanded that Germany spare civilians from attack. In the so-called *Sussex* pledge, Germany once again relented but warned that it might resume unrestricted submarine warfare if the United States did not prevail on Great Britain to permit neutral ships to pass through the naval blockade.

The German submarine attacks strengthened the hand of Theodore Roosevelt and others who had been arguing that war with Germany was inevitable and that the United States must prepare itself to fight. By 1916, Wilson could no longer ignore these critics. Between January and September of that year, he sought and won congressional approval for bills to increase the size of the army and navy, tighten federal control over National Guard forces, and authorize the building of a merchant fleet. Although Wilson had conceded ground to the pro-war agitators, he did not share their belief that war with Germany was either inevitable or desirable. To the contrary, he accelerated his diplomatic initiatives to secure peace, and he dispatched Colonel House to London in January 1916 to draw up a peace plan with the British foreign secretary, Lord Grey. This initiative resulted in the House-Grey memorandum of February 22, 1916, in which Britain agreed to ask the United States to negotiate a settlement between the Allies and the Central Powers. The British believed that the terms of such a peace settlement would favor the Allies. They were furious when Wilson revealed that he wanted an impartial, honestly negotiated peace in which the claims of the Allies and Central Powers would be treated with equal respect and consideration. Britain now rejected U.S. peace overtures, and relations between the two countries grew unexpectedly tense.

The Peace Movement

Underlying Wilson's 1916 peace initiative was a vision of a new world order in which relations between nations would be governed by negotiation rather than war and in which justice would replace power as the fundamental principle of diplomacy. In a major foreign policy address on May 27, 1916, Wilson formally declared his support for

what he would later call the League of Nations, an international parliament dedicated to the pursuit of peace, security, and justice for all the world's peoples.

Many Americans supported Wilson's efforts to commit national prestige to the cause of international peace rather than conquest and to keep the United States out of war. Carrie Chapman Catt, president of the National American Woman Suffrage Association, and Jane Addams, founder of the Women's Peace Party, actively opposed the war. In 1915, an international women's peace conference at The Hague (in the Netherlands) had drawn many participants from the United States. A substantial pacifist group emerged among the nation's Protestant clergy. Midwestern progressives such as Robert La Follette, Bryan, and George Norris urged that the United States steer clear of this European conflict, as did leading socialists such as Eugene V. Debs. In April 1916, many of the country's most prominent progressives and socialists joined hands in the American Union Against Militarism and pressured Wilson to continue pursuing the path of peace.

Wilson's peace campaign also attracted support from the country's sizable Irish and German ethnic populations, who wanted to block a formal military alliance with Great Britain. That many German ethnics, who continued to feel affection for their native land and culture, would oppose U.S. entry into the war is hardly surprising. And the Irish viewed England as an arrogant imperial power that kept Ireland subjugated. That view was confirmed when England crushed the Easter Rebellion that Irish nationalists had launched on Easter Monday 1916 to win their country's independence. The Irish in America, like those in Ireland, wanted to see Britain's strength sapped (and Ireland's prospects for freedom enhanced) by a long war.

Wilson's Vision: "Peace without Victory"

The 1916 presidential election revealed the breadth of peace sentiment. At the Democratic convention, Governor Martin Glynn of New York, the Irish American speaker who renominated Wilson for a second term, praised the president for keeping the United States out of war. His portrayal of Wilson as the "peace president" electrified the convention and made "He kept us out of war" a campaign slogan. The slogan proved particularly effective against Wilson's Republican opponent, Charles Evans Hughes, whose close ties to Theodore Roosevelt seemed to place him in the pro-war camp. Combining the promise of peace with a pledge to push ahead with progressive reform, Wilson won a narrow victory.

Emboldened by his electoral triumph, Wilson intensified his quest for peace. On December 16, 1916, he sent a peace note to the belligerent governments, entreating them to consider ending the conflict and, to that end, to state their terms for peace. Although Germany refused to specify its terms and Britain and France announced a set of conditions too extreme for Germany ever to accept, Wilson pressed ahead, initiating secret peace negotiations with both sides. To prepare the American people for what he hoped would be a new era of international relations, Wilson appeared before the Senate on January 22, 1917, to

ON A MISSION FOR PEACE

Members of the American Women's Peace Party pose on a ship taking them to The Hague (The Netherlands) for a 1915 meeting of the International Committee for Permanent Peace. These women were part of a large domestic movement that opposed U.S. involvement in the war. Jane Addams, one of the peace movement's leaders, is third from the right behind the banner.

outline his plans for peace. In his speech, he reaffirmed his commitment to the League of Nations, but for such a league to succeed, Wilson argued, it would have to be handed a sturdy peace settlement. This entailed a "peace without victory." Only a peace settlement that refused to crown a victor or humiliate a loser would ensure the equality of the combatants, and "only a peace between equals can last."

Wilson listed the crucial principles of a lasting peace: freedom of the seas; disarmament; and the right of every people to self-determination, democratic self-government, and security against aggression. He was proposing a revolutionary change in world order, one that would allow all of the world's peoples, regardless of their size or strength, to achieve political independence and to participate as equals in world affairs. These views, rarely expressed by the leader of a world power, stirred the despairing masses of Europe and elsewhere caught in deadly conflict.

German Escalation

Wilson's oratory came too late to serve the cause of peace. Sensing the imminent collapse of Russian forces on the eastern front, Germany had decided, in early 1917, to throw its full military might at France and Britain. On land it planned to launch a massive assault on the trenches, and at sea it prepared to unleash its submarines to attack all vessels heading for British ports. Germany knew that this last action would compel the United States to enter the war, but it was gambling on being able to strangle the British economy and leave France isolated before significant numbers of American troops could reach European shores.

On February 1, the United States broke off diplomatic relations with Germany. Wilson continued to hope for a negotiated settlement, however, until February 25, when the British intercepted and passed on to the president a telegram from Germany's foreign secretary, Arthur Zimmermann, to the German minister in Mexico. The infamous "Zimmermann telegram" instructed the minister to ask the Mexican government to attack the United States in the event of war between Germany and the United States. In return, Germany would pay the Mexicans a large fee and regain for them the "lost provinces" of Texas, New Mexico, and Arizona. Wilson, Congress, and the American public were outraged by the story.

In March, news arrived that Tsar Nicholas II's autocratic regime in Russia had collapsed and had been replaced by a liberal-democratic government under the leadership of Alexander Kerensky. As long as the tsar ruled Russia and stood to benefit from the Central Powers' defeat, Wilson could not honestly claim that America's going to war against Germany would bring democracy to Europe. The fall of the tsar and the need of Russia's fledgling democratic government for support gave Wilson the rationale he needed to justify American intervention.

Appearing before a joint session of Congress on April 2, Wilson declared that the United States must enter the war because "the world must be made safe for democracy." He continued:

> We shall fight for the things which we have always carried nearest our hearts—for democracy, for the right of those who submit to authority to have a voice in their own Governments, for the rights and liberties of small nations, for a universal dominion of right by such a concert of free peoples as shall bring peace and safety to all nations and make the world itself at last free. To such a task we dedicate our lives and our fortunes.

Inspired by his words, Congress broke into thunderous applause. On April 6, Congress voted to declare war by a vote of 373 to 50 in the House and 82 to 6 in the Senate.

The United States thus embarked on a grand experiment to reshape the world. Wilson had given millions of people around the world reason to hope, both that the terrible war would soon end and that their strivings for freedom and social justice would be realized. Although he was taking America to war on the side of the Allies, he stressed that America would fight as an "associated power," a phrase meant to underscore America's determination to keep its war aims separate from and more idealistic than those of the Allies.

Still, Wilson understood all too well the risks of his undertaking. A few days before his speech to Congress, he had confided to a journalist his worry that the American people, once at war, will "forget there ever was such a thing as tolerance. To fight you must be brutal and ruthless, and the spirit of ruthless brutality will enter into the very fibre of our national life, infecting Congress, the courts, the policeman on the beat, the man in the street."

🌏 American Intervention

The entry of the United States into the war gave the Allies the muscle they needed to defeat the Central Powers, but it came almost too late. Germany's resumption of unrestricted submarine warfare took a frightful toll on Allied shipping. From February through July 1917, German subs sank almost 4 million tons of shipping, more than one-third of Britain's entire merchant fleet. One of every four large freighters departing Britain in those months never returned; at one point, the British Isles were down to a mere four weeks of provisions. American intervention ended Britain's vulnerability in dramatic fashion. U.S. and British naval commanders now grouped merchant ships

into convoys and provided them with warship escorts through the most dangerous stretches of the North Atlantic. Destroyers armed with depth charges were particularly effective as escorts. Their shallow draft made them invulnerable to torpedoes, and their great acceleration and speed allowed them to pursue slow-moving U-boats. The U.S. and British navies had begun to use sound waves (later called "sonar") to pinpoint the location of underwater craft, and this new technology increased the effectiveness of destroyer attacks. By the end of 1917, the tonnage of Allied shipping lost each month to U-boat attacks had declined by two-thirds, from almost 1 million tons in April to 350,000 tons in December. The increased flow of supplies stiffened the resolve of the exhausted British and French troops.

The French and British armies had bled themselves white by taking the offensive in 1916 and 1917 and had scarcely budged the trench lines. The Germans had been content in those years simply to hold their trench position in the West because they were engaged in a huge offensive against the Russians in the East. The Germans intended first to defeat Russia and then to shift their eastern armies to the West for a final assault on the weakened British and French lines. Their opportunity came in the winter and spring of 1918.

A second Russian revolution in November 1917 had overthrown Kerensky's liberal-democratic government and had brought to power a revolutionary socialist government under Vladimir Lenin and his Bolshevik Party. Lenin pulled Russia out of the war on the grounds that the war did not serve the best interests of the working classes, that it was a conflict between rival capitalist elites interested only in wealth and power (and indifferent to the slaughter of soldiers in the trenches). In March 1918, Lenin signed a treaty at Brest-Litovsk that added to Germany's territory and resources and enabled Germany to shift its eastern forces to the western front.

Russia's exit from the war hurt the Allies. Not only did it expose French and British troops to a much larger German force, but it also challenged the Allied claim that they were fighting a just war against German aggression. Lenin had published the texts of secret Allied treaties showing that Britain and France, like Germany, had plotted to enlarge their

nations and empires through war. The revelation that the Allies were fighting for land and riches rather than democratic principles outraged large numbers of people in France and Great Britain, demoralized Allied troops, and threw the French and British governments into disarray.

The treaties also embarrassed Wilson, who had brought America into the war to fight for democracy, not territory. Wilson quickly moved to restore the Allies' credibility by unveiling, in January 1918, a concrete program for peace. His Fourteen Points reaffirmed America's commitment to an international system governed by laws rather than by might and renounced territorial aggrandizement as a legitimate war aim. This document provided the ideological cement that held the Allies together at a critical moment. (The Fourteen Points are discussed more fully in the section "The Failure of the International Peace.")

In March and April 1918, Germany launched its huge offensive against British and French positions, sending Allied troops reeling. A ferocious assault against French lines on May 27 met with little resistance; German troops advanced 10 miles a day—a faster pace than any on the western front since the earliest days of the war—until they reached the Marne River, within striking distance of Paris. The French government prepared to evacuate the city. At this perilous moment, a large American army—fresh, well-equipped, and oblivious to the horrors of trench warfare—arrived to reinforce what remained of the French lines.

The Granger Collections, New York.

THE ROCK OF THE MARNE

Mal Thompson's painting shows infantry units of the U.S. 30th and 38th regiments from the Third Division of the American Expeditionary Force engaging German troops in France in July 1918. Although he shows them under fire, Thompson depicts the soldiers as focused, calm, and determined against a landscape desolated by war.

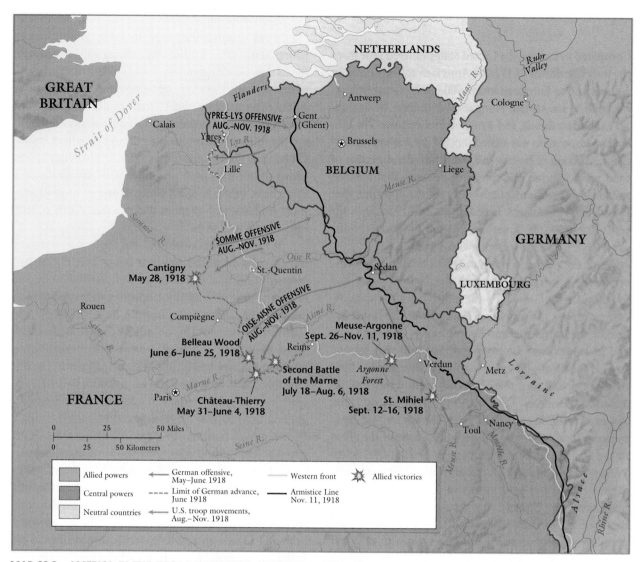

MAP 23.2 AMERICA IN THE FIRST WORLD WAR: WESTERN FRONT, 1918

In 1918, American forces joined the Allied forces in the climactic battles of the war. The red arrows show the major offensive by the Germans in the spring of 1918 and the blue arrows the decisive counteroffensive by the Allies in the fall of 1918. The fighting stopped along the black armistice line on November 11, 1918, after German capitulation.

In fact, these American troops, part of the American Expeditionary Force (AEF) commanded by General John J. Pershing, had begun landing in France almost a year earlier. During the intervening months, the United States had had to create a modern army from scratch, because its existing force was so small, ranking only 17th in the world. Men had to be drafted, trained, and supplied with food and equipment; ships for transporting them to Europe had to be found or built. In France, Pershing put his troops through additional training before committing them to battle. He was determined that the American soldiers—or "doughboys," as they were called—should acquit themselves well on the battlefield. The army he ordered into battle to counter the German spring offensive of 1918 fought well. Many American soldiers fell, but the German

offensive ground to a halt. Paris was saved, and Germany's best chance for victory slipped from its grasp.

Buttressed by this show of AEF strength, the Allied troops staged a major offensive of their own in late September. Millions of Allied troops (including more than a million from the AEF) advanced across the 200-mile-wide Argonne forest in France, cutting German supply lines. By late October, they had reached the German border. Faced with an invasion of their homeland and with rapidly mounting popular dissatisfaction with the war, German leaders asked for an armistice, to be followed by peace negotiations based on Wilson's Fourteen Points. Having forced the Germans to agree to numerous concessions, the Allies ended the war on November 11, 1918. The carnage was finally over.

Mobilizing for "Total" War

Compared to Europe, the United States suffered little from the war. The deaths of 112,000 American soldiers paled in comparison to European losses: 900,000 by Great Britain, 1.2 million by Austria-Hungary, 1.4 million by France, 1.7 million by Russia, and 2 million by Germany. The U.S. civilian population was spared most of the war's ravages—the destruction of homes and industries, the shortages of food and medicine, the spread of disease—that afflicted millions of Europeans. Only with the flu epidemic that swept across the Atlantic from Europe in 1919 to claim approximately 500,000 American lives did Americans briefly experience wholesale suffering and death.

Still, the war had a profound effect on American society. Every military engagement the United States had fought since the Civil War—the Indian wars, the Spanish-American War, the American-Filipino War, the Boxer Rebellion, the Latin American interventions—had been limited in scope. Even the troop mobilizations that seemed large at the time—the more than 100,000 needed to fight the Spanish and then the Filipinos—failed to tax severely American resources. The First World War was different. It was a "total" war to which every combatant had committed virtually all of its resources. The scale of the effort in the United States became apparent early in 1917 when Wilson asked Congress for a conscription law that would permit the federal government to raise a multimillion-man army. The United States would also have to devote much of its agricultural, transportation, industrial, and population resources to the war effort if it wished to end the European stalemate. Who would organize this massive effort? Who would pay for it? Would Americans accept the sacrifice and regimentation it would demand? These were vexing questions for a nation long committed to individual liberty, small government, and a weak military.

Organizing Industry

At first, Wilson pursued a decentralized approach to mobilization, delegating tasks to local defense councils throughout the country. When that effort failed, however, Wilson created several centralized federal agencies, each charged with supervising nationwide activity in its assigned economic sector.

The success of these agencies varied. The Food Administration, headed by mining engineer and executive Herbert Hoover (see Americans Abroad feature in this chapter), substantially increased production of basic foodstuffs and put in place an efficient distribution system that delivered food to millions of troops and European civilians. Treasury Secretary William McAdoo, as head of the

U.S. Railroad Administration, also performed well in shifting the rail system from private to public control, coordinating dense train traffic, and making capital improvements that allowed goods to move rapidly to eastern ports, where they were loaded onto ships and sent to Europe. At the other extreme, the Aircraft Production Board and Emergency Fleet Corporation did a poor job of supplying the Allies with combat aircraft and merchant vessels. On balance, the U.S. economy performed wonders in supplying troops with uniforms, food, rifles, munitions, and other basic items; it failed badly, however, in producing more sophisticated weapons and machines such as artillery, aircraft, and ships.

At the time, many believed that the new government war agencies possessed awesome power over the nation's economy and thus represented a near revolution in government. Most such agencies, however, were more powerful on paper than in fact. Consider, for example, the War Industries Board (WIB), an administrative body established by Wilson in July 1917 to harness manufacturing might to military needs. The WIB floundered for its first nine months, lacking the statutory authority to force manufacturers and the military to adopt its plans. Only the appointment of Wall Street investment banker Bernard Baruch as WIB chairman in March 1918 turned the agency around. Rather than attempting to force manufacturers to do the government's bidding, Baruch permitted industrialists to charge high prices for their products. He won exemptions from antitrust laws for corporations that complied with his requests. In general, he made war production too lucrative an activity to resist; however, he did not hesitate to unleash his wrath on corporations that resisted WIB enticements.

Baruch's forceful leadership worked reasonably well throughout his nine months in office. War production increased, and manufacturers discovered the financial benefits of cooperation between the public and private sectors. But Baruch's approach created problems, too. His favoritism toward the large corporations hurt smaller competitors. Moreover, the cozy relationship between government and corporation that he encouraged violated the progressive pledge to protect the people against the "interests." Achieving cooperation by boosting corporate profits, finally, was a costly way for the government to do business. The costs of the war soared to $33 billion, a figure more than three times expectations.

Securing Workers, Keeping Labor Peace

The government worried as much about labor's cooperation as about industry's compliance, for the best-laid

Herbert C. Hoover: International Mining Engineer and Businessman

From the time that he graduated from Stanford in 1897 at the age of 22 until he returned to America after the First World War, Herbert Hoover largely lived abroad, chiefly in Australia, China, and England. No other president, with the possible exception of Thomas Jefferson, brought such an impressive international résumé to the White House. Unlike Jefferson, Hoover had gone abroad not for culture or diplomacy but to seek his fortune as a businessman. He would be enormously successful in this quest.

Soon after graduating from Stanford with a geology degree, Hoover was sent by his employer, Bewick, Moreing, and Company of London, to Australia to look for gold. Enterprising, hardworking, and bold, he quickly made a name for himself by persuading Bewick to purchase a mine, known as the Sons of Gwalia, that would yield an immense amount of gold. "Boy Hoover," "Boy Wonder," and "Chief," as he came to be known, had quickly made himself a fortune.

Bewick next sent Hoover to China, where he shifted from gold to coal exploration. When the Boxer Rebellion broke out in 1900 (see chapter 22), Hoover took charge of the colony of Europeans, Americans, and Christian Chinese at Tientsin, to which the Boxers had laid siege. Hoover played a critical role in keeping his colony fed, united, and in good spirits until the rebellion had dissipated.

In 1901, Hoover moved to London, which would remain his base until the First World War. Working first for Bewick and then on his own, Hoover built a multinational mining business that, by the First World War, was extracting minerals on every one of the world's continents. Increasingly, Hoover turned his attention to politics. Raised a Quaker, he had always possessed a strong commitment to public service. He was particularly intrigued with American progressives such as

Theodore Roosevelt, who were attempting to help the United States find a solution to the turmoil of industrialization.

Hoover's opportunity came in the First World War. When war broke out in 1914, he took charge of getting the many Americans stranded in London home. Then he headed up the Committee for Relief in Belgium, somehow getting both the Allies and the Central Powers to support his efforts to get food to the Belgian people and thereby save them from starvation. And, finally, he became head of Woodrow Wilson's Food Administration, charged with organizing the production and distribution of American foodstuffs to feed millions of Allied soldiers and European civilians. He performed brilliantly at this task, continuing his efforts into the postwar period to stop the spread of famine in Europe.

In 1920, Hoover returned to America for good, becoming President Harding's secretary of commerce (see chapter 23). But for the misfortune of becoming president in 1929 just before the Great Depression struck, Hoover might be celebrated today as one of the most versatile men ever to occupy the Oval Office.

© Corbis.

HERBERT HOOVER, LOU HENRY HOOVER, AND FRIENDS IN CHINA, 1900

This photograph was taken shortly after Hoover had helped secure the safety of the European-American colony in Tientsin during the Boxer Rebellion. Hoover is standing on the far right in the back row, and his wife, Lou Henry Hoover, is seated on the left in the first row. They are surrounded by friends who, like Hoover, had graduated from Stanford University.

THE MIGRATION OF THE NEGRO, PANEL 40: "THE MIGRANTS ARRIVED IN GREAT NUMBERS," BY JACOB LAWRENCE (1940–1941)

This panel illustrates the rural origins of the black migrants who came north during the First World War.

Manufacturers responded to the labor shortage by recruiting new sources of labor from the rural South; a half million African Americans migrated to northern cities between 1916 and 1920. Another half million white southerners followed the same path during that period. Hundreds of thousands of Mexicans fled their revolution-ridden homeland for jobs in the Southwest and Midwest. Approximately 40,000 northern women found work as streetcar conductors, railroad workers, metalworkers, munitions makers, and in other jobs customarily reserved for men. The number of female clerical workers doubled between 1910 and 1920, with many of these women finding work in the government war bureaucracies. Altogether, a million women toiled in war-related industries.

production plans could be disrupted by a labor shortage or an extended strike. War increased the demand for industrial labor while cutting the supply. European immigrants had long been the most important source of new labor for American industry, and during the war they stopped coming. Meanwhile, millions of workers already in America were conscripted into the military and thus lost to industry.

These workers alleviated but did not eliminate the nation's labor shortage. Unemployment, which had hovered around 8.5 percent in 1915, plunged to 1.2 percent in 1918. Workers were quick to recognize the benefits of the tight labor market. They quit jobs they did not like and took part in strikes and other collective actions in unprecedented numbers. From 1916 to 1920, more than 1 million workers went on strike every year.

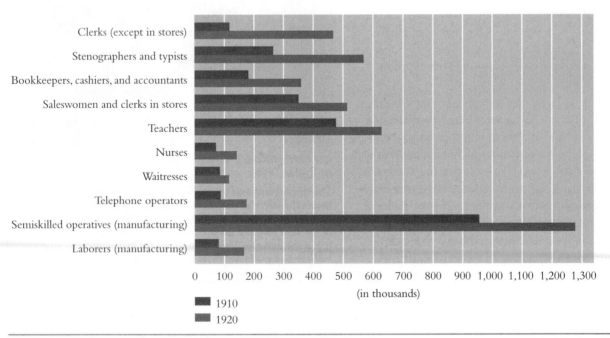

OCCUPATIONS WITH LARGEST INCREASE IN WOMEN, 1910–1920

Source: Joseph A. Hill, *Women in Gainful Occupations, 1870–1920*, U.S. Bureau of the Census, Monograph no. 9 (Washington, D.C.: Government Printing Office, 1929), p. 33.

Union membership almost doubled, from 2.6 million in 1915 to 5.1 million in 1920. Workers commonly sought higher wages and shorter hours through strikes and unionization. Wages rose an average of 137 percent from 1915 to 1920, although inflation largely negated these gains. The average workweek declined in that same period from 55 to 51 hours. Workers also struck in response to managerial attempts to speed up production and tighten discipline. As time passed, increasing numbers of workers began to wonder why the war for democracy in Europe had no counterpart in their factories at home. "Industrial democracy" became the battle cry of an awakened labor movement.

Wilson's willingness to include labor in his 1916 progressive coalition reflected his awareness of labor's potential power (see chapter 21). In 1918, he bestowed prestige on the newly formed National War Labor Board (NWLB)

by appointing former president William Howard Taft to be cochair alongside Samuel Gompers, president of the American Federation of Labor. The NWLB brought together representatives of labor, industry, and the public to resolve labor disputes.

Raising an Army

To raise an army, the Wilson administration committed itself to conscription—the drafting of most men of a certain age, irrespective of their family's wealth, ethnic background, or social standing. The Selective Service Act of May 1917 empowered the administration to do just that. By war's end, local Selective Service boards had registered 24 million young men age 18 and older and had drafted nearly 3 million of them into the military; another 2 million volunteered for service.

LINK TO THE PAST

"A Storm of Our People toward the North"

When jobs became available in the North during the First World War, African Americans from the South began journeying north in record numbers. Between 1916 and 1920, 500,000 made the journey, a population movement so large it became known as the Great Migration. That so many went north in such a brief period demonstrates how tough life was in the South for most African Americans and how ready they were to seize an opportunity to improve their situation. Many of the migrants were rural folk—tenant farmers, sharecroppers, and agricultural laborers—whose skills were not easily transferable to the urban and industrial economies of northern cities. They thus had to enter northern labor forces at the bottom—as unskilled industrial or service employees. But the Great Migration also counted educated African Americans in its ranks, as this excerpt from a letter sent to the *Chicago Defender,* a prominent black newspaper, demonstrates. The four letter writers were educated women from Florida who had been teachers in black schools and were now looking for jobs as domestic servants with well-off Chicago families. We do not know whether the *Chicago Defender* responded to this particular letter, but we do know that in general the newspaper played a key role in facilitating migration by providing important information to both southern migrants and northern employers.

We have several times read your noted newspaper and we are delighted with the same because it is a thorough Negro paper. There is a storm of our people toward the North and especially to your city. We have watched your want ad regularly and we are anxious for location with good families (white) where we can be cared for and do domestic work. We want to engage as cook, nurse, and maid. We have had some educational advantages, as we have taught in rural schools for few years but our pay so poor we could not continue. We can furnish testimonial of our honesty and integrity and moral standing. Will you please assist us in securing places as we are anxious to come but want jobs before we leave. Our chance here is so poor.

1. What, if anything, can we learn about these four potential migrants from this letter excerpt? In particular, how desperate were they to leave the South?
2. What steps had they taken to prepare for going north?
3. What risks were they willing to endure for the sake of gaining an opportunity for a better life?

For additional sources related to this feature, visit the *Liberty, Equality, Power* Web site at:

http://history.wadsworth.com/murrin_LEP4e

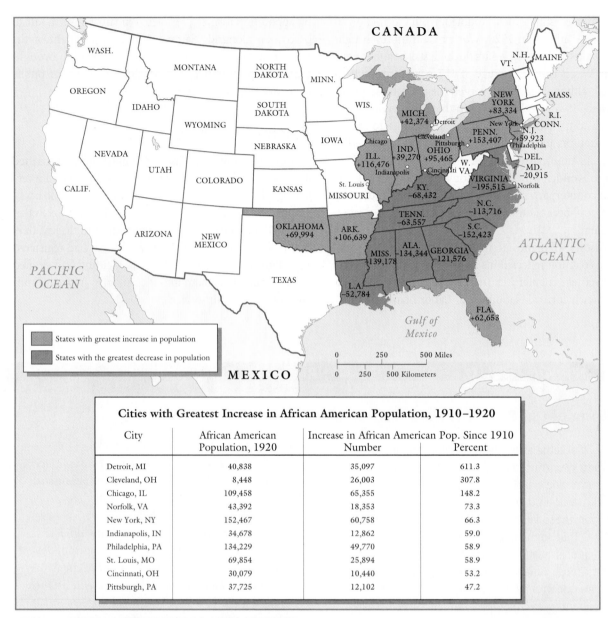

MAP 23.3 AFRICAN AMERICAN MIGRATION, 1910–1920

Most southern states lost 50,000 to 200,000 African Americans each during the years of the Great Migration, while many northern states, in the industrial belt stretching from Illinois through New York, gained 40,000 to 150,000 apiece. The table inset on the map shows the cities posting the biggest gains.

Relatively few men resisted the draft, even among recently arrived immigrants. Foreign-born men constituted 18 percent of the armed forces—a percentage greater than their share of the total population. Almost 400,000 African Americans served, representing approximately 10 percent, the same as the percentage of African Americans in the total population.

The U.S. Army, under the command of Chief of Staff Peyton March and General John J. Pershing, faced the difficult task of fashioning these ethnically and racially diverse millions into a professional fighting force. Teaching raw

recruits to fight was hard enough, Pershing and March observed; the generals refused the task of teaching them to put aside their prejudices. Rather than integrate the armed forces, they segregated black soldiers from white. Virtually all African Americans were assigned to all-black units and barred from combat. Being stripped of a combat role was particularly galling to blacks, who, in previous wars, had proven themselves to be among the best American fighters. Pershing was fully aware of the African American contribution. He had commanded African American troops in the 10th Cavalry, the all-black regiment that had distin-

guished itself in the Spanish-American War (chapter 22). Pershing's military reputation had depended so heavily on the black troops who fought for him that he had acquired the nickname Black Jack.

For a time, the military justified its intensified discrimination against blacks by referring to the results of rudimentary IQ (intelligence quotient) tests administered by psychologists to two million AEF soldiers. These tests allegedly "proved" that native-born Americans and immigrants from the British Isles, Germany, and Scandinavia were well endowed with intelligence, whereas African Americans and immigrants from Southern and Eastern Europe were poorly endowed. The tests were scientifically so ill-conceived, however, that their findings revealed nothing about the true distribution of intelligence in the population. Their most sensational revelation was that more than half of the soldiers in the AEF—white and black—were "morons," men who had failed to reach the mental age of 13. After trying to absorb the apparent news that most U.S. soldiers were feeble-minded, the military sensibly rejected the pseudo-science on which these intelligence findings were based. In 1919, it discontinued the IQ testing program.

National Archives.

WOMEN DOING "MEN'S" WORK
Labor shortages during the war allowed thousands of women to take industrial jobs customarily reserved for men. Here women operate pneumatic hammers at the Midvale Steel and Ordnance Company, Nicetown, Pennsylvania, 1918.

Given the racial and ethnic differences among American troops and the short time Pershing and his staff had to train recruits, the performance of the AEF was impressive. The United States increased the army from a mere 100,000 to 5 million in little more than a year. The Germans sank no troop ships, nor were any soldiers killed during the dangerous Atlantic crossing. In combat, U.S. troops became known for their sharpshooting skills.

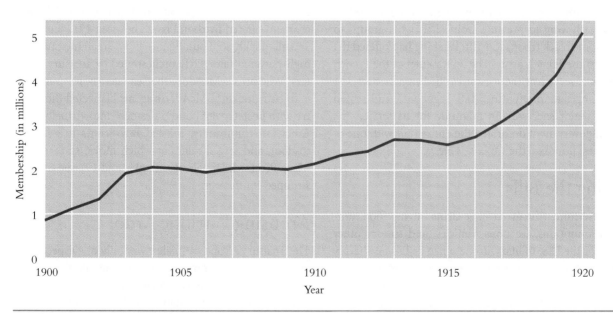

TOTAL MEMBERSHIP OF AMERICAN TRADE UNIONS, 1900–1920

Source: Leo Wolman, *The Growth of American Trade Unions, 1880–1923* (New York: National Bureau of Economic Research, 1924), p. 33.

RECRUITING POSTER, FIRST WORLD WAR, 1917

The government plastered public institutions with recruiting posters. This one represents navy work as glamorous, masculine, and brave, as a way of enticing more young men to join up.

The most decorated soldier in the AEF was Sergeant Alvin C. York of Tennessee, who captured 35 machine guns, took 132 prisoners, and killed 17 German soldiers with 17 bullets. York had learned his marksmanship hunting wild turkeys in the Tennessee hills. "Of course, it weren't no trouble nohow for me to hit them big [German] army targets," he later commented. "They were so much bigger than turkeys' heads." One of the most decorated AEF units was New York's 369th Regiment, a black unit recruited in Harlem. Bowing to pressure from civil rights groups to allow some black troops to fight, Pershing had offered the 369th to the French army. The 369th entered the French front line, served in the forward Allied trenches for 191 days (longer than any other U.S. regiment), and scored several major successes. In gratitude for its service, the French government decorated the entire unit with one of its highest honors—the *Croix de Guerre.*

Paying the Bills

The government incurred huge debts buying food, uniforms, munitions, weapons, vehicles, and sundry other items for the U.S. military. To help pay its bills, it sharply increased tax rates. The new taxes hit the wealthiest Americans the hardest: The richest were slapped with a 67 percent income tax and a 25 percent inheritance tax. Corporations were ordered to pay an "excess profits" tax. Proposed by the Wilson administration and backed by

Robert La Follette and other congressional progressives who feared that the "interests" would use the war to enrich themselves, these taxes were meant to ensure that all Americans would sacrifice something for the war.

Tax revenues, however, provided only about one-third of the $33 billion that the government ultimately spent on the war. The rest came from the sale of Liberty Bonds. These 30-year government bonds offered individual purchasers a return of 3.5 percent in annual interest. The government offered five bond issues between 1917 and 1920, and all quickly sold out, thanks, in no small measure, to a high-powered sales pitch, orchestrated by Treasury Secretary William G. McAdoo, that equated bond purchases with patriotic duty. McAdoo's agents blanketed the country with posters, sent bond "salesmen" into virtually every American community, enlisted Boy Scouts to go door-to-door, and staged rallies at which movie stars such as Mary Pickford, Douglas Fairbanks, and Charlie Chaplin stumped for the war.

Arousing Patriotic Ardor

The Treasury's bond campaign was only one aspect of an extraordinary government effort to arouse public support for the war. In 1917, Wilson set up a new agency, the Committee on Public Information (CPI), to popularize the war. Under the chairmanship of George Creel, a midwestern progressive and a muckraker, the CPI distributed 75

THE 369TH RETURNS TO NEW YORK

Denied the opportunity to fight in the U.S. Army, this unit fought for the French. For the length and distinction of its service in the front lines, this entire unit was awarded the *Croix de Guerre* by the French government.

National Archives.

million copies of pamphlets explaining U.S. war aims in several languages. It trained a force of 75,000 "Four-Minute Men" to deliver succinct, uplifting war speeches to numerous groups in their home cities and towns. It papered the walls of virtually every public institution (and many private ones) with posters, placed advertisements in mass-circulation magazines, sponsored exhibitions, and peppered newspaper editors with thousands of press releases on the progress of the war.

Faithful to his muckraking past (see chapter 21), Creel wanted to give the people the "facts" of the war, believing that well-informed citizens would see the wisdom of Wilson's policies. He also saw his work as an opportunity to achieve the progressive goal of uniting all Americans into a single moral community. Americans everywhere learned that the United States had entered the war "to make the world safe for democracy," to help the world's weaker peoples achieve self-determination, and to bring a measure of justice into the conduct of international affairs. Americans were asked to affirm those ideals by doing everything they could to support the war.

This uplifting message affected the American people, although not necessarily in ways anticipated by CPI propagandists. It imparted to many a deep love of country and a sense of participation in a grand democratic experiment. Among others, particularly those experiencing poverty and discrimination, it sparked a new spirit of protest. Workers, women, European ethnics, and African Americans began demanding that America live up to its democratic ideals at home as well as abroad. Workers rallied

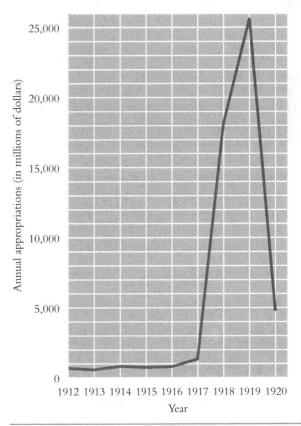

THE FIRST WORLD WAR AND THE FEDERAL BUDGET

Source: Data from *Statistical Abstract of the United States, 1919* (Washington, D.C.: Government Printing Office, 1920), p. 681.

to the cry of "industrial democracy." Women seized on the democratic fervor to bring their fight for suffrage to a successful conclusion (see chapter 21). African Americans began to dream that the war might deliver them from second-class citizenship. European ethnics believed that Wilson's support of their countrymen's rights abroad would improve their own chances for success in the United States.

Although the CPI had helped to unleash it, this new democratic enthusiasm troubled Creel and others in the Wilson administration. The United States, after all, was still deeply divided along class, ethnic, and racial lines. Workers and industrialists regarded each other with suspicion. Cultural differences compounded this class division, for the working class was overwhelmingly ethnic in composition, and the industrial and political elites consisted mainly of the native-born whose families had been "Americans" for generations. Progressives had fought hard to overcome these divisions. They had tamed the power of capitalists, improved the condition of workers, encouraged the Americanization of immigrants, and articulated a new, more inclusive idea of who could belong to the American nation. But their work was far from complete when the war broke out, and the war opened up new social and cultural divisions. German immigrants still formed the largest foreign-born population group—2.3 million. Another 2.3 million immigrants came from some part of the Austro-Hungarian Empire. And more than 1 million Americans—native-born and immigrants—supported the Socialist Party and the Industrial Workers of the World, both of which had opposed the war. The decision to authorize the CPI's massive unity campaign indicates that the progressives understood how widespread the discord was. Still, they had not anticipated that the promotion of democratic ideals at home would exacerbate, rather than lessen, the nation's social and cultural divisions.

Wartime Repression

By early 1918, the CPI's campaign had developed a darker, more coercive side. Inflammatory advertisements called on patriots to report on neighbors, coworkers, and ethnics whom they suspected of subverting the war effort. Propagandists called on all immigrants, especially those from Central, Southern, and Eastern Europe, to pledge themselves to "100 percent Americanism" and to repudiate all ties to their homeland, native language, and ethnic customs. The CPI aroused hostility toward Germans by spreading lurid tales of German atrocities and encouraging the public to see movies such as *The Prussian Cur* and *The Beast of Berlin*. The Justice Department arrested thou-

RENAMED GERMAN AMERICAN WORDS

Original German Name	Renamed "Patriotic" Name
hamburger	salisbury steak, liberty steak, liberty sandwich
sauerkraut	liberty cabbage
Hamburg Avenue, Brooklyn, New York	Wilson Avenue, Brooklyn, New York
Germantown, Nebraska	Garland, Nebraska
East Germantown, Indiana	Pershing, Indiana
Berlin, Iowa	Lincoln, Iowa
pinochle	liberty
German shepherd	Alsatian shepherd
Deutsches Hans of Indianapolis	Athenaeum of Indiana
Germania Maennerchor of Chicago	Lincoln Club
Kaiser Street	Maine Way

Source: From La Vern J. Rippley, *The German Americans* (Boston: Twayne, 1976), p. 186; and Robert H. Ferrell, *Woodrow Wilson and World War I, 1917–1921* (New York: Harper and Row, 1985), pp. 205–206.

sands of German and Austrian immigrants whom it suspected of subversive activities. Congress passed the Trading with the Enemy Act, which required foreign-language publications to submit all war-related stories to post office censors for approval.

German Americans became the objects of popular hatred. American patriots sought to expunge every trace of German influence from American culture. In Boston, performances of Beethoven's symphonies were banned, and the German-born conductor of the Boston Symphony Orchestra was forced to resign. Although Americans would not give up the German foods they had grown to love, they would no longer call them by their German names. Sauerkraut was rechristened "liberty cabbage," and hamburgers became "liberty sandwiches." Libraries removed works of German literature from their shelves, and Theodore Roosevelt and others urged school districts to prohibit the teaching of the German language. Patriotic school boards in Lima, Ohio, and elsewhere burned the German books in their districts.

German Americans risked being fired from work, losing their businesses, and being assaulted on the street. A St. Louis mob lynched an innocent German immigrant whom they suspected of subversion. After only 25 minutes of deliberation, a St. Louis jury acquitted the mob leaders, who had brazenly defended their crime as an act of patriotism. German Americans began hiding their ethnic identity, changing their names, speaking German only in the privacy of their homes, and celebrating their holidays only with trusted friends. This experience devastated the once-proud German American community; many would never

Imperial War Museum.

THE CAMPAIGN OF FEAR

By 1918, the government's appeal to Americans' best aspirations—to spread liberty and democracy—had been replaced by a determination to arouse fear of subversion and conquest. Here the German enemy is depicted as a terrifying brute who violates Lady Liberty and uses his *kultur* club to destroy civilization.

recover from the shame and vulnerability they experienced in those years.

The anti-German campaign escalated into a general anti-immigrant crusade. Congress passed the Immigration Restriction Act of 1917, over Wilson's veto, which declared that all adult immigrants who failed a reading test would be denied admission to the United States. The act also banned the immigration of laborers from India, Indochina, Afghanistan, Arabia, the East Indies, and several other countries within an Asiatic Barred Zone. This legislation marked the beginning of a movement in Congress that, four years later, would close the immigration door to virtually all transoceanic peoples. Congress also passed the 18th Amendment to the Constitution, which prohibited the manufacture and distribution of alcoholic beverages (see chapter 21). The crusade for prohibition was not new, but anti-immigrant feelings generated by the war gave it

added impetus. Prohibitionists pictured the nation's urban ethnic ghettos as scenes of drunkenness, immorality, and disloyalty. They also accused German American brewers of operating a "liquor trust" to sap people's will to fight. The states quickly ratified the 18th Amendment, and in 1919, Prohibition became the law of the land.

More and more, the Wilson administration relied on repression to achieve domestic unity. In the Espionage, Sabotage, and Sedition Acts passed in 1917 and 1918, Congress gave the administration sweeping powers to silence and even imprison dissenters. These acts went far beyond outlawing behavior that no nation at war could be expected to tolerate, such as spying for the enemy, sabotaging war production, and calling for the enemy's victory. Now citizens could be prosecuted for writing or uttering any statement that could be construed as profaning the flag, the Constitution, or the military. These acts constituted the most drastic restrictions of free speech at the national level since the Alien and Sedition Acts of 1798 (see chapter 8).

Government repression fell most heavily on the IWW and the Socialist Party. Both groups had opposed intervention before 1917. Although they subsequently muted their opposition, they continued to insist that the true enemies of American workers were to be found in the ranks of American employers, not in Germany or Austria-Hungary. The government responded by banning many socialist materials from the mails and by disrupting socialist and IWW meetings. By spring 1918, government agents had raided countless IWW offices and had arrested 2,000 IWW members, including its entire executive board. Many of those arrested would be sentenced to long jail terms. William Haywood, the IWW president, fled to Europe and then to the Soviet Union rather than go to jail. Eugene V. Debs, the head of the Socialist Party, received a 10-year jail term for making an antiwar speech in Canton, Ohio, in summer 1918.

This federal repression, carried out in an atmosphere of supercharged patriotism, encouraged local governments and private citizens to initiate their own antiradical crusades. In the mining town of Bisbee, Arizona, a sheriff with an eager force of 2,000 deputized citizens kidnapped 1,200 IWW members, herded them into cattle cars, and dumped them onto the New Mexico desert with little food or water. Vigilantes in Butte, Montana, chained an IWW organizer to a car and let his body scrape the pavement as they drove the vehicle through city streets. Next, they strung him up to a railroad trestle, castrated him, and left him to die. The 250,000 members of the American Protective League, most of them businessmen and professionals, routinely spied on fellow workers and neighbors. They opened mail and tapped phones and otherwise harassed

those suspected of disloyalty. Attorney General Thomas Gregory publicly endorsed the group and sought federal funds to support its "police" work.

The spirit of coercion even infected institutions that had long prided themselves on tolerance. In July 1917, Columbia University fired two professors for speaking out against U.S. intervention in the war. The National Americanization Committee, which before 1917 had pioneered a humane approach to the problem of integrating immigrants into American life, now supported surveillance, internment, and deportation of aliens suspected of anti-American sentiments.

Wilson bore responsibility for this climate of repression. He did attempt to block certain pieces of repressive legislation; for example, he vetoed both the Immigration Restriction Act and the Volstead Act (the act passed to enforce Prohibition), only to be overridden by Congress. But Wilson did little to halt Attorney General Gregory's prosecution of radicals or Postmaster General Burleson's campaign to exclude Socialist Party publications from the mail. He ignored pleas from progressives that he intervene in the Debs case to prevent the ailing 62-year-old from going to jail. His acquiescence in these matters cost him dearly among progressives and socialists. Wilson believed,

however, that once the Allies, with U.S. support, won the war and arranged a just peace in accordance with the Fourteen Points, his administration's wartime actions would be forgiven and the progressive coalition would be restored.

The Failure of the International Peace

In the month following Germany's surrender on November 11, 1918, Wilson was confident about the prospects of achieving a just peace. Both Germany and the Allies had publicly accepted the Fourteen Points as the basis for negotiations. Wilson's international prestige was enormous. People throughout the world were inspired by his dream of a democratic, just, and harmonious world order free of poverty, ignorance, and war. Poles, Lithuanians, and other Eastern Europeans whose pursuit of nationhood had been frustrated for 100 years or more now believed that independence might be within their reach. Zionist Jews in Europe and the United States dared to dream of a Jewish homeland within their lifetimes. Countless African and Asian peoples imagined achieving their freedom from colonial domination.

New York Times, 1919.

"THE SAVIOR OF HUMANITY"

Wherever he went in Europe, Woodrow Wilson was greeted by huge crowds eager to thank him for ending Europe's terrible war and to endorse his vision of a peaceful, democratic world. Here millions of Italians greet Wilson's arrival in Milan.

To capitalize on his fame and to maximize the chances for a peace settlement based on his Fourteen Points, Wilson broke with diplomatic precedent and decided to head the American delegation to the Paris Peace Conference in January 1919. Enormous crowds of enthusiastic Europeans turned out to hail Wilson's arrival on the Continent in December. Some 2 million French citizens—the largest throng ever assembled on French soil—lined the parade route in Paris to catch a glimpse of "Wilson, *le juste* [the just]." In Rome, Milan, and La Scala, Italians acclaimed him "The Savior of Humanity" and "The Moses from Across the Atlantic."

In the Fourteen Points, Wilson had translated his principles for a new world order into specific proposals for international peace and justice. The first group of points called for all nations to abide by a code of conduct that embraced free trade, freedom of the seas, open diplomacy, disarmament, and the resolution of disputes through mediation. A second group, based on the principle of self-determination, proposed redrawing the map of Europe to give the subjugated peoples of the Austro-Hungarian, Ottoman, and Russian empires national sovereignty. The last point called for establishing the League of Nations, an assembly in which all nations would be represented and in which all international disputes would be given a fair hearing and an opportunity for peaceful solutions.

The Paris Peace Conference and the Treaty of Versailles

Although representatives of 27 nations began meeting in Paris on January 12, 1919, to discuss Wilson's Fourteen Points, negotiations were controlled by the "Big Four": Wilson, Prime Minister David Lloyd George of Great Britain, Premier Georges Clemenceau of France, and Prime Minister Vittorio Orlando of Italy. When Orlando quit the conference after a dispute with Wilson, the Big Four became the Big Three. Wilson quickly learned that his negotiating partners' support for the Fourteen Points was much weaker than he had believed. The cagey Clemenceau mused: "God gave us the Ten Commandments, and we broke them. Wilson gives us Fourteen Points. We shall see." Clemenceau and Lloyd George refused to include most of Wilson's points in the peace treaty. The points having to do with freedom of the seas and free trade were omitted, as were the proposals for open diplomacy and Allied disarmament. Wilson won partial endorsement of the principle of self-determination: Belgian sovereignty was restored, Poland's status as a nation was affirmed, and the new nations of Czechoslovakia, Yugoslavia, Finland, Lithuania, Latvia, and Estonia were created. In addition, some lands of the former Ottoman Empire—Armenia,

Palestine, Mesopotamia, and Syria—were to be placed under League of Nations' trusteeships with the understanding that they would someday gain their independence. Wilson failed in his efforts to block a British plan to transfer former German colonies in Asia to Japanese control, an Italian plan to annex territory inhabited by 200,000 Austrians, and a French plan to take from Germany its valuable Saar coal mines.

Nor could Wilson blunt the drive to punish Germany for its wartime aggression. In addition to awarding the Saar basin to France, the Allies gave portions of northern Germany to Denmark and portions of eastern Germany to Poland and Czechoslovakia. Germany was stripped of virtually its entire navy and air force, and forbidden to place soldiers or fortifications in western Germany along the Rhine. It was allowed to keep an army of only 100,000 men. In addition, Germany was forced to admit its responsibility for the war. In accepting this "war guilt," Germany was, in effect, agreeing to compensate the victors in cash (reparations) for the pain and suffering it had inflicted on them.

Lloyd George and Clemenceau brushed off the protests of those who viewed this desire to prostrate Germany as a cruel and vengeful act. That the German people, after their nation's 1918 defeat, had overthrown the monarch (Kaiser Wilhelm II) who had taken them to war, and had reconstituted their nation as a democratic republic—the

PRESIDENT WOODROW WILSON IN PARIS, 1919
Wilson arrives at the Paris Peace Conference to begin negotiations on the treaty that would formally end the First World War and establish the League of Nations as a first step to a new world order.

first in their country's history—won them no leniency. On June 28, 1919, Great Britain, France, the United States, Germany, and other European nations signed the Treaty of Versailles. In 1921, an Allied commission notified the Germans that they were to pay the victors $33 billion, a sum well beyond the resources of a defeated and economically ruined Germany.

The League of Nations

The Allies' single-minded pursuit of self-interest disillusioned many liberals and socialists in the United States,

but Wilson seemed undismayed. He had won approval of the most important of his Fourteen Points—that which called for the creation of the League of Nations. The League, whose structure and responsibilities were set forth in the Covenant attached to the peace treaty, would usher in Wilson's new world order. Drawing its membership from the signatories to the Treaty of Versailles (except, for the time being, Germany), the League would function as an international parliament and judiciary, establishing rules of international behavior and resolving disputes between nations through rational and peaceful means. A nine-member executive council—the United States,

MAP 23.4 EUROPE AND THE NEAR EAST AFTER THE FIRST WORLD WAR

The First World War and the Treaty of Versailles changed the geography of Europe and the Near East. Nine nations in Europe, stretching from Yugoslavia in the south to Finland in the north, were created (or reformed) out of the defeated Austro-Hungarian and Ottoman Empires. In the Near East, meanwhile, Syria, Lebanon, Palestine, Transjordan, and Iraq were carved out of the Ottoman Empire, placed under British or French control, and promised eventual independence.

Britain, France, Italy, and Japan would have permanent seats on the council, while the other four seats would rotate among the smaller powers—was charged with administering decisions.

Wilson believed that the League would redeem the failures of the Paris Peace Conference. Under its auspices, free trade and freedom of the seas would be achieved, reparations against Germany would be reduced or eliminated, disarmament of the Allies would proceed, and the principle of self-determination would be extended to peoples outside Europe. Moreover, the Covenant (Article X) would endow the League with the power to punish aggressor nations through economic isolation and military retaliation.

Wilson versus Lodge: The Fight over Ratification

The League's success, however, depended on Wilson's ability to convince the U.S. Senate to ratify the Treaty of Versailles. Wilson knew that this would not be easy. The Republicans had gained a majority in the Senate in 1918, and two groups within their ranks were determined to frustrate Wilson's ambitions. One group was a caucus of 14 midwesterners and westerners known as the "irreconcilables." Most of them were conservative isolationists who wanted the United States to preserve its separation from Europe, but a few were prominent progressives—Robert La Follette, William Borah, and Hiram Johnson—who had voted against the declaration of war in 1917. The self-interest displayed by England and France at the peace conference convinced this progressive group that the Europeans were incapable of decent behavior in international matters.

Senator Henry Cabot Lodge of Massachusetts led the second opposition group. Its members rejected Wilson's belief that every group of people on earth had a right to form their own nation; that every state, regardless of its size, its economic condition, and the vigor and intelligence of its people, should have a voice in world affairs; and that disputes between nations could be settled in open, democratic forums. They subscribed instead to Theodore Roosevelt's vision of a world controlled by a few great nations, each militarily strong, secure in its own sphere of influence, and determined to avoid war through a carefully negotiated balance of power. These Republicans preferred to let Europe return to the power politics that had prevailed before the war rather than experiment with a new world order that might constrain and compromise U.S. power and autonomy.

This Republican critique was a cogent one that merited extended discussion. Particularly important were questions that Republicans raised about Article X, which gave the League the right to undertake military actions against aggressor nations. Did Americans want to authorize an international organization to decide when the United States would go to war? Was this not a violation of the Constitution, which vested war-making power solely in the Congress? Even if the constitutional problem could be solved, how could the United States ensure that it would not be forced into a military action that might damage its national interest?

It soon became clear, however, that several Republicans, including Lodge, were as interested in humiliating Wilson as in developing an alternative approach to foreign policy. They accused Wilson of promoting socialism through his wartime expansion of government power. They were angry that he had failed to include any distinguished Republicans, such as Lodge, Elihu Root, or William Howard Taft, in the Paris peace delegation. And they were still bitter about the 1918 congressional elections, when Wilson had argued that a Republican victory would embarrass the nation abroad. Although Wilson's electioneering had failed to sway the voters (the Republicans won a majority in both Houses), his suggestion that a Republican victory would injure national honor had infuriated Theodore Roosevelt and his supporters. Roosevelt died in

© Corbis.

REPUBLICAN ELDER STATESMEN
Henry Cabot Lodge is on the left; William Howard Taft is on the right. Lodge led the fight in the Senate against ratifying the Treaty of Versailles.

1919, but his close friend Lodge kept his rage alive. "I never thought I could hate a man as much as I hate Wilson," Lodge conceded in a moment of candor.

As chairman of the Senate Foreign Relations Committee, charged with considering the treaty before reporting it to the Senate floor, Lodge did everything possible to obstruct ratification. He packed the committee with senators who were likely to oppose the treaty. He delayed action by reading every one of the treaty's 300 pages aloud and by subjecting it to endless criticism in six long weeks of public hearings. When his committee finally reported the treaty to the full Senate, it came encumbered with nearly 50 amendments whose adoption Lodge made a precondition of his support. Some of the amendments expressed reasonable concerns—namely, that participation in the League not diminish the role of Congress in determining foreign policy, compromise American sovereignty, or involve the United States in an unjust or ill-advised war. But many were meant only to complicate the task of ratification.

Despite Lodge's obstructionism, the treaty's chances for ratification by the required two-thirds majority of the Senate remained good. Many Republicans were prepared to vote for ratification if Wilson indicated his willingness to accept some of the proposed amendments. Wilson could have salvaged the treaty and, along with it, U.S. participation in the League of Nations, but Wilson refused to compromise with the Republicans and announced that he would carry his case directly to the American people instead. In September 1919, he undertook a whirlwind cross-country tour that covered more than 8,000 miles with 37 stops. He addressed as many crowds as he could reach, sometimes speaking for an hour at a time, four times a day.

On September 25, after giving a speech at Pueblo, Colorado, Wilson suffered excruciating headaches throughout the night. His physician ordered him back to Washington, where on October 2 he suffered a near-fatal stroke. Wilson hovered near death for two weeks and remained seriously disabled for another six. His condition improved somewhat in November, but his left side remained paralyzed, his speech was slurred, his energy level low, and his emotions unstable. Wilson's wife, Edith Bolling Wilson, and his doctor isolated him from Congress and the press, withholding news they thought might upset him and preventing the public from learning how much his body and mind had deteriorated.

Many historians believe that the stroke impaired Wilson's political judgment. He refused to consider any of the Republican amendments to the treaty, even after it had become clear that compromise offered the only chance of winning U.S. participation in the League of Nations. When Lodge presented an amended treaty for a ratification vote on November 19, Wilson ordered Senate Democrats to vote against it; 42 (of 47) Democratic senators complied, and with the aid of 13 Republican irreconcilables, the Lodge version was defeated. Only moments later, the unamended version of the treaty—Wilson's version—received only 38 votes.

The Treaty's Final Defeat

As the magnitude of the calamity became apparent, supporters of the League in Congress, the nation, and the world urged the Senate and the president to reconsider. Wilson would not budge. A bipartisan group of senators desperately tried to work out a compromise without con-

---

WOODROW WILSON'S FOURTEEN POINTS, 1918: RECORD OF IMPLEMENTATION

1. Open covenants of peace openly arrived at	Not fulfilled
2. Absolute freedom of navigation upon the seas in peace and war	Not fulfilled
3. Removal of all economic barriers to the equality of trade among nations	Not fulfilled
4. Reduction of armaments to the level needed only for domestic safety	Not fulfilled
5. Impartial adjustments of colonial claims	Not fulfilled
6. Evacuation of all Russian territory; Russia to be welcomed into the society of free nations	Not fulfilled
7. Evacuation and restoration of Belgium	Fulfilled
8. Evacuation and restoration of all French lands; return of Alsace-Lorraine to France	Fulfilled
9. Readjustment of Italy's frontiers along lines of Italian nationality	Compromised
10. Self-determination for the former subjects of the Austro-Hungarian Empire	Compromised
11. Evacuation of Romania, Serbia, and Montenegro; free access to the sea for Serbia	Compromised
12. Self-determination for the former subjects of the Ottoman Empire; secure sovereignty for Turkish portion	Compromised
13. Establishment of an independent Poland with free and secure access to the sea	Fulfilled
14. Establishment of the League of Nations to secure mutual guarantees of independence and territorial integrity	Compromised

Source: From G. M. Gathorne-Hardy, *The Fourteen Points and the Treaty of Versailles,* Oxford Pamphlets on World Affairs, no. 6 (1939), pp. 8–34; and Thomas G. Paterson et al., *American Foreign Policy: A History,* 2nd ed. (Lexington, Mass.: Heath, 1983), vol. 2, pp. 282–93.

sulting him. When that effort failed, the Senate put to a vote, one more time, the Lodge version of the treaty. Because 23 Democrats, most of them southerners, still refused to break with Wilson, this last-ditch effort at ratification failed on March 8, 1920, by a margin of seven votes. Wilson's dream of a new world order died that day. The crumpled figure in the White House seemed to bear little resemblance to the hero who, barely 15 months before, had been greeted in Europe as the world's savior. Wilson filled out his remaining 12 months in office as an invalid, presiding over the interment of progressivism. He died in 1924.

The judgment of history lies heavily on these events, for many believe that the flawed treaty and the failure of the League contributed to Adolf Hitler's rise in Germany and the outbreak of a second world war more devastating than the first. It is necessary to ask, then, whether American participation in the League would have significantly altered the course of world history.

The mere fact of U.S. membership in the League would not have magically solved Europe's postwar problems. The U.S. government was inexperienced in diplomacy and prone to mistakes. Its freedom to negotiate solutions to international disputes would have been limited by the large number of American voters who remained strongly opposed to U.S. entanglement in European affairs. Even if such opposition could have been overcome, the United States would still have confronted European countries determined to go their own way.

Nevertheless, one thing is clear: No stable international order could have arisen after the First World War without the full involvement of the United States. The League of Nations required American authority and prestige in order to operate effectively as an international parliament. We cannot know whether the League, with American involvement, would have offered the Germans a less humiliating peace, allowing them to rehabilitate their economy and salvage their national pride; nor whether an American-led League would have stopped Hitler's expansionism before it escalated into full-scale war in 1939. Still, it seems fair to suggest that American participation would have strengthened the League and improved its ability to bring a lasting peace to Europe.

✒ The Postwar Period: A Society in Convulsion

The end of the war brought no respite from the forces convulsing American society. Workers were determined to regain the purchasing power they had lost to inflation. Employers were determined to halt or reverse the wartime gains labor had made. Radicals saw in this conflict between capital and labor the possibility of a socialist revolution. Conservatives were certain that the revolution had already begun. Returning white servicemen were nervous about regaining their civilian jobs and looked with hostility on the black, Hispanic, and female workers who had been recruited to take their places. Black veterans were in no mood to return to segregation and subordination. The federal government, meanwhile, uneasy over the centralization of power during the war, quickly dismantled such agencies as the War Industries Board and the National War Labor Board. By so doing, it deprived itself of mechanisms that might have enabled it to intervene in social conflicts and keep them from erupting into rage and violence.

Labor-Capital Conflict

Nowhere was the escalation of conflict more evident than in the workplace. In 1919, 4 million workers—one-fifth of the nation's manufacturing workforce—went on strike. In January 1919, a general strike paralyzed the city of Seattle when 60,000 workers walked off their jobs. By August,

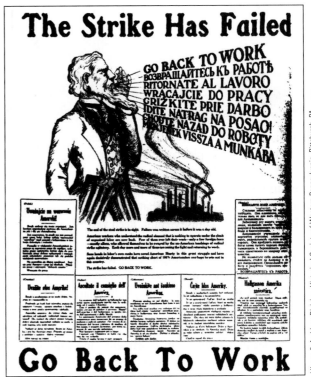

Library & Archives Division, Historical Society of Western Pennsylvania, Pittsburgh, PA.

THE 1919 STEEL STRIKE FAILS

The steel corporations were united in their opposition to the steelworkers' union and skillful in their use of media to demoralize the strikers. This poster reveals another reason for the strike's failure: a workforce so diverse that strike announcements had to be communicated in eight languages.

This black nationalist movement did not endure for long. Garvey entered into bitter disputes with other black leaders, including W. E. B. Du Bois, who regarded him as a flamboyant, self-serving demagogue. Garvey sometimes showed poor judgment, as when he expressed support for the Ku Klux Klan on the grounds that it shared his pessimism about the possibility of racial integration. Inexperienced in economic matters, Garvey squandered UNIA money on abortive business ventures. The U.S. government regarded his rhetoric as inflammatory and sought to silence him. In 1923, he was convicted of mail fraud involving the sale of Black Star stocks and was sentenced to five years in jail. In 1927, he was deported to Jamaica and the UNIA folded. Nevertheless, Garvey's philosophy of black nationalism endured.

Conclusion

The resurgence of racism in 1919 and the consequent turn to black nationalism among African Americans were signs that the high hopes of the war years had been dashed. Industrial workers, immigrants, and radicals also found their pursuit of liberty and equality interrupted by the fear, intolerance, and repression unleashed by the war. They came to understand as well that Wilson's commitment to these ideals counted for less than did his administration's and Congress's determination to discipline a people whom they regarded as dangerously heterogeneous and unstable. Of the reform groups, only woman suffragists made enduring gains—especially the right to vote—but, for the feminists in their ranks, these steps forward failed to compensate for the collapse of the progressive movement and, with it, their program of achieving equal rights for women across the board.

A similar disappointment engulfed those who had embraced and fought for Wilson's dream of creating a new and democratic world order. The world in 1919 appeared as volatile as it had been in 1914. More and more Americans—perhaps even a majority—were coming to believe that U.S. intervention had been a mistake.

In other ways, the United States benefited a great deal from the war. By 1919, the American economy was by far the world's strongest. Many of the nation's leading corporations had improved productivity and management during the war. U.S. banks were poised to supplant those of London as the most influential in international finance. The nation's economic strength triggered an extraordinary burst of growth in the 1920s, and millions of Americans rushed to take advantage of the prosperity that this "people's capitalism" had put within their grasp. But even affluence failed to dissolve the class, ethnic, and racial tensions that the war had exposed. And the failure of the peace process added to Europe's problems, delayed the emergence of the United States as a leader in world affairs, and created the preconditions for another world war.

SUGGESTED READINGS

On America's neutrality and road to war, consult **Arthur S. Link**, *Woodrow Wilson: Revolution, War and Peace* (1979), and **John Milton Cooper Jr.**, *The Vanity of Power: American Isolationism and the First World War, 1914–1917* (1969). **Roland C. Marchand**, *The American Peace Movement and Social Reform, 1898–1918* (1972), reconstructs the large and influential antiwar movement, while **John W. Chambers**, *To Raise an Army: The Draft Comes to Modern America* (1987), analyzes American efforts to prepare for war by raising a multimillion-man fighting machine. **David Kennedy**, *Over Here: The First World War and American Society* (1980), is a superb account of the effects of war on American society. For details on industrial mobilization, consult **Robert D. Cuff**, *The War Industries Board: Business-Government Relations during World War I* (1973). **David Montgomery**, *The Fall of the House of Labor: The Workplace, the State, and American Labor Activism, 1865–1925* (1987), expertly reconstructs the escalation of labor-management tensions during the war, but it should be read alongside **Joseph A. McCartin**, *Labor's Great War: The Struggle for Industrial Democracy and the Origins of Modern Labor Relations, 1912–1921* (1997). On the migration of African Americans to northern industrial centers and the movement of women into war production see **Joe William Trotter Jr.**, ed., *The Great Migration in Historical Perspective: New Dimensions of Race, Class, and Gender* (1991), and **Maurine W. Greenwald**, *Women, War and Work* (1980). **Stephen Vaughn**, *Holding Fast the Inner Lines: Democracy, Nationalism, and the Committee on Public Information* (1980), is an important account of the CPI, the government's central propaganda agency. **Harry N. Scheiber**, *The Wilson Administration and Civil Liberties, 1917–1921* (1960), analyzes the repression of dissent. On Wilson, Versailles, and the League of Nations, consult **Thomas J. Knock**, *To End All Wars: Woodrow Wilson and the Quest for a New World Order* (1992), **Arno Mayer**, *The Politics and Diplomacy of*

Peacemaking: Containment and Counterrevolution at Versailles, 1918–1919 (1967), **Lloyd C. Gardner,** *Safe for Democracy: The Anglo-American Response to Revolution, 1913–1923* (1984), **John Milton Cooper, Jr.,** *Breaking the Heart of the World: Woodrow Wilson and the Fight for the League of Nations* (2001), and **Katherine A. S. Siegel,** *Loans and Legitimacy: The Evolution of Soviet-American Relations, 1919–1933* (1996). On Republican opposition to the League of Nations, see **William C. Widenor,** *Henry Cabot Lodge and the Search for an American Foreign Policy* (1980). **Nell Irvin Painter,** *Standing at Armageddon: The United States, 1877–1919* (1987), offers a good overview of the class and racial divisions that convulsed American society in 1919. On the Red Scare, consult **Robert K. Murray,** *Red Scare: A Study in National Hysteria* (1955). **William Tuttle, Jr.,** *Race Riot: Chicago in the Red Summer of 1919* (1970), examines race conflict after the First World War, while **Judith Stein,** *The World of Marcus Garvey: Race and Class in Modern Society* (1986), explores the emergence of Marcus Garvey and the Universal Negro Improvement Association.

 AMERICAN JOURNEY ONLINE
AND
 INFOTRAC COLLEGE EDITION

Visit the source collections at www.ajaccess.wadsworth.com and infotrac.thomsonlearning.com and use the Search function with the following key terms to explore documents, images, audio and video clips, articles, and commentary related to the material in this chapter.

Woodrow Wilson	Red Scare
Lusitania	Sacco and Vanzetti
Fourteen Points	W. E. B. Du Bois
Treaty of Versailles	Marcus Garvey
League of Nations	black nationalism

GRADE AIDS

Visit the Liberty Equality Power Companion Web Site for resources specific to this textbook: http://history.wadsworth.com/murrin_LEP4e

 The CD in the back of this book and the U.S. History Resource Center at http://history.wadsworth.com/u.s./ offer a variety of tools to help you succeed in this course, including access to quizzes; images; documents; interactive simulations, maps, and timelines; movie explorations; and a wealth of other sources.

vacations became routine. Farmers and their families could now hop into their cars and head for the nearest town with its stores, movies, amusement parks, and sporting events. Suburbs proliferated, billed as the perfect mix of urban and rural life. Young men and women everywhere discovered that cars were a place where they could "make out," and even make love, without fear of reproach by prudish parents or prying neighbors.

In the 1920s, some Americans also discovered the benefits of owning stocks. The number of stockholders in AT&T, the nation's largest corporation, rose from 140,000 to 568,000. U.S. Steel stockholder numbers increased from 96,000 to 146,000. By 1929, as many as 7 million Americans owned stock, most of them people of middle-class means. This spread of stock ownership reflected the need for working capital among the nation's corporations. Because privately held wealth could not satisfy that need, corporations sought to sell their stocks and bonds to the general public. The New York Stock Exchange, first organized in 1792, assisted in processing complicated transactions.

A People's Capitalism

Capitalists boasted that they had created a "people's capitalism" in which virtually all Americans could participate. Now, everyone could own a piece of corporate America. Now, everyone could have a share of luxuries and amenities. Poverty, capitalists claimed, was banished and the gap between rich and poor all but closed. If every American could own a car and house, buy quality clothes, own stock, take vacations, and go to the movies, then economic inequality would cease to matter as a political issue.

Actually, although wages were rising, millions of Americans still earned too little to partake fully of the marketplace. The percentage of Americans owning stocks remained small. Social scientists Robert and Helen Lynd discovered, in their celebrated 1929 study of Muncie, Indiana, that working-class families who bought a car often lacked money for other goods. One housewife admitted, "We don't have no fancy clothes when we have the car to pay for. . . . The car is the only pleasure we have." Another declared, "I'll go without food before I'll see us give up the car." Many industrialists resisted pressure to increase wages, and workers lacked the organizational strength to force them to pay more.

One solution came with the introduction of consumer credit. Car dealers, home appliance salesmen, and other merchants began to offer installment plans that enabled consumers to purchase a product by making a down payment and promising to pay the rest in install-

ments. By 1930, 15 percent of all purchases—including 60 percent of all cars and 75 percent of all radios—were made on the installment plan.

Even so, many poor Americans benefited little from the consumer revolution. Middle-class Americans acquired a disproportionate share of consumer durables. They also could afford to purchase far more fresh fruits and vegetables and stocks than most working-class Americans.

The Rise of Advertising and Mass Marketing

But even middle-class consumers had to be wooed. How could they be persuaded to buy another car only a few years after they had bought their first one? General Motors had the answer. In 1926, it introduced the concept of the annual model change. GM cars took on a different look every year as GM engineers changed headlights and chassis colors, streamlined bodies, and added new features. The strategy worked. GM leaped past Ford and became the world's largest car manufacturer.

Henry Ford reluctantly introduced his Model A in 1927 to provide customers with a colorful alternative to the drab Model T. Having spent his lifetime selling a product renowned for its utility and reliability, Ford rejected the idea that sales could be increased by appealing to the intangible hopes and fears of consumers. He was wrong. The desire to be beautiful, handsome, or sexually attractive; to exercise power and control; to demonstrate competence and success; to escape anonymity, loneliness, and boredom; to experience pleasure—all such desires, once activated, could motivate a consumer to buy a new car even when the old one was still serviceable, or to spend money on goods that might have once seemed frivolous.

Arousing such desires required more than bright colors, sleek lines, and attractive packaging. It called for advertising campaigns intended to make a product seem to be the answer to the consumer's desires. To create those campaigns, corporations turned to a new kind of company: professional advertising firms. The new advertising entrepreneurs, people such as Edward Bernays, Doris Fleischmann, and Bruce Barton, tended to be well-educated, sensitive to public taste, and knowledgeable in human psychology. In their campaigns, these advertisers played on the emotions and vulnerabilities of their target audiences. One cosmetics ad decreed: "Unless you are one woman in a thousand, you must use powder and rouge. Modern living has robbed women of much of their natural color." A perfume manufacturer's ad pronounced: "The first duty of woman is to attract. . . . It does not matter how clever or independent you may be, if you fail to

Sunshine Mellows
Heat Purifies

LUCKIES
are always
kind to your
throat

The advice of your physician is: Keep out of doors, in the open air, breathe deeply; take plenty of exercise in the mellow sunshine, and have a periodic check-up on the health of your body.

Everyone knows that sunshine mellows—that's why the "TOASTING" process includes the use of the Ultra Violet Rays. LUCKY STRIKE—made of the finest tobaccos—the Cream of the Crop—THEN—"IT'S TOASTED"—an extra, secret heating process. Harsh irritants present in all raw tobaccos are expelled by "TOASTING." These irritants are sold to others. They are not present in your LUCKY STRIKE. No wonder LUCKIES are always kind to your throat.

"It's toasted"
Your Throat Protection—against irritation—against cough

The Granger Collection, New York.

SELLING BEAUTY AND HEALTH

This advertisement hints at the negative health effects of smoking, but touts "Luckies" as a healthful cigarette more appropriate for the delicate bodies of beautiful women.

influence the men you meet, consciously or unconsciously, you are not fulfilling your fundamental duty as a woman." A mouthwash ad warned about one unsuspecting gentleman's bad breath—"the truth that his friends had been too delicate to mention," while a tobacco ad matter-of-factly declared: "Men at the top are apt to be pipe-smokers. . . . It's no coincidence—pipe-smoking is a calm and deliberate habit—restful, stimulating. His pipe helps a man think straight. A pipe is back of most big ideas."

Advertising professionals believed they were helping people to manage their lives in ways that would increase their satisfaction and pleasure. American consumers responded enthusiastically. Their interest in fashion, their eagerness to fill their homes with the latest products, their alacrity to take up the craze of the moment (the mah-jongg card game, crossword puzzles, miniature golf)—all evidenced Americans' preoccupation with self-improvement and personal pleasure. The most enthusiastic of all were middle-class Americans, who could afford to buy what the advertisers were selling. Many of them were newcomers to middle-class ranks, searching for ways to affirm—or even create—their new identity. The aforementioned ad for pipe tobacco, for example, was targeted at the new middle-class man, imagined by advertisers to be someone holding a salaried position in a corporate office or bank, or working as a commission salesman, or owning a small business.

As male wage earners moved into the new middle class, their wives were freed from the necessity of outside work. Advertisers appealed to the new middle-class woman, too, as she refocused her attention toward dressing in the latest fashion, managing the household, and raising the children. Vacuum cleaners and other consumer

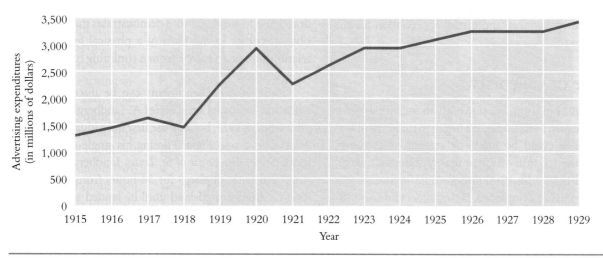

EXPENDITURES ON ADVERTISING, 1915–1929

Source: Data from *Historical Statistics of the United States, Colonial Times to 1970* (White Plains, N.Y.: Kraus International, 1989), p. 856.

The real purpose of these measures—collectively known as welfare capitalism—was to encourage employees to be loyal to their firm and to convince them—contrary to what labor union critics had been arguing—that industry did have the best interests of its employees at heart. Management had an understandable fear of union power, arising from the paralyzing strikes of 1919. As the decade proceeded and as prosperity rolled on, welfare capitalism reflected the confidence that capitalism had become more responsive to employee concerns and thus more humane.

Industrial Workers

Many industrial workers benefited from the nation's prosperity. Most of them enjoyed rising wages and a reasonably steady income. Skilled craftsmen in the older industries of construction, railroad transportation, and printing fared especially well. Their real wages rose by 30 to 50 percent over the decade. The several million workers employed in the large mass-production industries (such as automobile and electrical equipment manufacture) also did well. Their wages were relatively high, and they enjoyed good benefits—paid sick leave, paid vacations, life insurance, stock options, subsidized mortgages, and retirement pensions. Although all workers in companies with these programs were eligible for such benefits, skilled workers were in the best position to claim them.

Semiskilled and unskilled industrial workers had to contend with a labor surplus throughout the decade. As employers replaced workers with machines, the aggregate demand for industrial labor increased at a lower rate than it had in the preceding 20 years. Despite a weakening demand for labor, rural whites, rural blacks, and Mexicans continued their migration to the cities, stiffening the competition for factory jobs. Employers could hire and fire as they saw fit and could therefore keep wage increases lagging behind increases in productivity.

This softening demand for labor helps explain why many working-class families benefited little from the decade's prosperity or from its consumer revolution. An estimated 40 percent of workers remained mired in poverty, unable to afford a healthy diet or adequate housing, much less any of the more costly consumer goods. In 1930, for instance, only 25 to 40 percent of American households owned a washing machine, a vacuum cleaner, and a radio, and only 50 percent had a car.

The million or more workers who labored in the nation's two largest industries, coal and textiles, suffered the most during the 1920s. Throughout the decade, both industries experienced severe overcapacity. By 1926, only

half of the coal mined each year was being sold. Many New England textile cities experienced levels of unemployment that sometimes approached 50 percent. One reason was that many textile industrialists had shifted their operations to the South, where taxes and wages were lower. But the southern textile industry also suffered from excess capacity, exerting a downward pressure on prices and wages there as well. Plant managers pressured their workers to speed up production. Workers loathed the frequent "speed-ups" of machines and the "stretch-outs" in the number of spinning or weaving machines each worker was expected to tend. By the late 1920s, labor strife and calls for unionization were rising among disgruntled workers in both the South and the North.

Unionization of textiles and coal, and of more prosperous industries as well, would have brought workers a larger share of the decade's prosperity. Some labor leaders, such as Sidney Hillman of the Amalgamated Clothing Workers, argued that unionization would actually increase corporate profits by compelling employers to observe uniform wage and hour schedules that would restrain ruinous competition. Hillman pointed out—as Henry Ford had in the preceding decade—that rising wages would enable workers to purchase more consumer goods and thus increase corporate sales and revenues, but Hillman's views were ignored outside the garment industry.

Elsewhere, unions lost ground as business and government, backed by middle-class opinion, remained hos-

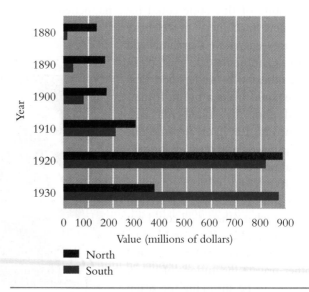

VALUE OF REGIONAL COTTON TEXTILE OUTPUT, 1880–1930

Source: Data from Nancy F. Kane, *Textiles in Transition: Technology, Wages, and Industry Relocation in the U.S. Textile Industry, 1880–1939* (New York: Greenwood Press, 1988), p. 29.

tile to labor organization. Employers attacked unions as un-American. A conservative Supreme Court whittled away at labor's legal protections. In 1921, it ruled that lower courts could issue injunctions against union members, prohibiting them from striking or picketing an employer. State courts also enforced what union members called "yellow dog" contracts, written pledges by which employees promised not to join a union while they were employed. Any employee who violated that pledge was subject to immediate dismissal.

These measures crippled efforts to organize trade unions. Membership fell from a high of 5 million in 1920 to less than 3 million in 1929, a mere 10 percent of the nation's industrial workforce. Other forces contributed to the decline, too. Many workers, especially those benefiting from welfare capitalist programs, decided they no longer needed trade unions. And the labor movement hurt itself by moving too slowly to open its ranks to semiskilled and unskilled factory workers.

Women and Work

Women workers experienced the same hardships as men in the industrial workforce and fewer of the benefits. They were largely excluded from the ranks of the skilled craftsmen and thus missed out on the substantial wage increases that the men in those positions enjoyed. Women also had trouble finding work in the automobile industry, the highest paying of the mass-production industries. They had better access to the electrical equipment and meat-

packing industries, although they were often segregated in departments given over to "women's work." Where women were allowed to compete for the same jobs as men, they usually earned less. Thus, a female trimmer in a meat-packing plant typically made 37 cents per hour, only two-thirds what a male trimmer earned. The textile industry had long been a major source of employment for women, but, in the 1920s, women and men alike in this ailing manufacturing sector suffered high rates of unemployment and declining wages.

White-collar work established itself, in the 1920s, as a magnet for women. This sector enjoyed rapid growth in a decade in which corporations expanded and refined their managerial and accounting practices. Discrimination prevented women from becoming managers, accountants, or supervisors, but they did dominate the lower level ranks of secretaries, typists, filing clerks, bank tellers, and department store clerks. By the 1930s, 2 million women, or 20 percent of the female workforce, labored in these and related occupations. Initially, these positions had a glamour that factory work lacked. Work environments were cleaner and brighter, and women had the opportunity—indeed were expected—to dress well and fashionably. But wages were low and managerial authority was absolute. Unions had virtually no presence in white-collar places of employment, and workers had difficulty finding alternative ways of protesting unfair managers or difficult working conditions.

Women with ambitious work aspirations had to pursue the "female" professions, such as teaching, nursing,

NEW OCCUPATIONS FOR WOMEN

By the 1920s, employers preferred women for the telephone operator jobs that were proliferating. The fancy dresses and high heels worn by the women in this photograph underscore the white-collar status of this job.

© Corbis.

social work, and librarianship. Opportunities in several of these fields, especially teaching and social work, were growing, and women responded by enrolling in college in large numbers. The number of female college students increased by 50 percent during the 1920s. Some of these college graduates used their new skills in new fields, such as writing for women's magazines. A few, drawing strength from their feminist forebears during the Progressive Era, managed to crack such male bastions of work as mainstream journalism and university research and teaching (see the Americans Abroad feature for chapter 25). In every field of endeavor, even such new and exotic ones as airplane flying, at least one woman arose to demonstrate that her sex had the necessary talent and drive to match or exceed what men had done. Thus in 1932, Amelia Earhart became the first woman to fly the Atlantic solo, matching Lindbergh's feat and inspiring women everywhere. Even so, Earhart's feat failed to substantially improve opportunities for women who wanted to work as pilots in the airline industry. In this industry, as in most lines of work, gender prejudices remained too entrenched. And the women who had broken the gender line remained, by and large, solitary figures.

The Women's Movement Adrift

Many supporters of the 19th Amendment to the Constitution, which, in 1920, gave women the right to vote, expected it to transform American politics. Women voters would reverse the decline in voter participation, cleanse politics of corruption, and launch a variety of reform initiatives that would improve the quality of life for women and men alike. This female-inspired transformation, however, failed to materialize. Voter participation rates did not increase nor did American politics become imbued with female-inspired virtue and honesty. The women's movement, instead, seemed to succumb to the same exhaustion and frustration as had the more general progressive movement from which it had emerged 20 years earlier. Younger women searching for independence and equality (such as the flappers discussed earlier in this chapter) often turned away from reform altogether, preferring a lifestyle that emphasized private achievement and personal freedom to a political career devoted to improving the collective status of America's women. Those who continued to agitate for reform found progress more difficult to achieve once the conservative Republican administrations of Harding and Coolidge came to power.

Despite the difficult political environment in which they had to work, some female reformers made significant strides in the 1920s. In 1921, one group succeeded in getting Congress to pass the Sheppard-Towner Act, a major social welfare program that provided federal funds for prenatal and child health care centers throughout the United States. It remained in effect until 1929. In 1923, Alice Paul, still head of the National Women's Party (NWP, see chapter 20), and her allies prevailed on Congress to consider an Equal Rights Amendment (ERA) to the Constitution, phrased as follows: "Men and women shall have equal rights throughout the United States and every place subject to its jurisdiction." And the National American Woman Suffrage Association, the major force behind the struggle for suffrage, transformed itself in 1920 into the League of Women Voters (LWV). During the next decade, the LWV launched numerous initiatives to encourage women to run for elective office, to educate voters about the issues before them, and to improve the condition of those Americans—the poor, female and child laborers, the mentally ill—who needed assistance.

Sometimes the women's movement was stymied not just by external opposition but also by internal division—as it was over the ERA. The NWP and other supporters of the ERA insisted that there could be no compromise with the proposition that women were the equals of men in every respect. But, the LWV countered, child-rearing and mothering duties did render women different from men in key respects and thus, in some instances, in need of special treatment by Congress and other lawmaking bodies.

The question of women's difference crystallized around the issue of protective labor legislation for women. Over the years, a series of state and federal laws had given women protections at the workplace—limitations on the hours of labor, prohibitions on overnight work, and other such measures—that men did not have. Many women reformers supported these measures, believing they were vital to protecting the masses of women workers from the worst forms of exploitation and thus enabling them to have enough time and energy to perform their vital roles as mothers and wives. Fearing that a successful ERA would render this protective legislation unconstitutional, the LWV and its allies opposed the ERA. But Alice Paul and her allies argued that female protective laws did not really benefit women. Instead, employers used these laws as an excuse to segregate women in stereotyped jobs that were mostly low status and low paying and thus to deny women the opportunities for advancement and fulfillment open to men.

This issue of whether women should be treated like men in all respects or offered some protections that no men enjoyed was a genuinely complicated one, and women activists would continue to argue about it with each other for decades. In the 1920s, however, their inability to speak with a single voice on this matter weakened their cause in the eyes of their adversaries.

☛ The Politics of Business

Republican presidents governed the country from 1921 to 1933. In some respects, their administrations resembled those of the Gilded Age, a time of mediocre presidents, rampant corruption, and government bent on removing obstacles to capitalist development. In other respects, however, the state-building tradition of Theodore Roosevelt lived on, although in somewhat altered form.

Harding and the Politics of Personal Gain

Warren Gamaliel Harding defeated Democrat James M. Cox for the presidency in 1920. From modest origins as a newspaper editor in the small town of Marion, Ohio, Harding had risen to the U.S. Senate chiefly because the powerful Ohio Republican machine knew it could count on him to do its bidding. He gained the presidency for the same reason. The Republican Party bosses believed that almost anyone they nominated in 1920 could defeat the Democratic opponent. They chose Harding because they could control him. Harding's good looks and geniality made him a favorite with voters, and he swept into office with 61 percent of the popular vote, the greatest landslide since 1820.

To his credit, Harding released the aging Socialist Party leader Eugene V. Debs from jail and took other measures to cool the passions unleashed by the Red Scare. Aware of his own intellectual limitations, Harding included talented men in his cabinet. His choices of Herbert Hoover as secretary of commerce, Charles Evans Hughes as secretary of state, and Andrew Mellon as secretary of the treasury were particularly impressive appointments. Still, Harding lacked the will to alter his ingrained political habits. He had built his political career on a willingness to please the lobbyists who came to his Senate office asking for favors and deals. He had long followed Ohio boss Harry M. Daugherty's advice and would continue to do so with Daugherty as his attorney general. Harding apparently did not consider men such as Daugherty self-serving or corrupt. They were his friends; they had been with him since the beginning of his political career. He made sure the "boys" had jobs in his administration, and he continued to socialize with them. Many a night he could be found drinking (despite Prohibition), gambling, and womanizing with the "Ohio Gang" at its K Street hangout. Sometimes the gang even convened in the White House. Alice Roosevelt Longworth, Theodore Roosevelt's daughter, once came into the White House study and found the air "heavy with tobacco smoke," its tables cluttered with "bottles containing every imaginable brand of whiskey, . . . [and] cards and poker chips at hand."

The K Street house was more than a place to carouse. It was a place of business where the Ohio Gang became rich selling government appointments, judicial pardons, and police protection to bootleggers. By 1923, the corruption could no longer be concealed. Journalists and senators began to focus public attention on the actions of Secretary of the Interior Albert Fall, who had persuaded Harding to transfer control of large government oil reserves at Teapot Dome, Wyoming, and Elk Hills, California, from the navy to the Department of the Interior. Fall had immediately leased the deposits to two oil tycoons, Harry F. Sinclair and Edward L. Doheny, who pumped oil from the wells in exchange for providing the navy with a system of fuel tank reserves. Fall had issued the leases secretly, without allowing other oil corporations to compete for them, and he had accepted almost $400,000 from Sinclair and Doheny.

Fall would pay for this shady deal with a year in jail. He was not the only Harding appointee to do so. Charles R. Forbes, head of the Veterans' Bureau, would go to Leavenworth Prison for swindling the government out of $200 million in hospital supplies. The exposure of Forbes's theft prompted his lawyer, Charles Cramer, to commit suicide; Jesse Smith, Attorney General Daugherty's close friend and housemate, also killed himself, apparently to avoid being indicted and brought to trial. Daugherty managed to escape conviction and incarceration for bribery by burning incriminating documents held by his brother's Ohio bank. Still, Daugherty left government service in disgrace.

WARREN G. HARDING, CAMPING PARTNER
This photo shows President Harding (on the right) participating in the kind of informal male gathering he so enjoyed. His "buddies" on this camping trip were Henry Ford (left) and Thomas Edison (center).

Brown Brothers.

Harding initially kept himself blind to the widespread use of public office for private gain that characterized his administration but grew depressed when he finally realized what had been going on. In summer 1923, in poor spirits, he left Washington for a West Coast tour. He fell ill in Seattle and died from a heart attack in San Francisco. The train returning his body to Washington attracted crowds of grief-stricken mourners who little suspected the web of corruption and bribery in which Harding had been caught. Even as the revelations poured forth in 1924 and 1925, few Americans seemed bothered. Some of this insouciance reflected the carefree atmosphere of the 1920s, but much of it had to do with the character of the man who succeeded Harding.

Coolidge and Laissez-Faire Politics

Calvin Coolidge rarely smiled. At the many dinners he attended as vice president, he said hardly a word. Silence was his public creed, much to the chagrin of Washington's socialites. He was never enticed into carousing with the "boys," nor did he ever stand by as liquor was being served. He believed that the best government was the government that governed least, and that the welfare of the country hinged not on politicians but on the people—their willingness to work hard, to be honest, and to live within their means.

Born in Vermont and raised in Massachusetts, Calvin Coolidge gained national visibility in September 1919, when as governor of Massachusetts he took a firm stand against Boston's striking policemen (see chapter 23). His reputation as a man who battled labor radicals earned him a place on the 1920 national Republican ticket. His image as an ordinary man helped convince voters in 1920 that the Republican Party would return the country to its commonsensical ways after eight years of reckless reforms. Coolidge won his party's presidential nomination handily in 1924 and easily defeated his Democratic opponent, John W. Davis. Coolidge's popularity remained strong throughout his first full term, and he probably would have been renominated and reelected in 1928, but he chose not to run.

Coolidge took greatest pride in those measures that reduced the government's control over the economy. The Revenue Act of 1926 slashed the high income and estate taxes that progressives had pushed through Congress during the First World War. Coolidge curtailed the power of the Federal Trade Commission to regulate business affairs and endorsed Supreme Court decisions invalidating Progressive Era laws that had strengthened organized labor and protected children and women from employer exploitation.

Brown Brothers.

A STERN YANKEE

In sharp contrast to Harding, President Calvin Coolidge did not enjoy informality, banter, or carousing. Here he fishes alone and in formal attire.

Hoover and the Politics of Associationalism

Republicans in the 1920s did more than simply lift government restraints and regulations from the economy. Some, led by Secretary of Commerce Herbert Hoover, conceived of government as a dynamic, even progressive, economic force. Hoover did not want government to control industry, but he did want government to persuade private corporations to abandon their wasteful, selfish ways and turn to cooperation and public service. Hoover envisioned an economy built on the principle of association. Industrialists, wholesalers, retailers, operators of railroad and shipping lines, small businessmen, farmers, workers, doctors—each of these groups would form a trade association whose members would share economic information, discuss problems of production and distribution, and seek ways of achieving greater efficiency and profit. Hoover believed that the very act of associating in this way—an approach that historian Ellis Hawley has called "associationalism"—would convince participants of the

superiority of cooperation over competition, of negotiation over conflict, of public service over selfishness.

A graduate of Stanford University, Hoover had worked first as a mining engineer and then as an executive in multinational mining corporations. During the war, he had directed the government's Food Administration (see chapter 23, especially the Americans Abroad feature on p. 709). From that experience, he had come to appreciate the role that government could play in coordinating the activities of thousands of producers and distributors scattered across the country.

Hoover's ambition as secretary of commerce was to make the department the grand orchestrator of economic cooperation. During his eight years in that post, from 1921 to 1929, he organized more than 250 conferences and brought together government officials, representatives of business, policy makers, and others who had a stake in strengthening the economy.

Hoover achieved some notable successes. He persuaded farmers to join together in marketing cooperatives, steel executives to abandon the 12-hour day for their employees, and some groups of bankers in the South to organize their institutions into regional associations with adequate resources and expertise. Hoover's dynamic conception of government did not endear him to Coolidge, who declared in 1927: "That man has offered me unsolicited advice for six years, all of it bad."

The Politics of Business Abroad

Republican domestic policy disagreements over whether to pursue laissez-faire or associationalism spilled over into foreign policy as well. Hoover had accepted the post of secretary of commerce thinking he would represent the United States in negotiations with foreign companies and governments. In fact, he intended to apply associationalism to international relations. He wanted the world's leading nations to meet regularly in conferences, to limit military buildups, and to foster an international environment in which capitalism could flourish. Aware that the United States must help create such an environment, Hoover hoped to persuade American bankers to adopt investment and loan policies that would aid European recovery. If they refused to do so, he was prepared to urge the government to take an activist, supervisory role in foreign investment.

In 1921 and 1922, Hoover helped to design the Washington Conference on the Limitation of Armaments. Although he did not serve as a negotiator at the conference—Secretary of State Charles Evans Hughes reserved that role for himself and his subordinates—Hoover did supply Hughes's team with a wealth of economic information. And he helped Hughes to use that information to design forceful, detailed proposals for disarmament. Those proposals gave U.S. negotiators a decided advantage

HERBERT HOOVER, SECRETARY OF COMMERCE

Hoover used his cabinet position to encourage innovation in American industry. In 1927, he participated in the nation's first television broadcast. Men in an ATT broadcast studio in New York speak and listen to Hoover and his associates in Washington.

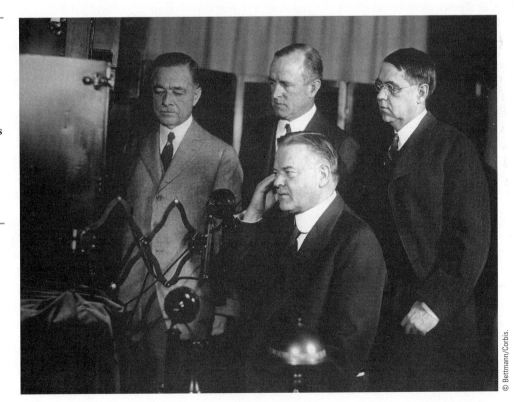

over their European and Asian counterparts and helped them win a stunning accord, the Five-Power Treaty, by which the United States, Britain, Japan, France, and Italy agreed to scrap more than 2 million tons of warships. Hughes also obtained pledges from all of the signatories that they would respect the "Open Door" in China, long a U.S. foreign policy objective (see chapter 22).

These triumphs redounded to Hughes's credit but not to Hoover's, and Hughes used it to consolidate his control over foreign policy. He rebuffed Hoover's efforts to put international economic affairs under the direction of the Commerce Department and rejected Hoover's suggestion to intervene in the international activities of U.S. banks.

Hughes was not entirely laissez faire in approach, as he demonstrated in his 1923 reaction to a crisis in Franco-German relations. The victorious Allies had imposed on Germany an obligation to pay $33 billion in war reparations (see chapter 23). In 1923, when the impoverished German government suspended its payments, France sent troops to occupy the Ruhr valley, whose industry was vital to the German economy. German workers retaliated by going on strike, and the crisis threatened to undermine Europe's precarious economic recovery. Hughes did not stand on the sidelines. He intensified American financial pressure on the French and compelled them to attend a U.S.-sponsored conference in 1924 to restructure Germany's debt obligation.

The conference produced the Dawes Plan (after the Chicago banker and chief negotiator, Charles G. Dawes), which reduced German reparations from $542 million to $250 million annually and called on U.S. and foreign banks to stimulate the German economy with a quick infusion of $200 million in loans. Within a matter of days, banker J. P. Morgan, Jr., raised more than $1 billion from American investors. Money poured into German financial markets, and the German economy appeared to stabilize.

The Dawes Plan won applause on both sides of the Atlantic, but soon the U.S. money flooding into Germany created its own problems. American investors were so eager to lend to Germany that their investments became speculative and unsound. At this point, a stronger U.S. government effort to direct loans to sound investments, a strategy that Hoover supported, might have helped. But neither Hughes nor his successor as secretary of state, Frank Kellogg, was interested in such initiatives, and neither was Secretary of the Treasury Mellon. The laissez-faire approach had reasserted itself, and Hoover's plan to involve the U.S. government directly in international economic matters had been rebuffed.

The Republicans' continued pursuit of disarmament and world peace seemed to diverge from their general re-

luctance to involve the U.S. government in foreign affairs. To follow up the success of the 1922 Five-Power treaty, Secretary of State Kellogg drew up a treaty with Aristide Briand, the French foreign minister, outlawing war as a tool of national policy. In 1928, representatives of the United States, France, and 13 other nations met in Paris to sign the Kellogg-Briand pact, an agreement that soon attracted the support of 48 other nations. Coolidge viewed Kellogg-Briand, however, not as a way of extending U.S. government power abroad but as a way of reducing further the size of the U.S. government at home. With the threat of war removed, the United States could scale back its military forces and eliminate much of the bureaucracy needed to support a large standing army and navy. Unfortunately, the pact contained no enforcement mechanism, thus rendering itself ineffective as a foreign policy tool.

The Republican administrations flexed U.S. power more effectively in Latin American affairs. U.S. investments in the region more than doubled from 1917 to 1929, and the U.S. government continued its policy of intervening in the internal affairs of Latin America to protect U.S. interests. Republican administrations did attempt initially to curtail American military involvement in the Caribbean. The Coolidge administration pulled American troops out of the Dominican Republic in 1924 and Nicaragua in 1925. In the case of Nicaragua, however, U.S. Marines returned in 1926 to end a war between liberal and conservative Nicaraguans and to protect American property; this time they stayed until 1934. U.S. troops, meanwhile, occupied Haiti continuously between 1919 and 1934, keeping in power governments friendly to U.S. interests. Opposition to such heavy-handed tactics continued to build in the United States, but they would not yield a significant change in U.S. policy until the 1930s (see chapter 25).

Farmers, Small-Town Protestants, and Moral Traditionalists

Although many Americans benefited from the prosperity of the 1920s, others did not. Overproduction was impoverishing substantial numbers of farmers. Beyond these economic hardships, many moral-traditionalist white Protestants, especially those in rural areas and small towns, believed that the country was being overrun by racially inferior and morally suspect foreigners.

Agricultural Depression

The 1920s brought hard times to the nation's farmers after the boom period of the war years. During the war, domes-

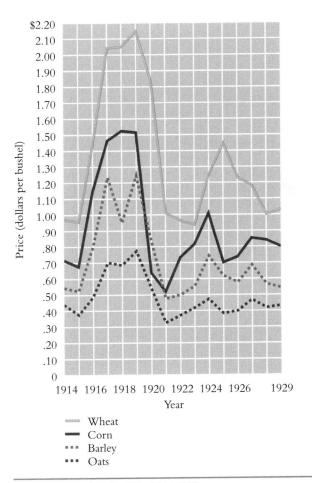

PRICE OF MAJOR CROPS, 1914–1929

Source: Data from *Historical Statistics of the United States, Colonial Times to 1970* (White Plains, N.Y.: Kraus International, 1989), pp. 511–12.

tic demand for farm products had risen steadily and foreign demand had exploded as the war disrupted agricultural production in France, Ukraine, and other European food-producing regions. Soon after the war, however, Europe's farmers quickly resumed their customary levels of production. Foreign demand for American foodstuffs fell precipitously, leaving U.S. farmers with an oversupply and depressed prices.

A rise in agricultural productivity made possible by the tractor also worsened the plight of many farmers. The number of tractors in use almost quadrupled in the 1920s, and 35 million new acres came under cultivation. Produce flooded the market. Prices fell even further, as did farm incomes. By 1929, the annual per capita income of rural Americans was only $223, one-quarter that of the nonfarm population. Hundreds of thousands had to sell their farms and either scrape together a living as tenants or abandon farming altogether. Many chose to abandon farm life, packed their belongings into jalopies or loaded them onto trains, and headed for the city.

Those who stayed on the land grew increasingly assertive in their demands. Early in the decade, radical farmers working through such organizations as the Nonpartisan League of North Dakota and farmer-labor parties in Minnesota, Wisconsin, and other midwestern states led the movement. By the second half of the decade, however, leadership had passed from farming radicals to farming moderates, and from small farmers in danger of dispossession to larger farmers and agribusinesses seeking to extend their holdings. By lobbying through such organizations as the Farm Bureau Federation, the more powerful agricultural interests brought pressure on Congress to set up economic controls that would protect them from failure. Their proposals, embodied in the McNary-Haugen Bill, called on the government to erect high tariffs on foreign produce and to purchase surplus U.S. crops. The government would then sell the surplus crops on the world market for whatever prices they fetched. Any money lost in international sales would be absorbed by the government rather than by the farmers. The McNary-Haugen Bill passed Congress in 1927 and in 1928, only to be vetoed by President Coolidge both times.

Cultural Dislocation

Added to the economic plight of the farmers was a sense of cultural dislocation among the majority who were white, Protestant, and of northwest European descent. These farmers had long perceived themselves as the backbone of the nation—hardworking, honest, God-fearing yeomen, guardians of independence and liberty.

The 1920 census challenged the validity of that view. For the first time, a slight majority of Americans now lived in urban areas. That finding in itself signified little because the census classified as "urban" those towns with a population as small as 2,500. But the census figures did reinforce the widespread perception that both the economic and cultural vitality of the nation had shifted from the countryside to the metropolis. Industry, the chief engine of prosperity, was an urban phenomenon. Commercialized leisure—the world of amusement parks, department stores, professional sports, movies, cabarets, and theaters—was to be enjoyed in cities; so too were flashy fashions and open sexuality. Catholics, Jews, and African Americans, who together outnumbered white Protestants in many cities, seemed to be the principal creators of this new world. They were also thought to be the purveyors of Bolshevism and other modes of radicalism. Cities, finally, were the home of secular intellectuals who had scrapped their belief in Scripture and in God and had embraced science as their new, unimpeachable authority.

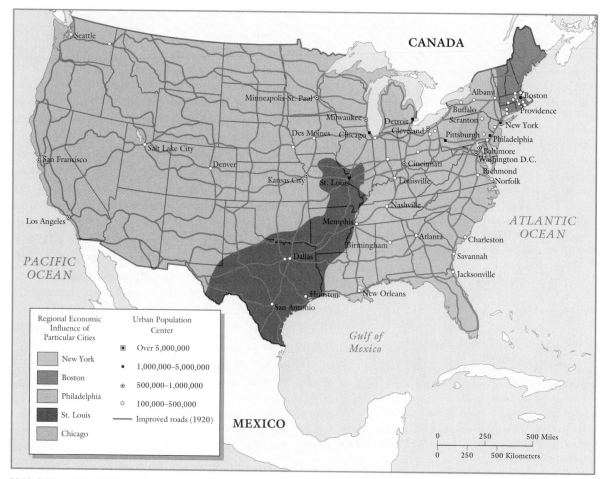

MAP 24.2 URBANIZATION, 1920

By 1920, New York City had surpassed 5 million people, and Boston, Philadelphia, Pittsburgh, Detroit, Chicago, and St. Louis had surpassed 1 million. Another 10 cities, from Los Angeles, California, to Buffalo, New York, had surpassed 500,000. This map, through its color coding, also shows the regions in which the country's five largest cities exercised economic influence.

All through the Progressive Era, rural white Americans had believed that the cities could be redeemed, that city dwellers could be reformed, that the Protestant values of rural America would triumph. War had crushed that confidence and had replaced it with the fear that urban culture and urban people would undermine all that "true" Americans held dear.

These fears grew even more intense with the changes brought by prosperity. Urban-industrial America increased in power and affluence and spread its consumer culture and its commodities to the countryside as never before. Even small towns now sported movie theaters and automobile dealerships. Radio waves carried news of city life into isolated farmhouses. The growth in the circulation of national magazines also broke down the wall separating country from city. Mail-order catalogs—Sears, Roebuck, and Company and others—invited farmers to fantasize that they too could fill their homes with refrigerators, RCA Victrolas, and Hoover vacuum cleaners.

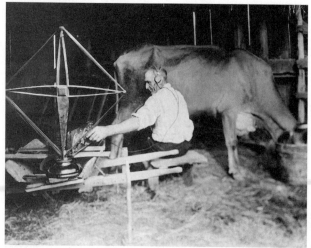

Brown Brothers.

CONSUMER CULTURE PENETRATES THE COUNTRYSIDE

By the 1920s, cars, Coca-Cola, radios, and other commodities had found their way to the country's smallest towns. Here a farmer tunes his radio as he milks his cow.

Rural white Americans showed ambivalence toward this cultural invasion. On the one hand, most country dwellers were eager to participate in the consumer marketplace. On the other hand, many worried that doing so would expose the countryside to atheism, immorality, and radicalism. They expressed their determination to protect their imperiled way of life in their support for Prohibition, the Ku Klux Klan, immigration restriction, and religious fundamentalism.

Prohibition

The 18th Amendment to the Constitution, which prohibited the manufacture and sale of alcohol, went into effect in January 1920. Initially it drew support from a large and varied constituency that included farmers, middle-class city dwellers, feminists, and progressive reformers who loathed the powerful "liquor trust" and who saw firsthand the deleterious effects of drink on the urban poor. It soon

---

M U S I C A L   L I N K   T O   T H E   P A S T

Women Singers and the Birth of Modern Country Music

Composer: A. P. Carter (credited as writer but probably was not)

Title: "Single Girl, Married Girl" (1927)

Performers: The Carter Family

Plaintive and never preachy, "Single Girl, Married Girl" explores women's roles and marriage in ways rarely seen in the country music of the 1920s. As she did throughout her career, Sara Carter, a country music pioneer, sang simply and passionately about the lives of common people, in this case women: "Single girl, single girl, she goes to the store and buys . . . Married girl, married girl, she rocks the cradle and cries . . . Single girl, single girl, she's going where she please . . . Married girl, married girl, baby on her knees." Is Sara sad or angry about the plight of this "married girl" tied down by her baby, or is she just plainly stating how women's lives change when children arrive? In either case, Sara Carter, in this song, offers us a glimpse of how country women of the 1920s, often thought to be conservative in outlook, were themselves struggling to balance traditional female responsibilities (in this case, motherhood) with the freedoms that modern society seemed to be offering young women.

The national commercialization of country and blues music in the 1920s opened up new, but still limited, roles for women in the mass media. The Carter Family was by far the most successful of the initial female country groups, producing hit recordings that sold throughout the United States, England, and South Africa, among other places. The group consisted of Sara, who played autoharp and contributed lead vocals; her sister-in-law Maybelle on guitar; and her husband A. P., who occasionally sang with them, but whose most important job was traveling in search of material for the group, which he often took unwarranted credit for, a common practice at the time. Victor Records's talent scout Ralph Peer discovered them at an open talent audition held in Bristol, Tennessee, on August 2, 1927. This recording, made at those sessions, provides us with a historic glimpse of the birth of modern country music.

The Carter women were relegated to the background in publicity concerning the group. Posters promised a "morally good" program in which a man (A. P.) appeared onstage, an important announcement because women performing popular music independently were viewed as morally suspect. Also, despite general agreement that Sara had a major hand in writing and arranging Carter Family material, her name rarely surfaced in the credits, where A.P.'s name typically dominated. Despite such caveats, the Carter Family represented an important example of the trend of women claiming new kinds of identities and expression in the modern mass media. Sara seemed to be an innovator in her personal life as well—her relatives described her as "very liberated" for a Southern woman in the 1920s and 1930s, wearing slacks, shooting big game, writing and arranging music, openly smoking, and divorcing A.P. in 1938.

---

1. Why do you think women performing music independently were frowned on and viewed by many as morally suspect during this period?

Listen to an audio recording of this music on the Musical Links to the Past CD.

became apparent, however, that Prohibition was doing as much to encourage law-breaking as abstinence. With only 1,500 federal agents to enforce the law, the government could not possibly police the drinking habits of 110 million people. With little fear of punishment, those who wanted to drink did so, either brewing liquor at home or buying it from speakeasies and bootleggers. Because the law prevented legitimate businesses from manufacturing liquor, organized crime added alcohol to its portfolio. Mobsters procured much of their liquor from Canadian manufacturers, smuggled it across the border, protected it in warehouses, and distributed it to speakeasies. Al Capone's Chicago-based mob alone employed 1,000 men to protect its liquor trafficking, which was so lucrative that Capone became the richest (and most feared) gangster in America. Blood flowed in the streets of Chicago and other northern cities as rival mobs fought one another to enlarge their share of the market.

These unexpected consequences caused many early advocates of Prohibition, especially in the cities, to withdraw their support. Not so for Prohibition's rural, white Protestant supporters, however. The violence spawned by liquor trafficking confirmed their view of alcohol as evil. The high-profile participation of Italian, Irish, and Jewish

gangsters in the bootleg trade reinforced their belief that Catholics and Jews were threats to law and morality. Many rural white Protestants became more, not less, determined to rid the country of liquor once and for all; some among them resolved to rid the country of Jews and Catholics as well.

The Ku Klux Klan

The original Ku Klux Klan, formed in the South in the late 1860s, had died out with the defeat of Reconstruction and the reestablishment of white supremacy (see chapter 17). The new Klan was created in 1915 by William Simmons, a white southerner who had been inspired by D. W. Griffith's racist film, *Birth of a Nation,* in which the early Klan was depicted as having saved the nation from predatory blacks. By the 1920s, control of the Klan had passed from Simmons to a Texas dentist, Hiram Evans, and its ideological focus had expanded from a loathing of blacks to a hatred of Jews and Catholics as well. Evans's Klan propagated a nativist message that the country should contain— or better yet, eliminate—the influence of Jews and Catholics and restore "Anglo-Saxon" racial purity, Protestant supremacy, and traditional morality to national life. This message swelled Klan ranks and expanded its visibility and influence in the North and South alike. By 1924, as many as 4 million Americans are thought to have belonged to the Klan, including the half-million members of its female auxiliary, Women of the Ku Klux Klan. Not only was the Klan strong in states of the Old Confederacy such as Louisiana and Texas and in border states such as Oklahoma and Kansas, but it thrived, too, in such northern states as Indiana, Pennsylvania, Washington, and Oregon. It even drew significant membership from the cities of those states. Indiana, for example, was home to 500,000 Klansmen and women, many of them in the Indianapolis area. In 1924, Indiana voters elected a Klansman to the governorship and sent several other Klan members to the statehouse.

In some respects, the Klan resembled other fraternal organizations. It offered its members friendship networks, social services, and conviviality. Its rituals, regalia, and mock-medieval language (the Imperial Wizard, Exalted Cyclops, Grand Dragons, and such) gave initiates a sense of superiority, valor, and mystery similar to what other fraternal societies, from the Masons to the Knights of Columbus, imparted to their members.

But the Klan also thrived on hate. It spread lurid tales of financial extortion by Jewish bankers and sexual exploitation by Catholic priests. The accusations were sometimes general, as in the claim that an international con-

AL CAPONE, CHICAGO MOB LEADER

Capone, in the first row on the right, sits with his son, Sonny, and chats with Chicago Cubs player Gabby Hartnett at a charity baseball event in 1931. Capone's presence at this charity event was part of his campaign to build a favorable public reputation for himself. He never strayed far from his gangsters, however, several of whom are seated behind him in the second row.

From the Collections of the Library of Congress.

WOMEN OF THE KU KLUX KLAN

Women made up a substantial portion of the Klan's membership in the 1920s. Here a group marches in an "America First" parade in Binghamton, New York.

© Bettmann/Corbis.

spiracy of Jewish bankers had caused the agricultural depression, or allegations that the pope had sent agents to the United States with instructions to destroy liberty and democracy. More common, and more incendiary, however, were the seemingly plausible, yet totally manufactured, tales of Jewish or Catholic depravity. Stories circulated of Jewish businessmen who had opened amusement parks and dance halls to which they lured innocent adolescents, tempting them with sexual transgression and profiting handsomely from their moral debasement. Likewise, Catholic priests and nuns were said to prey on Protestant girls and boys who had been forced into convents and Catholic orphanages. These outrageous stories sometimes provoked attacks on individual Jews and Catholics. More commonly, they prompted campaigns to boycott Jewish businesses and Catholic institutions, and to ruin reputations.

The emphasis on sexual exploitation in these stories reveals the anxiety Klan members felt about society's growing acceptance of sexual openness and sexual gratification. Many Klan supporters lived in towns suffused with these modern attitudes. That such attitudes might reflect the yearnings of Protestant children rather than the manipulation of deceitful Jews and Catholics was a truth some Protestant parents found difficult to accept.

Immigration Restriction

Although most white Protestants never joined the Klan, many of them did respond to the Klan's nativist argument that the country and its values would best be served by limiting the entry of outsiders. That was the purpose of the Johnson-Reed Immigration Restriction Act of 1924.

By the early 1920s, most Americans believed that the country could no longer accommodate the million immigrants who had been arriving each year before the war and the more than 800,000 who arrived in 1921. Industrialists no longer needed unskilled European laborers to operate their factories, their places having been taken either by machines or by African American and Mexican workers. Most labor movement leaders were convinced that the influx of workers unfamiliar with English and with trade unions had weakened labor solidarity. Progressive reformers no longer believed that immigrants could be easily Americanized or that harmony between the native-born and the foreign-born could be readily achieved. Congress responded to constituents' concerns by passing an immigration restriction act in 1921. In 1924, the more comprehensive Johnson-Reed Act imposed a yearly quota of 165,000 immigrants from countries outside the Western Hemisphere, effectively reducing total immigration to only 20 percent of the prewar annual average.

The sponsors of the 1924 act believed that certain groups—British, Germans, and Scandinavians, in particular—were racially superior and that, consequently, these groups should be allowed to enter the United States in greater numbers; however, because the Constitution prohibited the enactment of explicitly racist laws, Congress had to achieve this racist aim through subterfuge. Lawmakers established a formula to determine the annual immigrant quota for each foreign country, which was to be

ANNUAL IMMIGRANT QUOTAS UNDER THE JOHNSON-REED ACT, 1925–1927

Northwest Europe and Scandinavia		Eastern and Southern Europe		Other Countries	
Country	Quota	Country	Quota	Country	Quota
Germany	51,227	Poland	5,982	Africa (other than Egypt)	1,100
Great Britain and Northern Ireland	34,007	Italy	3,845	Armenia	124
Irish Free State (Ireland)	28,567	Czechoslovakia	3,073	Australia	121
Sweden	9,561	Russia	2,248	Palestine	100
Norway	6,453	Yugoslavia	671	Syria	100
France	3,954	Romania	603	Turkey	100
Denmark	2,789	Portugal	503	New Zealand and Pacific Islands	100
Switzerland	2,081	Hungary	473	All others	1,900
Netherlands	1,648	Lithuania	344		
Austria	785	Latvia	142		
Belgium	512	Spain	131		
Finland	471	Estonia	124		
Free City of Danzig	228	Albania	100		
Iceland	100	Bulgaria	100		
Luxembourg	100	Greece	100		
Total (number)	142,483	Total (number)	18,439	Total (number)	3,745
Total (%)	86.5%	Total (%)	11.2%	Total (%)	2.3%

Note: Total annual immigrant quota was 164,667

Source: From *Statistical Abstract of the United States* (Washington, D.C.: Government Printing Office, 1929), p. 100.

computed at 2 percent of the total number of immigrants from that country already resident in the United States in the year 1890. In 1890, immigrant ranks had been dominated by the British, Germans, and Scandinavians, so the new quotas would thus allow for a relatively larger cohort of immigrants from those countries. Immigrant groups that were poorly represented in the 1890 population—Italians, Greeks, Poles, Slavs, and Eastern European Jews—were effectively locked out. The Johnson-Reed Act also reaffirmed the long-standing policy of excluding Chinese immigrants, and it added Japanese and other groups of East and South Asians to the list of groups that were altogether barred from entry. The act did not officially limit immigration from nations in the Western Hemisphere, chiefly because agribusiness interests in Texas and California had convinced Congress that cheap Mexican labor was indispensable to their industry's prosperity. Still, the establishment of a Border Patrol along the U.S.–Mexican border and the imposition of a $10 head tax on all prospective Mexican immigrants made entry into the United States more difficult than it had been.

The Johnson-Reed Act accomplished Congress's underlying goal. Annual immigration from transoceanic nations fell by 80 percent. The large number of available slots for English and German immigrants regularly went unfilled, while the smaller number of available slots for Italians, Poles, Russian Jews, and others prevented hundreds of thou-

sands of them from entering the country. A "national origins" system put in place in 1927 further reduced the total annual quota to 150,000 and reserved more than 120,000 of these slots for immigrants from northwestern Europe. Except for minor modifications in 1952, the Johnson-Reed Act would dictate U.S. immigration policy until 1965.

Remarkably few Americans, outside of the ethnic groups being discriminated against, objected to these laws at the time they were passed—an indication of how broadly acceptable racism and nativism had become. In fact, racism and religious bigotry enjoyed a resurgence during the Jazz Age. The pseudoscience of eugenics, based on the idea that nations could improve the racial quality of their population by expanding its stronger racial strains and shrinking its weaker ones, found supporters not only in Congress but among prestigious scientists as well. Universities such as Harvard and Columbia set quotas similar to those of the Johnson-Reed Act to reduce the proportion of Jews among their undergraduates.

Fundamentalism versus Liberal Protestantism

Of all the movements protesting against the modern elements of urban life in the 1920s, Protestant fundamentalism was perhaps the most enduring. Fundamentalists

regarded the Bible as God's word and thus the source of all "fundamental" truth. They believed that every event depicted in the Bible, from the creation of the world in six days to the resurrection of Christ, happened exactly as the Bible described it. For fundamentalists, God was a deity who intervened directly in the lives of individuals and communities and who made known both his pleasure and his wrath to those who acknowledged his divinity. Sin had to be actively purged, and salvation actively sought.

The rise of the fundamentalist movement from the 1870s through the 1920s roughly paralleled the rise of urban-industrial society. Fundamentalists recoiled from the "evils" of the city—from what they perceived as its poverty, its moral degeneracy, its irreligion, and its crass materialism. Fundamentalism took shape in reaction against two additional aspects of urban society: the growth of liberal Protestantism and the revelations of science.

Liberal Protestants believed that religion had to be adapted to the skeptical and scientific temper of the modern age. No biblical story in which a sea opens up, the sun stands still, or a woman springs forth from a man's rib could possibly be true. The Bible was to be mined for its ethical values rather than for its literal truth. Liberal Protestants removed God from his active role in history and refashioned him into a distant and benign deity who watched over the world but did not intervene to punish or to redeem. They turned religion away from the quest for salvation and toward the pursuit of good deeds, social conscience, and love for one's neighbor. Although those with a liberal bent constituted only a minority of Protestants, they were articulate, visible, and influential in social reform movements. Fundamentalism arose in part to counter the "heretical" claims of the liberal Protestants.

Liberal Protestants and fundamentalists both understood that science was the source of most challenges to Christianity. Scientists believed that rational inquiry was a better guide to the past and to the future than prayer and revelation. Scientists even challenged the ideas that God had created the world and had fashioned humankind in his own image. These were assertions that many religious peoples, particularly fundamentalists, simply could not accept. Conflict was inevitable. It came in 1925, in Dayton, Tennessee.

The Scopes Trial

No aspect of science aroused more anger among fundamentalists than Charles Darwin's theory of evolution. There was no greater blasphemy than to suggest that man emerged from lower forms of life instead of being created by God. In Tennessee in 1925, fundamentalists succeeded in passing a law that forbade teaching "any theory that denies the story of the divine creation of man as taught in the Bible."

For Americans who accepted the authority of science, denying the truth of evolution was as ludicrous as insisting that the sun revolved around the earth. They ridiculed the fundamentalists, but they worried that the passage of the Tennessee law might signal the onset of a campaign to undermine First Amendment guarantees of free speech. The American Civil Liberties Union (ACLU), founded by liberals during the Red Scare of 1919 and 1920, began searching for a teacher who would be willing to challenge the constitutionality of the Tennessee law. They found their man in John T. Scopes, a 24-year-old biology teacher in Dayton, Tennessee. After confessing that he had taught evolution to his students, Scopes was arrested. The case quickly attracted national attention. William Jennings Bryan, the former Populist, progressive, and secretary of state, announced that he would help prosecute Scopes, and the famous liberal trial lawyer Clarence Darrow rushed to Dayton to lead Scopes's defense. That Bryan and Darrow had once been allies in the progressive movement only heightened the drama. A small army of journalists descended on Dayton, led by H. L. Mencken, a Baltimore-based journalist famous for his

Brown Brothers.

THE SCOPES TRIAL

Defense attorney Clarence Darrow (left) and prosecutor William Jennings Bryan take a break from their celebrated courtroom fight to enjoy each other's company. The two men had been allies in the Progressive era.

making big business subject to government control. The government could use its power to democratize corporations and to regulate the communications industry to ensure that every citizen had access to the facts needed to make reasonable, informed political decisions.

Dewey's views attracted the support of a wide range of liberal intellectuals and reformers, including Robert and Helen Lynd; Rexford Tugwell, professor of economics at Columbia; and Felix Frankfurter, a rising star at Harvard's law school. Some of these activists had ties to labor leaders and to New York Governor Franklin D. Roosevelt. They formed the vanguard of a new liberal movement committed to taking up the work the progressives had left unfinished.

But these reformers were utterly without power, except in a few states. The Republican Party had driven reformers from its ranks. The Democratic Party was a fallen giant, crippled by a split between its principal constituencies—rural Protestants and urban ethnics—over Prohibition, immigration restriction, and the Ku Klux Klan. The labor movement was moribund. The Socialist Party had never recovered from the trauma of war and Bolshevism. La Follette's Farmer-Labor Party had stalled after a promising debut. John Dewey and his friends tried to launch yet another third party, but they failed to raise money or arouse mass support.

Reformers took little comfort in the presidential election of 1928. Hoover's smashing victory suggested that the trends of the 1920s—the dominance of the Republicans, the centrality of Prohibition to political debate, the paralysis of the Democrats, the growing economic might of capitalism, and the pervasive influence of the consumer culture—would continue unabated.

Conclusion

Signs abounded in the 1920s that Americans were creating a new and bountiful society. The increased accessibility of cars, radios, vacuum cleaners, and other consumer durables; rising real wages, low unemployment, and installment buying; the widening circle of stock owners; the spread of welfare capitalism—all these pointed to an economy that had become more prosperous, more consumer-oriented, even somewhat more egalitarian. Moves to greater equality within marriage and to enhanced liberty for single women suggested that economic change was propelling social change as well.

Even so, many working-class and rural Americans benefited little from the decade's prosperity. Moreover, the decade's social changes aroused resistance, especially from white farmers and small-town Americans who feared that the rapid growth of cities and the large urban settlements of European and Mexican Catholics, Jews, and African Americans were rendering their Protestant America unrecognizable.

In the Democratic Party, farmers, small-town Americans, and moral traditionalists fought bitterly against the growing power of urban, ethnic constituencies. Elsewhere, the traditionalists battled hard to protect religion's authority against the inroads of science and to purge the nation of "inferior" population streams. In the process they arrayed themselves against American traditions of liberty and equality, even as they posed as the defenders of the best that America had to offer.

Their resistance to change caused many of the nation's most talented artists and writers to turn away from their fellow Americans in disgust. Meanwhile, although ethnic and racial minorities experienced high levels of discrimination, they nevertheless found enough freedom to create vibrant ethnic and racial communities and to launch projects—as in the case of African Americans in Harlem and Mexican Americans in Los Angeles—of cultural renaissance.

The Republican Party, having largely shed its reputation for reform, took credit for engineering the new economy of consumer plenty. It looked forward to years of political dominance. A steep and unexpected economic depression, however, would soon dash that expectation, revive the Democratic Party, and destroy Republican political power for a generation.

SUGGESTED READINGS

William Leuchtenberg, *The Perils of Prosperity, 1914–1932* (1958), and **Ellis Hawley**, *The Great War and the Search for a Modern Order: A History of the American People and Their Institutions, 1917–1933* (1979), offer useful overviews of the 1920s that stress political and economic developments. For an overview more attentive to culture and society, see **Nathan Miller**, *A New World Coming: The 1920s and the Making of Modern America* (2003). Important works on the consumer revolution include **Warren I. Susman**, *Culture as History: The Transformation of American Society in the Twentieth Century* (1984), **Roland Marchand**, *Advertising the American Dream: Making Way for Modernity, 1920–1940* (1985), and **Kathy Lee Peiss**, *Hope in a Jar: The Making of America's Beauty Culture* (1998). **John D. Hicks**, *Republican Ascendancy, 1921–1933* (1960), still serves as a good introduction to national politics, but consult, too, **Thomas B. Silver**, *Coolidge and the Historians* (1982), **Ellis Hawley, ed.**, *Herbert Hoover as Secretary of Commerce: Studies in New Era Thought and Practice* (1974), and **John W. Dean**, *Warren G. Harding* (2004). For a penetrating look at U.S. imperialism in the Caribbean in the 1920s, see **Mary A. Renda**, *Taking Haiti: Military Occupation and the Culture of U.S. Imperialism* (2001).

On agricultural distress and protest, see **Theodore Saloutos and John D. Hicks**, *Twentieth Century Populism: Agricultural Discontent in the Middle West, 1900–1939* (1951). For an examination of the economic and social effects of Prohibition, see **Norman Clark**, *Deliver Us From Evil: An Interpretation of American Prohibition* (1976). **John Higham**, *Strangers in the Land: Patterns of American Nativism, 1865–1925* (1955), remains an excellent work on the spirit of intolerance that gripped America in the 1920s. On the 1920s resurgence of fundamentalist movements and such reactionary groups as the Ku Klux Klan, consult **Nancy MacLean**, *Behind the Mask of Chivalry: The Making of the Second Ku Klux Klan* (1994), and **Ferenc Morton Szasz**, *The Divided Mind of Protestant America, 1880–1930* (1982), which expertly analyzes the split in Protestant ranks between liberals and fundamentalists. **Irving Bernstein**, *The Lean Years: A History of the American Worker, 1920–1933* (1960), remains the most thorough examination of 1920s workers. On ethnic communities, Americanization, and political mobilization in the 1920s, see **Gary Gerstle**, *Working-Class Americanism: The Politics of Labor in a Textile City, 1914–1960* (1989), **George J. Sánchez**, *Becoming Mexican American: Ethnicity, Culture and Identity in Chicano Los Angeles, 1900–1945* (1993), and **Kristi Andersen**, *The Creation of a Democratic Majority, 1928–1936* (1979). On the Harlem Renaissance, see **Nathan Huggins**, *Harlem Renaissance* (1971). **Malcolm Cowley**, *Exiles Return* (1934), is a marvelous account of the writers and artists who comprised the "Lost Generation." For a provocative interpretation of the intertwined character of white and black literary cultures in 1920s New York, see **Ann Douglas**, *Terrible Honesty: Mongrel Manhattan in the 1920s* (1995).

AMERICAN JOURNEY ONLINE AND INFOTRAC COLLEGE EDITION

Visit the source collections at www.ajaccess.wadsworth.com and infotrac.thomsonlearning.com and use the Search function with the following key terms to explore documents, images, audio and video clips, articles, and commentary related to the material in this chapter.

Warren G. Harding	Scopes Trial
Prohibition	Harlem Renaissance
Teapot Dome scandal	F. Scott Fitzgerald
Calvin Coolidge	Herbert Hoover
Dawes Plan	William Faulkner
Immigration Restriction Act	Johnson-Reed Act

GRADE AIDS

Visit the Liberty Equality Power Companion Web Site for resources specific to this textbook: http://history.wadsworth.com/murrin_LEP4e

The CD in the back of this book and the U.S. History Resource Center at http://history.wadsworth.com/u.s./ offer a variety of tools to help you succeed in this course, including access to quizzes; images; documents; interactive simulations; maps, and timelines; movie explorations; and a wealth of other sources.

Chapter 25

The Great Depression and the New Deal, 1929–1939

VICTIMS OF THE DEPRESSION
This image evokes the hardship of the 1930s in the form of a strong,
able-bodied man in the prime of his life who is unable to find work and
must depend on charity.

CHAPTER OUTLINE

The Great Depression began on October 29, 1929—"Black Tuesday"—with a spectacular stock market crash. On that one day, stock values plummeted $14 billion. By the end of that year, stock prices had fallen 50 percent from their September highs. By 1932, the worst year of the depression, they had fallen another 30 percent. In three years, $74 billion of wealth had simply vanished. Meanwhile, the unemployment rate had soared to 25 percent.

Many Americans who lived through the Great Depression could never forget the scenes of misery they saw everywhere. In cities, the poor meekly awaited their turn for a piece of stale bread and thin gruel at ill-funded soup kitchens. Scavengers poked through garbage cans for food, scoured railroad tracks for coal that had fallen from trains, and sometimes ripped up railroad ties for fuel. Hundreds of thousands of Americans built makeshift shelters out of cardboard, scrap metal, and whatever else they could find in the city dump. They called their towns "Hoovervilles," after the president whom they despised for his apparent refusal to help them.

The Great Depression brought cultural crisis as well as economic crisis. In the 1920s, American business leaders had successfully redefined the national culture in business terms, as Americans' values became synonymous with the values of business: economic growth, freedom of enterprise, and acquisitiveness. But the swagger and bluster of American businessmen during the 1920s made them vulnerable to attack in the 1930s, as jobs, incomes, and growth all disappeared. With the prestige of business and business values

From the Collections of the Library of Congress.

UNEMPLOYED MEN IN NEW YORK CITY

These unemployed men bow their heads, trying to get warm from the fire in the barrel and to ignore the devastation that everywhere surrounds them. Such scenes and experiences help to explain why the Great Depression seared itself into the memories of those who lived through it.

in decline, how could Americans regain their hope and recover their confidence in the future? The first years of the 1930s held no convincing answers.

The gloom broke in early 1933 when Franklin Delano Roosevelt became president and unleashed the power of government to regulate capitalist enterprises, to restore the economy to health, and to guarantee the social welfare of Americans who were unable to help themselves. Roosevelt called his pro-government program a "new deal for the American people," and it would dominate national politics for the next 40 years. Hailed as a hero, Roosevelt became (and remains) the only president to serve more than two terms. In the short term, the New Deal failed to restore prosperity to America, but the "liberalism" it championed found acceptance among millions, who agreed with Roosevelt that only a large and powerful government could guarantee Americans their liberty.

CHAPTER
FOCUS

♦ What caused the Crash of 1929, and why did the ensuing depression last so long?

♦ What were the First and Second New Deals? What were their similarities and differences? When and why did one give way to the other?

♦ Which groups in American society benefited most from the New Deal and which benefited least?

♦ In what ways did the Great Depression and New Deal shape American culture?

CHRONOLOGY

1929 Herbert Hoover assumes the presidency • Stock market crashes on "Black Tuesday"

1930 Tariff Act (Hawley-Smoot) raises tariffs

1931 More than 2,000 U.S. banks fail

1932 Unemployment rate reaches 25 percent • Reconstruction Finance Corporation established • Bonus Army marches on Washington • Roosevelt defeats Hoover for presidency

1933 Roosevelt assumes presidency • Hundred Days legislation defines First New Deal (March–June) • Roosevelt administration recognizes the Soviet Union • Good Neighbor Policy toward Latin America launched

1934 Father Charles Coughlin and Huey Long challenge conservatism of First New Deal • 2,000 strikes staged across country • Democrats overwhelm Republicans in off-year election • Radical political movements emerge in Wisconsin, Minnesota, Washington, and California • Indian Reorganization Act restores tribal land, provides funds, and grants limited right of self-government to American Indians • Reciprocal Trade Agreement lowers tariffs

1935 Committee for Industrial Organization (CIO) formed • Supreme Court declares NRA unconstitutional • Roosevelt unveils his Second New Deal • Congress passes Social Security Act • National Labor Relations Act (Wagner Act) guarantees workers' right to join unions • Holding Company Act breaks up utilities' near-monopoly • Congress passes Wealth Tax Act • Emergency Relief Administration Act passed; funds Works Progress Administration and other projects • Rural Electrification Administration established • Number of Mexican immigrants returning to Mexico reaches 500,000

1936 Roosevelt defeats Alf Landon for second term • Supreme Court declares AAA unconstitutional • Congress passes Soil Conservation and Domestic Allotment Act to replace AAA • Farm Security Administration established

1937 United Auto Workers defeat General Motors in sit-down strike • Roosevelt attempts to "pack" the Supreme Court • Supreme Court upholds constitutionality of Social Security and National Labor Relations acts • Severe recession hits

1938 Conservative opposition to New Deal does well in off-year election • *Superman* comic debuts

1939 75,000 gather to hear Marian Anderson sing at Lincoln Memorial

Causes of the Great Depression

America had experienced other depressions, or "panics," and no one would have been surprised if the boom of the 1920s had been followed by a one- or two-year economic downturn. No one was prepared, however, for the economic catastrophe of the 1930s.

Stock Market Speculation

In 1928 and 1929, the New York Stock Exchange had undergone a remarkable run-up in prices. In less than two years, the Dow Jones Industrial Average had doubled. Money had poured into the market, but many investors were buying on 10 percent "margin"—putting up only 10 percent of the price of a stock and borrowing the rest from brokers or banks. Few thought they would ever have to repay these loans with money out of their own pockets. Instead, investors expected to resell their shares within a few months at dramatically higher prices, pay back their loans from the proceeds, and still clear a handsome profit. And, for a while, that is exactly what they did. In 1928 alone, for example, RCA stock value increased 400 percent.

The possibility of making a fortune by investing only a few thousand dollars only intensified investors' greed. As speculation became rampant, money flowed indiscriminately into all kinds of risky enterprises. The stock market spiraled upward, out of control. When, in October 1929, confidence in future earnings finally faltered, creditors began demanding that investors who had bought stocks on margin repay their loans. The market crashed from its dizzying heights.

Still, the crash, by itself, fails to explain why the Great Depression lasted as long as it did. Poor decision making by the Federal Reserve Board, an ill-advised tariff that took effect soon after the depression hit, and a lopsided concentration of wealth in the hands of the rich deepened the economic collapse and made recovery more difficult.

Mistakes by the Federal Reserve Board

In 1930 and 1931, the Federal Reserve curtailed the amount of money in circulation and raised interest rates, thereby making credit more difficult for the public to secure. Although employing such a tight money policy during the boom years of 1928 or 1929 might have restrained the stock market and strengthened the economy, it was disastrous once the market had crashed. What the economy needed in 1930 and 1931 was an expanded money supply, lower interest rates, and easier credit. Such a course would have enabled debtors to pay their creditors. Instead, by choosing the opposite course, the Federal Reserve plunged an economy starved for credit deeper into depression. Higher interest rates also triggered international crisis, as the banks of Germany and Austria, heavily dependent on U.S. loans, went bankrupt. The German-Austrian collapse, in turn, spread financial panic through Europe and ruined many U.S. manufacturers and banks specializing in European trade and investment.

An Ill-Advised Tariff

The Tariff Act of 1930, also known as the Hawley-Smoot Tariff Act, accelerated economic decline abroad and at home. Throughout the 1920s, agricultural interests had sought higher tariffs to protect American farmers against foreign competition. But Hawley-Smoot not only raised tariffs on 75 agricultural goods from 32 to 40 percent (the highest rate in American history), it also raised tariffs by a similar percentage on 925 manufactured products. Industrialists had convinced their supporters in the Republican-controlled Congress that such protection would give American industry much-needed assistance. The legislation was a disaster. Angry foreign governments retaliated by raising their own tariff rates to keep out American goods. International trade, already weakened by the tight credit policies of the Federal Reserve, took another blow at the very moment when it desperately needed a boost.

A Maldistribution of Wealth

A maldistribution in the nation's wealth that had developed in the 1920s also stymied economic recovery. Although average income rose in the 1920s, the incomes of the wealthiest families rose higher than the rest. Between 1918 and 1929, the share of the national income that went to the wealthiest 20 percent of the population rose by more than 10 percent, while the share that went to the poorest 60 percent fell by almost 13 percent. The Coolidge administration contributed to this maldistribution by lowering taxes on the wealthy, thereby increasing the proportion of the national wealth concentrated in their hands. The deepening inequality of income distribution slowed consumption and held back the growth of consumer-oriented industries (cars, household appliances, processed and packaged foods, recreation), the most dynamic elements of the U.S. economy. Even when the rich spent their money lavishly—building huge mansions, buying expensive cars, vacationing on the French Riviera—they still spent a smaller proportion of their total incomes on consumption than wage earners did. The average 1920s wage earner, for example, might spend one-quarter to one-half of his annual earnings to buy a car.

Putting more of the total increase in national income into the pockets of average Americans during the 1920s would have steadied the demand for consumer goods and kept the newer consumer industries correspondingly stronger. Such an economy might have recovered relatively quickly from the stock market crash of 1929. Instead, recovery from the Great Depression lagged until 1941, more than a decade later.

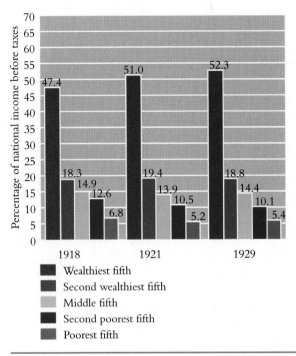

INCOME DISTRIBUTION BEFORE THE GREAT DEPRESSION

Source: From Gabriel Kolko, *Wealth and Power in America: An Analysis of Social Class and Income Distribution* (New York: Praeger, 1962), p. 14.

🌀 Hoover: The Fall of a Self-Made Man

In 1928, Herbert Hoover seemed to represent living proof that the American dream could be realized by anyone willing to work for it. A Stanford University geology major, a mining engineer, and a tireless and talented executive, Hoover rose quickly in corporate ranks. His government service had begun during the First World War, when he won an international reputation for his success in feeding millions of European soldiers and civilians. Then, in the 1920s, he became an active and influential secretary of commerce (see chapters 23 and 24). As the decade wound down, no American seemed better qualified to become president of the United States, an office that Hoover assumed in March 1929. Hoover was certain he could make prosperity a permanent feature of American life. "We in America today are nearer to the final triumph over poverty than ever before in the history of any land," he declared in August 1928. A little more than a year later, the Great Depression struck.

Hoover's Program

To cope with the crisis, Hoover first turned to the associational principles he had followed as secretary of commerce

(see chapter 24). He encouraged organizations of farmers, industrialists, and bankers to share information, bolster one another's spirits, and devise policies to aid economic recovery. He urged farmers to restrict output, industrialists to hold wages at predepression levels, and bankers to help each other remain solvent. The federal government would provide them with information, strategies of mutual aid, occasional loans, and morale-boosting speeches.

Hoover turned to other aggressive policies once he realized that associationalism was failing. To ease the European crisis, Hoover secured a one-year moratorium on loan payments that European governments owed American banks. He steered through Congress the Glass-Steagall Act of 1932, which was intended to help American banks meet the demands of European depositors who wished to convert their dollars to gold. And to ease the crisis at home, he began to expand the government's economic role. The Reconstruction Finance Corporation (RFC), created in 1932, made $2 billion available in loans to ailing banks and to corporations willing to build low-cost housing, bridges, and other public works. The RFC was the biggest federal peacetime intervention in the economy up to that point in American history. The Home Loan Bank Board, set up that same year, offered funds to savings and loans, mortgage companies, and other financial institutions that lent money for home construction and mortgages.

Despite this new government activism, Hoover was uncomfortable with the idea that the government should be responsible for restoring the nation's economic welfare. When RFC expenditures, in 1932, created the largest peacetime deficit in U.S. history, Hoover tried to balance the federal budget. He supported the Revenue Act of 1932, which aimed to erase the deficit by raising taxes. He also insisted that the RFC issue loans only to relatively healthy institutions that were capable of repaying them and that it favor public works, such as toll bridges, that were likely to become self-financing. As a result of these constraints, the RFC spent considerably less than Congress had mandated.

Hoover was especially reluctant to engage the government in providing relief to unemployed and homeless Americans. To give money to the poor, he insisted, would destroy their desire to work, undermine their sense of self-worth, and erode their capacity for citizenship.

Hoover saw no similar peril in extending government assistance to ailing banks and businesses. Critics pointed to the seeming hypocrisy of Hoover's policies. For example, in 1930, Hoover refused a request of $25 million to help feed Arkansas farmers and their families but approved $45 million to feed the same farmers' livestock. In 1932, shortly after rejecting an urgent request from the city of

Chicago for aid to help pay its teachers and municipal workers, Hoover approved a $90 million loan to rescue that city's Central Republic Bank.

The Bonus Army

In spring 1932, a group of army veterans mounted a particularly emotional challenge to Hoover's policies. In 1924, Congress had authorized a $1,000 bonus for First World War veterans in the form of compensation certificates that would mature in 1945. Now the veterans were demanding that the government pay the bonus immediately. A group of Portland, Oregon, veterans, calling themselves the Bonus Expeditionary Force, hopped onto empty boxcars of freight trains heading east, determined to stage a march on Washington. As the impoverished "army" moved eastward, its ranks multiplied, so that by the time it reached Washington its numbers had swelled to 20,000, including wives and children. The so-called Bonus Army set up camp in the Anacostia Flats, southeast of the Capitol, and petitioned Congress for early payment of the promised bonus. The House of Representatives agreed, but the Senate turned them down. Hoover refused to meet with the veterans. In July, federal troops led by Army Chief of Staff Douglas MacArthur and 3rd Cavalry Commander George Patton attacked the veterans' Anacostia

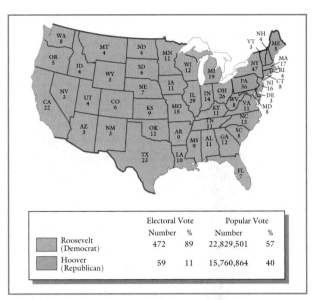

MAP 25.1   PRESIDENTIAL ELECTION, 1932

The trauma of the Great Depression can be gauged by the shifting fortunes of President Herbert Hoover. In 1928, he had won 444 electoral votes and carried all but eight states (see Map 24.3, p. 755). In 1932, by contrast, he won only 59 electoral votes and carried only seven states. His Democratic opponent, Franklin D. Roosevelt, was the big winner.

THE BONUS ARMY'S ENCAMPMENT SET ABLAZE

U.S. troops under the command of General Douglas MacArthur torched the tents and shacks that housed thousands of First World War veterans who had come to Washington to demand financial assistance from the government.

encampment, set the tents and shacks ablaze, and dispersed the protestors. In the process, more than 100 veterans were wounded and one infant was killed.

News that veterans and their families had been attacked in the nation's capital served only to harden anti-Hoover opinion. In the 1932 elections, the discredited Republicans were voted out of office after having dominated national politics (excepting Woodrow Wilson's two terms) for 36 years. Hoover received only 39.6 percent of the popular vote and just 59 (of 531) electoral votes. Hoover left the presidency in 1933 a bewildered man, reviled by Americans for his seeming indifference to suffering and his ineptitude in dealing with the economy's collapse.

A Culture in Crisis

The economic crisis of the early 1930s expressed itself not just in politics but also in culture, especially in the literature and cinema of the time. Many writers who, in the 1920s, had castigated ordinary Americas for their small-mindedness and crass materialism now felt compelled to travel among them, learn about their condition, and seek signs of social renewal. But writers found mostly

economic misery and a deep spiritual depression. Edmund Wilson, a leading literary critic, traveled the country in 1930 and 1931 and wrote numerous essays about how Americans had lost their way and knew not where to turn. When he reached San Diego, he got hold of the city's coroner reports on the numerous individuals who, in desperation, had taken their own lives. Wilson had believed that San Diego, that lovely outpost of the American frontier sitting astride the great and beckoning Pacific, would be a place where the American dream still thrived. But here, too, Wilson claimed, failure and death suffused life and snuffed out hope. He reported on the city's suicides in this fashion:

> They drive their cars into dark alleys, get into the back seat and shoot themselves; they hang themselves in hotel bedrooms, take overdoses of suphonal or barbital; they slip off to the municipal golf-links and there stab themselves with carving-knives; or they throw themselves into the bay, blue and placid, where gray battleships and cruisers guard the limits of their broad-belting nation.

A sense of aimlessness and hopelessness characterized one of the major literary works of the early 1930s, the Studs Lonigan trilogy (1932–35) written by the Chicago-born writer James T. Farrell. In another decade, one easily imagines that Farrell might have cast his scrappy Irish-American protagonist, Studs, as an American hero who, through pluck, guile, and force of character, rises from poverty to wealth, success, and influence. But Studs lacks the necessary focus and is too easily overcome by the harshness of his environment. He dies poor and alone, not even having reached the age of 30. The popular writer Nathaniel West, meanwhile, was publishing such novels as *Miss Lonelyhearts* (1933) and *A Cool Million* (1934), works similarly built around central characters succumbing to failure, drift, and even insanity.

One can detect parallel themes of despair in the period's cinema, especially in such movies as *Fugitive from a Chain Gang* (1932), in which an industrious and honorable man, James Allen, returns from Europe a war hero, only to sink into vagabondage. Caught by the police when he becomes an innocent accessory to a crime, Allen is sentenced to 10 years on a Georgia chain gang. Unable to tolerate the hardship and injustice of his punishment, Allen escapes from jail and uses his intelligence, determination, and good character to start a new life for himself under an alias. He finds satisfying work as an engineer and falls in love, but must abandon both once his true identity is revealed. His desire to stay out of prison condemns him to being a man always on the run, unable to prove his innocence or to earn a decent living or build enduring relationships. It is a powerful and utterly bleak cinematic work

that was, nevertheless, popular with moviegoers and given an Academy Award for Best Picture.

Less bleak but still sobering were the gangster movies of the early 1930s, especially *Little Caesar* (1930) and *The Public Enemy* (1931), which told stories of hard-nosed, crooked, and violent men who made themselves into figures of wealth and influence by living outside the law and bending the social environment in which they lived to their will. These gangsters usually had to pay for their sins by dying or going to jail, but, before that happened, they were often portrayed sympathetically, as individuals who, against all odds, found a way to succeed. Moviegoers were gripped by the intensity, suspense, and violence of gangster–police confrontations in these films but they were drawn, too, to the gangsters themselves, modern-day outlaws who demonstrated how tough it was to succeed in America and how necessary it might be to break the rules.

The lawlessness that was so integral to the gangster movies also surfaced in the wild comedy of Groucho, Chico, Harpo, and Zeppo Marx, entertainers who, in the 1920s and 1930s, made the transition from vaudeville stage to silver screen. In their films, the Marx Brothers ridiculed figures of authority, broke every rule of etiquette, smacked around their antagonists (and each other), and deliberately and delightfully mangled the English language. Anarchy ruled their world. Many of the moviegoers who went to see the Marx Brothers on the big screen simply wanted to enjoy 90 minutes of side-splitting laughter, if only to escape for a time the harsh realities of their daily lives.

But some of the Marx Brothers movies carried a more serious political message, perhaps none more so than *Duck Soup* (1933), a withering political satire set in the fictional nation of Fredonia. Fredonia's dictatorial leaders are pompous and small-minded, its legal system is a fraud, and its citizens are clueless and easily misled; by the movie's end, the latter are called to arms through spectacularly ludicrous song and dance scenes, and then led off to fight a meaningless but deadly war. In one of the film's most famous and controversial lines, Rufus T. Firefly, leader of Fredonia (played by Groucho Marx), declares to his troops: "And remember while you're out there risking life and limb through shot and shell, we'll be in here thinking what a sucker you are."

The Marx Brothers frame their critique of politics and war in their customary comedic style; the movie contains some of the funniest scenes the Marx Brothers ever filmed. But *Duck Soup* also delivers the dispiriting message that people could not hope to better themselves through politics, for politics had been emptied of all meaning and

Margaret Mead:
Studying the South Pacific

In the 1920s and 1930s, the practitioners of a relatively new intellectual discipline, cultural anthropology, began making research trips abroad an integral part of their work. Their ambition was to understand more about the diversity of the human experience and the power of culture to shape social life. These anthropologists rejected the notions that American culture was inherently superior to all others or that all the world's people should assimilate the values and beliefs that guided the West. Instead, these scholars delighted in the world's diversity and insisted on treating all cultures as fundamentally equal.

Few anthropologists were as influential in this quest as Margaret Mead. Born in Philadelphia in 1901, Mead received her B.A. from Barnard College in 1923 and then enrolled in Columbia University to study with the preeminent cultural anthropologist Franz Boas. Rather than travel to the American Southwest to conduct her initial field research, as most Boas students had done, Mead opted to study adolescents in the American Samoa of the South Pacific. This was a remarkable decision given that few young women in this era traveled such a long distance by themselves. In Samoa, Mead selected for study a T'au village on the least westernized Samoan island. Studying the transition of T'au children to adulthood, Mead discovered that young girls there did not experience as stormy an adolescence as did their counterparts in the United States and that this Samoan society, as a whole, seemed to be less convulsed by sexual anxiety than America. The book in which Mead published her findings, *Coming of Age in Samoa* (1928), became an overnight sensation and brought anthropology to the attention of the general American public. For Americans who were perturbed by what they perceived to be the limits of their own culture (see chapter 24),

Mead's work seemed to demonstrate that humans could develop alternative and more wholesome ways of living.

Mead's trip to Samoa was only the first of 24 expeditions to the South Pacific that she would undertake during her long and distinguished career. In the 1930s, she worked among no less than six different groups of Pacific Islanders: the Arapesh, Mundugumor, Chambri, Iatmul, Omaha, and Balinese. Everywhere she went, she explored how different cultures shaped gender roles, gender temperaments, sex, child rearing, and children's experience in particular ways. By the end of the 1930s, she had confirmed her initial claims and research about the variability of human experience and about how different societies assigned different roles and personalities to men and women, parents, and children. Culture, she insisted, mattered more than nature or biology in determining these roles and identities.

By the 1950s, Mead had become a public figure of great repute. In the 1960s, her arguments about the variability of human experience helped to propel a sexual revolution and the rebirth of feminism. In such ways did knowledge gained on faraway Pacific islands begin to shape American culture.

MARGARET MEAD

Mead in an intimate conversation with a Manus mother and child during a visit to the Admiralty Islands in 1953, one of Mead's many expeditions abroad to learn about peoples very different from those in America among whom she had grown up.

© Bettmann/Corbis.

honesty. This cinematic sentiment paralleled the conviction held by many Americans in 1932 and early 1933 that their own politicians, especially Hoover and the Republicans, had failed them in a time of need. In such ways did the political pessimism of the early 1930s seep into the era's culture.

🌐 The Democratic Roosevelt

Between 1933 and 1935, the mood of the country shifted sharply, and politics would, once again, generate hope rather than despair. This change was largely attributable to the personality and policies of Hoover's successor, Franklin D. Roosevelt, and to the social movements that emerged during his presidency.

An Early Life of Privilege

Roosevelt was born in 1882 into a patrician family descended, on his father's side, from Dutch gentry who in the 17th century had built large estates on the fertile land along the Hudson River. By the 1880s, the Hyde Park manor where Roosevelt grew up had been in the family for more than 200 years. His mother's family—the Delanos—traced its ancestry back to the Mayflower. Roosevelt's education at Groton, Harvard College, and Columbia Law School was typical of the path followed by the sons of America's elite.

The Roosevelt family was wealthy, although not spectacularly so by the standards of the late 19th century. His parents' net worth of more than $1 million was relatively small in comparison to the fortunes being amassed by the rising class of industrialists and railroad tycoons, many of whom commanded fortunes of $50 to $100 million or more. This widening gap in wealth disturbed families like the Roosevelts, who worried that the new industrial elite would dislodge them from their social position. Moreover, they took offense at the newcomers' vulgar displays of wealth, lack of taste and etiquette, indifference to the natural environment, and hostility toward those less fortunate than themselves. Theodore Roosevelt, an older cousin of Franklin Roosevelt, had called on the men of his gentry class to set a better example by devoting themselves to public service and the public good. Though young Franklin often said he wanted to follow in his famous cousin's footsteps, he showed little of Teddy's seriousness of purpose. He distinguished himself neither at school nor at law. Prior to the 1920s, he could point to few significant political achievements, and he owed his political ascent in the Democratic Party mostly to his famous name. He was charming and gregarious, and devoted a great deal of energy to sailing, partying, and enjoying the company of women other than his wife, Eleanor. Then, in 1921, at the age of 39, Roosevelt was both stricken and transformed by a devastating illness, polio, which paralyzed him from the waist down for the rest of his life.

During the two years that Roosevelt spent bedridden, he seemed to acquire a new determination and seriousness. He developed a compassion for those suffering misfortune that would later enable him to reach out to the millions caught in the Great Depression. Roosevelt's physical debilitation also transformed his relationship with Eleanor, with whom he had shared a testy and increasingly loveless marriage. Eleanor's dedication to nursing Franklin back to health forged a new bond between them. More conscious of his dependence on others, he now welcomed her as a partner in his career. Eleanor soon displayed a talent for political organization and public speaking that surprised those who knew her only as a shy, awkward woman. She was an indispensable player in the revival of Franklin's political fortunes, which began in 1928, with his election to the governorship of New York state. Eleanor would also become an active, eloquent First Lady, her husband's trusted ally, and an architect of American liberalism.

Roosevelt Liberalism

As governor of New York for four years (1929–33), Roosevelt had initiated various reform programs, and his success made him the front-runner for the 1932 Democratic presidential nomination. Even so, he had little assurance that he would be the party's choice. Since 1924, the Democrats had been sharply divided between southern and midwestern agrarians on the one hand and northeastern ethnics on the other. The agrarians favored government regulation—both of the nation's economy and of the private affairs of its citizens. Their support of government intervention in the pursuit of social justice marked them as economic progressives, while their advocacy of Prohibition revealed a cultural conservatism as well as a nativistic strain. By contrast, urban ethnics opposed Prohibition and other forms of government interference in the private lives of its citizens. Urban ethnics were divided over whether the government should regulate the economy, with former New York governor Al Smith increasingly committed to a laissez-faire policy and Senator Robert Wagner of New York and others supporting more federal control.

Roosevelt understood the need to carve out a middle ground. As governor of New York, and then as a presidential candidate in 1932, he surrounded himself with men and women who embraced the new reform movement

called liberalism. Frances Perkins, Harry Hopkins, Raymond Moley, Rexford Tugwell, Adolph Berle, Samuel Rosenman—all were interventionist in economic matters and libertarian on questions of personal behavior. They shared with the agrarians and Wagner's supporters a desire to regulate capitalism, but they agreed with Al Smith that the government had no business telling people how to live their lives. Although it seemed unlikely at first, Roosevelt did manage to unite the party behind him at the 1932 Democratic Party convention. In his convention acceptance speech, he declared: "Ours must be the party of liberal thought, of planned action, of enlightened international outlook, and of the greatest good for the greatest number of citizens." He promised "a new deal for the American people."

The First New Deal, 1933–1935

By the time Roosevelt assumed office in March 1933, the economy lay in shambles. From 1929 to 1932, industrial production had fallen by 50 percent, while new investment had declined from $16 billion to less than $1 billion. In those same years, more than 100,000 businesses went bankrupt. The nation's banking system was on the verge of collapse. In 1931 alone, more than 2,000 banks had shut their doors. The unemployment rate was soaring.

Some Americans feared that the opportunity for reform had already passed.

Not Roosevelt. "This nation asks for action, and action now," Roosevelt declared in his inaugural address. Roosevelt was true to his word. In his first Hundred Days, from early March through early June 1933, Roosevelt persuaded Congress to pass 15 major pieces of legislation to help bankers, farmers, industrialists, workers, homeowners, the unemployed, and the hungry. He also prevailed on Congress to repeal Prohibition. Not all of the new laws helped to relieve distress and promote recovery, but, in the short term, that seemed to matter little. Roosevelt had brought excitement and hope to the nation. He was confident, decisive, and defiantly cheery. "The only thing we have to fear is fear itself," he declared.

Roosevelt used the radio to reach out to ordinary Americans. On the second Sunday after his inauguration, he launched a series of radio addresses known as "fireside chats," speaking in a plain, friendly, and direct voice to the forlorn and discouraged. In his first chat, he explained the banking crisis in simple terms but without condescension. "I want to take a few minutes to talk with the people of the United States about banking," he began. An estimated 20 million Americans listened.

To hear the president speaking warmly and conversationally—as though he were actually there in the room— was riveting. An estimated 500,000 Americans wrote letters to Roosevelt within days of his inaugural address.

LEGISLATION ENACTED DURING THE "HUNDRED DAYS," MARCH 9–JUNE 16, 1933

Date	Legislation	Purpose
March 9	Emergency Banking Act	Provide federal loans to private bankers
March 20	Economy Act	Balance the federal budget
March 22	Beer-Wine Revenue Act	Repeal Prohibition
March 31	Unemployment Relief Act	Create the Civilian Conservation Corps
May 12	Agricultural Adjustment Act	Establish a national agricultural policy
May 12	Emergency Farm Mortgage Act	Provide refinancing of farm mortgages
May 12	Federal Emergency Relief Act	Establish a national relief system, including the Civil Works Administration
May 18	Tennessee Valley Authority Act	Promote economic development of the Tennessee Valley
May 27	Securities Act	Regulate the purchase and sale of new securities
June 5	Gold Repeal Joint Resolution	Cancel the gold clause in public and private contracts
June 13	Home Owners Loan Act	Provide refinancing of home mortgages
June 16	National Industrial Recovery Act	Set up a national system of industrial self-government and establish the Public Works Administration
June 16	Glass-Steagall Banking Act	Create Federal Deposit Insurance Corporation; separate commercial and investment banking
June 16	Farm Credit Act	Reorganize agricultural credit programs
June 16	Railroad Coordination Act	Appoint federal coordinator of transportation

Source: Arthur M. Schlesinger, Jr., *The Coming of the New Deal* (Boston: Houghton Mifflin, 1959), pp. 20–21.

FRANKLIN D. ROOSEVELT

A smiling, confident Roosevelt delivering a speech. The man on the left in the first row behind Roosevelt is Interior Secretary Harold Ickes.

Millions more would write to him and to Eleanor Roosevelt over the next few years. Many of the letters were simply addressed to "Mr. or Mrs. Roosevelt, Washington, D.C." Democrats began to hang portraits of Franklin Roosevelt in their homes, often next to a picture of Jesus or the Madonna.

Roosevelt was never the benign father figure he made himself out to be. He skillfully crafted his public image. Compliant news photographers agreed not to show him in a wheelchair or struggling with the leg braces and cane he used to take even small steps. His political rhetoric sometimes promised more than he was prepared to deliver in actual legislation. This was not simply a strategy meant to confuse his opponents and to sustain his own appeal. Roosevelt was struggling to keep together a party that was divided over a variety of issues. At the same time, he was attempting to establish a strong government in a society that had long been hostile to that idea. In America, unlike Great Britain, for example, relatively few individuals were experienced in public service. This lack of administrative expertise created dilemmas for Roosevelt and other New

Dealers, who often found it difficult to translate ambitious social programs into effective social policy.

Saving the Banks

Roosevelt's first order of business was to save the nation's financial system. By inauguration day, several states had already shut their banks. Roosevelt immediately ordered all of the nation's banks closed—a bold move he brazenly called a "bank holiday." At his request, Congress rushed through the Emergency Banking Act (EBA), which made federal loans available to private bankers, and followed that with the Economy Act (EA), which committed the government to balancing the budget.

Both the EBA and the EA were fiscally conservative programs that Hoover had proposed. The EBA made it possible for private bankers to retain financial control of their institutions, and the EA announced the government's intention of pursuing a fiscally prudent course. Only after the financial crisis had eased did Roosevelt turn to the structural reform of banking. A second Glass-Steagall Act (1933) separated commercial banking from investment banking. It also created the Federal Deposit Insurance Corporation (FDIC), which assured depositors that the government would protect up to $5,000 of their savings. The Securities Act (1933) and the Securities Exchange Act (1934) imposed long-overdue regulation on the New York Stock Exchange, both by reining in buying on the margin and by establishing the Securities and Exchange Commission (SEC) to enforce federal law.

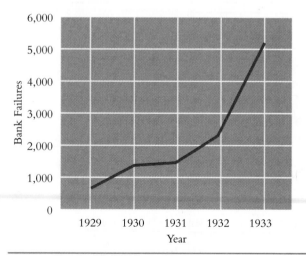

BANK FAILURES, 1929–1933

Source: From C. D. Bremer, *American Bank Failures* (New York: Columbia University Press, 1935), p. 42.

Economic Relief

Roosevelt understood the need to temper financial prudence with compassion. Congress responded swiftly in 1933 to Roosevelt's request to establish the Federal Emergency Relief Administration (FERA), granting it $500 million for relief to the poor. To head FERA, Roosevelt appointed a brash young reformer, Harry Hopkins, who disbursed $2 million during his first two hours on the job. Roosevelt next won congressional approval for the Civilian Conservation Corps (CCC), which put more than 2 million single young men to work planting trees, halting erosion, and otherwise improving the environment. The following winter, Roosevelt launched the Civil Works Administration (CWA), an ambitious work-relief program, also under Harry Hopkins's direction, which hired 4 million unemployed at $15 per week and put them to work on 400,000 small-scale government projects. For middle-class Americans threatened with the loss of their homes, Roosevelt won Congressional approval for the Homeowners' Loan Corporation (1933) to refinance mortgages. These direct subsidies to millions of jobless and home-owning Americans lent credibility to Roosevelt's claim that the New Deal would set the country on a new course.

Agricultural Reform

In 1933, Roosevelt expected economic recovery to come not from relief, but through agricultural and industrial cooperation. He regarded the Agricultural Adjustment Act, passed in May, and the National Industrial Recovery Act (NIRA), passed in June, as the most important legislation of his Hundred Days. Both were based on the idea that curtailing production would trigger economic recovery. By shrinking the supply of agricultural and manufactured goods, Roosevelt's economists reasoned, they could restore the balance of normal market forces. As demand for scarce goods exceeded supply, prices would rise and revenues would climb. Farmers and industrialists, earning a profit once again, would increase their investment in new technology and hire more workers, and prosperity and full employment would be the final result.

To curtail farm production, the Agricultural Adjustment Administration (AAA), which was set up by the Agricultural Adjustment Act, began paying farmers to keep a portion of their land out of cultivation and to reduce the size of their herds. The program was controversial; many farmers were skeptical of a government offer to pay more money for working less land and husbanding

HELPING DUST BOWL VICTIMS
This poster by the artist and New Deal supporter Ben Shahn dramatizes the plight of the Dust Bowl's victims while expressing the belief that relief is forthcoming from a New Deal agency, the Resettlement Administration.

fewer livestock, but few refused to accept payments. As one young Kansas farmer reported:

> There were mouthy individuals who seized every opportunity to run down the entire program . . . condemning it as useless, crooked, revolutionary, or dictatorial; but . . . when the first AAA payments were made available, shortly before Christmas, these same wordy critics made a beeline for the courthouse. They jostled and fell over each other in their mad scramble to be the first in line to receive allotment money.

The AAA had made no provision, however, for the countless tenant farmers and farm laborers who would be thrown out of work by the reduction in acreage. In the South, the victims were disproportionately black. A Georgia sharecropper wrote Harry Hopkins of his misery: "I have Bin farming all my life But the man I live with

Has Turned me loose taking my mule [and] all my feed. . . . I can't get a Job so Some one said Rite you." New Dealers within the Department of Agriculture, such as Rexford Tugwell and Jerome Frank, were sympathetic to the plight of sharecroppers, but they failed during the First New Deal to extend to them the government's helping hand.

The programs of the AAA also proved inadequate to Great Plains farmers, whose economic problems had been compounded by ecological crisis. Just as the depression rolled in, the rain stopped falling on the plains. The land, stripped of its native grasses by decades of excessive plowing, dried up and turned to dust. And then the dust began to blow, sometimes traveling 1,000 miles across open prairie. Dust became a fixed feature of daily life on the plains (which soon became known as the Dust Bowl), covering furniture, floors, and stoves, and penetrating people's hair and lungs. The worst dust storm occurred on April 14, 1935, when a great mass of dust, moving at speeds of 45 to 70 miles per hour, roared through Colorado, Kansas, and Oklahoma, blackening the sky, suffocating cattle, and dumping thousands of tons of topsoil and red clay on homes and streets.

The government responded to this calamity by establishing the Soil Conservation Service (SCS) in 1935. Rec-

SEARCHING FOR A BETTER LIFE

Scenes like this one were common in the 1930s as farm families in Oklahoma and Texas who had lost their land began heading to California. Here a family's entire belongings are packed onto a truck, and the mother tends to her baby on an isolated road. The woman's fur collar suggests that this family had once known better times.

ognizing that the soil problems of the Great Plains could not be solved simply by taking land out of production, SCS experts urged plains farmers to plant soil-conserving grasses and legumes in place of wheat. They taught farmers how to plow along contour lines and how to build terraces—techniques that had been proven effective in slowing the runoff of rainwater and improving its absorption into the soil. Plains farmers were open to these suggestions, especially when the government offered to subsidize those willing to implement them. Bolstered by the new assistance, plains agriculture began to recover.

Still, the government offered little assistance to the rural poor—the tenant farmers and sharecroppers. Nearly 1 million had left their homes by 1935, and another 2.5 million would leave after 1935. Most headed west, piling their belongings onto their jalopies, snaking along Route 66 until they reached California. They became known as Okies, because many, although not all, had come from Oklahoma. Their dispossession and forced migration disturbed many Americans, for whom the plight of these once-sturdy yeomen became a symbol of how much had gone wrong with the American dream.

In 1936, the Supreme Court ruled that AAA-mandated limits on farm production constituted an illegal restraint of trade. Congress responded by passing the Soil Conservation and Domestic Allotment Act, which justified the removal of land from cultivation for reasons of conservation rather than economics. This new act also called on landowners to share their government subsidies with sharecroppers and tenant farmers, although many landowners managed to evade this and subsequent laws that required them to share federal funds.

The use of subsidies, begun by the AAA, did eventually bring stability and prosperity to agriculture, but at high cost. Agriculture became the most heavily subsidized sector of the U.S. economy, and the Department of Agriculture grew into one of the government's largest bureaucracies. The rural poor, black and white, never received a fair share of federal benefits. Beginning in the 1930s, and continuing in the 1940s and 1950s, they would be forced off the land and into the cities of the North and West.

Industrial Reform

American industry was so vast that Roosevelt's administration never contemplated paying individual manufacturers direct subsidies to reduce, or even halt, production. Instead, the government decided to limit production through persuasion and association—techniques that Hoover had also favored.

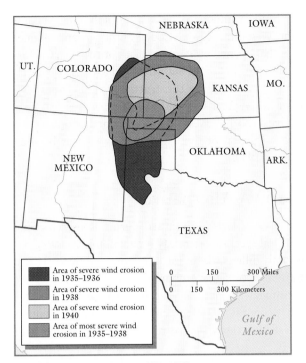

MAP 25.2 DUST BOWL, 1935–1940

This map shows the areas in six states—Texas, New Mexico, Oklahoma, Colorado, Kansas, and a bit of Nebraska—claimed by the Dust Bowl between 1935 and 1940. The light red color shows the area where the winds caused the worst damage.

To head the National Recovery Administration (NRA), authorized under the National Industrial Recovery Act, Roosevelt chose General Hugh Johnson, a participant in industrial planning experiments during the First World War. Johnson's first task was to persuade industrialists and businessmen to agree to raise employee wages to a minimum of 30 to 40 cents per hour and to limit employee hours to a maximum of 30 to 40 hours per week. The limitation on hours was meant to reduce the quantity of goods that any factory or business could produce.

Johnson launched a high-powered publicity campaign. He distributed NRA pamphlets and pins throughout the country. He used the radio to exhort all Americans to do their part. He staged an NRA celebration in Yankee Stadium and a parade down New York City's Fifth Avenue. He sent letters to millions of employers asking them to place a "blue eagle"—the logo of the NRA—on storefronts, at factory entrances, and on company stationery to signal their participation in the campaign to limit production and restore prosperity. Blue eagles soon sprouted everywhere, usually accompanied by the slogan "We Do Our Part."

Johnson understood, however, that his propaganda campaign could not by itself guarantee recovery. So he brought together the largest producers in every sector of manufacturing and asked each group (or conference) to work out a code of fair competition that would specify prices, wages, and hours throughout the sector. He also asked each conference to restrict production.

In summer and fall 1933, the NRA codes drawn up for steel, textiles, coal mining, rubber, garment manufacture, and other industries seemed to be working. The economy improved, and people began to hope for an end to the depression. But in winter and spring 1934, economic indicators plunged downward once again, and manufacturers began to evade the code provisions. Government

SELLING THE NRA THROUGH SEX AND SUNBURN

Americans were asked to display their support for the NRA by pasting eagles onto their factory entrances, storefronts, and even clothes. The young women in this photo dispensed with pasting, choosing instead to allow the sun to burn their bare backs around a stenciled blue eagle and NRA lettering, which were being applied by the woman in the white gown.

© Bettmann/Corbis.

committees set up to enforce the codes were powerless to punish violators. By fall 1934, it was clear that the NRA had failed. When the Supreme Court declared the NRA codes unconstitutional in May 1935, the Roosevelt administration allowed the agency to die.

Rebuilding the Nation's Infrastructure

In addition to establishing the NRA, the National Industrial Recovery Act launched the Public Works Administration (PWA). The PWA had a $3.3 billion budget to sponsor internal improvements that would strengthen the nation's infrastructure of roads, bridges, sewage systems, hospitals, airports, and schools. The labor needed for these projects would shrink relief rolls and reduce unemployment, but the projects could be justified in terms that conservatives approved: economic investment rather than short-term relief.

The PWA authorized the building of three major dams in the West—the Grand Coulee, Boulder, and Bonneville—that opened up large stretches of Arizona, California, and Washington to industrial and agricultural development. It funded the construction of the Triborough Bridge in New York City and the 100-mile causeway linking Florida to Key West. It also appropriated money for the construction of thousands of new schools between 1933 and 1939.

The TVA Alternative

One piece of legislation passed during Roosevelt's First New Deal specified a strategy for economic recovery significantly different from the one promoted by the NIRA. The Tennessee Valley Authority Act (1933) called for the government—rather than private corporations—to promote economic development throughout the Tennessee Valley, a vast river basin winding through parts of

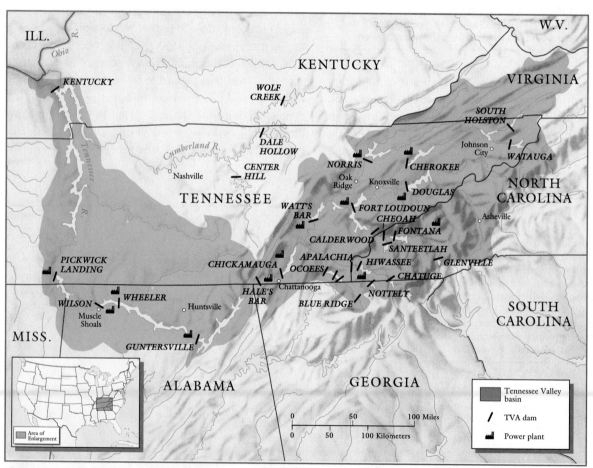

MAP 25.3 TENNESSEE VALLEY AUTHORITY

This map shows the vast scale of the TVA, and pinpoints the locations of 29 dams and 13 power plants that emerged from this project.

Kentucky, Tennessee, Mississippi, Alabama, Georgia, and North Carolina. The act created the Tennessee Valley Authority (TVA) to control flooding on the Tennessee River, harness its water power to generate electricity, develop local industry (such as fertilizer production), improve river navigability, and ease the poverty and isolation of the area's inhabitants. In some respects, the TVA's mandate resembled that of the PWA, but the TVA enjoyed even greater authority. The extent of its control over economic development reflected the influence of Rexford Tugwell and other New Dealers who were committed to a government-planned and government-operated economy. Although they rarely said so, these reformers were drawn to socialism.

The accomplishments of the TVA were many. It built, completed, or improved more than 20 dams, including the huge Wheeler Dam near Muscle Shoals in Alabama. At several of the dam sites, the TVA built hydroelectric generators and soon became the nation's largest producer of electricity. Its low rates compelled private utility companies to reduce their rates as well. The TVA also constructed waterways to bypass non-navigable stretches of the river, reduced the danger of flooding, and taught farmers how to prevent soil erosion and use fertilizers.

Although the TVA was one of the New Deal's most celebrated successes, it generated little support for more ambitious experiments in national planning. For the government to have assumed control of established industries and banks would have been quite a different matter from bringing prosperity to an impoverished region. Like Roosevelt, few members of Congress or the public favored the radical growth of governmental power that such programs would have entailed. Thus, the thought of replacing the NRA with a nationwide TVA, for instance, made little headway. The New Deal never embraced the idea of the federal government as a substitute for private enterprise.

The New Deal and Western Development

As the TVA showed, New Deal programs could make an enormous difference to a particular region's welfare. Other regional beneficiaries of the New Deal included the New York City area, which prospered from the close links of local politicians to the Roosevelt administration. The region that most benefited from the New Deal, however, was the West. Between 1933 and 1939, per capita payments for public works projects, welfare, and federal loans in the Rocky Mountain and Pacific Coast states outstripped those of any other region.

Central to this western focus was the program of dam building. Western real estate and agricultural interests wanted to dam the West's major rivers to provide water and electricity for urban and agricultural development. But the costs were prohibitive, even to the largest capitalists, until the New Deal offered to defray the expenses with federal dollars. Western interests found a government ally in the Bureau of Reclamation, a hitherto small federal agency (in existence since 1902) that became, under the New Deal, a prime dispenser of funds for dam construction, reservoir creation, and the provision of water to western cities and farms. Drawing on PWA monies, the bureau oversaw the building of the Boulder Dam (later renamed Hoover Dam), which provided drinking water for southern California, irrigation water for California's Imperial Valley, and electricity for Los Angeles and southern Arizona. It also authorized the Central Valley Project and the All-American Canal, vast water-harnessing projects in central and southern California meant to provide irrigation, drinking water, and electricity to California farmers and

© Lester Lefkowitz/Corbis.

IMPROVING THE NATION'S INFRASTRUCTURE

The federal government built several major dams in the West to boost agricultural and industrial development. This is a photograph of the mammoth Boulder Dam (later renamed the Hoover Dam) on the Colorado River.

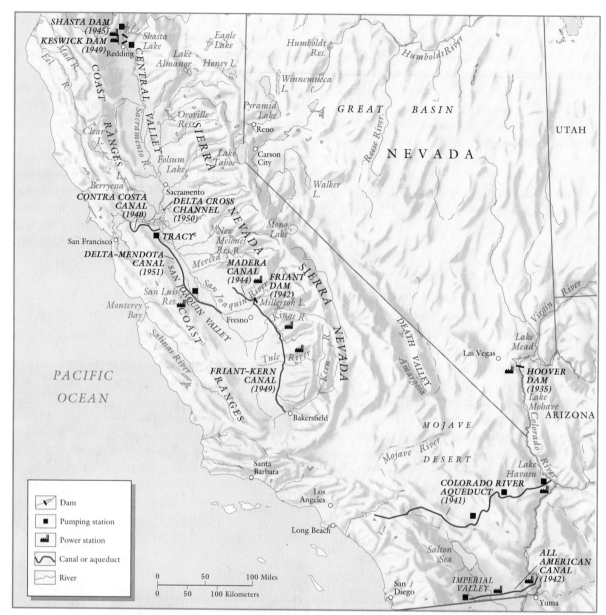

MAP 25.4 FEDERAL WATER PROJECTS IN CALIFORNIA BUILT OR FUNDED BY THE NEW DEAL

This map demonstrates how much California cities and agriculture benefited from water projects—dams, canals, aqueducts, pumping stations, and power plants—begun under the New Deal. The projects extended from the Shasta Dam in the northern part of the state to the All-American Canal that traversed the Imperial Valley south of San Diego, and included the Colorado River Aqueduct that would bring vital drinking water to Los Angeles.

towns. The greatest construction project of all was the Grand Coulee Dam on the Columbia River in Washington, which created a lake 150 miles long. Together with the Bonneville Dam (also on the Columbia), the Grand Coulee gave the Pacific Northwest the cheapest electricity in the country and created the potential for huge economic and population growth. Not surprisingly, these two dams also made Washington state the largest per capita recipient of New Deal aid.

These developments attracted less attention in the 1930s than the TVA because their benefits did not fully

materialize until after the Second World War. Also, dam building in the West was not seen as a radical experiment in government planning and management. Unlike the TVA, the Bureau of Reclamation hired private contractors to do the work. Moreover, the benefits of these dams were intended to flow first to large agricultural and real estate interests, not to the poor; they were intended to aid private enterprise, rather than bypass it. In political terms, dam building in the West was more conservative than it was in the Tennessee Valley. Even so, this activity made the federal government a key architect of the modern American West.

Political Mobilization, Political Unrest, 1934–1935

Although Roosevelt and the New Dealers quickly dismantled the NRA in 1935, they could not stop the political forces it had set in motion. Ordinary Americans now believed they could make a difference. If the New Dealers could not achieve economic recovery, the people would find others who could.

Populist Critics of the New Deal

Some critics were disturbed by what they perceived as the conservative character of New Deal programs. Banking reforms, the AAA, and the NRA, they alleged, all seemed to favor large economic interests. Ordinary people had been ignored.

In the South and Midwest, millions listened regularly to the radio addresses of Louisiana Senator Huey Long, a former governor of that state and an accomplished orator. In attacks on New Deal programs, he alleged that "not a single thin dime of concentrated, bloated, pompous

HUEY LONG, POPULIST

A spellbinding speaker, Long influenced millions with his calls for redistributing America's wealth in a more equitable manner.

© UPI-Bettmann/Corbis.

wealth, massed in the hands of a few people has been raked down to relieve the masses." Long offered a simple alternative: "Break up the swollen fortunes of America and . . . spread the wealth among all our people." He called for a redistribution of wealth that would guarantee each American family a $5,000 estate.

Long's rhetoric inspired hundreds of thousands of Americans to join the Share the Wealth clubs his supporters organized. Most came from middle-class ranks or from the ranks of skilled workers. Long's supporters worried that the big business orientation of New Deal programs would undermine their economic and social status. By 1935, Roosevelt regarded Long as the man most likely to unseat him in the presidential election of 1936. Before that campaign began, however, Long was murdered by an assassin.

Meanwhile, in the Midwest, Father Charles Coughlin, the "radio priest," delivered his stinging critique of the New Deal to a weekly radio audience of between 30 and 40 million listeners. Like Long, Coughlin appealed to anxious middle-class Americans and to privileged groups of workers who believed that middle-class status was slipping from their grasp. A devoted Roosevelt supporter at first—he had once called the New Deal "Christ's Deal"—Coughlin had become, by 1934, a harsh critic. He charged that the New Deal was run by bankers and the NRA simply aimed to resuscitate corporate profits without concern for the average working man. Coughlin called for a strong government to compel capital, labor, agriculture, professionals, and other interest groups to do its bidding. He founded the National Union of Social Justice (NUSJ) in 1934 as a precursor to a political party that would challenge the Democrats in 1936. Coughlin increasingly admired dictators such as Italy's Benito Mussolini who built their power and programs through decree rather than through democratic consent. If necessary, he admitted in 1936, he would "'dictate' to preserve democracy."

As Coughlin's disillusionment with the New Deal deepened, a strain of anti-Semitism became apparent in his radio talks, as in his accusation that Jewish bankers were masterminding a world conspiracy to dispossess the toiling masses. Although Coughlin was a compelling speaker, he failed to build the NUSJ into an effective political force. Its successor, the Union Party, attracted only a tiny percentage of voters in 1936. Embittered, Coughlin moved further to the political right. By 1939, his denunciations of democracy and Jews had become so extreme that some radio stations refused to carry his addresses. But millions of ordinary Americans continued to put their faith in the "radio priest."

Another popular figure was Francis E. Townsend, a California doctor who claimed that the way to end the depression was to give every senior citizen $200 per month

with the stipulation that seniors would spend that money, thus putting more money in circulation and reviving economic demand. The Townsend Plan also made clear the need for some kind of pension program to ease the plight of the nation's elderly. While the Townsend movement did not last long, it did prod a nervous Roosevelt administration to make relief for the elderly—a program that Roosevelt would label Social Security—an important component of the New Deal.

Labor Protests

The attacks by Long, Coughlin, and Townsend on the New Deal deepened popular discontent and inspired other insurgent movements. The most important of them was the labor movement. Workers began joining unions in response to the National Industrial Recovery Act, and especially its Clause 7 (a), which granted workers the right to join labor unions of their own choosing, and obligated employers to recognize unions and bargain with them in good faith. Union members made quite modest demands at first: They wanted employers to observe the provisions of the NRA codes; they wanted to be treated fairly by their foremen; and they wanted employers to recognize and negotiate with their unions.

Few employers, however, were willing to grant their employees any say in their working conditions. Many ignored the NRA's wage and hour guidelines altogether and even used their influence over NRA code authorities to thwart worker requests for wage increases and union recognition. Workers flooded Washington with letters addressed to President Roosevelt, Labor Secretary Frances Perkins, and General Hugh Johnson, asking them to force employers to comply with the law. A Rhode Island textile worker who had been fired for joining a union asked why the NRA had neither responded to his complaint nor punished the company that had fired him. "If people can be arrested for violating certain laws," he wondered, "why can't this company?"

When their pleas went unanswered, workers began to take matters into their own hands. In 1934, they staged 2,000 strikes, some of which escalated into armed confrontations between workers and police. In Toledo, Ohio, in May, 10,000 workers surrounded the Electric Auto-Lite plant, declaring that they would block all exits and entrances until the

company agreed to shut down operations and negotiate a union contract. Two strikers were killed in an exchange of gunfire. In Minneapolis, unionized truck drivers and warehousemen fought police, private security forces, and the National Guard in a series of street battles from May through July that left four dead and hundreds wounded. In San Francisco in July, skirmishes between longshoremen and employers killed two and wounded scores of strikers. This violence provoked a general strike in San Francisco that shut down the city's transportation, construction, and service industries for two weeks. In September, 400,000 textile workers at mills from Maine to Alabama walked off their jobs. Attempts by employers to bring in replacement workers triggered violent confrontations that caused several deaths, hundreds of injuries, and millions of dollars in property damages.

Anger at the Polls

By late September, textile union leaders had lost their nerve and called off the strike, but workers took their anger to the polls. In Rhode Island, they broke the Republican Party's 30-year domination of state politics. In the South Carolina gubernatorial race, working-class voters rejected a conservative Democrat, Coleman Blease, and chose instead Olin T. Johnston, a former mill worker and an ardent New Dealer. In the country as a whole, Demo-

Detroit Industry, North Wall, 1932–1933. Diego Rivera. Gift of Edsel B. Ford. Photograph © 1991 The Detroit Institute of Arts.

MEN AT WORK

This picture depicts part of the mural that the Mexican artist Diego Rivera painted for the walls of the Detroit Art Museum in 1932–33. The mural conveys both the awesome size of Detroit's industrial plants and the centrality of workers to their operation. Rivera's work, like that of other 1930s artists, suggested that industrial workers stood at the very heart of American civilization and that they would play a key role in rehabilitating an economy devastated by depression.

crats won 70 percent of the contested seats in the Senate and House. The Democrats increased their majority, from 310 to 319 (out of 432) in the House, and from 60 to 69 (out of 96) in the Senate. No sitting president's party had ever done so well in an off-year election.

The victory was not an unqualified one for Roosevelt and the First New Deal, however. The 74th Congress would include the largest contingent of radicals ever sent to Washington: Tom Amlie of Wisconsin, Ernest Lundeen of Minnesota, Maury Maverick of Texas, Vito Marcantonio of New York, and some 30 others. Their support for the New Deal depended on whether Roosevelt delivered more relief, more income security, and more political power to farmers, workers, the unemployed, and the poor.

Radical Third Parties

Radical critics of the New Deal also made an impressive showing in state politics in 1934 and 1936. They were particularly strong in states gripped by labor unrest. In Wisconsin, for example, Philip La Follette, the son of Robert La Follette (see chapter 21), was elected governor in 1934 and 1936 as the candidate of the radical Wisconsin Progressive Party. In Minnesota, discontented agrarians and urban workers organized the Minnesota Farmer-Labor (MFL) Party and elected their candidate to the governorship in 1930, 1932, 1934, and 1936. In Washington, yet another radical third party, the Commonwealth Builders, elected both senators and almost half the state legislators in 1932 and 1934. And in California, the socialist and novelist Upton Sinclair and his organization, End Poverty in California (EPIC), came closer to winning the governorship than anyone had expected.

A widespread movement to form local labor parties offered further evidence of voter volatility, as did the growing appeal of the Communist Party. The American Communist Party (CP) had emerged in the early 1920s with the support of radicals who wanted to adopt the Soviet Union's path to socialism. The CP began to attract attention in the early 1930s, as its organizers spread out among the poorest and most vulnerable populations in America—homeless urban blacks in the North, black and white sharecroppers in the South, Chicano and Filipino agricultural workers in the West—and mobilized them in unions and unemployment leagues. CP members also played significant roles in strikes described earlier, and they were influential in the Minnesota Farmer-Labor Party and in Washington's Commonwealth Builders. Once they stopped preaching world revolution in 1935 and began calling instead for a "popular front" of democratic forces against fascism (a term used to describe the new kinds of dictatorships appearing in Hitler's Germany and Mussolini's

Italy), their ranks grew even more. By 1938, approximately 80,000 Americans were thought to have been members of the Communist Party.

Although the Communist Party proclaimed its allegiance to democratic principles beginning in 1935, it nevertheless remained a dictatorial organization that took its orders from the Soviet Union. Many Americans feared the growing strength of the CP and began to call for its suppression. The CP, however, was never strong enough to gain power for itself. Its chief role in 1930s politics was to channel popular discontent into unions and political parties that would, in turn, force New Dealers to respond to the demands of the nation's dispossessed.

The Second New Deal, 1935–1937

The labor unrest of 1934 had taken Roosevelt by surprise. For a time, he kept his distance from the masses mobilizing in his name, but in spring 1935, with the 1936 presidential election looming, he decided to place himself at their head. He called for the "abolition of evil holding companies," attacked the wealthy for their profligate ways, and called for new programs to aid the poor and downtrodden. Rather than becoming a socialist, as his critics charged, Roosevelt sought to reinvigorate his appeal among poorer Americans and turn them away from radical solutions.

Philosophical Underpinnings

To point the New Deal in a more populist direction, Roosevelt turned increasingly to a relatively new economic theory, underconsumptionism. Advocates of this theory held that a chronic weakness in consumer demand had caused the Great Depression. The path to recovery lay, therefore, not in restricting production, as the architects of the First New Deal had tried to do, but in boosting consumer expenditures through government support for strong labor unions (to force up wages), higher social welfare expenditures (to put more money in the hands of the poor), and ambitious public works projects (to create hundreds of thousands of new jobs).

Underconsumptionists did not worry that new welfare and public works programs might strain the federal budget. If the government found itself short of revenue, it could always borrow additional funds from private sources. These reformers, in fact, viewed government borrowing as a crucial antidepression tool. Those who lent the government money would receive a return on their investment; those who received government assistance

would have additional income to spend on consumer goods; and manufacturers would profit from increases in consumer spending. Government borrowing, in short, would stimulate the circulation of money through the economy and end the depression. This fiscal policy, a reversal of the conventional wisdom that government should always balance its budget, would in the 1940s come to be known as Keynesianism, after John Maynard Keynes, the British economist who had been its most forceful advocate.

Many politicians and economists rejected the notion that increased government spending and the deliberate buildup of federal deficits would lead to prosperity. Roosevelt was not easily convinced that he should put aside his concern for fiscal restraint and balanced budgets. But in 1935, as the nation entered its sixth year of the depression,

he was willing to give the new ideas a try. Reform-minded members of the 1934 Congress were eager for a new round of legislation directed more to the needs of ordinary Americans than to the needs of big business.

Legislation

Congress passed much of that legislation in January to June 1935—a period that came to be known as the Second New Deal. Two of the acts were of historic importance: the Social Security Act and the National Labor Relations Act. The Social Security Act, passed in May, required the states to set up welfare funds from which money would be disbursed to the elderly poor, the unemployed, unmarried mothers with dependent children, and the disabled. It also enrolled a majority of working Americans in a pension

HISTORY THROUGH FILM

Mr. Deeds Goes to Town (1936)

Mr. Deeds Goes to Town was one of several films made by Frank Capra, the most popular director of the 1930s, in which he charmed audiences with fables of simple, small-town heroes vanquishing the evil forces of wealth and decadence. The heroic ordinary American in *Mr. Deeds* is Longfellow Deeds from Mandrake Falls, Vermont, who goes to New York City to claim a fortune left to him by a deceased uncle. Deciding to give the fortune away, he becomes the laughingstock of slick city lawyers, hardboiled newspapermen and women, cynical literati, and self-styled aristocrats. He also becomes a hero to the unemployed and downtrodden to whom he wishes to give the money. By making the conflict between the wealthy and ordinary Americans central to this story, Capra illuminated convictions that were popular in 1930s politics, as expressed by the New Deal.

The movie delivers its serious message, however, in an entertaining and often hilarious style. Capra was a master

Directed by Frank Capra. Starring Gary Cooper (Longfellow Deeds), Jean Arthur (Babe Bennett), Lionel Stander (Cornelius Cobb), George Bancroft (McWade), and H. B. Warner (Judge Walker).

of what became known as "screwball" comedy. Longfellow Deeds slides down banisters, locks his bodyguards in a closet, uses the main hall of his inherited mansion as an echo chamber, punches a famous intellectual in the "kisser" (face), and turns his own trial for insanity into a delightful attack on the pretensions and peculiarities of corporate lawyers, judges, and psychiatrists. Central to the story, too, is an alternately amusing and serious love story between Deeds and a newspaperwoman, Babe Bennett (Jean Arthur). Bennett insinuates herself into Deeds's life by pretending to be a destitute woman without work, shelter, family, or friends. Deeds has long dreamed about rescuing a "lady in distress," and he falls for the beautiful Bennett. Bennett, in turn, uses her privileged access to Deeds to learn about his foibles and to mock them (and him) in newspaper stories written for a ruthless and scandal-hungry public. But Deeds's idealism, honesty, and virtue overwhelm Bennett's cynicism and cause her to fall in love

program that guaranteed them a steady income upon retirement. A federal system of employer and employee taxation was set up to fund the pensions. Despite limitations on coverage and inadequate pension levels, the Social Security Act of 1935 provided a sturdy foundation on which future presidents and congresses would erect the American welfare state.

Equally historic was the passage, in June, of the National Labor Relations Act (NLRA). This act delivered what the NRA had only promised: the right of every worker to join a union of his or her own choosing and the obligation of employers to bargain with that union in good faith. The NLRA, also called the Wagner Act after its Senate sponsor, Robert Wagner of New York, set up a National Labor Relations Board (NLRB) to supervise union elections and to investigate claims of unfair labor

practices. The NLRB was to be staffed by federal appointees, who would have the power to impose fines on employers who violated the law. Union leaders hailed the act as their Magna Carta.

Congress also passed the Holding Company Act to break up the 13 utility companies that controlled 75 percent of the nation's electric power. It passed the Wealth Tax Act, which increased tax rates on the wealthy from 59 to 75 percent, and on corporations from 13.75 to 15 percent; and it passed the Banking Act, which strengthened the power of the Federal Reserve Board over its member banks. It created the Rural Electrification Administration (REA) to bring electric power to rural households. Finally, it passed the huge $5 billion Emergency Relief Appropriation Act. Roosevelt funneled part of this sum to the PWA and the CCC and used another part to create the National

with him. By movie's end, she has proclaimed her love and seems ready to return with Deeds to Mandrake Falls, where she will become his devoted wife and the nurturing mother of his children.

In Babe Bennett's conversion from tough reporter to female romantic, we can detect the gender conservatism of 1930s culture. The movie suggests that Bennett's early cruelty toward Deeds arose as a consequence of her inappropriate involvement in the rough, male realm of newspaper work. Only by abandoning this realm and returning to the "natural" female realm of hearth and home can she recover her true and soft womanly soul. Thus this movie is as rich a document for exploring attitudes toward male and female behavior as for examining relations between the rich and poor.

Gary Cooper as Longfellow Deeds (center of photo with hand on cheek) during his hilarious insanity trial. Cooper's bodyguard, Lionel Stander (Cobb) sits to the left of Cooper, and Cooper is looking at H. B. Warner (Judge Walker), who is presiding at the trial.

The Granger Collection

The Granger Collection.

WPA MURAL BY ANTON REFREGIER
The WPA funded a vast program of public art that employed thousands of artists and adorned public buildings with murals, paintings, and sculptures. This mural depicts an encounter between a Franciscan monk and Indians at a California mission during the era of Spanish rule.

SELECTED WPA PROJECTS IN NEW YORK CITY, 1938

Construction and Renovation	Education, Health, and Art	Research and Records
East River Drive	Adult education: homemaking, trade and technical skills, and art and culture	Sewage treatment, community health, labor relations, and employment trends surveys
Henry Hudson Parkway		
Bronx sewers	Children's education: remedial reading, lip reading, and field trips	Museum and library catalogs and exhibits
Glendale and Queens public libraries		Municipal office clerical support
King's County Hospital	Prisoners' vocational training, recreation, and nutrition	Government forms standardization
Williamsburg housing project	Dental clinics	
School buildings, prisons, and firehouses	Tuberculosis examination clinics	
Coney Island and Brighton Beach boardwalks	Syphilis and gonorrhea treatment clinics	
Orchard Beach	City hospital kitchen help, orderlies, laboratory technicians, nurses, doctors	
Swimming pools, playgrounds, parks, drinking fountains	Subsistence gardens	
	Sewing rooms	
	Central Park sculpture shop	

Source: John David Millet, *The Works Progress Administration in New York City* (Chicago: Public Administration Service, 1938), pp. 95–126.

Youth Administration (NYA), which provided work and guidance to the nation's youth.

Roosevelt directed most of the new relief money, however, to the Works Progress Administration (WPA) under the direction of Harry Hopkins, now known as the New Deal's "minister of relief." The WPA built or improved thousands of schools, playgrounds, airports, and hospitals. WPA crews raked leaves, cleaned streets, and landscaped cities. In the process, the WPA provided jobs to approximately 30 percent of the nation's jobless.

By the time the decade ended, the WPA, in association with an expanded Reconstruction Finance Corporation, the PWA, and other agencies, had built 500,000 miles of roads, 100,000 bridges, 100,000 public buildings, and 600 airports. The New Deal had transformed America's urban and rural landscapes. The awe generated by these public

works projects helped Roosevelt retain popular support at a time when the success of the New Deal's economic policies was uncertain. The WPA also funded a vast program of public art, supporting the work of thousands of painters, architects, writers, playwrights, actors, and intellectuals. Beyond extending relief to struggling artists, it fostered the creation of art that spoke to the concerns of ordinary Americans, adorned public buildings with colorful murals, and boosted public morale.

Victory in 1936: The New Democratic Coalition

Roosevelt described his Second New Deal as a program to limit the power and privilege of the wealthy few and to increase the security and welfare of ordinary citizens. In his 1936 reelection campaign, he excoriated the corporations as "economic royalists" who had "concentrated into their own hands an almost complete control over other people's property, other people's money, other people's labor—other people's lives." He called on voters to strip the corporations of their power and "save a great and precious form of government for ourselves and the world." American voters responded by handing Roosevelt the greatest landslide victory in the history of American politics. He received 61 percent of the popular vote; Alf Landon of Kansas, his Republican opponent, received only 37 per-

cent. Only two states, Maine and Vermont, representing a mere eight electoral votes, went for Landon.

The 1936 election won the Democratic Party its reputation as the party of reform and the party of the "forgotten American." Of the 6 million Americans who went

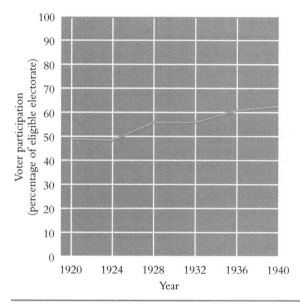

VOTER PARTICIPATION IN PRESIDENTIAL ELECTIONS, 1920–1940

Source: Data from *Historical Statistics of the United States, Colonial Times to 1970* (White Plains, N.Y.: Kraus International, 1989), p. 1071.

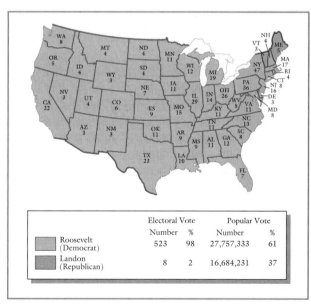

MAP 25.5 PRESIDENTIAL ELECTION, 1936

In 1936, Franklin D. Roosevelt's reelection numbers were overwhelming: 98 percent of the electoral vote, and more than 60 percent of the popular vote. No previous election in American history had been so one-sided.

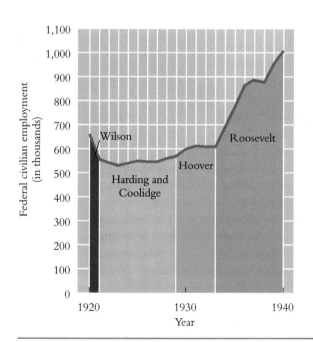

GROWTH IN FEDERAL CIVILIAN EMPLOYMENT, 1920–1940

Source: Data from *Historical Statistics of the United States, Colonial Times to 1970* (White Plains, N.Y.: Kraus International, 1989), p. 1102.

788 CHAPT

to the
nics,
Amer
Black
the "I
would
Roose
many
Act. T
coaliti
the D
ican p

Rhe

Roose
ical th
consic
was a
Comp
tact.
ered t
not co
Labor
Amer
tial n
South
The sl
crats
impro
blacks
effort
tect th
New

R
enthu
the Se
a cons
nevill
contra
a grou
cratic
west
cludec
Bamb
and tl
tions
Lehm
House
establ
the Ba

MAN OF STEEL

The comic book *Superman* debuted in 1938, with the cover that appears in this reproduction. The character Superman partook of the New Deal's commitment to help ordinary Americans in need while offering men a fantasy about unconquerable male power.

Many artists introduced a strident masculinism into their painting and sculpture. Mighty *Superman*, the new comic-strip hero of 1938, reflected the spirit of the times. Superman was depicted as a working-class hero who, on several occasions, saved workers from coal mine explosions and other disasters caused by the greed and negligence of villainous employers.

Superman's greatest vulnerability, however, other than kryptonite, was his attraction to the sexy and aggressive *working* woman, Lois Lane. He could never resolve his dilemma by marrying Lois and tucking her away in a safe domestic sphere, because the continuation of the comic strip demanded that Superman be repeatedly exposed to kryptonite and female danger. But the producers of male and female images in other mass media, such as the movies, faced no such technical obstacles. Anxious men could take comfort from the conclusion of the movie *Woman of the Year*, in which Spencer Tracy persuades the

ambitious Katharine Hepburn to exchange her successful newspaper career for the bliss of motherhood and home-making. From a thousand different points, 1930s politics and culture made it clear that a woman's proper place was in the home. Faced with such obstacles, it is not surprising that women activists failed to make feminism a major part of New Deal reform.

Labor in Politics and Culture

In 1935, John L. Lewis of the United Mine Workers, Sidney Hillman of the Amalgamated Clothing Workers, and the leaders of six other unions that had seceded from the American Federation of Labor (AFL) cobbled together a new labor organization: The Committee for Industrial Organization (CIO—later renamed the Congress of Industrial Organizations) aspired to organize millions of nonunion workers into unions that would strengthen labor's influence in politics. In 1936, Lewis and Hillman created a second organization, Labor's Non-Partisan League (LNPL), to develop a labor strategy for the 1936 elections. Although professing the league's nonpartisan-ship, Lewis intended from the start that the LNPL's role would be to channel labor's money, energy, and talent into Roosevelt's reelection campaign. Roosevelt welcomed the league's help, and labor would become one of the most important constituencies of the new Democratic coalition. The passage of the Wagner Act and the creation of the NLRB in 1935 enhanced the labor movement's status

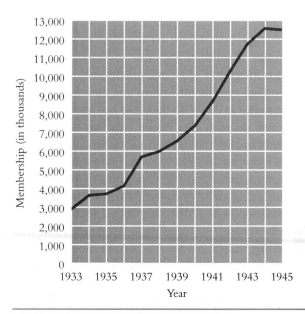

LABOR UNION MEMBERSHIP, 1933–1945

Source: From Christopher Tomlins, "AFL Unions in the 1930s," in Melvyn Dubofsky and Stephen Burwood, eds., *Labor* (New York: Garland, 1990), p. 1023.

and credibility. Membership in labor unions climbed steadily, and in short order, union members began flexing their new muscles.

In late 1936, the United Auto Workers (UAW) took on General Motors, widely regarded as the most powerful corporation in the world. Workers occupied key GM factories in Flint, Michigan, declaring that their sit-down strike would continue until GM agreed to recognize the UAW and negotiate a collective bargaining agreement. Frank Murphy, the pro-labor governor of Michigan, refused to use National Guard troops to evict the strikers, and Roosevelt declined to send federal troops. The 50-year-old practice of using soldiers to break strikes came to an end, and General Motors capitulated after a month of resistance. Soon, the U.S. Steel Corporation, which had defeated unionists in the bloody strike of 1919 (see chapter 23), announced that it was ready to negotiate a contract with the newly formed CIO steelworkers union.

The labor movement's public stature grew along with its size. Many writers and artists, funded through the WPA, depicted the labor movement as the voice of the people and the embodiment of the nation's values. Murals sprang up in post offices and other public buildings featuring portraits of blue-collar Americans at work. Broadway's most celebrated play in 1935 was Clifford Odets's *Waiting for Lefty,* a raw drama about taxi drivers who confront their bosses and organize an honest union. Audiences were so moved by the play that they often spontaneously joined in the final chorus of "Strike, Strike, Strike," the words that ended the play. *Pins and Needles,* a 1937 musical about the hopes and dreams of garment workers, performed by actual members of the International Ladies Garment Workers Union, became the longest-running play in Broadway history (until *Oklahoma!* broke its record of 1,108 performances in 1943).

Similarly, many of the most popular novels and movies of the 1930s celebrated the decency, honesty, and patriotism of ordinary Americans. In *Mr. Deeds Goes to Town* (1936) and *Mr. Smith Goes to Washington* (1939), Frank Capra delighted movie audiences with fables of simple, small-town heroes vanquishing the evil forces of wealth and decadence. Likewise, in *The Grapes of Wrath,* the best-selling novel of 1939, John Steinbeck told an epic tale of an Oklahoma family's fortitude in surviving eviction from their land, migrating westward, and suffering exploitation in the "promised land" of California. In 1940, John Ford turned Steinbeck's novel into one of that year's highest-grossing and most acclaimed movies. Moviegoers found special meaning in the declaration of one of the story's main characters, Ma Joad: "We'll go on forever . . . 'cause we're the people." In themselves and in one another, Americans seemed to discover the resolve they needed to

rebuild a culture that had surrendered its identity to corporations and business.

John Steinbeck wrote about the Okie migrants to California as an outsider. But the Okies produced a writer and musician of their own who became, in the late 1930s, a popular folk singer. Born in 1913 in Okemah, Oklahoma, Woody Guthrie grew up in nearby Pampa, Texas. He wasn't born poor—his father was a small businessman and a local politician—but by the time he reached his 20s, Guthrie had known a great deal of hardship: his father's business failed, three family homes burned down, one sister died from burns, and then the drought and dust storms struck. In the 1930s, Guthrie joined the large migration of Okies to California. There, his musical gifts were discovered, chiefly because radio stations, in particular, were keen to put "singing cowboys" on the air. Guthrie had emerged from a country music tradition in Texas and Oklahoma and found an immediate audience among the many people from those states who had gone to California. But Guthrie quickly developed a far broader appeal as he cast himself as the bard of ordinary Americans everywhere. He loved America for the beauty of its landscape and its people, sentiments he expressed in one of his most

From the Collections of the Library of Congress.

WOODY GUTHRIE

A bard from Okemah, Oklahoma, embraced by millions for his homespun melodies and lyrics and for his hopeful message that Americans could survive the Depression with their dignity and sense of humor intact.

popular songs, "This Land Is Your Land," which he wrote in 1940 in response to Irving Berlin's "God Bless America" (a song Guthrie did not like because he thought it comforted people with a false sense of complacency). Guthrie did not possess a refined singing voice, but his "hillbilly" lyrics, melodies, and humor were inventive and often inspiring. He would become a powerful influence on subsequent generations of musicians, including such major figures as Bob Dylan and Bruce Springsteen.

Most comfortable on the road and away from his family, Guthrie traveled ceaselessly in the 1930s, from Los Angeles to New York and from Texas to Washington state. The more he learned about the hardships of individual Americans, the angrier and more politically active he became. He drew close to the labor movement and to the Communist Party, and increasingly, in his writings and songs, he criticized the industrialists, financiers, and their political agents who, he believed, had brought the calamity of the Depression on America. But Guthrie always associated his criticism with the hope that the working people of America, if united, could take back their land—which is the message he meant to convey when he sang "This Land Is Your Land"—and restore its greatness. The optimism of his message underscored how much the cultural mood had changed since the early 1930s. In his focus on ordinary working Americans, in his hope for the future, and in his fusion of dissent and patriotism, Guthrie was emblematic of the dominant stream of culture and politics in the late 1930s.

🌐 America's Minorities and the New Deal

1930s reformers generally believed that issues of capitalism's viability, economic recovery, and the inequality of wealth and power outweighed problems of racial and ethnic discrimination; only in the case of American Indians did New Dealers pass legislation specifically designed to improve a minority's social and economic position. Because they were disproportionately poor, most minority groups did profit from the populist and pro-labor character of New Deal reforms, but the gains were distributed unevenly. Eastern and Southern European ethnics benefited the most, and African Americans and Mexican Americans advanced the least.

Eastern and Southern European Ethnics

Eastern and Southern European immigrants and their children had begun mobilizing politically in the 1920s in response to religious and racial discrimination (see chapter 24). Roosevelt understood their political importance well, for he was a product of New York Democratic politics, where men such as Robert Wagner and Al Smith had begun to organize the "ethnic vote" even before 1920 (see chapter 21). He made sure that a significant portion of New Deal monies for welfare, building and road construction, and unemployment relief reached the urban areas where most European ethnics lived. As a result, Jewish and Catholic Americans, especially those descended from Eastern and Southern European immigrants, voted for Roosevelt in overwhelming numbers. The New Deal did not eliminate anti-Semitism and anti-Catholicism from American society, but it did allow millions of European ethnics to believe, for the first time, that they would overcome the second-class status they had long endured.

Eastern and Southern European ethnics also benefited from their strong working-class presence. Forming one of the largest groups in the mass-production industries of the Northeast, Midwest, and West, they formed a large part of the labor movement's new membership. Roosevelt accommodated himself to their wishes because he understood and feared the power they wielded through their labor organizations.

African Americans

The New Deal did more to reproduce patterns of racial discrimination than to advance the cause of racial equality. African Americans who belonged to CIO unions or who lived in northern cities benefited from New Deal programs, but most blacks lived in the rural South, where they were barred from voting, largely excluded from AAA programs, and denied federal protection in their efforts to form agricultural unions. The CCC ran separate camps for black and white youth. The TVA hired few blacks. Those enrolled in the CWA and other work-relief programs frequently received less pay than whites for doing the same jobs. Roosevelt consistently refused to support legislation to make lynching a federal crime.

This failure to push a strong civil-rights agenda did not mean that New Dealers were racist. Eleanor Roosevelt spoke out frequently against racial injustice. In 1939, she resigned from the Daughters of the American Revolution when the organization refused to allow black opera singer Marian Anderson to perform in its concert hall. She then pressured the federal government into granting Anderson permission to sing from the steps of the Lincoln Memorial. On Easter Sunday, 75,000 people gathered to hear Anderson and to demonstrate their support for racial equality. The president did not attend.

Roosevelt did eliminate segregationist practices in the federal government that had been in place since Woodrow

Wilson's presidency. He appointed Mary McLeod Bethune, Robert Weaver, William Hastie, and other African Americans to important second-level posts in his administration. Working closely with each other in what came to be known as the Black Cabinet, these officials fought hard to end discrimination in New Deal programs.

Roosevelt, however, refused to support the Black Cabinet if it meant alienating white southern senators who controlled key congressional committees. He believed that pushing for civil rights would cost him the support of the white South. Meanwhile, African Americans and their supporters were not yet strong enough as an electoral constituency or as a reform movement to force Roosevelt to accede to their wishes.

Mexican Americans

The Mexican American experience in the Great Depression was particularly harsh. In 1931, Hoover's secretary of labor, William N. Doak, announced a plan for repatriating illegal aliens (returning them to their land of origin) and giving their jobs to American citizens. The federal campaign quickly focused on Mexican immigrants in California and the Southwest. The U.S. Immigration Service staged a

---

MUSICAL LINK TO THE PAST

An African American Rhapsody

Songwriter: Duke Ellington

Title: "Creole Rhapsody Parts One and Two" (1931—the second recording)

Performers: Duke Ellington and His Orchestra

By 1931, Duke Ellington had established himself as the premier African American bandleader, his hit songs airing nightly courtesy of a live national radio hook-up (the first for any black act) emanating from Harlem's Cotton Club. But Ellington was not satisfied with popularity and fame. "I have always been a firm believer in musical experimentation," he proclaimed during this period. "To stand still musically is equivalent to losing ground." Ellington wished to be viewed as a serious artist and composer, and "Creole Rhapsody" represented one of his first major bids to cultivate this image. Most pop records seldom broke the three-minute barrier, but "Creole" lasted nine minutes, spanning two sides of a 78-RPM record. While jazz and blues artists generally composed within 8-, 12-, and 16-bar forms, Ellington experimented with different phrase lengths. In an era when blacks were primarily associated with "torrid" dance records, the shifting tempos of "Creole" marked it as a record for concentrated listening. Ellington also composed the solos to ensure that they jelled with his elaborate arrangement, which did away with musical improvisation, a trademark of jazz and blues performances. Ellington was more involved with recording technique than most artists, sometimes placing microphones far away from his players to achieve a more evocative sound.

"Creole Rhapsody" reached only minor hit status, but Ellington and his manager Irving Mills took advantage of the event of this unprecedented recording to bolster Ellington's image as a serious artist, a status that no other African Americans of his period had achieved in the segregated white-dominated popular music marketplace. In contrast to the denigrating stereotypes that accompanied the appearance of most blacks in the mass media, Ellington was respectfully portrayed in the manner of a classical conductor, usually clad in a tuxedo and tails, baton in his hand.

Not all contemporary observers endorsed the idea of Ellington as a major composer. The English critic Constant Lambert wrote in 1934 that "Ellington is definitely a *petit maitre*," a "small master" not capable of extended composition. Many music lovers, however, embraced "Creole Rhapsody." The New York School of Music named it the best composition of the year because "it portrayed Negro life as no other piece had." Ellington attempted to keep the critics, both the laudatory and castigating ones, at a distance and to keep searching for musical innovation. He almost never took a formal political stand or made a speech demanding civil rights for blacks during the 1930s, choosing to let his music and his reputation as an innovative band leader speak for themselves.

1. From listening to "Creole Rhapsody," can you discern what the New York School of Music meant in celebrating this composition as a unique portrait of Negro life?

Listen to an audio recording of this music on the Musical Links to the Past CD.

series of highly publicized raids, rounded up large numbers of Mexicans and Mexican Americans, and demanded that each detainee prove his or her legal status. Those who failed to produce the necessary documentation were deported. Local and state governments pressured many more Mexicans into leaving. The combined efforts of federal, state, and local governments created a climate of fear in Mexican communities that prompted 500,000 to return to Mexico by 1935. This total equaled the number of Mexicans who had come to the United States in the 1920s. Los Angeles lost one-third of its Mexican population. Included in repatriate ranks were a significant number of legal immigrants who were unable to produce their immigration papers, the American-born children of illegals, and some Mexican Americans who had lived in the Southwest for generations.

The advent of the New Deal in 1933 eased but did not eliminate pressure on Chicano communities. New Deal agencies made more money available for relief, thereby lightening the burden on state and local governments. But federal laws, more often than not, failed to dissuade local officials from continuing their campaign against Mexican immigrants. Where Mexicans gained access to relief rolls, they received payments lower than those given to "Anglos" (whites) or were compelled to accept tough agricultural jobs that paid less than living wages.

Life grew harder for immigrant Mexicans who stayed behind. The Mexican cultural renaissance that had arisen in 1920s Los Angeles (see chapter 24) stalled. Hounded by government officials, Mexicans everywhere sought to escape public attention and scrutiny. In Los Angeles, where their influence had been felt throughout the city in the 1920s, they retreated into the separate community of East Los Angeles. To many, they became the "invisible minority." Mexicans and Mexican Americans who lived in urban areas and worked in blue-collar industries, however, did benefit from New Deal programs. In Los Angeles, for example, Chicanos employed in canneries, in garment and furniture shops, and on the docks responded to the New Deal's pro-labor legislation by joining unions in large numbers and winning concessions from their employers. Most Chicanos, however, lived in rural areas and labored in agricultural jobs, and the New Deal offered them little help. The National Labor Relations Act did not protect their right to organize unions, and the Social Security Act excluded them from the new federal welfare system.

American Indians

From the 1880s until the early 1930s, federal policy had contributed to the elimination of American Indians as a distinctive population. The Dawes Act of 1887 (see chap-

INDIAN CHILDREN

An Arnold Rothstein photograph depicting three Indian children on the Mescalero Reservation in New Mexico in 1936.

From the Collections of the Library of Congress.

ter 19) had called for tribal lands to be broken up and allotted to individual owners in the hope that Indians would adopt the work habits of white farmers. But American Indians had proved stubbornly loyal to their languages, religions, and cultures. Few of them succeeded as farmers, and many lost land to white speculators. By 1933, nearly half the American Indians living on reservations whose land had been allotted were landless, and many who retained allotments held land that was largely desert or semidesert.

The shrinking land base in combination with a growing population deepened American Indian poverty. The assimilationist pressures on American Indians, meanwhile, reached a climax in the intolerant 1920s when the Bureau of Indian Affairs (BIA) outlawed Indian religious ceremonies, forced children from tribal communities into federal boarding schools, banned polygamy, and imposed limits on the length of men's hair.

Government officials working in the Hoover administration began to question this draconian policy, but its reversal had to await the New Deal and Roosevelt's appointment of John Collier as the commissioner of the BIA. Collier pressured the CCC, AAA, and other New Deal agencies to employ Indians on projects that improved reservation land and trained Indians in land conservation methods. He prevailed on Congress to pass the Pueblo Relief Act of 1933, which compensated Pueblos for land taken from them in the 1920s, and the Johnson-O'Malley Act of 1934, which funded states to provide for Indian

health care, welfare, and education. As part of his campaign to make the BIA more responsive to American Indian needs, Collier increased the number of Indian employees of the BIA from a paltry few hundred in 1933 to a respectable 4,600 in 1940.

Collier also took steps to abolish federal boarding schools, encourage enrollment in local public schools, and establish community day schools. He insisted that American Indians be allowed to practice their traditional religions, and he created the Indian Arts and Crafts Board in 1935 to nurture traditional Indian artists and to help them market their works.

The centerpiece of Collier's reform strategy was the Indian Reorganization Act (also known as the Wheeler-Howard Act) of 1934, which revoked the allotment provisions of the Dawes Act. The IRA restored land to tribes, granted Indians the right to establish constitutions and bylaws for self-government, and provided support for new tribal corporations that would regulate the use of communal lands. This landmark act signaled the government's recognition that American Indian tribes possessed the right to chart their own political, cultural, and economic futures. It reflected Collier's commitment to "cultural pluralism," a doctrine that celebrated the diversity of peoples and cultures in American society and sought to protect that diversity against the pressures of assimilation. Collier hoped that the IRA would invigorate traditional Indian cultures and tribal societies and sustain both for generations. Cultural pluralism was not a popular creed in America during the depression years, which makes its acceptance as the rationale for the IRA all the more remarkable.

Collier encountered opposition everywhere: from Protestant missionaries and cultural conservatives who wanted to continue an assimilationist policy; from white farmers and businessmen who feared that the new legislation would restrict their access to Native American land; and even from a sizable number of Indian groups, some of which had embraced assimilation and others that viewed the IRA cynically, as one more attempt by the federal government to impose "the white man's will" on the Indian peoples. This opposition made the IRA a more modest bill than the one Collier had originally championed.

A vocal minority of Indians continued to oppose the act even after its passage. The Navajo, the nation's largest tribe, voted to reject its terms along with 76 other tribes. Still, 181 tribes, nearly 70 percent of the total, supported Collier's reform and began organizing new governments under the IRA. Although their quest for independence would suffer setbacks, as Congress and the BIA continued to interfere with their economic and political affairs, these tribes gained significant measures of freedom and autonomy during the New Deal.

The New Deal Abroad

When he first entered office, Roosevelt seemed to favor a nationalist approach to international relations. The United States, he believed, should pursue foreign policies to benefit its domestic affairs, without regard for the effects of those policies on world trade and international stability. Thus, in June 1933, Roosevelt abruptly pulled the United States out of the World Economic Conference in London, a meeting called by leading nations to strengthen the gold standard and thereby stabilize the value of their currencies. Roosevelt feared that the United States would be forced into an agreement designed to keep the gold content of the dollar high and U.S. commodity prices low, which would frustrate New Deal efforts to inflate the prices of agricultural and industrial goods.

Soon after his withdrawal from the London conference, however, Roosevelt put the United States on a more internationalist course. In November 1933, he became the first president to recognize the Soviet Union and to establish diplomatic ties with its Communist rulers. In December 1933, he inaugurated a Good Neighbor Policy toward Latin America by formally renouncing U.S. rights to intervene in the affairs of Latin American nations. To back up his pledge, Roosevelt ordered home the Marines stationed in Haiti and Nicaragua, scuttled the Platt Amendment that had given the United States control over the Cuban government since 1901, and granted Panama more political autonomy and a greater administrative role in operating the Panama Canal (see chapter 22).

None of this, however, meant that the United States had given up its influence over Latin America. When a 1934 revolution brought a radical government to power in Cuba, the United States ambassador there worked with conservative Cubans to replace it with a regime more favorable to U.S. interests. The United States did refrain from sending troops to Cuba. It also kept its troops at home in 1936 when a radical government in Mexico nationalized several U.S.-owned and British-owned petroleum companies. The United States merely demanded that the new Mexican government compensate the oil companies for their lost property—a demand that Mexico eventually met. Although the United States was still the dominant power in hemispheric affairs, its newfound restraint inspired Latin American hopes that a new era had dawned.

The Roosevelt administration's recognition of the Soviet Union and embrace of the Good Neighbor Policy can be seen as an international expression of the liberal principles that guided its domestic policies. These diplomatic initiatives, however, also reflected Roosevelt's interest in stimulating international trade. American businessmen wanted access to the Soviet Union's domestic market.

Latin America was already a major market for the United States, but one in need of greater stability. To win the support of American traders and investors, Roosevelt stressed how the Good Neighbor Policy would improve the region's business climate.

Roosevelt further expressed his interest in building international trade through his support for the Reciprocal Trade Agreement, passed by Congress in 1934. This act allowed his administration to lower U.S. tariffs by as much as 50 percent in exchange for similar reductions by other nations. By the end of 1935, the United States had negotiated reciprocal trade agreements with 14 countries. Roosevelt's emphasis on international trade—a move consonant with the Second New Deal's program of increasing the circulation of goods and money through the economy—further solidified support for the New Deal in parts of the business community, especially among those firms, such as United Fruit and Coca-Cola, with large overseas investments.

Actually increasing the volume of international trade was more difficult than passing legislation to encourage it. In Germany and Italy, belligerent nationalists Adolf Hitler and Benito Mussolini told their people that the solution to their ills lay not in foreign trade but in military strength and conquest. Throughout the world, similar appeals to national pride proved more popular than calls for tariff reductions and international trade. In the face of this historical current, the New Deal's internationalist economic policies made little headway.

Stalemate, 1937–1940

By 1937 and 1938, the New Deal had begun to lose momentum. One reason was an emerging split between working-class and middle-class Democrats. After the UAW's victory over General Motors in 1937, other workers began to imitate the successful tactics of the Flint, Michigan, militants. Sit-down strikes spread to many industries and regions, a development that many middle-class Americans found disturbing.

The Court-Packing Fiasco

The president's proposal on February 5, 1937, to alter the makeup of the Supreme Court exacerbated middle-class fears. Roosevelt asked Congress to give him the power to appoint one new Supreme Court justice for every member

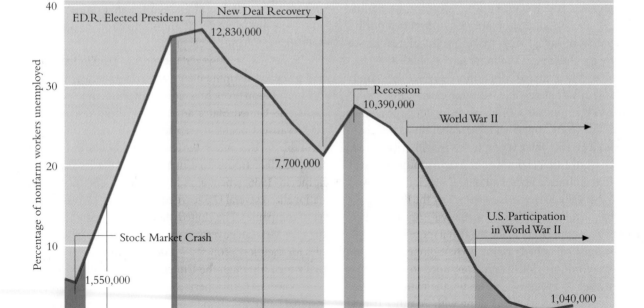

UNEMPLOYMENT IN THE NONFARM LABOR FORCE, 1929–1945

Source: Data from *Historical Statistics of the United States, Colonial Times to 1970* (White Plains, N.Y.: Kraus International, 1989), p. 126.

of the court who was older than age 70 and who had served for at least 10 years. His stated reason was that the current justices were too old and feeble to handle the large volume of cases coming before them. But his real purpose was to prevent the conservative justices on the court—most of whom had been appointed by Republican presidents—from dismantling his New Deal. His proposal, if accepted, would have given him the authority to appoint six additional justices, thereby securing a pro–New Deal majority.

The president seemed genuinely surprised by the storm of indignation that greeted his "court-packing" proposal. Roosevelt's political acumen had apparently been dulled by his 1936 victory. His inflated sense of power infuriated many who had previously been New Deal enthusiasts. Although working-class support for Roosevelt remained strong, many middle-class voters turned away from the New Deal. In 1937 and 1938, a conservative opposition took shape, uniting Republicans, conservative Democrats (many of them southerners), and civil libertarians who were determined to protect private property and government integrity.

Ironically, Roosevelt's court-packing scheme may have been unnecessary. In March 1937, just one month after he proposed his plan, Supreme Court Justice Owen J. Roberts, a former opponent of New Deal programs, decided to support them. In April and May, the Court upheld the constitutionality of the Wagner Act and Social Security Act, both by a 5-to-4 margin. The principal reforms of the New Deal would endure. Roosevelt allowed his court-reform proposal to die in Congress that summer. Within three years, five of the aging justices had retired, giving Roosevelt the opportunity to fashion a court more to his liking. Nonetheless, Roosevelt's reputation had suffered.

The Recession of 1937–1938

Whatever hope Roosevelt may have had for a quick recovery from the court-packing fiasco was dashed by a sharp recession that struck the country in late 1937 and 1938. The New Deal programs of 1935 had stimulated the economy, prompting Roosevelt to scale back relief programs. Meanwhile, new payroll taxes took $2 billion from wage earners' salaries to finance the Social Security pension fund even though the government did not intend to begin paying benefits until 1941. Thus, the government substantially shrunk the volume of dollars it was putting into circulation. Starved for money, the economy and stock market crashed once again. Unemployment, which had fallen to 14 percent, shot back up to 20 percent. In the 1938 elections, voters vented their frustration by electing many

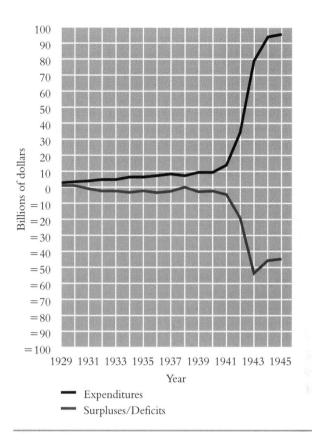

FEDERAL EXPENDITURES AND SURPLUSES/DEFICITS, 1929–1945

Source: Data from *Historical Statistics of the United States, Colonial Times to 1970* (White Plains, N.Y.: Kraus International, 1989), p. 1105.

conservative Democrats and Republicans who were opposed to the New Deal. These conservatives could not dismantle the New Deal reforms already in place, but they did block the passage of new programs.

Conclusion

Roosevelt first assumed the presidency in the same week that Adolf Hitler established a Nazi dictatorship in Germany. Some feared that Roosevelt, by accumulating more power into the hands of the federal government than had ever been held in peacetime, aspired to autocratic rule. Nothing of the sort happened. Roosevelt and the New Dealers not only strengthened democracy, they also inspired millions of Americans who had never before voted to go to the polls. Groups that had been marginalized—Eastern and Southern European ethnics, unskilled workers, American Indians—now believed that their political activism could make a difference.

Not everyone benefited to the same degree from the broadening of American democracy. Northern factory

workers, farm owners, European American ethnics, and middle-class consumers (especially homeowners) were among the groups who benefited most. In contrast, the socialist and communist elements of the labor movement failed to achieve their radical demands. Southern industrial workers, black and white, benefited little from New Deal reforms; so did farm laborers. Feminists made no headway. African Americans and Mexican Americans gained meager influence over public policy.

Of course, New Deal reforms might not have mattered to any group if the Second World War had not rescued the New Deal economic program. With government war orders flooding factories from 1941 on, the economy grew vigorously, unemployment vanished, and prosperity finally returned. The architects of the Second New Deal, who had argued that large government expenditures would stimulate consumer demand and trigger economic recovery, were vindicated.

The war also solidified the political reforms of the 1930s: an increased role for the government in regulating the economy and in ensuring the social welfare of those unable to help themselves; strong state support of unionization, agricultural subsidies, and progressive tax policies; and the use of government power and money to develop the West and Southwest. In sharp contrast to progressivism, the reforms of the New Deal endured. Voters returned Roosevelt to office for unprecedented third and fourth terms. And these same voters remained wedded for the next 40 years to Roosevelt's central idea: that a powerful state would enhance the pursuit of liberty and equality.

SUGGESTED READINGS

T. H. Watkins, *The Great Depression: America in the 1930s* (1993), provides a broad overview of society and politics during the 1930s. No work better conveys the tumult and drama of that era than **Arthur M. Schlesinger Jr.'s** three-volume *The Age of Roosevelt: The Crisis of the Old Order* (1957), *The Coming of the New Deal* (1958), and *The Politics of Upheaval* (1960). On Hoover's failure to restore prosperity and popular morale, see **David Burner, *Herbert Hoover: A Public Life*** (1979). The most complete biography of FDR, and one that is remarkably good at balancing Roosevelt's life and times, is **Kenneth S. Davis, *FDR*** (1972–1993), in four volumes. On Eleanor Roosevelt, see **Blanche Wiesen Cook, *Eleanor Roosevelt,*** vol. 1 (1992). On the New Deal, see **William E. Leuchtenberg, *Franklin D. Roosevelt and the New Deal, 1932–1940*** (1963), **Anthony J. Badger, *The New Deal: The Depression Years, 1933–1940*** (1989), and **Steve Fraser and Gary Gerstle, eds., *The Rise and Fall of the New Deal Order, 1930–1980*** (1989). **Ellis Hawley, *The New Deal and the Problem of Monopoly*** (1966), is essential to understand the First New Deal's industrial policy, while **Steven Fraser, *Labor Will Rule: Sidney Hillman and the Rise of American Labor*** (1991), examines the role of the labor movement in national politics. **Michael Denning, *The Cultural Front: The Laboring of American Culture in the Twentieth Century*** (1996), is essential reading on the centrality of labor and the "common man" to literary and popular culture in the 1930s,

as is **Lary May, *The Big Tomorrow: Hollywood and the Politics of the American Way*** (2000). For the economic and cultural ties between the New Deal and the rebirth of the labor movement, see **Lizabeth Cohen, *Making a New Deal: Industrial Workers in Chicago, 1919–1939*** (1990). **Irving Howe and Lewis Coser, *The American Communist Party: A Critical History, 1919–1957*** (1957), is still the best single-volume history of the Communist Party during the 1930s. **Harvard Sitkoff, *A New Deal for Blacks*** (1978), is a wide-ranging examination of the place of African Americans in New Deal reform. **Abraham Hoffman, *Unwanted Mexican Americans in the Great Depression: Repatriation Pressures, 1929–1939*** (1974), analyzes the repatriation campaign, while the problems of illegal alienage created by that campaign are expertly analyzed in **Mae Ngai, *Impossible Subjects: Illegal Aliens and the Making of Modern America*** (2004). The importance of John Collier and the Indian Reorganization Act are treated well in **Lawrence C. Kelly, *The Assault on Assimilation: John Collier and the Origins of Indian Policy Reform*** (1983). **James T. Patterson, *Congressional Conservatism and the New Deal*** (1967), expertly analyzes the growing opposition to the New Deal in the late 1930s, while **Alan Brinkley, *The End of Reform: New Deal Liberalism in Recession and War*** (1995), provocatively examines the efforts of New Dealers to adjust their beliefs and programs as they lost support, momentum, and confidence in the late 1930s.

AMERICAN JOURNEY ONLINE

AND

INFOTRAC COLLEGE EDITION

Visit the source collections at www.ajaccess.wadsworth.com and infotrac.thomsonlearning.com and use the Search function with the following key terms to explore documents, images, audio and video clips, articles, and commentary related to the material in this chapter.

Black Tuesday   Tennessee Valley Authority
The Great Depression   National Recovery Administration
Herbert Hoover   John L. Lewis
Bonus Army   Works Progress Administration
Franklin D. Roosevelt   Eleanor Roosevelt
New Deal

GRADE AIDS

Visit the Liberty Equality Power Companion Web Site for resources specific to this textbook: http://history.wadsworth.com/murrin_LEP4e

The CD in the back of this book and the U.S. History Resource Center at http://history.wadsworth.com/u.s./ offer a variety of tools to help you succeed in this course, including access to quizzes; images; documents; interactive simulations, maps, and timelines; movie explorations; and a wealth of other sources.

Chapter 26

America during the Second World War

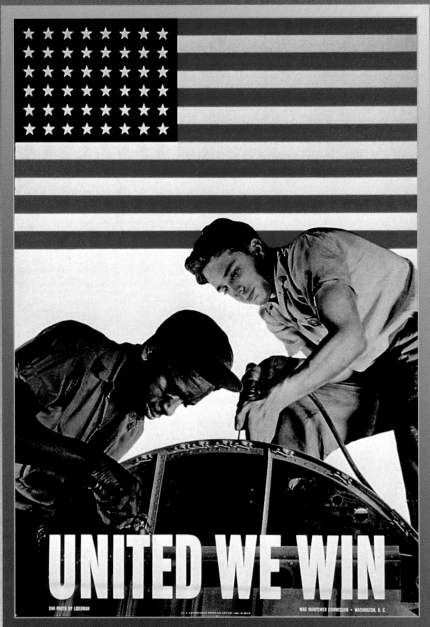

Hoover Institute Archives, Stanford University. U560.

"UNITED WE WIN"
Government posters during the Second World War attempted to mute class and racial divisions and offer images of Americans united against fascism.

CHAPTER OUTLINE

The Second World War, a struggle of unprecedented destruction that brought death to some *60 million* people worldwide, transformed American life. During a decade-long process, the United States abandoned isolationism, moved toward military engagement on the side of the Allies, and emerged triumphant in a global war in which U.S. forces fought and died in North Africa, Europe, and Asia.

To succeed militarily, the United States greatly expanded the power of its national government. The mobilization for war finally brought the country out of the Great Depression and produced significant economic and social change. The nation's productive capacity—spurred by new technologies and by a new working relationship among government, business, labor, and scientific researchers—dwarfed that of every other nation and provided the economic basis for military victory.

At home, citizens reconsidered the meanings of liberty and equality. A massive propaganda effort to bolster popular support for wartime sacrifice presented the conflict as a struggle to protect and preserve "the American way of life." This message inevitably raised questions about how to define the American way. How would America, while striving for victory, reorder its economy, its culture, and the social patterns that had shaped racial, ethnic, and gender relationships during the 1930s? What processes of reconstruction, at home and abroad, might be required to build a prosperous and lasting peace?

CHAPTER FOCUS

♦ How did events in Asia and in Europe affect the domestic debate over isolationism versus intervention in the war?
♦ What central strategic issues arose in fighting the war in both Europe and Asia?
♦ How did mobilization for war produce economic and social changes in American life?
♦ What major institutions and policies shaped the reconstruction of the postwar world?

🌐 The Road to War: Aggression and Response

The road to the Second World War began at least two decades before it started. Resentments growing out of the First World War, together with the worldwide depression of the 1930s, set the stage for international political instability. In Japan, Italy, and Germany, economic collapse and rising unemployment created political conditions that nurtured ultranationalist movements promising recovery through military buildup and territorial expansion. Elsewhere in Europe and in the United States itself, economic problems made governments turn inward, concentrating on domestic ills and avoiding expensive foreign entanglements. As international economic and political conditions deteriorated, Americans debated how to respond to acts of aggression overseas.

The Rise of Aggressor States

War began first in Asia. On September 18, 1931, Japanese military forces seized Manchuria and created a puppet state called Manchukuo. This action violated the League of Nations charter, the Washington treaties, and the Kellogg-Briand Pact (see chapter 24). Japanese military leaders, who had urged their nation to create an Asian empire, won their gamble: The international community was too preoccupied with domestic economic problems to counter Japan's move. In the United States, the Hoover-Stimson Doctrine declared a policy of "nonrecognition" of Manchukuo, and the League of Nations also condemned Japan's action. These stands were not backed by military force, however, and Japan first ignored them and then withdrew from the League of Nations in 1935.

Meanwhile, ultranationalist states in Europe also sought to alleviate domestic ills through military aggression. Adolf Hitler's National Socialist (Nazi) Party came to power in Germany in 1933 and instituted a fascist regime, a one-party dictatorial state. Hitler denounced the Versailles peace settlement of 1919, blamed Germany's plight on a Jewish conspiracy, proclaimed the genetic superiority of the Aryan race of German-speaking peoples, and promised to build a new empire (the Third Reich). The regime renounced the League of Nations in 1933 and reinstituted compulsory military service. Nearly doubling Germany's military expenditures (a blatant violation of the Treaty of Versailles), Hitler sought to create an air force and an army that would outnumber those of France, Germany's major European rival. The fascist government of Italy, headed by Benito Mussolini, who had come to power in 1922, also

C H R O N O L O G Y	
1931	Japanese forces seize Manchuria
1933	Hitler takes power in Germany
1936	Spanish Civil War begins • Germany and Italy agree to cooperate as the Axis Powers
1937	Neutrality Act broadens provisions of Neutrality Acts of 1935 and 1936 • Roosevelt makes "Quarantine" speech • Japan invades China
1938	France and Britain appease Hitler at Munich
1939	Hitler and Stalin sign Soviet–German nonaggression pact • Hitler invades Poland; war breaks out in Europe • Congress amends Neutrality Act to assist Allies
1940	Paris falls after German *blitzkreig* (June) • Battle of Britain carried to U.S. by radio broadcasts • Roosevelt makes "destroyers-for-bases" deal with Britain • Selective Service Act passed • Roosevelt wins third term
1941	Lend-Lease established • Roosevelt creates Fair Employment Practices Commission • Roosevelt and Churchill proclaim the Atlantic Charter • U.S. engages in undeclared naval war in North Atlantic • Congress narrowly repeals Neutrality Act • Japanese forces attack Pearl Harbor (December 7)
1942	Rio de Janeiro Conference (January) • President signs Executive Order 9066 for internment of Japanese Americans (February) • General MacArthur driven from Philippines (May) • U.S. victorious in Battle of Midway (June) • German army defeated at Battle of Stalingrad (August) • Operation TORCH begins (November)
1943	Axis armies in North Africa surrender (May) • Allies invade Sicily (July) and Italy (September) • "Zoot suit" incidents in Los Angeles; racial violence in Detroit • Allies begin drive toward Japan through South Pacific islands
1944	Allies land at Normandy (D-Day, June 6) • Allied armies reach Paris (August) • Allies turn back Germans at Battle of the Bulge (September) • Roosevelt reelected to fourth term • Bretton Woods Conference creates IMF and World Bank • Dumbarton Oaks Conference establishes plan for UN
1945	U.S. firebombs Japan • Yalta Conference (February) • Roosevelt dies; Truman becomes president (April) • Germany surrenders (May) • Hiroshima and Nagasaki hit with atomic bombs (August) • Japan surrenders (September) • United Nations established (December)

launched a military buildup and dreamed of an empire. In October 1935, Mussolini's armies invaded Ethiopia, an independent African kingdom that had never before succumbed to colonialist rule. Although Mussolini's forces met fierce Ethiopian resistance, Italy soon prevailed.

Isolationist Sentiment and American Neutrality

Many Americans wished to isolate their country from these foreign troubles. Many historians, writing after the First World War, had maintained that Woodrow Wilson manipulated the country into a war that had not been in the nation's best interests. Popular antiwar movies, such as *All Quiet on the Western Front* (1931) and *The Big Parade* (1925), portrayed the conflict as a selfish power game played by business and governmental elites, who used appeals to nationalism to dupe common people into serving as cannon fodder. Between 1934 and 1936, a Senate investigating committee headed by Republican Gerald P. Nye of North Dakota held well-publicized hearings on U.S. participation in the First World War. The Nye committee endorsed claims that the nation had been maneuvered into the war to preserve the profits of American bankers and munitions makers, who had developed a huge financial stake in an Anglo-French victory. By 1935, public opinion polls suggested that Americans overwhelmingly opposed involvement in foreign conflicts and feared being manipulated by what one writer called "merchants of death."

To prevent a repetition of the circumstances that had supposedly drawn the United States into the First World War, Congress enacted neutrality legislation to halt the growth of financial connections to warring countries. The Neutrality Acts of 1935 and 1936 mandated an arms embargo against belligerents, prohibited loans to them, and curtailed travel by Americans on ships belonging to nations at war. The Neutrality Act of 1937 further broadened the embargo to cover all trade with any belligerent, unless it paid in cash and carried the products away in its own ships. This "cash-and-carry" provision minimized damage to America's export sector while it reduced the risk that loans or the presence of American commerce in a war zone might entangle the United States in a conflict overseas.

The isolationist mood in the United States, matched by British policies of appeasing Hitler, encouraged Germany's expansionist designs. In March 1936, Nazi troops again violated the Versailles agreement by remilitarizing the Rhineland. A few months later, Hitler and Mussolini extended aid to General Francisco Franco, a fellow fascist who was seeking to overthrow Spain's republican government. By lending Franco sophisticated weaponry and soldiers, Italy and Germany used Spain's civil war as a training ground for fascist forces. Republicans in Spain appealed to antifascist nations for assistance, but only the Soviet Union responded. Britain, France, and the United States, fearing that the conflict would flare into world war if more nations took sides, adopted policies of noninvolvement.

The United States even extended its arms embargo to cover civil wars, a move that aided the well-armed fascist forces and crippled republican resistance.

Growing Interventionist Sentiment

Although the United States remained officially uninvolved, the Spanish Civil War precipitated a major debate over foreign policy. Many conservative groups in the United States applauded General Franco as a strong anticommunist whose fascist government would support religion and social stability in Spain. In contrast, the political left championed the cause of republican Spain and denounced the fascist repression sweeping Europe. Cadres of Americans, including the famed "Abraham Lincoln Brigade," crossed the Atlantic and joined Soviet-organized, international troops, which fought alongside republican forces from Spain. American peace groups, strong during the 1920s and early 1930s, split over how to avoid a wider war. Some continued to advocate neutrality and isolation, but others argued for a strong stand against fascist militarism and aggression. Increasingly, Americans separated into camps of isolationists and interventionists.

The administration of President Franklin Roosevelt, tilting cautiously toward interventionism, tried to influence the debate. In October 1937, Roosevelt called for international cooperation to "quarantine" aggressor nations, and he gingerly suggested some modification of America's neutrality legislation. Congress, however, remained adamant in maintaining the policy of noninvolvement.

The Mounting Crisis

As Americans debated strict neutrality versus cautious engagement, Japan attacked China. In summer 1937, after an exchange of gunfire between Japanese and Chinese troops at the Marco Polo Bridge southwest of Beijing, Japanese armies invaded and captured Shanghai, Nanjing, Shandong, and Beijing. Japan demanded that China become subservient politically and economically to Tokyo. It also announced a plan for an East Asian Co-Prosperity Sphere, a self-sufficient economic zone that would supposedly liberate peoples throughout Asia from Western colonialism. Toward the end of 1937, Japanese planes sank the American gunboat *Panay* as it evacuated American officials from Nanjing, but Japan's quick apology defused a potential crisis. Even so, the *Panay* incident and Japanese brutality in occupying Nanjing, where perhaps 300,000 Chinese were killed in an assault against civilians, alarmed Roosevelt. The president began to consult with Britain about planning for a possible war in Asia.

Further aggression heightened the sense of alarm among American interventionists, especially when the expansionist states began working together. In October 1936, Germany and Italy agreed to cooperate as the Axis Powers, and Japan joined them in alliance against the Soviet Union in November 1936. Italy followed Japan and Germany in withdrawing from the League of Nations. In March 1938, Hitler annexed Austria to the Third Reich and announced his intention to seize the Sudetenland, a portion of Czechoslovakia inhabited by 3.5 million people of German descent. In May, Roosevelt announced a program of naval rearmament that would increase the U.S. Navy beyond the treaty limits that Japan had already violated.

The Outbreak of War in Europe

French and British leaders, wishing to avoid a confrontation with Germany, met with Hitler in Munich in September 1938. They acquiesced to Germany's seizure of the Sudetenland in return for Hitler's promise to seek no more territory. Roosevelt expressed relief that the Munich Conference seemed to promise future peace in Europe.

The promise of peace did not last. In March 1939, Germans marched into Prague and, within a few months, annexed the rest of Czechoslovakia. In August 1939, Hitler secured Germany's eastern flank by signing a nonaggression pact with the Soviet Union. The most bitter of enemies, Stalin and Hitler nonetheless agreed to cooperate in carving up territory. In a secret protocol, they plotted to divide Poland and the Baltic states. By fall 1939, Germany was clearly preparing to attack Poland.

Britain and France were finally ready to draw the line. Both countries pledged to defend Poland, and on September 1, 1939, Hitler's invasion forced them into action. Two days after Hitler's armies stormed into Poland, Britain and France declared war on Germany. The Allies, however, were unable to mobilize in time to help the Poles. Outnumbered and outgunned, Polish forces fought valiantly but could not withstand Germany's unrelenting strikes on land and from the air. With Soviet troops moving in simultaneously from the east, Poland fell within weeks. Once the occupation of Poland was completed, Hitler's troops waited out the winter of 1939–40. Some observers dubbed this period a *sitzkrieg,* or "sitting war."

The lull proved only temporary. In April 1940, a German *blitzkrieg,* or "lightning war" of massed tank formations, motorized infantry and artillery, and air support, swiftly overran Denmark, Norway, the Netherlands, Belgium, Luxembourg, and France. The speed with which Hitler's well-trained army moved shocked Allied leaders in Paris and London. Britain barely managed to evacuate its troops, but not its equipment, from the French coastal town of Dunkirk, just before it fell to the German onslaught that began in late May. Early in June, Italy joined Germany by declaring war on the Allies. In June 1940, France fell, and Hitler installed a pro-Nazi government at Vichy in southern France. French officials were forced to surrender to Hitler in the same railway car used for the German surrender to France at the end of the First World War. In only six weeks, Hitler's army had seized complete control of Europe's Atlantic coastline, from the North Sea south to Spain, where Franco remained officially neutral but decidedly pro-Axis.

America's Response to War in Europe

In a somber, six-minute speech delivered on the day that Britain and France entered the war against Germany, President Roosevelt declared U.S. neutrality. But the tone of his speech was hardly neutral. Unlike Woodrow Wilson when the European war had broken out in 1914, Roosevelt did not urge Americans to be impartial. From 1939 to 1941, Roosevelt tried to mobilize public opinion against Congress's Neutrality Acts and in favor of what he called "measures short of war" that would bolster the Allied fight against the Axis.

At Roosevelt's urging, late in 1939, Congress did ease the Neutrality Act's ban on selling military armaments to either side by broadening the earlier "cash-and-carry" trade provision to allow arms sales to belligerents who could pay immediately and use their own ships for transport. Because Britain and France controlled the Atlantic sea lanes, they clearly benefited from this change in policy. Congress responded further to Roosevelt's requests, appropriating more funds for rearmament and passing the Selective Training and Service Act of 1940, the first peacetime draft in U.S. history. Abandoning any further pretense of neutrality, the United States began supplying war matériel directly to Great Britain. The appointment of two distinguished Republicans to the cabinet—Henry Stimson as secretary of war and Frank Knox as secretary of the navy—gave the new policies bipartisan overtones, if not fully bipartisan support.

Meanwhile, Hitler concentrated on Great Britain. From August through October 1940, Germany's *Luftwaffe* subjected British air bases to daily raids, coming close to knocking Britain's Royal Air Force (RAF) out of the war. Just as he was on the verge of success, however, Hitler lost patience with this strategy and ordered instead the bombing of London and other cities—first by day and then by night. In addition to giving the RAF time to recover, Ger-

MAP 26.1 GERMAN EXPANSION AT ITS HEIGHT

This map shows the expansion of German power from 1938 through 1942. Which countries fell to German control? Why might Americans have differed over whether these moves by Germany represented a strategic threat to the United States?

many's nighttime bombings of Britain's cities aroused sympathy in the United States. The use of airpower against civilians in the Battle of Britain, as it was called, shocked Americans, who heard the news in dramatic radio broadcasts from London. As writer Archibald MacLeish phrased it, radio journalist Edward R. Murrow "skillfully burned the city of London in our homes and we felt the flames."

In September 1940, Roosevelt ignored any possible constitutional questions about the limits of his authority and transferred 50 First World War–era naval destroyers to the British navy. In return, the United States gained the right to build eight naval bases in British territory in the Western Hemisphere. This "destroyers-for-bases" deal infuriated isolationist members of Congress. Even within the president's own party, opposition was strong. Democratic Senator Burton K. Wheeler of Montana distributed more than a million antiwar postcards, at government expense, an action that Secretary of War Stimson characterized as "very near the line of subversion . . . if not treason."

U.S. marines to Greenland and Iceland to relieve British troops, which had occupied these strategic Danish possessions after Germany's seizure of Denmark.

In August 1941, Roosevelt and British Prime Minister Winston Churchill met on the high seas off the coast of Newfoundland to work toward a formal wartime alliance. An eight-point declaration of common principles, called the Atlantic Charter, disavowed territorial expansion, endorsed free trade and self-determination, and pledged the postwar creation of a new world organization that would ensure "general security." Roosevelt agreed to Churchill's request that the U.S. Navy convoy American goods as far as Iceland. This step, aimed at ensuring the safe delivery of lend-lease supplies headed for Britain, inched the United States even closer to belligerence. Soon, in an undeclared naval war, Germany was using its formidable submarine "wolf packs" to attack U.S. ships.

By this time, Roosevelt and his advisers firmly believed that defeating Hitler would require U.S. entry into the war, but public support still lagged. The president urged Congress to repeal the Neutrality Act altogether to allow U.S. merchant ships to carry munitions directly to Britain. Privately, he may have hoped that Germany would commit some provocative act in the North Atlantic that would jar public opinion. The October 1941 sinking of the U.S. destroyer *Reuben James* did just that, and Congress repealed the Neutrality Act. The vote was so close and the debate so bitter, however, that Roosevelt knew he could not yet seek a formal declaration of war. By avoiding any further provocations at sea, Hitler made Roosevelt's task harder. In addition, since late June 1941, Hitler had been concentrating his attacks on the Soviet Union, a country for which Americans held far less sympathy than they did for Britain.

Pearl Harbor

As it turned out, Japan, rather than Germany, sparked America's formal entry into the war. In response to Japan's invasion of China in 1937, the United States sought to bolster China's defense by extending economic credits to China and halting sales of some U.S. equipment to Japan. In 1939, the United States abrogated its Treaty of Commerce and Navigation with Japan, an action that allowed for the possible future curtailment or even the outright prohibition of U.S. exports to the island nation.

These measures did little to deter Japanese aggression, and by 1940 Germany's successes in Europe had further raised the stakes in Asia. As the European war sapped their strength, France, Britain, and the Netherlands had more trouble maintaining links with their Southeast Asian colonies. Japan quickly mobilized to exploit the vacuum as Japanese expansionists called for the incorporation of Southeast Asia into their East Asian Co-Prosperity Sphere.

President Roosevelt hoped that a 1940 ban on the sale of aviation fuel and high-grade scrap iron to Japan would slow Japan's imminent military advance into Southeast Asia. Instead, this act intensified Japanese militancy. After joining the Axis alliance in September 1940, Japan pushed deeper into French Indochina to secure strategic positions and access to raw materials it could no longer buy from the United States. When Japan's occupation of Indochina went unopposed, its military forces prepared to launch attacks on Singapore, the Netherlands East Indies (Indonesia), and the Philippines. Roosevelt expanded the trade embargo against Japan, promised further assistance to China, and accelerated the U.S. military buildup in the Pacific.

In mid-1941, Roosevelt played his most important diplomatic card. He froze Japanese assets in the United States, effectively bringing under presidential control all commerce between the two countries, including trade in petroleum, which was vital to the Japanese economy. Faced with impending economic strangulation, Japanese leaders did not reassess their plan to create an empire. Instead, they began planning a preemptive attack on the United States.

On December 7, 1941, Japanese bombers swooped down without warning on Pearl Harbor, Hawaii, and destroyed much of the U.S. Pacific Fleet. Altogether, 19 ships were sunk or severely damaged; 188 aircraft were destroyed or disabled; and more than 2,200 Americans were killed. The attack could have been worse: The three American carriers and seven heavy cruisers were not in port at the time, and Japan's commander failed to destroy the navy's submarine base, fuel storage tanks, or repair facilities. The psychological effect galvanized the nation. Secretary of War Stimson remembered: "My first feeling was of relief that the indecision was over and that a crisis had come that would unite all our people." In a war message broadcast by radio on December 8, Roosevelt decried the attack and labeled December 7 "a date which will live in infamy," a phrase that served as a rallying cry throughout the war.

Japan's attack on Pearl Harbor was an act of desperation. The U.S. embargoes, especially on petroleum, had narrowed Japan's options. Negotiations between the two countries proved fruitless: Japan was unwilling to abandon its designs on China, the only concession that might have ended the embargoes. With limited supplies of raw materials, Japan had little hope of winning a prolonged war. Japanese military strategists decided to risk a surprise attack, gambling that a crippling blow might so weaken U.S. military power as to avoid a long war. "Sometimes a

man has to jump with his eyes closed," remarked General Hideki Tojo, who became Japan's prime minister.

A few Americans charged that Roosevelt had intentionally provoked Japan in order to open a "back door" to war. They pointed out that the fleet at Pearl Harbor, the nation's principal Pacific base, lay vulnerable at its docks, not even in a state of full alert. In actuality, the American actions and inactions that led to Pearl Harbor were more confused than devious. Beginning in 1934, the United States had gradually enlarged its Pacific fleet, and Roosevelt had also increased the number of B-17 bombers based in the Philippines. The president hoped that the possibility of aerial attacks would intimidate Japan and slow its expansion. This strategy of deterrence failed. It may also have contributed to the lack of vigilance at Pearl Harbor. Intelligence experts, who had broken Japan's secret diplomatic code (the decrypted messages were called MAGIC), expected Japan to move toward Singapore or other British or Dutch possessions. MAGIC intercepts, along with visual sightings of Japanese transports, seemed to confirm preparations for a strike in Southeast Asia (a strike that did occur). American leaders doubted that Japan would risk a direct attack on the United States and gravely underestimated the skill of Japan's military planners.

On December 8, 1941, Congress declared war against Japan. The lone dissenting vote came from Representative Jeannette Rankin, a longtime peace activist from Montana. Japan's allies, Germany and Italy, declared war on the United States three days later. Hitler, whose eastern offensive had stalled within sight of Moscow, mistakenly assumed that war with Japan would keep the United States preoccupied in the Pacific. The three Axis Powers had not foreseen America's ability to mobilize swiftly and effectively in a unified war effort.

Fighting the War in Europe

The first few months after America's entry into the war proved discouraging. German forces controlled most of Europe from Norway to Greece and had pushed eastward into the Soviet Union. Now they rolled across North Africa, threatening the strategically important Suez Canal, which remained under British control. In the Atlantic,

San Diego Historical Society.

IS THAT A WAR PLANT?
This photo from 1945 shows an aircraft plant bedecked with camouflage.

German submarines were endangering Allied supply lines, sinking 7 million tons of Allied shipping in the first 16 months after Pearl Harbor. Japan seemed unstoppable in the Pacific. Japanese forces overran Malaya, the Dutch East Indies, and the Philippines and drove against the British in Burma and the Australians in New Guinea. At home, Americans had been unprepared for war. Before Pearl Harbor, army morale was low, industrial production was still on a peacetime footing, and labor–management relations were contentious.

New government bureaucracies and technologies assisted rapid economic and military mobilization. Military priorities—acquiring naval bases, securing landing rights for aircraft, ensuring points for radio transmissions, and gaining access to raw materials—superseded all other demands. The newly formed Joint Chiefs of Staff, consisting of representatives from each of the armed services, became Roosevelt's major source of guidance on strategy. The War Department's new Pentagon complex dwarfed the State Department's cramped quarters. The giant five-story, five-sided building was completed in January 1943, after 16 months of around-the-clock work. In 1942, aircraft equipped with radar, a new technology developed in collaboration with Britain, proved effective against submarines. Although the army and navy engaged in months of bickering over who should conduct the antisubmarine warfare, the navy finally received official responsibility and performed well. During 1943, Germany's submarine capability faded "from menace to problem," in the words of Admiral Ernest King. Radar was one of the most important innovations of the war.

Code-breaking was another. In the 1920s, a private company had developed the complex ENIGMA encryption machine to encode radio messages. Realizing that radio communications would be essential to his war strategy, Hitler adapted the machine to military purposes. ENIGMA messages were considered unbreakable because the cipher keys changed once or twice a day, and the machine could be configured 150 million million million different ways for any message. Polish mathematicians, however, obtained an ENIGMA machine and made some key breakthroughs in the science of decryption. They escaped from Poland just as German armies overran the country. Their discoveries contributed to a massive Allied code-breaking operation that was established at Bletchley Park in England, an endeavor so secret that most records were destroyed after the war, and no open mention was allowed before 1974. At its height, Bletchley Park employed some 4,000 people, including many Americans. Gradually, cryptographers perfected decryption machines. Decoded German messages, called "Ultra" for "Ultra-secret," helped British defenses during the Battle of Britain and gave the Allies a crucial advantage in campaigns in North Africa and France. Throughout the war, the Germans never discovered that many of their radio communications were being forwarded to Allied commanders—occasionally even before they had made it to their German recipient. In the postwar world, the code-breaking technologies of Ultra would lead to the development of computer technology.

Campaigns in North Africa and Italy

Military strategy divided the Allied Powers, now consisting principally of the United States, Britain, and the Soviet Union. All agreed that the primary focus would be the European theater of the war, and Roosevelt and his military strategists immediately established a unified command with the British. The Soviet Union, facing 200 German divisions just west of Moscow and suffering hundreds of thousands of casualties, pleaded with Roosevelt and Churchill to open a second front in Western Europe, by an invasion across the English Channel into France, to relieve pressure on the USSR. Many of Roosevelt's advisers, including Stimson and General George C. Marshall, agreed. They feared that if German troops forced the Soviet Union out of the war, Germany could turn its full attention toward Britain.

Churchill, however, urged instead the invasion of French North Africa, which was under the control of Vichy France. Churchill's strategy sought to peck away at the edges of enemy power rather than strike at its heart. At a meeting between Roosevelt and Stalin at Casablanca,

Morocco, in January 1943, Roosevelt sided with Churchill, and the promised invasion of France was postponed. The risk of any cross-Channel assault was great, Roosevelt reasoned, and he wanted some rapid victories to build morale on the home front. To assuage Stalin's fears that his capitalist allies might sign a separate peace with Hitler, the two leaders announced that they would stay in the fight until Germany agreed to nothing less than unconditional surrender. Continuing disagreements over the timing of the cross-Channel invasion, however, still strained the alliance.

The North African operation, code-named TORCH, began with Anglo-American landings in Morocco and Algeria in November 1942. To ease resistance against this North African invasion, U.S. General Dwight D. Eisenhower struck a deal with French Admiral Jean Darlan, a Nazi sympathizer and the Vichy officer who controlled France's colonies in North Africa. Darlan agreed to break with the Vichy regime and stop resisting the Allied operation in return for Eisenhower's pledge that the United States would support his political aspirations. The deal outraged some Americans, who believed that it compromised the moral purpose of the war. Darlan's assassination in December 1942, called an "act of Providence" by one of Eisenhower's deputies, ended the embarrassment. Even so, the antagonism that Eisenhower's action had generated in the Free French movement, led by General Charles de Gaulle, had lasting consequences for postwar relations.

As TORCH progressed, assisted by Ultra intercepts, the Soviets suddenly turned the tide of battle at Stalingrad. They cut off and destroyed one German army in the city and sent other German armies reeling backward. Despite this defeat in the East, Hitler poured reinforcements into North Africa but could not stop either TORCH or the British, who were driving west from Egypt. About 200,000 Axis soldiers surrendered to the Allies in April and May 1943. In summer 1943, Allied troops followed up the successful North African campaign by overrunning the island of Sicily and fighting their way slowly north through Italy's mountains. Their successes boosted morale in the United States, but the Italian campaign drained badly needed resources for the upcoming cross-Channel invasion of France, while scarcely denting the German stranglehold on Europe.

Some American officials increasingly worried about the postwar implications of wartime strategy. Stimson, for example, warned that the peripheral campaigns through Africa and Italy might leave the Soviets dominating central Europe. Unless the western democracies confronted Germany in the heart of Europe, he argued, Germany would be left holding "the leg for Stalin to skin the deer

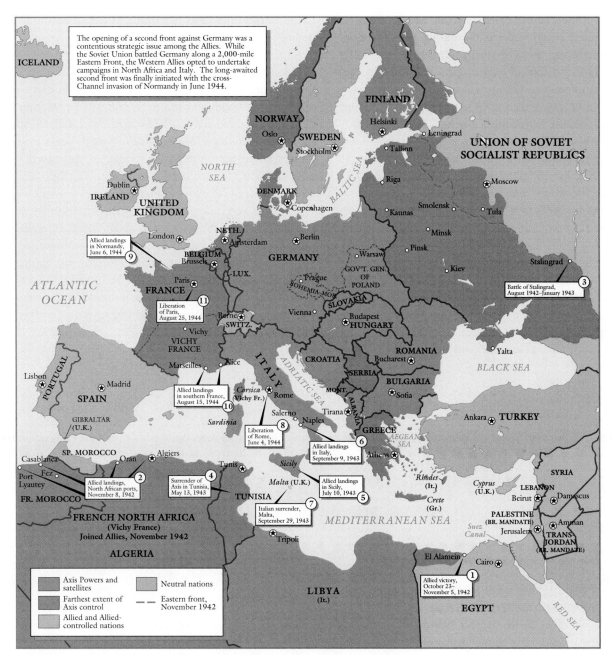

The opening of a second front against Germany was a contentious strategic issue among the Allies. While the Soviet Union battled Germany along a 2,000-mile Eastern Front, the Western Allies opted to undertake campaigns in North Africa and Italy. The long-awaited second front was finally initiated with the cross-Channel invasion of Normandy in June 1944.

MAP 26.2   ALLIED MILITARY STRATEGY IN NORTH AFRICA, ITALY, AND FRANCE

This map shows the European theater of war from 1942 through 1944. Note how the crucial Battle of Stalingrad and the North African campaign began a rollback of German power. Why did June 1944 appear to be a critical month for the Allied effort?

and I think that will be dangerous business for us at the end of the war." Acting on such advice, Roosevelt finally agreed to set a date for the cross-Channel invasion that Stalin had long been promised.

Operation OVERLORD

Operation OVERLORD, directed by Eisenhower, finally began on June 6, 1944, D-Day. During the months pre-ceding D-Day, probably the largest invasion force in history had been assembled in England. Allied double agents and diversionary tactics had fooled the Germans into expecting a landing at the narrowest part of the English Channel rather than in the Normandy region. Just five months earlier, a new decoding machine had dramatically increased the number of Ultra intercepts, and Allied intelligence officers therefore had the advantage of knowing that their deception had worked. After several delays,

because of the Channel's unpredictable weather, nervous commanders finally ordered the daring plan to begin. The night before, as naval guns pounded the Normandy shore, three divisions of paratroopers were dropped behind enemy lines to disrupt German communications. Then, at dawn, more than 4,000 Allied ships landed troops and supplies on Normandy's beaches. The first American troops to land at Omaha Beach met especially heavy German fire and took enormous casualties, but the waves of invading troops continued throughout the day and through the weeks that followed. Within three weeks, more than 1 million people had landed, secured the Normandy coast, and opened the long-awaited second front.

Just as the Battle of Stalingrad had reversed the tide of the war in the East, so Operation OVERLORD turned the tide in the West. Within three months, U.S., British, and Free French troops entered Paris. After repulsing a desperate German counteroffensive in Belgium, at the Battle of the Bulge in December and January, Allied armies swept eastward, crossed the Rhine, and headed toward Berlin.

The Allies disagreed on how to orchestrate the defeat of Germany. British strategists favored a swift drive, so as to meet up with Soviet armies in Berlin or even farther east. General Eisenhower favored a strategy that was militarily less risky and politically less provocative to the Soviets. He doubted that Allied troops could reach Berlin from the west before the Soviet armies arrived, and he knew that stopping short of Berlin would save lives among the troops under his command. He was also eager to end the war on a note of trust and believed that racing the Soviets to Berlin would undermine the basis for postwar Soviet–American cooperation. In the end, Eisenhower's views prevailed. The general moved cautiously along a broad front, halting his troops at the Elbe River, west of Berlin, and allowing Soviet troops to roll into the German capital. The Soviets, who suffered staggering casualties in taking Berlin, worked with the other Allies to establish joint administration of the city.

HISTORY THROUGH FILM

Saving Private Ryan (1998)

Directed by Steven Spielberg. Starring Tom Hanks (Captain John Miller), Matt Damon (Private James Ryan), Harve Presnell (General George Marshall).

Hollywood marked the 50th anniversary of the Allied effort in the Second World War with a series of films about "the good war." Although *Saving Private Ryan* invited comparison with *The Longest Day* (1962) because of its depiction of the D-Day invasion of Normandy, Steven Spielberg's battlefield sequences represented a considerable advance in the arts of waging war on film. His production team employed sophisticated computer graphics and nearly deafening Dolby sound to mount battle scenes so realistic that reviewers cautioned veterans susceptible to post-traumatic stress syndrome about watching the film.

The film also suggested the kind of family-centered melodrama that Spielberg had grafted onto the sci-fi genre in *E.T.: The Extra-Terrestrial* (1982). A heroic squad led by Captain John Miller is trying to locate a single U.S. soldier, Private James Ryan, whose mother has already lost her three other sons to the war. The film poses the question of whether such a family-related mission legitimates and sanctifies the sacrifices of the Second World War. *Private Ryan* answers "yes" to this question.

The major body of the film carefully justifies the rescue mission. Although Captain Miller wonders if his dangerous assignment is simply a public relations stunt, he quickly drops this idea and pursues his mission with the gallantry required of a Hollywood-commissioned officer. Later, his platoon members debate the morality of risking eight lives to save one, but the cause of Ryan's mother always seems overriding. General George Marshall cuts off debate over the appropriateness of the Ryan mission by invoking an earlier war leader, Abraham Lincoln, who once faced a similar dilemma. When Miller's troops finally locate Private Ryan, the film's audience discovers that he is the kind of clean-cut Iowa farm boy who

As the war in Europe drew to a close, the horrors perpetrated by the Third Reich became visible to the world. Hitler's campaign of extermination, now called the Holocaust, killed between 5 and 6 million Jews out of Europe's prewar population of 10 million; hundreds of thousands more from various other groups—especially gypsies, homosexuals, intellectuals, communists, and the physically and mentally challenged—were also murdered. Although only a military victory could close the German death camps, the Allies might have saved thousands of Jews by helping them escape and emigrate. Allied leaders, however, worried about how to deal with large numbers of Jewish refugees, and they also were reluctant to use scarce ships to transport Jews to neutral sanctuaries. In 1943, after Romania proposed permitting an evacuation of 70,000 Jews from its territory, for example, Allied leaders avoided any serious discussion of the plan. With few places to go, hundreds of thousands of people who might have been saved went to Nazi death camps.

The Allies would, in 1945 and 1946, bring 24 high German officials to trial at Nuremberg for "crimes against humanity." Large quantities of money, gold, and jewelry that Nazi leaders stole from victims of the Holocaust and deposited in Swiss banks, however, remained largely hidden from view for more than 50 years. Not until 1997 did Jewish groups and the U.S. government force an investigation of the Swiss banking industry's holdings of stolen "Nazi gold," an inquiry that finally prompted some restitution for victim's families.

With Hitler's suicide in April and Germany's surrender on May 8, 1945, the military foundations for peace in Europe were complete. Soviet armies controlled Eastern Europe; British and U.S. forces predominated in Italy and the rest of the Mediterranean; Germany and Austria fell under divided occupation. Governmental leaders now needed to work out a plan for transforming these military arrangements into a comprehensive political settlement for the postwar era. Meanwhile, the war in the Pacific was still far from over.

will stay with his would-be saviors rather than retreat to safety. Ryan survives, although most of his comrades perish. Captain Miller, dying, implores young Ryan to lead a "good" life, to justify the sacrifice of so many others.

The film *Private Ryan*, in contrast to its characters, takes few risks. It secures its emotional investment in the rescue effort by bracketing the Second World War segments with two brief framing sequences in which an aging Ryan, along with his own family, returns to Normandy and visits the grave of Captain Miller. In the final segment, Ryan's wife provides the final reassurance that the trauma of the Second World War served a good cause, because Private Ryan's own family life has justified Miller's sacrifice. "Tell me I've led a good life. Tell me I'm a good man," he implores his wife. After nearly three hours of this Spielberg epic, the question is rhetorical.

Saving Private Ryan, which garnered four Academy Award nominations, celebrated the heroism of what popular historians called America's "greatest generation."

© AFP/Corbis.

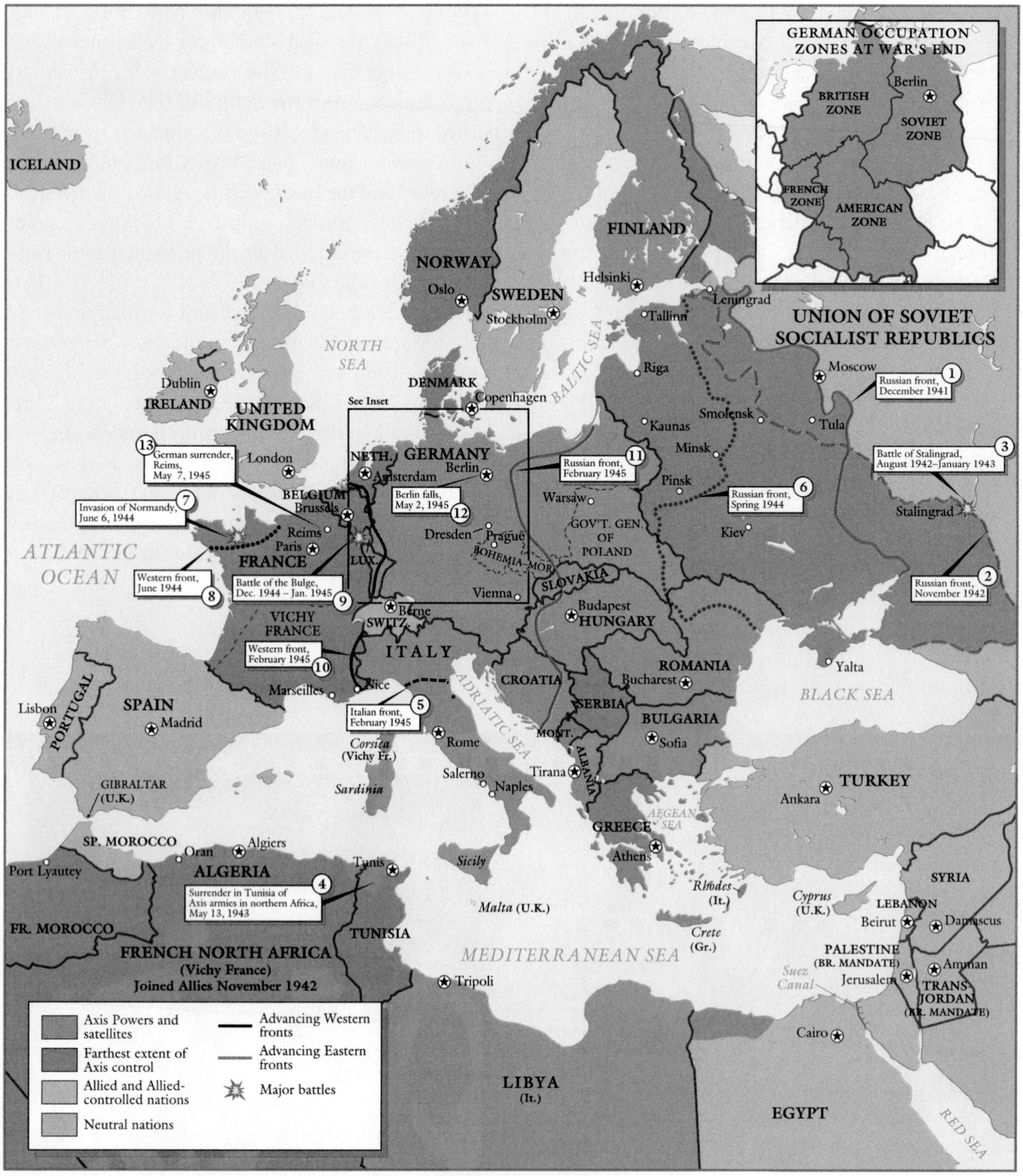

MAP 26.3   ALLIED ADVANCES AND COLLAPSE OF GERMAN POWER

This map depicts the final Allied advances and the end of the war in Germany. Through what countries did Soviet armies advance, and how might their advance have affected the postwar situation? How was Germany divided by occupying powers, and how might that division have affected postwar politics?

 View an animated version of this map or related maps at http://history.wadsworth.com/murrin_LEP4e.

The Pacific Theater

For six months after Pearl Harbor, nearly everything in the Pacific theater of the war went Japan's way. Britain's supposedly impregnable colony at Singapore fell easily. American naval garrisons in the Philippines and on Guam and Wake islands were overwhelmed, and American and Filipino armies were forced to surrender at Bataan and Corregidor in the Philippines. In one of the most notorious incidents of the war, the Bataan Death March, Japanese commanders forced many of their 70,000 American and Filipino captives to walk 60 miles with almost no food or water and then packed them tightly onto ships for transport to prison camps. Suffering from disease, hunger,

and cruelty, more than 7,000 soldiers died in the forced march. Elsewhere, Japanese forces streamed southward to menace Australia. Then the tide turned.

Seizing the Initiative in the Pacific

When Japan finally suffered its first naval defeat at the Battle of the Coral Sea in May 1942, Japanese naval commanders decided to hit back hard. They amassed 200 ships and 600 planes to destroy what remained of the U.S. Pacific fleet and to take Midway Island, a strategic location for Hawaii's security. U.S. Naval Intelligence, however, was able to break enough of the Japanese code to warn Admiral Chester W. Nimitz of the plan. Surprising the Japanese navy, U.S. planes sank four Japanese carriers, destroyed a total of 322 planes, and preserved the American presence at Midway. The U.S. Navy's losses were substantial, but Japan's were so much greater that its offensive capabilities were crippled.

Two months later, American forces splashed ashore at Guadalcanal in the Solomon Islands and successfully relieved the pressure on Australia and its military supply lines. The bloody engagements in the Solomons continued for months on both land and sea, but they accomplished one major objective: seizing the initiative against Japan. This success, combined with the delay in opening a second front in Europe, also affected grand strategy. According to prewar plans, the war in Europe was to have received highest priority, but by 1943 the two theaters were receiving roughly equal resources.

The bloody engagements in the Pacific dramatically illustrated that the conflict had become, in historian John Dower's phrase, a "war without mercy." It was one in which racial prejudice reinforced brutality. For Japan, the war was to establish forever the superiority of the divine Yamato race. Prisoners taken by the Japanese, mostly on the Asian mainland, were brutalized in unimaginable ways, and few survived. The Japanese army's Unit 731 tested bacteriological weapons in China and, like the Nazi doctors, conducted horrifying medical experiments on live subjects. American propaganda images also played on themes of racial superiority, portraying the Japanese as animalistic subhumans. American troops often rivaled Japan's forces in their disrespect for the enemy dead and sometimes killed Japanese soldiers rather than take prisoners. The longer the Pacific war lasted, the more it seemed to loosen the boundaries of acceptable violence against combatants and civilians alike.

China Policy

U.S. policy makers hoped that China would fight effectively against Japan and emerge from the war as a strong and united nation. Neither hope was realized.

General Joseph W. Stilwell, who had worked with the Chinese armies resisting the Japanese invasion in the late 1930s, undertook the job of turning China into an effective military force. Jiang Jieshi (formerly spelled Chiang Kai-shek) headed China's government and accepted the prickly Stilwell as his chief of staff, but friction between "Vinegar Joe" Stilwell and Jiang, fueled by disputes over military priorities, became so intense that in May 1943 Roosevelt bowed to Jiang's demand for Stilwell's dismissal. Meanwhile, Japan's advance into China continued, and in 1944 its forces captured seven of the principal U.S. air bases in China.

To complicate matters further, China was beset by civil war. Jiang's Nationalist government was incompetent, corrupt, and unpopular. It avoided engaging the Japanese invaders and still made extravagant demands for U.S. assistance. Meanwhile, a growing communist movement led by Mao Zedong was fighting effectively against the Japanese and enjoyed widespread support among Chinese peasants. Stilwell urged Roosevelt to cut off support to Jiang unless he fought with more determination. Roosevelt, however, feared that such actions would create even greater chaos and resisted strengthening Mao's position. He continued to provide moral support and matériel to Jiang's armies and even convinced Stalin to support Jiang rather than Mao. Moreover, pressed by a powerful "China lobby" in the United States, Roosevelt insisted that Jiang's China be permitted to stand alongside the major powers after victory had been won. By tying U.S. policy to Jiang's leadership and entertaining the pretense that China was a stable power, Roosevelt and the "China lobby" prepared the way for great difficulties in forging a China policy in the postwar period.

Pacific Strategy

In contrast to the war in Europe, there was no unified command to guide the war in the Pacific; consequently, military actions often emerged from compromise. General Douglas MacArthur, commander of the army in the South Pacific, favored an offensive launched from his headquarters in Australia through New Guinea and the Philippines and on to Japan. After Japan drove him out of the Philippines in May 1942, he had promised to return, and he was determined to keep his pledge. He argued that the United States needed to control the Philippines at war's end in order to preserve its strategic position in Asia. Admiral Nimitz disagreed. He favored a more direct route, advancing toward Japan via the smaller islands of the central Pacific and bypassing the Philippines. Unable to decide between the two strategies, the Joint Chiefs of Staff authorized both.

Marked by fierce fighting and heavy casualties, both offensives moved forward. MacArthur took New Guinea,

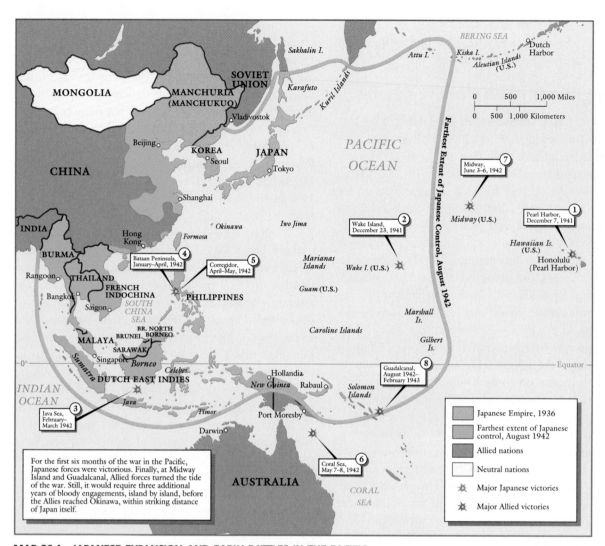

MAP 26.4   JAPANESE EXPANSION AND EARLY BATTLES IN THE PACIFIC

This map shows the expansion of Japanese power prior to the Battle of Midway. What countries were in the Japanese orbit? U.S. opinion polls from the late 1930s suggest that more Americans supported strong measures against this Japanese threat in Asia than against the German threat in Europe. What might be some explanations for this concern?

and Nimitz's forces liberated the Marshall Islands and the Marianas in 1943 and 1944. An effective radio communication system conducted by a Marine platoon of Navajo Indians made a unique contribution to success. On hundreds of Pacific beaches Navajo-speaking squads set up radio contact with headquarters and with supporting units. Navajo, a language unfamiliar to Japanese intelligence officers, provided a secure medium for sensitive communications. In late 1944, the fall of Saipan brought American bombers within range of Japan. The capture of the islands of Iwo Jima—18 square miles taken at the cost of 27,000 American casualties—and of Okinawa further shortened that distance during spring 1945. Okinawa illustrated the nearly unbelievable ferocity of the island campaigns: 120,000 Japanese soldiers died; 48,000 Americans. U.S. military planners extrapolated from these numbers when considering the dreaded prospect of an invasion of the home islands of Japan.

As the seaborne offensive proceeded, airpower also played a role. Before the war, Roosevelt had become convinced that aerial bombing offered almost magical military power. At one time, he even had hoped that the mere threat of bombing would be so frightening that airpower would be a deterrent to war rather than a means of conducting it. The effects of strategic bombing in Europe, however, had been ambiguous. The Nazi bombardment of British cities in 1940 and 1941 did heavy damage but only steeled British resolve, uniting the nation and boosting civilian morale. The Allies' strategic bombing of Germany, including the destruction of such large cities as Hamburg and Dresden, produced equally mixed results. Military historians continue to debate the relative merits of the

National Archives #127-N-69559-A.

NAVAJO SIGNAL CORPS

Sending messages in their native language, which neither the Japanese nor the Germans could decipher, Navajo Indians in the Signal Corps made a unique contribution to preserving the secrecy of U.S. intelligence.

strategic bombing in Europe, wondering whether the gains against military targets really offset the huge civilian casualties and the unsustainable losses of American pilots and aircraft.

Still, Roosevelt continued to believe that strategic bombing might provide the crucial advantage in the Pacific. In February 1944, General Henry Harley ("Hap") Arnold, commander of the newly formed 20th Army Air Force, presented Roosevelt with a plan for a systematic campaign of firebombing against Japanese cities, "not only because they are greatly congested but because they contain numerous war industries." Roosevelt approved the plan. In the month before bombing began, the Office of War Information lifted its ban on atrocity stories about Japan's treatment of American prisoners. As grisly reports swept across the country, officials expected that the American public would become more accepting of killing Japanese civilians. Arnold's original air campaign, operating from bases in China, turned out to be cumbersome and ineffective. It was replaced by an even more lethal operation, run by General Curtis LeMay from Saipan.

The official position was that the incendiary raids on Japanese cities constituted "precision" rather than "area"

bombing. In actuality, the success of a mission was measured in terms of the number of square miles it left scorched. Destroying Japan's industrial capacity by firebombing the workers who ran the factories and by systematically burning entire cities brought unprecedented civilian casualties. The number of Japanese civilians killed in the raids is estimated to have been greater than Japanese soldiers killed in battle. An attack on Tokyo on the night of March 9–10, 1945, inaugurated the new policy by leveling 16 square miles (one-fourth) of the city, destroying 267,000 buildings and inflicting 185,000 casualties. One by one, LeMay torched other cities. In his memoirs, LeMay summarized his strategy: "Bomb and burn them until they quit."

By the winter of 1944–45, a combined sea and air strategy had emerged: The United States would seek "unconditional surrender" by blockading Japan's seaports, continuing its bombardment of Japanese cities from the air, and perhaps invading Japan. Later critics of the policy of unconditional surrender have suggested that it may have hardened the determination with which Japan fought the war even after its ultimate defeat had become obvious. These critics have pointed out that many Japanese

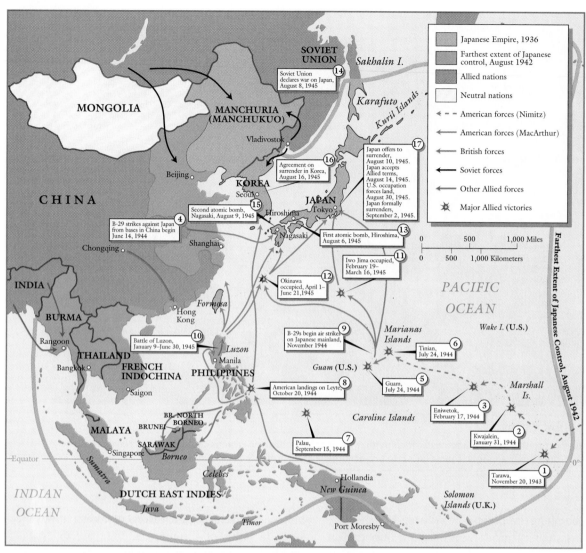

MAP 26.5 PACIFIC THEATER OFFENSIVE STRATEGY AND FINAL ASSAULT AGAINST JAPAN
This map suggests the complicated nature of devising a war strategy in the vast Pacific region. What tactics did the
United States use to advance upon and finally prevail over the island nation of Japan?

assumed that unconditional surrender would mean the
death of the emperor. Moreover, the policy prevented U.S.
negotiators from vigorously pursuing peace feelers, which
some Japanese leaders were trying to send through third
parties. With the unconditional surrender policy in place
and Japan's decision to fight even in the face of certain defeat, the strategy of American leaders seemed to require
massive destruction to achieve victory.

A New President

On April 13, 1945, just one month before Germany's formal surrender and five months before Japan's, newspaper
headlines across the country mourned, "President Roose-

velt Dead." FDR succumbed to a massive cerebral hemor-
rhage. Profound sorrow and shock spread through the
armed forces, where many young men and women had
hardly known any other president; through diplomatic
conference halls, where Roosevelt's personal magnetism
had often brought unity, if not clarity; and among factory
workers, farmers, and bureaucrats, for whom Roosevelt
had symbolized optimism and unity through depression
and war. Roosevelt had also accumulated a host of critics
and enemies. He had defeated Republican Thomas E.
Dewey in the 1944 presidential election by the smallest
popular vote margin in nearly 30 years. Still, FDR had
been the most popular president in modern history, and
he left an enduring imprint on American life. "He was

Commander-in-Chief, not only of the Armed Forces, but of our generation," wrote an editor of *Yank* magazine.

Compared with the legacy of Roosevelt, the stature of the new president, Harry S. Truman, seemed impossibly small. Born on a farm near Independence, Missouri, Harry Truman had served in France during the First World War. After the war, he went into politics, under the auspices of Thomas J. Pendergast's Democratic party machine in Kansas City, and was elected to the U.S. Senate in 1934. There, he made his reputation in the early years of the Second World War by fighting waste in spending programs and was chosen as Roosevelt's running mate in 1944. In contrast to Roosevelt, who was upper class, elite educated, and worldly, Truman was simply a "little man from Missouri." He prided himself on plain, direct talk. His critics considered him poorly prepared for the job of president. He had little background in international affairs. Moreover, because Roosevelt had not included him in high-level policy discussions, Truman knew little about any informal understandings Roosevelt may have made with foreign leaders. In fact, during the period between the inauguration following the 1944 election and the president's death, Truman had met with Roosevelt only three times.

Atomic Power and Japanese Surrender

At Los Alamos, New Mexico, scientists from all across the world had been secretly working on a new weapon. Advances in theoretical physics during the 1930s had suggested that splitting the atom (fission) would release a tremendous amount of energy that could fuel incredibly powerful bombs. Fearful that Germany was racing ahead of the United States in this area, Albert Einstein, a Jewish refugee from Germany, in 1939 had urged President Roosevelt to launch a secret program to build a bomb based on atomic research. The government subsequently enlisted top scientists in the Manhattan Project, the largest and most secretive military project yet undertaken. On July 16, 1945, after a succession of breakthroughs in physics research, the first atomic weapon was successfully tested at Trinity Site, near Alamogordo, New Mexico. The researchers notified Truman that the terrifying new weapon was ready.

Truman and his top policy makers assumed that the weapon should be put to immediate military use. They were eager to end the war, both because a possible land invasion of Japan might have cost so many American lives and because the Soviet Union was planning to enter the Pacific theater, and Truman wished to limit Soviet power

in that region. Secretary of War Stimson wrote: "It was our common objective, throughout the war, to be the first to produce an atomic weapon and use it. The possible atomic weapon was considered to be a new and tremendously powerful explosive, as legitimate as any other of the deadly explosive weapons of modern war." Churchill called the bomb a "miracle of deliverance" and a peace giver. Truman later claimed that he had never lost a night's sleep over its use because it saved lives.

Other advisers admitted to more qualms, and disagreement arose over where and how the bomb should be deployed. A commission of atomic scientists, headed by Jerome Franck, recommended a demonstration that would impress Japan with the bomb's power yet cause no loss of life. General George C. Marshall suggested using the bomb only on military installations or on some large manufacturing area where people would be warned away in advance. Most of Truman's advisers, however, agreed that simply demonstrating the bomb's power might not be enough. The purpose of the bomb, Stimson said, was to make "a profound psychological impression on as many inhabitants as possible."

In the context of the earlier aerial bombardment of Japanese cities, dropping atomic bombs on the previously unbombed cities of Hiroshima and Nagasaki on August 6 and 9, 1945, respectively, seemed simply an acceleration of existing policy rather than a departure from it. "Fat Man" and "Little Boy," as the two bombs were nicknamed, came to be viewed as merely bigger, more effective firebombs. Atomic weapons did, however, produce yet a new level of violence. Colonel Paul Tibbets, who piloted the plane that dropped the first bomb, reported that "the shimmering city became an ugly smudge . . . a pot of bubbling hot tar." Teams of U.S. observers who entered the two Japanese cities in the aftermath of their bombing were stunned at the immediate devastation, including the instantaneous incineration of both human beings and manmade structures, as well as the longer-lasting horror of radiation disease.

The mushroom clouds over Hiroshima and Nagasaki inaugurated a new "atomic age" in which dreams of peace were mingled with nightmares of Armageddon. But in those late summer days of 1945, most Americans sighed with relief. Although some of Japan's military leaders wanted to continue the fight, Emperor Hirohito summoned his cabinet and declared that, with the nation on the brink of destruction, "I cannot endure the thought of letting my people suffer any longer." News reports on August 15 proclaimed Japan's defeat. On September 2, dubbed V-J Day, Japan formally signed a surrender document aboard the battleship *Missouri* in Tokyo Bay.

National Archives.

RITA HAYWORTH SCRAPS HER BUMPERS
Movie stars aided the war effort by promoting the sale of war bonds and urging sacrifice. Here Hayworth urges Americans to scrap their unessential car parts.

course, became a matter of definition. Coca-Cola and Wrigley's chewing gum won precious sugar allotments by arguing that GIs overseas "needed" to enjoy these products. Both companies prospered. The Kaiser Corporation, whose spectacular growth in the 1930s had been spurred by federal dam contracts, now turned its attention to building ships, aircraft, and military vehicles, such as the famous "jeep." By 1943 the company was handling nearly one-third of the nation's military construction, establishing a new industrial base for southern California's previously agricultural economy. Federal subsidies, low-interest loans, and tax breaks enabled factories to expand and retool. A cost-plus formula built into government contracts guaranteed a profit for manufacturers.

The war concentrated power in the largest corporations. Roosevelt ordered his justice department to postpone enforcement of antitrust laws. Legal challenges that had been years in preparation, such as the case against America's great oil cartel, were tucked away. The renewal of some antitrust activity in 1944, when victory seemed assured, helped keep alive the concept of trust-busting but did little to curtail the growing power of giant enterprises. Congressional efforts to investigate alleged collusion in the awarding of government contracts and to increase assistance to small businesses similarly made little progress in Washington's crisis atmosphere. The top 100 companies, which had provided 30 percent of the nation's total manufacturing output in 1940, were providing 70 percent by 1943. Small businesses were left catering mainly to the civilian economy, which was plagued by erratic allocations, shortages, and stagnation.

The Workforce

During the first two years of military buildup, many workers who had been idled during the Great Depression found jobs. Employment in heavy industry invariably went to men, and most of the skilled jobs went to whites. Initially, administrators of newly established, government-sponsored vocational training centers focused their efforts on training white males. They refused to set up courses for women or, especially in the South, to admit minority workers. Employers, they said, would never hire from these groups. But as military service drained the supply of white male workers, women and minorities became more attractive candidates for production jobs. Soon, both private employers and government were encouraging women to go to work, southern African Americans to move to northern industrial cities, and Mexicans to enter the United States under the *bracero* guest farm-worker program. In response to labor shortages, the composition of the workforce changed dramatically.

conservative, anti–New Deal coalition in Congress. In 1943 Congress abolished the job-creation programs of the Works Progress Administration (WPA), the Civilian Conservation Corps (CCC), and the National Youth Administration (NYA) (see chapter 25). It also shut down the Rural Electrification Administration (REA) and Farm Security Administration (FSA), agencies that had assisted impoverished rural areas. The budget was drastically reduced for the National Recovery Planning Board, which was designed to introduce comprehensive national planning into America's market economy. As "dollar-a-year" business executives flocked to Washington, D.C., to run the new wartime bureaus, the Roosevelt administration adopted a more cooperative stance toward big business. Although many people in the business community never fully trusted Roosevelt, the war nevertheless nudged the president's New Deal to the right.

In win-the-war Washington, social programs withered as big businesses considered essential to victory flourished under government subsidies. What was essential, of

© Bettmann/Corbis.

WOMEN JOIN THE WAR EFFORT
Women employees at the Convair Company in California use a rivet gun and bucking bar, tools traditionally used only by men.

Hired for jobs never before open to them, women became welders, shipbuilders, lumberjacks, and miners. For the first time, women won places in prestigious symphony orchestras. As major league baseball languished from a lack of top-flight players, female teams sprang up to give new life to the national pastime; the owner of the Chicago Cubs organized a woman's league in 1943 that eventually fielded 10 teams. Many employers hired married women, who before the war were often banned even from such traditionally female occupations as teaching. Minority women, who before the war had worked mostly on farms or as domestic servants, moved into clerical or secretarial jobs, where they had not previously been welcome. Although most workplaces continued to be largely segregated by sex—women working with other women and men working with other men—the range of jobs open to women grew wider.

The character of unpaid labor, long provided mostly by women, also underwent significant change. Volunteer activities such as Red Cross projects, civil defense work, and recycling drives claimed more and more of the time of women, children, and older people. Government propaganda exhorted homemakers: "Wear it out, use it up, make it do, or do without." "Work in a garden this summer." "Save waste fats for explosives." Most Depression-era Americans were already used to scarcity, but the war now equated a parsimonious lifestyle with patriotism rather than with poverty. Both in the home and in the factory, women's responsibilities and workloads increased.

The new labor market improved the general economic position of African Americans as many moved into labor-scarce cities and into jobs previously off limits to them. By executive order in June 1941, the president created the Fair Employment Practices Commission (FEPC), which tried to ban discrimination in hiring. In 1943 the government announced that it would not recognize as collective bargaining agents any unions that denied admittance to minorities. The War Labor Board outlawed the practice of paying different wages to whites and nonwhites doing the same job. Before the war, the African American population had been mainly southern, rural, and agricultural; within a few years, a substantial percentage of African Americans had become northern, urban, and industrial. Although employment discrimination was hardly eliminated, twice as many African Americans held skilled jobs at the end of the war as at the beginning.

For both men and women, the war brought higher wages and longer work hours. Although in 1943 the government insisted that labor unions limit demands for wage increases to 15 percent, overtime often raised paychecks far more. During the war, average weekly earnings rose nearly 70 percent. Income derived from farming, which had lagged through the many years of low prices and overproduction, doubled and then doubled again.

Labor Unions

The scarcity of labor during the war substantially strengthened the union movement. Union membership rose by 50 percent. Women and minority workers joined unions in unprecedented numbers (women accounted for 27 percent of total membership by 1944), but the main beneficiaries of labor's new power were the white males who still comprised the bulk of union workers.

Especially on the national level, the commitment of organized labor to female workers was weak. Not a single woman served on the executive boards of either the American Federation of Labor (AFL) or the Congress of Industrial Organizations (CIO). The International Brotherhood of Teamsters even required women to sign a statement that their union membership could be revoked when the war was over. Unions did fight for contracts stipulating equal pay for men and women in the same job, but these benefited women only as long as they held "male" jobs. The unions' primary purpose in advocating equal pay was to maintain wage levels for the men who would return to their jobs after the war. During the first year of peace, as employers trimmed their workforces, both business and

Print advertising also contributed to the wartime propaganda effort. Roosevelt encouraged advertisers to sell the benefits of freedom. Most obliged, and "freedom" often appeared in the guise of new washing machines, ingenious kitchen appliances, improved automobiles, a wider range of lipstick hues, and automation in a hundred forms. As soon as the fighting ended, these wartime ads promised, American technological know-how would usher in a consumer's paradise. Ads sometimes suggested that Americans were fighting to restore the consumer society of the 1920s (see chapter 24).

The president initially resisted the creation of an official propaganda bureau, preferring to rely on a newly created Office of Facts and Figures (OFF) to disseminate information to the public. Poet Archibald MacLeish, who headed the OFF, however, acknowledged that his office most often resembled a "Tower of Babel" when it came to setting forth the aims and progress of the war. So, in spring 1942, Roosevelt created the Office of War Information (OWI) to coordinate policies related to propaganda and censorship. Democratic critics charged that the OWI was dominated by advertising professionals who dealt in slogans rather than substance. Republicans blasted it as a purveyor of crass political advertisements for causes favored by Roosevelt and New Deal Democrats. Despite such criticism, the OWI established branches throughout the world; published a magazine called *Victory;* and produced hundreds of films, posters, and radio broadcasts.

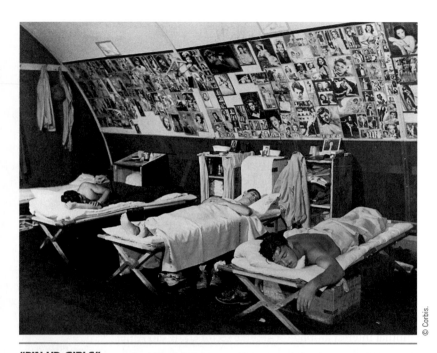

© Corbis.

"PIN-UP GIRLS"

Male GIs often surrounded themselves with "pin-up girls," images very different from that of the home front "Rosie-the-Riveter."

Gender Equality

Nostalgic portraits of an "American way of life" often clashed with the socioeconomic changes that wartime mobilization brought. Nowhere was this more apparent than in matters affecting the lives and status of women. As women took over jobs traditionally held by men, many people began to take more seriously the idea of gender equality. Some 350,000 women volunteered for military duty during the war; more than 1,000 women served as civilian pilots with the Women's Airforce Service Pilots (WASPs). Although they constituted only 2 percent of all military personnel, these women broke gender stereotypes. Not everyone approved. One member of Congress asked: "What has become of the manhood of America,

that we have to call on our women?" Still, Congress eventually authorized a women's corps, with full status, for each branch of the military, a step that had been thwarted during the First World War.

The military service of women, together with their new importance in the labor market, strengthened arguments for laws guaranteeing equal treatment. Congress seriously considered, but did not pass, an Equal Rights Amendment (ERA) to the Constitution and a national equal-pay law. Women's organizations, however, disagreed over how to advance equality. Organizations representing middle-class women strongly backed passage of the ERA, but other groups, which were more responsive to the problems of women who worked outside their homes, opposed its passage. They saw it as a threat to the protective legislation, regulating hours and hazardous conditions, which women's rights crusaders had struggled to win earlier in the century. Should women continue to be accorded "protected" status in view of their vulnerability to exploitation in a male-directed workplace? Or should they fight for "equal" status?

Even as the war temporarily narrowed gender differences in employment, governmental policies and propaganda frequently framed changes in women's roles in highly traditional terms. Women's expanded participation in the workplace was often portrayed as a short-term sacrifice, necessary to preserve women's "special" responsibilities—hearth and home. A typical ad suggesting that women take on farm work declared: "A woman can do

anything if she knows she looks beautiful doing it." Despite the acceptance of women into the armed services, most were assigned to stateside clerical and supply jobs; only a relatively few women served overseas. Day care programs for mothers working outside their homes received reluctant and inadequate funding. The 3,000 centers set up during the conflict filled only a fraction of the need and were swiftly shut down after the war. Social scientists and welfare experts, mostly male, blamed working mothers for an apparent rise in juvenile delinquency and in the divorce rate during the war years.

The war also widened the symbolic gap between "femininity" and "masculinity." Military culture often fostered a "pin-up" mentality toward women. Service publications contained pin-up sections, and tanks and planes were decorated with glossy images of female sexuality. Wartime fiction often associated manliness with brutality and casual sex. After the war, tough-guy fiction with a violent and misogynist edge, like Mickey Spillane's "Mike Hammer" series of detective novels, became one of the most successful genres of popular culture.

Racial Equality

Messages about race were as ambiguous as those related to gender; wartime culture both propelled yet firmly resisted change. Before the Second World War, America had been a sharply segregated society, with racial inequality enforced by law and custom. African Americans, disenfranchised in the South and only beginning to achieve voting power in the North, had only limited access to the political, legal, and economic systems. The fight against fascism, however, challenged this old order.

Nazism, based on the idea of racial inequality, exposed the racist underpinnings of much of 20th-century social science theory. "The Huns have wrecked the theories of the master race with which we were so contented so long," Frank Dixon, ex-governor of Alabama, remarked in 1944. The view that racial difference was not a function of biology but a function of culture—a view most American anthropologists had been advancing for a generation—gained wider popular acceptance during the war. The idea that a democracy could accommodate racial difference provided a basis for the postwar struggle against discrimination.

The northward migration of African Americans accelerated demands for equality. They found an outspoken advocate of civil rights within the White House. First Lady Eleanor Roosevelt repeatedly antagonized southern Democrats and members of her husband's administration (often including the president) by her support for civil rights and her participation in integrated social functions. The writer Clare Boothe Luce once remarked that Mrs. Roosevelt "enjoyed comforting the afflicted and afflicting the comfortable." Although the president often ignored her appeals for federal action against discrimination, her advocacy nevertheless dramatized the case for reform.

African Americans understood the irony of fighting overseas for a country that denied them equality at home. Many challenged the government to live up to its own rhetoric about freedom and democracy. The *Amsterdam News*, a Harlem newspaper, called for a "Double V" campaign—victory at home as well as abroad. In January 1941, even before the United States entered the war, the labor leader A. Philip Randolph promised to lead tens of thousands of frustrated black workers in a march on Washington to demand more defense jobs and integration of the military forces. With the support of major black organizations and other prestigious African American leaders, Randolph invited Roosevelt to address the planned gathering. The president, however, feared the event would embarrass his administration and urged that it be canceled. Randolph's persistence, however, forced Roosevelt to make concessions. In return for Randolph's canceling

A SEGREGATED MILITARY

This photo of an African American regiment eating in a mess hall during the Second World War illustrates racial segregation in the armed forces.

on Racial Equality (CORE), an organization founded in 1942 and composed of whites and blacks who advocated nonviolent resistance to segregation, devised new strategies during the war. CORE activists staged sit-ins to integrate restaurants, theaters, and even prison dining halls in Washington, D.C. These same tactics would serve in the 1950s and 1960s to force the desegregation of interstate buses and public accommodations. As the Swedish sociologist Gunnar Myrdal predicted in his influential study of American racial issues, *An American Dilemma* (1944), "fundamental changes" would soon have to come throughout the nation. Prominent African American novelist Richard Wright wrote that America had to do something about its "white problem."

People of Japanese descent faced a unique situation. During the two months after the attack on Pearl Harbor, fear of sabotage by pro-Japanese residents engulfed West Coast communities. One military report concluded that a "large, unassimilated, tightly knit racial group, bound to an enemy nation by strong ties of race, culture, custom, and religion . . . constituted a menace" that justified extraordinary action. Despite lack of evidence of disloyalty, the president in February 1942 issued Executive Order 9066, directing the relocation and internment of first- and second-generation Japanese Americans (called Issei and

Nisei, respectively) at inland camps. Curiously, in Hawaii, where the presumed danger of subversion might have been much greater, no such internment took place; there, people of Japanese ancestry constituted 37 percent of the population and were essential to the economy. Forced to abandon their possessions or sell them for a pittance, nearly 130,000 mainland Japanese Americans were confined in flimsy barracks, enclosed by barbed wire and under armed guard. Two-thirds of the detainees were native-born U.S. citizens. Many had been substantial landowners in California's agricultural industries.

Despite the internment, the courage and sacrifice of Japanese American soldiers became legendary. The 100th Battalion, composed of Nisei from Hawaii, was nearly wiped out; 57 percent of the famed 442nd Regimental Combat Team were killed or wounded in the mountains of Italy; and 6,000 members of the Military Intelligence Service provided invaluable service in the Pacific theater.

Racial hostilities reflected the underlying strains in America's social fabric, but other tensions pulled at Americans as well. Rifts developed between city dwellers and migrants from rural areas. Some Californians derided the "Okies," people who had fled the Dust Bowl in Oklahoma looking for agricultural work on the West Coast, as ignorant and unruly. In Chicago, migrants from Appalachia

INTERNMENT
Uniformed officials check the baggage of people of Japanese descent as they are being evacuated to internment camps.

FDR Library.

met similar derision. At the beginning of the war, more than one-third of white Americans were still either first- or second-generation immigrants. Many ethnic communities that had preserved the language and culture of their homelands felt the pressure to assimilate.

The symbol of the "melting pot," together with appeals to nationalism, grew more and more powerful in American culture. Wartime propaganda stressed the theme of national unity by calling the Second World War a "people's war," and it contrasted America's melting pot with German and Japanese obsessions about racial purity. Wartime movies, plays, and music reinforced a sense of national community by building on cultural nationalism and stressing historical themes. Many foreign-language broadcasts and publications ceased to exist during the war, and naturalization applications nearly doubled from what they had been only five years earlier.

The great movements of population during the war—rural to urban, south to north, east to west—helped erode distinctions based on geography, ethnicity, and race. Wartime demands for additional labor weakened the barriers to many occupations. As each of America's racial and ethnic minorities established records of distinguished military service, the claim of equality—"Americans All," in the words of a wartime slogan—took on greater moral force. The possibility for more equitable participation in the mainstream of American life, together with rhetoric extolling social solidarity and freedom, provided a foundation for the antidiscrimination movements of the decades ahead. The war for the American way of life, it turned out, carried many different meanings.

🌐 Shaping the Peace

The end of the war raised difficult questions about demobilization and peace. Truman built on Roosevelt's many wartime conferences and agreements to shape the framework of international relations for the next half-century. He participated in establishing the United Nations, creating new international economic institutions, and settling global political issues involving territory and governance.

International Organizations

In the Atlantic Charter of 1941 and at a conference in Moscow in October 1943, the Allies had already pledged to create an international organization to replace the defunct League of Nations. The new United Nations (UN) fulfilled Woodrow Wilson's vision of an international body to deter aggressor nations. At the Dumbarton Oaks Conference in Washington in August 1944 and at a subsequent

meeting in San Francisco in April 1945, the Allies worked out the organizational structure of the UN. It would have a General Assembly, in which each member nation would be represented and have one vote. It would also have a Security Council, whose makeup would include five permanent members—the United States, Great Britain, the Soviet Union, France, and China—and six rotating members. The Security Council would have primary responsibility for maintaining peace, but permanent members of the council enjoyed an absolute veto over any council decision. The inclusion of China in the Security Council was a victory for the United States, which hoped that Jiang's government could remain in power and would become an effective U.S. ally. A UN Secretariat would handle day-to-day business, and an Economic and Social Council would promote social and economic advancement throughout the world.

The U.S. Senate accepted the UN charter in July 1945 with only two dissenting votes. This resounding victory for internationalism contrasted sharply with the Senate's rejection of membership in the League of Nations after the First World War. Americans of an earlier generation had worried that internationalist policies might impinge on their country's ability to follow its own national interests. Following the Second World War, because U.S. power clearly dominated emerging organizations such as the UN, Americans thought it less likely that decisions of international bodies would impede their nation's foreign policies. In addition, Americans recognized that the war had partly resulted from the lack of a coordinated, international response to aggression during the 1930s and wanted to avoid the same situation again.

Eleanor Roosevelt, the former first lady and a domestic social activist, also played a prominent role in building the new postwar internationalist ethos. A delegate to the first meeting of the UN's General Assembly, she chaired the U.S. Commission on Human Rights and guided the drafting of a Universal Declaration of Human Rights, adopted by the UN in 1948. The Declaration set forth "inalienable" human rights and freedoms as cornerstones of international law.

Postwar economic settlements also illustrated a growing acceptance of other new international organizations. At the Bretton Woods (New Hampshire) Conference of 1944, assembled nations created the International Monetary Fund (IMF), which was designed to maintain stable exchange by ensuring that each nation's currency could be converted into any other national currency at a fixed rate. Exchange rates could be altered only with the agreement of the fund. (This international system of fixed exchange rates was replaced in 1971 by a system of floating rates.) The International Bank for Reconstruction and

Development, later renamed the World Bank, was also created at Bretton Woods to provide loans to war-battered countries and promote the resumption of world trade. In 1947 the General Agreement on Tariffs and Trade (GATT) created an institutional structure for breaking up closed trading blocs and implementing free and fair trade agreements. Policy makers hoped that these three institutions would preclude the currency devaluation and economic protectionism that had unsettled the world economy during the 1930s. American capital and American policies dominated the bodies, even though they were international bodies financed by member nations throughout the world. The Soviet Union, whose state-directed economy challenged the assumptions of western capitalism, did not participate.

Spheres of Interest and Postwar Settlements

Wartime conversations among Stalin, Churchill, and Roosevelt had often assumed that there would be special "spheres of influence," areas dominated by a single power, in the postwar world. As early as January 1942, the Soviet ambassador to the United States reported to Stalin that Roosevelt had tacitly assented to Soviet postwar control over the Baltic states of Lithuania, Latvia, and Estonia. The Soviets accepted British and U.S. dominance of Italy's post-fascist government. And in 1944 Stalin and Churchill agreed informally and secretly that Britain would continue its sway over Greece and that the Soviets could control Romania and Bulgaria.

Roosevelt had implied to Stalin that he understood the Soviet's need to create friendly states on its vulnerable western border, but, at the same time, he had talked about self-determination for small nations. For example, at the Tehran Conference of November 1943, held just one year before the 1944 presidential election, Roosevelt told Stalin that American voters of Polish, Latvian, Lithuanian, and Estonian descent expected their homelands to be independent after the war.

Precisely how Roosevelt intended to reconcile his contradictory positions on Soviet spheres of influence in the postwar world will never be known. Roosevelt, a master of finesse, probably believed that he could improvise a solution. As long as Soviet armies were essential to Germany's defeat—and the president also wanted the USSR to join the war against Japan—Roosevelt struck a tone of cooperation with Stalin. Flexibility, holding together unlikely coalitions, and taking contradictory positions simultaneously were Roosevelt's special strengths. On many critical international issues of the 1930s—the gold standard, tariff policy, and entry into the war—he had managed to straddle both sides of seemingly irreconcilable positions. On postwar issues, for which he seemed to have only vague policy ideas, Roosevelt likely thought he could perform a similar juggling act.

Roosevelt's contradictory policies toward a Soviet sphere of interest, however, bedeviled his successors. The military results of the war, particularly the USSR's powerful position in Eastern Europe, strongly influenced postwar territorial settlements. On issues of governance—particularly in Germany, Poland, and Korea—splits between U.S. and Soviet interests widened.

Germany, especially, became a focus and a symbol of bipolar tensions. Early in the war, both the United States and the Soviet Union had urged the dismemberment and deindustrialization of Nazi Germany after its defeat. Roosevelt endorsed a controversial plan proposed by Secretary of the Treasury Henry Morgenthau that would have turned Germany into a pastoral, agricultural country. At a conference held at Yalta, Ukraine, in early February 1945, the three Allied powers agreed to divide Germany into four zones of occupation (with France as the fourth occupying force). Later, as relations among the victors cooled, this temporary division of Germany permanently solidified into a Soviet-dominated zone in the East that faced off against the three other Allied zones in the West. Berlin, the German capital, also was divided, even though it lay totally within the Soviet zone. As fear of the Soviets began to replace earlier concerns of a revived Germany, Truman abandoned the Morgenthau plan in favor of efforts to rebuild the western zones of Germany.

Postwar rivalries for influence also focused on Poland. During the war, Poland had two governments: a government-in-exile based in London and a communist-backed one in Lublin. At the Yalta Conference, the Soviets agreed to permit free elections in postwar Poland and to create a government "responsible to the will of the people," but Stalin also believed that the other Allied leaders had tacitly accepted Soviet dominance over Poland. The agreement at Yalta was ambiguous at best, as many on the negotiating teams realized at the time. During Yalta, the war was still at a critical stage, and the western Allies chose to sacrifice clarity over the Polish issue in order to encourage cooperation with the Soviets. After Yalta, the Soviets assumed that Poland was to be in their sphere of influence, but many Americans charged the Soviets with bad faith for failing to hold free elections and for not relinquishing control.

In Asia, military realities likewise influenced postwar settlements. Roosevelt had long wanted to bring the USSR into the war against Japan to relieve pressure on U.S. forces in the Pacific. At Tehran in November 1943 and again at

Yalta, Stalin pledged to send troops to Asia as soon as Germany was defeated, but when U.S. policy makers learned that the atomic bomb was ready for use against Japan, they became eager to limit Soviet involvement in the Pacific theater. The first atomic bomb fell on Hiroshima just one day before the Soviets were to enter the war against Japan, and the United States took sole charge of the occupation and postwar reorganization of Japan. The Soviet Union and the United States split Korea, which had been controlled by Japan, into separate zones of occupation. Here, as in Germany, these zones later emerged as two antagonistic states (see chapter 27).

The fate of the European colonies seized by Japan in Southeast Asia was another issue that remained unresolved in the planning for peace. During the war, the United States had declared itself in favor of decolonization. Although the United States would have preferred to see the former British and French colonies become independent nations, with governments friendly to the West and especially to American interests, U.S. policy makers worried about the pro-communist politics of many anticolonial nationalist movements. After the war, as the United States developed an anticommunist foreign policy, it moved to support British and French efforts to reassemble their colonial empires. Long struggles would ensue over the independence and political orientation of postwar governments throughout the colonized world.

In its own colony of the Philippines, the United States honored a long-standing pledge to grant independence. A friendly government that agreed to respect U.S. economic interests and military bases took power in 1946 and enlisted American advisers to help suppress leftist rebels. The Mariana, Caroline, and Marshall Islands, all of which had been captured by Japan during the war, were designated Trust Territories of the Pacific by the United Nations and placed under U.S. administration in 1947.

Although the countries of Latin America had been only indirectly involved in military conflict or peace negotiations, the Second World War directly affected U.S. relations with them. During the 1930s the Roosevelt administration had sought to curb Nazi influence in Latin America. The Good Neighbor Policy, building on a 1928 pledge to carry out no more military interventions in the hemisphere, had helped improve U.S.–Latin American relations. The Office of Inter-American Affairs (OIAA), created in 1937, further expanded cultural and economic ties. Just weeks after the German invasion of Poland in 1939, at a Pan American Conference in Panama City, Latin American leaders showed that the hemisphere was nearly united behind the Allies. The conferees strengthened hemispheric economic cooperation and declared a 300-mile-wide band of neutrality in waters around the hemisphere (excepting

Canada). After U.S. entry into the war, at a January 1942 conference in Rio de Janeiro, all of the Latin American countries except Chile and Argentina broke off diplomatic ties with the Axis governments. When naval warfare in the Atlantic severed commercial connections between Latin America and Europe, Latin American countries became critical suppliers of raw materials to the United States, to the benefit of all.

Wartime conferences and settlements avoided clear decisions about creating a Jewish homeland in the Middle East, a proposal that England had supported, but not effected, after the First World War. The Second World War prompted survivors of the Holocaust and Jews from around the world to take direct action. Zionism, the movement to found a Jewish state in Palestine, their ancient homeland, attracted thousands of people, who began to carve out the new nation of Israel. Middle Eastern affairs, which had seldom concerned U.S. policy makers before 1941, would take on greater urgency after 1948, when the Truman administration formally recognized Israel as a sovereign state.

Conclusion

The world changed dramatically during the era of the Second World War. Wartime mobilization ended the Great Depression and shifted the New Deal's focus away from domestic social issues and toward international concerns. It brought victory over dictatorial, brutal regimes. As Europe lay in ruins, with at least 22 million people displaced from their homes, the United States emerged as the world's preeminent power, owning two-thirds of the world's gold reserves and controlling more than half of its manufacturing capacity.

At home, the war transformed the nation's economic structure. During the war emergency, a powerful national government, concerned with preserving national security, assumed nearly complete power over the nation's economy. New, cooperative ties were forged among government, business, labor, and scientific researchers. All sectors worked together to provide the seemingly miraculous growth in productivity that ultimately won the war.

The early 1940s sharpened debates over liberty and equality. Many Americans saw the Second World War as a struggle to protect and preserve the power and liberties they already enjoyed. Others, inspired by a struggle against racism and injustice abroad, insisted that a war for freedom should help secure equal rights at home.

News of Japan's surrender prompted joyous celebrations throughout the country, but questions remained about postwar policies. International conferences established a structure for the United Nations and for new,

global economic institutions. Still, Americans remained uncertain about postwar reconstruction of former enemies and about future relations with wartime allies, particularly the Soviet Union. Domestically, the wrenching dislocations of war—psychic, demographic, and economic—took their toll. Postwar adjustments would be difficult for all Americans. And, of course, the nation now faced the future without the charismatic leadership of Franklin D. Roosevelt, the only president that many Americans had ever known.

For the next 50 years, veterans of the Second World War remained relatively quiet about their combat experiences. "The reason they don't talk," a former tank commander commented, "is they couldn't get the picture over to somebody that wasn't there. He would think that you're making that story up." After the 50th anniversary of the war's end, however, with remaining veterans reaching old age, Americans suddenly rediscovered what journalist Tom Brokaw called the "greatest generation." Books about the war dominated bestseller lists during the late 1990s; Steven Spielberg's film *Saving Private Ryan* packed theaters; and Congress approved construction of a huge memorial on the grounds of the National Mall in Washington, D.C. The Second World War, through these popular representations, continued to stand as a powerful symbol of honor, unity, and common sacrifice.

SUGGESTED READINGS

On the United States and the coming of World War II, see **Robert Dallek**, *Franklin D. Roosevelt and American Foreign Policy, 1932–1945* (1979), and **Waldo H. Heinrichs**, *Threshold of War: Franklin D. Roosevelt and American Entry into World War II* (1988). For the war's military aspects, see **Gerhard L. Weinberg**, *A World at Arms: A Global History of World War II* (1994), and **Gerald F. Linderman**, *The World within War: America's Combat Experience in World War II* (1997). Few narrative histories can match the dramatic narrative sweep of **Stephen Ambrose's** many works, such as *D-Day: June 6, 1944: The Climactic Battle of World War II* (1994) and *Band of Brothers: E Company, 506th Regiment, 101st Airborne from Normandy to Hitler's Eagle's Nest* (2001). **Michael Beschloss**, *The Conquerors: Roosevelt, Truman and the Destruction of Hitler's Germany, 1941–1945* (2002) is also highly readable. The decision to drop atomic bombs on Japan is adroitly analyzed in **J. Samuel Walker**, *Prompt and Utter Destruction: Truman and the Use of the Atomic Bombs against Japan* (1997).

For overviews of America's wartime experience, **William L. O'Neill**, *A Democracy at War: American's Fight at Home and Abroad in World War II* (1993), and **Michael C. C. Adams**, *The Best War Ever: America and World War II* (1994) present contrasting perspectives.

On the home front, see the superb overview by **John Morton Blum**, *V Was for Victory: Politics and American Culture during World War II* (1976). It may be supplemented by essays from **Lewis A. Erenberg and Susan E. Hirsch, eds.**, *The War in American Culture: Society and Consciousness during World War II* (1996), and **Thomas Patrick Doherty**, *Projections of War: Hollywood, American Culture, and World War II* (1993). **Richard W. Steele**, *Free Speech and the Good War* (1999) examines governmental efforts to regulate dissent. **Karen Anderson**, *Wartime Women: Sex Roles, Family Relations, and the Status of Women during World War II* (1981) surveys women's roles during the war. **Ronald Takaki**, *Double Victory: A Multicultural History of America in World War II* (2000) is a good synthesis of issues related to race and ethnicity.

AMERICAN JOURNEY ONLINE
AND
 INFOTRAC COLLEGE EDITION

Visit the source collections at www.ajaccess.wadsworth.com and
infotrac.thomsonlearning.com and use the Search function with
the following key terms to explore documents, images, audio
and video clips, articles, and commentary related to the material
in this chapter.

Adolph Hitler	Dwight D. Eisenhower
Joseph Stalin	Navajo Signal Corps
Neutrality Act	Harry S. Truman
Franklin D. Roosevelt	Hiroshima
Lend-Lease	Women in World War II
Pearl Harbor	Japanese Internment

GRADE AIDS

**Visit the Liberty Equality Power Companion Web site for resources specific to
this textbook:** http://history.wadsworth.com/murrin_LEP4e

The CD in the back of this book and the U.S. History Resource Center at
http://history.wadsworth.com/u.s./ offer a variety of tools to help you succeed in
this course, including access to quizzes; images; documents; interactive simulations,
maps, and timelines; movie explorations; and a wealth of other sources.

🌐 Creating a National Security State, 1945–1949

The wartime alliance between the United States and the Soviet Union had been little more than a marriage of convenience. Defeat of the Axis powers had required the two nations to cooperate, but collaboration scarcely lasted beyond victory. Especially after President Franklin Roosevelt's death in April 1945, relations between the United States and the Soviet Union steadily degenerated into a Cold War of suspicion and tension.

Onset of the Cold War

Historians have discussed the origins of the Cold War from many different perspectives. The traditional interpretation, which gained new power after the collapse of the Soviet Union in 1991, focuses on Soviet expansionism, stressing a historic Russian appetite for new territory, or an ideological zeal to spread international communism, or some interplay between the two. According to this view, the United States needed to take as hard a line as possible. Other historians—generally called *revisionists*—argue that the Soviet Union's obsession with securing its borders was an understandable response to the invasion of its territory during both world wars. The United States, in this view, should have tried to reassure the Soviets by seeking accommodation, instead of pursuing policies that intensified Soviet fears. Still other scholars maintain that assigning blame obscures the clash of deep-seated rival interests that made postwar tensions between the two superpowers inevitable.

In any view, Harry Truman's role proved important. His brusque manner, in sharp contrast to Franklin Roosevelt's urbanity, brought a harsher tone to U.S.–Soviet meetings. Truman initially hoped that he could somehow cut a deal with Soviet Premier Joseph Stalin, much like his old mentor, "Boss" Tom Pendergast, struck bargains with rogue politicians back in Kansas City. "I like Stalin," Truman once wrote his wife. "[He] knows what he wants and will compromise when he can't get it." However, as disagreements between the two former allies mounted, Truman came to rely on his more hard-line advisers.

The atomic bomb provided an immediate source of friction. At the Potsdam Conference of July 1945, Truman had casually remarked to Stalin, "We have a new weapon of unusual destructive force." Calmly, Stalin had replied that he hoped the United States would make "good use" of it against Japan. Less calmly, Stalin immediately ordered a crash program to develop nuclear weapons of his own. After atomic bombs hit Japan, Stalin reportedly told his

scientists that "the equilibrium has been destroyed. Provide the bomb. It will remove a great danger from us." Truman hoped that the bomb would scare the Soviets, and it did. Stalin grew even more concerned about the Soviet Union's future security. Historians still debate whether "wearing the bomb ostentatiously on our hip," as Secretary of War Henry Stimson put it, frightened the Soviets into more cautious behavior or made them more fearful and aggressive.

In 1946 Truman authorized Bernard Baruch, a presidential adviser and special representative to the United Nations, to offer a proposal for the international control of atomic power. The Baruch Plan called for full disclosure by all UN member nations of nuclear research and materials, creation of an international authority to ensure compliance, and destruction of all U.S. atomic weapons once these first steps were completed. Andrei A. Gromyko, the Soviet ambassador to the UN, argued that the Baruch plan would require other nations to halt their atomic research and disclose their secrets to the UN (dominated by the United States) before the United States was required to do anything. Gromyko countered by proposing that the United States unilaterally destroy its atomic weapons first, with international disclosure and control to follow. The United States refused. Both sides used this deadlock to justify a stepped-up arms race.

Other sources of Soviet-American friction involved U.S. loan policies and the Soviet sphere of influence in Eastern Europe. Truman abruptly suspended lend-lease assistance to the Soviet Union in early September 1945, partly to pressure Moscow into holding elections in Poland. Subsequently, Truman's administration similarly linked extension of U.S. reconstruction loans to its goal of rolling back Soviet power in Eastern Europe. This linkage strategy never worked. Lack of capital and signs of Western hostility provided the Soviets with excuses for tightening their grip on Eastern Europe, a course of action that further discouraged the United States from extending economic assistance to countries dominated by Moscow. The Soviet sphere of influence in Eastern Europe, which Stalin called defensive and Truman labeled proof of communist expansionism, solidified. By 1946, the former allies were well on their way to becoming bitter adversaries.

From 1947 on, Harry Truman placed his personal stamp on the presidency by focusing on "national security," a relatively new and emotionally powerful term, and on an international fight against the spread of communism. His policy initiatives, in both foreign and domestic affairs, extended the reach and power of the executive branch of government.

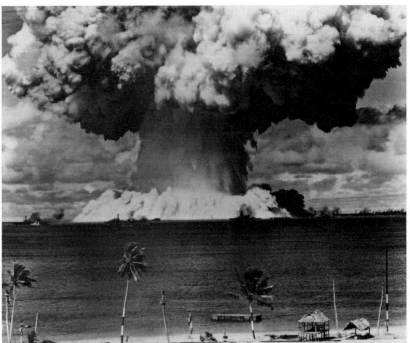

TESTING THE ATOMIC BOMB AT BIKINI ATOLL

This atomic test, one of 23 detonations at Bikini Atoll in the Marshall Islands during the late 1940s, raised a column of water 5,000 feet high. Although Bikini islanders were evacuated from the blast sites, the radiation still affected nearby people, including U.S. service personnel, and the area's ecology for years to come. As nuclear-related imagery spread through Cold War culture, new "bikini" swimsuits for "bombshell" women became a fashion rage.

The Granger Collection, New York.

Containment Abroad: The Truman Doctrine

In March 1947, the president announced what became known as the Truman Doctrine. He was addressing Congress concerning the civil war in Greece, a conflict in which communist-led insurgents were trying to topple a corrupt but pro-Western government. Historically, Greece had fallen within Great Britain's sphere of influence. Britain, however, was badly weakened by the Second World War and could no longer maintain its formerly strong presence there or in the Middle East. Truman's advisers claimed that a leftist victory in Greece would open neighboring Turkey, which they considered especially critical to U.S. interests, to Soviet subversion. Truman's policy makers doubted they enjoyed broad support, either among the public or in Congress, for a U.S. foreign aid program to Greece and Turkey. The president consequently made his case to Congress in especially dramatic terms. U.S. security interests, he said, were now worldwide, and the fate of "free peoples" everywhere, not simply the future of Greece and Turkey, hung in the balance. Unless the United States aided countries "who are resisting attempted subversion by armed minorities or by outside pressures," totalitarian communism would spread around the world and threaten the security of the United States.

Although the Truman Doctrine's global vision of national security encountered skepticism, the president got his request. Henry Wallace, the president's most visible Democratic critic, chided Truman for exaggerating the Soviet threat. Conservative Republicans looked suspiciously at the increase of executive power and the vast expenditures the Truman Doctrine seemed to imply. If Truman wanted to win support for his position, Republican Senator Arthur Vandenberg had already advised, he would need to "scare hell" out of people, something that Truman proved quite willing to do. With backing from both Republicans and Democrats, Congress passed Truman's request for $400 million in assistance to Greece and Turkey, most of it in military aid, in spring 1947. This vote signaled broad, bipartisan support for a national security policy that came to be called "containment."

The term containment had appeared in a 1947 article in the influential journal *Foreign Affairs*. The author, writing under the pseudonym "X," was George Kennan, the State Department's leading expert on Soviet affairs. Kennan argued that the "main element" in any U.S. policy "must be that of a long-term, patient but firm and vigilant containment of Russian expansive tendencies." Although Kennan later insisted that he had meant containment to be a series of discrete responses to specific moves by the Soviets and had never proposed an open-ended crusade, his broad prose lent itself to different interpretations. Whatever Kennan's precise intent, his "X" article quickly became associated with the alarmist tone of the Truman Doctrine.

Containment thus became the catchphrase for a global, anticommunist, national security policy. In the popular view, containment linked all leftist insurgencies, wherever they occurred, to a totalitarian movement controlled from Moscow that directly threatened, by its ideas as much as by military might, the United States. Although foreign policy debates regularly included sharp disagreements over precisely *how* to pursue the goal of containment, few Americans dared to question the basic premise that their country needed a global and activist foreign policy.

Truman's Loyalty Program

Nine days after proclaiming the Truman Doctrine, the president issued Executive Order 9835, which brought the containment of communism to the home front. Truman's order called for a system of loyalty boards empowered to determine if there were "reasonable grounds" for believing that any government employee belonged to an organization or held political ideas that might pose a "security risk" to the United States. People judged to be security risks would lose their government jobs. The Truman loyalty program also authorized the attorney general's office to identify organizations it considered subversive, and in December 1947 the first Attorney General's List was released.

The Truman administration's domestic loyalty program rested on its assessment of the extent of Soviet espionage activity in the United States, an issue that has generated great controversy over the years. Although few people ever doubted that Soviets were carrying out operations in the United States during the 1940s, sharp disagreement has persisted regarding their scope and success. Were Soviet agents operating only at the fringes, or had they penetrated the top levels of the U.S. government? Were they obtaining easily available information or stealing vital national secrets? Did the administration exaggerate, underestimate, or accurately assess the situation?

Such debates now take place in light of recently declassified evidence about Soviet activities in the United States. As early as 1943, a super-secret Army counterintelligence unit had begun intercepting transmissions between Moscow and the United States in 1943. Called the "Venona files" and finally released to the public in 1995, these intercepted messages suggested that the USSR gave financial support to America's Communist Party; had informants in wartime governmental agencies, including the Office of War Information (OWI) and the intelligence-gathering agency, the Office of Strategic Services (OSS); and began obtaining secret information about U.S. atomic work in 1944. The issue of Soviet espionage, in short, was a legitimate national security concern, but historians remain divided over the significance and reliability of specific pieces of the Venona evidence and over the extent of Truman's knowledge about the intercepts.

The president justified his loyalty program by claiming that the government faced relatively few security risks but that their potential to do harm demanded a response that was unprecedented in peacetime. Truman's position, however, failed to satisfy a wide range of critics. Some Republicans charged that hundreds, perhaps even thousands, of Communist Party members had been infiltrating the federal bureaucracy since the New Deal and stronger measures were required. On the other hand, the president's program worried civil liberties groups, who insisted that a limited internal security threat logically demanded an equally limited governmental response. Should not, for example, civil libertarians asked, any loyalty investigation distinguish between an atomic scientist with suspicious ties to the Soviet embassy and a clerical worker in the Interior Department with leftist political leanings? Truman's approach angered both fervent anticommunists, who accused the president of doing too little to fight the Red Menace at home, and civil libertarians, who charged him with going too far.

The National Security Act, the Marshall Plan, and the Berlin Crisis

The Truman Doctrine and the loyalty program only began the administration's national security initiatives. The National Security Act of 1947 created several new bureaucracies. It began the process that transformed the old Navy and War departments into a new Department of Defense, finally established in 1949. It instituted another new arm of the executive branch, the National Security Council, with broad authority over planning foreign policy.

It established the Air Force as a separate service equal to the Army and Navy. And it created the Central Intelligence Agency (CIA) to gather information and to undertake covert activities in support of the nation's newly defined security interests.

The CIA proved to be the most flexible arm of the national security bureaucracy. During the Second World War, the OSS had provided valuable intelligence and conducted espionage, but it was disbanded when the war was over because Americans generally opposed having a permanent secret agency devoted to spying in peacetime. Cold War fears about the spread of communism in Europe, however, had created pressure to reinstitute an intelligence agency, the CIA. Shrouded from public scrutiny, the new agency used its secret funds to gather information on Soviet activities and to encourage anticommunist activities around the globe. Between 1949 and 1952, the CIA's office for covert operations expanded its overseas stations from 7 to 47. The CIA cultivated ties with anti-Soviet groups in Eastern Europe and within the Soviet Union. It helped finance pro-U.S. labor unions in Western Europe to curtail the influence of leftist organizations. It orchestrated covert campaigns to prevent the Italian Communist Party from winning an electoral victory in 1948 and to bolster anticommunist parties in France, Japan, and elsewhere. From the beginning, the Truman administration encouraged the CIA to use its national security mandate broadly and aggressively.

Truman's White House also linked economic policies in Western Europe to the doctrine of containment. Concerned that the region's severe economic problems might embolden communist movements, Secretary of State George Marshall sought to strengthen the economies of Western Europe. Shortly after Congress approved funding for the Truman Doctrine, the secretary proposed the Marshall Plan. Under his plan, funds provided by the United States would enable governments in Western Europe to work together to design and carry out a broad program of postwar economic reconstruction. Between 1946 and 1951, the United States provided nearly $13 billion in assistance to 17 Western European nations. The Soviets were also invited to participate in the Marshall Plan, but American policy makers correctly anticipated that Moscow would avoid any program whose major goal was rebuilding capitalism in Europe. Instead, Stalin responded to the Marshall Plan by further consolidating the Soviets' sphere of influence in Eastern Europe.

The Marshall Plan proved a stunning success. When conservatives called it a "giveaway" program, the administration emphasized how it opened up both markets and investment opportunities in Western Europe to American

Courtesy of the George C. Marshall Research Library, Lexington, Virginia.

MARSHALL PLAN

This poster, by an artist from the Netherlands, was the winning entry in a contest run in Marshall Plan countries. It suggests how the plan encouraged a united Europe to transcend the divisions that had led to two World Wars.

businesses. Moreover, within its first few years the Marshall Plan helped stabilize the European economy by quadrupling industrial production. Improved standards of living enhanced political stability and, along with the CIA's covert activities, helped undermine the appeal of communist parties in Western Europe.

American policy makers believed that to revitalize Europe under the Marshall Plan they must first restore the economy of Germany, which was still divided into zones of occupation. In June 1948 the United States, Great Britain, and France announced a plan for currency reform that would be the first step in merging their sectors of occupation into a federal German republic. Soviet leaders were alarmed by the prospect of a revitalized German state under Western auspices. Having twice been invaded by Germany during the preceding 35 years, they wanted Germany reunited but weak. Hoping to sidetrack Western

plans for Germany, in June 1948 the Soviets cut off all highways, railroads, and water routes linking West Berlin, which was located within their zone, to West Germany.

This Soviet blockade of Berlin failed. American and British pilots, in what became known as the Berlin Airlift, made 250,000 flights, 'round-the-clock, to deliver a total of 2 million tons of supplies to the city's beleaguered residents. Truman, hinting at a military response, reinstated the draft and sent two squadrons of B-29 bombers to Britain. Conceding defeat, Stalin abandoned the blockade in May 1949. The Soviets then created the German Democratic Republic out of their East German sector. West Berlin survived as an enclave tied to the West. The "two Germanys" and the divided city of Berlin stood as symbols of Cold War divisions.

The Election of 1948

Concerns about national security helped Harry Truman win the 1948 presidential election, a victory that capped a remarkable political comeback. Truman had been losing the support of left-leaning Democrats, led by his Secretary of Commerce Henry A. Wallace, who thought his containment policies too militant. In September 1946, after Wallace criticized Truman's policies toward the Soviet Union, Truman had ousted him from the cabinet. Two months later, in the off-year national election of 1946, voters had given the Republicans control of Congress for the first time since 1928. Although Truman's standing in opinion polls had risen slowly in 1947 and 1948, most political pundits thought he had little chance to win the presidency in his own right in 1948. Truman waged a vigorous campaign against challenges from the left by a new Progressive Party, which nominated Wallace, and from the right by both the Republican nominee Thomas E. Dewey and the southern segregationist Strom Thurmond, the candidate of the States' Rights Party, or "Dixiecrats." Truman called the Republican-controlled Congress into special session, presented it with domestic policy proposals that were anathema to the GOP, and then denounced the "Republican Eightieth Congress, that do-nothing, good-for-nothing, worst Congress."

Thomas Dewey, who had been defeated by Franklin Roosevelt four years earlier, proved a cautious, lackluster campaigner in 1948. Even Republicans complained about his bland speeches and empty platitudes. A pro-Democratic newspaper caricatured Dewey's standard speech as four "historic sentences: Agriculture is important. Our rivers are full of fish. You cannot have freedom without liberty. The future lies ahead." When Dewey's campaign train, called "The Victory Special," reached Kansas City, Truman's old political base, Dewey was so confident of victory that he booked the hotel suite the president used whenever he was in town.

By contrast, Truman conducted an old-style, energetic campaign. He moved from town to town, stopping to denounce Dewey and Henry Wallace from the back of a railroad car. Dewey was plotting "a real hatchet job on the New Deal," he charged, and the Republican Party was controlled by a cabal of "cunning men" who were planning

WHISTLESTOP CAMPAIGN, 1948

Truman addressed cheering crowds from the back of a train, as captured in this photograph from Chillicothe, Ohio. How and why have electioneering techniques changed since 1948?

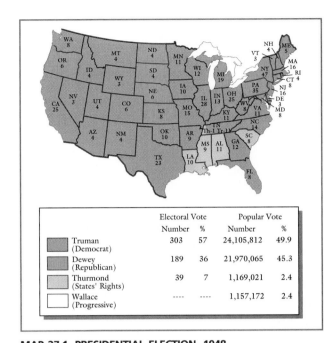

	Electoral Vote		Popular Vote	
	Number	%	Number	%
Truman (Democrat)	303	57	24,105,812	49.9
Dewey (Republican)	189	36	21,970,065	45.3
Thurmond (States' Rights)	39	7	1,169,021	2.4
Wallace (Progressive)	----	----	1,157,172	2.4

MAP 27.1 PRESIDENTIAL ELECTION, 1948
This electoral map helps show how, in this close election, Truman won the presidency with less than 50 percent of the popular vote.

"a return of the Wall Street economic dictatorship." "Give 'em hell, Harry!" shouted enthusiastic crowds. In November, Truman won only 49.6 percent of the popular vote but gained a solid majority in the electoral college. He, and not Thomas Dewey, would be moving back into the presidential suite in Kansas City—and into the White House in Washington, D.C.

Truman's victory now seems less surprising to historians than it did to political analysts in 1948. Despite Republican electoral gains in the congressional elections of 1946, the Democratic Party was hardly enfeebled. The Democrats running for Congress in 1948, who identified themselves with Franklin Roosevelt rather than with his successor, generally polled a higher percentage of the popular vote in their districts than did Truman. Still, voter loyalty to the memory of Roosevelt and to his New Deal coalition—labor union members, farmers, people of color, and social justice activists—helped Truman.

Truman also attracted a constituency of his own by virtue of his anticommunist policies. In this sense, Truman's presidency established a pattern that would persist for several decades: If Democratic candidates could avoid appearing "soft" or "weak" on national security issues, they stood a good chance of being elected president. The candidacies of both George McGovern in 1972 and Jimmy Carter in 1980 faltered on the issue of national security. Conversely, Harry Truman stood tough in 1948. His hard-line national security credentials proved especially effec-

tive against Henry Wallace. After the election, Wallace's Progressive Party, which had challenged Truman's national security policies and had promised to revive the New Deal at home, lay in shambles. Hampered by his refusal to reject support from the Communist Party, Wallace failed to win a single electoral vote and received less than 3 percent of the popular tally.

The Korean War Era, 1949–1952

To carry out the containment policy, the Truman administration marshaled the nation's economic and military resources and deepened its focus on national security issues. A series of Cold War crises in 1949 and the outbreak of war on the Korean peninsula heightened anticommunist fervor.

NATO, China, and the Bomb

Building on the Truman Doctrine, the Marshall Plan, the Berlin Airlift, and the 1949 creation of the Federal Republic of Germany (West Germany), the United States set about creating a worldwide system of military alliances. In April 1949 the United States, Canada, and 10 European nations formed the North Atlantic Treaty Organization (NATO). Members of NATO pledged that an attack against one would automatically be considered an attack against all and agreed to cooperate on economic and political, as well as military, matters. Some U.S. leaders worried about the implications of NATO. Republican Senator Robert Taft of Ohio declared that it was a provocation to the Soviet Union and an "entangling alliance" that defied common sense, violated the traditional U.S. foreign policy of nonentanglement, and threatened constitutional government by eclipsing Congress's power to declare war. The nation's use of military force, Taft warned, could be dictated by a response to events in other countries rather than shaped through its own policy-making processes. Even so, the NATO concept prevailed, and the United States expanded the idea of pursuing containment through such mutual security pacts during the 1950s.

Meanwhile, events in China aggravated Cold War tensions. Between 1945 and 1948, the United States had extended to Jiang Jieshi's government $1 billion in military aid and another billion in economic assistance. Jiang, however, steadily lost ground to the communist forces of Mao Zedong, who promised land reform and commanded wide support among China's peasantry. Although experienced U.S. diplomats privately predicted that Jiang's downfall was inevitable, the Truman administration continued

The cold war split Europe into two opposing alliances. Germany was divided into two countries: The Federal Republic of Germany (West Germany) and the German Democratic Republic (East Germany). Berlin, the former capital of Germany, was also divided. In 1949 NATO was formed, and in 1955 the Warsaw Pact came into existence.

THE DIVISION OF BERLIN

American Zone

British Zone

French Zone

Soviet Zone

(The American, British, and French zones were consolidated as West Berlin)

NATO Countries

Warsaw Pact Countries

Nonaligned Countries

MAP 27.2 DIVIDED GERMANY AND THE NATO ALLIANCE

This map shows the geopolitics of the Cold War. Which countries aligned with the United States through NATO? Which aligned with the Soviet Union through the Warsaw Pact? Note how Berlin became a divided city, although it was located within East Germany.

to publicly portray Jiang as a respected leader of "free China" and to prop up his regime.

In 1949, when Mao's armies forced Jiang off the mainland to the island of Formosa (Taiwan), many Americans wondered how communist forces could have triumphed. Republican opponents charged the Truman administration with a "sellout." Financed by conservative business leaders, the still powerful "China lobby" excoriated Tru-

man and his new secretary of state, Dean Acheson, for being soft on communism. Despite evidence of friction between Stalin and Mao, the detractors spoke of a global communist conspiracy directed from Moscow. Tainted by the "loss" of China, several State Department officials who had criticized Jiang or merely predicted his downfall were dismissed and discredited, depriving Washington of its most knowledgeable experts on China and Southeast Asia.

Meanwhile, responding to the criticism, Acheson and Truman escalated their anticommunist rhetoric. For more than 20 years, even after friction between China and the Soviet Union became evident, the United States refused to recognize or deal with Mao's "Red China." Jiang's anticommunist island of Taiwan, like Berlin, became a powerful symbol of the Cold War.

The communist threat seemed even more alarming when, in September 1949, the Soviets exploded a crude atomic device, marking the end of the U.S. nuclear monopoly. Already besieged by critics who saw a world filled with Soviet gains and American defeats, Truman issued reassuring public statements but privately took the advice of hard-line advisers and authorized the development of a new bomb based on the still unproven concept of nuclear fusion. The decision to build this "hydrogen bomb" wedded the doctrine of containment to the creation of ever more deadly nuclear technology.

NSC-68

Prompted by events of 1949, the Truman administration reviewed its foreign policy assumptions. George Kennan, worried that a simplistic and increasingly militaristic version of his containment concept was emerging, resigned from the State Department's policy planning staff. As a result, the task of conducting this review fell to Paul Nitze, a hard-liner who produced a top-secret policy paper officially identified as National Security Council document 68 (NSC-68). It provided a blueprint for both the rhetoric and the substance of future Cold War foreign policy.

NSC-68 opened with a melodramatic account of a global ideological clash between "freedom," spread by U.S. power, and "slavery," promoted by the Soviet Union as the center of "international communism." Warning against any negotiations with the Soviets, the report urged a full-scale offensive to enlarge U.S. power. It endorsed the more vigorous use of covert action, economic pressure, propaganda campaigns, and a massive military buildup. Because Americans might oppose larger military spending and budget deficits, the report warned, U.S. actions should be labeled as "defensive" and be presented as a stimulus to the economy rather than as a drain on national resources. Although NSC-68 remained classified for more than two decades, the early 1950s public heard its message well. Secretary of State Dean Acheson stumped the country preaching its tenets and elaborating on its portrayal of the Cold War as a global showdown between good and evil.

The Korean War

The dire warnings of NSC-68 seemed to be confirmed in June 1950 when communist North Korea attacked South Korea. The Truman administration portrayed the move as a simple case of Soviet-inspired aggression against a free state. An assistant secretary of state remarked that the relationship of the Soviet Union to North Korea was "the same as that between Walt Disney and Donald Duck." Truman again invoked the policy of containment: "If aggression is successful in Korea, we can expect it to spread through Asia and Europe to this hemisphere."

The Korean situation, however, was partly a civil war. Korea had been occupied by Japan between 1905 and 1945, and after Japan's defeat in the Second World War, Koreans had expected to establish their own independent state. Instead, the postwar Soviet and U.S. zones of occupation became separate political entities. Against the desires of both North and South Koreans, Korea became two states, split at the 38th parallel. The Soviet Union supported a North Korean communist government under the oppressive dictatorship of Kim Il-sung. The United States backed Syngman Rhee, who held a Ph.D. from Princeton University, to head the unsteady and autocratic government in South Korea. Despite being split along an arbitrary line, Korea remained a single society, divided by political factions and religious differences as much as by geography.

Both Korean leaders hoped that the patronage of a superpower might help bolster their control and advance their respective notions of how Korean society should be organized. Rhee's regime, protective of upper-class landholders, generated opposition in South Korea, a movement that Kim's communist dictatorship encouraged. As discontent spread in South Korea, Kim moved troops across the 38th parallel on June 25, 1950, to attempt unification. Earlier, he had consulted both Soviet and Chinese leaders about his plans and received their support, after assuring them that a U.S. military response was highly unlikely. Under attack, Rhee appealed to the United States to protect his government.

The fighting in Korea escalated into an international conflict. The Soviets, uninformed about the precise details of Kim's plans, were boycotting the UN on the day the invasion was launched. Consequently, they were not present to veto a U.S. proposal to send a peacekeeping force to Korea. Under UN auspices, the United States rushed assistance to Rhee, who moved to eliminate disloyal South Korean civilians as well as to repel the invading North Koreans.

U.S. goals in Korea were unclear. Should the United States seek to contain communism by driving the North Koreans back over the 38th parallel? Or should it try to reunify the country under Rhee's leadership? At first, that decision could be postponed because the war was going so badly. North Korean troops pushed their Soviet-made

Courtesy of the Truman Library.

REFUGEES MOVE SOUTH

The Korean War disrupted life on the peninsula. Here, refugees flee their homes after receiving evacuation orders from the South Korean army.

tanks rapidly southward; within three months, they took Seoul, the capital of South Korea, and reached the southern tip of the Korean peninsula. American troops seemed unprepared and, unaccustomed to the unusually hot Korean weather during these first months, many fell sick. Fearing the worst, U.S. generals laid contingency plans for a large-scale American evacuation from Pusan. American firepower, however, gradually took its toll on the elite troops who had spearheaded North Korea's rapid move southward. North Korea had to send fresh, untrained recruits to replace seasoned fighters. As supply lines stretched out, the North Korean effort became more vulnerable.

General Douglas MacArthur devised a plan that most other commanders considered crazy: an amphibious landing behind enemy lines at Inchon. MacArthur, now 70 years old, remained as bold and egotistical as he had been both during the Second World War and as head of the occupation government of Japan. Those stunned by his invasion proposal were even more astounded by its results.

On September 15, 1950, the Marines successfully landed 13,000 troops at Inchon, suffered only 21 deaths, and moved back into Seoul within 11 days.

The price of recovering the military offensive was devastation on the ground. The Korean War was called a "limited" war because the United States did not employ atomic weapons, but intense American bombing preceded every military move. The number of estimated dead and wounded reached perhaps one-tenth of Korea's total population. As armies contested for control of Seoul, the city became rubble, with only the Capitol building and a train station left standing.

As MacArthur's troops drove northward, Truman faced a crucial decision. MacArthur, emboldened by success, urged moving beyond containment to an all-out war of "liberation" and reunification. Other advisers warned Truman that China would retaliate if U.S. forces approached its border. Truman allowed MacArthur to carry the war into North Korea but ordered him to avoid antagonizing China.

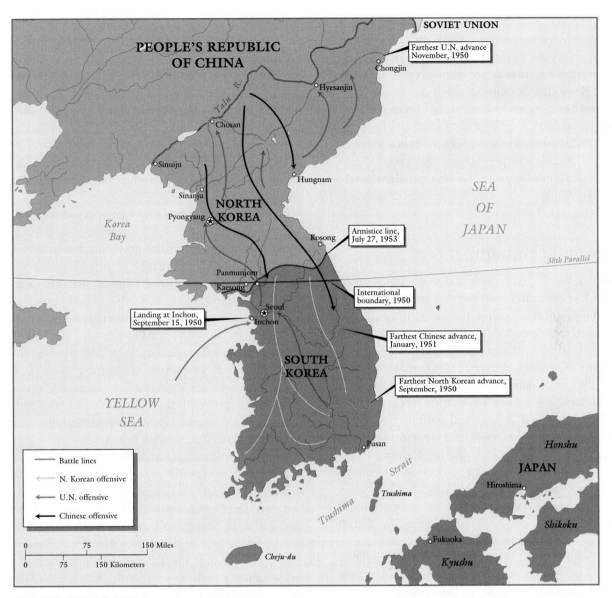

MAP 27.3 KOREAN WAR

This map shows the lines of battle and the armistice line that still divides the two Koreas. Note the advances made first by North Korea and then by UN (United States–led) troops.

 View an animated version of this map or related maps at http://history.wadsworth.com/murrin_LEP4e.

MacArthur pushed too far. Downplaying encounters between his troops and Chinese "volunteers," he continued to advance toward the Yalu River on the Chinese–Korean border. China responded by sending troops into North Korea and driving MacArthur back across the 38th parallel. With China now in the war, Truman again faced the question of military goals. When MacArthur's troops regained the initiative, Truman ordered his general to negotiate a truce at the 38th parallel. MacArthur, challenging the president, argued instead for all-out victory over North Korea—and over China, too. Truman thereupon relieved MacArthur of his command in April 1951, pointing out that the Constitution specified that mili-

tary officers must obey the orders of the president, the commander-in-chief.

MacArthur returned home as a war hero. New York City greeted him with a ticker-tape parade that drew a crowd nearly twice as large as the one that had greeted General Dwight Eisenhower at the end of the Second World War. One poll reported that less than 30 percent of the U.S. public supported Truman's actions. The China lobby portrayed MacArthur as a martyr to Truman's "no-win" containment policy. For a brief but intense moment, MacArthur seemed a genuine presidential possibility for 1952. This outpouring of admiration, however, reflected MacArthur's personal charisma rather than any

significant public support for a full-scale land war in Asia. During Senate hearings on the general's dismissal, military strategists expressed their opposition to a wider war, and most Americans apparently preferred a negotiated settlement in Korea. Truman now set about convincing North Korea and South Korea to meet at the conference table. Dwight Eisenhower, the Republican candidate for president in 1952, promised to go to Korea to hasten the peace process, if elected. The negotiations that eventually reestablished the borderline at the 38th parallel emerged as a major foreign policy task for the new Eisenhower administration in 1953.

Korea and Containment

The Korean War had repercussions throughout the world. It focused American foreign policy ever more narrowly on anticommunism and justified the global offensive that NSC-68 had recommended. The United States announced a plan to rearm West Germany, scarcely five years after Germany's defeat, and increased NATO's military forces. In 1951 the United States signed a formal peace treaty with Japan, and a Japanese-American security pact granted the United States bases on Okinawa and permission to station U.S. troops in Japan. The United States also acquired bases in Saudi Arabia and Morocco, bolstering its strategic position in the oil-rich Middle East. In 1950 direct military aid to Latin American governments, which had been voted down in the past, slid through Congress. In French Indochina, Truman provided assistance to strengthen French efforts against a communist-led independence movement. In the Philippines, the United States stepped up military assistance to suppress the leftist Huk rebels. And in 1951 the ANZUS collective security pact linked the United States strategically to Australia and New Zealand. Throughout the world, economic pressure, CIA covert activities, and propaganda campaigns helped forge anticommunist alliances. Truman's global "Campaign of Truth," an intensive informational and psychological offensive, used mass media and cultural exchanges to counter Soviet propaganda.

While the Truman administration fortified America's strategic position throughout the world, U.S. military budgets increased in order to fund ongoing weapons research and production. The Atomic Energy Commission had been created in 1946 to succeed the Manhattan Project in overseeing development of nuclear power; aviation had received special government funding for the first time in the 1946 budget; the army had joined with aircraft manufacturers in an effort to develop surface-to-surface missiles. To coordinate global strategy with the development of long-range weapons, a new "think

tank"—RAND, an acronym for Research and Development—was created. Expensive contracts for manufacturing military materials worried cost-conscious members of Congress, but the prospect that the contracts would create new jobs in their home districts muted their opposition. The Cold War, especially after Korea, thus intensified what historian Michael Sherry has called "the militarization of American life": a steady military buildup and an intermingling of military and economic policies, all justified by an emphasis on anticommunism at home and abroad.

Fearful of communist gains, U.S. policy makers opposed any movement that was left-leaning in its political orientation. The U.S. occupation government in Japan, for example, increasingly restricted the activities of labor unions, suspended an antitrust program that American officials had earlier implemented, brought back conservative wartime leaders, and barred communists from government offices and universities. As in Germany, the United States tried to contain communism by strengthening industrial elites and promoting economic growth. U.S. purchases during the Korean conflict stimulated Japan's economy and provided the foundation for the pro-capitalist, anticommunist Japanese government that succeeded the American occupation in 1952.

In Africa, anticommunism brought the United States into an alliance with South Africa. In 1948 the all-white Nationalist Party instituted a legal system based on elaborate rules of racial separation and subordination of blacks (called *apartheid*). Some State Department officials warned that supporting apartheid in South Africa would damage U.S. prestige, but the Truman administration decided to cement an alliance with South Africa nonetheless. That country, the Truman administration reasoned, possessed important raw materials (especially uranium for bombs and manganese for steel) and a large labor force. Moreover, South Africa's Nationalist Party was militantly anticommunist.

From 1947 to the early 1950s, U.S. citizens often felt embattled and insecure. Stalin in the Soviet Union and Mao in China, both ambitious dictators, denounced the United States and promoted communism in other countries. The American policy of containment invoked the rhetoric of defensiveness: the term "national security" replaced "national interest"; the War Department became the Department of Defense. Yet the United States, a regional power before the Second World War, was anything but passive. It moved rapidly during the early Cold War era to stake out a global military and strategic presence. The Truman administration extended U.S. power into the former British sphere of influence of Iran, Greece, and

Edward Lansdale: Psy-ops in the Cold War

EDWARD LANSDALE

America's best known super-spy stands here (second from left) with CIA director Allen Dulles (left) and Generals Charles P. Cabell and Nathan Twining.

Edward G. Lansdale (1908–1987) was one of America's most influential spies during the early Cold War. He introduced a strategy of psychological operations, or "psy-ops." Born in Detroit in 1908, Lansdale learned techniques of psychological persuasion as a young advertising executive and, during the Second World War, in the famed Office of Strategic Services (OSS). At the end of the war, Lansdale was sent to the Philippines, America's former colony, to rebuild security services. Returning there a few years later as the CIA's chief operative, he helped design the Philippine government's campaign, including psy-ops, against an uprising led by a communist-oriented peasant army called the Huks.

Lansdale had formed a close friendship with Ramón Magsaysay, who became president of the Philippines after an electoral battle marked by an influx of U.S. money. Lansdale's advertising expertise was also evident in the slogan "Magsaysay is my guy" and in an electoral theme song called the "Magsaysay Mambo." Lansdale tramped through the countryside, learning folktales and collecting songs. He later wrote that he came to understand that "the Huk battleground was a haunted place filled with ghosts and eerie creatures." He sought to design psy-ops to simulate vampire-like figures, malevolent eyes, and other supernatural events that he felt would strike fear into the Huk rebels. The anti-Huk campaign also featured intensive bombing and huge shipments of military equipment from the United States.

With Magsaysay's military victory over the Huks, Landale's reputation as a skilled anticommunist operative soared. In 1954, he worked with a team that went to Saigon, Vietnam, to mount a campaign modeled on the one in the Philippines. In Southeast Asia, he orchestrated a strategy that included distribution of documents purporting to show that communist forces under Ho Chi Minh were slaying civilian opponents, sabotage in North Vietnam, training a new South Vietnamese army, and helping to rig an election that installed Ngo Dinh Diem as president of South Vietnam. U.S. involvement in the South Vietnamese government of Diem steadily expanded.

Throughout the late 1950s and 1960s, Lansdale served in various posts in the U.S. government, once trying to organize a plan of psychological warfare against Fidel Castro in Cuba and returning again to Vietnam in 1965. In 1963, he received a Distinguished Service Medal for his work, which was becoming known as "counter-insurgency."

Lansdale's legacy of using secret psychological operations and daring, even ruthless, tactics in foreign nations attracted both defenders and critics. Some admirers have called him America's "greatest spy." To others, his assumption that the United States could manipulate other people's culture for political ends projected a hubris that could easily veer into disaster. Upon his death, Lansdale left an impressive, well-documented collection of songs, which he had taped in the Philippines and Vietnam, and had gathered from U.S. soldiers serving in Southeast Asia. Edward Lansdale will remain an enigmatic figure—part spy, part ethnomusicologist.

Turkey; initiated the Marshall Plan and NATO; and transformed former enemies—Italy, Germany, and Japan—into anti-Soviet states. Furthermore, the United States assumed control of hundreds of Pacific islands, launched research to develop the hydrogen bomb, winked at anticommunist ally South Africa's apartheid policies, solidified its sphere of influence in Latin America, acquired bases around the world, and devised a master plan for using military, economic, and covert action to fight any group that opposed U.S. interests. Beginning with the Truman Doctrine of 1947, the United States reinvented itself as a global superpower.

Containment at Home

Although containment abroad generally gained bipartisan support, Harry Truman's national security policies at home became increasingly divisive. An emotional debate over alleged communist influences in the United States raged from the late 1940s through the early 1950s. Taking their cue from Truman's anticommunist rhetoric, conservatives leveled more strident allegations of internal communist subversion, even charging Truman's own administration with harboring people who were disloyal or soft on communism. Civil libertarians, on the other side, complained that a witch-hunt was being conducted against people whose only sins were dissent or support for leftist, or pro-labor, political agendas. Many people, even devoted anticommunists, began to worry that irresponsible smear campaigns and wild goose chases after unlikely offenders only hampered the search for authentic Soviet agents. The search for supposed subversives affected many aspects of postwar life. Many politicians, professional organizations, labor unions, business corporations, and individual citizens found it prudent to join in the "red-baiting" to demonstrate their anticommunist credentials. A particularly aggressive group of anticommunists emerged in Congress.

Anticommunism and the Labor Movement

An unprecedented wave of labor strikes had swept across the country after the end of the Second World War. Militant workers had struck for increased wages and for a greater voice in workplace routines and production decisions. Strikes had brought both the auto industry and the electronics industry to a standstill. In Stamford, Connecticut, and Lancaster, Pennsylvania, general strikes had led to massive work stoppages that later spread to Rochester,

STEELWORKERS' STRIKE
Striking steelworkers picket their employer in 1946. During that year, strikes affected millions of American workers.

New York; Pittsburgh, Pennsylvania; Oakland, California; and other large cities. By 1947 labor militancy had begun to subside as Truman took a hard line. He warned oil refinery strikers to "cut out all the foolishness." He threatened to seize mines and railroads shut down by work stoppages, and ordered the strikers to return to their jobs.

The labor unrest of the immediate postwar years made unions a prominent target for anticommunist legislators. In 1947 congressional opponents of organized labor effectively tapped anticommunist sentiment to help pass the Labor-Management Relations Act, popularly known as the Taft-Hartley Act. The law negated some of the gains unions had made during the 1930s by limiting a union's power to conduct boycotts, to compel employers to accept "closed shops" in which only union members could be hired, and to conduct a strike that the president judged against the national interest. In addition, as a means of curtailing "wildcat" strikes, the law strengthened the power of union leaders to discipline their own members. Finally, Taft-Hartley required that these same union officials sign affidavits stating that they did not belong to the Communist Party or to any other "subversive" organization. A union that refused to comply was effectively denied protection under national labor laws when engaged in conflict with management. Truman vetoed Taft-Hartley, but Congress swiftly overrode him.

The issue of communists in the labor movement not only concerned Congress but, especially after Taft-Hartley, affected union politics as well. Anticommunist unionists had long charged that some communist organizers, despite their energetic work in grassroots campaigns, were

more loyal to the Communist Party than to their unions or to the nation. Differences over whether labor should endorse the Democratic Party or Henry Wallace's third-party effort in 1948 also heightened tensions within many unions. In the years following Truman's victory, the Congress of Industrial Organizations (CIO) expelled 13 unions—and a full third of its membership—for allegedly following Communist Party policies. Meanwhile, as red-hunters searched for subversives in the workplace, many workers found their jobs at risk because of their political ideas. Businesses that were hostile to worker demands often employed anticommunism as a tactic to lessen labor's power. By the end of the Truman era, some type of loyalty-security check had been conducted on about 20 percent of the American workforce, more than 13 million people.

HUAC and the Loyalty Program

Anticommunists also scrutinized the entertainment industry. In 1947, only three days after the unveiling of the Truman Doctrine, the House Un-American Activities Committee (popularly known as HUAC) opened hearings to expose alleged communist infiltration in Hollywood. Basking in the glare of newsreel cameras, committee members seized on the refusal of 10 screenwriters, producers, and directors who had been or still were members of the Communist Party to testify about their own political affiliations and those of other members of the film community. Known as "the Hollywood Ten," this group claimed that the First Amendment shielded their political activities from HUAC's scrutiny. After the federal courts upheld HUAC's power and denied the Hollywood Ten's First Amendment claim, members of the group went to prison for contempt of Congress.

Meanwhile, studio heads secretly drew up a blacklist of alleged subversives who could no longer work in the entertainment industry. Industry leaders denied the existence of such a list, but their disavowals were unconvincing. The actor John Wayne later explained, "The only thing our side did that was anywhere near blacklisting was just running a lot of people out of the business." By the mid-1950s hundreds of people in Hollywood and in the fledgling television industry—technicians who worked behind the scenes as well as performers who appeared in front of them—were unable to find jobs until they agreed to appear before HUAC and other investigative bodies. There, they were required to name people whom they had seen at some "communist meeting" some time in the past. Some well-known celebrities, such as writer Lillian Hellman, invoked the Fifth Amendment and refused to answer any questions. Others, such as Hollywood director Elia Kazan,

cooperated with the interrogation. Compliance or resistance to naming names created a split in the entertainment industry that lasted for decades.

Ronald Reagan and Richard Nixon, two future Republican presidents, first attracted the political spotlight through the HUAC hearings. Reagan, who was president of the Screen Actors Guild and also a secret informant for the FBI (identified as "T-10"), decried the communist presence in Hollywood. Nixon, then an obscure member of Congress from California, began his political ascent in 1948 when he associated himself with Whittaker Chambers, a journalist who had once been active in communist circles. Appearing before HUAC, Chambers charged Alger Hiss, a prominent New Deal Democrat who had a long career in government, with having links to the Communist Party and with divulging classified information to Soviet agents during the late 1930s.

The Hiss-Chambers-Nixon affair set off a raging controversy. Hiss maintained that he had been framed in an elaborate FBI plot and alleged that the Bureau had even rigged his typewriter so it would appear to be the source of incriminating evidence. Although the passage of time legally shielded Hiss from prosecution for any acts of espionage that might have occurred during the 1930s, he was charged with committing perjury in his Congressional testimony. Nixon and his supporters considered the exposure of Hiss, who had been one of Franklin Roosevelt's advisers during the Yalta Conference (see chapter 26), proof that the search for Soviet subversion required greater vigor than the Truman administration could provide. To HUAC's critics, however, the Hollywood Ten and Hiss cases suggested the consequences of overzealous witch-hunting. Debates over whether the Hiss case was an example of high-level espionage or anticommunist hysteria would continue for decades.

During the mid-1990s, the availability of long-classified documents, such as those in the Venona files, tilted the debate against Hiss. He died in 1996, at the age of 92, still maintaining his innocence and still attracting his defenders. Even so, a growing number of historians came to agree that the evidence suggested that Hiss (along with several other high-ranking public officials and certain lower-level government employees with ties to the American Communist Party) had passed some information to agents of the Soviet Union during the 1930s and 1940s. The precise circumstances surrounding each individual case, however, remained hotly contested.

Meanwhile, as controversy swirled around the Hiss episode, the Truman administration continued to pursue its own anticommunist policies. Under the president's loyalty program, hundreds of government employees were dismissed. Truman's attorney general Tom Clark (whom

As the effort to enact this part of the bill stalled, a scaled-down vision of domestic policymaking gradually emerged. The law that Congress finally passed, renamed the Employment Act of 1946, called for "maximum" (rather than full) employment and specifically acknowledged that private enterprise, not government, bore primary responsibility for economic decision making. Recognizing that the national government could play an ongoing role in economic management, however, the act created a new executive branch body, the Council of Economic Advisers, to help formulate long-range policy recommendations. The measure signaled that government would assume some yet to be defined responsibility for the performance of the economy.

A crucial factor in the gradual acceptance of Washington's new role was a growing faith that *advice* from economic experts, as an alternative to government *planning*, could guarantee a constantly expanding economy. An influential group of theorists, many of them disciples of the British economist John Maynard Keynes, insisted that the United States no longer needed to endure the boom-and-bust cycles that had long afflicted its economy. Instead of holding the economy hostage to the largely uncoordinated decisions of private individuals and business firms, economists with new theoretical expertise could advise the government on coherent policies most likely to produce uninterrupted economic growth. If the economy lagged, for example, government might help encourage growth by boosting its own spending.

The promise of economic growth as a permanent condition dazzled postwar leaders. Corporate executives, many of whom had feared that the end of the war would intensify labor unrest and trigger recession, viewed economic growth as a guarantee of social stability. The Truman administration embraced the idea that the government should encourage economic growth by updating, through measures such as the Employment Act of 1946, the cooperative relationship with both big business and organized labor that the Roosevelt administration had pursued during the Second World War. The president's advisers claimed that such cooperation would actually ease domestic policy making. Economic growth would produce increased tax revenues and, in turn, finance Washington's domestic programs. "With economic expansion, every problem is capable of solution," insisted George Soule, a celebrant of economic growth. Walter Heller, another leader of the postwar generation of economists, likened the promise of sustained growth to finding both the rainbow and its proverbial pot of gold. Using the relatively new measure of gross national product (GNP), postwar experts could actually calculate the nation's growing economic bounty. Developed in 1939, GNP—defined as the total dollar value of all goods and services produced in the nation during a given year—became the standard gauge of economic health.

Truman and his advisers soon began preaching the gospel of economic growth. This economic faith nicely complemented their foreign policy programs. Sharp increases in military spending stimulated the sluggish postwar economy without raising the opposition that costly domestic measures would have sparked. Rearmament and the Keynsian-style stimulus dovetailed in a policy that some historians now call "military Keynsianism." As *U.S. News and World Report* put it at the time, "government planners figure that they have found the magic formula for almost endless good times. [The] Cold War is an automatic pump primer." Cold War assistance programs, such as the Marshall Plan, also helped create markets and investment opportunities overseas. As Western Europe made its postwar recovery, sales of American products, such as Coca-Cola, soared. Economic growth at home was linked to development in the world at large—and to the all-pervasive concern with national security.

Shaping the Fair Deal

In his inaugural address of 1949, Truman unveiled a domestic agenda he had outlined during his 1948 presidential campaign: the "Fair Deal." He called for the extension of popular New Deal programs such as Social Security and minimum wage laws; enactment of long-stalled, Democratic-sponsored civil rights and national health care legislation; federal aid for education; and repeal of the Taft-Hartley Act of 1947. Charles Brannan, Truman's secretary of agriculture, proposed an ambitious new plan for supporting farm prices by means of additional governmental subsidies, and the president urged substantial spending on public housing projects. The assumption on which Truman built his Fair Deal—that enlarged domestic programs could be financed from economic growth—would dominate political discussions for years to come. Through the magic of constant economic growth, all Americans would enjoy progressively bigger pieces of an always expanding economic pie.

Two prominent government programs, both of which predated Truman's administration, illustrate the approach to domestic policy making that dominated the Fair Deal years. The first, the so-called GI Bill (officially entitled the Serviceman's Readjustment Act of 1944), had always enjoyed strong support in Congress. After the First World War, Congress had voted veterans cash pensions or bonuses. This time, Congress worked out a comprehensive set of benefits for the several million men and 40,000 women who had served in the armed forces. The GI Bill

GI JOES STORM CAMPUS, 1946
Men who had served in the Second World War, aided by the GI Bill, flooded colleges after war's end. This picture from the University of Minnesota shows the surge in male students along with the attire and the slightly older average age of college students in the late 1940s.

Courtesy of the Minnesota Historical Society.

encompassed several different programs, including immediate financial assistance for college and job-training programs for veterans of the Second World War. By 1947, the year of peak veteran enrollment, about half of the entire college and university population was receiving government assistance. In other provisions, veterans received preferential treatment when applying for government jobs; generous terms on loans when purchasing homes or businesses; and, eventually, comprehensive medical care in veterans' hospitals. The Veterans' Readjustment Assistance Act of 1952, popularly known as the GI Bill of Rights, extended these programs to veterans of the Korean War. In essence, although the Truman administration did not enact FDR's Second Bill of Rights in its entirety, the Fair Deal did grant many of its social and economic protections to veterans.

Social Security, the most popular part of Roosevelt's New Deal, expanded under Truman's Fair Deal. When conservatives attacked Social Security as an unwarranted extension of federal power, the Truman administration noted that the program included needed support for the disabled and the blind and that older people had earned the "income security" through years of work and monetary contributions withheld from their paychecks. Under the Social Security Act of 1950, the level of benefits increased significantly; the retirement portions of the program expanded; and coverage was extended to more than 10 million people, including agricultural workers. As subsequent debate would highlight, however, no new financing system accompanied this expansion—a consequence of a widespread faith that sustained growth could under-

write the cost of domestic programs and a belief that politically divisive adjustments could be postponed for a later day.

The more expansive (and expensive) Fair Deal proposals either failed or were scaled back. For instance, Truman's plan for a comprehensive national health insurance program ran into strong opposition. The American Medical Association (AMA) and the American Hospital Association (AHA) blocked any government intervention in the traditional fee-for-service medical system and steered Congress toward a less controversial alternative—federal financing of new hospitals under the Hill-Burton Act. Opinion polls suggested that most voters, many of whom were enrolling in private health insurance plans such as Blue Cross and Blue Shield, were either apathetic or confused about Truman's national health proposals.

Continued shortage of affordable housing in urban areas after the war stirred greater support for home-building programs, another part of Truman's Fair Deal. Private construction firms and real estate agents welcomed extension of federal home loan guarantees, such as those established under the GI Bill and through the Federal Housing Administration (FHA), but they lobbied against publicly financed housing projects. Yet even conservatives such as Senator Taft recognized the housing shortage and supported the Housing Act of 1949. This law promised "a decent home and a suitable living environment for every American family." It authorized construction of 810,000 public housing units (cutting back Truman's goal of 1.05 million). The same law also provided federal funds for "urban renewal" zones, areas to be

KIDS LINE UP FOR SHOTS

Polio was one of the most feared diseases of the Cold War period because it crippled young children. Its postwar history illustrated differences between the Canadian and U.S. medical systems. The Canadian government, with its national health care system, was heavily involved in funding research, testing new medicines, and ultimately distributing the new vaccine. In the United States, a nongovernmental organization called the March of Dimes—famous for its effective solicitation of small donations—took the lead. Dr. Jonas Salk, cooperating with Canadian researchers, developed an effective vaccine that was approved in 1954.

cleared of rundown dwellings and rebuilt with new construction. The Housing Act of 1949 set forth bold goals but provided only modest funding for its public housing component.

Fair Deal policy making ultimately focused on specific groups, such as veterans and older Americans, rather than on more extensive programs such as a national health care plan and a large-scale commitment to government-built, affordable housing projects. Opponents of economic planning and greater government spending considered the broader proposals of the Fair Deal—such as health care—to be "welfare," and the Truman administration found it easier to defend more narrowly targeted programs that could be hailed as economic security measures for specific groups. This approach to social policy making under the Fair Deal significantly narrowed the approach of Roosevelt's Second Bill of Rights, which had envisioned an array of constitutionally guaranteed entitlements for all citizens, even as it embraced the idea that government should play an active role in social and economic betterment.

Civil Rights

Truman, while modifying the New Deal's domestic policy assumptions, actually broadened its commitment to civil rights. In fact, he supported the fight against racial discrimination more strongly than any previous president.

During his 1948 presidential campaign, Truman had made a special appeal to African American voters. He had strongly endorsed proposals advanced by a civil rights committee he established in 1946. The committee's report, entitled "To Secure These Rights," called for federal legislation against lynching; a special civil rights division within the Department of Justice; antidiscrimination initiatives in employment, housing, and public facilities; and desegregation of the military. Although these proposals prompted many white southern Democrats to bolt to the short-lived Dixiecrat Party in the 1948 election, they won Truman significant support from African Americans.

The Dixiecrat Party episode of 1948, a reaction to Truman's stance on civil rights, portended significant political change among southern whites, who had been voting overwhelmingly Democratic since the late 19th century. Strom Thurmond, the Dixiecrats' presidential candidate, denounced Truman for offering a "civil wrongs" program and charged that "radicals, subversives, and reds" had captured the Democratic Party. Although Thurmond claimed that southerners did not oppose the concept of civil rights measures, he maintained that the Constitution required that they come from state governments and not from Washington, D.C. Other white southern Democrats pledged to fight any federal effort to end the pattern of legally enforced racial segregation. Thurmond carried four states in 1948, and his candidacy showed that the race issue was powerful enough to lead lifelong southern Democrats to abandon their party in national presidential elections.

Despite discord within Democratic ranks, Truman generally supported the civil rights movement. When successive Congresses failed to enact any civil rights legislation—including a law against lynching and a ban on the poll taxes that prevented most southern blacks from voting—the movement turned to a sympathetic White House and to the federal courts. After the labor leader A. Philip Randolph threatened to organize protests against continued segregation in the military, Truman issued an executive order calling for desegregation of the armed forces, a move that began to be implemented toward the end of the Korean War. Truman also endorsed the efforts of the Fair Employment Practices Commission (FEPC) to end racial discrimination in federal hiring.

Members of Truman's administration also spoke candidly of how segregation tarnished America's image abroad. "Communist propaganda twisted and distorted our civil-rights problems," argued one Democratic Sena-

© Bettmann/Corbis.

tor, and created an "enormous but little understood worldwide impact." In a world "which is 90 percent colored," said Truman, racial discrimination issued an invitation to communism. Cold War anxiety prompted the government to spy on some African American leaders with links to communism, but it also made segregation into a foreign policy liability by highlighting the limits of America's claim to represent liberty and equality.

Meanwhile, Truman's Justice Department regularly appeared in court on behalf of litigants who contested government-backed public school segregation and "restrictive covenants" (legal agreements that prevented racial or religious minorities from acquiring real estate). In 1946, the Supreme Court declared restrictive covenants illegal and began chipping away at the "separate but equal" principle used since *Plessy* v. *Ferguson* (1896) to justify segregated schools. In 1950, the Court ruled that under the 14th Amendment racial segregation in state-financed graduate and law schools was unconstitutional. In light of these decisions, all of the traditional legal arguments used since *Plessy* to legitimate racial segregation in public schools seemed open to a successful challenge. The challenge would finally come in 1954 (see chapter 28).

In summary, the years immediately after the Second World War marked a turning point in domestic policy making. The New Deal's hope for comprehensive socioeconomic planning gave way to the Fair Deal's view that the nation could expect uninterrupted economic growth. Henceforth, Washington could reap, through taxation, its own steady share of a growing economy and so finance programs targeted to assist specific groups, such as military veterans and older people. As one supporter of this new approach argued, postwar policy makers were sophisticated enough to embrace "partial remedies," such as the GI Bill, rather than to wait for fanciful "cure-alls," such as FDR's Second Bill of Rights.

☙ A Changing Culture

The postwar years brought dramatic changes in the daily life of most Americans. Encouraged by the advertising industry, most people seemed, at one level, to automatically view anything new as "progress." Yet, at another level, the pace and scope of change during these years brought a feeling of uneasiness into American life.

Jackie Robinson and the Baseball "Color Line"

The interplay between embracing and resisting change could be seen in the integration of organized baseball during the 1940s and 1950s. In 1947, major league baseball's

policy of racial segregation finally cracked when Jackie Robinson, who had played in the Negro National League, became the Brooklyn Dodgers' first baseman. Certain players, including several on Robinson's own club, had talked about a boycott. Baseball's leadership, needing new sources of players and aware of the steady stream of African American fans coming out to the parks, threatened to suspend any player who refused to play with Robinson. (Baseball's moguls, though, did relatively little to protect Robinson. He was ordered to endure, without protest, racist insults, flying spikes, and brush-back pitches during his rookie season.)

The pressure to integrate the national pastime became inexorable. Several months after Robinson's debut, the Cleveland Indians signed center fielder Larry Doby, and other African American stars quickly began leaving the Negro leagues for the American and National circuits. Eventually, the talents of Robinson—named Rookie of the Year in 1947 and the National League's Most Valuable Player in 1949—and other African American players

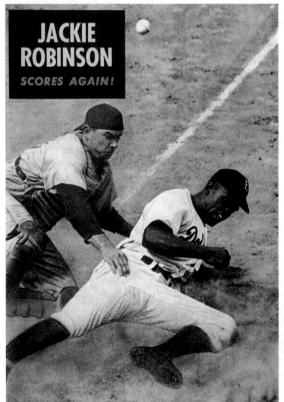

Michael Barson Collection/Past Perfect.

JACKIE ROBINSON

In 1947 Jackie Robinson joined the Brooklyn Dodgers and became the first African American since the 19th century to play major league baseball. He had served as a lieutenant in the Army during the Second World War. Racial integration of the national pastime of baseball became a powerful symbol of progress in race relations.

carried the day. By 1960 every major league team fielded African American players, and some began extensive re-cruiting in Puerto Rico and elsewhere in the Caribbean. During the 50th anniversary of Robinson's debut, major league baseball staged elaborate memorial ceremonies for Robinson, who had died in 1972, and congratulated the sport for having led the fight against racial prejudice dur-ing the Cold War years.

During the late 1940s and early 1950s, however, base-ball's leaders had also worked to limit the participation of African Americans. Several teams waited for years before fielding any black players, claiming they could find no talented prospects. More commonly, teams restricted the number of nonwhite players they would take on and

kept their managers, coaches, and front-office personnel solidly white. Even Jackie Robinson, a successful entrepre-neur outside of baseball, never received an offer to return to the game in a management capacity after he retired as a player.

Suburban Development

In suburbia, too, change was both celebrated and feared. Suburban living had long been a feature of the "American dream." The new Long Island, New York, suburb of Levit-town, which welcomed its first residents in October 1947, seemed to make that dream a reality, at affordable prices, for middle-income families.

MUSICAL LINK TO THE PAST

Big Band to Bebop

Songwriter: Charlie Parker
Title: "Koko" (1946)
Performers: Charlie Parker's Ri Bop Boys

The big band jazz craze of the late 1930s and 1940s drove the American record industry to new levels of profit. But it also inspired major corporate record compa-nies to adopt conservative musical policies. By the early 1940s, most big band recordings adhered to strict for-mulas based on previous sales successes, which pro-duced a lot of dull recordings. Because of this, it was left to independently owned, smaller companies to search out and present the next generation of innova-tive artists. Charlie "Bird" Parker, the most important artist to emerge from these labels in the mid-1940s, introduced a new kind of jazz called "bebop" with his recording of "Koko." Black bebop musicians such as Parker and Dizzy Gillespie broke the old big band formu-las by performing at a faster, near anarchic tempo with more notes per bar, playing songs that extended beyond the usual three-minute commercial barrier, disdaining formal arrangements, reducing the number of players in ensembles, and stressing individual expression through extended solos. As can be heard on "Koko," the music was also fun and exciting, requiring a technical profi-ciency beyond the reach of most big band musicians.

Many in the jazz world resisted bebop. Artists like Parker and Gillespie refused to play dance music or entertain audiences as previous jazz figures did. They emphasized their own musical advancement and played a harsh, challenging, and intellectual music that some-

times was not immediately enjoyable. Some historians have argued that bebop, with its anti-commercial and anti-assimilationist attitude, symbolized the increasing rebellion and resistance by black Americans during the postwar years that eventually led to the civil rights movement of the 1950s and 1960s.

Bebop's initial recordings were on small record labels such as Savoy (owned by an electronics retailer who released music as a sideline) and Dial (opened by a Hollywood record store entrepreneur to give beboppers wider exposure). Independent labels have played a sig-nificant role in introducing trailblazing American musical movements in the face of short-term corporate thinking and musical conservatism. Other examples include 1950s rock and roll (spearheaded by labels such as Sun and Chess) and hip-hop (labels included Tommy Boy and Sugar Hill).

1. Could a similar argument concerning big band music in the 1940s be made for hip-hop music in the 21st century?
2. Has the widespread popularity of hip-hop and its dominance of the best-seller charts induced major record companies to adopt a conservative, formulaic approach toward the hip-hop records they release? Can this historical pattern be found in other styles of American popular music during the 20th century?

Listen to an audio recording of this music on the Musical Links to the Past CD.

SUBURBIA

Builder William Levitt's opening of Levittown, New York, in the late 1940s set a pattern for mass-produced homes in suburban developments. Assistance from governmental financing programs, such as the GI Bill, and the benefits of standardized production methods brought the cost of such homes within the reach of millions of buyers and hastened the flight, particularly of whites, out of central cities and older suburbs.

© Archive Photos/Lambert.

Nearly everything about Levittown seemed unprecedented. A construction company that had mass-produced military barracks during the Second World War, Levitt & Sons bragged that it was completing a five-room bungalow every 15 minutes. Architectural critics sneered at these "little boxes," but potential buyers stood in long lines hoping to purchase one. By 1950, Levittown consisted of more than 10,000 homes and 40,000 residents, and bulldozers and construction crews were sweeping into other suburban developments across the country. One-quarter of all the houses that existed in 1960 were built after 1949.

To help buyers purchase these homes, the government offered an extensive set of programs. The Federal Housing Administration (FHA), established during the New Deal, helped private lenders extend credit to mass-production builders, who in turn sold houses on generous financing terms. Typically, people who bought FHA-financed homes needed only 5 percent of the purchase price as a down payment; they could finance the rest with a long-term, government-insured mortgage. Millions of war veterans enjoyed even more favorable terms under the GI loan program operated by the Veterans Administration. These government programs made it cheaper to buy a new house in the average suburb than to rent a comfortable apartment in most cities. Moreover, families could deduct from their federal income tax the interest they paid on their mortgages. This deduction could be seen as a disguised form of governmental subsidy for the building and lending industries and for homeowners. Because construction

never caught up with demand during the 1950s, many suburbanites could sell their first house at a profit and move up to a more spacious, more expensive dwelling.

The new suburban areas promised greater privacy and more amenities than crowded city neighborhoods or even older suburbs. Builders, quick to recognize the appeal of new housing developments, soon began to offer larger homes, including the sprawling, one-level "ranch" model. The joys of "easy and better" living often came with the house. A Levitt home, for example, contained an automatic washer and a built-in television set. Even the television, by being attached to the house itself, qualified as a "structural" component and could be financed under federally guaranteed loan programs.

The new postwar suburbs enjoyed a reputation for being ideal places in which to raise children, and many more families were having babies. After the war, a complex set of factors, including early marriages and rising incomes, helped produce a "baby boom" that would last well into the 1950s. With houses generally occupying only about 15 percent of suburban lots, large lawns served as private playgrounds. Nearby schools were as new as the rest of the neighborhood, and suburban school boards used their well-equipped, up-to-date buildings to attract both skilled teachers and middle-income families.

In many respects, the new suburban lifestyle epitomized an optimistic spirit of new possibilities, confidence in the future, and acceptance of change. In other respects, though, it represented an effort to create a material and

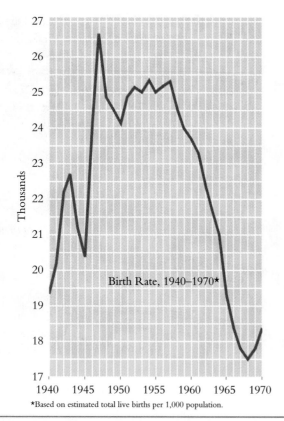

*Based on estimated total live births per 1,000 population.

THE BABY BOOM

psychological refuge. Most obviously, buying a new suburban home seemed a way of cushioning the impact of the social and demographic changes ushered in by the war. As African American families left the rural South in search of work in northern cities, "white flight" to suburbia quickened. Although Jackie Robinson, Larry Doby, and other talented athletes could find a place in professional baseball during the 1940s, not a single black person could buy a home in Long Island's Levittown until well into the 1960s.

Government and private housing policies helped structure and maintain the segregationist pattern of white suburbs and increasingly nonwhite urban neighborhoods. Federal laws allowed local groups to veto public housing projects in their communities. Although land and building costs would have been cheaper in the suburbs, public housing projects were concentrated on relatively expensive, high-density urban sites. More important, the lending industry channeled government loan guarantees away from most urban neighborhoods, and private lenders generally denied credit to nonwhites seeking new suburban housing.

No one in the postwar housing industry admitted intentional complicity in these discriminatory patterns. William Levitt could identify his private housing projects with the public crusade against communism. "No man

who owns his house and lot can be a Communist," he remarked in 1948. "He has too much to do." Levitt held himself blameless, however, for racial issues. He could help solve the nation's housing problem—and perhaps even the problem of domestic communism—but he insisted that his "private" construction choices had nothing to do with the public issue of race.

Similarly, the architects of this new suburbia saw nothing problematic with postwar gender patterns. William Levitt's confident identification of home ownership with men unconsciously reflected the fact that the lending industry generally would not extend loan guarantees to women. Single women simply could not obtain FHA-backed loans, a policy that the agency justified on the grounds that men were the family breadwinners and that women rarely made enough money to qualify as good credit risks. As a result, home ownership in the new suburbs was invariably limited to white males, with wives as co-owners at best.

Allure and Danger: Women on Film

As postwar suburbs boomed, initially symbolizing promise and affluence, movie moguls found that older urban areas provided rich sites for popular drama. During the 1940s and 1950s, Hollywood released a cycle of motion pictures that came to be called *film noir*. Nearly always filmed in black and white and often set at night in large cities, these movies peeked into the dark corners of postwar America and hinted at deep-seated anxieties and fears.

Many film noir pictures populated their dark cities with alluring femmes fatales: beautiful but dangerous women who challenged the prevailing order. The femme fatale represented the opposite of the nurturing, faithful wife and mother. Usually unmarried and childless, she posed a threat to both men and other women. In *The File on Thelma Jordan* (1949), for instance, the title character, played by Barbara Stanwyck, cynically destroys the marriage of a young, weak-willed district attorney. She initiates an illicit affair with him not because of love, or even lust, but as part of a complicated plot to manipulate the criminal justice system. The postwar era's most prominent female stars—such as Stanwyck, Joan Crawford, Rita Hayworth, and Lana Turner—achieved both popular and critical acclaim playing such roles. Film noir features developed a loyal audience among female viewers, suggesting that women, as well as men, were drawn to the image of independent women.

The fear of communism during the years from 1946 to 1953 accentuated pressures for conformity and often made it difficult to advocate significant change. Yet grow-

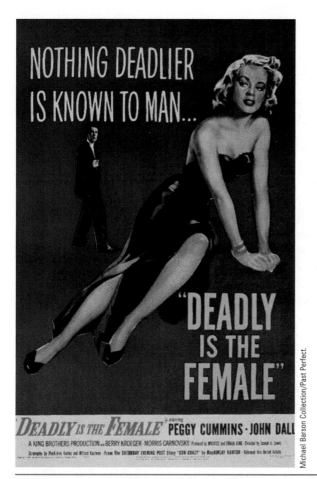

NOTHING DEADLIER
IS KNOWN TO MAN...

"DEADLY
IS THE
FEMALE"

DEADLY IS THE FEMALE PEGGY CUMMINS · JOHN DALL
A KING BROTHERS PRODUCTION

Michael Barson Collection/Past Perfect.

DEADLY IS THE FEMALE

Also called *Gun Crazy* (1949), this film noir played on fears of social breakdown and inspired the later movie *Bonnie and Clyde* (1967).

ing prosperity, new expectations stemming from the war, and demographic shifts, inevitably transformed many social and cultural patterns. The everyday lives of Americans—racial patterns and living arrangements and social expectations—were inexorably changing.

From Truman to Eisenhower

Harry Truman declined to run for another term in the presidential election of 1952. The Democrats were on the defensive, and denunciations of communism and Truman provided the focus of the Republican campaign.

The Election of 1952

Adlai Stevenson of Illinois, the Democratic presidential candidate in 1952, warned that "Soviet secret agents and

their dupes" had "burrowed like moles" into governments throughout the world. "We cannot let our guard drop for even a moment." Stevenson approved of the prosecution of the Communist Party's leaders and the dismissal of schoolteachers who were party members. A strong anti-communist stance, however, could not save Stevenson or the Democratic Party.

The Republicans assailed the unpopular Truman presidency and Stevenson. Their vice presidential nominee, Senator Richard Nixon of California, called Stevenson "Adlai the appeaser" and claimed he held a Ph.D. from "Dean Acheson's Cowardly College of Communist Containment." Republicans criticized Truman's handling of the Korean War and highlighted revelations about favoritism and kickbacks on government contracts in his administration. The GOP's successful election formula could be reduced to a simple equation, "K1C2": "Korea, corruption, and communism."

A Soldier-President

For their presidential candidate, Republicans turned to a hero of the Second World War, General Dwight David Eisenhower, popularly known as "Ike." Eisenhower had never sought elective office, but nearly a half-century of military service had made him a skilled politician. Ike grew up in Kansas; won an appointment to, and graduated from, West Point; rose through the army ranks under the patronage of General George Marshall; and directed the Normandy invasion of 1944 as supreme Allied commander. He served as army chief of staff from 1945 to 1948 and, after an interim period as president of Columbia University, returned to active duty as the commander of NATO, a post he held until May 1952.

Eisenhower seemed an attractive political leader. Although his partisan affiliations had always been so vague that some Democrats had courted him in 1948, he finally declared himself a Republican. Initially reluctant to seek the presidency in 1952, he became convinced that Robert Taft, his main GOP rival, leaned too far to the right on domestic issues and lacked a firm commitment to containment policies overseas. Perceived as a middle-of-the-road candidate, Ike appeared able to lead the nation during a cold war as firmly as he had during a hot one. Adlai Stevenson grumbled that the press had embraced the old war hero even before knowing "what his party platform would be" or "what would be the issues of the campaign."

The first military leader to gain the presidency since Ulysses S. Grant (1869–1877), Eisenhower achieved a great personal victory in 1952. The Eisenhower-Nixon ticket received almost 7 million more popular votes than the

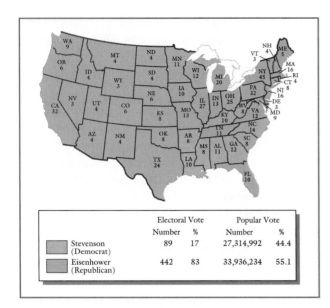

		Electoral Vote		Popular Vote	
		Number	%	Number	%
	Stevenson (Democrat)	89	17	27,314,992	44.4
	Eisenhower (Republican)	442	83	33,936,234	55.1

MAP 27.4 PRESIDENTIAL ELECTION, 1952

In this overwhelming victory for Eisenhower, Stevenson carried only a few states. Note that the so-called "solid South" was still solidly Democratic. This trend would shift substantially over the next two decades.

Democrats and won in the electoral college by a margin of 442 to 89. The Republican Party made more modest gains. The GOP gained a single-vote majority in the Senate and enjoyed only an eight-vote margin in the House of Representatives. The electoral coalition Franklin Roosevelt had put together during the 1930s still survived, even though it showed signs of fraying, especially in the South. There,

many of the white southern votes that had gone to the Dixiecrats in 1948 began moving toward the Republicans, and Eisenhower carried four states in the Democratic Party's once "solid South."

Conclusion

Efforts at containing communism dominated both domestic and foreign policy during the years after the Second World War. As worsening relations between the United States and the Soviet Union developed into the Cold War, the Truman administration pursued policies that expanded the power of the government, particularly the executive branch, to counter the threat. The militarization of foreign policy intensified when the United States went to war in Korea in 1950. At home, anticommunism focused on containing both the activities and ideas of alleged subversives. These initiatives raised difficult issues about how to protect legitimate national security interests while still safeguarding constitutional liberties.

Within this Cold War climate, struggles to achieve greater equality still emerged. Truman's Fair Deal promised that new economic wisdom would be able to guarantee economic growth and thereby provide the tax revenues to expand domestic programs. Truman also pressed for national measures against racial discrimination.

The election of Dwight D. Eisenhower in 1952 gave the Republicans the presidency for the first time in 20 years. Eisenhower's broad personal appeal, however, did not signal an imminent end to the power of the Democratic coalition that had held sway since the 1930s.

SUGGESTED READINGS

David Reynolds, *One World Divisible: A Global History since 1945* (2001) provides an international context for the emerging Cold War, while **Walter LaFeber,** *America, Russia, and the Cold War, 1945–2002* (9th rev. ed., 2002) offers an expert interpretive synthesis of U.S. policies. **Melvyn Leffler,** *The Specter of Communism* (1994) is a brief, critical account of the onset of the Cold War. **Leffler's** *A Preponderance of Power: National Security, the Truman Administration, and the Cold War* (1992) offers more detail, as does **Michael J. Hogan,** *A Cross of Iron: Harry S. Truman and the Origins of the National Security State, 1945–1954* (1998), and **Arnold A. Offner,** *Another Such Victory: President Truman and the Cold War, 1945–1953* (2002). **John Lewis Gaddis,** *We Now Know: Rethinking Cold War History* (1997) and his many other books present a less critical view. The most thorough and scholarly biography of

Harry Truman remains **Alonso L. Hamby,** *Man of the People: A Life of Harry S. Truman* (1995).

On the Korean War, **William Stueck,** *The Korean War: An International History* (1995) provides an overview, while **Bruce Cumings's many books, including** *Korea: The Unknown War* (coauthored with Jon Halliday) (1988), provide a more critical view. Postwar reconstruction of former enemies is expertly treated in **John Dower,** *Embracing Defeat: Japan in the Wake of World War II* (2000), and **Marc Trachtenberg,** *A Constructed Peace: The Making of the European Settlement, 1945–1963* (1999).

On communism and anticommunism in America during this period, **Allen Weinstein and Alexander Vassiliev,** *The Haunted Wood: Soviet Espionage in America, the Stalin Era* (1999) examines Soviet espionage. **Stanley I. Kutler,** *American*

Inquisition: Justice and Injustice in the Cold War (1982) and **Ellen Schrecker,** *The Age of McCarthyism* (2001) stress the excesses of anticommunist crusading.

The effect of the Cold War and containment on American culture is the subject of many excellent studies. **Michael S. Sherry,** *In the Shadow of War: The United States Since the 1930s* (1995), a broad synthesis, and **Stephen Whitfield,** *The Culture of the Cold War* (rev. ed., 1996) are good places to begin. **Tom Englehardt,** *The End of Victory Culture and the Disillusioning of a Generation* (1995) provides an influential interpretation. **Paul Boyer,** *By the Bomb's Early Light* (1985) and **Alan Nadel,** *Containment Culture: American Narrative, Postmodernism, and the Nuclear Age* (l995) examine diverse cultural effects of the atomic age. **Lary May,** *The Big Tomorrow: Hollywood and the Politics of the American Way* (2000) examines Hollywood film culture. **Jessica Wang,** *American Science in an Age of Anxiety: Scientists, Anticommunism, and the Cold War* (1999) stresses FBI pressure on scientists to support the Cold War. **Lizabeth Cohen,** *A Consumer's Republic: Mass Consumption in Postwar America* (2003) critically highlights the convergence of a number of important Cold War–era social and political forces.

 AMERICAN JOURNEY ONLINE
AND
INFOTRAC COLLEGE EDITION

Visit the source collections at www.ajaccess.wadsworth.com and infotrac.thomsonlearning.com and use the Search function with the following key terms to explore documents, images, audio and video clips, articles, and commentary related to the material in this chapter.

Harry S. Truman	General Douglas MacArthur
GI Bill	Dwight D. Eisenhower
House Un-American Activities Committee (HUAC)	Cold War
George Kennan (Mr. X)	Korean War
Containment	National Security Act
Jackie Robinson	Marshall Plan
NSC-68	A. Philip Randolph
Alger Hiss	Joseph McCarthy
North Atlantic Treaty Organization (NATO)	

GRADE AIDS

Visit the Liberty Equality Power Companion Web Site for resources specific to this textbook: http://history.wadsworth.com/murrin_LEP4e

 The CD in the back of this book and the U.S. History Resource Center at http://history.wadsworth.com/u.s./ offer a variety of tools to help you succeed in this course, including access to quizzes; images; documents; interactive simulations, maps, and timelines; movie explorations; and a wealth of other sources.

♦ How did the Eisenhower and Kennedy administrations respond to these issues?

♦ What foreign and domestic policies did Kennedy champion during his brief presidency?

♦ Why does Kennedy's presidency loom so large in popular memory?

Foreign Policy, 1953–1960

By 1953 the strident anticommunist rhetoric associated with McCarthyism and the Korean War era was beginning to subside. The dominant assumption of Cold War policy—that the United States must protect the "free world" and fight communism everywhere—remained unchanged, but the focus and tactics shifted. Bipolar confrontations between the United States and the Soviet Union over European issues gave way to greater reliance on nuclear deterrence and to more subtle and complex power plays in the "Third World": the Middle East, Asia, Latin America, and Africa.

Eisenhower Takes Command

Eisenhower honored a campaign pledge to travel to Korea as a means of ending U.S. military involvement there. Negotiations reached an apparent impasse, however, over whether North Korean and Chinese prisoners of war (POWs) wishing to remain in South Korea could forcibly be returned to North Korea and China. Hoping to end the stalemate, Eisenhower began to ruminate, in vague language heard in China and North Korea, about the use of nuclear weapons if diplomacy failed. Talks resumed, and on July 27, 1953, both sides signed a truce that established a special commission of neutral nations to handle the POW issue. (The POWs themselves were subsequently allowed to determine whether they wished to be repatriated.) A conflict in which more than 2 million Asians, mostly noncombatants, and 53,000 Americans died finally ended. A formal peace treaty remained unsigned, however, and the 38th parallel between North and South Korea became one of the most heavily militarized borders in the world.

At home, Ike gradually wrested control of the national security issue from Senator Joseph McCarthy and other extreme anticommunists. Congress did exceed the wishes of the Eisenhower administration when it passed the Communist Control Act of 1954, which barred the Communist Party from entering candidates in elections and extended the registration requirements established by the McCarran Act of 1950. But with a Republican president in the White House, most members of the GOP began to reject the McCarthyite style of anticommunism.

CHRONOLOGY

1953 Korean War ends • Julius and Ethel Rosenberg executed • *Playboy* magazine debuts

1954 Joseph McCarthy censured by U.S. Senate • Communist Control Act passed • *Brown v. Board of Education of Topeka* decision • SEATO formed • Arbenz government overthrown in Guatemala • Elvis Presley releases first record on Sun label • Geneva Peace Accords in Southeast Asia signed

1955 Montgomery bus boycott begins • *National Review* founded • *Brown II* decision

1956 Suez Crisis • Anti-Soviet uprisings occur in Poland and Hungary • Federal Highway Act passed • Eisenhower reelected

1957 Eisenhower sends troops to Lebanon • Eisenhower sends troops to Little Rock, Arkansas • Congress passes Civil Rights Act, first civil rights legislation in 80 years • Soviets launch *Sputnik* • Gaither Report urges more defense spending

1958 National Defense Education Act passed by Congress • *The Affluent Society* published

1959 Khrushchev visits United States

1960 Civil Rights Act passed • U-2 incident ends Paris summit • Kennedy elected president • Sit-in demonstrations begin

1961 Bay of Pigs invasion fails • Berlin Wall erected • Freedom rides begin in the South • Kennedy announces Alliance for Progress

1962 Cuban Missile Crisis • Kennedy sends troops to University of Mississippi to enforce integration

1963 Civil rights activists undertake march on Washington • Betty Friedan's *The Feminine Mystique* published • Kennedy assassinated (November 22); Lyndon Johnson becomes president

The erratic McCarthy careened completely out of control when he claimed that the U.S. Army was harboring subversives within its ranks. During spring 1954, a Senate committee conducted a televised investigation of his fantastic charge, and these Army–McCarthy Hearings brought him down. Under the glare of TV lights, McCarthy appeared as a crude, desperate bully who hurled slanders in every direction. In December 1954, a majority of the Senate, including colleagues who had once supported him, voted to censure him for conduct "unbecoming" a member. McCarthyism began to recede to the fringes of American politics. McCarthy faded from the limelight and died in obscurity in 1957, still holding onto a seat in the Senate.

Meanwhile, the Eisenhower administration expanded its own national security agenda. Compared to McCarthy's bombast, Eisenhower's low-key approach seemed eminently reasonable and moderate. The demonstrated un-

reliability of anticommunist zealots such as McCarthy strengthened the position of the White House when it successfully claimed a constitutional privilege to withhold from Congress classified information on national security matters. Relatively free from congressional and judicial oversight, the Eisenhower administration extended Truman's earlier programs of domestic surveillance, wiretapping, and covert action overseas. The president also backed a secret program to develop new aerial surveillance capabilities; by 1956, he enjoyed, courtesy of intelligence photographs taken from the new "U-2 spy planes," a clear view of the Soviet military arsenal.

Historians increasingly see Eisenhower as a skilled leader who could aggressively use the power of the presidency while often seeming to be doing very little. Eisenhower, in the words of one scholar, conducted a "hidden hand presidency." Mindful of how the ebullient Truman had become personally linked to popular controversies, Ike generally stayed in the background and projected an air of calm steadiness. In foreign policy, Eisenhower usually allowed John Foster Dulles, his secretary of state from 1953 to 1959, to take center stage; he encouraged the belief that George Humphrey, his secretary of the treasury, and Sherman Adams, his chief of staff, handled domestic issues.

The New Look and Summitry

Eisenhower quietly worked to reorient the nation's anticommunist foreign policy. The change of leadership in Moscow, following the 1953 death of Joseph Stalin, helped Ike make significant adjustments to U.S. policy. Nikita Khrushchev, who eventually emerged as the dominant Soviet leader, denounced Stalin's murderous despotism and talked of "peaceful coexistence" with capitalist nations. Seeking to free up resources to produce more consumer goods, Khrushchev began reducing Soviet armed forces.

U.S. military policy also underwent review. In December 1953, Admiral Arthur Radford, head of the Joint Chiefs of Staff, urged a reduction of the military budget and a fresh approach to defense strategy. Radford's "New Look" reflected Eisenhower's belief that unchecked military expenditures might eventually impede economic growth. The new strategy would look less to costly ground forces and more to airpower, advanced nuclear capabilities, and covert action.

The Eisenhower administration's doctrine of "massive retaliation" gambled that the threat of unleashing U.S. nuclear weaponry would check Soviet expansion. John Foster Dulles warned that Washington would not hesitate to launch an all-out nuclear attack on the Soviet Union if Moscow's actions, anywhere in the world, threatened

U.S. security. To make the U.S. nuclear umbrella more effective worldwide, Eisenhower expanded NATO to include West Germany in 1955 and added two other mutual defense pacts with noncommunist nations in Central and Southeast Asia. The Southeast Asia Treaty Organization (SEATO), formed in 1954, linked the United States to Australia, France, Great Britain, New Zealand, Pakistan, the Philippines, and Thailand. The weakly bonded Central Treaty Organization (CENTO), formed in 1959, included Pakistan, Iran, Turkey, Iraq, and Britain.

The Eisenhower administration elevated psychological warfare and "informational" programs into major Cold War weapons. The government-run Voice of America extended the geographic reach of its radio broadcasts and programmed in more languages. Washington also secretly funded Radio Free Europe, Radio Liberty (beamed to the Soviet Union), and Radio Asia. In 1953, Eisenhower persuaded Congress to create the United States Information Agency (USIA) to coordinate anticommunist informational and propaganda campaigns.

The United States and the Soviet Union, hoping to improve relations, began holding high-level "summit" meetings. In May 1955, an agreement was reached to end the postwar occupation of Austria and to transform it into a neutral country. Two months later, the United States, the Soviet Union, Britain, and France met in Geneva, Switzerland. Making little progress on arms reduction, the future of Germany, and other matters, this summit conference nonetheless inaugurated new cultural exchanges. Cold War tensions eased somewhat, and all sides hailed the conciliatory "spirit of Geneva." In fall 1959, to heal differences that had developed over Berlin, Khrushchev toured the United States, met with Eisenhower, and paid well-publicized visits to farmers in Iowa and Disneyland in California. Although a 1960 Paris summit meeting fell apart after the Soviets shot down a U-2 spy plane over their territory, the tone of cold-war rhetoric had grown less strident by the end of Eisenhower's presidency.

The superpowers also began to consider arms limitation. Eisenhower's "Open Skies" initiative of 1955 proposed that the two nations use reconnaissance flights over each other's territory to verify disarmament efforts. The Soviets balked, but some progress was made in limiting atomic tests. Responding to worries about the health hazards of atomic fallout, both countries slowed aboveground testing and discussed a broader test-ban agreement. For many Americans, efforts to curtail nuclear testing came too late. Government documents declassified in the 1980s confirmed what antinuclear activists had long suspected: People who had lived "downwind" from rural nuclear test sites during the 1940s and 1950s had suffered an unusual number of atomic-related illnesses. In the

Willis Conover:
Fighting the Cold War with Jazz

Willis Conover (1921–1996) was known as the most famous American that few other Americans had ever heard about. His radio program, *Music USA: The Jazz Hour,* went out over the U.S. government–run Voice of America radio station, which could not be heard within the United States. It attracted some 30 million regular listeners in Eastern Europe and the Soviet Union and perhaps 100 million fans throughout Asia, Africa, and Latin America.

Proclaiming jazz as "the music of freedom," Conover, literally, *was* America's voice during the height of the Cold War. Six nights a week for two hours each, Conover's program would, in the words of his *New York Times* obituary, "bombard Budapest with Billy Taylor, strafe Poland with Oscar Peterson and drop John Coltrane on Moscow." Conover may have been more effective in generating admiration for the United States, especially among young people, and in fomenting dissent against disapproving communist regimes than most other weapons in America's Cold War arsenal.

Born in Buffalo, New York, Conover developed an interest in radio as a young man and became a popular local disc jockey in Washington, D.C., where he hosted the city's only jazz program. After Duke Ellington toured the Soviet Union in 1954, to wildly enthusiastic audiences, the Voice of America decided that a regular slot devoted to jazz would attract listeners. Conover broadcast his first program in 1955. For the next 40 years, *The Jazz Hour,* one of Voice of America's most popular programs, ran in a prime evening spot between two news broadcasts. During the late 1950s, it claimed more than 1,400 fan clubs in almost every country in the world.

Although some members of Congress charged that jazz was "pure noise" and complained that the U.S. government should not spend money broadcasting something so trivial, officials who were fighting the Cold War knew the cultural value of jazz. It was genuinely *American* music; it symbolized individuality and free expression; and its global popularity (which greatly exceeded its recognition at home) seemed boundless. *Look* magazine proclaimed the usefulness of jazz as a Cold War weapon in these words: "Jazz is a door opener everywhere, a Pandora's box full of friendliness that totalitarians won't easily be able to close." Conover, opening his program each night with "Take the 'A' Train," brought American jazz to the world and nurtured an international fascination with American culture.

CONOVER SPINS JAZZ, 1959

From his Voice of America studio in Washington, D.C., Willis Conover brought the sounds of jazz greats such as Miles Davis and Duke Ellington to the world.

1990s, new revelations showed that the government had covertly conducted experiments with radioactive materials on unsuspecting American citizens.

Meanwhile, events in Eastern Europe during the middle of the 1950s underscored the danger of being drawn into a military confrontation with Moscow. The Soviet-dominated "satellite countries" were chafing under managed economies and police-state control. Seizing on the post-Stalinist atmosphere, insurgents in Poland staged a three-day rebellion in June 1956 and forced the Soviets to accept Wladyslaw Gomulka, an old foe of Stalin, as head of state. Hungarians then rallied in support of Imre Nagy, another anti-Stalinist communist, who pledged to create a multiparty democracy. The Soviets sought an accommodation that would preserve Moscow's power while allowing minimal political change, but armed rebellion spread throughout Hungary.

The Hungarian revolutionaries appealed for American assistance. They took hope from Secretary of State Dulles's talk about an anticommunist policy aimed at "liberation" rather than merely containment. The United States, however, could hardly launch military operations so close to the Soviet Union. Soviet armies crushed the Hungarian uprising and killed thousands of dissidents,

including Nagy. U.S. policy makers came to recognize that advocating freedom from communist rule might make good political rhetoric at home but could lead to tragedy abroad.

Covert Action and Economic Leverage

Increasingly, the U.S. battle against communism shifted its focus from Europe to the Third World. Covert action and economic leverage replaced overt military confrontation as the primary tools. These tactics proved both less expensive and less visible than military deployment, and therefore less likely to provoke public controversy at home or a military showdown with the Soviets overseas.

The CIA played a leading role in the new policy. In 1953, it helped bring about the election of Ramón Magsaysay, a strong anticommunist, as president of the Philippines. That same year, the CIA facilitated a coup that overthrew Mohammed Mossadegh's legitimate, although left-leaning, government in Iran and restored Shah Reza Pahlavi to power. The increasingly dictatorial Shah remained a firm ally of the United States and a friend of American oil interests in Iran until his ouster by Muslim fundamentalists in 1979. In 1954, the CIA, working closely with the United Fruit Company, secretly helped topple President Jacobo Arbenz Guzmán's elected government in Guatemala. Officials of the Eisenhower administration and officers of the fruit company saw Arbenz as a communist because he sought to nationalize and redistribute large tracts of land, including some owned by United Fruit. These successful covert actions gained the CIA, headed by Allen Dulles, brother of the U.S. secretary of state, even greater influence and power. In 1954, the National Security Council widened the CIA's mandate, and by 1960 it had approximately 15,000 agents (compared to about 6,000 when Eisenhower took office) deployed around the world.

Eisenhower also employed economic strategies—trade and aid—to fight communism and win influence for the United States in the Third World. These strategies aimed at opening new opportunities for American enterprises overseas, discouraging other countries from adopting state-directed economic systems, and encouraging trade expansion. U.S. policy makers came to identify "freedom" with the "free market" and thus regarded efforts of Third World nations to break old colonial bonds by creating government-controlled economies and nationalizing local industries as a threat to liberty. New governmental assistance programs offered economic aid to friendly nations, and military aid rose sharply as well. Under the Mutual Security Program and the Military Assistance Program,

the United States spent $3 billion annually and trained 225,000 representatives from nations around the world in anticommunism and domestic police tactics. The buildup of military allies in Third World nations strengthened the anticommunist resources of the United States but also contributed to the development of dictatorships in foreign nations.

America and the Third World

In pursuing its policies, the Eisenhower administration employed a broad definition of what counted as anticommunism. In many countries, groups seeking to change labor laws and land ownership patterns that might benefit large numbers of people had allied with communist movements. Economic elites and dictators could hope to win U.S. support against these internal political opponents simply by whispering the word communist.

Latin America

In Latin America, the White House talked about expanding freedom but regularly backed dictatorial regimes that welcomed U.S. investment and rejected leftist movements. Eisenhower awarded the Legion of Merit to unpopular dictators in Peru and Venezuela and privately confessed his admiration for the anticommunism of Paraguay's General Alfredo Stroessner, a tyrant who sheltered ex-Nazis and ran his country as a private fiefdom. Vice President Richard Nixon toasted Cuba's Fulgencio Batista, a corrupt despot beholden to illegal gambling syndicates in the United States, as "Cuba's Abraham Lincoln." The CIA secretly trained Batista's security forces. Surveying Eisenhower-era policies, America's disgruntled ambassador to democratic Costa Rica complained that Secretary of State Dulles had advised foreign service officers to "do nothing to offend the dictators; they are the only people we can depend on."

Such policies offended many Latin Americans. "Yankeephobia" spread, and events in Cuba dramatized the growth of anti-American sentiments. After a leftist movement led by Fidel Castro overthrew Batista in 1959, tried to curtail Cuba's dependence on the United States, and adopted policies that prompted many middle-class Cubans to flee to the United States, the Eisenhower administration imposed an economic boycott on the island. Castro turned to the Soviet Union for economic aid, declared himself a communist, further tightened his political grip over Cuba, and pledged to support Cuban-style insurgencies throughout Latin America. The CIA began formulating an

invasion to unseat Castro, and the Eisenhower administration ordered a review of the U.S. policies that were generating ill will throughout Latin America. This review recommended greater emphasis on encouraging democratic political processes, protection of human rights, and economic growth in Latin America.

Nasserism and the Suez Crisis of 1956

In the Middle East, distrust of nationalism and neutralism shaped U.S. policy. In 1954, when Colonel Gamal Abdel Nasser overthrew the corrupt monarchy of King Farouk and seized control of Egypt, he also promised to rescue other Arab nations from European domination and guide them toward "positive neutralism." Denouncing Israel and accepting aid from both the United States and the Soviet Union, Nasser boosted Egypt's economic and military power. He also purchased advanced weapons from communist Czechoslovakia and extended diplomatic recognition to communist China. Those actions prompted the United States to cancel loans that were to finance the huge Aswan Dam, a project designed to improve agriculture along the Nile River and provide hydroelectric power for new industries. Nasser responded in July 1956 by nationalizing the British-controlled Suez Canal, arguing that canal tolls would provide substitute financing for the dam. The Suez was still of economic and symbolic importance to Britain, and its forces, joined by those of France and Israel, attacked Egypt in October and seized control of the the waterway.

Eisenhower distrusted Nasser, but he opposed Britain's blatant attempt to retain its imperial position. The Soviets were, at that same time, crushing the Hungarian revolt, and Eisenhower could not effectively criticize the Soviets for maintaining a sphere of influence in Eastern Europe when Britain was using military force in the Middle East. Denouncing the Anglo-French-Israeli action, Ike threatened to use America's economic might to destabilize Britain's currency unless the invasion ended. Eventually, a plan supported by the United States and the United Nations allowed Egypt to regain the Suez Canal, but America lost prestige and power in the area as the Soviet Union took over financing of the Aswan Dam and strengthened its ties with Nasser.

Egypt's new links to the Soviets increased the Eisenhower administration's fear that "Nasserism" might spread throughout the energy-rich Middle East. In spring 1957, Congress endorsed the "Eisenhower Doctrine," the president's pledge to defend Middle Eastern countries "against overt armed aggression from any nation controlled by international communism." Although Moscow's machinations only began to account for the spread of Nasser-style nationalism and civil unrest in the area, anticommunist rhetoric did provide a handy justification for backing governments that supported America's need for petroleum and natural gas. Elites in Lebanon and Jordan, fearful of more Nasser-style revolts, after military coups toppled the monarchy in oil-rich Iraq and threatened that of Jordan, asked the United States and Britain for help. In the spirit of the Eisenhower doctrine (which was never formally invoked), Ike sent U.S. marines to Lebanon to protect an anti-Nasser government in Beirut and supported Britain's simultaneous move to help King Hussein retain his throne in Jordan. These actions furthered the U.S. policy of supporting friendly, conservative governments in the Middle East but also intensified Arab nationalism and fostered anti-Americanism.

The Eisenhower administration tried to derail left-leaning political movements elsewhere in the world. In 1958, the president approved a CIA plan to help unseat Achmed Sukarno, leader of Indonesia, who drew support from that nation's large Communist Party. When civil war broke out, the CIA furnished planes, pilots, and encouragement to the rebels. But after the rebellion collapsed, the United States abandoned its Indonesian allies, and Sukarno tightened his grip on power. Other CIA activities included various schemes to assassinate Fidel Castro (which failed) and Patrice Lumumba, a popular black nationalist in the Congo. (Assassins did get Lumumba in 1961, and scholars still debate the CIA's role in his death.)

Vietnam

Eisenhower's strategy of thwarting communism and neutralism in the Third World set the stage for steadily increasing U.S. involvement in Indochina. There, communist-nationalist forces led by Ho Chi Minh (born Nguyen Tat Thanh) sought independence from France. Ho Chi Minh had studied in the Soviet Union and in France before returning to Indochina in 1941 to fight against the Japanese armies that had overrun this French colony. When Japan withdrew at war's end, Ho Chi Minh had vainly appealed to the United States to support independence for Indochina. Despite wartime criticism of colonialism, U.S. leaders supported the return of French rule. In 1946, Ho Chi Minh and his Vietminh forces went to war against France and its ally, Bao Dai. Despite U.S. willingness to finance French military operations, a stunning Vietminh victory, orchestrated by General Nguyen Giap at Dien Bien Phu in 1954, convinced Paris to abandon Indochina. The Geneva Peace Accords of 1954, which the United States refused to sign, removed French forces and divided Indochina into three new countries: Laos, Cambodia, and Vietnam. The

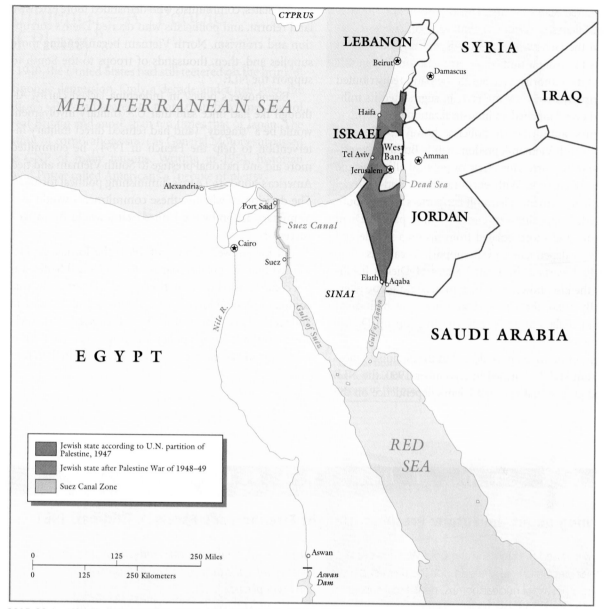

MAP 28.1 ISRAEL, THE MIDDLE EAST, AND THE SUEZ CRISIS, 1956

The creation of Israel and the Suez Crisis of 1956 shaped international politics in the Middle East in the postwar era. This map helps suggest some reasons why the establishment of Israel sharpened Arab nationalism and why the Suez Canal was considered to be such an important strategic location.

accords split Vietnam into two jurisdictions—North Vietnam and South Vietnam—until an election could unify the country under a single government.

Eisenhower's advisers expected that Ho Chi Minh would win any electoral contest and feared that a communist-nationalist victory in Vietnam could set off a geopolitical chain reaction. Using familiar Cold War language, the Eisenhower administration insisted that "the loss of any of the countries of Southeast Asia to Communist aggression" would ultimately "endanger the stability and security" of Europe and Japan, a formulation known

as the "domino theory." As a communist government took control of North Vietnam, Eisenhower supported a non-communist one in South Vietnam and ordered covert operations and economic programs to prevent Ho Chi Minh from becoming the head of a unified Vietnam.

Colonel Edward Lansdale, who had directed the CIA's campaign against a leftist insurgency in the Philippines from 1950 to 1953, arrived in Saigon, capital of South Vietnam, in 1954. Lansdale masterminded the creation of a pro-U.S. government in South Vietnam under Ngo Dinh Diem, an anticommunist Catholic who had been educated

SPLIT-LEVEL LIVING

This 1960 cartoon, by the *Washington Post*'s "Herblock" (Herbert Block), illustrates the growing critique of Eisenhower-era social policy. While suburbanites enjoy new affluence in a split-level home, public services and distressed people remain underfunded.

inner-directed citizenry. Riesman subsequently conceded that his autonomy-to-adjustment thesis might be overly broad but still insisted that it correctly identified a growing trend toward conformity in American life.

To illustrate the subtle manner in which children were taught conformist values, Riesman pointed to *Tootle, the Engine,* a popular children's book. When Tootle showed a preference for frolicking in the fields beside the tracks, people exerted peer pressure as a means of getting him to conform. If Tootle stayed on tracks laid down by others, they assured him, he would grow up to be a powerful and fast-moving streamliner. This message of adjusting to peer expectations in this "modern cautionary tale," Riesman argued, contrasted vividly with the conflict-filled fairy tales, such as *Little Red Riding Hood,* on which earlier generations of young people had been reared.

The critique of conformity reached its broadest audience through the best-selling books of journalist Vance Packard. *The Hidden Persuaders* (1957) argued that adver-

tising—especially through calculated, subtle appeals to the insecurities of consumers—produced conformity. The book, Packard claimed, could help its readers "to achieve a creative life in these conforming times" when so many people "are left only with the roles of being consumers or spectators."

Critics such as Whyte, Riesman, and Packard focused on the lives of middle-class men, but other writers such as Betty Friedan claimed to find an analogous psychological malaise among many women. Business corporations, for instance, expected that the wives of their male executives would help their husbands deal with the demands of corporate life, including the need for frequent moves to new locations. The organization man, it was said, should recognize that his ascent up the economic ladder could depend on how well his wife conformed to her informal duties in the corporate world.

Restive Youth

Concerns about young people, including their taste in culture, also intensified during the 1950s. Many criminologists attributed an alleged rise in juvenile delinquency to the burgeoning sales of comic books. Psychologist Frederick Wertham, in *The Seduction of the Innocent* (1954), blamed comics, especially those displaying sex and violence, for "mass-conditioning" children and for stimulating juvenile unrest. Responding to local legislation and to calls for federal regulation, the comic book industry quickly embraced self-censorship. Publishers who adhered to new, industry-developed guidelines for the portrayal of violence and deviant behavior could display a seal of approval on their comics. With this response, the great comic book scare faded away.

Critics of the youth culture, however, easily found other worrisome signs. In 1954, Elvis Presley, a former truck driver from Memphis, Tennessee, rocked the pop music establishment with a string of hits on the tiny Sun record label. In contrast to the people running the major record distributors, Sun's Sam Phillips correctly viewed rock as more than a passing fad. Presley's sensual, electric stage presence thrilled his young admirers. Presley ("The King") and other youthful rock stars—such as Buddy Holly from West Texas, Richard Valenzuela (Richie Valens) from East Los Angeles, and Frankie Lymon from Spanish Harlem—crossed cultural and ethnic barriers and shaped new musical forms from older ones, especially African American rhythm and blues (R & B) and the "hillbilly" music of southern whites.

The first rock 'n' rollers inspired millions of fans and thousands of imitators. They sang about the joys of "hav-

© Corbis.

ELVIS PRESLEY
A former truck driver from Memphis, "Elvis the Pelvis"
drew upon blues, gospel, hillbilly, and pop music traditions
to become the premier rock 'n' roll star of the 1950s.

ing a ball tonight"; the pain of the "summertime blues"; the torment of being "a teenager in love"; and the hope of deliverance, through the power of rock, from "the days of old." Songs such as "Roll Over Beethoven" by Chuck Berry (a black singer-songwriter who merged southern hillbilly music with the blues of his native St. Louis) became powerful teen anthems.

Guardians of older, family-oriented forms of commercial culture found rock 'n' roll far more frightening than comic books. They denounced its sparse lyrics, pulsating guitars, and screeching saxophones as an assault on the very idea of music. Religious groups condemned it as the sound of the devil; red-hunters detected a communist plan to corrupt youth; and segregationists saw it as part of a sinister plot by integrationists. The dangers of rock 'n' roll seemed abundantly evident in *The Blackboard Jungle* (1955), a hit movie about a racially mixed gang of high school students who terrorized teachers and mocked adult authority, which featured "Rock Around the Clock" on its soundtrack.

Rock 'n' roll music often spoke to the concerns of its young fans. The satirical "Charlie Brown" contrasted pieties about staying in school with the bleak educational opportunities open to many students. Chuck Berry sang of alienated teenagers riding around "with no particular place to go." This kind of implied social criticism, which older listeners invariably failed to decode, anticipated the more overtly rebellious rock music of the 1960s.

Rock music and the larger youth culture of the 1950s, however, gradually merged into the era's mass-consumption economy. Sun Records, lacking capital to distribute its music to a rapidly expanding market, sold Presley's contract to RCA and watched its other stars drift away. The major record labels and Top-40 radio stations quickly identified middle-class teenagers, whose average weekly income/allowance reached $10 by 1958, as a market worth targeting. Chuck Berry's "Sweet Little Sixteen" portrayed an affluent teenager eagerly chasing after the latest fashions, the next rock 'n' roll concert, and "about half-a million famed autographs." By 1960, record companies and disc jockeys were promoting performers such as the Beach Boys and songs that exalted the pursuit of "fun, fun, fun" with the help of clothes, cars, and rock 'n' roll records. Rock music—and the product-centered culture of youth—could easily embrace the ethic of a people of plenty.

The Mass Culture Debate

The criticism of conformity and of youth culture was part of a broader phenomenon becoming known as the mass culture debate. Much of the anxiety about the decline of individualism and the rise of rock 'n' roll could be traced to fears that "hidden persuaders" could apparently use the cultural marketplace to reach millions of people with standardized imagery and messages.

Cosmopolitan cultural critics, most of whom admired elite, European culture, decried mass-marketed products. They worried that the "bad"—such as rock music and Mickey Spillane's best-selling "Mike Hammer" detective novels—was driving anything "good" from the cultural marketplace and preventing people from distinguishing between them. In addition, by treating millions of consumers in the same manner, mass culture threatened to obscure meaningful differences under a blur of pleasant, superficial imagery. In a classic study of a small town in upstate New York, a team of sociologists articulated another common complaint: The presence of mass media was "so overwhelming that little scope is left for the expression of local cultural forms" in many parts of American life.

Television provided a prominent target. Evolving out of the structure of network radio, the television industry was dominated by three major corporations (NBC, CBS, and ABC) and sustained by advertisers, euphemistically called sponsors. Picturing millions of seemingly passive viewers gathered around "the boob tube," critics decried both the quality of mass-produced programming and its presumed impact on the public. Network television responded to pressure from advertisers and avoided controversial programs in favor of shows that, according to TV's critics, encouraged retreat into unrealities such as a mythical Old West. Television networks in 1958 were broadcasting 25 westerns during their prime-time hours. Newton Minow, appointed to head the Federal Communications Commission (FCC) in 1961, denounced TV as a "vast wasteland" and hinted that only federal regulation might improve network programming.

Critics also noted how television seemed to be transforming the fabric of everyday life. Architects were calling for the rearrangement of living space within middle-class homes so that the television set, serving as an electronic substitute for the traditional fireplace hearth, could become the focal point for family life. New products—such as the frozen TV dinner, the TV tray, the recliner chair, and the influential magazine *TV Guide*—became extensions of television culture. The TV set itself, initially encased in a substantial wooden cabinet, became an important symbol of postwar affluence.

The mass culture they decried, these critics recognized, remained embedded within the economic system they generally celebrated. Was it really possible to eliminate the curse of mass culture while still enjoying the benefits of affluence and liberty? If, for example, Congress were encouraged (as it had been during the comic book scare) to legislate against "dangerous" cultural products, censorship might end up curtailing free expression. If local communities were to step in (as some had done in the case of comics), the result might be even worse. The prospect of southern segregationists confiscating civil rights literature or of local censorship boards banning movies produced in Hollywood or books published in New York City hardly appealed to these cosmopolitan, elite-educated critics. Their critique of mass culture, in short, seemed to generate few solutions. More important, it did nothing to halt the flood of products, especially TV programs, aimed at an ever-expanding audience of eager consumers.

Meanwhile, amid the concern about mass culture, other questions about the direction of postwar life emerged. Americans were adjusting to new gender patterns and remained especially divided over issues related to racial discrimination and to government's role in confronting it.

Changing Gender Patterns

The 1950s significantly altered how and where people lived and worked. Women, in particular, found their lives changing.

The New Suburbs and Gender Ideals

In middle-class homes, especially those located in the new suburbs, wives and mothers discovered how consumer technology kept them busy. Shiny appliances and "modern conveniences"—such as automatic clothes washers, more powerful vacuum cleaners, and home freezers—eased old burdens but created new ones. Contrary to what advertisers promised, women could devote as much of their day to household tasks during the 1950s as had their grandmothers in the early 1900s. The time that women spent on domestic duties was not reduced but reallocated to new activities that involved the household gadgets that accompanied affluence.

Daily life in the new suburbs was structured by a broad pattern of "separate spheres": a public sphere of work and politics dominated by men and a private sphere of housework and child care reserved for women. Because few businesses located in these suburbs, men began spending a good portion of their day commuting from home to work. Women who wanted to hold a job outside their homes found nearby employment opportunities about as scarce as child-care facilities. Consequently, mothers spent a great deal of time taking care of their baby-boom children. In contrast to the urban neighborhoods or the rural communities where many suburban housewives had grown up, suburbs of the 1950s contained few older relatives or younger single women who could help with household and child-care duties.

Without mothers and grandmothers living close by, suburban women turned elsewhere for child-rearing advice. Local Parents and Teachers Associations (PTAs), connected to neighborhood schools, offered the chance to exchange information, as did women's organizations such as the La Leche League. Increasingly, though, both parents consulted child-care manuals. Dr. Benjamin Spock's *Baby and Child Care,* first published in 1946, sold millions of copies. Like earlier advice books, Spock's assigned virtually all child-care duties to women and underscored their nurturing role by stressing the need to constantly oversee a child's psychological growth. The future of the family and the nation itself, Spock implied, depended on how well mothers handled the daily traumas of childhood. Other manuals picked up where Dr. Spock left off and counseled

mothers on the care and feeding of teenagers. The alarmist tone of many of these books reflected—and helped generate—widespread concern over juvenile delinquency.

The ideal mother, according to most experts, did not work outside the home and devoted herself to rearing her own segment of the baby-boom generation and thereby fighting broader social dislocation. Delinquent children, according to a study of the early 1950s, sprang from a "family atmosphere not conducive to development of emotionally well-integrated, happy youngsters, conditioned to obey legitimate authority." It was up to parents, especially mothers, to rear good children. Women who sought careers outside of the home and marriage risked being labeled as lost, maladjusted, guilt-ridden, man-hating, or all of the above.

Versions of this message appeared nearly everywhere. Even the nation's prestigious women's colleges assumed a student would quickly pursue a man and a marriage rather than a career in the workplace. In his 1955 commencement address at Smith College, Adlai Stevenson, the Democratic Party's urbane presidential candidate in 1952 and 1956, told female graduates that it was the duty of each to keep her husband "truly purposeful, to keep him whole." Popular magazines, psychology literature, and pop-culture imagery suggested that understanding, supportive wives and mothers could help ensure social stability.

Some portraits of family life, however, were beginning to paint a more complicated view of gender arrangements. Most men told researchers that they preferred an active partner to a "submissive, stay-at-home" wife. Popular television shows, such as "Father Knows Best" or "Leave It to Beaver," suggested the hope that middle-class fathers would become more involved in family life than their own fathers had been. Experts on gender relationships still envisioned suburban men earning their family's entire income but increasingly urged them to be "real fathers" at home. Parenting literature emphasized "family togetherness," and institutions such as the Young Men's Christian Association (YMCA) began to offer courses on how to achieve it.

This call for family togetherness was partly a response to what some cultural historians have seen as an incipient "male revolt" against "family values." Hugh Hefner's *Playboy* magazine, which debuted in 1953, epitomized this trend. It saw men who neglected their own happiness in order to support a wife and children as suckers rather than saints. *Playboy*'s first issue proclaimed: "We aren't a 'family magazine.'" Hefner told women to pass it "along to the man in your life and get back to your *Ladies Home Companion*." In his version of the good life, the man rented a "pad" rather than owned a home; drove a sports car rather than a sedan or a station wagon; and courted the Playmate of the Month rather than the Mother of the Year.

Women's Changing Roles

Despite media images that depicted "the average woman" as a homebound wife and mother, economic realities were propelling more women into the job market. Female employment outside the home rose steadily during the late 1940s and throughout the 1950s. More married women were entering the labor force, many of them as part-time workers in the expanding clerical and "service" sectors. In 1948, about 25 percent of married mothers had jobs outside the home; at the end of the 1950s, nearly 40 percent did. With the introduction of a new, reliable oral contraception method in 1960—the birth control pill—women could enjoy greater control over family planning and career decisions. By 1964, one-quarter of the couples who used contraception relied on the pill.

Although more women were seeking jobs outside their homes, employment opportunities remained largely limited to well-defined, gender-segregated areas. Virtually all of the nation's nurses, telephone operators, secretaries, and elementary school teachers were women. Historically, pay scales in these areas lagged behind those paid to men in comparable fields, labor unions were rare, and chances for advancement were very limited. As the number of low-paid jobs for women expanded during the 1950s, better-paid professional opportunities actually narrowed. Medical and law schools and many professional societies admitted few, if any, women. When Sandra Day (who would later become Justice Sandra Day O'Connor of the U.S. Supreme Court) graduated with honors from a prestigious law school during the 1950s, not a single firm would extend her a job offer. The number of women on college faculties shrank back even from the low levels of the 1920s and 1930s.

Although employers still invoked the "family wage" ideal as a justification for disparities in pay and opportunity based on gender, more women were struggling to support a family on their own paychecks. This was especially true for women of color. By 1960, slightly more than 20 percent of black families were headed by women. Recognizing that images of domesticity hardly fit the lives of African American women, a large percentage of whom had always worked outside the home, *Ebony* magazine celebrated black women who combined success in parenting and at work. One story, for example, highlighted the only female African American mechanic at American Airlines; many others featured educators and prominent entertainers.

Mass-circulation magazines also carried mixed messages about domesticity. Although many social commentators labeled the pursuit of activities outside the home as "unnatural," any magazine that sought a broad readership

The Montgomery Bus Boycott and Martin Luther King, Jr.

In response to the uncertainty of judicial remedies, African Americans began supplementing legal maneuvering with aggressive campaigns of direct action. One of the first occurred, even before the *Brown* cases, in Baton Rouge, Louisiana. In 1953, a brief boycott of the local bus system ended after white officials agreed, while formally maintaining a token segregation system, to grant more seats to black riders. Two years later, activists in Montgomery, Alabama, raised the ante when Rosa Parks, an active member of the local NAACP chapter, was arrested for defying a local segregation ordinance. Montgomery's black community quickly demanded complete desegregation, began a boycott of public transportation, and organized a system of private carpools as alternative transit. Joining with Rosa Parks, many African American women spearheaded this broad-based effort. The resulting financial losses eventually convinced the city of the desirability of ending its separatist transit policy, and the U.S. Supreme Court weighed in by declaring the segregation of Montgomery's buses to be unconstitutional. Events in Montgomery during 1955 and 1956 showed other southern black communities that they could also mobilize against racial discrimination.

AP/Gene Herrick/Wide World Photos.

ROSA PARKS IGNITES DESEGREGATION CAMPAIGN

Rosa Parks's refusal to sit at the back of a segregated bus in 1955 sparked a campaign to integrate public transportation in Montgomery, Alabama. Here, Rosa Parks is fingerprinted by a law enforcement officer.

The Montgomery boycott vaulted Dr. Martin Luther King, Jr., one of its leaders, into the national spotlight. Born, raised, and educated in Atlanta, Georgia, with a doctorate in theology from Boston University, King and other black ministers followed up the victory in Montgomery by forming the Southern Christian Leadership Conference (SCLC). In addition to demanding desegregation of public facilities, the SCLC launched an effort to register African American voters throughout the South. More activist than the NAACP, the SCLC embodied Dr. King's broad vision of using passive civil disobedience to obtain social change. According to King, civil disobedience would dramatize, through both words and deeds, the moral evil of racial discrimination. The ultimate goal of the civil rights crusade was to bring "redemption and reconciliation" to American society. Aided by the national media, especially network television, King's powerful presence and religiously rooted rhetoric carried the antidiscrimination message out of the South to most parts of the nation and, eventually, to a wider world.

The Domestic and International Politics of Civil Rights

Political institutions in Washington, D.C., responded slowly. The Supreme Court lent its support at crucial times, as during the Montgomery bus boycott, but it always lacked the power to mandate the sweeping institutional changes needed to translate its expanded definition of civil rights into enforceable practices. Congress, with the ability to enact legislation, remained deeply divided on racial issues. With southern segregationists, all of them members of the Democratic majority, holding key posts on Capitol Hill, antidiscrimination measures faced formidable obstacles.

Even so, Congress passed its first civil rights measures in more than 80 years. The Civil Rights Act of 1957 established new procedures for expediting lawsuits by African Americans who claimed that their right to vote had been illegally abridged. It also created a permanent Commission on Civil Rights, although this was an advisory body empowered only to study alleged violations and recommend new remedies. In 1960, with the crucial support of Lyndon Johnson of Texas, the Democratic leader in the Senate, another act added additional federal support for blacks who were being barred from voting in the South. These civil rights initiatives, which became law against fierce opposition from southern Democrats, dramatized the difficulty of getting even relatively limited antidiscrimination measures through Congress.

President Eisenhower, who held the office with the power to enforce legislation and court orders, initially appeared reluctant to tackle racial discrimination head on. Ike supported the Civil Rights Act of 1957 but held back when some Republicans urged a dramatic presidential step—perhaps issuing an executive order barring racial discrimination on construction projects financed by federal funds. Always the gradualist, Eisenhower regarded the fight against discrimination as primarily a local matter, and he publicly doubted that the power of Washington could do much to change the attitudes of people opposed to the integration of public facilities or job sites.

In 1957, however, Eisenhower was forced to use the full power of his office to enforce a federal court order that mandated the desegregation of Central High School in Little Rock, Arkansas. Orval Faubus, the state's segregationist governor, promised his white supporters he would prevent black students from entering the school building. Ike allowed Faubus time to play to the white supremacist galleries of Arkansas, and the governor eventually deployed his state's National Guard to block the desegregation. Responding to this direct challenge to a court decision, Eisenhower put the Arkansas National Guard under federal control and augmented it with members of the U.S. Army. Black students, escorted by armed troops, finally entered Central High. The primary issue at stake, in Eisenhower's view, was a state's blatant defiance of the law of the land rather than school desegregation.

The confrontation in Little Rock underscored, as Eisenhower also recognized, the international dimension of civil-rights politics in the United States. Washington often found itself on the defensive when foreign critics pointed to the U.S. record on civil rights. The Soviet Union delighted in telling people around the world, particularly those in the Third World, how racial discrimination showed "the façade of the so-called 'American democracy.'" Secretary of State Dulles suggested that racial conflict at home was "not helpful to the influence of the United States abroad." When the U.S. Supreme Court, in *Cooper* v. *Aaron* (1958), unanimously invalidated an Arkansas law intended to block further integrationist efforts, newspapers around the world highlighted the decision. Events in Arkansas reaffirmed the image, carried throughout the world by the Eisenhower administration's informational campaign, of the United States as a powerful nation that supported liberty and equality.

Ike's initial indecision during the situation at Little Rock also suggested, however, how his grasp of domestic issues seemed to slip during his second term as president. In the election of 1956, he had achieved another landslide victory over Democrat Adlai Stevenson, but Ike's continued personal popularity did relatively little for his party. The Republicans failed to win back control of Congress from the Democrats. In fact, in this presidential election and in the off-year races of 1958, the GOP lost congressional seats as well as state legislatures and governors' mansions to the Democrats. After the 1958 elections, the Democrats outnumbered Republicans by nearly 2-to-1 margins in both the Senate and in the House. Meanwhile, Eisenhower, who had suffered a mild heart attack before the 1956 election, seemed progressively enfeebled, physically as well as politically. He appeared especially unsteady in his approach to racial issues.

American Indian Policy

The Eisenhower administration struggled with its policy toward American Indians. It attempted to implement two programs, "termination" and "relocation," that had been developed before it took office. The first called for Washington to terminate the status of Indians as "wards of the United States" and to grant them all the "rights and privileges pertaining to American citizenship." The long-term goals of termination, to be pursued on a tribe-by-tribe basis, were to abolish reservations, liquidate assets of the tribes, and curtail the services offered by the Bureau of Indian Affairs (BIA). In 1954, one year after this general policy had received congressional approval, six bills of termination were enacted. Immediately at stake were the legal status of more than 8,000 American Indians and more than 1 million acres of tribal land.

Under the relocation program, which had begun in 1951, Indians were encouraged to leave rural reservations and seek jobs in urban areas. In 1954, the BIA intensified its relocation efforts, with Minneapolis, St. Louis, Dallas, and several other cities joining Denver, Salt Lake City, and Los Angeles as relocation sites. This program, like termination, assumed that American Indians could rather easily become assimilated into urban life.

The initiatives quickly failed. As several more termination bills were enacted during the Eisenhower years, almost 12,000 people lost their status as tribal members, and the bonds of communal life for many Indians grew weaker. At the same time, more than 1 million acres of tribal lands, which often fell into the hands of real estate speculators, were lost. Indians from terminated tribes also lost both their exemption from state taxation and the social services provided by the BIA. They gained little in return. Most terminated Indians saw their economic prospects grow dimmer. Relocation went no better. Most of the relocated Indians found only low-paying, dead-end jobs and racial discrimination. In some cities, Indian

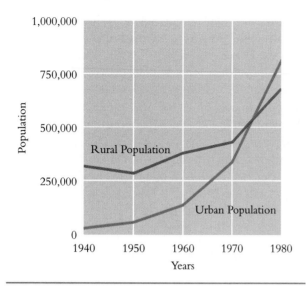

TOTAL URBAN AND RURAL INDIAN POPULATION IN THE UNITED STATES, 1940–1980

children who had left reservations found it difficult even to enter racially *segregated*, let alone integrated, public schools. Despite its problems, the relocation program nevertheless continued throughout the Eisenhower years.

Both Indians and their supporters soon mobilized against the termination and relocation policies. By 1957, the BIA had scaled back its initial timetable for liquidating every tribe within five years, and in 1960 the party platforms of both the Republicans and Democrats repudiated the policy entirely. In 1962, the policy was itself terminated. The relocation program continued, however, and by 1967 almost one-half of the nation's Indians lived in relocation cities. This policy neither touched the deep-rooted problems that many Indians confronted, including a life expectancy only two-thirds that of whites, nor provided significantly better opportunities for employment or education.

The Growth of Spanish-Speaking Populations

Millions of Spanish-speaking people, many of whom had recently arrived in the United States, also highlighted discrimination issues. Despite facing discriminatory practices in the job and housing markets in the United States, Puerto Ricans began moving in large numbers from their island commonwealth to the mainland during the 1950s. By 1960, New York City's Puerto Rican population was nearly 100 times greater than it had been before the Second World War. Chicago, Boston, and Hartford, Connecticut, also became the U.S. destinations for many Puerto Ricans during the 1950s. The government of Puerto Rico

encouraged this immigration as a way of easing population pressures but also urged the migrants to maintain cultural ties with the island. Although U.S. citizens, most of the newcomers spoke only Spanish, and the formation of social and cultural clubs helped link them with the Puerto Rican towns they had left behind and buffer the cultural impact of moving to the mainland. At the same time, Puerto Ricans began to organize against the discrimination they faced in the United States. The Puerto Rican–Hispanic Leadership Forum, organized in 1957, presaged the emergence of groups that looked more to social and economic conditions—and, ultimately, greater political clout—in the United States than to cultural affinities with Puerto Rico.

Meanwhile, large numbers of Spanish-speaking people from Mexico were moving to California and the Southwest, where they settled in long-established Mexican American communities. Beginning with the Second World War and continuing until 1967, the U.S. government sponsored the *bracero* (or farmhand) program, which brought nearly 5 million Mexicans northward, theoretically on short-term contracts, to fill agricultural jobs. Many *braceros* and their families remained in the United States after their contracts expired. Joining them were legal immigrants from Mexico and growing numbers of people who filtered across the border. These undocumented immigrants became the target of an ongoing government dragnet, begun in 1950 and intensified by the Eisenhower administration, called "Operation Wetback." ("Wetback" was a term of derision that implied people of Mexican ancestry had reached the United States by swimming across the Rio Grande River.) During a five-year period, the government claimed to have rounded up and deported to Mexico nearly 4 million people, allegedly all illegal immigrants. The operation helped stigmatize even citizens of Mexican heritage and justify discriminatory treatment by the government and employers.

People in long-established Mexican American communities mobilized to fight such discrimination. Labor organizers sought higher wages and better working conditions in the factories and fields, although the FBI labeled many of these efforts as "communist-inspired" and harassed unions—such as the United Cannery, Agricultural, Packing and Allied Workers of America (UCAPAWA)—that had large Mexican American memberships. A lengthy mining strike in New Mexico became the subject of the 1954 motion picture *Salt of the Earth*. Middle-class organizations, such as the League of United Latin American Citizens (LULAC) and the Unity League, sought to desegregate schools, public facilities, and housing in Southern California and throughout the Southwest. In 1940, Mexican Americans had been the most rural of all the major

ethnic groups; by 1950, in contrast, more than 65 percent of Mexican Americans were living in urban areas, a figure that would climb to 85 percent by 1970. As a result of this fundamental demographic shift, Mexican Americans began to become an important political force in many southwestern cities.

Urban-Suburban Issues

The growth of suburban areas during the 1950s created new urban issues, many of them related to race. Throughout the 1950s, both public and private institutions were shifting resources away from cities, especially away from neighborhoods in which Latinos and African Americans had settled. Adopting a policy called "red-lining," many banks and loan institutions denied funds for home-buying and business expansion in areas that were labeled "decaying" or "marginal" because they contained aging buildings, dense populations, and growing numbers of people who were not of European descent. The Federal Housing Administration (FHA) and other government agencies channeled most lending toward the suburbs. In 1960, for example, the FHA failed to put up a single dollar for home loans in Camden or Paterson, New Jersey, cities in which minority populations were growing, while it poured millions of dollars into surrounding, largely all-white suburbs.

"Urban renewal" programs, authorized by the Housing Act of 1949 (see chapter 27), often amounted to "urban removal." Although the law called for "a feasible method for the temporary relocation" of persons displaced by urban renewal projects, developers could generally ignore the housing needs of the people they displaced. During the 1950s, Robert Moses, who directed New York City's vast construction projects, effectively concealed the number of people dislocated by his urban renewal and highway building programs. In New York and other cities, office buildings and freeways replaced the living units that people with low-income jobs could afford.

Plans for new, federally built public housing quickly faltered. Although suburban areas, where land was abundant and relatively inexpensive, seemed the obvious place to locate affordable housing, middle-income homeowners used zoning laws to freeze out government-sponsored housing projects. Consequently, officials turned toward urban sites, where population density was high and land was expensive. At the same time, private housing interests lobbied to limit the number of public units actually constructed and to ensure that they would offer tenants few amenities. Originally conceived as a temporary alternative for families who would rather quickly move to their own homes, publicly built facilities became stigmatized as "the

projects," housing of last resort for people with chronically low incomes and meager prospects for rapid economic advancement.

By the end of the 1950s, the urban policies of both the Truman and Eisenhower eras seemed spectacular failures. Urban renewal projects not only disrupted urban housing patterns but also helped disperse industries that had long provided entry-level jobs for unskilled workers. Both major presidential candidates in 1960 pledged to create a new cabinet office for urban affairs and to expand Washington's role in addressing the dilemma of suburban growth and urban decay.

Debating the Role of Government

Controversy over urban-suburban issues was tied to larger debates of the late 1950s over how Washington might deal with a wide range of domestic issues. Although Eisenhower sometimes hinted that he favored rolling back the New and Fair Deals, he lacked both the will and the political support to do so. Actually, Eisenhower presided over a modest expansion of earlier Democratic initiatives: an expanded Social Security system, a higher minimum wage, better unemployment benefits, and a new Department of Health, Education, and Welfare (HEW). Still, as his stance on urban and racial issues most dramatically showed, he hesitated to enlarge governmental power. Eisenhower liked to call his stance one of "moderate Republicanism."

The New Conservatives

Eisenhower's centrist position on most domestic issues angered a growing group of people, who became known as the "new conservatives." Eisenhower was popular—and the first Republican president since Herbert Hoover—but did his administration really represent the conservative principles for which the GOP was supposed to stand?

Not to Arizona's Barry Goldwater. Ruggedly handsome and militantly anticommunist, Goldwater won election to the U.S. Senate in 1952 and emerged as the spokesperson for those Republicans who viewed Eisenhower's policies as insufficiently conservative. *The Conscience of a Conservative* (1960) summarized Goldwater's critique of postwar policies. By refusing to take stronger military measures against the Soviet Union and by not making "victory the goal of American policy," Eisenhower had likely endangered national security. Goldwater decried almost all domestic programs, including federal civil rights legislation, as grave threats to individual liberty.

The Eisenhower administration, he charged, was simply aping the Democratic Party's "New Deal antics" in its own domestic policy making.

While Goldwater was pressing the GOP to reject Eisenhower's moderate Republicanism, others, particularly the publisher William F. Buckley, Jr., were trying to frame a new conservative message. Buckley, a devout Roman Catholic, first gained national attention while still in his twenties. In his *God and Man at Yale* (1952), Buckley attacked what he saw as a "collectivist" and antireligious tilt in American higher education and defended capitalism and Christianity. In 1955, Buckley helped found the *National Review*, a weekly magazine that attracted a talented group of writers. It avoided positions, particularly the anti-Semitism of some old-line conservatives and the hysterical anticommunism of groups such as the John Birch Society, that could be seen as extremist. Although this new conservatism began amid considerable doubts about its immediate prospects, it sought a long-term strategy for building a right-of-center political and cultural movement. To that end, conservatives established Young Americans for Freedom (YAF) in 1960, several years before similar college-based youth organizations emerged on the political left.

Advocates of a More Active Government

While the new conservative movement was criticizing the Eisenhower administration for failing to repudiate policies of the Roosevelt and Truman years, a more eclectic group was pressing Washington to expand these earlier efforts. After Eisenhower suffered a second heart attack and a mild stroke during his second term, these critics talked about the need for more vigorous presidential leadership. They were especially disturbed at Eisenhower's reluctance to use Washington's power to attack racial discrimination. In addition, many economists, pointing to a severe economic downturn in 1958–59 when unemployment rose precipitously, ridiculed Eisenhower's commitment to a balanced budget. Even after conditions improved, economists such as John Kenneth Galbraith urged deficit spending by Washington, which Eisenhower stoutly resisted, as a spur to even greater economic expansion.

Other critics, although avoiding the strident anticommunism of conservatives such as Goldwater, dissected Eisenhower's national security policies. The 1957 Gaither Report, prepared by foreign policy analysts with close ties to defense industries, claimed that the Soviet Union's GNP was growing even more quickly than that of the United States and that much of this expansion came in its military

sector. The Gaither Report urged an immediate increase of about 25 percent in the Pentagon's budget and longer-term programs for building fallout shelters, developing intercontinental ballistic missiles (ICBMs), and expanding conventional military forces. Another report, written by a young political scientist named Henry Kissinger and issued by the Rockefeller Foundation, claimed that Eisenhower's New Look undermined national security by relying too heavily on massive nuclear retaliation and by downplaying non-nuclear options. It, too, called for greater spending on defense.

Eisenhower, who remained far more attentive to foreign policy than domestic issues, reacted cautiously. Although he agreed to accelerate the development of ICBMs, he opposed a crash effort to build fallout shelters or one to create the capability for fighting limited, non-nuclear wars around the globe. In fact, he reduced the size of several army and air force units and kept his defense budget well below the levels his critics were proposing. Eisenhower felt confident in pursuing this course because super-secret U-2 surveillance flights over the USSR revealed that the Soviets were lagging behind, rather than outpacing, the United States in military capability.

Concerns about national security and calls for greater government spending also surfaced in the continuing controversy over education. Throughout the 1950s, some critics complained that schools were emphasizing "life adjustment" skills—getting along with others and adapting to social change—instead of teaching traditional academic subjects. Rudolf Flesch's best-selling *Why Johnny Can't Read* anticipated books that asked why Johnny and his classmates couldn't add or subtract well either and why they lagged behind their counterparts in the Soviet Union in science. Washington's help in funding K–12 instruction seemed an obvious way to upgrade educational performance. Simultaneously, the nation's leading research universities were seeking greater federal aid for higher education; in summer 1957, a committee of prominent scientists implored the Defense Department to expand its support for basic scientific research. "Research is a requisite for survival" in the nuclear age, it declared. The case for increased spending on all levels of education suddenly gained new intensity when, in October 1957, the Soviets launched the world's first artificial satellite, a 22-inch sphere called *Sputnik.*

In 1958, using the magical phrase "national security," school administrators and university researchers obtained the federal dollars they had been seeking. The National Defense Education Act funneled money to college-level programs in science, engineering, foreign languages, and the social sciences. This act marked a milestone in the long battle to overcome congressional opposition, especially

© UPI-Bettmann/Corbis.

COLD WAR COMPETITION REACHES INTO SPACE

This "Space Race" card game was manufactured after the Soviet Union orbited its first *Sputnik* satellite in 1957. The fear that the Soviets were ahead of the United States in space technology prompted the nation to undertake a crash program of upgrading mathematics and science education and to accelerate its own space program, run by the newly created National Aeronautics and Space Administration (NASA). A fascination with space technology permeated popular culture in the late 1950s, but the cost implications of this initiative worried Eisenhower.

from southern representatives who feared that federal aid might bring pressures for racial integration, to educational spending by Washington. The Soviets' apparent superiority in satellite technology, seemingly confirmed by the launch of a second and much larger *Sputnik*, fueled a research-and-development (R&D) effort, overseen by a new National Aeronautics and Space Administration (NASA), to harness American educational and technological know-how so that outer space might be used for the benefit of "all mankind."

An effort to gain increased federal spending for social welfare programs also took root during the last years of Eisenhower's presidency. Galbraith's *The Affluent Society,* for instance, saw a dangerous tilt in the "social balance," away from "public goods." Affluent families could travel in

shiny new automobiles, but they needed to pass through shabby cities, motor along litter-filled roadsides, and speed by unsightly billboards. The researcher who developed a new carburetor is well rewarded, but anyone "who dreams up a new public service is [labeled] a wastrel," Galbraith's book sardonically noted.

Galbraith's analysis seemed mild in comparison to the jeremiads of Michael Harrington. In 1959, *Commentary,* one of several national magazines beginning to feature social criticism, published an article in which Harrington claimed that the problem of economic inequality remained as urgent as it had been during the 1930s. At least one-third of the nation's people—living in rural areas, small towns, and cities—barely subsisted in a land of supposed abundance. Avoiding the usual trappings of economic analysis, Harrington crafted dramatic stories about how poverty continued to ravage the bodies and spirits of people whose lives had been largely untouched by the economic growth of the 1940s and 1950s.

During the early 1960s, when addressing social and economic issues became a priority in Washington, critics such as Galbraith and Harrington became political celebrities. Their critiques, however, grew out of the political culture of the late 1950s. The Kennedy presidency of 1961–63 would in fact be rooted in the calls for more active foreign and domestic policies that had emerged during the Eisenhower years.

● The Kennedy Years: Foreign Policy

A wealthy, politically ambitious father had groomed John Fitzgerald Kennedy for the White House. After graduation from Harvard in 1940, the young Kennedy pursued both private passions (especially for Hollywood movie stars) and public service. After winning military honors while serving in the navy during the Second World War, Kennedy entered Democratic party politics. In 1946, he won election from Massachusetts to the House of Representatives; six years later, he captured a seat in the Senate. Kennedy became better known for his social life than for his command of legislative details, but he eventually gained a national political reputation, largely on the basis of his charm and youthful image. His 1953 marriage to Jacqueline Bouvier added yet another dash of glamour. A favorite of the media, Jackie won plaudits for her tastes in culture, her stylish dress, and her fluency in several foreign languages. After John Kennedy narrowly missed winning the vice presidential nomination in 1956, he immediately took aim at the top spot on the 1960 Democratic ticket.

The Election of 1960

Kennedy, often accompanied by Jackie and by his brothers (Robert and Ted), barnstormed across the country. This early presidential campaigning, along with a talented staff and his family's vast wealth, helped Kennedy overwhelm his primary Democratic challengers, Senators Hubert Humphrey of Minnesota and Lyndon Johnson. By pledging to separate his Catholic religion from his politics and by confronting those who appealed to anti-Catholic prejudice, Kennedy tried to defuse the religious issue that had doomed the candidacy of Al Smith in 1928 (see chapter 24).

Vice President Richard Nixon, obliged to seek the White House on Eisenhower's record even though Ike seemed lukewarm to a Nixon candidacy, remained on the defensive throughout the 1960 campaign. Nixon seemed notably off-balance during the first of several televised debates in which the cool, tanned Kennedy emerged, according to surveys of TV viewers, with a clear victory over the pale, nervous Nixon. (People who only listened on radio generally gave Nixon much higher marks.) Despite chronic and severe health problems, which Kennedy's entourage effectively concealed, JFK projected the image of a vigorous, energetic leader.

Kennedy's 1960 campaign highlighted issues from the 1950s that, taken together, became his "New Frontier" agenda. Although Senator Kennedy's civil rights record had been mixed, candidate Kennedy declared that his White House would press for new congressional legislation. In an important symbolic act, he dispatched aides to Georgia to assist Martin Luther King, Jr., who was facing a jail sentence for a minor traffic violation. Kennedy further promised to use the president's executive authority, which Eisenhower had refused to do, against racial discrimination. Kennedy also endorsed the kind of social programs that Eisenhower's critics had been advocating. These included federal spending to rebuild rural communities, to increase educational opportunities, and to improve urban conditions.

Kennedy highlighted two other central issues of the late 1950s: promoting greater economic growth and conducting a more aggressive foreign policy. Dismissing Eisenhower's cautious policies as timid and ineffectual, Kennedy embraced advisers who spoke of stimulating the economy by means of tax cuts and deficit spending measures. On foreign policy, he criticized Eisenhower for failing to rid the hemisphere of Castro in Cuba and for allowing a "missile gap" to develop in the arms race with the Soviet Union. By spending more on defense than Eisenhower, Kennedy claimed, he would create a "flexible response" against communism, especially in the Third

World. Adlai Stevenson, in his 1956 presidential campaign against Eisenhower, had claimed that Americans could no longer "drift, we must go forward." Reworking this phrase, Kennedy proclaimed that "the American people are tired of the drift in our national course . . . and that they are ready to move again."

The 1960 election defied easy analysis. Kennedy defeated Nixon by only about 100,000 popular votes, and his victory in the electoral vote rested on razor-thin margins in several states, including Illinois. Many Republicans urged Nixon to challenge Kennedy's triumph in Illinois as fraudulent, but the vice president chose to accept the disputed result. Anti-Catholic sentiment, especially in the South, resurfaced, and Kennedy won a smaller percentage of the popular vote than most of the Democrats who had competed for lesser offices in 1960. His election owed a great debt to his vice presidential running mate, Lyndon Johnson, whose regional appeal helped the Democratic ticket carry the Deep South and Johnson's home state of Texas. Democrats remained the majority party, but this did not translate into a groundswell of support for Kennedy and his New Frontier in 1960.

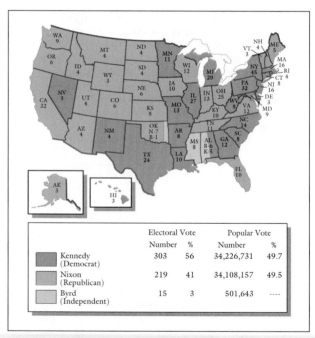

	Electoral Vote		Popular Vote	
	Number	%	Number	%
Kennedy (Democrat)	303	56	34,226,731	49.7
Nixon (Republican)	219	41	34,108,157	49.5
Byrd (Independent)	15	3	501,643	----

MAP 28.3 PRESIDENTIAL ELECTION, 1960

In one of the closest elections in American history in terms of the popular vote, Kennedy only narrowly out-polled Nixon. Kennedy's more commanding victory in the electoral vote produced some discussion about the consequences if the electoral college one day produced a president who had failed to carry the popular vote, a situation that did indeed occur in the election of 2000.

From the outset, JFK and Jackie riveted media attention on the White House. They hobnobbed with movie stars, and the new president welcomed prominent intellectuals to the administration. The Kennedy inaugural featured designer clothing, an appearance by the aged poet Robert Frost, and an oft-quoted speech in which JFK challenged people to "ask not what your country can do for you; ask what you can do for your country." The "best and the brightest," the name given to the hard-driving people who joined Kennedy's administration, promised to launch exciting and difficult crusades, even one to the frontier of outer space. Many of the administration's initiatives, including space exploration, drew from ideas developed during the 1950s.

Kennedy's Foreign Policy Goals

Kennedy promised vigorous action in foreign policy. Although Secretary of Defense Robert McNamara quickly found that the alleged "missile gap" did not exist, Kennedy raised the defense budget anyway. The White House strongly supported military assistance programs, propaganda agencies, and covert action plans. In one of his most popular initiatives, the president created the Peace Corps, a new program that sent Americans, especially young people, to nations around the world to work on development projects that might undercut communism's appeal.

Eisenhower's last-minute effort to reorient U.S. Latin American policy away from reliance on dictators and toward support of more broadly based socioeconomic programs was elaborated on and repackaged as Kennedy's "Alliance for Progress." Proposed in spring 1961 in hopes of checking the spread of anti-Americanism and Castro-like insurgencies, the Alliance offered $20 billion in loans over a 10-year period to Latin American countries that would undertake land reform and other economic development measures. The Alliance, which underestimated obstacles to rapid social and economic change in Latin America, rapidly failed.

Cuba and Berlin

The worst fiasco of the Kennedy presidency, a daring but ill-conceived CIA mission against Cuba, also had its roots in the Eisenhower administration. The CIA, looking back on earlier covert actions against anti-American governments in Iran and Guatemala, had been planning a secret, Eisenhower-endorsed invasion to oust Fidel Castro. Kennedy, overriding the doubts of some of his advisers, reaffirmed the operation. On April 17, 1961, however, when U.S.-backed and trained forces (mainly anticommunist Cuban exiles) landed at the Bahia de Cochinas (the Bay of Pigs) on the southern coast of Cuba, the expected popular uprising did not occur. Forces loyal to Castro quickly surrounded and imprisoned the invaders. Kennedy refused to provide the air support that the Cuban exiles had expected and, initially, tried to deny any U.S. involvement in the invasion. The CIA's role quickly became public, however, and anti-Yankee sentiment mounted throughout Latin America. Castro tightened his grip over Cuban life and strengthened his ties to the Soviet Union.

Kennedy responded to the Bay of Pigs by admitting error and by devising new anti-Castro strategies. "I have made a tragic mistake," Kennedy told one adviser. "Not only were our facts in error, but our policy was wrong." Stung by the failed invasion, the White House continued to target Castro with a covert program, "Operation Mongoose," which included efforts to destabilize Cuba's economy and several failed plots against Castro. During one of the attempts to kill the Cuban leader, the CIA worked directly with U.S. organized crime figures, who wanted revenge for Castro's closure of their casinos in Havana.

Another dramatic confrontation loomed in Berlin. In June 1961, Nikita Khrushchev and Kennedy met in Vienna, Austria, where the Soviets proposed ending the Western presence in Berlin and reuniting the city as part of East Germany. Khrushchev's offer responded to the steady flow of immigrants from East Germany into West Berlin, a migration that was both embarrassing and economically draining to the German communist regime. Kennedy refused to abandon West Berlin, and the East German government continued to press Khrushchev for help. In August 1961, the communist regime began to erect first a barbed-wire fence and then a concrete wall to separate East from West Berlin. East Germans attempting to escape into the West were shot down. The Berlin Wall became a symbol of communist repression. Kennedy's assertion, *"Ich bin ein Berliner"* ("I am a Berliner"), delivered in front of the wall to a cheering crowd of West Berliners, provided a memorable image of JFK's presidency.

Superpower confrontation escalated to a potentially lethal level during the Cuban Missile Crisis of October 1962. The Soviet Union, fulfilling a request from Castro, began sending sophisticated weapons to the island nation. After spy-plane flights showed missile-launching sites in Cuba, the Kennedy administration announced it would not allow the Soviet Union to place nuclear warheads so close to American soil. It demanded that the Soviets dismantle the missile silos and turn back supply ships, perhaps containing warheads, then heading for Cuba. After tense strategy sessions with his top advisers, Kennedy rejected a military strike against Cuba that might have taken the United States and the Soviet Union to war. Instead, he ordered the U.S. Navy to "quarantine" the island. The

to smear him, the FBI intensified surveillance and illegally wiretapped King's private conversations.

Events, however, forced the Kennedy administration to devise legislative initiatives. In early 1960, African American students at North Carolina A & T College in Greensboro sat down at a drugstore lunch counter and asked to be served in the same manner as white customers. It was the beginning of the "sit-in" movement, a new phase in the civil rights movement in which young activists challenged local segregation laws by demanding equal access to hitherto racially separated places. All across the South, demonstrators staged nonviolent sit-in demonstrations at restaurants, bus and train stations, and other public facilities.

The courage and commitment of these demonstrators reenergized the antidiscrimination movement. With songs such as "We Shall Overcome" and "Oh, Freedom" inspiring solidarity, young people pledged their talents, their resources—indeed, their lives—to the civil rights struggle. In 1961, interracial activists from the Congress of Racial Equality (CORE) and the Student Nonviolent Coordinating Committee (SNCC), a student group that emerged from the sit-in movement, risked racist retaliation by conducting "freedom rides" across the South. The freedom riders were challenging the Kennedy administration to enforce a series of federal court decisions that had declared state laws requiring segregation on interstate buses (and in bus stations) to be unconstitutional.

This grassroots activism prompted a response from the Kennedy administration. It first dispatched U.S. marshals to protect the freedom riders. In 1962 and again the following year, it called on National Guard troops and federal marshals to prevent segregationist mobs from blocking court-ordered integration at several educational institutions in the Deep South, including the universities of Mississippi and Alabama. In November 1962, Kennedy issued a long-promised executive order that banned racial discrimination in federally financed housing. The following February, in hopes of curtailing future confrontations, he sent Congress a limited civil rights bill that called for faster trial procedures in cases involving challenges to racial discrimination in voting practices.

Events in the South, however, continued to outpace the Kennedy administration's policies. In 1963, racial conflict convulsed Birmingham, Alabama. White police officers unleashed dogs and high-pressure water hoses on African Americans, including children, who were seeking to desegregate that city. Four young girls were later murdered (and 20 people injured) when racists bombed Birmingham's Sixteenth Street Baptist Church, a center of the civil rights campaign. When thousands of blacks took to the streets in protest—and two more children were killed, this time by police officers—the Kennedy administration decided it had to staunch the bloodletting.

The determination of civil rights activists to defy racist violence created a real-life drama that played to the entire world. The major television networks carried vivid images of the struggle, and Kennedy made an emotional plea on TV for a national commitment to the battle against discrimination. Recent events had raised "a moral issue . . . as old as Scriptures and . . . as clear as the Constitution." The time for "patience" and "delay," he declared, had passed. Racial violence was also "retarding our Nation's economic and social progress and weakening the respect with which the rest of the world regards us," the President insisted. Against the backdrop of a televised battle line that seemed to stretch across the South, the issue of civil rights dominated national politics during the last six months of Kennedy's presidency.

RACIAL CONFLICT IN BIRMINGHAM

Images such as this 1963 photograph of a confrontation in Birmingham, Alabama, in which segregationists turned dogs on youthful demonstrators, helped rally public support for civil rights legislation. Events in Birmingham, however, also presaged the increasingly violent clashes that would punctuate the efforts to end racial discrimination.

AP/Wide World Photos.

Kennedy still hoped to control the direction and pace of change. The White House crafted additional legislation designed to dampen the enthusiasm for civil rights demonstrations without further inflaming white segregationists. It supported a ban on racial discrimination in all public facilities and housing and new measures to protect the voting rights of African Americans in the South. When the administration recognized that its legislative proposals would not derail a "March on Washington for Jobs and Freedom," planned for the late summer of 1963, it belatedly endorsed the event.

On August 28, 1963, an integrated group of more than 200,000 people marched through the nation's capital to the Lincoln Memorial. There, Martin Luther King, Jr., delivered his famous "I Have a Dream" speech. A broad coalition of civil rights and labor organizations sponsored the march. Speakers generally applauded Kennedy's latest initiatives but also urged a broader agenda. Demands included a higher minimum wage and a federal program to guarantee new jobs. Well-organized and smoothly run, this one-day demonstration received overwhelmingly favorable coverage from the national media and put even greater political pressure on the White House and Congress to lend their assistance.

Women's Issues

The seeds of a resurgent women's movement were also being sown, although more quietly, during the Kennedy years. Kennedy's own call for people to enter public service in organizations such as the Peace Corps helped raise young women's expectations for lives that included more than marriage and child rearing.

All across the political spectrum, women were speaking out on contemporary issues. The energy of women such as Phyllis Schlafly, whose book *A Choice, Not an Echo* (1964) became one of the leading manifestos on the political right, helped fuel the new conservatism. African American activists such as Bernice Johnson Reagon (whose work with the Freedom Singers combined music and social activism) and Fannie Lou Hamer (who spearheaded the organization of a racially integrated Freedom Democratic Party in Mississippi) fought discrimination based on both race and gender.

Similarly, Chicana farm workers became key figures in the union activism that led to the organization of the United Farm Workers of America. Women also played an important role in protests, through the Committee for a Sane Nuclear Policy (Sane) and the Women's Strike for Peace, against the U.S.–Soviet arms race. During Kennedy's final year in office, 1963, Betty Friedan published *The Feminine Mystique*. Widely credited with helping to spark a new phase of the feminist movement, Friedan's book drew on her own social criticism from the late 1950s and articulated the dissatisfactions that many middle-class women felt about the narrow confines of domestic life and the lack of public roles available to them.

To address women's concerns, Kennedy appointed the Presidential Commission on the Status of Women, chaired by Eleanor Roosevelt. Negotiating differences between moderate and more militant members, the commission issued a report that documented discrimination against women in employment opportunities and wages. Kennedy responded with a presidential order designed to eliminate gender discrimination within the federal civil service system. His administration also supported the Equal Pay Act of 1963, which made it a federal crime for employers to pay lower wages to women who were doing the same work as men.

The Assassination of John F. Kennedy

By fall 1963, the Kennedy administration, although still worried about its ability to push legislation through a recalcitrant Congress, was preparing new initiatives on civil rights and economic opportunity. Then, on November 22, 1963, John F. Kennedy was shot down as his presidential motorcade moved through Dallas, Texas. Vice President Lyndon Johnson, who had accompanied Kennedy to Texas, took the oath of office and hurried back to Washington. The Dallas police quickly arrested Lee Harvey Oswald and pegged him as JFK's assassin. Oswald had ties to the Marcello crime family; had once lived in the Soviet Union; and had a bizarre set of political affiliations, including shadowy ones with groups interested in Cuba. Oswald, who declared his innocence, never faced trial. Jack Ruby, whose Dallas nightclub catered to powerful crime figures, killed Oswald on national television, while the alleged gunman was in police custody. A lengthy investigation by a special commission headed by Chief Justice Earl Warren concluded that both Oswald and Ruby had acted alone.

The Warren Commission's "lone gunman" report has come under increasing scrutiny. In 1978, a special panel of the House of Representatives speculated that Kennedy might have been the victim of a wider plot, perhaps involving organized crime, but produced little supporting evidence. Other theories of a conspiracy, including ones that pointed toward the CIA and high governmental officials, sprang up. Oliver Stone's *JFK* (1991) refocused attention on the flaws in the Warren Commission's report and prompted Congress to create the Assassinations

discrimination in the Deep South, was poised to transform political life.

In the post-Kennedy era, debate would become riveted on questions related to the government's exercise of power: Was the United States spreading liberty in Vietnam? Was it sufficiently active in pursuing equality for racial minorities and the poor? The troubled presidencies of Kennedy's successors, Lyndon Johnson and Richard Nixon, would turn on these questions.

SUGGESTED READINGS

James T. Patterson, *Grand Expectations: The United States, 1945–1974* (1996) provides an overview of the period. For accounts of presidential leadership, begin with **Fred I. Greenstein,** *The Hidden-Hand Presidency: Eisenhower as Leader* (rev. ed., 1994). **Chester Pach, Jr. and Elmo Richardson,** *The Presidency of Dwight D. Eisenhower* (1991) presents a fine, brief history. On John Kennedy, see **Robert Dallek,** *An Unfinished Life: John F. Kennedy, 1917–1963* (2003); **Richard Reeves,** *President Kennedy: Profile of Power* (1994); and **Seymour Hersh,** *The Dark Side of Camelot* (1997).

There are many studies of Eisenhower's foreign policy, but a good sense of the issues and scholarly debates can be gleaned from **Robert R. Bowie and Richard H. Immerman,** *Waging Peace: How Eisenhower Shaped an Enduring Cold War Strategy* (2000). **John Prados,** *Presidents' Secret Wars: CIA and Pentagon Covert Operations from World War II through the Persian Gulf* (1996), and **Zachary Karabell,** *Architects of Intervention: The United States, the Third World, and the Cold War, 1946–1962* (1999) put an important aspect of policy in a broad perspective. **Walter L. Hixson,** *Parting the Curtain: Propaganda, Culture, and the Cold War, 1945–1961* (1997) argues that cultural initiatives provided powerful weapons in the Cold War. **Lawrence Freedman,** *Kennedy's Wars: Berlin, Cuba, Laos, and Vietnam* (2000) illuminates the major international crises of the Kennedy years.

For events on the home front, **James B. Gilbert,** *A Cycle of Outrage: America's Reaction to the Juvenile Delinquent in the 1950s* (1986) discusses cultural fears; **Karal Ann Marling,** *As Seen on TV: The Visual Culture of Everyday Life in the 1950s* (1994) stresses the new emphasis on visuality; and **James B. Gilbert,** *Redeeming Culture: American Religion in an Age of Science* (1997) examines another aspect of America's changing culture. **W. T. Lhamon, Jr.,** *Deliberate Speed: The Origins of a Cultural Style in the American 1950s* (1990) advances a provocative interpretation. The highly readable examination of the struggle against racial discrimination by **Taylor Branch,** *Parting the Waters: America in the King Years, 1954–1963* (1988) may be augmented by **Mary L. Dudziak,** *Cold War Civil Rights: Race and the Image of American Democracy* (2000), which places concerns over civil rights in an international context; by **James Patterson,** *Brown v. Board of Education: A Civil Rights Milestone and Its Troubled Legacy* (2001); and by **David L. Chappell,** *A Stone of Hope: Prophetic Religion and the Death of Jim Crow* (2004).

On women and families during the 1950s, **Elaine Tyler May,** *Homeward Bound: American Families in the Cold War Era* (rev. ed., 1999) stresses the new emphasis on family life, while **Leila J. Rupp,** *Survival in the Doldrums: The American Women's Rights Movement, 1945 to the 1960s* (1987); **Joanne Meyerowitz, ed.,** *Not June Cleaver: Women and Gender in Postwar America, 1945–1960* (1994); and **Stephanie Coontz,** *The Way We Never Were: American Families and the Nostalgia Trip* (1992) work against that grain.

AMERICAN JOURNEY ONLINE
 AND
INFOTRAC COLLEGE EDITION

Visit the source collections at www.ajaccess.wadsworth.com and infotrac.thomsonlearning.com and use the Search function with the following key terms to explore documents, images, audio and video clips, articles, and commentary related to the material in this chapter.

Dwight D. Eisenhower
U-2 plane
Eisenhower Doctrine
Dr. Benjamin Spock
Baby Boom
Brown v. Board of Education
Rosa Parks
Civil Rights Act of 1957
Montgomery Bus Boycott
Martin Luther King, Jr.
Little Rock Central High School
Termination and relocation policies (Native Americans)

Sputnik
Highway Act of 1956
Consumerism
Elvis Presley
Chuck Berry
Rock 'n' roll
John F. Kennedy
Bay of Pigs
Cuban Missile Crisis
Student Nonviolent Coordinating Committee (SNCC)
Betty Friedan
The Feminine Mystique
Kennedy assassination

GRADE AIDS

Visit the Liberty Equality Power Companion Web Site for resources specific to this textbook: http://history.wadsworth.com/murrin_LEP4e

The CD in the back of this book and the U.S. History Resource Center at http://history.wadsworth.com/u.s./ offer a variety of tools to help you succeed in this course, including access to quizzes; images; documents; interactive simulations, maps, and timelines; movie explorations; and a wealth of other sources.

exacerbated by the escalating cost of the war in Vietnam, made greater federal expenditures on domestic programs a highly controversial policy.

Observers still disagree on the impact of Johnson's Great Society programs. Charles Murray's influential book *Losing Ground* (1984) charged that massive government expenditures, associated with Johnson's initiatives, encouraged antisocial behavior. Lured by welfare payments, this study argued, people abandoned the goals of marrying, settling down, and seeking jobs that would raise their income. In this view, the money appropriated for Great Society programs also created government deficits that slowed economic growth. Had this ill-advised spending not undermined personal initiative and the nation's economic structure, continued growth would have guaranteed virtually everyone a middle-class lifestyle. This conservative argument portrayed the Great Society as the cause of, not the remedy for, economic distress.

Others vigorously rejected this view. They found scant evidence for the proposition that millions of people preferred welfare to meaningful work. Moreover, spending for the military sector outstripped that for social programming and seemed the principal cause of the burgeoning government deficit. Funds actually spent on Great Society programs, these observers have noted, neither matched Johnson's promises nor reached the lavish total claimed in critical studies such as *Losing Ground.*

Most antipoverty activists continued to fault the Great Society for not seriously challenging the prevailing distribution of political and economic power. The Johnson administration, they argued, remained closely wedded to large-scale bureaucratic solutions, by people connected to Washington elites, for problems that had many local variations. The White House quickly jettisoned the CAP model of grassroots participation. Moreover, the Great Society, which assumed that economic growth would continue to finance federal initiatives, never even considered measures that might seek to redistribute income and wealth. Its promises were never implemented, this critique alleged, and the proposed War on Poverty became only a series of small skirmishes.

Although historians disagree on the Great Society's impact, there is broad agreement that Johnson's domestic program brought the kind of federal support for domestic social programs that recalled the New Deal of the 1930s. Washington's financial outlay, although never what Johnson had seemed to promise, increased more than 10 percent in every year of his presidency. In 1960, federal spending on social welfare constituted 28 percent of total government outlays; by 1970, this figure had risen to more than 40 percent. Moreover, Great Society programs such as Medicaid, legal services, and job training permitted many low-income families to have some of the services, such as medical care, that more affluent Americans had long taken for granted.

The Great Society, by extending national power, inflamed political passions. When trying to promote equality, could social policy makers make the distinction, which was becoming increasingly important in political rhetoric, between people who really merited assistance—those seeking a "hand up"—and people merely seeking a "handout"? Partisan controversy over social spending policies, reinvigorated by the Great Society, would shape political life during the years that followed Lyndon Johnson's presidency.

Escalation in Vietnam

Johnson's divisive crusade to build a Great Society at home had its counterpart abroad. The pledge to protect South Vietnam demanded ever more of the nation's energy, its resources, and its military personnel. Johnson's foreign policy alienated many Americans, especially among the young, divided the entire nation, and eventually contributed to economic disarray.

The Gulf of Tonkin Resolution

Immediately after John Kennedy's assassination in November 1963, Johnson had avoided widening the war in Vietnam. He did not wish, however, to be seen as "soft" on communism. Seeing no alternative to backing the South Vietnamese government in Saigon, Johnson accepted the recommendation of his military advisers that the United States could beat back enemy offensives in South Vietnam by ordering air strikes against North Vietnam. He prepared a congressional resolution authorizing such an escalation of hostilities.

Events in the Gulf of Tonkin, off the coast of North Vietnam, provided the rationale for taking this resolution to Capitol Hill. On August 1, 1964, the U.S. destroyer *Maddox,* while conducting an intelligence-gathering mission, exchanged fire with North Vietnamese torpedo boats. Three days later, the *Maddox* returned with the *Turner Joy* and, during severe weather, reported what could have been evidence of a failed torpedo attack. Although the *Maddox's* commander radioed that the episode needed further analysis, Johnson immediately claimed that North Vietnam had engaged in "unprovoked aggression" against U.S. forces. Congress overwhelmingly authorized Johnson to take "all necessary measures to repel armed attack." (A later study concluded that there had never been a North Vietnamese attack.) Johnson treated this Gulf of Tonkin

Resolution as tantamount to a congressional declaration of war and cited it as legal authorization for subsequent military action in Vietnam.

Despite Johnson's aggressive response to events in the Gulf of Tonkin, the president still positioned himself as a cautious moderate during the presidential campaign of 1964. When Republican candidate Barry Goldwater urged stronger measures against North Vietnam and hinted at possible use of tactical nuclear weapons, Johnson's campaign managers portrayed Goldwater as a threat to the survival of civilization. Johnson promised not to commit American troops to a land war in Asia.

Soon after the election, however, Johnson again escalated the war. The 1963 coup against Diem (see chapter 28) had left a political vacuum in South Vietnam. The incompetence of South Vietnam's military-led government was sparking growing popular discontent, and South Vietnamese soldiers were deserting at an alarming rate. In January 1965, this military regime fell, and factionalism stalled the emergence of a stable alternative.

Lacking an effective ally in South Vietnam, Johnson puzzled over his options. Did the nation's long-standing Cold War policy of containing communism mean that the conflict in Vietnam required full-fledged American involvement? What kind of backlash might a South Vietnamese defeat produce in the United States and around the world? Would a U.S. escalation against North Vietnam lead to confrontation with its communist allies, China and the Soviet Union?

Johnson's aides offered conflicting advice. National Security Adviser McGeorge Bundy predicted inevitable defeat unless the United States greatly increased its military role. Walt Rostow, a specialist in issues of economic development, assured Johnson that a broad-based effort would bring victory. Once the enemy recognized Johnson's determination to remain in Vietnam, he advised, they would give up their plans to overrun the South. Undersecretary of State George Ball, by contrast, warned that U.S. troops could not save South Vietnam. "The South Vietnamese are losing the war," he wrote, and "no one has demonstrated that a white ground force of whatever size can win a guerrilla war . . . in jungle terrain in the midst of a population that refuses cooperation to the white forces." Senate Majority Leader Mike Mansfield urged the president to devise a plan for reuniting Vietnam as a neutral country. The Joint Chiefs of Staff, afflicted by interservice rivalries, provided differing military assessments and no clear guidance.

Although privately doubting the chance for success, Johnson worried more about the political and diplomatic costs of a U.S. pullout. He feared that domestic criticism of any communist victory in South Vietnam would endanger his Great Society programs. Moreover, he accepted the familiar Cold War proposition that a U.S. withdrawal from a confrontation such as the one in South Vietnam would set off a "domino effect." It would encourage communist-leaning insurgencies in Latin America, increase pressure on West Berlin, and damage U.S. credibility around the world. Both Eisenhower and Kennedy had staked American prestige on the preservation of a noncommunist South Vietnam. Johnson either had to abandon that commitment or chart an uncertain course by ordering a massive infusion of U.S. troops into the Vietnam conflict.

Ultimately, Johnson decided he had no choice but to extend U.S. involvement. He ordered a sustained campaign of bombing in North Vietnam, code-named "Rolling Thunder." He also deployed U.S. ground forces to regain lost territory in the South, expanded covert operations, and stepped up economic aid to the beleaguered Saigon government. Only six months after the 1964 election, with his advisers still divided, Johnson committed the United States to war against not only the NLF but North Vietnam as well.

The War Widens

The war grew more intense throughout 1965. Trying to break the enemy's will, U.S. military commanders mounted an effort to inflict more casualties. Accordingly, the administration authorized the use of napalm, a chemical that charred both foliage and people, and allowed the Air Force to bomb new targets. Additional U.S. combat troops arrived to secure enclaves in the South against further enemy incursions. Every escalation seemed to require a further one. When North Vietnam rejected a Johnson "peace plan" that it viewed as a surrender, the United States again stepped up its military involvement. North Vietnam's leader, Ho Chi Minh, who was also playing a game of escalation and attrition, became convinced that Johnson commanded meager public and congressional support for continuing the costly war.

In April 1965, Johnson brought his Cold War, anticommunist crusade closer to home. Responding to exaggerated reports of a communist threat to the Dominican Republic, Johnson sent American troops to unseat a left-leaning elected president and to install a government favorable to U.S. interests in the Caribbean nation. This U.S. incursion violated a long-standing "good neighbor" pledge not to intervene militarily in the Western Hemisphere. Although the action raised criticism throughout Latin America, the successful overthrow of a leftist government in the Dominican Republic steeled the administration's determination to hold the line against communism in Vietnam.

the Vietnam War was undeclared, Johnson had to resort to informal, although initially effective, ways of managing information. With television reports making Vietnam into a "living room war"—one that citizens could watch in their own homes—Johnson kept three sets playing in his office in order to monitor what viewers were seeing. Sometimes he would phone network executives and castigate them for their broadcasts—the "Johnson treatment," some called it. After one report, Frank Stanton of CBS reportedly received this call: "Frank, are you trying to f— me? . . . This is your president, and yesterday your boys shat on the American flag." Increasingly sensitive to criticism, Johnson equated any question or doubt about his policy with a lack of patriotism.

Antiwar activists were equally disturbed by what they regarded as the media's uncritical reporting on the war. Most journalists, they claimed, relied on official handouts for their stories, spent their time in Saigon's best hotels, and kowtowed to the White House. Especially in the early years, few reporters filed critical stories. Although the press corps did not invite the American public to cheer on the military effort, as it had during the two world wars, neither did its coverage help to encourage dissent.

In time, however, the tone of news coverage began to change. Images of unrelenting destruction on the nightly TV news and in magazine photos inevitably eroded enthusiasm for the war. In addition, a few journalists forthrightly expressed their opposition. Harrison Salisbury of the *New York Times* sent reports from Vietnam that detailed the destructive power of U.S. bombing missions. Gloria Emerson's grim reports portrayed the war as a class-based effort in which poor and disproportionately non-white troops fought and died so that rich men, with draft-exempt "fortunate sons," might reap war-related profits.

As the war dragged on, the media began to talk about a "war at home," one between "hawks" and "doves." Johnson insisted that he was merely following the containment policy favored by Eisenhower and Kennedy. Secretary of State Dean Rusk spoke of the dangers of "appeasement." But influential politicians—including J. William Fulbright of Arkansas, chair of the powerful Senate Foreign Relations Committee—warned of misplaced priorities and of an "arrogance of power." Meanwhile, antiwar protestors began to challenge the structure of American politics and culture.

The War at Home

Millions came to oppose the war in Southeast Asia, and support eroded for the Great Society at home. By 1968, tensions escalated into confrontation and violence.

A New Left

During the early 1960s, small groups of people, many of them college students, came to reject the policies of the postwar years. In 1962, two years after conservative activists had formed Young Americans for Freedom (YAF), insurgents on the left established an organization they dubbed Students for a Democratic Society (SDS). While YAF worked quietly to build a "New Right," SDS captured the media's attention with its more flamboyant attempt to create a "New Left." Although SDS endorsed familiar political causes, especially the fight against racial discrimination, its "Port Huron Statement" of 1962 also spoke of novel, more spiritual and personal issues. SDS pledged to attack the "loneliness, estrangement, isolation" of postwar society.

The SDS became one part of a New Left. This movement tried to distance its politics from those of the Democratic Party and that of the "old" communist-inspired Left. Charging that the dominant culture valued bureaucratic

ANTIWAR DEMONSTRATION IN WASHINGTON, D.C.
Mass rallies against U.S. involvement in the Vietnam War became an important part of antiwar politics during the late 1960s and early 1970s.

Responses to the question: "Do you think that the United States made a mistake in sending troops to fight there?"

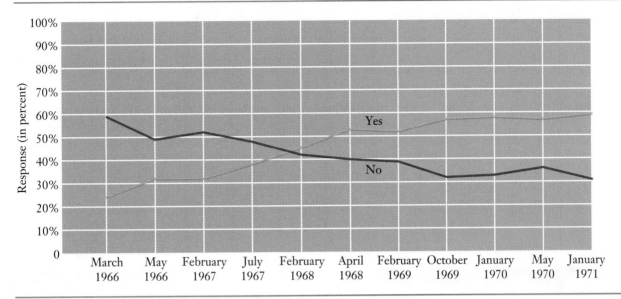

AMERICAN ATTITUDES TOWARD THE VIETNAM WAR

expertise over citizen engagement and economic growth over meaningful work, this New Left embraced an alternative socioeconomic vision. In politics, it called for "participatory democracy," grassroots activities, and institutions responsive to the wishes of local communities rather than the dictates of national elites. "We felt that we were different, and that we were going to do things differently," recalled one early SDS member. "It felt like the dawn of a new age."

During the early 1960s, the antidiscrimination movement in the Deep South inspired many young, white college students from the North. Risking racist violence, they went to the South and helped local political activists. Some remained there, working for civil rights; others returned to the North and joined neighborhood-based political projects. The New Left also tried to organize college campuses, mobilizing students on behalf of civil rights and against both the war in Southeast Asia and socioeconomic deprivation at home.

Even students not formally aligned with this New Left often saw colleges and universities as part of a vast "establishment" that blindly opposed change. On campus, young people had increasingly been complaining that required academic courses ignored relevant issues of the day and that college administrators imposed archaic restrictions, such as sex-segregated living arrangements and required dorm hours, from an authoritarian past when colleges acted *in loco parentis* (in place of parents). Giant universities, sustained by funds from government and corpora-

tions, seemed oblivious to the social and moral implications of their war-related research, dissenting students also claimed. During the "Berkeley student revolt" of 1964 and 1965, students and sympathetic faculty members protested restrictions on political organizing on campus and then began speaking out against the Vietnam War and racial discrimination. Although the long-running drama at Berkeley, which disrupted classes and polarized the university, was hardly the only or even the first example of student dissent, it came to symbolize the turmoil that the media called "the war on campus."

By 1966, the Vietnam issue convulsed many campuses. A young man's draft card signified a highly personal connection to U.S. involvement in Southeast Asia. Local draft boards usually granted an educational deferment to male students, but these always expired at graduation and could occasionally be revoked or denied. The burning of draft cards, as a symbolic protest against both the war and universal military service for men, became a central feature of antiwar demonstrations.

Bitter strife rocked many campuses after 1965. At "teach-ins," supporters and opponents of the war argued their positions. These debates soon gave way to less-structured demonstrations. As antiwar sentiment grew, students who supported the war began claiming that *their* rights were being restricted. Conservatives such as Ronald Reagan called on college administrators to return "civility" to the campus life and added opposition to student protests to their expanding political agenda.

The Counterculture

Accompanying the spread of New Left politics was the rise of a much-publicized "counterculture." Seen most broadly, this alternative culture helped support several ongoing causes—including the cooperative movement, environmentalism, and the fight against restrictions on lifestyle choices (see chapter 30)—but the mass media of the 1960s invariably highlighted only the most visible trappings of this insurgency. It focused on those individuals whose colorful, experimental approach to daily life defied traditional attitudes on matters such as clothing, hair style, and sexuality. The media liked to portray these people, caricatured as "hippies," as the vanguard of a supposedly massive "youth revolt." It detailed their association with drugs such as marijuana and LSD; communal living arrangements, especially rural communes; and new forms of music such as the folk-rock of the Byrds and the acid-rock of the Grateful Dead.

The media hailed young people linked to cultural innovation, particularly musicians, not simply as cultural symbols but, even if they shunned the role, as generational prophets. The reclusive singer-songwriter Bob Dylan, who had helped spur the revival of acoustic folk music during the early 1960s, became one such figure after his music "went electric" in 1965. Reworking idioms used by African American blues artists such as Muddy Waters, Dylan's "Like a Rolling Stone" (1965) exploded onto both the

---

MUSICAL LINK TO THE PAST

The Folk-Rock Moment

Songwriter: Bob Dylan
Title: "Subterranean Homesick Blues"
(1965)

From 1962 to 1964, Bob Dylan led the American folk music revival with Woody Guthrie–inspired original protest songs such as "Blowin' in the Wind," which Peter, Paul, and Mary made into a number-one single in 1963. Very rarely, if ever, in American popular music had songs that were so political become so popular. However, by 1965, Dylan decided to employ a more aggressive rock 'n' roll sound with electric guitar and drums, instead of the more rustic-sounding acoustic guitar. When he first "plugged in" publicly at the 1965 Newport Folk Festival, it was one of the iconic moments in American popular music history, both for the quality and intensity of Dylan's new songwriting style and because of the vehement negative response of the folk music community that had lauded him in years past. For the next year, audiences around the world booed when Dylan arrived on stage with an electric band.

"Subterranean Homesick Blues" was one of the first examples of Dylan's revamped musical direction. For many in his old audience, the electric amplification was perhaps less alarming than his new lyrical style. He dropped the relatively straightforward protest songs, which he then referred to as "finger-pointing songs," for a more free-form approach that used "chains of flashing images" in a manner reminiscent of 1950s Beat Generation writers Allen Ginsberg and Jack Kerouac. The words did not always immediately make sense, but

many of the phrases burned into the national lexicon and consciousness ("don't follow leaders, watch the parking meters"; "you don't need a weatherman to know which way the wind blows"). Dylan's 1964–1966 compositions combined alienation with a sense of humor and questioned American values ("please her, please him, buy gifts / don't steal, don't lift / twenty years of schooling and they put you on the day shift!"). As Paul Williams, Dylan's most perceptive critic, has written: "Some reacted by calling Dylan a 'sell-out,' not realizing, at least at first, that he was now making the most anti-establishment, revolutionary music of his or anyone's career." A new style of American songwriting had been born and would soon sweep the world.

---

1. Why do you think that important stylistic turning points in music history (such as Dylan's embrace of a rock sound, or the arrival of the waltz in the 1850s or hip-hop in the 1980s) have often engendered fierce resistance from certain elements of the public? Why, at these times, do people view music as something threatening, something more than just a source of entertainment?

2. Do you think that Dylan's new songwriting style had an influence on hip-hop music of the 1980s, such as "The Message" (see Chapter 31)?

Listen to an audio recording of this music on the Musical Links to the Past CD.

Top-40 charts of AM radio and the freewheeling playlists of the new, alternative FM stations. Rock-music writers and sociologists took up "Dylanology," a hybrid journalistic-academic enterprise that combed Dylan's lyrics and eclectic musical tastes in search of clues to broader values of the counterculture. New publications, including the long-running magazine *Rolling Stone,* dispatched youthful journalists to report on—and also participate in—this new cultural "scene."

Images and products from the counterculture soon found a ready market. Recognizing the appeal of bands such as San Francisco's Grateful Dead and the Jefferson Airplane, the culture industry welcomed them to a world in which rock 'n' roll was really "here to pay." The Rolling Stones cashed in with their ode to a "Street Fighting Man" (1968) and their pledge of "Sympathy for the Devil" (1968). The Beatles made even more money and attracted critical acclaim with their albums *Sgt. Pepper's Lonely Hearts Club Band* (1967) and *The Beatles* (popularly known as *The White Album*) (1968).

Hollywood increasingly abandoned its traditional, all-ages market in favor of attracting a youth-dominated audience. Building on a trend evident in movies of the 1950s, such as *Rebel without a Cause,* the film industry targeted younger viewers with movies such as *The Graduate* (1967) and *Bonnie and Clyde* (1967) and followed up with a brief cycle of films, including *Easy Rider* (1969) and *Wild in the Streets* (1968), which portrayed adult authority figures as vampire-like ravagers of the young. Films from this "new Hollywood" often featured graphic images of sexuality and violence. Almost any consumer product could be linked to an advertising campaign that suggested rebellious young people. Fully embracing imagery connected to the counterculture, automobile manufacturers eagerly used the notion of youthful dissent to entice car buyers of almost any age. A true rebel, Detroit suggested, could combat conformity by rejecting the bulky, family-oriented automobile of the 1950s for something like the Ford Mustang, a car as sleek and stylish as youthful clothing fashions. In a series of famous TV spots, young women in brightly colored miniskirts hailed "the Dodge Rebellion," and General Motors proudly announced the death of "your father's Oldsmobile."

Media coverage of the counterculture sparked lively, increasingly bitter debates. Conservative commentators, along with supporters of President Johnson, charged the media with spreading dangerous, antisocial images. In this view, a focus on demonstrations in which young radicals and countercultural musicians joined with older opponents of the Vietnam War exaggerated the strength of the antiwar movement. Conversely, some veterans of the early New Left claimed that media attention on the counterculture actually undercut their search for a new kind of politics.

A 1967 march on the Pentagon helped polarize this debate. Rejecting political speeches and draft-card burning as too tame, some of the marchers chanted mystical incantations and claimed they would levitate the Pentagon. In a similar vein, Abbie Hoffman, self-proclaimed leader of a nonexistent Youth International Party (the "Yippies"), facetiously urged "loot-ins at department stores to strike at the property fetish that underlies genocidal war" in Vietnam. The Pentagon march generated eye-catching TV footage and won novelist Norman Mailer a National Book Award for *Armies of the Night,* his personal account of this event. But the march's relationship to deepening antiwar sentiment seemed less certain. Could such a youth-dominated spectacle effectively convey the passionate moral stance of the variety of people who were coming, often for very different reasons, to oppose the war? Might not media images of colorful quipsters such as Hoffman help fuel cultural polarization rather than political action? Was the media's appetite for spectacular demonstrations and new celebrities helping to trivialize issues and pit cultural and political dissenters against one another?

From Civil Rights to Black Power

Meanwhile, sharp debate over the role of the media and its relationship to the political and cultural insurgencies began splintering the campaign against racial discrimination as well. Early on, leaders in the fight against discrimination, notably Dr. Martin Luther King, Jr., had recognized the value of media coverage. During King's 1965 drive to win easier access to the ballot box for African Americans, television pictures of the violence in Selma, Alabama, helped galvanize support for federal legislation. At one point, ABC television interrupted the anti-Nazi film *Judgment at Nuremberg* to show white Alabama state troopers beating peaceful, mostly African American, civil rights marchers. President Johnson used television to dramatize his support for voting-rights legislation and to promise that "we shall overcome" the nation's "crippling legacy of bigotry and injustice."

At the same time, the media became the forum for bitter arguments about what was increasingly being called a "racial crisis." Conservatives such as Goldwater and Reagan insisted that subversive agitators were provoking conflict and violence and that only a firm commitment to law and order would ease racial tensions. Social activists replied that racism, lack of educational and employment opportunities, and inadequate government remedies were producing the frustration and despair that burst forth in

Cassius Clay / Muhammad Ali: Champion of the Whole World

More than 3 billion people, from around the globe, were watching television on a summer night in 1996. Speculation centered on which American—ideally, one instantly recognizable throughout the world—would light the ceremonial fire for the Olympic Games in Atlanta. Might it be former president Jimmy Carter, a Georgia native whose personal, post-presidential diplomatic career had made him an international celebrity? The slightly stooped and graying middle-aged man who shuffled forward to light the flame, however, was better known to the world than any former U.S. president.

Muhammad Ali (born Cassius Marcellus Clay, Jr. in Louisville, Kentucky, 1942), who won an Olympic boxing championship in 1960, came to dominate what one TV network calls "the wide world of sports." After his Olympic triumph, Clay turned professional and gained the heavyweight championship in 1964. His first title defense attracted only several thousand people to a makeshift arena in Maine. When Ali concluded his career in 1978, however, he had fought before adoring crowds all over the world. Governments rather than sports promoters, Ali once bragged, negotiated his fights.

Once heavyweight champion, the twenty-two-year-old fighter set out to establish a global presence that transcended sports. He declared himself a member of the Muslim faith; officially changed his name; and pro-claimed that, as a world champion, he would "meet the people I am champion of." In 1967, Ali became the most prominent opponent of U.S. involvement in Vietnam by refusing induction into the military. Temporarily stripped of his boxing honors in the United States, Ali traveled widely, especially to Africa and the Middle East, and became as well known abroad as at home. Eventually returning to the ring, Ali staged his most memorable (and physically damaging) bouts in Zaire and the Philippines. Despite increasing physical ailments—the harsh legacy of his profession—Ali has continued to travel abroad and to reconfirm his reputation as one of the best-known Americans of his generation.

© Bettmann/Corbis.

ALI VISITS EGYPT, 1964
In this photo, taken during Ali's trip to the Middle East at the invitation of the Arab Boxing Union, Ali kisses a bust of President Gamal Abdel Nasser.

---

sporadic racial violence. This debate intensified in 1965 in the wake of a devastating racial conflict in Los Angeles. A confrontation between a white highway patrol officer and a black motorist escalated into six days of urban violence, centered in the largely African American community of Watts in south-central Los Angeles. Thirty-four people died; hundreds of businesses and homes were burned; the National Guard patrolled the streets; and television cameras framed the conflagration as an ongoing media spectacle. Violence erupted in many other U.S. cities during the remainder of the 1960s.

A new "Black Power" movement was emerging, heralded by a charismatic minister named Malcolm X. A member of the Nation of Islam, a North American–based group popularly known as the "Black Muslims," Malcolm X initially denounced the civil rights movement. He saw Dr. King's gradualist, nonviolent approach to political change as irrelevant to the social and economic problems of most African Americans and proclaimed that integration was unworkable. Although he never called for violent confrontation, he did endorse self-defense "by any means necessary." Malcolm X, a growing group of followers argued, was simply "telling it like it is."

Malcolm X offered more than angry rhetoric. He called for a renewal of pride in African American cultural practices and for economic reconstruction. In order to revitalize institutions of culture, he urged African Americans to "recapture our heritage and identity" and "launch a cul-

tural revolution to unbrainwash an entire people." Seeking a broad movement, Malcolm X eventually broke from the Nation of Islam, established his own Organization of Afro-American Unity, and explored alliances with other insurgent groups. Murdered in 1965 by enemies from the Nation of Islam, Malcolm X remained a powerful symbol of militant politics and renewed pride in African American culture.

A new generation assumed the mantle of Malcolm X. Disdaining the integrationist agenda, the youthful militants embraced the word *black* and a political-cultural agenda based on their racial identity. As "Black Power" replaced the old civil rights call for "Freedom Now," advocates soon caught the media's attention and began to gain support within African American communities. "Black Is Beautiful" became a watchword. James Brown, the "Godfather of Soul," captured this new cultural spirit with his 1965 hit song, "Papa's Got a Brand New Bag," which renounced old rules and restrictions. Later, his "Say It Loud, I'm Black and Proud" encapsulated the cultural message of the Black Power movement.

The Black Power insurgency challenged the civil rights movement philosophically and tactically. Frustrated by the slow pace of change, some younger African Americans—including Stokely Carmichael, who became head of the Student Nonviolent Coordinating Committee (SNCC) in 1966, and members of the Black Panther Party—criticized the gradualist approach of older organizations such as King's Southern Christian Leadership Conference (SCLC). A Black Panther manifesto called for community "self-defense" groups as protection against police harassment, the release from jail of all African American prisoners (on the assumption that none had received fair trials in racist courts), and guaranteed employment for all citizens. Although opinion surveys suggested that most African Americans still supported an integrationist agenda, the new modes of challenging discrimination upset the established black–white civil rights alliance.

Within this context, Congress passed the Civil Rights Act of 1968. One provision of this omnibus law, popularly known as the Fair Housing Act, sought to eliminate racial discrimination in the real estate market. But in response

VIOLENCE IN DETROIT, 1967

Outbreaks of violence, rooted in economic inequality and racial tension, swept through many U.S. cities between 1965 and 1969. The 1967 violence in Detroit, which federal troops had to quell, left many African American neighborhoods in ruin.

to charges that antidiscrimination efforts could invade the rights of landlords and realtors, the act provided exemptions that enfeebled its enforcement provisions. Moreover, another section in the law declared it a crime to cross state lines in order to incite a "riot." Its supporters hailed this provision as an effort to reestablish "law and order," while critics countered that it unconstitutionally invoked the power of the federal government against political activists, especially those supportive of the Black Power movement.

1968: The Violence Overseas

In 1968, several violent events abroad worsened political polarization in the United States. The first came in Vietnam. At the end of January, during a supposed truce in observance of Tet, the Vietnamese lunar new year celebration, troops of the National Liberation Front (NLF) and North Vietnamese forces mounted surprise attacks throughout South Vietnam. After sweeping through eight provincial capitals, they even seized the grounds of the U.S. embassy in Saigon for a few hours. Militarily, this so-called Tet offensive ended with the NLF and the North suffering heavy casualties and gaining relatively little territory. Supporters of the war blamed the media for exaggerating the effect of the early attacks and ignoring the heavy losses to the NLF and North Vietnamese and thereby turning a "victory" into a "defeat." Critics countered that the

Tet offensive had caught the U.S. military off guard and ill prepared to take advantage of enemy losses.

Tet turned out to be a serious psychological defeat for the United States because it undercut President Johnson's claims about an imminent South Vietnamese–United States victory. When General Westmoreland asked for 206,000 additional U.S. troops, most of Johnson's advisers, led by his new secretary of defense, Clark Clifford, insisted that South Vietnamese troops assume more of the military burden. Johnson accepted their argument, realizing that such a large increase in U.S. forces, even if troops could

have been spared from other duties, would have fanned antiwar opposition at home. In a way, the events of Tet contributed to the beginning of a policy that would become known as the "Vietnamization" of the war.

The Tet offensive also destroyed much of whatever political support Johnson still commanded among antiwar Democrats and threw his strategic planners into confusion. Faced with revolt in his own party, led by Senator Eugene McCarthy of Minnesota, Johnson suddenly declared on March 31, 1968, that he would not run for reelection. He halted the bombing of North Vietnam and

HISTORY THROUGH FILM

Malcolm X (1992)

**Directed by Spike Lee.
Starring Denzel Washington (Malcolm X), Angela Bassett (Betty Shabbaz), Al Freeman, Jr. (Elijah Muhammad).**

Spike Lee, the U.S. film industry's best-known African American director, campaigned actively to make a movie about *Malcolm X.* For nearly 25 years, Hollywood moguls had been trying to portray the charismatic leader who was gunned down in 1965 and whose *Autobiography,* published in 1963, had become a literary classic. Delays in obtaining financing, crafting a script, and finding a director always stymied production plans.

Lee, who had denounced the Hollywood establishment for passing over his celebrated (and controversial) *Do the Right Thing* (1989) for an Academy Award nomination, insisted that only he could do justice to the story of Malcolm X. Initially buoyed by a $34 million budget, Lee encountered problems of his own, including his insistence on releasing a movie that ran for more than three hours. Lee called *Malcolm X* "my interpretation of the man. It is nobody else's."

The finished film displays Lee's desire to show the presence of the past in the present. Produced by Lee's own independent production—whose name, "Forty Acres and a Mule," recalls the land-distribution program advanced by advocates of Radical Reconstruction after the Civil War—the movie argues for the continuing relevance of Malcolm X's ideas and initiatives.

The famous segments that begin and end the film feature a collage of iconic images. Against the backdrop of the

Warner Brothers logo, the soundtrack features the voice of Malcolm X decrying American history as the continuing story of racist actions. Malcolm's accusations continue as a giant American flag, perhaps a reference to the popular film *Patton* (1970), appears on screen. Then, the image of the flag is cut into pieces by jagged images from the homemade videotape of the 1991 incident in which Los Angeles police officers beat an African American named Rodney King. Next, the flag begins to burn until, revealed behind it, a giant "X," adorned with remnants of the flag, dominates the film frame. The ending uses substantial archival footage of Malcolm, along with images of South African freedom fighter Nelson Mandela, while the soundtrack features the voice of Ozzie Davis, the celebrated African American actor, giving a eulogy to Malcolm X.

The body of the film, borrowing its organizational structure from Malcolm's *Autobiography,* breaks into three parts. The movie first traces how the young Malcolm, born Malcolm Little and later known as "Detroit Red," financed a gaudy lifestyle through small-time criminal schemes. The second part covers how, following his imprisonment and his embrace of the Nation of Islam (a group popularly known as the "Black Muslims"), the flamboyant hustler became the almost ascetic rebel, Malcolm X. The final portion of the film, which takes roughly 90 minutes, races through the rest of his private and public life.

promised to devote his remaining time in office to seeking an end to the war. McCarthy, campaigning on a peace platform, continued his electoral bid against Johnson's vice president and party stalwart, Hubert H. Humphrey.

1968: The Violence At Home

One former supporter who rejoiced at Johnson's withdrawal was Martin Luther King, Jr. He hoped that the Democratic Party would now turn to an antiwar candidate, preferably Senator Robert Kennedy of New York, JFK's younger brother, who might embrace King's new program for confronting economic inequality at home. But on April 4, 1968, during a trip to Memphis, Tennessee, in support of a strike by African American sanitation workers, King was assassinated. Allegedly, a lone gunman named James Earl Ray pulled the trigger. Ray quickly pleaded guilty and received a 99-year sentence. Subsequently, though, he recanted, insisting that he was a pawn in a larger racist conspiracy and unsuccessfully lobbying for a jury trial. When he died in 1998, Ray still insisted on his innocence, a claim roundly rejected by most legal observers.

Denzel Washington stars as Malcolm X.

© Corbis.

Released near Thanksgiving, the film opened to packed houses and took in considerably more money than Oliver Stone's *JFK* had garnered when it had debuted during the same time period only one year earlier. Despite a multimedia publicity blitz, *Malcolm X*'s box-office revenues steadily declined. Reviewers and industry spokespeople reported that the lengthy, episodic movie seemed to tax the patience and attention span of most filmgoers.

Watching *Malcolm X* on video or DVD, however, can allow a viewer to concentrate on its many stunning sequences, speeding by ones that seem to drag, and returning to scenes that may seem unclear at first viewing. *Malcolm X* remains a fascinating cinematic history of the creation of the Black Power movement and, more generally, of the social turmoil that engulfed the nation during its longest war.

As news of King's murder spread, violence swept through urban neighborhoods around the country. More than 100 cities and towns witnessed outbreaks; 39 people died; 75,000 regular and National Guard troops were called to duty. When President Johnson proclaimed Sunday, April 7, as a day of national mourning for the slain civil rights leader, parts of the nation's capital city, not far from the White House, remained ablaze.

Meanwhile, Robert Kennedy had joined the race for the 1968 Democratic presidential nomination. Campaigning at a feverish pace, Kennedy battled Eugene McCarthy in a series of primaries, hoping to gain a majority of those convention delegates who were not already pledged to Hubert Humphrey by the party's old-line bosses such as Richard J. Daley, mayor of Chicago. Then, on June 5, only minutes after winning California's primary, Kennedy fell victim to an assassin's bullets. Los Angeles police immediately arrested Sirhan Sirhan, a Palestinian immigrant, who was later convicted of the killing. Kennedy's nationally televised funeral was a disturbing reminder of King's recent murder and the assassination of his own brother five years earlier.

The violence of 1968 continued. During the Republican national convention in Miami, as presidential candidate Richard Nixon was promising to restore "law and order," racial violence, during which four people died, wracked that city. Later that summer, in Chicago, thousands of antiwar demonstrators converged on the

L I N K   T O   T H E   P A S T

Singing for Freedom: "We Shall Overcome"

Music provided a mobilizing force wherever people gathered to protest racial discrimination during the 1960s. Singing in large groups and small ones, activists built a powerful sense of community and purpose. "We Shall Overcome" became perhaps the most famous and most frequently used of the many civil rights songs. Its lyrics derived from the gospel song "I'll Overcome Some Day" (1900), and portions of the melody came from the pre–Civil War spiritual, "No More Auction Block for Me."

1. *We shall overcome*
   We shall overcome
   We shall overcome some day

CHORUS: Oh, deep in my heart
　　　　　I do believe
　　　　　We shall overcome
　　　　　Some day

2. *We'll walk hand in hand*
   We'll walk hand in hand
   We'll walk hand in hand some day

CHORUS

3. *We shall all be free*
   We shall all be free
   We shall all be free some day

CHORUS

4. *We are not afraid*
   We are not afraid
   We are not afraid some day

CHORUS

5. *We are not alone*
   We are not alone
   We are not alone
   We are not alone some day

CHORUS

6. *The whole wide world around*
   The whole wide world around
   The whole wide world around
   　　some day

CHORUS

1. How does the structure of this song contribute to its usefulness in civil rights demonstrations? Why did it adapt well to group singing?
2. Although this song was closely associated with the struggle to end racial discrimination, it can have larger meanings as well. In what contexts have you encountered this song?
3. How do the messages of this song compare to the views associated with the culture of the Black Power movement?

For additional sources related to this feature, visit the CD accompanying this text or the *Liberty, Equality, Power* Web site at:

http://history.wadsworth.com/murrin_LEP4e

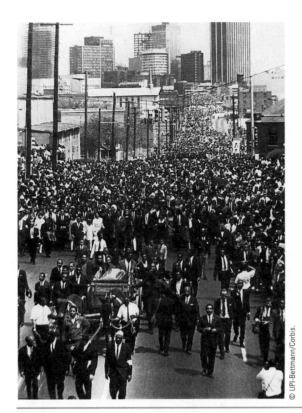

MARTIN LUTHER KING, JR.'S FUNERAL CORTEGE

Martin Luther King, Jr.'s assassination in 1968 sparked both violent protests and solemn mourning for the slain civil rights leader. Thousands of his grieving supporters followed the cart, drawn by mules, which carried King's body through the streets of his native Atlanta.

Democratic Party's convention to protest the nomination of Humphrey, who was still supporting Johnson's policy in Vietnam. Responding to acts of provocation by youthful demonstrators, who seemed to welcome confrontation, some police officers struck back with indiscriminate attacks on antiwar forces and some members of the media. Although an official report later talked about a "police riot," opinion polls showed that most Americans supported the use of force in Chicago. Hubert Humphrey easily captured the Democratic presidential nomination, but differing views of Johnson's Vietnam policy and the violence in Chicago left his party bitterly divided.

The Election of 1968

Both Humphrey and Nixon faced a serious challenge from the political right, spearheaded by Alabama's George Wallace, a southern Democrat who ran for president as a third-party candidate in 1968. A grassroots campaign eventually placed his American Independent Party on the presidential ballot in every state. Because Wallace's opposition to civil rights efforts was well established, he could

concentrate his fire on other controversial targets, particularly the counterculture and the antiwar movement. He bragged that if any "hippie" ever blocked his motorcade, "it'll be the last car he'll ever lay down in front of." Moreover, Wallace recognized that many voters were turning against Great Society programs and seeing themselves as victims of an aloof, "tax-and-spend" bureaucracy in Washington.

Wallace's candidacy hoped to tap the polarization of 1968. If neither major-party candidate won a majority of the electoral votes, the presidential election would rest with the House of Representatives, and Wallace might act as a power broker. (A president had last been selected by the House in 1824.) Hoping to court voters who wanted a U.S. victory in Vietnam, Wallace chose a militant hawk, the retired Air Force General Curtis LeMay, as his running mate. LeMay almost immediately self-destructed when he complained that too many Americans had a "phobia" about using nuclear weapons. Critical pundits lampooned Wallace and LeMay as the "Bombsey Twins."

Nixon narrowly prevailed in November. Although the former vice president won 56 percent of the electoral vote in 1968, he outpolled Humphrey in the popular vote by less than 1 percent. Humphrey had benefited when

ROBERT F. KENNEDY'S FUNERAL

An elaborately staged funeral also followed the 1968 assassination of Robert Kennedy. The shootings of the two beloved leaders—King and Kennedy—prompted widespread concern about the stability of America's social and political fabric and added to the tensions of this tumultuous year.

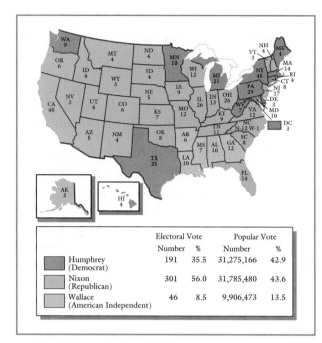

MAP 29.2 PRESIDENTIAL ELECTION, 1968
George Wallace's independent, third-party candidacy influenced the election of 1968. Compare this map with ones of earlier and later election years to see how the southern states gradually left the Democratic column and, in time, became a base of Republican power.

Johnson ordered a pause in the bombing of North Vietnam and pledged to begin peace talks in Paris, and he had helped his own cause with a belated decision to distance himself from the president's overall policy in Vietnam. Still, Humphrey carried only Texas in the South, losing the grip that the Democratic Party had held on that region since Reconstruction. George Wallace picked up 46 electoral votes, all from the Deep South, and 13.5 percent of the popular vote nationwide. Nixon won five key southern states and attracted, all across the country, those whom he called "the forgotten Americans, the nonshouters, the nondemonstrators." Hinting at a plan for ending the war in Vietnam, Nixon predicted he would restore tranquility to the domestic front, but his policies proved every bit as divisive as those of Lyndon Johnson.

The Nixon Years, 1969–1974

Raised in a modest Quaker home in southern California, Richard Nixon graduated from Whittier College, a small Quaker school. Three years of legal studies at Duke University, a hitch in the navy during the Second World War, and a job in Franklin Roosevelt's wartime bureaucracy gave Nixon a taste of new, cosmopolitan worlds. After the war, however, he returned to a small-town California law practice before beginning a meteoric political career that took him to the House of Representatives in 1946, the Senate in 1950, and the vice presidency in 1952.

Nixon seemed to thrive on seeking out enemies, at home and abroad, and on confronting a constant series of personal challenges. He entitled an early memoir of his political life *Six Crises*. Devastated by his narrow loss to Kennedy in 1960, Nixon seemed crushed politically when, in 1962, he failed to win the California governorship. At a post-election press conference, Nixon angrily denounced the press for distorting his record and announced his retirement from politics. Although Barry Goldwater's 1964 defeat and Johnson's problems had revived Nixon's political fortunes, during his turbulent presidency (1969–74), he frequently seemed preoccupied with settling old scores and with confronting new enemies.

The Economy

Nixon's presidency coincided with a series of economic problems that had been unthinkable only a decade earlier. No simple cause can account for these difficulties, but most analyses begin with the war in Vietnam. This expensive military commitment, along with fundamental changes in the international economy, brought an end to the economic growth of the previous two decades.

Lyndon Johnson, determined to stave off defeat in Indochina without cutting Great Society programs, had concealed the rising costs of the war from the country and even from his own advisers. Johnson bequeathed Nixon a deteriorating (although still favorable) balance of trade and rising inflation rate. Between 1960 and 1965, consumer prices had risen an average of only about 1 percent per year; by 1968, the rate exceeded 4 percent.

Nixon hoped to check inflation by cutting government expenditures. He recovered some costs by reducing U.S. troop levels and expanding the use of bombing, but this strategy still drained economic resources. Moreover, although Nixon spoke about slashing domestic spending, many programs still enjoyed support in the Democratic-controlled Congress and among voters. During Nixon's first years in office, the percentage of federal funds that went to domestic programs increased steadily.

Meanwhile, unemployment soared, topping 6 percent by 1971. According to conventional wisdom, expressed in a technical economic concept called "the Phillips curve," when unemployment rises, prices should remain constant or even decline. Yet *both* unemployment and inflation were rising. Economists coined the term *stagflation* to describe this puzzling, unprecedented convergence of eco-

nomic stagnation and price inflation. Along with stagflation, U.S. exports were becoming less competitive in international markets, and in 1971, for the first time in the 20th century, the United States ran a trade deficit, importing more products than it exported.

Long identified as an opponent of government regulation of the economy but now fearful of the political consequences of stagflation and the trade deficit, Nixon needed a quick cure for the nation's economic ills. In a reversal that one media commentator likened to a religious conversion, Nixon suddenly proclaimed himself a believer in governmental remedies. Hoping to relieve inflationary pressures before the 1972 election, he announced a "new economic policy" in August 1971. It mandated a 90-day freeze on any increase in wages and prices, to be followed by government monitoring to detect "excessive" increases in either.

To try to reverse the trade deficit, Nixon also revised the United States' relationship to the world monetary structure. Dating from the 1944 Bretton Woods agreement (see chapter 26), the value of the U.S. dollar had been tied to the value of gold at $35 for every ounce. This meant that the United States, in order to provide an anchor for world currencies, would exchange its dollars for gold at that rate if any other nation's central bank requested it to do so. Other countries had fixed their own exchange rates against the dollar. But U.S. trade deficits

undermined the value of the American dollar, enabling foreign banks to exchange U.S. dollars for gold at highly favorable rates.

In response to this situation, in August 1971, the Nixon administration abandoned the fixed gold-to-dollar ratio. It announced that the U.S. dollar would be free to "float" in value against the prevailing market price of gold and against all other currencies. In 1973, Nixon devalued the dollar, thereby reducing the price of American goods overseas in hopes of making them more competitive on the world market. The strategy fundamentally altered the international economic order but had little immediate impact on the deterioration of U.S. trade balances. Over the next decade, U.S. exports more than tripled in value, but imports more than quadrupled.

Social Policy

At the urging of Daniel Patrick Moynihan, a maverick Democrat who advised Nixon on domestic issues, the president pondered a drastic revision in welfare policy. Moynihan insisted that Nixon, while remaining identified as a conservative Republican, could radically change political life. After heated debates within his inner circle, Nixon unveiled his Family Assistance Plan (FAP). A complex package of different programs, FAP would replace most welfare measures, including the controversial Aid to Families with

As a Percentage of Total Spending

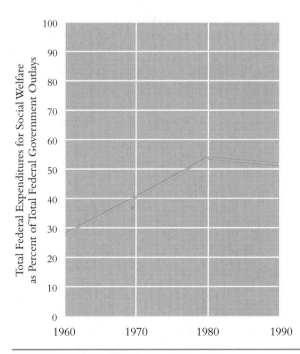

Total Expenditures

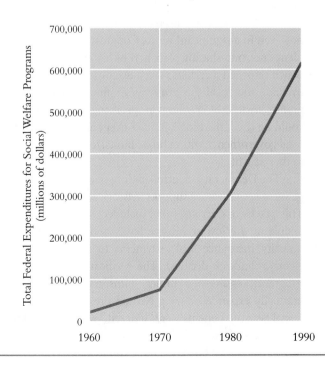

SOCIAL WELFARE SPENDING, 1960–1990

Dependent Children (AFDC), with a guaranteed annual income for all families. AFDC provided government payments to cover basic costs of care for low-income children who had lost the support of a bread-winning parent. By 1970, half of all persons in families headed by women were receiving AFDC payments.

Under Nixon's proposal, the government would guarantee a family of four an annual payment of $1,600, with the possibility of further assistance based on how much income the family earned. In one bold stroke, FAP would supplant existing welfare arrangements, which provided services and assistance *only* to those with special circumstances (such as low-income mothers with small children or people who were unemployed) with a new system of government aid for *all* low-income families. Even a family with an annual income of nearly twice the $1,600 level, according to one projection, would still benefit from Nixon's plan because of the tax refund and food stamp provisions included in the FAP proposal.

FAP attracted tepid support. Conservatives blasted it, claiming that income supplements for families that had a regularly employed, although low-paid, wage earner would be too costly. In contrast, proponents of more generous government assistance programs saw a guaranteed income of $1,600 as too miserly. The House of Representatives approved a modified version of FAP in 1970, but a Senate alliance that included people both to the right and to the left of Nixon blocked its passage. Beset by economic problems and the lingering war in Vietnam, Nixon simply abandoned FAP, and the nation's welfare system would not be comprehensively overhauled until the 1990s.

Some changes in domestic programs were enacted, however. In a significant move, Congress passed the president's revenue-sharing plan, part of his "new federalism," which returned a certain percentage of federal tax dollars to state and local governments in the form of "block grants." Instead of Washington specifying how these funds could be used, the block grant concept allowed state and local governments, within broad limits, to spend the funds as they saw fit.

The Democratic-controlled Congress also stitched together a revised social support network in the early 1970s. This patchwork arrangement included rent subsidies for people at the lowest income levels and Supplementary Security Insurance (SSI) payments to those who were elderly, blind, or disabled. The Medicare and Medicaid programs, established under Johnson's Great Society, gradually expanded during Nixon's presidency. In 1972, Social Security benefits were "indexed," which meant they would rise with the inflation rate. Less comprehensive than Nixon's FAP proposal, these congressional initiatives substantially extended the nation's income-support programs, albeit only for specific groups, especially older Americans. Between 1970 and 1980, the federal government's spending for social welfare rose from 40.1 percent of total government outlays to slightly more than 53 percent.

Environmentalism

A relatively new phenomenon, environmentalism became a significant force during Nixon's presidency; its roots reached back to the earlier conservation and preservation movements. During the first four decades of the 20th century, the conservation movement had begun to promote the "wise use" of water, forests, and farmlands by urging government to promote scientific resource management and to designate areas as national parks and forests (see chapter 21). A preservation movement—spearheaded by the Sierra Club, the Audubon Society, the Wilderness Society, and local advocacy groups—had been primarily concerned with the aesthetics of nature and had worked to preserve the natural environment in a state as pristine as possible. Lyndon's Johnson's Great Society proved to be particularly supportive of preservationism. Landmark legislation of the 1960s—the Wilderness Act of 1964, the National Wild and Scenic Rivers Act of 1968, and the National Trails Act of 1968—set aside new areas, protecting them from development. Lady Bird Johnson, the president's wife, championed a Commission on Natural Beauty that spurred the nation's growing interest in its natural habitat.

By 1970, the conservation and preservation movements had merged into a broader environmental crusade that focused on improving people's health and on maintaining an ecological balance. Accounts such as Rachel Carson's *Silent Spring* (1962) raised concern that the pesticides used in agriculture, especially DDT, threatened bird populations. Air pollution in cities such as Los Angeles became so bad that the simple act of breathing became equivalent to smoking several packs of cigarettes per day. Industrial processes polluted water systems, and atomic weapons testing and the proliferation of nuclear power plants prompted fear of overexposure to cancer-causing, radioactive materials. In response to all of these concerns, environmentalists tried to focus national attention on toxic chemicals and the adverse impact of industrial development on air, water, and soil quality. The Environmental Defense Fund, a private organization formed in 1967, took the crusade against DDT and other dangerous toxins to the courts. And in an event linked to the counterculture, environmental activists came together in 1970 for Earth Day. This one-day "happening"—which featured art, music, and countercultural theatre—aimed to

raise awareness about environmental degradation and popularize the science of ecology, an area of biology concerned with the interrelationship between living organisms and their physical environments.

The Nixon administration, although not a sponsor of Earth Day, did take environmental issues seriously. The president established the Environmental Protection Agency (EPA) and signed major pieces of environmental legislation: the Resources Recovery Act of 1970 (dealing with waste management), the Clean Air Act of 1970, the Water Pollution Control Act of 1972, the Pesticides Control Act of 1972, and the Endangered Species Act of 1973. During Nixon's presidency, national parks and wilderness areas were further expanded, and a new law required that "environmental impact statements" be prepared in advance of any major government project.

The new environmental standards brought both unanticipated problems and significant improvements. The Clean Air Act's requirement for higher smokestacks for factories, for example, moved pollutants higher into the atmosphere, where they produced a dangerous byproduct, "acid rain." Still, the act's restrictions on auto and smokestack emissions cleared smog out of city skies and benefited people with respiratory ailments. It reduced six major airborne pollutants by one-third in a single decade. Lead emissions into the atmosphere declined by 95 percent.

Controversies over Rights

New legislation on social and environmental concerns came against the backdrop of debate over how to define the federal government's responsibility to protect constitutional rights. The struggle to define these rights embroiled the U.S. Supreme Court in controversy.

A majority of the Justices, who supported the Great Society's political vision, sought to bring an expanding list of rights under constitutional protection. As this group charted the Court's path through the 1960s, two Eisenhower appointees, Chief Justice Earl Warren and Associate Justice William Brennan, often led the way. Although nearly all of the Warren Court's decisions involving the issue of rights drew critical fire, perhaps the most emotional cases raised claims by people accused of violent crime. *Miranda* v. *Arizona* (1966) held that the Constitution required police officers to advise anyone arrested for a felony offense of their constitutional rights to remain silent and to consult an attorney, including one provided to indigents by the government. Defenders of the decision, which inspired the famous "Miranda warning," saw it as the logical extension of settled judicial precedents; the Court's critics, in contrast, accused the Court's majority of

simply inventing rights not found in the Constitution. Amid rising public concern over crime, political conservatives made *Miranda* a symbol of the judicial "coddling" of criminals and the Warren Court's supposed disregard for constitutional law.

Richard Nixon campaigned for president as an opponent of the Warren Court and promised to appoint federal judges who would "apply" rather than "make" the law. Before the 1968 election, Chief Justice Warren announced his resignation, but Lyndon Johnson's plan to elevate his close confidante, Associate Justice Abe Fortas, stalled. Consequently, the victorious Nixon could appoint a Republican loyalist, Warren Burger, as Chief Justice. Subsequently, Nixon appointed three other Republicans—Harry Blackmun, William Rehnquist, and Lewis Powell—to the High Court.

This new Burger Court soon faced difficult rights-related cases of its own. Lawyers sympathetic to the Great Society vision advanced the controversial argument that access to adequate economic assistance from the federal government was a constitutionally protected right, one every bit as fundamental as, say, that of voting. The Supreme Court, however, rejected this claim when deciding *Dandridge* v. *Williams* (1970). A majority of Justices held that state laws capping the amount paid to welfare recipients did not violate the constitutional requirement of equal protection of the law. It drew a sharp distinction between the government's responsibility to protect the traditional liberties of all citizens, such as the right to vote and freedom of speech, and its discretionary ability to make distinctions in the administration of social-spending programs such as AFDC. In short, the Court flatly rejected the idea that welfare was a national right.

Other rights-related disputes involved health and safety. A vigorous consumer movement, initially drawing inspiration from Carson's *Silent Spring* and Ralph Nader's exposé about auto safety (*Unsafe at Any Speed,* 1965), joined with environmentalists in seeking to protect the right to safety in the workplace, the right to safe consumer products, and the right to a healthy environment. Their effort, overcoming strong opposition from many business groups, found expression in such legislation as the Occupational Safety Act of 1973, stronger consumer protection laws, and measures to protect the environment. The Burger Court invariably supported the constitutionality of health and safety laws.

At the same time, a newly energized women's rights movement pushed another set of issues. The National Organization for Women (NOW), founded in 1966, backed an Equal Rights Amendment (ERA) that would explicitly guarantee women the same legal rights as men. Easily passed by Congress in 1972 and quickly ratified by

MARCH FOR WOMEN'S RIGHTS
Demonstrations such as this one down New York City's Fifth Avenue in 1971 became a familiar part of politics during the 1960s and early 1970s. Modeled on earlier civil-rights and antiwar rallies, these marches helped focus attention on the issue of gender equality.

more than half the states, the ERA suddenly became controversial. Conservative women's groups, such as Phyllis Schlafly's "Stop ERA," charged that this change in the Constitution would undermine traditional "family values" and expose women to new hazards. Anti-ERA rallies featured children carrying signs such as "Please Don't Send My Mommy to War." As a result of such opposition, the ERA, which once seemed assured of passage, failed to attain approval from the three-quarters of states needed for ratification. Ultimately, women's groups abandoned the ERA effort in favor of using the courts to adjudicate equal rights claims on a case-by-case, issue-by-issue basis.

One of these issues, whether a woman could claim a constitutional right to terminate a pregnancy, became far more controversial than the ERA. In *Roe v. Wade* (1973), the Supreme Court narrowly ruled that a state law making abortion a criminal offense violated a woman's right to privacy. The *Roe* decision outraged conservatives. Rallying under the "Right to Life" banner and focusing on the rights of the unborn fetus, antiabortion groups denounced *Roe v. Wade*. In 1976, they succeeded in persuading Congress to ban the use of federal funds to finance abortions for women with low incomes. Standing behind the right to privacy—and behind the right of a woman to have access to a safe, medically supervised abortion—feminist groups made the issue of individual choice in reproductive decisions a principal rallying point. Invoking rights-based arguments of their own, antiabortion forces provided new support for the steadily expanding conservative wing of the Republican Party.

Richard Nixon had promised an administration that, in contrast to Lyndon Johnson's, would "bring us together."

Instead, divisions over economic policy, government spending programs, and the meaning of basic constitutional rights made Nixon's presidency a time of increasing, rather than decreasing, polarization.

Foreign Policy under Nixon and Kissinger

Even as it wrestled with divisive domestic concerns, the Nixon administration was far more preoccupied with international affairs. Henry Kissinger, a political scientist from Harvard, became Nixon's national security adviser and turned the National Security Council (NSC) into the most powerful shaper of U.S. foreign policy within the government. In 1973, Nixon appointed Kissinger as Secretary of State, a position he held until 1977. Working with Nixon, Kissinger orchestrated a grand strategy for foreign policy: détente with the Soviet Union, normalization of relations with China, and disengagement from direct military involvement in Southeast Asia and other parts of the world.

Détente

Although Nixon had built his political career on hard-line anticommunism, the Nixon-Kissinger team worked to ease tensions with the two major communist nations: the Soviet Union and China. Kissinger surmised that, as both nations began to seek favor with the United States, they might reduce their support for North Vietnam, facilitating

America's ability to withdraw from the war that was dividing the nation.

Arms-control talks took top priority in U.S.–Soviet relations. In 1969, the two superpowers opened the Strategic Arms Limitation Talks (SALT), and after several years of high-level diplomacy they signed an agreement (SALT I) that limited further development of both antiballistic missiles (ABMs) and offensive intercontinental ballistic missiles (ICBMs). SALT I's impact on the arms race was negligible because it said nothing about the number of nuclear warheads that one missile might carry. Still, the very fact that the two superpowers could conclude any pact on arms control signaled improving relations between Washington and Moscow. Moreover, to increase the possibility for new arms agreements, the Nixon administration offered the Soviets greater access to U.S. trade and technology for their faltering economy.

Nixon's overtures toward the People's Republic of China brought an even more dramatic break with the Cold War past. Supported by the China lobby, Nixon had been one of the most vocal critics of the communist regime established in China in 1949. Now, tentative conversations secretly arranged through embassies in Poland led to a slight easing of U.S. trade restrictions against China in early 1971 and then to an invitation from China for Americans to compete in a table tennis match. This much-celebrated ping-pong exhibition presaged more significant exchanges. In 1972, Nixon visited China, posing for photos with Mao Zedong and strolling along the Great Wall. Relations between the two countries remained difficult, especially over the status of Taiwan, which the United States still recognized as the legitimate government of China. A few months after Nixon's visit, however, the United Nations admitted the People's Republic as the representative of China, and in 1973 the United States and China exchanged informal diplomatic missions.

Vietnamization

In Vietnam, Nixon and Kissinger decided to start the withdrawal of U.S. ground forces (the policy called "Vietnamization") while stepping up the air war and intensifying diplomatic efforts to reach a settlement. In July 1969, the president announced the "Nixon Doctrine," which pledged that the United States would provide military assistance to anticommunist governments in Asia but would require them to provide their own combat forces. The goal of Vietnamization was the gradual removal of U.S. ground troops without accepting compromise or defeat. While officially adhering to Johnson's 1968 bombing halt over the North, Nixon and Kissinger accelerated both the ground and air wars by launching new offensives in South

Vietnam and by approving a military incursion into Cambodia, an ostensibly neutral country. The Cambodian decision underscored Kissinger's crucial role in shaping foreign policy; both Secretary of State William Rogers and Secretary of Defense Melvin Laird had counseled against such a drastic step.

The move into Cambodia set off a new wave of protest at home. Many campuses exploded in anger, and bomb threats led some colleges to close early for the 1970 summer recess. White police officers fatally shot two students at the all-black Jackson State College in Mississippi, and National Guard troops at Kent State University in Ohio fired on demonstrators and killed four students. As growing numbers of protestors took to the streets, business and political leaders became alarmed by how war-related passions were polarizing the country.

The continuing controversy over the "My Lai" incident was also spreading disillusionment about the war.

© UPI-Bettmann/Corbis.

JACKSON STATE

In 1970, the violence associated with America's longest war came home. In May, police gunfire killed 2 students and wounded 15 others at Jackson State University in Mississippi. This picture was taken through a bullet-riddled window in a women's dorm.

Shortly after the 1968 Tet episode, troops led by U.S. Lieutenant William Calley had entered the small hamlet of My Lai and shot more than 200 people, mostly women and children. This massacre of South Vietnamese civilians became public in 1969 and sparked new discussions about U.S policy. In 1971, a military court convicted Calley and, in a controversial decision, sentenced him to life imprisonment. The military was using Calley, many argued, as a scapegoat for a failed strategy that emphasized body counts. In 1974, Nixon pardoned Calley.

Meanwhile, the Nixon administration was conducting a widening war in Cambodia and Laos. Although it denied waging any such campaign, large areas of those agricultural countries were ravaged by U.S. bombing. As the number of Cambodian refugees swelled and food supplies dwindled, the communist guerrilla force in Cambodia—the Khmer Rouge—grew into a well-disciplined army. The Khmer Rouge eventually came to power and, in a murderous attempt to eliminate potential dissent, turned Cambodia into a "killing field." It murdered more than 1 million Cambodians. While Nixon continued to talk about U.S. troop withdrawals and peace negotiations with North Vietnam proceeded in Paris, the Vietnam War actually broadened into a conflict that destabilized all of Indochina.

Even greater violence was yet to come. In spring 1972, a North Vietnamese offensive approached within 30 miles of Saigon, and U.S. generals warned of imminent defeat. Nixon responded by resuming the bombing of North Vietnam and by mining its harbors. Just weeks before the November 1972 election, Kissinger again promised peace and announced a cease-fire. After the election, however, the United States unleashed even greater firepower. During the so-called Christmas bombing of December 1972, the heaviest bombardment in history, B-52 planes pounded military and civilian targets in North Vietnam around the clock.

By this time, however, much of the media, Congress, and the public had lost the desire to continue the bloodshed. Many were sickened by the violence in Asia and apprehensive about how the Nixon administration seemed to be expanding its power in the attempt to control dissent at home. Others simply decided that the United States should abandon a conflict that it seemed unable to conclude. Perhaps most important, sagging morale among troops in the field began to undermine the U.S. military's role in Indochina. Many soldiers questioned the larger purpose of their sacrifices, some refused to engage the enemy, and a few openly defied their own superiors. At home, Vietnam Veterans against the War (VVAW), a new organization, joined the antiwar coalition. During one dramatic demonstration, several thousand highly decorated combat vets returned their war medals. Testifying before Congress, a VVAW leader and later senator, John Kerry, wondered, "How do you ask a man to be the last man to die in Vietnam? How do you ask a man to be the last man to die for a mistake?"

Running out of options, Nixon proceeded with full-scale Vietnamization. In January 1973, North Vietnam and the United States signed peace accords, in Paris, which provided for the withdrawal of U.S. troops from South Vietnam. As American ground forces departed, the South Vietnamese government, headed by Nguyen Van Thieu, continued to fight, although it was growing increasingly demoralized and ineffectual.

In spring 1975, nearly two years after the Paris accords, South Vietnam's army could no longer withstand the forces of North Vietnam's skilled general Nguyen Giap. Thieu's government in Saigon collapsed, North Vietnamese armies entered South Vietnam's capital, soon to be renamed Ho Chi Minh City, while U.S. helicopters scrambled to airlift the last remaining officials out of the besieged U.S. embassy. America's longest war ended in defeat.

The Aftermath of War

Between 1960 and 1973, approximately 3.5 million American men and women served in Vietnam: 58,000 died, 150,000 were wounded, and 2,000 remained missing. In the aftermath of this costly, divisive war, Americans struggled to understand why their country failed to prevail over a small, barely industrialized nation. Those still supporting the war argued that it had been lost on the home front. They blamed an irresponsible media, a disloyal antiwar movement, and a Congress beset by a "failure of will." The war, they insisted, had been for a laudable cause; politicians, setting unrealistic limits on the military, had denied the country the means to attain victory. By contrast, those who had opposed the war stressed the overextension of American power, the misguided belief in U.S. omnipotence, the deceitfulness of governmental leaders, and the incompetence of bureaucratic processes. For them, the war had been waged in the wrong place for the wrong reasons. The human costs to the United States, and to the people of Indochina, outweighed any possible gain.

Regardless of their position on the war, most Americans seemed to agree on one proposition: There must be "no more Vietnams." The United States should not undertake another military involvement that lacked clear and compelling political objectives, demonstrable public support, and the provision of adequate means to accomplish the goal. Eventually, the people who wanted to aggressively reassert U.S. power in the world criticized this widely held position as "the Vietnam Syndrome."

Expanding the Nixon Doctrine

Although the Nixon Doctrine initially applied to the Vietnamization of the war in Indochina, Richard Nixon and Henry Kissinger extended its premise to other areas of the world. In molding foreign policy, Kissinger relied increasingly on pro-U.S. anticommunist allies to police their own regional spheres. Kissinger made it clear that the United States would not dispatch troops to oppose revolutionary insurgencies but would generously aid anticommunist regimes or factions willing to fight their own battles.

During the early 1970s, U.S. Cold War strategy came to rely on supporting staunchly anticommunist regional powers. These included nations such as Iran under Shah Reza Pahlavi, South Africa with its apartheid regime, and Brazil with its repressive military dictatorship. All of these countries built large military establishments trained by the United States. U.S. military assistance, together with covert CIA operations, also incubated and protected anticommunist dictatorships in South Korea, the Philippines, and much of Latin America. U.S. arms sales to the rest of the world skyrocketed from $1.8 billion in 1970 to $15.2 billion six years later. In one of its most controversial foreign policies, the Nixon administration employed covert action against the elected socialist government of Salvador Allende Gossens in Chile in 1970. After Allende took office, Kissinger gave top priority to encouraging destabilization of his government, and in 1973 Allende was overthrown by the Chilean military, who immediately suspended democratic rule and announced that Allende had committed suicide.

Critics charged that the United States, in the name of anticommunism, too often wedded its diplomatic fortunes to questionable covert actions and unpopular military governments. In 1975, Senator Frank Church conducted widely watched Senate hearings into possible abuses by the CIA (including the action in Chile). Supporters of the Nixon Doctrine, however, applauded the administration's systematic support of anticommunist allies. In many circles, Nixon received high marks for a pragmatic foreign policy that combined détente toward the communist giants with containment directed toward the spread of revolutionary regimes.

The Wars of Watergate

Nixon's presidency ultimately collapsed as a result of fateful decisions made in the president's Oval Office. Nixon arrived at the White House inclined to see nearly every person and institution in Washington as his enemy. He pressed the Internal Revenue Service (IRS) to harass prominent Democrats with expensive audits and suspected the IRS of disloyalty when it seemed to be moving too slowly on his request. Nixon's enmity focused on antiwar activists and old political opponents, but likely allies, such as J. Edgar Hoover, the staunchly conservative director of the FBI, could also come under suspicion. Isolated behind a close-knit group of advisers, Nixon ultimately created his own secret intelligence unit, which set up shop in the White House.

This group quickly acted on the president's behalf. During summer 1971, Daniel Ellsberg, a dissident member of the national security bureaucracy, leaked to the press a top-secret history of U.S. involvement in the Vietnam War, subsequently known as the "Pentagon Papers." Nixon responded by seeking, unsuccessfully, a court injunction to stop publication of the study and, more ominously, by unleashing his secret intelligence unit, now dubbed "the plumbers," to stop information leaks to the media. Looking for something that might discredit Ellsberg, the plumbers burglarized his psychiatrist's office. Thus began a series of "dirty tricks" and outright crimes, often financed by funds illegally solicited for Nixon's 1972 reelection campaign, which would culminate in the constitutional crisis known as "Watergate."

The Election of 1972

Nixon's political strategists worried that economic troubles and the war in Vietnam might deny the president another term. Creating a campaign organization separate from that of the Republican Party, with the ironic acronym of CREEP (Committee to Re-elect the President), they secretly raised millions of dollars, much of it from illegal contributions.

As the 1972 campaign proceeded, Nixon's chances of reelection dramatically improved. An assassin's bullet crippled George Wallace. Senator Edmund Muskie of Maine, initially Nixon's leading Democratic challenger, made a series of blunders (some of them, perhaps, precipitated by Republican "dirty tricksters") that derailed his campaign. Eventually, Senator George McGovern of South Dakota, an outspoken opponent of the Vietnam War but a lackluster campaigner, won the Democratic nomination.

McGovern never seriously challenged Nixon. He called for higher taxes on the wealthy, a guaranteed minimum income for all Americans, amnesty for Vietnam War draft resisters, and the decriminalization of marijuana—positions that angered many old-line Democrats. In foreign policy, McGovern called for deep cuts in defense spending and for vigorous efforts to achieve peace in Vietnam—proposals that Nixon successfully portrayed as signs of weakness.

upheaval that surrounded the conflict in Vietnam. In this sense, the Watergate episode tends to blend into a broader picture of political, social, economic, and cultural turmoil that accompanied U.S. involvement in the nation's longest war.

Conclusion

The power of the national government grew steadily during the 1960s. Lyndon Johnson's Great Society provided a blueprint for expanding domestic programs and waging a War on Poverty. Johnson's escalation of the war in Vietnam, a struggle that consumed more of the nation's wealth and energy, eventually dominated his presidency.

This growth of governmental power prompted divisive debates that polarized the country. During Johnson's term, both the war effort and the economy faltered, top leaders became discredited, and his presidency collapsed. Johnson's Republican successor, Richard Nixon, let loose an abuse of power that ultimately drove him from office in disgrace. The hopes of the early 1960s—that the U.S. government could promote liberty and equality both in America and throughout the rest of the world—ended in frustration.

The era of America's longest war was a time of high political passions, of generational and racial conflict, of differing definitions of patriotism. It saw the slow convergence of an antiwar movement, along with the emergence of youthful dissent, of Black Power, of "women's liberation," and of contests over what constituted the basic rights of Americans. Different groups invoked different explanations of the failures of both the Great Society and the war effort, and the divisions from these years shaped the fault lines of politics for years to come. Most Americans became much more skeptical, many even cynical, about further enlarging the power of the federal government in the name of expanding liberty and equality.

SUGGESTED READINGS

On Lyndon Johnson, see **Robert J. Dallek, *Flawed Giant: Lyndon Johnson and His Times, 1961–1973*** (1998). **Irving Bernstein, *Guns or Butter: The Presidency of Lyndon Johnson*** (1996) is a detailed synthesis.

The many outstanding overviews of U.S. involvement in Vietnam include **George Herring, *America's Longest War: The United States and Vietnam, 1950–1975*** (rev. ed., 2001); **Robert D. Schulzinger, *A Time for War: The United States and Vietnam, 1941–1975*** (1997); **Robert J. McMahon, *The Limits of Empire: The United States and Southeast Asia Since World War II*** (1999); **David Kaiser, *American Tragedy: Kennedy, Johnson, and the Origins of the Vietnam War*** (2000); and **Fredrik Logevall, *The Origins of the Vietnam War*** (2001). **Christian G. Appy, *Working-Class War: American Combat Soldiers and Vietnam*** (1993) focuses on soldiers, and his ***Patriots: The Vietnam War Remembered from All Sides*** (2003) provides a wider range of perspectives.

The social and cultural ferment of the 1960s can be surveyed, from diverse vantage points, in **David W. Levy, *The Debate over Vietnam*** (rev. ed., 1994); **Lynn Spigel and Michael Curtain, *The Revolution Wasn't Televised: Sixties Television and Social Conflict*** (1997); **Maurice Isserman and Michael Kazin, *America Divided: The Civil War of the 1960s*** (1999); and **Edward K. Spann and David L. Anderson, eds., *Democracy's Children: The Young Rebels of the 1960s and the Power of Ideals*** (2003). On the civil rights movement, **Taylor Branch** continues his multivolume history with ***Pillar of Fire: America in the King Years, 1963–1965*** (1998), while **William L. Van Deburg, *New Day in Babylon: The Black Power Movement and American Culture, 1965–1975*** (1992) examines the emergence of the Black Power movement.

Different sides of the women's movement emerge from **Sara Evans, *Personal Politics: The Roots of Women's Liberation in the Civil Rights Movement and the New Left*** (1979); **Alice Echols, *Daring to Be Bad: Radical Feminism in America, 1967–75*** (1990); and **Susan Hartman, *The Other Feminists: Activists in the Liberal Establishment*** (1999). The background to the influential ***The Feminine Mystique*** (1963) emerges in **Daniel Horowitz, *Betty Friedan and the Making of the Feminine Mystique: The American Left, the Cold War, and Modern Feminism*** (1998).

For a series of very useful, encyclopedia-style sketches, see **David R. Farber and Beth Bailey, eds., *The Columbia Guide to America in the 1960s*** (2001).

AMERICAN JOURNEY ONLINE
AND
INFOTRAC COLLEGE EDITION

Visit the source collections at www.ajaccess.wadsworth.com and
infotrac.thomsonlearning.com and use the Search function with
the following key terms to explore documents, images, audio
and video clips, articles, and commentary related to the material
in this chapter.

Vietnam War
The Great Society
Lyndon B. Johnson
Civil Rights Act of 1964
Gulf of Tonkin Resolution
Malcolm X
Black Power movement
Voting Rights Act
Antiwar demonstrations
The Beatles
Tet Offensive
Civil Rights Act of 1968
Richard M. Nixon
Environmentalism

Sierra Club
Audobon Society
Rachel Carson
Silent Spring
Environmental Protection Agency
Détente
Vietnamization
Kent State
Jackson State
Equal Rights Amendment (ERA)
Roe v. *Wade*
Watergate
Gerald R. Ford

GRADE AIDS

Visit the Liberty Equality Power Companion Web Site for resources specific to this textbook: http://history.wadsworth.com/murrin_LEP4e

The CD in the back of this book and the U.S. History Resource Center at http://history.wadsworth.com/u.s./ offer a variety of tools to help you succeed in this course, including access to quizzes; images; documents; interactive simulations, maps, and timelines; movie explorations; and a wealth of other sources.

their assembly work and parts procurement outside of the United States; by 1990, more than 50 percent of the sticker price on most "American" models went to foreign businesses and workers. Moreover, the trend toward privatization (the sale of government-owned industries to private business) in many economies worldwide provided firms based in the United States with new opportunities for overseas acquisitions. Foreign interests also purchased many U.S. companies and real estate holdings. In the early 1990s, RCA, Doubleday, Mack Truck, Goodyear, and Pillsbury were just some of the traditionally American brands owned by foreign-based corporations. In the late 1990s, German automaker Daimler took over the venerable Chrysler Corporation. Even the entertainment industry, which the United States had dominated for decades, attracted significant foreign investment. A Japanese conglomerate, for example, owned Columbia Pictures during the early 1990s, and Mexico's Televiso took over U.S.-owned Univision. So many industrial giants had become global by the early 21st century that it was often difficult to define what constituted an American company or a foreign one. Drinking the most prominent brands of "Mexican" beer, after a 1997 deal, actually meant drinking a product of Anheuser-Busch. The task of assembling a Honda may have employed more U.S. workers than assembling a Pontiac.

Postindustrial Restructuring

New technologies and economic globalization helped change the American business structure and the workforce. In the 1970s, citing pressure from international competition and declining profits, many companies began cutting back their workforce and trimming their management staff, a move known as "downsizing." More than a dozen major steel plants closed, and the auto industry laid off thousands of workers. In the 1980s and 1990s, the steel and auto industries regained profitability, and other sectors took their turn at downsizing. Business restructuring, together with the government's deregulation of major industries, touched off another merger boom. During the prosperity of the late 1990s, huge mergers, with acquisitions totaling more than $1.6 trillion per year, brought a concentration in corporate power unseen since the 1890s. The 2001 merger of America Online (AOL) with Time Warner, a company that had earlier acquired CNN, exemplified the new environment in which bigger promised to be better.

Meanwhile, the kinds of jobs Americans held shifted. As employment slots in traditional manufacturing and extractive sectors (such as mining) decreased, jobs in ser-

vice, high technology, and information and entertainment sectors increased. Computing and other high-tech sectors offered high salaries, but most jobs in the expanding service sector—clerks, servers, cleaners—were often low paying, part time, and nonunionized. Wal-Mart's enormous workforce, for example, was not unionized, earned an average of $7 to $8 per hour in 2003, and had limited health benefits. Moreover, manufacturers wanting to lower costs to attract the huge Wal-Mart contracts moved their plants into labor environments abroad, where wages were cheap. Such moves further contributed to the decline of relatively better-paid manufacturing jobs in the United States.

Labor union membership, traditionally highest in the manufacturing occupations that were coming to constitute a decreasing proportion of jobs in the restructuring economy, dropped dramatically. In the 1950s, 35 percent of American workers belonged to a union. By 2003, the figure stood at only 13 percent. While union membership rolls and labor's political clout steadily slipped, the union movement struggled to make inroads into new sectors of the economy. Some union locals around the country, for example, launched organizing drives in occupations held predominantly by women, such as clerical, restaurant, and hotel work. Businesses adamantly fought unionization, claiming that it would raise labor costs.

Efforts to organize agricultural workers, who were largely of Mexican and Filipino descent, also dramatized the difficulties of expanding the union movement into new, nonunionized sectors. Cesar Chavez, a charismatic leader who emulated the nonviolent tactics of Martin Luther King, Jr., vaulted the United Farm Workers (UFW)

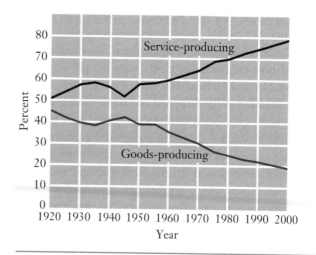

GROWTH OF SERVICE SECTOR JOBS, 1920–2000

Source: U.S. Census Bureau.

seemed unlikely prospects for the multiplex mall theaters. In time, movies that did especially well at Landmark theaters might earn a run on the mall circuit, a trend that encouraged the major studios to create special divisions, such as Paramount Classics, which financed and distributed so-called independent films. The Internet first welcomed filmmakers who were experimenting with digital technology; by 2004, digital movies that dispensed with traditional film stock regularly played in commercial movie theaters.

The New Hollywood became increasingly intertwined with the changing television establishment, once its feared rival, and with the emerging VCR and DVD industries. Hollywood gained badly needed revenue by licensing its theatrical films to broadcast and cable TV and, later, for VCR and DVD distribution. Film fans could easily convert their own home, upgraded with ever-larger video screens and new technologies, into a movie palace. During the 1980s and early 1990s, before a few video-store chains cornered the market, the United States claimed more video-rental outlets than movie theaters. During the same period, sales of VCRs soared, but digital video discs (DVDs) eventually won out. DVD technology gave viewers improved visual imagery; bonus attractions, such as footage cut from the theatrical release; wide-screen prints; and the kind of expert commentary hitherto only available at a film school. The DVD version of *Something About Mary* (1998), a lightweight comedy, featured nearly six hours of extra material and commentary. As Hollywood studios discovered that DVD sales easily matched theatrical receipts, they sought movies, such as action films with elaborate special effects, that promised to sell well on DVD.

The Changing Media Environment

CATV, VCRs, and ultimately digital technology also transformed the pop music industry. The Music Television channel (MTV), initially offering a 24-hour supply of rock range of Hollywood genres, including science fiction, combat films, westerns, and the Saturday morning serials of the 1930s and 1940s.

The film's major event, the triumph of individual effort and resourcefulness—not sophisticated technology—over an evil enemy, arguably attempts to replace the traumatic history of U.S. involvement in Southeast Asia with a heroic folktale. Similarly, the alliance between youthful Skywalker and aging Obi-Wan Kenobi seems a parable about the need to repudiate the "generation gap" that had emerged during the cultural conflict of the 1960s.

Seen another way, though, the market logic that shaped a film product such as *Star Wars* focused less and less on crafting a story, even the kind of political-historical allegory found in Cold War–era movies such as *High Noon* (1952). Instead, a successful blockbuster primarily needed to create opportunities for inserting eye-filling special effects (often portraying considerable violence and mayhem) and

Star Wars' C-3PO and R2-D2, a droid and a robot with personalities, generated considerable nonfilm revenue from product tie-ins.

Kobal Collection/Lucasfilm/20th Century Fox.

for devising imagery (such as cute robots and cuddly creatures) that could be remarketed in various offscreen forms. In this sense, spectacles such as *Star Wars* merit attention less as representations of specific episodes in the past than as historical events in their own right.

videos, debuted in 1981. Critics immediately charged it with portraying women as sex objects and with excluding artists of color. Eventually, however, MTV defused complaints, especially after featuring Michael Jackson's 29-minute video based on his hit single "Thriller" (1983). By 2004, MTV and other CATV channels regularly programmed videos that represented the increasingly multiethnic nature of the music industry.

Performers such as Madonna used MTV to forge a new relationship between music and visual imagery, the "MTV aesthetic." This fast-paced visual style fed off its musical soundtrack; played with traditional ideas about time and space; recycled images from movies and TV programs; and often carried a sharp, satirical edge. The MTV aesthetic crossed over among video, television, and motion pictures. In the 1990s, MTV abandoned its all-video format and developed a wide range of youth-oriented programming. Its cult classic, "The Real World," anticipated the run of controversial "reality" shows such as "Survivor" on network and cable television.

Entertainment conglomerates such as Sony began marketing musical packages in a variety of different, constantly updated formats. The 45-rpm record and the long-play album (LP), which had propelled the musical revolutions of the 1950s and 1960s, all but disappeared. Digital compact discs (CDs) changed not only the technology through which pop music was delivered but also the nature of the product and the listening experience. The classic LPs of the late 1960s and early 1970s, such as The Beatles' *Abbey Road* (1969) or Willie Nelson's *The Red-Headed Stranger* (1975), had ideally featured 10 to 12 songs, split between the two sides and organized around a core theme or concept. The turn-of-the-21st-century CD, able to hold 15 or 20 minutes more music than an LP, was rarely structured thematically and often contained a hodgepodge of songs, several casually tossed in as "bonus tracks." Thematic coherence became increasingly irrelevant with the introduction of players that could shuffle back and forth between the tracks on a hundred different CDs. Listeners could program their machine according to their own whims or simply let songs play randomly.

The Internet also promised to change how people obtained and listened to music. First, it allowed access to commercial and noncommercial radio stations far beyond the range of any radio. More important, the Internet and digital technology permitted people to obtain, preserve, and exchange music in entirely new ways. Celebrants of the Internet proclaimed that they would break the hold of the commercial music companies and make a wide array of sounds instantly available to consumers. In reply, the music industry and various artists complained that people were using the Internet to "pirate" copyrighted material.

Although the U.S. Supreme Court, in 1986, had endorsed the home copying of television programs on VCRs, experts in copyright law joined the various interested parties in debating how this decision affected the downloading of music from the Internet. After years of indecisive legal sparring, while revenues from CD sales slumped and file-swapping soared, the music industry tried a carrot-and-stick approach. In 2003, it began selling songs online and filed an unprecedented number of lawsuits, for copyright infringement, against ordinary people who were sharing music files from their personal computers. Corporate executives seemed determined to bury the claim that the Internet provided a medium in which ordinary people could freely distribute music.

The New Mass Culture Debate

New trends in mass commercial culture generated other controversies. In 1975, the Federal Communications Commission (FCC) ordered the television networks to dedicate the first 60 minutes of prime time each evening to "family" programming free of violence or "mature" themes. Eventually, the courts struck down this family-hour requirement as a violation of the First Amendment's guarantee of free speech. Demands that Congress regulate rock lyrics and album covers also ran afoul of complaints that this kind of legislation would amount to unconstitutional censorship. Eventually, TV programmers and record companies, pressed by private organizations and the threat of new governmental action, adopted "warning labels," similar to the ones pioneered by the movie industry during the 1960s, that supposedly informed parents about products with violent and sexually explicit imagery.

Meanwhile, popular reviewers and university professors were paying serious attention to works of commercial culture. Unlike the critics of the 1950s, who had dismissed mass culture as trivial and condemned its effect on daily life, these writers often seemed to be unabashed fans of the cultural products they were studying. Instead of critically comparing mass culture to "high" culture (the "classical" works of Western civilization), this new generation jettisoned the distinction between lowbrow and highbrow. The music of The Beatles could be studied along with that of Beethoven; moreover, the lyrics of Chuck Berry and Bob Dylan merited academic analysis. Academics similarly pondered the meaning of the MTV aesthetic and wrote scholarly studies about pop celebrities such as Madonna, Nirvana's Kurt Cobain, and Britney Spears.

These analysts, who gravitated to the new academic field of "cultural studies," looked at how people merged the products of commercial culture into their daily lives. Again rejecting the cultural criticism of the 1950s—which

had seen consumers as cultural dupes who passively soaked up worthless products—they stressed people's creative interaction with commercial culture. Scholarly studies of "Star Trek," for example, examined how loyal fans had kept this popular 1960s television series alive in syndication and had subsequently prompted a succession of motion pictures and new TV programs. Moreover, through self-produced magazines (called "fanzines"), conventions, and the Internet, these Trekkies created a grassroots subculture that used "Star Trek" as the launching pad for discussions of social and political issues, especially ones that touched on race, gender, and sexuality.

Academics associated with cultural studies tended to embrace multiculturalism. They urged new attention to works produced by women, political outsiders, and non-Western writers and artists. They also encouraged students to see traditional texts, such as those attributed to Shakespeare, in light of their political and historical contexts rather than as timeless works. Traditionalists condemned this "cultural turn" as a legacy of the counterculture of the 1960s and blamed it for eroding settled ideas of artistic quality and value.

☙ Social Activism

The activism associated with the 1960s became embedded in most areas of American life and rippled through the decades that followed. After 1970, an ever-increasing amount of activity aimed at advancing particular social, political, and cultural agendas. By the early 21st century, virtually every public forum, from neighborhood newspapers to the streets of the nation's capital, featured the influence, and the clash, of activists who claimed to represent some particular constituency or goal.

Mounting a mass demonstration, reminiscent of those against the Vietnam War, remained one tool of advocacy and protest. The nation's capital still provided a stage for rallies aimed at attracting the attention of national lawmakers and the media. Both anti-abortion and pro-choice forces, for example, intermittently sponsored demonstrations in Washington, D.C. In October 1995, the Million Man March sought to mobilize African American men behind a campaign of social reconstruction in their own communities; two years later, an evangelical men's group called the Promise Keepers filled Washington's Mall.

Increasingly, though, activists focused on smaller, more targeted demonstrations. During the 1980s, the Clamshell Alliance conducted a campaign of civil disobedience against a nuclear reactor being built in Seabrook, New Hampshire, and a broad coalition of West Coast activists waged a lengthy, unsuccessful struggle to close the University of California's Lawrence Livermore National Laboratory, which was developing nuclear weapons. In many cities, women's groups staged annual Take Back the Night rallies to protest the rising tide of sexual assaults. Beginning in the late 1990s, people representing workers' rights and environmental causes mobilized to disrupt meetings, in both the United States and overseas, of the World Trade Organization (WTO).

The media seldom covered demonstrations, unless they sparked violent conflict, as did some of those against the WTO. In 1991, for example, 30,000 Korean Americans staged a march for racial peace in Los Angeles. Although it was the largest demonstration ever conducted by any Asian American group, even the local media ignored it. Similarly, few people learned from newspapers and television that 75,000 California high school students staged a walkout in 1994 to denounce a state measure aimed at curtailing education, welfare, and medical care for undocumented immigrants. Even the 24/7 cable news operations, such as CNN and Fox, failed to track protests in the way that major networks had done during the civil-rights and Vietnam-war eras. Only C-Span, a niche network devoted to public-affairs programming, provided regular coverage of events of social protest.

Women's Issues

In this new environment, women's groups puzzled over how to rally new supporters and re-energize their core constituencies. Struggles over gender-related issues had emerged within the civil-rights and antiwar movements of the 1960s. Initially, most men attracted to these causes saw no contradiction between women's second-class status and their own egalitarian pronouncements. Male leaders of these movements often expected women to be available for secretarial services or sexual liaisons and complained that issues of gender equality interfered with the fight to redirect racial and foreign policies. Spread of the birth control pill, introduced in 1960, simultaneously gave women greater control over reproductive choices and complicated the meaning of "sexual freedom."

The new feminism that emerged during the last decades of the 20th century encompassed a wide range of movements. The National Organization for Women (NOW) became generally identified with the rights-based agenda of the mainstream of the Democratic Party. African American women often formed separate organizations that looked at issues of cultural and ethnic identity; Chicana groups coalesced within the UFW movement and many Mexican American organizations; lesbians organized their own groups, often allying with an emerging gay

rights movement; and many feminist organizations based in the United States began exploring the possibility of joining with groups in other nations, an effort that viewed women's issues as international in scope.

Beginning in the 1970s, women promoted "consciousness-raising" sessions to discuss issues and share perspectives. Consciousness-raising produced a growing conviction that women's concerns about *political* empowerment were inseparable from *personal* power relationships involving housework, child-rearing, sexuality, and economic independence. Although this post-1960s generation of feminists still pursued traditional public issues, such as fighting discrimination in the workplace, "the personal is political" became its watchword.

Economic self-sufficiency remained a pressing issue. An increase in Aid to Families with Dependent Children (AFDC) payments and an expansion of the Food Stamp program had boosted the average social welfare "package" for single mothers with children during the 1960s, but the economic dislocations of the following decades inexorably undercut the value, measured in constant dollars, of these benefits. In 1972, a family of four, headed by a woman, received governmental benefits that, on average, totaled about $577 per month. Two decades later, the monthly value (in real dollars) of the same benefits had fallen to about $430. Homeless shelters, which once catered almost exclusively to single men, increasingly tried to meet the needs of women and children. Activists tried to highlight

LINK TO THE PAST

Cultural Disagreements: Equality for Women?

The changing role of women in America dramatically altered family and civic life during this era. Many of the cultural and political disputes of these years revolved around issues related to gender. Advocates of "full equality" for women, such as the National Organization for Women (NOW), clashed with New Right activists, who opposed gender equality as an affront to the "natural" order.

The purpose of NOW is to take action to bring women into full participation in the mainstream of American society now, exercising all the privileges and responsibilities thereof in truly equal partnership with men. . . . We reject the current assumptions that a man must carry the sole burden of supporting himself, his wife, and family, and that a woman is automatically entitled to lifelong support by a man upon her marriage, or that marriage, home and family are primarily woman's world and responsibility. . . . We believe that a true partnership between the sexes demands a different concept of marriage, an equitable sharing of the responsibilities of home and children and of the economic burdens of their support. . . .

We will strive to ensure that no party, candidate, president, senator, governor, congressman, or any public official who betrays or ignores the principle of full equality between the sexes is elected or appointed to office.

NATIONAL ORGANIZATION FOR WOMEN (NOW)
Statement of Purpose, 1966

I believe that at the foundation of the women's liberation movement there is a minority core of women who were once bored with life, whose real problems are spiritual problems. Many women have never accepted their God-given roles. . . . God Almighty created men and women biologically different and with differing needs and roles.

He made men and women to complement each other and to love each other. Not all the women involved in the feminist movement are radicals. Some are misinformed, and some are lonely. . . . I believe that women deserve more than equal rights. . . . Men and women have differing strengths. . . . Because a woman is weaker does not mean that she is less important.

JERRY FALWELL
calling for a "moral majority" in his 1980 book,
Listen America!

1. Different assumptions about gender roles led to public policy disputes, especially in areas related to military service, families and reproduction, and labor rights. What specific social and political issues seem to be grounded in the contest over women's rights?

For additional sources related to this feature, visit the CD accompanying this text or the *Liberty, Equality, Power* Web site at:

http://history.wadsworth.com/murrin_LEP4e

the feminization of poverty and to urge greater public assistance for the growing number of children reared in low-income, female-headed families. Proposals for reshaping the pattern of governmental support increasingly sought to limit so-called entitlements and to emphasize moving women, even those with young children, into the workforce.

The job market, however, was laced with inequalities. Women constituted 30 percent of the labor force in 1950 and more than 45 percent in 2001. Although women increasingly entered the professions and gained unionized positions (by 2000 nearly 45 percent of union members were women, compared with 18 percent in 1960), the average female worker still made less than 70 cents for every dollar earned by the average male worker. "Glass ceilings" limited women's chances for promotion, and child-care expenses often fell disproportionately on women who worked outside the home.

With so many issues to address—and with agendas often varying along lines of class, race, ethnicity, and religion—the women's movement remained highly diverse. Women from different backgrounds increasingly cooperated to build new institutions and networks that addressed a wide range of economic, social, and cultural matters. Their efforts included battered-women's shelters, health and birthing clinics specializing in women's medicine, rape crisis centers, economic development counseling for women-owned businesses, union-organizing efforts led by women, organizations of women in specific businesses or professions, women's studies programs in colleges and universities, and academic journals devoted to research on women's issues.

Pressure for gender equity also affected existing institutions. Country clubs and service organizations, such as Rotary International, faced pressure to admit women, and most began to do so. Many of the Protestant denominations, after some hesitation, accepted women into the ministry. Reform Judaism placed women in its pulpits. Educational institutions began to adopt "gender-fair" hiring practices and academic curricula. American women by the beginning of the 21st century lived in an environment significantly different from that of their mothers.

Sexual harassment, one of the most publicized of the new concerns, became a highly charged issue. To a few activists, such as Camille Paglia, a focus on sexuality—or on the related issue of pornography—tended to identify feminism with a puritanical spirit that the women's movement of the 1960s had pledged to end. Most women's groups, however, pressed government and private employers to regulate sexually charged behavior that they saw demeaning women and exploiting their lack of power vis-à-vis male supervisors and coworkers. In 1986, the U.S. Supreme Court ruled that sexual harassment constituted a form of discrimination covered under the 1964 Civil Rights Act.

In 1991, the issue gained national attention when Anita Hill, an African American law professor, accused Clarence Thomas, an African American nominee for the Supreme Court, of having sexually harassed her when both had worked for the federal government. Feminists denounced the all-male Senate Judiciary Committee, which was responsible for considering Thomas's nomination, for its apparent inability to understand the issue of sexual harassment. Although the Senate narrowly approved Thomas for the Supreme Court, women's groups gained new converts. Political observers credited the Thomas-Hill hearings with mobilizing female voters and electing four women as U.S. Senators in 1992. The numbers of women in public office continued to rise slowly, as the political gender gap—a difference in the way men and women voted—became a feature of most electoral contests.

Sexual harassment also became a controversial issue within the U.S. military, which began to recruit women more actively. The service academies accepted female cadets, and women found places within the military hierarchy. Soon, however, revelations about harassment and even sexual assaults against female naval officers by their male comrades revealed problems. Attempts by navy officials to cover up sexual harassment during the 1991 "Tailhook" convention provoked outrage, and several high-ranking officers were forced to step down. More than a decade later, an investigation revealed both widespread evidence of harassment, including sexual assaults, at the Air Force Academy and apparent indifference among the institution's male-dominated leadership.

Sexual Politics

The politics of sexuality entered an entirely new phase with the emergence of public issues involving gays and lesbians. Some homosexuals, especially gay men affiliated with the left-leaning Mattachine Society and lesbians who organized the Daughters of Bilitis, had already begun to claim a right to nondiscriminatory treatment during the 1950s (see chapter 27). Insurgency spread during the 1960s. In 1969, New York City police raided the Stonewall Inn, a bar in Greenwich Village. Patrons resisted arrest, and the confrontation pitted the bar's largely homosexual patrons, who claimed to be the victims of police harassment, against law enforcement officials.

"Stonewall" marked an important turning point in sexual politics. Borrowing ideas and rhetoric from the civil-rights movement, New York City's Gay Liberation Front (GLF) provided a model for similar groups across

the country. During the decades after the Stonewall episode, thousands of gay and lesbian advocacy groups sprang up, and many individuals "came out of the closet," proudly proclaiming their sexual orientation. During the 1990s, a group called Act Up introduced a new style of in-your-face protests that challenged what it saw as systematic discrimination against homosexuals.

Newspapers, theaters, nightspots, and religious groups identifying themselves with homosexual communities became part of daily life, particularly in larger cities. Specific forms of popular entertainment, such as the disco club scene of the late 1970s and early 1980s, became identified with the gay and lesbian subcultures, which benefited significantly from a general relaxation of legal and cultural controls over the portrayal and practice of explicit sexuality.

Homosexuals joined with civil-liberties groups in demanding that state and local governments enact laws pro-

hibiting discrimination against gays and lesbians in housing and jobs. They also demanded that the police treat attacks on homosexuals no less seriously than they handled other forms of violent crime. In addition, gay and lesbian activists joined with heterosexual supporters in insisting that private associations, such as church groups, drop discriminatory bylaws and practices. As gays and lesbians gained a voice in public and private life, however, their activism met determined opposition from cultural conservatives.

One issue, with international implications, initially overrode all others: acquired immune deficiency syndrome (AIDS), a generally fatal and contagious disease that attacks the body's immune system. First identified in the early 1980s, AIDS became an intensely contested medical and political issue. Before the emergence of AIDS, the medical establishment argued that improvements in vaccination, sanitation, and drug treatment would limit the

© Bettmann/Corbis.

AIDS "ACT UP" CAMPAIGN

Health care issues increasingly galvanized grassroots activists in the late 20th century. In 1989, members of Act Up, a group that represented militant homosexuals, protested what they saw as the federal government's inattention to the issue of AIDS during the 1980s.

spread of any viral infection. Epidemiologists soon identified the AIDS virus, human immunodeficiency virus (HIV), as a grave threat for which medicine offered little in the way of prevention or cure. The disease could be transmitted through the careless use of intravenous drugs, tainted blood supplies, and unprotected heterosexual intercourse.

At first, the incidence of AIDS in the United States was primarily limited to gay men. AIDS activists charged that, as a consequence of this association, cultural and social conservatives placed a low priority on medical efforts to understand its causes, to check its spread, or to devise a cure. The resultant controversy over the level of medical funding galvanized gay and lesbian activists to voice their concern with ever-greater force. With the development of drugs that could combat AIDS, most public figures, even many who did not support other concerns involving gays and lesbians, came to support anti-AIDS efforts both at home and overseas, particularly in Africa. "AIDS has taught us both the power of science and its limitations," concluded one prominent physician.

Gay rights remained a rallying cry for activists—and a challenge to their conservative opponents. In response to legal tests, in 2003 a divided U.S. Supreme Court declared that state laws criminalizing sodomy were in violation of the Constitution. Even supporters of these anti-sodomy measures, enforceable only by the kind of intrusive policing that most Americans opposed, recognized their largely symbolic character, but the Supreme Court's opinion contained the hint that it might deploy the same reasoning to strike down bans against same-sex marriages. When a Canadian province and, in 2003, Vermont formally authorized homosexual unions, conservative activists in the United States rallied around a constitutional amendment that would protect the "sanctity of marriage."

Race, Ethnicity, and Social Activism

The emphasis on group identity as the fulcrum for social activism became especially strong among various racial and ethnic communities. In movements that recalled, and extended, the activism of the 1960s, groups emphasized pride in their distinctive traditions and declared that cultural differences should be affirmed rather than feared, celebrated rather than merely tolerated. Especially with the influx of new immigrants (by 2000, 1 of every 10 Americans was foreign born), identity politics and multiculturalism took on growing importance.

African American Activism

African Americans had developed a strong sense of cultural identity during the civil-rights and black power struggles of the 1960s (see chapters 28 and 29). As battles against discrimination and for cultural pride continued, controversies over future directions also emerged.

Activism often looked inward to stress pride in distinctively African American cultural practices. A variant of this impulse, popularly known as "Malcolmania," accelerated with the appearance of Spike Lee's film *Malcolm X* (1991). The emphasis on racial pride also showed in rap and hip-hop music and in the hundreds of schools established in order to offer students an "Afrocentric" curriculum. More broadly, the Black Entertainment Television network (BET) aimed its programming specifically to African American viewers but also attracted a multicultural audience, especially for its musical and comedy offerings.

Similarly, academics such as Henry Lewis Gates, Jr., who became head of Harvard's Afro-American Studies Department in 1991, made attention to the black experience part of a larger push toward multiculturalism. Gates and a colleague published *Africana: The Encyclopedia of the African and African American Experience* (1999). This project, which had been started by W. E. B. DuBois, brought together more than 200 contributors, who offered the latest scholarly perspective on thousands of issues and individuals. African American culture, in the view of Gates and other academics, was not "a thing apart, separate from the whole, having no influence on the shape and shaping of American culture." Gates and other supporters of multiculturalism insisted that African American authors, such as Toni Morrison (who won the Nobel Prize for Literature in 1993) and Alice Walker, be viewed as writers who take "the blackness of the culture for granted" and use this as "a springboard to write about those human emotions that we share with everyone else, and that we have always shared with each other." The cultural works of African Americans, in short, could simultaneously be seen as unique and different, *and also* be viewed in relationship to broader cultural traditions.

People of African descent expressed a broad spectrum of views on most public issues. The clash between Clarence Thomas and Anita Hill, for instance, split African Americans, just as it divided others. Many black feminists saw Hill's testimony against Thomas as evidence of pervasive sexism within African American life, but others focused on the racial implications of this episode. No nominee of European descent, they argued, would have ever faced the kind of personal scrutiny that Thomas confronted.

Opinion polls suggested that African Americans tended to see protecting Thomas's position as a successful male professional as more important than attacking his conservative politics or pressing the gender issues raised by Hill and her supporters.

The story of sports star and media personality O. J. Simpson, who starred in the longest-running legal spectacle in U.S. history, sparked another emotional, and longer-lasting, debate about the relationship between racial identity and law. In 1995, authorities in Los Angeles prosecuted Simpson for two brutal murders, including that of his former wife. His defense team successfully focused the trial on alleged misconduct by purportedly racist officers within the L.A. police department, and a largely black jury declared Simpson not guilty. Polls indicated that African Americans overwhelmingly supported this verdict and that members of other ethnic groups rejected it. (A subsequent civil trial for monetary damages, a judicial proceeding in which the laws of evidence and burden of proof differ from those in a criminal prosecution, resulted in another jury, largely white, finding Simpson monetarily liable for the murders.) The Simpson episode, which resurfaced whenever a prominent African American (such as basketball player Kobe Bryant in 2004) faced legal liability, continued to mark a significant gulf stemming from distrust of the police and the legal system in African American communities. Efforts to develop "community policing" and more racially diverse police forces failed to erase this kind of distrust.

Issues of equal treatment in the legal and criminal justice systems remained part of the agenda for African American activists. A post-Simpson investigation of the L.A. police department featured allegations that that some of its officers regularly manufactured evidence against people who were African American. Differences in the sentencing of convicted felons, in most parts of the country, raised a broader concern. In general, it appeared, courts imposed harsher sentences for crimes involving crack cocaine, a drug consumed in African American neighborhoods, than for those involving the more expensive varieties of cocaine favored by white, suburban drug users. The fact that, by the late 1990s, more African American men sat in jails and prisons than attended colleges and universities, activists claimed, could partly be explained by sentencing disparities such as the one involving different kinds of cocaine. In addition, statistical evidence also indicated that African Americans convicted of potential capital crimes were more likely to receive the death penalty than were prison inmates from other ethnic and racial backgrounds.

"Racial profiling," a practice that could touch anyone of African descent, also remained a prominent issue. Repeated studies suggested that police detained African Americans as criminal suspects and stopped black motorists far more often than members of any other ethnic group. Activists called this practice DWB, or "driving while black." (In Hispanic communities, DWB came to stand for "driving while brown.") Some police officials explained such statistics as merely reflecting probabilities based on crime data, but most recognized that the practice raised legitimate questions about equal protection and hardly engendered respect for the criminal justice system. Even if someone of non-European descent were released immediately, critics of policing practices argued that the mere fact of having been detained represented a serious, race-related affront to a person's dignity. Profiling seemed a symbolic reminder of the days of slavery and legally sanctioned discrimination.

Other practices that symbolized racism of the past also became the target of activists. At the beginning of the 1990s, several southern states and many institutions, such as colleges and private clubs, still flew the flag of the Confederacy. The battle over the flags, and over other memorials relating to the Civil War, could become highly charged. Groups that defended symbols of the Confederacy argued that they merely honored the people who had supported the southern cause in the mid-19th century, not the system of chattel slavery. Civil libertarians wondered how campaigns to remove symbolic forms that carried multiple meanings could be squared with the First Amendment's guarantee of free speech. Activists, however, countered that the cause of the Confederacy could not be separated from that of preserving slavery and that the Confederate flag had long provided a powerful symbol of racist resistance to efforts to attack racial discrimination during the civil-rights era of the 1950s and 1960s.

By the beginning of the 21st century, many African American activists no longer worked from outside of the country's dominant institutions. In 1970, 13 African American members of Congress established the Congressional Black Caucus (CBC) as a means of providing a common front on a wide range of foreign and domestic issues. By 2004, nearly 40 members of the House, all Democrats, supported the CBC. It issued a hypothetical "Alternative Budget," which targeted far more money toward social initiatives than the ones being passed by Congress; campaigned on behalf of better relations with African nations and other countries with large populations of African descent, such as Cuba and Haiti; and took stands on issues, such as racial profiling and drug sentencing, that particularly affected African Americans.

American Indian Activism

American Indians conducted their activism along two broad fronts. Indians had, of course, long-standing identities based on their tribal affiliation, and many issues, par-

AP/Wide World Photos.

CONGRESSIONAL BLACK CAUCUS

The Congressional Black Caucus frequently took collective stands on issues they felt would be of special importance to African Americans.

ticularly those involving land and treaty disputes, turned on specific, tribal-based claims. Other questions, which seemed to require strategies that extended beyond a single tribe, became identified as "pan-Indian" in nature. In 1969, people from several tribes began a two-year sit-in, designed to dramatize a history of broken treaty promises, at the former federal prison on Alcatraz Island in San Francisco harbor. Expanding on this tactic, the American Indian Movement (AIM), created by young activists from several Northern Plains tribes, adopted a similarly confrontational approach. Violent clashes, with both federal officials and older American Indian leaders, eventually erupted in early 1973 on the Pine Ridge Reservation in South Dakota. In response, federal officials targeted members of AIM for illegal surveillance and for controversial criminal prosecutions.

Meanwhile, important legal and social changes were taking place. The omnibus Civil Rights Act of 1968 contained several sections that became known as the "Indian Bill of Rights." In these sections, Congress finally extended most of the provisions of the constitutional Bill of Rights to American Indians on reservations while still upholding the legitimacy of tribal laws. Federal legislation and several Supreme Court decisions in the 1970s subsequently reinforced the principle of "tribal self-determination." In 1978, Congress passed the Tribally Controlled College Assistance Act, which supported educational institutions that would build job skills and preserve tribal cultures. Tribal identification itself required legal action. By the early 21st

century, the federal government officially recognized more than 550 separate tribes and bands; another 150 were seeking such recognition; and 30 others had secured recognition from individual states. Tribes were not always geographical entities. Three-quarters of American Indians lived in urban areas, and about half of the people residing on reservations did not officially identify themselves as Indians.

Following the suggestion of American Indian lawyers and tapping the expertise of the Native American Rights Fund (NARF), tribes aggressively used the legal system. They pressed demands that derived from old treaties with the U.S. government and from the unique legal status of tribal nations. Some tribal representatives sought recognition of specific fishing and agricultural rights, a campaign that often provoked resentment among non-Indians, who argued that these special claims, based on federal authority, should not take precedence over state and local laws. At the same time, American Indians also sued to protect tribal water rights and traditional religious ceremonies (some of which included the ritualistic use of drugs such as peyote) and to secure repatriation of Indian skeletal remains that were being displayed or stored in museums across the country. (At one point, the Smithsonian Institution was housing the remains of more than 18,000 Indians, supposedly for historical and scientific purposes.) Pressure from American Indian rights groups led Congress to pass the Native American Graves Protection and Repatriation Act (1990), which required universities and museums to return human remains and sacred objects to any tribe that requested them.

Tribes also sued to obtain Las Vegas–style gaming privileges. Claiming exemption from state gambling laws, American Indians opened bingo halls and, then, full-blown casinos. In 1988, the U.S. Supreme Court ruled that states could not prohibit gaming operations on tribal land within their borders, and Congress responded with the Indian Gaming Regulatory Act, which gave a federal seal of approval to casino operations. As gambling emerged as one of the most lucrative sectors of the nation's entertainment business, American Indian–owned casinos became a major part of this phenomenon. In states such as Connecticut and Minnesota, American Indian gaming establishments employed growing numbers of Indians and non-Indians alike.

© Gary A. Conner/PhotoEdit.

GAMING AT MYSTIC LAKE CASINO IN MINNESOTA
By the mid-1990s, legal gambling had become one of the nation's leading economic enterprises. Native Americans saw casinos as an important way to generate jobs and capital on Indian reservations.

The competition to establish casinos in prime locations prompted intertribal political and legal conflict.

Ironically, the glitzy, tribal-owned casinos existed alongside tribal powwows and other efforts to nurture older cultural practices. The Mashantucket Pequot tribe in Connecticut earmarked some of the profits from its lucrative Foxwoods casino to finance one of the nation's largest powwows, which offered nearly $1 million in prizes for entrants in its American Indian dance contests.

Powwows were only one part of the attempt to build a stronger sense of identity through the promotion of cultural practices viewed as traditional. To forestall the disappearance of native languages, American Indian activists urged bilingualism and the renewed attention to tribal rituals. By 2000, only about 175 native languages were spoken at all; of these, less than two dozen were used between parents and children. Indian groups denounced the use of stereotypical nicknames, such as "Chiefs" and "Redskins," and Indian-related logos in amateur and professional sports. The federal government assisted this cultural-pride movement by appropriating funds for two National Museums of the American Indian, one in New York and another in the nation's capitol. The National Park Service changed the name of "Custer Battlefield" in Montana to

Bill Pugliano/Gamma-Liaison Network.

LOS ANGELES POWWOW
Tribal dancers participate in a powwow in Los Angeles. Many Native Americans in the late 20th century embraced the rediscovery of traditional ways.

"Little Bighorn Battlefield," shifting the site's historical emphasis and redesigning its exhibits to help celebrate American Indian culture. Activists also forged links with aboriginal peoples throughout the Americas and the South Pacific to draw international attention to the problems facing aboriginal peoples around the globe.

Activism in Spanish-Speaking Communities

Spanish-speaking Americans, who constituted the fastest-growing ethnic group in the United States, highlighted the complexity of ethnic identity. Many Spanish-speaking people, especially in the Southwest, prefer the umbrella term "Latino," whereas others, particularly in Florida, use the term "Hispanic." At the same time, people whom the U.S. Census began (in 1980) labeling Hispanic more frequently identified themselves according to the Spanish-speaking country or commonwealth from which they or their ancestors had immigrated.

Beneath these general designations and a common Spanish language lay great diversity. The Cuban Americans who came to South Florida during the 1960s, for example, generally enjoyed greater access to education and higher incomes than did most Latinos who came later, even from Cuba. The initial wave of Cuban immigrants also tended to be more politically conservative than other Latinos; they generally voted Republican and espoused a hard-line stance against the communist government of Cuba's Fidel Castro. Émigrés from Puerto Rico focused some of their political energy on the persistent "status" question—that is, whether Puerto Rico should hope for independence, strive for statehood, or retain a commonwealth connection to the mainland. Immigrants from the Dominican Republic and Central America (both legal and undocumented) were among the most recent and economically deprived newcomers.

Mexican Americans, members of the oldest and most numerous Spanish-speaking group in the United States, could tap a long tradition of social activism. The 1960s saw an emerging spirit of *Chicanismo*, a populistic pride in a heritage that could be traced back to the ancient civilizations of Middle America. Young activists made "Chicano/a," once terms of derision that older Mexican Americans had generally avoided, a rallying cry. In cities in the Southwest, advocates of *Chicanismo*, although still a minority force in Mexican American politics, gained considerable cultural influence. Attempts by the police to crack down on Chicano activism during the 1970s backfired, especially in Los Angeles, and increasing numbers of young Mexican Americans identified with the new spirit of insurgency.

Beginning in the 1970s, cities and towns in the Southwest with large Mexican American populations experienced considerable cultural ferment and political-social change. Members of La Raza Unida, a movement founded in 1967, began to win local elections. At the same time, Mexican American communities experienced a cultural flowering. Although Catholic priests generally avoided militancy, many of them opened their churches to groups devoted to ethnic dancing, mural painting, poetry, and literature. Spanish-language newspapers and journals, too, reinforced the growing sense of pride. Mexican Americans pushed for programs in Chicano/a Studies at colleges and universities.

Developments in San Antonio, a city with a large Mexican American population, suggested the potential fruits

MURAL ART IN CHICAGO

Themes in Mexican history and culture, inspired by the great Mexican muralists, appeared in Mexican American communities throughout the country.

of grassroots political organizing. In the 1970s, Ernesto Cortes, Jr., took the lead in founding Communities Organized for Public Service (COPS), a group that focused on achieving concrete, tangible changes that touched the everyday lives of ordinary citizens. In San Antonio this strategy meant that Mexican American activists worked with Anglo business leaders and with Democratic politicians such as Henry Cisneros, who became the city's mayor in 1981. COPS brought many Mexican Americans, particularly women, into the public arena for the first time.

By the early 21st century, Mexican American activism was becoming increasingly diverse. La Raza Unida continued its activities but never became a national force. Instead, the Mexican American Legal Defense and Educational Fund (MALDEF), established in 1968 with funding from the Ford Foundation, emerged as the most visible national group, one ready to lobby or litigate on behalf of Mexican Americans. At the local level, organizations formed on the model of COPS, such as United Neighborhood Organization (UNO) in Los Angeles, continued to work on community concerns. The booming U.S. economy of the 1990s offered expanding employment and educational opportunities, especially for women. Yet most new jobs, Mexican American advocacy groups complained, offered low wages and few benefits. Mexican Americans often spearheaded labor-organizing efforts, particularly in the rapidly expanding service sector of the economy. Women continued to join organizations such as the National Network of Hispanic Women, which represented Chicanas who had been successful in professional and business life. Conservatives such as Linda Chavez—a Republican activist who moved among the worlds of business, politics, and public policy—joined Democrats such as Henry Cisneros as symbols of Mexican American mobility.

Social activism among Puerto Ricans in the United States emerged more slowly than among Mexican Americans. Much of the effort during the 1960s went toward strengthening existing community-based institutions and building new ones. New York City's Puerto Rican Day Parade, an important focus of cultural pride that had begun during the 1950s, became the city's largest ethnic celebration. Despite the formation of activist groups, such as the Young Lords, however, the social programs of the Great Society often bypassed Puerto Ricans. A 1976 report by the U.S. Commission on Civil Rights concluded that Puerto Ricans remained "the last in line" for government-funded benefits and opportunity programs. By the 1980s, activists were focusing on legal and political issues. The Puerto Rican Legal Defense and Education Fund and allied groups obtained courtroom victories that helped Puerto Ricans surmount obstacles to the ballot box and to political office. Puerto Rican voters provided important support for insurgent, grassroots politics in Chicago and in many cities on the East Coast.

Even after leaving the Caribbean, Puerto Ricans continued to address issues there as well. In 2000, the Puerto Rican Legal Defense and Education Fund joined other groups to organize a well-publicized, ultimately successful campaign to stop the U.S. Navy from using the small island of Vieques as a target range, thereby creating health and ecological hazards for Puerto Rico.

Americans of Cuban origin increasingly wrestled with how much energy they should devote to affairs in their homeland. Although Cuban Americans became active in southern Florida politics and civic affairs, critics noted the persistent "exile mentality" that revolved around anti-Castro activities. The issue of how to focus activism emerged most vividly in 2000 over a familial struggle involving a young Cuban boy whom U.S. authorities had picked up in the Atlantic after his mother, fleeing from the island, had drowned. Although most people in Miami's Little Havana seemed to rally behind the effort of the boy's U.S. relatives to contest the federal government's decision to return him to his father in Cuba, some Cuban Americans argued that this media-saturated spectacle misrepresented a diverse community whose involvement in American life increasingly overshadowed the one-time obsession with the fate of Castro's regime.

Asian American Activism

People with diverse ancestral roots in Asia increasingly adopted the term "Asian American" as a way of signifying a new identity consciousness. During the 1970s, Asian American studies programs took shape at colleges and universities on the West Coast. By the early 1980s, political activists were gaining influence, especially within the Democratic Party, and more Asian American politicians won election to public office during the late 1980s and 1990s. Meanwhile, older Japanese Americans finally began to talk about what had long been unspoken—their experiences in internment camps during the Second World War (see chapter 26). Talk eventually turned to political agitation, and in 1988, Congress issued a formal apology and voted a reparations payment of $20,000 to every living Japanese American who had been confined in the camps.

The new Asian American vision encouraged Americans of Chinese, Japanese, Korean, Filipino, and other backgrounds to join together in a single pan-Asian movement. Organizations such as the Asian Pacific Planning

Council (APPCON), founded in 1976, lobbied to obtain government funding for projects that benefited Asian American communities. The Asian Law Caucus, founded in the early 1970s by opponents of U.S. intervention in Vietnam, and the Committee Against Anti-Asian Violence, created a decade later in response to a wave of racist attacks, mobilized to fight a wide range of legal battles. Beginning in 1997, the National Asian Pacific American Network Council, the first civil-rights group to be formed by Asian Americans, began to lobby on issues related to immigration and education.

Emphasizing this broad, pan-Asian identity, however, raised questions of inclusion and exclusion. Filipino American activists, members of the second largest Asian American group in the United States in 1990, often resisted the Asian American label because they believed that Chinese Americans or Japanese Americans dominated groups such as APPCON. Many people of Filipino descent focused on specific goals, particularly an effort to obtain citizenship and veteran's benefits for former soldiers of the Second World War who had fought against Japan in the Philippines. Similarly, Hmong groups often pursued matters specific to their own particular concerns. In 2000, for instance, they and their allies succeeded in obtaining the Hmong Veterans Naturalization Act, which allowed Hmong immigrants (and their spouses and widows) to use an interpreter when taking the test to obtain U.S. citizenship. At the same time, as new arrivals continued to come from Asia, groups such as Filipinos for Affirma-

tive Action agreed to cooperate with other organizations in opposing efforts to deny social services to legal immigrants.

As a result of pressure from different ethnic groups, the federal government finally decided to designate "Asian or Pacific Islanders" (API) as a single pan-ethnic category in the censuses of 1990 and 2000. It also provided, however, nine specifically enumerated subcategories (such as Hawaiian or Filipino) and allowed other API groups (such as Hmong or Samoan) to write in their respective ethnic identifications.

Socioeconomic differences also made it difficult to frame a single Asian American agenda. Although in the late 1980s and early 1990s many Asian American groups showed remarkable upward mobility, demonstrating both economic and educational achievement, others such as Hmong immigrants and Chinese American garment workers struggled to find jobs that paid more than the minimum wage. Thus, the term Asian American—which, by the beginning of the 21st century, applied to more than 10 million people and dozens of different ethnicities—both reflected, and was challenged by, the new emphasis on ethnic identity.

The Dilemmas of Antidiscrimination Efforts

How might governmental power best advance the cause of equality? Between the end of the Second World War and about 1970, the antidiscrimination movement had demanded that the government not categorize individuals according to group identities based on race or ethnicity. On matters such as education, housing, or employment, the law must remain "color-blind" and treat people equally. The courts stood increasingly ready to strike down discriminatory laws and practices and to guarantee at least formal equality for all individuals.

Gradually, ideas about the relationship between group identities and moves toward greater equality began to change. By the 1970s, the new social-activist agenda envisioned that governmental power could do more than simply eliminate discriminatory barriers to *individual* opportunity. Social justice, according to this view, required government to take "affirmative action" so that *groups* that had historically faced discrimination could begin to receive an equitable share of the nation's jobs, public spending, and educational programs. It was not enough, in short, that individual members of ethnic minorities theoretically be permitted to compete for jobs and educational opportunities; rather, government needed to make sure

VIETNAMESE AMERICAN BUSINESSES IN LOS ANGELES
New Asian immigrants, especially from Southeast Asia, established a growing economic presence in many U.S. cities and helped revitalize older urban neighborhoods.

that a representative number of people from different groups had a reasonable chance of acceptance. Affirmative action, supporters argued, would help compensate for past discrimination and for hidden prejudices that continued to thwart members of particular ethnic groups.

Affirmative action sparked controversy. Some people, generally in the Republican ranks, saw affirmative action as a dangerous form of "interest-group politics." Any program that appeared to "set aside" jobs or openings in educational institutions for certain racial or ethnic groups, they charged, smacked of racist "quotas." Moreover, was not affirmative action *on behalf of* some groups inevitably also "reverse discrimination" *against* others? The claim of reverse discrimination became particularly emotional when members of one ethnic group received jobs or entry to educational institutions despite lower scores on admissions exams. Even some beneficiaries of compensatory programs began to claim that the derogatory label of "affirmative action hire" demeaned their individual talents and accomplishments.

Courts struggled to square affirmative action programs with legal precedents, from the civil-rights era, against discrimination. They tended to strike down, as unconstitutional, any affirmative action plan that seemed to contain inflexible quotas and to uphold less rigid ones designed to remedy "past patterns" of discrimination and to make ethnicity only one of several criteria for making hiring or educational decisions.

A drive to eliminate or radically scale back affirmative action plans gained momentum during the 1990s. In 1996, after a hotly contested referendum campaign, voters in California passed Proposition 209, which aimed at ending most affirmative action measures in California by abolishing racial or gender preference in state hiring, contracting, and college admissions. The number of African Americans and Latinos admitted to the state's most prestigious law and medical schools temporarily dropped as most of those who were admitted chose to go elsewhere. Proponents of affirmative action challenged Proposition 209 as discriminatory. New programs that boosted ethnic

AP/Wide World Photos.

RACIAL TENSION IN BROOKLYN, 1990

In 1990, African American demonstrators staged a four-month boycott of a Brooklyn grocery store, owned by Korean Americans, after a black customer allegedly was assaulted by the store's employees. Tensions among racial and ethnic groups were part of the new diversity during the late 20th century.

diversity were subsequently devised, in California and elsewhere. These emphasized income or high school ranking, rather than race or ethnicity, in the design of affirmative action programs.

Ironically, the debates over identity politics and affirmative action coincided with a rise in racial and ethnic intermarriage—a trend that might, in time, change the entire basis of discussion about equality. The 2000 census suggested that growing numbers of people identified themselves as "mixed race" and could, or would, not claim a single ethnic-racial identity. In 1997, the media hailed Eldrick ("Tiger") Woods as the first African American golfer to win the prestigious Masters tournament, but Woods, whose mother was from Thailand, fiercely resisted the label. In an official statement, Woods said he was "equally proud" to be "both African American and Asian!" But he hoped that he could also "be just a golfer and a human being."

The New Right

Beginning in the mid-1970s, a diverse coalition called the "New Right" began to mobilize. By the early 21st century, its vision of conservatism eventually captured the imagination of millions.

Several different constituencies made up the New Right. Older activists, who had rallied around William F. Buckley's *National Review* during the 1950s and Barry Goldwater during the mid-1960s, contributed continuity

ANTI-ABORTION PROTEST, 1989
Legalized abortions became a major political issue after the 1973 Supreme Court decision in *Roe* v. *Wade.* Here, on the 16th anniversary of *Roe,* protesters assemble in front of the Supreme Court building.

(see chapter 28). Espousing anticommunism and denouncing domestic spending programs, they also spoke out on a widening range of social and cultural issues. Phyllis Schlafly assumed a prominent role in successfully mobilizing opposition to ratification of the Equal Rights Amendment, and Buckley's broad-ranging *Firing Line* became one of public television's most successful programs during the 1970s and 1980s.

New Conservative Institutions

These established activists teamed up with a group of intellectuals called the "neoconservatives" or "neocons." The first neoconservatives, writers such as Norman Podhoretz and Gertrude Himmelfarb, had been anticommunist liberals during the 1950s and early 1960s. Unsettled by the insurgencies of the 1960s, they saw the Democratic Party abandoning an anticommunist foreign policy and catering to social activists. Most neocons supported Democrat Hubert Humphrey over Republican Richard Nixon in 1968, but some began moving steadily rightward during the 1970s and embraced the Republicans during the 1980s.

The neoconservatives of this era remained true to their political and cultural roots. Their lively essays, written for established organs of conservatism such as *National Review* and the *Wall Street Journal* and for neoconservative publications such as *Commentary* and the *New Criterion,* denounced any movement associated with the 1960s, including affirmative action. Neoconservatives offered intellectual sustenance to a new generation of conservative thinkers, who worked to reinvigorate the nation's anticommunist foreign policy and celebrate its capitalist economic system.

A new militancy among conservative business leaders also helped build the New Right. Denouncing the Great Society and even criticizing Richard Nixon's Republican administration, some business spokespeople claimed that health and safety regulations and environmental legislation endangered "economic freedom." They urged rededication to the idea of limited government. Generous funding by corporations and philanthropic organizations helped staff conservative research institutions (such as the American Enterprise Institute and The Heritage Foundation) and finance new lobbying organizations (such as the Committee on the Present Danger). Conservatism also gained considerable ground on college campuses, which had been incubators of the New Left and the counterculture during the 1960s.

The New Religious Right

The New Right of the 1970s also attracted important grassroots support from Protestants in fundamentalist and evangelical churches. (Fundamentalists preach the necessity of fidelity to a strict moral code, of an individual commitment to Christ, and of a faith in the literal truth of the Bible. Evangelicals generally espouse the same doctrinal tenets as fundamentalists but place more emphasis on converting non-Christians and less on defending the literal truth of the Bible.) Since the 1920s, fundamentalist and evangelical Protestants had generally stayed clear of partisan politics, but the Supreme Court's abortion decision in *Roe* v. *Wade* (1973) mobilized their leaders. They joined with anti-abortion Catholics in opposing the *Roe* ruling. Reverend Jerry Falwell of the Thomas Road Baptist Church and the *Old Time Gospel Hour* television ministry declared that *Roe* showed that it was time to fight back on the political front because "liberals have been imposing morality on us for the last fifty years." Leaders of the New Religious Right, particularly in the South, also embarked on a lengthy legal battle to prevent the Internal Revenue Service from denying tax-exempt status to private Christian colleges and academies that opposed racial integration.

This chart shows the self-described religious affiliations of the American people compiled through sampling techniques.

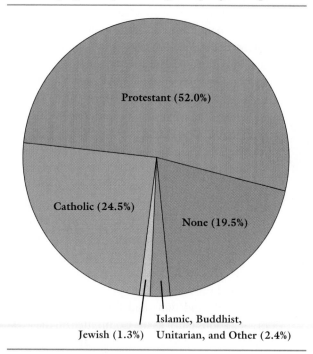

RELIGION IN AMERICA, 2001

Source: Data adapted from *The American Religious Identification Survey,* Graduate Center, City University of New York.

This wing of the New Right sought to redefine the relationship between religious and political action. During the 1950s, many mainstream religious leaders had supported the civil-rights crusade, and some joined in the antiwar movement of the 1960s. Those associated with the New Right went further in insisting that religious values should actively shape day-to-day political policy making. The insistence on a clear separation between church and state, a guiding principle of American constitutionalism during the era of Earl Warren's Supreme Court, struck the New Right as a violation of the right to the "free exercise of religion" that the First Amendment guaranteed. Going beyond this claim, some activists on the New Right declared that churches could provide the kind of divinely inspired assistance to people in need that secular institutions, such as social welfare agencies, could never dispense. Challenging older constitutional precedents against state aid to religious institutions, they urged that government, at all levels, should use tax monies to help fund church-centered education and "faith-based" social programming.

The New Right's Agenda

Political developments also contributed to the emergence of the New Right. Many on the right ultimately judged Richard Nixon to be more of an Eisenhower-style moderate than a Goldwater-style conservative, and the end of Nixon's presidency in 1974 intensified the desire to identify a "real" conservative leader. This search became a crusade after Nixon's successor, Gerald Ford, selected the old enemy of Goldwater Republicans, Nelson Rockefeller, as his vice president. "I could hardly have been more upset if Ford had selected Teddy Kennedy," one outraged conservative fumed.

It soon became apparent that opposition to a wide range of federal social programs and to cultural change could energize millions of voters. In 1975, New Right activists formed the National Conservative Political Action Committee (NCPAC), the first of many similar organizations, including the Conservative Caucus, The Committee for the Survival of a Free Congress, and Jerry Falwell's Moral Majority. Although these organizations initially focused on lobbying in Washington and backing conservative Republican candidates, they also looked to broader cultural and social goals. As one architect of this new coalition put it, they fervently believed that "God's truth ought to be manifest politically."

Increasingly, the New Right mobilized behind a defense of "family values." Its leaders opposed what they called "degenerate lifestyles," particularly those espoused

by feminists and homosexuals. Jerry Falwell's *Listen America!* (1980) suggested that the nation's military establishment was "under the complete control of avid supporters of the women's liberation movement." Because homosexuality was "one of the gravest sins condemned in the Scriptures," argued Paul Weyrich of NCPAC, the issue of gay and lesbian rights was not a matter of private lifestyles but a "question of morality which . . . affects the society as a whole." American institutions, particularly the male-headed nuclear family, needed protection. More broadly, parents needed to protect their children from educational "experiments." School boards and liberal educators, the New Right argued, were not only challenging Biblical precepts by teaching evolution but were also advancing dangerous new ideas such as multiculturalism and feminism. These activists saw educational bureaucrats forcing students to accept values that violated the religious and cultural values of their churches and families.

The New Right also condemned innovations associated with the 1960s in college curricula and in cultural life. Colleges were contributing to "the closing of the American mind" (the title of a best-selling 1987 book by Allan Bloom) by exposing students only to what was trendy and "politically correct" (or PC). The new attention to multicultural works, educational traditionalists charged, would soon debase intellectual life. In the broader public realm, the government-funded National Endowment for the Humanities (NEH) and the National Endowment for the Arts (NEA) came under fire for backing projects that focused on diversity and on politically sensitive cultural productions. The New Right, led by educational activists such as William Bennett and Lynn Cheney, championed what they called traditional cultural values and crusaded against multiculturalism. Their broad campaign won an important legal victory in 1998 when the U.S. Supreme Court ruled that the NEA's denial of a governmental grant, which had been supported by a preliminary review panel, to a controversial "performance artist" did not violate First Amendment guarantees of free speech.

The New Right adeptly publicized its positions. Well-funded conservative organizations sponsored academic conferences, popular gatherings, and radio and television programs. The religious wing of the New Right embraced the electronic media. Pat Robertson capitalized on the expansion of CATV to build a multimedia empire that, at one time, even included its own 24/7 Christian Broadcasting Network. Sexual and financial scandals overtook some religious broadcasters, but Robertson's "700 Club," a program that continually adapted his conservative evangelical style to new TV formats, flourished.

More important, conservative broadcasters, such as Rush Limbaugh, used the talk-radio genre, at both the local and national levels, to spread the New Right's message. Other conservative activists used television and, later, eagerly embraced the Internet. By the early 21st century, the fast-growing Fox News Channel (FNC), while proclaiming its news to be more "fair" and "balanced" than arch-rival CNN, also cultivated a conservative audience with commentators, such as Bill O'Reilly, who highlighted New Right perspectives.

The New Right, much like other activist groups, hardly moved in lockstep. More traditional members of the New Right coalition, such as the journalist and sometimes presidential candidate Patrick Buchanan, saw a new generation of neocons hijacking their cause and urging a "radical" turn in U.S. foreign policy during the 1990s. Buchanan and his followers denounced the free trade policies and the global military strategy that other conservatives promoted.

While remaining a coalition of disparate parts, the New Right became a powerful force in both American politics and culture. It successfully challenged the once-dominant political agenda of the Democratic Party, propelled the mainstream of the Republican Party decidedly rightward, established a strong foothold in public-policy and media discussions, and succeeded in remapping the nation's cultural and informational landscape.

Conclusion

Sweeping changes occurred in demographics, economics, culture, and society during the last quarter of the 20th century. The nation aged, and more of its people gravitated to the Sunbelt. Sprawling urban corridors and edge cities challenged older central cities as sites for commercial, as well as residential, development. Rapid technological change fueled the growth of globalized industries, restructuring the labor force to fit a postindustrial economy.

The most prominent development in American popular culture was the proliferation of the video screen. Television, motion pictures, and the Internet increasingly targeted specific audiences, and the fragmented nature of cultural reception was exemplified by the rise of new, particularistic media ventures.

Meanwhile, American society also seemed to fragment into specialized identifications. Social activism often organized around sexual, ethnic, and racial identities. Multiculturalists celebrated this fragmentation, while another activist movement, the New Right, argued that identity

politics was dividing the nation. The New Right's stress on limiting the power of government and promoting conservative values increasingly set the terms for political debate during the 1980s and 1990s, reconfiguring discussions about whether government power advanced, or worked against, greater liberty and equality in American life.

SUGGESTED READINGS

The economic ferment of the late 20th and early 21st centuries may be surveyed, from differing perspectives, in **Daniel Yergin,** *The Commanding Heights: The Battle between Government and the Marketplace That Is Remaking the Modern World* (1998); **Robert N. McCauley, Judith Ruud, and Frank Iacano, eds.,** *Dodging Bullets: Changing U.S. Corporate Structure in the 1980s and 1990s* (1999); **Randall E. Stross,** *Eboys: the First Inside Account of Venture Capitalists at Work* (2001); **Jeffrey A. Frankel and Peter R. Orszas, eds.,** *American Economic Policy in the 1990s* (2002); **Kevin Phillips,** *Wealth and Democracy: A Political History of the American Rich* (2003); and **Paul Krugman,** *The Great Unraveling: Losing Our Way in the New Century* (2003).

An overview of major social issues can be gleaned, again from very different viewpoints, in studies such as **Stephen Steinberg,** *Turning Back: The Retreat from Racial Justice in American Thought and Policy* (1995); **David Hollinger,** *Post-Ethnic America: Beyond Multiculturalism* (1995); **David M. Reimers,** *Unwelcome Strangers: American Identity and the Turn against Immigration* (1998); **Debra L. DeLaet,** *U.S. Immigration Policy in an Age of Rights* (2000); **Joseph Nevins,** *Operation Gatekeeper: The Rise of the "Illegal Alien" and the Remaking of the U.S.-Mexico Boundary* (2001); **Alice O'Connor,** *Poverty Knowledge: Social Science, Social Policy, and the Poor in Twentieth-Century U.S. History* (2001); and **Hugh Davis Graham,** *Collision Course: The Strange Convergence of Affirmative Action and Immigration Policy in America* (2002).

The much-contested cultural scene comes into view in **Lawrence Grossberg,** *We Gotta Get Out of This Place: Popular Conservatism and Postmodern Culture* (1992); **Alan Nadel,** *Flatling on the Field of Dreams: Cultural Narratives in the Films of President Reagan's America* (1995); **Fred Goodman,** *Mansion on the Hill: Dylan, Young, Geffen, Springsteen, and the Head-On Collision of Rock and Commerce* (1997); **Robert Kolker,** *Cinema of Loneliness: Penn, Kubrick, Scorsese, Spielberg, Altman* (rev. ed., 2000); **Robert Brent Toplin,** *Reel History: In Defense of Hollywood* (2002); and **Virginia Postel,** *The Substance of Style: How the Rise of Aesthetic Value is Remaking Commerce, Culture, and Consciousness* (2003).

The many other excellent and suggestive studies relevant to themes in this chapter include **Juan P. Garcia, ed.,** *Mexican Americans in the 1990s* (1997); **John D'Emilio, William B. Turner, and Urvashi Vaid, eds.,** *Creating Change: Sexuality, Public Policy, and Civil Rights* (2000); **Ellen Messer-Davidow,** *Disciplining Feminism: From Social Action to Academic Discourse* (2002); **Frank Wu,** *Yellow: Race in America Beyond Black and White* (2002); **Rickie Sollinger,** *Beggars and Choosers: How the Politics of Choice Shapes Adoption, Abortion, and Welfare in the United States* (2002); and **Sara Evans,** *Tidal Wave: How Women Changed America at Century's End* (2003).

AMERICAN JOURNEY ONLINE

 AND

 INFOTRAC COLLEGE EDITION

Visit the source collections at www.ajaccess.wadsworth.com and infotrac.thomsonlearning.com and use the Search function with the following key terms to explore documents, images, audio and video clips, articles, and commentary related to the material in this chapter.

Immigration Act of 1965	Indian Bill of Rights
Refugee Act of 1980	Native American Rights Fund
Information Revolution	Chicano/Chicana
Bill Gates	La Raza Unida
Human Genome Project	Asian Pacific Planning Council
Cesar Chavez	(APPCON)
United Farm Workers	National Asian Pacific American
AIDS	Network Council
Racial profiling	Affirmative Action
Congressional Black Caucus	Neoconservatives
(CBC)	Religious Right

GRADE AIDS

Visit the Liberty Equality Power Companion Web Site for resources specific to this textbook: http://history.wadsworth.com/murrin_LEP4e

The CD in the back of this book and the U.S. History Resource Center at http://history.wadsworth.com/u.s./ offer a variety of tools to help you succeed in this course, including access to quizzes; images; documents; interactive simulations, maps, and timelines; movie explorations; and a wealth of other sources.

promised an administration that would restore political tranquility. The close election of 2000, a sharp economic downturn, and increasingly bitter partisan debates, however, further polarized American life.

Disagreements also focused on foreign policy. Should the United States set aside anticommunism to pursue other goals, as Democratic President Jimmy Carter (1977–81) initially urged, or should it wage the Cold War even more vigorously, as his successor, Republican Ronald Reagan (1981–89), advocated? After 1989, when the Cold War ended unexpectedly, the United States needed to reshape its foreign policy for a new post–Cold War world, one that after the attacks of September 11, 2001, in New York City and Washington, D.C., seemed as dangerous as ever before.

CHAPTER FOCUS

◆ How were the presidencies of Gerald Ford (1974–77) and Jimmy Carter shaped by the legacies of Watergate and the Vietnam War?

◆ What conservative agenda, in both domestic and foreign policy, did Ronald Reagan's Republican administration construct?

◆ What forces and events contributed to the end of the Cold War?

◆ Around what policies and appeals did President Bill Clinton reorient the Democratic Party's domestic appeal? What was Clinton's post–Cold War agenda in foreign policy?

◆ How did the presidency of George W. Bush seek to change both domestic and foreign policy, especially in the wake of the attacks of September 11, 2001?

The Caretaker Presidency of Gerald Ford (1974–1977)

When Richard Nixon resigned from the presidency in August 1974, Gerald Ford became the first person to serve as vice president and then as president without having been elected to either office. Ford promised to salve the wounds of the 1960s and early 1970s. Drawing on political ties from his long career in the House of Representatives, Ford hoped to reestablish the presidency as a focus of national unity. But Ford's ability to "heal the land," as he put it, proved limited. A genial, unpretentious former football star who preferred his public entries to be accompanied by the fight song of his alma mater, the University of Michigan, rather than by "Hail to the Chief," Ford appeared a weak, indecisive president.

CHRONOLOGY

1974	Nixon resigns and Ford becomes president; Ford soon pardons Nixon
1975	South Vietnam falls to North Vietnam • Ford asserts U.S. power in *Mayaguez* incident
1976	Jimmy Carter elected president • OPEC sharply raises oil prices
1978	Carter helps negotiate Camp David peace accords on Middle East
1979	Soviet Union invades Afghanistan • Sandinista party comes to power in Nicaragua • U.S. hostages seized in Iran
1980	Reagan elected president • U.S. hostages in Iran released
1981	Reagan tax cut passed
1983	U.S. troops removed from Lebanon • U.S. troops invade Grenada • Reagan announces SDI ("Star Wars") program
1984	Reagan defeats Walter Mondale
1986	Reagan administration rocked by revelation of Iran-*Contra* affair
1988	George H. W. Bush defeats Michael Dukakis in presidential election
1989	Communist regimes in Eastern Europe collapse; Berlin Wall falls • Cold War, in effect, ends
1990	Bush angers conservative Republicans by agreeing to a tax increase
1991	Bush orchestrates Persian Gulf War against Iraq
1992	Bill Clinton defeats Bush and third-party candidate Ross Perot in presidential race
1993	Congress approves North American Free Trade Agreement (NAFTA)
1994	Republicans gain control of both houses of Congress and pledge to enact their Contract with America • Special prosecutor Kenneth Starr takes over the investigation of Whitewater allegations
1995	World Trade Organization (WTO) created
1996	The Personal Responsibility and Work Opportunity Reconciliation Act becomes the first major overhaul of the national welfare system since the 1930s • Clinton defeats Robert Dole in the presidential race
1997	Congress and the White House agree on legislation aimed at reducing taxes and rolling back the federal deficit
1998	Republicans lose House seats in off-year election • Republican-controlled House impeaches Clinton
1999	Senate fails to convict Clinton on impeachment charges • Clinton orders bombing campaign against Serbia
2000	Longest economic expansion in U.S. history continues • George W. Bush defeats Gore in close, hotly disputed election
2001	Large tax cuts passed • Al Qaeda suicide squads crash passenger airplanes into World Trade Center and Pentagon on September 11 • Patriot Act passed • U.S. military campaign ousts Taliban from power in Afghanistan
2002	Midterm elections strengthen Republican majorities in House and Senate
2003	U.S. invades Iraq and overthrows Saddam Hussein • Huge federal budget deficits return

Trying to Whip Stagflation

Ford's plan to rebuild his own party around an updated version of the moderate Republicanism of the 1950s quickly foundered. His appointment of Nelson Rockefeller as vice president infuriated the New Right, and his granting of a presidential pardon to former President Nixon, in September 1974, proved widely unpopular. Ford's approval rating plummeted.

Economic problems dominated the domestic side of the 865-day Ford presidency. Focusing on rising prices, rather than on increasing unemployment, the Ford administration touted a program called "Whip Inflation Now" (WIN). It offered a one-year income tax surcharge and cuts in federal spending as solutions to inflation. Prices, however, defied the predictions of prevailing economic wisdom and crept higher. As both prices and unemployment rose—continuing the condition known during Nixon's presidency as "stagflation"—Ford abandoned WIN. Unemployment reached 8.5 percent, and the inflation rate topped 9 percent during 1975.

Meanwhile, Ford clashed with the Democratic-controlled Congress over how to deal with stagflation. Ford, who vetoed nearly 40 spending bills during his brief presidency, eventually acquiesced to a congressional economic program that included a tax cut, an increase in unemployment benefits, an unbalanced federal budget, and a limited set of controls over oil prices. Democrats charged that Ford could not implement coherent programs of his own, and many Republicans complained that he could not stand up to Democrats in Congress.

Foreign Policy

As he struggled with economic problems at home, Ford steered the nation through its final involvement in the war in Southeast Asia. After assuming office, Ford pledged a renewal of U.S. military support to the government in South Vietnam if it ever became directly menaced by North Vietnam. The antiwar mood in Congress and throughout the country, however, made fulfilling this commitment impossible. North Vietnam's armies, sensing final victory, moved rapidly through the South in March 1975, and Congress, relieved that U.S. troops had finally been withdrawn after the 1973 Paris peace accords, refused to reintroduce U.S. military personnel.

Spring 1975 brought new communist victories. In early April, Khmer Rouge forces in Cambodia drove a U.S.-backed government from the capital of Phnom Penh, and on April 30, 1975, North Vietnamese troops overran the South Vietnamese capital of Saigon, renaming it Ho Chi Minh City. Debate over U.S. policy in Indochina again became contentious. Former "doves" lamented the lives lost and money wasted, while former "hawks" derided their country's "failure of will."

Within this charged atmosphere, Ford tried to demonstrate that the United States could still assert its power. In May 1975, a contingent of Khmer Rouge boarded a U.S. ship, the *Mayaguez,* and seized its crew. Secretary of State Henry Kissinger, declaring that it was time to "look ferocious," convinced Ford to order a rescue mission and bombing strikes against Cambodia. This military response, along with pressure on the Khmer Rouge from China, secured the release of the *Mayaguez* and its crew. The president's approval ratings briefly shot up, but the incident did little to allay doubts about Ford's leadership. The White House seemed primarily interested in looking tough, and the United States lost more men than it saved during the *Mayaguez* rescue. Meanwhile, the president's other foreign policy initiatives, which included extending Nixon's policy of détente with the Soviet Union and pursuing a peace treaty for the Middle East, achieved little. Gerald Ford increasingly appeared a caretaker president.

The Election of 1976

Conservative Republicans rallied behind Ronald Reagan and nearly denied Ford the GOP presidential nomination in 1976. Reagan, once a movie actor and the governor of California from 1966 to 1974, ignited his campaign by abandoning specific policy proposals and by highlighting his image as a "true conservative" who, unlike Ford, stood apart from political insiders in Washington. Ford had already won just enough delegates in the early primaries, however, to eke out a narrow, first-ballot victory at the Republican Party's national convention.

The Democrats did turn to an outsider, James Earl (Jimmy) Carter, the former governor of Georgia. A retired naval officer, with a degree in engineering, Carter had worked on the nuclear submarine program before abandoning a military career to return to Plains, Georgia, and run his family's peanut farming business. Later, Carter entered state politics, gaining the reputation of being a social moderate and a fiscal conservative. When he announced his presidential candidacy in 1976, few people took notice; no governor, after all, had captured the White House since Franklin Roosevelt in 1932.

With Watergate still a vivid memory, Carter's campaign emphasized personal character. Highlighting his small-town roots, Carter pledged to "give the government of this country back to the people of this country." A devout Baptist, Carter campaigned as a born-again Christian. Touting his record as a successful governor, he asked people to "help me evolve an efficient, economical, purposeful, and manageable government for our nation." In order to balance the Democratic ticket, he picked a member of the

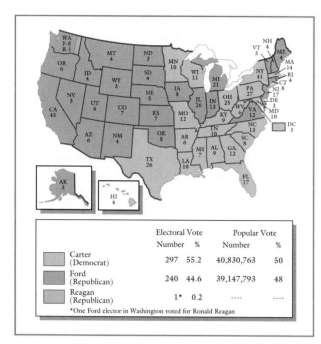

MAP 31.1 PRESIDENTIAL ELECTION, 1976

This map shows the low voter turnout and the very close election that made Jimmy Carter president. Notice how Carter, from Georgia, drew votes from Southern states.

U.S. Senate, Walter Mondale of Minnesota, as his running mate. In November, Carter won a narrow victory over Ford.

Carter's triumph rested on a diverse, transitory coalition. Tapping his regional appeal, Carter carried every southern state except Virginia. Although he ran well among southern whites who belonged to fundamentalist and evangelical churches, his victory in the South depended on a strong turnout among African Americans, the beneficiaries of federal voter protection measures enacted during the 1960s. Carter courted younger voters by promising to pardon most Vietnam-era draft resisters. With the floundering economy a major concern, Walter Mondale's appeal to party loyalists helped Carter narrowly capture three key states that had long been Democratic strongholds—New York, Pennsylvania, and Ohio. Even so, Carter defeated Ford by less than 2 million popular ballots and by only 56 electoral votes. Voter turnout in 1976 hit its lowest mark since the end of the Second World War; only about 54 percent of eligible voters went to the polls.

Jimmy Carter's One-term Presidency (1977–1981)

Jimmy Carter's lack of a popular mandate and his outsider image posed serious handicaps. Powerful constituencies, including both business and labor, feared that Carter might

prove an unpredictable leader. Moreover, many Democratic members of Congress, especially those first elected in the aftermath of Watergate, stressed their independence from the White House. In 1976, most of them, after all, rolled up higher vote totals in their states than the Carter-Mondale ticket. Carter also seemed a regional, rather than a national, figure. Although some veteran Washington people joined his cabinet, he relied on the Georgians on his White House staff, a small cadre of advisers that the Washington press corps dubbed the Georgia Mafia. After leaving government, Carter reflected on his difficulties: "I had a different way of governing. . . . I was a southerner, a born-again Christian, a Baptist, a newcomer."

Welfare and Energy Initiatives

Carter found himself caught between advisers who claimed that the national government was already exercising too much power and ones who argued that Washington was doing too little to address social and economic problems at home.

In contrast to Richard Nixon, who had unveiled a bold Family Assistance Plan (FAP) before retreating, Carter immediately temporized on welfare policy. His staff split over offering a revised version of FAP, which would have emphasized monetary assistance to low-income families, and creating several million new public service jobs, which would be underwritten by Washington. Opposed to increasing federal spending, Carter nonetheless asked Congress for a compromise program that included both additional spending on existing social programs and job creation but nothing that resembled Nixon's FAP initiative. Carter's proposal failed in Congress, and the drive to overhaul the social welfare system stalled for nearly a decade.

Carter pushed harder on energy issues. The United States obtained 90 percent of its energy from fossil fuels, and this dependence, especially on petroleum imported from abroad, worried policy makers. In 1973 and again in 1976, the Organization of Petroleum Exporting Countries (OPEC), a cartel dominated by oil-rich nations in the Middle East, dramatically raised the price of crude oil and precipitated acute shortages across the globe, particularly in the United States. As gasoline became both expensive and scarce, drivers quickly wearied of high prices and long lines at service stations. Carter promised to make the United States less dependent on imported fossil fuel.

The President charged James Schlesinger, a veteran of the Nixon and Ford administrations and head of a new Department of Energy, with developing a sweeping energy plan. Schlesinger outlined ambitious goals: (1) decrease U.S. reliance on foreign oil and natural gas; (2) expand

domestic energy production through new tax incentives and deregulation of natural gas production; (3) levy new taxes to discourage gasoline use; (4) foster conservation by encouraging energy-saving measures; and (5) promote nonpetroleum energy sources, especially coal and nuclear power. Neither Carter nor Schlesinger consulted Congress or even some members of the president's own administration. Instead, in April 1977, the president suddenly announced an energy proposal that included more than 100 interrelated provisions.

Congress quickly rejected the plan. Legislators from oil-producing states opposed higher taxes on gasoline, and critics of corporate power blocked deregulation of domestic oil and natural gas production. Meanwhile, environmentalists charged that greater use of coal would consequently increase air pollution. Most Americans, meanwhile, ignored Carter's plea that the struggle with energy problems amounted to "the moral equivalent of war." Carter continued to press for energy conservation; for development of renewable sources, such as solar and wind-generated energy; and for greater use of nuclear power.

The nuclear option generated sharp controversy. Boosters of atomic research programs during the early days of the Cold War had promised that giant nuclear reactors would provide a cheap, almost limitless supply of energy. The cost of building and maintaining them, however, far exceeded the original estimates, and critics saw the reactors as grave safety risks. A 1979 incident seemingly offered a graphic illustration of the danger when the malfunction of a reactor at Three Mile Island, Pennsylvania, nearly produced a nuclear meltdown. Responding to growing public concern, power companies canceled orders for new reactors, and nuclear power industry expansion halted. Meanwhile, OPEC oil prices continued to skyrocket, from $1.80 a barrel in 1971 to nearly $30 a decade later, at the end of Carter's presidency.

A Faltering Economy

Carter inherited economic problems—especially stagflation—from the Nixon and Ford years, but rising oil prices heightened inflationary pressures during his own presidency. Carter pledged to lower both unemployment and inflation, to stimulate greater economic growth, and to balance the federal budget (which showed a deficit of about $70 billion in 1976). Instead, by 1980 the economy had virtually stopped expanding, unemployment (after temporarily dipping) was again rising, and inflation was topping 13 percent. Most voters told opinion pollsters that their own economic conditions had dramatically deteriorated while Carter occupied the White House.

Economic difficulties spread beyond individuals. New York City, beset by long-term economic and social problems and short-term fiscal mismanagement, faced bankruptcy. The nation's largest city could neither meet its financial obligations nor borrow new money through the normal channels. Private bankers and public officials had to secure congressional "bailout" legislation that granted federal loan guarantees to New York City.

The Big Apple's troubles, although different in scale from those of other cities, were hardly unique. According to one estimate, Chicago lost 200,000 manufacturing jobs during the 1970s. Bricks from demolished, industrial-era buildings in St. Louis became one of that city's leading exports. Increasing numbers of people living in central cities across the country could find only low-paying, short-term jobs with no fringe benefits. Many found no employment at all. Rising crime rates, deteriorating downtowns, and shrinking tax revenues afflicted most urban areas, even as inflation further eroded the buying power of city budgets.

What explains the economic dislocation of the late 1970s? Tax cuts, increased governmental spending on

"IS CAPITALISM WORKING?"

In 1980, even *Time* magazine wondered about the economic future of the United States. Persistent economic problems—especially high rates of inflation and unemployment—dominated the Ford and Carter presidencies.

public works projects, and actions by the Federal Reserve Board were aimed at stimulating recovery. These measures, however, also drove price inflation. Meanwhile, ever-rising international oil prices triggered a series of increases for gasoline and home heating fuel that rippled through the economy. These severe inflationary pressures brought high interest rates and a loss of confidence and investment, choking off productivity and economic growth.

Conservative economists and business groups charged that domestic programs favored by most congressional Democrats contributed to economic distress. Increasing the minimum wage and vigorously enforcing safety and antipollution regulations, they argued, drove up the cost of doing business and forced companies to raise prices to consumers. During his last two years in office, Carter seemed to agree, in part, with this analysis. Defying most Democrats in Congress, he cut spending for many social programs; sought to reduce capital gains taxes to encourage investment; and inaugurated a process of "deregulating" various industries, beginning with the transportation sector.

Negotiating Foreign Disputes

In foreign, as in domestic policy, Carter promised new directions. On his first day in office, he granted amnesty to most Vietnam-era draft resisters. He soon declared that he would not be afflicted by an "inordinate fear of communism" and would place concern for human rights at the center of U.S. foreign policy. After four years, however, his foreign policy initiatives were in disarray. Republican Ronald Reagan's "get-tough-again" presidential campaign of 1980 would link Carter with ineptitude in foreign affairs.

Although skillful in small-group negotiations, Carter had little experience working with long-term foreign policy issues. Furthermore, his top advisers—Cyrus Vance as secretary of state and Zbigniew Brzezinski as national security adviser—pursued contradictory agendas. Brzezinski favored a hard-line, anti-Soviet policy with an emphasis on military muscle; Vance preferred to avoid confrontations and to engage in quiet diplomacy. Pulled in divergent directions, Carter's foreign policy seemed to waffle. Still, Carter set some important new directions, emphasizing negotiation in particular trouble spots of the world and making human rights a priority.

Carter's faith in negotiations and in his personal skill as a facilitator yielded some success in Latin America and the Middle East. On the issue of the Panama Canal, which had been the object of diplomatic negotiations for 13 years, Carter adroitly secured treaties that granted Panama increasing authority over the waterway to culminate in full Panamanian control in 2000. U.S. ownership of the canal, a legacy of turn-of-the-20th century expansionism, he argued, continued to fuel anti-Yankee sentiment not just in Panama but throughout Latin America. In addition, Carter convinced skeptical U.S. senators, whose votes he needed to secure any treaty, that the canal was no longer the economic and strategic necessity it had once been.

Carter's personal touch also emerged during the Camp David peace talks of 1978. Relations between Egypt and Israel had been strained since the Yom Kippur War of 1973, when Israel had repelled an Egyptian attack and had seized the Sinai Peninsula and territory along the West Bank (of the Jordan River). Reviving earlier Republican efforts to mediate the Arab-Israeli conflict, Carter brought Menachem Begin and Anwar Sadat, leaders of Israel and Egypt, respectively, to the presidential retreat at Camp David. After 13 days of bargaining, the three leaders announced the framework for a negotiating process and a peace treaty. Middle East tensions hardly vanished, but these Camp David Accords kept alive high-level discussions, lowered the level of acrimony between Egypt and Israel, and bound both nations to the United States through Carter's promises of economic aid.

In Asia and Africa, the Carter administration also emphasized accommodation. Building on Nixon's initiative, Carter expanded economic and cultural relations with China and finally established formal diplomatic ties with the People's Republic on New Year's Day 1979. In Africa, Carter abandoned Kissinger's reliance on white colonial regimes and supported the transition of Zimbabwe (formerly Rhodesia) to a government run by its black majority.

Campaigning for Human Rights Abroad

Carter's foreign policy became best known for an emphasis on human rights. Cold War alliances with anticommunist dictatorships, Carter believed, were undermining U.S. influence in the world. In the long run, Carter's policy helped encourage worldwide support for human rights issues. The trend toward democratization, which occurred in many nations during the 1980s and 1990s, could be partly traced back to Carter's stress on human rights.

The immediate impact of Carter's human rights policy, however, proved ambiguous. Because his administration sometimes ignored this matter in specific circumstances, many of America's most repressive allies, such as Ferdinand Marcos in the Philippines, continued their dictatorial ways. Moreover, Carter's own rhetoric about human rights helped justify uprising against other long-

standing dictator-allies in Nicaragua and Iran. Revolutions in these countries, fueled by resentment against the United States, brought anti-American regimes to power and presented Carter with difficult choices.

In Nicaragua, the Sandinista movement toppled the repressive regime of Anastasio Somoza, whom the United States had long supported. The Sandinistas, initially a coalition of moderate democrats and communists, soon tilted toward a militant Marxism and began to expropriate private property. Carter opposed this turn in Nicaragua but concluded he could not immediately change it. Republican critics charged that Carter's policies had given a green light to communism throughout Central America and pledged to oust Nicaragua's Sandinista-controlled government.

Confronting Problems in Iran and Afghanistan

If events in Nicaragua eroded Carter's standing, those in Iran and Afghanistan all but shattered it. The United States had steadfastly supported Shah Reza Pahlavi, who had reigned in Iran since an American-supported coup in 1953, with military and economic aid. The Shah's overthrow, in January 1979, by revolutionary movement spearheaded by Islamic fundamentalists thus signaled a massive rejection of U.S. influence in oil-rich Iran. When the Carter administration allowed the deposed Shah to enter the United States for medical treatment in November 1979, a group of Iranians (with the tacit support of their government) seized the U.S. embassy compound in Tehran and 66 American hostages. Iranians demanded the return of the Shah in exchange for the release of the Americans.

Carter's critics saw this "hostage crisis" as proof of his incompetence. In response, Carter talked tough; levied economic reprisals against Iran; and, over the objections of Cyrus Vance (who subsequently resigned), sent a military mission to rescue the hostages. The effort proved an embarrassing failure, and Carter never could resolve the situation. After his defeat in the 1980 election, diplomatic efforts finally freed the hostages, but the United States and Iran remained at odds.

Criticism of Carter also focused on the Soviet Union's invasion of Afghanistan in December 1979, a move primarily sparked by Soviet fear of the growing influence of Islamic fundamentalists along its borders. Carter's opponents, however, saw this episode as a sign that Soviet leaders viewed the United States, under Carter's leadership, as too weak to contain their expansionism. Charged with suffering from the "post-Vietnam syndrome," a failure to act decisively in foreign affairs, Carter tried to respond in

nonmilitary ways. He halted grain exports to the Soviet Union (angering his farm constituency), organized a boycott of the 1980 Olympic Games in Moscow, withdrew a new Strategic Arms Limitation Treaty (SALT) from the Senate, and revived registration for the military draft. Still, Republicans (along with some Democrats) charged Carter with allowing American power and prestige to decline.

The Election of 1980

For a time, when Senator Edward Kennedy of Massachusetts entered the party's 1980 presidential primaries, it seemed that Democrats themselves might deny Carter a second term. Although Kennedy's challenge eventually fizzled, it did underscore Carter's vulnerability. Kennedy popularized anti-Carter themes that Republicans gleefully embraced. "It's time to say no more hostages, no more high interest rates, no more high inflation, and no more Jimmy Carter," went one of Kennedy's stump speeches. More than one-third of the Democrats who supported Kennedy in the final Democratic primaries (most of which Kennedy won) told pollsters they probably would vote Republican in the general election. As Carter entered the fall campaign, he seemed a sure loser.

Republican candidate Ronald Reagan exuded confidence. He stressed his opposition to many domestic social programs and his support for a stronger national defense. His successful primary campaign glossed over specific details, promised massive tax cuts, and highlighted an optimistic vision of a rejuvenated America and a supply of movie-inspired quips. To remind voters of the economic problems associated with Carter's presidency, Reagan asked repeatedly, "Are you better off now than you were four years ago?" He would quickly answer his own question by invoking what he called a "misery index," which added the rate of inflation to the rate of unemployment.

Reagan seized an issue that the Democratic Party had long regarded its own: economic growth. In 1979, one of Jimmy Carter's advisers had gloomily portrayed the nation's economic problems as so severe that there was "no way we can avoid a decline in our standard of living. All we can do is adapt to it." In contrast, Reagan promised that sharp tax cuts would bring back the kind of economic expansion the nation had enjoyed during the 1950s and 1960s. During a crucial television debate, when Carter charged that Reagan's upbeat proposals lacked specificity, a smiling Reagan spotlighted Carter's apparent pessimism by repeatedly quipping, "There you go again!"

Reagan (and his running mate, George H. W. Bush) won the November presidential election with slightly more than 50 percent of the popular vote. (John Anderson, a middle-of-the-road Republican who ran an independent

campaign for the White House, won about 7 percent.) Reagan's vote total in the Electoral College, however, overwhelmed Carter's: 489 to 49. Moreover, Republicans took 12 Senate seats away from Democrats, gaining control of the Senate for the first time since 1954.

Noting Reagan's slim majority in the popular vote, old-line Democrats underestimated his political clout. They portrayed 1980 as more of a defeat for Carter than a victory for the Republicans and the New Right. By reducing expenditures for domestic programs and lowering taxes on capital gains, according to their analysis, Carter had alienated traditional Democrats. Moreover, these Democrats told themselves that Reagan's sophisticated media campaign temporarily misled voters; in due course,

they claimed, Reagan would be unmasked as a media-manufactured president.

These same Democrats, however, refused to recognize that their party's domestic agenda had been steadily losing support for more than a decade and failed to acknowledge the appeal of the New Right. In 1980, voters ousted seven prominent Democratic senators, including former presidential candidate George McGovern. The real income of the average American family, which had advanced at an annual rate of nearly 3 percent per year between 1950 and 1965, rose only 1.7 percent per year between 1965 and 1980, with the worst times coming after 1973. In this economic climate, middle-income taxpayers who were struggling to make ends meet found Democratic social

---

M U S I C A L   L I N K   T O   T H E   P A S T

Hip-hop Leaps In

Songwriters: E. Fletcher, M. Glover, C. Chase, S. Robinson

Title: "The Message" (1982)

Performers: Grandmaster Flash and the Furious Five

Black radio formats in the early 1980s were staid and conservative, favoring easy listening, corporate-associated artists such as Lionel Richie. According to Nelson George, New York–based black music professionals "were so office-bound, taking meetings with managers and listening to tapes from song publishers [in midtown Manhattan], that they failed to venture up the road to Harlem and the South Bronx, where, in the middle of the nation's most depressing urban rot, something wonderful was happening." That "wonderful" innovation was hip-hop music, which began in the mid-1970s with DJs utilizing other artists' records (Chic's "Good Times" was a perennial favorite) as instrumental backing tracks for live rappers. Hip-hop assembled elaborate rhyming stories, messages, and braggings—often improvised on the spot.

Although early hits such as the Sugar Hill Gang's 1979 "Rapper's Delight" promoted a lightweight party mood, "The Message" presented a sobering litany of inner-city ghetto life: police brutality, junkies, pimps, homeless people "pissing on the stairs," and random violence, punctuated with the mantra of "sometimes it makes me wonder, how I keep from going under." It presaged the even harder-edged, more politically minded and economically successful rap artists, such as Public Enemy, NWA, and KRS-One. Despite commercial

success ("The Message" was a top-five R&B hit), major label executives veered away from the angry black, mostly male performers of rap music until the mid-1980s. Like other controversial American music innovations such as bebop and rock 'n' roll, rap was initially confined to independent label distribution.

Hip-hop also introduced revolutionary musical approaches. DJ Grandmaster Flash, who was unable to afford studio recording time in the mid-1970s, created his own backing tracks by manipulating turntables and vinyl records in new ways. He, along with DJ Kool Herc, pioneered the effects of "scratching" (turning records manually to make the needle repeat brief lengths of groove) and "phasing" (altering turntable speeds to change the sound of recordings). These and other new technologies helped construct the soundscapes that brought a harsh urban atmosphere to life in "The Message."

---

1. Can a turntable be viewed as a musical instrument?
2. If so, what does this use of a century-old technology say about the historical atmosphere that gave birth to hip-hop?
3. What might it say about the role of technology in musical change?

For additional sources related to this feature, visit the CD accompanying this text or the *Liberty, Equality, Power* Web site at:

http://history.wadsworth.com/murrin_LEP4e

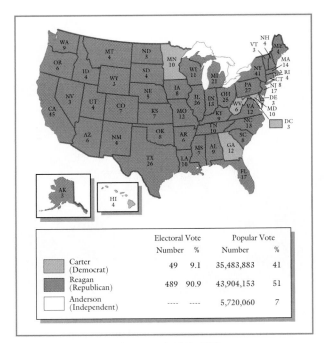

		Electoral Vote		Popular Vote	
		Number	%	Number	%
	Carter (Democrat)	49	9.1	35,483,883	41
	Reagan (Republican)	489	90.9	43,904,153	51
	Anderson (Independent)	----	----	5,720,060	7

MAP 31.2   PRESIDENTIAL ELECTION, 1980

Compare this map with the one showing the election of Jimmy Carter four years earlier. What factors might explain such a sudden downturn in Democratic fortunes?

welfare measures far less palatable than during more prosperous times.

The 1970s had dampened support for ambitious domestic programming. Still, most traditional Democrats continued to talk about how to improve, and even expand, the social welfare system they had constructed since the New Deal of the 1930s. The New Right, on the other hand, advocated a significant reduction in government spending programs. It decried public housing, for example, as a waste of tax dollars and denounced Aid to Families with Dependent Children (AFDC) and food stamps as socially debilitating for their recipients and a drag on the nation's economy. The New Right's antigovernment rhetoric increasingly resonated with voters, including some longtime Democrats.

Ronald Reagan's "New Morning in America" (1981–1989)

Ronald Reagan's advisers quickly crafted a bold conservative agenda. A taxpayer revolt that had swept through California politics during the late 1970s provided a model for his administration's attack on "tax-and-spend" policy making at the federal level. (The situation was ironic, however, because California's tax revolt had emerged in

response to increases while Reagan had served as the state's governor.) Across the country, people increasingly responded to the tax-reduction message.

In addition, Reagan courted the New Right. He opposed abortion, advocated prayer in school, extolled "family values," urged radical tax reductions, and offered new approaches to affirmative action and energy policy. Conservative religious figures, including Jerry Falwell and Pat Robertson, former Democrats, joined Reagan's new Republican coalition. Even Jimmy Carter's own Southern Baptists, who had rallied behind him in 1976, along with born-again Christians across the country, began flocking to Reagan. By touting "color-blind" social policies and by bringing conservative African Americans and Hispanics into his administration, the president could effectively court white (especially male) voters who were upset over affirmative action, while avoiding the charge that he was making racially charged appeals. "Guaranteeing equality of treatment is the government's proper function," Reagan proclaimed at one of his first presidential press conferences.

Pursuing Supply-Side Economics

To justify cutting taxes, Reagan touted "supply-side economics." This economic theory held that sizable tax reductions would stimulate growth by putting more money in the hands of both producers and consumers, thereby curing the economic stagnation of the 1970s. Reagan pushed a tax-reduction plan through Congress during summer 1981. It significantly reduced taxes for people who earned high incomes and already possessed significant wealth. Taxes on businesses also were slashed to encourage investment in new facilities and equipment. Most Democrats, who had supported more limited tax reductions during Carter's presidency, endorsed Reagan's plan. At the same time, the Federal Reserve Board under Paul Volcker, a Carter appointee, kept interest rates high in hopes of driving down inflation.

After a severe economic downturn in 1981 and 1982, the worst since the Great Depression of the 1930s, the economy rebounded and entered a vibrant period of non-inflationary growth. Between 1983 and 1986, the economy added more than 11 million new jobs. By 1986, the GNP was steadily climbing, and the inflation rate rested at less than 2 percent. Although unemployment figures stubbornly refused to drop, Reagan's supporters called the turnaround an "economic miracle" and hailed a "Reagan revolution."

This revival sparked debate over several issues, particularly the cumulative impact of Reagan's budget deficits and the consequences of the economic expansion. On the first issue—budget deficits—Reagan's critics complained

that he had not matched tax cuts with budget reductions. Although Reagan constantly inveighed against budget deficits and big spenders, his administration rolled up an extraordinary record of deficits and spending. Despite some upward revision in tax rates after his first round of tax-cutting, annual deficits tripled to nearly $300 billion during Reagan's eight-year presidency. To finance such spending, the United States borrowed abroad and piled up the largest foreign debt in the world. Reagan's "revolution," critics charged, brought short-term recovery for some people by courting a long-term budget crisis that harmed low-income people who relied more heavily on government programs. Future generations, these observers argued, would pay dearly for the soaring government debt of the 1980s.

FARM FORECLOSURES

During the early 1980s, many Midwest farmers endured hard times. Farm foreclosures—followed by auctions of land, equipment, and personal property—swept across the Farm Belt during Ronald Reagan's first term as president.

On the second issue—the grassroots impact of the expansion—Reagan's supporters and opponents argued over the distribution of the new economic growth. Reagan partisans insisted that a booming economy would ultimately benefit all Americans. In contrast, critics saw a "Swiss-cheese" economy, one full of holes. Farmers in the Midwest, especially battered during the 1981–82 recession, watched falling crop prices hamper their ability to pay back the high-interest loans they had contracted during the inflation-ridden 1970s. The value of land, a small farmer's primary asset, plummeted. A series of mortgage foreclosures, reminiscent of the 1930s, hit the farm states, and the ripple effect decimated the economies of small towns. At the same time, those urban families who found only low-paying jobs and declining welfare benefits also puzzled over talk of a booming economy. Many jobs created during the 1980s came in the service sector and offered relatively low wages and few, if any, fringe benefits. In 1981, the average weekly paycheck was $270; measured in constant dollars, the same check was worth only $254 in 1991. The minimum wage, when adjusted for inflation, fell in value throughout Reagan's presidency.

The economic changes of the Reagan era fell especially hard on disadvantaged groups. People with educational credentials and marketable skills could make significant economic gains. The number of African American families earning a solid middle-class income more than doubled between 1970 and 1990. College graduates of African descent could expect incomes comparable to those of

their white classmates, partly as a result of affirmative action hiring plans put in place by the Nixon and Carter administrations. Many people, therefore, could afford to leave problem-plagued inner-city neighborhoods. The story of mobility looked very different, however, for those who remained persistently unemployed, an underclass who seemed trapped in declining urban centers. At the end of the 1980s, one-third of all African American families lived in poverty, and the number earning less than $15,000 per year had doubled since 1970. In inner cities, less than half of African American children were completing high school, and more than 60 percent were unemployed. Throughout America, the gap between the well-off and the disadvantaged widened significantly during the 1980s.

Broadening the New Right Agenda

Reagan moved aggressively on several domestic issues. In 1981, he summarily fired the nation's air traffic controllers when their union refused to halt a nationwide strike. Overall, union membership continued to decline, as both the Reagan administration and most large businesses pursued aggressive antiunion strategies during the 1980s. The percentage of unionized workers fell to just 16 percent by the end of Reagan's presidency. Workers recognized that the balance of power was tilting against them and increasingly turned away from strikes as an economic weapon.

The president also placed a conservative stamp on the federal legal system. Almost immediately, he nominated a Supreme Court justice, Sandra Day O'Connor (the first woman to sit on the Court), who initially seemed a staunch conservative, particularly on social questions and criminal justice matters. During Reagan's first term, when the Republican Party controlled the Senate, Reagan also named prominent conservative jurists, such as Robert Bork and Antonin Scalia, to lower federal courts. The New Right, which had decried the "rights revolution" of the Supreme Court, welcomed the influx of judges from the political right. Civil libertarians complained that the federal courts were becoming less hospitable to legal claims made by criminal defendants, labor unions, and political dissenters. By 1990, because of retirements, about half of all federal judges had reached the bench during Ronald Reagan's presidency. Reagan also looked for staunch conservatives to fill nonjudicial appointments. He staffed his department of justice with lawyers who were eager to end the rights revolution and—in line with the "color-blind" approach to racial issues—to sidetrack affirmative action programs.

Reagan, who had campaigned in 1980 on a promise not only to halt the growth of government power but to roll back its reach, could claim only limited success in fulfilling this pledge. He appointed James Watt, an outspoken critic of environmental legislation, as secretary of the interior, the department that guides the nation's conservation policy. Watt angered environmentalists by supporting the "sagebrush rebellion," in which western states demanded fewer restrictions on the use of public land within their borders. Emotional battles broke out over private use of resources in federal wilderness areas. Particularly in the timber states of the Pacific Northwest, people hotly debated whether endangered species, such as rare bird populations, should be protected to the detriment of economic activities such as timber cutting. Reagan's first two appointees to the Department of Energy actually proposed eliminating the cabinet office they headed—an idea that Congress blocked. Reagan mused about abolishing the Department of Education and often criticized programs espoused by his own secretary of education. Able to fill most of the administrative agencies with conservatives, the president sought to ease regulations on businesses by relaxing enforcement of the safety and environmental laws that conservative economists continued to blame for driving up costs.

After taking office in 1981, Reagan promised to break OPEC's oil monopoly by encouraging the development of new sources of supply. Ignoring environmentalists' calls to break U.S. dependence on fossil fuels by promotion of renewable sources, Reagan and his successor George H. W. Bush followed a "cheap oil" policy. The tapping of new supplies of oil at home, together with rivalries among OPEC members, weakened OPEC's hold on the world market and reduced energy costs, which remained moderate throughout the economic boom of the 1990s.

Reagan tinkered with social welfare policy. He eliminated funding for some programs, most notably the Comprehensive Employment and Training Act (CETA), established during Richard Nixon's first term, and reduced funding for others, such as food stamps. Reagan proved to be much more conservative on domestic issues than Nixon, who had allowed social expenditures to increase, had courted some labor union leaders, and had advanced his guaranteed income program, FAP. Nevertheless, Reagan pledged that Washington would maintain a "safety net" for those in true need of governmental assistance.

Controversy surrounded the reach of this safety net. Critics complained about the increasing number of people whose total package of income and public benefits fell below what the federal government defined as the "poverty level." The burden of Reagan-era cutbacks seemed to fall disproportionately on female-headed households and on children. By the end of the 1980s, one of every five children was being raised in a household whose total income fell below the official poverty line. Meanwhile, many older people continued to benefit from a revision, during the 1970s, in the nation's most popular welfare program, Social Security. As a consequence of the arrangement called "indexing," Social Security payments automatically increased along with the rate of inflation. Larger Social Security checks, along with Medicare benefits, enabled millions of older Americans to do relatively well during the Reagan years.

Despite sometimes sharp debate, especially over the economic downturn of 1981–82 and the soaring federal deficit, Reagan remained a popular leader. His genial optimism seemed unshakable. He even appeared to rebound quickly—although close observers noted a clear decline in his energies—after being shot by a would-be assassin in March 1981. No matter what problems beset his administration, criticism never stuck to Reagan, whom one frustrated Democrat dubbed the "Teflon president."

Routing the Democrats, 1984

Democrats continually underestimated the appeal of Reagan and his policies—a miscalculation that doomed their own 1984 presidential effort. Walter Mondale, Jimmy Carter's vice president, ran on a platform calling for "the eradication of discrimination in all aspects of American life" and for an expansion of national social welfare programs. Mondale also proposed higher taxes to fund his agenda.

REAGAN RIDES

A latecomer to politics, the former motion picture star often used cowboy imagery to counter charges that he was too old for national leadership.

Courtesy, Ronald Reagan Library.

seemed eager to implement this goal or the larger one of reducing the still-soaring government deficit. Second, the Family Support Act of 1988 required states to inaugurate work training programs and to move people, including mothers receiving AFDC payments, off the welfare rolls. This law, its critics worried, failed to guarantee that its work training provision would actually result in people finding—and keeping—jobs. Yet, despite their limitations, Gramm-Rudman-Hollings and the Family Support Act set policy makers on a course that culminated in comprehensive budget-reduction and welfare-overhaul packages nearly a decade later.

Conservatives would eventually hail Ronald Reagan as the Moses of the New Right, but during his second term, some early supporters on the New Right looked balefully at his domestic record. The 1986 resignation of Warren Burger allowed Reagan to elevate William Rehnquist to the Chief Justice position and to tap Antonin Scalia, an even more conservative jurist, to replace Rehnquist as an

associate justice on the Supreme Court. In 1987, however, the Senate rebuffed Reagan's attempt to nominate Robert Bork, a particular favorite of the New Right, to the High Court. Bork's rejection enraged conservatives, some of whom blamed Reagan for not working hard enough on Bork's behalf. Meanwhile, the religious wing of the New Right chafed at what it considered Reagan's tepid support of its antiabortion crusade. Reagan also appeared to show little interest in altering the structure of Social Security or social welfare arrangements.

Although never lacking for critics, the "Reagan revolution" succeeded in advancing much of the New Right's agenda and in significantly changing the nation's political vocabulary. "Liberalism" no longer connoted a set of government programs that would stimulate the economy and build prosperity for all. Instead, Republicans made "liberal" a code word for wasteful social programs devised by a bloated federal government that gouged hardworking people and squandered their dollars. The term "conservative," as used by New Right Republicans, came to mean economic growth, curtailment of governmental power, and support for traditional sociocultural values. The once-dominant Democratic Party seemed to face an uncertain future.

☭ Renewing the Cold War

Reagan quickly established foreign policy themes that emphasized building American power in the world. Carter's policies, he claimed, represented a "Vietnam syndrome" of passivity and a "loss of will." In contrast to Carter's grant of amnesty for Vietnam War resisters, Reagan declared that the war had been a "noble cause" that the government had refused to win. Although Reagan did not repudiate Carter's human rights policy, he employed it in a renewed Cold War, highlighting the Soviet Union's mistreatment of its Jewish population and ethnic minorities.

The Defense Buildup

The United States, Reagan claimed, had "unilaterally disarmed" during the 1970s, while the Soviets had staged a massive military buildup. He denounced the "evil empire" of the Soviet Union and dismissed critics of his foreign policy as the "Blame-America-First Crowd." They were "the strangest collection of misfits, loony tunes, and squalid criminals since the advent of the Third Reich."

Closing what Reagan called America's "window of vulnerability" against Soviet military power proved expensive. Even though Reagan's tax cuts reduced government revenues, the White House sought dramatic increases in

military spending. The Pentagon launched programs to enlarge the Navy and to modernize strategic nuclear forces. It also deployed new missiles throughout Western Europe. At the height of Reagan's military buildup, the Pentagon was purchasing about 20 percent of the nation's manufacturing output.

In 1984, Reagan proposed the most expensive defense system in history—a space-based shield against any missile hurled toward the United States. Beginning as a nebulous hope, the Strategic Defense Initiative (SDI) soon had its own Pentagon agency that sought $26 billion, over five years, just for start-up research. Controversy swirled around SDI. Critics dubbed it "Star Wars" and shuddered at its astronomical costs. Although most scientists dismissed the initiative as impossible to implement, Congress voted appropriations for SDI, and Reagan steadfastly clung to the idea of a defensive shield. SDI dominated both strategic debates at home and arms talks with the Soviet Union.

Greater defense spending had another strategic dimension. Secretary of Defense Caspar Weinberger predicted that, as the Soviets increased the burden on their own faltering economy in order to compete in the accelerating arms race, the Soviet Union might collapse under the economic strain. This scenario, an implicit goal of the containment policy since the NSC-68 blueprint of 1950, increasingly tantalized the Reagan administration.

Reagan's foreign policy agenda included many nonmilitary initiatives. In a new "informational" offensive, the administration funded a variety of conservative groups around the world and established Radio Martí, a Florida station beamed at Cuba and designed to discredit Fidel Castro's communist government. When the United Nations agency UNESCO adopted an anti-American tone and called for a New World Information Order that would reduce the influence of U.S.-originated news and information, Reagan cut off U.S. contributions to UNESCO and demanded changes in UN operations. The Reagan administration also championed free markets, urging other nations to minimize tariffs and restrictions on foreign investment. The Caribbean Basin Initiative, for example, rewarded with U.S. aid those small nations in the Caribbean region that adhered to free-market principles.

The CIA, now headed by William Casey, stepped up its "covert" activities. Some of these became so obvious that they hardly qualified as covert. It was no secret, for example, that the United States sent aid to anticommunist forces in Afghanistan, many of them radical Muslim fundamentalist groups, and to the opponents of the Sandinista government in Nicaragua, the *contras*. At the time, however, Washington acknowledged neither the extent nor the nature of its assistance.

Deploying Military Power

In renewing a global Cold War, Reagan promised vigorous military support to "democratic" revolutions anywhere, a move designed to constrain the Soviet Union's sphere of influence. Reagan's UN representative, Jeane Kirkpatrick, wrote that "democratic" forces included almost any movement, no matter how autocratic, that was noncommunist. The United States thus funded opposition military movements in countries aligned with the Soviet Union: Ethiopia, Angola, South Yemen, Cambodia, Grenada, Cuba, Nicaragua, and Afghanistan. Reagan called the participants in such anticommunist insurgencies "freedom fighters," although few had any visible commitment to democratic values or institutions.

The Reagan administration also deployed U.S. military power, first in southern Lebanon in 1982. Here, Israeli troops were facing off against Lebanese Muslims supported by Syria and the Soviet Union. Alarmed by Muslim gains, the Reagan administration convinced Israel to withdraw and sent 1,600 American marines as part of a "peacekeeping force" to restore stability. Muslim fighters, however, turned against the Americans. After a suicide commando mission into a U.S. military compound killed 241 marines, Reagan decided that this ill-defined undertaking could never win public support. He subsequently pulled out U.S. troops and disengaged from Lebanon. Another military intervention seemed more successful. In October 1983, Reagan sent 2,000 U.S. troops to the tiny Caribbean island of Grenada, whose socialist leader was forging ties with Castro's Cuba. U.S. troops overthrew the government and installed one that was friendly to American interests.

Buoyed by Grenada, the Reagan administration fixed its sights on Nicaragua. Here, the Sandinista government was trying to strengthen ties with Cuba and to break Nicaragua's historic dependence on the United States. The Reagan administration responded by augmenting U.S. military forces in neighboring Honduras, conducting training exercises throughout Central America, stepping up a campaign of economic pressure and anti-Sandinista propaganda. Most important, it gave increased support to the *contras*. Meanwhile, the Reagan administration supported the harsh dictatorships in nearby El Salvador and Guatemala in order to prevent other leftist insurgencies from gaining ground in Central America.

These initiatives in Central America became the most controversial aspect of Reagan's foreign policy. Regimes supported by the Reagan administration were clearly implicated in human-rights abuses, not only against their own people but also against American nuns, journalists, and humanitarian-aid workers. Mounting evidence of brutality

and corruption among the Nicaraguan *contras* fueled growing criticism. In 1984, the Democratic-controlled Congress broke with the president's policy and barred further military aid to the *contras*.

The Reagan administration quickly sought to avoid the congressional ban. It encouraged wealthy American conservatives and foreign governments to donate money to the *contras*. In June 1984, at a top-secret meeting of the National Security Planning Group, Reagan and his top advisers discussed the legality of pressing "third parties" to contribute to the *contra* cause. Reagan ended the meeting with a bid for secrecy: "If such a story gets out, we'll all be hanging by our thumbs in front of the White House."

Meanwhile, violence continued to escalate throughout the Middle East. Militant Islamic groups increased attacks against Israel and Western powers; bombings and the kidnapping of Western hostages became more frequent. Apparently, Libya's Muammar al-Qaddafi and Iranian leaders encouraged such activities. In spring 1986, the United States launched an air strike into Libya against Qaddafi's personal compound. The bombs killed Qaddafi's young daughter, but Qaddafi and his government survived. Despite what looked like a long-range assassination attempt against a foreign leader (an action outlawed by Congress), Americans generally approved of using strong measures against sponsors of terrorism and hostage-taking.

The Iran-*Contra* Controversy

In November 1986, a magazine in Lebanon claimed that the Reagan administration was selling arms to Iran in order to secure the release of Americans being held hostage by Islamic militants. The alleged deal stood in clear conflict with the Reagan administration's pledge that it would not sell arms to Iran and would never reward hostage-taking by negotiating for the release of captives. During the 1980 campaign, Reagan had made hostages in Iran a symbol of U.S. weakness under Carter. When Iranian-backed groups continued to kidnap Americans during his presidency, it seemed that Reagan had begun seeking a clandestine way to recover hostages.

As Congress began to investigate the arms-for-hostages charge, matters turned even more bizarre. It appeared that the Reagan administration had not only sold arms to Iran but had channeled profits from these deals to the *contra* forces in Nicaragua as a means of circumventing the congressional ban on U.S. military aid. Oliver North, who worked in the office of the national security adviser, had directed the effort, working with shadowy international arms dealers and private go-betweens. North's covert machinations seemingly violated both the stated

policy of the White House and an act of Congress. Pundits soon dubbed the episode, reminiscent of the constitutional crisis of the Nixon era, as Irangate.

In the end, however, the Iran-*Contra* controversy never reached the proportions of Watergate. In contrast to Richard Nixon, who had temporized, Ronald Reagan stepped forward and testified (through a deposition) that he could remember no details about either the release of hostages or the funding of the *contras*. His management skills might deserve criticism, Reagan admitted, but he had intended to break no law or to violate any presidential promise. Meanwhile, Vice President George H. W. Bush, whom investigators initially linked to some of North's machinations, steadfastly claimed ignorance about any arms deals. Oliver North even became a New Right celebrity as a result of his artful dodging during televised hearings into the Iran-*Contra* affair. North had destroyed so many documents and had left so many false paper trails that congressional investigators struggled even to compile a simple narrative of events. North and several others connected to the Reagan administration were convicted of felonies, including falsification of documents and lying to Congress, but appellate courts later overturned these verdicts. Finally, in 1992, just a few days before the end of his presidency, George H. W. Bush pardoned six former Reagan-era officials connected to the Iran-*Contra* controversy.

The Beginning of the End of the Cold War

Although Reagan's first six years in office had revived the Cold War confrontation, his last two years saw a sudden thaw in U.S.–Soviet relations. The economic cost of superpower rivalry was burdening both nations. Moreover, changes within the Soviet Union were eliminating the reasons for confrontation. Mikhail Gorbachev, who became general secretary of the Communist Party in 1985, was a new style of Soviet leader. Gorbachev understood the challenge of technological change in Western democracies, as their economies and communications became globally integrated. He also realized that his isolated country faced economic stagnation and an environmental crisis brought on by decades of poorly planned industrial development. To redirect the Soviet Union's course, he withdrew Soviet troops from Afghanistan, reduced commitments to Cuba and Nicaragua, proclaimed a policy of *glasnost* ("openness"), and began to implement *perestroika* ("economic liberalization") at home.

Gorbachev's policies brought him acclaim throughout the West and stirred winds of change. He began summit meetings with the United States to discuss arms control. At Reykjavik, Iceland, in October 1986, Reagan shocked

both Gorbachev and his own advisers by proposing a wholesale ban on nuclear weapons. Although negotiations at Reykjavik stumbled over Gorbachev's insistence that the United States abandon its Star Wars program, the next year Gorbachev dropped that condition. In December 1987, Reagan and Gorbachev signed a major arms treaty that reduced each nation's supply of intermediate-range missiles and allowed for on-site verification, which the Soviets had never before permitted. The next year, Gorbachev scrapped the policy that forbade any nation under Soviet influence from renouncing communism. In effect, Gorbachev declared an end to the Cold War. Within the next few years, the Soviet sphere of influence—and the Soviet Union itself—would cease to exist.

The First Bush Presidency (1989–1993)

During his first term, Ronald Reagan became America's most popular president since Franklin Roosevelt, but even before the Iran-*Contra* affair, his presidential image and influence were beginning to fade. Even as some members of the New Right were criticizing the president for failing to vigorously support their agenda, economic problems—especially the growing federal deficit and disarray in the financial sector—sparked calls for more assured leadership from the White House. Despite criticism of Reagan's leadership at home, Cold War détente boosted the 1988 presidential prospects of his heir-apparent, Vice President George H. W. Bush.

The Election of 1988

Bush easily gained the Republican nomination. Born into a prominent Republican family and educated at Yale, Bush had moved from Connecticut to Texas and entered the oil business as a young man. His lengthy political résumé included time in the House of Representatives and a stint as director of the CIA. To court the New Right, which was decidedly lukewarm to his candidacy, Bush chose Senator J. Danforth Quayle, a staunch conservative better known for his golfing prowess than his legislative skills, as a running mate. Suddenly elevated into the national spotlight, the youthful senator from Indiana delighted political comedians, who found his verbal blunders a rich source for new material.

Governor Michael Dukakis of Massachusetts emerged as the Democratic presidential candidate. Hoping to distance himself from the disastrous Democratic effort in 1984, Dukakis avoided talk of new domestic programs and higher taxes. Instead, he spoke about bringing competence and honesty to the White House and boasted of knowing, as a result of his gubernatorial experience, how to mobilize private expertise and to handle economic matters. Dukakis gambled that a cautious campaign, devoid of bold promises, could defeat Bush, who lacked Reagan's charisma.

The election of 1988, the last of the Cold War era, became best known for its negative campaigning, especially by Republican strategists. Pro-Bush television commercials usually presented Dukakis bathed in shadows and always showed him with a frown on his face. The campaign's most infamous ad linked Dukakis to Willie Horton, an African American inmate who had been charged with rape while on furlough from a Massachusetts prison. While seeming to play "the race card," the ad charged that Dukakis, whom Bush identified as a "card-carrying member of the American Civil Liberties Union," was soft on crime. As one media analyst quipped, the Bush campaign almost made it appear that Willie Horton was Dukakis's running mate.

Bush did emerge the winner in 1988 but by a relatively narrow margin. A quick glance at the 1988 returns might suggest that he had comfortably carried both the popular vote and the electoral college. Yet, the Republican ticket carried so many states by such a small margin that several relatively minor shifts in voter turnouts, especially among black and Latino voters who failed to support Dukakis as enthusiastically as they had backed Mondale four years earlier, could have given the victory to the Democrats. Dukakis bested Mondale's 1984 performance with 111 electoral votes. Outside the South, which Bush swept, Dukakis carried more than 500 counties that had supported Reagan in 1984. Overall, voter turnout was the lowest of any national election since 1924, and polls suggested that many voters considered neither George H. W. Bush nor Michael Dukakis worthy of being president. At the same time, their ballots allowed the Democrats to retain control of both houses of Congress.

Although the New Right hoped Bush would build on the Reagan presidency, his campaign prompted distrust about his commitment to its agenda. Might not his campaign slogan about a "kinder, gentler America" imply a veiled criticism of Reagan's domestic policies? Could conservatives believe Bush when he promised "no new taxes"? Once in the White House, Bush angered the New Right by agreeing to an increase in the minimum wage and by failing to veto the Civil Rights Act of 1991, a law that critics charged with establishing "quotas" for the "preferential hiring" of women and people of color in business and government. Most important, in 1990, Bush apparently broke his antitax pledge, the issue on which New Right leaders came to judge his worthiness as Reagan's successor, when

he agreed to an upward revision in tax rates in order to deal with the rising federal deficit. Although Bush's move began a process that would eventually temporarily eliminate the deficit, the New Right bitterly denounced his decision.

Meanwhile, the national government, divided between a Democratic-controlled Congress and a Republican-occupied White House, increasingly appeared to suffer from gridlock. Any hope of addressing key domestic issues, especially reorganization of the health care and social welfare systems, vanished. Worse, the economic growth of the Reagan years began slowing, and the budget deficit continued expanding. George H. W. Bush's chances for a second term seemed to depend on his record in foreign, rather than domestic, policy.

The End of the Cold War

During the first Bush presidency, the Soviet Union collapsed. As other communist states toppled like dominoes, the international order underwent its greatest transformation since the end of the Second World War.

Beginning in 1989, political change swept through Eastern and Central Europe. In Poland, the anticommunist labor party, Solidarity, ousted the pro-Soviet regime. The pro-Moscow government in East Germany fell in November 1989, and both West and East Germans hacked down the Berlin Wall. Divided since the Second World War, Germany began the difficult process of reunification. Popular movements similarly forced out communist governments throughout Eastern Europe. Yugoslavia quickly disintegrated, and warfare ensued as rival ethnic groups re-created separate states in Slovenia, Serbia, Bosnia, and Croatia. The Baltic countries of Latvia, Lithuania, and Estonia, which had been under Soviet control since the Second World War, declared their independence. Most dramatic, the major provinces that had constituted the Soviet Union assumed self-government. The president of the new state of Russia, Boris Yeltsin, put down a coup by hard-line communists in August 1991, and he soon solidified his political position. In December 1991, the Russian Parliament ratified Yeltsin's plan to abolish the Soviet Union and replace it with 11 republics, loosely joined in a commonwealth arrangement.

As the map of Europe changed, the United States needed to create diplomatic relations with the new countries. In December 1991, Congress authorized $400 million for helping the Soviet Union's successor states, especially Ukraine, dismantle their nuclear weaponry, and it later allotted an equivalent amount for promoting democracy in the new European states.

More broadly, the administration of George H. W. Bush pressed a program of international economic integration. During the mid-1980s, huge debts that Third World nations owed to U.S. banks had threatened the international banking system, but most of these obligations had been renegotiated by 1990. Market economies, which replaced centrally controlled ones, began to emerge in the former communist states; Western Europe moved toward economic integration; and the nations of the Pacific Rim were seeing steady economic growth. At the same time, President Bush pressed for the North American Free Trade

BERLIN WALL, 1989

Berliners celebrated the end of the Cold War by chiseling away at the Berlin Wall, which the communist East German state had erected in 1962 to prevent the flow of refugees to West Berlin. Pieces of the Berlin Wall became coveted symbols of the fall of communism.

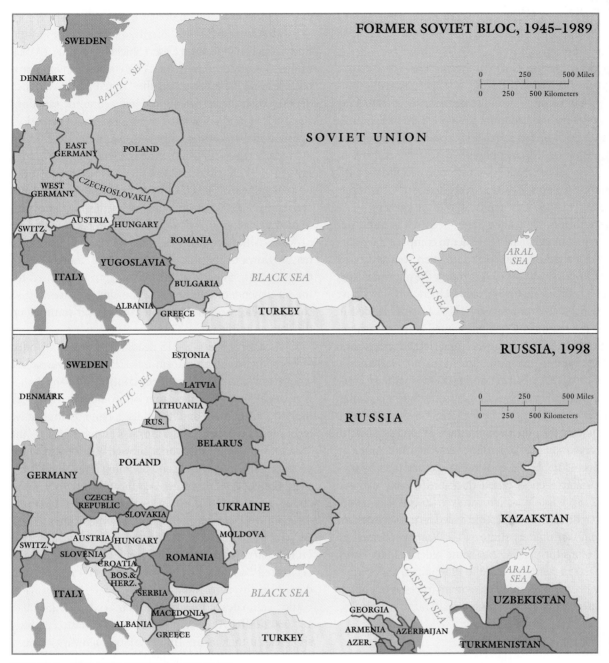

MAP 31.3 COLLAPSE OF THE SOVIET BLOC

These contrasting maps show the Soviet Union and the countries it dominated before and after the fall of communist governments. What countries in Eastern Europe escaped Russian control after 1989? What new countries emerged out of the old Soviet Union?

Agreement (NAFTA), which would eliminate tariff barriers and join Canada, the United States, and Mexico in the largest free-market zone in the world.

As the likelihood of armed conflict with the Soviet Union faded, the Bush administration also set about redefining national security. The end of the Cold War weakened support for the leftist insurgencies in Central America that had preoccupied the Reagan administration.

Nicaraguans voted the Sandinistas, who became just another political party in a multiparty system, out of office. Supported by the United States, the United Nations assisted both El Salvador and Guatemala in turning their armed conflicts into electoral ones. The Pentagon pondered new missions for its military forces. Future action, its planners predicted, would take the form of rapid, sharply targeted strikes rather than lengthy military campaigns.

The armed forces might even serve in the "war against drugs," an effort that Bush had promised during his 1988 presidential campaign.

General Manuel Noriega, the president of Panama, was deeply involved in the drug trade. The Reagan administration had secured an indictment for drug trafficking against Noriega and had mounted a program of economic pressure, which only deepened his reliance on drug revenue. Confronting Noriega posed a potentially embarrassing problem for the Bush administration because the anticommunist general had been recruited as a CIA "asset" during the mid-1970s, when Bush was the agency's director. Nevertheless, the United States needed a friendly, stable government in Panama in order to complete the transfer of the Panama Canal to Panamanian sovereignty by 2000, and Bush finally decided to topple the mercurial Noriega. In a military incursion called Operation Just Cause and broadcast live on television, U.S. Marines landed in Panama in December 1989, pinpointed Noriega's whereabouts, and laid siege to his headquarters. Noriega soon surrendered, faced extradition to Florida, and was imprisoned in 1992 after a conviction for trafficking in cocaine.

Although a relatively minor episode, the Panamanian operation carried major implications. On the one hand, using military force in a region that was long sensitive to U.S. intervention sparked controversy in Latin America, and deposing the leader of a foreign government by unilateral military action raised questions of international law. Yet, this episode, which involved 25,000 U.S. troops but brought few casualties, provided a new model for post–Cold War military strategy. The Pentagon firmed up existing plans for phasing out some older military bases, particularly in Germany and the Philippines, and for creating highly mobile, rapid deployment forces. A test of this new strategy came in the Persian Gulf War.

The Persian Gulf War

On August 2, 1990, President Saddam Hussein of Iraq ordered his troops to occupy the neighboring, oil-rich emirate of Kuwait. Within a day, Iraq's forces had taken control of Kuwait, a move that caught the United States off guard. Although Iraq had been moving troops to its border with Kuwait and denouncing Kuwaiti producers for cooperating with U.S. oil interests, American intelligence forecasters had not expected an immediate invasion. Now, however, they warned that Iraq's next target might be Saudi Arabia, the largest oil exporter in the Middle East and a longtime ally of the United States.

Moving swiftly, Bush orchestrated a multilateral, international response. He convinced the Saudi government, initially concerned about allowing Western troops on sacred Islamic soil, to accept a U.S. military presence in Saudi Arabia. Four days after Iraq's invasion of Kuwait, Bush launched Operation Desert Shield by sending 230,000 troops to protect Saudi Arabia. After consulting with European leaders, he approached the United Nations, which denounced Iraqi aggression, ordered economic sanctions against Iraq, and authorized the United States to lead an international force to restore the government of Kuwait if Saddam Hussein's troops had not withdrawn by January 15, 1991. Bush assembled a massive coalition force, ultimately nearly 500,000 troops from the United States and some 200,000 from other countries. He also persuaded Congress to approve a resolution backing the use of force. Although Bush claimed a moral obligation to rescue Kuwait, his policy makers spoke frankly about the economic threat that Hussein's aggression posed for the oil-dependent economies of the United States and its coalition allies. Secretary of State James Baker summed up the danger in one word: "Jobs."

Just after the January 15 deadline passed, the United States launched an air war on Iraq. "Pools" of journalists, whose movements were carefully controlled by the Pentagon, highlighted the new role of women in America's modernized military and hailed its apparently innovative technology, especially the antimissile missile called the "Patriot." Television networks showed Patriots, in video game fashion, intercepting and downing Iraqi "Scud" missiles. (Later, careful studies significantly revised claims about the stellar performance of the Patriot missiles.) After six weeks of devastating aerial bombardment, General Colin Powell ordered a ground offensive against Iraq on February 24. Coalition forces, enjoying air supremacy, decimated Saddam Hussein's armies over the next four days. U.S. casualties were relatively light (148 deaths in battle). Estimates of Iraqi casualties ranged from 25,000 to 100,000 deaths. Although the conflict had lasted scarcely six weeks, it took an enormous toll on highways, bridges, communications, and other infrastructure facilities in both Iraq and Kuwait.

In a controversial decision, Bush stopped short of ousting Saddam Hussein, a goal that the UN had never approved and that military advisers had considered costly to achieve. Instead, the United States, backed by the UN, maintained its economic pressure, ordered the dismantling of Iraq's nuclear and bacteriological capabilities, and enforced "no-fly" zones over northern and southern Iraq to help protect the Kurds and Shi'a Muslims from Hussein's continued persecution. The Persian Gulf War temporarily boosted George H. W. Bush's popularity and seemed to assure his reelection in 1992.

Yet, with a second term resting on his international record, Bush seemed increasingly unable to articulate

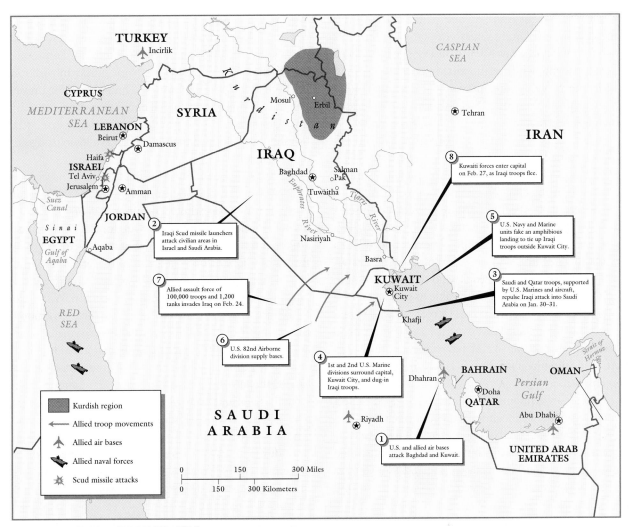

MAP 31.4 PERSIAN GULF WAR, 1991

After Iraq invaded Kuwait, the United States marshaled forces in neighboring areas to attack. Notice the positioning of U.S. air, naval, and land forces. What countries hosted American bases?

long-term strategic goals for a post–Cold War world. Turmoil broke out in some of the former Soviet provinces, and Russia struggled to develop an economy based on private property and market mechanisms. Full-scale warfare erupted among the states of the former Yugoslavia, with Serbs launching a brutal campaign of territorial aggrandizement and "ethnic cleansing" against Bosnian Muslims. In the Far East, Japan's still-growing economy prompted Americans to grumble about "unfair" competition. In Africa, when severe famine struck the country of Somalia, Bush ordered U.S. troops to establish humanitarian supply lines, but the American public remained wary of this military mission.

Ultimately, voters judged Bush's record on foreign affairs as something of a muddle. He assembled and held together an international coalition against Iraq, construc-

tively assisted the transition in Russia and Eastern Europe at the end of the Cold War, and advanced a global process of economic integration. As the old reference points of containing the Soviet Union disappeared between 1989 and 1992, however, George H. W. Bush failed to effectively articulate a new vision that could inspire people and firmly establish his reputation as a world leader.

The Election of 1992

The inability to portray a coherent vision of either domestic or foreign policy threatened Bush's reelection and forced concessions to the New Right. Dan Quayle, although clearly a liability with voters outside his conservative constituency, returned as Bush's running mate. The president allowed New Right activists, who talked about "a religious

war" for "the soul of America" and pictured Democrats as the enemies of "family values," to dominate the 1992 Republican national convention. Conservative Democrats and independents, who had supported Ronald Reagan and Bush in the previous three presidential elections, found this rhetoric no substitute for policies that addressed domestic concerns, particularly the sluggish economy.

Bush's Democratic challenger, Governor William Jefferson Clinton of Arkansas, zeroed in on economic issues. Bill Clinton promised to increase governmental spending for job creation and long-term economic growth. Addressing a concern that cut across partisan lines, he promised a comprehensive revision of the nation's health care system. On other domestic issues, Clinton almost sounded like a Republican. "It's time to end this [welfare] system as we know it," Clinton insisted. "People who can work ought to go to work, and no one should be able to stay on welfare forever." He campaigned as a "new Democrat" who would reduce taxes for middle-class Americans, cut the federal deficit, and shrink the size of government. Clinton, in short, made it difficult for Bush to label him as a "big government liberal."

A focus on economic questions also helped deflect attention from the sociocultural issues on which Bill Clinton was vulnerable. As a college student, he had not only avoided service in Vietnam but had also demonstrated against the Vietnam War while in England as a Rhodes Scholar. When Bush, a decorated veteran of the Second World War, challenged Clinton's patriotism, Clinton countered by emphasizing, rather than repudiating, his roots in the 1960s. He campaigned on MTV and touted his affection for (relatively soft) rock music. In addition, he chose Senator Albert Gore of Tennessee, a Vietnam veteran, as his running mate. Bill and Hillary Rodham Clinton acknowledged past problems in their personal relationship but defended their marriage as a loving, ongoing partnership.

The 1992 election brought Bill Clinton a surprisingly easy victory. The quixotic campaign of Ross Perot, a billionaire from Texas who spent more than $60 million of his own money on a third-party run for the White House, attracted 19 million popular, but no electoral, votes. Perot's candidacy, which denounced the "mess" in Washington and urged people to "take back our country," likely hurt insider Bush more than outsider Clinton. With Perot in the race, Clinton garnered only 43 percent of the popular vote but won 370 electoral votes by carrying 32 states and the District of Columbia. Bush won a majority only among white Protestants in the South. In contrast, Clinton carried the Jewish, African American, and Latino vote by large margins and even gained a plurality among people who had served in the Vietnam War. He also ran well among independents who had supported Reagan and Bush during the 1980s. Perhaps most surprising, about 55 percent of eligible voters went to the polls, a turnout that reversed 32 years of steady decline in voter participation.

🌐 The Presidency of Bill Clinton (1993–2001)

Bill Clinton, the first Democratic president in 12 years and the first chief executive from the baby boom generation, brought an image of youth, vitality, and cultural diversity to Washington. The inaugural celebration included different balls for different musical tastes; one (broadcast live on MTV) featured rock 'n' roll from the Vietnam War era. Clinton's initial cabinet included three African Americans and two Latinos; three cabinet posts went to women. His first nominee to the Supreme Court was Ruth Bader Ginsburg, only the second woman to sit on the Court. As representative to the United Nations, Clinton named Madeleine Albright, who would become the country's first female secretary of state during his second term.

Clinton's First Two Years

Clinton gave his supporters several victories on domestic issues. He ended the Reagan era's ban on abortion counseling in family planning clinics; pushed through Con-

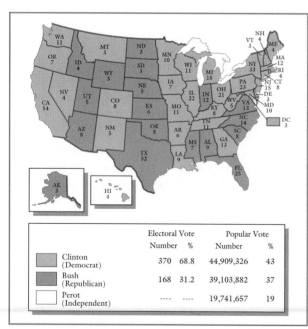

MAP 31.5 PRESIDENTIAL ELECTION, 1992

Notice the substantial number of votes cast for an independent candidate, Ross Perot. How did Perot's vote totals affect the mandate that Bill Clinton had as president?

		Electoral Vote		Popular Vote	
		Number	%	Number	%
	Clinton (Democrat)	370	68.8	44,909,326	43
	Bush (Republican)	168	31.2	39,103,882	37
	Perot (Independent)	----	----	19,741,657	19

CLINTON WAILS SAX DURING HIS PRESIDENTIAL CAMPAIGN

Bill Clinton eagerly identified himself as a New Democrat and as a member of the rock 'n' roll generation.

included a provision that expanded an existing governmental program, called the earned tax credit, which provided annual cash bonuses to low-income workers with children.

In contrast, Clinton's hope of reshaping the nation's health care system quickly collapsed. Hillary Rodham Clinton led a task force that produced a complex plan that few people understood; even worse, virtually no one liked what they could decipher. Republicans effectively used the health care proposal, which quickly died in Congress, to paint Clinton as just another advocate of big government. Meanwhile, talk-radio shows, especially that of arch-conservative Rush Limbaugh, featured nonstop criticism of the Clinton White House for bungling the health care issue and for raising taxes. As the welfare rolls soared to an all-time high of 14.4 million people in 1994, Clinton delayed any effort at an overhaul.

Clinton also faced personal problems. Hillary Rodham Clinton's prominent role in the failed heath care effort fueled criticism of her public activities. The Clintons' joint involvement in financial dealings in Arkansas—particularly those connected to a bankrupt savings and loan institution and to a failed land development called Whitewater—drew criticism. In August 1994, a three-judge panel appointed Kenneth Starr, a conservative Republican, to replace the independent prosecutor appointed in January. Charged with investigating the Whitewater affair, Starr moved aggressively to expand his inquiry into new allegations and seemed intent on securing an indictment against at least one of the Clintons.

A Republican Congress, A Democratic White House

The November 1994 elections brought a dramatic, unexpected GOP victory that was spearheaded by New Right strategists, particularly Newt Gingrich, a member of Congress from Georgia. Republicans secured control of both houses of Congress for the first time in 40 years; they won several new governorships, gained ground in most state legislatures, and made significant headway in many city and county elections, particularly across the South. Newt Gingrich hailed these gains as a mandate for an ambitious agenda that the New Right called a Contract with America. It aimed at rolling back federal spending and a variety of governmental programs and regulations.

Congressional Republicans, however, soon overplayed their hand. Opinion polls suggested that people distrusted Gingrich, who became Speaker of the House of Representatives, more than they did Clinton. Moreover, surveys also showed little support for the immediate "revolution" against federal programs that Gingrich and the New Right

gress a family leave program for working parents; established the Americorps program, which allowed students to repay their college loans through community service; and secured passage of the Brady Bill, which instituted a five-day waiting period on handgun purchases. Limited college-loan and youth training programs also received funding. An anticrime bill, passed in 1994, provided federal funds to put more police officers on the streets; it also contained more money for prison construction and a controversial "three strikes and you're out" provision, which mandated a lifetime prison sentence for a third felony conviction.

Clinton obtained new economic legislation. His 1993 deficit-reduction plan, which required a tie-breaking vote of Vice President Al Gore to pass the Senate, featured a tax-increase and spending-cut package aimed at reducing the federal deficit and eventually lowering interest rates as a means of stimulating economic growth. The plan also

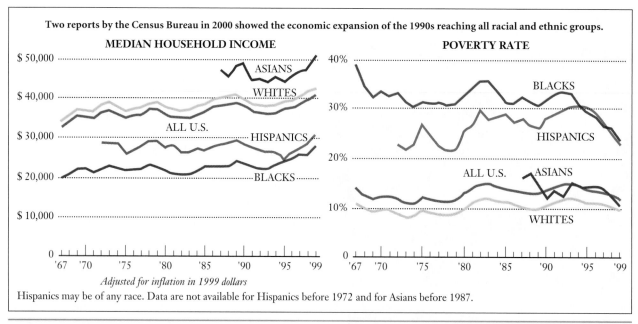

Two reports by the Census Bureau in 2000 showed the economic expansion of the 1990s reaching all racial and ethnic groups.

Adjusted for inflation in 1999 dollars

Hispanics may be of any race. Data are not available for Hispanics before 1972 and for Asians before 1987.

INCOME AND POVERTY IN THE LATE 20TH CENTURY

were seeking. When conflict between the Democratic president and the GOP Congress over budget issues led to two brief shutdowns of many government agencies, most people blamed congressional Republicans, rather than the Clinton White House, for the situation.

Most important, a revived U.S. economy buoyed Clinton's presidency. Alan Greenspan, chairman of the Federal Reserve Board, gained a reputation for economic wizardry, particularly for his ability to keep inflation in check through adroit management of interest rates. Low rates of inflation, accompanied by steady economic growth, spurred millions of new jobs. The stock market, before forming a speculative "bubble" at the end of the 1990s, soared. Old-line Democrats often complained that benefits of this Clinton-era expansion were distributed unequally. The agricultural economy continued to push smaller farmers off the land; the gap between earnings of corporate executives and ordinary workers grew steadily larger; and the wealthiest 10 percent of households still owned 90 percent of the nation's stockholdings. Yet, most people did see their economic fortunes improve. Unemployment figures fell steadily, and real income began to grow for the first time in nearly 15 years.

An overhaul of the social welfare system boosted Clinton's political capital. The president, whose 1996 State of the Union address declared that "the era of big government is over," and congressional Republicans cooperated on the long-delayed welfare issue. The Personal Responsibility and Work Opportunity Reconciliation Act of 1996 represented a series of compromises that pleased Republicans more than Democrats. Relatively uncontroversial

sections of the law tightened collection of child support payments and reorganized nutrition and child-care programs. Clinton, while voicing concern about provisions that cut the food stamp program and benefits for recent immigrants, embraced the law's central feature. It replaced the AFDC program, which provided funds and basic social services to poor families headed by single unemployed women, with a flexible system of block grants to individual states. Under the new program, entitled Temporary Assistance to Needy Families (TANF), the 50 states were to design, under broad federal guidelines, their own welfare-to-work programs.

TANF, which effectively replaced the national welfare system created during the New Deal and Great Society, provoked bitter controversy. Its proponents claimed that TANF would encourage states to experiment with new programs that would reduce their welfare costs and create job opportunities. Critics worried that its provisions, including those that limited a person to five years of government assistance during his or her lifetime and authorized states to cut off support if recipients failed to find employment within two years, underestimated the difficulty that people without job skills faced. They also feared the impact that TANF might have on the daily lives of children, especially if states provided inadequate child care, nutritional, and medical care programs. By deferring any protracted debate over these difficult issues, however, the new welfare law effectively removed several potential domestic issues from the political campaign of 1996, a turn that especially helped Bill Clinton.

The huge growth in the productivity of workers, partly due to the computer revolution, buttressed the economic boom of the late 1990s.

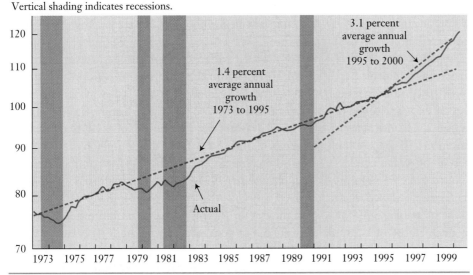

Output per hour in the nonfarm business sector
Index, 1992 = 100
Vertical shading indicates recessions.

PRODUCTIVITY GROWTH, 1973–2000

Sources: Department of Commerce (Bureau of Economic Analysis) and Department of Labor (Bureau of Labor Statistics).

Victory and Impeachment

The election of 1996 capped Clinton's political comeback. Clinton and Gore, riding the economic expansion, defeated Republicans Robert Dole and Jack Kemp by about the same margin they had beaten George H. W. Bush and Dan Quayle in 1992. Clinton, the first Democratic president since Franklin Roosevelt to win back-to-back terms, continued to run especially well among African Americans, women, and Hispanic voters. Republicans did retain control of Congress and gained several new governorships, but Democrats still held a majority of the seats in the 50 state legislatures, a sign that many voters believed that ticket-splitting (voting for both Democrats and Republicans) need not produce gridlock.

After the election, Clinton and congressional Republicans cooperated by passing legislation that established a timetable for reducing the federal deficit. Clinton's 1998 State of the Union address proclaimed that the budget deficit would inevitably disappear, and the president began to negotiate with congressional Republicans about what to do with potential surpluses. He also launched a "national conversation" about racial issues, pressed for programs to improve education, and secured a measure extending health care coverage to several million children from low-income families. The White House even seemed poised, in early 1998, to work with congressional Republicans on reshaping Social Security and Medicare programs.

The nation's political life during 1998 and early 1999, however, revolved not around legislative initiatives but around charges about the president's personal behavior. Kenneth Starr's inquiry finally narrowed to the question of whether the president had been concealing sexual encounters with female employees. Although Clinton unequivocally denied wrongdoing, Republicans pressed forward, claiming that Clinton's efforts to fend off Starr amounted to "obstruction of justice." In response, the president's defenders charged Starr with pursuing a partisan vendetta and with coordinating his efforts with that of New Right activists, especially those bankrolling a civil lawsuit that charged Clinton with sexual harassment while serving as governor of Arkansas. Internet sites and 24/7 cable news channels—relatively new additions to the informational matrix—competed to provide the latest tidbits on the Clinton-Starr battle. Meanwhile, with economic statistics continuing to show solid growth, Clinton's approval ratings rose, while Starr's plummeted.

The president's denials of any personal indiscretion crumbled after Starr obtained irrefutable evidence of his relationship with a young intern named Monica Lewinsky. Facing both a widening criminal investigation and a lingering civil lawsuit, the president's problems went beyond personal embarrassment. Republican opponents insisted that his public actions, particularly a deposition in the lawsuit for sexual harassment (which a federal judge had actually dismissed in April 1998), justified his ouster from the White House. Democrats denounced Clinton's behavior

but insisted that his private failings hardly merited removal from public office. Partisan passions, both inside Congress and in the media, intensified as political invective mingled with legal debate over what constituted the kind of "high crimes and misdemeanors" that the Constitution required for the impeachment of a president.

Throughout all of the controversy, Clinton's approval rating, which remained consistently higher than those of any of his Republican critics, provided a formidable barrier against his ouster from the presidency. After making Clinton their primary target during the off-year election of 1998, the GOP actually lost five seats in the House of Representatives. (For the first time since 1934, the opposition party failed to gain House seats in an off-year election.) Even worse for the New Right, Clinton's main antagonist in Congress, House Speaker Newt Gingrich, resigned when a long-term extramarital affair became public. Still, the Republican majority in the lame-duck House of Representatives sent two articles of impeachment (one for perjury and another for obstruction of justice) against Clinton to the Senate on December 19, 1998. Although no one expected that Republicans could attract enough Democratic senators to secure the two-thirds vote required by the Constitution to remove Clinton, only the second president in U.S. history to face an impeachment trial, bipartisan attempts to find an alternative sanction failed. After a month-long trial, which concluded on February 12, 1999, Republican senators failed to muster even a bare majority on either article of impeachment.

Clinton's popularity actually grew during and after the impeachment imbroglio. Economic growth, carefully watched over by Alan Greenspan, continued. Unemployment dropped under 4 percent for the first time in more than 30 years, and the economic expansion that began during the Bush presidency and lasted more than eight years ranked as the longest in U.S. history. Crime statistics dropped dramatically, and the welfare rolls shrank to one-seventh of their 1994 high, or 2.2 million families. The earned income tax credit, whose expansion the president had obtained in 1993, provided more than $30 billion in federal assistance to low-income workers with families. On the eve of Clinton's departure from office, nearly 70 percent of poll respondents believed he had been an effective political leader.

On the surface, the national political climate seemed to change between 1992 and 2000. Clinton and other New Democrats succeeded in reviving their party's fortunes. Once reviled by Ronald Reagan as the party of the "misery index," the Democrats became associated with economic growth, full employment, low inflation, and fiscal responsibility. The White House and congressional Republicans even found common ground on issues such as overhauling the welfare system and reducing the federal deficit. A person who generated bitter enemies, Clinton also engendered equally fervent support, particularly from African Americans. Author Toni Morrison joked that Clinton, who had grown up in a multiracial community, might be considered the nation's first "black president." The success of the earned income tax credit allowed Clinton to retain a strong base among low-income families. Polls indicated that, overall, Americans lost some of their previous cynicism about government.

The percentage of the public who approved of the way the presidents handled the economy clearly correlates with the unemployment rate. Note the rise in unemployment around 1982, 1992, and 2002, and the presidential approval ratings for those same years.

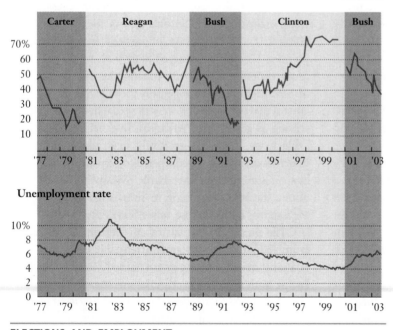

ELECTIONS AND EMPLOYMENT

Environmental Policy

Clinton's years in office expanded environmental protection. His administration negotiated plans to manage and protect old-growth forests in the Pacific Northwest, to implement a conservation framework in nine national forests in the Sierra Nevada,

and to handle the crowds of tourists in Yosemite National Park. In more controversial moves, Clinton's secretary of the interior, Bruce Babbitt, set aside 16 new national monuments and blocked road construction and logging in 58 million acres of wild areas in national forests. Building on records of his Republican predecessors, his administration placed 5.6 million new surface and underwater acres under federal protection. New approaches to environmental management often sought to promote change through incentives rather than penalties. In 1997, for example, the Conservation Reserve Program, a farm subsidy program that previously paid farmers to remove land from tillage, now extended payment to farmers who would restore wetlands on their properties in order to decrease polluted runoff into streams and preserve wildlife habitat.

The U.S. government, however, often seemed to be one of the country's most flagrant polluters. Toward the end of the Reagan administration, the secretary of energy had admitted that the government's nuclear facilities had been lax in enforcing safety measures and estimated that cleanup would cost more than $1 billion. The revelation of hazardous conditions at sites where atomic weapons had been produced shocked nearby residents, who feared they might have suffered radiation poisoning. Workers at the sites had been inadequately warned about radiation, even though government officials knew of its dangers. Moreover, medical records, long suppressed by the government, revealed that people living downwind of nuclear test sites in the 1940s and 1950s had experienced an abnormally high incidence of cancer, leukemia, and thyroid disorders. In 1993, Clinton's new energy secretary released records relating to radiation testing and experimentation and promised programs to inform and compensate victims. The legacy of other kinds of military-related toxic pollutants also became evident as many of the nation's bases were closed down during the 1990s.

The environmental movement increasingly focused on international, as well as national, ecological dangers. Those hazards included global warming (the "greenhouse effect"); holes in the ozone layer caused by chlorofluorocarbons (CFCs); massive deforestation and desertification with accompanying climatic changes; pollution of the oceans; and the rapid decline of biological diversity among both plant and animal species. A so-called Earth Summit was held in Brazil in 1992, and a conference in Cairo in 1994 took up global population issues. Fear that environmental restrictions could harm economic growth and disagreements over mechanisms to measure and enforce agreed-on targets, however, slowed the progress of the international environmental movement. Solutions to global problems required worldwide cooperation toward "sustainable development," and international meetings on environmental issues became more frequent. Conventions in Vienna in 1985, Montreal in 1987, London in 1990, Kyoto in 1997, and The Hague in 2000 worked toward establishing international standards on emissions of CFCs and greenhouse gases.

AIR QUALITY IN LOS ANGELES: GOOD DAYS AND BAD

During the 1960s, before the introduction of federal air-quality laws, a layer of thick smog that endangered public health hung over the Los Angeles basin 80 percent of the time. By the late 1990s, *left,* **the bad old days seemed to be over. Yet, enough bad days still occurred,** *right,* **that during two of every five days the air quality level failed to meet minimum safety levels, despite the introduction of pollution controls.**

Post–Cold War Foreign Policy

For nearly a half century, anticommunism and rivalry with the Soviet Union had shaped U.S. foreign policy. The United States now began to redefine national security. Throughout his presidency, Bill Clinton articulated an expansive, internationalist vision: promoting free-market policies, improving relations with the UN, expanding NATO, advancing human rights and democracy abroad, reducing nuclear threats, and working on global environmental and health concerns. Critics charged that his administration lacked any overall vision or framework; defenders claimed that Clinton's apparent flexibility was a virtue in the fragmented post–Cold War world.

One of the most perplexing issues involved when, and under what conditions, to use U.S. military power in localized conflicts. Several trouble spots sparked debate. In Somalia, U.S. troops, under the umbrella of a UN mission, had been assisting a humanitarian effort to provide food and relief supplies for that African nation since May 1992. The effort, however, cost the lives of 18 American servicemen, who were killed in factional fighting. Under heavy domestic criticism for undertaking an ill-defined mission, Clinton ordered a pullout during spring 1994. The next year, recalling criticism over Somalia, Clinton withheld support from a UN peacekeeping effort in Rwanda, where 500,000 Tutsis died during a genocidal civil war.

In Haiti, closer to home, U.S. interests seemed clearer, and Clinton vowed to help reinstall the ousted president, Jean-Bertrand Aristide. In September 1994, U.S. troops, in cooperation with the UN, landed in Haiti. Last-minute negotiations by former president Jimmy Carter persuaded the Haitian military to step aside. After six months, with Aristide back in office, the United States handed over responsibility for keeping civil order to UN forces.

The United States, through NATO, also sent troops into former Yugoslavia to stop Bosnian Serbs from massacring Bosnian Muslims. The U.S. military remained in Bosnia to oversee a cease-fire and peace-building process in the U.S.-brokered Dayton (Ohio) accords of 1995.

In March 1999, Clinton supported a NATO bombing campaign in Kosovo, a province of Serbia. NATO leaders and Clinton insisted that this controversial use of military force was necessary to protect ethnic Albanian Muslims, who constituted nearly 90 percent of Kosovo's population, from an "ethnic cleansing" program directed by Serbia's president Slobodan Milosevic. As NATO's bombs systematically decimated Serbia's economic infrastructure, Milosevic stepped up his campaign and forced hundreds of thousands of ethnic Albanians to flee from Kosovo into neighboring countries. Finally, in June 1999, after 78 days

of bombardment, Serbia withdrew its forces and, watched over by NATO troops, ethnic Albanians returned to Kosovo. In fall 2000, Serbs repudiated Milosevic, turned him out of office, and elected a president who was more friendly to multiethnic democracy and to the West. As in Bosnia, however, American and other allied troops remained as peacekeepers.

These military initiatives provoked controversy in the United States. Republican critics accused Clinton of an erratic policy with no clear guiding principles about when and how to employ force. They were especially suspicious of cooperation with UN forces and sought clearer exit strategies. Defenders of Clinton's policy continued to argue that flexibility and working with allied forces were strengths, not weaknesses, in the post–Cold War world. In 2000, disputes over a military assistance operation called Plan Colombia, undertaken to combat drug cartels and guerrilla fighters in that country, suggested that the issue of when and how to organize military intervention would remain a contentious one.

Clinton's post–Cold War agenda also included working to promote accords among antagonists in the trouble spots of Northern Ireland and the Middle East. In summer 2000, Clinton brought Israeli and Palestinian heads of state to Camp David in an unsuccessful effort to broker peace, an issue to which he devoted his energy in the closing hours of his administration.

Clinton sought to shape new policies on weapons of mass destruction and terrorism. He dismantled some of the U.S. nuclear arsenal and tried to curtail the potential danger from other nuclear powers. When the former Soviet Union's nuclear stockpile became dispersed among several independent states, the Clinton administration feared dangerous weapons might find their way onto the black market and into the hands of terrorists. In early 1994, it increased economic aid to Ukraine, then the third greatest nuclear power in the world, in return for promises to disarm its 1,600 warheads. In the same year, highly secret Project Sapphire transferred enriched uranium stocks from Kazakhstan to storage facilities in the United States. Jimmy Carter helped negotiate a complicated agreement with North Korea over nuclear weapons, signed in 1994. In return for American help in constructing safe, light-water nuclear reactors for its energy needs, North Korea agreed to begin dismantling its nuclear program and permit international inspections, promises it later violated. The United States also successfully pressed many nations to sign a new Nuclear Nonproliferation Treaty in spring 1995. In early 1998, Clinton went to the brink of war with Iraq to maintain international inspections of Saddam Hussein's weapons programs, but after enduring punishing air

Madeleine Albright: A Woman on the World Stage

The second woman to represent the United States as its ambassador to the United Nations and the first to serve as Secretary of State, Madeleine Albright (1937–) took a circuitous route to diplomatic fame. Born Marie Jana Korbel in Czechoslovakia, she left for Great Britain during the 1930s when her father, a prominent Czech diplomat, took his family out of the reach of the Nazis. After the communist coup of 1948 ended a brief return to Czechoslovakia, the family of Joseph Korbel settled in Denver, Colorado, where he became a college professor. Madeleine, now a teenager, attended a private school for girls.

After graduating from Wellesley College, Madeleine married journalist Joseph Albright in 1959 and devoted much of the 1960s to raising three children. At the same time, though, she began graduate study at Columbia University under the tutelage of Zbigniew Brzezinski. Initially a firm supporter of U.S. involvement in the Vietnam War, Madeleine gradually came to see American intervention as a disastrous mistake. Finally receiving her Ph.D. in international studies in 1976, she went to work for Brzezinksi, then Jimmy Carter's National Security Adviser. Shortly after Carter's 1980 defeat left Madeleine Albright without a political position, her husband's decision to seek a divorce left her, at age 45, with the need to pursue new options. On returning to Wellesley in 1984, for the 25th anniversary of her graduation, she listed "Divorce and Ronald Reagan" as the "lows" in an otherwise successful life.

Madeleine Albright soon plunged into the interlocking worlds of Democratic Party politics and foreign affairs. Bill Clinton's eight-year presidency gave her the chance to serve as UN ambassador and, then, as Secretary of State during the 1990s. Shortly after becoming Secretary of State, Madeleine Albright, raised a Catholic, learned that three of her grandparents had been Jewish and had died in Nazi concentration camps. This news,

she later observed, inclined her to see international issues, especially those related to genocide, in a more intensely personal light.

Albright gained the reputation of being a shrewd, tough-minded negotiator—and an often witty observer of the diplomatic scene. One of her most poignant moments, she recalled, was her first flight into Prague, Czechoslovakia, with President Clinton. Visiting there and listening to a band play the Czech national anthem, "Where Is My Home," she recalled the strange international journey she had taken to become America's top policy maker.

© Reuters NewMedia Inc./Corbis.

MADELEINE ALBRIGHT RETURNING TO HER NATIVE CZECHOSLOVAKIA, 2000

The secretary of state speaks under a statue of Tomas Masaryk, president of Czechoslovakia before the Second World War, in a celebration to mark the 150th anniversary of his birth.

strikes, Iraq still expelled the investigators. International terrorists bombed the World Trade Center in New York City in 1993, the U.S. embassies in Kenya and Tanzania in 1998, and a U.S. battleship docked in Yemen in 2000. These escalating attacks by Islamic militants raised alarm about future plots.

Globalization

The Clinton administration placed high priority on lowering trade barriers and expanding the global marketplace—a process called "globalization." Building on the Reagan-Bush legacy, Clinton argued that globalization would boost prosperity and foster democracy around the world.

Clinton enthusiastically backed the North American Free Trade Agreement (NAFTA), which projected cutting tariffs and eliminating other trade barriers between the United States, Canada, and Mexico over a 15-year period. After adding weak new provisions on labor and environmental issues, in December 1993 he muscled NAFTA through Congress in a close vote that depended on Republican support and faced fierce opposition from labor unions. Then, in early 1995, Mexico's severe debt crisis and a dramatic devaluation of its peso prompted Clinton to extend a $20 billion loan from America's Exchange Stabilization Fund. Although unprecedented and controversial, this loan stabilized the Mexican economy and, within a few years, had been repaid with $1 billion in interest.

Clinton's administration frequently used economic enticements to persuade other nations to embrace globalization and the more than 300 trade agreements signed between 1993 and 2001. His trade negotiators completed the so-called Uruguay Round of the General Agreement on Tariffs and Trade (GATT) in late 1993, and in early 1995, GATT was replaced by a more powerful World Trade Organization (WTO), created to enlarge world trade by implementing new agreements and mediating disputes. Anxious to move China toward capitalism, Clinton reversed his election-year position and granted China, despite its dismal record on human rights, equal trading status with other nations. In October 1999, the Clinton administration agreed to back China's entry into the WTO in exchange for a promise to liberalize its policies toward the United States and other potential trading partners. Clinton argued that increased trade with China would contribute to long-term pressures for democratization there. Similarly, in February 1994, the United States ended its 19-year-old trade embargo against Vietnam.

Clinton claimed that the effort to expand trade, along with the emerging free-market economies in Eastern Europe and Latin America, provided the framework for global prosperity. When Asian economies faltered during 1998, he supported acting with the International Monetary Fund (IMF) to provide huge emergency credits to reform and restore financial systems from Korea to Indonesia. Everywhere he went, Clinton extolled the "new century" in which "liberty will spread by cell phone and cable modem."

● The Presidency of George W. Bush (2001–)

Bill Clinton's popularity in the polls remained high as he neared the end of his term. After one of the closest elections in U.S. history, however, his Republican successor began to take the country in very different directions. George W. Bush, son of the nation's 41st president, assumed the mantle of Ronald Reagan and determined to vigorously pursue the New Right agenda that Clinton's presidency had interrupted.

The Long Election

A retro aura surrounded the presidential campaign of 2000. Al Gore reappeared, this time as the Democratic presidential nominee. The Republican ballot, for the fifth time in the last six elections, bore the name of Bush—that of George W. Bush. The younger Bush selected Richard (Dick) Cheney, who had served in his father's administration, as the GOP's vice-presidential running candidate. The presidential ballot also included a third-party challenger: Ralph Nader, the veteran activist. Nader ran as the candidate of the Green Party and ultimately attracted less than 3 percent of the popular vote, a far less impressive showing than Ross Perot's in 1996.

The tepid campaign stirred few passions. George W. Bush cited his record as governor of Texas as a sign that he could work with Democrats, attract a following among African Americans and Hispanics, and pursue "compassionate conservatism." While the Bush camp stayed "on message," Gore's disorganized campaign struggled to articulate coherent themes. By distancing himself from Clinton, the vice president likely squandered his primary asset, eight years of economic prosperity. The turnout was relatively light; barely 50 percent of the eligible voters went to the polls. Following a pattern that had been in place since the Reagan era, the popular vote highlighted the gender, racial, and ethnic differences between the two parties. According to exit polls, Bush attracted 54 percent of the votes cast by men but only 43 percent of those from women. He received 38 percent of his votes from Latinos,

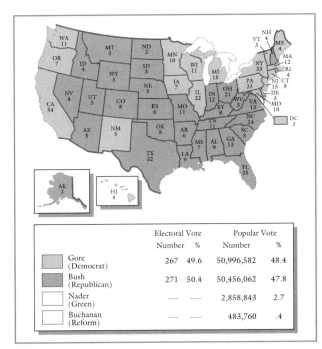

MAP 31.6 PRESIDENTIAL ELECTION, 2000

Although Gore won the popular vote, Bush won the electoral vote after a bitter dispute involving ballots in Florida. Note the possible impact of third-party candidates.

RECOUNTING VOTES IN PALM BEACH COUNTY, FLORIDA

The slow process of interpreting voters' intentions from improperly punched ballots with "hanging chads" helped complicate the effort to recount votes in Florida.

37 percent from Asian Americans, and 9 percent from African Americans.

The election of 2000 produced a near dead heat. Republicans narrowly maintained control of the House of Representatives, and the Senate ended up evenly split between the two parties. Gore carried the popular vote by about 500,000 ballots. The only tally that mattered, the one in the electoral college, remained so close that the identity of the next president turned on who had gained the 25 electoral votes from Florida, where about 1,000 votes separated the candidates and where Bush's brother Jeb served as governor and Republicans controlled the legislature.

Partisan fervor, which was muted during the campaign, suddenly flared as, for a month, no clear winner emerged in Florida. After counting all absentee ballots, Republican officials in Florida declared Bush, by a margin of 930 votes, to be the winner. Democrats complained that many circumstances, particularly antiquated voting machines, had distorted the count, and they sued to force hand recounts in several counties where the Gore total seemed abnormally low. More than 50 lawsuits, by both Democrats and Republicans, soon dotted court dockets; both parties, particularly the GOP, flooded Florida with cadres of lawyers and demonstrators; and an even greater number of media personnel saturated the Sunshine State. When the early recounts seemed to be reducing Bush's

already slim margin, Republicans charged that Democrats were "stealing" his victory. Statisticians advised that no procedure for hand counting so many disputed ballots, in such a close election, could ever yield a universally agreed-upon result.

Finally, the U.S. Supreme Court, in two 5–4 opinions, chose the new president. After first issuing a temporary injunction, halting all manual recounts in Florida, the Court's conservative Republicans (over the dissents of two moderate Republicans and two Democrats) declared, on December 12, 2000, that conducting these recounts only in the contested counties violated the Constitution. In addition, the same justices insisted that, because of Florida's timetable for reporting to the electoral college, there could not be any statewide recount of the November ballots. At this point, Gore conceded defeat, and George W. Bush became the 43rd president of the United States.

A Conservative Domestic Agenda

Several divisive domestic issues soon dominated Bush's presidency. First, signs of a downturn in the overall economy, accompanied by a plunge in a badly overvalued and fraud-plagued stock market, seemed to herald the end of the Clinton-era boom. The revenue surpluses of the late 1990s, at both the national and state levels, began dwindling and promised to become, once again, growing

the self-proclaimed liberators encountered more resistance than the Bush administration initially predicted, Saddam's regime fell in less than two months. On May 1, President Bush landed on the deck of the aircraft carrier *Abraham Lincoln* and proclaimed an end to the combat phase of his Iraqi mission. This carefully crafted media event quickly rebounded against the president as resistance to the American-dominated occupation, which aimed at creating a pro-U.S. government and an economic order closely tied to U.S. companies in post-Saddam Iraq, grew steadily wider and increasingly more lethal. By fall 2003, more Americans had died from hostile fire *after* Bush's landing on the *Abraham Lincoln* than *before* his declaration.

Meanwhile, attacks on Americans in Iraq expanded to include deadly assaults against aid workers from the United Nations, the Red Cross, and various other international relief agencies. Anti-Western groups from outside Iraq, it appeared, were joining the battle there as well as in Afghanistan, where the U.S.-backed government in Kabul retained a tenuous hold on power. Although early supporters of action against Saddam Hussein had suggested that Iraqi oil revenues could pay for the costs of any U.S. military action there, by fall 2003, the president had to ask Congress for $87 billion to fund just the immediate costs of the fighting and rebuilding activity in Iraq and Afghanistan. The lack of international support for U.S. action meant that, unlike in the 1991 Persian Gulf War, most of the costs would be borne by American taxpayers.

The White House insisted that the political and economic reconstruction of Iraq remained on track, but public opinion polls revealed growing doubts in the United States about the Bush policy. Had the administration misinterpreted or exaggerated intelligence information about Saddam's supposed cache of weapons of mass destruction, which could not be found after his fall? Did its claim that American-led forces would be hailed as liberators badly misread the situation in Iraq? Had there been an appropriate planning process for postwar stabilization in Iraq? As spokespeople for the Bush administration portrayed their goal of building a democratic Iraq as being similar to the successful operations in Japan and Germany during the 1940s, critics saw the Iraqi situation looking more like the failed crusade in Vietnam during the 1960s. As the cost of the occupation in both money and human life escalated, discussion in both the United States and overseas

U.S. SOLDIERS IN BAGHDAD, NOVEMBER 2003
After a relatively short military campaign to overthrow Saddam Hussein, U.S. forces struggled to bring stability to Iraq. Here, troops respond to a rocket attack on the Iraqi Oil Ministry and two hotels in central Baghdad.

slowly turned to whether the Bush administration could devise alternative policies to achieve its overly optimistic goals for a post-invasion Iraq.

Conclusion

Two outsized personalities dominated American political life in the late 20th century: Ronald Reagan and Bill Clinton. The "Reagan revolution" of the 1980s saw the emergence of a new conservative movement that had been born in the shadow of Lyndon Johnson's Great Society. New Right Republicans distrusted extending federal government power, advocated sharp tax cuts, and stressed a sociocultural agenda emphasizing traditional values. The dozen years of Republican dominance in the White House from 1980 to 1992 significantly shifted the terms of political debate to the right. The once-proud label of "liberal" became a term that politicians of both parties sought to avoid.

During the 1990s, the Republican agenda met its match in Bill Clinton, a New Democrat. Clinton blunted the Republican surge by adopting a fairly conservative economic agenda (e.g., slashing the federal deficit, reshaping the welfare system, and downsizing the federal bureaucracy). At the same time, he supported other issues that were heatedly opposed by many Republicans: abortion rights, gun control, affirmative action, and environmental protection. During his presidency, Clinton moved the Democratic Party away from its big-government agenda of the 1960s and 1970s.

In foreign policy, Reagan's military buildup coincided with the last years of the Cold War. By contrast, Clinton's emphasis on economic globalization addressed the post–Cold War environment.

The first president to take office in the 21st century, George W. Bush, recalled and built on the policies of the Reagan years. Polling data in early 2004, however, suggested that the electorate remained evenly split in their party loyalties.

Reagan and Clinton, both charismatic, media-savvy, two-term presidents, inspired intense adoration and passionate dislike. Together, their administrations tried to redraw the political landscape. In their shadows, Americans continued to negotiate the difficult balances among liberty, equality, and power.

SUGGESTED READINGS

For differing views of the political trends that came together during the 1980s, see **Garry Wills**, *Reagan's America: Innocents at Home* (1987); **Thomas Byrne and Mary D. Edsall**, *Chain Reaction: The Impact of Race, Rights, and Taxes on American Politics* (1992); **Burton J. Kaufman**, *The Presidency of James Earl Carter* (1993); **John W. Sloan**, *The Reagan Effect: Economics and Presidential Leadership* (1999); **Frances Fitzgerald**, *Way Out There in the Blue: Reagan and Star Wars and the End of the Cold War* (2000); **Lisa McGirr**, *Suburban Warriors: The Origins of the New American Right* (2001); **John Schoenwald**, *A Time for Choosing: The Rise of Modern American Conservatism* (2001); and **W. Carl Biven**, *Jimmy Carter's Economy: Policy in an Age of Limits* (2002).

Very different perspectives on the post-Reagan political scene appear in **Bob Woodward**, *The Agenda: Inside the Clinton White House* (1994) and *The Choice* (1996); **Theodore Lowi and Benjamin Ginsburg**, *Embattled Democracy: Politics and Policy in the Clinton Era* (1995); **David Mervin**, *George Bush and the Guardian Presidency* (1996); **Kenneth Baer**, *Reinventing Democrats: The Politics of Liberalism from Reagan to Clinton* (2000); **Steven F. Schier**, ed., *The Postmodern Presidency: Bill Clinton's Legacy in U.S. Politics* (2000); **John Robert Greene**, *The Presidency of George Bush* (2000); **Haynes Johnson**, *The Best of Times: America in the Clinton Years* (2001); **David Halberstam**, *War in a Time of Peace* (2001); **Joe Conanson and Gene Lyons**, *The Hunting of the President: The Ten-Year Campaign to Destroy Bill and Hillary Clinton* (2001); and **Sidney Blumenthal**, *The Clinton Wars* (2003).

The electoral contest that elevated George W. Bush to the presidency is analyzed in **Gerald M. Pomper, et al.**, *The Election of 2000: Reports and Interpretations* (2000); **Richard Posner**, *Breaking the Deadlock: The 2000 Election and the Courts* (2001); and **Jeffrey Toobin**, *Too Close to Call* (2001).

The controversy surrounding George W. Bush's early tenure in the White House, and especially its relationship to the attacks of 9/11, is reflected in titles such as **Fred H. Halliday**, *Two Hours That Shook the World: September 11, 2001: Causes and Consequences* (2002); **Bob Woodward**, *Bush At War* (2002); **Craig Calhoun, Paul Price, and Ashley Timmer**, eds., *Understanding September 11* (2002); **David Frum**, *The Right Man: The Surprise Presidency of George W. Bush* (2003); **Stephen Hess and Marvin Kalb**, eds., *The Media and the War on Terrorism* (2003); **Gerald Posner**, *Why America Slept: The Failure to Prevent 9/11* (2003); **Williamson Murray and Major General Robert H. Scales, Jr.**, *The Iraq War: A Military History* (2003); and **Joanne Meyerowitz**, ed., *History and September 11th* (2003).

 AMERICAN JOURNEY ONLINE
AND
INFOTRAC COLLEGE EDITION

Visit the source collections at www.ajaccess.wadsworth.com and infotrac.thomsonlearning.com and use the Search function with the following key terms to explore documents, images, audio and video clips, articles, and commentary related to the material in this chapter.

Gerald R. Ford	North American Free Trade
Jimmy Carter	Agreement (NAFTA)
Ronald Reagan	Kenneth Starr
Iran-*Contra*	Clinton impeachment
Star Wars (SDI)	George W. Bush
Persian Gulf War	September 11, 2001
Bill Clinton	War on Terrorism
Ross Perot	

GRADE AIDS

Visit the Liberty Equality Power Companion Web Site for resources specific to this textbook: http://history.wadsworth.com/murrin_LEP4e

 The CD in the back of this book and the U.S. History Resource Center at http://history.wadsworth.com/u.s./ offer a variety of tools to help you succeed in this course, including access to quizzes; images; documents; interactive simulations, maps, and timelines; movie explorations; and a wealth of other sources.

The Declaration of Independence

THE UNANIMOUS DECLARATION OF
THE THIRTEEN UNITED STATES OF AMERICA

When in the Course of human events it becomes necessary for one people to dissolve the political bands which have connected them with another, and to assume among the Powers of the earth, the separate and equal station to which the Laws of Nature and of Nature's God entitle them, a decent respect to the opinions of mankind requires that they should declare the causes which impel them to the separation.

We hold these truths to be self-evident, that all men are created equal, that they are endowed by their Creator with certain unalienable Rights, that among these are Life, Liberty and the pursuit of Happiness. That to secure these rights, Governments are instituted among Men, deriving their just Powers from the consent of the governed. That whenever any Form of Government becomes destructive of these ends, it is the Right of the People to alter or to abolish it, and to institute new Government, laying its foundation on such principles and organizing its Powers in such form, as to them shall seem most likely to effect their Safety and Happiness. Prudence, indeed, will dictate that Governments long established should not be changed for light and transient causes; and accordingly all experience hath shewn, that mankind are more disposed to suffer, while evils are sufferable, than to right themselves by abolishing the forms to which they are accustomed. But when a long train of abuses and usurpations, pursuing invariably the same Object evinces a design to reduce them under absolute Despotism, it is their right, it is their duty, to throw off such Government, and to provide new Guards for their future security. Such has been the patient sufferance of these Colonies; and such is now the necessity which constrains them to alter their former Systems of Government. The history of the present King of Great Britain is a history of repeated injuries and usurpations, all having in direct object the establishment of an absolute Tyranny over these States. To prove this, let Facts be submitted to a candid world.

<hr>

Text is reprinted from the facsimile of the engrossed copy in the National Archives. The original spelling, capitalization, and punctuation have been retained. Paragraphing has been added.

He has refused his Assent to Laws, the most wholesome and necessary for the public good.

He has forbidden his Governors to pass Laws of immediate and pressing importance, unless suspended in their operation till his Assent should be obtained; and when so suspended, he has utterly neglected to attend to them.

He has refused to pass other Laws for the accommodation of large districts of people, unless those people would relinquish the right of Representation in the Legislature, a right inestimable to them and formidable to tyrants only.

He has called together legislative bodies at places unusual, uncomfortable, and distant from the depository of their Public Records, for the sole Purpose of fatiguing them into compliance with his measures.

He has dissolved Representative Houses repeatedly, for opposing with manly firmness his invasions on the rights of the People.

He has refused for a long time, after such dissolutions, to cause others to be elected; whereby the Legislative Powers, incapable of Annihilation, have returned to the People at large for their exercise; the State remaining in the mean time exposed to all the dangers of invasion from without, and convulsions within.

He has endeavoured to prevent the Population of these States; for that purpose obstructing the Laws for Naturalization of Foreigners; refusing to pass others to encourage their migrations hither, and raising the conditions of new Appropriations of Lands.

He has obstructed the Administration of Justice, by refusing his Assent to Laws for establishing Judiciary Powers.

He has made Judges dependent on his Will alone, for the tenure of their offices, and the amount and payment of their salaries.

He has erected a multitude of New Offices, and sent hither swarms of Officers to harass our People, and eat out their substance.

He has kept among us, in times of peace, Standing Armies without the Consent of our legislatures.

He has affected to render the Military independent of and superior to the Civil Power.

He has combined with others to subject us to a jurisdiction foreign to our constitution, and unacknowledged by our laws; giving his Assent to their Acts of pretended Legislation:

For Quartering large bodies of armed troops among us:

For protecting them, by a mock Trial, from Punishment for any Murders which they should commit on the Inhabitants of these States:

For cutting off our Trade with all parts of the world:

For imposing Taxes on us without our Consent:

For depriving us in many cases, of the benefits of Trial by Jury:

For transporting us beyond Seas to be tried for pretended offences:

For abolishing the free System of English Laws in a neighbouring Province, establishing therein an Arbitrary government, and enlarging its Boundaries so as to render it at once an example and fit instrument for introducing the same absolute rule into these Colonies:

For taking away our Charters, abolishing our most valuable Laws, and altering fundamentally the Forms of our Governments:

For suspending our own Legislatures, and declaring themselves invested with Power to legislate for us in all cases whatsoever.

He has abdicated Government here, by declaring us out of his Protection, and waging War against us.

He has plundered our seas, ravaged our Coasts, burnt our towns, and destroyed the lives of our people.

He is at this time transporting large Armies of foreign Mercenaries to compleat the works of death, desolation and tyranny, already begun with circumstances of Cruelty and perfidy scarcely paralleled in the most barbarous ages, and totally unworthy the Head of a civilized nation.

He has constrained our fellow Citizens taken Captive on the high Seas to bear Arms against their Country, to become the executioners of their friends and Brethren, or to fall themselves by their Hands.

He has excited domestic insurrections amongst us, and has endeavoured to bring on the inhabitants of our frontiers, the merciless Indian Savages, whose known rule of warfare, is an undistinguished destruction of all ages, sexes and conditions.

In every stage of these Oppressions We have Petitioned for Redress in the most humble terms: Our repeated Petitions have been answered only by repeated injury. A Prince, whose character is thus marked by every act which may define a Tyrant, is unfit to be the ruler of a free People.

Nor have We been wanting in attentions to our British brethren. We have warned them from time to time of attempts by their legislature to extend an unwarrantable jurisdiction over us. We have reminded them of the circumstances of our emigration and settlement here. We have appealed to their native justice and magnanimity, and we have conjured them by the ties of our common kindred to disavow these usurpations, which, would inevitably interrupt our connections and correspondence. They too have been deaf to the voice of justice and of consanguinity. We must, therefore, acquiesce in the necessity, which denounces our Separation, and hold them, as we hold the rest of mankind, Enemies in War, in Peace Friends.

WE, THEREFORE, the Representatives of the UNITED STATES OF AMERICA, in General Congress, Assembled, appealing to the Supreme Judge of the world for the rectitude of our intentions, do, in the Name, and by Authority of the good People of these Colonies, solemnly publish and declare, That these United Colonies are, and of Right ought to be FREE AND INDEPENDENT STATES; that they are Absolved from all Allegiance to the British Crown, and that all political connection between them and the State of Great Britain, is and ought to be totally dissolved; and that, as Free and Independent States, they have full Power to levy War, conclude Peace, contract Alliances, establish Commerce, and to do all other Acts and Things which Independent States may of right do. And for the support of this Declaration, with a firm reliance on the protection of divine Providence, we mutually pledge to each other our Lives, our Fortunes and our sacred Honor.

The Constitution of the United States of America

We the People of the United States, in Order to form a more perfect Union, establish Justice, insure domestic Tranquility, provide for the common defence, promote the general Welfare, and secure the Blessings of Liberty to ourselves and our Posterity, do ordain and establish this Constitution for the United States of America.

ARTICLE I.

SECTION 1. All legislative Powers herein granted shall be vested in a Congress of the United States, which shall consist of a Senate and House of Representatives.

SECTION 2. The House of Representatives shall be composed of Members chosen every second Year by the People of the several States, and the Electors in each State shall have the Qualifications requisite for Electors of the most numerous Branch of the State Legislature.

No Person shall be a Representative who shall not have attained to the Age of twenty five Years, and been seven Years a Citizen of the United States, and who shall not, when elected, be an Inhabitant of that State in which he shall be chosen.

Representatives and direct Taxes[1] shall be apportioned among the several States which may be included within this Union, according to their respective Numbers, which shall be determined by adding to the whole Number of free Persons, including those bound to Service for a Term of Years, and excluding Indians not taxed, three fifths of all other Persons.[2] The actual Enumeration shall be made within three Years after the first Meeting of the Congress of the United States, and within every subsequent Term of ten Years, in such Manner as they shall by Law direct. The Number of Representatives shall not exceed one for every thirty Thousand, but each State shall have at Least one Representative; and until such enumeration shall be made, the State of New Hampshire shall be entitled to chuse three; Massachusetts eight; Rhode Island and Providence Plantations one; Connecticut five; New York six; New Jersey four; Pennsylvania eight; Delaware one; Maryland six; Virginia ten; North Carolina five; South Carolina five; and Georgia three.

When vacancies happen in the Representation from any State, the Executive Authority thereof shall issue Writs of Election to fill such Vacancies.

The House of Representatives shall chuse their Speaker and other Officers; and shall have the sole Power of Impeachment.

SECTION 3. The Senate of the United States shall be composed of two Senators from each State, chosen by the Legislature thereof, for six Years; and each Senator shall have one Vote.[3]

Immediately after they shall be assembled in Consequence of the first Election, they shall be divided as equally as may be into three Classes. The Seats of the Senators of the first Class shall be vacated at the Expiration of the second Year, of the second Class at the Expiration of the fourth Year, and of the third Class at the Expiration of the sixth Year, so that one third may be chosen every second Year; and if Vacancies happen by Resignation, or otherwise, during the Recess of the Legislature of any State, the Executive thereof may make temporary Appointments until the next Meeting of the Legislature, which shall then fill such Vacancies.[4]

No Person shall be a Senator who shall not have attained to the Age of thirty Years, and been nine Years a Citizen of the United States, and who shall not, when elected, be an Inhabitant of that State for which he shall be chosen.

The Vice President of the United States shall be President of the Senate, but shall have no Vote, unless they be equally divided.

The Senate shall chuse their other Officers, and also a President pro tempore, in the Absence of the Vice President, or when he shall exercise the Office of President of the United States.

Text is from the engrossed copy in the National Archives. Original spelling, capitalization, and punctuation have been retained.
[1]Modified by the Sixteenth Amendment.
[2]Replaced by the Fourteenth Amendment.
[3]Superseded by the Seventeenth Amendment.
[4]Modified by the Seventeenth Amendment.

The Senate shall have the sole Power to try all Impeachments. When sitting for that Purpose, they shall be on Oath or Affirmation. When the President of the United States is tried, the Chief Justice shall preside: And no Person shall be convicted without the Concurrence of two thirds of the Members present.

Judgment in Cases of Impeachment shall not extend further than to removal from Office, and disqualification to hold and enjoy any Office of honor, Trust or Profit under the United States: but the Party convicted shall nevertheless be liable and subject to Indictment, Trial, Judgment and Punishment, according to Law.

SECTION 4. The Times, Places and Manner of holding Elections for Senators and Representatives, shall be prescribed in each State by the Legislature thereof, but the Congress may at any time by Law make or alter such Regulation, except as to the Places of chusing Senators.

The Congress shall assemble at least once in every Year, and such Meeting shall be on the first Monday in December, unless they shall by Law appoint a different Day.[5]

SECTION 5. Each House shall be the Judge of the Elections, Returns and Qualifications of its own Members, and a Majority of each shall constitute a Quorum to do Business; but a smaller Number may adjourn from day to day, and may be authorized to compel the Attendance of absent Members, in such Manner, and under such Penalties as each House may provide.

Each House may determine the Rules of its Proceedings, punish its Members for disorderly Behaviour, and, with the Concurrence of two thirds, expel a Member.

Each House shall keep a Journal of its Proceedings, and from time to time publish the same, excepting such Parts as may in their Judgment require Secrecy; and the Yeas and Nays of the Members of either House on any question shall, at the Desire of one fifth of those Present, be entered on the Journal.

Neither House, during the Session of Congress, shall, without the Consent of the other, adjourn for more than three days, nor to any other Place than that in which the two Houses shall be sitting.

SECTION 6. The Senators and Representatives shall receive a Compensation for their Services, to be ascertained by Law, and paid out of the Treasury of the United States. They shall in all Cases, except Treason, Felony and Breach of the Peace, be privileged from Arrest during their Attendance at the Session of their respective Houses, and in going to and returning from the same; and for any Speech or Debate in either House, they shall not be questioned in any other Place.

No Senator or Representative shall, during the Time for which he was elected, be appointed to any civil Office under the Authority of the United States, which shall have been created, or the Emoluments whereof shall have been encreased during such time; and no Person holding any Office under the United States, shall be a Member of either House during his Continuance in Office.

SECTION 7. All Bills for raising Revenue shall originate in the House of Representatives; but the Senate may propose or concur with Amendments as on other Bills.

Every Bill which shall have passed the House of Representatives and the Senate shall, before it become a Law, be presented to the President of the United States; If he approve he shall sign it, but if not he shall return it, with his Objections to that House in which it shall have originated, who shall enter the Objections at large on their Journal, and proceed to reconsider it. If after such Reconsideration two thirds of that House shall agree to pass the Bill, it shall be sent, together with the Objections, to the other House, by which it shall likewise be reconsidered, and if approved by two thirds of that House, it shall become a Law. But in all such Cases the Votes of both Houses shall be determined by yeas and Nays, and the Names of the Persons voting for and against the Bill shall be entered on the Journal of each House respectively. If any Bill shall not be returned by the President within ten Days (Sundays excepted) after it shall have been presented to him, the Same shall be a Law, in like Manner as if he had signed it, unless the Congress by their Adjournment prevent its Return, in which Case it shall not be a Law.

Every Order, Resolution, or Vote to which the Concurrence of the Senate and House of Representatives may be necessary (except on a question of Adjournment) shall be presented to the President of the United States; and before the Same shall take Effect, shall be approved by him, or being disapproved by him shall be repassed by two thirds of the Senate and House of Representatives, according to the Rules and Limitations prescribed in the Case of a Bill.

SECTION 8. The Congress shall have power To lay and collect Taxes, Duties, Imposts and Excises, to pay the Debts and provide for the common Defence and general Welfare of the United States; but all Duties, Imposts and Excises shall be uniform throughout the United States;

To borrow Money on the credit of the United States;

To regulate Commerce with foreign Nations, and among the several States, and with the Indian Tribes;

To establish an uniform Rule of Naturalization, and uniform Laws on the subject of Bankruptcies throughout the United States;

To coin Money, regulate the Value thereof, and of foreign Coin, and fix the Standard of Weights and Measures;

----

[5]Superseded by the Twentieth Amendment.

To provide for the Punishment of counterfeiting the Securities and current Coin of the United States;

To establish Post Offices and post Roads;

To promote the Progress of Science and useful Arts, by securing for limited Times to Authors and Inventors the exclusive Right to their respective Writings and Discoveries;

To constitute Tribunals inferior to the supreme Court;

To define and punish Piracies and Felonies committed on the high Seas, and Offences against the Law of Nations;

To declare War, grant Letters of Marque and Reprisal, and make Rules concerning Captures on Land and Water;

To raise and support Armies, but no Appropriation of Money to that Use shall be for a longer Term than two Years;

To provide and maintain a Navy;

To make Rules for the Government and Regulation of the land and naval Forces;

To provide for calling forth the Militia to execute the Laws of the Union, suppress Insurrections and repel Invasions;

To provide for organizing, arming, and disciplining, the Militia, and for governing such Part of them as may be employed in the Service of the United States, reserving to the States respectively, the Appointment of the Officers, and the Authority of training the Militia according to the discipline prescribed by Congress;

To exercise exclusive Legislation in all Cases whatsoever, over such District (not exceeding ten Miles square) as may, by Cession of particular States, and the Acceptance of Congress, become the Seat of the Government of the United States, and to exercise like Authority over all Places purchased by the Consent of the Legislature of the State in which the Same shall be, for the Erection of Forts, Magazines, Arsenals, dock-Yards, and other needful Buildings;—And

To make all Laws which shall be necessary and proper for carrying into Execution the foregoing Powers, and all other Powers vested by this Constitution in the Government of the United States, or in any Department or Officer thereof.

SECTION 9. The Migration or Importation of such Persons as any of the States now existing shall think proper to admit, shall not be prohibited by the Congress prior to the Year one thousand eight hundred and eight, but a Tax or duty may be imposed on such Importation, not exceeding ten dollars for each Person.

The Privilege of the Writ of Habeas Corpus shall not be suspended, unless when in Cases of Rebellion or Invasion the public Safety may require it.

No Bill of Attainder or ex post facto Law shall be passed.

No Capitation, or other direct, Tax shall be laid, unless in Proportion to the Census or Enumeration herein before directed to be taken.

No Tax or Duty shall be laid on Articles exported from any State.

No Preference shall be given by any Regulation of Commerce or Revenue to the Ports of one State over those of another: nor shall Vessels bound to, or from, one State, be obliged to enter, clear, or pay Duties in another.

No Money shall be drawn from the Treasury, but in Consequence of Appropriations made by Law, and a regular Statement and Account of the Receipts and Expenditures of all public Money shall be published from time to time.

No Title of Nobility shall be granted by the United States: And no Person holding any Office of Profit or Trust under them, shall, without the Consent of the Congress, accept of any present, Emolument, Office, or Title, of any kind whatever, from any King, Prince, or foreign State.

SECTION 10. No State shall enter into any Treaty, Alliance, or Confederation; grant Letters of Marque and Reprisal; coin Money; emit Bills of Credit; make any Thing but gold and silver Coin a Tender in Payment of Debts; pass any Bill of Attainder, ex post facto Law, or Law impairing the Obligation of Contracts, or grant any Title of Nobility.

No State shall, without the Consent of the Congress, lay any Imposts or Duties on Imports or Exports, except what may be absolutely necessary for executing its inspection Laws: and the net Produce of all Duties and Imposts, laid by any State on Imports or Exports, shall be for the Use of the Treasury of the United States; and all such Laws shall be subject to the Revision and Controul of the Congress.

No State shall, without the Consent of Congress, lay any Duty of Tonnage, keep Troops, or Ships of War in time of Peace, enter into any Agreement or Compact with another State, or with a foreign Power, or engage in War, unless actually invaded, or in such imminent Danger as will not admit of delay.

ARTICLE II.

SECTION 1. The executive Power shall be vested in a President of the United States of America. He shall hold his Office during the Term of four Years, and, together with the Vice President, chosen for the same Term, be elected, as follows:

Each State shall appoint, in such Manner as the Legislature thereof may direct, a Number of Electors, equal to

two thirds of the several States, shall call a Convention for proposing Amendments, which, in either Case, shall be valid to all Intents and Purposes, as Part of this Constitution, when ratified by the Legislatures of three fourths of the several States, or by Conventions in three fourths thereof, as the one or the other Mode of Ratification may be proposed by the Congress; Provided that no Amendment which may be made prior to the Year One thousand eight hundred and eight shall in any Manner affect the first and fourth Clauses in the Ninth Section of the first Article; and that no State, without its Consent, shall be deprived of its equal Suffrage in the Senate.

ARTICLE VI.

All Debts contracted and Engagements entered into, before the Adoption of this Constitution, shall be as valid against the United States under this Constitution, as under the Confederation.

This Constitution, and the Laws of the United States which shall be made in Pursuance thereof; and all Treaties made, or which shall be made, under the Authority of the United States, shall be the supreme Law of the Land; and the Judges in every State shall be bound thereby, any Thing in the Constitution or Laws of any State to the Contrary notwithstanding.

The Senators and Representatives before mentioned, and the Members of the several State Legislatures, and all executive and judicial Officers, both of the United States and of the several States, shall be bound by Oath or Affirmation, to support this Constitution; but no religious Test shall ever be required as a Qualification to any Office or public Trust under the United States.

ARTICLE VII.

The Ratification of the Conventions of nine States, shall be sufficient for the Establishment of this Constitution between the States so ratifying the Same.

Done in Convention by the Unanimous Consent of the States present the Seventeenth Day of September in the Year of our Lord one thousand seven hundred and Eighty seven and of the Independence of the United States of America the Twelfth. In witness whereof We have hereunto subscribed our Names,

Articles in Addition to, and Amendment of, the Constitution of the United States of America, Proposed by Congress, and Ratified by the Legislatures of the Several States, Pursuant to the Fifth Article of the Original Constitution.

AMENDMENT I [9]

Congress shall make no law respecting an establishment of religion, or prohibiting the free exercise thereof; or abridging the freedom of speech, or of the press; or the right of the people peaceably to assemble, and to petition the Government for a redress of grievances.

AMENDMENT II

A well regulated Militia, being necessary to the security of a free State, the right of the people to keep and bear Arms shall not be infringed.

AMENDMENT III

No Soldier shall, in time of peace, be quartered in any house, without the consent of the Owner, nor in time of war, but in a manner to be prescribed by law.

AMENDMENT IV

The right of the people to be secure in their persons, houses, papers, and effects, against unreasonable searches and seizures, shall not be violated, and no Warrants shall issue, but upon probable cause, supported by Oath or affirmation, and particularly describing the place to be searched, and the persons or things to be seized.

AMENDMENT V

No person shall be held to answer for a capital or otherwise infamous crime, unless on a presentment or indictment of a Grand Jury, except in cases arising in the land or naval forces, or in the Militia, when in actual service in time of War or public danger; nor shall any person be subject for the same offence to be twice put in jeopardy of life or limb; nor shall be compelled in any criminal case to be a witness against himself, nor be deprived of life, liberty, or property, without due process of law; nor shall private property be taken for public use, without just compensation.

AMENDMENT VI

In all criminal prosecutions, the accused shall enjoy the right to a speedy and public trial, by an impartial jury of the State and district wherein the crime shall have been

---

[9]The first ten amendments were passed by Congress September 25, 1789. They were ratified by three-fourths of the states December 15, 1791.

committed, which district shall have been previously ascertained by law, and to be informed of the nature and cause of the accusation; to be confronted with the witnesses against him; to have compulsory process for obtaining witnesses in his favor, and to have the Assistance of Counsel for his defence.

AMENDMENT VII

In suits at common law, where the value in controversy shall exceed twenty dollars, the right of trial by jury shall be preserved, and no fact tried by a jury, shall be otherwise reexamined in any Court of the United States, than according to the rules of the common law.

AMENDMENT VIII

Excessive bail shall not be required, nor excessive fines imposed, nor cruel and unusual punishments inflicted.

AMENDMENT IX

The enumeration in the Constitution, of certain rights, shall not be construed to deny or disparage others retained by the people.

AMENDMENT X

The powers not delegated to the United States by the Constitution; nor prohibited by it to the States, are reserved to the States respectively, or to the people.

AMENDMENT XI[10]

The Judicial power of the United States shall not be construed to extend to any suit in law or equity, commenced or prosecuted against one of the United States by Citizens of another State, or by Citizens or Subjects of any Foreign State.

AMENDMENT XII[11]

The Electors shall meet in their respective States and vote by ballot for President and Vice-President, one of whom, at least, shall not be an inhabitant of the same State with themselves; they shall name in their ballots the person voted for as President, and in distinct ballots the person voted for as Vice-President, and they shall make distinct lists of all persons voted for as President, and of all persons voted for as Vice-President, and of the number of votes for each, which lists they shall sign and certify, and transmit sealed to the seat of the government of the United States, directed to the President of the Senate;—The President of the Senate shall, in the presence of the Senate and House of Representatives, open all the certificates and the votes shall then be counted;—The person having the greatest number of votes for President, shall be the President, if such number be a majority of the whole number of Electors appointed; and if no person have such majority, then from the persons having the highest numbers not exceeding three on the list of those voted for as President, the House of Representatives shall choose immediately, by ballot, the President. But in choosing the President, the votes shall be taken by states, the representation from each state having one vote; a quorum for this purpose shall consist of a member or members from two-thirds of the states, and a majority of all the states shall be necessary to a choice. And if the House of Representatives shall not choose a President whenever the right of choice shall devolve upon them, before the fourth day of March next following, then the Vice-President shall act as President, as in the case of the death or other constitutional disability of the President.—The person having the greatest number of votes as Vice-President, shall be the Vice-President, if such number be a majority of the whole number of Electors appointed, and if no person have a majority, then from the two highest numbers on the list, the Senate shall choose the Vice-President; a quorum for the purpose shall consist of two-thirds of the whole number of Senators, and a majority of the whole number shall be necessary to a choice. But no person constitutionally ineligible to the office of President shall be eligible to that of Vice-President of the United States.

AMENDMENT XIII[12]

SECTION 1. Neither slavery nor involuntary servitude, except as a punishment for crime whereof the party shall have been duly convicted, shall exist within the United States, or any place subject to their jurisdiction.

SECTION 2. Congress shall have power to enforce this article by appropriate legislation.

AMENDMENT XIV[13]

SECTION 1. All persons born or naturalized in the United States, and subject to the jurisdiction thereof, are citizens of the United States and of the State wherein they

---

[10]Passed March 4, 1794. Ratified January 23, 1795.
[11]Passed December 9, 1803. Ratified June 15, 1804.

[12]Passed January 31, 1865. Ratified December 6, 1865.
[13]Passed June 13, 1866. Ratified July 9, 1868.

reside. No State shall make or enforce any law which shall abridge the privileges or immunities of citizens of the United States; nor shall any State deprive any person of life, liberty, or property, without due process of law; nor deny to any person within its jurisdiction the equal protection of the laws.

SECTION 2. Representatives shall be apportioned among the several States according to their respective numbers, counting the whole number of persons in each State, excluding Indians not taxed. But when the right to vote at any election for the choice of electors for President and Vice-President of the United States, Representatives in Congress, the Executive and Judicial officers of a State, or the members of the Legislature thereof, is denied to any of the male inhabitants of such State, being twenty-one years of age, and citizens of the United States, or in any way abridged, except for participation in rebellion, or other crime, the basis of representation therein shall be reduced in the proportion which the number of such male citizens shall bear to the whole number of male citizens twenty-one years of age in such State.

SECTION 3. No person shall be a Senator or Representative in Congress, or elector of President and Vice-President, or hold any office, civil or military, under the United States, or under any State, who, having previously taken an oath, as a member of Congress, or as an officer of the United States, or as a member of any State legislature, or as an executive or judicial officer of any State, to support the Constitution of the United States, shall have engaged in insurrection or rebellion against the same, or given aid or comfort to the enemies thereof. But Congress may by a vote of two-thirds of each House, remove such disability.

SECTION 4. The validity of the public debt of the United States, authorized by law, including debts incurred for payment of pensions and bounties for services in suppressing insurrection or rebellion, shall not be questioned. But neither the United States nor any State shall assume or pay any debt or obligation incurred in aid of insurrection or rebellion against the United States, or any claim for the loss or emancipation of any slave; but all such debts, obligations, and claims shall be held illegal and void.

SECTION 5. The Congress shall have the power to enforce, by appropriate legislation, the provisions of this article.

AMENDMENT XV[14]

SECTION 1. The right of citizens of the United States to vote shall not be denied or abridged by the United States or by any State on account of race, color, or previous conditions of servitude—

SECTION 2. The Congress shall have power to enforce this article by appropriate legislation.

AMENDMENT XVI

The Congress shall have power to lay and collect taxes on incomes, from whatever source derived, without apportionment among the several States, and without regard to any census or enumeration.

AMENDMENT XVII[15]

The Senate of the United States shall be composed of two Senators from each State, elected by the people thereof, for six years; and each Senator shall have one vote. The electors in each State shall have the qualifications requisite for electors of the most numerous branch of the State legislatures.

When vacancies happen in the representation of any State in the Senate, the executive authority of such State shall issue writs of election to fill such vacancies: *Provided,* That the legislature of any State may empower the executive thereof to make temporary appointments until the people fill the vacancies by election as the legislature may direct.

This amendment shall not be so construed as to affect the election or term of any Senator chosen before it becomes valid as part of the Constitution.

AMENDMENT XVIII[16]

SECTION 1. After one year from the ratification of this article the manufacture, sale, or transportation of intoxicating liquors within, the importation thereof into, or the exportation thereof from the United States and all territory subject to the jurisdiction thereof for beverage purposes is hereby prohibited.

SECTION 2. The Congress and the several States shall have concurrent power to enforce this article by appropriate legislation.

SECTION 3. This article shall be inoperative unless it shall have been ratified as an amendment to the Constitution by the legislatures of the several States, as provided in the Constitution, within seven years from the date of the submission hereof to the States by the Congress.

---

[14]Passed February 26, 1869. Ratified February 2, 1870.

[15]Passed May 13, 1912. Ratified April 8, 1913.
[16]Passed December 18, 1917. Ratified January 16, 1919.

AMENDMENT XIX[17]

The right of citizens of the United States to vote shall not be denied or abridged by the United States or by any State on account of sex.

Congress shall have power to enforce this article by appropriate legislation.

AMENDMENT XX[18]

SECTION 1. The terms of the President and Vice-President shall end at noon on the 20th day of January, and the terms of Senators and Representatives at noon on the 3d day of January, of the years in which such terms would have ended if this article had not been ratified; and the terms of their successors shall then begin.

SECTION 2. The Congress shall assemble at least once in every year, and such meeting shall begin at noon on the 3d day of January, unless they shall by law appoint a different day.

SECTION 3. If, at the time fixed for the beginning of the term of the President, the President elect shall have died, the Vice-President elect shall become President. If a President shall not have been chosen before the time fixed for the beginning of his term, or if the President elect shall have failed to qualify, then the Vice-President elect shall act as President until a President shall have qualified; and the Congress may by law provide for the case wherein neither a President elect nor a Vice-President elect shall have qualified, declaring who shall then act as President, or the manner in which one who is to act shall be selected, and such person shall act accordingly until a President or Vice-President shall have qualified.

SECTION 4. The Congress may by law provide for the case of the death of any of the persons from whom the House of Representatives may choose a President whenever the right of choice shall have devolved upon them, and for the case of the death of any of the persons from whom the Senate may choose a Vice-President whenever the right of choice shall have devolved upon them.

SECTION 5. Sections 1 and 2 shall take effect on the 15th day of October following the ratification of this article.

SECTION 6. This article shall be inoperative unless it shall have been ratified as an amendment to the Constitution by the legislatures of three-fourths of the several States within seven years from the date of its submission.

AMENDMENT XXI[19]

SECTION 1. The eighteenth article of amendment to the Constitution of the United States is hereby repealed.

SECTION 2. The transportation or importation into any State, Territory, or possession of the United States for delivery or use therein of intoxicating liquors, in violation of the laws thereof, is hereby prohibited.

SECTION 3. This article shall be inoperative unless it shall have been ratified as an amendment to the Constitution by conventions in the several States, as provided in the Constitution, within seven years from the date of the submission hereof to the States by the Congress.

AMENDMENT XXII[20]

No person shall be elected to the office of the President more than twice, and no person who has held the office of President, or acted as President, for more than two years of a term to which some other person was elected President shall be elected to the office of the President more than once.

But this Article shall not apply to any person holding the office of President when this Article was proposed by the Congress, and shall not prevent any person who may be holding the office of President, or acting as President, during the term within which this Article becomes operative from holding the office of President or acting as President during the remainder of such term.

AMENDMENT XXIII[21]

SECTION 1. The District constituting the seat of Government of the United States shall appoint in such manner as the Congress may direct:

A number of electors of President and Vice President equal to the whole number of Senators and Representatives in Congress to which the District would be entitled if it were a State, but in no event more than the least populous State; they shall be in addition to those appointed by the States, but they shall be considered, for the purposes of the election of President and Vice President, to be electors appointed by the State; and they shall meet in the District and perform such duties as provided by the twelfth article of amendment.

SECTION 2. The Congress shall have power to enforce this article by appropriate legislation.

---

[17]Passed June 4, 1919. Ratified August 18, 1920.
[18]Passed March 2, 1932. Ratified January 23, 1933.

[19]Passed February 20, 1933. Ratified December 5, 1933.
[20]Passed March 12, 1947. Ratified March 1, 1951.
[21]Passed June 16, 1960. Ratified April 3, 1961.

Amendment XXIV[22]

SECTION 1. The right of citizens of the United States to vote in any primary or other election for President or Vice President, or for Senator or Representative in Congress, shall not be denied or abridged by the United States or any State by reason of failure to pay any poll tax or other tax.

SECTION 2. The Congress shall have power to enforce this article by appropriate legislation.

Amendment XXV[23]

SECTION 1. In case of the removal of the President from office or of his death or resignation, the Vice President shall become President.

SECTION 2. Whenever there is a vacancy in the office of the Vice President, the President shall nominate a Vice President who shall take office upon confirmation by a majority vote of both Houses of Congress.

SECTION 3. Whenever the President transmits to the President pro tempore of the Senate and the Speaker of the House of Representatives his written declaration that he is unable to discharge the powers and duties of his office, and until he transmits them a written declaration to the contrary, such powers and duties shall be discharged by the Vice President as Acting President.

SECTION 4. Whenever the Vice President and a majority of either the principal officers of the executive department or of such other body as Congress may by law provide, transmit to the President pro tempore of the Senate and the Speaker of the House of Representatives their written declaration that the President is unable to discharge the powers and duties of his office, the Vice President shall immediately assume the powers and duties of the office of Acting President.

Thereafter, when the President transmits to the President pro tempore of the Senate and the Speaker of the House of Representatives his written declaration that no inability exists, he shall resume the powers and duties of his office unless the Vice President and a majority of either the principal officers of the executive department or of such other body as Congress may by law provide, transmit within four days to the President pro tempore of the Senate and the Speaker of the House of Representatives their written declaration that the President is unable to discharge the powers and duties of his office. Thereupon Congress shall decide the issue, assembling within forty-eight hours for that purpose if not in session. If the Congress, within twenty-one days after receipt of the latter written declaration, or, if Congress is not in session, within twenty-one days after Congress is required to assemble, determines by two-thirds vote of both Houses that the President is unable to discharge the powers and duties of his office, the Vice President shall continue to discharge the same as Acting President; otherwise, the President shall resume the powers and duties of his office.

Amendment XXVI[24]

SECTION 1. The right of citizens of the United States, who are eighteen years of age or older, to vote shall not be denied or abridged by the United States or by any State on account of age.

SECTION 2. The Congress shall have power to enforce this article by appropriate legislation.

Amendment XXVII[25]

No law, varying the compensation for the service of the Senators and Representatives, shall take effect, until an election of Representatives shall have intervened.

---

[22]Passed August 27, 1962. Ratified January 23, 1964.
[23]Passed July 6, 1965. Ratified February 11, 1967.

[24]Passed March 23, 1971. Ratified July 5, 1971.
[25]Passed September 25, 1789. Ratified May 7, 1992.

ADMISSION OF STATES

Order of admission	State	Date of admission	Order of admission	State	Date of admission
1	Delaware	December 7, 1787	26	Michigan	January 26, 1837
2	Pennsylvania	December 12, 1787	27	Florida	March 3, 1845
3	New Jersey	December 18, 1787	28	Texas	December 29, 1845
4	Georgia	January 2, 1788	29	Iowa	December 28, 1846
5	Connecticut	January 9, 1788	30	Wisconsin	May 29, 1848
6	Massachusetts	February 6, 1788	31	California	September 9, 1850
7	Maryland	April 28, 1788	32	Minnesota	May 11, 1858
8	South Carolina	May 23, 1788	33	Oregon	February 14, 1859
9	New Hampshire	June 21, 1788	34	Kansas	January 29, 1861
10	Virginia	June 25, 1788	35	West Virginia	June 20, 1863
11	New York	July 26, 1788	36	Nevada	October 31, 1864
12	North Carolina	November 21, 1789	37	Nebraska	March 1, 1867
13	Rhode Island	May 29, 1790	38	Colorado	August 1, 1876
14	Vermont	March 4, 1791	39	North Dakota	November 2, 1889
15	Kentucky	June 1, 1792	40	South Dakota	November 2, 1889
16	Tennessee	June 1, 1796	41	Montana	November 8, 1889
17	Ohio	March 1, 1803	42	Washington	November 11, 1889
18	Louisiana	April 30, 1812	43	Idaho	July 3, 1890
19	Indiana	December 11, 1816	44	Wyoming	July 10, 1890
20	Mississippi	December 10, 1817	45	Utah	January 4, 1896
21	Illinois	December 3, 1818	46	Oklahoma	November 16, 1907
22	Alabama	December 14, 1819	47	New Mexico	January 6, 1912
23	Maine	March 15, 1820	48	Arizona	February 14, 1912
24	Missouri	August 10, 1821	49	Alaska	January 3, 1959
25	Arkansas	June 15, 1836	50	Hawaii	August 21, 1959

POPULATION OF THE UNITED STATES

Year	Total population	Number per square mile	Year	Total population	Number per square mile	Year	Total population	Number per square mile
1790	3,929	4.5	1808	6,838		1826	11,580	
1791	4,056		1809	7,031		1827	11,909	
1792	4,194		1810	7,224	4.3	1828	12,237	
1793	4,332		1811	7,460		1829	12,565	
1794	4,469		1812	7,700		1830	12,901	7.4
1795	4,607		1813	7,939		1831	13,321	
1796	4,745		1814	8,179		1832	13,742	
1797	4,883		1815	8,419		1833	14,162	
1798	5,021		1816	8,659		1834	14,582	
1799	5,159		1817	8,899		1835	15,003	
1800	5,297	6.1	1818	9,139		1836	15,423	
1801	5,486		1819	9,379		1837	15,843	
1802	5,679		1820	9,618	5.6	1838	16,264	
1803	5,872		1821	9,939		1839	16,684	
1804	5,065		1822	10,268		1840	17,120	9.8
1805	6,258		1823	10,596		1841	17,733	
1806	6,451		1824	10,924		1842	18,345	
1807	6,644		1825	11,252		1843	18,957	

Figures are from *Historical Statistics of the United States, Colonial Times to 1957* (1961), pp. 7, 8; *Statistical Abstract of the United States: 1974*, p. 5, Census Bureau for 1974 and 1975; and *Statistical Abstract of the United States: 1988*, p. 7.

Note: Population figures are in thousands. Density figures are for land area of continental United States.

(continued)

PRESIDENTIAL ELECTIONS, CONTINUED

Year	Number of states	Candidates	Parties	Popular vote	Electoral vote	Percentage of popular vote[1]
1836	26	**Martin Van Buren**	Democratic	765,483	170	50.9
		William H. Harrison	Whig		73	
		Hugh L. White	Whig	739,795	26	
		Daniel Webster	Whig		14	
		W. P. Mangum	Whig		11	
1840	26	**William H. Harrison**	Whig	1,274,624	234	53.1
		Martin Van Buren	Democratic	1,127,781	60	46.9
1844	26	**James K. Polk**	Democratic	1,338,464	170	49.6
		Henry Clay	Whig	1,300,097	105	48.1
		James G. Birney	Liberty	62,300		2.3
1848	30	**Zachary Taylor**	Whig	1,360,967	163	47.4
		Lewis Cass	Democratic	1,222,342	127	42.5
		Martin Van Buren	Free Soil	291,263		10.1
1852	31	**Franklin Pierce**	Democratic	1,601,117	254	50.9
		Winfield Scott	Whig	1,385,453	42	44.1
		John P. Hale	Free Soil	155,825		5.0
1856	31	**James Buchanan**	Democratic	1,832,955	174	45.3
		John C. Frémont	Republican	1,339,932	114	33.1
		Millard Fillmore	American	871,731	8	21.6
1860	33	**Abraham Lincoln**	Republican	1,865,593	180	39.8
		Stephen A. Douglas	Democratic	1,382,713	12	29.5
		John C. Breckinridge	Democratic	848,356	72	18.1
		John Bell	Constitutional Union	592,906	39	12.6
1864	36	**Abraham Lincoln**	Republican	2,206,938	212	55.0
		George B. McClellan	Democratic	1,803,787	21	45.0
1868	37	**Ulysses S. Grant**	Republican	3,013,421	214	52.7
		Horatio Seymour	Democratic	2,706,829	80	47.3
1872	37	**Ulysses S. Grant**	Republican	3,596,745	286	55.6
		Horace Greeley	Democratic	2,843,446	[2]	43.9
1876	38	**Rutherford B. Hayes**	Republican	4,036,572	185	48.0
		Samuel J. Tilden	Democratic	4,284,020	184	51.0
1880	38	**James A. Garfield**	Republican	4,453,295	214	48.5
		Winfield S. Hancock	Democratic	4,414,082	155	48.1
		James B. Weaver	Greenback-Labor	308,578		3.4
1884	38	**Grover Cleveland**	Democratic	4,879,507	219	48.5
		James G. Blaine	Republican	4,850,293	182	48.2
		Benjamin F. Butler	Greenback-Labor	175,370		1.8
		John P. St. John	Prohibition	150,369		1.5
1888	38	**Benjamin Harrison**	Republican	5,477,129	233	47.9
		Grover Cleveland	Democratic	5,537,857	168	48.6
		Clinton B. Fisk	Prohibition	249,506		2.2
		Anson J. Streeter	Union Labor	146,935		1.3

[1]Candidates receiving less than 1 percent of the popular vote have been omitted. For that reason the percentage of popular vote given for any election year may not total 100 percent.

[2]Greeley died shortly after the election; the electors supporting him then divided their votes among minor candidates.

Year	Number of states	Candidates	Parties	Popular vote	Electoral vote	Percentage of popular vote[1]
1892	44	**Grover Cleveland**	Democratic	5,555,426	277	46.1
		Benjamin Harrison	Republican	5,182,690	145	43.0
		James B. Weaver	People's	1,029,846	22	8.5
		John Bidwell	Prohibition	264,133		2.2
1896	45	**William McKinley**	Republican	7,102,246	271	51.1
		William J. Bryan	Democratic	6,492,559	176	47.7
1900	45	**William McKinley**	Republican	7,218,491	292	51.7
		William J. Bryan	Democratic; Populist	6,356,734	155	45.5
		John C. Wooley	Prohibition	208,914		1.5
1904	45	**Theodore Roosevelt**	Republican	7,628,461	336	57.4
		Alton B. Parker	Democratic	5,084,223	140	37.6
		Eugene V. Debs	Socialist	402,283		3.0
		Silas C. Swallow	Prohibition	258,536		1.9
1908	46	**William H. Taft**	Republican	7,675,320	321	51.6
		William J. Bryan	Democratic	6,412,294	162	43.1
		Eugene V. Debs	Socialist	420,793		2.8
		Eugene W. Chafin	Prohibition	253,840		1.7
1912	48	**Woodrow Wilson**	Democratic	6,296,547	435	41.9
		Theodore Roosevelt	Progressive	4,118,571	88	27.4
		William H. Taft	Republican	3,486,720	8	23.2
		Eugene V. Debs	Socialist	900,672		6.0
		Eugene W. Chafin	Prohibition	206,275		1.4
1916	48	**Woodrow Wilson**	Democratic	9,127,695	277	49.4
		Charles E. Hughes	Republican	8,533,507	254	46.2
		A. L. Benson	Socialist	585,113		3.2
		J. Frank Hanly	Prohibition	220,506		1.2
1920	48	**Warren G. Harding**	Republican	16,143,407	404	60.4
		James N. Cox	Democratic	9,130,328	127	34.2
		Eugene V. Debs	Socialist	919,799		3.4
		P. P. Christensen	Farmer-Labor	265,411		1.0
1924	48	**Calvin Coolidge**	Republican	15,718,211	382	54.0
		John W. Davis	Democratic	8,385,283	136	28.8
		Robert M. La Follette	Progressive	4,831,289	13	16.6
1928	48	**Herbert C. Hoover**	Republican	21,391,993	444	58.2
		Alfred E. Smith	Democratic	15,016,169	87	40.9
1932	48	**Franklin D. Roosevelt**	Democratic	22,809,638	472	57.4
		Herbert C. Hoover	Republican	15,758,901	59	39.7
		Norman Thomas	Socialist	881,951		2.2

[1]Candidates receiving less than 1 percent of the popular vote have been omitted. For that reason the percentage of popular vote given for any election year may not total 100 percent.

(continued)

PRESIDENTIAL ELECTIONS, CONTINUED

Year	Number of states	Candidates	Parties	Popular vote	Electoral vote	Percentage of popular vote[1]
1936	48	**Franklin D. Roosevelt**	Democratic	27,752,869	523	60.8
		Alfred M. Landon	Republican	16,674,665	8	36.5
		William Lemke	Union	882,479		1.9
1940	48	**Franklin D. Roosevelt**	Democratic	27,307,819	449	54.8
		Wendell L. Willkie	Republican	22,321,018	82	44.8
1944	48	**Franklin D. Roosevelt**	Democratic	25,606,585	432	53.5
		Thomas E. Dewey	Republican	22,014,745	99	46.0
1948	48	**Harry S Truman**	Democratic	24,105,812	303	49.5
		Thomas E. Dewey	Republican	21,970,065	189	45.1
		J. Strom Thurmond	States' Rights	1,169,063	39	2.4
		Henry A. Wallace	Progressive	1,157,172		2.4
1952	48	**Dwight D. Eisenhower**	Republican	33,936,234	442	55.1
		Adlai E. Stevenson	Democratic	27,314,992	89	44.4
1956	48	**Dwight D. Eisenhower**	Republican	35,590,472	457	57.6
		Adlai E. Stevenson	Democratic	26,022,752	73	42.1
1960	50	**John F. Kennedy**	Democratic	34,227,096	303	49.9
		Richard M. Nixon	Republican	34,108,546	219	49.6
1964	50	**Lyndon B. Johnson**	Democratic	43,126,506	486	61.1
		Barry M. Goldwater	Republican	27,176,799	52	38.5
1968	50	**Richard M. Nixon**	Republican	31,785,480	301	43.4
		Hubert H. Humphrey	Democratic	31,275,165	191	42.7
		George C. Wallace	American Independent	9,906,473	46	13.5
1972	50	**Richard M. Nixon**	Republican	47,169,911	520	60.7
		George S. McGovern	Democratic	29,170,383	17	37.5
1976	50	**Jimmy Carter**	Democratic	40,827,394	297	50.0
		Gerald R. Ford	Republican	39,145,977	240	47.9
1980	50	**Ronald W. Reagan**	Republican	43,899,248	489	50.8
		Jimmy Carter	Democratic	35,481,435	49	41.0
		John B. Anderson	Independent	5,719,437		6.6
		Ed Clark	Libertarian	920,859		1.0
1984	50	**Ronald W. Reagan**	Republican	54,281,858	525	59.2
		Walter F. Mondale	Democratic	37,457,215	13	40.8
1988	50	**George H. Bush**	Republican	47,917,341	426	54
		Michael Dukakis	Democratic	41,013,030	112	46
1992	50	**William Clinton**	Democratic	44,908,254	370	43.0
		George H. Bush	Republican	39,102,343	168	37.4
		Ross Perot	Independent	19,741,065		18.9
1996	50	**William Clinton**	Democratic	45,628,667	379	49.2
		Robert Dole	Republican	37,869,435	159	40.8
		Ross Perot	Reform	7,874,283		8.5
2000	50	**George W. Bush**	Republican	50,456,062	271	47.9
		Albert Gore	Democratic	50,996,582	266	48.4
		Ralph Nader	Green	2,858,843		2.7

[1]Candidates receiving less than 1 percent of the popular vote have been omitted. For that reason the percentage of popular vote given for any election year may not total 100 percent.

PRESIDENTIAL ADMINISTRATIONS

President	Vice President	Secretary of State	Secretary of Treasury	Secretary of War	Secretary of Navy	Postmaster General	Attorney General
George Washington 1789–1797	John Adams 1789–1797	Thomas Jefferson 1789–1794 Edmund Randolph 1794–1795 Timothy Pickering 1795–1797	Alexander Hamilton 1789–1795 Oliver Wolcott 1795–1797	Henry Knox 1789–1795 Timothy Pickering 1795–1796 James McHenry 1796–1797		Samuel Osgood 1789–1791 Timothy Pickering 1791–1795 Joseph Habersham 1795–1797	Edmund Randolph 1789–1794 William Bradford 1794–1795 Charles Lee 1795–1797
John Adams 1797–1801	Thomas Jefferson 1797–1801	Timothy Pickering 1797–1800 John Marshall 1800–1801	Oliver Wolcott 1797–1801 Samuel Dexter 1801	James McHenry 1797–1800 Samuel Dexter 1800–1801	Benjamin Stoddert 1798–1801	Joseph Habersham 1797–1801	Charles Lee 1797–1801
Thomas Jefferson 1801–1809	Aaron Burr 1801–1805 George Clinton 1805–1809	James Madison 1801–1809	Samuel Dexter 1801 Albert Gallatin 1801–1809	Henry Dearborn 1801–1809	Benjamin Stoddert 1801 Robert Smith 1801–1809	Joseph Habersham 1801 Gideon Granger 1801–1809	Levi Lincoln 1801–1805 John Breckinridge 1805–1807 Caesar Rodney 1807–1809
James Madison 1809–1817	George Clinton 1809–1813 Elbridge Gerry 1813–1817	Robert Smith 1809–1811 James Monroe 1811–1817	Albert Gallatin 1809–1814 George Campbell 1814 Alexander Dallas 1814–1816 William Crawford 1816–1817	William Eustis 1809–1813 John Armstrong 1813–1814 James Monroe 1814–1815 William Crawford 1815–1817	Paul Hamilton 1809–1813 William Jones 1813–1814 Benjamin Crowninshield 1814–1817	Gideon Granger 1809–1814 Return Meigs 1814–1817	Caesar Rodney 1809–1811 William Pinkney 1811–1814 Richard Rush 1814–1817
James Monroe 1817–1825	Daniel D. Tompkins 1817–1825	John Quincy Adams 1817–1825	William Crawford 1817–1825	George Graham 1817 John C. Calhoun 1817–1825	Benjamin Crowninshield 1817–1818 Smith Thompson 1818–1823 Samuel Southard 1823–1825	Return Meigs 1817–1823 John McLean 1823–1825	Richard Rush 1817 William Wirt 1817–1825
John Quincy Adams 1825–1829	John C. Calhoun 1825–1829	Henry Clay 1825–1829	Richard Rush 1825–1829	James Barbour 1825–1828 Peter B. Porter 1828–1829	Samuel Southard 1825–1829	John McLean 1825–1829	William Wirt 1825–1829
Andrew Jackson 1829–1837	John C. Calhoun 1829–1833 Martin Van Buren 1833–1837	Martin Van Buren 1829–1831 Edward Livingston 1831–1833 Louis McLane 1833–1834 John Forsyth 1834–1837	Samuel Ingham 1829–1831 Louis McLane 1831–1833 William Duane 1833 Roger B. Taney 1833–1834 Levi Woodbury 1834–1837	John H. Eaton 1829–1831 Lewis Cass 1831–1837 Benjamin Butler 1837	John Branch 1829–1831 Levi Woodbury 1831–1834 Mahlon Dickerson 1834–1837	William Barry 1829–1835 Amos Kendall 1835–1837	John M. Berrien 1829–1831 Roger B. Taney 1831–1833 Benjamin Butler 1833–1837
Martin Van Buren 1837–1841	Richard M. Johnson 1837–1841	John Forsyth 1837–1841	Levi Woodbury 1837–1841	Joel R. Poinsett 1837–1841	Mahlon Dickerson 1837–1838 James K. Paulding 1838–1841	Amos Kendall 1837–1840 John M. Niles 1840–1841	Benjamin Butler 1837–1838 Felix Grundy 1838–1840 Henry D. Gilpin 1840–1841

(continued)

PRESIDENTIAL ADMINISTRATIONS, CONTINUED

President	Vice President	Secretary of State	Secretary of Treasury	Secretary of War
William H. Harrison 1841	John Tyler 1841	Daniel Webster 1841	Thomas Ewing 1841	John Bell 1841
John Tyler 1841–1845		Daniel Webster 1841–1843 Hugh S. Legaré 1843 Abel P. Upshur 1843–1844 John C. Calhoun 1844–1845	Thomas Ewing 1841 Walter Forward 1841–1843 John C. Spencer 1843–1844 George M. Bibb 1844–1845	John Bell 1841 John C. Spencer 1841–1843 James M. Porter 1843–1844 William Wilkins 1844–1845
James K. Polk 1845–1849	George M. Dallas 1845–1849	James Buchanan 1845–1849	Robert J. Walker 1845–1849	William L. Marcy 1845–1849
Zachary Taylor 1849–1850	Millard Fillmore 1849–1850	John M. Clayton 1849–1850	William M. Meredith 1849–1850	George W. Crawford 1849–1850
Millard Fillmore 1850–1853		Daniel Webster 1850–1852 Edward Everett 1852–1853	Thomas Corwin 1850–1853	Charles M. Conrad 1850–1853
Franklin Pierce 1853–1857	William R. King 1853–1857	William L. Marcy 1853–1857	James Guthrie 1853–1857	Jefferson Davis 1853–1857
James Buchanan 1857–1861	John C. Breckinridge 1857–1861	Lewis Cass 1857–1860 Jeremiah S. Black 1860–1861	Howell Cobb 1857–1860 Philip F. Thomas 1860–1861 John A. Dix 1861	John B. Floyd 1857–1861 Joseph Holt 1861
Abraham Lincoln 1861–1865	Hannibal Hamlin 1861–1865 Andrew Johnson 1865	William H. Seward 1861–1865	Salmon P. Chase 1861–1864 William P. Fessenden 1864–1865 Hugh McCulloch 1865	Simon Cameron 1861–1862 Edwin M. Stanton 1862–1865
Andrew Johnson 1865–1869		William H. Seward 1865–1869	Hugh McCulloch 1865–1869	Edwin M. Stanton 1865–1867 Ulysses S. Grant 1867–1868 John M. Schofield 1868–1869
Ulysses S. Grant 1869–1877	Schuyler Colfax 1869–1873 Henry Wilson 1873–1877	Elihu B. Washburne 1869 Hamilton Fish 1869–1877	George S. Boutwell 1869–1873 William A. Richardson 1873–1874 Benjamin H. Bristow 1874–1876 Lot M. Morrill 1876–1877	John A. Rawlins 1869 William T. Sherman 1869 William W. Belknap 1869–1876 Alphonso Taft 1876 James D. Cameron 1876–1877

Secretary of Navy	Postmaster General	Attorney General	Secretary of Interior
George E. Badger 1841	Francis Granger 1841	John J. Crittenden 1841	
George E. Badger 1841 Abel P. Upshur 1841–1843 David Henshaw 1843–1844 Thomas Gilmer 1844 John Y. Mason 1844–1845	Francis Granger 1841 Charles A. Wickliffe 1841–1845	John J. Crittenden 1841 Hugh S. Legaré 1841–1843 John Nelson 1843–1845	
George Bancroft 1845–1846 John Y. Mason 1846–1849	Cave Johnson 1845–1849	John Y. Mason 1845–1846 Nathan Clifford 1846–1848 Isaac Toucey 1848–1849	
William B. Preston 1849–1850	Jacob Collamer 1849–1850	Reverdy Johnson 1849–1850	Thomas Ewing 1849–1850
William A. Graham 1850–1852 John P. Kennedy 1852–1853	Nathan K. Hall 1850–1852 Sam D. Hubbard 1852–1853	John J. Crittenden 1850–1853	Thomas McKennan 1850 A. H. H. Stuart 1850–1853
James C. Dobbin 1853–1857	James Campbell 1853–1857	Caleb Cushing 1853–1857	Robert McClelland 1853–1857
Isaac Toucey 1857–1861	Aaron V. Brown 1857–1859 Joseph Holt 1859–1861 Horatio King 1861	Jeremiah S. Black 1857–1860 Edwin M. Stanton 1860–1861	Jacob Thompson 1857–1861
Gideon Welles 1861–1865	Horatio King 1861 Montgomery Blair 1861–1864 William Dennison 1864–1865	Edward Bates 1861–1864 James Speed 1864–1865	Caleb B. Smith 1861–1863 John P. Usher 1863–1865
Gideon Welles 1865–1869	William Dennison 1865–1866 Alexander Randall 1866–1869 William M. Evarts 1868–1869	James Speed 1865–1866 Henry Stanbery 1866–1868 O. H. Browning 1866–1869	John P. Usher 1865 James Harlan 1865–1866
Adolph E. Borie 1869 George M. Robeson 1869–1877	John A. J. Creswell 1869–1874 James W. Marshall 1874 Marshall Jewell 1874–1876 James N. Tyner 1876–1877	Ebenezer R. Hoar 1869–1870 Amos T. Akerman 1870–1871 G. H. Williams 1871–1875 Edwards Pierrepont 1875–1876 Alphonso Taft 1876–1877	Jacob D. Cox 1869–1870 Columbus Delano 1870–1875 Zachariah Chandler 1875–1877

(continued)

PRESIDENTIAL ADMINISTRATIONS, CONTINUED

President	Vice President	Secretary of State	Secretary of Treasury	Secretary of War	Secretary of Navy
Rutherford B. Hayes 1877–1881	William A. Wheeler 1877–1881	William M. Evarts 1877–1881	John Sherman 1877–1881	George W. McCrary 1877–1879 Alexander Ramsey 1879–1881	R. W. Thompson 1877–1881 Nathan Goff, Jr. 1881
James A. Garfield 1881	Chester A. Arthur 1881	James G. Blaine 1881	William Windom 1881	Robert T. Lincoln 1881	William H. Hunt 1881
Chester A. Arthur 1881–1885		F. T. Frelinghuysen 1881–1885	Charles J. Folger 1881–1884 Walter Q. Gresham 1884 Hugh McCulloch 1884–1885	Robert T. Lincoln 1881–1885	William E. Chandler 1881–1885
Grover Cleveland 1885–1889	T. A. Hendricks 1885	Thomas F. Bayard 1885–1889	Daniel Manning 1885–1887 Charles S. Fairchild 1887–1889	William C. Endicott 1885–1889	William C. Whitney 1885–1889
Benjamin Harrison 1889–1893	Levi P. Morton 1889–1893	James G. Blaine 1889–1892 John W. Foster 1892–1893	William Windom 1889–1891 Charles Foster 1892–1893	Redfield Procter 1889–1891 Stephen B. Elkins 1891–1893	Benjamin F. Tracy 1889–1893
Grover Cleveland 1893–1897	Adlai E. Stevenson 1893–1897	Walter Q. Gresham 1893–1895 Richard Olney 1895–1897	John G. Carlisle 1893–1897	Daniel S. Lamont 1893–1897	Hilary A. Herbert 1893–1897
William McKinley 1897–1901	Garret A. Hobart 1897–1899 Theodore Roosevelt 1901	John Sherman 1897–1898 William R. Day 1898 John Hay 1898–1901	Lyman J. Gage 1897–1901	Russell A. Alger 1897–1899 Elihu Root 1899–1901	John D. Long 1897–1901
Theodore Roosevelt 1901–1909	Charles Fairbanks 1905–1909	John Hay 1901–1905 Elihu Root 1905–1909 Robert Bacon 1909	Lyman J. Gage 1901–1902 Leslie M. Shaw 1902–1907 George B. Cortelyou 1907–1909	Elihu Root 1901–1904 William H. Taft 1904–1908 Luke E. Wright 1908–1909	John D. Long 1901–1902 William H. Moody 1902–1904 Paul Morton 1904–1905 Charles J. Bonaparte 1905–1906 Victor H. Metcalf 1906–1908 T. H. Newberry 1908–1909
William H. Taft 1909–1913	James S. Sherman 1909–1913	Philander C. Knox 1909–1913	Franklin MacVeagh 1909–1913	Jacob M. Dickinson 1909–1911 Henry L. Stimson 1911–1913	George von L. Meyer 1909–1913
Woodrow Wilson 1913–1921	Thomas R. Marshall 1913–1921	William J. Bryan 1913–1915 Robert Lansing 1915–1920 Bainbridge Colby 1920–1921	William G. McAdoo 1913–1918 Carter Glass 1918–1920 David F. Houston 1920–1921	Lindley M. Garrison 1913–1916 Newton D. Baker 1916–1921	Josephus Daniels 1913–1921

Postmaster General	Attorney General	Secretary of Interior	Secretary of Agriculture	Secretary of Commerce and Labor	
David M. Key 1877–1880 Horace Maynard 1880–1881	Charles Devens 1877–1881	Carl Schurz 1877–1881			
Thomas L. James 1881	Wayne MacVeagh 1881	S. J. Kirkwood 1881			
Thomas L. James 1881 Timothy O. Howe 1881–1883 Walter Q. Gresham 1883–1884 Frank Hatton 1884–1885	B. H. Brewster 1881–1885	Henry M. Teller 1881–1885			
William F. Vilas 1885–1888 Don M. Dickinson 1888–1889	A. H. Garland 1885–1889	L. Q. C. Lamar 1885–1888 William F. Vilas 1888–1889	Norman J. Colman 1889		
John Wanamaker 1889–1893	W. H. H. Miller 1889–1893	John W. Noble 1889–1893	Jeremiah M. Rusk 1889–1893		
Wilson S. Bissel 1893–1895 William L. Wilson 1895–1897	Richard Olney 1893–1895 Judson Harmon 1895–1897	Hoke Smith 1893–1896 David R. Francis 1896–1897	J. Sterling Morton 1893–1897		
James A. Gary 1897–1898 Charles E. Smith 1898–1901	Joseph McKenna 1897–1898 John W. Griggs 1898–1901 Philander C. Knox 1901	Cornelius N. Bliss 1897–1898 E. A. Hitchcock 1898–1901	James Wilson 1897–1901		
Charles E. Smith 1901–1902 Henry C. Payne 1902–1904 Robert J. Wynne 1904–1905 George B. Cortelyou 1905–1907 George von L. Meyer 1907–1909	Philander C. Knox 1901–1904 William H. Moody 1904–1906 Charles J. Bonaparte 1906–1909	E. A. Hitchcock 1901–1907 James R. Garfield 1907–1909	James Wilson' 1901–1909	George B. Cortelyou 1903–1904 Victor H. Metcalf 1904–1906 Oscar S. Straus 1906–1909	

				Secretary of Commerce	Secretary of Labor
Frank H. Hitchcock 1909–1913	G. W. Wickersham 1909–1913	R. A. Ballinger 1909–1911 Walter L. Fisher 1911–1913	James Wilson 1909–1913	Charles Nagel 1909–1913	
Albert S. Burleson 1913–1921	J. C. McReynolds 1913–1914 T. W. Gregory 1914–1919 A. Mitchell Palmer 1919–1921	Franklin K. Lane 1913–1920 John B. Payne 1920–1921	David F. Houston 1913–1920 E. T. Meredith 1920–1921	W. C. Redfield 1913–1919 J. W. Alexander 1919–1921	William B. Wilson 1913–1921

(continued)

PRESIDENTIAL ADMINISTRATIONS, CONTINUED

President	Vice President	Secretary of State	Secretary of Treasury	Secretary of War	Secretary of Navy	Postmaster General	Attorney General
Warren G. Harding 1921–1923	Calvin Coolidge 1921–1923	Charles E. Hughes 1921–1923	Andrew W. Mellon 1921–1923	John W. Weeks 1921–1923	Edwin Denby 1921–1923	Will H. Hays 1921–1922 Hubert Work 1922–1923 Harry S. New 1923	H. M. Daugherty 1921–1923
Calvin Coolidge 1923–1929	Charles G. Dawes 1925–1929	Charles E. Hughes 1923–1925 Frank B. Kellogg 1925–1929	Andrew W. Mellon 1923–1929	John W. Weeks 1923–1925 Dwight F. Davis 1925–1929	Edwin Denby 1923–1924 Curtis D. Wilbur 1924–1929	Harry S. New 1923–1929	H. M. Daugherty 1923–1924 Harlan F. Stone 1924–1925 John G. Sargent 1925–1929
Herbert C. Hoover 1929–1933	Charles Curtis 1929–1933	Henry L. Stimson 1929–1933	Andrew W. Mellon 1929–1932 Ogden L. Mills 1932–1933	James W. Good 1929 Patrick J. Hurley 1929–1933	Charles F. Adams 1929–1933	Walter F. Brown 1929–1933	J. D. Mitchell 1929–1933
Franklin Delano Roosevelt 1933–1945	John Nance Garner 1933–1941 Henry A. Wallace 1941–1945 Harry S Truman 1945	Cordell Hull 1933–1944 E. R. Stettinius, Jr. 1944–1945	William H. Woodin 1933–1934 Henry Morgenthau, Jr. 1934–1945	George H. Dern 1933–1936 Harry H. Woodring 1936–1940 Henry L. Stimson 1940–1945	Claude A. Swanson 1933–1940 Charles Edison 1940 Frank Knox 1940–1944 James V. Forrestal 1944–1945	James A. Farley 1933–1940 Frank C. Walker 1940–1945	H. S. Cummings 1933–1939 Frank Murphy 1939–1940 Robert Jackson 1940–1941 Francis Biddel 1941–1945
Harry S Truman 1945–1953	Alben W. Barkley 1949–1953	James F. Byrnes 1945–1947 George C. Marshall 1947–1949 Dean G. Acheson 1949–1953	Fred M. Vinson 1945–1946 John W. Snyder 1946–1953	Robert P. Patterson 1945–1947 Kenneth C. Royall 1947 Secretary of Defense James V. Forrestal 1947–1949 Louis A. Johnson 1949–1950 George C. Marshall 1950–1951 Robert A. Lovett 1951–1953	James V. Forrestal 1945–1947	R. E. Hannegan 1945–1947 Jesse M. Donaldson 1947–1953	Tom C. Clark 1945–1949 J. H. McGrath 1949–1952 James P. McGranery 1952–1953
Dwight D. Eisenhower 1953–1961	Richard M. Nixon 1953–1961	John Foster Dulles 1953–1959 Christian A. Herter 1957–1961	George M. Humphrey 1953–1957 Robert B. Anderson 1957–1961	Charles E. Wilson 1953–1957 Neil H. McElroy 1957–1961 Thomas S. Gates 1959–1961		A. E. Summerfield 1953–1961	H. Brownell, Jr. 1953–1957 William P. Rogers 1957–1961
John F. Kennedy 1961–1963	Lyndon B. Johnson 1961–1963	Dean Rusk 1961–1963	C. Douglas Dillon 1961–1963	Robert S. McNamara 1961–1963		J. Edward Day 1961–1963 John A. Gronouski 1961–1963	Robert F. Kennedy 1961–1963
Lyndon B. Johnson 1963–1969	Hubert H. Humphrey 1965–1969	Dean Rusk 1963–1969	C. Douglas Dillon 1963–1965 Henry H. Fowler 1965–1968 Joseph W. Barr 1968–1969	Robert S. McNamara 1963–1968 Clark M. Clifford 1968–1969		John A. Gronouski 1963–1965 Lawrence F. O'Brien 1965–1968 W. Marvin Watson 1968–1969	Robert F. Kennedy 1963–1965 N. deB. Katzenbach 1965–1967 Ramsey Clark 1967–1969

Secretary of Interior	Secretary of Agriculture	Secretary of Commerce	Secretary of Labor	Secretary of Health, Education and Welfare	Secretary of Housing and Urban Development	Secretary of Transportation
Albert B. Fall 1921–1923 Hubert Work 1923	Henry C. Wallace 1921–1923	Herbert C. Hoover 1921–1923	James J. Davis 1921–1923			
Hubert Work 1923–1928 Roy O. West 1928–1929	Henry C. Wallace 1923–1924 Howard M. Gore 1924–1925 W. J. Jardine 1925–1929	Herbert C. Hoover 1923–1928 William F. Whiting 1928–1929	James J. Davis 1923–1929			
Ray L. Wilbur 1929–1933	Arthur M. Hyde 1929–1933 Roy D. Chapin 1932–1933	Robert P. Lamont 1929–1932 William N. Doak 1930–1933	James J. Davis 1929–1930			
Harold L. Ickes 1933–1945	Henry A. Wallace 1933–1940 Claude R. Wickard 1940–1945	Daniel C. Roper 1933–1939 Harry L. Hopkins 1939–1940 Jesse Jones 1940–1945 Henry A. Wallace 1945	Frances Perkins 1933–1945			
Harold L. Ickes 1945–1946 Julius A. Krug 1946–1949 Oscar L. Chapman 1949–1953	C. P. Anderson 1945–1948 C. F. Brannan 1948–1953	W. A. Harriman 1946–1948 Charles Sawyer 1948–1953	L. B. Schwellenbach 1945–1948 Maurice J. Tobin 1948–1953			
Douglas McKay 1953–1956 Fred Seaton 1956–1961	Ezra T. Benson 1953–1961	Sinclair Weeks 1953–1958 Lewis L. Strauss 1958–1961	Martin P. Durkin 1953 James P. Mitchell 1953–1961	Oveta Culp Hobby 1953–1955 Marion B. Folsom 1955–1958 Arthur S. Flemming 1958–1961		
Stewart L. Udall 1961–1963	Orville L. Freeman 1961–1963	Luther H. Hodges 1961–1963	Arthur J. Goldberg 1961–1963 W. Willard Wirtz 1962–1963	A. H. Ribicoff 1961–1963 Anthony J. Celebrezze 1962–1963		
Stewart L. Udall 1963–1969	Orville L. Freeman 1963–1969	Luther H. Hodges 1963–1965 John T. Connor 1965–1967 Alexander B. Trowbridge 1967–1968 C. R. Smith 1968–1969	W. Willard Wirtz 1963–1969	Anthony J. Celebrezze 1963–1965 John W. Gardner 1965–1968 Wilbur J. Cohen 1968–1969	Robert C. Weaver 1966–1968 Robert C. Wood 1968–1969	Alan S. Boyd 1966–1969

(continued)

PRESIDENTIAL ADMINISTRATIONS, CONTINUED

President	Vice President	Secretary of State	Secretary of Treasury	Secretary of Defense	Postmaster General[1]	Attorney General	Secretary of Interior	Secretary of Agriculture
Richard M. Nixon 1969–1974	Spiro T. Agnew 1969–1973 Gerald R. Ford 1973–1974	William P. Rogers 1969–1973 Henry A. Kissinger 1973–1974	David M. Kennedy 1969–1970 John B. Connally 1970–1972 George P. Schultz 1972–1974 William E. Simon 1974	Melvin R. Laird 1969–1973 Elliot L. Richardson 1973 James R. Schlesinger 1973–1974	Winton M. Blount 1969–1971	John M. Mitchell 1969–1972 Richard G. Kleindienst 1972–1973 Elliot L. Richardson 1973 William B. Saxbe 1974	Walter J. Hickel 1969–1971 Rogers C. B. Morton 1971–1974	Clifford M. Hardin 1969–1971 Earl L. Butz 1971–1974
Gerald R. Ford 1974–1977	Nelson A. Rockefeller 1974–1977	Henry A. Kissinger 1974–1977	William E. Simon 1974–1977	James R. Schlesinger 1974–1975 Donald H. Rumsfeld 1975–1977		William B. Saxbe 1974–1975 Edward H. Levi 1975–1977	Rogers C. B. Morton 1974–1975 Stanley K. Hathaway 1975 Thomas D. Kleppe 1975–1977	Earl L. Butz 1974–1976
Jimmy Carter 1977–1981	Walter F. Mondale 1977–1981	Cyrus R. Vance 1977–1980 Edmund S. Muskie 1980–1981	W. Michael Blumenthal 1977–1979 G. William Miller 1979–1981	Harold Brown 1977–1981		Griffin Bell 1977–1979 Benjamin R. Civiletti 1979–1981	Cecil D. Andrus 1977–1981	Robert Bergland 1977–1981
Ronald W. Reagan 1981–1989	George H. Bush 1981–1989	Alexander M. Haig, Jr. 1981–1982 George P. Shultz 1982–1989	Donald T. Regan 1981–1985 James A. Baker 1985–1988 Nicholas F. Brady 1988–1989	Caspar W. Weinberger 1981–1987 Frank C. Carlucci 1987–1989		William French Smith 1981–1985 Edwin Meese 1985–1988 Richard Thornburgh 1988–1989	James G. Watt 1981–1983 William P. Clark 1983–1985 Donald P. Hodel 1985–1989	John R. Block 1981–1986 Richard E. Lyng 1986–1989
George H. Bush 1989–1993	J. Danforth Quayle 1989–1993	James A. Baker 1989–1992 Lawrence S. Eagleburger 1992–1993	Nicholas F. Brady 1989–1993	Richard Cheney 1989–1993		Richard Thornburgh 1989–1990 William Barr 1990–1993	Manuel Lujan 1989–1993	Clayton Yeutter 1989–1990 Edward Madigan 1990–1993
William Clinton 1993–2001	Albert Gore 1993–2001	Warren M. Christopher 1993–1996 Madeleine K. Albright 1997–2001	Lloyd Bentsen 1993–1994 Robert E. Rubin 1994–1999 Lawrence H. Summers 1999–2001	Les Aspin 1993–1994 William J. Perry 1994–1996 William S. Cohen 1997–2001		Janet Reno 1993–2001	Bruce Babbitt 1993–2001	Mike Espy 1993–1994 Dan Glickman 1995–2001
George W. Bush 2001–	Richard B. Cheney 2001–	Gen. Colin L. Powell 2001–	Paul H. O'Neill 2001–2002 John W. Snow 2003–	Donald H. Rumsfeld 2001–		John Ashcroft 2001–	Gale A. Norton 2001–	Ann M. Veneman 2001–

[1]On July 1, 1971, the Post Office became an independent agency. After that date, the postmaster general was no longer a member of the Cabinet.
[2]Acting secretary.

Secretary of Commerce	Secretary of Labor	Secretary of Health, Education and Welfare / Secretary of Health and Human Services	Secretary of Education	Secretary of Housing and Urban Development	Secretary of Transportation	Secretary of Energy	Secretary of Veterans Affairs	Secretary of Homeland Security
Maurice H. Stans 1969–1972 Peter G. Peterson 1972 Frederick B. Dent 1972–1974	George P. Shultz 1969–1970 James D. Hodgson 1970–1973 Peter J. Brennan 1973–1974	Robert H. Finch 1969–1970 Elliot L. Richardson 1970–1973 Caspar W. Weinberger 1973–1974		George W. Romney 1969–1973 James T. Lynn 1973–1974	John A. Volpe 1969–1973 Claude S. Brinegar 1973–1974			
Frederick B. Dent 1974–1975 Rogers C. B. Morton 1975 Elliot L. Richardson 1975–1977	Peter J. Brennan 1974–1975 John T. Dunlop 1975–1976 W. J. Usery 1976–1977	Caspar W. Weinberger 1974–1975 Forrest D. Matthews 1975–1977		James T. Lynn 1974–1975 Carla A. Hills 1975–1977	Claude S. Brinegar 1974–1975 William T. Coleman 1975–1977			
Juanita Kreps 1977–1981	F. Ray Marshall 1977–1981	Joseph Califano 1977–1979 Patricia Roberts Harris 1979–1980		Patricia Roberts Harris 1977–1979 Moon Landrieu 1979–1981	Brock Adams 1977–1979 Neil E. Goldschmidt 1979–1981	James R. Schlesinger 1977–1979 Charles W. Duncan, Jr. 1979–1981		
		Patricia Roberts Harris 1980–1981	Shirley M. Hufstedler 1980–1981					
Malcolm Baldridge 1981–1987 C. William Verity, Jr. 1987–1989	Raymond J. Donovan 1981–1985 William E. Brock 1985–1987 Ann Dore McLaughlin 1987–1989	Richard S. Schweiker 1981–1983 Margaret M. Heckler 1983–1985 Otis R. Bowen 1985–1989	Terrell H. Bell 1981–1985 William J. Bennett 1985–1988 Lauro Fred Cavazos 1988–1989	Samuel R. Pierce, Jr. 1981–1989	Drew Lewis 1981–1983 Elizabeth H. Dole 1983–1987 James H. Burnley 1987–1989	James B. Edwards 1981–1982 Donald P. Hodel 1982–1985 John S. Harrington 1985–1989		
Robert Mosbacher 1989–1991 Barbara Franklin 1991–1993	Elizabeth Dole 1989–1990 Lynn Martin 1992–1993	Louis Sullivan 1989–1993	Lamar Alexander 1990–1993	Jack Kemp 1989–1993	Samuel Skinner 1989–1990 Andrew Card 1990–1993	James Watkins 1989–1993	Edward J. Derwinski 1989–1993	
Ronald H. Brown 1993–1996 William M. Daley 1997–2000 Norman Y. Mineta 2000–2001	Robert B. Reich 1993–1996 Alexis M. Herman 1997–2001	Donna E. Shalala 1993–2001	Richard W. Riley 1993–2001	Henry G. Cisneros 1993–1996 Andrew M. Cuomo 1997–2001	Federico F. Peña 1993–1996 Rodney E. Slater 1997–2001	Hazel O'Leary 1993–1996 Federico F. Peña 1997–1998 Bill Richardson 1998–2001	Jesse Brown 1993–1997 Togo D. West, Jr.[2] 1998–2001	
Donald L. Evans 2001–	Elaine L. Chao 2001–	Tommy G. Thompson 2001–	Roderick R. Paige 2001–	Melquiades R. Martinez 2001–	Norman Y. Mineta 2001–	Spencer Abraham 2001–	Anthony Principi 2001–	Tom Ridge 2001–

JUSTICES OF THE U.S. SUPREME COURT

Name	Term of Service	Years of Service	Appointed By	Name	Term of Service	Years of Service	Appointed By
John Jay	1789–1795	5	Washington	Rufus W. Peckham	1895–1909	14	Cleveland
John Rutledge	1789–1791	1	Washington	Joseph McKenna	1898–1925	26	McKinley
William Cushing	1789–1810	20	Washington	Oliver W. Holmes, Jr.	1902–1932	30	T. Roosevelt
James Wilson	1789–1798	8	Washington	William R. Day	1903–1922	19	T. Roosevelt
John Blair	1789–1796	6	Washington	William H. Moody	1906–1910	3	T. Roosevelt
Robert H. Harrison	1789–1790	—	Washington	Horace H. Lurton	1910–1914	4	Taft
James Iredell	1790–1799	9	Washington	Charles E. Hughes	1910–1916	5	Taft
Thomas Johnson	1791–1793	1	Washington	Willis Van Devanter	1911–1937	26	Taft
William Paterson	1793–1806	13	Washington	Joseph R. Lamar	1911–1916	5	Taft
John Rutledge[1]	1795	—	Washington	**Edward D. White**	1910–1921	11	Taft
Samuel Chase	1796–1811	15	Washington	Mahlon Pitney	1912–1922	10	Taft
Oliver Ellsworth	1796–1800	4	Washington	James C. McReynolds	1914–1941	26	Wilson
Bushrod Washington	1798–1829	31	J. Adams	Louis D. Brandeis	1916–1939	22	Wilson
Alfred Moore	1799–1804	4	J. Adams	John H. Clarke	1916–1922	6	Wilson
John Marshall	1801–1835	34	J. Adams	**William H. Taft**	1921–1930	8	Harding
William Johnson	1804–1834	30	Jefferson	George Sutherland	1922–1938	15	Harding
H. Brockholst Livingston	1806–1823	16	Jefferson	Pierce Butler	1922–1939	16	Harding
Thomas Todd	1807–1826	18	Jefferson	Edward T. Sanford	1923–1930	7	Harding
Joseph Story	1811–1845	33	Madison	Harlan F. Stone	1925–1941	16	Coolidge
Gabriel Duval	1811–1835	24	Madison	**Charles E. Hughes**	1930–1941	11	Hoover
Smith Thompson	1823–1843	20	Monroe	Owen J. Roberts	1930–1945	15	Hoover
Robert Trimble	1826–1828	2	J. Q. Adams	Benjamin N. Cardozo	1932–1938	6	Hoover
John McLean	1829–1861	32	Jackson	Hugo L. Black	1937–1971	34	F. Roosevelt
Henry Baldwin	1830–1844	14	Jackson	Stanley F. Reed	1938–1957	19	F. Roosevelt
James M. Wayne	1835–1867	32	Jackson	Felix Frankfurter	1939–1962	23	F. Roosevelt
Roger B. Taney	1836–1864	28	Jackson	William O. Douglas	1939–1975	36	F. Roosevelt
Philip P. Barbour	1836–1841	4	Jackson	Frank Murphy	1940–1949	9	F. Roosevelt
John Catron	1837–1865	28	Van Buren	**Harlan F. Stone**	1941–1946	5	F. Roosevelt
John McKinley	1837–1852	15	Van Buren	James F. Byrnes	1941–1942	1	F. Roosevelt
Peter V. Daniel	1841–1860	19	Van Buren	Robert H. Jackson	1941–1954	13	F. Roosevelt
Samuel Nelson	1845–1872	27	Tyler	Wiley B. Rutledge	1943–1949	6	F. Roosevelt
Levi Woodbury	1845–1851	5	Polk	Harold H. Burton	1945–1958	13	Truman
Robert C. Grier	1846–1870	23	Polk	**Fred M. Vinson**	1946–1953	7	Truman
Benjamin R. Curtis	1851–1857	6	Fillmore	Tom C. Clark	1949–1967	18	Truman
John A. Campbell	1853–1861	8	Pierce	Sherman Minton	1949–1956	7	Truman
Nathan Clifford	1858–1881	23	Buchanan	**Earl Warren**	1953–1969	16	Eisenhower
Noah H. Swayne	1862–1881	18	Lincoln	John Marshall Harlan	1955–1971	16	Eisenhower
Samuel F. Miller	1862–1890	28	Lincoln	William J. Brennan, Jr.	1956–1990	34	Eisenhower
David Davis	1862–1877	14	Lincoln	Charles E. Whittaker	1957–1962	5	Eisenhower
Stephen J. Field	1863–1897	34	Lincoln	Potter Stewart	1958–1981	23	Eisenhower
Salmon P. Chase	1864–1873	8	Lincoln	Byron R. White	1962–1993	31	Kennedy
William Strong	1870–1880	10	Grant	Arthur J. Goldberg	1962–1965	3	Kennedy
Joseph P. Bradley	1870–1892	22	Grant	Abe Fortas	1965–1969	4	Johnson
Ward Hunt	1873–1882	9	Grant	Thurgood Marshall	1967–1994	24	Johnson
Morrison R. Waite	1874–1888	14	Grant	**Warren E. Burger**	1969–1986	18	Nixon
John M. Harlan	1877–1911	34	Hayes	Harry A. Blackmun	1970–1994	24	Nixon
William B. Woods	1880–1887	7	Hayes	Lewis F. Powell, Jr.	1971–1987	15	Nixon
Stanley Matthews	1881–1889	7	Garfield	**William H. Rehnquist**[2]	1971–	—	Nixon
Horace Gray	1882–1902	20	Arthur	John P. Stevens III	1975–	—	Ford
Samuel Blatchford	1882–1893	11	Arthur	Sandra Day O'Connor	1981–	—	Reagan
Lucius Q. C. Lamar	1888–1893	5	Cleveland	Antonin Scalia	1986–	—	Reagan
Melville W. Fuller	1888–1910	21	Cleveland	Anthony M. Kennedy	1988–	—	Reagan
David J. Brewer	1890–1910	20	B. Harrison	David Souter	1990–	—	Bush
Henry B. Brown	1890–1906	16	B. Harrison	Clarence Thomas	1991–	—	Bush
George Shiras, Jr.	1892–1903	10	B. Harrison	Ruth Bader Ginsburg	1993–	—	Clinton
Howell E. Jackson	1893–1895	2	B. Harrison	Stephen G. Breyer	1994–	—	Clinton
Edward D. White	1894–1910	16	Cleveland				

Note: Chief justices appear in bold type.

[1] Acting chief justice; Senate refused to confirm appointment.

[2] Chief justice from 1986 on (Reagan administration).

Photo Credits

Images not referenced below are in the public domain.

Chapter 1

p. 2 (left): © Bettmann/Corbis; **p. 2 (right):** Bibliotheque Nationale de France; **p. 10:** © Jon Adkins/National Geographic Society; **p. 11 (top):** © Genevieve Leaper; Ecoscene/Corbis; **p. 11 (bottom):** © Werner Forman/Art Resource, NY; **p. 13:** © Archivo Iconografico, S.A./Corbis; **p. 14:** Leonardo Torriani, Die Kanarischen Inseln und Ihre Urbewohner [1590], ed. Dominik Wolfel (Leipzig: K. F. Koehler, 1940), Plate X; **p. 18 (top left):** © North Wind Picture Archives; **p. 18 (top right):** © Stock Montage, Inc.; **p. 18 (bottom):** © Historical Picture Archive/Corbis; **p. 19 (top):** Courtesy of the John Carter Brown Library at Brown University; **p. 22 (bottom):** © Boltin Picture Library; **p. 22 (top):** © Werner Forman/Art Resource, NY; **p. 23 (top):** Reconstruction by Tatiana Proskouriakoff. From The Fall of the Ancient Maya by David Webster, published by Thames & Hudson, London and New York; **p. 23 (bottom):** © Boltin Picture Library; **p. 25 (left):** Image taken from exhibit produced by the Florida Museum of Natural History; **p. 25 (right):** © Boltin Picture Library; **p. 26 (bottom):** © Richard A. Cooke/Corbis; **p. 28:** Painting by Lloyd K. Townsend; **p. 29:** © David Muench; **p. 30:** North Wind Picture Archives; **p. 31:** Moctezuma's Mexico, by David Carrasco and Eduardo Mato Moctezuma, © 1992 University Press of Colorado. Photographs by Salvador Guil'liem Arroyo; **p. 32 (top):** Fray Bernardinode Sahagun, General History of the Things of New Spain; **p. 32 (bottom):** Folding Screen: The Encounter of Cortes and Moctezuma (obverse); The Four Continents (reverse) Collection Banco Nacional de Mexico, Mexico City; **p. 33:** York Public Library. Astor, Lenox and Tilden Foundations, Rare book Division; **p. 35:** © Picture Desk/Kobal Collection/Warner Bros; **p. 37:** © Hulton Archive/Getty Images

Chapter 2

p. 42: © SEF/Art Resource, NY; **p. 45:** Theodore DeBry; **p. 47:** © Picture Desk/Kobal Collection/Alliance/Goldwyn; **p. 48:** Theodore DeBry; **p. 56:** © Bettmann/Corbis; **p. 57:** William C. Clements Library, University of Michigan, Ann Arbor; **p. 59:** Courtesy of the John Carter Brown Library at Brown University; **p. 60:** Image courtesy of Historic St. Mary's City; **p. 62:** The Library Company of Philadelphia; **p. 64:** Museum of the American Indian/Heye Foundation, NY; **p. 68:** Photograph © 2003 Museum of Fine Arts, Boston; **p. 69:** From the Collection of the Library of Congress; **p. 70:** © Bettmann/Corbis; **p. 76:** North Wind Picture Archives; **p. 78:** © Bettmann/Corbis; **p. 79 (left):** Hans Oswald Wild/TimePix; **p. 79 (right):** From the Collections of the Library of Congress

Chapter 3

p. 82: © The Granger Collection, New York; **p. 90:** © The British Museum; **p. 92:** Houghton Library, Harvard University, Cambridge, Ma; **p. 94:** Courtesy, American Antiquarian Society; **p. 95:** Patrick M. Malone, The Skulking Way of War, Madison Books c 1991; **p. 97:** © Wendell Metzen/Bruce Coleman Inc.; **p. 98:** The Virginia Journals of Benjamin Henry Latrobe (2 vols., New Haven, 1977) I, 181-82, 247, plate 21; **p. 102 (left):** Thomas B. Macaulay, History of England from the Accession of James II, ed. by Charles H. Firth (London: Macmillan, 1914); **p. 10 (right):** Thomas B. Macaulay, History of England from the Accession of James II, ed. by Charles H. Firth (London: Macmillan, 1914); **p. 104:** PBS Home Video; **p. 105:** © Hulton Archive/Getty Images; **p. 108:** Yale University Art Gallery; **p. 109 (left):** Hampton Court Palace "A View of Hampton Court" by Leonard Knyff, c.1703 (detail). The Royal Collection © 1998 Her Majesty The Queen. The Royal Picture Library, Windsor Castle; **p. 109 (right):** Dixon Harvesters, c.1725. by English School, (18th century) Cheltenham Art Gallery & Museums, Gloucestershire, U.K./The Bridgeman Art Library; **p. 111:** Archives Nationales; **p. 115 (left):** Courtesy Massachusetts Historical Society; **p. 115 (right):** Illustrated London News

Chapter 4

p. 118: 1963.6.1 (1904)/PA: Copley, John Singelton, "Watson and the Shark", Ferdinand Lammot Belin Fund © 1998 Board of Trustees, National Gallery of Art, Washington, 1778, oil on canvas, 1.82 x 2.297 (71 3/4 x 90 1/2); framed: 2.413 x 2.642 x .101 (95 x 104 x 4); **p. 122:** Chicago Historical Society; **p. 123:** after John Barbot, from Churchill's Voyages; **p. 124:** © The Granger Collection; **p. 125:** North Wind Picture Archives; **p. 126:** © Corbis; **p. 128:** Copyright © 1965 by Edwin Tunis. Copyright renewed 1993 by David Hutton, Executor for

the Estate of Edwin Tunis. Illustrations from Colonial Craftsmen and the beginnings of American Industry, now published by Johns Hopkins University Press. Reprinted by permission of Curtis Brown, Ltd.; **p. 130:** The Saint Louis Museum Purchase; **p. 131:** from the Collections of the Library of Congress; **p. 133:** Hargrett Rare Book and Manuscript Library/University of Georgia Libraries, Athens; **p. 138:** Colonial Williamsburg Foundation; **p. 142 (bottom):** Peabody Museum, Harvard University. Photograph by Hillel Burger; **p. 145:** Collection of the New-York Historical Society; **p. 147:** North Wind Picture Archives; **p. 149:** © Hulton Archive/Getty Images; **p. 151:** © Picture Desk/Kobal Collection/20th Century Fox/Morgan Creek; **p. 155:** Clements Library, University of Michigan, Ann Arbor

Chapter 5

p. 158: © The Granger Collection; **p. 163:** Colonial Williamsburg Foundation; **p. 165:** 05.003 New York Public Library; **p. 167:** © Philadelphia Museum of Art/Corbis; **p. 168:** Courtesy of the John Carter Brown Library at Brown University; **p. 171:** The Granger Collection, New York; **p. 173:** Colonial Williamsburg Foundation; **p. 179 (top):** From the Collections of the Library of Congress; **p. 179 (bottom):** American Antiquarian Society; **p. 180:** Courtesy of the John Carter Brown Library at Brown University; **p. 181:** Courtesy, American Antiquarian Society; **p. 182:** From the Collections of the Library of Congress; **p. 183 (left):** © North Wind Picture Archives; **p. 183 (right):** © The Granger Collection; **p. 185:** The Granger Collection, New York; **p. 189:** © Picture Desk/Kobal Collection/Columbia

Chapter 6

p. 192: Gift of the Owners of the Old Boston Museum Courtesy, Museum of Fine Arts, Boston © 2002/All Rights Reserved; **p. 197:** Lewis Walpole Library, Yale University; **p. 199:** Fairfield Historical Society; **p. 200:** © Alon Reininger/Woodfin Camp; **p. 205:** Courtesy, American Antiquarian Society; **p. 206:** National Archives of Canada/C-002001; **p. 207 (left):** Fenimore Art Museum, New York State Historical Association, Cooperstown, New York; **p. 207 (right):** Chicago Historical Society; **p. 209 (top):** Courtesy, American Antiquarian Society; **p. 209 (bottom):** Colonial Williamsburg; **p. 212:** Yale University Art Gallery, Gift of Ebenezer Baldwin, B.A. 1808; **p. 214:** From the Collections of the Library of Congress; **p. 217:** © J. Gilbert Harrington; **p. 219 (bottom):** Missouri Historical Society; **p. 224:**

© Bettmann/Corbis; **p. 225:** © North Wind Picture Archives

Chapter 7

p. 230: The Historical Society of Pennsylvania, Preparation for War to Defend Commerce, by William Russell Birch(BD61B531.2pl.29); **p. 235:** PBS Home Video; **p. 236:** Lewis Miller (1796-1882). The Historical Society of York County, The York County Heritage Trust, PA.; **p. 237:** New Bedford Whaling Museum; **p. 240:** The Granger Collection, New York; **p. 241:** "Old Homestead, Late Residence of R. H,. Constant." From Illustrated Atlas Map of Sangamon County, Ill. (Springfield, Ill.: Brink, McComrick & Co., 1874); **p. 243:** Abby Aldrich Rockefeller Folk Art Center, Williamsburg, VA; **p. 245:** Collection of the Maryland Historical Society, Baltimore; **p. 246:** The Granger Collection, New York; **p. 247:** Collection of the New-York Historical Society; **p. 248:** Courtesy, Gore Place; **p. 250:** The Historical Society of Pennsylvania, Procession of the Victuallers, by John Lewis Krimmel (Bc85 K89); **p. 251:** John Lewis Krimmel, American, 1786-1821 Village Tavern, 1813-14, oil on canvas, 16 7/8 x 22 1/2 in. (42.8 x 56.9 cm) The Toledo Museum of Art, Toledo, Ohio; Purchased with funds from the Florence Scott Libbey Bequest in Memory of her Father, Maurice A. Scott; **p. 257:** New Bedford Whaling Museum; **p. 258:** Historical Commission, Mother Bethel AME Church, Philadelphia, PA

Chapter 8

p. 262: collections of Davenport West, Jr.; **p. 265:** National Portrait Gallery/Smithsonian Institution/Art Resource, NY; **p. 269:** © Gianni Dagli/Corbis; **p. 273:** © North Wind Picture Archives; **p. 278 (top):** © Bettmann/Corbis; **p. 278 (bottom):** The Granger Collection, New York; **p. 280:** Architect of the Capitol; **p. 281:** A View of New Orleans Taken from the Plantation of Marigny, November, 1803 by Boqueto de Woiserie, Chicago Historical Society; **p. 284:** North Wind Picture Archives; **p. 285:** North Wind Picture Archives; **p. 286:** Courtesy of the Royal Ontario Museum, Toronto, Canada; **p. 288:** From the Collections of the Library of Congress; **p. 289:** Allyn Cox, 1974 Architect of the Capitol; **p. 291:** © Picture Desk/Kobal Collection/Paramount

Chapter 9

p. 294: from the Collections of the Library of Congress; **p. 297:** The Library Company of Philadelphia; **p. 300:** Thomas L. McKenney, Sketches of a Tour to the Lakes

(1827); **p. 301:** The Granger Collection; **p. 306:** Old Sturbridge Village, Photo by: Thomas Neill, #25.K74if.1994.2.1; **p. 307:** Chicago Historical Society; **p. 308:** © Bettmann/Corbis; **p. 309:** Smithsonian Institution; **p. 310:** The Granger Collection, New York; **p. 311:** American Textile History Museum. Lowell, Mass; **p. 312:** © Hulton-Deutsch Collection/Corbis; **p. 315:** © Kobal/Picture Desk; **p. 316:** The Library Company of Philadelphia; **p. 318:** The Historic New Orleans Collection, Accension #1975.931 & 2; **p. 320:** The Historic New Orleans Collection, Accension # 1977.13734311

Chapter 10

p. 322: National Portrait Gallery, Smithsonian Institution/Art Resource, NY; **p. 325:** © Bettmann/Corbis; **p. 326:** Abby Aldrich Rockefeller Folk Art Center, Williamsburg, VA; **p. 329:** Frederic Edwin Church NIAGARA, 1857. oil on canvas, 42 1/2 x 90 1/2 in. (107.95 x 229.87 cm) In the Collection of the Corcoran Gallery of Art, Museum Purchase, Gallery Fund. 76.15; **p. 331:** Courtesy American Antiquarian Society; **p. 335:** From the Collections of the Library of Congress; **p. 336:** © Museum of the City of New York/Corbis; **p. 337 (both):** Courtesy, American Antiquarian Society; **p. 338:** Hunter Museum of American Art, Chattanooga, Tennessee, Gift of Mr. and Mrs. Thomas B. Whiteside; **p. 341:** From the Collections of the Library of Congress; **p. 343:** Reproduced form the Collections of the Library of Congress; **p. 345:** © Picture Desk/Kobal Collection/Regan, Ken/Touchstone

Chapter 11

p. 350: The Nelson-Atkins Museum of Art, Kansas City, Missouri (Purchase: Nelson Trust) 54-9; **p. 353:** The Saint Louis Art Museum, Purchase; **p. 358:** North Wind Picture Archives; **p. 359:** The Granger Collection, New York; **p. 360:** North Wind Picture Archives; **p. 364:** From the Collections of the Library of Congress; **p. 365:** A Black Oyster Seller in Philadelphia, 1814, Watercolor by John Lewis Krimmel. The Metropolitan Museum of Art, Rogers Fund, 1942 (42.95.18) Photograph © 1989 The Metropolitan Museum of Art; **p. 367:** © Bettmann/Corbis; **p. 368:** The Library Company of Philadelphia; **p. 371:** Old Sturbridge Village, photo by Henry E. Peach; **p. 374:** PBS Home Video

Chapter 12

p. 378: National Portrait Gallery, Smithsonian Institution/Art Resource, NY; **p. 384:** The Granger Collection;

p. 385: From the Collections of the Library of Congress; **p. 387:** U.S. Naval Historical Center Photograph; **p. 388:** The Hermitage: Home of President Andrew Jackson, Nashville, TN; **p. 390:** White House Collection; **p. 392:** © Picture Desk/Kobal Collection/Cooper, Andrew/Dreamworks LLC; **p. 394:** Woolaroc Museum; **p. 396:** From the Collection of the Library of Congress; **p. 400:** Collection of the New-York Historical Society; **p. 401:** North Wind Picture Archives; **p. 403:** Reproduced from the collections of the Library of Congress

Chapter 13

p. 406: From the collections of the Library of Congress; **p. 410:** North Wind Picture Archives; **p. 412:** Joseph Mustering the Nauvoo Legion, C.C.A. Christensen. © Courtesy Museum of Art, Brigham Young University. All Rights reserved. Photographer: David W. Hawkinson; **p. 415:** © John Springer Collection/Corbis; **p. 417:** Yale Collection of Western Americana, Beinecke Rare Book and Manuscript Library; **p. 420:** Missouri Historical Society. MHS art acc# 1939.3.1; **p. 421:** James Smith Noel Collection, Noel Memorial Library. Louisiana State University in Shreveport; **p. 423:** The Granger Collection, New York; **p. 426:** Courtesy of The Trustees of Boston Public Library; **p. 427:** "The Underground Railroad" painting by Charles T. Webber (1893) from the Cincinnati Art Museum (#1927.26); **p. 428:** The Granger Collection, New York

Chapter 14

p. 432: The Granger Collection, New York; **p. 435 (left):** Reproduced from the Collections of the Library of Congress; **p. 435 (right):** © Bettmann/Corbis; **p. 439:** Maryland Historical Society, Baltimore; **p. 440:** Kansas State Historical Society; **p. 442:** Prints Division, The New York Public Library. Astor, Lenox and Tilden Foundations; **p. 445:** © The Granger Collection; **p. 447:** © Corbis; **p. 449:** Reproduced from the Collections of the Library of Congress; **p. 450:** © Bettmann/Corbis; **p. 453 (top):** From the Collections of the Library of Congress; **p. 453 (bottom):** The Granger Collection; **p. 455:** © Bettmann/Corbis; **p. 458:** North Wind Picture Archives; **p. 459:** © Bettmann/Corbis; **p. 460:** Courtesy of the Illinois State Historical Library; **p. 462:** Kansas State Historical Society

Chapter 15

p. 464: Thomas C. Linday, Hornet's Nest, Cincinnati Historical Society; **p. 466:** Reproduced from the

Collections of the Library of Congress; **p. 468:** From the Ralph E. Becker Collection of Political Americana, The Smithsonian Institution; **p. 470:** Courtesy of The South Carolina Historical Society; **p. 474:** From the Collections of the Library of Congress; **p. 479:** © Springer/Corbis; **p. 480:** Cook Collection, Valentine Museum, Richmond, Virginia; **p. 482:** Photo by Timothy O'Sullivan, Chicago Historical Society, ICHi-08091; **p. 484:** From the Collections of the Library of Congress; **p. 485:** Historical Society of Pennsylvania; **p. 486 (top):** From the Collections of the Library of Congress; **p. 486 (bottom):** © Bettmann/Corbis

Chapter 16

p. 498: Eastman Johnson 1824-1906 A RIDE FOR LIBERTY-THE FUGITIVE SLAVES, circa 1862. Oil on board The Brooklyn Museum 40.59. A Gift of Miss Gwendolyn O.L. Conkling; **p. 501:** From the collections of the National Archives; **p. 504 (top):** Reproduced from the Collections of the Library of Congress; **p. 504 (bottom):** © Bettmann/Corbis; **p. 505:** Architect of the Capitol; **p. 509 (top):** The Library of Virginia; **p. 509 (bottom):** Collection of the New-York Historical Society; **p. 511:** Reproduced from the Collections of the Library of Congress; **p. 512 (left):** Reproduced from the Collections of the Library of Congress; **p. 512 (right):** Courtesy of the Illinois State Historical Library; **p. 514:** National Park Service, Harpers Ferry Center; **p. 518:** From the Collections of the Library of Congress; **p. 519:** © Picture Desk/Kobal Collection/Tri Star; **p. 522:** Brown Brothers; **p. 524:** From the Collections of the Library of Congress; **p. 525:** Reproduced from the Collections of the Library of Congress; **p. 527:** Reproduced from the Collections of the Library of Congress; **p. 530:** Reproduced from the Collections of the Library of Congress; **p. 531:** Reproduced from the Collections of the Library of Congress

Chapter 17

p. 534: Winslow Homer, Sunday Morning in Virginia, 1877. Cincinnati Art Museum John J. Emery Fund. Acc.#1924.247; **p. 537:** Courtesy Chicago Historical Society; **p. 539 (left):** Reproduced from the Collections of the Library of Congress; **p. 539 (right):** Reproduced from the Collections of the Library of Congress; **p. 541 (top):** Reproduced from the Collections of the Library of Congress; **p. 541 (bottom):** © Bettmann/Corbis; **p. 542:** Reproduced from the Collections of the Library of Congress; **p. 543 (left):** © Stock Montage, Inc.; **p. 543 (right):** From the Collections of the Library of Congress; **p. 545:**

From the Collections of the Library of Congress; **p. 548:** © Corbis; **p. 553:** © Bettmann/Corbis; **p. 554:** From the Collections of the Library of Congress; **p. 556:** © Bettmann/Corbis; **p. 558:** The Granger Collection, New York

Chapter 18

p. 562: Frederic Remington, "A Dash for Timber" oil on canvas, 1889. 1961.381. © Amon Carter Museum, Fort Worth, Texas; **p. 564:** Nebraska State Historical Society; **p. 568:** Erwin E. Smith Collection of the Library of Congress on deposit at the Amon Carter Museum, Fort Worth; **p. 569:** By courtesy of the National Portrait Gallery, London; **p. 570:** Smithsonian Institution, Bureau of American Ethnology; **p. 571:** © John Springer Collection/Corbis; **p. 577:** © The Granger Collection

Chapter 19

p. 582: The Kansas State Historical Society Topeka, Kansas; **p. 586:** The Museum of the City of New York; **p. 587:** © Bob Krist/Corbis; **p. 591:** From the Collections of the Library of Congress; **p. 593:** © Bettmann/Corbis; **p. 595:** © Bettmann/Corbis; **p. 598:** North Wind Picture Archives; **p. 599:** © Bettmann/Corbis; **p. 600:** Kansas State Historical Society; **p. 603:** From the Collections of the Library of Congress

Chapter 20

p. 608: John Sloan, The City from Greenwich Village, 1922. National Gallery of Art. Gift of Helen Farr Sloan, 1970.I. I.; **p. 611:** © Lake County Museum/Corbis; **p. 614:** © Bettmann/Corbis; **p. 615:** © Bettmann/Corbis; **p. 617:** State Historical Society of Wisconsin; **p. 618:** Brown University Archives; **p. 622:** © Bettmann/Corbis; **p. 624:** Victor Joseph Gatto Triangle Fire, March 25, 1911. Oil on canvas, 19 x 28 inches. Museum of the City of New York, 54.75, Gift of Mrs. Henry L. Moses; **p. 626:** © Bettmann/ Corbis; **p. 628:** From the Collections of the Library of Congress; **p. 631:** Underwood Photo Archives; **p. 632:** The Granger Collection, New York; **p. 633:** © Bettmann/ Corbis; **p. 635:** © Picture Desk/ Kobal Collection/20th Century Fox; **p. 636:** © Bettmann/ Corbis

Chapter 21

p. 638: Culver Pictures; **p. 641:** Culver Pictures; **p. 642:** George Bellows, "Cliff Dwellers" 1913. oil on canvas. Los Angeles County Museum of Art, Los Angeles County Fund; **p. 643:** Brown Brothers; **p. 645:** Columbia University Library; **p. 648:** © Hulton Artchive/Getty Images;

p. 652: Reproduced from the Collections of the Library of Congress; **p. 654:** © Bettmann/Corbis; **p. 656:** © Bettmann/Corbis; **p. 657:** © Bettmann/Corbis; **p. 659:** From the Collections of the Library of Congress; **p. 662:** Brown Brothers; **p. 664:** Reproduced from the Collections of the Library of Congress; **p. 667:** © Picture Desk/Kobal Collection/20th Century Fox

Chapter 22

p. 670: Culver Pictures; **p. 673:** Smithsonian Institution Photo No. 85-14366; **p. 674:** © Hulton-Deutsch Collection/Corbis; **p. 676:** The Granger Collection, New York; **p. 677:** Chicago Historical Society; **p. 679:** From the Collections of the Library of Congress; **p. 680 (top):** © Bettmann/Corbis; **p. 680 (bottom):** The Granger Collection; **p. 682:** © Corbis; **p. 684:** The Granger Collection, New York; **p. 685:** The Granger Collection, New York; **p. 689:** © Bettmann/Corbis; **p. 690:** © Underwood & Underwood/Corbis; **p. 691:** North Wind Picture Archives; **p. 694:** Brown Brothers

Chapter 23

p. 698: Mary Evans Picture Library; **p. 702:** Imperial War Museum, London; **p. 704:** Records of the Women's International League for Peace and Freedom, U.S. Section, Swarthmore College Peace Collection; **p. 706:** The Granger Collections, New York; **p. 709:** © Corbis; **p. 710:** © Digital Images © The Museum of Modern Art/ Licensed by Scala/Art Resource, NY; **p. 713:** National Archives photo; **p. 714:** Reproduced from the Collections of the Library of Congress; **p. 715:** National Archives; **p. 717:** Imperial War Museum; **p. 718:** New York Times, 1919; **p. 719:** © UPI-Bettmann/Corbis; **p. 721:** © Corbis; **p. 723:** Library & Archives Division, Historical Society of Western Pennsylvania, Pittsburgh, Pa; **p. 725:** © Picture Desk/Kobal Collection/Paramount; **p. 726:** © 1995 Estate of Ben Shahn/VAGA, New York. Collection of Whitney Museum of American Art; **p. 727:** From the Collections of the Library of Congress

Chapter 24

p. 730: The Dance Club, or The Jazz Party, 1923 (oil on canvas) by Roberts, William Patrick (1895–1980) Leeds Museums and Galleries (City Art Gallery)/The Bridgeman Art Library. Reproduced by permission of the Treasury Solicitor (administrator of the estate of John David Roberts); **p. 735:** The Granger Collection, New York; **p. 737 (top):** From the Collections of the Library of Congress; **p. 737 (bottom):** © Bettmann/Corbis; **p. 739:** © Corbis; **p. 741:** Brown Brothers; **p. 742:** Brown Brothers; **p. 743:** © Bettmann/Corbis; **p. 746:** Brown Brothers; **p. 748:** From the Collections of the Library of Congress; **p. 751:** Brown Brothers; **p. 753:** The Granger Collection; **p. 755:** National Portrait Gallery, Smithsonian Institution/Art Resource, NY; **p. 756:** © Bettmann/Corbis; **p. 759:** Security Pacific Colleciton/Los Angeles Public Library; **p. 760:** © Leonard de Selva/Corbis; **p. 761:** The Granger Collection, New York

Chapter 25

p. 764: The Granger Collection, New York; **p. 766:** From the Collections of the Library of Congress; **p. 769:** © Bettmann/Corbis; **p. 771:** © Bettmann/Corbis; **p. 774:** From the Collections of the Library of Congress; **p. 775:** From the Collections of the Library of Congress; **p. 776:** FDR Library; **p. 777:** © Bettmann/Corbis; **p. 779:** © Lester Lefkowitz/Corbis; **p. 781:** © UPI-Bettmann/Corbis; **p. 782:** Detroit Industry, North Wall, 1932-1933, Diego Rivera. Gift of Edsel B. Ford. Photograph © 1991 The Detroit Institute of Arts; **p. 785:** The Granger Collection; **p. 786:** The Granger Collection, New York; **p. 789:** AP/Wide World Photos; **p. 790:** Michael Barson Collection/Past Perfect; **p. 791:** From the Collections of the Library of Congress; **p. 794:** From the Collections of the Library of Congress

Chapter 26

p. 800: Hoover Institute Archives, Stanford University. U560; **p. 806:** © Bettmann/Corbis; **p. 807:** © UPI-Bettmann/Corbis; **p. 809:** San Diego Historical Society; **p. 813:** © AFP/Corbis; **p. 817:** National Archives #127-N-69559-A; **p. 820 (both):** © UPI-Bettmann/Corbis; **p. 822:** National Archives; **p. 823:** © Bettmann/Corbis; **p. 824:** Reproduced from the Collections of the Library of Congress; **p. 825:** From the Collections of the Library of Congress; **p. 826:** © Corbis; **p. 827:** © Bettmann/Corbis; **p. 830:** FDR Library

Chapter 27

p. 836: Michael Barson Collection/Past Perfect; **p. 839:** The Granger Collection, New York; **p. 841:** Courtesy of the George C. Marshall Research Library, Lexington, Virginia; **p. 842:** Courtesy of the Truman Library; **p. 846:** Courtesy of the Truman Library; **p. 850:** © Archive Photos; **p. 853:** © Sunset Boulevard/Corbis Sygma; **p. 854:** From the Collections of the Library of Congress; **p. 859:** Courtesy of the Minnesota Historical Society; **p. 860:** © Bettmann/Corbis; **p. 861:** Michael Barson Collection/Past Perfect; **p. 865:** Michael Barson Collection/Past Perfect

Chapter 28

p. 868: The Granger Collection, New York; **p. 872:** © AP/Wide World Photo; **p. 877 (top):** © UPI-Bettmann/ Corbis; **p. 877 (bottom):** © Elliott Erwitt/Magnum Photos Inc.; **p. 879:** © Joe Munroe/Photo Researchers; **p. 882:** From the Collections of the Library of Congress; **p. 883:** © Corbis; **p. 886:** © UPI-Bettmann/Corbis; **p. 888:** AP/Wide World; **p. 893:** © UPI-Bettmann/Corbis; **p. 896:** © UPI-Bettmann/Corbis; **p. 897:** © Danny Lyon/Magnum Photos, Inc.; **p. 898:** AP/Wide World Photos; **p. 901:** © John Springer Collection/Corbis

Chapter 29

p. 904: © Joseph Sohm; ChromoSohm Inc./Corbis; **p. 907 (both):** George Tames/NYT Pictures; **p. 913:** AP/Wide World Photos; **p. 914:** The Granger Collection, New York; **p. 918:** © Bettmann/Corbis; **p. 919:** © UPI-Bettmann/Corbis; **p. 921:** © Corbis; **p. 923 (top):** © UPI-Bettmann/Corbis; **p. 923 (bottom):** © UPI-Bettmann/ Corbis; **p. 928:** © Bettmann/Corbis; **p. 929:** © UPI-Bettmann/Corbis

Chapter 30

p. 936: © Richard Nowitz/Corbis; **p. 941:** © Paul Conklin/PhotoEdit; **p. 944 (all):** California Department of Transportation; **p. 946:** © Ted Streshinsky/Corbis; **p. 947:** © Karen Su/Corbis; **p. 950:** © Archive Photos/Fotos International; **p. 953:** © Picture Desk/Kobal Collection/ Lucasfilm/20th Century Fox; **p. 958:** © Bettmann/Corbis; **p. 961:** AP/Wide World Photos; **p. 962 (top):** Bill Pugliano/Gamma-Liaison Network; **p. 962 (bottom):** © Gary A. Conner/PhotoEdit; **p. 963:** © Ralf-Finn Hestoft/Corbis; **p. 965:** © Nik Wheeler/Corbis; **p. 966:** AP/Wide World Photos; **p. 967:** © Bettmann/Corbis

Chapter 31

p. 972: © James L. Amos/Corbis; **p. 977:** © 1980 Time Inc, Reprinted by permission; **p. 982:** © Jeff Lowenthal/Woodfin Camp; **p. 985:** © Bettmann/Corbis; **p. 986:** Courtesy, Ronald Reagan Library; **p. 990:** © Owen Franken/Corbis; **p. 995:** © Reuters NewMedia Inc/Corbis; **p. 999 (both):** © Tom Prettyman/PhotoEdit; **p. 1001:** © Reuters Newmedia Inc/Corbis; **p. 1003:** © Corbis; **p. 1004:** AP/Wide World Photos; **p. 1005:** © Lee Snider/ Corbis; **p. 1006:** © Damir Sagolj/Reuters Newmedia Inc/Corbis

Civil War in, 492
constitution of, 202
Creoles in, 63
dependency patterns in, 121
electing governor of, 91
expansion by, 57–58, 144, 145
House of Burgesses in, 57
Indian war in, 97–98
Jamestown colony in, 55–56
land cession by, 204, 221 (map)
land in, 176
population growth in, 85
religion in, 60
reorganization of, 57–58
in Revolution, 213, 214, 215 (map)
as royal colony, 101
secession of, 475
in 1675, 61
slavery in, 86, 218, 243
Statute for Religious Freedom in, 217
Thunderbird dig in, 4
tobacco and, 56, 57, 59
Turner, Nat, in, 346–347
voters in, 650
Virginia (*Merrimac,* ironclad), 486–487
Virginia and Kentucky Resolves, 274–275, 394
Virginia Company, 55
area of charter, 58 (map)
Virginia Gazette, 130
Virginia (large state) Plan, 225–226
Virginia Tobacco Inspection Act (1730), 139
Virgin Islands, purchase of, 694
Virginius (ship), 548
Virtue
Adams, John, on, 201
republican, 249
Virtuous electorate, 650
VISTA. *See* Volunteers in Service to America (VISTA)
Vitamins, in 1920s, 733
V-J Day, 819
Voice of America, 871
jazz program on, 872
Voice of the Negro, The (magazine), 589
Volstead Act, 718
Voluntaristic ethic, 113–114, 145
Volunteers
in antebellum South, 478
in Civil War, 475, 480, 502
in Continental Army, 195
in Second World War, 823
women as Civil War, 511
Volunteers in Service to America (VISTA), 907
Voting. *See also* Elections; specific elections
African Americans and, 254, 536, 537, 545, 650–651, 886–887, 888
Australian ballot and, 650

bulldozing and, 558
in colonies, 105
constituencies and, 352–354
in Continental Congress, 204
disenfranchisement and, 650–651
electioneering and, 350
European American ethnics and, 754
Fifteenth Amendment and, 547
Fourteenth Amendment and, 544
in Kansas Territory, 441, 446
in Massachusetts, 103, 203
Mississippi Plan and, 555–556
native-born vs. foreign-born voters, 437
in New South, 575, 577
in 1936 election, 788
in 1992, 994
in North and West, 352–353
participation in presidential elections (1920–1940), 787
in Pennsylvania, 202
personal registration laws and, 650
in presidential elections (1876–1920), 652
by propertied widows, 254
qualifications for, 253
during Reconstruction, 538, 544
in South, 353–354
women and, 218, 219, 652–654, 740
Voting Rights Act (1965), 909
Voyages of exploration. *See also* Portugal; Spain; specific explorers
of Cabot, 51
of Columbus, 14–17, 16 (map)
of Verrazano, 45

Wade, Benjamin, 537, 538
Wade-Davis reconstruction bill (1864), 537–538
Wage labor, 250
vs. self-employment, 595
vs. slavery, 451–454
social mobility and, 457
Wages, 949
between 1922 and 1929, 732
of artisans, 250
during First World War, 711
at Ford, 616
in manufacturing, 629–630
in Massachusetts Bay, 66
in mass-production industries, 738
in 1950s and 1960s, 880
in 1980s, 982
in Panic of 1837, 403
real, 594
in seaport cities, 249
in Second World War, 823
of women, 590, 739
of workers in manufacturing, 623–624

Wage system
AFL and, 596
Knights of Labor and, 596
Wagner, Fort, assault on, 518, 519
Wagner, Robert F., 655, 772, 785, 792
Wagner Act (1935). *See* National Labor Relations Act (NLRA, 1935)
Wagner-Rogers Bill, 807
Waiting for Lefty (Odets), 790
Wake Island, 814
Wald, Lillian, 655
Walden (Thoreau), 326
Walker, Alice, 959
Walker, David, 366
Walker, Madame C. J., 629
Walker, Maggie Lena, 589
Walker, Robert J., 420
Walker, William, 430
Walker tariff, 420
Walking cities, demise of, 586
Wallace, George
election of 1964 and, 908
election of 1968 and, 923
Wallace, Henry A., 839, 851
election of 1948 and, 842, 843, 843 (map)
Waller, Fats, 757
Walling, William English, 656
Walloons (Netherlands), 50, 51
Wall Street Journal, 967
Wal-Mart, 947, 948
Walpole, Robert, 109, 139
Waltham system, 311–313
Walton, Sam, 947
Waltz, controversy over, 454
Wampanoag Indians, 64, 94
Wanamaker, John, 588
Wanamaker's department store, 589
War agencies, in First World War, 708
War bonds
in Civil War North, 483, 600–601
in Second World War, 821
War Department, 265, 266
Pentagon and, 809
"War for democracy," 699
War guilt, of Germany, 719
War Hawk Congress, 285–286
War Industries Board (WIB), 708
War Labor Board, 821, 823
War Manpower Commission, 821
Warner, Charles Dudley, 549
Warner, Susan, 326
"Warning out" system, in Massachusetts, 66
War of 1812, 287 (map)
British offensive in (1814), 289–290
Tecumseh's confederacy in, 241
War Hawks and, 285–286
War of Jenkins's Ear, 115, 141–144
War of the Austrian Succession. *See* King George's War

in New York, 655
in 1990s, 996
Nixon and, 925–926
Reagan and, 983, 985–986
for single mothers, 956
Truman and, 860
in West, 779
in Wisconsin, 655
Welfare capitalism, 737–738
Welles, Gideon, 505
Wellesley, 590
Wells, Ida B., 655, 656
Wentworth, Benning, 139
We Owe Allegiance to No Crown, 262
Wertham, Frederick, 882
"We Shall Overcome," 898, 922
Wesley, John, 134–135, 178, 257
West
    British threats in, 270–272
    Chinese labor in, 622–623
    Civil War in, 489–492
    dams in, 778
    expansion into, 380–381
    Indians in, 829
    land claims during Revolution, 221
        (map)
    lands in, 204
    New Deal and development in,
        779–780
    political parties in, 352–353
    preservation of, 659–660
    1790–1796, 271 (map)
    state claims in, 204
    transportation and trade in, 304
    transportation in, 299
    white population increase in, 563
    woman suffrage in, 652
West, Benjamin, 78, 155
West, Nathaniel, 770
West, Thomas (baron de la Warr). *See*
    De la Warr, baron (Thomas West)
West Africa
    agricultural work in, 246
    Dutch and, 50
    European trade and colonies in,
        10–12
    slave trade in, 11–12
West Bank (of Jordan River), 978
West Berlin, Kennedy, John F., and, 895
Western Delaware Indians, 148
Western Europe
    immigrants from, 749
    Truman and, 841
Western Federation of Miners, 565
Western front, in First World War, 700,
    707 (map)
Western Hemisphere
    Monroe Doctrine and, 386
    native populations of, 18
    naval bases in, 805
    papal division of, 16

Portugal in, 13
Roosevelt, Theodore, and, 687–690
U.S. influence in, 671, 684–685, 695
West Florida, cession to Spain, 201
West Germany (Federal Republic of
    Germany), 842, 843 (map)
    in NATO, 871
    rearmament of, 848
West India Companies, 50, 51
West Indies
    English migrants to, 55
    after French and Indian War, 156
    French in, 49
    Jay's Treaty and, 272
    New England molasses trade and,
        127
    Panama Canal labor from, 690
    principal colonies in 17th century,
        63 (map)
    purchase of Danish, 694
    royal governments in, 87
    slaves in, 86
Westinghouse (company), 592, 613
Westinghouse, George, 610
West Jersey Concessions and Agree-
    ments, 78
Westmoreland, William, 920
West New Jersey, 72, 77, 78 (map)
West Point
    military academy at, 278
    southerners from, 478
West Virginia, creation of, 477
Westward movement, 219–222, 232,
    238, 406. *See also* Louisiana Pur-
    chase (1803)
    into backcountry, 241–242
    depression of 1837–1843 and, 409
    environmental impact of, 580
    frontier thesis and, 673
    Indians and, 206, 567–574
    Mexican Americans and, 574–575
    mining frontier and, 565
    Northwest Ordinance and, 220–221
    overland trails and, 410–412, 411
        (map)
    in post-Civil War era, 563
    railroads and, 564
    ranching frontier and, 565–567
    to 1790, 222 (map)
Wetback, use of term, 890
Wetlands, 999
Weyler, Valeriano "Butcher," 676, 677
Weyrich, Paul, 969
Whaling industry, 127
Wheat, 125, 126
    blight in, 127
    in Middle Atlantic region, 87
    in Northwest, 307
Wheatley, Phillis, 179
Wheel, among Indians, 19
Wheeler, Burton K., 805, 807

Wheeler Dam, 779
Wheeler-Howard Act (1934). *See* Indian
    Reorganization Act (1934)
Wheeling, West Virginia, 477
Wheelock, Eleazer, 137
Wheelwright, Esther, 114, 115
Wherry, Kenneth, 855
Whig Party, 351, 352–353, 376, 401, 433.
    See also Politics; specific issues
    American Party and, 438
    American System and, 379
    banking and, 356
    beginnings of, 400–401
    Conscience Whigs and, 422
    demise of, 407, 436, 465
    on economic development, 354–355
    educational reform and, 357
    election of 1836 and, 402
    election of 1840 and, 403–404
    election of 1848 and, 422
    evangelicals of, 370
    internal improvements and, 356
    Mexican War and, 416–417
    politics of social reform and,
        357–364
    prohibition and, 362–363
    sexual politics and, 372
    in South, 353–354
Whigs (England), 100, 109
Whip Inflation Now (WIN) program,
    975
Whipping post, 360
Whiskey. *See also* Alcohol and alco-
    holism; Temperance
    production of, 251–252
Whiskey Rebellion, 267, 270–271
Whistle-stop campaign, of Bryan, 604
White, George, 345
White, Hugh Lawson, 354
    election of 1836 and, 402
White, John, 53, 90
White, William Allen, 807
White Citizens Council, 887
White-collar workers, 313
    women as, 590, 739
White Eyes (Delaware), 206
Whitefield, George, 134, 135, 136
White flight, 864, 886
White Leagues, 555, 558
Whites
    anti-Asian attitudes of, 622, 623
    in backcountry, 241
    black assaults on, 655
    civil rights issues and, 656, 860,
        915
    classes of, 73
    conceptions of racial difference
        among, 368–369
    Cubans as, 677–678
    migration to free states, 455
    population increase in West, 563

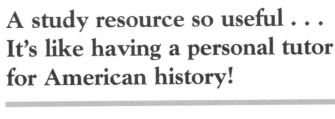

A study resource so useful . . . It's like having a personal tutor for American history!

Also accessible from this CD-ROM: a free preview of HistoryNOW: Interactive Explorations in American History, an innovative and [...] way to expe[...] from your ou[...]

The *History Interactive* CD-ROM

Packaged free with every new copy of this text, the **History Interactive CD-ROM** makes it easier to succeed on quizzes and tests. Simply insert the CD-ROM into your computer for instant access to features that enhance each chapter of the book:

▶ A **Chapter Summary** highlights key points—perfect for a quick review of the chapter's core ideas, trends, people, events, and dates.

▶ **Study Tips** comment on important subjects, documents, maps, and art illustrations, and connect you with "The Main Idea"—a brief commentary that helps you improve and test your knowledge on the significance of each source. In addition, map exercises link you to interactive and timeline maps, as well as activities that further your understanding of what the maps represent.

▶ **Review Questions** repeat the questions that appear at the beginning of each chapter of the text—and answer them with bulleted points that let you see if your answers meet the criteria instructors might look for on quizzes and tests.

▶ **Interactive Content** links you to interactive maps, two free interactive modules covering different points in history, as well as the full text of additional primary documents—yet another way to experience the past.

▶ **Chapter Quizzing** lets you test your knowledge—helping you quickly identify those areas where you need to spend extra time reviewing. Quizzing focuses on people, events, and other details covered in the chapter.

▶ **Global Links** take you to additional free resources on the Thomson Wadsworth History pages—including photographs, interactive simulations, and more that bring history to life.

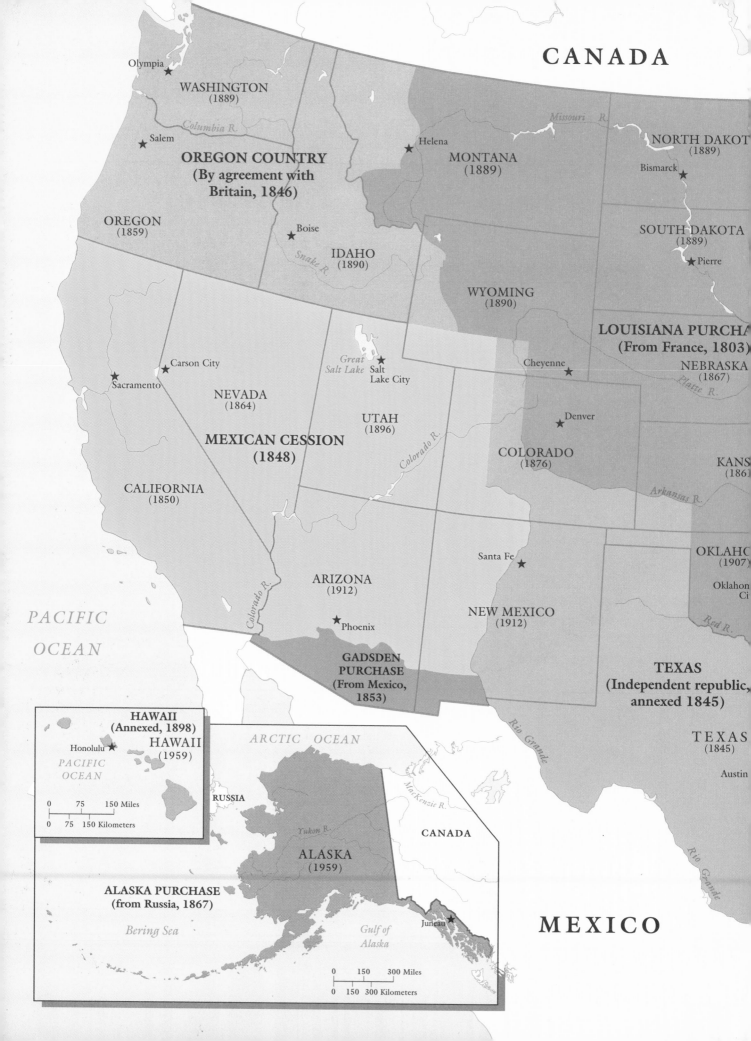

CANADA

Olympia
WASHINGTON
(1889)

Salem

Columbia R.

OREGON COUNTRY
(By agreement with
Britain, 1846)

OREGON
(1859)

Boise

Helena

MONTANA
(1889)

Missouri R.

NORTH DAKOT
(1889)

Bismarck

SOUTH DAKOTA
(1889)

Pierre

Snake R.

IDAHO
(1890)

WYOMING
(1890)

LOUISIANA PURCHA
(From France, 1803)

Carson City

Sacramento

NEVADA
(1864)

*Great
Salt Lake* Salt
Lake City

UTAH
(1896)

Cheyenne

Denver

NEBRASKA
(1867)

Platte R.

MEXICAN CESSION
(1848)

Colorado R.

COLORADO
(1876)

KANS
(186

Arkansas R.

CALIFORNIA
(1850)

PACIFIC

OCEAN

Colorado R.

ARIZONA
(1912)

Phoenix

GADSDEN
PURCHASE
(From Mexico,
1853)

Santa Fe

NEW MEXICO
(1912)

OKLAHO
(1907)

Oklahom
Ci

Red R.

TEXAS
(Independent republic,
annexed 1845)

TEXAS
(1845)

Austin

Rio Grande

HAWAII
(Annexed, 1898)
HAWAII
(1959)

Honolulu

*PACIFIC
OCEAN*

0   75   150 Miles

0   75   150 Kilometers

ARCTIC OCEAN

RUSSIA

MacKenzie R.

CANADA

Yukon R.

ALASKA
(1959)

ALASKA PURCHASE
(from Russia, 1867)

Bering Sea

*Gulf of
Alaska*

Juneau

MEXICO

Rio Grande

0   150   300 Miles

0   150   300 Kilometers